ANNUAL REVIEW OF PSYCHOLOGY

EDITORIAL COMMITTEE (1988)

ALBERT BANDURA
GORDON H. BOWER
FRANCES D. HOROWITZ
LYMAN W. PORTER
MARK R. ROSENZWEIG
JANET T. SPENCE
AUKE TELLEGEN

Responsible for organization of Volume 39
(Editorial Committee, 1985)

NORMAN GARMEZY
FRANCES K. GRAHAM
BERT F. GREEN
EDWARD E. JONES
JEANNE S. PHILLIPS
LYMAN W. PORTER
MARK R. ROSENZWEIG
GORDON H. BOWER (Guest)

Production Editor   IKE BURKE
Indexing Coordinator   MARY A. GLASS
Subject Indexer   STEVEN SORENSEN

ANNUAL REVIEW OF PSYCHOLOGY

VOLUME 39, 1988

MARK R. ROSENZWEIG, *Editor*

University of California, Berkeley

LYMAN W. PORTER, *Editor*

University of California, Irvine

ANNUAL REVIEWS INC.   4139 EL CAMINO WAY   P.O. BOX 10139   PALO ALTO, CALIFORNIA 94303-0897

Ⓡ ANNUAL REVIEWS INC.
Palo Alto, California, USA

International Standard Serial Number: 0066–4308
International Standard Book Number: 0–8243–0239–7
Library of Congress Catalog Card Number: 50-13143

Typesetting by Kachina Typesetting Inc., Tempe, Arizona; John Olson, President
Typesetting coordinator, Janis Hoffman

PRINTED AND BOUND IN THE UNITED STATES OF AMERICA

PREFACE

Eleanor J. Gibson, author of this year's Prefatory Chapter, is a distinguished psychologist who has received deserved recognition for her research on perception and its development in children. Her chapter, on "Exploratory Behavior in the Development of Perceiving, Acting, and the Acquiring of Knowledge" is a stimulating account of empirical and conceptual milestones in this field. Another view of this topic, largely limited to recent contributions, is presented in the chapter by Richard N. Aslin and Linda B. Smith.

Another pair of chapters in this volume also shows the perspective of different authors on topics that are shared by more than one field. Specifically, both the chapter on "Human Behavior Genetics" and that on "Addictive Behaviors" consider hereditary factors in alcohol and drug abuse.

Because the XXIV International Congress of Psychology will take place August 28–September 3, 1988, in Sydney, this volume includes a chapter on "Psychology in Australia." Written by Ronald Taft and Ross Day, it will be of special interest to psychologists who plan to attend the Congress and to those who follow the international development of psychology. Volume 41 will include an article on psychology in Japan, which has been selected to be the host country for the next International Congress of Applied Psychology in 1990 (to be held in Kyoto).

This year we have three "Timely Topic" chapters, reviews written with shorter deadlines and covering topics not included in our Master List. Arnold Binder reviews research on "Juvenile Delinquency;" G. Alan Marlatt, John S. Baer, Dennis M. Donovan, and Daniel R. Kivlahan take on "Addictive Behaviors: Etiology and Treatment," and Richard L. Gorsuch focuses on "The Psychology of Religion." The Master List is reflected in the five-year cumulative index of chapter titles at the back of this volume.

In 1987 Edward E. Jones completed his five-year period of dedicated service on the Editorial Committee. Ned contributed greatly to the volumes published during his term, through his keen knowledge and evaluations of psychology and psychologists, not only in his own special field of social psychology but also in many other areas.

The Editorial Committee is pleased to welcome as our new member Auke Tellegen, whose term began in 1987.

M.R.R.
L.W.P.

Ann. Rev. Psychol.
Volume 39, 1988

CONTENTS

SOME RELATED ARTICLES IN OTHER *ANNUAL REVIEWS*

From the *Annual Review of Anthropology,* Volume 16 (1987)

> *Some Reflections on Fifty Years in Biological Anthropology,* Joseph B. Birdsell
> *Foraging Strategies Among Living Primates,* Paul A. Garber
> *Hominid Paleoneurology,* Dean Falk
> *Current Generative Approaches to Syntax,* Sandra Chung
> *The Relation Between Written and Spoken Language,* Wallace Chafe and Deborah Tannen
> *Cross-Cultural Surveys Today,* Michael L. Burton and Douglas R. White
> *Anthropology and Alcohol Studies: Current Issues,* Dwight B. Heath
> *The Cross-Cultural Study of Human Sexuality,* D. L. Davis and R. G. Whitten

From the *Annual Review of Pharmacology and Toxicology,* Volume 28 (1988)

> *Regulation of the Release of Coexisting Neurotransmitters,* T. Bartfai, K. Iverfeldt, G. Fisone, and Peter Serfözö
> *Pharmacology of Dynorphin,* Andrew P. Smith and Nancy M. Lee
> *Neuromodulatory Actions of Peptides,* L.-M. Kow and Donald W. Pfaff

From the *Annual Review of Public Health,* Volume 9 (1987)

> *Preventing Cigarette Smoking Among School Children,* J. Allan Best, Shirley J. Thompson, Suzanne M. Santi, Edward A. Smith, K. Stephen Brown
> *A Public Health Approach to the Prevention of Alcohol-Related Health Problems,* Mary Jane Ashley and James G. Rankin
> *Organic Solvent Neurotoxicity,* Edward L. Baker
> *Health Hazards of Passive Smoking,* Michael P. Eriksen, Charles LeMaistre, and Guy R. Newell

From the *Annual Review of Neuroscience,* Volume 11 (1988)

> *Some Aspects of Language Processing Revealed Through the Analysis of Acquired Aphasia: The Lexical System,* A. Caramazza
> *Behavioral Studies of Pavlovian Conditioning,* R. A. Rescorla
> *Excitatory Amino Acid Neurotransmission: NMDA Receptors and Hebb-Type Synaptic Plasticity,* C. W. Cotman, D. T. Monaghan, and A. H. Ganong
> *Anatomical Organization of Macaque Monkey Striate Visual Cortex,* J. S. Lund
> *Formation of Topographic Maps,* S. B. Udin and J. W. Fawcett

From the *Annual Review of Medicine,* Volume 39 (1988)

From the *Annual Review of Sociology,* Volume 13 (1987)

For the convenience of readers, a detachable order form/envelope is bound into the back of this volume.

Eleanor J. Gibson

Ann. Rev. Psychol. 1988. 39:1–41

EXPLORATORY BEHAVIOR IN THE DEVELOPMENT OF PERCEIVING, ACTING, AND THE ACQUIRING OF KNOWLEDGE*

Eleanor J. Gibson

Department of Psychology, Cornell University, Ithaca, New York 14853

CONTENTS

TRADITIONS IN THE STUDY OF CHILDREN'S EXPLORATORY BEHAVIOR

Interest in exploratory behavior, especially when such behavior is manifest as play, curiosity, or reactions to strangeness, is nothing new in psychology. Its role in the development of young mammals was recognized by the early

---

*This is the ninth in a series of prefatory chapters written by eminent senior psychologists.

0066-4308/88/0201-0001$02.00

behavioral biologists inspired by Darwin, such as Romanes; by the baby biographers a little later; and by pioneer psychologists such as G. Stanley Hall. It has been studied in primates, including human infants, intensively (e.g. Welker 1961). In Piaget's *Origins of Intelligence in Children* (1937; transl. 1952), it emerged as a mechanism of primary theoretical importance in accounting for a child's development. It took several decades for Piaget's theory of cognitive development to penetrate the thinking of American developmental psychologists, but as the shift away from behaviorist theories took place, new concepts relevant to exploratory activity were introduced. With each wave of conceptual change, newly oriented studies of exploratory behavior appeared. A brief mention of some of these changes will establish their significance in the rapid progress of developmental psychology in recent years.

One of the first concepts to be attacked and revised was the notion of motivation as a homeostatic process tied firmly to organic needs and drives, and linked to reinforcement in explaining behavior change. White (1959) in a much-cited paper urged that "competence" provided a natural motive in young children—a need to learn about the environment and how to deal with it. The notion was not revolutionary, since it was highly reminiscent of Woodworth's functional approach and his emphasis on a direct perceptual motive—an organism needs to "see clearly, to hear distinctly" so as to cope adequately with its environment (Woodworth 1947, 1958). But the climate of the times was finally right for reintroduction of such a motive. "Intrinsic" motivation was coming into its own. Berlyne (1966) proposed two types of exploration, one "specific" and one "diversive," motivated not by hunger or thirst or the like, but by something more like a need to know. These concepts were followed up with a large number of experiments by Berlyne and others, and led to further notions to be linked to exploration, such as "novelty" (e.g. Hutt 1970).

In the 1970s the literature of early childhood was enriched by large-scale studies of exploratory manipulation of objects (e.g. McCall 1974; Fenson et al 1976). The relevant concept that inspired these studies was cognition, as the study of cognitive development emerged with the new focus on cognitive psychology. Emphasis was placed on a change toward the end of the first year of a child's life from relatively random action on objects, to cognitively directed "functional" activities, such as drinking from a toy cup or talking into a toy telephone instead of banging them on somelhing. McCall suggested that early exploration was "largely an investigation of the raw sensory-perceptual feedback of the objects" (1974, p. 77), which changed progressively toward greater cognitive control and imaginative play with the object. Fenson et al (1976) similarly stressed emergence of new "cognitive capacities" following nonspecific manipulation:

Although 9-month-olds generally showed the ability to relate to objects and 7-month-olds did not, at both ages play was nonrelational and nonaccommodative and was characterized by close visual and tactual inspection of individual objects, usually accompanied by mouthing and chewing and the application of more or less indiscriminate motor schemes (shaking, banging, turning the object over and over, and shifting it from hand to hand). . . . The emergence of relational acts in the latter part of the first year and the emergence of symbolic acts in the first half of the second year dramatically change the structure of the child's play, mirroring the development of important new cognitive capacities (pp. 234 ff).

It is interesting to read that the play mirrors the development of new cognitive capacities, rather than that the manipulative play has a key role in cognitive development, as Piaget would have suggested.

A quite different concept, the idea of "attachment" bonds belween an infant and a carelaker, led to a different line of research on exploration. Researchers studied not manipulation but the child's exploration of the larger environment as its capacity for self-initiated locomotion matured. Rheingold and her colleagues (Rheingold & Eckerman 1969; Ross 1974; Ross et al 1972) were the pioneers in this work. What happens to the child's intellectual growth when his physical growth enables him to enlarge his scope of observation on his own? The question is now being readdressed, and I return to it below. Rheingold thought of familiarity and novelty (as well as relationships with its mother) as having an important role in the child's ventures into new territory (Rheingold & Eckerman 1970; Rheingold 1985). Her research did not lead her to overstress the role of attachment and dependence on maternal help; she was impressed by the strength of the infant's urge to explore new territory on its own initiative. All this had to do with learning about the world.

Few psychologists were writing about action in the 1970s, but Jerome Bruner devoted a series of papers to the topic and made the development of skilled action in infancy the subject of a number of studies (Bruner 1968, 1973). Exploratory activities played a prominent role for him in understanding action, and so did intentionality (Kalnins & Bruner 1973). Bruner studied the "attainment of competence." "In the growth of such competence in infants, three themes are central—intention, feedback, and the patterns of action that mediate between them" (Bruner 1973, p. 1). Bruner's description of an infant's actions in capturing an object differed from earlier descriptions of reaching and grasping because he emphasized the intentional, unified character of the action. Bruner quoted Bernstein's model (Bernstein 1967) for programming an action, one that emphasizes neither reflexes nor random responses but "future requirements." [I return to this point below in considering the experiments of von Hofsten (1983).] Exploratory activity, even at a very early age, is controlled by some anticipation of an outcome, presumably an adaptive one. Bruner thought one of the principal steps in the development of any skill was an objectivized representation, or image ["a constructed space that is independent of action" (Bruner 1968, p. 47)]. But anticipation must have been there earlier, too, in some form. Indeed, in concluding a series of lectures on achievement of skilled actions, Bruner said that

> cognition—the achievement, retention, and storage of information—is inherent or immanent in the functional enterprises of organisms. . . . So, when we study the changing responses of the three-week-old infant to changes in the pay-off for sucking, we are studying not just sucking but the infant's mode of coping cognitively with a changing environment (1968, p. 68).

Bruner's emphasis on function, and on actions as systems, gave a new character to the study of even such simple exploratory behaviors as reaching for things. This emphasis exists in stronger form at the present time in work such as Thelen's on development of locomotion (Thelen 1984, 1987). Reaching and locomotion are not necessarily exploratory activities, but they must be regarded as prominent in the service of exploring the world and its furnishings, as I argue below.

THE CONCEPT OF AFFORDANCE AND EXPLORATION

Why, in view of this rich background of theory and research, should we turn again to the topic of exploration? Is there anything new to be said theoretically, or is there a new body of facts to be related? As Jane Austen made Mary Crawford say in *Mansfield Park*, "Every generation has its improvements." The years since 1975 have garnered a vast harvest of research in infant cognition and development, and a significant new concept has arisen. It is thus time to look at exploratory activity again, and to link it to *perceptual* development, to development of *action* (motor skill, if anyone prefers that term), and to *cognitive* development, all three.

The relevant concept is the notion of affordance, introduced by J. J. Gibson (1966, 1979). *Affordance* links perception to action, as it links a creature to its environment. It links both to cognition, because it relates to meaning. Meaning is in the world, as much as in the mind, because meaning involves the appropriateness of an organism's actions to its surroundings. The concept of affordance implies a special approach to psychology, particularly to perception—the ecological approach (J. J. Gibson 1979). An animal, human or otherwise, has evolved and lives in an environment and occupies an ecological niche that it is uniquely specialized for and with which it maintains reciprocal relations. Gibson emphasized the mutuality of animal and environment, as he did also the mutuality of perceiving and acting. The environment affords animals such necessities for existence as terrain, shelters, tools, and other animals. We perceive affordances of the ground to be walked on, of the cup to be drunk from, of the noises, fumes, and onrush of a truck in our path to be avoided.

> The *affordances* of the environment are what it *offers* the animal, what it *provides* or *furnishes,* either for good or ill. The verb to *afford* is found in the dictionary, but the noun

affordance is not. I have made it up. I mean by it something that refers to both the environment and the animal in a way that no existing term does. It implies the complementarity of the animal and the environment (Gibson 1979, p. 127).

Elsewhere I have discussed the term further, with developmental applications (E. J. Gibson 1982). Here I want to link this notion to the development of exploratory activities. When and how do we come to perceive affordances of surfaces, things, places, and events? As a developmental psychologist, I want to know how a child comes to perceive the world so as to keep in touch with the things and events in his environment that afford actions like going places and making use of the objects and people that serve his needs. Perception guides his actions (I take that as given); it tells him what to do, where to go, and how to go where he wants to go. After a decade of research and thought on this problem, I have come to some (to me) rather obvious conclusions. First, nature has not endowed the infant with the ability to perceive these things immediately; babies spend nearly all of their first year finding out a lot about the affordances of the world around them. (Of course, we keep on finding out ever after, though not quite so assiduously.) Second, learning about affordances entails exploratory activities. I develop this idea more fully below and then trace the development of exploratory behavior in the light of recent research.

Implications for Perception, Action, and Cognition

The point of view of this essay is functional, in the old sense, but also in a modern sense that incorporates systems theory. I assume that both information about the environment and action occur over time in a sequence related by some common factor. A sequence of acts termed exploratory will have some outcome and will not be random. It will have a perceptual aspect, a motor aspect, and a knowledge-gathering aspect.

Why is exploratory behavior implicit in perception, in fact an essential part of it? The old view of perception was that "input" from stimuli fell upon the retina, creating a meaningless image composed of unrelated elements. Static and momentary, this image had to be added to, interpreted in the light of past experiences, associated with other images, etc. Such a view of perception dies hard, but die it must. There is no shutter on the retina, no such thing as a static image. Furthermore, perceiving is active, a process of *obtaining* information about the world (J. J. Gibson 1966). We don't simply see, we look. The visual system is a motor system as well as a sensory one. When we seek information in an optic array, the head turns, the eyes turn to fixate, the lens accommodates to focus, and spectacles may be applied and even adjusted by head position for far or near looking. This is a point long emphasized by functional psychologists such as Dewey (1896) and Woodworth (1958). It was developed in detail by Gibson—e.g. in his experiments on active touch

(1962). These adjustments of the perceptual system are often, especially in early life, exploratory in nature because the young creature is discovering optimal means of adjustment. But they may be exploratory even in a skilled observer, because they are used to seek information. We live in interaction with a world of happenings, places, and objects. We can know it only through perceptual systems equiped to pick up information in an array of energy, such as the optical array. Furthermore, time is required for the adjustment of the perceptual system, for the monitoring of the information being acquired, and for the scanning required by most perceptual systems to pick up information (perceiving an object by touching, for example, or locating a sound source through hearing). Information, accordingly, is picked up over time. Thus if a stable world is to be discovered, there must be temporal invariants of some kind that make constancy of perception possible. I take for granted that perceptual acts extend over time. Perceiving and acting go on in a cycle, each leading to the other.

Perception occurs over time and is active. Action participates in perception. Active adjustments in the sensory systems are essential. But action itself may be informative, too. Information about things and events exists in ambient arrays of energy. Actions have consequences that turn up new information about the environment. They also provide information about the actor—about where he is, where he is going, what he is doing. All actions have this property; but it is useful to distinguish *executive* action from action that is *information-gathering*. We tend to think of some perceptual systems and the activities that go on within them as primarily information-gathering. The visual and auditory systems, in particular, seem to have little or no executive function. (There are exceptions. The eyes, for example, are used socially in an executive fashion to signal approbation, displeasure, surprise and so on). Some systems, on the other hand, have on the surface a primary executive function, such as the haptic systems of the mouth and of the hand. The mouth is used for tasting and testing for substantial properties as well as for sucking, eating, and speaking. The hand is used for examining textures, substantial properties of objects, shape, and location, as well as for holding, carrying, and lifting. Because executive functions like lifting can be informative, the distinction between exploratory and executive actions has sometimes been questioned. But it is a useful distinction for a developmental approach. The possibilities of executive action are minimal in very young infants, but research in recent years has made it clear that exploratory activities are available and are used in functional ways even in the newborn.

Executive actions, such as reaching, grasping, and locomotion have their own role in perceptual and cognitive development because they change the affordances of things and places, providing new occasions for information-gathering and for acquiring knowledge about what Tolman referred to as the "causal texture" of the environment (Tolman & Brunswik 1935). Cognition, I suggest, rests on a foundation of knowledge acquired as a result of early exploration of events, people, and things. As the baby's perceptual systems develop, exploratory activities are used to greater and greater advantage to discover the affordances that are pertinent to each phase of development. As new action systems mature, new affordances open up and new "experiments on the world" can be undertaken, with consequences to be observed.

The active obtaining of information that results from the spontaneous actions of the infant is a kind of learning. To say that learning occurs only when actions are repeatedly "reinforced" is to blind ourselves to the most important kind of learning that underlies our accumulation of knowledge about the world and ourselves. Spontaneous self-initiated actions have consequences, and observation of these is supremely educational. Affordances of things generally have to be learned, with the aid of the perceptual systems and exploratory behavior. External reinforcement plays a small role, if any. Intellectual development is built on information-gathering, and this is what young creatures (not only human ones) are predestined to do. They have structures, action patterns, and perceptual systems that are either ready to start doing this at birth or grow into it in a highly adaptive sequence during the first year (in human infants). These activities continue as play through the pre-school years and as deliberate learning in later life, but the serious role they fill is most obvious as they are coming into being. Cognition begins as spontaneous exploratory activity in infancy. Piaget said this long ago. But now research puts a new face on the story.

THE COURSE OF EXPLORATORY DEVELOPMENT: AN OVERALL PERSPECTIVE

A baby is provided by nature with some very helpful equipment to start its long course of learning about and interacting with the world. A baby is provided with an urge to use its perceptual systems to explore the world; and it is impelled to direct attention outward toward events, objects and their properties, and the layout of the environment. A baby is also provided with a few ready-to-go exploratory systems, but these change and develop as sensory processes mature and as new action systems emerge. There is an order in this development that has interesting implications for cognitive growth. As new actions become possible, new affordances are brought about; both the information available and the mechanisms for detecting it increase.

Exploratory development during the first year of life occurs as a sequence of phases that build the infant's knowledge of the permanent features of the world, of the predictable relations between events, and of its own capacities for acting on objects and intervening in events. The three phases that I am about to suggest are not stages, in a Piagetian sense. They overlap, change is not "across the board," and absolute timing varies tremendously from one infant to another. They depend heavily in at least one case on growth in anatomical structure. Nevertheless, an order is apparent that gives direction to development and makes clear how perceptual and action systems cooperate in their development to promote cognitive growth.

The first phase extends from birth through about four months. During this phase the neonate focuses attention on events in the immediate visual surround, within the layout commanded by its limited range of moving gaze. Sensory capacities and exploratory motor abilities are geared to this task, and some serendipitous possibilities for preliminary learning about features of the grosser layout exist. Visual attention to objects is minimal, but discovery of some basic properties of objects is made possible by visual attention to motion and by the active haptic system of mouthing. Sounds accompanying events are attended to. It is most impressive that these early exploratory systems, rudimentary as they seem, appear well coordinated.

The second phase, beginning around the fifth month, is a phase of attention to objects. Development of the manual exploratory system makes reaching and grasping possible. By the same time visual acuity has increased, and stereoscopic information for depth is available. Objects, though presented in a static array, can be explored and their affordances and distinctive features learned.

The third phase, beginning around the eighth or ninth month, expands attention to the larger layout, which can only be explored as the baby becomes ambulatory. Spontaneous, self-initiated locomotion makes possible discovery of properties of the extended environment around corners, behind obstacles, and behind oneself. Affordances of places for hiding, escaping, and playing are open for investigation. Watching a two-year-old on a playground is a relevation of attention to affordances of things like swings, ladders, bridges, and ropes.

After the first year, other phases might be identified—e.g. exploring devices that have complicated affordances like mirrors, and tools that must be carried to other objects as well as manipulated. Research is still scanty in this area. There is also the whole domain of speech development, in which exploratory activity plays an extensive role during the first year (see chapters by Stark, and by Oller in Yeni-Komshian et al 1980). This domain I reluctantly leave to the experts.

Phase 1: Neonates Explore Events

Very young infants attend preferentially to visually presented movement (e.g. an object moving across the field of view, or a flickering light) Static objects or scenes generally arouse little interest. An infant's visual acuity for static two-dimensional displays is poor for the first several months and increases only gradually during the first year (Banks & Salapatek 1983). This handicap was long thought to incapacitate the young infant almost to the point of blindness and prevent it from learning much about the world. We know now that this is by no means the case; not only are other perceptual systems functioning, but the baby picks up information from motion in the optical array as it regards events taking place before it, such as a caretaker approaching, or things receding, disappearing behind other things, and reappearing as the baby is carried or wheeled about. I describe briefly what kinds of exploratory activity are possible over the first few months and then consider three basic questions about the meaning and value of this activity. First, is the neonate's activity externally directed; is it really exploring the world? Second, is this activity in any way controlled by the infant, or is it compulsory reflexive response to stimulation? And third, are there any cognitive consequences of the activity? Is a rudimentary foundation of knowledge being acquired, or is the baby merely exercising its receptor organs as it awaits maturation of cognitive competence? If it is acquiring knowledge, knowledge about what?

What can infants before the fifth month do by way of exploratory action? From birth, infants can scan the layout visually by moving the head and eyes, albeit relatively unskillfully. Studies of scanning movements of the eyes in newborns suggest that they are preprogrammed to "search" and are spontaneously active, rather than stimulated reflexly (Haith 1980). The evidence has been presented in detail elsewhere (Banks & Salapatek 1983; Gibson & Spelke 1983; Haith 1980). The eyes are sufficiently coordinated to maintain a gaze on a moving target, and on a static one when the baby is being moved itself (Owen & Lee 1986). Neonates are most likely to look at a moving object and are able to track it. Although visual pursuit and head movements are jerky at first, the movements of head and eyes are aimed and coordinated (Tronick & Clanton 1971). The neonate's visual field when the head is still and the eyes fixate a stationary display is limited peripherally, both vertically and horizontally (only 15–20° to either side of the line of regard), and is limited as to the distance of the target. However, the field is wider and the distance can be greater for a moving object of regard (Tronick 1972), and the head moves to keep the object in view (Bullinger 1977). Tronick concluded, after extensive research on looking patterns in infants 2–10 weeks old,

> The infant's effective visual field is directly related to the nature of events available for registration. Motion is a more effective producer of attention—more easily registered in the peripheral field, more compelling in the focal field. Initially, the field is quite small, but motion is already more effective in either the periphery or the center of the field. With increasing age, the areal limits increase, but only in relation to the stimulus conditions (Tronick 1972, p. 375).

Visual "capture" of a moving object improves during early infancy (Burnham & Dickinson 1981) and is affected by various conditions, such as the speed of the target. Very likely it is also affected by other aspects of events, such as accompanying sounds.

Events can usually be heard as well as seen, and the baby's exploratory head and eye movements may be elicited by such sounds as a human voice. The head turns toward a sound source, and the eyes open (Butterworth & Castillo 1976; Field et al 1980; Alegria & Noirot 1978). The looking and listening systems appear coordinated from the start and unite in attending to the same event. Further evidence for coordinated auditory-visual exploration comes from research using a looking-preference method. Spelke (1976) found that four-month-old infants presented with two filmed events placed side by side looked preferentially at the one matching a sound track, although the sound source was midway between the two. There is some evidence that infants in the second month look preferentially at the face of a person simultaneously articulating an appropriate speech sound (Kuhl & Meltzoff 1982) given a choice of two faces.

In addition to the eye-head exploratory system, neonates have a haptic exploratory system. The mouth is a versatile organ, used for tasting, sucking, vocalizing, and examining the textures and substantial properties of things placed in it. Rochat (1983) demonstrated that infants explore with this system soon after birth. He observed sucking and exploratory responses to an intra-oral stimulus in one-, two-, and three-month-old infants, and described the perceptual activity of the mouth and tongue as "a distinct pattern of oral behavior corresponding to movements and scannings of tongue and lips relative to the intra-oral stimulus" (p. 124). At one month, infants distinguished differences in the texture or substance of a nipple, but not in its shape. At three months, infants distinguished nipples that varied in global shape. Rochat concluded that there was a "distinctly perceptual function of the mouth, inherent in the exploratory response." This activity is not reflexive, since it is modulated in character and varies in response to context.

Like visual and auditory exploration, oral exploration is probably pre-coordinated with other systems to some extent. A study of hand-to-mouth activity in newborns (Butterworth et al 1985) showed that spontaneous arm movements consist in a direct motion of the hand to the mouth about 15% of the time; the mouth is held wide open from the start of the movement, apparently in anticipation of the hand. It might be thought that the mouth and the hand, because they are both haptic exploratory organs, have a similar function and substitute for one another. This is not the case at an early age, however. The hand only achieves exploratory skill at around five months, and it is used for transferring objects to the mouth for examination until the end of the first year. Rochat & Gibson (1985) compared discrimination of two substances (one hard, one soft) by neonates (newborns and babies two and three months old) when the object was placed in the mouth and when it was placed in the hand. The substances appeared to be discriminated in both cases, but the patterns of exploration were different. The hand squeezed the hard object more often; the mouth pressed harder on the soft one.

The visual system may be able to obtain some of the same information as the oral exploratory system in another form of precoordination. Meltzoff & Borton (1979) reported evidence that infants of 29 days could visually discriminate objects previously explored orally when the objects differed in shape and texture. This study has proved hard to replicate, perhaps because stationary visually presented shapes are poorly attended to by infants of this age. However, Gibson & Walker (1984) found that infants of one month, given a hard or a soft substance to explore orally, and subsequently given a visual preference test with two objects moving either in a pattern characteristic of rigid objects or in one characteristic of flexible, squeezy objects, prefered the novel substance. Type of motion produced by exerting pressure on different substances is both visually and haptically perceptible. Information for the different affordances may be represented amodally.

It seems likely that oral exploration of gustatory stimuli occurs in neonates, since there is evidence for some taste discrimination (e.g. preference for sweetened fluids); but the activity itself has been little studied. It was found in our laboratory (Andrea Messina 1985; unpublished manuscript) that infants of three months presented orally with a small plastic cylinder dipped in fruit juice tend actively to lick the cylinder. Habituation may be demonstrated using this spontaneous activity, and dishabituation may occur to a novel compound.

IS EXPLORATION EXTERNALLY DIRECTED?   Now, consider the first of my three questions. Are these systems externally directed in early infancy? Or, as Piaget held, are young infants egocentric, not differentiating themselves from external, objective things and happenings? Can any factual argument be made that neonates can explore the world?

Evidence from the visual system alone supports such an argument. Infants from eight weeks up (perhaps earlier) have been found to track an object visually only when it moves relative to a background. If the background moves along with the object, tracking is disrupted (Harris et al 1974). The object is evidently seen as located in, and moving with respect to, a spatial layout. The baby is not just responding to motion as such (see also Owen & Lee 1986). Action of a limb in coordination with the tracking or fixation is even more convincing evidence that the event is placed in the external environment. The ability to reach for and grasp an object, in the sense of an executive action, does not mature until about the fifth month. But experiments have been reported which assert that neonates may extend an arm and even a hand toward a stationary object, occasionally managing to touch it, as if attempting to grasp the object. A picture of the same object did not elicit similar reaching. (Bower 1972; Bower et al 1979). Attempts to replicate these experiments did not find evidence of reaching or grasping at the object, nor evidence of reaching more toward object than picture, although the infants expressed interest through visual exploration (Dodwell et al 1976, 1979). But as early as 15 weeks, infants reach to nearer targets more often than farther ones, and look significantly longer at an object than at a picture of it (Field 1976). More recently, arm extensions and grasping by young infants during the presentation of *moving* target objects have extended these results. Von Hofsten & Lindhagen (1979) found, surprisingly, that by the time infants had mastered reaching for stationary objects, they also reached successfully for moving ones and caught them at a speed of 30 cm/sec. These infants were about 18 weeks of age. Von Hofsten later studied arm extensions of infants during the very first week of life in response to a moving object (von Hofsten 1982). While these infants certainly did not catch the moving object, meticulous analysis of the spatiotemporal characteristics of the infants' arm extensions as they followed the object with their eyes gave evidence of aim at the object. Von Hofsten concluded that this was an attentional, orienting response rather than an attempt to grasp, but that the coordinated action was unmistakably externally directed.

The coordination of two perceptual systems in response to the same external event is particularly convincing evidence of externally directed attention. It has often been argued that detection of an external event that creates a disturbance in the optic array and results in retinal stimulation is only evidence of sensitivity to proximal stimulation of the receptor and does not necessarily indicate perception of the distal source, the event in the world. But when two systems, such as the auditory and the visual system, cooperate in eliciting exploratory activity, with two different receptor mechanisms involved, such an argument does not apply. The two systems are both locating the event somewhere in the world, uniting in detecting its affordance. The same argument applies for visual-haptic coordination. Oral haptic exploration of an object followed by visual exploration that results in detection of the same property of the object, such as rigidity of substance, indicates perception of an external, objective property of the object, since the perception is not modality (i.e. receptor) specific. There is evidence for such recognition at one month of age.

The ultimate argument for perception of events as external distal happenings in the world is appropriate, adaptive response to them in the face of changing context. This brief survey of exploratory activity in neonates can be supplemented by evidence from a number of studies of response to an approaching object on a collision course. Bower et al (1971) and Ball & Tronick (1971) found that very young infants (2 months or less) responded defensively to an approaching object that filled the optic array with an accelerating expansion pattern. This response (head retraction, raising of hands, etc) did not occur for an expansion pattern on a "miss" course. Yonas (1981) has summarized the developmental course of this defensive behavior. It increases over several months in differentiation and organization, but it occurs in a primitive form soon after birth, providing an example of perception of the affordance of an external event at a very early age.

ARE INFANTS' EXPLORATORY RESPONSES REFLEXIVE OR CONTROLLED? The S-R psychologists in the first half of this century generally viewed activity of the neonate as composed of reflexes, compulsory responses to stimuli. Although Piaget would not willingly have allied himself with their view, he nevertheless felt that activity began with reflexes and that controlled spontaneous exploration developed only later as intentional activity. My view in this essay differs; early exploratory activities are immature and unskilled, but they do appear to be spontaneous and directed. They may be controlled appropriately very early by contextual factors.

Methods for studying perception in infants only began to bear fruit when experimenters realized that they could use natural exploratory activity to tell them whether the infants were or were not capable of extracting information from events presented to them. Two behaviors—turning the head and eyes to look, and exploratory mouthing—were found to be appropriate and useful indicators of perceptual competence (or lack of it). Looking responses have been used as indicators with preference paradigms (Fantz 1961), habituation paradigms (Horowitz 1974), and contingent-learning paradigms in which infants learned to turn their heads appropriately to look at an interesting display (Papoušek 1967; Siqueland & Lipsitt 1966). Sucking has also been used in contingent-learning paradigms in which infants learned to suck at high amplitudes to elicit an interesting visual or vocal event (Siqueland & DeLucia 1969; Eimas et al 1971). Innumerable ingenious variations of these paradigms have resulted in our present rich accumulation of data on infant perception. All these paradigms have been used successfully well before infants are capable of grasping and handling objects, and they demonstrate neonatal control of exploratory activity.

A few examples suffice to demonstrate control.[1] Siqueland & DeLucia

---

[1]Many other examples of early establishment of control of exploratory behavior could be given. For example, a spontaneous action system, kicking, can play a role in directed exploratory behavior. A ten-week-old infant learns in a few moments to double or triple the amplitude of kicks in order to view a mobile over its head in motion (Rovee & Rovee 1969).

(1969) performed experiments with infants from three weeks to one year of age in which high-amplitude nonnutritive sucking resulted in appearance of a projected slide of a cartoon figure, geometric pattern, or human face. Four-month-old infants quickly learned to suck at criterion rates to look at the slides, and reduced the rate when slides were withdrawn. After an extinction phase (no slides), the rate rose again at once on reintroduction of slides. Similar experiments with visual consequences ensuing upon control of sucking rate demonstrated "motivated exploratory behavior with infants as young as 3 weeks of age" (Siqueland & DeLucia 1969, p. 1146).

Very young infants not only want to look at interesting events, they like to see them as clearly as possible. They detect an out-of-focus presentation and show a preference for one in focus (Atkinson et al 1977). Kalnins & Bruner (1973) showed that infants would even act spontaneously to control clarity of a visual scene presented to them. They showed infants aged 5–12 weeks a color film whose clarity of focus was made contingent on sucking rate. When the baby sucked for a clear focus, the rate increased very fast and remained high as long as focus was maintained. When sucking resulted in a blur, no such increase occurred. When the condition was reversed, sucking rate dropped. The authors concluded:

> What is striking about the adaptation we have observed is its swiftness in establishment and its equally great swiftness in being transformed when conditions change. In all the above respects it seems reasonable to suppose that, just as the sensory-perceptual and sensory-motor capacities of the very young infant have been seriously underestimated because of failure to use the correct behavioural repertory for measurement, so too, and for the same reason, has the voluntarily-controlled problem-solving activity of the infant been similarly underestimated (p. 313).

The actions observed in these experiments do not savor of anything reflex or random, but rather show modulation due to observation of the consequences of exploratory activity of the kind that we expect of intentionally controlled behavior. This quality of the activity reminds us of control of attention in adults. As adults we can select what we choose to attend to. Can an infant explore the environment with sufficient competence to ignore one visually presented event and observe another selected one when the events are literally superimposed on one another, as adults are able to do (Neisser & Becklen 1975)? The question was explicitly addressed in an experiment by Bahrick et al (1981) with four-month-old infants. An intermodal preference paradigm (Spelke 1976) was used. Two films of interesting events were presented superimposed, while one soundtrack was played to influence the selective attention to one of them. If the baby could attend primarily to one film, ignoring the other, it should have become more familiar with that event. Following the superimposed presentation, the two films were presented side by side, in silence. If the baby looked preferentially now at the film that had been unaccompanied by sound, it might be inferred that it was selecting a novel event to look at. This was the case. Bahrick et al concluded that four-month-old infants can selectively attend to one complex visual event while ignoring another superimposed upon it, a remarkable example of controlled exploratory activity.

CONSEQUENCES FOR COGNITION   What does this motivation and ability to observe external events buy the neonate in terms of acquiring knowledge about the world? Does he perceive anything that gives him knowledge of objects and the spatial layout of things? What can his limited exploratory skill and relative dependence on movement in the visual surround permit him to discover for founding a knowledge base? Despite poor visual acuity for stationary displays, little if any functional use of binocular disparity, and inability to handle objects and bring them close in front of the eyes, sensitivity to motion in the optic array provides a surprising amount of useful information for an actively exploring perceiver. Retinal disparity does not provide the only information about depth and about where things are in relation to the perceiver and to one another. Kinetic information is useful, and young infants do use it before they can use either stereoscopic or so-called pictorial cues for the solidity and distance of things (Yonas & Granrud 1984). As an infant moves his head or as things move around in the area accessible to his gaze, motion parallax provides optical information about depth. As one thing goes behind another, accretion and deletion at edges provide information about which item is behind the other. This information is used to determine that one surface is in front of another by infants at five months, according to a study using preferential reaching as a response indicator (Granrud et al 1984). Using the habituation method, younger infants (three months) were shown to discriminate one form from another on the basis of kinetic information (Kaufmann-Hayoz et al 1986). The form's outline was delineated by motion through a field of random dots, producing accretion and deletion of texture at contours. Habituated infants were shown to transfer recognition of the form's outline to a static black and white drawing of it by remaining habituated, and by dishabituating to the drawing of a different form. Thus kinetic information serves to reveal structure by way of contours at three months. Common motion of dots in the form's contours could also contribute to perceived unity of the figure. When a static-to-moving order of habituation was compared, no recognition was found. At this age, static forms are less likely to be attended to and perceived as a whole; perception of them may even depend on preceding detection by means of kinetic information.

Can infants use information provided by motion to detect three-dimensional solid form at this age? Kellman (1984) demonstrated that at 16 weeks they can. His subjects were habituated to a videotaped three-dimensional object rotating successively on two axes of rotation in depth, thus giving rise to a sequence of optical projective transformations. After habituation, they were tested with the same object rotating around a third, new axis, and with an object of a different shape. The infants generalized habituation to the same object, showing that they recognized it even in different transformations; but they dishabituated to the new one. By contrast, infants who were shown stationary views of the object taken from the same transformation sequences did not generalize to the new transformations of the same object, showing the importance of kinetic information.

Can infants obtain the same information by moving their gaze themselves so as to achieve kinetic optical information in the case of spontaneous visual exploration? Kellman & Short (1986) in a later experiment moved the infant in an arc around a static target object. The axes were alternated as before by changing the attachment of the object to the axis on which it was mounted. As before, when motion perspective was available in the optical transformations, the object's shape was recognized and discriminated from another, but not when only static views of successive transformations were available. Furthermore, the infants' looking times did not differ in the moving and static conditions, strong evidence that they perceived the object as stationary and themselves as moving. A third point to note from these experiments is that the infants were exhibiting object constancy, since they recognized the object as the same despite presentation of varied transformations. It is possible, though not so likely, that shape constancy may be perceived under static conditions at this age, but it surely is when optical motion is involved in presentations.

A question that has been little addressed in research on perceptual development is that of how perceived unity of objects comes about. There seems little doubt that infants perceived as units the objects presented under conditions of optical motion in the experiments just described, since there was generalization of habituation to new presentations that varied in the specific retinal image projected. What are the conditions for perceived unity? Kellman & Spelke (1983; Kellman et al 1986) investigated this question by presenting infants with partly occluded objects and testing whether the objects were perceived as whole and unitary by observing generalization of habituation to a complete, unoccluded object in contrast to the object broken so as to present a gap between the two parts that were visible during occlusion. In one condition of habituation, the object moved behind its occluder, translating either laterally, vertically, or in depth, but in another it did not. Infants of four months perceived the occluded object as a connected unit when it moved behind the occluder, but not when it remained static. Common motion of parts thus serves as information for unity of objects, and separates them perceptually from surrounding objects. It will be noted that the condition of common motion was present and may have played a role in the experiments on perception of the shape of moving figures and objects described above.

These points are underlined and extended in an elegant experiment by Kellman et al (1987) performed with four-month-old subjects. Another question is addressed as well. Kellman et al asked whether the infant could distinguish between its own motion and motion of an object in the layout, making use of their method of investigating perception of object unity. It is a fact described by J. J. Gibson forty years ago (Gibson 1947) that movement of an observer results in optical motion of a deforming character (e.g. expansion or contraction) over the total optical array, while motion of an object in the layout results in a local displacement relative to its background. An adult easily distinguishes the two, even when both occur together. The disturbance of the whole array specifies motion of the self, while the local displacement specifies motion of an object within the layout, relative to its background. Kellman et al placed the infant in a seat that moved in an arc around a partially occluded facing object, a stick. When the stick was moved to and fro behind the partially occluding screen, the baby could be moved conjugately. Would the baby perceive itself as moving separately from the stick, or would it perceive egocentrically, detecting only one movement to and fro? The babies did indeed differentiate self from object motion, since they perceived the object as a unit when it moved, whether they themselves were moved conjugately or not, and perceived it as broken when it did not move, again whether they were moving or not. They also looked longer at a moving stick, whether or not they themselves were in motion. This competence has important implications. Infants at 16 weeks show position constancy as regards the layout of things around them (that is, ability to locate themselves in relation to it), and perceive real object motion during self-movement. They use the motion of the object, at the same time, to establish the unity of a partly occluded object.

The kind of optical motion elicited by self-movement is generally referred to as "optical flow." It has great usefulness for guiding movement through an environmental layout because it can at the same time specify where things are as an observer moves and provide information about the observer himself (Gibson 1979). There is only scanty research to date on the development of the ability to use such information. Deliberate exploratory use of body movement that produces optical flow has not been studied in infants, although they have been informally observed to use appropriate head and torso motions to "see around" things in, for example, peekaboo games (E. J. Gibson 1969). A recent line of research has established that optic flow from head and body movements is used to monitor and maintain postural equilibrium by infants just beginning to walk (Lee & Aronson 1974; Stoffregen et al 1987) and even by considerably younger ones (Butterworth & Hicks 1977). Butterworth & Pope (1982) observed such an effect at two months. This use of optic flow is automatic, rather than exploratory, but it is another indication of competence in the perceptual use of optical motion at a very early age.

Another cognitive consequence of the neonate's competence in perceiving events involving movement is the opportunity for detecting sequential, potentially causal relations between events—what follows what, as Tolman would have put it (Tolman & Brunswik 1935). Causal relations between events, both self-perpetrated and entirely objective, are an important basis of knowledge about happenings in the world, and provide the foundation for discovering order and regularity. Piaget (1954) argued that the young infant's "feeling of efficacy" of his own actions was the beginning of causal perception. Certainly the earliest convincing evidence relevant to causal understanding lies in the neonate's quick detection of the consequences of his own actions when an outcome is made contingent on them, as described in the Siqueland & DeLucia (1969) and the Kalnins & Bruner (1973) studies. The infant perceives the relation of *affordance* between his own actions and the outcome. Habituation experiments using looking behavior frequently allow the infant subject to set its own criterion for trial length, a method referred to as "infant control" (Horowitz 1974); this procedure works as early as three months. The infant presumably learns to time its exploratory activities so as to control exposure of the displays offered by the experimenter.

What about observing order in the world in totally objective events? If two structurally and temporally related events are presented to an infant observer with sufficient repetition, will a potentially causal relationship be detected? This question is necessarily moot, since the implications of the word "causal" are fraught with philosophical ambiguities. However, a few experimenters have tried presenting infants with displays of a mechanical event similar to the spatiotemporal impact events used by Michotte (1963) to demonstrate direct perception of causality in adults (launching, entraining, etc). In Michotte's experiments, the event presented involved spatial contact of one moving object with another and transmission of force (momentum) from one to the other. A causal event maintained an invariant relation through conservation of momentum—as one object gained velocity, the other lost it. An infringement of this invariant relation achieved by some trick of the experimenter should be perceived as noncausal, while the original event should be perceived as causal. In any case, a violation of the invariant relation should be detected if causal relations can be perceived. An experiment by Leslie (1982) illustrates an application of this idea in an experiment with 13–38-week-old infants. Infants in one group were habituated to a filmed display of a red brick moving toward, colliding with, and launching a green brick (causal event). In another group, the subjects were habituated to a film of the red brick striking the green one, which then moved off only after a short delay (noncausal event). Following habituation, half the subjects were presented with a film in which the red brick collided with the green one, which remained stationary. The other half were presented with a film in which the green brick moved away from the red one, without any impact. All the films except the first were noncausal, showing either no exchange of momentum or a violation of conservation of momentum. Presumably the group that had first habituated to a direct-launching film should dishabituate to the others, if causal relations were detected, whereas the other (noncausal) habituation group should not. The highest level of dishabituation occurred when the direct-launching film was followed by the film in which the green brick moved away from the red without any impact (red brick didn't move). It is difficult to draw conclusions about perception of causality from this complex experiment. Leslie concluded that the infants distinguished a spatiotemporally continuous movement from a temporally discontinuous one. Leslie's experiments have since been extended to a more natural scene of a hand moving toward a doll to pick it up, with varied spatiotemporal conditions (Leslie 1984).

It is perhaps unreasonable to expect that a very young infant could perceive an objective causal relation directly, without experience. More likely, one learns the rule of conservation of momentum through observation of events involving two objects in a dynamic relation of transmission of energy. It has become fashionable to suppose that human beings, even as infants, are endowed by way of an evolutionary program with prior implicit knowledge of some natural laws of dynamics. However that may be, the neonate's natural tendency to engage in active visual exploration of events presents a magnificent opportunity to detect dynamic relations between moving objects in the environment. The information is available, and as the infant becomes able to differentiate the structure of a complex event he may perceive the affordances for dynamic change within it (E. J. Gibson 1984). Perceiving affordances for action precedes understanding of objective causal relations and possibly plays a role in it. Affordances begin to be perceived early, whereas the ability to distinguish causal relations from other types of events is a long-time cognitive development that has its foundation in early exploratory activity.

Phase 2: Attention to Affordances and Distinctive Features of Objects

Beginning around four to five months, the exploratory activities of infants take on a new aspect, one that appears revolutionary to observant parents and caretakers. An elaborate system for examining objects comes into its own. The appearance of revolutionary change is not deceptive, but that is not to say that there is no continuity of development. The new exploratory system depends on maturation of a number of contributing factors, each with its own time course when considered separately, but they come together at this point to make possible the discovery of a whole new set of affordances.[2] The

[2]This way of viewing the emergence of a radical new achievement is discussed in detail by Thelen (1987).

coordination of the various factors involved and the spontaneity and determination of the action greatly increase the apparent intentionality of an infant's behavior from this time. What are the parts that arrive at this conjunction? The major components are increasing capabilities of the visual system, and development of muscular components involved in reaching, grasping, and fingering. Visual acuity and motor components of tracking and fixating have improved greatly by two months of age (Banks & Salapatek 1983) and by four months are quite competent for visual exploration; at four months or thereabouts, stereopsis is generally mature, and retinal disparity can provide precise information for depth at close hand. At around three months, reaching out toward an object shows signs of readiness, but grasping takes longer and independent fingering longer still. The period between four and five months sees these components getting organized into a superb exploratory strategy that includes oral exploration (already quite competent) as well as visual and manual activity. Objects can be seized and brought before the eyes for close-up visual examination and to the mouth for proficient haptic search. This is the time when babies become interested in objects and reach for them, eager to examine them. The infant is no longer dependent on motion to provide information in an optic array, nor on actions of others to bring things close enough for oral exploration. As the hands become active and controllable, a whole new set of affordances is opened up for the baby's discovery; things can be displaced, banged, shaken, squeezed, and thrown—actions that have informative consequences about an object's properties.

There have been numerous studies of exploratory manipulation of objects during this period—classic older studies and more recent ones that emphasize the kind of information that can be obtained, and the coordination of modal information. Kopp (1974) summarized work of her own and earlier work on exploratory activities around eight months as follows:

> There is no question that manipulative activities do have attentional and informative value for infants. It has also been suggested that modulated motor behaviors free the organism to focus attention on the object of interest, with consequent additional information input. Nevertheless, it is obvious that a considerable amount of learning and information-processing does go on during infancy, mainly through use of the eyes (p. 635).

This observation foreshadows some questions that underlie much of the recent work on development of exploratory activities between five and nine months. Few studies question whether the baby's activities and perception are externally oriented in this period; very recent research confirms that they are (Keating et al 1986). No one questions whether they are intentional. It seems obvious that they are. The questions debated center on (a) what is the relation between various modal systems, or types of information, especially visual and haptic; (b) what is it that the baby is learning; and (c) whether exploratory activity in this period predicts future cognitive development. I do not summarize studies of detailed development of motor skill during this period, although skill obviously increases. Instead I consider these questions.

INTERMODAL ASPECTS OF EXPLORATORY ACTIVITY   Some of the questions about intermodal relations are old ones. When do babies make use of sounds in search behavior (Uzgiris & Benson 1980; Freedman et al 1969)? Does touch teach vision, or does vision dominate everything else? Are modal systems "integrated" to build, finally, a coordinated schema (Piaget 1954)? Today the questions seem to be asked in a less general style and with more emphasis on defining the information, control of behavior, and cognitive outcome.

Intermodal exploration is not new to this period of growth, as we noted in surveying exploratory behavior in the earlier period; but with increasing skill and new coordinations available, it may be different. A number of studies have confirmed earlier findings that novel objects motivate exploration (e.g. Willats 1983; Ruff 1984), but will the recognition of novelty persist over a shift in the mode of the pick-up system? There was some evidence that it did in one-month-old infants (e.g. Gibson & Walker 1984), but availability of multiple systems may bring about specialization of modes of exploration as experience with them is gained. Studies have reported intermodal transfer in four- to five-month-old infants (Streri & Pêcheux 1986b; Streri & Spelke, in press). Streri & Pêcheux showed that five-month-old infants were capable of intra-modal tactual discrimination of shape by manual exploration (1986a) and then went on to examine cross-modal recognition of the object explored (1986b). They found evidence of generalization of habituation from visual exploration to manual, but not vice versa. Five months is about as early as active manual exploration can be expected in infants, and it is obviously far from its peak of skill at that time. It is noteworthy that Streri & Pêcheux (1986a) found that tactual habituation required much more time than visual (about three times as long), possibly because infants at this age may simply hold the object some of the time without actively exploring it. Even a month of experience with manual exploration may bring greater skill and change results, since other experimenters have found transfer from touch to vision at six months (Ruff & Kohler 1978; Rose et al 1981). The fact of transfer from vision to touch but not vice versa at five months suggests that skill in pick-up of information in one mode may facilitate the process in a less-developed mode, analogous to visual discrimination of a stationary form following observation of a dynamic, moving presentation of the same form in younger infants (Kaufmann-Hayoz et al 1986).

A developmental process of another kind may be at work here, as well. As infants acquire skill in manipulating an object, and bring it before the eyes for visual examination of its properties, opportunities occur for differentiating unique experiential qualities that arise via haptic versus visual exploration. Infants at about six months do not always show consistent novelty preferences in cross-modal experiments where touch precedes vision. There are modality-specific attributes of objects, such as color, and these specificities may begin to be differentiated about this time. Walker-Andrews & Gibson (1986) described experiments with 1-, 6-, and 12-month-old subjects that tend to support this suggestion. The 1-month-old infants were familiarized with a substance (rigid or deformable) orally and were then given a visual preference test with two objects that differed in type of motion presented, one moving rigidly, the other deforming. The infants looked reliably more often to the one exhibiting the novel type of movement. Twelve-month-old infants were given either a rigid or deformable substance for manual exploration, followed by a visual preference test presented pictorially (a movie of two objects moving appropriately). These older infants looked reliably more often at the familiarized type of motion, not the novel one. Infants of six months, with real objects to look at, tended to show a novelty preference, but not all did. Infants of 12 months, with a real object to look at, showed a shift toward a familiarity preference, though not as pronounced as when the presentation was pictured. It appeared that the older infants detected modality-specific properties that made the haptic and visual experiences different, but also recognized the similar affordance that both haptic and visual information specified and were concerned with *congruence* as well as novelty.[3]

The influence of modality-specific properties on exploratory activity and resulting novelty or familiarity preferences was the subject of research by Bushnell et al (1985). Earlier studies investigating the concordance of visual and tactual exploration produced conflicting results, but a study by Steele & Pederson (1977) suggested an explanation. Presented with a novel object following familiarization, an infant's exploratory activities, visual or tactual, may be guided by the type of new information introduced. If the new object differs from the old one in only one property, and that one modality-specific (e.g. color), an infant old enough to differentiate modal properties might be expected to apply only the most appropriate exploratory system. Bushnell et al investigated the differential sensitivity of six-month-old infants to modality-specific properties (color and temperature) combined in a single object, a plastic vial containing warm or cool water, covered with either red or blue paper. The infants were familiarized with a single vial, which they could examine both visually and haptically, and then given two test trials, one

---

[3]"Duality" of perception, detection of both similarity and differences, occurs in a somewhat analogous situation with three-dimensional objects and two-dimensional representations of them in six-month-old infants (Rose 1977; 1986).

familiar and one novel. The novel trial was a vial differing in only one respect, either color or temperature, from the familiarized vial. When temperature was the property changed, there was a significant increase in both touching and looking; but when color was changed, there was no increase in either type of exploratory behavior. These infants had at six months a coordinated pattern of looking and touching that was applied when a novel "tactual" property was introduced, so visual and haptic attentive processes were not differentiated in this respect. The coordinated exploratory pattern is just at its peak, and the little vials afford handling, which in this case was accompanied by looking as well. The curious fact that a color change elicited no fresh burst of exploration is not totally unexpected. Color receptivity is mature well before six months, but color does not appear to be an important factor in defining affordances of objects at this stage and was not differentiated as specifying anything important. Indeed, when one considers the action repertory of a six-month-old, what could color signify? Finding and securing something warm to the touch is a different matter. This does not mean that visual information is not important—optical specification of substance, shape, and where something is located certainly is important. Perception is selective at six months, but not in purely sensory respects; exploratory activity is geared to affordances of objects.

There is evidence that exploration is refined and differentiated with respect to object properties during the period from 6 to 12 months. Ruff (1984) performed experiments on 6-, 9-, and 12-month-old infants, studying their manipulative exploration of objects varying in shape, texture, and color, and making detailed observations of specific behaviors during visual and haptic examination (e.g. looking at an object while rotating it) and mouthing (e.g. taking an object out of the mouth and turning it or looking at it before mouthing it again). The general method was to allow the infants to become familiarized with an object and then present them with one differing in a single property. There were age differences, such as a decrease in mouthing and an increase in fingering between 6 and 12 months, and the influence of specific object characteristics was particularly apparent. For example, more fingering (rubbing fingers over the object) occurred when texture changed. Mouthing and transferring from hand to hand were prominent with shape change. The older infants dramatically increased the amount of rotation for a shape change, thus enhancing the opportunity to observe new object features both visually and haptically. In short, the infants appeared to maximize opportunities for picking up information about a specific change, varying their actions for different object properties. There was no suggestion that one method of exploration or one sensory system had priority, but rather that differentiation of exploratory methods was developing in relation to distinctive properties of objects.

The question about differentiation of specific (including modality-specific) properties can be asked with respect to affordances. Does an infant learn to differentiate affordances of objects as this period of active manipulation goes on? Some objects afford banging (especially if they are rigid, make a sharp impact on a rigid surface, and create a noise), some are squeezable because they are elastic and yielding, changing shape when pressed. Gibson & Walker (1984) noted the appropriate occurrence of such differential exploratory activity in 12-month-old infants presented with rigid or elastic objects in the dark. Palmer (1985) asked this question in a program of research with infants 6, 9, and 12 months of age. The babies were presented (in the light) with objects differing in texture, size, and other properties that afforded varied actions or had different consequences (e.g. a bell with and without a clapper). There was indication of exploration, both visual and haptic, relevant for acquiring knowledge of and exploiting appropriate uses of the objects (but not necessarily imitative of adult uses). The specificity of actions relevant to properties of objects increased during the 6- to 12-month interval. The evidence suggested that as manual exploration becomes more expert, it becomes less redundant with visual exploration of an object, the two exploratory systems being used to supplement one another with respect to modality-specific properties.

Along with maximization of actions suited to object properties, motor skills of manipulation increase—for example, skill in using two hands in parallel for manipulation (Willats 1985) and skill in catching moving objects (von Hofsten 1983; von Hofsten & Lindhagen 1979). Von Hofsten showed that infants were capable of catching a moving object as soon as they could reach and grasp a stationary object, and that their reaches correctly predicted the velocity of the distal object. But motor skills improved, enabling capture of faster-moving objects along with more economical movements of the catcher. Affordances depend both on information available to the perceiver and on the developmental status of the perceiver's action system.

WHAT IS LEARNED? COGNITIVE CONSEQUENCES   What is the infant learning during this period of object exploration about the things in the world around it? I have already suggested that active exploration of objects, leading to observable consequences and more specialized exploratory activities, has important results for learning about what an object affords, what can be done with it, its functional possibilities and uses. It also provides the optimal conditions for learning about distinctive features of objects—what figural features make them unique and how they resemble or do not resemble other knowledge is the basis, potentially, for classifying things. I (E. J. Gibson 1969) that learning the distinctive features of sets of objects (like faces) and pictured things (like letters) was the principal means of perceptual learning. I would now put this notion in a perspective that includes active exploration and observation of consequences leading to detection of affordances. Functional properties may be recognized by acquaintance with an object's distinctive features. Simply learning about identities of things is important, too. Recognition of things as the same when they are represented, as having a certain identity and uniqueness, is cognitively extremely economical. Abstractions about the dimensional properties by which objects differ (e.g. size, color, and weight) become apparent as the process of differentiating and identifying objects goes on, a useful kind of knowledge in its own right. In short, the cognitive consequences of this phase of intensive exploration of the objects at hand are enormous. The process of learning to identify objects, learning what can be done with them, and learning how categories of objects that share affordances can be formed furnishes the world with meaningful things.

All this knowledge is about things, however. Does learning about objects and their properties have any cognitive consequences for the understanding of events and causal relations? I think it may. As Leslie (1982) pointed out in studies of detection of causal relations by young infants, perceiving that one object propels another or "launches" it implies perceiving two movement components as distinguishable. Events may be perceived very early as dynamic changes over time, but much then remains to be learned—i.e. how to differentiate the structure of events and the roles of objects within them. Perceiving the role of an object implies detection of a potential affordance by means of active exploration. Discovering the uses of tools is a case in point. Using even a simple tool is at a minimum a two-step event—an action that serves as a means to a further step of reaching something desirable, perhaps. Piaget's observations of his own children included many such cases.

A recent study by Willats (1985), in the Piagetian tradition, investigated learning to pull on a piece of fabric underneath an object in order to bring the object within reach. The fabric supporting the object can be thought of as a simple tool, to be used as a means to a desired end. Willats presented babies at six, seven, and eight months with a toy placed on a reachable cloth, the toy either 30 or 60 cm distant. At six months, few infants showed evidence of intentional use of the supporting cloth by pulling on it, although they often retrieved the toy in the nearer position as a result of playing with the cloth in an exploratory fashion. By eight months, nearly all the infants rapidly retrieved the toy in both conditions with a single pull, or with rapidly executed short ones. The infants (the same ones, observed longitudinally) had learned the affordance of the cloth as a tool, and thereby gained knowledge about the function of supports in potential events.

ASSESSMENT AND EVALUATIVE USES OF EXPLORATORY ACTIVITY   It is often reported by people who work with a retarded population that these individuals lack normal exploratory motives and do not spontaneously seek out new information as we expect normal children to do. Attempts to teach them the uses of unfamiliar objects seem more successful when routines resembling classical conditioning or repetition with application of external rewards are adopted. One can surmise that, in evolutionary terms, exploratory activity insures cognitive development. This observation has led to research comparing exploratory activities in normally developing infants and infants at risk (e.g. preterms) or infants with delayed development linked to genetic or other defects.

Studies of preterm infants tend to find a negative relationship between premature birth and exploratory activity, but only when qualified by the degree of risk involved. Ruff et al (1984) compared 30 preterms, aged nine months, with 20 nine-month-old full-term infants. The preterm infants were divided into high- and low-risk groups on the basis of respiration at birth, neurological patterns, and neurobehavioral assessment. The low-risk group resembled the full-term infants in patterns of exploratory activity. The high-risk group differed from both the other groups, engaging in less handling of objects and less fingering, rotation, and transferral of objects from hand to hand. A summary exploration score correlated very significantly with measures of cognitive functioning at 24 months. It is possible, as Ruff et al (1984) speculate, that the less infants learn by active exploration of object properties, the less they will engage in categorization of objects, which in turn could lead to retardation of language development.

A study by MacTurk et al (1985) compared infants with Down Syndrome (mean age 9.2 months) with nondelayed infants (mean age 6 months) on tasks involving manipulation of complex commercial toys. They reported that the nondelayed sample displayed a significantly greater number of exploratory and social behaviors, while the Down Syndrome infants looked at the toys more frequently without manipulation. The nondelayed infants exhibited more persistence in achieving some outcome afforded by the toy, such as securing a small object from a hole or behind a barrier, or producing sounds from the object. Nevertheless, both groups exhibited persistent, goal-directed behaviors. Behavior of the Down group appeared to be organized around looking, while social behavior apparently played a greater role for the nondelayed group.

A study by Loveland (1987) provides a detailed analysis of exploritory activity in older Down Syndrome children (mental age 16–32 months) in a task exploiting discovery of the affordances of a mirror. This process requires perceptual learning that takes place in the course of exploration, and eventually results in knowledge such as rules governing what to do to locate objects reflected in the mirror. Exploration must eventually involve more sophisticated strategies than the manipulatory activities characteristic of infants in the second half of their first year. Nevertheless, Loveland's results parallel those from studies of exploration in younger children. The exploratory activities engaged in when searching for a toy reflected in the mirror do not differ spectacularly between the Down sample and a nondelayed comparison group, but strategies of exploration are different. When presented with the reflection of their mother or a toy in the mirror, the nondelayed children looked back and forth comparing the person or toy with the image significantly more often than the Down Syndrome children. Exploratory patterns characteristic of object manipulation occurred in both groups, but the mirror task is essentially one of spatial exploration and involves moving in the layout and observing changing relations in the mirror in relation to the self. This behavior is more closely related to Phase 3, ambulatory exploration (below), which begins only after exploration of objects has been going on for about four months.

Studies such as these appear to support the conclusion that exploratory activities have important cognitive consequences, expanding the child's knowledge of the world as his repertoire and competence in using exploratory strategies increase.

Phase 3: Ambulatory Exploration—Discovering the Layout

By nine months, an infant is highly competent in looking at, listening to, mouthing, touching, and manipulating objects—all active modes of discovering their properties. But what he can learn is severely limited by his dependence on caretakers to move him from place to place. He can explore his surroundings visually only to the degree that he can turn his head and trunk, although from being carried or wheeled about he may learn some of the consequences of changing position, such as what happens when one moves around a barrier. Nevertheless, a kind of cognitive revolution must result when an infant's horizons are expanded by the acquisition of self-initiated, self-controlled locomotion. A new field of knowledge is opened up and a whole new set of skills must be mastered. A new kind of activity that is both exploratory and performatory becomes available for learning about the larger world.

GUIDING LOCOMOTION   A primary function of perception is the guidance of locomotion. For the crawler, who proceeds with his weight distributed on four limbs except during brief forward pushes, there are two major perceptual requirements: steering around obstacles and through apertures between objects that may clutter the layout, and detecting a safe surface of support for traversal.

Steering   Must steering around obstacles and aiming for openings be learned from scratch when a baby makes her first trips crawling around the layout? Certainly not entirely. We know from a considerable body of research on the "looming" experiment that even pre-reaching infants show avoidance responses as objects approach them on a collision course (Bower et al 1971; Yonas 1981). They may retract their heads, raise their hands, and blink. The behavior does not occur if the object approaches on a "miss" course (Ball & Tronick 1971). The information for the event of imminent collision is a contour expanding in magnitude at an accelerated rate. The expanding flow pattern specifies an approaching obstacle, in the case of the looming experiment an object approaching the subject, as might a vehicle bearing down on a pedestrian. This expansion pattern is not produced by locomotion of the subject, but a similar flow pattern would be produced by locomotion at a constant rate toward an object in one's path. In the latter case, the advancing perceiver must stop, or shift direction toward an aperture or open space. It seems reasonable to suppose that there is transfer on the basis of the expanding flow pattern from early avoidance behavior to locomotion, but it is also likely that a certain amount of exploratory practice in changing course would be required before precision steering is attained. I know of no research on the question.

What about aiming for the gaps between things? An experiment by Carroll & Gibson (1981) with three-month-old infants contrasted the usual looming situation (a solid obstacle approaching) with a similar situation in which a contour identical with that of the obstacle surrounded an aperture. In the case of the obstacle, approach coincided with increasing occlusion of background, while in the case of the aperture, approach coincided with disocclusion, opening up a "vista" (J. J. Gibson 1979, p. 234). Avoidance responses occurred, as would be expected, to the obstacle, but not to approach of the aperture. Instead of retracting the head, babies tended to release head pressure as the aperture came near. Something more is involved in locomotion toward and through an aperture, however. Its size must be estimated. Is it big enough to get through? Is the gap wide enough for this particular body? Such a judgment requires knowing the width of one's own body, in relation to the aperture. This is an important affordance, which must be perceived in analogous situations by adults (e.g. is the ring big enough for the finger; is the opening big enough to get one's hand through?). It seems highly likely that exploratory activity would result in increased skill in this locomotor situation, but research on the problem is only beginning (Palmer 1987).

We know little about steering through a cluttered environment [but see J. J. Gibson (1979) for the rules guiding locomotion]. Aiming toward the center of the flow pattern during locomotion specifies direction of locomotion, and we know that even adults cannot walk in a straight line toward a straight-ahead goal for more than a few seconds with eyes closed. Small children can do this even less well (remember the game of "Pin the tail on the Donkey"?), so they may be even more dependent on optic flow patterns for aiming toward a goal. As yet, there is no research on acquiring the skill in the early stages of walking. Babies solve a detour problem when they must reach around a barrier to secure a toy before they can crawl around it for the same objective (Lockman 1984), so there is some domain specificity linked to putting a new action system to use, despite potential transfer from a familiar affordance. Exploratory trials with the new action system are bound to play a role in developing the new skill.

What the ground affords   Besides keeping on the path to a destination and steering around obstacles and through openings, locomotion over a ground surface requires monitoring of the surface. Does the ground extend ahead, without bumps, drop-offs, or holes? Is it firm and rigid? How do infants engaging in their first solo trips find out what the surface affords for traversal? Earlier studies with the visual cliff (Gibson & Walk 1960) showed that most infants with the ability to crawl will avoid crossing over a simulated drop-off, even though a firm, rigid glass surface extends over it. Optical information specifies a drop-off, and the conflicting haptic evidence for a solid supporting surface is generally insufficient to tempt the infant to move out on it. But what of opaque surfaces that are unfamiliar? The problem has been investigated in a series of experiments with crawling and newly walking infants (Gibson et al 1987). The infants were presented with walkways stretching ahead of them. A baby was placed, seated, at one end of the walkway with the mother serving as the baby's destination at the other. The surface of the walkway could be changed so as to vary its properties. Rigidity of the surface was the major variable. Bipedal locomotion, as compared with crawling, imposes constraints on properties that underlie the affordance of a surface for traversal. The surface rigidity—its resistance to deformation—is such a property. It is potentially specified both optically and haptically, so both visual and haptic exploratory activity could be observed in infant subjects. A rigid surface (strong plywood) was compared with a waterbed, gently agitated. Both were covered with the same patterned fabric. Maintaining upright posture and walking was difficult on the waterbed, although crawling was perfectly feasible. The question was whether the infants capable of bipedal locomotion would explore the surface and detect the difference in affordances, as compared with those only capable of crawling.

Observations of exploratory behavior showed that the walking infants differentiated the two surfaces by longer periods of haptic and visual exploration. They also differentiated them by a longer delay of locomotion, more displacement and evasive activity, and by choosing to walk (rather than crawl) more often over the rigid surface than over the waterbed. The crawlers, however, did not differentiate the two surfaces, except by somewhat longer visual exploration. Infants at both stages of locomotor development did actively explore these surfaces and other unfamiliar surfaces presented in further experiments, but the walking infants also observed the consequences of their exploration in relation to the constraints imposed by bipedal locomotion.

Standing up and walking   What are the constraints imposed by maintaining equilibrium when standing upright, and when moving forward with only one foot on the ground? How does perception facilitate this remarkable feat? Again information in flow patterns plays an essential role, activating compensatory movements that maintain stability. Experiments in a "moving room" subjected infants to optical flow simulating the flow pattern characteristic of falling forward or backward. Infants newly standing alone and even pre-locomotor infants use optical flow to maintain their posture (Lee & Aronson 1974; Butterworth & Hicks 1977). Recent research has shown that flow in the peripheral area of the optic array is critical for compensatory postural adjustment (Stoffregen et al 1987). The affordance of peripheral flow for maintaining stability appears to be differentiated from the affordance of central radial outflow for steering in adults and children over two years, but the differentiation may not be complete much before this time and may depend on exploratory locomotion and practice in walking.

Schmuckler and Gibson (Schmuckler 1987) have investigated the performances of novice and more experienced walkers both standing and walking to a destination where optical flow is imposed in a moving hallway. Subjects were two groups of infants under two years of age, with either a mean of three months experience or a mean of over five months experience walking. They walked to their mothers at the end of either an uncluttered hallway, requiring minimal steering, or a hallway in which two sets of obstacles had to be circumnavigated. Compensatory responses to imposed optical flow were significantly greater with both groups of infants in the case requiring steering. It would seem that a considerable period of exploratory locomotion is needed to perfect skills of upright walking in a cluttered environment such as generally characterizes even a newly walking infant's route in exploring an unfamiliar place.

WHAT IS AROUND THE CORNER   This is the time when an infant turns its attention to the layout of the world that contains itself and other objects and provides the background for events. The furnishings of the layout, unless they are animate or vehicular, generally stay where they are, providing stable landmarks no matter what the small human's viewing point. A child may learn from being carried about that even though he is moved around, the room and what it contains are fixed. But he can learn it far better when he crawls around the chair, peeks out from one side or the other, and moves himself to obtain continuously changing perspectives. He can observe the layout and search 360 degrees around him, and he may become much more aware that the area in which he is moving extends behind him. Optical flow patterns are generated by one's own movements in the layout. These flow patterns provide a kind of interface between the self and the world, because they contain information that specifies both at the same time, permitting "coperception" of the self and the layout. Differentiation of oneself from the surrounding layout has occurred long before this, if it is not innate (Kellman et al 1987), but now multiple opportunities are available for perceiving that *I* am *here, you* are *there,* and *I* can *go* there, a kind of differentiation that underlies learning important cognitive and linguistic distinctions (Loveland 1984).

There is an exhaustive literature on so-called "perspective-taking," inspired by pioneer studies of Piaget and Inhelder. Earlier work assigned development of the ability to appreciate another person's point of view (that it was different from one's own and that what might be visible or occluded for that person was not the same as for oneself) to a rather late age, but as better ways of testing the activities and knowledge of younger children were found, the age was progressively lowered. McKenzie et al (1984) found that six- and eight-month-old infants could locate an anticipated event from a novel direction after rotation, and did not search always in a constant direction relative to themselves. The rotations were 30 or 60 degrees to the right or left of the child's original position. Butterworth & Cochran (1980) presented evidence that infants detected something about what someone else can see from changes of the other's gaze direction, and searched for the visual target; but up to 18 months exploratory scanning was often improperly directed when the other person looked behind the infant. Observing another person changing gaze direction, young infants will search for the target of the gaze peripherally, but generally not accurately behind themselves. The ability to act so as to take account of what someone else can see (for example, turning a picture so that someone else can see it although it is then occluded from oneself) is apparently perfected only after skilled locomotion has been attained. Locomotor exploration of the layout undoubtedly plays a role in this development.

COGNITIVE MAPPING   Attaining different perspectives is a consequence of locomotion; as one moves continuously around the layout, one's point of observation is continuously changing, providing different views of a room or a scene. Exploratory locomotion is identifiable with such continuously changing perspectives, and thus forms the foundation for detecting what path leads where, what object or landmark is nearest what other, what wall or object occludes another and will shortly be occluded by one's own body or some barrier about to be passed. J. J. Gibson wrote many years ago that "knowing the possibilities of locomotion *outside* the limits of momentary vision, that is to say the *cognitive mapping of the extended environment,* can be explained in part by the recurrent, constant, or invariant properties of such stimulation [continuous change of points of observation] which are discovered during exploratory behavior" (Gibson 1958, p. 193). Research on acquisition of cognitive maps by toddlers bears on whether knowledge of places presently out of view depends on previous exploration of the territory.

Finding a once-seen-but-now-hidden target by advancing toward it along the shortest route has been used as a test of a cognitive map. What conditions must be satisfied to make this achievement possible? Rieser and his colleagues performed experiments on this question with toddlers and older children. The situation usually involved showing the subject a target from one point of observation and then moving the subject to a position from which the target was hidden. The subject was then required to move through the expermental space to the target, or to point to it. The task required a "spatial inference" for accurate response. Children of 18 months could do this by moving to a target in a simple layout (Rieser & Heiman 1982). Children of 24 months could point in the correct direction more often than chance when they had been walked through an experimental layout, even though there were no landmarks available (Rider & Rieser 1987). But the younger subjects made many errors. Exactly what kind of learning goes on when children are not given an opportunity for free ambulatory exploration is not clear. Most of the studies allowed their subjects no opportunity of this sort, and furthermore presented them with homogeneous featureless environments, such as a circular or perfectly square area with symmetrically placed doors or windows. The ability to make inferences in such situations (e.g. inferring the shortest route, or the direction of a concealed target) not surprisingly increases with age. The reason for this could be the dawning of a new cognitive faculty, but it could also be the need for spontaneous exploratory walks through real environments, observing the continuities of paths and the reversibility of vistas.

Few of us as grown-ups are competent at finding a building in a new neighborhood without preliminary exploration. Special devices like maps and street numbers can help us, but the problem for the toddler is a more immediate one. Menzel (1973) showed that chimpanzees develop a cognitive map of a well-known terrain and proceed to targets via economical routes, but in this study the terrain had previously been well travelled daily for months. Familiarity with an environment enhances even very young children's ability to locate a target (Acredolo 1979). Rider & Rieser (1987) found that their youngest subjects made errors in locating unseen targets because they "aimed their responses in the direction of the visibly open, most direct route to the target." That such behavior should precede inference about shortest routes, especially without previous free exploration, seems almost inevitable.

An experiment by Hazen (1982) examined directly the relationship between self-initiated exploration of a playhouse of three rooms and later competence to find a route through it by reversing a previously learned one or by selecting a detour to a goal. The subjects were children of 1.8–2.4 years, and children of 3.0–3.8 years. Half were given the opportunity to explore the playhouse rooms freely on their own before performing the route-finding tasks. Older children were better at performing the tasks, but the main finding was that active exploration of the playhouse was related to accurate knowledge of its spatial layout. Sheer quantity of exploration (passive and guided exploration included) was not associated with such knowledge; what mattered was the extent to which the children had explored on their own. Perhaps the active explorers were detecting landmarks, which have the affordance of indicating what path leads to another landmark and thus which way to go.

CARRYING: EMERGENCE OF A NEW AFFORDANCE   The achievement of bipedal locomotion brings with it entirely new potential affordances to be learned by making possible a quite new activity—carrying things to a destination. Theories of the evolution of bipedal locomotion in man have sometimes proposed that the advantage of being able to carry food, young, materials for shelter, tools, etc greatly favored the emergence of walking on two legs. Observing the joy of a novice walker in carrying small objects around, often handing them to someone and then retrieving them to transport again, the possibility does not seem fanciful. Research has not yet been focussed directly on carrying things in young walkers, but a few suggestive observations have been reported. In experiments with the moving hallway, Schmuckler and Gibson (Schmuckler 1987) had young walkers move back and forth along the hallway carrying a colored golf ball (sometimes the young walker collected several to carry) to a parent at one end. The task consisted entirely in carrying the ball to the parent, handing it to them, and going back to the other end for another to carry in the same way. This simple "game" proved astonishingly motivating.

In research on exploring new territory where a number of toys could be found, Jones (1983) found that young walkers would leave their mothers to go off after toys. Rather than stopping to play with the toys, they frequently picked them up and carried them to the parent and then went after another, to follow the same routine. The pure motive of carrying something somewhere because a new affordance has emerged no doubt wears out fairly soon, but it seems to go through a self-motivating exploratory stage that permits a child to refine her perceptions of what she can carry—how large an object, what substances are feasible to transport, how heavy the burden can be, and so on. Anecdotal evidence abounds that toddlers sometimes attempt to carry a toy or a piece of furniture almost as large as themselves. Whether the stories are true or not, exploratory carrying is a sure way of learning about the affordance of "transportability" of objects and how much effort must be put into the act—once again a cognitive advantage that leads eventually to expertise.

Carrying is especially interesting to the developmental psychologist who wishes to relate detection of new affordances to developing cognition because it suggests a spiralling process, beginning with perception of the simplest affordances, such as separability and contactability, then moving on to chewability and graspability, then to reachability, to hideability, and eventually to all the refinements of transportability. With each new coil of the spiral, new properties of surfaces, objects, and events are perceived as consequences of exploratory activity, building an ever richer cognitive world. Detecting new affordances provides the means of differentiating the properties of things.

EXPLORATION IN THE SERVICE OF ACQUIRING KNOWLEDGE

The Grounding of Knowledge

In the final accounting, what is the significance of exploratory activity and its perceptual consequences? May it not be the essential ingredient for building a foundation of knowledge about the world? Or does intelligence emerge as a separate force that pulls action—even exploratory activity—along behind it? I have not discussed the latter idea at all, but the notion that intelligence develops and action somehow follows along has been fairly prevalent during the so-called "cognitive revolution." Beliefs about and representations of the world and the self presumably come first and actions follow after them. This notion is clearly opposed to the points I have been trying to make. Perhaps knowledge eventually becomes a system of representations and beliefs about the world (and oneself as an inhabitant of it), but it seems to me that representations and beliefs must be grounded by detection of the surfaces, events, and objects of the layout—the "stuff" of knowledge must somehow be obtained from the world. Furthermore, as living beings we act in the world and necessarily interact with the events and furnishings of the layout surrounding us. Our knowledge cannot consist of general abstract properties alone but must relate to the affordances for action that the world provides, not only in general beliefs but also in intimate everyday situations whose ever-changing circumstances demand great flexibility. I have been trying to show that the young organism, as it grows, has the capability to discover what the world affords and what to do about it. The foundations of the organism's knowledge evolve in an orderly fashion, with something new around the corner in each phase in a kind of spiralling evolution. What kind of knowledge could result, other than flexible means of interaction?

Predications About the World

The knowledge that results from learning affordances for action through exploratory activity and observation of its consequences is, in the beginning, probably entirely utilitarian. Meanings may be confined to situations where interactions are occurring and then can reoccur. It seems to me that this utilitarian, early, simple knowledge constitutes the beginning of ability to make predications about the world. For example, objects rest on a ground (but can be lifted from it, if they are the right size and substance). Ground is always underneath them. Some things are in front of other things. Things can be bumped into. Things can move in the surrounding layout. Some things make sounds. Some of these things are responsive (can eventually be categorized as animate). One can oneself control these responses by one's own actions (cooing, smiling). These are simple examples, but with expanding exploratory and action systems they may become much more elaborate as means available through grasping, manipulation, and later locomotion open up new possibilities of learning affordances.

Controlled manipulation accompanied by increasingly mature capabilities of visual observation provides a mechanism for differentiating affordances and qualitative properties of things and thus furnishes the material for categorizing, yielding more refined and more general predications. Locomotion with ensuing exploration of places and territories firms up incomplete knowledge and makes possible predications about the objectivity and permanence of the layout and the movability of oneself and others. Events, both external and self-perpetrated, present the opportunity for learning about consequences of movement, impact, and applying pressures, and thus provide the foundation for discovering causal relations.

I am not suggesting that predications of the kind I have illustrated have been formulated as anything like verbal propositions. Rather, knowledge has been attained that can function as a basis for further categorization and inference. Learning a vocabulary and a syntax for verbal representation of predications and events is an achievement that presupposes knowledge (something to talk about). It may well have rules of its own, but I doubt that these rules determine or even select what the infant first attends to and discovers about its early environment (cf Gelman 1986). I see little profit for the scientist in arguments about the mental representation of knowledge that cannot be talked about, but I think it must be conceded that such knowledge exists, even in adults, and certainly in the preverbal child.

Other questions—e.g. how knowledge is organized—are well worth asking and have a good chance of being answered. An important one has to do with the generalizability of knowledge, sometimes referred to as "domain specificity." After an infant has discovered an affordance pertaining to one action system, will it transfer appropriately across action systems? Is the affordance of a substance detected by mouthing detected as the same when the hands become active in exploring it? Is the differentiation of an aperture and an obstacle by a three-month-old in a looming situation generalized immediately to guiding locomotion by a crawler? I doubt that such transfer is automatic in early life, because new action systems bring new affordances, and some exploratory practice with them seems essential. But the role of practice would diminish as maturation winds down. Proliferation of tasks, however, increases as possibilities of action increase, bringing new opportunities for generalization. So do tasks proliferate with social expectations of caretakers, and these may engender a new kind of domain specificity as "training" by society begins. Still more affordances must be learned and the question of flexibility of generalization over domains can reappear on a new level.

Ontogenesis of Perceptually Based Knowledge

The course of development of perceptually based knowledge (knowledge based on exploratory perceptual systems) is an orderly one, as I have tried to show. As the phases of development evolve in the individual, with a focus in each phase, there is a progressive fanning out. New exploratory systems develop and new action systems emerge, making new tasks (e.g. carrying something somewhere) possible. Still, one sees evidence of earlier phases implying the later ones, as in the case of the aperture-obstacle distinction. The process does not look like disconnected shoots growing out in different directions, but rather like a spiralling course, an echoing of earlier abilities of affordance detection plus strengthened opportunities for discovering new meanings. Perhaps a system of meanings begins its evolution thus.

Differentiation is the key process in the kind of development I have been describing—differentiation of organs of both perception and action, and differentiation of perceived affordances. But the process is always related to the environment—its resources and its constraints. In the case of the looming experiment in the three-month-old, the information in the optical array, an expanding occluding contour increasing at an accelerated rate, has the affordance of imminent collision, calling for such avoidance behavior as the child can muster (head retraction, raising of hands). When a crawler's own locomotion produces an expansion pattern of an object in its path, the information has the affordance of potential imminent collision, but not in the same way, because the crawler can stop or detour. Furthermore, the information, while similar, is not the same. In the case of the approaching object, the expansion pattern characterizes only a part of the total array; but in the case of the infant's advance by way of its own locomotion, the expansion encompasses the total array. The cases call for differentiation, and yet they are closely related; the consequences of failing to perceive the affordance are the same because important environmental conditions are the same. The system that must be referred to for understanding the organization of perceived affordances is not the child's own organism alone, despite its manifold relations between perceptual and action systems, but an organism-environment system. Understanding behavioral and cognitive development requires consideration of both as reciprocal entities, a requirement for both the developing child and the psychologist.

Summing Up

If I did not make my theme clear in describing what I have called the three phases of exploration, I hope the last few paragraphs have enlightened the reader. My objective was a quite general one, allied with an ecological approach to biological science. The young organism grows up in the environment (both physical and social) in which his species evolved, one that imposes demands on his actions for his individual survival. To accommodate to his world, he must detect the information for these actions—that is, perceive the affordances it holds. How does the infant creature manage this accomplishment? Has evolution somehow provided him with representations of the world, and rules for how to act? I doubt this very much. But I think evolution has provided him with action systems and sensory systems that equip him to discover what the world is all about. He is "programmed" or motivated to use these systems, first by exploring the accessible surround, then acting on it, and (as spontaneous locomotion becomes possible) extending his explorations further. The exploratory systems emerge in an orderly way that permits an ever-spiralling path of discovery. The observations made possible via both exploratory and performatory actions provide the material for his knowledge of the world—a knowledge that does not cease expanding, whose end (if there is an end) is understanding. I like these lines from T. S. Eliot,

> We shall not cease from exploration
> And the end of all our exploring
> Will be to arrive where we started
> And know the place for the first time.

Four Quartets: Little Gidding

Literature Cited

Acredolo, L. P. 1979. Laboratory versus home: The effect of environment on the 9-month-old infant's choice of spatial reference system. *Dev. Psychol.* 14:224–34

Alegria, J., Noirot, E. 1978. Neonate orientation behaviour towards human voice. *Int. J. Behav. Dev.* 1:291–312

Atkinson, J., Braddick, O., Moar, K. 1977. Infants' detection of image defocus. *Vis. Res.* 17:1125–26

Bahrick, L. E., Walker, A. S., Neisser, U. 1981. Selective looking by infants. *Cogn. Psychol.* 13:377–90

Ball, W. A., Tronick, E. 1971. Infant responses to impending collisions: Optical and real. *Science* 171:818–20

Banks, M. S., Salapatek, P. 1983. Infant visual perception. In *Handbook of Child Psychology*, ed. P. H. Mussen, Vol. 2. New York: Wiley. 1244 pp.

Berlyne, D. E. 1966. Curiosity and exploration. *Science* 153:25–33

Bernstein, N. 1967. *The Coordination and Regulation of Movement*. New York: Pergamon

Bower, T. G. R. 1972. Object perception in infants. *Perception* 1:15–30

Bower, T. G. R., Broughton, J., Moore, M. K. 1971. Infant responses to approaching objects: an indicator of response to distal variables. *Percept. Psychophys* 9:193–96

Bower, T. G. R., Dunkeld, J., Wishart, J. G. 1979. Infant perception of visually presented objects. *Science* 203:1137–38

Bruner, J. S. 1968. *Processes of Cognitive Growth: Infancy*, Vol. 3. Heinz Werner Lect. Ser. Barre, Mass: Clark Univ. Press/ Barre Publishers

Bruner, J. S. 1973. Organization of early skilled action. *Child Dev.* 44:1–11

Bullinger, A. 1977. Orientation de la tête du nouveau-né en présence d'un stimulus visuel. *Ann. Psychol.* 77:357–64

Burnham, D. K., Dickinson, R. G. 1981. The determinants of visual capture and visual pursuit in infancy. *Infant Behav. Dev.* 4:359–72

Bushnell, E. W., Shaw, L., Strauss, D. 1985. Relationship between visual and tactual exploration by 6-month-olds. *Dev. Psychol.* 21:591–600

Butterworth, G., Castillo, M. 1976. Coordination of auditory and visual space in newborn human infants. *Perception* 5:155–60

Butterworth, G., Cochran, E. 1980. Towards a mechanism of joint visual attention in human infancy. *Int. J. Behav. Dev.* 3:253–72

Butterworth, G., Henshall, C., Johnston, S., Abd-Fattah, N., Hopkins, B. 1985. *Hand to mouth activity in the newborn baby: evidence for innate sensory-motor coordination.* Presented at Ann. Conf. Dev. Psychol. Sect., Brit. Psychol. Soc., Belfast

Butterworth, G., Hicks, L. 1977. Visual proprioception and postural stability in infancy: a developmental study. *Perception* 6:255–62

Butterworth, G., Pope, M. J. 1982. *Origin and functions of visual perception in human infants.* Presented at Int. Conf. Infant Stud., Austin, Texas

Carroll, J., Gibson, E. J. 1981. *Differentiation of an aperture from an obstacle under conditions of motion by three-month-old infants.* Presented at Meet. Soc. Res. Child Dev., Boston

Dewey, J. 1896. The reflex arc concept in psychology. *Psychol. Rev.* 3:357–70

Dodwell, P. C., Muir, D., DiFranco, D. 1976. Responses of infants to visually presented objects. *Science* 194:209–11

Dodwell, P. C., Muir, D., DiFranco, D. 1979. Infant perception of visually presented objects. *Science* 203:1138–39

Eimas, P. D., Siqueland, E. R., Jusczyk, P. W., Vigorito, J. 1971. Speech perception in infants. *Science* 171:303–6

Fantz, R. L. 1961. The origin of form perception. *Sci. Am.* 204:66–72

Fenson, L., Kagan, J., Kearsley, R., Zelazo, P. 1976. The developmental progression of manipulative play in the first two years. *Child Dev.* 47:232–36

Field, J. 1976. Relation of young infants' reaching behavior to stimulus distance and solidity. *Dev. Psychol.* 12:444–48

Field, J., Muir, D., Pilon, R., Sinclair, M., Dodwell, P. 1980. Infants' orientation to lateral sounds from birth to three months. *Child Dev.* 51:295–98

Freedman, D. A., Fox-Kolenda, B. J., Margileth, D. A., Miller, D. H. 1969. The development of the use of sound as a guide to affective and cognitive behavior—a two-phase process. *Child Dev.* 40:1099–1105

Gelman, R. 1986. *First principles for structuring cognition.* Presented at Ann. Meet. Am. Psychol. Assoc., Washington, DC

Gibson, E. J. 1969. *Principles of Perceptual Learning and Development*. New York: Appleton, Century, Crofts

Gibson, E. J. 1982. The concept of affordances in development: the renascence of functionalism. In *The Concept of Development: The Minnesota Symposia on Child Psychology*, Vol. 15, ed. W. A. Collins. Hillsdale, NJ: Erlbaum

Gibson, E. J. 1984. Reflections on awareness of causality: what develops? In *Advances in*

Infancy Research, Vol. 3, ed. L. P. Lipsitt, C. Rovee-Collier. Norwood, NJ: Ablex

Gibson, E. J., Riccio, G., Schmuckler, M., Stoffregen, T., Rosenberg, D., Taormina, J. 1987. Detection of the traversability of surfaces by crawling and walking infants. *J. Exp. Psychol.: Hum. Percept. Perform.* In press

Gibson, E. J., Spelke, E. S. 1983. Development of perception. In *Handbook of Child Psychology*, Vol. 3, ed. P. H. Mussen. New York: Wiley. 942 pp.

Gibson, E. J., Walk, R. D. 1960. The "visual cliff." *Sci. Am.* 202:64–71

Gibson, E. J., Walker, A. S. 1984. Development of knowledge of visual-tactual affordances of substance. *Child Dev.* 55:453–60

Gibson, J. J., ed. 1947. *Motion Picture Testing and Research.* (Rep. No. 7, A.A.F. Aviation Psychol. Res. Rep.). Washington: US Government Printing Office

Gibson, J. J. 1958. Visually controlled locomotion and visual orientation in animals. *Brit. J. Psychol.* 49:182–94

Gibson, J. J. 1962. Observations on active touch. *Psychol. Rev.* 69:477–491

Gibson, J. J. 1966. *The Senses Considered as Perceptual Systems.* Boston: Houghton-Mifflin

Gibson, J. J. 1979. *The Ecological Approach to Visual Perception.* Boston: Houghton Mifflin. Reprinted 1986, Erlbaum

Granrud, C. E., Yonas, A., Smith, I. M., Arterbury, M. E., Glicksman, M. L., Sorknes, A. C. 1984. Infants' sensitivity to accretion and deletion of texture as information for depth at an edge. *Child Dev.* 55:1630–36

Haith, M. M. 1980. *Rules That Babies Look By.* Hillsdale, NJ: Erlbaum

Harris, P. L., Cassel, T. Z., Bamborough, P. 1974. Tracking by young infants. *Brit. J. Psychol.* 65:345–49

Hazen, N. L. 1982. Spatial exploration and spatial knowledge: individual and developmental differences in very young children. *Child Dev.* 53:826–33

Horowitz, F. D., ed. 1974. Visual attention, auditory stimulation, and language discrimination in young infants. *Monogr. Soc. Res. Child Dev.* 39(158):140

Hutt, C. 1970. Specific and diversive exploration. In *Advances in Child Development and Behavior*, Vol. 5, ed. H. W. Reese, L. P. Lipsitt. New York: Academic

Jones, S. S. 1983. *On the motivational bases for proximity-seeking: "attachment behavior" in the second year.* PhD thesis. Univ. Pennsylvania

Kalnins, I. V., Bruner, J. S. 1973. The coordination of visual observation and instrumental behavior in early infancy. *Perception* 2:307–14

Kaufmann-Hayoz, R., Kaufmann, F., Stucki, M. 1986. Kinetic contours in infants' visual perception. *Child Dev.* 57:292–99

Keating, M. B., McKenzie, B. E., Day, R. H. 1986. Spatial localization in infancy: position constancy in a square and circular room with and without a landmark. *Child Dev.* 57:115–24

Kellman, P. J. 1984. Perception of three-dimensional form by human infants. *Percept. Psychophys.* 36:353–58

Kellman, P. J., Gleitman, H., Spelke, E. S. 1987. Object and observer motion in the perception of objects by infants. *J. Exp. Psychol.: Hum Percept. Perform.* In press

Kellman, P. J., Short, K. R. 1986. The more things change the more they stay the same: infant perception of three-dimensional form from information given by observer movement. *Abstr. Infant Behav. Dev.* 9:196

Kellman, P. J., Spelke, E. S. 1983. Perception of partly occluded objects in infancy. *Cogn. Psychol.* 15:483–524

Kellman, P. J., Spelke, E. S., Short, K. R. 1986. Infant perception of object unity from translatory motion in depth and vertical translation. *Child Dev.* 57:72–86

Kopp, C. B. 1974. Fine motor abilities of infants. *Dev. Med. Child Neurol.* 16:629–36

Kuhl, P., Meltzoff, A. N. 1982. The bimodal perception of speech in infancy. *Science* 218:1138–41

Lee, D. N., Aronson, E. 1974. Visual proprioceptive control of standing in human infants. *Percept. Psychophys.* 15:529–32

Leslie, A. M. 1982. The perception of causality in infants. *Perception* 11:173–86

Leslie, A. M. 1984. Infant perception of a manual pick-up event. *Brit. J. Dev. Psychol.* 2:19–32

Lockman, J. J. 1984. The development of detour ability during infancy. *Child Dev.* 55:482–91

Loveland, K. A. 1984. Learning about points of view: spatial perception and the acquisition of "I/You". *J. Child Lang.* 11:535–56

Loveland, K. A. 1987. Behavior of young Down Syndrome children before the mirror. I. Exploration. *Child Dev.* In press

McCall, R. B. 1974. Exploratory manipulation and play in the human infant. *Monogr. Soc. Res. Child Dev.* 39(155):88

McKenzie, B. E., Day, R. H., Ihsen, E. 1984. Localization of events in space: Young infants are not always egocentric. *Brit. J. Dev. Psychol.* 2:1–9

MacTurk, R. H., Vietze, P. M., McCarthy, M. E., McQuiston, S., Yarrow, L. J. 1985. The organization of exploratory behavior in Down Syndrome and nondelayed infants. *Child Dev.* 56:573–81

Meltzoff, A., Borton, R. W. 1979. Intermodal matching by human neonates. *Nature* 282:403–4

Menzel, E. W. 1973. Chimpanzee spatial memory organization. *Science* 182:943–45

Michotte, A. 1963. *The Perception of Causality*. New York: Basic Books

Neisser, U., Becklen, R. 1975. Selective looking: attending to visually-specified events. *Cogn. Psychol.* 7:480–94

Owen, B. M., Lee, D. N. 1986. Establishing a frame of reference for action. In *Motor Development: Aspects of Coordination and Control*, ed. M. G. Wade, H. T. A. Whiting. Dordrecht: Martinus Nijhoff

Palmer, C. 1985. *Infants' exploration of objects: relations between perceiving and acting*. PhD thesis. Univ. Minnesota

Palmer, C. 1987. *Between a rock and a hard place: babies in tight spaces*. Presented at Meet. Soc. Res. Child Dev., Baltimore

Papoušek, H. 1967. Experimental studies of appetitional behavior in human newborns and infants. In *Early Behavior*, ed. H. W. Stevenson, E. H. Hess, H. L. Rheingold. New York: Wiley

Piaget, J. 1937, 1952. *The Origins of Intelligence in Children*. New York: Int. Univ. Press

Piaget, J. 1954. *The Construction of Reality in the Child*. New York: Basic Books

Rheingold, H. L. 1985. Development as the acquisition of familiarity. *Ann. Rev. Psychol.* 36:1–17

Rheingold, H. L., Eckerman, C. O. 1969. The infant's free entry into a new environment. *J. Exp. Child Psychol.* 8:271–83

Rheingold, H. L., Eckerman, C. O. 1970. The infant separates himself from his mother. *Science* 168:78–83

Rider, E. A., Rieser, J. J. 1987. Pointing at objects in other rooms: young children's sensitivity to perspective after walking with and without vision. *Child Dev.* In press

Rieser, J. J., Heiman, M. L. 1982. Spatial self-reference systems and shortest-route behavior in toddlers. *Child Dev.* 53:524–33

Rochat, P. 1983. Oral touch in young infants: response to variations of nipple characteristics in the first months of life. *Int. J. Behav. Dev.* 6:123–33

Rochat, P., Gibson, E. J. 1985. Early mouthing and grasping: development and cross-modal responsiveness to soft and rigid objects in young infants. Abstr. Ann. Meet. Can. Psychol. Assoc. *Can. Psychol.* 26(2):452

Rose, S. A. 1977. Infants' transfer of response between two-dimensional and three-dimensional stimuli. *Child Dev.* 48:1086–91

Rose, S. A. 1986. Abstraction in infancy: evidence from cross-modal and cross-dimensional transfer. In *Advances in Infancy Research*, Vol. 4, ed. L. P. Lipsitt, C. Rovee-Collier. Norwood, NJ: Ablex

Rose, S. A., Gottfried, A. W., Bridger, W. H. 1981. Cross-modal transfer in 6-month-old infants. *Dev. Psychol.* 17:661–69

Ross, H. S. 1974. The influence of novelty and complexity on exploratory behavior in 12-month-old infants. *Exp. Child Psychol.* 17:436–51

Ross, H. S., Rheingold, H. L., Eckerman, C. O. 1972. Approach and exploration of a novel alternative by 12-month-old infants. *Exp. Child Psychol.* 13:85–93

Rovee, C. K., Rovee, D. T. 1969. Conjugate reinforcement of infant exploratory behavior. *J. Exp. Child Psychol.* 8:33–39

Ruff, H. A. 1984. Infants' manipulative exploration of objects: effects of age and object characteristics. *Dev. Psychol.* 20:9–20

Ruff, H. A., Kohler, C. J. 1978. Tactual-visual transfer in six-month-old infants. *Infant Behav. Dev.* 1:259–64

Ruff, H. A., McCarton, C., Kurtzberg, D., Vaughn, H. G. 1984. Preterm infants' manipulative exploration of objects. *Child Dev.* 55:1166–73

Schmuckler, M. 1987. *The effect of imposed optical flow on guided locomotion in young walkers*. Presented at Meet. Soc. Res. Child Dev., Baltimore

Siqueland, E. R., DeLucia, C. A. 1969. Visual reinforcement of sucking in human infants. *Science* 165:1144–46

Siqueland, E. R., Lipsitt, L. P. 1966. Conditioned head-turning behavior in newborns. *Exp. Child Psychol.* 3:356–76

Spelke, E. S. 1976. Infants' intermodal perception of events. *Cogn. Psychol.* 8:553–60

Steele, D., Pederson, D. R. 1977. Stimulus variables which affect the concordance of visual and manipulative exploration in six-month-old infants. *Child Dev.* 48:104–11

Stoffregen, T., Schmuckler, M., Gibson, E. J. 1987. Development of use of optical flow in stance and locomotion in young walkers. *Perception*. In press

Streri, A., Pêcheux, M. 1986a. Tactual habituation and discrimination of form in infancy: a comparison with vision. *Child Dev.* 57:100–4

Streri, A., Pêcheux, M. 1986b. Vision-to-touch and touch-to-vision transfer of form in 5-month-old infants. *Brit. J. Dev. Psychol.* 4:161–67

Streri, A. S., Spelke, E. 1987. Haptic perception of objects in infancy. *Cogn. Psychol.* In press

Thelen, E. 1984. Learning to walk: ecological demands and phylogenetic constraints. In *Advances in Infancy Research*, Vol. 3, ed. L. P. Lipsitt. Norwood, NJ: Ablex

Thelen, E. 1987. Development of coordinated movement: implications for early human development. In *Motor Skills Acquisition,* ed. H. T. A. Whiting, M. G. Wade. Amsterdam: North Holland. In press

Tolman, E. C., Brunswik, E. 1935. The organism and the causal texture of the environment. *Psychol. Rev.* 42:43–77

Tronick, E. 1972. Stimulus control and the growth of the infant's effective visual field. *Percept. Psychophys.* 11:373–76

Tronick, E., Clanton, C. 1971. Infant looking patterns. *Vis. Res.* 11:1479–86

Uzgiris, I. C., Benson, J. 1980. *Infants' use of sound in search for objects.* Presented at Int. Conf. Infant Stud., New Haven, Conn.

von Hofsten, C. 1982. Eye-hand coordination in newborns. *Dev. Psychol.* 18:450–61

von Hofsten, C. 1983. Catching skills in infancy. *J. Exp. Psychol.* 9:75–85

von Hofsten, C., Lindhagen, K. 1979. Observations on the development of reaching for moving objects. *J. Exp. Child Psychol.* 28:158–73

Walker-Andrews, A. S., Gibson, E. J. 1986. What develops in bimodal development? In *Advances in Infancy Research,* Vol. 4, ed. L. P. Lipsitt, C. Rovee-Collier. Norwood, NJ: Ablex

Welker, W. I. 1961. An analysis of exploratory and play behavior in animals. In *Functions of Varied Experience,* ed. D. W. Fiske, S. R. Maddi. Homewood, Ill: Dorsey

White, R. W. 1959. Motivation reconsidered: the concept of competence. *Psychol. Rev.* 66:297–333

Willats, P. 1983. Effects of object novelty on the visual and manual exploration of infants. *Infant Behav. Dev.* 6:145–49

Willats, P. 1985. *Development and rapid adjustment of means-end behavior in infants aged six to eight months.* Presented at Meet. Int. Soc. Stud. Behav. Dev., Tours, France

Willats, P. 1985. *Learning to do two things at once: coordination of actions with both hands by young infants.* Presented at Meet. Int. Soc. Stud. Behav. Dev., Tours, France

Woodworth, R. S. 1947. Reinforcement of perception. *Am. J. Psychol.* 60:119–24

Woodworth, R. S. 1958. *Dynamics of Behavior.* New York: Henry Holt & Co.

Yeni-Komshian, G., Kavanaugh, J., Ferguson, C., eds. 1980. *Child Phonology, Vol. 1: Production.* New York: Academic

Yonas, A. 1981. Infants' responses to optical information for collision. In *Development of Perception: Psychobiological Perspectives, Vol. 2: The Visual System,* ed. R. N. Aslin, J. R. Alberts, M. R. Peterson. New York: Academic

Yonas, A., Granrud, C. E. 1984. The development of sensitivity to kinetic, binocular and pictorial depth information in human infants. In *Brain Mechanisms and Spatial Vision,* ed. D. Ingle, D. Lee, M. Jeannerod. Amsterdam: Martinus Nijhoff

Ann. Rev. Psychol. 1988. 39:43–68

ETHOEXPERIMENTAL APPROACHES TO THE BIOLOGY OF EMOTION

D. C. Blanchard and R. J. Blanchard

Pacific Biomedical Research Center and Department of Psychology, University of Hawaii, Honolulu, Hawaii 96822

CONTENTS

INTRODUCTION

While it is difficult to decide which should be termed "thesis" and which "antithesis," the two major traditions in the study of animal behavior have clearly had opposing positions on many aspects of research in this area (Eibl-Eibesfeldt 1979). The tradition of experimental psychology has emphasized stringent control of extraneous variables, the systematic manipulation of independent variables, and objective, often instrument-mediated, measurement of behavior. The ethological tradition emphasizes study of behavior in natural settings, or in laboratory settings specifically designed to include whatever natural features are necessary to support a fully developed action pattern. Ethological measures typically involve descriptions of these naturally occurring behavior patterns, and usually require observation by a trained observer rather than measurement with instruments. These differences reflect other disparities in the two traditions. The ethological tradition shows much greater interest in differences between species, and in the evolutionary aspect of behavior; the experimental tradition exhibits more concern for physiological mechanisms and greater interest in relationships that might be generalized across species.

Recent years have brought something of a rapprochement, focused on several areas in which progress toward understanding behavior is facilitated by a judicious combination of features, procedural and philosophical, from both traditions. The "ethoexperimental analysis" of behavior (Blanchard & Blanchard 1986; Brain 1987) combines an emphasis on laboratory-based research, along with explicit concern for manipulation of independent variables and control of extraneous variables, with attention to the description and measurement of naturally occurring behavior patterns. It is concerned with both the evolutionary functions of these behaviors and the degree to which they may be generalized across species. This approach has been extensively combined with investigations of the biological bases of aggression (Blanchard & Blanchard 1984; Brain & Benton 1981) and sexual behavior (Barfield 1984) and the pharmacological control of a variety of social and emotional behaviors (Miczek et al 1984). However, ethoexperimental analysis has a more general applicability: Although it is labor intensive, requiring attention to the adequacy of both the laboratory environments and the behaviors measured, it provides the possibility of greatly improved understanding of complex behavior patterns, and more appropriate use of lower mammals as models for research on human behavior.

NATURAL PATTERNS OF OFFENSE AND DEFENSE MANIPULATED AND MEASURED IN LABORATORY SETTINGS

Conspecific Attack and Self-Defense

The view that natural defensive and aggressive behaviors of lower animals may provide an analogue to human emotions began with the pioneering work of Darwin (1872). Extensive work (Barnett 1958; Ewer 1971; Eibl-Eibesfeldt 1961; Leyhausen 1979; Scott & Fredericson 1951), using a variety of species, delineated different sets of behaviors for animals attacking a conspecific (attack), and for animals under attack (self-defense). The good agreement between behaviors seen in a relatively barren laboratory setting (Grant 1963) and those seen in field studies (Ewer 1971) strongly suggested that these patterns may be well investigated under laboratory conditions.

The typical field situations in which ethologists have described conspecific aggressive and defensive behaviors involve social interactions between dominant and subordinate animals, and encounters between territorial residents and intruders. These situations may be reproduced in a laboratory setting by placing mixed-sex groups of animals in larger-than-normal enclosures, and introducing intruders into these established colonies (Blanchard & Blanchard 1980). In rats conspecific offensive attack is most characteristic of one—the dominant—male in a given group, and is directed either toward subordinate male group members or toward strange male intruders. In the case of resident-intruder interactions, the resident male usually sniffs the intruder's perianal area, then erects its body hairs, which results in an apparent increase in size. The resident male rat chases the intruder and crowds laterally against it if the intruder is upright, or stands "on top" if it lies on its back. The attacker's bites are directed at the intruder's back. With reference to defense, the intruder may flee, rear up with its forepaws extended toward the attacking male to push it away, or roll backwards into a supine position. While being bitten, or immediately afterwards, the intruder may direct a retaliatory bite at the snout of the attacker. During the intervals between attacks the intruder tends to freeze (Blanchard & Blanchard 1980).

The mouse pattern of attack and defense is close to that of the rat, while other species (e.g. cats: Leyhausen 1979) show functionally, though not always topographically, similar patterns of attack and defense (Blanchard & Blanchard 1984). For these and other species, attack and defensive behaviors are organized in terms of specific functions.

Organizational Principles of Conspecific Attack and Self-Defense

In rats, attack upon intruders is directed toward the back (Blanchard et al 1977). Wound data from field-trapped rats show excellent agreement with laboratory results: About 80% of wounds occur on the back (Blanchard et al 1985). The consistency of these target-site preferences suggests that conspecific defensive behaviors such as "boxing" and "lying on the back" have evolved as "back-defense" strategies. They are adaptive in that they conceal the specific target of offensive bites. The corresponding offensive "back-attack" strategies are the "lateral attack" and "standing on top," each an active behavior pattern serving to counter a particular back-defense and to gain biting access to the target (Blanchard & Blanchard 1984).

Since these specific defensive strategies work only because of the strict targeting of bites, they would be maladaptive in the context of antipredator defense. Thus the "back-defense" behaviors are seen almost exclusively in the context of conspecific attack, while the other components of defense occur against all major classes of threatening stimuli.

It should be emphasized that the offensive and defensive patterns are very different from each other, not only in rats but in every species in which they have been studied (Blanchard & Blanchard 1984). However, one consistent difficulty in conveying the difference between the two patterns is that they occur in the same encounters, with offensive and defensive behaviors dyadically organized: When the defender flees, the attacker chases; the other two common dyads are lateral attack vs boxing, and on-top-of vs on-the-back. In real-world agonistic encounters lasting for any length of time, both combatants usually have some offensive motivations: If this were not true, then the purely defensive animal would flee as soon as possible, ending the encounter. Thus real-world combatants all typically show some mixture of offense and defense. One particular value of laboratory situations is that flight availability can be manipulated, and the motivations of opponents strongly polarized. This provides a much cleaner situation for analysis of effects of independent variables on the two systems.

Antipredator Behavior

In contrast to offense, which is rarely seen outside a conspecific context, there is a second ethoexperimental model for the study of defense: antipredator behavior (Edmunds 1974). Most elements of the antipredator defense pattern—flight, freezing, and defensive threat and attack—are similar among vertebrate species, although the mixture of these varies with the species and situation. In wild rats antipredator behavior is organized as a joint function of the availability of escape and the distance between the predator and the prey. Flight is the predominant response when escape is possible and the predator approaches within flight distance. When flight is not possible, freezing is the initial defense, followed by defensive threat (vocalization with display of teeth) when about 1 m separates the two, and by an explosive jump attack should the predator continue to approach. This jump attack may involve a bite at the predator's eye-snout area, followed immediately by flight (Blanchard & Blanchard 1987).

Although laboratory rats will display some antipredator behaviors, there is considerable evidence that the process of domestication has involved systematic selection by breeders against defensive threat and attack, as well as a general reduction in flight (Blanchard & Blanchard 1987). Thus wild rats (or other undomesticated species) may prove to be superior subjects for the study of defensive behaviors.

Assessment of Predatory Risk

Both attacking conspecifics and predators are discrete and relatively easily discriminated stimuli. Indeed, many of the adaptations of predators (e.g. cryptic coloration) function in reducing this discriminability, to facilitate access to prey. Both conspecific defenses and antipredator defenses, as outlined, function best in the context of a discrete, highly discriminable stimulus (Edmunds 1974). With the exception of freezing, each of these behaviors has a specific orientation in space that requires some information about the location and nature of the opponent in order to be reasonably effective. In fact, when a discrete threat stimulus is present even freezing is an oriented response: Freezing animals focus sight, hearing, and smell receptors directly on the threat source.

However, many potentially threatening situations do not present a discrete, easily discriminated threat source. Such situations may contain odors or other traces of potential opponents; they may be unfamiliar, too dark, too bright, or too open, or they may involve unexpected noises, movement, or other potential dangers. In these situations, where specific defensive behaviors cannot be used effectively until the danger is located and perhaps identified, an elaborate pattern of assessment of predatory risk is initiated. This pattern is highly motivated, just as defense is highly motivated, and it is aimed at assessing the danger in a stimulus or situation while simultaneously avoiding that danger. There are two major variants of the pattern of predatory risk assessment, each involving a sort of best fit between the opposing demands of risk avoidance and risk assessment. When an escape route or place of concealment is available, the animal tends to flee or seek concealment, which avoids risk but does little to gain information. After the passage of time with no further evidence of danger, the animal may systematically reenter the danger zone to explore it. This involves brief, cautious forays, followed by rapid retreat: If the danger signals are absent, the forays grow longer and the periods of retreat or concealment are shorter. While in the threatening area the animal moves with agonizing slowness, clings to walls (thigmotaxis), and refrains from any unnecessary movements or activities. Objects may be explored using a "stretched attention" motion of leaning far forward to sniff, then rapidly withdrawing. As the animal becomes more familiar with the situation and its contents, and if there is no further indication of danger, this pattern of cautious movement and exploration gives way slowly to more normal activities, usually beginning with compensatory grooming. However, even rather high probability activities such as offensive attack, sexual behavior, and eating may take hours or days to reappear.

When escape or concealment is impossible, freezing is the only effective method of avoiding risk. This may involve total immobility (high avoidance of risk, low assessment of risk) or freezing with scanning movements of the head and vibrissae (which somewhat decreases risk avoidance, while increasing risk assessment). As the apparent risk declines over time without further incident, freezing gives way to exploration, and finally to a return to normal behavior (eating, drinking, aggression, and sexual activity, as described above). What must be reemphasized for either situation is that the return to normalcy takes a long time. When potential threat stimuli recur on a poorly predictable basis, this pattern of movement arrest, slow but intense exploration, and suppression of other activities could go on indefinitely. Thus freezing, the most dramatic single response in this pattern, is only the tip of the iceberg with reference to the motivated behaviors of the risk assessment pattern.

The suggestion that reactions to poorly discriminable threat stimuli may be related to anxiety (as opposed to fear of definite threat objects or events) is an old one (Blanchard & Blanchard 1969). Descriptions of anxiety based on the patterns of changes produced by anxiolytic drugs (Gray 1982) reveal much the same set of behavioral elements as found in the predatory risk pattern. In fact, some of these risk-assessment reactions have recently been used as models for testing anxiolytic drugs (Treit 1985; Johnston & File 1986).

The Use of Offense and Defense as Ethoexperimental Models for the Study of Fear, Anxiety, and Aggression

Both offensive and defensive behaviors occur in socially and experimentally naive rats, suggesting that these may represent basic, in large part unlearned neurobehavioral systems in animals at this level. Certainly these behaviors, and the circumstances in which they occur, appear to be highly adaptive and functional under normal conditions of life for individuals of virtually all mammalian species. Specifically, offense increases access to breeding females, with dominant males reproducing at a higher rate than subordinates (DeFries & McClearn 1970). Depending on species and situations, dominant males may also have priority of access to other important natural resources such as food (especially preferred foods) and territories or nest sites.

Defense is, if anything, more immediately necessary than offensive attack. Risk assessment is perhaps the most common and prevalent behavior pattern for any higher animal, occurring in situations involving any considerable degree of unfamiliarity or unpredictability, in addition to danger from predation, conspecific attack, or natural hazards. After a threat source has been localized, appropriate defensive behaviors remove the animal from danger, or act to shield vulnerable attack sites on the defender's body. The threat of defensive (retaliatory) attack can also discourage a predator or attacking conspecific (see Blanchard & Blanchard 1987 for a review). Fear reactions are easily conditioned to salient stimuli paired with pain, and the specific defensive behaviors to such conditioned threat stimuli involve many of the same components that would be seen in response to unconditioned threat stimuli with the same features in similar circumstances. This strongly suggests that the same patterns of defense used against conspecifics and predators are also adaptive in reacting to learned threat stimuli and situations.

An Emotional Cost/Benefit Analysis

While each of these patterns is beneficial under the appropriate circumstances, there is in each case a cost as well. The cost of the risk-assessment pattern is perhaps the best known, since a particular learning paradigm—habituation—has evolved largely on the basis that it contains this cost. Offense and the specific defenses, too, can be costly if they occur too persistently or under incorrect circumstances. What is especially notable about these three patterns—offense, defense, and risk assessment—is that they commonly interact under normal circumstances for most animals, a fact that introduces additional complications into the cost/benefit analyses of these situations. Thus offense and defense both occur in conspecific agonistic encounters; risk assessment and specific defenses may both be required in particular danger situations; or the demands of risk assessment may conflict with offensive tendencies under a variety of circumstances. We have analyzed (Blanchard & Blanchard 1984) emotions as providing the proximate mechanism for the cost/benefit analyses required by such conflicting demands, with the strength of these emotions (e.g. anger, fear, anxiety) depending on both the specifics of the eliciting situation and relevant internal features of the animal (e.g. hormonal status, previous learning).

There is no evidence of any discontinuity in the adaptive values of either offense or defense for people as opposed to lower mammals. Moreover, analyses of human responses to fear and dominance/resource competition (the factors eliciting defense and offense, respectively, in lower mammals) suggest that very different human behavior patterns likewise occur in these situations, with numerous specific agreements between these and the lower mammalian offense and defense patterns (for reviews see Archer 1979; Blanchard & Blanchard 1984; Plutchik & Kellerman 1986). Finally, some degree of preprogramming of behaviors is associated with these emotions: The facial patterns characteristic of fear and anger are recognizable across noncontacting cultures (Izard 1972).

These lines of evidence, here briefly summarized, suggest that offense and defense, as elicited and measured in subhuman animals, may also be represented in human behavior, and that these measures in lower mammals may serve as the most appropriate models for ethoexperimental investigations of human angry aggression and fear/anxiety.

If these behavior patterns of lower mammals do indeed serve as analogues of human emotional behavior, then investigation of the biological bases of these patterns becomes especially important. In the remainder of this paper we therefore briefly survey current information on the neuroanatomical, pharmacological, and hormonal control of these behavior patterns.

Several organizing caveats should be mentioned. First, some of these brain-behavior relationships have been extensively investigated, while for others serious investigation is just beginning. Second, a number of important related behavior patterns (e.g. predatory attack and maternal attack) are not treated. Finally, no rigid one-to-one correspondence between a specific behavior seen in lower mammals and a human emotion is intended: In many cases the emotions are no more clearly defined than are the lower mammalian behavior patterns, and neither common usage or scientific analysis yet permits a satisfactory definition. As an example, when applied to human behavior the term "aggressiveness" often denotes both angry aggression and defensive or retaliatory attack. What follows, then, is an overview of some of the biological factors differentially contributing to this set of highly adaptive, indeed crucial behaviors that have evolved from lower mammals to people in ways just coming to be understood.

THE BIOLOGICAL BASES OF DEFENSE AND OFFENSE

The acceptance of an ethoexperimental distinction between offense and defense quickly led to consideration of the differential biological systems involved in these behavior patterns. Thorough reviews by Adams (1979) and by Ursin (1981) suggested that most studies of the neuroanatomic organization of "aggression"—based largely on reactions to handling or shock-elicited fighting—were in fact studies of defensive behavior. These two reviews, and work done since, provide a relatively consistent view of the brain systems involved in defense, using primarily rat and cat subjects. The general conclusion that much more is known about the biological basis of defense than of offense also remains true, and the disproportionateness of our knowledge of defense, in comparison to offense, has probably increased in the past several years.

The Neural Control of Defense

Ethoexperimental analyses of defense suggest that the neural systems underlying defensive behavior must do a number of things.

These systems must process (perceive and actively seek to identify) a variety of dangerous or potentially dangerous stimuli or situations. If the stimulus/situation is ambiguous, a risk-assessment pattern is instituted that involves intense investigation accompanied by suppression of other behaviors.

Upon identification/localization of the danger source, specific defensive behaviors appropriate to the situation must be selected; these must be changed in accord with momentary alterations of the subject's relationship to the environment and to the attacking conspecific or predator. Diverse mechanisms are involved here, including changing levels of attention to specific features of the stimulus situation, and perhaps coordinated reflexes to specific features of the opponent and its movements.

At some point (probably early) in the above processes, defensive motivational states are engendered. These likely involve two partially separable systems: (*a*) risk assessment and avoidance (with its primary goal of identification of the threatening stimulus or event) elicited by partial stimuli or potential threat situations, and (*b*) defense elicited by specific threat stimuli.

In addition, relatively specific patterns of cardiovascular and other sympathetic changes occur in response to threat stimuli. Feedback from these may also become a factor in the modulation of the behavior pattern.

It is becoming increasingly possible to suggest some of the brain systems involved in the preceding activities. There is a venerable and relatively consistent literature linking structures in the amygdala, hypothalamus, and midbrain to the elicitation, modulation, and organization of defensive behavior, including defensive threat and attack. This material has been beautifully reviewed by Bandler (1987). In addition, a system involving the bed nucleus of the stria terminalis, the lateral septal area, and the nucleus accumbens appears to be involved in the active inhibition of some aspects of defense.

THE AMYGDALA   Defensive reactions of wild or laboratory rats to predators and human handling are virtually eliminated following amygdala lesions (Ursin 1981). Lesions or electrical stimulation of the amygdala may alter various components of the defensive pattern, with some indication of regional differentiation of flight from defensive threat and attack (Ursin 1965). Although the precise localization of these effects within the amygdala or adjacent structures is still an open question, the central and medial nuclei and the stria terminalis appear to be most specifically involved in active defenses (cf fear-potentiated startle: Hitchcock & Davis 1986; see also Watson et al 1983).

There is considerable evidence that the functions of the amygdala include an analysis and integration of complex sensory input leading to emotional arousal (Aggelton & Mishkin 1986). This multisensory integration may not be limited to defense: Rolls (1986) suggests that damage to the amygdala produces a range of problems with the identification of complex natural stimuli. It is notable also that electrical stimulation of the human amygdala typically elicits reports of fear or anxiety with little or no anger (Halgren 1981).

THE HYPOTHALAMUS   The hypothalamus has long been regarded as one of the key structures in emotion. Lesions of the ventromedial nuclei increase defensive threat and attack during human handling but do not increase "social aggression" (Albert & Walsh 1981). An important complication in the interpretation of these results is that stimulation of this area also elicits "affective defense," a similarity of lesion and stimulation effects that has not yet been satisfactorily explained (Bandler 1987). Combined stimulation-labelling studies indicate that the defense-related systems in the hypothalamus are mediated via the midbrain periaqueductal gray (PAG), although there is some disagreement about the specific route (Bandler 1987). One intriguing possibility (Fuchs et al 1985a, b) is that ventromedial hypothalamic (VMH) fibers actually project forward to a medial preoptic, medial anterior hypothalamic site (MPOA,AH), which also receives major input from the amygdala, as well as input from a septal area system (to be described below) that may inhibit defense. The result of the integration of these diverse inputs is then seen as passing caudally from this MPOA,AH site to the PAG.

Although this system has not appeared in all labelling studies (Bandler 1987), its hypothesized existence provides an attractive basis for explaining some of the relationships among diencephalic and forebrain structures involved in defense. First, this configuration provides a satisfying view of the excitatory-inhibitory interactions involved in defense (about which more later below). Second, it fits strikingly with information on the distribution of testosterone uptake in brain, linking the putative anatomy of defense to an additional factor in the biology of defense.

With reference to this last factor, the VMH takes up labelled testosterone at an extremely high rate (Rees & Michael 1982; Rees et al 1986). Moreover, testosterone propionate (TP) implants in this area selectively restore "male social aggression" that has been reduced by castration of male rats (Albert et al 1987). It is thus tempting to speculate that this area may be involved with hormonal or visceral factors modulating fear or defensive reactions, an input that is then integrated (in the MPOA,AH?) with the releasing stimulus from the amygdala.

THE MIDBRAIN PERIAQUEDUCTAL GRAY   The crucial structure for defense is in the periaqueductal gray (PAG) of the midbrain, an area Bandler (1987) has called the "final common path" for affective defensive behavior. The importance of this area is indicated by a number of findings (Bandler 1987): After removal of the entire forebrain, painful stimulation elicits a complete defensive display; stimulation of the PAG in animals with isolation or lesions of the "upstream" hypothalamic areas still produces a defensive reaction that includes directed attacking and biting; lesions of the PAG virtually eliminate most defensive responses to stimulation of amygdala and hypothalamic sites that normally elicit defense. PAG lesions also eliminate defensive responses to naturally threatening stimuli (Edwards & Adams 1974; Blanchard et al 1981). These results suggest that the PAG can produce a coordinated defense pattern against pain. However, higher forebrain centers may be required for "recognition" of nonpainful threatening stimuli, as well as for some complex modulatory effects.

The relevant structure appears to consist of a rostrodorsal, caudoventral column of cells in the PAG underlying the posterior half of the superior colliculus: Studies of microinjections of excitatory amino acids (Bandler et al 1985) indicate that the effective cells are largely within the PAG itself, not extending to adjacent tegmental areas. The view of an intimate connection between activity here and defensive behavior is supported by single-unit studies. Bandler and his colleagues have traced projections from the PAG to a number of midbrain and hindbrain nuclei that appear to be involved in the actual motor elements of the defense pattern.

Finally, the PAG (and at least one other midbrain site) is also involved with the cardiovascular components of the defensive response. A pattern of increases in heart rate and blood pressure, with vasoconstriction of renal, mesenteric, and cutaneous beds but vasodilation of skeletal beds, is characteristic of naturally elicited defense, doubtless serving as a form of physiological preparation for vigorous action. This pattern accompanies PAG stimulation that elicits defense, and Bandler and his colleagues, in addition to detailing skeletal motor outflow paths for defense from the PAG, have outlined efferent connections of the PAG in the hindbrain that are likely responsible for these cardiovascular effects. An additional bit of evidence linking hypothalamic sites to the behavioral and cardiovascular correlates of defense is that the hypothalamic-midbrain fiber system ending in part in the PAG also has terminations in the ventral tegmentum. Stimulation of this latter site, while not producing a behavioral defense pattern, does result in the appropriate cardiovascular changes.

Although the full cardiovascular pattern typical of defense is elicited by the PAG stimulation that produces defense, PAG lesions that eliminate defensive responses to higher-brain stimulation do not abolish this cardiovascular response. However, when lesions are made in both PAG and sites in the ventrolateral tegmentum, these cardiovascular changes are abolished (Bandler 1987). This architecture appears to provide an anatomical separation of the oriented defensive behaviors and cardiovascular changes in defense. Such a separation may reflect the involvement of the latter in very different behaviors, such as those involved in assessment of predatory risk.

THE "DEFENSE INHIBITORY SYSTEM"   While the above-described structures (i.e. specific areas of amygdala, preoptic area, hypothalamus, and midbrain central gray) all appear to be considerably involved with the initiation, modulation, integration, and organization of defensive behaviors, there is another brain system that also strongly influences this behavior pattern. For many years Albert and his colleagues (Albert & Richmond 1975; Albert & Walsh 1982, 1984) have studied a "defense inhibitory system" involving the lateral septal nucleus, the bed nucleus of the stria terminalis (BNST), and [only in rats (Albert & Walsh 1984)] the nucleus accumbens. Damage to these structures produces a transient or longer-lasting "release" of a number of defensive responses (including defensive threat and attack) to stimuli such as human handling, conspecific attack, or electric shock. This "release" of defensiveness is relatively consistent across species (Albert & Walsh 1984), but not all defensive behaviors are equally facilitated: In rats and cats, the animals most used in studies of brain localization, lesions in these areas (*a*) produce a striking increase in defensive threat and attack (Blanchard et al 1981), (*b*) apparently have little effect on flight, and (*c*) either decrease or do not change freezing behavior (in wild cats: Ursin et al 1981). A view of these areas as inhibitory of defensive behavior is supported by the finding that stimulation of the BNST reduces flight behaviors elicited by hypothalamic stimulation (Shaikh et al 1985).

Additional evidence for the involvement of this "defense inhibitory system" comes from combined stimulation-labelling studies which indicate (Fuchs et al 1985a; Watson et al 1983) that stimulation of flight and affective defense-eliciting areas in the medial nucleus of the amygdala and in the VMH produce activity in precisely the same set of structures as those implicated in the septal-area defense inhibitory system—lateral septal nuclei, the BNST, and an area around the anterior commissure as it diverges rostrally. The target for these inhibitory septal-area influences appears to be the MPOA,AH (Brutus et al 1984), which thus provides a possible site of confluence and interaction for input from the amygdala, the hypothalamus, and the septal-area inhibitory system.

When it is noted that the septal area, notably the lateral nucleus, is intimately tied to the hippocampal system, a somewhat different view of the action of this area becomes possible. Gray has suggested (1982) that the septo-hippocampal system underlies "anxiety" with specific functions that overlap considerably with those here described for the risk-assessment aspects of defense. The behaviors involved include movement arrest and tonic inhibition, as well as inhibition of behaviors that might compete with the risk-assessment pattern. Hippocampal damage produces a change in motor movement patterns and reduces freezing and latencies to engage in behaviors normally suppressed in risk situations (Blanchard & Blanchard 1969; Blanchard & Blanchard 1972). Many of these effects are seen also with septal-area lesions, overlaid with the higher defensive attack propensities associated with damage to the latter site. This configuration suggests that some aspects of the risk-assessment pattern—movement inhibition and the suppression of competing responses—may be particularly associated with the functioning of the hippocampus. The information-gathering aspect of this pattern is additionally compatible with O'Keefe & Nadel's (1978) view of the hippocampus as the substrate for "mapping" of the environment.

A DEFENSE SYSTEM SUMMARY   A preliminary analysis of the brain systems underlying defense suggests that some amygdala-area mechanism is involved in integration of complex, multisensory inputs underlying the perception of threatening "releasing stimuli" such as predators. This information passes to cells in the MPOA,AH, where it is integrated with information from VMH elements, possibly concerning the animal's hormonal status. Meanwhile, both the stimulus and the hormonal inputs have been processed also by the septal-area "defense inhibitory" system, which may promote shifts from one component of the defense pattern to another, in addition to changes in a general level of defensiveness. Some of the dense interaction of amygdala and hippocampus may be involved with analysis of stimuli leading to a "choice" between a risk-assessment pattern and an oriented-defense pattern. The output of this inhibitory system terminates in the same MPOA,AH area as the amygdala and hypothalamic components, and all three inputs are there integrated into a diffuse path. This path passes through the perifornical and lateral hypothalamus and the midbrain tegmentum (its tegmental terminations concerned with cardiovascular correlates of defensiveness) to terminate on the "final common path" PAG system, which is capable of controlling both behavioral and visceral components of defense.

Most of the work on defensive behaviors elicited by electrical brain stimulation has involved "affective defense," a choice that may in part reflect the salience of some aspects of this pattern in cats. Flight has also been studied, although to lesser degree, and many aspects of the neuroanatomic systems underlying flight seem to be similar to those subsuming affective defense. However, some brain sites apparently related to the flight system [e.g. the nucleus of the diagonal band of Broca and the centrum-medianum, parafascicular complex (Fuchs & Siegel 1984)] are not. Ursin (1965) and Kemble et al 1984 have also reported a differentiation between flight and affective defenses in the amygdala. Thus although a flight system has certainly not been mapped with the thoroughness of the affective defense system, and even though these two systems appear to overlap with reference to many specific sites, the possibility of a physiological differentiation between flight and affective defense should be seriously considered.

The Neural Control of Offense

FOREBRAIN   Compared to the detailed picture that can be presented for defense, little is known about the neural systems underlying offensive attack. Although the amygdala has long been regarded as an area in which stimulation can elicit, and lesions reduce, "rage" or "aggression," studies permitting a clear differentiation of the two have suggested that amygdala lesions reduce defense (Blanchard et al 1979) while offensive attack is not changed (Busch & Barfield 1977; D. C. Blanchard and S. Nakamura, unpublished results). Septal-area lesions also sharply reduce offense while increasing defensive attack (Lau & Miczek 1977; Blanchard & Blanchard 1977). However, since defensiveness, however elicited (Blanchard et al 1984), tends to strongly suppress offensive attack, the effect of these lesions is likely to be indirect.

Lesions in the MPOA,AH have also been reported to reduce intermale "social aggression" in the rat (Albert et al 1986a). Since such lesions decrease affective defense in cats (Fuchs et al 1985b), this is not likely to reflect increased fear. However, the decreased social aggression reported in that study largely involved biting rather than the initial segments of the offense pattern, raising the possibility that mechanisms related to biting (also a component of "affective defense") may be particularly represented in this area. Also, the MPOA (like the VMH) selectively takes up testosterone, and these same animals showed a decrease in sexual behavior (note the covariance of male offense and male sexual behavior after these manipulations), suggesting another mechanism for this effect.

HYPOTHALAMUS   In addition to producing a clear and consistent increase in defense, VMH lesions have been reported to increase some offensive attack elements (lateral attacks), but only in the context of reactivity to being attacked by another animal. Lesioned resident rats approached, investigated, and attacked intruders less, not more (Colpaert & Wiepkema 1976). Some component of this mixed picture may be due to an anterior/posterior division within the VMH. Olivier reported (1977) that anterior VMH lesions increase defensive attack, while posterior VMH lesions increase offense. Olivier et al (1983) reported a striking increase of offense by even more posterior medial hypothalamic lesions involving the area of the mammillary bodies.

A considerable amount of work has been done on attack behaviors elicited by electrical stimulation of hypothalamic sites lateral to the VMH, the importance of such a medial-lateral distinction having been recognized since early work by Adams (1971). These behaviors again appear to combine elements of offense and defense (Kruk et al 1979; Wiepkema et al 1980), but they respond appropriately to manipulations that influence male offense, such as administration of fluprazine (Kruk et al 1984). However, lesions of the

PAG, which totally block defensive behaviors (including defensive attack) from hypothalamic or amygdaloid stimulation, in some cases increased but in other cases decreased the hypothalamic stimulation current required to elicit these attack behaviors. Moreover, these same PAG lesions did not block spontaneously occurring territorial attack (Mos et al 1983). Thus although stimulation in the perifornical and lateral hypothalamus does appear to elicit some elements of offense, the PAG is not an essential element in the downward projections of this system.

MIDBRAIN   Adams has recently (1987) reported that lesions of the ventromedial tegmentum, adjacent to the medial raphe nuclei, do abolish offense, while defense and predation remain. This finding provides clear evidence that offense has a discrete substrate in the midbrain, and it agrees with the Mos et al study (1983) in indicating that the midbrain substrate for offense is very different from that of the defense system. As yet, however, the essential forebrain input to this area remains to be clarified.

Hormonal Influences on Offense and Self-Defense

Hormones in general are regarded as modulating agents, rather than as a direct and specific "cause" of a particular action pattern (Brain 1983). For both attack and defense there are appropriate eliciting stimuli or situations that are necessary for the appearance of the behavior, regardless of the presence or amount of the relevant hormone. This modulatory influence may be more or less robust and specific, however, and it may involve effects at different points in the elicitation and integration of an action pattern.

GONADAL HORMONES   Testosterone has been extensively investigated in conjunction with male offense patterns. Castration reduces male attack (Barfield et al 1972) while TP (testosterone propionate) replacement restores it (Barr et al 1976; DeBold & Miczek 1981). During the formation of rat colonies, castration and TP replacement therapies have the expected effects of reducing and restoring male attack (Albert et al 1986b). The potentiation of male attack by testosterone may also be a factor in the potentiation of male attack by sexual experience (Flannelly et al 1982) since copulation increases male testosterone levels (Kamel et al 1975).

Schuurman (1980) found a substantial and reliable correlation between individual male testosterone levels and attack on an intruder. This relationship involves influences in both directions, with defeat lowering testosterone levels. Testosterone level in the opponent animal also appears to be an important consideration in male offensive attack. Thor & Flannelly (1976) reported that resident males attack castrated male intruders less than intact animals, while attack toward intruder males of different ages appears to vary with the testosterone levels of these intruders, a level that is ascertained by the attacker through extensive olfactory investigation. It might here be mentioned that testosterone per se may not be the hormone involved in potentiation of male offense. Testosterone is converted in brain to estrogenic metabolites, and estrogen therapy following castration has many of the same restorative effects on male offense as TP replacement (Brain 1983).

Despite these consistent findings, gonadal hormones may not be a necessary condition for male offense. First, castrated males do attack intruders, although they are much more likely to be defeated by intact intruders than are intact residents (Christie & Barfield 1979). Also, the decline in attack seen after castration is much more dramatic in a novel situation than in the subject's home cage (Schuurman 1980), where castrated males may continue to attack intruders indefinitely.

In fact, in addition to its specific roles in the elicitation of male offense and sexual behavior, testosterone might well be viewed as having a more general energizing and behavior-organizing function, which extends also to defensive attack situations. Baenninger (1974) paired neonatally castrated to intact males in a reflexive fighting situation and found that although castrates showed the same pattern of activities, including biting, as intact rats, they were inclined to "give up" sooner, assuming the "on the back" posture and ceasing to make further active movements in response to shock. On the face of it, this finding suggests that castration may be a factor in the onset of "defeat" as defined by Miczek et al (1984). It seems likely that this difference in the persistence of active defense accounts for the frequent finding that castration reduces shock-induced fighting somewhat, and rather inconsistently (see Conner et al 1983 for a review).

An additional method of assessing the specificity of the relationship between hormones and attack/defensive behaviors is to examine the specific brain regions where these hormones are taken up. In both male and female primates (Rees & Michael 1982; Rees et al 1986), the major sites for testosterone uptake are: medial preoptic area, anterior hypothalamic area, ventromedial nucleus, bed nucleus of stria terminalis, lateral septal nucleus, and (in males only, but females were not examined in this area) periaqueductal gray. The congruence of this uptake pattern with the brain areas implicated in the control of affective defense is striking. Even more specifically, each of these areas is among those activated by VMH stimulation, and/or stimulation of the MPOA,AH, earlier postulated to be involved with hormonal/visceral modulation of agonistic behavior. What is also interesting is that the diagonal band of Broca and the centrum medianum, parafascicular complex, both linked to flight as opposed to defensive attack systems (Fuchs

& Siegel 1984), do not take up testosterone in the same way as do the areas implicated in the control of affective defense.

Luttge (1983) presents data suggesting that gonadal hormones may modulate aggression and defense through alterations of regional neurotransmitter systems. While this material is too complex to be meaningfully described here, it is notable that the areas involved are familiar (medial amygdala, septum, MPOA,AH, ventral tegmental area) and that many of the specific neurotransmitter systems influenced are those with independent evidence of influence on the behaviors we are examining.

ADRENOCORTICOIDS   The other set of hormones extensively investigated in conjunction with attack and defense are the adrenocorticoids. The effects of ACTH and corticosterone (the two major hormones of the pituitary-adrenocortical axis) on agonistic behaviors are complex, showing variation from species to species, variation with chronic as opposed to acute doses (ACTH), and nonmonotonic variation with dose level (ACTH) (Leshner 1983). An overview suggests that, on a short-term basis, variations in ACTH influence aggressiveness through alterations of corticosterone levels, but that on a long-term basis ACTH tends to decrease attack either through its direct action on brain function or through some mechanism other than corticosterone, or behavioral fearfulness, or testosterone changes (Leshner 1983).

Of the two hormones, corticosterone is more often linked to defeat and the effects of defeat on future attack and defensive behaviors. For both resident and intruder rats, corticosterone rises rapidly during an encounter, but it remains elevated for some time in the defeated intruder while quickly returning to normal in the victorious resident (Schuurman 1980). This effect may be rapidly conditioned and does not require pain; once defeated, male rats show a pronounced corticosterone surge in the presence of another male (Schuurman 1980). Corticosterone is also sensitive to housing- or situation-related stress or fear (DeWied 1969), and this stress or fear in an unfamiliar place is likely to be one of the factors reducing offense in intruders. Finally, both chronic and acute administration of corticosterone increases "submissiveness" components of the defense pattern (Leshner 1981; see Heller 1984a, b for some complications of this picture).

Corticosteroid uptake in brain (Luttge 1983) involves the hippocampus, the lateral septal area, and the corticomedial nuclei of the amygdala, plus the prefrontal area. This distribution is clearly congruent with Gray's suggestion that the hippocampal-septal system is involved in "anxiety" and with the present view that it is a risk-assessment pattern that is being described. The specific amygdala-area (and prefrontal) uptake suggests an effect of corticosterone-mediated emotional arousal on the processing of complex information.

The Involvement of Neurotransmitter Systems in Offense and Self-Defense

Because of an explosive increase in studies of the pharmacological control of emotion-related behaviors, the recent literature in this area is perhaps more extensive than that on all other aspects of the biology of emotion combined. This literature has been extensively summarized elsewhere (Miczek et al 1984; Panksepp 1986; Shepard 1986), and we mention only selected aspects here. A reasonable overview of the pharmacology of aggression may be found in the statement (Miczek et al 1984) that "Neither a specific 'aggressive' neuroamine or neuropeptide [has] been found nor a profile or constellation of neurotransmitter activity has been identified that is unique to aggressive behavior. . . ." This statement is true also for defense/anxiety. However, despite complications stemming from complexity and lack of knowledge involving both the behavioral and the pharmacological aspects of these putative relationships, some evidence suggests that certain classes of neurotransmitters may have relatively consistent differential effects on these behaviors.

BENZODIAZEPINE/GABA   The benzodiazepines (BZP) have been used widely and, in general, effectively as anxiolytic drugs over a period of 20 or more years. Recent evidence (Costa et al 1983) linking BZP action and the functioning of the GABA system provides a possible mechanism for influence on "behavioral inhibition" systems. Gray (1982) has also proposed that the BZP system mediates the activity of the behavioral inhibition system he identifies with anxiety. It is interesting to note that in rats bred for a polarization of "fearfulness" the fearful rats had a significantly lower number of [^{3}H]-Diazepam binding sites than the nonfearful ones (Robertson et al 1978).

Nonetheless, experimental evidence on an animal model linking BZP to anxiety is still preliminary. File (1985) has recently summarized work on BZP and "BZP-like" compounds in the context of exploratory and nose-poking behaviors in novel environments, activities that appear to be related to the assessment of predatory risk pattern. In this context, specific profiles of behavior change for the various compounds are often different, with subject-species effects, sedative effects, and the like producing complications. Some component of this difference may reflect differential actions of BZP type 1 and type 2 receptors with reference to stimulant and sedative effects (File & Cooper 1985). Recent clinical trials of a partial BZP agonist (Merz et al 1986) suggest greatly improved efficacy among patients not requiring sedation, which is consonant with the view that the anxiolytic and sedative aspects of BZP function may be separable. Such findings suggest that both improved behavioral models and increased understanding of the complex structure and function of the BZP/GABA system will be necessary before a clear set of relationships emerge in this area.

There is an additional mass of evidence on BZP and social behavior. Much of this has been reviewed recently by Rodgers & Waters (1985), who indicate that BZP consistently reduces defense, including defensive attack, in a number of species and contexts. BZP receptors also appear to be intimately involved in the non-opioid analgesia induced by defeat experience in male mice (Rodgers & Randall 1986), an interpretation that fits well with the interpretation of some of these non-opioid analgesic states as anxiety. Krsiak et al (1984), after testing the effects of 50 psychoactive drugs on attack and defense, found that only the BZP group (7 compounds) consistently reduced defense at dosages that did not alter offensive behaviors (although offense generally decreased at higher doses). In fact, BZP has very inconsistent effects on offense (Rodgers & Waters 1985). While there is an occasional report of enhanced offense following low doses of BZP, high doses consistently (and low doses sometimes) reduce offensive behavior.

THE OPIOIDS   Since the discovery of opiate receptors and endogenous opioid peptides in the 1970s, brain opioid systems have consistently been implicated in organismic responses to stress (Amir et al 1980). Both opiate agonists (such as morphine) and antagonists (e.g. naloxone) tend to suppress aggressive behavior, while either reducing or having no effect on defense (Miczek & Krsiak 1979; Olivier & van Dalen 1982; Puglisi-Allegra et al 1984; see Rodgers & Hendrie 1984 for a review of this area). However, the opioid system involves a number of different receptors, and high doses of either morphine or naloxone may affect all of these, perhaps with confounding effects. Benton has recently (1985) suggested that mu and kappa receptors have opposite effects on "timid/defensive" behaviors, with kappa additionally suppressing resident male aggression through its enhancement of defense.

However, the major focus of work on opioids and agonistic behavior has involved "defeat analgesia." Mice and rats under severe conspecific attack tend to assume a relatively immobile upright posture, failing to respond by body adjustments to further attack, and squealing when approached. These animals show substantially elevated thresholds for tail-flick in response to heat, indicating pain analgesia. Naloxone, an opioid-blocking agent, significantly decreased defeat analgesia without reliably altering other aspects of defense (Miczek & Thompson 1984). Tolerance to the effects of defeat was seen to develop with repeated testing, and withdrawal jumps occurred in response to naloxone administration after 7 days of testing. The arcuate nucleus and the periaqueductal gray appear to be particularly sensitive sites for these opioid effects. Direct injections of naloxone into these areas block the analgesia response (Miczek et al 1984).

Rodgers & Hendrie (1984) point out that isolated male mice are strongly analgesic compared to group-housed intruders before any encounter takes place; this difference is not responsive to naloxone and is therefore presumably not mediated by opioid mechanisms, although the defeat analgesia seen for intruders after defeat is opioid mediated. They interpret some aspects of these differences as reflecting variations in the controllability of the situation. This interpretation suggests it might be profitable to examine these phenomena in terms of a fear-anxiety distinction.

SEROTONIN   5-HT systems are regarded as important elements in the neurochemical substrate of reactivity to reward and punishment (see Panksepp 1986 for a review), and as inhibitors of aggression and a range of other behaviors (Reis 1974). Sheard (1983) found a good deal of support for the view that 5-HT inhibits many forms of "aggression," including predation as well as both offensive and defensive attack. It might be noted, however, that the major sources of brain 5-HT, the dorsal and medial nuclei of the raphe, appear to be differentially involved with aggressive behaviors. Both electrolytic (Jacobs & Cohen 1976) and neurotoxic [5,7 DHT (File et al 1981)] lesions of these two structures have produced very different effects on defensive attack, general activity, and behaviors related to dominance and submission.

In recent years the focus of 5-HT work has shifted toward anxiety. This trend may reflect an implicit view that the general (though by no means invariant) inhibitory effects of the serotonin system on aggression and other behaviors may be mediated by changes in an anxiety-linked inhibitory system. The evidence linking 5-HT to anxiety-related behaviors has been reviewed recently by Johnston & File (1986). The recent identification of subtypes of 5-HT receptors (5-HT1A,B,C; 5-HT2), together with the development of more selective 5-HT compounds, has given a fresh impetus to interest in the possible role of 5-HT pathways in the control of anxiety (Johnston & File 1986). In particular, several novel agonists that act primarily at 5-HT1A sites [e.g. buspirone, TVX Q7821 (Smith & Peroutka 1986)] have recently been reported to display nonsedative anxiolytic profiles in a number of animal models. These different subtypes of receptors appear to have diverse, and even opposite, effects on other behaviors [e.g. lordosis (Mendelson & Gorzalka 1986)], suggesting that the use of receptor-selective 5-HT compounds may quickly bring order to the many conflicting findings in this area.

THE SERENICS   A recently introduced class of "serenics" includes phenylpiperazine compounds such as fluprazine, DU 27716, and DU 28412. These compounds reduce offense of male rats and mice in a variety of situations (social isolation, resident-intruder, after stimulation of lateral hypothalamic areas) while not altering either the defensiveness of an intruder or general activity, at doses that influence offense. This finding makes their action considerably more specific than many other "antiaggressive" compounds (Olivier et al 1984). However, some lack of specificity of action is apparent for these compounds. They also reduce sexual behavior of male rats (Flannelly et al 1985), mouse-killing by rats, and "shock-induced aggression" (Bradford et al 1984). Van de Poll et al have recently (1986) reported a number of effects of fluprazine on both sexual and aggressive responses in testosterone-treated female rats, including an increase in offense toward other females. The effects of fluprazine may be mediated in large part through actions on the serotonin (5-HT) system. If so, it seems likely that the serenics selectively interact with specific subtypes of 5-HT receptors, and that an understanding of the pharmacological action of these compounds will be tied up with further analyses of the functions of the various serotonin receptors.

THE BIOLOGY OF THE EMOTIONS

The preceding sections on the relationship of certain biological systems to aggression, anxiety, and fear clearly represent only sketchy summaries of what are in each case research areas of moderate to considerable size. What these summaries suggest is that a large number of investigators representing a variety of biological and physiological research interests are coming to agree that careful attention to specific patterns of behavior—to the "architecture" of behavior, as it were—is prerequisite to an understanding of the relationship between biological and behavioral systems. This view emphasizes also that an adequate description of behavior must include reference to the stimuli and situations that normally produce that behavior, and to its normal consequences in the environment. This process of conceptualization of the essential stimulus-response-effect relationships in behavior should both produce and be enlightened by a view of the adaptive functions of the behavior pattern. This represents, in short, an ethoexperimental analysis.

Such analyses have produced dramatic changes in the concepts of aggression and fear, stemming from animal research. Aggression is conceptualized as offensive attack, which occurs in the context of resource or dominance disputes, and is adaptive because it facilitates access to important resources. Defensive attack, which is seen in reaction to pain or other immediate forms of danger from a predator or conspecific, is regarded as an important component of the self-defense pattern elicited by the types of discrete and discriminable stimuli that permit active, oriented defenses to be effective. Flight would also appear to fit this definition, but there are tantalizing hints that the neural substrate for flight may be so systematically different from defensive threat and attack that it is misleading to regard them as part of the same neurobehavioral system. Finally, the risk-assessment pattern is also related to defense, but it occurs in the context of unclear or partial threat stimuli and has the primary goal of acquiring information needed either to make the defense pattern effective or to make it unnecessary. While the use of appropriate models of risk assessment is recent, the clinical importance of pharmacological control of anxiety is now strongly boosting research in this area.

Ethoexperimental analysis is coming to be an important paradigm in the study of brain-behavior relationships at a time when physiological and pharmacological sophistication is increasing at an even faster pace than the analysis of behavior. Even the necessarily sketchy information presented here should make it clear that substantial progress is being made in the analysis of brain systems underlying emotional behaviors, and that this progress involves a description of systems separable on anatomical and pharmacological as well as behavioral grounds. This area is far from the sort of closure that will permit optimal use of this information in the alleviation of human problems. But with more appropriate models becoming available, it seems reasonable to expect a significant improvement in understanding of the biology of these emotional systems in the near future.

ACKNOWLEDGMENTS

Our gratitude to F. Robert Brush and Kevin Hori for their helpful comments on this manuscript. Support from NIH Research Grant AA06220 to R.J.B. and NIH RCMI Grant RR003061 to the Pacific Biomedical Research Center is gratefully acknowledged.

Literature Cited

Adams, D. B. 1971. Defense and territorial behavior dissociated by hypothalamic lesions in the rat. *Nature* 232:573–74

Adams, D. B. 1979. Brain mechanisms for offense, defense, and submission. *Behav. Brain Sci.* 2:201–41

Adams, D. 1987. Ventromedial tegmental lesions abolish offense without disturbing predation or defense. *Physiol. Behav.* In press

Aggleton, J. P., Mishkin, M. 1986. The amygdala: sensory gateway to the emotions. See Plutchik & Kellerman 1986, pp. 281–99

Albert, D. J., Dyson, E. M., Walsh, M. L. 1987. Intermale social aggression: reinstatement in castrated rats by implants of testosterone propionate in the medial hypothalamus. *Physiol. Behav.* 38. In press

Albert, D. J., Richmond, S. E. 1975. Septal hyperreactivity: a comparison of lesions within and adjacent to the septum. *Physiol. Behav.* 15:339–47

Albert, D. J., Walsh, M. L. 1981. Medial hypothalamic lesions in the rat enhance reactivity and mouse killing but not social aggression. *Physiol. Behav.* 28:791–95

Albert, D. J., Walsh, M. L. 1982. The inhibitory modulation of agonistic behavior in the rat brain: a review. *Neurosci. Biobehav. Rev.* 6:125–43

Albert, D. J., Walsh, M. L. 1984. Neural systems and the inhibitory modulation of agonistic behavior: a comparison of mammalian species. *Neurosci. Biobehav. Rev.* 8:5–24

Albert, D. J., Walsh, M. L., Gorzalka, B. B., Mendelson, S., Zalys, C. 1986a. Intermale social aggression: suppression by medial preoptic area lesions. *Physiol. Behav.* 38:169–73

Albert, D. J., Walsh, M. L., Gorzalka, B. B., Siemens, Y., Louie, H. 1986b. Testosterone removal in rats results in a decrease in social aggression and a loss of social dominance. *Physiol. Behav.* 36:401–7

Amir, S., Brown, Z. W., Amit, Z. 1980. The role of endorphins in stress: evidence and speculations. *Neurosci. Biobehav. Rev.* 4: 77–86

Archer, J. 1979. Behavioural aspects of fear. In *Fear in Animals and Man,* ed. W. Sluckin, 1:56–85. New York: Van Nostrand Reinhold

Baenninger, R. 1974. Effects of day one castration on aggressive behaviors of rats. *Bull. Psychonom. Soc.* 3:189–90

Bandler, R. 1987. Brain mechanisms of aggression as revealed by electrical and chemical stimulation: suggestion of a central role for the midbrain periaqueductal grey region. In *Progress in Psychobiology and Physiological Psychology,* ed. A. N. Epstein, R. Morrison. New York: Academic

Bandler, R., Depaulis, A., Vergnes, M. 1985. Identification of midbrain neurons mediating defensive behavior in the rat by microinjections of excitatory amino acids. *Behav. Brain Res.* 15:107–19

Barfield, R. J. 1984. Reproductive hormones and aggressive behavior. See Flannelly et al 1984, pp. 105–34

Barfield, R. J., Busch, D. E., Waleen, K. 1972. Gonadal influence on agonistic behavior in the male domestic rat. *Horm. Behav.* 3:247–59

Barnett, S. A. 1958. Social behaviour in wild rats. *Proc. Zool. Soc. London* 130:107–52

Barr, G. A., Gibbons, J. L., Moyer, K. E. 1976. Male-female differences and the influence of neonatal and adult testosterone on intraspecies aggression in rats. *J. Comp. Physiol. Psychol.* 90:1169–83

Benton, D. 1985. Mu and kappa opiate receptor involvement in agonistic behavior in mice. *Pharmacol. Biochem. Behav.* 23: 871–76

Blanchard, D. C., Blanchard, R. J. 1972. Innate and conditioned reactions to threat in rats with amygdaloid lesions. *J. Comp. Physiol. Psychol.* 81:281–90

Blanchard, D. C., Blanchard, R. J. 1984. Affect and aggression: an animal model applied to human behavior. In *Advances in the Study of Aggression,* ed. R. J. Blanchard, D. C. Blanchard, 1:1–58. New York: Academic

Blanchard, D. C., Blanchard, R. J., Lee, E. M. C., Nakamura, S. 1979. Defensive behaviors in rats following septal and septal-amygdala lesions. *J. Comp. Physiol. Psychol.* 93:378–90

Blanchard, D. C., Blanchard, R. J., Lee, E. M. C., Williams, G. 1981. Taming in the wild Norway rat following lesions in the basal ganglia. *Physiol. Behav.* 27:995–1000

Blanchard, D. C., Lee, E. M. C., Williams, G., Blanchard, R. J. 1981. Taming of *Rattus norvegicus* by lesions of the mesencephalic central gray. *Physiol. Psychol.* 9:157–63

Blanchard, R. J., Blanchard, D. C. 1969. Crouching as an index of fear. *J. Comp. Physiol. Psychol.* 67:370–75

Blanchard, R. J., Blanchard, D. C. 1980. The organization and modelling of aggressive behavior. In *The Biology of Aggression,* ed. P. F. Brain, D. Benton, pp. 529–62. Alphen aan den Rijn: Noordhoof/Sijthoff

Blanchard, R. J., Blanchard, D. C. 1986. Ethoexperimental models of fear and aggression. *Clin. Neuropharmacol.* 9:383–85

Blanchard, R. J., Blanchard, D. C. 1987. Ethoexperimental approaches to the study of fear. *Psychol. Rec.* In press

Blanchard, R. J., Blanchard, D. C., Takahashi, T., Kelley, M. J. 1977. Attack and defensive behaviour in the albino rat. *Anim. Behav.* 25:622–34

Blanchard, R. J., Kleinschmidt, C. K., Flannelly, K. J., Blanchard, D. C. 1984. Fear and aggression in the rat. *Aggress. Behav.* 10:309–15

Blanchard, R. J., Pank, L., Fellows, D., Blanchard, D. C. 1985. Conspecific wounding in free-ranging *Rattus norvegicus* from stable and unstable populations. *Psychol. Rec.* 35:329–35

Bradford, L. D., Olivier, B., van Dalen, D., Schipper, J. 1984. Serenics: the pharmacology of fluprazine and DU 28412. See Miczek et al 1984b, pp. 191–208

Brain, P. F. 1987. Ethoexperimental approaches to the study of behavior. Symp. presented at the European meetings of the Int. Soc. for Res. on Aggression, Seville

Brain, P. F., Benton, D., eds. 1981. *A Multidisciplinary Approach to Aggression Research.* Amsterdam: Elsevier/North Holland

Brain, P. F. 1983. Pituitary gonadal influences on social aggression. See Svare 1983, pp. 3–26

Brain, P. F., Benton, D. 1983. Conditions of housing, hormones, and aggressive behavior. See Svare 1983, pp. 351–72

Brutus, M., Shaikh, M. B., Siegel, H. E., Siegel, A. 1984. An analysis of the mechanisms underlying septal area control of hypothalamically elicited aggression in the cat. *Brain Res.* 310:235–48

Busch, D. E., Barfield, R. J. 1974. A failure of amygdaloid lesions to alter agonistic behavior in the laboratory rat. *Physiol. Behav.* 12:887–92

Christie, M. H., Barfield, R. J. 1979. Effects of castration and home cage residency on aggressive behavior in rats. *Horm. Behav.* 13:85–91

Colpaert, F., Wiepkema, P. R. 1976. Effects of ventromedial hypothalamic lesions on spontaneous intraspecies aggression in male rats. *Behav. Biol.* 166:117–25

Conner, R. L., Constantino, A. P., Scheuch, G. C. 1983. Hormonal influences on shock-induced fighting. See Svare 1983, pp. 119–44

Costa, E., Corda, M. G., Epstein, B., Forchetti, C., Guidotti, A. 1983. GABA-benzodiazepine interactions. In *The Benzodiazepines: From Molecular Biology to Clinical Practice*, ed. E. Costa, pp. 117–36. New York: Raven

Darwin, C. 1872. *The Expression of the Emotions in Man and Animals.* London: John Murray

DeBold, J. F., Miczek, K. A. 1981. Sexual dimorphism in the hormonal control of aggressive behavior of rats. *Pharmacol. Biochem. Behav.* 14:89–93

DeFries, J. C., McClearn, G. E. 1970. Social dominance and Darwinian fitness in the laboratory mouse. *Am. Nat.* 104:408–11

DeWied, D. 1969. Effects of peptide hormones on behavior. In *Frontiers in Neuroendocrinology*, ed. W. F. Ganong, L. Martini. New York: Oxford Univ. Press

Edmunds, M. 1974. *Defense in Animals.* Essex: Longmans

Edwards, M. A., Adams, D. B. 1974. Role of midbrain central gray in pain-induced defensive boxing of rats. *Physiol. Behav.* 13:113–21

Eibl-Eibesfeldt, I. 1961. The fighting behavior of animals. *Sci. Am.* 205:112–22

Eibl-Eibesfeldt, I. 1979. Human ethology: concepts and implications for the sciences of man. *Behav. Brain Sci.* 2:1–57

Ewer, R. F. 1971. The biology and behavior of a free-living population of black rats (*Rattus rattus*). *Anim. Behav. Monogr.* 4:127–74

File, S. E., Cooper, S. J. 1985. Benzodiazepines and behavior. *Neurosci. Biobehav. Rev.* 9:1–3

File, S. E., James, T. A., MacLeod, N. K. 1981. 5,7-Dihydroxytryptamine lesions of dorsal and medial raphe nuclei and performance in the social interaction test of anxiety and in a home-cage aggression test. *J. Affect. Dis.* 1:115–22

File, S. E. 1985. What can be learned from the effects of benzodiazepines on exploratory behavior? *Neurosci. Biobehav. Rev.* 9:45–54

Flannelly, K. J., Blanchard, R. J., Blanchard, D. C. 1984. *Biological Perspectives on Aggression.* New York: Alan R. Liss

Flannelly, K. J., Blanchard, R. J., Muraoka, M. Y., Flannelly, L. 1982. Copulation increases offensive attack in male rats. *Physiol. Behav.* 29:381–85

Flannelly, K. J., Lim, H. L., Diamond, M., Blanchard, D. C., Blanchard, R. J. 1985. Fluprazine hydrochloride decreases copulation in male rats. *Pharmacol. Biochem. Behav.* 22:1–4

Fuchs, S. A. G., Siegel, A. 1984. Neural pathways mediating hypothalamically elicited flight behavior in the cat. *Brain Res.* 306:263–81

Fuchs, S. A. G., Edinger, H. M., Siegel, A. 1985a. The organization of the hypothalamic pathways mediating affective defense behavior in the cat. *Brain Res.* 330:77–92

Fuchs, S. A. G., Edinger, H. M., Siegel, A. 1985b. The role of the anterior hypothalamus in affective defense behavior elicited from the ventromedial nucleus of the cat. *Brain Res.* 330:77–92

Grant, E. C. 1963. An analysis of the social behavior of the male laboratory rat. *Behaviour* 21:260–81

Gray, J. A. 1982. *The Neuropsychology of Anxiety: An Enquiry into the Functions of the Septo-Hippocampal System.* Oxford: Oxford Univ. Press

Halgren, E. 1981. The amygdala contribution to emotion and memory: current studies in humans. In *The Amygdaloid Complex*, ed. Y. Ben Ari, pp. 395–408. Amsterdam: Elsevier

Heller, K. E. 1984a. Role of the pituitary-adrenocortical axis in the control of agonistic behaviour after single and repeated footshock in castrated male mice. *Behav. Proc.* 9:323–38

Heller, K. E. 1984b. Effects of repeated exposure to electric footshock on subsequent agonistic behaviour and adrenocortical secretion in male mice of different androgen status. *Behav. Proc.* 9:61–72

Hitchcock, J., Davis, M. 1986. Lesions of the amygdala, but not of the cerebellum or red nucleus, block conditioned fear as measured with the potentiated startle paradigm. *Behav. Neurosci.* 100:11–22

Izard, C. E. 1972. *Patterns of Emotions: A New Analysis of Anxiety and Depression.* New York: Academic

Jacobs, B. L., Cohen, A. 1976. Differential behavioral effects of lesions of the median or dorsal raphe nuclei in rats' open field and pain-elicited aggression. *J. Comp. Physiol. Psychol.* 90:102–8

Johnston, A. L., File, S. E. 1986. 5-HT and anxiety: promises and pitfalls. *Pharmacol. Biochem. Behav.* 24:1467–70

Kamel, F., Mock, E. J., Wright, W. W., Frankel, A. I. 1975. Alterations in plasma concentrations of testosterone, LH, and prolactin associated with mating in the male rat. *Horm. Behav.* 6:277–88

Kemble, E. D., Blanchard, D. C., Blanchard, R. J., Takushi, R. 1984. Taming in wild rats following medial amygdaloid lesions. *Physiol. Behav.* 32:131–34

Krsiak, M., Sulcova, A., Donat, P., Tomasikova, Z., Dlohozkova, N., Kosar, E., Masek, K. 1984. Can social and agonistic interactions be used to detect anxiolytic activity of drugs? See Miczek et al 1984b, pp. 93–114

Kruk, M. R., van der Poel, A. M., de vos-Frerichs, T. P. 1979. The induction of aggressive behavior by electrical stimulation in the hypothalamus of male rats. *Behaviour* 70:292–322

Kruk, M. R., Van der Laan, C. E., Meelis, W., Phillips, R. E., Mos, J., Van der Poel, A. M. 1984. Brain-stimulation induced agonistic behavior: a novel paradigm in ethopharmacological aggression research. See Miczek et al 1984b, pp. 157–78

Lau, P., Miczek, K. A. 1977. Differential effects of septal lesions on attack and defensive submissive reactions during interspecies aggression in rats. *Physiol. Behav.* 19:479–85

Leshner, A. I. 1981. The role of hormones in the control of submissiveness. See Brain & Benton 1981, pp. 309–22

Leshner, A. I. 1983. Pituitary-adrenocortical effects on intermale agonistic behavior. See Svare 1983, pp. 27–38

Leyhausen, P. 1979. *Cat Behavior: the Predatory and Social Behavior of Domestic and Wild Cats.* New York: Garland STPM Press

Luttge, W. G. 1983. Molecular mechanisms of steroid hormone actions in the brain. See Svare 1983, pp. 247–312

Mendelson, S. D., Gorzalka, B. B. 1986. 5-HT1A receptors: differential involvement in female and male sexual behavior in the rat. *Physiol. Behav.* 37:345–51

Merz, W. A., Stabl, M., Ballmer, U. 1986. Prediction of treatment outcome with Ro 16-6028, a partial benzodiazepine agonist. Presented at the 15th C.I.N.P. Congress, San Juan, Puerto Rico

Miczek, K. A., DeBold, J. F., Thompson, M. L. 1984a. Pharmacological, hormonal, and behavioral manipulations in the analysis of aggressive behavior. See Miczek et al 1984b, pp. 1–26

Miczek, K. A., Kruk, M. R., Olivier, B. 1984b. *Ethopharmacological Aggression Research.* New York: Alan R. Liss

Miczek, K. A., Krsiak, M. 1979. Drug effects on agonistic behavior. In *Advances in Behavioral Pharmacology, Vol. 2,* ed. T. Thompson, P. B. Dews, pp. 87–162. New York: Academic

Miczek, K. A., Thompson, M. L. 1984. Analgesia resulting from defeat in a social confrontation: the role of endogenous opioids in the brain. In *Modulation of Sensorimotor Activity During Altered Behavioural States,* ed. R. Bandler. New York: Alan R. Liss

McConnell, P. S., Boer, G. J., Romijn, H. J., van de Poll, N. E., Corner, M. A. 1980. *Adaptive Capabilities of the Nervous System.* Amsterdam: Elsevier/North Holland.

Mos, J., Lammers, J. H. C. M., van der Poel, A. M., Bermond, B., Meelis, W., Kruk, M. R. 1983. Effects of midbrain central gray lesions on spontaneous and electrically induced aggression in the rat. *Aggress. Behav.* 9:133–55

O'Keefe, J., Nadel, L. 1978. *The Hippocampus as a Cognitive Map.* Oxford: Oxford Univ. Press

Olivier, B. 1977. The ventromedial hypothalamus and aggressive behavior in rats. *Aggress. Behav.* 3:47–56

Olivier, B. et al. 1984. Effects of a new psychoactive drug (DU27716) on different models of rat agonistic behavior and EEG. See Flannelly et al 1984, pp. 261–80

Olivier, B., Olivier-Aardema, R., Wiepkema, P. R. 1983. The effects of anterior hypothalamic and mammillary area lesions on territorial aggressive behavior in male rats. *Behav. Brain Res.* 9:59–81

Olivier, B., van Dalen, D. 1982. Social behavior in rats and mice: an ethologically based model for differentiating psychoactive drugs. *Aggress. Behav.* 8:163–68

Panksepp, J. 1986. The neurochemistry of behavior. *Ann. Rev. Psychol.* 37:77–107

Plutchik, R., Kellerman, H. 1986. *Emotion: Theory, Research, and Experience. Vol. III: Biological Foundations of Emotion.* New York: Academic

Puglisi-Allegra, S., Mele, A., Cabib, S. 1984. Involvement of endogenous opioid systems in social behavior of individually-housed mice. See Miczek et al 1984b, pp. 209–26

Rees, H. D., Bonsall, R. W., Michael, R. P. 1986. Sites of action of testosterone in the brain of the female primate. *Exp. Brain Res.* 63:67–75

Rees, H. D., Michael, R. P. 1982. Brain cells of the male rhesus monkey accumulate 3H-testosterone or its metabolites. *J. Comp. Neurol.* 206:273–77

Reis, D. J. 1974. Central neurotransmitters in aggression. *Res. Publ. Assoc. Res. Nerv. Ment. Disord.* 52:119–48

Robertson, H. A., Martin, I. L., Candy, J. M. 1978. Differences in benzodiazepine receptor binding in Maudsley reactive and Maudsley nonreactive rats. *Eur. J. Pharmacol.* 50:455

Rodgers, R. J., Hendrie, C. A. 1984. On the role of endogenous opioid mechanisms in offense, defense, and nociception. See Miczek et al 1984b, pp. 27–42

Rodgers, R. J., Randall, J. I. 1986. Acute non-opioid analgesia in defeated male mice. *Physiol. Behav.* 36:947–50

Rodgers, R. J., Waters, A. J. 1985. Benzodiazepines and their antagonists: a pharmacoethological analysis with particular reference to their actions on 'aggression'. *Neurosci. Biobehav. Rev.* 9:21–36

Rolls, E. T. 1986. Neural systems involved in primates. See Plutchik & Kellerman 1986, pp. 125–43

Schuurman, T. 1980. Hormonal correlates of agonistic behavior in adult male rats. See McConnell et al 1980, pp. 415–20

Scott, J. P., Fredericson, E. 1951. The causes of fighting in mice and rats. *Physiol. Zool.* 26:273–309

Shaikh, M. B., Brutus, M., Siegel, H. E., Siegel, A. 1985. Forebrain structures regulating flight behavior in the cat. *Brain Res. Bull.* 14:217–21

Sheard, M. H. 1983. Aggressive behavior: effects of neural modulation by serotonin. In *Aggressive Behavior: Genetic and Neural Approaches,* ed. E. C. Simmel, M. E. Hahn, J. K. Walters. Hillsdale: Erlbaum

Shepard, R. A. 1986. Neurotransmitters, anxiety and benzodiazepines: a critical review. *Neurosci. Biobehav. Rev.* 10:449–61

Simmel, E. C., Hahn, M. E., Walters, J. K., eds. 1983. *Aggressive Behavior: Genetic and Neural Approaches.* Hillsdale: Lawrence Erlbaum

Smith, L. M., Peroutka, S. J. 1986. Differential effects of 5-hydroxytryptamine 1A selective drugs on the 5-HT behavioral syndrome. *Pharmacol. Biochem. Behav.* 24:1513–18

Svare, B., ed. 1983. *Hormones and Aggressive Behavior.* New York: Plenum

Thor, D. H., Flannelly, K. J. 1976. Intruder gonadectomy and elicitation of territorial aggression in the rat. *Physiol. Behav.* 17:725–27

Treit, D. 1985. Animal models for the study of anti-anxiety agents: A review. *Neurosci. Biobehav. Rev.* 9:203–22

Ursin, H. 1965. The effect of amygdaloid lesions on flight and defense behavior in cats. *Exper. Neurol.* 11:61–79

Ursin, H. 1981. Neuroanatomical basis of aggression. See Brain & Benton 1981, pp. 269–94

Ursin, H., Blanchard, D. C., Blanchard, R. J., Ursin, R. 1981. Flight and defense in cats with septal lesions. *Bull. Psychon. Soc.* 17:206–8

van de Poll, N. E., Eerland, E. M. J., de-Jonge, F. H. 1986. Effects of fluprazine (DU 27716) upon aggressive and sexual behavior of testosterone-treated female rats. *Aggress. Behav.* 12:293–302

Watson, R. E., Troiano, R., Poulakos, J., Weiner, S., Block, C. H., Siegel, A. 1983. A (14C) 2-deoxyglucose analysis of the functional neural pathway to the limbic forebrain in the rat. I. The amygdala. *Brain Res. Rev.* 5:1–44

Wiepkema, P. R., Koolhaas, J. M., Olivier-Aardema, R. 1980. Adaptive aspects of neuronal elements in agonistic behavior. See McConnell et al 1980, pp. 369–85

Ann. Rev. Psychol. 1988. 39:69–100

COLOR VISION

Robert M. Boynton

University of California at San Diego, La Jolla, California 92093

CONTENTS

INTRODUCTION[1]

To understand color vision, one must pay attention first to the physics of light and its interaction with objects perceived, and then to the reception of photic input by the eye considered as an optical device, photon detector, and initial

---

[1]The following abbreviations are used in this chapter: CIE—Commission Internationale de l'Éclairage (International Commission on Illumination); deg—degree; ERG—electroretinogram; Hz—hertz; LGN—lateral geniculate nucleus; L-cone—longwavelength-sensitive cone photoreceptor (the other two are M and S); MSP—microspectrophotometry; nm—nanometer; td—troland; $V(\lambda)$—photopic spectral luminous efficiency function (spectral sensitivity of the light-adapted eye for the CIE standard observer).

0066-4308/88/0201-0069$02.00

processor of the resulting neural signals. Next comes extensive manipulation by the brain of what it receives from the eye, resulting finally in sensations and perceptions, the reports of which—when appropriately correlated with physical measures of the stimuli being viewed—constitute psychophysical data.

The study of the physiological bases of color vision, about which virtually nothing was known before the second half of the twentieth century, has for the most part advanced slowly and steadily since 1950, accompanied by the revival of opponent-color theory, spearheaded by the psychophysicists L. M. Hurvich and D. Jameson, and reinforced by the first physiological evidence of opponent responses in the retinas of fish and the LGNs of monkeys. Today, opponent-color concepts, contained within broader theories that also pay proper attention to trichromacy at the receptor stage, provide the dominant theoretical structure within which the largest number of color-related psychophysical experiments, and a substantial proportion of physiological ones, are currently being conducted.

During the period under review, substantial progress has been made on many fronts, with the most spectacular advances occurring at the receptor level, where the methods of molecular biology have revealed previously unknown details concerning the genetic basis for the cone pigments, and electrophysiological records have been obtained for the first time from single primate photoreceptors, including a few human cones. The discovery of ever more regions of the brain's cortex that are visually active has continued, although clear correlates of color perception in wavelength-dependent physiological activity recorded beyond the receptors are not yet easy to discern, probably because the chromatic problems that seem to be solved so easily by the visual system are in reality extremely difficult ones. For example, the color that seems so unambiguously attached to an object isn't really there; it exists only as a latent property of the object's surface, one that remains closely related to its spectral reflectance even under considerable variations in illumination that change the physical input to the eye. This phenomenon of color constancy, long studied but far from solved, is now being treated with rigor as part of the promising new field of computational vision. Logic, physiology, and psychophysics combine to show that color perception involves profound lateral influences, so that a color seen in the fixated central area (where we enjoy our best acuity and color vision) depends upon the radiance and spectral distribution of light received from many, and perhaps all, parts of the visual field.

As seems fitting for a psychological review, I have placed special emphasis on psychophysical experiments, choosing papers from selected areas of color science related to human color vision that have been published since the previous review of Mollon (1982); more than 90% of the references are to publications in the 1980s. Important areas not covered include comparative and developmental aspects, peripheral color vision, color deficiencies, and applications. The section to follow should help the reader locate some of this literature.

Books and Reviews

An unusual number of relevant books have been published during the period under review. In the category of textbooks are those of Hurvich (1981), Overheim & Wagner (1982), and a second edition of Billmeyer & Saltzman (1981). Hurvich's book is probably the best for most undergraduate psychology students; physics students might prefer Overheim & Wagner. Although Billmeyer & Saltzman speak primarily to industrial colorists, their text provides a useful introduction for others as well. In the handbook category, certain additions to the second edition of *Color Science* by Wyszecki & Stiles (1982) will interest psychologists. The first of two huge volumes called the *Handbook of Human Performance and Perception* (Boff et al 1986) includes two chapters on color. Some of the chapters in the new edition of the *IES Lighting Handbook* (Kaufman 1981) and two volumes of *Optical Radiation and Measurement* (Grum & Bartleson 1980; Bartleson & Grum 1984) also include relevant survey material.

Three excellent specialty books are Jacobs's (1981) *Comparative Color Vision,* Nassau's (1983) *The Physics and Chemistry of Color,* and Sherman's (1981) *Colour Vision in the Nineteenth Century.* Verriest's *Colour Deficiencies* Volumes (1980, 1982, 1984) summarize papers from the biennial meetings of the International Research Group on Color Vision Deficiencies. An introduction to that subject is provided by Fletcher & Voke's (1985) *Defective Colour Vision.* Two multiauthored volumes present material from a personal-historical viewpoint: Of interest here are five chapters in *Foundations of Sensory Science,* edited by Dawson & Enoch (1984), and four chapters in *Vision Research Retrospective: 1981–1986,* which I edited (Boynton 1987). On the physiological side, see Zrenner's (1983) monograph on *Neurophysiological Aspects of Color Vision in Primates* and a volume edited by Ottoson & Zeki (1985) on *Central and Peripheral Mechanisms of Colour Vision.*

During the summer of 1982, more than 100 color scientists gathered at the University of Cambridge to participate in an international conference on color vision. The proceedings were published in the form of 55 papers contained in a valuable book of more than 600 pages edited by Mollon & Sharpe (1983).

The only American journal dealing exclusively with color is the eclectic *Color Research and Application,* whose successful founding editor, F. W.

Billmeyer, Jr. concluded his tour of duty at the end of 1986 after 11 years. At least one third of what has been published in *CR&A* should be of interest to psychologists, and it is a good place to gain an entry into a wide variety of colorful subjects, including many that cannot be covered in this review. For example, the evaluation of color differences and formulas for their prediction runs like a thread tying together the 46 issues of the journal published through 1986. And there is much more. A wealth of historical material is contained within 20 articles in volumes 6 through 11. Articles on chromatic adaptation will be found in the Fall, 1981 (Vol. 6, No. 3) issue. A critical assessment of the evidence concerning popular views about the effects of color on humans (those fuzzy kinds of things that most laypeople think you must be studying if you are a psychologist interested in human color vision) has been prepared by Kaiser (1983, 1984). The Third Taniguchi Symposium, on "Neurobiological and Psychophysical Aspects of Color Vision," makes up Part 2 of Vol. 7, No. 2. Color vision models are presented and discussed by Benzschawel & Guth (1984), Hunt (1982), and Vos (1982). Volume 9, No. 4 features color order systems.

Instrumentation and Analytic Techniques

The use of raster displays permits spatial, temporal, and chromatic variables to be manipulated in almost any desired configuration. However, problems of calibration, linearity, stability, quantization, and unwanted spatial interactions have delayed their widespread use for serious color research. These problems are discussed in four papers starting on page 131 of Mollon & Sharpe (1983) and in more than a dozen papers in a special issue of *Color Research and Application* (Cowan 1986). It seems probable that raster displays will be used for most of the studies that will be cited in the next *Annual Review of Psychology* chapter on color vision in 1994. Meanwhile, the Maxwellian view continues to be important for experiments requiring high-intensity monochromatic radiation, and for displays that must be spatially and temporally continuous, rather than quantized. Whereas four- and five-channel systems were once rarities, these are now commonplace; most such apparatuses are now under computer control.

Instruments that take advantage of Zeiss fundus camera optics (van Norren & van der Kraats 1981; Faulkner & Kemp 1984) have approximately doubled the density difference recorded between a fully bleached and dark-adapted retina as compared to earlier retinal densitometers. Krauskopf et al (1981) have described a computer-controlled color mixer that uses laser primaries. Although limited to much weaker stimuli, the La Jolla Analytic Colorimeter (Boynton & Nagy 1982) permits straightforward control of stimuli along the cardinal axes of color space at constant luminance.

STRUCTURE AND FUNCTION OF PRECORTICAL PATHWAYS

Photopigments

DIRECT MEASUREMENTS   Suction electrodes permit recordings from single primate receptors (Nunn et al 1984). Within the range of variation attributable to self-screening and wavelength-selective preretinal absorption (Smith et al (1983), the most recent action spectra from macaque monkey cones (Bowmaker 1984; Baylor et al 1984) are in satisfactory agreement with estimates from psychophysics and microspectrophotometry obtained by Dartnall et al (1983). Data from six longwave-sensitive human cones (Schnapf et al 1987) agree closely with those from monkeys.

The first reports concerning the genetic basis of the visual photopigments have been published by Nathans et al (1986a, b). Whereas the DNA sequences of the L- and M-cone pigments are 99% homologous, the percentage of sequence homology between either of these and S-cone pigment is less than 50%. As expected, the genes for L- and M-cone pigments are found on the X chromosome; not anticipated was the finding that the X chromosomes of color normals may have more than one M-cone pigment gene. Human S-cone pigment derives from chromosome 7, consistent with the autosomal mode of inheritance of visual deficiencies ascribed to S-cone abnormality. Rhodopsin, the rod photopigment, derives from chromosome 3. Useful brief reviews of this work have been prepared by Botstein (1986) and Mollon (1986).

PSYCHOPHYSICS   Various psychophysical estimates suggest a small variation in the wavelengths of peak sensitivity within cone classes (MacLeod & Webster 1983; Nagy et al 1981; Neitz & Jacobs 1986), most of which seems to occur between subjects. Nevertheless, when self-screening and the role of inert pigments are taken into account, mean color-matching data should be linear transformations of mean cone action spectra. Burns & Elsner (1985) studied failures of linearity in color matching at high illuminances, showing changes in the Rayleigh match of more than twofold over a range from about 4–5 log td, in good quantitative agreement with the known bleaching range and what would be expected from associated changes in self-screening by L- and M-cone pigments.

In 1959, Stiles & Burch published mean "pilot" data for 10 subjects who made matches with 2-deg fields as part of a larger project that used a much larger cadre of observers of 10-deg fields. Estévez (1982) has been the principal spokesman for those who have regarded the average values from the Stiles-Burch study as the best small-field color-matching data against which to compare cone action spectra. Only average data were published, and for many years the individual 2-deg data were believed to have been irretrievably lost. Thanks to the efforts of Trezona (1987), they have been recovered and are now available.

Many studies, including those of Goldberg et al (1983), Buck (1985a,b), and Coletta & Adams (1986) show rod-cone interactions, some of very great magnitude. Consequently rods influence color appearance even at photopic levels (McCann & Benton 1969), although matches remain trichromatic, implying that trichromacy is not fully determined at the receptor stage unless rods are selectively eliminated by one of the psychophysicist's tricks: a bleach, very fast flicker, or the use of stimuli confined to the rod-free foveola.

The pigment-loss explanation of dichromacy, which is still adequate to explain small-field results, requires serious modification where large fields are concerned. The results indicate that most dichromats experience the sensation of red, which according to conventional wisdom is supposed to be lacking. In support of this view, Pokorny & Smith (1982) review psychophysical evidence from seven studies (their references 25 to 31) authored by various combinations of R. M. Boynton, M. E. Breton, W. B. Cowan, F. S. Frome, D. H. Kelly, A. L. Nagy, J. Pokorny, V. C. Smith, and T. P. Piantanida. These investigators used a variety of methods including color naming, matching, bleaching, and flicker to reach common conclusions: With large fields, most dichromats enjoy a limited anomalous trichromacy based partially on signals from rods, with the remainder coming from cones, two of which are of the normal type. The anomalous third type does not exhibit itself in small-field tests, or with prolonged adaptation, which is why it has been thought to be missing entirely in dichromats. Because these new findings complicate an otherwise straightforward and well-publicized story, they probably will not be included at the textbook level for some years.

Receptors

TERMINOLOGY   No consensus has been reached for naming the three classes of cones. The following designations have been most widely used and are equivalent within categories: S, SWS, B, blue; M, MWS, G, green; L, LWS, R, red. The S-M-L designation is used here to designate receptors whose action spectra peak in the short-, middle-, and long-wavelength regions of the visible spectrum.

S-CONE DISTRIBUTION   Because all cones from a particular region of the retina look much alike, the probability of finding an S-cone for direct study is low and commensurate with their relatively small numbers in the retina. Light microscopy reveals a sprinkling of retinal cones that are a bit larger and more circular than the others (Borwein et al 1980; Ahnhelt et al 1987); these seem to be the same ones that selectively stain (McCrane et al 1983). On the basis of a comparison with psychophysical data showing regions of high S-cone sensitivity showing a similar topography (Williams et al 1981a,b), the identification of the selectively stained receptors as S cones seems established. As long suspected, S cones are absent, or nearly so, in the foveola. Their density reaches a maximum in a ring about 1 deg out, falling to a low and uniform level beyond that. This pattern bears no resemblance at all to the classical function of G. Oesterberg showing a cone density that peaks sharply at the foveola, attributable to L and M cones (De Monasterio et al 1985). The S cones are too widely spaced to play an important role in spatial vision, but they are capable of mediating weak border perception (Kaiser & Boynton 1985; Boynton et al 1985; Kaiser & Ayama 1985).

L/M RATIO   Given a lack of direct evidence about the distribution of L and M cones that make up most of the hexagonal receptor array, recent speculations about the L/M ratio, put forth in the context of broader models, have varied from 0.67 [Paulus & Kröger-Paulus (1983)] to 1.6 [Ingling & Martinez-Uriegas (1983a)]. An estimate of about 2 has been derived from analysis of the slopes of psychometric functions by Cicerone & Nerger (1985), although they find substantial individual differences. Table 1, which shows L/M values from MSP and suction-electrode studies, suggests that there may also be sampling biases and species differences. Older work that also indicates appreciable individual differences among humans is discussed by Ingling & Martinez-Uriegas (1983a); see also Akita et al (1982).

RECEPTOR INTERACTIONS   Baron (1980, 1982) has found evidence in the waveforms of cone-dominated local ERGs from cynomolgus of a difference signal believed to result from interactions between L and M cones. Although the interpretation of local ERGs as pure cone potentials can be questioned, primate retinal anatomy supports the possibility of such interactions, and electrophysiological data from other animals (for example, the carp, summa-

Table 1 Numbers of L and M cones, and their ratios, found in microspectrophotometric (MSP) and suction-electrode (SE) studies.

Method	Species	L	M	L/M	Study
MSP	cynomolgus	21	14	1.50	Bowmaker 1984
MSP	rhesus	121	89	1.36	Bowmaker 1984
MSP	baboon	59	44	1.34	Bowmaker 1984
SE	cynomolgus	306	300	1.02	Baylor et al 1984
MSP	human	45	58	0.78	Dartnall et al 1983
Total		552	505	1.09	

rized by Toyoda et al 1982) support the concept of interactions between L and M cones that depend upon tight junctions between receptors and/or horizontal-cell feedback. Although Naka & Rushton's (1966) Principle of Univariance need not be repealed where photopigments are concerned, perhaps it should at least have its capitals lowered when applied to the description of signals from cone photoreceptors. Nevertheless, Abraham et al (1985), working with the human electroretinogram, provide convincing evidence that field sensitivity functions can be obtained that depend only upon the most-sensitive L or M cone type. They ascribe observed phase differences between L and M cones to the receptors themselves, rather than to interactions between them.

Beyond the Receptors

For generalization to human vision, Old World monkeys are the subjects of choice (Harwerth & Smith 1985); for this reason, unless noted otherwise, reference to animal work in this review refers only to macaques. In the primate retina, details of horizontal, bipolar, amacrine, and interplexiform cell function remain obscure because records from these neurons have yet to be obtained. Records from primate retinal ganglion and LGN cells, first obtained about 25 years ago, require invasive procedures that cannot be used on humans. Cynomolgus and rhesus have been most commonly used, without substantial differences being found between them. Gouras & Zrenner (1981a) report 13 kinds of retinal ganglion cells. Double-opponent retinal ganglion or LGN cells are not found distal to the cortex. Instead, neurons of the center-surround, single-opponent type, discovered by Wiesel & Hubel in 1966, vastly predominate, and it has become generally accepted that they play a role in pattern perception whose importance at least equals that for color.

Zrenner & Gouras (1981) report that ganglion cells receiving S-cone input are always excitatory, forming the centers of receptive fields that show surround inhibition from L and M cones. In sharp contrast to this, Valberg et al (1986) find cells that receive excitation from M and inhibition from S cones, with coextensive excitatory and inhibitory pools. Such discrepancies must relate somehow to methodological differences. Although Valberg et al recorded from the LGN rather than from retinal ganglion cells, this difference is probably trivial compared to the influence of stimulus conditions. Whereas Zrenner & Gouras present their stimuli against a dark background, the Valberg group replaces an otherwise steady white adapting field with brief, monochromatic test pulses, and they plot curves showing impulses/sec versus the luminance ratio between test and adapting fields. These functions reach a maximum just beyond unity and then decrease. Ratios less than unity, which allow the study of colors darker than the prevailing adapting level, have seldom been assessed by electrophysiologists. By using the full range of ratios, the Valberg team has been able to develop a model relating their results to human surface-color perception; the model is also able to account for the complex shapes of their experimental functions.

For the brain to sort out the signals it receives, its visual parts beyond the LGN face a formidable task: A given class of neuron, even assuming a labeled line, carries an ambiguous code much like a single class of cone at the initial stage. Having two types of center-surround ganglion cells, rather than just one, may simplify the decoding problem. Ingling & Martinez-Uriegas (1983a) propose that the discrepancy between the crossover wavelengths for L and M sensitivity curves required to account for color balance around 570 nm as compared to that needed to predict luminance by their sum (about 490 nm) can be explained on the hypothesis that M-center cells predominate by a ratio of about $2:1$.

Channels

The concept of chromatic-opponent and achromatic-nonopponent channels in the visual system, which was already well established prior to the current review period (Boynton 1979), has inspired a large body of recent research that has in general strongly supported this important division of function while filling in many interesting details. However, as defined by psychophysics, a channel is not isomorphic with a unique neuronal pathway, and many textbooks will need revision on this important point. Zrenner & Gouras first reported at ARVO in 1978 that red-green ganglion cells lose their opponency as frequency is increased to about 30 Hz. Ingling & Martinez-Uriegas (1983b) call attention to the idea that the Y-cell system (magnocellular, phasic, and nonlinear) cannot logically mediate the vision of small details, which must therefore be handled by the same X-cell (parvocellular, tonic, and linear) units responsible for carrying the opponent-color code. They have produced a plausible model to show how such multiplexing might occur (Ingling & Martinez-Uriegas 1985; see also Kelly 1983).

BASIC CHANNEL CHARACTERISTICS   It is well established that modulation transfer functions of chromatic channels are low-pass both in time and space, whereas those of achromatic channels are band-pass with much higher cutoff frequencies (Kelly 1983; Mullen 1985). Stripes that appear to alternate between red and green appear as lighter and darker yellow at intermediate spatial frequencies, beyond which a uniform field is seen. Pulses that clearly alternate between red and green at low temporal frequencies fuse into a flickering yellow as frequency is increased to about 20 Hz, becoming steady only at yet higher frequencies. Wisowaty (1981) has shown that extreme care must be taken to eliminate achromatic artifacts if the temporal characteristics of red-green opponent channels are to be examined validly using flicker; chromatic aberration complicates the spatial picture.

EFFECT OF TEST WAVEFORM   Test lights that are small and brief tend to isolate achromatic channels. However, Finkelstein & Hood (1982, 1984) and Kaiser & Ayama (1986) have shown that such isolation is incomplete. Large and long flashes tend to favor chromatic channels, especially if superimposed on a white background, for which purpose 1000 td is often used. Better isolation is achieved by shaping the test pulses to avoid abrupt edges in space and transients in time (Thornton & Pugh 1983).

ADDITIVITY AND CANCELLATION   Spectral sensitivity functions with peaks in the orange, green, and violet spectral regions are often used as a signature of opponent-channel activity (for example, see Foster & Snelgar 1983). Such functions are held to result from additivity failure related to chromatic cancellation. Total isolation of an opponent channel would imply that a test flash at a crossover wavelength, where excitatory and inhibitory cone inputs cancel, should remain invisible even at the highest intensities. However, unlike the familiar and complete cancellation of the component hues of suprathreshold stimuli that otherwise remain clearly visible, cancellation is only partial for thresholds, implying that, with detection as the criterion, the complete isolation of chromatic channels by the manipulation of stimulus parameters is probably impossible.

Results using the color-cancellation method introduced 30 years ago by L. M. Hurvich and D. Jameson have been compared with those for red-green cancellation at threshold by Akita et al (1985), who find reasonable agreement. Takahashi & Ejima (1984) show that reducing field size increases the red and yellow chromatic responses relative to those for green and blue, in accord with the classical view of small-field tritanopia. Ejima & Takahashi (1984, 1985) demonstrate nonlinearities of hue cancellation as a function of intensity which they attribute to interactions between S cones and either L or M cones at the opponent site. They also cite evidence for interactions between the yellow-blue and red-green opponent systems.

TRANSIENT DESENSITIZATION   Evidence of chromatic channel function is also provided by transient desensitization following the extinction of an adapting field (see the discussion of transient tritanopia by Mollon 1982). Originally thought to be limited to the blue-yellow system, it also occurs, although less spectacularly, in the red-green channels (Reeves 1981a–c; Reeves 1983). These "second stage" effects have also been studied for flickering adapting fields (Jameson et al 1979; Benzschawel & Guth 1982). Transient desensitization is greatly reduced when a preadapting field is flickered, rather than being presented as a steady light. Flicker adaptation also lessens the disruption of red-green equilibrium, although the time required to recover equilibrium is extended.

LINEARITY TESTS   Linearity of opponent cancellation, a characteristic feature of several models, would imply that an equilibrium color (unique hue) should remain so over a wide range of intensities; also, loci for unique hues should plot as straight lines through the white point in a chromaticity diagram. Pokorny et al (1981) have given an account of how to treat and consider nonlinearities in the yellow-blue pathway, but their summary requires updating on the basis of subsequent studies, many of them from their own laboratory. These show that nonlinearities, which are very obvious in the yellow-blue channel, occur also in the red-green channel (Burns et al 1984). Elsner et al (1987) find changes in constant-hue loci with spatial frequency that they feel cannot be explained by optical factors, chromatic induction, or changes in the relative sensitivity of the opponent channels. Larimer (1981) finds that, for nonequilibrium adapting fields, linearity fails for low-intensity test stimuli.

King-Smith & Kranda (1981), measuring thresholds, also observe nonlinearities. Elzinga & de Weert (1984), in a complicated theoretical paper, ascribe nonlinearities at threshold to the S-cone system. Ejima & Takahashi (1985), who have extensively tested shifts of unique hues with intensity, also find nonlinearities in both opponent systems, although these tend to stabilize above 500 td: They posit an S-cone input into the red-green channel as well as second-stage influences.

The question of whether unique white remains so with intensity variations has been tested over a 4 log unit range in separate studies with starkly conflicting results: Ejima et al (1986) say no, Walraven & Werner (1986) say yes; the reason for this discrepancy is unclear.

NEW PSYCHOPHYSICAL TECHNIQUES   Piantanida (1985) used a field that ordinarily would be achromatic, but which appears yellow only because of the filling-in of a stabilized retinal image. He then demonstrated that such a field will alter the modulation sensitivity of S cones in a manner similar to a field that appears yellow for the ordinary reason. Krauskopf et al (1982) used a 1-Hz sinusoidal "habituation" stimulus followed by test pulses exhibiting a Gaussian shape in time, and found evidence of three underlying channels, two of which were conventional—red-green and luminance. The third lay along a tritanopic axis (which differs significantly from a yellow-blue one). At first they attributed their results to second-stage processing, but a later analysis (Krauskopf et al 1986a) has also implicated higher-order color mechanisms thought to exist in great variety, each with its own characteristic color preference.

Foster (1981) and Foster & Snelgar (1983) show that the peaks and dips of spectral sensitivity functions are exaggerated if the test flash is superimposed upon a fixed white pedestal of equal area, rather than upon the more common extended background. Stromeyer (1983) also finds large threshold elevations caused by the use of small adapting fields. By contrast, Laxar et al (1984) show that spectral sensitivity measured by flicker photometry is unaffected by reducing the size of a steady chromatic adapting field until it equals that of the alternating test stimuli, even though the larger field produces the usual simultaneous contrast effects; this disassociation of flicker sensitivity and color appearance reinforces the idea that flicker photometry selectively taps achromatic pathways.

Reeves (1983) is able to distinguish contributions of chromatic channels in early dark adaptation. Stromeyer et al (1985) show how chromatic adaptation selectively influences the spectral sensitivity of opponent channels.

PHYSIOLOGICAL BASIS   It is not easy to understand the physiological basis for psychophysical data of the sort just described. Derrington et al (1984), recording from the LGN in response to perturbations in various chromatic and combined chromatic-achromatic directions around a white point, support the bipartite distinction between chromatic cell types but do not find evidence for the chromatic-achromatic distinction; also they do not observe habituation of the type seen psychophysically. Lennie & D'Zmura (1987; see also Lennie, 1984 and 1986 for briefer reviews) stress such discrepancies between LGN records and psychophysics, and make the point (also stated by Gouras & Eggers, 1984) that the neurons of the primate retinogeniculate pathway, taken one at a time, cannot distinguish color from brightness; therefore they must play a dual role in pattern vision as well as hue perception.

LUMINANCE, BRIGHTNESS, AND PHOTOMETRY

Isoluminance

DEFINITION   The term *isoluminant,* which seems to have been coined by Gregory in 1977, has come into general use to describe a condition that occurs when the relative luminances of two stimuli are adjusted in an effort to null the achromatic visual channels. Doing so provides a test of residual capacity of the opponent-color channels to mediate the activity under test. Unfortunately, there have been frequent disagreements in reported results that seem attributable to one or more of the following: (*a*) differences between studies in the amount of chromatic contrast remaining at isoluminance, (*b*) which of the two opponent-color channels is most active, (*c*) differing response criteria, or (*d*) failure to eliminate achromatic artifacts.

DEPTH   Lu & Fender (1972) and Gregory (1977) reported that the sensation of depth in random-dot stereograms disappeared at isoluminance. De Weert & Sadza (1983) were unable to confirm this; also, according to Grinberg &

Williams (1985), depth does not disappear at the null point for the isolated S-cone system which theoretically feeds only opponent channels. On the other hand Troscianko (1987), using uncorrelated dynamic surrounds and a response criterion that required the observer to discriminate the shape of an apparently moving target, did find that depth disappeared at isoluminance (although the perception of random-dot symmetry remained).

MOTION   Ramachandran & Gregory (1978) reported that motion perception disappeared at isoluminance. They concluded (p. 56) that "colour and motion are handled separately by the human visual system and . . . colour provides only a weak 'cue', at best, to movement perception." This conclusion is at odds with findings of Derrington & Badcock (1985), who reported transfer of the motion aftereffect between systems, and of Mullen & Baker (1985), who observed a motion aftereffect from an isoluminant stimulus. Also, Cavanagh & Favreau (1985) report that an equiluminant target can be used to null the perceived motion of a luminance-based target, provided that the equiluminant one is moving about five times faster.

METACONTRAST   Flashes can be produced at isoluminance by hue substitution. On the basis of experiments with such stimuli, Bowen et al (1977) concluded that metacontrast masking requires luminance contrast for its occurrence. Foster (1979) found metacontrast masking for all combinations of masks and tests that were selectively active on π_1 and π_5 mechanisms. A condition where pi-1 is exclusively involved should be isoluminant; yet this condition actually produced the largest metacontrast effects. Reeves (1981d) also found metacontrast masking at isoluminance. His conclusion, which seems reasonable, is simply that Bowen's group used a hue difference that was too small to reveal the effect.

LOCALIZATION   Morgan & Aiba (1985) found that spatial localization, evaluated by vernier acuity, was less accurately performed at equiluminance than with a luminance boundary, and that the result was specific to the isoluminant situation and not merely dependent on a loss of effective stimulus contrast. They attribute their result to the differing spatial filtering characteristics of luminance and opponent-color units.

CHROMATIC VS ACHROMATIC CONTRAST   No general agreement exists concerning how isoluminant (chromatic) and luminance (achromatic) contrasts can be validly compared. An effort to measure this for short and steadily fixated borders is that of Frome et al (1981), who studied the resistance to fading of such borders, when steadily fixated, as a function of chromatic contrast, luminance contrast, and luminance level. Tritanopic purity differences characterized the salient aspect of chromatic contrast very well, indicating as expected that S cones play no significant role in this situation.

"Brightness/Luminance" Ratio

Two stimuli that match for CIE-defined luminance may differ radically in brightness; it is typically the more saturated of the two that appears brighter (Uchikawa et al 1984). The effect is usually evaluated by having an observer adjust the luminance of a white light until it matches a chromatic one for brightness. The ratio of the two luminances is often called a "brightness/ luminance" (B/L) ratio, although it is actually the luminance ratio required for equal brightness. Quantitative studies of the phenomenon by Burns et al (1982) and Booker (1981) have yielded results that agree qualitatively, though not in detail. Surprisingly, Fry (1984) finds the ratio to be constant for pairs of wavelengths used for his method of distimulus photometry, including 680 nm and 520 nm, for which saturations differ substantially. Ikeda & Nakano (1986) have examined the effects of stimulus parameters by culling data from several studies. As field size is reduced, the values of B/L become smaller; in the limiting case of point sources they approach unity, provided that the Judd-corrected $V(\lambda)$ function is used to make the calculation. The implication is that brightness contributed by the luminance channels increases more slowly with area than that contributed by the opponent-color channels.

At the prompting of a CIE committee working on the problem, Ware & Cowan (1983) found 63 studies of the brightness-luminance phenomenon in the literature; after applying reasonable criteria for selecting data from these, they fitted a fourth-order polynomial that can be used to calculate B/L for any chromaticity. In contrast to this atheoretical approach, Howett (1986a), using a linear opponent-color model in which the chromatic channels carry the extra brightness signals, attempted to account for a more limited set of data. The brightness-luminance relation for spectral lights has also been examined theoretically by Elzinga & de Weert (1986).

Photometry

SIGNIFICANCE OF BRIGHTNESS   Howett (1986b), basing his argument largely on the inability of $V(\lambda)$ to predict brightness, has written about a "coming redefinition of photometry." Although this may be in prospect, it is not unreasonable to ask just what significance brightness really has, and whether it is even worthwhile to develop an alternative photometric scheme that attempts to predict it. Not often emphasized is the fact that the extra brightness added by unbalancing the opponent-color channels surely must keep saturated surface colors from looking as dark as they otherwise would.

In particular, red, which is generally regarded as a bright surface color, is nevertheless produced by surfaces of low reflectance. On the other hand, luminance, rather than brightness, predicts many things, including the strength of contours (Boynton 1978), level of visual acuity (Olzak & Thomas 1986, pp. 7–47), limits of temporal resolution (see the next section), reaction time (Guth 1964), and quite possibly other aspects of visually mediated performance.

FLICKER   The established method of photometric measurement that discounts both brightness and S-cone contributions is that of flicker photometry, selected originally because of the linearity of the resulting data. Strong disagreement exists concerning whether the resulting photometric values can be explained in terms of additive combinations of the same receptor outputs upon which colorimetric specification can be based. For examples of contrasting views, see MacLeod (yes, 1982) vs Estévez (no, 1982). For dichromats, Nagy et al (1984) show that spectral sensitivity, as determined by flicker photometry, can be accounted for by the action spectrum of the remaining normal pigment; Eisner & MacLeod (1981), using a chromatic adaptation method, found that it was unexpectedly easy to isolate either the L- or M-cone inputs to the visual systems of normal observers, although Swanson et al (1986) question this because of phase shifts observed under similar conditions. Individual differences are modest: Luria & Neri (1986) find standard deviations of less than 0.1 log unit, over most of the spectrum, for the flicker-photometric settings of 52 normal observers. Using a sensitive test, Ikeda (1983) has found only slight departures from linearity, and these exceptions occur only at a low flicker frequency, with dark adaptation, and using red-green combinations. Cushman & Levinson (1983) and Lindsey et al (1986) have found phase dependencies in heterochromatic flicker, but these do not seem to complicate the use of the method in practice.

MESOPIC PHOTOMETRY   It has long been recognized that, because of a gradual shift from cone to rod vision in the mesopic region, photometric matches obtained at photopic luminance levels fail badly at scotopic ones. Sagawa & Takeichi (1986) have obtained extensive new data, limited to spectral stimuli, which they fit using the equation

$$\log V(\lambda) = a \log V(\lambda) + (1 - a) \log V(\lambda),$$

where the value of a shifts gradually from zero at 100 photopic td to unity at 0.01 photopic td. (Slightly different values of a are used depending upon whether wavelength is greater or less than 570 nm.) Trezona (1986) is continuing to develop a system of general photometry, also aimed at the mesopic region, based on her newly obtained 10-deg brightness-matching data. Using a triple silent-substitution technique, Verdon & Adams (1987) have shown that S cones make no significant contribution to mesopic luminosity.

PROPOSED PHOTOPIC SYSTEM   I have proposed an alternative system of photopic colorimetry and photometry that relates more closely to underlying physiology than does the CIE system (Boynton 1986). In particular, it makes use of an equal-luminance chromaticity diagram developed by MacLeod & Boynton (1979). The system assumes no S-cone contribution to luminance, a concept that remains controversial and that depends upon exactly what one means by "luminance."

SPACE, TIME, AND COLOR DISCRIMINATION

Spatial Masking

K. K. DeValois & Switkes (1983) have studied masking interactions between chromatic and luminance gratings. All conditions showed symmetrical spectral tuning on a log-log plot of contrast sensitivity versus mask/test frequency ratio. For the condition of maximum masking, which occurred consistently when the mask/test ratio was unity, sensitivity for achromatic test gratings was reduced approximately sixfold when presented with either type of mask; for chromatic test gratings, the reduction was about half as much, and also was roughly independent of the type of mask used, although cross-masking by achromatic gratings was somewhat more effective. One of the functions of color vision may be to enhance the visibility of environmental details that otherwise might be lost because of masking. The extent to which chromatic contrast would have this salutary effect when added to an existing achromatic contrast has not been tested.

Induction

DISCOUNTING THE BACKGROUND   When a yellow test light is added to a red spot of the same size, shape, duration, and retinal location, its yellow hue shifts toward orange, as expected on the basis of colorimetric addition. When the same yellow test light is superimposed upon a red adapting field that is created by enlarging the red spot, its yellow hue will shift instead toward green, as also would happen were it fitted into the otherwise dark center of a red annulus—a standard arrangement for producing chromatic induction. The greening of yellow for the large-background case implies that induction is stronger than colorimetric addition; indeed, Walraven (1976) claimed that induction was so much stronger that the influence of that part of the background underlying the test stimulus was entirely "discounted." This contention was examined quantitatively by Drum (1981), who rejected it because, for three of his five subjects, adding a sufficient intensity of steady red background to a flashing test that appeared initially green could shift its appearance to yellow. (However, the other two subjects always saw the test as green.)

Adelson (1981), using a penlight to produce a veil of reddish light over his retina by means of scatter from localized transscleral illumination, thereby looked at the world, as he put it, "through a rose colored Ganzfeld." He noted that many regions of the scene, especially those that were initially dark or blue, took on a reddish cast, indicating that the background veil surely was not discounted in those instances. Shevell (1982) examined the influence of red backgrounds on the appearance of an initially yellow test by having his subjects add sufficient green to maintain an equilibrium yellow, and concluded that Walraven's generalization was only approximate at best. Shevell favors a two-process theory that includes von Kries–type adaptation within the test area, as well as an opposed "restoring effect" which must be attributable mainly to the surround. On the other hand, Davies et al (1983) found support for the discounting hypothesis in an experiment much like Shevell's, except that the test stimulus was flashed (2 sec on, 1 sec off) rather than being presented steadily. Except for a few cases at the lowest contrast, 25 subjects confirmed Walraven's results.

Putting the pieces of this puzzle together, the results seem to imply that for a small test stimulus superimposed upon a large background, both colorimetric addition and lateral induction are normally at work, but induction prevails when the test is flashed. Also, individual differences may be important for steady test lights, possibly complicated by varying patterns of eye movements.

NONLINEARITIES   Other recent studies of chromatic induction agree that the strength of an induced hue is nonlinearly related to the strength of the inducing stimulus (Valberg & Seim 1983; Takahashi & Ejima 1983b). Fuld & Otto (1985) show that induced hue is intensity dependent; Takahashi & Ejima (1983a) have compared the effects of cancellation stimuli used with ordinary colors with those used to cancel hue resulting from induction, finding that the two results do not agree. Krauskopf et al (1986b) investigated the effects of a sinusoidally varying inducing stimulus, also using a nulling procedure, as did DeValois et al (1986), who note that large induction effects observed at low frequencies fall virtually to zero with temporal modulations above about 2.5 Hz.

Dichoptic Phenomena

S CONES REVISITED   Sagawa (1981) has reported on the threshold amount of light required for color rivalry in various dichoptically viewed stimulus pairs. The results can be accounted for in terms of the orthogonal vector sum of two opponent responses, provided that those of the red-green opponent system are weighted ten times more heavily than those of the yellow-blue. In a paper titled "Is the binocular rivalry mechanism tritanopic?" Rogers & Hollins (1982) concluded that it was, but their methodology may not have been sensitive enough to detect a small contribution of S cones implicit in Sagawa's result. Also, Stalmeier & De Weert (1986) described a binocular rivalry technique that shows promise as a metric for assessing large color differences, including those that depend entirely or in part upon S cones. Other kinds of binocular interactions involving S cones occur: Grinberg & Williams (1985) find that the S-cone system is capable of mediating stereopsis, while Boynton & Wisowaty (1984) report that for dichoptic transient masking of the Crawford type, the S-cone system plays a dominant role.

AVERAGING   Another experiment by Sagawa (1982) used fused dichoptic fields, initially matched. The wavelength of the lower half of the field in just one eye was varied to determine a threshold of hue difference. The experimentally supported hypothesis was that, because binocular mixture of the lower fields is an average, the perceived difference between the upper and lower fields should be less than if the contralateral lower field were not used. Humanski & Shevell (1985), using a test stimulus in only one eye, studied color perception with binocularly fused adapting fields of different wavelengths, with complex results: Adding an adapting stimulus of another color in the nontest eye changes the perceived color of the fused background, but the perceived color does not predict the appearance of the test, nor do the combined effects of contralateral and ipsilateral adaptation.

CENTRAL PROCESSING   Although much of the older literature implies that chromatic induction is a retinal phenomenon, it now appears that the underlying mechanisms are mostly central. In support of this viewpoint, Olson & Boynton (1984) showed that monoptic chromatic induction could be severely inhibited by a metacontrast mask delivered to the other eye which had been shown to be directly effective only upon the inducer. Land et al (1983) report that the expected change in appearance of a test spot seen on the vertical meridian by both eyes, caused by changing the illumination of a flanking Mondrian, did not occur in a split-brain patient when signals initiated by the Mondrian were delivered to the right hemisphere, whereas the change did occur in the opposite case. The result, which is held by the authors to imply that the cortex is necessary for long-range color computations, seems also to indicate that only the left hemisphere in this right-handed patient is capable of carrying out the computations.

Color Discrimination

EFFECTS OF SPACE AND TIME   Using combinations of 7 temporal and 6 spatial frequencies, at 5 reference chromaticities, Noorlander & Koenderink (1983) used the CIE chromaticity diagram to compare their results (equiluminant slices through the discrimination ellipsoids) with the classical data of W. R. J. Brown and D. L. MacAdam. These venerable but sturdy results, obtained using free viewing of steady fields, resemble the new data only for low spatial and temporal frequencies. Similarly, Uchikawa & Ikeda (1985) find that when wavelength discrimination is studied using alternating stimuli, traditional curves result only for low temporal frequencies.

When S-cone excitation levels are held constant or nearly so, a convenient data format shows L-cone excitation increasing along one coordinate, with M-cone excitation increasing along the orthogonal one. Thresholds reveal additive effects (135-deg ellipse) or subtractive ones (45-deg ellipse), depending upon the combinations of spatial and temporal frequencies used. Noorlander et al (1981) found that a combination of low temporal and spatial frequencies reliably elicited the 45-deg ellipse indicative of chromatic-opponent interaction. Their highest temporal frequency (15 Hz) produced the 135-deg ellipse indicative of achromatic discrimination. Wandell (1985) studied such discrimination and detection contours using pulses that were temporally shaped either as Gaussian or Gabor functions (which provide low and high spatial frequencies, respectively) for stimuli of limited temporal durations. Gaussian functions produce the expected chromatic contour at a 45-deg orientation. Gabor functions were interpreted as exciting achromatic channels, but they yielded rather round discrimination contours of a sort that Cowan et al (1984) ascribe instead to a combination of excitations from both kinds of channels. Wandell's achromatic discriminations were to some degree categorical, whereas the chromatic ones were not. His chromatic discrimination contours were predictable from detection data.

In the more conventional split-field situation, Hita et al (1982) show that 1 sec of viewing time is optimal for discriminating between simultaneously viewed fields. With variable delays between the stimuli to be compared, Uchikawa (1983), Uchikawa & Ikeda (1986), and Romero et al (1986) show that delay reduces discriminability in a general fashion for all dimensions of chromatic and achromatic variation tested.

REFERENCE CHROMATICITY   An approach toward reducing the enormous general problem of predicting the size of chromatic discrimination steps is given by Nagy et al (1987), who have reanalyzed constant-luminance discrimination data in terms of cardinal-axis concepts, showing that if the sizes of discrimination steps are known along these axes, then the shape of the entire discrimination ellipse, if suitably normalized, is largely independent of reference chromaticity and other variables. Boynton & Kambe (1980) developed formulas that characterize the variations in the size of chromatic discrimination steps measured along the cardinal axes, with data that agree with those of Rich & Billmeyer (1983) who, using specially prepared color samples, concluded that there is a proportionality between threshold and somewhat larger steps of color difference that holds, at least roughly, for all reference chromaticities and directions of difference.

METAMERISM   Beginning with the work of D. L. MacAdam nearly 50 years ago, investigators of color-difference thresholds have avoided metamerism at the match point. Taking this precaution allows a physical specification of a match and circumvents subjective difficulties related to the fact that metameric matches are seldom perfect. Hita et al (1986) show that the problem with the use of a metameric match is not so much that the shapes of the resulting ellipsoids differ from those based on isomeric matches, but that their centers shift, suggesting small failures of colorimetric additivity.

COLOR CONTEXT

Color Constancy and Computational Vision

To explain color constancy, it is necessary to understand how the visual system can evaluate and then discount the spectral character of an illuminant and thereby recover information related to the spectral reflectance of a surface. Otherwise the two variables are hopelessly confounded.

THE COMPUTATIONAL APPROACH   The most explicit examination of this problem is attributable to practitioners of computational vision, a burgeoning field whose arrival was signaled for many of us by the posthumous publication in 1982 of David Marr's *Vision*. Subsequently Buchsbaum & Gottschalk (1983) have shown that, for the most efficient transmission of color signals in the visual system (given absorption bandwiths on the order of those found for actual photopigments) the optimal number of receptors is three, opponent-color coding is required, and von Kries–type chromatic adaptation is useful. Also, the computational approach has focused attention on ecological factors long ignored by most basic vision researchers, leading for example to the resurrection of a valuable and long-neglected work by Jozef Cohen (1964), who had demonstrated that the spectral reflectances of Munsell color samples can be accurately represented as additive combinations of only three fixed basis functions [although Maloney (1986) shows that natural objects usually require more].

Many light sources—especially the ones under which color constancy is best maintained—are adequately described by the weighted sum of as few as two such basis functions. Such insights serve to simplify and focus the task of the computational modeler. Maloney & Wandell (1986), who argue that color constancy would be impossible otherwise, proceed to show (a) how the number of classes of photoreceptors limit the gamut of surface reflectances that can be potentially recovered, and (b) that the solution to the color-constancy problem logically requires the presence of a minimum number of distinct surface reflectances in the scene.

In an 89-page paper seemingly ignored by other computational theorists, Cohen & Kappauf (1985) make use of a concept originally introduced by G. Wyszecki, that any radiometric spectral distribution may be regarded as the product of a fundamental metamer and a metameric black (the latter always has negative as well as positive values as a function of wavelength, summing to zero tristimulus values). Given any spectral distribution, Cohen & Kappauf show how to calculate the fundamental metamer and eject the metameric black uniquely associated with that distribution. To accomplish this, they use a so-called "Matrix R," which is the ordered collection of the fundamental metamers of visible monochromatic lights. They also show how, given only tristimulus values, the fundamental metamer corresponding to those values can be calculated although—because many spectral distributions can produce the same tristimulus values—no unique metameric black is implicated. This system might be of use to computational vision theorists who are looking for more general and visually meaningful ways to represent spectral power distributions.

Fourier analysis of stimuli and receptor sensitivities along the dimension of spectral wavelength provides another new perspective (Barlow 1982, Benz-schawel et al 1986). Buchsbaum & Gottschalk (1984) show that the gamut of surface colors corresponding to the sum of three independent positive sinusoidal functions of spectral frequency, all free to vary in phase but limited to 15 cycles per 300 nm (which is about all the receptors can handle), includes all Munsell samples with a bit of room to spare. Given that monochromatic lights require much higher spectral frequencies for their complex Fourier representation, it is perhaps counterintuitive that the same visual apparatus that seems to have evolved to analyze the gently sloped spectral distributions of natural surface reflectances is nevertheless capable of discriminating very small differences between the wavelengths of monochromatic lights almost never seen in the natural setting.

No doubt many other sources of information are typically used by the visual system to solve the constancy problem to the extent that it does (the limits of this ability need further experimental testing). D'Zmura & Lennie (1986), who consider the roles of specular reflection and eye movements, propose a physiological model with two stages of adaptation. Gershon et al (1986) distinguish among three components of reflection and two of illumination, of which the ambient, or indirect kind is given special emphasis. Worthey & Brill (1986) emphasize the selective adaptability of the three kinds of cones (von Kries adaptation), which oddly is ignored by some computational theorists. Brill & West (1986) suggest, on the other hand, that color constancy and chromatic adaptation may be distinct processes, given that a considerable degree of constancy seems to occur almost immediately with change of illuminant, whereas at least some components of adaptation develop slowly.

In general, unless they are isomeric, two surface color samples that match under one illuminant will not match under a different one, and the degree to which they will exhibit color constancy will also differ. Berns et al (1985) provide an approach to the calculation of spectral reflectance functions that will describe samples of a desired chromaticity, when seen under a reference illuminant, that exhibit the best color constancy. These cannot generally be the same as Cohen & Kappauf's fundamental metamers because some of the latter, having negative values, cannot be physically realized.

"DISCOUNTING" REVISITED   A wholly different outlook is supplied by Werner & Walraven (1982). They repeatedly adjusted bichromatic mixture components of test flashes, seen against various backgrounds, to appear as psychologically unique white. The background was found to affect the state of chromatic adaptation without adding colorimetrically to the appearance of the test flash (the "discounting" principle mentioned above). The behavior of their adaptational mechanisms, which turn out to have the spectral sensitivities of π-mechanisms, implies crosstalk among receptors. Their work points to a paradox between chromatic induction in the lab and color constancy in the real world (p. 942):

> The significance of the von Kries type of sensitivity control is self-evident for all theories of chromatic adaptation, since it provides a mechanism for maintaining the approximate color constancy of the visual system. However, the functional significance of the discounting principle seems less obvious in this respect. . . . It may thereby introduce "artifacts," as can be observed in demonstrations of simultaneous color contrast, but it may also provide the eye with important information. . . . such a differencing mechanism may enable the visual system to . . . separate reflectance distributions from illuminance distributions.

CONTEXT AND CONSTANCY   Models of color constancy require that the visual system assimilate information from all over the visual scene. Color figures on pages 87–90 of the September, 1986 issue of *Scientific American*

(Brou et al 1986) dramatically illustrate this theme. For more than 25 years, Edwin Land has emphasized the importance of color context; he has buttressed his arguments with elaborate demonstrations, all the while fine-tuning his retinex model (for recent versions, see Land 1983 and 1986). Hurlbert (1986) has examined similarities among algorithms (some unpublished) proposed by several workers including Land, and a "multiple scales" model of her own. Assuming a two-dimensional Mondrian and smoothly varying illumination, all of these models split the intensity signal into two components by (*a*) differentiating the signal over space and thresholding the derivative, and (*b*) integrating the "thresholded" derivative to recover surface reflectance. Whether human vision works this way is, in her opinion, an open question. Brainard & Wandell (1986) think not: They have criticized Land's model because it is dependent upon physically measured surface reflectances, whereas the human visual system is not privy to such information.

Categorical Color Perception

We seem to have emerged from an earlier era, when matching was regarded as the only acceptable means for gauging color appearance, to a realization that absolute color judgments can be made with high precision and with the added advantage of eliminating a comparison stimulus whose very presence may affect what is being assessed. Such judgments can be used indirectly, as in some of the studies cited in the section on channels or in the Werner & Walraven study just mentioned, but the idea of basic colors is also of interest in its own right.

LANDMARK COLORS   Fuld et al (1981) examined the use of the category purple in a color-scaling experiment, and concluded that purple could be fully described by mixtures of a pair of more fundamental hues—in this case red and blue. Orange, which was similarly examined by C. E. Sternheim and the author more than 20 years ago, can be described as a blend of red and yellow. The quartet of red, green, yellow, and blue—also the opponent colors of Ewald Hering—have been called "landmark" colors by Miller & Johnson-Laird (1976).

BASIC COLOR TERMS   Although it may be true that there are only four landmark chromatic colors that contain no trace of any other hue, the anthropologists Berlin & Kay proposed in 1969 that there are eleven basic color terms, each related to a unique sensation. These include but are not restricted to the landmark colors. In addition to the the landmark chromatic colors and the achromatic colors (white, gray, and black), the other four basic surface colors are orange, purple, pink, and brown. Ratliff (1976) marshaled evidence of many kinds that led him not only to agree with this position but also to suggest that there must be a definite physiological substrate of some kind that underlies the use of each basic color term. In a color-naming experiment, using the OSA Uniform Color Scales samples (Nickerson 1981), Boynton & Olson (1987) found that the eleven basic color terms were in a class by themselves as judged by three different response measures: response time, within-subjects consistency, and between-subjects consensus of color naming. Although the centroids of the eleven basic colors in the OSA space occupy unique positions when projected into the chromatic plane, lightness is also an important determinant of their locations.

Electrophysiology and Color Perception

WHAT WE DON'T KNOW   Several excellent reviews of the literature concerned with the electrophysiology of color vision and its relation to human color perception have appeared in recent years (Gouras & Zrenner 1981b; Zrenner 1983; Foster 1984; Lennie 1984; Lennie & D'Zmura 1987); these should be consulted for references to a substantial primary literature not cited here. Despite the rapid accumulation of detailed information, there remain many unanswered questions, some of which seem fundamental. We do not know, for example, what differs in the brain when we see a red object rather than a green one. We have no evidence concerning how the activity in multiple cortical areas, with color being represented in many of them, becomes integrated to form one aspect of a unitary perception [although Barlow (1986) and Cowey (1981) have provided some interesting speculations]. We do not understand the brain mechanisms underlying color constancy. It is not evident why the division of function so strongly suggested by the psychophysically derived channel concept is so confusingly related to physiological data that seem inordinately complex and frequently contradictory. (Surely a continuing lack of agreement about how to classify and label cells according to function has not helped.)

BLOBS   This is not to say that important advances have been lacking. When Gouras & Zrenner (1981a) wrote their review, they seemed convinced that there was a separate columnnar organization in area V1 for hue versus luminance contrast detection. Subsequently, Livingstone & Hubel (1984) reported in detail on regions within established cortical columns revealed by staining for a mitochondrial enzyme, cytochrome oxydase. These regions, which lacked directional sensitivity and seemed to be specifically concerned with color, were called "blobs." In extending this work, DeValois (1987) argues instead that luminance and color are processed similarly, with low spatial frequencies (rather than color per se) represented inside, and high frequencies outside, such modules. Thus many cells within the blobs respond to slow spatial variations in both color and luminance. Projections from blobs to extrastriate cortex are discussed by Zeki (1985) and Van Essen (1986).

WHAT IMMEDIATELY UNDERLIES COLOR EXPERIENCE? Perceived basic colors are correlated with broad spectral ranges that overlap with those of adjacent colors. The results of Vautin & Dow (1985) and Dow & Vautin (1987), based on single-unit records from V1 in awake macaques, have produced results that are in line with this correlation. Yet it seems unlikely that primary visual cortex is the best place to look for whatever it is that lies immediately beneath the conscious experience of color.

Fifteen years ago, Zeki (1973) identified a cortical area called V4 that he thought was exclusively comprised of wavelength-selective cells. Desimone et al (1985) have provided a review of subsequent work that has laid this extreme claim to rest. Nevertheless, the spatial organization of units in V4 suggests that they could be importantly involved in chromatic context effects.

The psychological relevance of much chromatic electrophysiology has been limited because little effort has been made to search systematically for the physiological correlates of color context effects. A striking exception is a study by Zeki (1983), who displayed Mondrians to monkeys and reported cells in V4 selectively responsive to colors of particular hues regardless of how these were produced using various combinations of illumination and Mondrianal geometry. Recording from the LGN, Northdurft & Lee (1982) also used Mondrians but did not find such evidence of the effects of chromatic context. Nor did Zeki (1983) when recording from V1 or, for that matter, some of the cells in V4; he suggests that a clear distinction should be drawn between "wavelength selective" cells of the sort found in LGN and V1, and "colour-coded" cells of the sort found in V4.

Zeki's effort represents an important attempt to find brain activity that might be related intimately to the immediately underlying neurophysiological substrate of chromatic sensation, as opposed to the bulk of chromatic electrophysiology which seems instead to have tapped into the pathways at various places along the way between the receptors and the final locus. Such work has been valuable, because even if the answer at the final stage were known, one would want to understand the mechanisms that produced it. However, as Gouras & Eggers (1984) have pointed out, lower-level neurophysiological data have often been seriously misinterpreted as explaining very high-level perceptual effects. Zeki's pioneering experiment, although an important step in the right direction, was of limited value because his monkeys were anesthetized, meaning that in addition to feeling no pain they were seeing no colors; moreover, there are possible artifacts associated with his casually reported psychophysics. This is an important area of research that would profit from the use of behaving monkeys and double-blind procedures.

ACKNOWLEDGMENTS

I thank the National Eye Institute for its support of the preparation of this review and of my research program, the latter over many years; and I gratefully acknowledge the help of Donald MacLeod, who provided useful suggestions based on an earlier draft. Kathleen Purl helped to verify references. This review is dedicated to Professor Lorrin Riggs of Brown University, who introduced me to visual science 40 years ago and has continued ever since to serve as a superb role model and continuing source of inspiration.

Literature Cited

Abraham, F. A., Alpern, M., Kirk, D. B. 1985. Electroretinograms evoked by sinusoidal excitation of human cones. *J. Physiol.* 363:135–50

Adelson, E. H. 1981. Looking at the world through a rose-colored ganzfeld. *Vision Res.* 21:749–50

Ahnhelt, P. K., Kolb, H., Pflug, R. 1987. Identification of a subtype of cone photoreceptor, likely to be blue sensitive, in the human retina. *J. Comp. Neurol.* 255:18–34

Akita, M., Ejima, Y., Takahashi, S. 1982. Differences of unique-yellow between individuals. *Color Res. Appl.* 7:168–72

Akita, M., Takahashi, S., Ejima, Y. 1985. Red-green opponency in the detection and the perceptual hue cancellation. *Vision Res.* 25:1129–1135

Barlow, H. B. 1982. What causes trichromacy? A theoretical analysis using comb-filtered spectra. *Vision Res.* 22:635–43

Barlow, H. B. 1986. Why have multiple cortical areas? *Vision Res.* 26:81–90

Baron, W. S. 1980. Cone difference signal in foveal local electroretinogram of primate. *Invest. Ophthalmos. Vis. Sci.* 19:1442–1448

Baron, W. S. 1982. Chromatic adaptation and flicker-frequency effects on primate R-G cone difference signal. *J. Opt. Soc. Am.* 72:1008–13

Bartleson, C. J., Grum, F. 1984. *Optical Radiation Measurements.* Vol. 5, *Visual Measurements.* New York: Academic. 662 pp.

Baylor, D. A., Nunn, B. J., Schnapf, J. 1984. Spectral sensitivity of cones of the monkey *Macaca fascicularis. Nature* 309:264–66

Benzschawel, T., Brill, M. H., Cohn, T. E. 1986. Analysis of human color mechanisms using sinusoidal spectral power distributions. *J. Opt. Soc. Am. A* 3:1713–25

Benzschawel, T., Guth, S. L. 1982. ATDN: Post-receptor chromatic mechanisms revealed by flickering vs. fused adaptation. *Vision Res.* 22:69–75

Benzschawel, T., Guth, S. L. 1984. Toward a uniform color space. *Color Res. Appl.* 9:133–41

Berlin, B., Kay, P. 1969. *Basic Color Terms: Their Universality and Evolution.* Berkeley: Univ. Calif. Press. 178 pp.

Berns, R. S., Billmeyer, F. W. Jr., Sacher, R. S. 1985. Methods for generating spectral reflectance functions leading to color-constant properties. *Color Res. Appl.* 10: 73–83

Billmeyer, F. W., Saltzman, M. 1981. *Principles of Color Technology.* New York: Wiley. 240 pp. 2nd ed.

Boff, K. R., Kaufman, L., Thomas, J. P. 1986. *Handbook of Perception and Human Performance.* Vol. I: *Sensory Processes and Perception.* New York: Wiley. 1360 pp.

Booker, R. L. 1981. Luminance-brightness comparisons of separated circular stimuli. *J. Opt. Soc. Am.* 71:139–44

Borwein, B., Borwein, D., Medeiros, J., McGowan, J. W. 1980. The ultrastructure of monkey foveal photoreceptors, with special reference to the structure, shape, size, and spacing of foveal cones. *Am. J. Anat.* 159:125–46

Botstein, D. 1986. The molecular biology of color vision. *Science* 232:142–43

Bowen, R. W., Pokorny, J., Cacciato, D. 1977. Metacontrast masking depends on luminance transients. *Vision Res.* 17:971–75

Bowmaker, J. K. 1984. Microspectrophotometry of vertebrate photoreceptors. *Vision Res.* 24:1641–50

Boynton, R. M. 1978. Ten years of research with the minimally-distinct border. In *Visual *Psychophysics and Physiology*, ed. J. C. Armington, J. Krauskopf, B. R. Wooten. New York: Academic. 488 pp.

Boynton, R. M. 1979. *Human Color Vision*. New York: Holt, Rinehart & Winston. 438 pp.

Boynton, R. M. 1986. A system of photometry and colorimetry based on cone excitations. *Color Res. Appl.* 11:244–52

Boynton, R. M., ed. 1987. *Vision Research Retrospective: 1981–1986*. Oxford: Pergamon

Boynton, R. M., Eskew, R. T. Jr., Olson, C. X. 1985. Blue cones contribute to border distinctness. *Vision Res.* 25:1349–52

Boynton, R. M., Kambe, N. 1980. Chromatic difference steps of moderate size measured along theoretically critical axes. *Color Res. Appl.* 5:13–23

Boynton, R. M., Nagy, A. L. 1982. La Jolla analytic colorimeter. *J. Opt. Soc. Am.* 72:666–67

Boynton, R. M., Olson, C. X. 1987. Locating basic colors in the OSA space. *Color Res. Appl.* In press

Boynton, R. M., Wisowaty, J. J. 1984. Selective color effects in dichoptic masking. *Vision Res.* 24:667–75

Brainard, D. H., Wandell, B. A. 1986. Analysis of the retinex theory of color vision. *J. Opt. Soc. Am. A* 3:1651–61

Brill, M. H., West, G. 1986. Chromatic adaptation and color constancy: a possible dichotomy. *Color Res. Appl.* 11:196–204

Brou, P., Sciascia, T. R., Linden, L., Lettvin, J. Y. 1986. The colors of things. *Sci. Am.* 255(3):84–91

Buchsbaum, G., Gottschalk, A. 1983. Trichromacy, opponent colours coding and optimum colour information transmission in the retina. *Proc. R. Soc. B* 220:89–113

Buchsbaum, G., Gottschalk, A. 1984. Chromaticity coordinates of frequency-limited functions. *J. Opt. Soc. Am. A* 1:885–87

Buck, S. L. 1985a. Cone-rod interaction over time and space. *Vision Res.* 25:907–16

Buck, S. L. 1985b. Determinants of the spatial properties of cone-rod interaction. *Vision Res.* 25:1277–84

Burns, S. A., Elsner, A. E. 1985. Color matching at high illuminances: the color-match-area effect and photopigment bleaching. *J. Opt. Soc. Am. A* 2:698–704

Burns, S. A., Elsner, A. E., Pokorny, J., Smith, V. C. 1984. The Abney effect: chromaticity coordinates of unique and other constant hues. *Vision Res.* 24:479–89

Burns, S. A., Smith, V. C., Pokorny, J., Elsner, A. E. 1982. Brightness of equal-luminance lights. *J. Opt. Soc. Am.* 72:1225–31

Cavanagh, P., Favreau, O. E. 1985. Color and luminance share a common motion pathway. *Vision Res.* 25:1595–1601

Cicerone, C., Nerger, J. 1985. The ratio of long-wavelength-sensitive to middle-wavelength-sensitive cones in the human fovea. *Invest. Ophthalmos.* 26 Suppl: 11 (Abstr.)

Cohen, J. B. 1964. Dependency of the spectral reflectance curves of the Munsell color chips. *Psychon. Sci.* 1:369–70

Cohen, J. B., Kappauf, W. E. 1985. Color mixture and fundamental metamers: theory, algebra, geometry, application. *Am. J. Psychol.* 98:171–259

Coletta, N. J., Adams, A. J. 1986. Spatial extent of rod-cone and cone-cone interactions for flicker detection. *Vision Res.* 26:917–25

Cowan, W. B., ed. 1986. Proceedings of the 1986 AIC interim meeting on color in computer-generated displays. *Color Res. Appl.* 11 (Suppl.):S1–S90

Cowan, W. B., Wyszecki, G., Yaguchi, H. 1984. Probability summation among color channels. *J. Opt. Soc. Am. A* 1:1307–8 (Abstr.)

Cowey, A. 1981. Why are there so many cortical areas? In *The Organization of the Cerebral Cortex*, ed. F. O. Schmitt, G. Worden, G. Adelman. Cambridge, Mass: MIT Press

Cushman, W. B., Levinson, J. Z. 1983. Phase shift in red and green counterphase flicker at high frequencies. *J. Opt. Soc. Am.* 73:1557–61

Dartnall, H. J. A., Bowmaker, J. K., Mollon, J. D. 1983. Human visual pigments: microspectrophotometric results from the eyes of seven persons. *Proc. R. Soc. B* 220:115–30

Davies, S. E., Faivre, I. A., Werner, J. S. 1983. Transient processing in chromatic induction. *Vision Res.* 23:707–12

Dawson, W. W., Enoch, J. M., eds. 1984. *Foundations of Sensory Science*. New York: Springer-Verlag. 577 pp.

De Monasterio, F. M., McCrane, E. P., Newlander, J. K., Schein, S. J. 1985. Density profile of blue-sensitive cones along the horizontal meridian of macaque retina. *Invest. Ophthalmos. Vis. Sci.* 26:289–302

Derrington, A. M., Badcock, D. R. 1985. The low level motion system has both chromatic and luminance inputs. *Vision Res.* 25:1879–84

Derrington, A. M., Krauskopf, J., Lennie, P. 1984. Chromatic mechanisms in lateral geniculate nucleus of macaque. *J. Physiol.* 357:241–65

Desimone, R., Schein, S. J., Moran, J., Ungerleider, L. G. 1985. Contour, color, and shape analysis beyond the striate cortex. *Vision Res.* 25:441–52

DeValois, K. K., Switkes, E. 1983. Simultaneous masking interactions between chromatic and luminance gratings. *J. Opt. Soc. Am.* 73:11–18

De Valois, R. L. 1987. *Color and luminance processing by the geniculo-striate system.* Presented at Western Eye Res. Conf., Pacific Grove, Calif., Feb. 25

DeValois, R. L., Webster, M. A., De Valois, K. K., Ingelbach, B. 1986. Temporal properties of brightness and color induction. *Vision Res.* 26:887–97

de Weert, C. M. M., Sadza, K. J. 1983. New data concerning the contribution of colour differences to stereopsis. See Mollon & Sharpe 1983, pp. 553–62

Dow, B. M., Vautin, R. G. 1987. Horizontal segregation of color information in the middle layers of foveal striate cortex. *J. Neurophysiol.* In press

Drum, B. 1981. Additive effect of backgrounds in chromatic induction. *Vision Res.* 21:959–61

D'Zmura, M., Lennie, P. 1986. Shared pathways for rod and cone vision. *Vision Res.* 26:1273–80

Eisner, A., MacLeod, D. I. A. 1981. Flicker photometric study of chromatic adaptation: selective suppression of cone inputs by colored backgrounds. *J. Opt. Soc. Am.* 71:705–18

Ejima, Y., Takahashi, S. 1984. Bezold-Brucke hue shift and nonlinearity in opponent-color process. *Vision Res.* 24:1897–1904

Ejima, Y., Takahashi, S. 1985. Interaction between short- and longer-wavelength cones in hue cancellation codes: nonlinearities of hue cancellation as a function of stimulus intensity. *Vision Res.* 25:1911–1922

Ejima, Y., Takahashi, S., Akita, M. 1986. Achromatic sensation for trichromatic mixture as a function of stimulus intensity. *Vision Res.* 26:1065–71

Elsner, A. E., Burns, S. A., Pokorny, J. 1987. Changes in constant-hue loci with spatial frequency. *Color Res. Appl.* 12:42–50

Elzinga, C. H., de Weert, C. M. M. 1984. Nonlinear codes for yellow/blue mechanism. *Vision Res.* 24:911–22

Elzinga, C. H., de Weert, C. M. M. 1986. Spectral sensitivity functions derived from brightness matching: implications of intensity invariance for color-vision models. *J. Opt. Soc. Am. A* 3:1173–81

Estévez, O. 1982. A better colorimetric standard observer for color-vision studies: the Stiles and Burch 2 deg. color-matching functions. *Color Res. Appl.* 7:131–34

Faulkner, D. J., Kemp, C. M. 1984. Human rhodopsin measurement using a TV-based imaging fundus reflectometer. *Vision Res.* 24:221–31

Finkelstein, M. A., Hood, D. C. 1982. Opponent-color cells can influence detection of small, brief lights. *Vision Res.* 22:89–95

Finkelstein, M. A., Hood, D. C. 1984. Detection and discrimination of small, brief lights; variable tuning of opponent channels. *Vision Res.* 24:175–81

Fletcher, R., Voke, J. 1985. *Defective Colour Vision.* Bristol: Hilger. 608 pp.

Foster, D. H. 1979. Interactions between blue-and red-sensitive colour mechanisms in metacontrast masking. *Vision Res.* 19:921–31

Foster, D. H. 1981. Changes in field spectral sensitivities of red-, green- and blue-sensitive colour mechanisms obtained on small background fields. *Vision Res.* 21:1433–55

Foster, D. H. 1984. Colour vision. *Contemp. Physiol.* 25:477–97

Foster, D. H., Snelgar, R. S. 1983. Test and field spectral sensitivities of colour mechanisms obtained on small white backgrounds: action of unitary opponent-colour processes? *Vision Res.* 23:787–97

Frome, F. S., Buck, S. L., Boynton, R. M. 1981. Visibility of borders: separate and combined effects of color differences, luminance contrast, and luminance level. *J. Opt. Soc. Am.* 71:145–50

Fry, G. A. 1984. The distimulus method of assessing luminous efficiency of the spectrally pure stimuli. *Color Res. Appl.* 9:142–46

Fuld, K., Otto, T. A. 1985. Colors of monochromatic lights that vary in contrast-induced brightness. *J. Opt. Soc. Am. A* 2:76–83

Fuld, K., Wooten, B. R., Whalen, J. J. 1981. The elemental hues of short-wave and extraspectral lights. *Percept. Psychophys.* 29:317–22

Gershon, R., Jepson, A. D., Tsotsos, J. K. 1986. Ambient illumination and the determination of material changes. *J. Opt. Soc. Am. A* 3:1700–7

Goldberg, S. H., Frumkes, T. E., Nygaard, R. W. 1983. Inhibitory influence of unstimulated rods in the human retina: evidence provided by examining cone flicker. *Science* 221:180–82

Gouras, P., Eggers, H. 1984. Hering's opponent color channels do not exist in the primate retinogeniculate pathway. *Ophthalmic Res.* 16:31–35

Gouras, P., Zrenner, E. 1981a. Color coding in primate retina. *Vision Res.* 21:1591–98

Gouras, P., Zrenner, E. 1981b. Color vision: a review from a neurophysiological perspective. *Prog. Sensory Physiol.* 1:139–79

Gregory, R. L. 1977. Vision with isoluminant colour contrast: I. A projection technique and observations. *Perception* 6:113–19

Grinberg, D. L., Williams, D. R. 1985. Stereopsis with chromatic signals from the blue-sensitive mechanism. *Vision Res.* 25: 531–37

Grum, F., Bartleson, C. J. 1980. *Optical Radiation Measurements*, Vol. 2: *Color Measurement*. New York: Academic. 372 pp.

Guth, S. L. 1964. The effect of wavelength on visual perceptual latency. *Vision Res.* 4:567–78

Harwerth, R. S., Smith, E. L. III. 1985. Rhesus monkey as a model for normal vision of humans. *Am. J. Optom. Physiol. Opt.* 62:633–41

Hita, E., Jiménez del Barco, L., Romero, J. 1986. Differential color thresholds from metameric matches: experimental results concerning failures of colorimetric additivity. *J. Opt. Soc. Am. A* 3:1203–9

Hita, E., Romero, L., Jiménez del Barco, L., Martinez, R. 1982. Temporal aspects of color discrimination. *J. Opt. Soc. Am.* 72:578–82

Howett, G. L. 1986a. Linear opponent-colors model optimized for brightness prediction. *NBSIR 85-3202.* Gaithersberg, Md: Natl. Bur. Stand. US Dept. Commerce

Howett, G. L. 1986b. The coming redefinition of photometry. *J. Illum. Eng. Soc.* 15:5–18

Humanski, R. A., Shevell, S. K. 1985. Color perception with binocularly fused adapting fields of different wavelengths. *Vision Res.* 25:1923–35

Hunt, R. W. G. 1982. A model of colour vision for predicting colour appearance. *Color Res. Appl.* 7:95–112

Hurlbert, A. 1986. Formal connections between lightness algorithms. *J. Opt. Soc. Am. A* 3:1684–93

Hurvich, L. 1981. *Color Vision.* Sunderland, Mass: Sinauer. 328 pp.

Ikeda, M. 1983. Linearity law reexamined for flicker photometry by the summation-index method. *J. Opt. Soc. Am.* 73:1055–61

Ikeda, M., Nakano, Y. 1986. Spectral luminous-efficiency functions obtained by direct heterochromatic brightness matching for point sources and for 2 deg and 10 deg fields. *J. Opt. Soc. Am. A* 3:2105–8

Ingling, C. R. Jr., Martinez-Uriegas, E. 1983a. Simple-opponent receptive fields are asymmetrical; G-cone centers predominate. *J. Opt. Soc. Am.* 73:1527–32

Ingling, C. R. Jr., Martinez-Uriegas, E. 1983b. The relationship between spectral sensitivity and spatial sensitivity for the primate r-g X-channel. *Vision Res.* 23:1495–1500

Ingling, C. R. Jr., Martinez-Uriegas, E. 1985. The spatiotemporal properties of the r-g X-cell channel. *Vision Res.* 25:33–38

Jacobs, G. H. 1981. *Comparative Color Vision.* New York: Academic. 209 pp.

Jameson, D., Hurvich, L. M., Varner, F. D. 1979. Receptoral and postreceptoral visual processes in recovery from chromatic adaptation. *Proc. Natl. Acad. Sci. USA* 76:3034–38

Kaiser, P. K. 1983. Nonvisual color perception: a critical review. *Color Res. Appl.* 8:137–44

Kaiser, P. K. 1984. Physiological response to color: a critical review. *Color Res. Appl.* 9:29–36

Kaiser, P. K., Ayama, M. 1985. Just noticeable inhomogeneity criterion for determining wavelength discrimination functions. *Vision Res.* 25:1327–30

Kaiser, P. K., Ayama, M. 1986. Small, brief foveal stimuli: an additivity experiment. *J. Opt. Soc. Am. A* 3:930–34

Kaiser, P. K., Boynton, R. M. 1985. Role of the blue mechanism in wavelength discrimination. *Vision Res.* 25:523–29

Kaufman, J. E., ed. 1981. *IES Lighting Handbook.* New York: Illuminating Eng. Soc. North America. 2 vols.

Kelly, D. H. 1983. Spatiotemporal variation of chromatic and achromatic contrast thresholds. *J. Opt. Soc. Am.* 73:742–50

King-Smith, P. E., Kranda, K. 1981. Photopic adaptation in the red-green spectral range. *Vision Res.* 21:565–72

Krauskopf, J., Williams, D. R., Heeley, D. W. 1981. Computer controlled color mixer with laser primaries. *Vision Res.* 21:951–53

Krauskopf, J., Williams, D. R., Heeley, D. W. 1982. Cardinal directions of color space. *Vision Res.* 22:1123–31

Krauskopf, J., Williams, D. R., Mandler, M. B., Brown, A. M. 1986a. Higher order color mechanisms. *Vision Res.* 26: 23–32

Krauskopf, J., Zaidi, Q., Mandler, M. B. 1986b. Mechanisms of simultaneous color induction. *J. Opt. Soc. Am. A* 3:1752–57

Land, E. H. 1983. Recent advances in retinex theory and some implications for cortical computations: color vision and the natural image. *Proc. Natl. Acad. Sci. USA* 80: 5163–69

Land, E. H. 1986. Recent advances in retinex theory. *Vision Res.* 26:7–21

Land, E. H., Hubel, D. H., Livingstone, M. S., Perry, S. H., Burns, M. M. 1983. Colour-generating interactions across the corpus callosum. *Nature* 303:616–18

Larimer, J. 1981. Red/green opponent color equilibria measured on chromatic adapting fields: evidence for gain changes and restoring forces. *Vision Res.* 21:501–12

98   BOYNTON

Laxar, K., Kass, D., Wooten, B. R. 1984. Flicker-photometric spectral sensitivity in the presence of chromatic surrounds. *J. Opt. Soc. Am. A* 1:888–92

Lennie, P. 1984. Recent developments in the physiology of color vision. *Trends Neurosci.* 7:243–48

Lennie, P. 1986. Central pathways for color vision. *J. Opt. Soc. Am. A* 3:P43 (Abstr.)

Lennie, P., D'Zmura, M. 1987. Mechanisms of color vision. In press

Lindsey, D. T., Pokorny, J., Smith, V. C. 1986. Phase-dependent sensitivity to heterochromatic flicker. *J. Opt. Soc. Am. A* 3:921–27

Livingstone, M. S., Hubel, D. H. 1984. Anatomy and physiology of a color system in the primate visual cortex. *J. Neurosci.* 4:309–56

Lu, C., Fender, D. H. 1972. The interaction of color and luminance in stereoscopic vision. *Invest. Ophthalmos. Vis. Sci.* 11:482–89

Luria, S. M., Neri, D. F. 1986. Individual differences in luminous efficiency measured by flicker photometry. *Color Res. Appli.* 11:72–75

MacLeod, D. I. A. 1982. The estimation of cone spectral sensitivities. *Color Res. Appl.* 7:142–45

MacLeod, D. I. A., Boynton, R. M. 1979. Chromaticity diagram showing cone excitation by stimuli of equal luminance. *J. Opt. Soc. Am.* 69:1183–86

MacLeod, D. I. A., Webster, M. A. 1983. Factors influencing the color matches of normal observers. See Mollon & Sharpe 1983, pp. 81–92

Maloney, L. T. 1986. Evaluation of linear models of surface spectral reflectance with small numbers of parameters. *J. Opt. Soc. Am. A* 3:1673–83

Maloney, L. T., Wandell, B. A. 1986. Color constancy: a method for recording surface spectral reflectance. *J. Opt. Soc. A* 3:29–33

Marr, D. 1982. *Vision.* San Francisco: Freeman. 397 pp.

McCann, J. J., Benton, J. K. 1969. Interaction of the long-wave cones and the rods to produce color sensations. *J. Opt. Soc. Am.* 59:103–7

McCrane, E. P., De Monasterio, F. M., Schein, S. J., Caruso, R. C. 1983. Nonfluorescent dye staining of primate blue cones. *Invest. Ophthalmos. Vis. Sci.* 24:1449–55

Miller, G. A., Johnson-Laird, P. N. 1976. *Language and Perception.* Cambridge, Mass: Harvard Univ. Press. 760 pp.

Mollon, J. D. 1982. Color vision. *Ann. Rev. Psychol.* 33:41–85

Mollon, J. D. 1986. Understanding colour vision. *Nature* 321:12–13

Mollon, J. D., Sharpe, L. T., eds. 1983. *Colour Vision: Physiology and Psychophysics.* New York: Academic. 613 pp.

Morgan, M. J., Aiba, T. S. 1985. Positional acuity with chromatic stimuli. *Vision Res.* 25:689–95

Mullen, K. T. 1985. The contrast sensitivity of human colour vision to red-green and blue-yellow chromatic gratings. *J. Physiol.* 359:381–400

Mullen, K. T., Baker, C. L. Jr. 1985. A motion aftereffect from an isoluminant stimulus. *Vision Res.* 25:685–88

Nagy, A. L., Eskew, R. T. Jr., Boynton, R. M. 1987. Analysis of color discrimination ellipses in a cone excitation space. *J. Opt. Soc. Am.* In press

Nagy, A. L., Harami, E., Purl, K. F. 1984. Flicker photometric sensitivity and chromatic adaptation in color-deficient and normal observers. *Color Res. Appl.* 9:206–12

Nagy, A. L., MacLeod, D. I. A., Heyneman, N., Eisner, A. 1981. Four cone pigments in women heterozygous for color deficiency. *J. Opt. Soc. Am.* 71:719–29

Naka, K. I., Rushton, W. A. H. 1966. S-potentials from colour units in the retina of fish (Cyprinidae). *J. Physiol.* 185:536–55

Nassau, K. 1983. *The Physics and Chemistry of Color.* New York: Wiley-Interscience. 454 pp.

Nathans, J., Piantanida, T. P., Eddy, R. L., Shows, T. B., Hogness, D. S. 1986a. Molecular genetics of inherited variation in human color vision. *Science* 232:203–10

Nathans, J., Thomas, D., Hogness, D. S. 1986b. Molecular genetics of human color vision: the genes encoding blue, green, and red pigments. *Science* 232:193–202

Neitz, J., Jacobs, G. H. 1986. Polymorphism of the long-wavelength cone in normal human colour vision. *Nature* 323:623–25

Nickerson, D. 1981. OSA uniform color scale samples: a unique set. *Color Res. Appl.* 6:7–28

Noorlander, C., Heuts, M. J. G., Koenderink, J. J. 1981. Sensitivity to spatiotemporal combined luminance and chromaticity contrast. *J. Opt. Soc. Am.* 71:453–59

Noorlander, C., Koenderink, J. J. 1983. Spatial and temporal discrimination ellipsoids in color space. *J. Opt. Soc. Am.* 73:1533–43

Northdurft, H. C., Lee, B. B. 1982. Responses to coloured patterns in the macaque lateral geniculate nucleus: analysis of receptive field properties. *Exp. Brain Res.* 48:55–65

Nunn, B. J., Schnapf, J. L., Baylor, D. A. 1984. Spectral sensitivity of single cones in the retina of *Macaca fascicularis.* *Nature* 309:264–66

Olson, C. X., Boynton, R. M. 1984. Dichoptic metacontrast masking reveals a central basis for monoptic chromatic induction. *Percept. Psychophys.* 35:295–300

Olzak, L. A., Thomas, J. P. 1986. Seeing spatial patterns. See Boff et al. 1986, pp. 7-1, 7-56

Ottoson, D., Zecki, S., eds. 1985. *Central and Peripheral Mechanisms of Colour Vision.* London: MacMillan. 239 pp.

Overheim, R. D., Wagner, D. L. 1982. *Light and Color.* New York: Wiley. 269 pp.

Paulus, W., Kröger-Paulus, A. 1983. A new concept of retinal color coding. *Vision Res.* 23:529–40

Piantanida, T. 1985. Temporal modulation sensitivity of the blue mechanism: measurements made with extraretinal chromatic adaptation. *Vision Res.* 25:1439–44

Pokorny, J., Smith, V. C. 1982. New observations concerning red-green color defects. *Color Res. Appl.* 7:159–64

Pokorny, J., Smith, V. C., Burns, S. A., Elsner, A. E., Zaidi, Q. 1981. Modeling blue-yellow opponency. In *Proc. 4th Int. Congr. Int. Color Assoc. (AIC),* ed. M. Richter. Berlin

Ramachandran, V. S., Gregory, R. L. 1978. Does colour provide an input to human motion perception? *Nature* 275:55–56

Ratliff, F. 1976. On the psychophysical basis of universal color terms. *Proc. Am. Philos. Soc.* 120:311–30

Reeves, A. 1981a. Transient tritanopia after flicker adaptation. *Vision Res.* 21:657–64

Reeves, A. 1981b. Transient tritanopia: its abolition at high intensities. *Vision Res.* 21:665–72

Reeves, A. 1981c. Metacontrast in hue substitution. *Vision Res.* 21:907–12

Reeves, A. 1981d. Transient desensitization of a red-green opponent site. *Vision Res.* 21:1267–77

Reeves, A. 1983. Distinguishing opponent and non-opponent detection pathways in early dark adaptation. *Vision Res.* 23:647–54

Rich, D. C., Billmeyer, F. W. Jr. 1983. Small and moderate color-differences. IV. Color-difference perceptibility ellipses in surface-color space. *Color Res. Appl.* 8:31–39

Rogers, D. C., Hollins, M. 1982. Is the binocular rivalry mechanism tritanopic? *Vision Res.* 22:515–20

Romero, J., Hita, E., Jiménez del Barco, L. 1986. A comparative study of successive and simultaneous methods in colour discrimination. *Vision Res.* 26:471–76

Sagawa, K. 1981. Minimum light intensity required for color rivalry. *Vision Res.* 21:1467–74

Sagawa, K. 1982. Dichoptic color fusion studied with wavelength discrimination. *Vision Res.* 22:945–52

Sagawa, K., Takeichi, K. 1986. Spectral luminous efficiency functions in the mesopic range. *J. Opt. Soc. Am. A* 3:71–75

Schnapf, J. L., Kraft, T. W., Baylor, D. A. 1987. Spectral sensitivity of human cone photoreceptors. *Nature* 325:439–41

Sherman, P. D. 1981. *Colour Vision in the Nineteenth Century.* Bristol: Hilger. 233 pp.

Shevell, S. K. 1982. Color perception under chromatic adaptation: equilibrium yellow and long-wavelength adaptation. *Vision Res.* 22:279–92

Smith, V. C., Pokorny, J., Zaidi, Q. 1983. How do sets of color-matching functions differ? See Mollon & Sharpe 1983, pp. 93–105

Stalmeier, P. F. M., De Weert, C. M. M. 1986. Large colour differences measured with binocular rivalry. *Perception* 15:A26 (Abstr.)

Stiles, W. S., Burch, J. M. 1959. N.P.L. colour-matching investigation: final report (1958). *Optica Acta* 6:1–26

Stromeyer, C. F. III. 1983. Spatial sensitization and desensitization with small adapting fields: interactions of signals from different classes of cones. *Vision Res.* 23:621–30

Stromeyer, C. F. III, Cole, G. R., Kronauer, R. E. 1985. Second-site adaptation in the red-green chromatic pathways. *Vision Res.* 25:219–37

Swanson, W. H., Pokorny, J., Smith, V. C. 1986. Heterochromatic flicker with chromatic adaptation: cone isolation? *Invest. Ophthalmos. Vis. Sci.* 27:293 (Abstr.)

Takahashi, S., Ejima, Y. 1983a. Chromatic induction as a function of wavelength of inducing stimulus. *J. Opt. Soc. Am.* 73:190–97

Takahashi, S., Ejima, Y. 1983b. Functional relationship between chromatic induction and luminance of the inducing stimulus. *J. Opt. Soc. Am.* 73:198–207

Takahashi, S., Ejima, Y. 1984. Spatial properties of red-green and yellow-blue perceptual opponent-color response. *Vision Res.* 24:987–94

Thornton, J. E., Pugh, E. N. Jr. 1983. Relationship of opponent-colours cancellation measures to cone-antagonistic signals deduced from increment threshold data. See Mollon & Sharpe 1983, pp. 361–73

Toyoda, J., Kujiraoka, T., Fujimoto, M. 1982. The role of L-type horizontal cells in the opponent-color process. *Color Res. Appl.* 7:152–54

Trezona, P. W. 1987. Individual observer data for the 1955 Stiles-Burch 2° pilot investigation. *J. Opt. Soc. Am. A* 4:769–82

Trezona, P. W. 1986. An investigation into mesopic photometry. *Perception* 15:A26 (Abstr.)

Troscianko, T. 1987. Perception of random-dot symmetry and apparent movement at or near isoluminance. *Vision Res.* In press

Uchikawa, K. 1983. Purity discrimination: Successive vs. simultaneous comparison method. *Vision Res.* 23:53–58

Uchikawa, K., Ikeda, M. 1985. Wavelength discrimination with chromatically alternating stimuli. *Color Res. Appl.* 10:204–9

Uchikawa, K., Ikeda, M. 1986. Accuracy of memory for brightness of colored lights measured with successive comparison method. *J. Opt. Soc. Am. A* 3:34–39

Uchikawa, K., Uchikawa, H., Kaiser, P. K. 1984. Luminance and saturation of equally bright colors. *Color Res. Appl.* 9:5–14

Valberg, A., Lee, B. B., Tigwell, D. A. 1986. Neurones with strong inhibitory S-cone inputs in the macaque lateral geniculate nucleus. *Vision Res.* 26:1061–64

Valberg, A., Lee, B. B., Tigwell, D. A., Creutzfeldt, O. D. 1985. A simultaneous contrast effect of steady remote surrounds on responses of cells in macaque lateral geniculate nucleus. *Exp. Brain Res.* 58:604–8

Valberg, A., Seim, T. 1983. Chromatic induction: responses of neurophysiological double opponent units? *Biol. Cybern.* 46:149–58

Van Essen, D. C. 1986. Functional organization of primate visual cortex. In *Cerebral Cortex*, ed. A. Peters, E. G. Jones. New York: Plenum

van Norren, D., van der Kraats, J. 1981. A continuously recording retinal densitometer. *Vision Res.* 21:897–905

Vautin, R. G., Dow, B. M. 1985. Color cell groups in foveal striate cortex of the behaving macaque. *J. Neurophysiol.* 54:273–92

Verdon, W., Adams, A. J. 1987. Short-wavelength-sensitive cones do not contribute to mesopic luminosity. *J. Opt. Soc. Am. A* 4:91–95

Verriest, G., ed. 1980. *Colour Deficiencies V.* Bristol: Hilger. 410 pp.

Verriest, G., ed. 1982. *Colour Deficiencies VI.* The Hague: Junk. 521 pp.

Verriest, G., ed. 1984. *Colour Deficiencies VII.* The Hague: Junk. 424 pp.

Vos, J. J. 1982. On the merits of model making in understanding color-vision phenomena. *Color Res. Appl.* 7:69–77

Walraven, J. 1976. Discounting the background—the missing link in the explanation of chromatic induction. *Vision Res.* 16:289–95

Walraven, J., Werner, J. S. 1986. The invariance of unique white: implications for normalizing cone spectral-sensitivity functions. *Perception* 15:A27 (Abstr.)

Wandell, B. A. 1985. Color measurement and discrimination. *J. Opt. Soc. Am. A* 2:62–71

Ware, C., Cowan, W. B. 1983. Specification of heterochromatic brightness matches: a conversion factor for calculating luminances of stimuli that are equal in brightness. *NRC Tech. Rep. 26055.* Nat. Res. Council, Ottawa, Canada

Werner, J. S., Walraven, J. 1982. Effect of chromatic adaptation on the achromatic locus: the role of contrast, luminance and background color. *Vision Res.* 22:929–43

Wiesel, T. N., Hubel, D. H. 1966. Spatial and chromatic interactions in the lateral geniculate body of the rhesus monkey. *J. Neurophysiol.* 29:1115–56

Williams, D. R., MacLeod, D. I. A., Hayhoe, M. M. 1981a. Foveal tritanopia. *Vision Res.* 21:1341–56

Williams, D. R., MacLeod, D. I. A., Hayhoe, M. M. 1981b. Punctate sensitivity of the blue-sensitive mechanism. *Vision Res.* 21:1357–75

Wisowaty, J. J. 1981. Estimates for the temporal response characteristics of chromatic pathways. *J. Opt. Soc. Am.* 71:970–77

Worthey, J. A., Brill, M. H. 1986. Heuristic analysis of Von Kries color constancy. *J. Opt. Soc. Am. A* 3:1708–12

Wyszecki, G., Stiles, W. S. 1982. *Color Science.* New York: Wiley. 950 pp. 2nd ed.

Zeki, S. M. 1973. Color coding in rhesus monkey prestriate cortex. *Brain Res.* 53:422–27

Zeki, S. 1983. Color coding in the cerebral cortex: the responses of wavelength-selective and colour-coded cells in monkey visual cortex to changes in wavelength composition. *Neuroscience* 9:767–81

Zeki, S. 1985. Colour pathways and hierarchies in the cerebral cortex. See Ottoson & Zeki 1985, pp. 19–44

Zrenner, E. 1983. *Neurophysiological Aspects of Color Vision in Primates.* Berlin: Springer-Verlag. 218 pp.

Zrenner, E., Gouras, P. 1978. Retinal ganglion cells lose color opponency at high flicker rates. *Invest. Ophthalmos. Vis. Sci. Suppl.* 17:130 (Abstr.)

Zrenner, E., Gouras, P. 1981. Characteristics of the blue sensitive cone mechanism in primate retinal ganglion cells. *Vision Res.* 21:1605–9

Ann. Rev. Psychol. 1988. 39:101–33

HUMAN BEHAVIOR GENETICS

John C. Loehlin, Lee Willerman, and Joseph M. Horn

Department of Psychology, University of Texas, Austin, Texas 78712

CONTENTS

INTRODUCTION

What is the current status of human behavior genetics as a distinct discipline? It is still distinct: Experimental, clinical, personality, social, and developmental psychologists are not yet routinely incorporating genetic varia-

101

0066-4308/88/0201-0101$02.00

tion into their research designs. However, an increasing number of psychologists are at least recognizing the potential role of the genes in their specialties, and a few are doing much more than that. Not many are yet following Plomin's (1986a) prescription: Do whatever research you would do anyway, using a sample of twins, adoptees, or other informative groups, and study genetic variation simultaneously with whatever else you have in mind.

In any event, human behavior genetics continues as an active research area. In this chapter we look at the roughly six years' worth of publication since Henderson's *Annual Review* chapter of 1982 (the Wimers' 1985 chapter concentrated on behavior genetic studies with nonhuman animals). Given limited space, we have been unable to mention—let alone discuss—many interesting topics and worthwhile papers. Often we have cited a recent summary paper or chapter in which further references may be found to a relevant body of earlier work.

A few recent behavior genetics textbooks may be helpful in filling in gaps: a general text by Hay (1985), a text on developmental behavior genetics by Plomin (1986b), and one on the heredity of behavior disorders by Vandenberg et al (1986).

We begin our review with work on intellectual abilities and disabilities, proceed to personality and psychopathology, and wind up with a brief consideration of models and model-fitting.

INTELLECTUAL ABILITIES AND DISABILITIES

General Intelligence

At the time of the last *Annual Review* chapter on human behavior genetics, Henderson (1982), following Plomin et al (1980), noted that heritability estimates for general intelligence were a function of date of publication. Studies published before 1963 produced estimates as high as 80%, while those in print after 1975 seemed to converge on a figure closer to 50%. The then-recent family, twin, and adoption studies were in substantial agreement: Each methodology yielded lower heritability estimates. Loehlin (1980), and indirectly Reed & Rich (1982), suggested that restriction of range in the recent IQ data could be responsible, but it was also possible that changes in the environment over the previous 50 years had made an appreciable difference.

One of the major discrepancies between the early and recent data sets involved the lower family correlations (parent-child and among siblings) in the recent research. Plomin et al (1980) noted that these lower correlations support the idea of an increase in the strength or number of factors operating within the family to make family members different. Critics of genetic explanations for individual differences have traditionally emphasized the importance of the other major theoretical source of environmental influences: between-family factors that make family members more similar to one another but different from people in other families. Such influences increase family correlations. Since family correlations had fallen, a more potent between-family environment could not be responsible for the lower heritabilities observed in 1982.

It now appears that heritability estimates of general intelligence are back up again, although perhaps not to the highest figures from the early data. Henderson's review did not include data from separated identical twins because no recent data were then available. However, in 1982, Lykken presented the first results from the Minnesota Study of Twins Reared Apart. Lykken and his colleagues' 29 pairs of adult monozygotics reared apart had a correlation of .71 for adult general intelligence compared to .78 for a control group of monozygotic twins reared together. Since the intraclass correlation between separated identicals is itself an estimate of heritability, these data suggest an upward revision of heritability estimates.

Follow-up and new studies of monozygotic (MZ) and dizygotic (DZ) twins reared together are also yielding higher heritabilities. In a study of middle-aged twins (Tambs et al 1984), the IQ correlations were .88 and .47 for MZs and same-sex DZs, respectively. For younger twins, age seems to be important. Wilson (1983, 1986) reports higher MZ correlations and lower DZ correlations as twins mature. At 9 years of age, his identical twins showed a correlation of .83, the fraternals one of .65. Those twins retested at age 15 had correlations of .88 and .54, respectively. Fischbein's (1981) longitudinal study of adolescent twins also showed larger differences between MZ and DZ correlations with increasing age. Segal (1985) even found a low DZ correlation for younger twins. Her twins were 8 years old on the average, and the MZ's correlation was .85 while the DZs was .46. Nathan & Guttman (1984) worked with twins 8–13 years old and found a median MZ correlation of .80 for a battery of five tests, while the corresponding figure for DZs was only .38. The only new twin study with a DZ correlation close to the average DZ correlation of .62 in Henderson's review was that of Stevenson et al (1987). Their 13-year-old twins showed a correlation of .84 for MZs and .61 for DZs on the WISC-R. Since genetic assortative mating increases DZ correlations but does not affect the similarity of MZs, corrections for assortative mating would increase MZ-DZ differences and make typical estimates of heritability for general intelligence from these new studies of twins reared together at least as high as the new estimate from separated twins.

Age also appears to make a difference in the adoption studies, in this case lowering shared family environmental effects. Scarr & Weinberg (1983) compared unrelated siblings reared together in their Transracial Adoption Study to the same category of individuals in their Adolescent Adoption Study.

The unrelated siblings in the transracial study averaged 7 years of age and were as similar as the biologically related sibs. However, among the unrelated sibs (18 years old on the average) in the adolescent study the correlation was close to zero. Their interpretation was that "older children escape the influence of the family and are freer to select their own environments."

Scarr & Weinberg's finding of near zero correlations for older unrelated siblings has been supported in a study from Denmark. Teasdale & Owen (1984) located a small sample of pairs of unrelated adoptees who had been reared together and been tested by their draft boards. Their correlation for intelligence was .02. Data from the Texas Adoption Project 10-year follow-up (J. M. Horn et al, in preparation) also shows near zero IQ correlations for unrelated, reared-together pairs averaging 18 years of age, correlations down about .15 points from 10 years earlier.

To summarize the results for general intelligence since 1982: Separated identical twins are almost as similar as identicals reared together; in studies of twins reared together, DZ correlations are lower; and in adoption studies, unrelated children become less similar the longer they live together. On the whole, these studies appear to have reversed the trend toward lower heritability estimates reported by Plomin et al and Henderson. Several of the studies suggest that older subjects reveal genetic influences more strongly than younger ones. If this difference is real, it will profit behavior geneticists to add age parameters to their analyses (Gourlay 1979). It will also be important to know if between-family environmental influences simply decline in potency as children mature, or if they are overshadowed by new within-family or genetic factors that come into play.

The Colorado Adoption Project (Plomin & DeFries 1985) is an important new longitudinal study involving 182 adopted infants and 165 matched nonadopted control infants who have so far been tested each year through age 4. In addition to almost all of the adoptive parents and biological mothers, about one fourth of the biological fathers were also tested. DeFries et al (1987) used their path models on these data plus the twin data of Loehlin & Nichols (1976) and Wilson (1983) to estimate heritabilities for both children and adults. The adult heritability was .55 and the childhood heritabilities rose from .10 at age 1 to .26 at age 4. Estimates of the genetic correlation from childhood to adulthood varied from .42 among 1 year olds to .75 for the 4 year olds, indicating for the latter group "that about half of the phenotypic stability between childhood and adulthood is mediated genetically." This means that a significant proportion of the genetic factors contributing to individual differences on the Stanford-Binet at age 4 are the same genetic factors influencing individual differences in adult IQ—and that a significant proportion are not. Another interesting finding was that the fathers' correlations with their adoptive and natural children showed more of a genetic pattern than the correlations for the mothers. This result agrees with that of Horn et al (1979, 1982) in the Texas Adoption Project.

One particularly valuable component of the Colorado Adoption Project is the sizeable number of measures of the environments and behavior of both the adoptive and control parents. Hardy-Brown & Plomin (1985) have used these measures to study correlates of infant communicative competence at one year of age. For this very young sample, the findings were essentially negative; all the significant correlations between maternal behavior or parents' environment and infant competence were no longer significant after the relationship to parental IQ was controlled. Scarr (1985) also studied child communication skills but at a later age (42–48 months). The results were the same; after maternal IQ was partialled out, the mother's behavior was not a significant predictor of child IQ or communication skills.

Twin and adoption studies have provided most of the data for behavior genetic analyses over the past decades, but studies of the offspring from consanguineous matings yield results that confirm the importance of genetic factors in individual differences. Daniels et al (1982) found that children from first-cousin matings averaged about one tenth of a standard deviation lower than control children on cognitive measures as well as on anthropometric and behavioral characters. This inbreeding depression is to be expected only when genes show directional dominance. Another effect of dominance is to increase the variance of the trait. Agrawal et al (1984) found both inbreeding depression (averaging greater than one half standard deviation) and a larger variance on Raven's Progressive Matrices for Indian Muslim boys when their parents were first cousins.

Some adoption projects have focused on demonstrating environmental effects on average IQ and scholastic performance (Schiff et al 1978; Schiff et al 1982; Dumaret 1985). These investigators do not have IQ data on biological parents but have relied on biological parent occupational status to identify 35 adopted-away children genetically at risk for lower IQ and poor academic performance. These children are compared to other children who were reared by the same mothers who gave the at-risk group of children up for adoption. Both of these groups are then compared to SES-matched children or other controls. All biological parents were of low occupational status, while the adoptive fathers were all middle or higher level managers. Results indicated that IQs were significantly higher and school failures significantly lower than predicted from biological parent status. Duyme (1985) obtained a similar result for school success in a separate study of 87 adopted children.

These are not surprising findings. Many studies have found higher IQs for adoptive children than would have been expected if the children had remained with their biological mothers (Horn 1983). Significant increases in average IQ appear to be possible through radical environmental intervention (adoption).

But individual differences remain large, and the evidence is that these are substantially influenced by genetic factors.

Separate Abilities

The question of whether intelligence is one general ability or, rather, a collection of relatively separate abilities is one of the more venerable debates in psychology (Spearman 1927; Thurstone 1938). Vernon (1950) proposed a hierarchical model that includes both general and specific factors with intermediate group factors that allow for the intercorrelations among subgroups of specific abilities. His two major group factors correspond roughly to verbal and performance IQ. The biological validity of this partition of intelligence is supported by chromosomal anomalies. Turner syndrome women (45X) lack one X chromosome and show performance IQs that are depressed by one standard deviation. Their verbal IQs are unaffected (Netley 1983). The opposite pattern is found for men with an extra X (47XXY). These men average one standard deviation below the norm for verbal IQ, but their performance IQs are close to the population mean. Thus, chromosomal alterations appear to have independent effects on the two major components of intelligence.

Are verbal and performance test scores influenced differentially by allelic as well as chromosomal variations? The new twin studies included in this review are inconclusive on this point. Four studies of twins reared together measured intelligence with the WAIS or WISC so that verbal and performance scores were available (Segal 1985; Stevenson et al 1987; Tambs et al 1984; Wilson 1986), but only two (Stevenson and Tambs) showed appreciably different MZ-DZ discrepancies in heritability for verbal and performance IQs. This failure to find consistent differential heritability is in accord with an earlier review of twin data on cognitive abilities by Nichols (1978).

One interesting possibility is that different sets of genes influence different abilities. The degree of influence might be approximately the same for each major component of intelligence but different genes would be responsible. In order to determine if such a situation exists, it is necessary to examine the covariance among measures of different abilities. Martin & Eaves (1977) did this using twin data from Thurstone's Primary Mental Abilities test, and Martin et al (1984) analyzed twin scores from the five subtests of the National Merit Scholarship Qualifying Test. In the first study, nearly all the within-family environmental variance appeared to be specific to particular abilities, while a large general environmental factor operated between families. On the genetic side there was a large general factor and sizeable ability-specific factors. Similar results were obtained in the second study, although the largest specific genetic factor was for word fluency in the first study and mathematics in the second investigation, and there was a verbal group factor as well in the second study. If different genes are affecting different abilities to different degrees, there nevertheless does exist a set of genes (the general genetic factor) that influences all intellectual abilities. Thurstone's and Vernon's theories about the organization of intelligence are both partially supported by these results.

Language and Learning Disabilities

Two excellent publications summarizing earlier results in this area have appeared recently (Ludlow & Cooper 1983; Pennington & Smith 1983), and we will only attempt to highlight a few of the major subsequent findings.

The importance of parental reading disability as an indication of risk for their children was investigated by Vogler et al 1985. Depending on what is accepted as the overall incidence of reading disability (RD) in the general population, the ratio of probabilities for a RD male child if a father is disabled versus normal (relative risk) was between 4.9 and 9.7. The corresponding figures for a female child were between 10.2 and 13.3. Relative risks are slightly lower if the mother rather than the father was RD. These risks could be seen as a reflection of an environmental liability if parents with reading problems are less encouraging of reading in their offspring. However, RD parents have more normal children than RD children, a fact that encourages the search for a genetic diathesis.

Stevenson et al (1987) used a twin sample to assess genetic influences on reading and spelling ability (and disability). The measures of reading and spelling levels showed moderate heritabilities even when intelligence was controlled, but reading backwardness and specific reading retardation did not show significant MZ-DZ differences. In the area of disabilities, only spelling disability provided a clear indication of genetic effects. The failure to find the usual genetic influences for disability in reading was considered in the light of the weaknesses of previous studies and the narrow age range for the children used by Stevenson et al.

Pennington et al (1986) have looked at spelling errors on the Wide Range Achievement Test from adults "with an apparent autosomal dominant form of dyslexia." These errors were compared to those from normal adult relatives and spelling-age matched normal controls (children). The findings indicated that this form of dyslexia is characterized by phonological rather than orthographic inaccuracies. Data from other types of dyslexics were not included in their report. Hay (1985) urges caution in accepting the autosomal dominant classification used in this research, but if other types of dyslexics show different patterns of spelling errors in future research, it will confirm the utility of such a category.

PERSONALITY, ATTITUDES, TEMPERAMENT

There have been several recent efforts to place personality psychology within a broad evolutionary-biological framework (e.g. Buss 1984; Rushton 1984). Buss & Barnes (1986) examined gender differences in the qualities preferred in mates, and interpreted these as reflecting cues to reproductive potential that differ for the two sexes (youth is more critical for reproductive success in females, for example). Rushton (1985) interpreted various social class, race, and individual differences in terms of "differential K theory," the contrast between reproductive strategies that lead to many offspring with little investment in each or to a few offspring carefully nurtured. However, most behavior genetic work on personality continues to fall within the traditional categories of twin and adoption studies.

Identical and Fraternal Twins

Several substantial studies comparing MZ and DZ twins on a range of personality measures have been reported during the period under review. One is based on an Australian sample of 3810 adult pairs tested by mailed questionnaires (Martin & Jardine 1986). The tests used were the Eysenck Personality Questionnaire (EPQ), a conservatism scale, and scales measuring symptoms of anxiety and depression. Martin & Jardine fit biometric models to variances and covariances. They estimated 35–50% genetic variance on the various scales, largely additive except for EPQ Extraversion, which had a substantial genetic dominance component ($\approx$30%). Several scales showed sex differences. EPQ Lie and the conservatism scale had more genetic variance in females; EPQ Psychoticism had more in males. Only the conservatism scale had a detectable family environment component, and it was modest ($\approx$20%).

Thus the Australian study supports the earlier US and British twin studies reviewed by Henderson in his 1982 *Annual Review* chapter in finding heritabilities in the 40–50% range for most personality traits, with the remaining environmentally caused variation almost entirely idiosyncratic (i.e. unshared by the twins of a pair). It also supports the tendency noted by Henderson for extraversion measures to show DZ correlations less than half those for MZs, which could represent the effect of nonadditive genetic variation (Martin & Jardine's genetic dominance component) but might alternatively reflect special shared MZ environments, contrast or competition between DZ twins, or other factors Henderson discusses.

The presence of shared cultural variation for the conservatism scale also confirms previous studies reviewed by Henderson, although the Martin & Jardine data show a larger genetic component than has sometimes been reported for such measures. Moreover, in a separate analysis of the conservatism scale along with similar data from a British twin sample (Martin et al 1986), it is suggested that the apparent shared environment factor might even be spurious—an artifact of the strong assortative mating characteristic of social attitudes.

Another twin study, done in the United States, involved 133 twin pairs tested twice, five years apart, at ages 20 and 25 years (Pogue-Geile & Rose 1985). Six scales based on the Minnesota Multiphasic Personality Inventory (MMPI) were used, covering ground similar to that of the Martin & Jardine study. Results were similar, except that the DZ correlations tended to be less than half the MZ correlations for most scales–not just for extraversion– suggesting a widespread presence of nonadditive genetic variation or twin method artifacts. Changes in the traits over the five-year period were also assessed. They appeared predominantly to reflect specific environmental rather than genetic or shared environmental factors.

Another substantial twin study of 573 adult pairs in Great Britain measured social or interpersonal aspects of personality: altruism, empathy, nurturance, aggressiveness, and assertiveness (Rushton et al 1986). Results for these traits were like those reported for the EPQ or MMPI: around 40–50% genetic variance, mostly additive, with little or no evidence for the effect of shared environments. On another aspect of social behavior, a study by Rowe (1983a) of 265 Ohio adolescent twin pairs' self-reported delinquencies arrived at generally similar conclusions. A model with only additive genetic and non-shared environmental effects provided an adequate fit to the data.

Thus standard twin studies continue to find evidence of medium-sized and similar heritabilities for most personality traits (40–50%); some evidence of nonadditive genetic variance, especially for extraversion; and some evidence of shared environmental variance in the domain of social attitudes, with a suggestion by Martin and his colleagues that the latter may at least in part reflect assortative mating rather than the effects of shared environment proper.

Adoption and Family Studies

The Texas Adoption Project contributed the principal new adoption data on personality during the period under review. An unusual result was reported from the original sample of 300 adoptive families, tested when the children averaged about 8 years of age. Birth mothers' emotional adjustment, as measured by the MMPI, tended to relate negatively to their adopted-away childrens' adjustment, although positive resemblance seemed to be present in the extraversion domain (Loehlin et al 1982). The authors speculate that a genotype-environment interaction might be involved, in which these children responded exceptionally strongly to their environments, in this case the highly supportive climate of the adoptive homes. If so, problems might emerge later as the children moved out into a wider environment, and indeed a change of this kind seemed to have occurred in two older adoptive samples, one a separate sample from the same adoption agency (Loehlin et al 1985), and one a ten-year follow-up of the original adoptees (J. C. Loehlin et al, under review).

Data from the adoptive families in these last two samples generally agreed with the earlier results of Scarr and her colleagues (1981): modest biologically based correlations, on the order of .10–.15, and near-zero adoptive correlations. As in the case of the twin data, there seems to be little evidence of shared family environmental effects on personality but some genetic effects, although the latter may be smaller in the adoption data. This difference might reflect the expression of different genes at different ages lowering familial correlations, the presence of nonadditive genetic variance raising MZ twin correlations, or various possible artifacts of the adoption or twin designs.

If it is indeed the case that the influences of shared family environment are negligible for most personality traits, then ordinary families should be as informative for behavior genetic work as more exotic groups like twins and adoptees. Not much advantage seems so far to have been taken of this. One major exception is the Hawaii Family Study of Cognition, for which familial regressions and correlations have been published for 54 scales from 5 personality inventories administered to subsamples of 100–669 families (Ahern et al 1982). These results also suggest lower heritabilities than do the twin studies, presumably for similar reasons.

Another implication of the twin and adoption data is that within-family environmental variation must be very important for personality development (Plomin & Daniels 1987), and this is beginning to be studied systematically (e.g. Daniels 1986; Daniels et al 1985; Rowe 1983b).

Separated Twins

As noted, personality scale correlations for DZ twins often are less than half those for MZ twins. Such a phenomenon is ambiguous. It might reflect nonadditive genetic variance shared by MZ twins or it might reflect one or another environmental mechanism, such as an unusual degree of commonality of MZ twin environments, contrast or competition between DZ twins, or the like. One group that can help resolve such ambiguities is twins reared apart. For such twins, presumably, the special environmental mechanisms mentioned do not come into play, and if DZ rs are still less than half MZ rs, some direct or indirect genetic explanation would seem to be required. In addition, direct comparisons of twins reared together and apart speak to the importance of shared environment: If twins reared together are not more similar in personality than are twins reared apart, shared environment would not seem to make a major contribution to resemblance.

Tellegen and his colleagues in the Minnesota study of separated twins (A.

Tellegen et al, under review) have obtained correlations on the 11 scales of the Multidimensional Personality Questionnaire (MPQ) for 44 MZ and 27 DZ pairs reared apart, as well as for a comparison group of 217 MZ and 114 DZ pairs reared together. While there is some evidence of common environmental effects, on the whole correlations for twins reared together and apart are more alike than different. The data do not suggest either that MZs reared together show grossly inflated correlations for environmental reasons, or that DZs reared together show depressed ones. In both the reared-together and reared-apart samples, there are interesting differences between the two second-order MPQ factors Tellegen calls Positive and Negative Emotionality, factors that are related respectively to Eysenck's Extraversion and Neuroticism dimensions. Positive Emotionality shows a pattern suggestive of genetic nonadditivity (DZ correlations decidedly less than half MZ correlations), whereas Negative Emotionality looks much more like a genetically additive trait.

MZ twins with varying degrees of separation also represent a potentially informative design. While most of the evidence we have reviewed has pointed to little influence of shared environment on personality traits, Rose & Kaprio (1987) present data in which they read a different message. A Finnish sample of 2320 adult MZ pairs was classified by degree of social contact, from twins living together to those who rarely communicated. Intraclass twin correlations on a short version of Eysenck's Neuroticism scale decreased with decreasing contact, from around .60 for pairs living together to around .20 for twins rarely communicating. Since these are MZ twins, genetic differences cannot be responsible. However, the causal sequences among environmental events remain ambiguous. Do twins who happen to be unlike each other—perhaps by virtue of chance events occurring early in development—tend as a consequence to associate less? Or does the lack of shared experience in members of rarely associating pairs permit their personalities to drift apart? Or both? It will likely take longitudinal studies to sort these matters out.

Another study involving length of separation, this time among members of 78 Melbourne families (Hopper & Culross 1983), also concluded that separation might affect personality resemblance, but in this case in the opposite direction: Mothers and their children tended to grow more alike on Cattell's Factor A (outgoing versus reserved) with longer separation. However, preliminary results for a measure of anxiety (Hopper 1983) suggest that this trait may behave in Australia as it does in Finland, with less resemblance associated with more separation.

Combinations of Groups

Several papers appeared during the period under review that have fit models simultaneously to data from several groups (e.g. twins, adoptees, ordinary families). Cattell, who originally proposed this approach under the name of

Multiple Abstract Variance Analysis (MAVA), summarizes the results of a major MAVA study in his book *The Inheritance of Personality and Ability* (Cattell 1982). The study involved MZ and DZ twins and ordinary and adoptive siblings, all boys aged 12–18 years. He reports results for 10 questionnaire and 9 objective test scales. Averaged across several different methods of analysis, the heritabilities ranged from a low of 12% to a high of 65% genetic variance, with median values in the .30s for both the questionnaire and test measures. A distinctive feature of Cattell's work is the attempt to estimate heredity-environment correlations for the various traits. These often emerged as quite large numerically, but statistical tests failed to show them as differing significantly from zero, so apparently his methods have little statistical power for the estimation of such correlations.

Other studies have involved two-generational data. Carey & Rice (1983) fit models using data from twin, adoptive, and familial relationships for three traits in the extraversion domain. Social Closeness fit an additive genetic model, and Social Potency and Impulsivity could be fit either by allowing nonadditive genetic variance or special MZ environments. Allowing for differences in parameters between the sexes often yielded significant improvements in fit. Loehlin (1985, 1986a) reported two analyses, one of the California Psychological Inventory (CPI) scales using two twin studies and an adoption study, and one for the Thurstone Temperament Schedule (TTS) based on two studies of twins, a twin-family study, and an adoption study. Very small shared-environment components were typical, and estimates of additive genetic variation in the range 40–55%. However, not all traits were alike–heritability varied over both the CPI and TTS scales. Finally, Price and his colleagues (1982) analyzed six Eysenck and Comrey scales in a Swedish sample of MZ twins and their families. They fit a 13-parameter model for each of the scales; but in a reanalysis, Hewitt (1984) showed that the data could be fit by simple 1-parameter models involving additive genes and no family environment. Hewitt's solutions yielded estimates of genetic variation in the range 37–51% for the six scales.

Infant Temperament

Can genetic variation be demonstrated in the temperament of infants as expressed during the first year of life? Several attempts to answer this question have been made during the period under review, with mostly negative results.

The Louisville Twin Study (Wilson & Matheny 1986) carried out laboratory assessments of temperament at 9 and 12 months on about 30 pairs of each zygosity, and found little evidence of heritability. Neonatal temperament assessments (Riese et al 1985) based on hospital observation of about 20 pairs of each zygosity yielded similar results. However, laboratory assessments during the second year began to show higher MZ than DZ correlations (Wilson & Matheny 1986), as did age-to-age changes during the second year. In a second study of temperament in infant twins (Goldsmith & Campos 1986), in which about 35 pairs of each zygosity have been studied in laboratory situations at about 9 months of age, preliminary results provide only weak evidence for genetic variation. Parents were also measured, but no substantial, replicated parent-infant correlations on putatively corresponding traits were obtained.

Parent-infant correlations were also obtained in the Colorado Adoption Project (Plomin & DeFries 1985) in both adoptive families and matched control families, and for birth parents of the adopted children. At age 12 months, based on roughly 150–170 infants, there appeared to be no appreciable correlations between the infants' temperaments, as rated by their adoptive parents or by independent observers, and the birth parents' personalities, as measured by questionnaire or as rated by self or partner. There were, however, a handful of significant correlations of infants with their adoptive parents, or of infants and parents in control families, suggesting that environmental factors might be capable of producing some parent-offspring resemblances during the first year of life. By age 24 months–as in the Louisville study–there is occasionally a suggestion of genetic effects. Birth mothers' self-ratings of sociability correlate .15 with infants' rated sociabilities; a neuroticism factor score correlates .20 with infant emotionality ratings. However, the bulk of the correlations still hover around zero.

Thus, several efforts during the past six years have not provided much evidence of identifiable genetic components underlying individual differences in temperament during the first year of life. By the second year or so, however, some signs of the patterns characteristic of later ages are beginning to emerge.

PSYCHOPATHOLOGY

Schizophrenia

Genetic research on schizophrenia continues apace, but no new discoveries have galvanized investigation along a particular line. A blind reanalysis of the Kety adoption study of schizophrenia using modified DSM-III criteria (Kendler & Gruenberg 1984) has confirmed earlier observations that the disorder is heritable in this sample. A preliminary report of a Finnish study of the adopted-away offspring of schizophrenic and control mothers has already found five of the high-risk offspring and only one control offspring to be probably or certainly schizophrenic (Tienari et al 1985). This study also provides a detailed examination of adoptive family functioning and may eventually shed light on social-environmental factors that can precipitate schizophrenia. The adoptees are quite young and have not yet passed through much of the risk period–one third are less than 20 years old–and follow-ups will be necessary.

Many family studies (Baron et al 1985; Kendler et al 1985; Loranger 1981; Tsuang et al 1983, 1985b) have indicated that schizophrenia seems to "breed true," though there is usually some elevation in the rate of schizoaffective (mainly schizophrenic) disorder and schizotypal personality disorder in the relatives. However, schizophrenia is not associated with family excesses of affective disorder, anxiety disorder, or alcoholism. While there is evidence for homotypia (i.e. affected relatives tend to have the same subtype of schizophrenia), there are numerous exceptions (Farmer et al 1984). Indeed, a follow-up of the Genain quadruplets, who were all concordant for schizophrenia, revealed just how variable the symptom picture could be (DeLisi et al 1984). Some experts have concluded that the different subtypes (e.g. paranoid vs nonparanoid) indicate different degrees of severity on the same underlying dimension of liability (McGuffin et al 1987), which is not inconsistent with the idea that environmental liabilities may be a major influence on the severity of the disorder's expression.

A large twin study of American veterans has confirmed a strong genetic component to schizophrenia (Kendler & Robinette 1983). These authors also computed twin concordances for five common medical conditions, finding the heritability of schizophrenia to exceed that for diabetes, ulcers, chronic obstructive pulmonary disease, hypertension, and ischemic heart disease, each of which also showed significant heritabilities.

A single major genetic locus model for schizophrenia cannot be successfully fitted. Reanalyses of large sets of family data have either been unable to demonstrate the presence of a single major recessive or dominant "schizogene" (Tsuang et al 1982), or have made dubitable the existence of a single major gene that accounts for the presence or absence of schizophrenia (O'Rourke et al 1982; McGue et al 1983; Faraone & Tsuang 1985). The preeminent surviving hypotheses are that schizophrenia is a genetically heterogeneous (i.e. different single major genes each can cause schizophrenia) or a multifactorial (multiple genetic and environmental factors) disorder. Attempts to discover linkages with known genetic markers thus far have been unsuccessful, although several studies have suggested that the A9 locus of the HLA complex on chromosome 6 is weakly associated with paranoid schizophrenia (see McGuffin & Sturt 1986). In the absence of evidence for a single major gene, not to mention the chromosome on which it may reside, these linkage studies are working against long odds. If a single major schizogene exists, however, the rapidly accumulating number of genetic markers with which to perform linkage studies will eventually yield something of value (White et al 1985).

The failure to discover convincing genetic linkage has prompted some experts to ask whether schizophrenia is a single entity or a heterogeneous group of genetic and nongenetic diseases, each of which affects the common final pathway for the symptoms of schizophrenia. This is not implausible since aspects of the phenylketonuria phenotype can be produced by different genetic abnormalities at different loci (Murphey 1983). On the genetic side, Propping (1983) has identified 27 different genetic disorders that may initially produce schizophrenic symptoms. These "symptomatic schizophrenias" are fairly rare, however, and it seems doubtful that they contribute to the typical forms of schizophrenia in which an organic abnormality never becomes apparent over the life course of the disorder (Farmer et al 1984).

In twin sets discordant for schizophrenia, the unaffected co-twin (Holzman 1985) or unaffected parents often manifest eye tracking abnormalities (Siegel et al 1984). This has prompted a latent-trait model in which the same putative schizogene can produce schizophrenia, and/or eye tracking abnormalities, depending on which areas of the brain are affected (Matthysse et al 1986). The meaning of eye tracking abnormalities in schizophrenia, however, remains ambiguous. It is not known whether it is just an interesting indicant of an attention-information processing deficit (Mather 1986) or is associated with an as yet obscure specific neurological abnormality.

High-risk longitudinal studies of the young offspring of schizophrenics are described comprehensively in a book edited by Watt et al (1984). These studies are predicated on the idea that early signs of vulnerability are likely to be present in a subset of high-risk children of schizophrenic vs other psychiatric and normal control parents. Some evidence on behalf of that view is found, especially global signs of attentional abnormality (Cornblatt & Erlenmeyer-Kimling 1985) and motor dysfunction or variability (Marcus et al 1984). But if schizophrenia can arise like puberty does in adolescence or Huntington's disease in middle age, it sometimes may be impossible to see phenotypic manifestations of the genetic liability very early in life.

Affective Disorders

Definitional problems have plagued research on affective disorders. Population prevalence rates for depression across studies vary many-fold, compromising attempts to assess its inheritance. Experts recognize that affective disorders can arise from multiple mechanisms, some of which are nongenetic, and that inclusion of such phenocopies in genetic analyses is likely to lead to ambiguities. The term "depression" for even minor dysphoria is now used so widely that it is in danger of losing its distinctiveness as a psychopathological concept. Consequently, there are efforts to produce more homogeneous categories. Winokur (1983) has shown, for example, that depressives with a positive family history of depression are much more likely than depressives with a negative family history to show early escape from dexamethasone suppression.

Moreover, striking differences in the sex ratios in bipolar and unipolar depression (with approximately equal numbers of males to females in bipolar and a great excess of females among the unipolar depressed) suggest complexities in the interpretation of familial transmission as well as some heterogeneity among the causes of affective disorder (Winokur & Crowe 1983). Unfortunately, while personal interviews identify many more affectively disordered individuals than second-hand reports or hospitalization records (Orvaschel et al 1982), even personal interviews miss some cases. Corroborating evidence comes from observations of a higher rate of depression in younger than older interviewed samples (Price et al 1985b), suggesting that older people often forget or misinterpret earlier affective episodes.

Efforts to characterize the inheritance of affective disorder have often faltered because of diagnostic definitions and etiological heterogeneity. Even if the diagnoses are reliably precise, there is no assurance that nature is being cleaved at its joints. An understanding of genetic vs nongenetic forms of depression will surely become clarified with the advent of more comprehensive diagnoses that take into account not only behavioral signs of depression but also family history, drug responsiveness, and biochemical factors.

Bertelsen (1985) studied the offspring of MZ and DZ twins discordant for manic-depressive illness, finding the same 10% risk of affective disorder in the offspring of MZ twins, whether the co-twin was the affected or unaffected parent. In contrast, the offspring of the unaffected DZ co-twin had only a small (2.4%) risk for affective disorder, while 17% of the offspring of the affected DZ co-twin had an affective disorder. This pattern of results suggests the transmission of an affective liability that is largely genetic in nature and does not depend on being reared by a manifestly affectively disturbed parent.

Three adoption studies of affective disorder have appeared since 1983. One Swedish study of the biological and adoptive relatives of proband adoptees with depression found no evidence for the specific inheritance of depression (von Knorring et al 1983). Unfortunately, only 16 of their 56 affectively disordered probands had psychotic depressions (suggestive of greater severity); the bulk had neurotic depressions, for which the evidence of heritability is much weaker. Ascertainment of affected biological relatives also could easily have missed affected family members had they been treated privately. Only one of the 26 biological relatives of the bipolar, cycloid, or unipolar probands was also affected, a proportion lower than any family study in which relatives are directly examined (Gershon 1987). Von Knorring et al did find that the biological mothers of the female probands had an excess of registered treatment for some psychiatric illness, however. Of additional interest was the observation that the adoptive fathers of the probands had more often been treated for a psychiatric illness, especially affective disorder. There was no concordance between the specific diagnosis of the proband and the adoptive father, however. From this the investigators inferred the absence of parental modeling of the specific illness, though help-seeking behavior in the context of distress may have been modeled.

A second adoption study in Iowa also failed to find statistically significant evidence for the specific genetic transmission of affective disorder, but the rate of depressive disorder in the biological parents of the depressed probands was more than twice the rate in probands without depression (Cadoret et al 1985). A major problem with interpreting these results is that the biological parents were only in their teens or early twenties at the time the proband was adopted and therefore had not passed through a significant portion of the risk period for depression. Paralleling the Swedish study, there appeared to be an excess of psychiatric problems (e.g. alcoholism, antisocial behavior) in the adoptive families of the affected probands.

Finally, a Danish study of the biological and adoptive families of affectively ill and control probands revealed evidence for heritable transmission of affective disorder (Wender et al 1986). The biological relatives of the affectively ill probands had a higher rate of definite and uncertain affective disorder, but not a higher rate of neurotic depression. Moreover, the biological relatives of the affected probands had a much greater rate of alcoholism. Perhaps the most dramatic finding in this study was the relatively high rate of suicide and attempted suicide in the biological relatives of the depressed adoptee probands. More than 7% of the biological relatives of the affected probands had attempted or committed suicide, in comparison to only 1.5% of the biological relatives of control adoptees. Unlike the von Knorring and Cadoret studies, there was no excess of psychopathology in the adoptive relatives of the ill vs the control adoptees. That suicide runs in families has also been shown by Egeland & Sussex (1985) who found that 73% of the suicides in the last 100 years among the Old Order Amish came from just 16% of the families.

By modern research standards the precision of psychiatric diagnoses in the adoption studies was limited, although the investigators did about as well as can be expected given the necessary reliance on official records. In light of diagnostic limitations, provable genetic heterogeneity, and nongenetic depressive phenocopies, it is not surprising that attempts to fit models to the inheritance of affective disorder have yielded ambiguous results (Price et al 1985b; Tsuang et al 1985a).

In the last year manic-depressive illness has been unambiguously linked to a region on the short arm of chromosome 11 in the Old Order Amish, using restriction fragment length polymorphisms (RFLPs) (Egeland et al 1987).

Model-fitting suggests that the dominant gene has a penetrance of 63% so that not everyone with the gene will manifest the disorder, thus leaving open other possible genetic and environmental influences that affect penetrance. The linkage of manic-depression to chromosome 11 has also been reported in a small pedigree study showing that the gene for thalassemia minor (on chromosome 11) was inherited simultaneously with bipolar affective disorder (Joffe et al 1986). Other evidence indicates that manic-depression is also linked to color blindness and to G6PD deficiency on the X chromosome in four Israeli families of non-European origin (Baron et al 1987). These data thus confirm the general observation of genetic heterogeneity in depression, even in bipolar affective disorder.

It is worth keeping in mind that the two identified genetic causes of bipolar disorder (on chromosome 11 and on the X chromosome) do not exhaust all the genetic and nongenetic possibilities. Studies using RFLPs in Icelandic and non-Amish North American pedigrees have shown that some bipolar disorders are *not* associated with a gene on the same region of chromosome 11 (Hodgkinson et al 1987; Detera-Wadleigh et al 1987).

Alcoholism

The case for heredity as an etiological factor in alcoholism can be regarded as fairly secure. The adoption and cross-fostering studies (Schuckit et al 1972; Goodwin et al 1973; Cadoret et al 1980; Cloninger et al 1981) all point convincingly to an important role for heredity. With one exception, Gurling et al (1984), the twin studies also point to the importance of genetics. The focus of much of the recent research is on the problem of genetic heterogeneity and the possibility of interactions between genes and the postnatal environment, including cultural influences on drinking habits.

The expression of an inherited vulnerability for alcoholism may be somewhat regulated by factors associated with social class. Sigvardsson et al (1985) found that a mild manifestation of alcohol abuse (a single registration for abuse) among biological fathers did not lead to increases of single or recurrent episodes of abuse among their adopted-away sons whose adopted fathers were in skilled occupations. However, when the adopted fathers had unskilled jobs, mild abuse in the biological fathers significantly increased the rates of recurrent abuse among the adopted sons. Furthermore, each level of abuse among biological fathers (none, one, or recurrent) was associated with higher rates of recurrent abuse for adopted-away sons when the adopted fathers were unskilled rather than skilled.

Cloninger et al (1981) had earlier identified two distinct subgroups of alcoholics: the milieu-limited form and the male-limited form. The risk factors are different in the two forms, and the rates of alcoholism for those at risk compared to those not at risk (relative risk) vary with postnatal provocation only in the milieu-limited form. Milieu-limited alcoholism appears in adopted men whose biological fathers and mothers showed mild alcohol abuse and mimimal criminality. If these men experienced postnatal provocation (e.g. late adoptive placement, lower occupational status of adoptive parents), their relative risk for alcoholism was doubled. The male-limited form of alcoholism occurs in men whose biological fathers showed severe alcohol abuse and severe criminality but whose mothers were normal. Regardless of the postnatal environment, the men with these biological risk factors had a rate of alcoholism nine times that of men without them.

Most genetic analyses begin with the identification of affected probands. If the group of probands is not homogeneous, subsequent analysis is clouded by the inclusion of nongenetic or genetically heterogeneous types of the disorder in question. Cloninger & Reich (1983) have shown that this is a particularly acute problem in the study of alcoholism because so many individuals with antisocial personality (ASP) are also alcoholics and will be selected as probands in a genetic investigation. Results from such studies indicate that alcoholism and ASP are both found at elevated rates among the relatives of the probands. This has led to the conclusion that alcoholism and ASP are alternative manifestations of the same underlying liability, an idea that now appears to be erroneous. Using only data where both probands and family members were interviewed, Cloninger & Reich have shown that when the primary diagnosis of an alcoholic proband is alcoholism, there is an elevated risk of alcoholism among the first-degree relatives but no elevation of risk for a primary diagnosis of ASP. Elevated rates of alcoholism were found among the relatives of ASP probands, and this could be due to partial overlap of the liabilities for alcoholism and ASP. Another explanation could be higher rates of heavy drinking in families with ASP probands. Vaillant's (1983) prospective investigation of Core City men supports the idea that alcoholism alone is different from alcoholism in sociopaths. He found that "many sociopaths later abuse alcohol as part of their antisocial behavior; but most alcoholics are not premorbidly sociopathic."

Ethnic differences in alcoholism continue to be investigated, with some progress being made at the level of genetic bases for ethnic variations. Reed (1985) concluded that ethnic variations in the first aldehyde dehydrogenase isozyme account for the unpleasant response to alcohol ingestion on the part of many Asians and, consequently, reduce their rate of alcoholism. Harada et al (1982) found that only 2.3% of Japanese alcoholics had the low-activity allele that confers protection against heavy drinking; whereas, 44% of the general population in Japan have this gene. Reed notes, however, that allelic variations cannot explain alcoholism in European populations since all Europeans have the high-activity alleles. Among Europeans, Vaillant's (1983) finding may prove more germane. He found that an alcoholic heredity was much more predictive of alcoholism in Americans of Mediterranean heritage, where drinking is widely accepted but drunkenness uncommon, than among the Irish, where fewer people drink but drunkenness is more frequent than in Mediterranean cultures.

Antisocial Personality

The definition of antisocial personality in adoption and twin studies has most often depended on criminal convictions rather than personality diagnosis. Because of the correlation of criminal convictions with alcoholism and drug abuse, inferences about independent genetic transmission of each of these disorders have been uncertain. It now appears from adoption studies, however, that petty criminality (as inferred from property crimes) has a heritable component independent of alcoholism (Baker 1986; Bohman et al 1982; Cadoret et al 1986; Cloninger et al 1982; Mednick et al 1984; Sigvardsson et al 1982). Antisocial personality diagnosed solely from the MMPI (Willerman et al 1987) also appears to be heritable. By stringent standards, no recent study has established the inheritance of antisocial personality disorder using current DSM-III or classic Cleckley criteria. Apparently, only half of incarcerated felons meet DSM-III criteria for antisocial personality (Hare 1983), implying a need for a genetic study of antisocial personality disorder per se, rather than criminality, before we can be confident about what specifically is being transmitted.

In a review of the world literature on juvenile delinquency and adult criminality in twins, Cloninger & Gottesman (1987) have shown that DZ twin concordance rates for juvenile delinquency reliably exceed .50, suggesting a considerable influence of shared family environment. In contrast, twin studies of adult criminality point to substantial heritability with much less indication of shared family environmental influences on the twins. One implication of these findings is that the bulk of juvenile delinquency arises from environmental factors but that a subgroup of juvenile delinquents who go on to become adult criminals may have a genetic liability.

Longitudinal studies indicate that primary-grade children with a diagnosis of attention deficit disorder are at high risk for later juvenile delinquency, drug abuse, and a teenage diagnosis of conduct disorder, the childhood version of antisocial personality disorder (Satterfield et al 1982; Gittelman et al 1985). How this relates to adult antisocial personality disorder is unclear, however.

Briquet's Syndrome

This syndrome is characterized by the dramatic presentation of multiple recurrent and inexplicable symptoms in many different organ systems as well as psychological complaints such as depression and anxiety. Individuals with the syndrome, almost always women, have a disproportionate number of unnecessary surgical operations, perhaps because physicians are reluctant to make a psychiatric diagnosis in the face of the many medical complaints. Objective criteria for diagnosing Briquet's syndrome, first proposed by Perley & Guze in 1962, were simplified in the DSM-III as somatization disorder. It has been argued that Briquet's syndrome is to be preferred to the somatization disorder of DSM-III because it represents a more homogeneous category and may constitute a distinctive constellation from a hereditary standpoint (Cloninger et al 1986). Briquet's syndrome is of interest, not only in its own right, but because it runs in families and is associated with an excess of male relatives with antisocial personality (Guze et al 1986). The familial association of Briquet's with antisocial personality is surprising because there are no symptoms in common for the two diagnoses and may therefore represent sex-specific expression of the same underlying genetic liability.

While there have been no twin or adoption studies of Briquet's syndrome, an adoption study in Sweden has indicated two types of somatization (Bohman et al 1984). Female adoptees with the "diversiform" type had biological fathers with a history of petty criminality and moderate alcoholism. They had an average of two sick leaves per year since the age of 16 with multiple bodily complaints across many different organ systems. A second type of somatization, "high-frequency," was associated with symptoms mainly involving the abdomen, urogenital system, backaches, and psychiatric complaints. The high-frequency adoptees averaged five sick leaves per year since age 16 and had biological fathers with an excess of early onset recidivism for violent crimes in the absence of alcoholism. The relation of Briquet's syndrome to these two forms of somatization is currently unclear, but the fact that biological parents of these two types of somatizers differ from each other and from the parents of control adoptees suggests that something about multiple medical complaints is being genetically transmitted.

Anorexia Nervosa

Anorexia nervosa, an eating disorder predominantly affecting females, is characterized by a fear of fatness, the preoccupation with and pursuit of thinness, and amenorrhea. There have been scattered reports suggesting a genetic component to anorexia and a connection to affective disorder both in the anorexic and her relatives. Family studies of anorexic probands generally confirm the link to affective disorder (e.g. Gershon et al 1984; Hudson et al 1983), and the previously scattered data on anorexic twins were consistent with a hereditary factor for anorexia. Now for the first time a twin series of anorexic probands has been reported, with concordance rates of 55% and 7% for 16 MZ and 14 DZ twin pairs, respectively (Holland et al 1984).

Infantile Autism

The autistic triad, originally described by Kanner in 1937, included autistic aloneness, speech and language disturbances, and an obsessive desire for sameness, occurring before 30 months of age. While asseverations that faulty maternal childrearing figured importantly in the genesis of the disorder have now been discounted, the origins of the disorder remain mysterious. The current view is that the disorder has heterogeneous causation, including prenatal rubella and neurofibromatosis. There is no doubt that infantile autism runs in families, being perhaps 50 or 100 times more frequent in relatives of probands than in the general population (Rutter & Garmezy 1983). High rates of pregnancy complications and minor physical anomalies point to prenatal orgins, and high rates of epilepsy in adolescence suggest an organic abnormality (Rutter & Garmezy 1983). A recent twin study found con-cordance rates of 96% and 23% for MZ and DZ twins, respectively (Ritvo et al 1985), suggesting a strong genetic component. But only 1.7% of the singleton siblings of the twins were also affected, implying an important role for shared intrauterine factors as contributing to the disorder. There was no linkage to any of 30 genetic markers in a study of families with at least two autistic members (Spence et al 1985). Analyses of chromosomal aberrations in a total population of Swedish children with infantile autism and other psychotic conditions revealed that 25% of those with infantile autism had the fragile X marker (Gillberg & Wåhlstrom 1985). No control group was employed, but the results suggest that infantile autism is associated with a higher proportion of chromosome abnormalities than heretofore believed. Moreover, 35% of the children in their study had epileptic seizures.

Tourette's Syndrome

First described in 1885 by Gilles de la Tourette, the syndrome is characterized by multiple complex vocal and motor tics. DSM-III criteria require the presence of these tics for more than one year and that they can be voluntarily suppressed for short periods. Tourette's has an onset somewhere between 2 and 15 years of age. The frequency of Tourette's in the general population is estimated to be about 1 per 2000, but motor tics alone may occur at three times that frequency. Although the idea of a hereditary basis to Tourette's has been around from the inception of its delineation, only in the past few years have data been systematically collected in sufficient amounts to clarify not only its hereditary basis, but its mode of transmission. Two observations have assisted in this clarification: the recognition that motor tics alone and obses-sive-compulsive disorder (OCD) could be expressions of the same liability underlying Tourette's.

Comings et al (1984) analyzed pedigrees from 250 consecutive unselected families using complex segregation analysis, allowing for Tourette's and motor tics alone. Results indicated that the best-fitting model to the pedigrees was of a rare autosomal dominant gene in which most of the affected members were heterozygotes and the penetrance (i.e. the likelihood that the trait would be expressed given the presence of the dominant gene) was about 50%. Pauls & Leckman (1986) allowed the presence of OCD as an expression of the Tourette's diathesis and also concluded that genetic transmission behaved as an autosomal dominant with penetrances of 100% and 71% in males and females, respectively. About 10% of Tourette's cases were judged to be phenocopies.

About half of all Tourette's cases meet DSM criteria for OCD (Pauls et al 1986a), and 63% meet criteria for attention deficit disorder with hyperactivity (ADDH) (Pauls et al 1986b). OCD may be an alternative or partial expression of Tourette's, but ADDH is not. The reason for this conclusion is that the absence of obsessive-compulsive disorder in Tourette probands is still associated with elevated OCD rates in relatives, while the absence of ADDH in probands is not associated with elevated rates of ADDH in relatives. A twin study of Tourette's is also consistent with estimates of fairly high penetrance (Price et al 1985a). While only 55% of MZ twins were fully concordant for the syndrome, broadening criteria to include the presence of motor tics alone produced a concordance rate of 77% for MZ twins and 23% for DZ twins. Diagnosis of OCD was not made in this study. It would be of interest to know what proportion of OCD probands in other studies have a family history of Tourette's or tics alone. In a study of 171 relatives of 10 patients with OCD, none was reported to meet DSM-III criteria for OCD, but only the 43 first-degree relatives were personally interviewed (Hoover & Insel 1984). One case study of a patient with early adult onset obsessive-compulsive behavior and an inability to sit still did show a deletion on the long arm of chromosome 18 (Donnai 1987), consistent with a hypothesis that the defect in Tourette's is at that location (Comings et al 1986).

Alzheimer's Disease

The senile dementias constitute a personal and societal burden of enormous and increasing proportions. Alzheimer's disease (AD), characterized by global cognitive deterioration, neuropathological abnormalities (e.g. intracellular neurofibrillary tangles and extracellular neuritic plaques both composed of beta amyloid filaments), and neurotransmitter deficiencies (Francis et al 1985), is believed to be the single most frequent cause of dementia. The identical amyloid filaments appear to be present in people over 40 years of age with Down's syndrome and in a variety of aged individuals in species including monkeys and dogs (Selkoe et al 1987). The gene coding for the amyloid, presumably the major cause of AD, has been characterized (Goldgaber et al 1987) and assigned to the proximal portion of the long arm of chromosome 21 (Kang et al 1987; Tanzi et al 1987; Robakis 1987). Familial cases of AD are associated with a defect in this region of chromosome 21 (St.

George-Hyslop et al 1987), as are nonfamilial or "sporadic" cases (Delabar et al 1987). These researchers have demonstrated that sporadic AD patients and translocation (chromosomally nontrisomic) Down's patients have 50% more activity than normal for this gene product, exactly as predicted by a hypothesis of an extra copy of the amyloid gene. Identifying a common genetic cause for sporadic and familial cases could eliminate the problem of heterogeneity in AD, but there is good evidence of nonconcordance for AD in many MZ sets (Nee et al 1987; Renvoize et al 1986), suggesting that somatic mutations after cleavage and nongenetic factors also figure in the disorder.

Conclusions

We are witnessing major breakthroughs in identifying the genes coding for some mental disorders. In the last year genes coding for one form of bipolar affective disorder and for Alzheimer's disease have been assigned to specific chromosomes. With the advent of a remarkable technology based on restriction fragment length polymorphisms (RFLPs), it seems only a matter of time before specific DNA sequences associated with many of these disorders will be precisely characterized (White et al 1985). Where single major genes for the disorders can be identified, it seems quite possible that in some instances an effective replacement therapy can be initiated based on incorporating a normal version of the gene via a harmless virus. Thus, it is reasonable to think that some mental disorders associated with identifiable genes will be correctable, provided that the genetic defect has not already produced irreversible structural changes in the brain.

MODELS AND MODEL-FITTING

It is perhaps too early to claim that the fitting of explicit heredity-environment models to observed correlations or other statistics is standard practice in human behavior genetics, but at least such procedures are no longer only in the province of the modeling specialist. The great merit of such models is that they can deal simultaneously, elegantly, and objectively with a volume of information that would be difficult to assimilate in other ways. Their most serious shortcoming may be that users seem occasionally to forget that complex computer programming works no magic. In the end, the results can be no better than the assumptions built into the models or the data to which they are applied.

Path and Variance Component Models

These appear to be the method of choice for dealing simultaneously with data from several groups, such as twins, adoptees, and so forth. A number of examples in the area of personality were discussed earlier. Also numerous have been applications of path and biometrical models to twin data.

It is always important to remember that because one model can be fit to a set of data, this does not mean that alternative models, with quite different implications, might not also fit. As a simple case in point, twin data can often be equally well fit by models assuming nonadditive genetic variance or by models assuming unequal twin environments. As a more extreme instance, there is the Price et al (1982) study, in which a 13-parameter model was fit to twin-family data for which a simple 1-parameter model was later shown to suffice.

There have been a number of methodological developments connected with model building. Vogler (1985) presents a multivariate approach to path analysis, whereby a path model can be used to deal simultaneously with a set of intercorrelated variables simply by substituting matrices for single variables in the model. Boomsma & Molenaar (1986) describe a clever method for using the computer program LISREL to fit models to twin data. Heath et al (1985) consider the sample sizes required in various multiple-group designs. McGue & Bouchard (1984) look at age and sex corrections for twins, and McGue et al (1984) examine the consequences of assuming independence among family correlations when dependence actually exists. Relatively pessimistic (Loehlin 1986b) and optimistic (Neale et al 1986) views have been expressed concerning model-fitting at the level of individual questionnaire items, as opposed to scales. Finally, proponents or opponents of path models might wish to look at a slashing attack on such models by Karlin et al (1983) and an equally energetic defense by Cloninger and his colleagues (1983).

Hierarchical Multiple Regression

An alternative approach to twin data is based on multiple regressions in which one twin's score is predicted from the other twin's score and an index of zygosity. Other variables such as age, sex, and degree of separation may also be included. An interaction of twin score with zygosity constitutes evidence of genetic effects, given ordinary twin method assumptions. Interactions of score and zygosity with other variables indicate modulation of the genetic effects by these variables. Both significance tests and estimates of variance components may be obtained (DeFries & Fulker 1985). The approach has special advantages in dealing with restricted samples, such as those selected via a proband suffering from some disability. Multiple regression has been used in studying children's fears (Rose & Ditto 1983), in examining the effects of length of separation among adult MZ twins (Rose & Kaprio 1987), and in a twin study of reading disability (LaBuda et al 1986).

Developmental Models

Eaves and his colleagues (1986) have proposed a fairly general developmental model in which variation may persist and accumulate over time from either genetic or environmental sources or their phenotypic consequences. Both constant and time-specific influences can be represented. Variations of this model were applied to cognitive data from the Louisville Twin Study. In fact, none of the fits was very good, but a model with an initially small (6%) but persisting and accumulating genetic effect and an appreciable (39%) but occasion-specific family environmental effect did as well as any. Such a model resembles the "amplification model" discussed by Plomin & DeFries (1985), in which initially small genetic differences in infancy become amplified during development into large effects in adulthood.

A somewhat different approach to developmental modeling is proposed by McArdle (1986), who allows for genetic and environmental influences on level and shape parameters governing growth curves, which are fit to means as well as covariances. Attempts with some of the Louisville data were again not spectacularly successful. Some of the better-fitting models showed a strong shared-environment component and rather small genetic and specific environmental effects.

Developmental behavior-genetic models seem almost certain to multiply. No doubt they will be elaborated to incorporate some of the complexities of genotype-environment correlation and interaction expressed in such theories as that of Scarr & McCartney (1983) in which genotypes actively select the environments that in turn shape phenotypic growth.

CONCLUSIONS

In reviewing different areas within human behavior genetics, it is clear that progress is being made on a variety of fronts.

Concern with the degree to which general intelligence is heritable continues, with recent estimates somewhat higher than those of six or eight years ago. While IQ controversies in some form seem destined to go on forever, there is at least some emerging consensus among informed individuals. In a survey of 1020 US experts on intelligence and intelligence testing (Snyderman & Rothman 1987) most respondents believed that there was evidence that IQ was significantly heritable. Interest in specific intellectual abilities and disabilities also continues. One could make a case that this area provides unusual promise for progress during the next decade.

With only a few exceptions, the last six years have provided continued support for a moderate genetic contribution to normal personality variation, and for the much more radical view that essentially none of the environmental contribution to adult personality is from shared family environment. Evidence is beginning to accumulate regarding differences among personality traits—for example, that genetic nonadditivity may be especially important in extraversion.

A major conclusion of recent behavior genetic research in both the ability and personality domains is that age is an important moderating variable, and—more speculatively—that age changes in the genetic contributions to trait variation may turn out to be fully as important as age changes in the environmental contributions.

While interesting developments are taking place in all of the areas we have surveyed, perhaps it is in psychopathology that further exciting breakthroughs seem most imminent. We temper our enthusiasm slightly by noting that this has tended to be a chronic condition in this area; but now, surely, the breakup of a glacial phenotype like manic-depressive illness into nice little genetic icebergs must at last really be under way. We shall, of course, see.

Twenty-eight years ago, Fuller (1960) concluded the very first chapter on behavior genetics in the *Annual Review of Psychology* by writing: "Adequate consideration of genetic factors may help to eliminate some current disagreements in the literature." This is still our hope.

Literature Cited

Agrawal, N., Sinha, S. N., Jensen, A. R. 1984. Effects of inbreeding on Raven Matrices. *Behav. Genet.* 14:579–84

Ahern, F. M., Johnson, R. C., Wilson, J. R., McClearn, G. E., Vandenberg, S. G. 1982. Family resemblances in personality. *Behav. Genet.* 12:261–80

Baker, L. A. 1986. Estimating genetic correlations among discontinuous phenotypes: an analysis of criminal convictions and psychiatric-hospital diagnoses in Danish adoptees. *Behav. Genet.* 16:127–42

Baron, M., Gruen, R., Rainer, J. D., Kane, J., Asnis, L., et al. 1985. A family study of schizophrenic and normal control probands: implications for the spectrum concept of schizophrenia. *Am. J. Psychiatry* 142:447–55

Baron, M., Risch, N., Hamburger, R., Mandel, B., Kushner, S., et al. 1987. Genetic linkage between X-chromosome markers and bipolar affective illness. *Nature* 326:289–92

Bertelsen, A. 1985. Controversies and consistencies in psychiatric genetics. *Acta Psychiatr. Scand.* 71:61–75

Bohman, M., Cloninger, C. R., von Knorring, A-L., Sigvardsson, S. 1984. An adoption study of somatoform disorders. III. Cross-fostering analysis and genetic relationship to alcoholism and criminality. *Arch. Gen. Psychiatry* 41:872–78

Bohman, M., Cloninger, C. R., Sigvardsson, S., von Knorring, A.-L. 1982. Predisposition to petty criminality in Swedish adoptees. I. Genetic and environmental heterogeneity. *Arch. Gen. Psychiatry* 39:1233–41

Boomsma, D. I., Molenaar, P. C. M. 1986. Using LISREL to analyze genetic and environmental covariance structure. *Behav. Genet.* 16:237–50

Buss, D. M. 1984. Evolutionary biology and personality psychology: toward a conception of human nature and individual differences. *Am. Psychol.* 39:1135–47

Buss, D. M., Barnes, M. 1986. Preferences in human mate selection. *J. Pers. Soc. Psychol.* 50:559–70

Cadoret, R. J., Cain, C. A., Grove, W. M. 1980. Development of alcoholism in adoptees raised apart from alcoholic biologic relatives. *Arch. Gen. Psychiatry* 37:561–63

Cadoret, R. J., O'Gorman, T. W., Heywood, E., Troughton, E. 1985. Genetic and environmental factors in major depression. *J. Affect. Disord.* 9:155–64

Cadoret, R. J., Troughton, E., O'Gorman, T. W., Heywood, E. 1986. An adoption study of genetic and environmental factors in drug abuse. *Arch. Gen. Psychiatry* 43:1131–36

Carey, G., Rice, J. 1983. Genetics and personality temperament: simplicity or complexity? *Behav. Genet.* 13:43–63

Cattell, R. B. 1982. *The Inheritance of Personality and Ability: Research Methods and Findings.* New York: Academic

Cloninger, C. R., Bohman, M., Sigvardsson, S. 1981. Inheritance of alcohol abuse: cross-fostering analysis of adopted men. *Arch. Gen. Psychiatry* 38:861–68

Cloninger, C. R., Gottesman, I. I. 1987. Genetic and environmental factors in antisocial behavior disorders. In *The Causes of Crime*, ed. S. Mednick, T. Moffit, S. Stack, pp. 92–109. New York: Cambridge Univ. Press

Cloninger, C. R., Martin, R. J., Guze, S. B., Clayton, P. J. 1986. A prospective follow-up and family study of somatization in men and women. *Am. J. Psychiatry* 143:873–78

Cloninger, C. R., Rao, D. C., Rice, J., Reich, T., Morton, N. E. 1983. A defense of path analysis in genetic epidemiology. *Am. J. Hum. Genet.* 35:733–56

Cloninger, C., Reich, T. 1983. Genetic heterogeneity in alcoholism and sociopathy. In *Genetics of Neurological and Psychiatric Disorders,* ed. S. Kety, L. Rowland, R. Sidman, S. Matthysse, pp. 145–66. New York: Raven

Cloninger, C. R., Sigvardsson, S., Bohman, M., von Knorring, A.-L. 1982. Predisposition to petty criminality in Swedish adoptees. II. Cross-fostering analysis of gene-environment interaction. *Arch. Gen. Psychiatry* 39:1242–47

Comings, D. E., Comings, B. G., Devor, E. J., Cloninger, C. R. 1984. Detection of major gene for Gilles de la Tourette Syndrome. *Hum. Genet.* 36:586–600

Comings, D. E., Comings, B. G., Diez, G., et al. 1986. Evidence the Tourette syndrome gene is at 18q22.1. *7th Int. Congr. Hum. Genet, Berlin,* Part II:620 (Abstr.)

Cornblatt, B. A., Erlenmeyer-Kimling, L. 1985. Global attentional deviance as a marker of risk for schizophrenia: specificity and predictive validity. *J. Abnorm. Psychol.* 94:470–86

Daniels, D. 1986. Differential experiences of siblings in the same family as predictors of adolescent sibling personality differences. *J. Pers. Soc. Psychol.* 51:339–46

Daniels, D., Dunn, J., Furstenberg, F. F. Jr., Plomin, R. 1985. Environmental differences within the family and adjustment differences within pairs of adolescent siblings. *Child Dev.* 56:764–74

Daniels, D., Plomin, R., McClearn, G., Johnson, R. C. 1982. "Fitness" behaviors and anthropometric characters for offspring of first-cousin matings. *Behav. Genet.* 12:527–34

DeFries, J. C., Fulker, D. W. 1985. Multiple regression analysis of twin data. *Behav. Genet.* 15:467–73

DeFries, J. C., Plomin, R., LaBuda, M. C. 1987. Genetic stability of cognitive development from childhood to adulthood. *Dev. Psychol.* 23:4–12

Delabar, J.-M., Goldgaber, D., Lamour, Y., Nicole, A., Huret, J.-L., et al. 1987. β Amyloid gene duplication in Alzheimer's disease and karyotypically normal Down syndrome. *Science* 235:1390–92

DeLisi, L. E., Mirsky, A. F., Buchsbaum, M. S., van Kammen, D. P., Berman, K. F., et al. 1984. The Genain Quadruplets 25 years later: a diagnostic and biochemical follow-up. *Psychiatry Res.* 13:59–76

Detera-Wadleigh, S. D., Berrettini, W. H., Goldin, L. R., Boorman, D., Anderson, S., Gershon, E. S. 1987. Close linkage of c-Harvey-ras-1 and the insulin gene to affective disorder is ruled out in three North American pedigrees. *Nature* 325:806–8

Donnai, D. 1987. Gene location in Tourette syndrome. *Lancet* 1:627

Dumaret, A. 1985. IQ, scholastic performance and behavior of sibs raised in contrasting environments. *J. Child Psychol. Psychiatry* 26:553–80

Duyme, M. 1985. Scholastic achievement as a function of parental social class: an adoption study. In *Developmental Psychology,* ed. C. J. Brainero, V. F. Reyna, pp. 319–25. Amsterdam: Elsevier Science

Eaves, L. J., Long, J., Heath, A. C. 1986. A theory of developmental change in quantitative phenotypes applied to cognitive development. *Behav. Genet.* 16:143–62

Egeland, J. A., Gerhard, D. S., Pauls, D. L., Sussex, J. N., Kidd, K. K., et al. 1987. Bipolar affective disorders linked to DNA markers on chromosome 11. *Nature* 325:783–87

Egeland, J. A., Sussex, J. N. 1985. Suicide and family loading for affective disorders. *J. Am. Med. Assoc.* 254:915–18

Faraone, S. V., Tsuang, M. T. 1985. Quantitative models of the genetic transmission of schizophrenia. *Psychol. Bull.* 98:41–66

Farmer, A. E., McGuffin, P., Gottesman, I. I. 1984. Searching for the split in schizophrenia: a twin study perspective. *Psychiatry Res.* 13:109–18

Fischbein, S. 1981. Heredity-environment influences on growth and development during adolescence. In *Twin Research 3 (Part B): Program in Clinical and Biological Research,* ed. L. Gedda, P. Parisi, W. E. Nance, pp. 211–26. New York: Liss

Francis, P. T., Palmer, A. M., Sims, N. R., Bowen, D. M., Davison, A. N., et al. 1985. Neurochemical studies of early-onset Alzheimer's disease. *N. Engl. J. Med.* 313:7–11

Fuller, J. L. 1960. Behavior genetics. *Ann. Rev. Psychol.* 11:41–70

Gershon, E. S. 1987. Genetics. In *Manic-Depressive Illness,* ed. F. K. Goodwin, K. R. Jamison. Oxford: Oxford Univ. Press

Gershon, E. S., Schreiber, J. L., Hamovit, J. R., Dibble, E. D., Kaye, W. 1984. Clinical findings in patients with anorexia nervosa and affective illness in their relatives. *Am. J. Psychiatry* 141:1419–22

Gillberg, C., Wåhlstrom, J. 1985. Chromosomal abnormalities in infantile autism and other childhood psychoses: a population study of 66 cases. *Dev. Med. Child Neurol.* 27:293–304

Gittelman, R., Mannuzza, S., Shenker, R., Bonagura, N. 1985. Hyperactive boys almost grown up. *Arch. Gen. Psychiatry* 42:937–47

Goldgaber, D., Lerman, M. I., McBride, O. W., Saffiotti, U., Gajdusek, D. C. 1987. Characterization and chromosomal localization of a DNA encoding brain amyloid of Alzheimer's disease. *Science* 235:877–80

Goldsmith, H. H., Campos, J. J. 1986. Fundamental issues in the study of early temperament: the Denver Twin Temperament Study. In *Advances in Developmental Psychology*, ed. M. E. Lamb, A. L. Brown, B. Rogoff, 4:231–83. Hillsdale, NJ: Erlbaum

Goodwin, D. W., Schulsinger, F., Hermansen, L., Guze, S. B., Winokur, G. 1973. Alcohol problems in adoptees raised apart from biological parents. *Arch. Gen. Psychiatry* 28:238–43

Gourlay, N. 1979. Heredity versus environment—an integrative analysis. *Psychol. Bull.* 86:596–615

Gurling, H., Oppenheim, B. E., Murray, R. M. 1984. Depression, criminality and psychopathology associated with alcoholism: evidence from a twin study. *Acta Genet. Med. Gemellol.* 33:333–39

Guze, S. B., Cloninger, C. R., Martin, R. L., Clayton, P. J. 1986. A follow-up and family study of Briquet's syndrome. *Br. J. Psychiatry* 149:17–23

Harada, S., Agarwal, D. P., Goedde, H. W., Tagaki, S., Ishikawa, B. 1982. Possible protective role against alcoholism for aldehyde dehydrogenase isozyme deficiency in Japan. *Lancet* 2:827

Hardy-Brown, K., Plomin, R. 1985. Infant communicative development: evidence from adoptive and biological families for genetic and environmental influences on rate differences. *Dev. Psychol.* 21:378–85

Hare, R. D. 1983. Diagnosis of antisocial personality disorder in two prison populations. *Am. J. Psychiatry* 140:887–90

Hay, D. A. 1985. *Essentials of Behaviour Genetics*. Melbourne: Blackwell

Heath, A. C., Kendler, K. S., Eaves, L. J., Markell, D. 1985. The resolution of cultural and biological inheritance: informativeness of different relationships. *Behav. Genet.* 15:439–65

Henderson, N. D. 1982. Human behavior genetics. *Ann. Rev. Psychol.* 33:403–40

Hewitt, J. K. 1984. Normal components of personality variation. *J. Pers. Soc. Psychol.* 47:671–75

Hodgkinson, S., Sherrington, R., Gurling, H., Marchbanks, R., Reeders, S., et al. 1987. Molecular genetic evidence for heterogeneity in manic depression. *Nature* 325:805–6

Holland, A. J., Hall, A., Murray, R., Russell, G. F. M., Crisp, A. H. 1984. Anorexia nervosa: a study of 34 twin pairs and one set of triplets. *Br. J. Psychiatry* 145:414–19

Holzman, P. S. 1985. Eye movement dysfunctions and psychosis. *Int. Rev. Neurobiol.* 27:179–205

Hoover, C. F., Insel, T. R. 1984. Families of origin in obsessive-compulsive disorder. *J. Nerv. Ment. Dis.* 172:207–15

Hopper, J. L. 1983. The utility of a multivariate normal model for studying familial patterns in medical and psychiatric data. *Aust. NZ J. Psychiatry* 17:342–48

Hopper, J. L., Culross, P. R. 1983. Covariation between family members as a function of cohabitation history. *Behav. Genet.* 13: 459–71

Horn, J. M. 1983. The Texas Adoption Project: adopted children and their intellectual resemblance to biological and adoptive parents. *Child Dev.* 54:268–75

Horn, J. M., Loehlin, J. C., Willerman, L. 1979. Intellectual resemblance among adoptive and biological relatives: the Texas Adoption Project. *Behav. Genet.* 9:177–207

Horn, J. M., Loehlin, J. C., Willerman, L. 1982. Aspects of the inheritance of intellectual abilities. *Behav. Genet.* 12:479–516

Hudson, J. I., Pope, H. G., Jonas, J. M., Yurgelun-Todd, D. 1983. Family history study of anorexia nervosa and bulimia. *Br. J. Psychiatry* 142:133–38

Joffe, R. T., Horvath, Z., Tarvydas, I. 1986. Bipolar affective disorder and thalassemia minor. *Am. J. Psychiatry* 143:933

Kang, J., Lemaire, H.-G., Unterbeck, A., Salbaum, J. M., Masters, C. L., et al. 1987. The precursor of Alzheimer's disease amyloid A4 protein resembles a cell surface receptor. *Nature* 325:733–36

Karlin, S., Cameron, E. C., Chakraborty, R. 1983. Path analysis in genetic epidemiology: a critique. *Am. J. Hum. Genet.* 35:695–732

Kendler, K. S., Gruenberg, A. M. 1984. An independent analysis of the Danish Adoption Study of Schizophrenia. VI. *Arch. Gen. Psychiatry* 41:555–64

Kendler, K. S., Gruenberg, A. M., Tsuang, M. T. 1985. Psychiatric illness in first-degree relatives of schizophrenics and surgical control patients: a family study using DSM-III criteria. *Arch. Gen. Psychiatry* 42:770–79

Kendler, K. S., Robinette, C. D. 1983. Schizophrenia in the National Academy of Sciences–National Research Council twin registry: a 16-year update. *Am. J. Psychiatry* 140:1551–63

LaBuda, M. C., DeFries, J. C., Fulker, D. W. 1986. Multiple regression analysis of twin data obtained from selected samples. *Genet. Epidemiol.* 3:425–33

Loehlin, J. C. 1980. Recent adoption studies of IQ. *Hum. Genet.* 55:297–302

Loehlin, J. C. 1985. Fitting heredity-environment models jointly to twin and adoption data from the California Psychological Inventory. *Behav. Genet.* 15:199–221

Loehlin, J. C. 1986a. Heredity, environment, and the Thurstone Temperament Schedule. *Behav. Genet.* 16:61–73

Loehlin, J. C. 1986b. Are California Psychological Inventory items differently heritable? *Behav. Genet.* 16:599–603

Loehlin, J. C., Nichols, R. C. 1976. *Heredity, Environment, and Personality: A Study of 850 Sets of Twins.* Austin: Univ. Texas Press

Loehlin, J. C., Willerman, L., Horn, J. M. 1982. Personality resemblances between unwed mothers and their adopted-away offspring. *J. Pers. Soc. Psychol.* 42:1089–99

Loehlin, J. C., Willerman, L., Horn, J. M. 1985. Personality resemblances in adoptive familes when the children are late-adolescent or adult. *J. Pers. Soc. Psychol.* 48:376–92

Loranger, A. W. 1981. Genetic independence of manic-depression and schizophrenia. *Acta Psychiatry Scand.* 63:444–52

Ludlow, C. L., Cooper, J. A., eds. 1983. *Genetic Aspects of Speech and Language Disorders.* New York: Academic

Lykken, D. T. 1982. Research with twins: the concept of emergenesis. *Psychophysiology* 19:361–73

Marcus, F., Auerbach, J., Wilkinson, L., Burack, C. M. 1984. Infants at risk for schizophrenia: the Jerusalem Infant Development Study. See Watt et al 1984, pp. 440–64

Martin, N. G., Eaves, L. J. 1977. The genetical analysis of covariance structure. *Heredity* 38:79–95

Martin, N. G., Eaves, L. J., Heath, A. C., Jardine, R., Feingold, L. M., Eysenck, H. J. 1986. Transmission of social attitudes. *Proc. Natl. Acad. Sci. USA* 83:4364–68

Martin, N., Jardine, R. 1986. Eysenck's contributions to behaviour genetics. In *Hans Eysenck: Consensus and Controversy*, ed. S. Modgil, C. Modgil, pp. 13–47. Philadelphia: Falmer

Martin, N. G., Jardine, R., Eaves, L. J. 1984. Is there only one set of genes for different abilities? A reanalysis of the National Merit Scholarship Qualifying Test (NMSQT) data. *Behav. Genet.* 14:355–70

Mather, J. A. 1986. Saccadic eye movements to seen and unseen targets: oculomotor errors in normal subjects resembling those of schizophrenics. *J. Psychiatry Res.* 20:1–8

Matthysse, S., Holzman, P. S., Lange, K.

1986. The genetic transmission of schizophrenia: application of Mendelian latent structure analysis to eye tracking dysfunctions in schizophrenia and affective disorder. *J. Psychiatr. Res.* 20:57–76

McArdle, J. J. 1986. Latent variable growth within behavior genetic models. *Behav. Genet.* 16:163–200

McGue, M., Bouchard, T. J. Jr. 1984. Adjustment of twin data for the effects of age and sex. *Behav. Genet.* 14:325–43

McGue, M., Gottesman, I. I., Rao, D. C. 1983. The transmission of schizophrenia under a multifactorial threshold model. *Am. J. Hum. Genet.* 35:1161–78

McGue, M., Wette, R., Rao, D. C. 1984. Evaluation of path analysis through computer simulation. *Genet. Epidemiol.* 1:255–69

McGuffin, P., Farmer, A. E., Gottesman, I. I. 1987. Is there really a split in schizophrenia? The genetic evidence. *Br. J. Psychiatry* 150:581–92

McGuffin, P., Sturt, E. 1986. Genetic markers in schizophrenia. *Hum. Hered.* 36:65–88

Mednick, S. A., Gabrielli, W. F. Jr., Hutchings, B. 1984. Genetic influences in criminal convictions: evidence from an adoption cohort. *Science* 224:891–94

Murphey, R. M. 1983. Phenylketonuria (PKU) and the single gene: an old story retold. *Behav. Genet.* 13:141–57

Nathan, M., Guttman, R. 1984. Similarities in test scores and profiles of kibbutz twins and singletons. *Acta Genet. Med. Gemellol.* 33:213–18

Neale, M. C., Rushton, J. P., Fulker, D. W. 1986. Heritability of item responses on the Eysenck Personality Questionnaire. *Pers. Individ. Differ.* 7:771–79

Nee, L. E., Eldridge, R., Sunderland, T., Thomas, C. B., Katz, D., et al. 1987. Dementia of the Alzheimer type: clinical and family study of 22 twin pairs. *Neurology* 37:359–63

Netley, C. 1983. Sex chromosome abnormalities and the development of verbal and nonverbal abilities. See Ludlow & Cooper 1983, pp. 179–95

Nichols, R. C. 1978. Twin studies of ability, personality, and interests. *Homo* 29:158–73

O'Rourke, D. H., Gottesman, I. I., Suarez, B. K., Rice, J., Reich, T. 1982. Refutation of the general single-locus model for the etiology of schizophrenia. *Am. J. Hum. Genet.* 34:630–49

Orvaschel, H., Thompson, W. D., Belanger, A., Prusoff, B. A., Kidd, K. K. 1982. Comparison of the family history method to direct interview: factors affecting the diagnosis of depression. *J. Affect. Disord.* 4:49–59

Pauls, D. L., Leckman, J. F. 1986. The inheritance of Gilles de la Tourette's syndrome and associated behaviors. *N. Engl. J. Med.* 315:993–97

Pauls, D. L., Hurst, C. R., Kruger, S. D., Leckman, J. F., Kidd, K. K., et al. 1986a. Gilles de la Tourette's syndrome and attention deficit disorder with hyperactivity: evidence against a genetic relationship. *Arch. Gen. Psychiatry* 43:1177–79

Pauls, D. L., Towbin, K. E., Leckman, J. F., Zahner, G. E. P., Cohen, D. J. 1986b. Gilles de la Tourette's syndrome and obsessive compulsive disorder: evidence supporting a genetic relationship. *Arch. Gen. Psychiatry* 43:1180–82

Pennington, B. F., McCabe, L., Smith, S. D., Lefly, D. L., Bookman, M. O., et al. 1986. Spelling errors in adults with a form of familial dyslexia. *Child Dev.* 57:1001–13

Pennington, B. F., Smith, S. D. 1983. Genetic influences on learning disabilities and speech and language disorders. *Child Dev.* 54:369–87

Perley, M., Guze, S. B. 1962. Hysteria—the stability and usefulness of clinical criteria. *N. Engl. J. Med.* 266:421–26

Plomin, R. 1986a. Behavioral genetic methods. *J. Pers.* 54:226–61

Plomin, R. 1986b. *Development, Genetics, and Psychology.* Hillsdale, NJ: Erlbaum

Plomin, R., Daniels, D. 1987. Why are children in the same family so different from one another? *Behav. Brain Sci.* 10:1–16

Plomin, R., DeFries, J. C. 1985. *Origins of Individual Differences in Infancy: The Colorado Adoption Project.* Orlando, Fla: Academic

Plomin, R., DeFries, J. C., McClearn, G. E. 1980. *Behavioral Genetics: A Primer.* San Francisco: Freeman

Pogue-Geile, M. F., Rose, R. J. 1985. Developmental genetic studies of adult personality. *Dev. Psychol.* 21:547–57

Price, R. A., Vandenberg, S. G., Iyer, H., Williams, J. S. 1982. Components of variation in normal personality. *J. Pers. Soc. Psychol.* 43:328–40

Price, R. A., Kidd, K. K., Cohen, D. J., Pauls, D. L., Leckman, J. F. 1985a. A twin study of Tourette syndrome. *Arch. Gen. Psychiatry* 42:815–20

Price, R. A., Kidd, K. K., Pauls, D. L., Gershon, E. S., Prusoff, B. A., et al. 1985b. Multiple threshold models for the affective disorders: the Yale-NIMH Collaborative Family Study. *J. Psychiatry Res.* 19:533–46

Propping, P. 1983. Genetic disorders presenting as "schizophrenia": Karl Bonhoeffer's early view of the psychoses in the light of medical genetics. *Hum. Genet.* 65:1–10

Reed, S. C., Rich, S. S. 1982. Parent-offspring correlations and regressions for IQ. *Behav. Genet.* 12:535–42

Reed, T. E. 1985. Ethnic differences in alcohol use, abuse, and sensitivity: a review with genetic interpretation. *Soc. Biol.* 32:195–209

Renvoize, E. B., Mindham, R. H. S., Stewart, M., McDonald, R., Wallace, D. R. D. 1986. Identical twins discordant for presenile dementia of the Alzheimer type. *Br. J. Psychiatry* 149:509–12

Riese, M. L., Wilson, R. S., Matheny, A. P. Jr. 1985. Multimethod assessment of temperament in twins: birth to six months. *Acta Genet. Med. Gemellol.* 34:15–31

Ritvo, E. R., Freeman, B. J., Mason-Brothers, A., Mo, A., Ritvo, A. M. 1985. Concordance for the syndrome of autism in 40 pairs of affected twins. *Am. J. Psychiatry* 142:74–77

Robakis, N. K., Wisniewski, H. M., Jenkins, E. C., Devine-Gage, E. A., Houck, G. E., et al. 1987. Chromosome 21q21 sublocalisation of gene encoding beta-amyloid peptide in cerebral vessels and neuritic (senile) plaques of people with Alzheimer's disease and Down syndrome. *Lancet* 1:384–85

Rose, R. J., Ditto, W. B. 1983. A developmental-genetic analysis of common fears from early adolescence to early adulthood. *Child Dev.* 54:361–68

Rose, R. J., Kaprio, J. 1987. Shared experience and similarity of personality: positive data from Finnish and American twins. *Behav. Brain Sci.* 10:35–36

Rowe, D. C. 1983a. Biometrical genetic models of self-reported delinquent behavior: a twin study. *Behav. Genet.* 13:473–89

Rowe, D. C. 1983b. A biometrical analysis of perceptions of family environment: a study of twin and singleton sibling kinships. *Child Dev.* 54:416–23

Rushton, J. P. 1984. Sociobiology: toward a theory of individual and group differences in personality and social behavior. In *Annals of Theoretical Psychology*, ed. J. R. Royce, L. P. Mos, 2:1–48. New York: Plenum

Rushton, J. P. 1985. Differential K theory: the sociobiology of individual and group differences. *Pers. Individ. Differ.* 6:441–52

Rushton, J. P., Fulker, D. W., Neale, M. C., Nias, D. K. B., Eysenck, H. J. 1986. Altruism and aggression: the heritability of individual differences. *J. Pers. Soc. Psychol.* 50:1192–98

Rutter, M., Garmezy, N. 1983. Developmental psychopathology. In *Socialization, Personality and Social Development*, ed. E. M. Hetherington, pp. 775–911. New York: Wiley

Satterfield, J. H., Hoppe, C. M., Schell, A.

M. 1982. A prospective study of delinquency in 110 adolescent boys with attention deficit disorder and 88 normal adolescent boys. *Am. J. Psychiatry* 139:795–98

Scarr, S. 1985. Constructing psychology: making facts and fables for our times. *Am. Psychol.* 40:499–512

Scarr, S., McCartney, K. 1983. How people make their own environments. *Child Dev.* 54:424–35

Scarr, S., Webber, P. L., Weinberg, R. A., Wittig, M. A. 1981. Personality resemblance among adolescents and their parents in biologically related and adoptive families. *J. Pers. Soc. Psychol.* 40:885–98

Scarr, S., Weinberg, R. A. 1983. The Minnesota adoption studies: genetic differences and malleability. *Child Dev.* 54:260–67

Schiff, M., Duyme, M., Dumaret, A., Stewart, J., Tomkiewicz, S., Feingold, J. 1978. Intellectual status of working class children adopted into upper-middle class families. *Science* 200:1503–4

Schiff, M., Duyme, M., Dumaret, A., Tomkiewicz, S. 1982. How much could we boost scholastic achievement and IQ scores: a direct answer from a French adoption study. *Cognition* 12:165–96

Schuckit, M. A., Goodwin, D. W., Winokur, G. 1972. A half-sibling study of alcoholism. *Am. J. Psychiatry* 128:1132–36

Segal, N. L. 1985. Monozygotic and dizygotic twins: a comparative analysis of mental ability profiles. *Child Dev.* 56:1051–58

Selkoe, D. J., Bell, D. S., Podlisny, M. B., Price, D. L., Cork, L. C. 1987. Conservation of brain amyloid proteins in aged mammals and humans with Alzheimer's disease. *Science* 235:873–77

Siegel, C., Waldo, M., Miznor, G., Adler, L. E., Freedman, R. 1984. Deficits in sensory gating in schizophrenic patients and their relatives. *Arch. Gen. Psychiatry* 41:607–12

Sigvardsson, S., Cloninger, C. R., Bohman, M. 1985. Prevention and treatment of alcohol abuse: uses and limitations of the high risk paradigm. *Soc. Biol.* 32:185–94

Sigvardsson, S., Cloninger, C. R., Bohman, M., von Knorring, A.-L. 1982. Predisposition to petty criminality in Swedish adoptees. III. Sex differences and validation of the male typology. *Arch. Gen. Psychiatry* 39:1248–53

Snyderman, M., Rothman, S. 1987. Survey of expert opinion on intelligence and aptitude testing. *Am. Psychol.* 42:137–44

Spearman, C. 1927. *The Abilities of Man.* New York: MacMillan

Spence, M. A., Ritvo, E. R., Marazita, M. L., Funderburk, S. J., Sparkes, R. S., et al. 1985. Gene mapping studies with the syndrome of autism. *Behav. Genet.* 15:1–13

St. George-Hyslop, P. H., Tanzi, R. E., Polinsky, R. J., Haines, J. L., Nee, L., et al. 1987. The genetic defect causing familial Alzheimer's disease maps on chromosome 21. *Science* 235:885–90

Stevenson, J., Graham, P., Fredman, G., McLoughlin, V. 1987. A twin study of genetic influences on reading and spelling ability and disability. *J. Child Psychol. Psychiatry.* In press

Tambs, K., Sundet, J. M., Magnus, P. 1984. Heritability analysis of the WAIS subtests: a study of twins. *Intelligence* 8:283–93

Tanzi, R. E., Gusella, J. F., Watkins, P. C., Bruns, G. A. P., St. George-Hyslop, P. H., et al. 1987. Amyloid β protein gene: cDNA, mRNA distribution, and genetic linkage near the Alzheimer's locus. *Science* 235:880–84

Teasdale, T. W., Owen, D. R. 1984. Heredity and familial environment in intelligence and educational level—a sibling study. *Nature* 309:620–22

Thurstone, L. L. 1938. Primary mental abilities. *Psychometr. Monogr.* No. 1

Tienari, P., Sorri, A., Lahti, I., Naarala, M., Wahlberg, K., et al. 1985. The Finnish Adoptive Study of Schizophrenia. *Yale J. Biol. Med.* 58:227–37

Tsuang, M. T., Bucher, K. D., Fleming, J. A. 1982. Testing the monogenic theory of schizophrenia: an application of segregation analysis to blind family study data. *Br. J. Psychiatry* 140:595–99

Tsuang, M. T., Bucher, K. D., Fleming, J. A. 1983. A search for "schizophrenic spectrum disorders": an application of a multiple threshold model to blind family study data. *Br. J. Psychiatry* 143:572–77

Tsuang, M. T., Bucher, K. D., Fleming, J. A., Faraone, S. V. 1985a. Transmission of affective disorders: an application of segregation analysis to blind family study data. *J. Psychiatr. Res.* 19:23–29

Tsuang, M. T., Kendler, K. S., Gruenberg, A. M. 1985b. DSM-III schizophrenia: Is there evidence for familial transmission? *Acta Psychiatr. Scand.* 71:77–83

Vaillant, G. E. 1983. *The Natural History of Alcoholism.* Cambridge: Harvard Univ. Press

Vandenberg, S. G., Singer, S. M., Pauls, D. L. 1986. *The Heredity of Behavior Disorders in Adults and Children.* New York: Plenum

Vernon, P. E. 1950. *The Structure of Human Abilities.* New York: Wiley

Vogler, G. P. 1985. Multivariate path analysis of familial resemblance. *Genet. Epidemiol.* 2:35–53

Vogler, G. P., DeFries, J. C., Decker, S. N. 1985. Family history as an indicator of risk for reading disability. *J. Learn. Disabil.* 18:419–21

von Knorring, A.-L., Cloninger, C. R., Bohman, M., Sigvardsson, S. 1983. An adoption study of depressive disorders and substance abuse. *Arch. Gen. Psychiatry* 40:943–50

Watt, N. F., Anthony, J., Wynne, L. C., Rolf, J. E., eds. 1984. *Children at Risk for Schizophrenia: A Longitudinal Perspective.* New York: Cambridge Univ. Press

Wender, P. H., Kety, S. S., Rosenthal, D., Schulsinger, F., Ortmann, J., et al. 1986. Psychiatric disorders in the biological and adoptive families of adopted individuals with affective disorders. *Arch. Gen. Psychiatry* 43:923–29

White, R., Leppert, M., Bishop, T., Barker, D., Berkowitz, J., et al. 1985. Construction of linkage maps with DNA markers for human chromosomes. *Nature* 313:101–5

Willerman, L., Loehlin, J. C., Horn, J. M. 1987. An MMPI study of parent-child re-semblance for antisociality. *J. Child. Psychol. Psychiatry.* In press

Wilson, R. S. 1983. The Louisville twin study: developmental synchronies in behavior. *Child Dev.* 54:298–316

Wilson, R. S. 1986. Continuity and change in cognitive ability profile. *Behav. Genet.* 16:45–60

Wilson, R. S., Matheny, A. P. Jr. 1986. Behavior-genetics research in infant temperament: the Louisville Twin Study. In *The Study of Temperament,* ed. R. Plomin, J. Dunn, pp. 81–97. Hillsdale, NJ: Erlbaum

Wimer, R. E., Wimer, C. C. 1985. Animal behavior genetics. *Ann. Rev. Psychol.* 36:171–218

Winokur, G. 1983. The validity of familial subtypes in unipolar depression. *McLean Hosp. J.* 8:17–37

Winokur, G., Crowe, R. R. 1983. Bipolar illness: the sex-polarity effect in affectively ill family members. *Arch. Gen. Psychiatry* 40:57–58

Ann. Rev. Psychol. 1988. 39:135–68
Copyright © 1988 by Annual Reviews Inc. All rights reserved

NEURONAL UNIT ACTIVITY PATTERNS IN BEHAVING ANIMALS: Brainstem and Limbic System

Dennis McGinty and Ronald Szymusiak

Neurophysiology Research, Sepulveda Veterans Administration Medical Center, Sepulveda, California 91343; and Department of Psychology, University of California, Los Angeles, California 90024

CONTENTS

INTRODUCTION

This review summarizes studies concerned with neuronal coding of behavior in selected brainstem, hypothalamic, and limbic system sites. Behavioral experiments based on lesion, stimulation, and biochemical methods have firmly established the critical role of these regions in regulation of various "drive-related" behaviors (e.g. feeding, drinking, sleep, thermoregulation, sexual behavior, etc). As a step toward a mechanistic understanding of these

135

0066-4308/88/0201-0135$02.00

functions, we can ask how discharge of neurons within these regions is related to the occurrence of these behaviors. Brainstem and limbic system mechanisms are only partially understood, but recent findings show a surprising fit between unit discharge patterns and hypothesized behavioral functions.

A variety of approaches are required in analyzing neuronal mechanisms underlying behavior, but methods that apply to large populations of neurons are limited. Thus, regional lesion techniques, electrical or chemical stimulation, and metabolic labeling yield only general information about neuronal mechanisms. Of course, these methodologies are useful. Through their application it has become clear that control of specific behaviors is not localized to specific brain regions—i.e. to "centers." Rather, control mechanisms for even seemingly simple behaviors are distributed among several brain regions at various levels of the neuraxis. How can we examine the contributions of neuronal types within a given region, and the nature of the interactions among cells in functionally related brain areas?

Precise information about the behavioral functions of particular cell types can be obtained from neuronal unit recording techniques, particularly as they are applied in unanesthetized behaving animals. This approach focuses on the temporal sequence of neuronal events underlying behavior. If a cell plays a role in, for example, feeding, it should exhibit increased or decreased discharge during exposure to food, ingestion of food, or some component of the feeding-related regulatory process (see below). If cell discharge is examined during a variety of natural behaviors, meaningful inferences about selectivity of discharge for a particular behavior can be made. Insights into the type of influence coded in neuronal discharge are also possible—e.g. phasic time-locked coding versus tonic modulatory influence. Analysis of behaviorally categorized cell groups can be extended to include determination of input-output relationships using well-developed techniques for classifying anti- and orthodromic responses. No other neurobiological tool is capable of providing such temporally and anatomically discrete information in the behaving animal.

There is an extensive and varied literature on the neurophysiology of the brainstem, hypothalamus, and limbic system. Our review is necessarily selective and, to some extent, idiosyncratic. The degree of behavioral selectivity of neuronal discharge can be greatly overestimated in cells studied in restrained animals (see below), so we focus on regions that have been extensively studied in unanesthetized and unrestrained animals. The material considered also reflects our enduring interests in neural mechanisms of sleep and arousal. Some cell types are included (e.g. hypothalamic feeding-related neurons, hippocampal place cells) because they demonstrate how a detailed behavioral characterization of cell discharge reveals the surprising ability of single neurons to integrate complex sensory, motor, cognitive, and motivational variables. The intent is not to be comprehensive, but rather to highlight experimental strategies that appear to us to be the most powerful and most productive in the analysis of the neuronal coding of complex behaviors.

THE RETICULAR FORMATION

The reticular formation (RF) has been hypothesized to participate in a wide variety of functional mechanisms including arousal, nociception, habituation, anticipation of reward, fear of shock, and REM sleep as well as multimodal sensory processing (see Siegel 1979 for review). Siegel noted that there was extensive overlap in the localization of the pontine RF regions thought to mediate these various functions and that each investigator attributed a majority of cells in the overlapping sites to the hypothesized functions. An explanation for these conflicting views was developed from results of long-term unit recording studies in unrestrained animals. These conceptual developments illustrate well the scientific issues involved in the choice of unit recording strategies.

The earliest studies of RF units, carried out in anesthetized animals, demonstrated sensory responses from all modalities and emphasized the multimodal responses of cells and a characteristic response decrement or habituation with repeated stimulus presentation (e.g. Scheibel 1980). These findings were integrated with the classical studies of Moruzzi & Magoun (1949) showing that RF stimulation could cause cortical EEG activation and behavioral arousal; the RF constituted the headwaters of the ascending reticular activating system. RF neuronal multiunit discharge in chronic animals was found to increase during arousal (Podvoll & Goodman 1967). When investigators subsequently expanded the hypothesized functions of the RF, they typically studied unit discharge in relation to a specific experimental paradigm, such as the conditioned emotional response (Umemoto et al 1970), or REM sleep (McCarley & Hobson 1971). A reasonable objective was usually to minimize potential contributions to experimental variability. Conventional unit recordings were easiest in restrained animals, since movements could result in loss of unit isolation.

Studies in our lab utilized the microwire unit recording procedure employing 25–32 μ diameter wires, permitting extracellular unit recording in unrestrained animals during periods of several hours or more (Harper & McGinty 1973). We showed that pontine RF cells exhibit increased discharge in relation to specific movements (McGinty et al 1974; Siegel & McGinty 1977; Siegel et al 1979; Siegel & Tomaszewski 1983; Siegel et al 1980). Individual cellular discharge was augmented during movements of the eyes, pinna, facial muscles, movements involving the head, neck or back, or proximal limb. Most cells exhibited discharge in relation to ipsilateral directionally specific movement. Cellular activity related to head or neck movements was most common, constituting nearly 25% of the sample.

These findings were consistent with anatomical data. Most pontine and medullary neurons distribute axons within the ventromedial or ventrolateral funiculi of the spinal cord to make monosynaptic connections with motoneurons (Nyberg-Hansen 1965; Grillner & Lund 1968; Peterson et al 1975, 1978). The projection pattern exhibits specific topographic organization; projections to cervical motoneurons (controlling head and neck movements) are prominent. Both excitatory and inhibitory postsynaptic potentials (PSPs) can be evoked in spinal motoneurons by focal RF stimulation, depending on stimulation site (Peterson et al 1978). Reticular projections to oculomotor neurons have also been demonstrated (Graybiel 1977).

Siegel (1979) has argued that some previous results may reflect the correlated movements of animals in various behavioral paradigms. Subtle or gross movements are associated with anticipation of reward, anticipation of punishment, response to painful stimuli, and motor responses decline during "habituation." Thus, the apparent overlap in behavioral functions attributed to the RF neuron could be explained by the movements associated with the experimental situation. If an animal moves in a characteristic way during a behavior, one can expect that RF discharge will show a "significant" temporally discrete correlation. However, this does not constitute evidence that these cells are specifically involved in the behavior being studied.

An example of the potential difficulty resulting from use of movement-restricted animals was found in an analysis of REM sleep control, based on an observation of apparent REM-specific discharge of neuronal units in the medial pontine RF, detected in head-restrained animals (McCarley & Hobson 1971). However, there is now a consensus that medial RF cells are equally active during waking, when head movements are permitted (Vertes 1977; Corner & Bour 1984; see above). All types of supraspinal neurons discharging during movement are also active in REM sleep (McGinty & Drucker-Colin 1982). The origin of REM-related discharge in motor systems is not known, but it is a correlative phenomenon and does not constitute evidence for a causal role in REM sleep control. The extensive evidence bearing on the role of the pons in REM control in reviewed elsewhere (Siegel 1985; Sakai 1985; Jones 1985).

The discovery of specific movement-related discharge in RF cells was based on open-ended experimental strategy. Once cellular discharge is isolated (following advancement of the microdrive), the experimenter presents a variety of stimuli and induces a wide range of movements to learn whether or not discharge varies during such manipulations. In the case of pontine or medullary RF neurons, 2–50-fold variations in discharge rate associated with movement were observed in almost every cell encountered; this is a virtual signature of RF neurons. The next step was to induce more and more specific movements to refine the understanding of the unit discharge-movement correlation. The ability to record unit discharge in unrestrained animals over extended periods is crucial. Several hours of observation and manipulation may be necessary to identify subtle movement unit discharge correlations, such as those involving the tongue or pinna.

In the freely moving animal sensory and motor processes are always interacting; movements produce proprioceptive and vestibular feedback and changing visual, somatosensory, and auditory stimuli. However, the potential role of direct sensory activation of RF neurons could be assessed by systematic removal of visual, somatic (by local anesthesia), auditory (by ear plugs), or vestibular or proprioceptive stimuli (by restraint). Such manipulations had little effect on neural activity, if associated muscle contractions persisted (Siegel & McGinty 1977).

The specificity of movement-related discharge was further demonstrated by operant conditioning of increased unit discharge, using hypothalamic stimulation as a reward. That is, the behavior that was rewarded was a train of unit activity. Cellular discharge was greatly augmented during periods with reward, diminished during periods with extinction (Breedlove et al 1979). Frame-by-frame photographic analysis showed that cats achieved augmented unit discharge during rewarded periods by emitting a directionally specific movement, very similar to the movement initially identified by the experimenter as correlated with unit discharge. This result is consistent with the hypothesis of specific movement–RF unit discharge relationships. Thus, while the open-ended observational experiment is initially ambiguous with respect to possible correlates of unit discharge, the specificity can be refined in follow-up studies. Most crucially, the experimenter has not biased the conclusion of the study by predetermining the possible outcome through his experimental paradigm. The conception of the pontine and medullary RF as a motor system was consistent with certain previous studies of RF function, including studies relating the RF to control of eye movements (e.g. Fuchs & Luschei 1972), locomotion (Grillner & Shik 1973; Orlovskii 1970; Garcia-Rill et al 1983), and respiratory muscles (von Euler et al 1973). It would appear that these classes of movement represent subdivisions within the RF motor system.

The midbrain RF has not yet been carefully analyzed in terms of possible movement correlates, although movement-related discharge is prominent. Ray et al (1982) and Pragay et al (1978) have studied MRF units in head-restrained rhesus monkeys in a go/no-go task. While many cells showed discharge related to movement, roughly half of their cells exhibited increased discharge during the period of stimulus presentation that was unrelated to the specific button-push response on "go" trials. They hypothesized that these cells mediate attention to stimuli, although they acknowledge that discharge may be related to subtle changes in muscle tension accompanying the event sequence of the trained performance. Attention-related cells were widely distributed in the midbrain and pontine RF. Steriade et al (1982) have distinguished a subset of midbrain RF neurons, recorded in head-restrained cats, that are tonically active in waking and show greatly reduced discharge in SWS. Some of these cells exhibited increased discharge several seconds before arousal from sleep, and many were found to project to the medial intralaminar thalamus or subthalamic area. These findings suggested that such cells may be substrates of the ascending reticular activating system. However, Steriade et al noted that these cells were more active, as a group, during waking with movements. Older studies in unrestrained rats reported many midbrain RF cells exhibiting discharge during locomotion, sniffing, orientation, and other movements (Komisaruk & Olds 1968). Thus, there continues to be uncertainty about the behavioral specificity of midbrain RF neuronal activity; and the possibility that discharge is related to movement cannot be excluded until a careful "open-ended" analysis, like that applied in the pons and medulla, is completed. Midbrain RF neurons differ from those at the pontine and medullary levels in that they do not project directly to motoneurons, although widespread connections from midbrain to lower RF areas are known (Edwards 1975). Ascending projections from midbrain are prominent. It is possible that movement and drive or arousal-related inputs are jointly expressed in the midbrain RF.

SEROTONIN-CONTAINING NEURONS

The role of serotonin in the brain has been studied extensively, owing primarily to the development of theories relating this substance to control of virtually every class of behavior, psychiatric disorder, endocrine mechanism, and to the actions of most psychoactive drugs. The study of discharge patterns of serotonin-containing neurons in unanesthetized animals has played a central role in the evaluation of these theories, as summarized in several reviews (Jacobs & Gelperin 1981; Baumgarten & Lachenmayer 1985; Jacobs 1985). The present discussion is limited to the issue of possible behavioral coding in the discharge of this type of neuron.

Neurophysiological studies were initially stimulated by the finding that serotonin-containing neurons were restricted to well-defined nuclei in the brainstem, the raphe nuclei (Dahlstrom & Fuxe 1964). Within these incompletely homogeneous nuclei, further identification was based on the unique discharge pattern of these cells, and their responses to pharmacological probes and histological markers (Aghajanian et al 1977; Trulson & Jacobs

1979b). The slow, regular discharge pattern that characterizes these cells is not found in cell types bordering on the raphe nuclei. The use of these criteria to identify serotonin-containing neurons has been confirmed by many groups (Cespuglio et al 1981; Trulson 1984). Thus, at least within circumscribed regions of the brain, discharge pattern may be used as a marker for neuronal types.

The characteristics of serotonin-containing neuronal discharge in relation to behavior are as follows. Within waking, units maintain a regular discharge pattern at a typical rate of about 3 spikes per second with small variation during a wide variety of ongoing behaviors. Units do not exhibit consistent changes in relation to movement, social or nociceptive stimuli, manipulations of drive state, or within a homogeneous state, across the 24-hr day (McGinty 1973; Trulson & Jacobs 1983). In one study 72% of rat dorsal raphe nucleus (DRN) neurons were unresponsive to a powerful nociceptive stimulus [subcutaneous formalin injection (Shima et al 1986)]. Most DRN neurons exhibit a single spike at relatively long latency (about 40 msec) in response to auditory (clicks) or visual (flashes) stimuli, but no continuous sensory responses (Heym et al 1982a; Trulson & Trulson 1983a). In cats, some DRN neurons discharge at slightly higher (+5–10%) rates during active waking (periods with intensive movements) as compared with quiet waking (Trulson & Jacobs 1979a), but this activation response occurs in response to a variety of arousing stimuli. The most impressive aspect of these cells is their lack of discharge variation in relation to behavior.

In contrast to waking, sleep in both rats and cats is associated with pronounced changes in raphe unit discharge (McGinty 1973; McGinty & Harper 1976; Trulson & Jacobs 1979a; Cespuglio et al 1981; Lydic et al 1983; Shima et al 1986). SWS is associated with a 50% reduction in discharge rate, while REM is marked by a greater than 90% reduction. Thus, within the normal behavioral repertoire of rats and cats, serotonin-containing neurons show large changes in discharge rate only during sleep stages. Similar results have been reported for four major raphe nuclei, including the nucleus centralis superior (NCS, Rasmussen et al 1984), nucleus raphe magnus (NRM; Fornal et al 1985), and nucleus raphe pallidus (NRP, Heym et al 1982a; Trulson & Trulson 1982), in addition to the DRN. Within SWS, many DRN and NCS neurons exhibit pauses in discharge before the occurrence of ponto-geniculo-occipital (PGO) waves and before sleep spindles (McGinty et al 1973; Trulson & Jacobs 1979a); NRP and NRM neurons do not exhibit this feature (Heym et al 1982a; Trulson & Trulson 1982). An early report that NRP and NCS neurons exhibit increased discharge in REM may have been in error (Sheu et al 1974).

Serotonin turnover is lowest (serotonin levels highest) during the inactive phase of the 24-hr day (light period in the rat), and rises with the onset of activity (e.g. Hery et al 1972; Agren et al 1986). However, there is no circadian variation in discharge rate of cat DRN neurons *within* a state (Trulson & Jacobs 1983). Nevertheless, circadian variations in serotonin turnover could be explained by the distribution of sleep-waking stages. Turnover may be low during the inactive period because the animal is asleep. If this hypothesis is correct, circadian turnover patterns would be minimized by sleep deprivation. Another possibility is that release of serotonin from nerve terminals is not determined solely by discharge rate. Using a semi-quantitative voltametric method, Trulson (1985b) found that REM sleep-related release of serotonin was reduced less than was predicted by impulse flow; on the other hand, LSD (see below) produced a greater decrement in release than predicted by impulse flow.

The findings reviewed above are based on data obtained in unmedicated and otherwise normal animals. Serotonin-containing neurons are strongly affected by a variety of psychoactive drugs. DRN discharge is reduced by 10–90%, depending upon dose, by benzodiazepines (Trulson et al 1982), the novel anxiolytic buspirone (Trulson & Trulson 1986), MAO-inhibitors (Trulson & Trulson 1985), a centrally acting muscle relaxant agent mephenesin (Steinfels et al 1983c), the antidepressant chlorimipramine (Trulson & Trulson 1983b), and hallucinogens such as LSD or 5-methoxy-N,N-dimethyltryptamine (Trulson & Jacobs 1979b; Trulson 1986). Obviously, the behavioral effects of these different drugs vary widely, and no conclusion concerning the mechanisms of action of drugs relative to the discharge of serotonin-containing neurons seems warranted. The prominent effects of various drugs on monoaminergic neurons is often used as a basis for inferring that these neurons *normally* regulated the behaviors affected by the drugs. Since unit recording studies do not indicate specific correlations with behavior, drugs effects must be interpreted with caution. Anesthesia has been found to greatly alter the responses of DRN neurons to drugs. At a given dose many drugs produce far more potent inhibition of DRN unit discharge in anesthetized animals (McGinty 1973; Heym et al 1984; Trulson & Trulson 1983b). However, benzodiazepines had no effect in anesthetized rats, in contrast to the those noted above (Trulson & Trulson 1983b). Anesthesia also blocks the response of DRN neurons to auditory or visual stimuli and electrical stimulation of the pontine RF (Heym et al 1984).

There have been attempts to provide a conceptual framework for understanding the decrease in raphe unit discharge during sleep. DRN discharge is also greatly depressed following micro-injection of the cholinergic agonist carbachol into the medial pontine reticular formation (Steinfels et al 1983c). Discharge suppression is associated with the prolonged muscle atonia resulting from these injections. On the other hand, after dorsomedial pontine lesions that result in "REM without atonia," DRN discharge is reduced less in REM [50% instead of >90% (Trulson et al 1981)]. Muscle atonia is among the most prominent correlates of the normal REM sleep state. These observations have led Jacobs, Trulson, and associates to hypothesize that DRN discharge may be a correlate of CNS-controlled muscle tonus. This hypothesis is consistent with some drug effects, such as the response to benzodiazepines, which also produce muscle hypotonia. However, as noted above, other drugs, particularly hallucinogens, that result in DRN discharge suppression are associated with concomitant behavioral activation. Further, DRN discharge is not correlated with degree of motor activity across the sleep cycle (Lydic et al 1983). Therefore, the serotonin-tonus motor activity hypothesis needs modification.

Lydic et al (1983) have quantified the cyclic progressive decrease in DRN discharge in SWS, and suggested the DRN cells participate in a cyclic process controlling SWS-REM cycles. McGinty & Drucker-Colin (1982) proposed that cyclic changes in receptor—perhaps autoreceptor (Vandermaelen & Aghajanian 1983)—sensitivity during sleep account for REM-SWS cycles. These hypotheses have not been tested. However, it is significant that DRN discharge returns to its waking pattern immediately upon behavioral arousal, but decreases slowly after sleep onset. Thus, raphe unit discharge seems to be strongly controlled by waking mechanisms.

The system of serotoninergic neurons has several unusual features (Baumgarten & Lachenmayer 1985). The projections of these neurons are widespread and diffuse. Almost all CNS regions receive serotoninergic afferents, including neocortex, limbic system and basal ganglia, hypothalamus, and medial thalamus. Within the brainstem sensory relay and visceromotor nuclei, substantia nigra and locus coeruleus receive fibers. However, conventional junctional contacts constitute only about 5% of the terminals in neocortex, and nonjunctional contacts predominate in the spinal cord (Descarriers et al 1975). Cerebral blood vessels appear to receive serotoninergic innervation. Serotonin is hypothesized to have a primarily modulatory influence on target cells. For example, in the spinal cord serotonin facilitates responses of motoneurons to glutamate but has no direct effect (Aghajanian 1981).

In summary, the following tentative conclusions are suggested by the available data. The discharge of serotonin-releasing neurons is minimally responsive to behavioral events; it shows remarkable constancy during waking and is depressed during sleep. Changes in sleeping/waking state are the primary behavioral events controlling discharge. The neurons have a diffuse and widespread projection pattern with relatively few conventional synaptic junctions. The effects of serotonin on targets are considered to be modulatory (modifications of response to other transmitters are more important than direct effects). Since the disturbance of the serotoninergic network by lesions or with drugs influences virtually every type of behavior, the functional role of this system is likely to be nonspecific, modulatory, and related to some aspect of the "state" of the nervous system.

NORADRENERGIC NEURONS—THE LOCUS COERULEUS

Norepinephrine-containing neurons, particularly those of the largest cluster of these cells, the locus coeruleus (LC) of the dorsal pontine reticular formation, have been studied extensively. The functions of this cell group have also been the subject of much theorizing: The LC has been implicated in the biology of depression (Schildkraut 1965), regulation of cerebral blood flow and metabolism (Owman & Edvinsson 1977), neural basis of reward (Wise & Stein 1969), memory processes (Anlezark et al 1973), anxiety and nociception (Redmond & Huang 1979), REM sleep (Hobson et al 1975), attention, central nervous system "sympathetic" functions, and arousal mechanisms (see Aston-Jones et al 1984 for review). The anatomy of LC neurons has several unique and fascinating features (see Amaral & Sinnamon 1977). This well-delineated group of cells, estimated at 1600 in the rat and 20,000 in man, projects to every major CNS region. In neocortex, terminals were recently found to be geometrically organized and to make conventional synaptic junctions (Morrison et al 1978). Individual neurons may project to disparate CNS sites.

The identification of norepinephrine locus coeruleus (NE-LC) cellular activity is based on several features: a slow, fairly regular discharge rate at 1 to 2 spikes per second, somewhat like raphe neurons; long-duration action potential (>2 msec); suppression of discharge by administration of the α-adrenergic agonist clonidine; and, of course, a correspondence between detection of cells with these properties and the histological identification of noradrenergic cells (Graham & Aghajanian 1971; Svensson et al 1975). In the rat, noradrenergic cells form a homogeneous group. Thus, definitive correspondence between physiological and anatomical markers is possible. In the cat, the LC is not homogeneous, but an inference about cell identity can be made on the basis of electrophysiological features.

NE-LC cells exhibit a distinct patterns of changes in discharge rate during sleep. During SWS, discharge rate is reduced about 50% from quiet waking levels. During REM, unit discharge is almost totally absent. This pattern of discharge rate changes across states, first reported in the cat (Hobson et al 1975; McGinty et al 1974; Chu & Bloom 1974; Saito et al 1977; Sakai 1980; Reiner 1986; Rasmussen et al 1986), has now been confirmed for the homogeneous NE-LC group in the rat (Foote et al 1980; Aston-Jones et al 1981a). The identification of these "REM-off" cells in the cat as NE-LC cells was recently supported by the finding that discharge of such cells is suppressed by administration of the α-adrenergic agonist clonidine (Reiner 1985), as in the anesthetized rat (Svennson et al 1975). In the cat, REM-off cells are reported as being mixed with cells having different discharge patterns, in agreement with the anatomical distribution of NE cells in this species. Initial studies of LC cells, which failed to identify the suppression of discharge in REM (Chu & Bloom 1974), seemed to have focused on the non-NE cells of the LC, although we cannot exclude the possibility that some fraction of NE-LC cells in the cat exhibit different discharge patterns. This disagreement illustrates the importance of identification of cell types within heterogeneous sites.

Although the waking-sleep discharge profile of NE-LC cells is similar to that of raphe neurons, REM-off LC cells do not show suppression of discharge during sleep spindles (Aston-Jones & Bloom 1981a; Rasmussen et al 1986). However, a subset do exhibit cessation of discharge preceding PGO waves (McGinty et al 1974; Sakai 1980). In the rat, Aston-Jones & Bloom (1981a) have reported that NE-LC cells exhibit systematic changes in rate that anticipate sleep onset. During sustained waking, discharge rate gradually declined prior to sleep onset, perhaps contributing to decreased arousal (see below). However, there was no change in NE-LC discharge prior to the end of REM sleep, in contradiction to predictions of the Hobson et al (1975) theory of REM sleep control.

During waking, NE-LC neurons respond with short-duration (about 100 msec) groups of 1–4 spikes to mild nociceptive stimuli (tail pinch), and to auditory clicks, flashes, and nonaversive somatosensory stimuli (Foote et al 1980; Aston-Jones & Bloom 1981b; Rasmussen et al 1986). LC neuronal responses to sensory stimuli decline with repeated presentation, probably in relation to the arousing quality of the stimulus (Aston-Jones & Bloom 1981b). More arousing stimuli such as the threat of a blow (leading to a cowering response) yield greater increases in unit discharge (Rasmussen & Jacobs 1986). The neutral stimulus conditioned to presentation of an aversive air puff (conditioned emotional response paradigm) produced a >500% increase in discharge rate (Rasmussen & Jacobs 1986). On the other hand, conditioned presentation of food did not result in increased discharge compared to an active waking baseline. The largest response occurs during the roughly 30-sec period prior to emesis induced by administration of clonidine. LC discharge is significantly time-locked to the EKG during quiet waking, although this coupling accounts for only a fraction of spikes (Morilak et al 1986).

There is no evidence that LC neuronal responses are specific to particular forms of stimulation, learning, or other complex behavioral processes (Aston-Jones et al 1984; Jacobs 1986; German & Fetz 1976; Elam et al 1984). Jacobs and associates have concluded that NE-LC neurons are involved in adaptive response to physiological challenge, and Aston-Jones et al have suggested that these cells assist behavioral orientation to external events of phasically high priority. These concepts have in common the idea that the LC participates in nonspecific behavioral activation. This interpretation is consistent with the nonspecific behavioral activation induced by drugs such as amphet-amines that increase release of norepinephrine.

DOPAMINE-CONTAINING NEURONS

The dopamine(DA)-containing neurons of the substantia nigra (SN) pars compacta, projecting to the caudate nucleus, are implicated in the regulation of movement since their degeneration is the primary pathology in the motor disorder Parkinson's disease. Damage to the DAergic nigrostriatal pathway has profound effects on a variety of behaviors including feeding, learning, reward, and sleep, as well as movement (Ungerstedt 1971; Beninger 1983; see Horn et al 1979). As demonstrated by intracellular labeling studies, these cells can be identified in electrophysiological recordings by their very long compound action potentials (2–5 msec), relatively low regular discharge rate (1–10 spikes/sec), and response to pharmacological probes such as apomor-phine and haloperidol (Bunney et al 1973; Guyenet & Aghajanian 1978; Grace & Bunney 1980). DA neurons also exhibit spike bursts with decreasing spike amplitude. Identical spike patterns are seen in anesthetized and un-anesthetized animals.

In contrast to the findings in other aminergic neurons, DA-SN neurons exhibit only slight discharge rate modulation during the sleep-waking cycle (Trulson et al 1981; Steinfels et al 1981; Miller et al 1983; Trulson 1985c). The behaviors described above are also observed in DA-containing neurons recorded in the ventral tegmental area (Trulson & Preussler 1984). In the cat there is no circadian (24-hr) variation in discharge rate within a uniform quiet waking state (Trulson 1985c). These cells discharge slightly faster during active waking, compared to quiet waking, but they do not show relationship to movement per se. The latter finding has been confirmed in rats, cats, and monkeys (Miller et al 1981; Steinfels et al 1983a; DeLong et al 1983). These observations have led to the interpretation that DA may play a modulatory role in the regulation of movement by the caudate. Such an interpretation is consistent with the finding that deficits produced by DA pathway damage may be reversed by intra- or peristriatal implants of DA-secreting cells (Bjorklund et al 1980; Madrazo et al 1987). These neurons may act as synthesizing and releasing pumps, conveying no discrete information. Direct measurement of DA release using voltametric methods showed a reduction in DA release during sleep, and an increased release during movement was not predicted by impulse rates (Trulson 1985a). DA release from nerve terminals may be partially regulated by presynaptic modulation.

There is evidence that the DA nigrostriatal pathway has limited sensory function. In response to auditory (clicks) or visual (flashes) stimuli as well as olfactory and somatosensory stimuli, most DA-SN cells exhibit brief long-latency excitatory responses, followed by short-lasting inhibition (Steinfels et al 1983b; Strecker & Jacobs 1985; Trulson 1985c). Sustained sensory responses conveying information about the quality of the stimulus were not observed. Sensory responses do not habituate, but they disappear during sleep, feeding, or grooming (Strecker & Jacobs 1985; Steinfels et al 1983a,b). More complex sensory stimuli, such as those eliciting an orienting response, produce a 1–10 sec period of discharge suppression (Steinfels et al 1983b; Trulson 1985c).

DA-SN cellular discharge is not altered by manipulations affecting feeding, including food deprivation, changes in blood glucose, or insulin administration (Trulson et al 1983; Strecker et al 1983). The latter studies were carried out to evaluate hypotheses concerning the role of DA neurons in feeding behavior, as suggested by the aphagia resulting from nigrostriatal pathway damage. This result suggests that DA effects on feeding, like those on motor behavior, depend only on DA secretion rather than on DA release guided by nerve impulse traffic.

DA-SN neuronal discharge rate is reduced by apomorphine, L-Dopa, amphetamine, and the DA-reuptake blocker buproprion—all agents that augment DA receptor stimulation. Conversely, haloperidol increased DA-SN neuronal unit discharge (Trulson 1985c). Indeed, the number of DA-SN cells encountered during electrode passes was increased by haloperidol treatment, suggesting that some units may normally be silent in the untreated animal (Miller et al 1981).

In summary, evidence from unit-recording studies suggests that DAergic neurons, like serotoninergic neurons, play a modulatory role in behavior. The widespread behavioral consequences of interrupting the nigrostriatal pathway must result from the loss of DA secretion rather than information coded by nerve impulse patterns.

HYPOTHALAMIC NEURONAL DISCHARGE AND FEEDING BEHAVIOR

Stimulation and lesion studies have implicated the hypothalamus as an important locus of control for ingestive behaviors. Lesions of the ventromedial hypothalamus (VMH) reliably result in hyperphagia and obesity (Hetherington & Ranson 1942), and the area has been hypothesized to contain a satiety mechanism. Lesions of the lateral hypothalamic area (LHA) lead to a syndrome of behavioral deficits including aphagia and adipsia (Teitelbaum & Epstein 1962), and the LHA has been implicated in the active initiation of ingestive behaviors. Subsequent work on the hypothalamic control of feeding has demonstrated that the disturbances that result from hypothalamic ablations are more complex than simple abnormalities in feeding behavior (e.g. Marshall & Teitelbaum 1974) and that damage to the axons of brainstem monoaminergic cells contributes to the observed behavioral deficits (Stricker & Zigmond 1976). Nevertheless, there is good evidence that neurons intrinsic to the hypothalamus participate in the control of feeding, and much of this evidence comes from single-unit recordings.

The earliest neurophysiological studies focused on the responsiveness of hypothalamic neurons to internal stimuli related to hunger and satiety in anesthetized animals. For example, in rats, LHA neuronal discharge was suppressed by systemic or local infusions of glucose (Anand et al 1964; Oomura et al 1969a) or free fatty acids (Oomura et al 1975; Oomura 1976). Systemic infusion of insulin decreased hypothalamic unit discharge (Hernandez & Gottberg 1980). Hypothalamic neurons also respond to activation of gastric (Anand & Pillai 1967; Barone et al 1979) and intestinal (Maddison & Horrell 1979) stretch receptors.

With the advent of techniques permitting single-unit recordings in unanesthetized animals, correlations between hypothalamic discharge and feeding behaviors became possible. Recording in unanesthetized and unrestrained cats, Oomura et al (1969b) reported that LHA neurons responded with an initial brief rate increase, followed by a sustained decrease during food consumption. Cells in the VMH exhibited the opposite response during eating—i.e. an initial decrease followed by an increase in discharge rate (Oomura et al 1969b). In rats chronically implanted with microwires for unit recordings, 43% of the cells recorded in the LHA exhibited decreases in discharge rate during the ingestion of food, while cells in the medial hypothalamus were unaffected (Hamburg 1971). Ono et al (1981b) made long-term (>24 hr) recordings of LHA unit activity of freely moving rats using the microwire technique. They found that 43% of the LHA cells exhibited suppression of discharge during ingestion of food. These cells had low spontaneous discharge rates and did not show circadian changes in either spontaneous rate or responses to food. In monkeys, LHA neurons were found to either increase or decrease discharge during eating and drinking (Burton et al 1976). The disparate results obtained in different species may reflect either true species differences or sampling among different cell populations.

Feeding and drinking are associated with characteristic postures and movements, and the above examples may reflect a motor involvement of LHA cells. For example, movement-related LHA cells might exhibit discharge suppression during feeding if an animal becomes less active once food has entered its mouth. One strategy to overcome this problem is to conduct a detailed behavioral characterization of cell responsiveness in which the same cell is studied in a variety of sensory, behavioral, and motivational contexts. This approach has been used successfully in the study of the neurophysiology of feeding behavior in primates. Recordings have been made in unanesthetized monkeys restrained in a primate chair; the head may or may not be rigidly fixed. This arrangement permits the study of unit activity during the controlled presentation of stimuli, discrimination of food or nonfood objects, appetitive behaviors (e.g. bar pressing for food), and ingestion of food. A shortcoming of the method is that restraint is too extensive to permit an open-ended analysis of the movement correlates of neuronal discharge.

Rolls et al (1976) were the first to describe neurons in the LHA and substantia innominata (SI) of the monkey that respond to the sight of food. Such cells accounted for 12% of the sample. Some LHA cells increased discharge rate at the sight of food, while others decreased rate. These cells did not respond when monkeys were presented with food in the dark, nor did they respond to nonfood objects. LHA neuronal discharge did not appear to be correlated with gross movement; cells did not respond during startle movements evoked by a puff of air in the face, and discharge was not tightly coupled to feeding-related movements (e.g. reaching for food, chewing), in contrast to cells in the globus pallidus. However, the possibility that the cells were responding to subtle movements associated with the anticipation of food could not be entirely ruled out (Rolls et al 1976).

In subsequent reports, it was demonstrated that LHA cells were not purely sensory but that their responses to food depended on the animal's internal state. Cell responsiveness to the sight of food diminished when animals were fed to satiety (Burton et al 1976). The effects of satiety on these cells was sensory specific—i.e. cells ceased to respond to the sight of a food on which they had been fed to satiety, but continued to respond to other preferred foods (Ono et al 1984; Rolls et al 1986). The magnitude of response was also related to food preference (Ono et al 1984). Cognitive variables could influence cell discharge. For example, LHA cells began to respond to nonfood objects that had been repeatedly paired with food (Mora et al 1976).

Some LHA cells discharge in association with operant responses that lead to food reward. In monkeys, from a total sample of 144 LHA neurons, 18 responded to the sight of food, 23 during ingestion of food, and 10 to the sight of food and during bar pressing to obtain the food (Ono et al 1981a). Cells had either elevated or suppressed discharge rates during bar-press responses. Cells with similar discharge correlates were also recorded in the monkey caudate nucleus (Nishino et al 1981). Discharge of cells recorded in primate nucleus basalis of Meynert (NBM), a region located ventral to the globus pallidus and closely related to the SI, is correlated with various aspects of food-rewarded tasks. In a visuomotor tracking task, cells in the NBM discharged most reliably to delivery of juice reward, although many neurons discharged tonically during arm movements. This contrasted with more dorsally located cells of the globus pallidus, which responded phasically during arm movements and did not respond to juice reward (DeLong 1971; Richardson et al

1983). In macaque monkeys, 83% of NBM neurons responded to delivery of juice, and 57% responded phasically during reaching for juice (Mitchell et al 1982). In a delayed-response task, rhesus monkey NBM neurons responded most reliably during the choice phase and the reward phase of the task (Richardson & DeLong 1986). Responses during the cueing phase were less common and less vigorous, and changes in rate during the delay phase were even less frequent. The authors concluded that the best stimulus for NBM neurons was the delivery of juice, and that responses during the choice phase were common because this phase immediately preceded juice delivery (Richardson & DeLong 1986).

Cells with behavioral correlates similar to those of LHA/SI neurons in primates have been identified in the LHA of sheep (Maddison & Baldwin 1983). Sheep were head-restrained with their bodies suspended in a hammock during unit recordings. A subpopulation of LHA cells either increased or decreased discharge at the sight of food and/or during the approach of food to the mouth. They did not respond to the sight of nonfood objects. Such cells comprised 16% of the total sample (Maddison & Baldwin 1983). The magnitude of the response evoked in LHA neurons by the sight of food in sheep was proportional to the animal's preference for the food (Kendrick & Baldwin 1986a). Responses were attenuated when the animal was fed to satiety. Cells could be trained to respond to nonfood objects that had been repeatedly paired with food (Kendrick & Baldwin 1986a). Food-related neurons in sheep were more caudally distributed than those in primates, extending from the LHA to the zona incerta (Kendrick & Baldwin 1986a). One subtype of zona incerta neurons in sheep responded during ingestion of food, not to the sight of food (Kendrick & Baldwin 1986b). Inferences about behavioral correlates of zona incerta neurons recorded during head restraint should be made with caution. In cats, the majority of neurons in the zona incerta/subthalamic nucleus discharge maximally during waking movement; many in association with head movements (Steriade et al 1980; Szymusiak & McGinty 1986c). Since normal feeding behavior in sheep involves moving the head toward food (Kendrick & Baldwin 1986a), the motor correlates of putative food-related neurons should be examined in freely moving animals.

Other evidence suggests that LHA neurons related to the sight and/or taste of food may participate in the perception of reinforcement or reward associated with brain stimulation. In monkeys, many food-related LHA neurons responded to single-pulse stimulation at several brain sites that supported self-stimulation (Rolls et al 1980). In rats, the majority of LHA neurons that exhibited discharge suppression during ingestion of a glucose solution were also suppressed during rewarding brain stimulation of the median forebrain bundle (MFB), caudal to the LHA (Sasaki et al 1984; Nakamura & Ono 1986). These results support the hypothesis that stimulation at some brain sites is rewarding because it mimics the effect of food on LHA neuronal discharge (Rolls et al 1980).

In summary, a large body of neurophysiological evidence, gathered in several species, demonstrates that neurons in the LHA exhibit altered discharge in relation to several important aspects of feeding behavior. Individual cells may alter discharge during visual discrimination of food objects, during appetitive behaviors to obtain access to food, during the tasting and ingestion of food, and may participate in the perception of the rewarding effects of food. Furthermore, motivational and cognitive variables known to exert powerful effects on feeding behavior also modulate LHA neuronal discharge. The correlations between LHA unit discharge and feeding behavior provide compelling evidence of a role for these cells in the control of food intake.

The LHA, SI, and NBM are anatomically complex areas. In addition to being richly innervated by axons of the MFB, the area is now known to be the origin of the major cholinergic projection to the limbic system and cortex (Woolf et al 1983, 1984; Mesulam et al 1983; Saper 1984). Furthermore, ascending and descending noncholinergic projection systems also originate within the LHA/SI (Swanson et al 1984; Saper 1985; Saper et al 1986; Woolf et al 1986). One of the most intriguing problems for neuroscientists interested in hypothalamic function is understanding the functional correlates of these long-axoned projection systems. This type of analysis will require identification of the projection sites of recorded cells by antidromic activation. With few exceptions (e.g. Nakamura & Ono 1986), the elegant behavioral characterizations of food-responsive LHA neurons have not been accompanied by attempts to determine neural connectivity. We hope that this will be a focus of future research. Are food-responsive neurons primarily projection or interneurons? Do they have primarily ascending or descending projections? Do cells responsive to the sight of food have different patterns of connectivity from those responsive to the taste of food? Do cells in a particular projection pathway behave similarly in rats, monkeys, sheep, and other species? Answers to questions such as these should further our understanding of how internal stimuli, external stimuli, motivational state, and cognitive factors related to feeding are integrated in the hypothalamus, and how changes in LHA unit discharge are translated into behavioral action.

HYPOTHALAMIC AND BASAL FOREBRAIN SLEEP-WAKING NEURONAL DISCHARGE

The hypothalamus and surrounding basal forebrain (BF) have been prominently implicated in the control of sleep. In rats, transections through the posterior hypothalamus resulted in somnolence, whereas total, or near-total sleeplessness followed transections placed through the preoptic/anterior hypothalamic area (POAH; Nauta 1946). High- or low-frequency electrical stimulation of the BF, including the horizontal limb of the diagonal bands of Broca (DBB) and the lateral preoptic/substantia innominata (LPO/SI), can evoke cortical synchrony and sleep in cats (Sterman & Clemente, 1962a,b). Activation of medial POAH warm receptors by local warming (Roberts & Robinson 1969; Parmeggiani et al 1983, 1986) or via chemical stimulation (Benedek et al 1982) has sleep-promoting effects. Electrolytic lesions of the medial (McGinty & Sterman 1968) or the lateral POAH (Lucas & Sterman 1975) in cats, and of the medial POAH in rats (Szymusiak & Satinoff 1984), leads to persistent decreases in the amount of slow-wave sleep (SWS). Kainic acid lesions placed in the DBB and the LPO/SI in cats were followed by persistent hyposomnolence, with deep SWS undergoing the largest reductions (Szymusiak & McGinty 1986b). In rats with POAH damage, a portion of the sleep disturbance, particularly of the REM sleep disturbance, is secondary to abnormalities in body temperature regulation (Szymusiak & Satinoff 1984). While the above evidence strongly suggests that an active sleep-promoting mechanism is, at least partially, localizable to the POAH and BF, is there any neurophysiological evidence that identifiable cell types within this region participate in sleep onset and maintenance processes?

Before reviewing the literature on hypothalamic and BF neuronal discharge during sleep, let us consider what unit discharge characteristics putative sleep-promoting neurons might possess. Many cells in many brain areas undergo changes in spontaneous discharge rate or in spike-train characteristics during transitions from waking to sleep (Steriade & Hobson 1976; Paisley & Summerlee 1984). In addition, many sensory and motor functions are altered during sleep, and changes in spontaneous discharge rate may be secondary to such state-related changes. Therefore, alterations in spontaneous discharge rate alone can never provide definitive evidence of a cell's role in state control. However, in a region where a variety of experimental techniques have indicated an involvement in state control (such as the POAH and BF), analysis of single-unit discharge is the only neurobiological technique with sufficient resolution to evaluate the possible contribution of specific cell types to these state-controlling functions. Obviously the discharge of putative sleep-promoting cells should be highly correlated with the change from a waking to a sleeping state (Steriade & Hobson 1976); the more selective the discharge for sleep, the potentially more important its contribution. In addition, changes in discharge should anticipate changes in state (Steriade & Hobson 1976). In practice, cells with a variety of sleep-wake discharge profiles, and with varying degrees of state-selectivity, will be encountered on a given microelectrode pass. Therefore, it is preferable to be able to identify cells on the basis of characteristics other than discharge rate.

Findlay & Hayward (1969) first examined unit discharge during sleep and waking in several hypothalamic areas, including the POAH, of un-anesthetized and unrestrained rabbits. They found that the discharge of hypothalamic neurons was heterogeneous with respect to state. Out of a total of 144 cells studied during SWS and compared to waking, 39% decreased mean firing rate, 21% increased mean firing rate, and the discharge rates of 40% were not significantly altered. Of the cells examined during waking, SWS, and REM sleep, 78% had highest rates in REM sleep. There was no obvious anatomical segregation of the different cell types within the hypothalamus, and the cells were not otherwise identified. Parmeggiani & Franzini (1973) recorded unit discharge in unrestrained cats from a variety of diencephalic and mesencephalic sites. For most hypothalamic (including POAH, dorsal hypothalamic area, and LHA) units recorded, there was little difference in discharge rate during quiet waking and SWS. In contrast to the results of Findlay & Hayward (1969), most cells exhibited significant decreases during REM sleep compared to SWS. In head-restrained cats, the majority (84%) of cells recorded in the POA had higher discharge rates during SWS or REM sleep than during waking (Kaitin 1984). In addition, 19% of the recorded cells exhibited a bursting pattern of discharge during SWS but not during waking and REM. The SWS discharge rate of these bursting cells was, on the average, 35% above rates during waking. It was hypothesized that these SWS-bursting cells are hypnogenic neurons (Kaitin 1984). The discharge of these cells during transitions from waking to sleep was not described. In cats with C1–C2-level spinal transections (so-called *encéephale isolé* cats, which remain capable of exhibiting alternating synchronized and desynchronized EEG), 62.5% of the cells recorded in the preoptic area had higher discharge rates during periods of EEG synchrony than during period of EEG desynchrony (Mallick et al 1983). In *encéphale isolé* cats, high-frequency stimulation of the midbrain reticular formation that produced EEG activation also suppressed POAH unit discharge (Mallick et al 1986). In freely moving kangaroo rats, approximately 25% of cells recorded in the POA had higher spontaneous discharge rates in SWS than in waking (Glotzbach & Heller 1984).

Although there is disagreement about the REM sleep discharge of hypothalamic cells, there is some consensus that a significant proportion of POAH neurons have elevated discharge rates during SWS compared to waking. Unfortunately, the behavior of these cells during transition states has not been well described. Also, no other characterization of POAH sleep-related cells has been attempted either in terms of projection patterns or by examination of other behavioral correlates. The discharge of one functionally identified cell type, POAH temperature-sensitive neurons, is not highly correlated with transitions from waking to SWS (Parmeggiani et al 1983, 1986; Glotzbach & Heller 1984).

Few studies have examined the sleep-waking discharge of neurons in the areas lateral to the midline hypothalamus that have been implicated in the control of sleep by stimulation and lesion studies. These areas include the olfactory tubercle (OT), DBB, LPO, and SI. Detari et al (1984) recorded neurons in the OT and LPO of freely moving cats with the microwire technique employing somewhat larger diameter wire (75 μ). They found that waking and SWS discharge rates were similar in most cells, and that rates increased in REM sleep. These authors found no evidence for SWS-selective discharge within the BF. In contrast, Szymusiak & McGinty (1986a) did locate neurons with SWS-related discharge throughout the ventrolateral BF in cats. Using chronically implanted microwires for unit recordings in freely moving animals, we found 24% of the recorded cells had extremely low discharge rates (average of <1 spike/sec) during epochs of alert wakefulness and exhibited maximal discharge rates during deep SWS (average of >9 spikes/sec). These cells were labeled sleep-active neurons (SANs). The discharge of SANs anticipated transitions from waking to sleep; SANs discharge increased 1–5 sec prior to the initial signs of EEG synchrony, and rates during the transitional state between waking and deep SWS (light SWS or drowsiness) were significantly higher than waking rates. Discharge of SANs in REM sleep was lower than SWS rates, although cell discharge did not anticipate transitions from SWS to REM. The remaining 76% of cells were classified as either waking-active (waking rates ⩾2 times SWS rates), or state-indifferent (waking rates <2 times SWS rates). In the latter cell types as in SANs, REM sleep rates were similar to waking rates. SANs were recorded throughout the ventrolateral BF, in the horizontal limb of the DBB, the LPO/SI, and more caudally in the ventral globus pallidus (VGP), dorsal to the medial nucleus of the amygdala.

The distribution of SANs corresponded to sites of origin of BF long-axoned projection systems (see previous section). A subsequent experiment attempted to determine if SANs project to distant targets (Szymusiak & McGinty 1987). Cats were prepared for chronic unit recordings of the LPO/SI and VGP, and with stimulating electrodes in the midbrain reticular formation, external capsule, and anterior cingulate bundle; the latter two structures are known to contain axons of ascending BF efferents (Saper 1984, 1985). Of 128 recorded cells, 59 were antidromically driven from one of the three sites; all but two antidromic responses were recorded in the VGP. The sleep-wake discharge profiles of driven cells was highly correlated with antidromic latency (ADL). Cells with ADLs <5 msec were of the waking-active or state-indifferent type. Cells with latencies >5 msec had extremely low discharge rates during waking. Many long-ADL cells were silent during extended epochs of exploratory locomotion or other spontaneous behaviors. Cells were not responsive to startle stimuli, or to the site and ingestion of palatable foods. Approximately 25% of long-ADL neurons had elevated discharge rates during grooming, compared to other waking behaviors. Mean peak discharge rates occurred during SWS. However, several long-ADL neurons had peak rates <1 spike/sec, and average SWS rates were lower than in the previous population of unidentified SANs (Szymusiak & McGinty 1986a).

In summary, neurons in the ventrolateral BF have a discharge pattern consistent with a role in the sleep onset process. A population of SANs located in the VGP is the source of both ascending and descending projections. Thus, this cell type could potentially modulate activity in a variety of brainstem, limbic system, and neocortical sites during the transitions from waking to sleep. In addition, these cells are uniquely characterized by their antidromic latency, a fact that could be exploited in acute neurophysiological experiments. The connectivity of SANs in other BF subregions (e.g. POAH, DBB, and LPO/SI) and their relationship to cells of the VGP remain unknown.

HIPPOCAMPUS

Among the most fascinating cell types recognized in the behaving animal are hippocampal "place" cells. These neuronal types, first identified by O'Keefe & Dostrovsky (1971), exhibit increased discharge when an animal is located in a restricted part of the physical space confining the animal for the purposes of study (Ranck 1973; O'Keefe 1976; Olton et al 1978a; O'Keefe & Conway 1978; Best & Ranck 1982; McNaughton et al 1983). This physical space associated with increased discharge, called the "place field," may encompass a small part of a T-maze or the tip of one arm of an 8-arm radial maze, or it may include a somewhat larger area. For the rat, which has been the subject of virtually all experiments, the following tentative conclusions have been reached in a variety of follow-up studies (a detailed review may be found in O'Keefe 1979).

Place-specific discharge is a response to field cues—that is, stimuli that indicate the animal's position in the room as a whole. For example, place fields in a T-maze persist in the initial position of an arm after rotation of the maze, rather than follow the particular arm of initial discharge (O'Keefe & Conway 1978). Thus, local odors or textures are not critical to place-cell discharge. Similarly, specific motor behaviors in a particular location in the apparatus do not underlie this phenomenon, nor does the motivational state of the animal (Hill 1978; Olton et al 1978a). Further, most place cells retain their specificity when room orientation cues are removed individually; all such cues must be removed before the majority of cells are "disoriented" (O'Keefe & Conway 1978). Further, place-cell behavior does not depend on any particular sensory modality (Hill 1978; Hill & Best 1981). Thus, place-specific discharge is not a specific sensory or motor response, but a more integrated, multimodal response suggestive of a integrative function.

Place-cell behavior is found in virtually all hippocampal unit recordings exhibiting occasional complex spikes—i.e. bursts of 2–7 spikes at high frequency, usually with declining spike amplitude. This identifying cell signature has allowed different investigators to study the same cell type. Complex spike cells probably constitute a majority of hippocampal cells, and include primarily or exclusively pyramidal cells (Fox & Ranck 1975, 1981). So-called θ cells, which increase discharge during locomotion, rearing, and other nonstereotyped behaviors (behaviors associated with hippocampal EEG θ rhythm), do not exhibit place fields. Place cells are found in the fascia dentata and in the CA1 and CA3 fields. CA1 place fields appear to have more dependence on the animal's direction of movement (as well as position), at least as shown on the 8-arm radial maze (McNaughton et al 1983). While less directional overall, CA3 cells usually had a "preference" for an inward movement on the radial maze. These data do not fit easily into a concept that place fields become more specific as one proceeds along the sequential hippocampal processing path from dentate to CA3 to CA1, but much more data is needed.

Most complex spike cells encountered in recording experiments exhibit place fields in a given test apparatus. Place-cell behavior is seen on the first exposure of animals to an apparatus (Hill 1978). Thus, this phenomenon does not seem to depend on learning. The same cell may exhibit place fields in two different pieces of apparatus in the same room, but the two fields do not have the same relative position (O'Keefe & Conway 1978). That is, a cell may encode the north arm of a radial maze and the west part of another surface. The place fields of adjacent cells within the hippocampus appear to have no obvious relationship. Thus, if place fields are encoding spatial position, the structure of this coding does not follow the most reasonable geometric hypotheses.

Complex spike-cell discharge is also increased substantially during SWS, a possible reflection of disinhibition (Ranck 1973). The principal excitatory input to the hippocampus from the entorhinal cortex appears to be enhanced during SWS (Winson & Abzug 1977) and, as noted above, the inhibitory input (Segal & Bloom 1974) from NE-containing neurons is reduced. These state-related changes in afferent input could explain enhanced CS spike-cell discharge in SWS. An interesting finding is that, in some cases, the elimination of spatial cues increased the discharge of place cells throughout the maze (O'Keefe & Conway 1978). Thus, it would appear that spatial localization of discharge may depend on inhibition related to "nonpreferred" positions.

The discovery of cells with place fields within the hippocampus is consistent with results of lesion studies showing that this structure is required for spatial discrimination learning (Maut 1972; O'Keefe et al 1975; Olton et al

1978b). The loss of spatial orientation in Alzheimer's Disease patients, who exhibit extensive loss of hippocampal and entorhinal cortical neurons (Hyman et al 1984), can also be understood through these findings.

However, recent results dispute the hypothesis that hippocampal CS cells code only spatial representation (Wible et al 1986). Hippocampal lesions produce severe deficits in tasks requiring "working memory"—that is, use of cues in a recent temporal context. Tasks such as delayed alternation or delayed match-to-sample require working memory. In rats trained to perform such tasks a majority of cells exhibited increased discharge in relation to specific relevant "mnemonic" cues, sometimes in combination with spatial location. Spatial location alone was a significant predictor of elevated unit discharge for only a minority of cells (Wible et al 1986). Studies in monkeys performing delayed matching responses found that hippocampal unit discharge was related to cues pertinent to task performance (Watanabe & Niki 1985). About 10% of recorded cells exhibited discharge potentially related to memory functions, including differential cue responses or differential delay spanning. Other possible aspects of neuronal coding were not readily tested in these chaired, head-restrained monkeys. However, it appears that both memory and spatial functions may be understood in terms of hippocampal unit discharge. It may be possible to predict behavioral performance on the basis of information from unit discharge studies; this would provide a strong test of hypotheses concerning the role of spatial or cue-related coding by hippocampal neurons.

AMYGDALA AND INFERIOR TEMPORAL LOBE CORTEX

The existence of a subset of amygdala neurons responding to specific complex stimuli has been known for some time (Sawa & Delgado 1963; O'Keefe & Bouma 1969, Jacobs & McGinty 1972). In unrestrained cats, otherwise very slowly discharging neurons exhibited bursts of discharge in response to unique stimuli such as a "meow" sound, the smell of smoke, or the sound of the lab door opening (O'Keefe & Bouma 1969; Jacobs & McGinty 1972). These cells did not respond strongly to other stimuli, although arousing stimuli could reduce their discharge.

Recently, cells with specific responses have been studied in the amygdala and nearby inferior temporal lobe (ITL) cortex in the unanesthetized rhesus monkey. Of particular interest is a subset of cells (3–10% of encountered cells) responding selectively to "faces" (Rolls et al 1977; Sanghera et al 1979; Perrett et al 1982; Leonard et al 1985). Face-responsive cells were also found in anesthetized animals (Bruce et al 1981; Desimone et al 1984). These cells did not respond to a wide variety of other stimuli (up to 1000 objects tested), but increased their discharge rate more than 5-fold, on average, to faces presented as photos, on video, or real faces. Some face cells respond to a variety of faces, but many amygdala and ITL face cells responded most strongly to a particular familiar face, that is, an identity (Leonard et al 1985; Perrett et al 1984; Baylis et al 1985). When the elements of the faces were tested to determine the critical stimuli needed for "face" recognition, the eyes or mouth were often sufficient to elicit a response. A three-dimensional stimulus (real face) usually provided the strongest response. Face cells show relatively stable responses with changes in stimulus distance—that is, the size of the retinal image (Rolls & Baylis 1986). This is a quality expected of cells coding a complex perception. Systematic attempts to progressively distort the stimulus (high- or low-pass filtering, rotation, contrast reversal, etc) generally caused a loss of response at about the same level of distortion that causes human subjects to fail to recognize a face, under the same conditions. Interestingly, changes in facial expression to simulate emotion (threat, for example) did not usually modify cellular responses. In cortex, cells responding maximally to particular views of the head were grouped in columns (Perrett et al 1984). Thus, the columnar organization that characterizes other cortical regions may apply to ITC.

In the amygdala, 75% of encountered neurons were unresponsive to all stimuli presented (Jacobs & McGinty 1972; Sanghera et al 1979). Possibly, the experimenter does not have available for presentation many of the stimuli relevant to an animal. The anatomical connections of face cells or other cells responding to complex stimuli have not been established.

These studies provide an explanation for the "psychic blindness" following temporal or amygdala lesions (Kluver-Bucy syndrome). The social deficits of monkeys with such lesions can be most readily explained by failure to recognize socially significant facial expressions—e.g. threat, kinship, or position in dominance hierarchy. Indeed, some humans with temporal lobe damage have a specific deficit in face recognition—prosopagnosia (Damasio et al 1982).

SUMMARY

1. We have reviewed studies based on neuronal unit recording in unanesthetized animals in selected sites historically thought to be implicated in control of arousal and drive-related behaviors: the reticular formation, monoaminergic neurons, hypothalamus and adjacent basal forebrain, amygdala, and hippocampus. Neurons in these sites that regulate arousal or drive states should exhibit changes in discharge temporally coincident with the behaviors they are thought to control. Relatively simple methods for studying neuronal unit discharge in unanesthetized animals are available; these method lie within the tech-

nical and economic reach of most investigations and allow the measurement of unit discharge within sophisticated behavioral paradigms.

2. Studies that limit the possible outcomes by restricting data collection to the confines of a particular paradigm are subject to critical errors. If neurons exhibit discharge correlated with movement, significant temporally patterned discharge correlations will emerge in a variety of behavioral tests, but these do not show a specific role for the neuron in the behavior. Examples of this were found in the study of the pontine and medullary reticular formation. However, movement-related discharge is found throughout the brainstem and limbic system. An open-ended experiment can be used initially to explore the significant discharge-behavior correlations within a site. Sometimes results unexpected on the basis of theory will emerge.

3. All brainstem and limbic sites contain a variety of neuronal types. Progress in understanding is greatly increased when neuronal types can be identified, so that successive investigations provide the accumulation of a fund of information about a homgeneous group of cells. The study of identified neurons typically makes it possible to integrate anatomical, biochemical, and electrophysiological data with behavioral information. An example of important progress is found in the review of the behavior of serotonin-containing neurons, which have usually been identified. Progress has been slower in analysis of hypothalamic neurons, since most studies have dealt simply with encountered, but unidentified, neurons. A variety of methods can be used to identify homogeneous neuronal groups. In some cases a combination of histological and acute electrophysiological studies provides the documentation for neuronal classification in terms of spike-train patterns. Slow, regular discharge patterns are used to identify monoaminergic neurons; the occurrence of a complex spike identifies hippocampal pyramidal cells. Neurons can also be identified by antidromic or orthodromic responses produced by stimulation of remote sites. Other possibilities include the profile of discharge rate or pattern changes occurring during the waking-SWS-REM cycle, or the correlation between discharge rate and behaviors, including movements. Application of such methods is of vital importance in future studies of hypothalamic neurons.

4. Anesthetic-induced modifications in behavior of serotonin-containing neurons are well documented. Effects of anesthesia in other neuronal groups have been studied less. Anesthetic-induced distortions of neuronal responsiveness are recognized in identified neurons, for only in this case can differences between results in anesthetized and unanesthetized preparations be recognized.

5. The following tentative conclusions describe the state of knowledge of brainstem and limbic neurons. The pontine and medullary medial reticu-

lar core appears to be a primarily descending organized motor system, potentially utilized in any motor behavior. This system probably integrates complex but instinctive motor patterns: quadrupedal locomotion, head-on-neck reflexes, oculomotor reflexes, startle and orienting responses, etc. The degree of plasticity within this system is unknown. The ascending serotoninergic, noradrenergic, and dopaminergic neurons exhibit many similarities, including slow, regular discharge that shows surprisingly little response in behavioral situations. Slightly increased discharge during aroused states is noted, but this increase is nonspecific—i.e. there is no evidence that any specific behavior is coded by these neuronal types. These systems are thought to play nonspecific roles in maintaining "neurophysiological" integrity during waking and in adaptations to arousal or physiological challenge. This interpretation is consistent with the fact that virtually every type of behavior is disturbed when these systems are altered, and with the observation that lesion effects may be reversed with tissue explants.

At the headwaters of the limbic system, in the hippocampus, inferior temporal cortex, and amygdala, many neurons appear to be coded for very specific "cognitive" elements, including "perceptual" elements such as specific complex stimuli, faces or sounds, mnemonic cues, or spatial locations. These findings fit well with the known effects of lesions in these structures.

Within the basal forebrain, one system of partially identified projection neurons may mediate the SWS-regulatory functions of this region, in agreement with lesion and stimulation experiments. In the lateral hypothalamic area, many neurons exhibit responses consistent with a role in control of feeding, but these cells are unidentified, and discrepant results in different species are unexplained. Movement-related discharge, observed by some investigators, is ignored by others. However, some cells are responsive to variations in motivational state. Drive and movement-related behavioral functions may be integrated in these sites.

In spite of the awesome complexity of the mammalian brain, studies of neuronal discharge in behaving animals have revealed some comprehensible insights into control of behavior and surprising consistencies with neuropathological findings.

Literature Cited

Aghajanian, G. K. 1981. Modulatory role of serotonin at multiple receptors in brain. In *Serotonin Neurotransmission and Behavior*, ed. B. L. Jacobs, A. Gelperin, pp. 156–83. Cambridge, Mass: MIT Press

Aghajanian, G. K., Cedarbaum, J. M., Wang, R. Y. 1977. Evidence for norepinephrine-mediated collateral inhibition of locus coeruleus neurons. *Brain Res.* 136:570–77

Agren, H., Koulu, M., Saavedra, J. M., Potter, W. Z., Linnoila, M. 1986. Circadian covariation of norepinephrine and serotonin in the locus coeruleus and dorsal raphe nucleus in the rat. *Brain Res.* 397:353–58

Amaral, D. G., Sinnamon, H. M. 1977. The locus coeruleus: neurobiology of a central noradrenergic nucleus. *Prog. Neurobiol.* 9:147–96

Anand, B. K., Chhina, G. S., Sharma, K. N.,

Dua, S., Singh, B. 1964. Activity of single neurons in the hypothalamic feeding centers: effect of glucose. *Am. J. Physiol.* 207:1146–54

Anand, B. K., Pillai, R. V. 1967. Activity of single neurons in the hypothalamic feeding centers: effect of gastric distension. *J. Physiol.* 192:63–77

Anlezark, G. M., Crow, T. J., Greenway, A. P. 1973. Impaired learning and decreased cortical norepinephrine after bilateral locus coeruleus lesions. *Science* 181:682–84

Aston-Jones, G., Bloom, F. E. 1981a. Activity of norepinephrine-containing locus coeruleus neurons in behaving rats anticipates fluctuations in the sleep-waking cycle. *J. Neurosci.* 1:876–86

Aston-Jones, G., Bloom, F. E. 1981b. Norepinephrine-containing locus coeruleus neurons in behaving rats exhibit pronounced responses to non-noxious environmental stimuli. *J. Neurosci.* 1:887–900

Aston-Jones, G., Foote, S. L., Bloom, F. E. 1984. Anatomy and physiology of locus coeruleus neurons: functional implications. In *Norepinephrine,* ed. M. G. Ziegler, C. R. Lake, pp. 92–116. Baltimore: William & Wilkins

Barone, F. C., Wayner, M. J., Weiss, C. S., Almli, C. R. 1979. Effects of intragastric water infusion and gastric distension on hypothalamic neuronal activity. *Brain Res. Bull.* 4:267–82

Baumgarten, H. G., Lachenmayer, L. 1985. Anatomical features and physiological properties of central serotonin neurons. *Pharmacopsychiatry* 18:180–87

Baylis, G. C., Rolls, E. T., Leonard, C. M. 1985. Selectivity between faces in the responses of a population of neurons in the cortex in the superior temporal sulcus. *Brain Res.* 342:91–102

Benedek, G., Obal, F. Jr., Lelkes, Z., Obal, F. 1982. Thermal and chemical stimulations of the hypothalamic heat detectors: the effects on the EEG. *Acta Physiol. Acad. Sci. Hung.* 60:27–35

Beninger, R. J. 1983. The role of dopamine in locomotor activity and learning. *Brain Res. Rev.* 6:173–96

Best, P. J., Ranck, J. B. Jr. 1982. Reliability of the relationship between hippocampal unit activity and sensory-behavioral events in the rat. *Exp. Neurol.* 75:652–64

Breedlove, S. M., McGinty, D. J., Siegel, J. M. 1979. Operant conditioning of pontine gigantocellular units. *Brain Res. Bull.* 4: 663–67

Bruce, C. J., Desimone, R., Gross, C. G. 1981. Visual properties of neurons in a polysensory area in superior temporal sulcus of the macaque. *J. Neurophysiol.* 46:369–84

Bjorklund, A., Schmid, R. H., Stenevi, U. 1980. Functional reinnervation of the neostriatum in the adult rat by use of intraparenchymal grafting of dissociated cell suspensions from the substantia nigra. *Cell Tissue Res.* 212:39

Bunney, B. S., Aghajanian, G. K., Roth, R. H. 1973. Comparison of effects of L-dopa, amphetamine and apomorphine on firing rate of rat dopaminergic neurons. *Nature* 245:123–25

Burton, M. J., Rolls, E. T., Mora, F. 1976. Effects of hunger on the responses of neurons in the lateral hypothalamus to the sight and taste of food. *Exp. Neurol.* 51:668–77

Cespuglio, R., Faradji, H., Gomez, M. E., Jouvet, M. 1981. Single unit recordings in the nuclei raphe dorsalis and magnus during the sleep-waking cycle of semichronic prepared cats. *Neurosci. Lett.* 24:133–38

Chu, N. S., Bloom, F. E. 1974. Activity patterns of catecholamine-containing pontine neurons in the dorso-lateral tegmentum of unrestrained cats. *J. Neurobiol.* 5:527–44

Corner, M. A., Bour, H. L. 1984. Postnatal development of spontaneous neuronal discharges in the pontine reticular formation of freely-moving rats during sleep and wakefulness. *Exp. Brain Res.* 54:66–77

Dahlstrom, A., Fuxe, K. 1964. Evidence for the existence of monoamine-containing neurons in the central nervous system. I. Demonstration of monoamines in cell bodies of brainstem neurons. *Acta Physiol. Scand.* 62:3–55

Damasio, A. R., Damasio, H., van Hoesen, G. W. 1982. Prosopagnosia: anatomical basis and neurobehavioral mechanism. *Neurology* 32:331–41

DeLong, M. R. 1971. Activity of pallidal neurons during movement. *J. Neurophysiol.* 34:414–27

DeLong, M. R., Crutcher, M. D., Georgopoulos, A. P. 1983. Relations between movement and single cell discharge in the substantia nigra of the behaving monkey. *J. Neurosci.* 3:1599–1606

Descarriers, L., Beaudet, A., Watkins, K. C. 1975. Serotonin nerve terminals in adult rat neocortex. *Brain Res.* 100:563–88

Desimone, R., Albright, T. D., Gross, C. G., Bruce, C. 1984. Stimulus-selective properties of inferior temporal neurons in the macaque. *J. Neurosci.* 4:2051–62

Detari, L., Juhasz, G., Kukorelli, T. 1984. Firing properties of cat basal forebrain neurones during sleep-wakefulness cycle. *Electroencephalogr. Clin. Neurophysiol.* 58:362–68

Edwards, S. B. 1975. Autoradiographic studies of the projections of the midbrain reticular formation: descending projections of nucleus cuneiformis. *J. Comp. Neurol.* 161:341–58

Elam, M., Yao, T., Svensson, T. H., Thoren, P. 1984. Regulation of locus coeruleus neurons and splanchnic sympathetic nerves by cardiovascular afferents. *Brain Res.* 290:281–87

Findlay, A. R., Hayward, J. N. 1969. Spontaneous activity of single neurones in the hypothalamus of rabbits during sleep and waking. *J. Physiol.* 201:237–58

Foote, S. L., Aston-Jones, G., Bloom, F. E. 1980. Impulse activity of locus coeruleus neurons in awake rats and monkeys is a function of sensory stimulation and arousal. *Neurobiology* 77:3033–37

Fornal, C., Auerbach, S., Jacobs, B. L. 1985. Activity of serotonin-containing neurons in nucleus raphe magnus in freely moving cats. *Exp. Neurol.* 88:590–608

Fox, S. E., Ranck, J. B. Jr. 1975. Localization and anatomical identification of theta and complex spike cells in dorsal hippocampal formation of rats. *Exp. Neurol.* 49:299–313

Fox, S. E., Ranck, J. B. Jr. 1981. Electrophysiological characteristics of hippocampal complex-spike cells and theta cells. *Exp. Brain Res.* 41:399–410

Fuchs, A. F., Luschei, E. S. 1972. Unit activity in the brainstem related to eye movement: possible inputs to the motor nuclei. *Bibl. Ophthalmol.* 82:17–27

Garcia-Rill, E., Skinner, R. D., Fitzgerald, J. A. 1983. Activity in the mesencephalic locomotor region during locomotion. *Exp. Neurol.* 82:609–22

German, D. C., Fetz, E. E. 1976. Responses of primate locus coeruleus and subcoeruleus neurons to stimulation at reinforcing brain sites and to natural reinforcers. *Brain Res.* 109:497–514

Glotzbach, S. F., Heller, H. C. 1984. Changes in the thermal characteristics of hypothalamic neurons during sleep and wakefulness. *Brain Res.* 309:17–26

Grace, A. A., Bunney, B. S. 1980. Nigral dopamine neurons: intracellular recording and identification with L-dopa injection and histofluorescence. *Science* 210:654–56

Graham, A. W., Aghajanian, G. K. 1971. Effects of amphetamine on single cell activity in a catecholamine nucleus, the locus coeruleus. *Nature* 234:100–2

Graybriel, A. M. 1977. Direct and indirect preoculomotor pathways of the brainstem: an autoradiographic study of the pontine reticular formation in the cat. *J. Comp. Neurol.* 175:37–78

Grillner, S., Lund, S. 1968. The origin of a descending pathway with monosynaptic action on flexor motorneurons. *Acta Physiol. Scand.* 74:274–84

Grillner, S., Shik, M. L. 1973. On the descending control of the lumbosacral spinal cord from the 'mesencephalic locomotor region'. *Acta Physiol. Scand.* 87:320–33

Guyenet, P. G., Aghajanian, G. K. 1978. Antidromic identification of dopaminergic and other output neurons of the rat substantia nigra. *Brain Res.* 150:69–84

Hamburg, M. D. 1971. Hypothalamic unit activity and eating behavior. *Am. J. Physiol.* 220:980–85

Harper, R. M., McGinty, D. J. 1973. A technique for recording single neurons from unrestrained animals. In *Brain Unit Activity During Behavior*, ed. M. I. Phillips, pp. 80–104. Springfield, Ill: Thomas

Hernandez, L., Gottberg, E. 1980. Systemic insulin decreases lateral hypothalamic unit activity. *Physiol. Behav.* 25:981–84

Hery, F., Rover, E., Glowinski, J. 1972. Daily variations of central 5-HT metabolism in the rat brain. *Brain Res.* 43:445–65

Hetherington, A. W., Ranson, S. W. 1942. The spontaneous activity and food intake of rats with hypothalamic lesions. *Am. J. Physiol.* 136:609–17

Heym, J., Steinfels, G. F., Jacobs, B. L. 1982a. Activity of serotonin-containing neurons in the nucleus raphe pallidus of freely moving cats. *Brain Res.* 251:259–76

Heym, J., Steinfels, G. F., Jacobs, B. L. 1984. Chloral hydrate anesthesia alters the responsiveness on central serotonergic neurons in the cat. *Brain Res.* 291:63–72

Heym, J., Trulson, M. E., Jacobs, B. L. 1982b. Raphe unit activity in freely moving cats: effects of phasic auditory and visual stimuli. *Brain Res.* 232:29–39

Hill, A. J. 1978. First occurrence of hippocampal spatial firing in a new environment. *Exp. Neurol.* 62:282–97

Hill, A. J., Best, P. J. 1981. Effects of deafness and blindness on the spatial correlates of hippocampal unit activity in the rat. *Exp. Neurol.* 74:204–17

Hobson, J. A., McCarley, R. W., Wyzinski, P. W. 1975. Sleep cycle oscillation: reciprocal discharge by two brainstem neuronal groups. *Science* 189:55–58

Horn, A. S., Korf, J., Westerink, B. H. C. 1979. *The Neurobiology of Dopamine*. New York: Academic

Hyman, B. T., van Hoesen, G. W., Damasio, A. R., Barnes, C. L. 1984. Alzheimer's disease: cell-specific pathology isolates the hippocampal formation. *Science* 225:1168–70

Jacobs, B. L. 1985. Overview of the activity of brain monoaminergic neurons across the sleep-wake cycle. In *Sleep: Neurotransmitters and Neuromodulators*, ed. A. Wauquier, pp. 1–14. New York: Raven

Jacobs, B. L. 1986. Single unit activity of

locus coeruleus neurons in behaving animals. *Prog. Neurobiol.* 27:183–94

Jacobs, B. L., Gelperin, A. 1981. *Serotonin Neurotransmission and Behavior.* Cambridge, Mass: MIT Press

Jacobs, B. L., McGinty, D. J. 1972. Participation of the amygdala in complex stimulus recognition and behavioral inhibition: evidence from unit studies. *Brain Res.* 36:431–36

Jones, B. E. 1985. Neuroanatomical and neurochemical substrates of mechanisms underlying paradoxical sleep. In *Brain Mechanisms of Sleep,* ed. D. J. McGinty, R. Drucker-Colin, A. R. Morrison, P. L. Parmeggiani, pp. 139–56. New York: Raven

Kaitin, K. I. 1984. Preoptic area unit activity during sleep and wakefulness in the cat. *Exp. Neurol.* 83:347–57

Kendrick, K. M., Baldwin, B. A. 1986a. The activity of neurons in the lateral hypothalamus and zona incerta of the sheep responding to the sight approach of food is modified by learning and satiety and reflects food preference. *Brain Res.* 375:320–28

Kendrick, K. M., Baldwin, B. A. 1986b. Characterization of neuronal responses in the zona incerta of the subthalamic region of the sheep during ingestion of food and liquid. *Neurosci. Lett.* 63:237–42

Komisaruk, B. R., Olds, J. 1968. Neuronal correlates of behavior in freely moving rats. *Science* 161:810–12

Leonard, C. M., Rolls, E. T., Wilson, F. A. W., Baylis, G. C. 1985. Neurons in the amygdala of the monkey with responses selective for faces. *Behav. Brain Res.* 15:159–76

Lucas, E. A., Sterman, M. B. 1975. Effect of a forebrain lesion on the polycyclic sleep-wake cycle and sleep-wake patterns in the cat. *Exp. Neurol.* 46:368–88

Lydic, R., McCarley, R. W., Hobson, J. A. 1983. The time-course of dorsal raphe discharge, PGO waves, and muscle tone averaged across multiple sleep cycles. *Brain Res.* 274:365–70

Maddison, S., Baldwin, B. A. 1983. Diencephalic neuronal activity during acquisition and ingestion of food in sheep. *Brain Res.* 278:195–206

Maddison, S., Horrell, R. I. 1979. Hypothalamic unit responses to alimentary perfusions in the anesthetized rat. *Brain Res. Bull.* 4:259–66

Madrazo, I., Drucker-Colin, R., Diaz, V., Martinez-Mata, J., Jones, C., Becerril, J. J. 1987. Open microsurgical autocraft of adrenal medulla to the right caudate nucleus in two patients with intractable Parkinson's disease. *N. Engl. J. Med.* 316:831–34

Mallick, B. N., Chhina, G. S., Sundaram, K.

R., Singh, B., Kumar, V. M. 1983. Activity of preoptic neurons during synchronization and desynchronization. *Exp. Neurol.* 81:586–97

Mallick, B. N., Kumar, V. M., Chhina, G. S., Singh, B. 1986. Comparison of rostrocaudal brain stem influence on preoptic neurons and cortical EEG. *Brain Res. Bull.* 16:121–25

Marshall, J. F., Teitelbaum, P. 1974. Further analysis of sensory inattention following lateral hypothalamic damage in rats. *J. Comp. Physiol. Psychol.* 86:375–95

Maut, H. 1972. A selective spatial deficit in monkeys after transection of the fornix. *Neuropsychologia* 10:65–74

McCarley, R. W., Hobson, J. A. 1971. Single neuron activity in cat gigantocellular tegmental field: selectivity of discharge in desynchronized sleep. *Science* 174:1250–52

McGinty, D. J. 1973. Neurochemically defined neurons: behavioral correlates of unit activity of serotonin-containing neurons. In *Brain Unit Activity During Behavior,* ed. M. I. Phillips, pp. 244–67. Springfield, Ill: Thomas

McGinty, D. J., Drucker-Colin, R. 1982. Sleep mechanisms: biology and control of REM sleep. *Int. Rev. Neurobiol.* 23:391–436

McGinty, D. J., Harper, R. M. 1976. Dorsal raphe neurons: depression of firing during sleep in cats. *Brain Res.* 101:569–75

McGinty, D. J., Harper, R. M., Fairbanks, M. K. 1973. 5-HT-containing neurons: unit activity in behaving cats. In *Serotonin and Behavior,* ed. J. Barchas, E. Usdin, pp. 267–79. New York: Academic

McGinty, D. J., Harper, R. M., Fairbanks, M. K. 1974. Neuronal unit activity and the control of sleep states. In *Advances in Sleep Research,* ed. E. D. Weitzman, pp. 173–216. New York: Spectrum

McGinty, D. J., Sterman, M. B. 1968. Sleep suppression after basal forebrain lesions in the cat. *Science* 160:1253–55

McNaughton, B. L., Barnes, C. A., O'Keefe, J. 1983. The contributions of position, direction, and velocity to single unit activity in the hippocampus of freely-moving rats. *Exp. Brain Res.* 52:41–49

Mesulam, M.-M., Mufson, E. J., Levey, A. I., Wainer, B. H. 1983. Cholinergic innervation of cortex by the basal forebrain: cytochemistry and cortical connections of the septal area, diagonal band nuclei, nucleus basalis (substantia innominata), and hypothalamus in the rhesus monkey. *J. Comp. Neurol.* 214:170–97

Miller, J. D., Farber, J., Gatz, P., Roffwarg, H., German, D. C. 1983. Activity of mesencephalic dopamine and non-dopamine neurons across stages of sleep and waking in the rat. *Brain Res.* 273:133–41

Miller, J. D., Sanghera, M. K., German, D. C. 1981. Mesencephalic dopaminergic unit activity in the behaviorally conditioned rat. *Life Sci.* 29:1255–63

Mitchell, S. J., Richardson, R. T., Baker, F. H., DeLong, M. R. 1982. Electrophysiological and functional characteristics of neurons in the nucleus basalis of Meynert in macaque monkeys. *Soc. Neurosci. Abstr.* 8:212

Mora, F., Rolls, E. T., Burton, M. J. 1976. Modulation during learning of the responses of neurons in the lateral hypothalamus to the sight of food. *Exp. Neurol.* 53:508–19

Morilak, D. A., Fornal, C., Jacobs, B. L. 1986. Single unit activity of noradrenergic neurons in locus coeruleus and serotonergic neurons in the nucleus raphe dorsalis of freely moving cats in relation to the cardiac cycle. *Brain Res.* 399:262–70

Morrison, J. H., Grzanna, R., Molliver, M. E., Coyle, J. T. 1978. The distribution and orientation of noradrenergic fibers in neocortex of the rat: an immunofluorescence study. *J. Comp. Neurol.* 181:17–40

Moruzzi, G., Magoun, H. W. 1949. Brain stem reticular formation and activation of the EEG. *Electroencephalogr. Clin. Neurophysiol.* 1:455–73

Nakamura, K., Ono, T. 1986. Lateral hypothalamus neuron involvement in integration of natural and artificial rewards and cue signals. *J. Neurophysiol.* 55:163–81

Nauta, W. J. H. 1946. Hypothalamic regulation of sleep in rats: an experimental study. *J. Neurophysiol.* 9:285–316

Nishino, H., Ono, T., Fukuda, M., Sasaki, K., Muramoto, K. 1981. Single unit activity in monkey caudate nucleus during operant bar pressing feeding behavior. *Neurosci. Lett.* 21:105–10

Nyberg-Hansen, R. 1965. Sites and mode of termination of reticulo-spinal fibers in the cat: an experimental study with silver impregnation methods. *J. Comp. Neurol.* 124:71–100

O'Keefe, J. 1976. Place units in the hippocampus of the freely moving rat. *Exp. Neurol.* 51:78–109

O'Keefe, J. 1979. A review of the hippocampal place cells. *Prog. Neurobiol.* 13:419–39

O'Keefe, J., Bouma, H. 1969. Complex sensory properties of certain amygdala units in the freely moving cat. *Exp. Neurol.* 23:384–98

O'Keefe, J., Conway, D. H. 1978. Hippocampal place units in the freely moving rat: why they fire where they fire. *Exp. Brain Res.* 31:573–90

O'Keefe, J., Dostrovsky, J. 1971. The hippo-

campus as a spatial map. Preliminary evidence from unit activity in the freely-moving rat. *Brain Res.* 34:171–75

O'Keefe, J., Nadel, L., Keightly, S., Kill, D. 1975. Fornix lesions selectively abolish place learning in the rat. *Exp. Neurol.* 48:152–66

Olton, D. S., Branch, M., Best, P. K. 1978a. Spatial correlates of hippocampal unit activity. *Exp. Neurol.* 58:387–409

Olton, D. S., Walker, J. A., Gage, F. H. 1978b. Hippocampal connections and spatial discrimination. *Brain Res.* 139:295–308

Ono, T., Nishino, H., Fukuda, M., Sasaki, K. 1984. Monkey amygdala, lateral hypothalamus and prefrontal cortex roles in food discrimination, motivation to bar press, and ingestion reward. In *Modulation of Sensorimotor Activity During Alterations in Behavioral States*, ed. R. Bandler, pp. 251–68. New York: Liss

Ono, T., Nishino, H., Sasaki, K., Fukuda, M., Muramoto, K. 1981a. Monkey lateral hypothalamic neuron response to sight of food, and during bar press and ingestion. *Neurosci. Lett.* 21:99–104

Ono, T., Nishino, H., Sasaki, K., Fukuda, M., Muramoto, K. 1981b. Long-term lateral hypothalamic single unit analysis and feeding behavior in freely moving rats. *Neurosci. Lett.* 26:79–83

Oomura, Y. 1976. Significance of glucose, insulin and free fatty acid on the hypothalamic and satiety neurons. In *Hunger: Basic Mechanisms and Clinical Implications*, ed. D. Novin, W. Wrywicka, G. A. Bray, pp. 145–58. New York: Raven

Oomura, Y., Nakamuara, T., Sugimori, M., Yamada, Y. 1975. Effect of free fatty acid on rat lateral hypothalamic neurons. *Physiol. Behav.* 14:483–86

Oomura, Y., Ono, T., Ooyama, H., Wayner, M. J. 1969a. Glucose and osmosensitive neurons of the rat hypothalamus. *Nature* 222:77

Oomura, Y., Ooyama, H., Naka, F., Yamamoto, T., Ono, T., Kobayashi, N. 1969b. Some stochastical patterns of single unit discharges in the cat hypothalamus under chronic conditions. *Ann. NY Acad. Sci.* 157:666–89

Owman, C., Edvinsson, L. 1977. *Neurogenic Control of the Brain Circulation*. New York: Pergamon

Paisley, A. C., Summerlee, A. J. S. 1984. Relationships between behavioural states and activity of the cerebral cortex. *Prog. Neurobiol.* 22:155–84

Parmeggiani, P. L., Azzaroni, A., Cevolani, D., Ferrari, G. 1983. Responses of anterior hypothalamic-preoptic neurons to direct thermal stimulation during wakefulness and sleep. *Brain Res.* 269:382–85

Parmeggiani, P. L., Azzaroni, A., Cevolani, D., Ferrari, G. 1986. Polygraphic study of anterior hypothalamic-preoptic neuron thermosensitivity during sleep. *Electroencephalogr. Clin. Neurophysiol.* 63:289–95

Parmeggiani, P. L., Franzini, C. 1973. On the functional significance of subcortical single unit activity during sleep. *Electroencephalogr. Clin. Neurophysiol.* 34:495–508

Orlovskii, G. N. 1970. Work of the reticulospinal neurons during locomotion. *Biophysics* 15:761–71

Perrett, D. I., Rolls, E. T., Caan, W. 1982. Visual neurons responsive to faces in the monkey temporal cortex. *Exp. Brain Res.* 47:329–42

Perrett, D. I., Smith, P. A. J., Potter, D. D., Mistlin, A. J., Head, A. S., et al. 1984. Neurones responsive to faces in the temporal cortex: studies of functional organization, sensitivity to identity and relation to perception. *Hum. Neurobiol.* 3:197–208

Peterson, B. W., Maunz, R. A., Pitts, N. G., Mackel, R. G. 1975. Patterns of projection and branching of reticulospinal neurons. *Exp. Brain Res.* 23:333–51

Peterson, B. W., Pitts, N. G., Fukushima, K., Mackel, R. 1978. Reticulospinal excitation and inhibition of neck motoneurons. *Exp. Brain Res.* 32:471–89

Podvoll, E. M., Goodman, S. J. 1967. Averaged neural electrical activity and arousal. *Science* 155:223–25

Pragay, E. B., Mirsky, A. F., Ray, C. L., Turner, D. F., Mirsky, C. V. 1978. Neuronal activity in the brain stem reticular formation during performance of a 'go-no-go' visual attention task in the monkey. *Exp. Neurol.* 60:83–95

Ranck, J. B. Jr. 1973. Studies on single neurons in dorsal hippocampal formation and septum in unrestrained rats. Part 1. Behavioral correlates and firing repertoires. *Exp. Neurol.* 41:461–555

Rasmussen, K., Heym, J., Jacobs, B. L. 1984. Activity of serotonin-containing neurons in nucleus centralis superior of freely moving cats. *Exp. Neurol.* 83:302–17

Rasmussen, K., Jacobs, B. L. 1986. Single unit activity of locus coeruleus neurons in the freely moving cat. II. Conditioning and pharmacologic studies. *Brain Res.* 371:335–44

Rasmussen, K., Morilak, D. A., Jacobs, B. L. 1986. Single unit activity of locus coeruleus neurons in the freely moving cat. I. During naturalistic behaviors and in response to simple and complex stimuli. *Brain Res.* 371:324–34

Ray, C. L., Mirsky, A. F., Pragay, E. B. 1982. Functional analysis of attention-related unit activity in the reticular forma-

tion of the monkey. *Exp. Neurol.* 77:544–62

Redmond, D. E. Jr., Huang, Y. H. 1979. Current concepts. II. New evidence for a locus coeruleus-norepinephrine connection with anxiety. *Life Sci.* 25:2149–62

Reiner, P. B. 1985. Clonidine inhibits central noradrenergic neurons in unanesthetized cats. *Eur. J. Pharmacol.* 115:249–57

Reiner, P. B. 1986. Correlational analysis of central noradrenergic neuronal activity and sympathetic tone in behaving cats. *Brain Res.* 378:86–96

Richardson, R. T., DeLong, M. R. 1986. Nucleus basalis of Meynert neuronal activity during a delayed response task in monkey. *Brain Res.* 399:364–68

Richardson, R. T., Mitchell, S. J., Baker, F. H., DeLong, M. R. 1983. Activity of neurons in the macaque nucleus basalis of Meynert in a visuomotor tracking task. *Soc. Neurosci. Abstr.* 9:951

Roberts, W. W., Robinson, T. C. L. 1969. Relaxation and sleep induced by warming of the preoptic region and anterior hypothalamus in cats. *Exp. Neurol.* 25:282–94

Rolls, E. T., Baylis, G. C. 1986. Size and contrast have only small effects on the responses to faces of neurons in the cortex of the superior temporal sulcus of the monkey. *Exp. Brain Res.* 65:38–48

Rolls, E. T., Burton, M. J., Mora, F. 1976. Hypothalamic neuronal responses associated with the sight of food. *Brain Res.* 111:53–66

Rolls, E. T., Burton, M. J., Mora, F. 1980. Neurophysiological analysis of brain-stimulation reward in the monkey. *Brain Res.* 194:339–57

Rolls, E. T., Judge, S. J., Sanghera, M. K. 1977. Activity of neurons in the inferotemporal cortex of the alert monkey. *Brain Res.* 130:229–38

Rolls, E. T., Murzi, E., Yaxley, S., Thorpe, S. J., Simpson, S. J. 1986. Sensory-specific reduction in responsiveness of ventral forebrain neurons after feeding in the monkey. *Brain Res.* 368:79–86

Saito, H., Sakai, K., Jouvet, M. 1977. Discharge patterns of the nucleus parabrachialis lateralis neurons of the cat during sleep and waking. *Brain Res.* 134:59–72

Sakai, K. 1980. Some anatomical and physiological properties of ponto-mesencephalic tegmental neurons with special reference to the PGO waves and postural atonia during paradoxical sleep in the cat. In *The Reticular Formation Revisited*, ed. J. A. Hobson, M. A. Brazier, pp. 427–47. New York: Raven

Sakai, K. 1985. Anatomical and physiological basis of paradoxical sleep. In *Brain Mechanisms of Sleep*, ed. D. J. McGinty, R.

Drucker-Colin, A. R. Morrison, P. L. Parmeggiani, pp. 111–38. New York: Raven

Sanghera, M. K., Rolls, E. T., Roper-Hall, A. 1979. Visual responses of neurons in the dorsolateral amygdala of the alert monkey. *Exp. Neurol.* 63:610–26

Saper, C. B. 1984. Organization of cerebral cortical afferent systems in the rat: I. Magnocellular basal nucleus. *J. Comp. Neurol.* 222:313–42

Saper, C. B. 1985. Organization of cerebral cortical afferent systems in the rat. II. Hypothalamocortical projections. *J. Comp. Neurol.* 237:21–46

Saper, C. B., Akil, H., Watson, S. J. 1986. Lateral hypothalamic innervation of the cerebral cortex: immunoreactive staining for a peptide resembling but immunochemically distinct from pituitary/arcuate alpha-melanocyte stimulating hormone. *Brain Res. Bull.* 16:107–20

Sasaki, K., Ono, T., Muramoto, K., Nishino, H., Fukuda, M. 1984. The effects of feeding and rewarding brain stimulation on lateral hypothalamic unit activity in freely moving rats. *Brain Res.* 322:201–11

Sawa, M., Delgado, J. M. R. 1963. Amygdala unitary activity in the unrestrained cat. *Electroencephalogr. Clin. Neurophysiol.* 15:637–50

Scheibel, A. B. 1980. Anatomical and physiological substrates of arousal: a view from the bridge. In *The Reticular Formation Revisited: Specifying Function for a Nonspecific System*, ed. J. A. Hobson, M. A. B. Brazier, pp. 55–66. New York: Raven

Schildkraut, J. J. 1965. The catecholamine hypothesis of affective disorders: a review of supportive evidence. *Am. J. Psychiatry* 122:509–22

Segal, M., Bloom, F. E. 1974. The action of norepinephrine in the rat hippocampus. I. Iontophoretic studies. *Brain Res.* 72:79–97

Sheu, Y. S., Nelson, J. P., Bloom, F. E. 1974. Discharge patterns of cat raphe neurons during sleep and waking. *Brain Res.* 73:263–76

Shima, K., Hiroshi, N., Yamamoto, M. 1986. Firing properties of two types of nucleus raphe dorsalis neurons during the sleep-waking cycle and their responses to sensory stimuli. *Brain Res.* 399:317–26

Siegel, J. M. 1979. Behavioral functions of the reticular formation. *Brain Res. Rev.* 1:69–105

Siegel, J. M. 1985. Pontomedullary interactions in the generation of REM sleep. In *Brain Mechanisms of Sleep*, ed. D. J. McGinty, R. Drucker-Colin, A. R. Morrison, P. L. Parmeggiani, pp. 157–74. New York: Raven

Siegel, J. M., McGinty, D. J. 1977. Pontine

reticular formation neurons: relationship of discharge to motor activity. *Science* 196: 678–80

Siegel, J. M., Tomaszewski, K. S. 1983. Behavioral organization of reticular formation: studies in the unrestrained cat. I. Cells related to axial, limb, eye, and other movements. *J. Neurophysiol.* 50:696–716

Siegel, J. M., Tomaszewski, K. S., Wheeler, R. L. 1983. Behavioral organization of reticular formation: studies in the unrestrained cat: II. Cells related to facial movements. *J. Neurophysiol.* 50:717–23

Siegel, J. M., Wheeler, R. L., Breedlove, S. M., McGinty, D. J. 1980. Brainstem units related to movements of the pinna. *Brain Res.* 202:183–88

Siegel, J. M., Wheeler, R. L., McGinty, D. J. 1979. Activity of medullary reticular formation neurons in the unrestrained cat during waking and sleep. *Brain Res.* 179:49–60

Steinfels, G. F., Heym, J., Jacobs, B. L. 1981. Single unit activity of dopaminergic neurons in freely moving cats. *Life Sci.* 29:1435–42

Steinfels, G. F., Heym, J., Strecker, R. E., Jacobs, B. L. 1983a. Behavioral correlates of dopaminergic unit activity in freely moving cats. *Brain Res.* 258:217–28

Steinfels, G. F., Heym, J., Strecker, R. E., Jacobs, B. L. 1983b. Response of dopaminergic neurons in cat to auditory stimuli presented across the sleep-waking cycle. *Brain Res.* 277:150–54

Steinfels, G. F., Heym, J., Strecker, R. E., Jacobs, B. L. 1983c. Raphe unit activity in freely moving cats is altered by manipulations of central but not peripheral motor systems. *Brain Res.* 279:77–84

Steriade, M., Hobson, J. A. 1976. Neuronal activity during the sleep-waking cycle. *Prog. Neurobiol.* 6:155–376

Steriade, M., Oakson, G., Ropert, N. 1982. Firing rates and patterns of midbrain reticular neurons during steady and transitional states of the sleeping-waking cycle. *Exp. Brain Res.* 46:37–51

Steriade, M., Ropert, N., Kitsikis, A., Oakson, G. 1980. Ascending activating neuronal networks in midbrain reticular core and related rostral systems. In *The Reticular Formation Revisited*, ed. J. A. Hobson, M. A. B. Brazier, pp. 125–67. New York: Raven

Sterman, M. B., Clemente, C. D. 1962a. Forebrain inhibitory mechanisms: sleep patterns induced by basal forebrain stimulation. *Exp. Neurol.* 6:103–17

Sterman, M. B., Clemente, C. D. 1962b. Forebrain inhibitory mechanisms: cortical synchronization induced by basal forebrain stimulation. *Exp. Neurol.* 6:91–102

Strecker, R. E., Jacobs, B. L. 1985. Substantia nigra dopaminergic unit activity in behaving cats: effect of arousal on spontaneous discharge and sensory evoked activity. *Brain Res.* 361:339–50

Strecker, R. E., Steinfels, G. F., Jacobs, B. L. 1983. Dopaminergic unit activity in freely moving cats: lack of relationship to feeding, satiety, and glucose injections. *Brain Res.* 260:317–21

Stricker, E. M., Zigmond, M. J. 1976. Recovery of function after damage to central catecholamine-containing neurons: a neurochemical model of the lateral hypothalamic syndrome. In *Progress in Psychobiology and Physiological Psychology*, ed. J. M. Sprague, A. N. Epstein, pp. 121–89. New York: Academic

Svensson, T. H., Bunney, B. S., Aghajanian, G. K. 1975. Inhibition of both noradrenergic and serotonergic neurons in brain by the alpha-adrenergic agonist clonidine. *Brain Res.* 92:291–306

Swanson, L. W., Mogenson, G. J., Gerfen, C. R., Robinson, P. 1984. Evidence for a projection from the lateral preoptic area and substantia innominata to the mesencephalic locomotor region in the rat. *Brain Res.* 295:161–78

Szymusiak, R., McGinty, D. 1986a. Sleep-related neuronal discharge in the basal forebrain of cats. *Brain Res.* 370:82–92

Szymusiak, R., McGinty, D. 1986b. Sleep suppression following kainic acid–induced lesions of the basal forebrain. *Exp. Neurol.* 94:598–614

Szymusiak, R., McGinty, D. 1986c. Posterior lateral hypothalamic neurons: sleep-waking discharge, projection patterns, and evoked responses. *Soc. Neurosci. Abstr.* 12:159

Szymusiak, R., McGinty, D. 1987. Sleep-waking discharge of basal forebrain projection neurons in cats. *Sleep Res.* 16:33

Szymusiak, R., Satinoff, E. 1984. Ambient temperature-dependence of sleep disturbances produced by basal forebrain damage in rats. *Brain Res. Bull.* 12:295–305

Teitelbaum, P., Epstein, A. 1962. Recovery of feeding and drinking after lateral hypothalamic lesions. *Psychol. Rev.* 69:74–90

Trulson, M. E. 1984. Method for the identification of serotonin-containing neurons in single unit studies in freely moving cats. *J. Electrophysiol. Tech.* 11:205–14

Trulson, M. E. 1985a. Simultaneous recording of substantia nigra neurons and voltammetric release of dopamine in the caudate of behaving cats. *Brain Res. Bull.* 15:221–23

Trulson, M. E. 1985b. Simultaneous recording of dorsal raphe unit activity and seroto-

in release in the striatum using voltammetry in awake, behaving cats. *Life Sci.* 37:2199–2204

Trulson, M. E. 1985c. Activity of dopamine-containing substantia nigra neurons in freely moving cats. *Neurosci. Biobehav. Rev.* 9:283–97

Trulson, M. E. 1986. Dissociations between the effects of hallucinogens on behavior and raphe unit activity in behaving cats. *Pharmacol. Biochem. Behav.* 24:351–57

Trulson, M. E., Crisp, T., Trulson, V. M. 1983. Dopamine-containing substantia nigra units are unresponsive to changes in plasma glucose levels induced by dietary factors, glucose infusions or insulin administration in freely moving cats. *Life Sci.* 32:2555–64

Trulson, M. E., Jacobs, B. L. 1979a. Raphe unit activity in freely moving cats: correlation with level of behavioral arousal. *Brain Res.* 163:135–50

Trulson, M. E., Jacobs, B. L. 1979b. Effects of 5-methoxy-n,n-dimethyltryptamine on behavior and raphe unit activity in freely moving cats. *Eur. J. Pharmacol.* 54:43–50

Trulson, M. E., Jacobs, B. L. 1983. Raphe unit activity in freely moving cats: lack of diurnal variation. *Neurosci. Lett.* 36:285–90

Trulson, M. E., Jacobs, B. L., Morrison, A. R. 1981. Raphe unit activity during REM sleep in normal cats and in pontine lesioned cats displaying REM sleep without atonia. *Brain Res.* 226:75–91

Trulson, M. E., Preussler, D. W. 1984. Dopamine-containing ventral tegmental area neurons in freely moving cats: activity during the sleep-waking cycle and effects of stress. *Exp. Neurol.* 83:367–77

Trulson, M. E., Preussler, D. W., Howell, G. A. 1981. Activity of substantia nigra units across the sleep-waking cycle in freely moving cats. *Neurosci. Lett.* 26:183–88

Trulson, M. E., Preussler, D. W., Howell, G. A., Frederickson, C. J. 1982. Raphe unit activity in freely moving cats: effects of benzodiazepines. *Neuropharmacol.* 21:1045–50

Trulson, M. E., Trulson, V. M. 1982. Activity of nucleus raphe pallidus neurons across the sleep-waking cycle in freely moving cats. *Brain Res.* 237:232–37

Trulson, M. E., Trulson, V. M. 1983a. Chloral hydrate anesthesia blocks the excitatory responses of dorsal raphe neurons to phasic auditory and visual stimuli in cats. *Brain Res.* 265:129–33

Trulson, M. E., Trulson, V. M. 1983b. Chloral hydrate anesthesia alters the responsiveness of dorsal raphe neurons to psychoactive drugs. *Life Sci.* 32:949–56

Trulson, M. E., Trulson, V. M. 1985. Unit activity in the dorsal raphe in freely-moving cats. Effects of monomamine oxidase inhibitors. *Neuropharmacology* 24:473–78

Trulson, M. E., Trulson, V. M. 1986. Buspirone decreases the activity of serotonin-containing neurons in the dorsal raphe in freely-moving cats. *Neuropharmacology* 25:1263–66

Umemoto, M., Murai, Y., Kodama, M., Kido, R. 1970. Neuronal discharge patterns in conditioned emotional response. *Brain Res.* 24:347–51

Ungerstedt, U. 1971. Adipsia and aphagia after 6-hydroxydopamine induced degeneration of the nigro-striatal dopamine system. *Acta Physiol. Scand.* 82 (Suppl. 367):92–122

Vandermaelen, C. P., Aghajanian, G. K. 1983. Electrophysiological and pharmacological characterization of serotonergic dorsal raphe neurons recorded extracellularly in rat brain slices. *Brain Res.* 289:109–19

Vertes, R. P. 1977. Brainstem gigantocellular neurons: patterns of activity during behavior and sleep in the freely moving rat. *J. Neurophysiol.* 42:214–28

von Euler, C., Hayward, J. N., Marttila, I., Wyman, R. J. 1973. The spinal connections of the inspiratory neurons of the ventrolateral nucleus of the cat's tractus solitarius. *Brain Res.* 61:23–33

Watanabe, T., Niki, H. 1985. Hippocampal unit activity and delayed response in the monkey. *Brain Res.* 325:241–54

Wible, C. G., Findling, R. L., Shapiro, M., Lang, E. J., Crane, S., Olton, D. S. 1986. Mnemonic correlates of unit activity in the hippocampus. *Brain Res.* 399:97–110

Winson, J., Abzug, C. 1977. Gating of neuronal transmission in the hippocampus: efficacy of transmission varies with behavioral state. *Science* 196:1223–25

Wise, C. D., Stein, L. 1969. Facilitation of brain self-stimulation by central administration of norepinephrine. *Science* 163:299–301

Woolf, N. J., Eckenstein, F., Butcher, L. L. 1983. Cholinergic projections from the basal forebrain to the frontal cortex: a combined fluorescent tracer and immunohistochemical analysis in the rat. *Neurosci. Lett.* 40:93–98

Woolf, N. J., Eckenstein, F., Butcher, L. L. 1984. Cholinergic systems in the rat brain: I. Projections to the limbic telencephalon. *Brain Res. Bull.* 13:751–84

Woolf, N. J., Hernit, M. C., Butcher, L. L. 1986. Cholinergic and non-cholinergic projections from the rat basal forebrain revealed by combined choline acetyltransferase and phaseolus vulgaris leucoagglutinin immunohistochemistry. *Neurosci. Lett.* 66:281–86

Ann. Rev. Psychol. 1988. 39:169–200

PSYCHOPHYSICAL SCALING

George A. Gescheider

Psychology Department, Hamilton College, Clinton, New York 13323

CONTENTS

The fundamental problem in psychophysics, the measurement of sensation magnitude, is as old as psychophysics itself. It is now 138 years since Gustav Theodor Fechner, on October 22, 1850, had his insightful idea that arithmetic increases in sensation magnitude result from geometric increases in stimulus intensity. Fechner's proposed psychophysical function (Fechner 1860), soon to become known as Fechner's Law, was widely accepted for over 100 years, having tremendous impact on a number of fields, including engineering, neurophysiology, and psychology. Fechner's logarithmic law was strongly challenged in the 1950s when S. S. Stevens proposed a power function based on magnitude-estimation data, later to become known as Stevens' Power Law, as an alternative to Fechner's Law. Stevens' law has been said to be based on direct measurement of sensation magnitude, as compared to Fechner's Law, which was based on discriminability of stimuli—an indirect measure of sensation magnitude.

It is now clear that sensation magnitude, being an intervening variable, cannot be measured directly with any method. It must instead be inferred from observation of subjects' responses to stimuli presented in the psychophysical experiment (e.g. McKenna 1985). It has also become widely accepted in the past few years that the validity of such indirect measurements of sensation magnitude cannot be established independent of psychophysical theory. Instead, the validity of a psychophysical scale can be established only through examination of how well the psychophysical responses of subjects can be predicted from theories of sensory and cognitive processes. In this review, I attempt to establish some links between theory and the psychophysical responses of subjects that have bearing on the validity of psychophysical scales.

The last general review of psychophysical scaling was that of Cliff (1973), the reviews of Carroll & Arabie (1980) and Young (1984) being focused on multidimensional scaling and related methods. Because these topics have been thoroughly reviewed recently they are not treated here. I have elected to focus on scaling procedures that have enhanced our understanding of sensory and perceptual processes. In recent years, many of these methods have also been more broadly applied to problems ranging from clinical psychology (see Grossberg & Grant 1978) to social judgment (see Wegener 1982).

COMPONENTS OF THE SCALING EXPERIMENT

Before turning to experimental results as they relate to specific theories, let us examine how psychophysicists have come to view the basic components of the psychophysical scaling experiment. The psychophysical scaling task requires that the subject make sensory responses to stimuli. Generally, such responses can be divided into three types: (a) those that require the subject to make simple ordinal discrimination judgments of stimuli (e.g. Fechner 1860; Thurstone 1927), (b) those that require subjects to adjust stimuli to partition the sensory continuum into subjectively equal intervals (e.g. bisection or equisection), and (c) those that require subjects to assign numbers to stimuli that presumably represent sensation magnitude (e.g. magnitude estimation or category scaling) or to adjust stimuli to match numbers presented by the experimenter (magnitude production). With each of these methods, the unobservable sensation magnitude intervening between stimulus and response must be inferred from observations of subject's responses as they relate to properties of the stimulus and to psychophysical theory. Much recent work has consisted of attempts to analyze the psychophysical scaling task into its basic components with the aim of refining experimental procedures to enable valid inferences of sensation magnitude. Such analyses indicate that responses in the scaling task are a joint function of cognitive and sensory factors. A central theme of this review is the struggle of sensory and cognitive scientists to understand the complex interactions between these two classes of factors in psychophysical judgment.

MAGNITUDE ESTIMATION

Magnitude estimation is one of the most frequently used scaling methods in psychophysics. In a magnitude estimation experiment, the subject is required to make numerical estimations of the sensory magnitude produced by various stimuli. S. S. Stevens, whose name is most closely associated with this method, conducted early experiments using magnitude estimation to study brightness and loudness (S. S. Stevens 1953, 1955). He (1957) argued that the power function observed for the relationship between magnitude estimation and stimulus intensity was a direct measure of the relationship between sensation magnitude and stimulus intensity. The experimental finding that assigned numbers (N) were related to stimulus intensity (ϕ) by a power function has become a general law in psychology. It applies to dozens of sensory continua (see Gescheider 1985; Stevens 1975) and is expressed as

$$N = k \phi^a,$$

1.

where k is a constant determined by the absolute size of assigned numbers and a is the power exponent the value of which depends on the sensory modality and stimulus conditions (for statistical considerations see Coleman et al 1981; Elzinga 1985; Thomas 1981). Stevens (1956, 1957) contended that assigned numbers, N, were directly proportional to sensation magnitude (ψ) and that it was therefore permissible to substitute ψ for N and formulate a psychophysical law describing a power-function relationship between sensation magnitude and stimulus intensity:

$$\psi = k \phi^a.$$

2.

Several investigators (e.g. Attneave 1962; MacKay 1963; Treisman 1964) were later to argue that Stevens' contention about the validity of magnitude estimation data was based largely on faith rather than fact.

Components of the Magnitude Estimation Task

Recently, Shepard (1981) has argued that there are major limitations in the use of magnitude estimation and that Stevens' contention is logically flawed. The limitations of the method became apparent only when the investigator interprets the experimentally determined functional relationship (f_3) between stimulus (S) and response (R),

$$R = f_3 (S), \hspace{4cm} 3.$$

to be the *stimulus transformation function* describing the functional relationship (f_1) between the intervening variable, sensation magnitude (ψ), and the stimulus

$$\psi = f_1(S). \hspace{4cm} 4.$$

Shepard pointed out that this formulation is incomplete. He indicated that we must also consider a second transformation, the *response transformation function,* which determines the final response. This second transformation is the functional relationship (f_2) between the response and the intervening variable, ψ. The first transformation between the stimulus and sensation, $\psi = f_1 (S)$, being followed by the second transformation,

$$R = f_2(\psi), \hspace{4cm} 5.$$

results in the experimentally observed relationship, $R = f_3 (S)$, between stimulus and response.

As noted earlier by Treisman (1964), Shepard pointed out that, since the intervening variable, ψ, is not itself observable, the equation for R must be written as

$$R = f_3(S) = f_2[f_1(S)] \hspace{3cm} 6.$$

in which equation 4 does not explicitly appear.

Unless one of the two component functions of f_3 (i.e. f_1 or f_2) is known, it is impossible to determine the other by knowledge of the experimentally determined f_3. According to Shepard, the conclusion drawn by Stevens from magnitude estimation data, namely, that f_1 is a power function, depends on the assumption that instructions to the subject have ensured that f_2 is a linear function with zero intercept of the form

$$R = a\psi . \hspace{4cm} 7.$$

Shepard pointed out that the grounds for Stevens' assumption that instructions would have exactly this effect were never adequately explained. The general concept of a *two-stage model* of magnitude estimation in which the first stage is sensory and the second is cognitive has its origin in the work of Attneave (1962) and Curtis et al (1968) (see Rule & Curtis 1982 for a review).

In his criticism of Stevens, Shepard added that the subject's response in magnitude estimation is really only a discrete verbal response that itself possesses no definite quantitative magnitude. As noted by Shepard and others (Garner 1954; Graham 1958; Luce & Galanter 1963; McGill 1960; Oyamo 1968) it is questionable how legitimate it is to speak of ratios of and differences between such responses and to compute statistics such as geometric means when magnitude estimations are simply verbal responses with no inherent quantitative properties.

Shepard concluded his argument by saying that, although subjects are able to assign numbers consistently to stimuli, the results reveal only the form of the S into R transformation and not the form of the S into ψ transformation. He further points out that to be able to measure the intervening sensory magnitude from the observed $S\text{-}R$ relationship it is necessary to link this observation to acceptable psychophysical theory.

Establishing Validity

Advocates as well as critics of magnitude estimation have become aware of the inadequacy of merely assuming the validity of psychophysical data obtained by the method. Within the framework of Shepard's (1981) analysis, the validity of the method is reduced to considerations of the response transformation $R = f_2(\psi)$. Thus, one way to validate a set of judgments would be to establish a case for the linearity of the response transformation function. If this cannot be done, the judgments of the subject cannot be considered valid measures of sensation magnitude. A second way of obtaining a valid set of judgments would be to correct invalid judgments by using the nonlinear response transformations to convert responses into units of sensation magnitude. In this case the problem becomes one of experimentally determining the response transformation function. But how can this correction procedure be applied when this transformation, $R = f_2(\psi)$, involves the intervening variable sensation magnitude, ψ, which cannot be directly measured? As will be seen, the response transformation must be estimated from the responses of subjects as they relate to theory.

Evidence for the Validity of Magnitude Estimation Data

SENSATION MAGNITUDE MATCHING   A minimal requirement for the validity of a psychophysical scale is that stimuli having the same scale values should be judged to be subjectively equal when they are directly matched. Cross-modality matches, in which the subject adjusts the intensities of stimuli from different modalities to match their sensation magnitudes, have been successfully predicted from magnitude estimation scales [see Stevens (1975) for a review, and for more recent work on individual subjects see Collins & Gescheider (submitted for publication), Daning (1983), and Zwislocki et al (submitted for publication)]. A formal model of magnitude estimation and cross-modality matching is presented by Krantz (1972). Within-modality matches, in which the subject adjusts the intensities of qualitatively different stimuli (e.g. different frequencies of sound) so that their sensation magnitudes match, have also been successfully predicted from magnitude estimation scales (Gescheider & Joelson 1983; Hellman 1976; Hellman & Zwislocki 1964; Marks 1966; Verrillo et al 1969). Satisfying the requirement of consistency between magnitude estimation and direct matching does not guarantee scale validity since subjects could simply have been assigning numbers to sensations in a nonlinear but consistent way (i.e. when sensations are equal the same wrong number is assigned).

ADDITIVITY OF SCALE VALUES   Several experiments have supported the hypothesis that magnitude estimations are additive measures of sensation magnitude (e.g. Cain 1976; Dawson 1971; Hellman & Zwislocki 1963; Marks 1978a,b, 1979c, 1987; Marks & Bartoshuk 1979; Murphy et al 1977; Zwislocki 1983b). In these cases the average magnitude estimation of two stimuli presented together is equal to the sum of the average magnitude estimation of the stimuli presented alone. A strong case was also made for summation of loudness in simultaneous heterofrequency tone pairs (Marks 1979a) in which nonmetric conjoint measurement (Luce & Tukey 1964) was used. Research on binaural and binocular summation of sensation magnitude also has supported the additivity model of magnitude estimation. The results of Hellman & Zwislocki (1963) and Marks (1978a, 1987) are consistent with the hypothesis that total loudness is the linear sum of the loudness of the individual left-ear and right-ear components. Recently, Bolanowski (1987) found linear binocular summation in a uniform visual field (Ganzfeld).

Other evidence for additivity in magnitude estimation comes from studies of summation in which matching procedures were used to measure the amount of summation. In these studies subjects were required to match the subjective magnitude of a comparison stimulus to the overall subjective magnitude of a pair of equally intense stimuli. In the case of hearing, Zwislocki et al (1974) and Zwislocki & Sokolich (1974) found matches to the pair to be 10 dB higher than matches to the individual stimuli. The 10-dB difference corresponds to a doubling of magnitude estimation values on the loudness scale. In a similar vein, Verrillo & Gescheider (1975) found that matches to a pair of vibrotactile stimuli, each member of the pair being in different vibrotactile channels, was 6 dB higher than matches to individual members of the pair. In this case the

6-dB difference corresponds to a doubling of magnitude estimation on the vibratory subjective-magnitude scale.

Although these studies support the notion that additivity exists for average magnitude estimations for a group of subjects, it is less certain that additivity of magnitude estimations applies to the results of individual subjects. Zwislocki's (1983b) study is an example of how additivity of magnitude estimations may be found in the group data but not always in the data of individual subjects. In this study the subjects made judgments of the overall loudness of two brief tones with frequencies in different critical bands. Consistent with the hypotheses that loudness summates linearly in the nervous system and that subjects are capable of making valid judgments of loudness, magnitude estimations of the tone pair were equal to the sum of the magnitude estimations of the individual tones. Although additivity was evident in the average data for the group of subjects, it was absent in the data of some of the individual subjects.

In subjects where additivity is absent, either loudness summation in the nervous system is nonlinear, the response transformation function in which loudness is transformed to magnitude-estimation responses is nonlinear, or there exists some combination of the two nonlinear functions. If it is assumed that loudness summation is linear, it is possible to determine the nonlinear response transformations that were responsible for the lack of additivity of the magnitude estimations. The hypothesis that loudness summation is linear was supported by applying the rules of monotonicity and double cancellation of the conjoint measurement (Luce & Tukey 1964). Using this approach, Zwislocki (1983b) determined the response transformation functions of individual subjects and found them to be power functions with exponents ranging from .83 to 1.33 with a mean of 1.08. A power function with an exponent of 1.0 is a linear function. Thus, the average data indicate a nearly linear response transformation function, but analysis of the data of individuals indicates that some subjects deviated slightly from the ideal.

Zwislocki (1983b) also obtained data from his subjects on their magnitude estimations of line length. The average data in this experiment, as well as those of many earlier experiments (Teghtsoonian & Beckwith 1976, Verrillo 1981, Zwislocki & Goodman 1980), indicate that magnitude estimation of line length is proportional to actual line length (power function exponent = 1.0). Assuming that the sensory experience of line length is directly proportional to actual length, the exponent of 1.0 indicates that, on the average, the response transformation function is linear (power function with exponent of 1.0). It is particularly significant that, in Zwislocki's experiment, the results of individual subjects sometimes deviated from the ideal exponent of 1.0 for magnitude estimations of line length. This finding suggests that the response transformations of individual subjects for judging line length are sometimes nonlinear. Perhaps the most important finding in the study was the high correlation (r = .95) between the exponents for line length and the theoretical response transformation exponents calculated from the loudness summation data. Thus, similar estimates of the response transformation function from loudness and line-length estimations indicate that systematic errors in assigning numbers to sensation magnitudes carry over from one modality to another.

The finding of Zwislocki that it may be possible to estimate a generalized response transformation function from an individual subject's magnitude estimation of line length opens the possibility of using such estimations of the response transformation function to obtain unbiased estimations of the stimulus transformation function (the psychophysical law). The exponent of the stimulus transformation can be estimated by dividing the exponent for magnitude estimation of stimuli in a particular modality by the exponent for magnitude estimation of line length [see Zwislocki (1983b) for derivation].

Intersubject Variability

Collins & Gescheider (submitted for publication) used Zwislocki's correction procedure to correct the loudness exponents of individual subjects. In this study it was found that the intersubject variance of exponents for loudness was substantially reduced by dividing each individual loudness exponent by the line-length exponent of the same subject. The reduction in intersubject variability was interpreted as an indication that the correction procedure had removed a source of variability of loudness exponents attributable to differences in the response transformation functions of individual subjects.

Algom & Marks (1984), in their study of binaural summation and temporal summation, also attributed most of the individual differences in exponents to differences in the ways people assign numbers to sensation rather than to differences in sensory processes.

J. C. Stevens & Marks (1980), in pursuit of the goal of reducing and/or correcting for intersubject variability, developed a new method called *magnitude matching,* also referred to as mixed-modality psychophysical scaling (for a review see Bartoshuk & Marks 1986). In this method the subject, within the same experimental session, makes magnitude estimations of stimuli presented in an irregular order for two modalities. Based on the magnitude estimation data, a cross-modality matching function is plotted using pairs of stimuli from the two modalities that produce the same magnitude estimation values. This procedure, like the correction procedure described above, reduced intersubject variability. Magnitude matching has been used to normalize the judgments of individuals so that their absolute response values can be compared and differences interpreted as differences in sensory magnitude. In one of these studies the normalized magnitude estimations of odor intensity made by a group of young and a group of old subjects were compared (J. C. Stevens et al 1982), and in another the normalized magnitude estimations of patients with taste disorders were measured for comparison with normal subjects (Bartoshuk et al 1983). The method has also been used to assess the effects of aging on taste sensation (Bartoshuk et al 1986), and to evaluate individual differences in perceived exertion during dynamic work (Marks et al 1983).

Individual Differences

That response transformations tend to be unique characteristics of individual subjects is also supported by the finding of high correlations between exponents determined in separate experimental sessions for the same group of subjects (Collins & Gescheider, submitted for publication; Hellman 1981; Künnapas et al 1973; Logue 1976; Wanschura & Dawson 1974). The high correlation of line-length exponents across sessions reported by Collins & Gescheider (submitted for publication), however, are in disagreement with the results of Teghtsoonian & Teghtsoonian (1971), who reported little consistency of individual exponent values for line length and area over experimental sessions. The finding that individual differences in exponents are substantial and stable over sessions supports the hypothesis that subjects have individual ways of assigning numbers to sensations (response transformation) that tend to persist over time. Reports of high correlations between exponents obtained for different modalities (Collins & Gescheider, submitted for publication; Duda 1967, 1975; Ekman et al 1968; Künnapas et al 1973; Rule 1966) support the hypothesis that these unique response transformations tend to generalize across modalities. Because response transformations of individual subjects tend to be unique, identifiable, persistent over time, and to generalize across modalities, hope is now held out for the possibility of reducing or even eliminating the contaminating effects of nonlinear response transformation in attempts to measure sensory transformations through magnitude estimation.

The finding of Dawson & Waterman (1976) that the correlation of exponents across sessions was not influenced by number of repetitions within a session was interpreted as an indication that memory factors alone could not explain the reliability of individual exponents. Teghtsoonian & Teghtsoonian (1983) however, favor the view that persistence of patterns of individual differences over sessions is due to memory of specific responses made in the earlier session rather than to enduring modes of responding. Perhaps it is the case that both memory factors and enduring response patterns are involved in the high correlation of exponents across sessions and across modalities.

Models of Magnitude Estimation

In recent years, various models have been proposed to account for several characteristics of magnitude estimation data including sequential dependencies (for reviews see Luce et al 1980; Marley & Cook 1986). Some of these characteristics were recently summarized by Marley & Cook (1986):

1. Average magnitude estimations are approximately a power function of stimulus intensity.
2. Exponents are inversely proportional to the log of the dynamic range of the stimulus.
3. Standard deviation of the log response decreases with increases in log stimulus intensity.
4. The coefficient of variation (standard deviation divided by the mean) is a decreasing function of log stimulus intensity.
5. The coefficient of variation of the ratio of responses on successive trials as a function of stimulus separation is nearly constant except when successive stimuli are close, in which case it dips to a lower value than observed outside this region.
6. The correlations of successive log responses decreases as a function of the separation between successive stimuli.
7. Coefficients of variation and correlations between successive responses are affected by the range of stimuli presented in the experiment.

Models of magnitude estimation have met with varying degrees of success in accounting for these characteristics. The attention-band model (Baird et al 1980; Green et al 1977; Green et al 1980; Luce et al 1976; Luce et al 1980; Luce et al 1982) assumes a roving attention band within which stimuli are represented more accurately. The attention band tends to be centered on the previous stimulus and on end stimuli. This model accounts for both sequential effects and end effects in judgment. Ward developed a fuzzy-judgment model proposing category decisions and a guessing strategy that accounts for sequential effects. Petzold (1981) also accounts for sequential dependencies with a model in which a guessing strategy is influenced by the previous response. A criterion-setting model has been developed (Treisman & Faulkner 1984; Treisman & Williams 1984) that applies to a wide range of psychophysical paradigms including magnitude estimation, cross-modality matching (Treisman 1984), and absolute judgment (Treisman 1985). In this model, sequence effects are attributed to the operation of a Thurstonian-based criterion-setting process. A rehearsal model originally developed for absolute identification data (Marley & Cook 1984) has recently been applied to the loudness magnitude estimation data of Baird et al (1980) and of Green et al (1980) (Marley & Cook 1986). In this model, it is assumed that the subject must rehearse the psychological continuum in which the stimulus is presented. The subject's response is determined by the location of the stimulus perceived on the continuum relative to various possible anchors. The rehearsal model appears to be able to predict many of the results of magnitude

estimation experiments and seems also to be applicable to magnitude production. Marley & Cook (1986) suggest that the model may also account for
magnitude matching and cross-modality matching results. They noted,
however, that the rehearsal model may better account for sequential dependencies by incorporating ideas of Ward's fuzzy-judgment and Treisman's
criterion-change models. Marley & Cook also point out that their model, with
its roving range in which performance is facilitated by rehearsal, is similar to
the attention-band model in which performance is facilitated within a stimulus
range by attention, and is similar to the perceptual-anchor model of context
coding (Braida et al 1984).

ABSOLUTE MAGNITUDE ESTIMATION

Even if the response transformation function can be determined and the
subject's judgments corrected accordingly, other biasing factors such as those
produced by stimulus context, range, and sequential dependency effects may
make it difficult to infer measures of sensory magnitude from the subject's
responses. *Absolute magnitude estimation* is a method designed (Hellman &
Zwislocki 1961, 1963; Zwislocki 1978; Zwislocki & Goodman 1980) to
reduce or eliminate the effects of such biasing factors.

Psychophysical scales obtained by magnitude estimation were regarded by
Stevens and his associates to be ratio scales of sensation magnitude. According to this interpretation, scale values of sensation could be arbitrarily multiplied by a constant without violating the numerical significance of the scale
(e.g. S. S. Stevens 1951). It is also true, according to the ratio-scaling
hypothesis, that such a linear transformation of scale values is the only
permissible transformation that will leave the sensation magnitude scale
invariant. The work of S. S. Stevens (1956) and Hellman & Zwislocki (1961,
1963, 1964, 1968) on loudness scaling, in which the effects of using a
standard stimulus with a particular modulus (assigned sensation magnitude
value) as a reference were investigated, casts doubt on the ratio-scaling
hypothesis. These investigators found that the value of the modulus had a
substantial effect on the form of the sensation-magnitude function. Specifically, the scale values obtained with one modulus were not linearly related to
scale values obtained with a different modulus. If subjects in these experiments had been capable of making ratio judgments of sensation magnitude, the value of the modulus assigned to the standard stimulus should have
affected the subjects' judgments only by changing them by some multiplicative constant in accordance with properties of ratio scales of measurement. Hellman & Zwislocki interpreted these findings as evidence that subjects make judgments of sensation magnitude on an absolute rather than a
ratio scale. According to the absolute-scaling hypothesis, subjects tend to

assign numbers to stimuli in such a way that their impression of the size of the number matches their impression of the sensation magnitude of the stimulus. Using a standard stimulus with a defined modulus may force the subject to use numbers the perceived sizes of which do not match the sensation magnitudes of the stimuli and, as a consequence, the form of the psychophysical scale is distorted. One attempt to solve this problem has been to eliminate the use of the standard stimulus in magnitude estimation experiments (Hellman & Zwislocki 1961, 1963, 1964, 1968; S. S. Stevens 1956; Zwislocki & Goodman 1980). In this procedure, called absolute magnitude estimation, the subject is instructed to assign a number to a stimulus in such a way that the impression of how large the number is matches the impression of how intense the stimulus is. To reduce possible biases due to self-imposed restricted response ranges, the subject is told that any positive number that appears appropriate— whole numbers, decimals, or fractions—can be used. To discourage attempts to judge stimuli relative to one another, the subject is told to ignore numbers assigned to preceding stimuli when judging a particular stimulus.

Using the method of absolute magnitude estimation, Zwislocki & Goodman (1980) found that the judgments of subjects were remarkably free from stimulus-context effects. This finding contrasts with results obtained with conventional magnitude estimation instructions where strong context effects have typically been found (Poulton 1968, 1979).

The data of Ward (1987) also support the hypothesis that stimulus-context effects in absolute magnitude estimation are relatively small. Ward, however, argues that under most conditions, judgments tend to be relative rather than absolute.

The hypothesis that subjects have a strong tendency to assign numbers to sensations on a natural absolute scale is also suggested from the results of Ward (1973). In his experiment, subjects made magnitude estimations of the loudness of tones. The subject was told at the start of the experiment that a tone 56 dB above threshold had a subjective value of 10. This and other stimuli were presented throughout the session, but no further mention was made by the experimenter of the subjective value of the standard stimulus. By the end of the session, the average value assigned to the standard stimulus had changed from 10 to 2.08. Zwislocki & Goodman (1980) pointed out that 2.08 is almost exactly what their subjects assigned to this stimulus by absolute magnitude estimation. It seems that Ward's subjects eventually began to use their own natural numbers.

Zwislocki & Goodman (1980) contend that the tendency to make absolute judgments of sensation magnitude may be established at an early age. As support for this hypothesis they reported that the average judgments of line lengths by a group of adults and a group of 5–6-year-old children were the same. Zwislocki & Goodman pointed out that when children learn numbers, they learn them not as abstractions but instead by counting objects. Thus the first associations of numbers are with impressions of numerosity, and since numerosity is an absolute scale, numerical judgments of sensory impressions may also be an absolute scale.

Verrillo (1983) found the numbers used in absolute-magnitude estimation of line length to be stable over time even when the delay between testing sessions was as long as 1 or 2 years. However, no analysis of the results of individual subjects was provided.

Two recent studies support the hypothesis that subjects make magnitude-estimation judgments on an absolute scale (Collins & Gescheider, submitted for publication; Zwislocki et al, submitted for publication). In these studies, subjects made absolute-magnitude estimations of stimuli in two modalities and also made cross-modality matches of stimuli in these modalities. The critical finding in these two studies was that two stimuli presented to two different sense modalities, if given the same number in magnitude estimation, will be matched to have equal sensation magnitudes in cross-modality matching. Zwislocki's finding of the additivity of absolute magnitude estimations described earlier (Zwislocki 1983b) also supports the validity of the method.

The issue of whether magnitude estimations are absolute or relative has also been addressed by Marks et al (1986) using the method of magnitude matching. Relativity was exhibited by some subjects whose responses were affected by the values of other stimuli presented in the session. On the other hand, the responses of other subjects were close to absolute in that they were little affected by such stimulus context. It should be pointed out, however, that the term "absolute" as used by Zwislocki & Goodman (1980) and Zwislocki (1983b) in describing absolute scaling does not mean insensitivity to context. Instead it derives from S. S. Stevens' (1951) definition of scale types in terms of permissible mathematical transformations. An absolute scale is one that remains invariant only to transformations by multiplication by unity.

Applications of Absolute-Magnitude Estimation

Verrillo (1982) had old and young subjects make absolute-magnitude estimations of 25 Hz and 250 Hz vibratory stimuli of varied intensity presented to the thenar eminence of the hand. The magnitude-estimation functions in which average magnitude estimations were plotted as a function of intensity were essentially identical for old and young subjects when the frequency of vibration was 25 Hz, a frequency known to stimulate a receptor system that is little affected by age. On the other hand, the magnitude-estimation function of the old subjects was much lower than that of the young subjects when the vibration frequency was 250 Hz, a frequency that stimulates a receptor system known to lose its sensitivity with age.

In another experiment on individual differences, Verrillo (1979) found the absolute-magnitude estimations of vibrotactile stimuli to be greater for women than for men. That this difference was due to differences in the sensory transformations rather than to the response transformations of men and women was supported by the finding that magnitude estimations of line length were virtually identical for men and women.

The earliest study using absolute-magnitude estimation to measure suprathreshold responses to vibration was that of Verrillo et al (1969) in which subjects made magnitude estimations of the intensity of vibration for various frequencies of vibration. From the resulting family of magnitude-estimation functions it was possible to construct equal-sensation contours analogous to the equal-loudness contours of hearing. One contour resulted from plotting the intensity of vibration producing the same magnitude estimation at various frequencies. The validity of the scales produced by absolute-magnitude estimation was supported by the finding that equal-sensation contours constructed from magnitude-estimation data were consistent with those constructed by sensation-magnitude matching.

In a similar vein, the validity of loudness scales for 1000-Hz and 3000-Hz tones obtained by Hellman (1976) was supported by the finding that absolute-magnitude estimation data correctly predicted loudness matches across the two frequencies. Specifically, intensities of the 1000 Hz and 3000 Hz tone that were assigned the same numbers in magnitude estimation were judged to be equally loud in a heterofrequency matching experiment. Versions of absolute-magnitude estimation have also been used to study loudness adaptation (Scharf 1983) and brightness (Barlow & Verrillo 1976; Bolanowski 1987).

Criticism of Absolute-Magnitude Estimation

Mellers (1983a) has been critical of the method of absolute-magnitude estimation. In an experiment using standard absolute-magnitude estimation instructions, she required subjects to judge the darkness of dot patterns of varying density and found the scale values to be influenced by stimulus context. In her article, Mellers emphasized the view taken by Birnbaum (1974, 1975, 1982a,b) and Mellers & Birnbaum (1982, 1983) that all psychophysical judgments, including absolute-magnitude estimation judgments, are relative and occur in a context. Context includes the experimenter's choice of stimuli, order of presentation, etc, and also events that happened to the subject outside the laboratory before the experiment. Mellers explains the context effects produced by the distribution of stimuli in her experiment in terms of the range-frequency theory of Parducci (Parducci 1968, 1974, 1982).

Zwislocki (1983a) wrote a critique of Mellers' conception of scales of measurement. According to Zwislocki, a scale type is called "absolute" not because it cannot be biased but because it has the formal mathematical property of having a fixed unit, with no transformation of scale values possible that leaves the scale invariant. Zwislocki argues that realization of a scale type depends on experimental procedures; bias in psychophysical experiments means that subjects do not follow the instructions of the experimenter. He places the responsibility on the experimenter to arrange the conditions so that his or her subjects are able to follow the imposed rules.

Mellers (1983b) replied to Zwislocki's comments on her work by (a) claiming that Zwislocki's definition of an absolute scale requires that subjects' responses be taken at face value rather than being evaluated within the framework of theory such as the two-stage model of judgment in the tradition of Attneave (1962), Shepard (1981), Birnbaum (1974), Anderson (1974), and others; (b) claiming that Zwislocki, with no theory and a single demonstration of absolute scaling, in making his statement that the burden is on other investigators to achieve such a scale, has set himself in a position that is impossible to refute; and (c) making the case again that all psychophysical judgments are relative.

What does this all mean? I think the disagreement between Mellers and Zwislocki results from two fundamentally different approaches to research on psychophysical scaling. The work of Zwislocki & Goodman (1980) represents the approach of the sensory scientist whose goal is to obtain unbiased scales of sensory magnitude to study sensory processes such as summation, inhibition, adaptation, and sensory channels (see Marks 1974b). The study by Mellers (1983a), on the other hand, more represents the approach of the cognitive scientist whose goal is to understand the process of judgment. To these investigators, biased responses influenced by context are interesting—even welcome—and no doubt represent the way most people make judgments outside the laboratory. Obviously both approaches are important; but it should be recognized that the goals in the two approaches are different, each concentrating on understanding different stages of the two-stage judgment process.

RESPONSE BIAS

Responses in the psychophysical scaling experiment can be biased in many ways. Some of the major biases are described below.

Sequential Effects

Ideally, in the psychophysical scaling task, the response made to a stimulus is independent of both the physical values of stimuli presented on previous trials and responses given to those stimuli. Sequential effects, however, are often present in psychophysical scaling, creating a serious problem for the sensory scientist who, in his/her attempt to measure sensation magnitude, must eliminate them either through experimental procedures or through calculation. For the cognitive scientist, sequential effects are interesting in themselves in that they reflect basic characteristics of the judgment process. The general finding has been that, in magnitude estimation, category judgment, and absolute-identification experiments, responses on a particular trial tend to be biased toward (positively correlated with) responses on the previous trial (assimilation) and sometimes slightly biased away from (negatively correlated with) responses made before the previous trial (contrast) (Cross 1973; Holland & Lockhead 1963; Jesteadt et al 1977; Lockhead & King 1983; McKenna 1984; Staddon et al 1980; Ward 1972, 1973, 1975; Ward & Lockhead 1970).

Cross (1973) demonstrated that the influence of sequential effects in magnitude estimation tended to reduce the exponent of the power function describing the relationship between assigned numbers and stimulus intensity. The reduced exponent, seen in a reduction of the slope of the log-log plot of magnitude estimation and stimulus intensity, was due to assimilation of responses in the direction of the immediately preceding stimulus. Because a high-intensity stimulus is most frequently preceded by stimuli of lower intensity, assimilation tends to reduce the response to this stimulus. On the other hand, because a low-intensity stimulus is most frequently preceded by stimuli of higher intensity, assimilation tends to increase the response to this stimulus. The consequence of assimilation of responses toward the center of the response range is to reduce the response range, producing a power function exponent that is biased toward being too low. Cross suggested that unbiased exponents can be obtained by plotting only data where a response was made to a stimulus immediately preceded by itself or to correct the biased exponent by the measured magnitude of the sequential bias.

Using multiple regression analysis, Jesteadt et al (1977) found that sequential effects in magnitude estimation do not extend beyond the trial preceding the test trial. After these investigators examined the data of Ward & Lockhead (1971) and Luce et al (1976), they concluded that sequential effects in an absolute-identification task must also be limited to the preceding trial. These investigators also found that as the difference in intensity between the test stimulus and the preceding stimulus increased, the correlation between the responses to the two stimuli decreased.

Staddon et al (1980) contended that, in the absolute-identification task, sequential effects extend as far back as 7 or 8 previous trials. Specifically, the subject's response on trial n will exhibit assimilation toward the response on the previous trial, trial $n-1$, and exhibit contrast with trials $n-2$ and earlier. Staddon et al claimed that Jesteadt et al (1977) were in error in claiming that sequential effects in absolute identifications are confined entirely to the events of the previous trial. These investigators, using a regression analysis similar to that used by Jesteadt et al, found sequential effects extending over several trials.

King & Lockhead (1981) found that sequential effects in judgment have the same form for various response ranges created by varying the feedback given subjects about their performance on each trial. Giving feedback to subjects generally results in assimilation of responses to the just-previous stimulus and response and in contrast with earlier stimuli and responses (e.g. King & Lockhead 1981; Staddon et al 1980). When feedback is not given, assimilation alone may occur, or both assimilation and contrast several trials removed may occur (e.g. Wagner & Baird 1981; Ward & Lockhead 1971). As a result of their trial-to-trial analysis, Lockhead & King (1983) rejected the hypothesis that assimilation is due to neural integration of successive stimuli (Elmasian et al 1980) and proposed a memory model of sequence effects. They also rejected the hypothesis that assimilation is due to simple regression of responses toward the midpoint of the stimulus series but is instead a result of the tendency of subjects to bias their judgments toward the response on the previous trial.

Two classes of models have been developed to explain sequence effects. In one class of models, assimilation and contrast are assumed to be generated by a single mechanism (e.g. Jesteadt et al 1977; Luce et al 1980). In a second, assimilation and contrast are generated by separate mechanisms (e.g. Ward 1979). Ward (1982), in demonstrating sequential effects in judgments made in the magnitude matching task (Stevens & Marks 1980), concluded that separate mechanisms exist for assimilation and contrast. In his experiment, current responses were assimilated to previous responses regardless of modality, whereas current responses were contrasted with previous stimuli of the same modality only. In addition, Ward (1985), using magnitude matching, found the correlation between current and previous responses as a function of the difference between stimuli to be the usual inverted V both within and across modalities. On the other hand, the dependency of the coefficient of variation of the ratio of current to previous responses on the difference between stimuli was found only within a stimulus modality.

It is yet to be determined whether results from the method of absolute-magnitude estimation, in which subjects are instructed to ignore the stimuli and responses of previous trials, will be free of the potentially biasing effects of sequential dependencies. Ward (1987), however, did report sequential dependencies for this method under conditions in which subjects were required to make a large number of judgments at each stimulus intensity.

Other Biases

In addition to sequential dependencies, a number of other sources of response bias in psychophysical judgment have been studied extensively. Instructions to the subject is one such factor. Robinson (1976) found that numerical examples given in magnitude estimation instructions strongly influence judgments. Mention of 2:1 ratios in instructions, for example, yields much smaller exponents of the psychophysical function than does mention of 7.5 : 1 ratios.

Poulton (1979) has continued to identify sources of bias in the judgment of sensory magnitude. He proposed that responses that are closely linked to the stimulus by well-known rules are less easy to bias than those that are loosely related. For example, judgments of stimuli in familiar physical units are affected minimally by biasing factors. Poulton identified several stimulus-response tendencies that produce bias in psychophysical experiments. The *centering bias* is a tendency for subjects to center their response range on the range of stimuli presented in the experiment. Poulton points out that when controlling for the centering bias, care must be taken to avoid transfer bias from previous exposure to stimulus ranges (Bowsher et al 1966; Von Wright & Kekkinen 1970). The centering bias, along with the *stimulus-spacing bias*, accounts for Helson's (1964) level of adaptation (Parducci 1963; Parducci & Perrett 1971). The stimulus-spacing bias is a tendency for the subject to respond as if the stimuli were subjectively equally spaced regardless of their actual physical spacing. In category rating, categories tend to be used equally often, and the form of the psychophysical magnitude function is distorted (e.g. Montgomery 1975). The insertion of extra stimuli in a set tends to cause the subject to accommodate by expanding the response range. The effect is to increase the slope of the psychophysical magnitude function (Montgomery 1975; Stevens 1958).

Another source of bias is *stimulus-frequency bias*, a special case of stimulus-spacing bias in which, because categories are used equally often, the responses to stimuli a little stronger than a frequently presented stimulus are too large and responses to stimuli a little weaker than a frequently presented stimulus are too small. Poulton points out that the centering bias and the stimulus-spacing bias with its special case, the stimulus-frequency bias, form the bases for Parducci's range-frequency model for bias in category scaling (Parducci 1963, 1974, 1982; Parducci & Perrett 1971). The *logarithmic bias* is a tendency for subjects to assign numbers to equally spaced sensation magnitudes logarithmically rather than linearly. Banks & Hill (1974) demonstrated that a subject's use of numbers is often a compromise between the linear and logarithmic modes. The data of Gibson & Tomko (1972) suggest that this biased use of numbers may play a role in category ratings and magnitude estimations of sensory stimuli. The magnitude of this bias, however, has yet to be determined experimentally. In *contraction bias* the subject's responses are closer to the middle of the response range than they should be. In magnitude estimation, regression effects are due at least in part to sequential dependencies and tend to reduce the slope of the psychophysical function (Cross 1973). On the other hand, in magnitude production, the slope of the psychophysical function is increased by the contraction bias. These regression effects can be reduced by averaging psychophysical scales obtained by magnitude estimation and production (S. S. Stevens 1958; Hellman & Zwislocki 1963).

The *stimulus-equalizing bias* is the tendency of the subject to use the full range of responses, whatever the size of the range of stimuli. When the stimulus range is changed, the effect of this factor on psychophysical magnitude functions is to increase the slope for narrow stimulus ranges and to decrease the slope for wide stimulus ranges (Frederiksen 1975; Montgomery 1975). Teghtsoonian (1973), however, found the stimulus range to have little influence on magnitude estimation of apparent distance, apparent length, and loudness. In a later paper, Teghtsoonian & Teghtsoonian (1978) reported stimulus-range effects for magnitude estimation and magnitude production of loudness and perceived distance. In both cases, there was a decrease in the exponent of the psychophysical magnitude function with increasing stimulus range. The effect of intramodality-stimulus range, however, was not large enough to support the hypothesis, previously proposed by Poulton (1968), that variations of exponents among modalities could be explained by the stimulus-equalizing bias. If variations in exponents across modalities were simply due to the subject's producing a fixed range of numbers regardless of the stimulus range, magnitude estimation would be a useless psychophysical method for distinction among the stimulus transformations of sensory systems. Based on estimates of how the intramodality-stimulus bias decreased with stimulus range, Teghtsoonian & Teghtsoonian recommended that the widest possible stimulus ranges be used because under these conditions less biased estimates of the power function exponents can be obtained. Teghtsoonian & Teghtsoonian (1986), in their criticism of Poulton's (1984) claim that the loudness scale for white noise is a logarithmic function rather than the widely accepted power function, argued that Poulton's use of a very small stimulus range (5 dB) produced biased results. In addition, they pointed out that this range was so small as to make it impossible to distinguish between how well the logarithmic and power-function equations fit the experimental data.

The final bias that Poulton (1979) describes is the *response-equalizing bias,* which is a tendency for subjects to use the full range of available responses in responding to any particular stimulus range. This bias is built into the category-rating procedure in which subjects are asked to place stimuli in categories ranging from the lowest to highest.

Poulton et al (1980), in a systematic attempt to eliminate from ratio judgments of loudness all sources of bias described above, determined that a doubling or halving of loudness is produced by changing sound intensity by 11.5 dB—a value corresponding to a power function exponent of .26. The 11.5 dB for doubling of loudness is only slightly greater than Marks' (1974a) estimate of 11 dB (implied exponent of .27) or S. S. Stevens' (1955) estimate of 10 dB. The value, however, is substantially higher than the 6 dB (implied exponent of .5) value reported by Warren et al (1958) as support for the hypothesis that subjects make judgments of sensation from known physical correlates of the stimulus, such as distance between sound sources.

Subjective Magnitude of Numbers

If magnitude estimation is considered to be another case of cross-modality matching in which the subjective magnitudes of numbers are matched to the subjective magnitudes of stimuli, the subjective-magnitude function for numbers must be known for correct interpretation of magnitude-estimation data. Rule & Curtis (1982) pointed out that the exponent of the subjective-number function is the same as the reciprocal of that of the response-transformation function in the two-state model of magnitude estimation. Based on results from a number of studies (Banks & Hill 1974; Birnbaum 1974; McKelvie & Shepley 1977; Rule 1969, 1971, 1972; Rule & Curtis 1973; Schneider et al 1974a), Rule & Curtis estimated the subjective-number exponent to be .68. If this exponent for subjective numbers operates in magnitude estimation, then the response-transformation function for magnitude estimation of stimuli is a power function with an exponent of $1/.68 = 1.47$. If magnitude estimation of a set of stimuli can be described as a power function with exponent α, the exponent of the stimulus transformation, θ (psychophysical law), could be obtained by $\theta = \alpha/1.47$. All of the currently known exponents for magnitude estimation would have to be reduced to approximately 2/3 of the presently accepted values to provide estimates of stimulus-transformation functions. If Wagenaar's (1982) estimate of .14–.48 for the exponent for subjective number were correct, exponents for sensory modalities would have to be reduced even further.

Is this correction of exponents necessary; and if so, is it necessary for all modalities and stimulus conditions? For example, is it necessary in the case of line length, where it is generally accepted that the perception of line length is veridical with actual line length? Since the value of α measured experimentally is approximately 1.0, the value of θ would become $1.0/1.47 = .68$—a value that implies a lack of correspondence between perceived and actual line length. Perhaps, as suggested by Poulton (1979), response bias, in this case distortion in number usage, decreases as responses become linked to the stimulus through well-known rules such as those provided by knowledge of physical units of length.

Wendt (1982) has suggested that the psychological magnitude of numbers may be a logarithmic function of actual numbers (Fechner's Law). If this is true, the finding that assigned numbers (N) in magnitude estimation are related to stimulus intensity (I) by a power function implies that the relationship between sensation magnitude and stimulus intensity (the psychophysical law) is logarithmic (Fechner's Law) rather than a power function (Stevens' Law). This follows from the well-established fact that log N is linearly related to log I in magnitude-estimation studies, which becomes equivalent to the statement that psychological magnitude, log N, is proportional to log I (Fechner's Law).

Inverse Attributes

The results of experiments on magnitude estimation of a sensory attribute and the inverse of the attribute, such as loudness and its inverse softness, seem to indicate response bias in the use of very small numbers (Dawson & Miller 1978). The well-known steepening of the psychophysical magnitude function at low-stimulus intensities has traditionally been explained in terms of sensory factors such as the detection threshold and physiological noise (see Marks & Stevens 1968). Since inverse functions, in which large numbers are assigned to low-intensity stimuli, do not show this steepening at low intensities, Dawson & Miller (1978) rejected the physiological noise and threshold hypotheses. Response bias in the use of small numbers seems to be further indicated by the presence of a steepening in the inverse function at high stimulus intensities where small numbers are used.

Number of Categories

For some time it was commonly believed that, in category rating, the number of categories is unimportant in determining the form of the psychophysical scale. Recently, Parducci (1982) and Parducci & Wedell (1986) reported results to the contrary. These investigators found that the well-known biasing effects in category scaling produced by skewing the frequency of presentation of stimuli toward low or high values decrease as the number of categories increases (the category effect). It was also found that this bias increased as the number of stimulus values increased (the stimulus effect). Both the category and stimulus effects were described by changes in a single weighted parameter of Parducci's (1965) range frequency theory (see Parducci 1983 for a review). Although increasing the number of categories and decreasing the number of stimuli reduces or eliminates the bias due to frequency skewing of the number of stimulus presentations to low or high values, bias due to spatial skewing of the stimulus distribution was unaffected by changing either the number of categories or the number of stimuli. To explain the category and stimulus effects more fully, the range-frequency model was elaborated by adding the *principle of consistency,* which states that a subject, over the course of the experiment, resists applying more than a single category to the same stimulus—a process that depends on memory (Wedell & Parducci 1985).

That the number of categories in category rating has an influence on the psychophysical function was also reported by Foley et al (1983). In their study, the relationship between judgments and stimulus intensity (line length and sound intensity) was best described as a power function, as has been claimed by others (Marks 1968, 1974a; Schneider et al 1978). Moreover, exponents increased as the number of categories increased and stimulus range decreased. Comparison with magnitude estimation data indicated that the well-known concave curvilinear relation between category and magnitude-estimation judgments (Stevens & Galanter 1957) is most pronounced when there is a large disparity between the ranges of available responses in the two tasks.

The effects of varying stimulus range while holding the number of stimuli constant on category judgments of loudness were investigated by Payne & Corso (1985). Consistent with earlier findings of Poulton (1975) and contrary to S. S. Stevens (1975), these investigators found that the stimulus value corresponding to the midpoint of the subjective estimations made on a category scale depended on the range of stimuli judged.

Stimulus Context and Sensory and Cognitive Processes

Context effects in psychophysical scaling, such as those described above, can be found with the use of every psychophysical-scaling procedure. Investigators respond to this situation in two distinct ways. On the one hand, the sensory scientist in pursuit of pure sensory functions has attempted to eliminate context from the measurement situation. Birnbaum (1982a) argues that this approach is futile since judgments are always made in a stimulus context. In contrast to the sensory scientist, the cognitive scientist welcomes context effects in scaling because they supply a wealth of information about judgment processes. If psychophysical scales are to be useful in understanding sensory processes, and often they are, context effects that influence the response-transformation function, $R = f_2(S)$, must be eliminated from measurement or corrected for so that unconfounded stimulus transformations, $\psi = f_1(S)$, can be studied. The stimulus contexts that are of great interest to the sensory scientist are not those that affect judgment but those that affect sensation. Stimulus-contextual effects on sensory responses, such as those observed in masking, summation, and other sensory interactions, are of primary interest (Marks 1986).

RELATION BETWEEN DIFFERENT SCALES

Marks (1974a) has argued that there is strong evidence for the validity of ratio scales of sensory magnitude. He cites as evidence internal consistency of the data as determined by cross-modality matching and intramodality matching.

He also argues that the validity of magnitude-estimation data is supported by what he refers to as *psychosensory laws* in which measures of sensory magnitude enter into simple lawful relationships such as loudness summation and the multiplicative relation between measures of density and volume to produce loudness. Thus, the requirement that valid psychophysical measurements must interrelate with one another in laws in the same way that valid physical measurements do (Luce 1972) seems to be met in these instances.

A second type of psychophysical scale, referred to by Marks (1974a) as an interval scale, involves the subject's judgments of sensory differences between stimuli. These scales include bisection, category, and magnitude scales of the subjective differences between stimuli. Typically, the same stimuli scaled by ratio procedures and interval procedures result in psychophysical power functions, but the exponents are generally smaller for the interval procedures. Thus, the scale values obtained for the two types of scale are nonlinearly related, and consequently the validity of both scales is cast in doubt.

Although Marks and others make a strong case for the valid measurement of sensory magnitude by magnitude estimation and other ratio scaling procedures, Anderson (e.g. 1970, 1976, 1982) and others have argued for the validity of interval scales such as those produced by category judgments. Furthermore, McBride (1983a) argues for the validity of category scales of taste from their agreement with JND scales (discrimination scales) of the same stimuli, from their ability to predict taste matches (McBride 1983b) and from their descriptions of taste mixture (McBride 1986). In Anderson's functional-measurement approach (Anderson 1981), the sensory scale and the psychosensory law are simultaneously determined in experimental designs in which different dimensions of the stimulus are factorially manipulated (also see Bogartz 1980). It is Anderson's view that psychosensory (psychological) laws obey simple algebraic rules such as addition, averaging, and multiplication. In functional measurement any type of scaling procedure can be used, including magnitude estimation, as Marks has done with his work on loudness summation (e.g. Marks 1982), and as Algom and his associates have done in studying visual velocity (Algom & Cohen-Raz 1984), visual area (Algom et al 1985), and pain (Algom et al 1986). Generally, however, advocates of the method have used interval-type scaling procedures such as Anderson's twenty-point category scales. It is significant that category ratings are almost always nonlinearly related to magnitude estimations. Because category ratings and magnitude estimations yield different results, it has been frequently argued that the results of one method are valid while those of the other are invalid. Anderson and his associates have consistently argued that since the results of category scaling reveal psychosensory (psychological) laws that can be described by simple algebraic equations of information integration, the category scale is valid. Moreover, magnitude-estimation scales, because of their nonlinear relation with the category scale, must be invalid. It is noteworthy, however, that the recent studies mentioned above, in which magnitude estimation was used in a functional-measurement design, yielded simple algebraic equations of information integration.

The problem is that the two scaling methods yield scales that pass a variety of validity tests yet are nonlinearly related. It would appear that something must be wrong with the validity test or, as Marks (1974a) first proposed, each of the two types of scales produces valid measurements but of fundamentally different psychophysical processes. Marks' proposal is that ratio-scaling methods, when applied correctly, yield valid measures of sensory magnitude, and interval scaling methods, when applied correctly, yield valid measures of sensory dissimilarity. The sensory magnitudes and sensory dissimilarities of stimuli are considered to be equally meaningful dimensions of perceptual experience, each being tapped most effectively by a different scaling procedure.

Marks (1979a) continued his argument with his work concerning the differences between the sone scale of loudness, with its exponent of .6 determined by ratio-scaling methods (S. S. Stevens 1955), and the lambda scale of loudness, with its exponent of .3 determined by fractionation and equisection of loudness differences (Carterette & Anderson 1979; Garner 1959). Marks developed a theory in which sensation magnitude is processed at an earlier (sensory) stage of the auditory system and loudness differences are processed at a more central (cognitive) stage. Marks rejected the idea that judgments of loudness differences, because they pass validity testing, provide scales of loudness (Birnbaum & Elmasian 1977; Parker & Schneider 1974). Alternatively, according to Marks, both the loudness scale (L-scale) and the loudness difference scale (D-scale) provide valid scales of auditory perception but, in the case of the L-scale, it is loudness that is measured, while in the case of the D-scale, it is the perception of a loudness difference that is measured. The concept of loudness applies to the perception of a single stimulus and the concept of loudness differences applies to situations where the listener is presented with more than one sound for comparison.

In the case of loudness summation of simultaneously presented sounds, summation of loudness is sensory, whereas sequentially presented sounds result in cognitive summation (Marks 1979b). Marks' model is supported by his data and the data of Popper et al (1986), which indicate that magnitude estimation of loudness and loudness differences produce different power function exponents. Other studies using other methods have also found different scales of loudness judgments and loudness-difference judgments (Beck & Shaw 1967; Birnbaum & Elmasian 1977; Schneider et al 1974b; Schneider et al 1978). Although a unified theory of loudness and loudness-difference scales is needed, there are those who argue that Marks' model is too complex, requiring too many assumptions and, therefore, may not be correct (e.g. Birnbaum 1982a; Carterette & Anderson 1979).

Whether or not his account of the difference between L-scales and D-scales is correct, I think we need to consider Marks' suggestion that the underlying psychological representation—the scale—may in many circumstances depend on the task (Marks 1982). Marks (1982) also makes the point that we need to question the functional roles of scales in sensory, perceptual, and behavioral processes, so that the psychophysical procedures become a tool of the investigator.

Can Subjects Judge What They Are Instructed to Judge?

Torgerson (1961) proposed that differences between magnitude-estimation and category-rating scales might be due to an inability of subjects to follow instructions and make judgments of sensory ratios in magnitude estimation and judgments of sensory differences in category rating. Instead of following instructions, the same judgment process is thought to occur when a pair of stimuli are presented regardless of whether the subject is told to judge the sensory ratio or the sensory difference. The results of several studies on a wide variety of sensory continua seem to support this hypothesis (Birnbaum 1978; Birnbaum & Elmasian 1977; Birnbaum & Mellers 1978; Birnbaum & Veit 1974; Elmasian & Birnbaum 1984; Hagerty & Birnbaum 1978; Mellers et al 1984; Rose & Birnbaum 1975; Schneider et al 1976; Veit 1978). In these studies, the finding that judgments of differences and ratios in pairs of stimuli were monotonically related was taken as evidence that the same process mediates ratio and difference judgments. The theoretical model of Krantz et al (1971) dictates that ratio and difference judgments, if based on separate operations, should not be monotonically related but, instead, should have different rank orders that are predictably interrelated. Several investigators have argued from results in which subjects are required to make complex judgments of stimulus relationships (such as differences between ratios, ratios between ratios, difference between differences, and ratios between differences) that the underlying operation in all judgments is subtraction (Birnbaum 1978; Veit 1978). According to this view, when members of stimulus pairs are separated by the same subjective magnitude, the pairs are correctly given the same judgment of subjective difference between stimuli. On the other hand, these same pairs of stimuli are incorrectly given the same judgment of subjective ratio between stimuli (e.g. sensation magnitudes of 20 and 30 are judged correctly to differ by the same amount and judged incorrectly to differ by the same ratio as sensation magnitudes 5 and 15). It has been thought that judging sensory differences when told to judge differences (category scaling) and also when told to judge ratios (ratio scaling) could account for why scales are nonlinearly related. In conflict with this hypothesis are the results of Parker et al (1975) and Rule et al (1981), who found evidence for judgment of subjective ratios as well as subjective differences of line length and heaviness, respectively.

Generally, this type of scaling research is consistent with what is known as relation theory in scaling (Fagot 1978; Junge 1966; Krantz 1972; Shepard 1978, 1981). Schneider (1982) has recently argued that valid interval- or ratio-psychophysical scales probably require relational judgments from the subject. Whether or not this is true of absolute-magnitude estimation, in which subjects are instructed to judge each stimulus independently, is yet to be determined.

Schneider (1982) points out that one advantage of the relational approach is the opportunity to use nonmetric analysis (Shepard 1966) in which only the rank orders of difference judgments of pairs of stimuli are used to construct interval scales in which the nonlinear use of numbers by subjects is eliminated. Furthermore, since the results are insensitive to monotonic biases, one should obtain the same results with category- and magnitude-estimation procedures (e.g. Schneider et al 1978).

CONCLUSION

Here I have reviewed mainly the work of experimentalists with interests in the sensory and cognitive factors that affect psychophysical behavior. I have not described the work of measurement theorists, although it is equally important; many of their major contributions can be found in earlier reviews by Cliff (1973), Carrol & Arabie (1980), and Young (1984).

One trend to be seen in the experimental study of psychophysical scaling is the study of individual differences, and from this approach a better understanding of the role of sensory, perceptual, and cognitive factors in psychophysical judgment should emerge. Particularly important is a better understanding of how stimulus context influences judgments. Perhaps the most perplexing and certainly one of the oldest problems in psychophysics is the observed nonlinear relations between scales obtained by different methods. Whether these nonlinearities are due to cognitive-judgment factors or to sensory-perceptual factors is yet to be determined. Two scaling procedures applied to the same perceptual dimension cannot both be valid if one is a nonlinear function of the other. Of course, if the perceptual dimensions are different, both scales could be valid and nonlinearly related. Solution of this fundamental problem may be facilitated by the study of the judgments of individual subjects and their differences, an approach that would follow a tradition in psychophysics that has led to success in the past.

Literature Cited

Algom, D., Cohen-Raz, L. 1984. Visual velocity input-output functions: the integration of distance and duration onto subjective velocity. *J. Exp. Psychol. Hum. Percept. Perform.* 10:486–501

Algom, D., Marks, L. E. 1984. Individual differences in loudness processing and loudness scales. *J. Exp. Psychol. Gen.* 113:571–93

Algom, D., Raphaeli, N., Cohen-Raz, L. 1986. Integration of noxious stimulation across separate somatosensory communication systems: a functional theory of pain. *J. Exp. Psychol. Hum. Percept. Perform.* 12:92–102

Algom, D., Wolf, Y., Bergman, B. 1985. Integration of stimulus dimensions in perception and memory: composition rules and psychophysical relations. *J. Exp. Psychol. Gen.* 114:451–71

Anderson, N. H. 1970. Functional measurement and psychophysical judgment. *Psychol. Rev.* 77:153–70

Anderson, N. H. 1974. Algebraic models in perception. In *Handbook of Perception*, ed. E. C. Carterette, M. P. Friedman, 2:215–98. New York: Academic

Anderson, N. H. 1976. Integration theory, functional measurement, and the psychological law. In *Advances in Psychophysics*, ed. H. G. Geisslerl, Yu. M. Zabrodin, pp. 93–130. Berlin: VEB Deutscher Verlag

Anderson, N. H. 1981. *Foundation of Information Integration Theory.* New York: Academic

Anderson, N. H. 1982. Cognitive algebra and social psychophysics. See Wegener 1982, pp. 123–48

Attneave, F. 1962. Perception and related areas. In *Psychology: A Study of a Science*, ed. S. Koch, 4:619–59. New York: McGraw-Hill

Baird, J. C., Green, D. M., Luce, R. D. 1980. Variability and sequential effects in cross-modality matching of area and loudness. *J. Exp. Psychol. Hum. Percept. Perform.* 6:277–89

Banks, W. P., Hill, D. K. 1974. The apparent magnitude of number scaled by random production. *J. Exp. Psychol.* 102:353–76

Barlow, R. B., Verrillo, R. T. 1976. Brightness sensation in a Ganzfeld. *Vision Res.* 16:1291–97

Bartoshuk, L. M., Gent, J., Catalanotto, F. A., Goodspeed, R. B. 1983. Clinical evaluation of taste. *Am. J. Otolaryngol.* 4:257–60

Bartoshuk, L. M., Marks, L. E. 1986. Ratio scaling. In *Clinical Measurement of Taste and Smell*, ed. H. L. Meiselman, R. S.

Rivlin, pp. 50–65. New York: Macmillian

Bartoshuk, L. M., Rifkin, B., Marks, L. E., Bars, P. 1986. Taste and aging. *J. Gerontol.* 41:51–57

Beck, J., Shaw, W. A. 1967. Ratio-estimation of loudness-intervals. *Am. J. Psychol.* 80:59–65

Birnbaum, M. H. 1974. Using contextual effects to derive psychophysical scales. *Percept. Psychophys.* 15:89–96

Birnbaum, M. H. 1975. Expectancy and judgment. In *Cognitive Theory*, ed. F. Restle, R. M. Shiffrin, N. J. Castellan, H. R. Lindman, D. B. Pisoni, 1:107–18. Hillside, NJ: Erlbaum

Birnbaum, M. H. 1978. Differences and ratio in psychological measurement. In *Cognitive Theory*, ed. N. J. Castellan, F. Restle, 3:33–74. Hillsdale, NJ: Erlbaum

Birnbaum, M. H. 1982a. Controversies in psychological measurement. See Wegener 1982, pp. 401–85

Birnbaum, M. H. 1982b. Problems with so-called "direct" scaling. In *Selected Sensory Methods: Problems and Approaches to Hedonics* (ASTM STP773), ed. J. T. Kuznicki, R. A. Johnson, A. F. Rutkiewic, pp. 34–38. Philadelphia: Am. Soc. Test. Mater.

Birnbaum, M. H., Elmasian, R. 1977. Loudness "ratios" and "differences" involve the same psychophysical operation. *Percept. Psychophys.* 22:383–91

Birnbaum, M. H., Mellers, B. A. 1978. Measurement and the mental map. *Percept. Psychophys.* 23:403–8

Birnbaum, M. H., Veit, C. T. 1974. Scale convergence as a criterion for rescaling: information integration with difference ratio and averaging tasks. *Percept. Psychophys.* 15:7–15

Bogartz, R. 1980. Some functional measurement procedures for determining the psychophysical law. *Percept. Psychophys.* 27:284–94

Bolanowski, S. J. Jr. 1987. Contourless stimuli produce binocular brightness summation. *Vision Res.* In press

Bowsher, J. M., Johnson, D. R., Robinson, D. W. 1966. A further experiment on judging the noisiness of aircraft in flight. *Acustica* 17:245–67

Braida, L. D., Lim, J. S., Berliner, J. E., Durlach, N. I., Rabinowitz, W. M., Purks, S. R. 1984. Intensity perception XIII. Perceptual anchor model of context coding. *J. Acoust. Soc. Am.* 76:722–31

Cain, W. S. 1976. Olfaction and the common chemical sense: some psychophysical contrasts. *Sensory Process.* 1:57–67

Carroll, J. D., Arabie, P. 1980. Multidimensional scaling. *Ann. Rev. Psychol.* 31:607–49

Carterette, E. C., Anderson, N. H. 1979. Bisection of loudness. *Percept. Psychophys.* 26:265–280

Cliff, N. 1973. Scaling. *Ann. Rev. Psychol.* 21:473–506

Coleman, B. J., Graf, R. G., Alf, E. 1981. Assessing power function relationships in magnitude estimation. *Percept. Psychophys.* 29:178–80

Cross, D. V. 1973. Sequential dependencies and regression in psychophysical judgments. *Percept. Psychophys.* 14:547–52

Curtis, D. W., Attneave, F., Harrington, T. L. 1968. A test of a two-stage model of magnitude judgment. *Percept. Psychophys.* 3:25–31

Daning, R. 1983. Intraindividual consistencies in cross-modal matching across several continua. *Percept. Psychophys.* 33:516–22

Dawson, W. E. 1971. Magnitude estimation of apparent sums and differences. *Percept. Psychophys.* 9:368–74

Dawson, W. E., Miller, M. E. 1978. Inverse attribute functions and the proposed modifications of the power law. *Percept. Psychophys.* 24:457–65

Dawson, W. E., Waterman, S. P. 1976. Effects of session and intrasession repetition on individual power law exponents. *Bull. Psychon. Soc.* 7:306–8

Duda, P. D. 1967. Effects of procedural differences in ratio scaling techniques. *Can. Psychol.* 8:161(Abstr.)

Duda, P. D. 1975. Tests of the psychological meaning of the power law. *J. Exp. Psychol. Hum. Percept. Perform.* 104:188–94

Ekman, G., Hosman, B., Lindman, R., Ljungberg, L., Akesson, C. A. 1968. Interindividual differences in scaling performance. *Percept. Mot. Skills* 26:815–23

Elmasian, R., Birnbaum, M. 1984. Harmonious note on pitch: Scale of pitch derived from subtractive model of comparison agrees with the musical scale. *Percept. Psychophys.* 36:531–37

Elmasian, R., Galambos, R., Bernheim, A. 1980. Loudness enhancement and decrement in four paradigms. *J. Acoust. Soc. Am.* 67:601–7

Elzinga, C. H. 1985. A note on estimation in the power law. *Percept. Psychophys.* 37:175

Fagot, R. F. 1978. A theory of relative judgment. *Percept. Psychophys.* 24:243–52

Fechner, G. T. 1860. *Element der Psychophysik.* Leipzig: Breitkopf & Härterl

Foley, H. J., Cross, D. V., Foley, A., Reeder, R. 1983. Stimulus range, number of categories and the "virtual" exponent. *Percept. Psychophys.* 34:505–12

Frederiksen, J. R. 1975. Two models for psychological judgment: scale invariance with changes in stimulus range. *Percept. Psychophys.* 17:147–57

Garner, W. R. 1954. Context effects and the validity of loudness scales. *J. Exp. Psychol.* 48:218–24

Garner, W. R. 1959. On the lambda loudness function, masking, and the loudness of multicomponent tones. *J. Acoust. Soc. Am.* 31:602–7

Gescheider, G. A. 1985. *Psychophysics: Method, Theory, and Application.* Hillsdale, NJ: Erlbaum. 2nd ed.

Gescheider, G. A., Joelson, J. M. 1983. Vibrotactile temporal summation for threshold and suprathreshold level of stimulation. *Percept. Psychophys.* 33:156–62

Gibson, R. H., Tomko, D. L. 1972. The relation between category and magnitude estimations of tactile intensity. *Percept. Psychophys.* 12:135–38

Graham, C. H. 1958. Sensation and perception in an objective psychology. *Psychol. Rev.* 65:65–76

Green, D. M., Luce, R. D., Duncan, J. E. 1977. Variability and sequential effects in magnitude production and estimation of auditory intensity. *Percept. Psychophys.* 22:450–56

Green, D. M., Luce, R. D., Smith, A. F. 1980. Individual magnitude estimates for various distributions of signal intensity. *Percept. Psychophys.* 27:483–88

Grossberg, J. M., Grant, B. F. 1978. Clinical psychophysics: applications of ratio scaling and signal detection methods to research on pain, fear, drugs, and medical decision making. *Psychol. Bull.* 85:1154–76

Hagerty, M., Birnbaum, M. H. 1978. Nonmetric tests of ratio vs. subtractive theories of stimulus comparison. *Percept. Psychophys.* 24:121–29

Hellman, R. P. 1976. Growth of loudness at 1000 and 3000 Hz. *J. Acoust. Soc. Am.* 60:672–79

Hellman, R. P. 1981. Stability of individual loudness functions obtained by magnitude estimation and production. *Percept. Psychophys.* 29:63–70

Hellman, R. P., Zwislocki, J. J. 1961. Some factors affecting the estimation of loudness. *J. Acoust. Soc. Am.* 33:687–94

Hellman, R. P., Zwislocki, J. J. 1963. Monaural loudness function at 1000 cps and interaural summation. *J. Acoust. Soc. Am.* 35:856–65

Hellman, R. P., Zwislocki, J. J. 1964. Loudness function of a 1000 cps tone in the presence of a masking noise. *J. Acoust. Soc. Am.* 36:1618–27

Hellman, R. P., Zwislocki, J. J. 1968. Loudness determination at low sound frequencies. *J. Acoust. Soc. Am.* 43:60–64

Helson, H. 1964. *Adaptation-Level Theory.* New York: Harper & Row

Holland, M. K., Lockhead, G. R. 1963. Sequential effects in absolute judgments of loudness. *Percept. Psychophys.* 3:409–14

Jesteadt, W., Luce, R. D., Green, D. M. 1977. Sequential effects in judgments of loudness. *J. Exp. Psychol. Hum. Percept. Perform.* 3:92–104

Junge, K. 1966. *Some Problems of Measurement in Psychophysics.* Oslo: Universitetsforlaget

King, M. C., Lockhead, G. R. 1981. Response scale and sequential effects in judgment. *Percept. Psychophys.* 30:599–603

Krantz, D. H. 1972. A theory of magnitude estimation and cross-modality matching. *J. Math. Psychol.* 9:168–99

Krantz, D. H., Luce, R. D., Suppes, D., Tversky, A. 1971. *Foundations of Measurement.* New York: Academic

Künnapas, T., Hallsten, L., Söderberg, G. 1973. Interindividual differences in homomodal and heteromodal scaling. *Acta Psychol.* 37:31–42

Lockhead, G. R., King, M. C. 1983. A memory model of sequential effects in scaling tasks. *J. Exp. Psychol. Hum. Percept. Perform.* 9:461–73

Logue, A. W. 1976. Individual differences in magnitude estimation of loudness. *Percept. Psychophys.* 19:279–80

Luce, R. D. 1972. What sort of measurement is psychophysical measurement? *Am. Psychologist* 27:96–106

Luce, R. D., Baird, J. C., Green, D. M., Smith, A. F. 1980. Two classes of models of magnitude estimation. *J. Math. Psychol.* 22:121–48

Luce, R. D., Galanter, E. 1963. Psychophysical scaling. In *Handbook of Mathematical Psychology,* ed. R. D. Luce, R. R. Bush, E. Galanter, 1:245–307. New York: Wiley

Luce, R. D., Green, D. M., Weber, D. L. 1976. Attention bands in absolute identification. *Percept. Psychophys.* 20:49–54

Luce, R. D., Nosofsky, R. M., Green, M. D., Smith, A. F. 1982. The bow and sequential effects in absolute identification. *Percept. Psychophys.* 32:397–408

Luce, R. D., Tukey, J. 1964. Simultaneous conjoint measurement: a new type of fundamental measurement. *J. Math. Psychol.* 1:1–27

MacKay, D. M. 1963. Psychophysics of perceived intensity: a theoretical basis for Fechner's and Stevens' Laws. *Science* 139:1213–16

Marks, L. E. 1966. Brightness as a function of retinal locus. *Percept. Psychophys.* 1:335–41

Marks, L. E. 1968. Stimulus-range, number of categories, and form of the category scale. *Am. J. Psychol.* 81:467–79

Marks, L. E. 1974a. On scales of sensation: prolegomena to any future psychophysics that will come forth as science. *Percept. Psychophys.* 16:358–76

Marks, L. E. 1974b. *Sensory Processes.* New York: Academic

Marks, L. E. 1978a. Binaural summation of the loudness of pure tones. *J. Acoust. Soc. Am.* 64:107–13

Marks, L. E. 1978b. Phonion: translation and annotations concerning loudness scales and processing of auditory intensity. In *Cognitive Theory,* ed. N. J. Castellan Jr., F. Reske, 3:1–31. Hillsdale, NJ: Erlbaum

Marks, L. E. 1979a. A theory of loudness and loudness judgments. *Psychol. Rev.* 86:256–85

Marks, L. E. 1979b. Sensory and cognitive factors in judgments of loudness. *J. Exp. Psychol. Hum. Percept. Perform.* 5:426–43

Marks, L. E. 1979c. Summation of vibrotactile intensity: an analog to auditory critical bands? *Sensory Process.* 3:188–203

Marks, L. E. 1982. Psychophysical measurement: procedures, tasks, scales. See Wegener 1982, pp. 43–71

Marks, L. E. 1986. Context and sensory processes: in search of basic laws. *Cah. Psychol. Cognit.* 2:121–36

Marks, L. E. 1987. Binaural versus monaural loudness: supersummation of tone partially masked by noise. *J. Acoust. Soc. Am.* 81:122–28

Marks, L. E., Bartoshuk, L. M. 1979. Ratio scaling of taste intensity by a matching procedure. *Percept. Psychophys.* 26:335–39

Marks, L. E., Borg, G., Ljunggren, G. 1983. Individual differences in perceived exertion assessed by two new methods. *Percept. Psychophys.* 34:280–88

Marks, L. E., Stevens, J. C. 1968. The form of the psychophysical function near threshold. *Percept. Psychophys.* 4:315–18

Marks, L. E., Szczesiul, R., Ohlott, P. 1986. On the cross-modality perception of intensity. *J. Exp. Psychol. Hum. Percept. Perform.* 12:517–34

Marley, A. A. J., Cook, V. T. 1984. A fixed rehearsal capacity interpretation of limits on absolute identification performance. *Br. J. Math. Stat. Psychol.* 37:136–51

Marley, A. A. J., Cook, V. T. 1986. A limited capacity rehearsal model for psychophysical judgments applied to magnitude estimation. *J. Math. Psychol.* 30:339–90

McBride, R. L. 1983a. A JND-scale category-scale convergence in taste. *Percept. Psychophys.* 34:77–83

McBride, R. L. 1983b. Category scales of sweetness are consistent with sweetness-matching data. *Percept. Psychophys.* 34: 175–79

McBride, R. L. 1986. Sweetness of binary mixtures of sucrose, fructose, and glucose. *J. Exp. Psychol. Hum. Percept. Perform.* 12:584–91

McGill, W. 1960. The slope of the loudness function: a puzzle. In *Psychological Scaling: Theory and Application,* ed. H. Gulliksen, S. Messick, pp. 67–81. New York: Wiley

McKelvie, S. J., Shepley, K. 1977. Comparisons of intervals between subjective numbers, an extension. *Percept. Mot. Skills* 45:1157–58

McKenna, F. P. 1984. Assimilation and contrast in perceptual judgments. *Q. J. Exp. Psychol.* 36A:531–48

McKenna, F. P. 1985. Another look at the 'new psychophysics.' *Br. J. Psychol.* 76: 97–109

Mellers, B. A. 1983a. Evidence against "absolute" scaling. *Percept. Psychophys.* 33: 523–26

Mellers, B. A. 1983b. Reply to Zwislocki's views on "absolute" scaling. *Percept. Psychophys.* 34:405–8

Mellers, B. A., Birnbaum, M. H. 1982. Loci of contextual effects in judgment. *J. Exp. Psychol. Hum. Percept. Perform.* 8:582–601

Mellers, B. A., Birnbaum, M. H. 1983. Contextual effects in social judgment. *J. Exp. Soc. Psychol.* 19:157–71

Mellers, B. A., Davis, D., Birnbaum, M. H. 1984. Weight of evidence supports one operation for "ratios" and "differences" of heaviness. *J. Exp. Psychol. Hum. Percept. Perform.* 10:216–30

Montgomery, H. 1975. Direct estimation: effect of methodological factors on scale type. *Scand. J. Psychol.* 16:19–29

Murphy, C., Cain, W. S., Bartoshuk, L. M. 1977. Mutual action of taste and olfaction. *Sensory Process.* 1:204–11

Oyamo, T. 1968. A behavioristic analysis of Stevens' magnitude estimation method. *Percept. Psychophys.* 3:317–20

Parducci, A. 1963. Range-frequency compromise in judgment. *Psychol. Monogr.* 77:(2, Whole No. 565)

Parducci, A. 1965. Category judgment: a range frequency model. *Psychol. Rev.* 72:407–18

Parducci, A. 1968. The relativity of absolute judgment. *Sci. Am.* 219:84–90

Parducci, A. 1974. Contextual effects: a range-frequency analysis. In *Handbook of Perception,* ed. E. C. Carterette, M. P. Friedman, 2:123–41. New York: Academic

Parducci, A. 1982. Category ratings: still more contextual effects! See Wegener 1982, pp. 89–105

Parducci, A. 1983. Category rating and the relational character of judgment. In *Modern Trends in Perception,* ed. H. G. Geissler, V. Sarris, pp. 89–105. Berlin: VEB Deutscher Verlag Der Wissenschaften

Parducci, A., Perrett, L. F. 1971. Category rating scales: effect of relative spacing and frequency of stimulus values. *J. Exp. Psychol. Monogr.* 89:427–52

Parducci, A., Wedell, D. 1986. The category effect with rating scales: number of categories, number of stimuli, and method of presentation. *J. Exp. Psychol. Hum. Percept. Perform.* 12:496–516

Parker, S., Schneider, B. 1974. Non-metric scaling of loudness and pitch using similarity and difference estimates. *Percept. Psychophys.* 15:238–42

Parker, S., Schneider, B., Kanow, G. 1975. Ratio scale measurement of the perceived length of lines. *J. Exp. Psychol. Hum. Percept. Perform.* 1:195–204

Payne, M. C., Corso, G. M. 1985. Effects of range on category scaling of loudness judgments. *Percept. Mot. Skills* 60:619–24

Petzold, P. 1981. Distance effects on sequential dependencies on categorial judgments. *J. Exp. Psychol. Hum. Percept. Perform.* 7:1371–85

Popper, R., Parker, S., Galanter, E. 1986. Dual loudness scales in individual subjects. *J. Exp. Psychol. Hum. Percept. Perform.* 12:61–69

Poulton, E. C. 1968. The new psychophysics: six models for magnitude estimation. *Psychol. Bull.* 69:1–19

Poulton, E. C. 1975. Range effects in experiments on people. *Am. J. Psychol.* 88:3–32

Poulton, E. C. 1979. Models for biases in judging sensory magnitude. *Psychol. Bull.* 86:777–803

Poulton, E. C. 1984. A linear relation between loudness and decibels. *Percept. Psychophys.* 36:338–42

Poulton, E. C., Edwards, R. S., Fowler, T. J. 1980. Eliminating subjective biases in judging the loudness of a 1-kHz tone. *Percept. Psychophys.* 27:93–103

Robinson, G. H. 1976. Biasing power law exponents by magnitude estimation instructions. *Percept. Psychophys.* 19:80–84

Rose, B. J., Birnbaum, M. H. 1975. Judgments of differences and ratios of numerals. *Percept. Psychophys.* 18:194–200

Rule, S. J. 1966. Subject differences in exponents of psychophysical power functions. *Percept. Mot. Skills* 23:1125–26

Rule, S. J. 1969. Equal discriminability scale of number. *J. Exp. Psychol.* 79:35–38

Rule, S. J. 1971. Discriminability scales of number for multiple and fractional estimates. *Acta Psychol.* 35:328–33

Rule, S. J. 1972. Comparisons of intervals between subjective numbers. *Percept. Psychophys.* 11:97–98

Rule, S. J., Curtis, D. W. 1973. Conjoint scaling of subjective number and weight. *J. Exp. Psychol.* 97:305–9

Rule, S. J., Curtis, D. W. 1982. Levels of sensory and judgmental processing: strategies for the evaluation of a model. See Wegener 1982, pp. 107–22

Rule, S. J., Curtis, D. W., Mullin, L. C. 1981. Subjective ratios and differences in perceived heaviness. *J. Exp. Psychol. Hum. Percept. Perform.* 7:459–66

Scharf, B. 1983. Loudness adaptation. In *Hearing Research and Theory*, ed. J. V. Tobias, E. D. Schubert, 2:1–56. New York: Academic

Schneider, B. 1982. The nonmetric analysis of difference judgments in social psychophysics: scale validity and dimensionality. See Wegener 1982, pp. 317–77

Schneider, B., Parker, S., Kanow, G., Farrell, G. 1976. The perceptual basis of loudness ratio judgments. *Percept. Psychophys.* 10:309–20

Schneider, B., Parker, S., Ostrosky, D., Stein, D., Kanow, G. 1974a. A scale for the psychological magnitude of number. *Percept. Psychophys.* 16:43–46

Schneider, B., Parker, S., Stein, D. 1974b. The measurement of loudness using direct comparisons of sensory intervals. *J. Math. Psychol.* 11:259–73

Schneider, B., Parker, S., Valenti, M., Farrell, G., Kanow, G. 1978. Response bias in category and magnitude estimation of difference and similarity for loudness and pitch. *J. Exp. Psychol. Hum. Percept. Perform.* 4:483–96

Shepard, R. N. 1966. Metric structures in ordinal data. *J. Math. Psychol.* 3:287–315

Shepard, R. N. 1978. On the status of "direct" psychophysical measurement. In *Minnesota Studies in the Philosophy of Science*, ed. C. W. Savage, 9:441–90. Minneapolis: Univ. Minnesota Press

Shepard, R. N. 1981. Psychological relations and psychophysical scales: on the status of "direct" psychophysical measurement. *J. Math. Psychol.* 24:21–57

Staddon, J. E. R., King, M. C., Lockhead, G. R. 1980. On sequential effects in absolute judgment experiments. *J. Exp. Psychol. Hum. Percept. Perform.* 6:290–301

Stevens, J. C. 1958. Stimulus spacing and the judgment of loudness. *J. Exp. Psychol.* 56:246–50

Stevens, J. C., Marks, L. E. 1980. Cross-modality-matching functions generated by magnitude estimation. *Percept. Psychophys.* 27:379–89

Stevens, J. C., Plantinga, A., Cain, W. S. 1982. Reduction of odor and nasal pungency associated with aging. *Neurobiol. Aging* 3:125–32

Stevens, S. S. 1951. Mathematics, measurement and psychophysics. In *Handbook of Experimental Psychology*, ed. S. S. Stevens, pp. 1–49. New York: Wiley

Stevens, S. S. 1953. On the brightness of lights and loudness of sounds. *Science* 118:576(Abstr.)

Stevens, S. S. 1955. The measurement of loudness. *J. Acoust. Soc. Am.* 27:815–29

Stevens, S. S. 1956. The direct estimation of sensory magnitude—loudness. *Am. J. Psychol.* 69:1–25

Stevens, S. S. 1957. On the psychophysical law. *Psychol. Rev.* 64:153–81

Stevens, S. S. 1958. Problems and methods of psychophysics. *Psychol. Bull.* 55:177–96

Stevens, S. S. 1975. *Psychophysics: Introduction to Its Perceptual, Neural, and Social Prospects*. New York: Wiley

Stevens, S. S., Galanter, E. H. 1957. Ratio scales and category scales for a dozen perceptual continua. *J. Exp. Psychol.* 54:377–410

Teghtsoonian, M., Beckwith, J. B. 1976. Children's size judgments when size and distance vary: Is there a developmental trend to overconstancy? *J. Exp. Child Psychol.* 22:23–39

Teghtsoonian, M., Teghtsoonian, R. 1971. How repeatable are Stevens' Power Law exponents for individual subjects? *Percept. Psychophys.* 10:147–49

Teghtsoonian, M., Teghtsoonian, R. 1983. Consistency of individual exponents in cross-modal matching. *Percept. Psychophys.* 33:203–14

Teghtsoonian, R. 1973. Range effects in psychophysical scaling and a revision of Stevens' Law. *Am. J. Psychol.* 86:3–27

Teghtsoonian, R., Teghtsoonian, M. 1978. Range and regression effects in magnitude scaling. *Percept. Psychophys.* 24:305–14

Teghtsoonian, R., Teghtsoonian, M. 1986. Scaling loudness over short ranges: a reply to Poulton. *Percept. Psychophys.* 39:73–75

Thomas, H. 1981. Estimation in the power law. *Psychometrika* 46:29–34

Thurstone, L. L. 1927. A law of comparative judgment. *Psychol. Rev.* 34:273–86

Torgerson, W. S. 1961. Distances and ratios in psychological scaling. *Acta Psychol.* 19:201–5

Treisman, M. 1964. Sensory scaling and the psychophysical law. *Q. J. Exp. Psychol.* 16:11–12

Treisman, M. 1984. A theory of criterion setting: an alternative to the attention band and response ratio hypothesis in magnitude estimation and cross-modality matching. *J. Exp. Psychol. Gen.* 113:442–63

Treisman, M. 1985. The magical number seven and some other features of category scaling: properties of a model for absolute judgment. *J. Math. Psychol.* 29:175–230

Treisman, M., Faulkner, A. 1984. The setting and maintenance of criteria representing levels of confidence. *J. Exp. Psychol. Hum. Percept. Perform.* 10:119–39

Treisman, M., Williams, T. C. 1984. A theory of criterion setting with an application to sequential dependencies. *Psych. Bull.* 91:68–111

Veit, C. T. 1978. Ratio and subtractive processes in psychophysical judgment. *J. Exp. Psychol. Gen.* 102:81–107

Verrillo, R. T. 1979. Comparison of vibrotactile threshold and suprathreshold responses in men and women. *Percept. Psychophys.* 26:20–24

Verrillo, R. T. 1981. Absolute estimation of line length in three age groups. *J. Gerontol.* 36:625–27

Verrillo, R. T. 1982. Effects of aging on the suprathreshold response to vibration. *Percept. Psychophys.* 32:61–68

Verrillo, R. T. 1983. Stability of line-length estimates using the method of absolute magnitude estimation. *Percept. Psychophys.* 33:261–65

Verrillo, R. T., Fraioli, A. J., Smith, R. L. 1969. Sensory magnitude of vibrotactile stimuli. *Percept. Psychophys.* 6:366–72

Verrillo, R. T., Gescheider, G. A. 1975. Enhancement and summation in the perception of two successive vibrotactile stimuli. *Percept. Psychophys.* 18:128–36

Von Wright, J. M., Kekkinen, R. 1970. Stimulus range and the estimated ratio between two stimuli. *Percept. Mot. Skills* 31:294

Wagenaar, W. A. 1982. Misperception of exponential growth and the psychological magnitude of numbers. See Wegener 1982, pp. 379–99

Wagner, M., Baird, J. C. 1981. A quantitative analysis of sequential effects with numerical stimuli. *Percept. Psychophys.* 29:359–64

Wanschura, R. G., Dawson, W. E. 1974. Regression effect and individual power functions over sessions. *J. Exp. Psychol.* 102:806–12

Ward, L. M. 1972. Category judgments of loudnesses in the absence of an experimenter-induced identification function: sequential effects and power function fit. *J. Exp. Psychol.* 94:179–84

Ward, L. M. 1973. Repeated magnitude estimations with a variable standard: sequential effects and other properties. *Percept. Psychophys.* 13:193–200

Ward, L. M. 1975. Sequential dependencies and response range in cross-modality matches of duration to loudness. *Percept. Psychophys.* 18:217–23

Ward, L. M. 1979. Stimulus information and sequential dependencies in magnitude estimation and cross-modality matching. *J. Exp. Psychol. Hum. Percept. Perform.* 5: 444–59

Ward, L. M. 1982. Mixed-modality psychophysical scaling: sequential dependencies and other properties. *Percept. Psychophys.* 31:53–62

Ward, L. M. 1985. Mixed-modality psychophysical scaling: inter- and intramodality sequential dependencies as a function of lag. *Percept. Psychophys.* 38:512–22

Ward, L. M. 1987. Remembrance of sounds past: memory and psychophysical scaling. *J. Exp. Psychol. Hum. Percept. Perform.* 13:216–227

Ward, L. M., Lockhead, G. R. 1970. Sequential effects and memory in category judgments. *J. Exp. Psychol.* 84:27–34

Ward, L. M., Lockhead, G. R. 1971. Response system processes in absolute judgment. *Percept. Psychophys.* 9:73–78

Warren, R. M., Sersen, E., Pores, E. 1958. A basis for loudness judgment. *Am. J. Psychol.* 71:700–9

Wedell, D. H., Parducci, A. 1985. Category and stimulus effects: a process model for contextual memory in judgment. In *Cognition, Information Processing, and Motivation*, ed. G. d'Ydewalle, pp. 55–70. Amsterdam: North-Holland

Wegener, B., ed. 1982. *Social Attitudes and Psychophysical Measurement*. Hillsdale, NJ: Erlbaum

Wendt, D. 1982. On S. S. Stevens' psychophysics and the measurement of subjective probability and utility. See Wegener 1982, pp. 303–14

Young, F. W. 1984. Scaling. *Ann. Rev. Psychol.* 35:55–81

Zwislocki, J. J. 1978. Absolute scaling. *J. Acoust. Soc. Am.* 63:S16(Abstr.)

Zwislocki, J. J. 1983a. Absolute and other scales: question of validity. *Percept. Psychophys.* 33:593–94

Zwislocki, J. J. 1983b. Group and individual relations between sensation magnitude and their numerical estimates. *Percept. Psychophys.* 33:460–68

Zwislocki, J. J., Goodman, D. A. 1980. Absolute scaling of sensory magnitude: a validation. *Percept. Psychophys.* 28:28–38

Zwislocki, J. J., Ketkar, I., Cannon, M. W., Nodar, R. H. 1974. Loudness enhancement and summation in pairs of short sound bursts. *Percept. Psychophys.* 16:91–95

Zwislocki, J. J., Sokolich, W. G. 1974. On loudness enhancement of a tone burst by a preceding tone burst. *Percept. Psychophys.* 16:87–90

Ann. Rev. Psychol. 1988. 39:201–21

PSYCHOLOGY OF RELIGION

Richard L. Gorsuch

Department of Psychology, Graduate School of Psychology, Fuller Theological Seminary, Pasadena, California 91101

CONTENTS

Since this is the first review of the psychology of religion to occur in the *Annual Review of Psychology* series, the paper's first section relates the prominence of psychology of religion in early psychology, notes the decline of interest in it, and outlines the rebirth of attention in recent years. Also considered are possible explanations for this set of changes.

Some research on religion has occurred within other areas of psychology, and samples of such areas are noted in the second section. Other research has focused on religion per se, including mysticism, religious development, and the relationship of religion to prejudice, psychopathology, and other vari-

201

0066-4308/88/0201-0201$02.00

ables. These studies are reviewed in the third section. The last section of this review suggests how research on religion might be appropriate to the discipline of psychology.[1]

THE SHIFTING FORTUNES OF THE PSYCHOLOGY OF RELIGION

A Brief History

The "founding parents" of American psychology were deeply interested in the psychology of religion. William James's *The Varieties of Religious Experience* (James 1902) was of major importance when it first appeared and as an acknowledged classic is still widely read (Gorsuch & Spilka 1987). G. Stanley Hall was also interested in religious phenomena. In addition to being the first PhD in psychology and the first president of the American Psychological Association, he also established a journal on religious psychology that survived until 1915. Hall's concern with religion can also be seen in such articles as "The moral and religious training of children and adolescents" (Hall 1891).

The era also saw a number of major research studies published. People such as Starbuck (1899) and Leuba (1912) conducted massive studies involving thousands of people to establish such facts as the modal age of religious conversion.

While Hall's journal died in 1915, psychology of religion continued as an active area for another decade. But from 1930 to 1960, psychology of religion was almost extinct.

In 1959 the *Review of Religious Research* was started by the Religious Research Association. This "review" principally publishes empirical research, and the sponsoring society includes people employed by religious organizations to do basic and applied research. In 1961 the Society for the Scientific Study of Religion—composed principally of sociologists but with some psychologists—began publishing the *Journal for the Scientific Study of Religion,* and that journal continues to be the preeminent one for scientific investigations of religion; it functions identically to APA journals (e.g. blind

---

[1]Here I review studies upon which the current psychology of religion is based—principally studies in English of Protestant Christians. Hence "Christianity" could be substituted for "religion" throughout this discussion. Psychology always hopes that the principles found operating in one population will generalize to other populations, but this is not necessarily so. Being intrinsically committed to Protestant Christianity may produce relationships radically different from those produced by intrinsic commitment to another set of religious norms. Psychologists from other cultures and anthropologists (e.g. Heelas 1985) may be instrumental in distinguishing the psychology of American Protestantism from the psychology of other religions, and in helping us find conclusions that generalize across several religions.

reviews, 80% rejection rate, etc). At the time of the founding of these journals, it was still rare to see articles on the psychology of religion in the major psychological journals—one of the reasons the new societies were founded. With the establishment of Division 36 of APA, Psychologists Interested in Religious Issues, the psychology of religion is considered to have come of age; it now has a home within its parent organization (Sexton 1986).

There is considerable contemporary activity in the psychology of religion. The activity has produced major bibliographies (e.g. Capps et al 1976; Summerlin 1980; Vande Kemp 1984). Major summaries of the literature in the psychology of religion can be found in Argyle & Beit-Hallahmi (1975), Batson & Ventis (1982), and Spilka et al (1985a). More introductory treatments include Meadow & Kahoe (1984) and Paloutzian (1983). It has also led to what seems to be the inevitable book marking continuing activity in a substantive area: *Advances in the Psychology of Religion* (Brown 1985).

The current activity should not, however, be interpreted to mean that the psychology of religion is well integrated within psychology in general. As Ruble (1985) notes, introductory texts for the psychology of religion generally ignore the existence of religion itself. And when religion is considered, treatment is usually brief and seldom bears any relationship to the accumulating empirical studies of religion. As noted below, much material exists that could be included at this level, both about the relationship of religion to other areas of psychology and about the study of religion per se.

Theories Regarding the Decline and Rebirth of Psychology of Religion

American psychology has developed steadily since its founding, but the psychology of religion has not. What is different about this area of psychology? Does its phoenix history have implications for understanding the appropriate study of religion by current psychology?

THE SCHOLARLY DISTANCE HYPOTHESIS   This hypothesis was developed principally to explain why people in the social sciences are less religious than those in the physical and natural sciences (e.g. Beit-Hallahmi 1977). Teaching investigators to study people objectively, it suggests, produces both a lack of personal commitment to such things as religion and a lack of interest in studying them. The decline in interest in the study of religion might thus result from a coming to preeminence of psychologists taught to distance themselves from religious phenomena. But while this hypothesis could account for the decline of interest in the psychology of religion, it fails to account for the rebirth of interest in this area.

THE PERSONAL RELEVANCE HYPOTHESIS   A hypothesis could start from the fact that psychologists are less likely to be personally involved in a religion than are other academics, including physical scientists (Beit-Hallahmi 1977). Since psychologists find it irrelevant to their own lives, they may be inclined to assume that religion is irrelevant to other people's lives as well. If so, then studying religion would seem a waste of time.

A further development of this hypothesis would suggest that nonreligious people choose to enter psychology as a way of helping others. But religious people with the same concerns would enter theological studies or the ministry, thus leading to their underrepresentation in psychology. Such a process of self-selection could account for the decline in the study of the psychology of religion, and it might explain the initial rebirth in the area, for that occurred after the 1950s, a decade in which religion became more prominent in the United States. But the psychology of religion continued to develop from the 1960s till now even though mainline religious groups suffered a major decline during part of that time.

THE "BACKLASH" HYPOTHESIS   Sexton (1986) has documented the interaction between Roman Catholics and psychology. She shows that many Roman Catholic leaders had a negative reaction to psychology. It is probable that such a "backlash" occurred in Protestantism as well. These religious people had deemed human development and interaction to be primarily a matter of religion and saw the new science of psychology as encroaching upon their area. Such a concern would cause the withdrawal of religious people from the area of psychology as suggested in the previous theory. However, as an explanation of the decline and rebirth of the psychology of religion, the backlash hypothesis has an advantage over the previous one. It suggests that some Catholics and Protestants became psychologists themselves and interacted with the religious leadership, causing the leadership to believe that the threat from psychology was not as great as the threat from ignoring it. Hence the rebirth of interest in the psychology of religion might have resulted from a decrease in the backlash as religious leaders came to terms with psychology. This resurgence of acceptance led to establishment of such groups as the Catholic organization that was a precursor of Division 36 of the APA and to the founding of the Graduate School of Psychology at Fuller Theological Seminary.

THE COMING OF AGE OF PSYCHOLOGY HYPOTHESIS   A number of similar areas in psychology experienced decline and rebirth at approximately the same time as the psychology of religion. The course of cognitive psychology has parallelled that of the psychology of religion. I have suggested elsewhere (Gorsuch 1986) that both courses are functions of the same general movement, namely, the coming of age of psychology as a separate discipline.

The coming of age hypothesis suggests that psychologists from World War I to World War II turned away from both the psychology of religion and cognitive psychology because these resembled the discipline psychology was leaving: philosophy. During that period the study of anything that resembled philosophy was strongly discouraged in order to help psychology establish its separate identity as a science; hence psychology shifted from the study of mind and spirit to the study of behavior. But by the 1960s, psychologists had generally been trained after psychology was established as a discipline and so did not feel that the boundaries of psychology needed to be defended by eliminating topics resembling philosophy. Considerations of the activities of the mind—including both cognitive psychology and the psychology of religion—again became permissible topics, and both were reborn.

These hypotheses about the changing fortunes of the psychology of religion are based upon the personal concerns of psychologists. For example, the personal relevance theory and the coming of age theory both imply that psychologists have, for reasons unique to them as persons, often overlooked religion. The former posits that psychologists who are not religious themselves are not interested in finding out why others embrace religion, possibly because such discoveries might threaten their own personal noninvolvement. The latter suggests that psychologists may have restricted the area of psychology to prevent being personally misunderstood as philosophers rather than scientists. If such personal dynamics influence the relationship between psychology and religion, some problems in the psychology of religion may arise from psychologists' world views, a point to which I return below.

Is Religion An Important Psychological Variable?

Since psychology has functioned for a number of years without studying religion, it is reasonable to ask whether recent analyses have found evidence that religion is a variable worthy of mainstream research. Reviews that collate information on the relationship of religion to several psychological topics are available (e.g. Argyle & Beit-Hallahmi 1975; Spilka et al 1985a). In keeping with the behaviorist orientation of psychology for the past 50 years, these reviews concern either attitudes deemed directly relevant to behavior or behavior itself. Religion relates consistently to, for example, reductions in use of illegal drugs, in prejudicial attitudes, and in nonmarital sexual behavior. In areas such as these it is now apparent that psychological analysis is incomplete unless it includes information on the religiousness of the people being studied and how that affects the focal behavior.

Granted that religion is an important variable in people's lives, it could be argued that it is a part of sociology rather than psychology. Certainly religious institutions have been and remain a central focus in sociology. But to say that religion is only relevant to sociology would be to deny the impact of the internalized beliefs, attitudes, and values characteristic of religious people.

Such distinctive characteristics must be part of psychological analysis. Of course, sociological analyses may help us understand why particular beliefs, attitudes, values, and practices are found in particular religious people at a particular point in culture and history, but once they are within the life sphere of the individual they are legitimate psychological data.

But perhaps it is not necessary to demonstrate the importance of religion in people's lives. Psychology is a science, and any area within its general domain is legitimate for investigation. The results of such investigation vary in relevance according to the situation, and the relevance of a line of research may not become apparent until years later. Knowledge about religion is as worthwhile as any other addition to the knowledge base of psychology.

RESEARCH ON RELIGION WITHIN OTHER PSYCHOLOGICAL AREAS

While religion may not be the focal point of an investigation, religion as a variable may be included within a study for a variety of reasons. For example, religion may be an easy area in which to collect data to test a basic theory. Or it may be that it is gathered as one of the "background variables," as are age and social class. This section touches upon research in several areas of psychology that have included religion in such a manner. (The current section differs from the next one in that the latter reviews research where religion has been the focal point of the study.)

It is difficult to review the general psychological literature with regard to religion. Studies often include religion as a nonfocal variable without indexing it in abstracting systems. And since religion is nonfocal, studies seldom reference prior studies in the same area or focal studies of religion by which they might be retrieved through a citation search.

The difficulties can be illustrated from a review I conducted (Gorsuch & Butler 1976). Since the review was on substance abuse, we ran the indexing and citation searches accordingly. In examining the resulting articles, the variable most often included was religion, which correlated significantly with substance abuse. But these studies had not been indexed under religion. No one reviewing religion would have found them.

Therefore instead of being definitive, this section is illustrative. It notes the literature I have happened across in social psychology in which religion was included as a variable. It will probably illustrate the major possibilities and problems of other areas as well.

Attitudes and Behavior

Religious variables have been used for basic research on attitudes. Thurstone researched his equal-appearing-intervals method of attitude measurement with religion. Indeed, a set of scales (subsequently ignored) were developed by

Thurstone & Chave (1929) to cover the many facets of religion. This tradition of using religion to investigate basic attitude scaling was followed by Fishbein & Ajzen (1974). This study included religious attitude scales developed by several methods: Thurstone equal-appearing interval, Likert summative scaling, Osgood semantic differential technique, Guttman scaling, and self-rating. All these techniques correlated at the maximum allowed by their reliabilities, and hence the various attitude scales give the same result. One conclusion for the psychology of religion is that we need not be concerned with which of the well-established methods of attitude scaling is employed. A further conclusion, reinforced in the psychology of religion literature noted below, is that a single self-rating item can do as well as a traditional multi-item attitude scale when it comes to measuring religion.

Religion was also used by Fishbein & Ajzen (1974) to document a principle of central importance to social psychology. It has been known at least since Hartshorne & May (1929) that attitudes correlate only .2–.3 with an individual behavior. This has been a continuing embarrassment to a social psychology that defines itself as primarily concerned with behavior.

The study by Fishbein & Ajzen (1974) identified a condition that leads to a strong correlation between religious attitudes and religious behaviors. They had 100 self-reports of religious behaviors as well as religious-attitude scales. When they correlated the religious-attitude scales with any individual behavior, the median correlation was .14; but when they correlated the religious-attitude scale with the sum of 100 religious behaviors, the median correlation was .64, a value almost as high as it could be given the reliability of the scales. Religious-attitude scales are seldom about one behavior in one situation; rather, they measure aggregated attitudes toward aggregated religious behaviors. Hence they will predict aggregated religious behaviors. Fishbein and associates then moved into proving the corollary of this, namely, that to predict individual behavior in a particular situation one needs attitudes that match that behavior in terms of setting, time, and other such variables. While not using religion in these studies, they have nevertheless shown the principle clearly (Fishbein 1980). A literature review (Rushton et al 1983) has documented this *aggregation principle* in numerous areas of psychology. In order to predict a number of behaviors, one needs attitudes or other such scales that cut across the breadth of all of the behaviors to be predicted. To predict an individual behavior in a particular situation, one needs scales as specific as the behavior to be predicted. While we do not yet know how to move from aggregated to specific behavior, it is apparent that this principle must always be taken into account when designing any contemporary study involving a religious attitude or value and behavior.

Rokeach (1973, 1979, 1984) and Scott (1965) have both measured religion as a value. Rokeach subjectively analyzed a wide range of writings and derived his instrumental and terminal values therefrom. One of these is the item "salvation," which is then used to represent religion (even though it "pulls for" a conservative and personally oriented type of religiousness). Scott utilized an empirical method to determine what values college students held, among which was religion. His scale defines religion more broadly than did Rokeach but also measures values rather than attitudes. In the case of Rokeach, value is defined as that which is important, and in the case of Scott it is defined as that which one finds admirable. Considerable work has been done with Rokeach's scale, and every such study therefore has some data on one aspect of religion, namely, the item salvation.

Social Attitudes and Behavior

Research has considered religion in the context of other social-psychological variables. One fairly long tradition has considered the dimensionality of a number of social attitudes, of which religion is one. Ferguson (1939) was one of the first of that tradition and has been followed by Eysenck (1953, chapter 10), Wilson (1973), and Kerlinger (1984). The conclusion is that religion is often a part of a general second-order "conservative" factor, where conservative is defined as supporting traditional democratic culture and opposing socialist/communist cultures. These studies do not, however, account for either religion or conservatism in terms of the other and, due to their high level of aggregation resulting from such broad factors, can only be expected to predict highly aggregated behavior.

Social psychologists also often include religion as a nonfocal variable when they study sex. They conclude that the frequency of sexual intercourse among married couples is the same for religious and nonreligious people. However, the religious people have been involved in premarital and extramarital sex at a rate approximately half that of the nonreligious people (Spilka et al 1985a:60–264).

In the area of drug abuse and alcohol use, one also finds major differences between the religious and nonreligious. Religion is one of the most consistent correlates of drug noninvolvement (Gorsuch 1980; Spilka et al 1985a:64–270). In alcohol use, differences are also found across denominations, with those traditionally opposed to alcohol using it less; all denominations use less alcohol than the nonreligious. Of those who *do* drink, the religious abuse alcohol *less* than do the nonreligious [a widely quoted finding to the contrary has never been replicated even when a sample was drawn by identical methods by the same organization and analyzed using the same items (Gorsuch 1976)].

Critique

In most of the areas referred to above, religion has been a nonfocal variable and so has been measured at a primitive level despite the Thurstone and

Fishbein uses of religion in attitude scaling research. There has been heavy reliance upon either religious membership or religious preference as a single-item measure of religiousness. The fact that such measures combine the religiously inactive who have behaviorally rejected their faith with the religiously active suggests that they are relatively insensitive. (Research with more differentiated variables underscores that these variables are indeed relatively weak.) Despite mediocre measurement, large differences were still found in areas such as substance abuse and sexual behavior.

Better measurement is available for inclusion in studies when religion is a nonfocal variable. Two or three items, such as church attendance and religious preference, can give considerably more sophisticated measurement at virtually no extra cost in data collection or analysis. (See Gorsuch & McFarland 1972 for examples of such items.)

Another shortcoming of the studies including religions as a nonfocal variable is that the studies themselves have not taken religion seriously. Of course the fact that religion was originally included as a *non*focal variable suggests that the authors had no direct hypothesis regarding it and, thus, before the studies started, no reason to take the variable seriously. Unfortunately, the studies have often not taken religion seriously even after it has been empirically found to be a major variable. For example, when Gorsuch & Butler (1976) reviewed substance abuse, they found religion to be the most consistently replicated correlate of nonabuse. It was not unusual to find religion the most significant predictor in the study and yet have it ignored in both the discussion and the abstract. At that time not a single study had considered religion per se. Certainly any variable found to be a consistent predictor should be a focal point for discussion and new research, and yet religion continues to be ignored in studies of drug abuse (Gorsuch 1980) except for an occasional article in the psychology of religion (cf Perkins 1985).

ACTIVE RESEARCH AREAS

The Nature of Religion

Studies using religion as the focal dependent variable have little problem finding a scale. Instead the problem is of selecting among the many candidates. Chave (1939) extended the work with Thurstone by publishing 52 different measures of aspects of religion. Strommen et al (1972) have published 78 different scales, which represent almost every concept that others had attempted to scale before them, with factor analyses showing their interrelationships. In addition, there are scales particular to certain lines of research, such as analyses of concepts of God. These scales have been found to have reasonable reliabilities and validities (Gorsuch 1984).

There is little pressure in the psychology of religion towards one universal definition of religion. Instead religion is viewed as multifaceted, with facets that often interrelate. The facet most critical to the line of research being conducted is chosen for measurement. Of course, the reader must not assume that the results apply to other specific definitions of religion.

Generally, religion scales intercorrelate, and some can be considered interchangeable for exploratory purposes. But a scientist may need more specific data, and then particular religious scales, which only correlate moderately with each other, can be used to tap into different aspects of religiousness. Thus there tends to be a factor of religious conservatism/fundamentalism that is distinct from the factor of traditional Christianity. Likewise a separate factor of individualism (as opposed to institutionalism) can be readily found.

The most empirically useful definitions of religion so far are the intrinsic (*I*) and extrinsic (*E*) concepts introduced by Allport. Allport defined intrinsic religion as religion that serves as its own end or goal—i.e. as a terminal value. Extrinsic religion is used in the service of other goals and needs—i.e. as an instrumental value. Operational definitions of these constructs were given by Allport & Ross (1967) and have resulted in a generally useful scale (Gorsuch & Venable 1983; note that item 1 in the appendix is mislabeled as an *E* item, when it is actually scored as an *I* item). Donahue (1985) provides an overview of the research using *I* and *E*.

An approach to measuring religion that has seldom been used is that based on beliefs. Despite the fact that most religions make truth claims, religion itself is generally seen by psychologists as motivational. Cattell (Cattell & Child 1975) sees religion as a sentiment subsidiary to basic drives. Spiro (1966) sees religion as based upon needs which, having little other mode of satisfaction, are satisfied through religious activity. Psychologists of religion have been conceptualizing religion in terms of attitudinal measures, thus implicitly agreeing with such positions. However, it is apparent that many religious leaders see religion as based upon a certain understanding of the world—that is, upon beliefs about the nature of reality. Since beliefs have been critical in the thinking of many religious leaders, it would seem useful to examine beliefs specifically as a further development within the psychology of religion.

Religious Experience and Mysticism

Personal religious experiences involve encountering transcendence, and may also meet the criteria for mystical experiences (i.e. may be noetic, ineffable, holy, positive, and paradoxical) (Hood 1973). Several factors leading to such experiences include personal discontent and its resolution, on the one hand, and situational factors, on the other. The latter might be religious symbols and imagery or an unusual situation that confronts one in a unique way. For example, people report mystical experiences when they find encounters with nature either unexpectedly easy or unexpectedly difficult. Hood in Spilka et al (1985a, chapters 7 and 8) summarizes this line of research.

Religious Development

Several theories of religious development have continued to be of interest although research based upon any one of them has been sporadic at best. The theoretical approaches include projection theories, socialization theories, and cognitive-development theories.

Projection theories have been principally investigated using concepts of God and concepts of parental figures. This line of research has produced negligible results for two reasons. First, the correlations have been low even when they are significant and, second, they suffer from a methodological problem. Concepts of "good beings" are by definition highly similar. The correlation between the "good parent" concept and a concept of God (also presumably judged as good) is thus artificial. Within a general domain, any two elements that both meet a criterion of good will by definition correlate (Spilka et al 1985a:80–82), a suggestion supported by Schoenfeld (1987). Kirkpatrick (1986a) suggests that projection theories are so loosely defined they provide inadequate theoretical basis for research, and I concur.

The socialization approach to religious development investigates the impact upon the individual of others in the psychological field—namely, parents, teachers, and peers. The research finds correlations between parents' and children's approaches to religion. For example, parents' approach to religion correlates highly with children's attending parochial school, as does parents' religiousness with the religiousness of children's peers. In fact it has been methodologically difficult to establish whether children's religiousness is affected by factors other than religiousness of their parents. The correlation between children's religiousness and parochial school attendance may result from parents' choice of a school, or that between children's religiousness and the religiousness of peers may result from parental pressure to select certain types of peers; hence these correlations may not indicate causation (see Spilka et al 1985a, chapter 4).

Cognitive developmental approaches have been used to understand how children's views of, for example, prayer, God, and historicity change as they grow up. The conclusions are basically in keeping with the Piagetian approach: Young children view religion concretely whereas teenagers approach the materials more abstractly and symbolically. A methodological problem has plagued this developmental research: Studies of religious development have been sporadic and cross-sectional. Few advances will be made in this area until longitudinal and experimental approaches are brought into it.

Religion and Social Behavior

Studies of how religion affects prejudice or pro-social behavior are summarized in Batson & Ventis (1982, chapter 8) and Spilka et al (1985a, chapter 11). The area continues to be an active one, marked by varying interpretations of socially relevant variables.

Research relating religion to social behavior first centered upon prejudice toward minorities. This line of research began shortly after World War II and was the area in which Allport first conceptualized the intrinsic/extrinsic distinction. Gorsuch & Aleshire (1974) summarized that line of research in a metaanalysis. Their conclusions were:

1. Active church members were among the least prejudiced in society, and inactive church members were among the most prejudiced in society.

2. Religious behavior such as church attendance is curvilinearly related to prejudice, with the most prejudiced being those who are peripherally involved in religion and the less prejudiced being those who are heavily involved.

3. Those with an intrinsic orientation towards religion are relatively unprejudiced, whereas those with an extrinsic view are relatively prejudiced.

The Batson et al (1985) summary of the research supports the same conclusions.

Several variations upon relating I (i.e. intrinsic) and E (i.e. extrinsic) religiousness to prejudice have been noted recently that may be useful in understanding why E relates to variables such as prejudice. Kirkpatrick (1986b) shows that the E scale consists of two factor-analytically distinct subscales, along with some miscellaneous items. One subscale groups personal items (called here E_p) whereas the other groups items with a social orientation (labeled E_s). A further development is to look more closely at the interaction formed by the intrinsic and extrinsic scales—what Allport & Ross (1967) called the indiscriminately proreligious (high on both scales) versus the indiscriminately antireligious (low on both scales). The current recommendation for measuring the indiscriminately pro- and indiscriminately antireligious attitudes is to rescale the scores on I and E (dividing by the number of items in each scale) and then multiply the two scores together (i.e. $I \cdot E$). A high score can then only occur if a person is high on both scales, a low score if low on both. Following Kirkpatrick's distinction of E_p from E_s, there would be two such interactions—$I \cdot E_p$ and $I \cdot E_s$. In addition to the $I \cdot E$ approach, Pargament et al (1987) have made substantial progress in developing another direct measure of indiscriminate proreligiousness as well. The usefulness of E_p, E_s, and $I \cdot E$, or of the Pargament measure in further theory and research has yet to be explored, but this is currently considered the cutting edge in the utilization of these scales.

Batson has also suggested that a "quest" dimension be added to the intrinsic and extrinsic ones (e.g. Batson 1976; Batson & Ventis 1982). He has measured this through factor analysis in which his Interactional Scale loads a separate factor from several measures of *I* and *E* (Batson & Ventis 1982, chapter 5). The quest factor is problematic. Its reliability is low when measured by the Interactional Scale, the factor's only unique defining variable. For example, Snook & Gorsuch (1985) found an internal consistency reliability of .2. The fact that quest occasionally correlates at a low level with some other variable despite the low reliability probably means that one or two of the scale's items relate. Such a correlation should be followed by relating each item of the Interactional Scale to the other variable. However, this has seldom been done. (Batson's scoring of quest as a factor scale does, of course, preclude such subdividing of the items, and so is not recommended.) Until studies accrue that use more reliable measures of quest, such as that recently developed by Kojetin et al (1987), few conclusions can be theoretically meaningful.

With regard to the relationship of religiousness and pro-social behavior, Batson et al (1985) note that the literature consistently shows that (*a*) religious people report more helpfulness towards others (1985, p. 198) and (*b*) more religious people help others, owing to the institutionalized help programs provided by religious organizations (1985, p. 205). Spilka et al (1985a, p. 286) generally agree with this but point out that these studies are all correlational and hence cannot be interpreted causally.

A debate continues over interpretation of the relationships between religion and pro-social behavior. The interpretations have generally used terms from social psychology that have both operational definitions and judgmental overtones. For example, an investigator might borrow from Asch's (1951) conformity research the definition of conformity as one person following the suggestion of another (a confederate of the experimenter) in contradiction of his/her own perceptions. That definition might then be used to interpret a finding in research on religiousness and helping behavior. The finding might be, as Darley & Batson (1973) suggest, that religious people who stopped to help another could be divided into two groups. The first would contain those who, having heard the person they had stopped to help (the experimenter's confederate) suggest that no help was needed, quickly hurried on. The second would comprise those who, despite the confederate's statement, held to their own perception of the situation and persisted in helping. The first group could be interpreted as more "conforming." Such an interpretation accords with the definition of conformity found in the Asch studies and is consistent with the report of Darley & Batson (1973).

Readers familiar with the line of research begun by Darley & Batson's study have probably noted an anomaly: No investigator in this area has utilized an interpretation of conformity. Instead Batson (e.g. Batson & Ventis 1982; Batson et al 1985) has used another term from the social-psychological literature. He suggests that religious people who try to help a person they perceive to be in need despite a denial of that need are responding in a "socially desirable" manner. The conformity interpretation for the nonhelpers, an equally legitimate one, is not considered by Batson. I suggested it above not because I believe it is the appropriate interpretation but rather to point out how readily multiple value-laden terms such as "socially desirable" can be applied.

Research studies do not answer the kinds of question that some would like psychology to answer, such as whether "religion is on our side." That question can only be answered if one has already theologically or philosophically defined what it means "to be on our side," and then the result is usually tautological. Moving from simple descriptions of results to value-laden interpretive terms moves the discussion from psychology into philosophy.

Batson and associates have continued to test whether the intrinsically motivated religious person is interested in "socially desirable" results (see Batson et al 1985 for an overview of these studies). Intrinsic motivation, I, correlates with a set of self-reported helping behaviors but has not been found to correlate with specific helping behavior. Thus, for example, religiousness did not correlate with attempts to help in experiments where subjects had reason to believe a person in a neighboring room might have been injured by a falling ladder (Annis 1975, 1976). Batson heavily weights this *lack* of a statistically significant relationship between aggregated religious scores and a specific behavior. However, given the aggregation principle noted above, we must reconsider those studies. One seldom finds that any aggregated variable relates to an individual behavior, because the level of aggregation is inappropriate. Hence all studies comparing a religiousness scale to an individual behavior must be discounted, and cannot be used to suggest that the intrinsically motivated person says one thing and lives another. Only when those studies are redone with appropriate situationally specific variables or aggregated behaviors [following, for example, models like Fishbein's (1980)] can any conclusions be drawn on this topic.

A second line of evidence suggested by Batson has been the correlation of I with scores on a social desirability scale. Watson et al (1986), however, show that such correlations seem to be a unique function of only the Crowne & Marlowe (1964) measure of social desirability, which they hold to be confounded by religiously relevant content. Spilka et al (1985b) found no relationship between I and several measures of social desirability.

Batson uses the social desirability data to infer that intrinsically motivated people only appear low on measures of prejudice because this is the "socially desirable" thing to do. However, there is research evidence against this interpretation. Gorsuch & Aleshire (1974) did a metaanalysis of the work on this correlation and found two relevant facts. First, the date of the research—

and the years varied from the late 1940s to the early 1970s—was unrelated to the findings. Second, the region of the country in which each study was done was unrelated to the findings. These facts are important because the social desirability of a nonprejudiced position varied greatly across those years. In the 1940s and early 1950s, prejudice was socially desirable, particularly in the South. Hence if Batson is correct, early studies using church attendance or other such variables should have found that highly religious people were more prejudiced. However, that was not the case: the results in Texas, for example, showed the highly religious to be less prejudiced.[2]

One trouble with the notion of social desirability is that the question "Desirable to whom?" has gone unanswered. For example, is it to be desirable according to the values of anyone with whom one is in contact or according to the values of society at large? Discussions often ignore the technical literature that suggests multiple definitions are appropriate (e.g. Spilka et al 1966; Watson et al 1986) and that Protestants show little social desirability shift even on topics of central importance to them and society (Charters & Newcomb 1958). It should also be noted, in fairness to Batson and his associates, that Batson includes important modifiers of the position, pointing to considerable evidence on the other side of the argument (e.g. Batson et al 1985, pp. 204–5). This dialogue in the literature does suggest, however, that terms such as "conformity" and "social desirability" seem less than helpful in developing scientific understandings of religion. Instead these terms produce discussions in the area of moral philosophy, not empirical questions.

An interpretation that intrinsically religious people (I's) are trying to follow the internalized norms of their group is consistent with the past literature. American Christianity has contained a theme of the equality of all people, and those who are most involved in it–the high attenders and intrinsics–attempt to carry out that theme. But the fact that they primarily adhere to their group's norms is underscored by Snook & Gorsuch (1985), who investigated the relationship of religion to prejudice in South Africa. The Dutch Afrikaans church's documents have long contained strong theological statements supporting segregation of blacks and whites. Afrikaaner I's were found to be more prejudiced than the non-I's, and thus met their group's norms. The norms of the I's have gone unexamined to date because existing studies have treated a relatively homogeneous culture, principally American Protestantism, and so there was no variation in the norms to raise the question.

---

[2]I feel such an interpretation has lingered on in the journals only because today's young psychologists did not live through that era. For one such as myself who was involved in church work and the civil rights movement during that period, the losses to the church in terms of finances and church membership because of the pro-integration stance of most religious denominations were obvious. Few in the ministry saw favoring integration and being nonprejudiced as socially desirable in the eyes of their congregations until at least the late 1960s or early 1970s (e.g. Thomas 1985).

The problem of interpretation of the relationship of religion to a scale normally seen as undesirable occurs in another area: the positive correlation between religiousness and the MMPI Lie scale. Francis (1985, pp. 179–80) summarizes that literature. The Lie scale consists of a number of peccadillos the authors assume everyone will have engaged in and will report if they are honest. The authors note that people vary on the degree to which they have committed these peccadillos; lying is indicated by a threshold score. But studies relating religion to lying ignore the need to use a threshold score. Such studies generally conclude that religious people lie more because their L-scale scores are higher but do not test if they are above the threshold. Richardson (1985, pp. 214ff) reports that Wolfgang Kuner (who replicated the correlation) concluded that it is appropriate for religious people to have a higher L-scale score because they control their behaviors more than others do. This is, of course, in keeping with the evidence noted previously that religious people report a higher level of personal morality. It seems that most who interpret this correlation assume everyone always commits these peccadillos, and hence the L-scale scores of religious people may be high only because they lie or repress memories of what they have done. Another hypothesis, however, is that they commit fewer peccadillos. Presenting either interpretation as the only one seems premature.

In sum, religiously active and intrinsically religious people are among the least prejudiced in our society and report more helping of others. On the other hand, the extrinsically religious person, who seldom attends religious services, is among the most prejudiced and reports less helping of others. The latter are people to whom the church has little access, and so it cannot be blamed for their attitudes or behaviors. But neither can religious people use these conclusions to take credit. We have so little data on what happens to people who join churches that we do not yet know whether those who are pro-socially oriented join churches or whether people become pro-socially oriented as a result of their church joining.

Physical and Mental Health

A major study (Comstock & Partridge 1972) suggests that religious people are healthier and less suicidal than nonreligious people. Bernard Spilka (personal communication) confirms this result, even after partialling out the fact that religious people smoke and drink less. While there has been little investigation in this area, this finding is consistent with the fact that older people are more religious. Does age produce religiousness or do the religious outlive the nonreligious? Studies showing older people to be more religious are cross-sectional and thus consistent with either interpretation.

With regard to mental health, reviewers (Batson & Ventis 1982, chapter 7; Spilka et al 1985a, chapter 12) agree that the results are mixed owing to a scarcity of theoretical guidance. Definitions of positive mental health differ. If better health is identified with lower guilt and anxiety, then religious people appear more mentally healthy. But Batson & Ventis (1982) point out that a measure of mental health centered on openness and flexibility finds people highly committed to a particular value—such as the *I*'s—to score lower. Note that the question of ideal mental health is as much philosophical and theological as it is psychological. Psychology as a science cannot determine whether low anxiety is better than openness or vice versa. Bergins' review (1983) is recommended reading in this area as well as Batson & Ventis (1982) and Spilka et al (1985a).

Richardson (1985) summarizes the literature on whether those who enter cults are "maladjusted." He concludes that they are not. Indeed, the frequency with which people who join cults have rejected a life-style involving substance abuse and other behaviors commonly at variance with our cultural norms suggests the contrary conclusion. People who join cults are shifting towards the cultural norm of mental health (although they are often shifting away from the cultural norm of religiousness).

Attribution Research

Attribution research has been suggested as a major direction for movement in the psychology of religion. Articles by Proudfoot & Shaver (1975) and Spilka et al (1985c) lay some foundations for a psychology of religion based upon attribution theory, as does the book by Spilka et al (1985a). Unfortunately, too few studies using attribution approaches have accumulated to be reviewed at present.

Other Research Areas

Several minor areas within the psychology of religion deserve mention. One is the study of the process of conversion. Although cross-sectional studies have established such facts as the normal age of conversion, the factors underlying the process remain poorly understood. A major methodological problem in this area is the difficulty in finding appropriate subjects for longitudinal study. Ideally research in this area would involve designs tracking people across time as they do or do not experience conversion. A set of such studies might ferret out the conditions producing conversion and some of its major effects. However, except for occasional studies such as that by Lovekin & Malony (1977), there has been little longitudinal research. Classical research has established that the average age of conversion is between 12 and 17, that conversion may be either sudden or gradual, and that sudden conversions are typified by a definite emotional crisis (Spilka et al 1985a, chapter 9).

Another line of research has investigated attitudes toward death. The best research uses a variety of attitudes-toward-death scales and several measures of religiousness. Studies such as Spilka et al (1977) and Cerny & Carter (1977) typically find more concern with death among E's (i.e. extrinsically religious people) and less concern, particularly about death as the unknown or death as failure, among the I's.

In Western culture religiousness is usually expressed through social institutions, but surprisingly little social-psychological research has been done on religious groups. The most famous study of a religious group (Festinger et al 1964) was not replicated in the only known attempt to do so (Weiser 1974). However, Pargament and associates (e.g. Pargament et al 1979) have been investigating the psychological climate of congregations and synagogues and relating that to other psychological factors. One hopes that work will be expanded and replicated.

CONCLUDING COMMENTS

Psychologists generally have strong pro- or antireligious convictions, which they bring with them to their investigations and interpretations. Some of those convictions may have caused the decline of the psychology of religion, and some may influence how the data are interpreted by psychologists. In the worst cases, investigators have ignored or proceeded beyond the data to draw conclusions in keeping with their own philosophical positions.

While this is always a problem for any science, the personal involvement with which people approach religion means that personal distortions must be guarded against more carefully in this area than in most others. For example, Heelas (1985) provides a clear example of the difference between rational and irrational thinking. But to do so, Heelas must use a physical example; when the topic is religion, the area is much more complex, and what is one person's rationality is another's irrationality. Long ago Thomas Aquinas held that the truly rational person must conclude God exists, but Aquinas used his own definition of rational. Psychologists do not escape this problem just because they are psychologists.

As Collins (1986) notes, neutral objectivity towards religion is difficult to achieve (in part because the religious define neutrality as antireligious). The psychology of religion, then, is an example of the difficulty of complete objectivity in science.

Given the difficulties of objectivity, is a psychology of religion impossible? To say yes would claim that science should be carried out only where total objectivity can be achieved. As Kuhn (1970) shows, most natural sciences also have been far from completely objective and would need to be abandoned if science required complete objectivity.

Instead, the purpose of psychological science is to increase objectivity.

This occurs when each psychologist attempts to establish clear decision rules for conclusions before data are collected, and tests theories by those decision rules. The scientist attempts to define variables clearly, objectively, and nontautologically. Better science is typified by clearer definitions, research designs that eliminate more alternative explanations, and a willingness to state cases where data could refute one's theory. These cases must, of course, be as sophisticated as possible (thus, for example, avoiding violations of the aggregation principle). This is scarcely a new plea, for James (1902) also made this point while demonstrating an integration of his contemporary psychology of religion with his philosophy of pragmatism. (James however, gives a *philosophical* defence of his use of pragmatism in evaluating the results of religiousness.) Freud (1927), on the other hand, commits the genetic fallacy even though James had pointed out the need to avoid it some 25 years earlier.

Encouraging objectivity in psychology hardly means that the personal interests and values of the investigator must be left out of psychology as a science. Indeed, such factors determine the area in which a psychologist labors and lead to the development of good theories and hypotheses. All these elements are and should be influenced by what one feels is important and how one views the nature of reality.

Any study involving religion even as a nonfocal variable should use more sophisticated measurement than religious membership or preference. It is easy to include measures of church attendance and to use intrinsic and extrinsic religiousness scales. These should be the minimum standard for measuring religiousness.

Literature Cited

Allport, G. W., Ross, J. M. 1967. Personal religious orientation and prejudice. *J. Pers. Soc. Psychol.* 5:432–43

Annis, L. V. 1975 Study of values as a predictor of helping behavior. *Psychol. Rep.* 37:717–18

Annis, L. V. 1976. Emergency helping and religious behavior. *Psychol. Rep.* 39:151–58

Argyle, M., Beit-Hallahmi, B. 1975. *The Social Psychology of Religion.* London: Routledge & Kegan Paul. Rev. ed.

Asch, S. E. 1951. Effects of group pressure upon the modification and distortion of judgment. In *Groups, Leadership and Men,* ed. H. Guetzkow. Pittsburgh: Carnegie

Baker, M., Gorsuch, R. 1982. Trait anxiety and intrinsic-extrinsic religiousness. *J. Sci. Study Relig.* 21(2):119–22

Batson, C. D. 1976. Religion as prosocial agent or double agent. *J. Sci. Stud. Relig.* 15:29–45

Batson, C. D., Naifeh, S. J., Pate, S. 1978. Social desirability, religious orientation, and racial prejudice. *J. Sci. Study Relig.* 17:31–41

Batson, C. D., Schoenrade, P. A., Pych, V. 1985. Brotherly love or self-concern? Behavioural consequences of religion. See Brown 1985, pp. 185–208

Batson, C. D., Ventis, W. L. 1982. *The Religious Experience: A Social-Psychological Perspective.* New York: Oxford Univ. Press

Beit-Hallahmi, C. B. 1977. Curiosity, doubt, devotion: the beliefs of psychologists and the psychology of religion. In *Current Perspectives in the Psychology of Religion,* ed. H. N. Malony, pp. 381–91. Grand Rapids, Mich: Wm. B. Eerdmans

Bergin, A. E. 1983. Religiosity and mental health: a critical reevaluation and meta-analysis. *Prof. Psychol: Res. & Pract.* 14:170–84

220   GORSUCH

Brown, L. B., ed. 1985. *Advances in the Psychology of Religion*. Oxford: Pergamon Press

Capps, D., Rambo, L., Ransohoff, P. 1976. *Psychology of Religion: A Guide to Information Sources*. Detroit: Gale Research

Cattell, R. B., Child, D. E. 1975. *Motivation and Dynamic Structure*. New York: Wiley

Cerny, L. J. II, Carter, J. D. 1977. *Death perspectives and religious orientation as a function of Christian faith*. Presented at Ann. Meet. Soc. Sci. Stud. Relig., Chicago

Charters, W. W. Jr., Newcomb, T. M. 1958. Some attitudinal effects of experimentally increased salience of a membership group. In *Readings in Social Psychology*, ed. E. E. Maccoby, T. M. Newcomb, E. L. Hartley, pp. 276–81. New York: Henry Holt. 3rd ed.

Chave, E. J. 1939. *Measure Religion: Fifty-Two Experimental Forms*. Chicago: Univ. Chicago Press

Collins, G. R. 1986. The psychology of religion today. *J. Psychol. Christianity* 5:26–30

Comstock, G. W., Partridge, K. B. 1972. Church attendance and health. *J. Chronic Dis.* 25:665–72

Crowne, D., Marlowe, D. 1964. *The Approval Motive*. New York: Wiley

Darley, J., Batson, C. D. 1973. From Jerusalem to Jericho: a study of situational and dispositional variables in helping behaviour. *J. Pers. Soc. Psychol.* 27:100–8

Donahue, M. J. 1985. Intrinsic and extrinsic religiousness: review and meta-analysis. *J. Pers. Soc. Psychol.* 42:400–19

Eysenck, H. J. 1953. *The Structure of Human Personality*. New York: Wiley

Ferguson, L. W. 1939. Primary social attitudes. *J. Psychol.* 8:217–23

Festinger, L., Riecken, H. W., Schachter, S. 1964. *When Prophecy Fails*. New York: Harper & Row

Fishbein, M. 1980. A theory of reason and action: some applications and implications. In *Nebraska Symposium on Motivation, 1979*, ed. M. Page, pp. 65–116. Lincoln, Neb: Univ. Nebraska Press

Fishbein, M., Ajzen, I. 1974. Attitudes towards objects as predictors of single and multiple behavioral criteria. *Psychol. Rev.* 81:59–74

Francis, L. J. 1985. Personality and religion: theory and measurement. See Brown 1985, pp. 171–84

Freud, S. 1927. *The Future of an Illusion*. Garden City, NY: Anchor Books. Transl. J. Sterachey, 1961; rev. ed. 1964

Gorsuch, R. L. 1976. Religion as a significant predictor of important human behavior. In *Research in Mental Health and Religious Behavior*, ed. W. J. Donaldson Jr., pp. 206–21. Atlanta: Psychol. Stud. Inst.

Gorsuch, R. L. 1980. An interactive, multiple model approach to illicit drug use. In *Theories of Drug Use*, ed. D. J. Lettieri, pp. 18–23, 383–85. Washington, DC: Natl. Inst. Drug Abuse

Gorsuch, R. L. 1984. Measurement: the boon and bane of investigating religion. *Am. Psychol.* 39:228–36

Gorsuch, R. L. 1986. Psychology and religion, beliefs, and values. *J. Psychol. Christianity* 5:38–44

Gorsuch, R. L., Aleshire, D. 1974. Christian faith and ethnic prejudice: a review and interpretation of research. *J. Sci. Study Relig.* 13:81–307

Gorsuch, R. L., Butler, M. 1976. Initial drug abuse: a review of predisposing social psychological factors. *Psychol. Bull.* 81:120–37

Gorsuch, R. L., McFarland, S. 1972. Single- vs. multiple-item scales for measuring religious values. *J. Sci. Study Relig.* 11:53–65

Gorsuch, R. L., Spilka, B. 1987. *The Varieties* in historical and contemporary contexts. *Contemp. Psychol.* In press

Gorsuch, R. L., Venable, G. D. 1983. Development of an "age universal" I-E scale. *J. Sci. Study Relig.* 22:181–87

Hall, G. S. 1981. The moral and religious training of children and adolescents. *Pedagog. Semin.* 1:196–210

Hartshorne, H., May, M. A. 1929. *Studies in Service and Self-control*. New York: Macmillan

Heelas, P. 1985. Social anthropology and the psychology of religion. See Brown 1985, pp. 34–51

Hood, R. W. Jr. 1973. Religious orientation and the experience of transcendence. *J. Sci. Study Relig.* 12:441–48

James, W. 1902. *Varieties of Religious Experience*. New York: Longmans, Green

Kerlinger, F. N. 1984. *Liberalism and Conservatism: The Nature and Structure of Social Attitudes*. Hillsdale, NJ: Erlbaum

Kirkpatrick, L. A. 1986a. Empirical research on images of God: a methodological and conceptual critique. Presented at Ann. Meet. Soc. Sci. Stud. Relig., Savanna, Georgia

Kirkpatrick, L. A. 1986b. *Multidimensionality of extrinsic religiousness*. Presented at Ann. Meet. Am. Psychol. Assoc., Washington DC

Kojetin, B. A., McIntosh, D. N., Bridges, R. A., Spilka, B. 1987. Quest: constructive search or religious conflict? *J. Sci. Study Relig.* 26:111–15

Kuhn, T. S. 1970. *The Structure of Scientific Revolutions*. Chicago: Univ. Chicago Press. 2nd ed.

Leuba, J. H. 1912. *A Psychological Study of Religion*. New York: Macmillan

Lovekin, A., Malony, H. N. 1977. Religious glossolalia: a longitudinal study of personality changes. *J. Sci. Study Relig.* 16:383–93
Meadow, M. J., Kahoe, R. 1984. *Psychology of Religion: Religion in Individual Lives.* New York: Harper & Row
Paloutzian, R. F. 1983. *Invitation to the Psychology of Religion.* New York: Scott Foresman
Pargament, K. I., Brannick, M., Adamakos, H., Ensing, D., Kelemen, M. L., Warren, R., et al. 1987. Indiscriminate proreligiousness: conceptualization and measurement. *J. Sci. Study Relig.* 26:182–200
Pargament, K. I., Tyler, F. B., Steele, R. E. 1979. Is Fit it? The relationship between the church/synagogue member Fit and the psychosocial competence of the member. *J. Commun. Psychol.* 7:243–52
Perkins, H. W. 1985. Religious traditions, parents, and peers as determinants of alcohol and drug use among college students. *Rev. Relig. Res.* 27:15–31
Proudfoot, W., Shaver, P. 1975. Attribution theory and the psychology of religion. *J. Sci. Study Relig.* 14:317–30
Richardson, J. T. 1985. Psychological and psychiatric studies on new religions. See Brown 1985, pp. 209–23
Rokeach, M. 1973. *The Nature of Human Values.* New York: Free Press
Rokeach, M. 1979. *Understanding Human Values: Individual and Societal.* New York: Free Press
Rokeach, M. 1984. *The Great American Values Test: Influencing Belief and Behavior through Television.* New York: Free Press
Ruble, R. 1985. How introductory psychology textbooks treat religion. *J. Am. Sci. Affil.* 37:180–82
Rushton, J., Brainerd, C., Pressley, N. 1983. Behavioral development and construct validation: the principle of aggregation. *Psychol. Bull.* 94:18–38
Schoenfeld, E. 1987. Images of God and man: an exploratory study. *Rev. Relig. Res.* 28:224–35
Scott, W. A. 1965. *Values and Organizations: A study of Fraternities and Sororities.* Chicago: Rand McNally
Sexton, V. S. 1986. Psychology of religion: some accomplishments and challenges. *J. Psychol. Christianity* 5:79–83
Snook, S. C., Gorsuch, R. L. 1985. *Religious orientation and racial prejudice in South*

Africa. Presented at Ann. Meet. Am. Psychol. Assoc., 93rd, Los Angeles
Spilka, B., Hood, R. W. Jr., Gorsuch, R. L. 1985a. *The Psychology of Religion: An Empirical Approach.* Englewood Cliffs, NJ: Prentice-Hall
Spilka, B., Horn, J., Langenderfer, L. 1966. Social desirabilities among measures of social desirability. *Educ. Psychol. Meas.* 16:111–20
Spilka, B., Kojetin, B. A., McIntosh, D. 1985b. Forms and measures of personal faith: questions, correlates, and distinctions. *J. Sci. Stud. Relig.* 24:437–42
Spilka, B., Shaver, P., Kirkpatrick, L. A. 1985c. A general attribution theory for the psychology of religion. *J. Sci. Study Relig.* 24:1–20
Spilka, B., Stout, L., Minton, B., Sizemore, D. 1977. Death and personal faith: a psychometric investigation. *J. Sci. Study Relig.* 16:169–78
Spiro, M. 1966. Religion: problems of definition and explanation. In *Anthropological Approaches to the Study of Religion,* ed. M. Banton, pp. 85–126. London: Tavistock
Starbuck, E. 1899. *The Psychology of Religion.* New York: Charles Scribner's Sons
Strommen, M. P., Brekke, M. L., Underwager, R. C., Johnson, A. L. 1972. *A Study of Generations.* Minneapolis: Augsburg
Summerlin, F. A., ed. 1980. *Religion and Mental Health: A Bibliography.* Brockville, Md: Natl. Inst. Mental Health, US Dept. Health and Human Serv.
Thomas, C. B. Jr. 1985. Clergy in racial controversy: a replication of the Campbell and Pettigrew study. *Rev. Relig. Res.* 26:379–90
Thurstone, L. L., Chave, E. J. 1929. *The Measurement of Attitude.* Chicago: Univ. Chicago Press
Vande Kemp, H. 1984. *Psychology and Theology in Western Thought 1672–1965: A Historical and Annotated Bibliography.* Millwood, NY: Kraus Int. Publ.
Watson, P. J., Morris, R. J., Foster, J. E., Hood, R. W. Jr. 1986. Religiosity and social desirability. *J. Sci. Study Relig.* 25:215–32
Weiser, N. 1974. The effect of prophetic disconfirmation of the committee. *Rev. Relig. Res.* 16:19–30
Wilson, G. D., ed. 1973. *The Psychology of Conservatism.* New York: Academic

Ann. Rev. Psychol. 1988. 39:223–52

ADDICTIVE BEHAVIORS: ETIOLOGY AND TREATMENT

G. Alan Marlatt and John S. Baer

Department of Psychology, NI-25, University of Washington, Seattle, Washington 98195

Dennis M. Donovan and Daniel R. Kivlahan

Seattle Veterans Administration Medical Center, Department of Psychiatric and Behavioral Sciences, University of Washington, ZB-20, Seattle, Washington 98195

CONTENTS

0066-4308/88/0201-0223$02.00

INTRODUCTION AND OVERVIEW

Here we provide a selective review of significant evolving trends in the study of addictive behavior, especially those deriving from psychology and the behavioral sciences. As clinical psychologists, we focus on contributions having significant implications for the prevention and treatment of addiction problems. We therefore highlight studies involving human subjects over animal studies. Another bias is our common theoretical orientation, a perspective based on social-learning theory and on cognitive-behavioral principles. We embrace a commonalities approach for a variety of addictive behaviors, but emphasize alcohol abuse and alcoholism, the most costly of addiction problems in terms of frequency of usage and potential for harm. We refer to other substance abuses for illustrative purposes. Finally, we have limited our coverage to literature since 1980, and to review articles when these are available.

The chapter begins with an overview of the domain of addictive behaviors. Examples of these behaviors are provided, along with some of their defining characteristics. Various conceptual models of addiction are then outlined and critiqued. An emerging *biopsychosocial model* is described that posits multiple etiological determinants. One important component of this model is a *stages-of-change* analysis, based on the assumption that processes associated with becoming addicted and with the subsequent modification of this behavior appear to fall into discrete developmental stages. The bulk of our literature review is organized in terms of the stages-of-change model.

CONCEPTUAL MODELS OF ADDICTIVE BEHAVIOR

A spate of recent books describes a variety of addictive behaviors, including drinking, smoking, other forms of substance abuse, eating, gambling, compulsive sexual behaviors, and sometimes even "addictive relationships" (Levison et al 1983; Miller 1980; Mule 1981; Orford 1985; Peele 1985). These authors delineate the "addictive" potential of these behaviors by the use of adjectives such as compulsive, excessive, impulsive, uncontrolled, indulgent, etc. We define addictive behavior as a repetitive habit pattern that increases the risk of disease and/or associated personal and social problems. Addictive behaviors are often experienced subjectively as "loss of control"— the behavior continues to occur despite volitional attempts to abstain or moderate use. These habit patterns are typically characterized by immediate gratification (short-term reward), often coupled with delayed, deleterious effects (long-term costs). Attempts to change an addictive behavior (via treatment or by self-initiation) are typically marked by high relapse rates.

A variety of approaches to the development (etiology) of addiction and to the modification of these behaviors have been described (e.g. Peele 1985; Shaffer 1985). A model of helping and coping outlined by Brickman et al (1982) clarifies various conceptual approaches to understanding addictive behavior. In their analysis, Brickman and his colleagues posed the following two questions: (*a*) To what extent is the person considered responsible for the initial development of the problem? (*b*) To what extent is the person held responsible for changing the behavior or solving the problem? Based on responses to these two attributional questions, four general models were derived: the *moral model* (person is held responsible for both acquiring and solving the problem), the *medical/disease model* (person is held responsible neither for the etiology nor for the solution), the *enlightenment model* (person is responsible for development of the addiction but is incapable of changing without the help of a "higher power"), and the *compensatory model* (although the person is not held responsible for etiology, change is considered to be a personal responsibility).

The moral model has little support in the contemporary addictions literature, although this approach was predominant during Prohibition (Strug et al 1986). From the perspective of the moral model, addiction is viewed as a sign of weak character; addicts are urged to exercise greater willpower to overcome their sins. In the enlightenment model, so-called because it emphasizes enlightening people about the "true nature" of their addiction, change is possible only by relinquishing personal control to a higher power or collective entity. Brickman places the various anonymous self-help groups (e.g. Alcoholics Anonymous and Narcotics Anonymous) in this category. The self-help literature has recently been reviewed by Gartner & Riessman (1984).

The disease model of addiction developed as an alternative to the victim-blaming orientation of the moral and enlightenment models. First applied to alcoholism (e.g. Milam & Ketcham 1981; Royce 1981; Wallace 1985a), the disease model has been extended to include other forms of addiction (e.g. Norwood 1985). In conjunction with A.A., the disease model represents the dominant approach in American treatment programs (e.g. S. Brown 1985). Most recent advocates of a disease model hypothesize an underlying disease process with an emphasis on physical dependency (Tabakoff & Rothstein 1983), genetic predisposition (e.g. Crabbe et al 1985; Murray et al 1983; Murray & Stabenau 1982; Petrakis 1985; Schuckit 1983; Swinson 1983), and the assumption that the disease is progressive (Knott et al 1987; Mandell 1983).

Despite advantages of the clinical application of the disease model (e.g. allowing people to seek help without being blamed for their addictive behavior), there are several shortcomings associated with using this model as a scientific theory of addiction (Shaffer 1985; Peele 1986). Initially, because of notions about biological/genetic specificity, disease models of addiction fail to account for *commonalities* among addictions, including addictions that do not involve substance use (e.g., compulsive gambling or sexual behavior). Furthermore, disease models of etiology suggest that individuals are not responsible for changing their behavior, and thus these models stop short of explaining how and why many people appear to overcome their addictions without any treatment or professional assistance (Armor & Meshkoff 1983; Perri 1985) or why they seem to benefit from a variety of different treatment approaches (Cox 1987a; Miller & Heather 1986; Perri 1985).

The final model outlined by Brickman is the compensatory model. Here individuals are not considered responsible for the initial development of the problem (since the etiology of the problem involves biological and learning factors beyond individual control) but are assumed to be capable of "compensating" for the addiction by taking an active, responsible role in the change process. Central to the compensatory model is the notion that addiction can best be understood as learned adaptive or functional behavior in the context of personal and environmental factors—i.e. that drug use or other addictive activity is motivated by the individual's attempt to adapt to stress (including stress associated with the consequences of drug use) rather than by simple exposure to addictive substances (Alexander & Hadaway 1982; Peele 1985; Pohorecky & Brick 1983). Recognizing that addiction has multiple determinants, some theorists have suggested that addiction is best described as a biopsychosocial problem (e.g. Collins & Marlatt 1983; Donovan 1987; Ewing 1980; Galizio & Maisto 1985b; Zucker & Gomberg 1986).

Such a conceptualization of addiction attempts to study commonalities across addictive behaviors. In brief, biological processes may increase the risk of developing a dependency in the context of environmental factors (Connors & Tarbox 1985). Learning factors, such as classical and operant conditioning, observational and social learning, and higher-order cognitive processes such as beliefs, expectancies, and attributions are all apparently common to addictive processes. The development of conditioned responses to drug cues (L. H. Baker et al 1987) and conditioned tolerance effects (Tiffany & Baker 1986) are examples. Assessment of outcome expectancies associated with alcohol use has provided a wealth of information critical to understanding how psychological dependency develops (Goldman et al 1987; Lang & Michalec 1987; Marlatt 1987). Addictive behavior is often characterized by biphasic reinforcement effects (an initial positive response followed by subsequent negative responses) (Marlatt 1987), and can be understood using opponent process theories (Shipley 1987). Hedonic responses to drugs may have common neurological bases (Bloom 1983; Simon 1983). Finally, addictive behaviors are not continuous processes but follow common stages of change (Prochaska & DiClemente 1985, 1986). Although terminology differs among investigators, the usual sequence includes the initiation of the addictive behavior (experimentation and the acquisition of dependency), the transition to maintenance of ongoing use (sometimes called the "precontemplation stage"), and active change itself (attempts at reduction or cessation of addictive behavior). The behavior-change sequence (if it occurs) is further divided into three component stages: contemplation and motivation for change, active commitment to change (either self-initiated or treatment-aided), and finally postchange maintenance (successful change vs relapse). In the following sections, each of these stages is examined in greater detail with illustrations from the recent literature.

INITIATION PHASE

We assume a broad definition of initiation, encompassing biological, social, and physiological issues related to risk and initial use of addictive agents. We begin with research related to risk of addiction, before any substance has been encountered. Research on initial use and abuse of drugs is reviewed next, followed by interventions directed at early developmental stages of drug use. More complete reviews of this literature can be found in Galanter (1983, 1985) and Silbereisen et al (1986).

Genetic and Heritability Studies

The current literature frequently states that children of alcoholics are four times as likely to develop alcoholism as children of nonalcoholics, based on data derived from adoption and twin studies (Murray et al 1983; Peele 1986; Schuckit 1987).

The magnitude and dimensionality of this relationship continues to be a research question, however (Peele 1986). The operational definition of alcohol-related problems is a key issue (Alterman & Tarter 1986; Murray et al 1983). Some studies report strong heritability for heavy drinking, but little heritability for "loss of control" or social complications (Cloninger 1983). Other studies suggest heritability of dependency but not abusive drinking. The relatively high level of heritability is seen most clearly in the male children of male alcoholics, and less strongly in female children, when either parent is an alcoholic (Peele 1986).

These inconsistencies have led several authors to suggest typologies of heritability (Alterman & Tarter 1986; Cloninger 1983; reviewed below). Genetic effects are thought to be polygenic, interacting with environmental factors (McClearn 1983). Exposure to an extended period of heavy drinking appears necessary for development of the syndrome (Cloninger et al 1985; Stabenau 1984).

To determine how this apparent genetic vulnerability to alcoholism is physiologically mediated, researchers usually have compared children of alcoholics (so-called high-risk populations) to matched controls who have no alcoholism in their family. Data assessed via self-reports of subject intoxication and body sway (static ataxia) when blood alcohol levels and expectations have been controlled have documented that sons of alcoholics, on average, respond less intensely to moderate doses of ethanol (O'Malley & Maisto 1985; Schuckit 1984). Such group differences in subjective response may indicate increased initial tolerance to ethanol, and may be related to differential cortisol and/or prolactin responses (Schuckit et al 1987a,b). Children of alcoholics tend to have decreased EEG alpha rhythms, a characteristic of practicing alcoholics (Propping et al 1981). Sons of alcoholics also appear to have decreased event-related potentials (P300), with and without challenges of ethanol (Begleiter et al 1984). These results may suggest attentional or orienting differences. No conclusive data differentiate metabolic differences between high-risk populations and controls, although studies have found that high levels of acetaldehyde usually protect against development of alcoholism in certain ethnic groups (e.g. Asians) (Schuckit 1987).

Other research has examined behavioral and neuropsychological characteristics of children of alcoholics. Sons of alcoholics show poorer language-related functioning and learning achievement (Hedegus et al 1984), poorer verbal intellectual performance (Gabrielli & Mednick 1983), and general neuropsychological differences (Schaeffer et al 1984). Not all studies find differences, however (Hesselbrock et al 1985). The most meaningful differences are found when sociopathy is controlled in both high-risk and control samples (Alterman & Tarter 1986).

There is considerable evidence that the alcohol problems of alcoholics with and without a family history of alcoholism have somewhat different courses. Alcoholic children of alcoholics are thought to show symptoms earlier (Penick et al 1978) and to have more severe symptomology (Frances et al 1984), more binge and morning drinking (Valicer et al 1984), and less control over drinking (Stabenau 1984). However, these differences may reflect characteristics of an antisocial personality syndrome, which may represent one type of alcoholism problem (Alterman & Tarter 1986; Cadoret et al 1987; see reviews of typologies below).

Studies of Adolescent Drug Use and Abuse

Since 1960, there have been several large-scale panel studies of the initiation of drug use among adolescents; the reader is referred to Chassin (1984), Long & Scherl (1984), Jessor (1986), Kaplan (1985), and Sadava (1987). A number of consistent predictors of drug-use initiation and drug abuse have been found, including peer drug use, parent drug use, delinquency, parental sociopathy, poor self-esteem, lack of social conformity, and stressful life changes. [For a compendium of 43 theories of drug abuse, see Lettieri et al

(1980).] Recently, research emphasis has begun to focus on multivariate models of drug use in adolescence to determine patterns of drug use and interrelationships of these psychosocial factors.

Adolescent drug use appears to be one component of a syndrome of problem behaviors that may reflect a deviant or unconventional developmental pattern. Bivariate relationships among these variables, predictions from composite indexes, as well as recent factor analyses support this conceptualization (Donovan & Jessor 1985). Drug involvement develops in stages, beginning with beer and wine, moving to liquor and cigarettes, then to marijuana and other illicit drugs. Different social and psychological factors differentially predict initiation of different kinds and levels of drug use (Yamaguchi & Kandel 1984).

Complex models of family and social influences are being explored. Zucker & Noll (1982) have suggested that drug use is influenced directly by intraindividual (genetic and/or temperamental) factors, which are secondarily influenced by social variables (family and peers) and sociocultural and community factors. Predictive relationships are hypothesized to shift with developmental stages. For example, peer influences may be minimal at early ages but highly important at later adolescent stages (Zucker 1979). More recently, Zucker has suggested that some factors may be continuously related to drug and alcohol use (i.e. sociopathy, see below), whereas other factors are important only at certain developmental periods (Zucker 1987). Further research efforts have been directed at early parental influences on childhood knowledge of alcohol and its effects (see Zucker & Noll 1987 for a review).

Huba & Bentler (1982) have proposed a DOMAIN model of drug use development, which defines risk factors within biological, sociological, interpersonal, and intrapersonal domains of influence. This "metatheory" is a framework using latent-variable modeling procedures to define empirically the relative and causal roles of various risk factors. These techniques have been useful in describing, for example, that maternal drug use does not directly influence adolescent drug use, but appears to influence drug use indirectly through the development of deviant attitudes (Newcomb & Bentler 1987). Relatedly, Brook et al (1986) have suggested that certain positive characteristics of family and personality can ameliorate the risk factors stemming from peer involvement.

A host of other studies have begun to specify the roles of stressful life issues (P. Baer et al 1987; Newcomb & Harlow 1986), self-derogation (Kaplan 1985), and role status and social environments (Bachman et al 1984) within broad multivariate frameworks. The many correlates of drug abuse have also been used in a risk-factor analysis of drug involvement (Bry et al 1982; Newcomb et al 1986). In both studies, strong relationships were obtained between the number of risk factors present for an individual and the amount of drug use.

Primary and Secondary Intervention

A great deal of national interest and money has recently been directed at interventions to prevent initiation of adolescent drug and alcohol use. These clinical programs are generally considered primary interventions, organized for entire schools or communities (see Glynn et al 1983; Nathan & Niaura 1987; Schaps et al 1981 for reviews). Programs generally derived from successful anti-smoking campaigns in schools (Flay 1985), health promotion programs for cardiovascular risk (Johnson & Solis 1983), and personal competency training with adolescents (Botvin 1983). The vast majority of intervention programs are poorly evaluated, and most show only minor effectiveness in changing attitudes and behavior (Schaps et al 1981).One carefully controlled study with a two-year follow-up (Project Smart) supports the use of social-skills training programs over values clarification and personal/stress coping approaches (W. B. Hansen et al 1987, unpublished). Other skills-training programs have been adapted with some success to specific ethnic groups, such as Native Americans (Gilchrist et al 1987). Large-scale media campaigns have varying impact (Flay & Sobel 1983).

Recently some attempts have been directed at high-risk groups (secondary prevention) within families. Both Zucker (Zucker 1987, Zucker & Noll 1982) and Patterson (Dishion et al 1987) have developed programs designed for families with conduct-disordered youth. Conduct disorder is highly associated with drug abuse and is thought to be characteristic of chaotic family patterns. Parent-training programs are used to facilitate better parental monitoring and control of adolescent drug use.

Two large-scale information and intervention campaigns directed at alcohol and drug use on college campuses were generally unsuccessful (Kraft 1984; Mills & McCarty 1983). On the other hand, cognitive-behavioral skills-training programs designed specifically for college students who drink at high levels have yielded encouraging initial results (Kivlahan et al 1987).

TRANSITION AND MAINTENANCE OF ADDICTIVE BEHAVIOR

An important factor in the addictive process is the transition from social to deviant drinking patterns (Edwards 1984). Factors likely to be involved in these processes are related to (a) the pharmacological effects of the drug; (b) the user's psychological set (including personality function, attitudes, mood states, and expectations concerning the drug's effect on physical function, feelings, thinking, and behavior); and (c) the complex system of physical and social stimuli that comprise the setting in which the drug is used (Donovan 1987; Galizio & Maisto 1985a; Peele 1985; Wallace 1985b; Zinberg 1984).

This section briefly reviews the salient factors that may contribute both to the transition from initial to problematic use of alcohol and drugs and to the maintenance and escalation of problematic use. Broader and more detailed reviews of such factors are available in a number of recent books (T. B. Baker & Cannon 1987; Blane & Leonard 1987; Chaudron & Wilkinson 1987; Cox 1987b; Donovan & Marlatt 1987; Galanter 1986, 1987; Galizio & Maisto 1985b; Miller & Heather 1986).

Epidemiological Studies

The few long-term prospective studies that exist indicate that most adolescents who drink heavily moderate their alcohol use in later life (Donovan et al 1983; Fillmore & Midanik 1984; Kandel & Logan 1984). By age 21, those who have not initiated use of cigarettes, alcohol, or marijuana are unlikely to do so. Initiation of cocaine continues in the 20s, but this finding may reflect period or cohort effects (Raveis & Kandel 1987).

Recently, Newcomb (1987) has reviewed theory and relevant data pertaining to the effects of adolescent drug use. He concludes that only modest data exist to document the socially held notion that experimentation with drugs is dangerous for long-term physical and mental health. Of primary interest to us here are the characteristics of adolescent drug use that may be associated with later problem use. Intensity of prior use has significantly predicted later use in one sample (Raveis & Kandel 1987). In other samples, the breadth or range of involvement with alcohol (Fillmore & Midanik 1984) and the degree of problem involvement (Donovan et al 1983) have been suggested as better predictors of future alcohol problems. Such longitudinal studies, if continued into the next decade, will no doubt provide valuable prospective information about the transition from adolescent use to adult problem use.

Personality

Researchers have continued to focus on the personality structure of individuals who ultimately develop problems with alcohol and drugs. Cox (1985) noted over 1500 references in the PsyINFO data base related to personality and alcoholism, drug abuse, and other addictive behaviors, but he and others have found a number of methodological problems in research on personality and addiction (Cox 1985; Donovan et al 1986). Measured features of personality or psychopathology may represent antecedents, concomitants, or consequences of substance abuse (or be independent of it), but these features further complicate the interpretation of the underlying relationship (Meyer 1986; Nathan 1987).

The most consistent finding is that many substance abusers have a history of antisocial behavior (e.g. nonconformity, acting out, and impulsivity) and a high level of depression and/or low self-esteem (Cox 1985; Nathan 1987; Tarter et al 1985; Vaillant 1983; Vaillant & Milofsky 1982; Zucker &

Gomberg 1986). Depression and low self-esteem are more likely to be concomitants of either the social conditions surrounding the substance abuse or the pharmacological effects of the substances themselves. Although anti-social behavior may precede the initial signs of alcohol problems and is relatively specific as a precursor to this disorder, Nathan (1987) questions the viability of personality as the determining factor. He notes that a constellation of behaviors and overt acts are predictive of later substance use problems. Nathan finds that the base rates of such acts in the general population are high, that a large number of abusers have never demonstrated antisocial behavior, and that many individuals who have manifested such behaviors in their earlier life do not develop addictive behaviors. He concludes that the predictive utility of antisocial behavior, as a personality construct, is uncertain at best.

An additional inference to be drawn from his conclusion is that individuals at risk exhibit excessive behaviors reflecting their lack of appropriate self-control and coping skills. This, in turn, may contribute to their subsequent substance abuse by providing both a psychological set and social setting in which they are exposed to a variety of role models for the use of alcohol and drugs as part of a general life-style, as a method of gaining social inclusion and reinforcement, and as a means of trying to cope with and exert control over certain areas of their lives (Donovan & O'Leary 1983; Orford 1985; Rodin et al 1984; Wills & Shiffman 1985). This behavior at pattern of drug and alcohol abuse may represent one subtype of drug-related problems (reviewed below).

Drug Effects

Once a substance has been ingested, a number of psychopharmacological factors become operative in determining whether the individual will continue to use the drug (Bardo & Risner 1985; Barrett 1985; Matuschka 1985). Any model of addictive behavior must consider the direct tropic effects of alcohol and drugs of abuse and distinguish them from the indirect behavioral manifestations of these substances (Kaufmann et al 1985; Peele 1985; Zinberg 1984). Distinguishing tropic effects from behavioral manifestations is difficult for three reasons. First, the same drug will have differing pharmacological actions at different dose levels and at different phases of its intake/excretion (e.g. ascending versus descending blood alcohol levels). Second, different drugs within the same class share similar pharmacological properties and behavioral manifestations. Third, the pattern of changes at an affective level may vary across time but appear to be similar across different classes of drugs (Bardo & Risner 1985; Barrett 1985; Donegan et al 1983; Matuschka 1985; Shipley 1987; Solomon 1980; Stewart et al 1984).

The most notable feature of drugs of abuse is that they appear to produce an initial positive affective state or reinforcement (Barrett 1985; Hunt 1987a,b). A corollary is that all psychoactive drugs that are abused produce some alteration in the chemical signals transmitted within the central nervous system. Changes in these neurotransmitters or their receptor sites may mediate the positively reinforcing properties of such substances; the most promising candidates to date are the catecholamines, particularly dopamine and serotonin, and the endogenous opioids (Bardo & Risner 1985; Hunt 1987a,b).

The initial pleasurable feelings associated with drugs of abuse appear to motivate people to continue using them—the positive "hedonic" state that immediately follows drug use is preferred to the state that existed prior to the use (Barrett 1985). Haertzen et al (1983) found that the degree of perceived reinforcement associated with the first drug experience was directly related to the magnitude of the subsequent drug habit; this relationship held for all classes of drugs sampled except for caffeine and nicotine. Barrett (1985) concluded that it is unnecessary for drug users to feel good or to experience euphoria to motivate continued use, but only that they feel better shortly after taking the drug than they did immediately before. This suggests that an important parameter is the relative mood-enhancing properties of the drug, even after chronic use, rather than the absolute level of the resultant mood state.

Stewart et al (1984) and Cox (1987b) have presented incentive models of drug use based on approach behavior and the acquisition of positive affective motivational states. Through conditioning processes, those social and environmental stimuli, as well as the pharmacological effects of an initial dose of a drug after a period of not using it, acquire the power of conditioned positive incentive stimuli, which will generate a desire for the positive effects of the substance and motivate continued use.

Expectancy Factors

Pharmacological effects, by themselves, may be insufficient either to develop or maintain an abusive use pattern (Marlatt & Donovan 1981). As Lindesmith (1968) noted, addiction appears to be an interactive product of social learning in a situation involving physiological events as they are interpreted, labeled, and given meaning by the individual. Important in the latter process, representing the individual's "set" (Zinberg 1984), are the individual's expectations concerning the direct pharmacological and indirect behavioral, interpersonal, and social effects of the drug.

Two primary forms of expectancies have received considerable research attention in the addictions (Adesso 1985; Critchlow 1986; Donovan & Marlatt 1980; Goldman et al 1987; Lang & Michalec 1987; Oei & Jones 1986). Outcome expectancies represent an individual's belief that alcohol or drugs will produce a desired outcome, typically by providing a positive effect or by allowing him or her to avoid, minimize, or escape negative emotions or situations. Brown et al (1980) have found that a wide range of beliefs are held about alcohol's effects. The most notable and global is that alcohol serves as a positive transforming agent or a "magic elixir" (Marlatt 1987). Alcohol is expected to enhance social and physical pleasure, enhance sexual perfor- mance and responsiveness, increase power and aggression, increase social assertiveness, and reduce tension. These findings, based upon a self-report scale, parallel the results of a variety of early laboratory studies on the influence of alcohol and expectancies on behavior (Marlatt & Rohsenow 1980). The findings are also consistent with more recent theoretical and empirical perspectives concerning alcohol's tension-reducing or stress- response dampening effects (Cappell & Greeley 1987; Langenbucher & Nathan 1987; Marlatt 1987; Sher 1987; West & Sutker 1987).

Individuals may acquire their beliefs about alcohol's effects even before beginning to drink (Christiansen et al 1982). These early expectancies appear to be powerful predictors of both adolescent drinking status (Christiansen & Goldman 1983) and adult alcoholism (Christiansen et al 1985). However, drinking behavior may further reinforce and stabilize these beliefs. Both the nature and strength of alcohol-related outcome expectancies vary as a function of a family history of alcoholism (O'Malley & Maisto 1985), drinking status (e.g., Brown et al 1985; Connors et al 1986; Rohsenow 1983), dose levels or perceived levels of intoxication (Connors et al 1987; Southwick et al 1981), and the setting in which the drinking occurs (Sher 1985). In general, heavier drinkers expect more positive and fewer negative consequences from alcohol consumption than do light drinkers (Oei & Jones 1986). Also, the expectan- cies move from generalized to specific with increased drinking experiences (Adesso 1985).

A second form of expectancy that may play an important role in the maintenance of substance use are beliefs in self-efficacy (Bandura 1977). Self-efficacy is defined as an individual's belief about his or her ability to generate a behavior necessary to produce a desired outcome. Efficacy ex- pectancies are important components in a number of theories of substance use and relapse (e.g. Donovan & Chaney 1985; Litman 1986; Marlatt & Gordon 1985; Rollnick & Heather 1982). These theories state that individuals are more likely to use a drug when they feel unable or incompetent to cope with stress or negative mood states. Although the construct of efficacy expectan- cies appears to be valuable heuristically, theoretically, and clinically, it has been less well researched than the construct of outcome expectancies. Most research using the construct of self-efficacy has been in smoking relapse (e.g. Baer et al 1986); the role of self-efficacy in the development and maintenance of substance use is less clear.

Tolerance and Dependence

The diminished response to a particular dose of a drug, or tolerance, is a central construct in addiction (Tabakoff & Rothstein 1983; Tiffany & Baker 1986). Less tolerance appears to develop to the reinforcing effects of drugs, whereas more tolerance may develop to certain aversive effects (Tiffany & Baker 1986). There is no consensus on the basic physiological or biochemical processes responsible for tolerance effects (Tabakoff & Rothstein 1983; Tiffany & Baker 1986). A number of psychological models, based upon the classical conditioning of compensatory responses (e.g. Newlin 1985; Shapiro & Nathan 1986; Siegel 1983) and habituation processes (Baker & Tiffany 1985), have been proposed. Although most assume that both tolerance and withdrawal are mediated by the same physiological mechanisms, this assumption has not been supported by recent findings (Tabakoff & Rothstein 1983; Tiffany & Baker 1986). Again, classical conditioning processes play an important role in the development and elicitation of withdrawal and the experience of craving (Baker et al 1987; Donegan et al 1983; Tabakoff & Rothstein 1983; Tiffany & Baker 1986). Increased drinking is predicted to achieve a previously obtained drug-related effect or to avoid the aversiveness of withdrawal distress.

Tolerance and withdrawal distress have been cornerstones in the definition of addiction and are necessary components in the differential diagnosis of alcohol abuse and dependence (American Psychiatric Association 1980, DSM-III). This distinction between abuse and dependence has not been empirically supported (Schuckit et al 1985). A multiple-syndrome approach to alcohol and drug dependence has gained in prominence (Wanberg & Horn 1983). Dependence is viewed as a multidimensional construct involving a system of subjective, behavioral, physiological, and biochemical components (Hodgson & Stockwell 1985). The dependence syndrome (Edwards 1986; Hodgson & Stockwell 1985) is described as a clustering of a number of key elements, including a narrowing of one's drinking or drug-using repertoire, an increased salience of alcohol- or drug-seeking behavior, increased tolerance, repeated withdrawal symptoms, relief or avoidance of withdrawal symptoms by further drinking or drug use, subjective awareness of a compulsion to drink or use drugs, and a tendency to relapse following abstinence.

The syndrome is not an all-or-none phenomenon, but rather occurs with graded intensity. Not all of the elements need always be present or present at the same degree within the clustering; however, as the intensity of the syndrome increases, there is a greater coherence among the elements. Once limited to describing alcohol dependence, the syndrome concept has been extended to and validated for drug dependence as well (Babor et al 1987a; Skinner & Goldberg 1986).

Skinner (1986) has suggested that there are both state- and trait-like components of the dependence syndrome. The psychobiological elements (e.g. withdrawal, tolerance, relief drinking) appear to fluctuate in severity across situations as a function of the quantity of alcohol consumed and the time since a last drink. The behavioral and subjective elements (e.g. impaired control over drinking, compulsive drinking style, craving) appear to remain relatively consistent across situations and long periods. The basic construct of an alcohol dependence syndrome, as well as those self-report scales developed to measure it, have been validated for the desire or craving for alcohol, the impact of an initial "priming dose" of alcohol, the likelihood of and speed of taking a drink, the amount of medication required for detoxification, and the likelihood of relapse (Babor et al 1987a; Cooney et al 1986; Edwards 1986; Hodgson & Stockwell 1985).

Integrative Typologies of Etiology

An approach consistent with heterogeneous and multiple risk factors for transition to addiction is the development of subtypes within the population of abusers (e.g. Alterman & Tarter 1986; Hesselbrock 1986; Meyer et al 1983; Morey & Blashfield 1981; Morey & Skinner 1986; Nerviano & Gross 1983). The idea of subtypes of alcoholics was originated over 100 years ago (Babor & Meyer 1986). However, this approach has previously been limited by an exclusive reliance on personality variables to derive subtypes (Donovan et al 1986; Meyer et al 1983; Morey & Blashfield 1981). The identification of meaningful subgroups is theoretically and clinically important, especially to match patients more adequately to the most effective treatments. However, it appears necessary to increase the breadth of assessment beyond the scope of personality, employing instead a multiple-domain approach, including drug, set, and setting factors, if such subtyping is to be of practical utility (Donovan et al 1986; Meyer et al 1983).

Several authors have recently suggested typologies of alcohol problems that attempt to incorporate genetic and developmental perspectives. Cloninger et al (1985) have suggested that there are at least two different types of alcoholism heritability. The most common form occurs in both men and women and appears to interact with environmental factors (e.g. unskilled occupational status of parents). A second, less common type may be limited to males. Independent of environment, this type is more related to sociopathy in fathers and somataform disorders in daughters. Zucker (1987) proposes four types of alcoholism, including antisocial, primary (nonenvironmental), developmental limited (abusive-temporary), and negative affect, each with different etiological pathways. He argues that most genetic and drug initiation research has been conducted on only one of the subtypes, and that high predictability of alcoholism may be true for only certain subgroups. Alterman & Tarter (1986) have similarly suggested that sociopathy represents one subtype of alcohol-related problems.

Such fine-grained etiological problems can only be addressed using longitudinal, multivariate studies in which the comparative and interactive relationships of genetic, psychological, and social processes can be studied. For example, Cadoret et al (1987) suggest that heritability of alcoholism and sociopathy may be distinct, and that alcohol problems result from both heredity and alcohol abuse in the environment (adoptive family). Most noteworthy is the 33-year longitudinal study by Vaillant (Vaillant & Milofsky 1982; Vaillant 1983). Although this study did not make use of fine-grained subtyping of alcohol problems, Vaillant was able to compare the prospective predictive power of measures of ethnicity, social class, adolescent delinquency, family integration, adolescent drug use, and family history of alcoholism. Vaillant concluded that, whereas ethnicity and alcohol heredity are predictive of later drinking, personality factors of competence, truancy, and emotional problems appear to be the result of alcoholism, rather than its cause. Among others, Peele (1985) and Zucker & Gomberg (1986) have reinterpreted Vaillant's data, and they argue that Vaillant overlooked certain personality characteristics of sociopathy that they reason are consistently related to later alcohol problems. Future research efforts will no doubt elaborate on these important integrative issues.

INITIATION OF THE CHANGE PROCESS

Many individuals with problematic drinking styles or at early stages of the dependence syndrome do not perceive themselves as having significant problems. They are in a precontemplation stage of change (DiClemente & Prochaska 1982; Prochaska & DiClemente 1986). However, as individuals increasingly experience difficulties in a variety of areas of life function, they often begin to contemplate the need to change their use patterns and to initiate a process of self-change.

Self-Change

The ability to change without the assistance of formal treatment is often described as "spontaneous" remission. Many individuals choose not to seek treatment because they perceive themselves as having been responsible for the development of their problem and assume that they are capable of overcoming it on their own; others have negative attitudes toward treatment and also wish to avoid the labeling process (e.g. alcoholic, addict) and its related stigmatization (Tuchfeld 1981). However, self-change does not appear to be spontaneous, for a number of factors have been found to be related to the initiation of change efforts (Ludwig 1985; Stall & Biernacki 1986; Tuchfeld 1981). These factors include a personal illness or accident, hitting a personal "bottom" (involving real or perceived humiliation, shame, despair, or loss), some meaningful religious experience, direct support from or intervention by family or friends, financial and/or legal problems related to substance use, or the alcohol-related death or illness of another person. The common feature of these factors is that the apparent internal psychological commitment appears to be mediated by external events or aspects of the individual's social environment.

The initial level of commitment to change may be tenuous in contrast to the relative power of the biopsychosocial factors that have maintained the substance use. The individual must actively engage in a set of coping behaviors to maintain motivation, initially disengage from substance use, and persist in this change. Factors associated with successful self-change include public announcements, social support, alterations in one's social and leisure-time activities, general life-style changes to avoid cues that may elicit conditioned craving, strategies for coping with stress, and the generation of negative expectations of continued use and positive expectations concerning continued abstinence (DiClemente & Prochaska 1985; Litman 1986; Ludwig 1985; Marlatt & Gordon 1985; Perri 1985; Prochaska & DiClemente 1985; Stall & Biernacki 1986; Tuchfeld 1981; Wills & Shiffman 1985). For example, Perri (1985) found that individuals who were successful in their self-change attempts had higher levels of motivation and commitment to change, set higher goals and standards for change, and reported more frequent and persistent use of coping strategies and self-reinforcement methods than did their unsuccessful counterparts.

Seeking Treatment

Individuals seeking treatment may well represent a biased sampling of individuals attempting to quit alcohol or drug use; namely those who are unsuccessful with self-change (Fillmore & Midanik 1984; Schacter 1982; Vaillant 1983). When an individual seeks treatment, he or she appears to have a high level of ambivalence and a tenuous commitment similar to that noted in the initial stages of the self-change process. Kanfer (1986) has suggested that one's initial commitment when seeking treatment is usually based on a desire to change the negative consequences of the addiction rather than the behavior itself.

How the clinician affectively, cognitively, and behaviorally approaches the client, the addictive behavior, and the ambivalence around change will affect the client's level of motivation and commitment. The clinician's task is to 'hook" the side of the individual's ambivalence that is positively inclined toward change (Donovan 1987) by a number of interventions, the primary goals of which are awareness-building, consciousness-raising, and developing or reinforcing a state of dissonance between the continued engagement in the addictive behavior and one's personal beliefs, attitudes, values, and feelings (Miller 1985). Methods relevant to these goals include a comprehensive assessment, the provision of objective feedback concerning the extent and severity of one's addiction, the provision of advice to change, the elicitation of self-motivational statements from the client, and the establishment of appropriate target goals or standards of behavior (Appel 1986; Donovan 1987; Kanfer 1986; Kristenson 1987; Miller 1985; Prochaska & DiClemente 1986).

ACTIVE CHANGE PROCESS

Studies evaluating the effectiveness of treatment for addictive behaviors have increased in quality and quantity during the 1980s. Reviews of treatment outcome research typically focus on separate classes of addictive behaviors— i.e. smoking (Fielding 1985; Flay 1985; Lichtenstein 1982), opiate dependence (Tims & Ludford 1984), cocaine use (Washton & Gold 1987), and non-opiate dependence (Brown 1984).

The most extensive literature exists on evaluation of treatment for alcoholism. Reviews on outcome of undifferentiated (i.e. not matched to individual patient characteristics) alcoholism treatment yield a number of consistent conclusions. A particularly influential statement of this consensus comes from a Congressional report sponsored by the Office of Technology Assessment (Saxe et al 1983, pp. 4–5; more recent reviews focusing on elements of these conclusions have been added in brackets):

> Despite methodological limitations [Maisto & Connors 1987; Nathan & Skinstad 1987; Sobell et al 1987], the available research evidence indicates that any treatment of alcoholism is better than no treatment [Lettieri et al 1985]. However, there is little definitive evidence that any one treatment or treatment setting is better than any other. Furthermore, controlled studies have typically found few differences in outcome according to intensity or duration of treatment [Miller & Hester 1986a]. . . . With respect to treatment setting, there is little evidence for the superiority of either inpatient or outpatient care alone [Miller 1986], although some evidence exists for the importance of continuing aftercare as an adjunct to short-term intensive rehabilitation (usually in an inpatient setting) [Ito & Donovan 1986]. Further research is needed both to specify how to match patient to treatment and setting and to test competing claims of effectiveness [Miller & Hester 1986c].

Factors Affecting Outcome

TREATMENT FACTORS   Miller & Hester (1986a) have written the most comprehensive review of specific treatment modalities. They identify nine major classes of interventions. Consistent with a two-stage treatment process, they found aversion therapies (Cannon et al 1986) and behavioral self-control training (Miller 1987) generally effective for initial change in drinking behavior; whereas social-skills training (Hay & Nathan 1982) and marital/family therapy (McCrady et al 1986; O'Farrell 1987), and a combination of these elements with disulfiram use (Azrin et al 1982), increased the probability of prolonged sobriety. They noted with concern the lack of overlap between these empirically supported interventions and the list of treatment approaches that are currently "standard practice" in alcoholism programs, such as A.A. (cf Glaser & Ogborne 1982), alcoholism education (Braucht & Braucht 1984), confrontation, group and individual therapy, disulfiram use (Antabuse; Fuller et al 1986), and other pharmacotherapy (Liskow & Goodwin 1987).

PATIENT FACTORS   At the beginning of the decade it was stated that "The best predictor of patient outcome is the patient" (Institute of Medicine 1980, p. 145). Conclusions about specific patient characteristics previously thought to be related to outcome have since been disputed, including gender (Vanicelli 1984), motivation (Miller 1985), age (Janik & Dunham 1983), severity of alcohol dependence (Schuckit et al 1985), and personality (Nathan 1987).

In general, good prognosis is consistently associated with social stability (Ornstein & Cherepon 1985) and higher cognitive and psychosocial functioning (McLellan et al 1983a; Rounsaville et al 1987). Treatment factors and patient characteristics accounted for between 4% and 70% of outcome variance (Moos & Finney 1983). Consideration of extra-treatment or life-context factors such as work and family setting (cf Jacob & Seilhamer 1987) or life stressors accounted for an increment of between 7% and 27% of the variance in treatment outcome beyond that related to patient and treatment factors.

Evaluation Methodology

Conclusions about treatment effectiveness are reached within a context of the prevailing evaluation methodology. Several recent reviews have addressed the methodological state of the art within alcoholism treatment outcome research (Emrick & Hansen 1983; Maisto & Connors 1987; Moos & Finney 1983; Nathan & Skinstad 1987; Sobell et al 1987).

The selection of outcome criteria has generated intense debate since the first Rand Report (cf Polich et al 1981). Conflicts surrounding the appropriateness and possibility of successful non-abstinent (i.e. controlled drinking) treatment outcome have led to polarization within both the research and clinical communities (Cook 1985). Much of the controversy involved one early program of research (Roizen 1987). Whereas other long-term outcome studies (Helzer et al 1985; Nordstrom & Berglund 1987) and reviews (Heather & Robertson 1983; Miller 1987) reached somewhat different conclusions about the frequency and clinical predictors of controlled-drinking outcomes, most studies continue to include information about nonproblem drinking in reports of treatment outcome.

In addition to drinking outcome, a number of other areas of life function have been identified as outcome dimensions (Emrick & Hansen 1983), including treatment completion, readmission to treatment, mortality, other health care utilization, physical health, other substance abuse, legal problems, vocational functioning, family/social functioning, emotional functioning, and life stressors. Assessment of this more comprehensive set of indexes is based on the assumption that treatment outcome varies along a number of relatively independent dimensions. One recent investigation (Babor et al 1987b) provided limited support for both the unidimensional and multidimensional approaches; it concluded that treatment outcomes should be evaluated using specific indicators of drinking behavior and other areas of life functioning as well as a global dimension of outcome.

A criterion receiving increasing attention is the cost-effectiveness of alcoholism treatment. Recent estimates place the direct treatment costs for alcoholism at approximately $13.5 billion in 1983, with only $1 billion of that spent for specialized alcoholism treatment as opposed to general medical settings (NIAAA 1987). Recent large-scale studies have documented significant reductions in other health care utilization after alcoholism treatment (Holder & Blose 1986; Saxe et al 1983). These savings were sufficient to offset the costs of treatment within two to three years. McCrady et al (1986) found equivalent clinical effectiveness of partial hospitalization and inpatient treatment; they concluded the former was the treatment of choice because of its substantially lower cost.

To increase the proportion of alcoholics who receive treatment beyond the current estimated 15% (NIAAA 1987) and to improve cost-effectiveness, a graduated or stepped-care approach to treatment has been recommended (Babor et al 1986; Ritson 1986). Beginning with minimal intervention (e.g. Kristenson 1987), more intensive and expensive methods would be used only if conservative strategies were insufficient.

Once criteria for cost and effectiveness have been selected, issues of measurement and reporting can be addressed. The validity of patient self-report has been a central concern (Babor et al 1987c; Sobell & Sobell 1986). Data show acceptable validity of self-report relative to a variety of other criteria, none of which are without limitations. Recommendations include use of multiple corroborative data sources as well as other specific strategies to enhance self-report.

Because of evidence of the variability of drinking outcomes over time, Nathan & Skinstad (1987) recommended follow-up data be available for at least the first two years after treatment. Sobell et al (1987) called for reporting data over the entire follow-up interval rather than a limited period prior to the final assessment. Recommendations for lengthy follow-up increase the problem of subject attrition. A reduction in the attrition rate has been reported in studies published since 1980 (Sobell et al 1987).

Patient-Treatment Matching

Nearly 50 years have elapsed since Jellinek (Bowman & Jellinek 1941) called for research on matching alcoholic patients with optimal forms of treatment. Since 1980, some reference to "matching" has become a fixture in discussions of alcohol treatment outcome research.

The matching hypothesis challenges implicit assumptions about the uniformity of alcoholics and alcoholism treatment. Recognition of the wide variability that exists along many dimensions among individuals with alcohol problems has led to the search for clinically meaningful subtypes (reviewed above). Similarly, there are a number of variables to be differentiated within the treatment domain (Moos & Finney 1986). Based on a review of the above evidence, which found few powerful main effects for patient or treatment variables, the matching hypothesis posits significant interaction effects between patient subtype and treatment (i.e. differential effectiveness of a treatment intervention among subsets of patients).

Glaser (1980) identified three major variations of the matching hypothesis. Most of the limited empirical research on matching has tested the match between characteristics of clients and characteristics of therapists. The match between characteristics of clients and goals of treatment has focused primarily on controlled drinking vs abstinence outcomes (Ogborne et al 1982; Polich et al 1981; Sanchez-Craig et al 1984). Considerable recent research has investigated the match between severity or type of client problems (e.g. severity of alcohol dependence, degree of psychopathology, concurrent psychiatric diagnosis, level of cognitive functioning) and the specific focus or intensity of treatment received (McLellan et al 1983b; Meyer 1986; Walker et al 1983).

McLellan et al (1983a), using a 10-item measure of "psychiatric severity," reported an interaction with treatment intensity among those with intermediate levels of severity. Those with high levels of severity did uniformly poorly and those with low levels of severity did well regardless of treatment intensity. In a nonrandom prospective design, the investigators attempted to match the intensity of treatment to the psychiatric severity. Matched cases showed significantly better outcomes than mismatched cases.

Miller & Hester (1986b) reviewed evidence suggesting that clients may benefit from the opportunity to match themselves to treatment. They tentatively concluded that clients permitted to choose the treatment approach from among alternatives show greater acceptance of, compliance with, and improvement following treatment. Similarly, Sanchez-Craig & Lei (1986) identified disadvantages of imposing abstinence goals on problem drinkers.

Although the number of empirical tests of the matching hypothesis remains smaller than the number of reviews calling for such work, important issues have been clarified. Finney & Moos (1986) identified three methodological issues to be resolved prior to conducting effective matching research. They discussed five strategies for selecting relevant patient and treatment matching variables: (*a*) clinical judgment, (*b*) "cafeteria-style" patient selection, (*c*) post hoc exploratory data analysis, (*d*) empirical data reduction techniques (e.g. cluster analysis), and (*e*) theoretical analysis. They noted alternative criteria of effectiveness that matching might attempt to optimize. As we noted earlier, these criteria include drinking and nondrinking outcomes, and cost-effectiveness. A third conceptual issue is the need to consider matching as a multistage process, consistent with the stages-of-change perspective. Methodologically, three often overlooked and increasingly complex effects were noted: nonlinear, higher-order interaction, and multilevel (i.e. contextual or subject-within-group) effects. These effects encouraged investigators to maintain realistic expectations because of the complexity of the matching task and to appreciate that even affecting a small proportion of patients could have an impact on large numbers of individuals.

MAINTENANCE OF SUCCESSFUL CHANGE

Findings of major longitudinal studies (Helzer et al 1985; Fillmore 1987; Nordstrom & Berglund 1987; Polich et al 1981; Vaillant 1983) document the instability of drinking patterns and the low probability of complete abstinence over the long term.

Riley et al (1987) reviewed 68 alcoholism treatment outcome studies published from 1978–1983 involving 14,546 subjects followed over 6–144 months after treatment. Of the total sample, 2% were reported as deceased, 22% were lost to follow-up, 34% were "successful," and 40% continued to drink with associated problems. Varying definitions of "successful" typically included nonproblem drinking as well as abstinence outcomes, with more extensive follow-up studies finding nonproblem drinking at least as likely as abstinence (Helzer et al 1985; Polich et al 1981). In both studies, fewer than 15% of subjects were completely abstinent following treatment. Similarly high rates and patterns of relapse are found across addictive behaviors (Tims & Leukefeld 1986).

An emerging approach to the understanding and prevention of relapse focuses on the process by which single lapses or mistakes develop into a more problematic relapse outcome. Marlatt & Gordon (1985) present a cognitive-behavioral model of the relapse process that assumes that risk for relapse is determined by an interaction of individual, situational, and physiological factors.

A number of research questions remain to be investigated, including natural history of relapse, various effects of lapses and relapses, determinants and predictors of relapse, and effectiveness of methods for relapse prevention (Brownell et al 1986). Despite the need for further research, several clinical implications consistent with the stages-of-change model follow from available relapse research (Marlatt & Gordon 1985; Rounsaville 1986), including recognition of the likelihood of relapse; training in identification of and preparation for early signs and increased risk of relapse; and efforts to provide aftercare and/or enhance supports in the posttreatment environment.

CONCLUDING COMMENT

The field of addictive behavior has been dominated until recently by contributions from disciplines other than psychology—particularly from medicine and the neurosciences. A glut of popular and lay books has appeared on the topic of addiction, many written by individuals who are themselves recovering from addictions. The frequent discrepancies between the "professional" and "craft" literatures have added fuel to ongoing debates and have contributed to the divisive nature of the field. Recently psychology and its allied behavioral disciplines have been increasingly recognized for their contributions in helping to understand addiction and its treatment. We have presented a selective review of different research programs that illustrate an emerging integration of biological, psychological, and sociological approaches to etiology and treatment. This emerging biopsychosocial model will no doubt be refined and elaborated through the remainder of this century. We hope that research-based refinements of this model will reduce divisiveness and improve treatment outcomes in the field of addictive behavior.

ACKNOWLEDGMENTS

We wish to thank all our colleagues who responded to our request for publications in press. We also gratefully appreciate Don Wood for his editorial assistance and diligent effort in the preparation of this manuscript. This paper was supported in part by a grant to the first author from the National Institute on Alcohol Abuse and Alcoholism (Grant #2 R01 AA05591–04).

Literature Cited

Adesso, V. J. 1985. Cognitive factors in alcohol and drug use. See Galizio & Maisto 1985, pp. 179–208

Alexander, B. K., Hadaway, P. F. 1982. Opiate addiction: the case for an adaptive orientation. *Psychol. Bull.* 92:367–81

Alterman, A. I., Tarter, R. E. 1986. An examination of selected typologies: hyperactivity, familial, and antisocial alcoholism. See Galanter 1986, pp. 169–89

American Psychiatric Association. 1980. *Diagnostic and Statistical Manual of Mental Disorders: DSM-III*. Washington, DC: Am. Psychiatric Assoc., 494 pp. 3rd ed.

Appel, C-P. 1986. From contemplation to determination: contributions from cognitive psychology. See Miller & Heather 1986a, pp. 59–89

Armor, D. J., Meshkoff, J. E. 1983. Remission among treated and untreated alcoholics. See Mello 1983, pp. 239–70

Azrin, N. H., Sisson, R. W., Meyers, R., Godley, M. 1982. Alcoholism treatment by disulfiram and community reinforcement therapy. *J. Behav. Ther. Exp. Psychiatry* 13:105–12

Babor, T. F., Cooney, N. L., Lauerman, R. J. 1987a. The dependence syndrome concept as a psychological theory of relapse behaviour: an empirical evaluation of alcoholic and opiate addicts. *Br. J. Addict.* 82:393–406

Babor, T. F., Dolinsky, Z., Rounsaville, B., Jaffe, J. 1987b. Unitary versus multidimensional models of alcoholism treatment outcome: an empirical study. *J. Stud. Alcohol.* In press

Babor, T. F., Meyer, R. E. 1986. Overview. See Galanter 1986, pp. 107–12

Babor, T. F., Ritson, E. B., Hodgson, R. J. 1986. Alcohol-related problems in the primary health care setting: a review of early intervention strategies. *Br. J. Addict.* 81:23–46

Babor, T. F., Stephens, R. S., Marlatt, G. A. 1987c. Verbal report methods in clinical research on alcoholism: response bias and its minimization. *J. Stud. Alcohol.* In press

Bachman, J. G., O'Malley, P. M., Johnston, L. D. 1984. Drug use among young adults: the impacts of roles status and social environment. *J. Pers. Soc. Psychol.* 47:629–45

Baer, J. S., Holt, C. S., Lichtenstein, E. 1986. Self-efficacy and smoking reexamined: construct validity and clinical utility. *J. Consult. Clin. Psychol.* 54:846–52

Baer, P. E., Garmezy, L. B., McLaughlin, R. J., Pokorny, A. D., Wernick, M. J. 1987. Stress, coping, family conflict, and adolescent alcohol use. *J. Behav. Med.* In press

Baker, L. H., Cooney, N. L., Pomerleau, O. F. 1987. Craving for alcohol: theoretical processes and treatment procedures. See Cox 1987a, pp. 183–202

Baker, T. B., Cannon, D., eds. 1987. *Addictive Disorders: Psychological Research on Assessment and Treatment.* New York: Praeger

Baker, T. B., Tiffany, S. T. 1985. Morphine tolerance as habituation. *Psychol. Rev.* 92:78–108

Bandura, A. 1977. Self-efficacy: toward a unifying theory of behavioral change. *Psychol. Rev.* 84:191–215

Bardo, M. T., Risner, M. E. 1985. Biochemical substrates of drug abuse. See Galizio & Maisto 1985, pp. 65–99

Barrett, R. J. 1985. Behavioral approaches to individual differences in substance abuse: drug-taking behavior. See Galizio & Maisto 1985, pp. 125–75

Begleiter, H., Porjesz, B., Bihari, B., Kissin, B. 1984. Event-related brain potentials in boys at risk for alcoholism. *Science* 225:1493–95

Blane, H. T., Leonard, K. E., eds. 1987. *Psychological Theories of Drinking and Alcoholism.* New York: Guilford. 403 pp.

Bloom, F. E. 1983. Endorphins: cellular and molecular aspects for addictive phenomena. See Levison et al 1983, pp. 261–96

Botvin, G. J. 1983. Prevention of adolescent substance abuse through the development of personal and social competence. See Glynn et al. 1983, pp. 115–41

Bowman, K. M., Jellinek, E. M. 1941. Alcohol addiction and its treatment. *Am. J. Stud. Alcohol.* 2:98–176

Braucht, G. N., Braucht, B. 1984. Prevention of problem drinking among youth: evaluation of educational strategies. In *Prevention of Alcohol Abuse*, ed. P. M. Miller, T. D. Nirenberg, 7:253–80. New York: Plenum. 520 pp.

Brickman, P., Rabinowitz, V. C., Karuza, J., Coates, D., Cohn, E., et al. 1982. Models of helping and coping. *Am. Psychol.* 37:368–84

Brook, J. S., Whiteman, M., Gordon, A. S., Cohen, P. 1986. Some models and mechanisms for explaining the impact of maternal and adolescent characteristics on adolescent stage of drug use. *Dev. Psychol.* 22:460–67

Brown, B. S. 1984. Treatment of non-opiate dependency: issues and outcomes. In *Research Advances in Alcohol and Drug Problems*, ed. R. Smart et al, Vol. 8, Ch. 10:291–308. New York: Plenum. 333 pp.

Brown, S. 1985. *Treating the Alcoholic: A Developmental Model of Recovery.* New York: Wiley. 227 pp.

Brown, S. A., Goldman, M. S., Christiansen, B. A. 1985. Do alcohol expectancies mediate drinking patterns of adults? *J. Consult. Clin. Psychol.* 53:512–19

Brown, S. A., Goldman, M. S., Inn, A., Anderson, L. 1980. Expectations of reinforcement from alcohol: their domain and relation to drinking patterns. *J. Consult. Clin. Psychol.* 48:419–26

Brownell, K. D., Marlatt, G. A., Lichtenstein, E., Wilson, G. T. 1986. Understanding and preventing relapse. *Am. Psychol.* 41:765–82

Bry, B. H., McKeon, P., Pandina, R. J. 1982. Extent of drug use as a function of number of risk factors. *J. Abnorm. Psychol.* 91:273–79

Cadoret, R. J., Troughton, E., O'Gorman, T. W. 1987. Genetic and environmental factors in alcohol abuse and antisocial personality. *J. Stud. Alcohol* 48:1–9

Cannon, D. S., Baker, T. B., Gino, A., Nathan, P. E. 1986. Alcohol-aversion therapy: relation between strenth of aversion and abstinence. *J. Consult. Clin. Psychol.* 54:825–30

Cappell, H., Greeley, J. 1987. Alcohol and tension reduction: an update on research and theory. See Blane & Leonard 1987, pp. 15–54

Chassin, L. 1984. Adolescent substance use and abuse. *Adv. Child Behav. Anal. Ther.* 3:99–152

Chaudron, C. D., Wilkinson, D. A., eds. 1987. *Theories of Alcoholism.* Toronto: Addiction Res. Found. In press

Christiansen, B. A., Goldman, M. S. 1983. Alcohol-related expectancies vs. demographic/background variables in the prediction of adolescent drinking. *J. Consult. Clin. Psychol.* 51:249–57

Christiansen, B. A., Goldman, M. S., Brown, S. A. 1985. The differential development of adolescent alcohol expectancies may predict adult alcoholism. *Addictive Behav.* 10:299–306

Christiansen, B. A., Goldman, M. S., Inn, A. 1982. The development of alcohol-related expectancies in adolescents: separating pharmacological from social learning influences. *J. Consult. Clin. Psychol.* 50:336–44

Cloninger, C. R. 1983. Genetic and environmental factors in the development of alcoholism. *J. Psychol. Treat. Eval.* 5:487–96

Cloninger, C. R., Bohman, M., Sigvardsson, S., Von Knorring, A-L. 1985. Psychopathology in adopted-out children of alcoholics: the Stockholm adoption study. *Recent Dev. Alcohol.* 3:37–51

Collins, R. L., Marlatt, G. A. 1983. Psychological correlates and explanations of alcohol use and abuse. In *Medical and Social Aspects of Alcohol Abuse,* ed. B. Tabakoff, P. B. Sutker, C. L. Randall, 10:273–308. New York: Plenum

Connors, G. J., O'Farrell, T. J., Cutter, H. S. G., Thompson, D. L. 1986. Alcohol expectancies among male alcoholics, problem drinkers, and nonproblem drinkers. *Alcohol. Clin. Exp. Res.* 10:667–71

Connors, G. J., O'Farrell, T. J., Cutter, H. S. G., Thompson, D. L. 1987. Beliefs regarding alcohol's dose-related effects among alcoholics, problem drinkers, and nonproblem drinkers. *J. Stud. Alcohol.* In press

Connors, G. J., Tarbox, A. R. 1985. Macroenvironmental factors as determinants of substance use and abuse. See Galizio & Maisto 1985, pp. 283–316

Cook, D. R. 1985. Craftsman versus professional: analysis of the controlled drinking controversy. *J. Stud. Alcohol* 46:433–42

Cooney, N. L., Meyer, R. E., Kaplan, R. F., Baker, L. H. 1986. A validation study of four scales measuring severity of alcohol dependence. *Br. J. Addict.* 81:223–29

Cox, W. M. 1985. Personality correlates of substance abuse. See Galizio & Maisto 1985, pp. 209–46

Cox, W. M., ed. 1987a. *Treatment and Pre-vention of Alcohol Problems: A Resource Manual.* New York: Academic. 365 pp.

Cox, W. M., ed. 1987b. *Why People Drink: Parameters of Alcohol as a Reinforcer.* New York: Gardner. In press

Crabbe, J. C., McSwigan, J. D., Belknap, J. K. 1985. The role of genetics in substance abuse. See Galizio & Maisto 1985, pp. 13–64

Critchlow, B. 1986. The powers of John Barleycorn: beliefs about the effects of alcohol on social behavior. *Am. Psychol.* 41:751–64

DiClemente, C. C., Prochaska, J. O. 1985. Processes and stages of self-change: coping and competence in smoking behavior change. See Shiffman & Wills 1985, pp. 319–43

DiClemente, C. C., Prochaska, J. O. 1982. Self-change and therapy change of smoking behavior: a comparison of processes of change of cessation and maintenance. *Addict. Behav.* 7:133–42

Dishion, T. J., Reid, J. B., Patterson, G. R. 1987. Empirical guidelines for a family intervention for adolescent drug use. *Family Context of Adolescent Drug Use,* ed. R. H. Coombs. New York: Haworth. In press

Donegan, D. H., Rodin, J., O'Brien, C. P., Solomon, R. L. 1983. A learning-theory approach to commonalities. See Levison et al 1983, pp. 111–56

Donovan, D. M. 1987. Assessment of addictive behaviors: implications of an emerging biopsychosocial model. See Donovan & Marlatt 1987. In press

Donovan, D. M., Chaney, E. F. 1985. Alcoholic relapse prevention and intervention: models and methods. See Marlatt et al 1985, pp. 351–416

Donovan, J. E., Jessor, R. 1985. Structure of problem behavior in adolescence and young adulthood. *J. Consult. Clin. Psychol.* 53:890–904

Donovan, J. E., Jessor, R., Jessor, L. 1983. Problem drinking adolescence and young adulthood: a follow-up study. *J. Stud. Alcohol* 44:109–37

Donovan, D. M., Kivlahan, D. R., Walker, R. D. 1986. Alcoholic subtypes based on multiple assessment domains: validation against treatment outcome. See Galanter 1986, pp. 207–22

Donovan, D. M., Marlatt, G. A., eds. 1987. *Assessment of Addictive Behaviors: Behavioral, Cognitive, and Physiological Procedures.* New York: Guilford. In press

Donovan, D. M., Marlatt, G. A. 1980. Assessment of expectancies and behaviors associated with alcohol consumption: a cognitive-behavioral approach. *J. Stud. Alcohol* 41:1153–85

Donovan, D. M., O'Leary, M. R. 1983. Control orientation, drinking behavior and alcoholism. In *Research with the Locus of Control Construct. Vol. 2: Development and Social Problems*, ed. H. M. Lefcourt, 4:107–54. New York: Academic. 286 pp.

Edwards, G. 1986. The alcohol dependence syndrome: A concept as stimulus to inquiry. *Br. J. Addict.* 81:171–83

Edwards, G. 1984. Drinking in longitudinal perspective: career and history history. *Br. J. Addict.* 79:175–83

Emrick, C. D., Hansen, J. 1983. Assertions regarding the effectiveness of treatment for alcoholism: fact or fantasy? *Am. Psychol.* 38:733–38

Ewing, J. A. 1980. Biopsychosocial approaches to drinking and alcoholism. In *Phenomenology and Treatment of Alcoholism*, ed. W. E. Fann, I. Karacan, A. D. Pokorny, R. L. Williams, 1:1–19. New York: Spectrum. 328 pp.

Fielding, J. E. 1985. Smoking: health effects and control. *N. Engl. J. Med.* 313:555–61

Fillmore, K. M. 1987. Prevalence, incidence, and chronicity of drinking patterns and problems among men as a function of age: a longitudinal and cohort analysis. *Br. J. Addict.* 82:77–83

Fillmore, K. M., Midanik, L. 1984. Chronicity of drinking problems among men: a longitudinal study. *J. Stud. Alcohol* 45:228–36

Finney, J. W., Moos, R. H. 1986. Matching patients with treatments: conceptual and methodological issues. *J. Stud. Alcohol* 47:122–34

Flay, B. R. 1985. Psychosocial approaches to smoking prevention: a review of findings. *Health Psychol.* 4:449–88

Flay, B. R., Sobel, J. L. 1983. The role of mass media in preventing adolescent substance abuse. See Glynn et al 1983, pp. 5–35

Frances, R. J., Backy, S. T., Alexopoulos, G. A. 1984. Outcome study of familial and nonfamilial alcoholism. *Am. J. Psychiatry* 141:1469–71

Fuller, R. K., Branchey, L., Brightwell, D. R., Derman, R. M., Emerick, C. D., et al. 1986. Disulfiram treatment of alcoholism: a Veterans Administration cooperative study. *J. Am. Med. Assoc.* 256:1449–55

Gabrielli, W., Mednick, S. 1983. Intellectual performance in children of alcoholics. *J. Nerv. Ment. Dis.* 171:444–47

Galanter, M., ed. 1983. *Recent Developments in Alcoholism*, Vol. 1. New York: Plenum. 484 pp.

Galanter, M., ed. 1985. *Recent Developments in Alcoholism*, Vol. 3. New York: Plenum. 323 pp.

Galanter, M., ed. 1986. *Recent Developments*

in *Alcoholism*, Vol. 4. New York: Plenum. 453 pp.

Galanter, M., ed. 1987. *Recent Developments in Alcoholism*, Vol. 5. New York: Plenum. 457 pp.

Galizio, M., Maisto, S. A., eds. 1985a. *Determinants of Substance Abuse Treatment: Biological, Psychological, and Environmental Factors*. New York: Plenum. 429 pp.

Galizio, M., Maisto, S. 1985b. Toward a biopsychosocial theory of substance abuse. See Galizio & Maisto 1985a, pp. 425–29

Gartner, A., Riessman, F. 1984. *The Self-Help Revolution*. New York: Human Sciences Press. 266 pp.

Gilchrist, L. D., Schinke, S. P., Bobo, J. K., Trimble, J. E., Cvetkovich, G. T. 1987. Skills enhancement to prevent substance abuse among American Indian adolescents. *Int. J. Addict.* In press

Glaser, F. B. 1980. Anybody got a match? Treatment research and the matching hypothesis. In *Alcoholism Treatment in Transition*, ed. G. Edwards, M. Grant, 11:178–96. Baltimore: Univ. Park Press. 327 pp.

Glaser, F. B., Ogborne, A. C. 1982. Does A.A. really work? *Br. J. Addict.* 77:123–29

Glynn, T. J., Leukefeld, C. G., Ludford, J. P., eds. 1983. *Preventing Adolescent Drug Abuse: Intervention Strategies*. Washington, DC: NIDA. 255 pp.

Goldman, M. S., Brown, S. A., Christiansen, B. A. 1987. Expectancy theory: thinking about drinking. See Blane & Leonard 1987, pp. 181–226

Haertzen, C. A., Kocher, T. R., Miyasato, U. 1983. Reinforcements from the first drug experience can predict later drug habits and/or addiction: results with coffee, cigarettes, alcohol, barbiturates, minor and major tranquilizers, stimulants, marijuana, hallucinogens, heroin, opiates, and cocaine. *Drug Alcohol Depend.* 11:147–65

Hay, W., Nathan, P. E., eds. 1982. *Clinical Case Studies in Behavioral Treatment of Alcoholism*. New York: Plenum. 305 pp.

Heather, N., Robertson, I. 1983. *Controlled Drinking*. London: Methuen. Rev. ed.

Hedegus, A. M., Alterman, A. I., Tarter, R. E. 1984. Learning achievement in sons of alcoholics. *Alcohol. Clin. Exp. Res.* 8:330–33

Helzer, J. E., Robins, L. N., Taylor, J. R., Carey, K., Miller, R. H., et al. 1985. The extent of long-term moderate drinking among alcoholics discharged from medical and psychiatric treatment facilities. *N. Engl. J. Med.* 312:1678–82

Hesselbrock, M. N. 1986. Alcoholic typologies: a review of empirical evaluations of common classification schemes. See Galanter 1986, pp. 191–206

Hesselbrock, V. M., Stabenau, J. R., Hesselbrock, M. N. 1985. Minimal brain dysfunction and neurological test performance in offspring of alcoholics. See Galanter & Goodwin 1985a, pp. 65–82

Hodgson, R., Stockwell, T. 1985. The theoretical and empirical basis of the alcohol dependence model: a social learning perspective. In *The Misuse of Alcohol*, ed. N. Heather, I. Robertson, P. Davies, 1:17–34. London: Croom Helm. 284 pp.

Holder, H. D., Blose, J. D. 1986. Alcoholism treatment and total health care utilization and costs. *J. Am. Med. Assoc.* 256:1456–60

Huba, G. J., Bentler, P. M. 1982. A developmental theory of drug use: derivation and assessment of a causal modeling approach. In *Life-Span Development and Behavior*, ed. B. P. Baltes, O. G. Brim, 4:147–203. New York: Academic.

Hunt, W. A. 1987a. Biochemical bases for the reinforcing effects of ethanol. See Cox 1987b. In press

Hunt, W. A. 1987b. Brain mechanisms that underlie the reinforcing effects of ethanol. See Cox 1987b. In press

Institute of Medicine. 1980. *Alcoholism, Alcohol Abuse, and Related Problems: Opportunities for Research: Report of a Study.* Washington, DC: Natl. Acad. Press. 195 pp.

Ito, J. R., Donovan, D. M. 1986. Aftercare in alcoholism treatment: a review. In *Treating Addictive Behaviors: Processes of Change*, ed. W. R. Miller, N. Heather, 22:435–56. New York: Plenum. 464 pp.

Jacob, T., Seilhamer, R. A. 1987. Alcoholism and family interaction. In *Family Interaction and Psychopathology: Theories, Methods, and Findings*, ed. T. Jacob. New York: Plenum. In press

Janik, S. W., Dunham, R. G. 1983. A nationwide examination of the need for specific alcoholism treatment programs for the elderly. *J. Stud. Alcohol* 44:307–17

Jessor, R. 1986. Adolescent problem drinking: psychosocial aspects and developmental outcomes. See Silbereisen et al 1986, pp. 241–64

Johnson, C. A., Solis, J. 1983. Comprehensive community programs for drug abuse prevention: implications of the Community Heart Disease Prevention Programs for future research. See Glynn et al 1983, pp. 76–114

Kandel, D. B., Logan, J. A. 1984. Patterns of drug use from adolescence to young adulthood: I. Period of risk for initiation, continued use, and discontinuation. *Am. J. Public Health* 74:660–66

Kanfer, F. H. 1986. Implications of a self-regulation model of therapy for treatment of addictive behaviors. See Miller & Heather 1986a, pp. 29–47

Kaplan, H. B. 1985. Testing a general theory of drug abuse and other deviant adaptations. *J. Drug Issues* 15:477–92

Kauffman, J. F., Shaffer, H., Burglass, M. E. 1985. The biological basics: Drugs and their effects. In *Alcoholism and Substance Abuse: Strategies for Clinical Intervention*, ed. T. E. Bratter, G. G. Forrest, 4:107–36. New York: Free Press

Kivlahan, D. R., Coppel, D. B., Fromme, K., Williams, E. M., Marlatt, G. A. 1987. Secondary prevention of alcohol-related problems in young adults at risk. In *Prevention and Early Intervention: Biobehavioral Perspectives*, ed. K. D. Craig, S. M. Weiss. New York: Springer. In press

Knott, D. H., Beard, J. D., Fink, R. D. 1987. Medical aspects of alcoholism. See Cox 1987a, pp. 57–72

Kraft, D. P. 1984. A comprehensive prevention program for college students. In *Prevention of Alcohol Abuse*, ed. P. M. Miller, T. D. Nirenberg, 9:327–70. New York: Plenum. 520 pp.

Kristenson, H. 1987. Methods of intervention to modify drinking patterns in heavy drinkers. See Galanter 1987, pp. 403–24

Lang, A. R., Michalec, E. M. 1987. Expectancy effects in reinforcement from alcohol. See Cox 1987b. In press

Langenbucher, J. W., Nathan, P. E. 1987. The tension reduction hypothesis: a reanalysis of some crucial early data from chronic alcohol administration studies in humans. See Cox 1987b. In press

Lettieri, D. J., Sayers, M., Nelson, J. E., eds. 1985. *Treatment Handbook Series: Summaries of Alcoholism Treatment Assessment Research*, Vol. 1. Rockville, Md: NIAAA. 290 pp.

Lettieri, D. J., Sayers, M., Pearson, H. W. 1980. *Theories on Drug Abuse: Selected Contemporary Perspectives*. Rockville, Md: NIDA. 290 pp.

Levison, P. K., Gerstein, D. R., Maloff, D. R., eds. 1983. *Commonalities in Substance Abuse and Habitual Behavior*. Lexington, Mass: Lexington Books. 355 pp.

Lichtenstein, E. 1982. The smoking problem: a behavioral perspective. *J. Consult. Clin. Psychol.* 50:804–19

Lindesmith, A. R. 1968. *Addiction and Opiates*. Chicago: Aldine

Liskow, B. I., Goodwin, D. W. 1987. Pharmacological treatment of alcohol intoxication withdrawal and dependence. *J. Stud. Alcohol*. In press

Litman, G. K. 1986. Alcoholism survival: the prevention of relapse. See Miller & Heather 1986, pp. 294–303

Long, J. V. F., Scherl, D. J. 1984. Developmental antecedents of compulsive drug use: a report on the literature. *J. Psychoactive Drugs* 16:169–82

Ludwig, A. M. 1985. Cognitive processes associated with "spontaneous" recovery from alcoholism. *J. Stud. Alcohol* 46:53–58

Maisto, S. A., Connors, G. J. 1987. Assessment of treatment outcome in the addictive behaviors. See Donovan & Marlatt 1987. In press

Mandell, W. 1983. Types and phases of alcohol dependence illness. See Galanter 1983, pp. 415–48

Marlatt, G. A. 1987. Alcohol, the magic elixir: stress, expectancy, and the transformation of emotional states. In *Stress and Addiction*, ed. E. Gottheil, K. A. Druly, S. Pashko, S. P. Weinstein. New York: Brunner/Mazel. In press

Marlatt, G. A., Donovan, D. M. 1981. Alcoholism and drug dependence: cognitive social-learning factors in addictive behaviors. In *Behavior Modification: Principles, Issues, and Applications*, ed. W. E. Craighead, A. E. Kazdin, M. J. Mahoney, 14:264–85. Boston: Houghton Mifflin. 618pp. 2nd ed.

Marlatt, G. A., Gordon, J. R., eds. 1985. *Relapse Prevention: Maintenance Strategies in the Treatment of Addictive Behaviors*. New York: Guilford

Marlatt, G. A., Rohsenow, D. J. 1980. Cognitive processes in alcohol use: expectancy and balanced-placebo design. In *Advances in Substance Abuse: Behavioral and Biological Research*, ed. N. K. Mello, 3:159–99. Greenwich, Conn: JAI Press. Vol. 1, 376 pp.

Matuschka, P. R. 1985. The psychopharmacology of addiction. In *Alcoholism and Substance Abuse: Strategies for Clinical Intervention*, ed. T. E. Bratter, G. G. Forrest, 2:49–73. New York: Free Press

McClearn, G. E. 1983. Commonalities in substance abuse: a genetic perspective. See Levison et al 1983, pp. 323–42

McCrady, B. S., Noel, N. E., Abrams, D. B., Stout, R. L., Nelson, H. F., Hay, W. M. 1986. Comparative effectiveness of three types of spouse involvement in outpatient behavioral alcoholism treatment. *J. Stud. Alcohol* 47:459–67

McLellan, A. T., Luborsky, L., Woody, G. E., O'Brien, C. P., Druley, K. A. 1983a. Predicting response to alcohol and drug abuse treatments: role of psychiatric severity. *Arch. Gen. Psychiatry* 40:620–25

McLellan, A. T., Woody, G. E., Luborsky, L., O'Brien, C. P., Druley, K. A. 1983b. Increased effectiveness of substance abuse treatment: a prospective study of patient-treatment "matching." *J. Nerv. Ment. Dis.* 171:597–605

Meyer, R. E. 1986. How to understand the relationship between psychopathology and addictive behaviors: another example of the chicken and the egg. In *Psychopathology and Addictive Disorders*, ed. R. E. Meyer, 1:3–16. New York: Guilford. 362 pp.

Meyer, R. E., Babor, T. F., Mirkin, P. M. 1983. Typologies in alcoholism: an overview. *Int. J. Addict.* 18:235–49

Milam, J. R., Ketcham, K. 1981. *Under the Influence*. Seattle: Madrona. 210 pp.

Miller, W. R., ed. 1980. *The Addictive Behaviors*. Oxford: Pergamon Press. 353 pp.

Miller, W. R. 1983. Motivational interviewing with problem drinkers. *Behav. Psychother.* 11:147–72

Miller, W. R. 1985. Motivation for treatment: a review with special emphasis on alcoholism. *Psychol. Bull.* 98:84–107

Miller, W. R. 1987. Techniques to modify hazardous drinking patterns. See Galanter 1987, pp. 425–38

Miller, W. R., Heather, N., eds. 1986. *Treating Addictive Behaviors: Processes of Change*. New York: Plenum. 464 pp.

Miller, W. R., Hester, R. K. 1986a. The effectiveness of alcoholism treatment: what research reveals. See Miller & Heather, 1986, pp. 121–74

Miller, W. R., Hester, R. K. 1986b. Inpatient alcoholism treatment: who benefits? *Am. Psychol.* 41:794–805

Miller, W. R., Hester, R. K. 1986c. Matching problem drinkers with optimal treatments. See Miller & Heather 1986, pp. 175–203

Mills, K. C., McCarty, D. 1983. A data based alcohol abuse prevention program in a university setting. *J. Alcohol Drug Educ.* 28:15–27

Moos, R. H., Finney, J. W. 1983. The expanding scope of alcoholism treatment evaluation. *Am. Psychol.* 38:1036–44

Moos, R. H., Finney, J. W. 1986. The treatment setting in alcoholism program evaluations. *Ann. Behav. Med.* 8:33–39

Morey, L. C., Blashfield, R. K. 1981. Empirical classifications of alcoholism: a review. *J. Stud. Alcohol.* 42:925–37

Morey, L. C., Skinner, H. A. 1986. Empirically derived classifications of alcohol-related problems. See Galanter 1986, pp. 145–68

Mule, S. J., ed. 1981. *Behavior in Excess: An Examination of the Volitional Disorders*. New York: Free Press. 396 pp.

Murray, R. M., Clifford, C. A., Gurling, H. M. D. 1983. Twin adoption studies: How good is the evidence for a genetic role? See Galanter 1983, pp. 25–48

Murray, R. M., Stabenau, J. R. 1982. Genetic factors in alcoholism predisposition. In

Encyclopedic Handbook of Alcoholism, ed. E. M. Pattison, E. Kaufmann, 9:135–46. New York: Gardner Press

Nathan, P. E. 1987. The addictive personality: How valid? How useful? *J. Consult. Clin. Psychol.* In press

Nathan, P. E., Niaura, R. S. 1987. Prevention of alcohol problems. See Cox 1987a, pp. 333–54

Nathan, P. E., Skinstad, A.-H. 1987. Outcomes of treatment for alcohol problems: current methods, problems, and results. *J. Consult. Clin. Psychol.* 55:332–40

National Institute on Alcohol Abuse and Alcoholism. 1987. *6th Special Rep. US Congr. Alcohol and Health.* Washington, DC: US GPO. In press

Nerviano, V. J., Gross, H. W. 1983. Personality types of alcoholics on objective inventories: a review. *J. Stud. Alcohol* 44:837–51

Newcomb, M. D. 1987. Consequences of teenage drug use: the transition from adolescence to young adulthood. *Drugs Soc.* In press

Newcomb, M. D., Bentler, P. M. 1987. The impact of family context, deviant attitudes, and emotional distress on adolescent drug use: longitudinal latent-variable analyses of mothers and their children. *J. Res. Pers.* In press

Newcomb, M. D., Harlow, L. L. 1986. Life events and substance use among adolescents: mediating effects of perceived loss of control and meaninglessness in life. *J. Pers. Soc. Psychol.* 51:564–77

Newcomb, M. D., Maddahian, E., Bentler, P. M. 1986. Risk factors for drug use among adolescents: concurrent and longitudinal analyses. *Am. J. Public Health* 76:525–31

Newlin, D. B. 1985. Human conditioned compensatory response to alcohol cues: initial evidence. *Alcohol* 2:507–9

Nordstrom, G., Berglund, M. 1987. A prospective study of successful long-term adjustment in alcohol dependence: social drinking versus abstinence. *J. Stud. Alcohol* 48:95–103

Norwood, R. 1985. *Women Who Love Too Much: When You Keep Wishing and Hoping He'll Change.* Los Angeles: Tarcher. 266 pp.

O'Farrell, T. J. 1987. Marital therapy in the treatment of alcoholism. See Cox 1987a, pp. 205–34

Ogborne, A. C., Annis, H. M., Miller, W. R. 1982. Discriminant analysis and the selection of patients for controlled drinking programs: a methodological note. *J. Clin. Psychol.* 38:213–16

Oei, T. P. S., Jones, R. 1986. Alcohol-related expectancies: Have they a role in the understanding and treatment of problem drinking? *Adv. Alcohol Subst. Abuse* 6:89–105

O'Malley, S. S., Maisto, S. A. 1985. Effects of family drinking history and expectancies on response to alcohol in men. *J. Stud. Alcohol* 46:289–97

Orford, J. 1985. *Excessive Appetites: A Psychological View of Addictions.* Chichester: Wiley. 367 pp.

Ornstein, P., Cherepon, J. A. 1985. Demographic variables as predictors of alcoholism treatment outcome. *J. Stud. Alcohol* 46:425–32

Peele, S. 1986. The implications and limitations of genetic models of alcoholism and other addictions. *J. Stud. Alcohol* 47:63–73

Peele, S. 1985. *The Meaning of Addiction: Compulsive Experience and Its Interpretation.* Lexington, Mass: Lexington Books

Penick, E., Read, R., crowley, P., et al. 1978. Differentiation of alcoholics by family history. *J. Stud. Alcohol* 39:1944–48

Perri, M. G. 1985. Self-change strategies for the control of smoking, obesity, and problem drinking. See Shiffman & Wills 1985, pp. 295–317

Petrakis, P. 1985. *Alcoholism: An Inherited Disease.* Rockville, Md: NIAAA

Pohorecky, L., Brick, J., eds. 1983. *Stress and Alcohol Use.* New York: Elsevier. 452 pp.

Polich, J. M., Armor, D. J., Braiker, H. B. 1981. *The Course of Alcoholism: Four Years After Treatment.* New York: Wiley

Prochaska, J. O., DiClemente, C. C. 1985. Common processes of self-change in smoking, weight control, and psychological distress. In *Coping and Substance Use,* ed. S. Shiffman, T. A. Wills, 14:345–63. New York: Academic. 408 pp.

Prochaska, J. O., DiClemente, C. C. 1986. Toward a comprehensive model of change. See Miller & Heather 1986, pp. 3–27

Propping, P., Krueger, J., Mark, N. 1981. Genetic predisposition to alcoholism: an EEG study in alcoholics and relatives. *Hum. Genet.* 59:51–59

Raveis, V. H., Kandel, D. B. 1987. Changes in drug behavior from the middle to the late twenties: initiation, persistence, and cessation of use. *Am. J. Public Health.* 77:607–11

Riley, D. M., Sobell, L. C., Leo, G. I., Sobell, M. B., Klajner, F. 1987. Behavioral treatment of alcohol problems: a review and a comparison of behavioral and nonbehavioral studies. See Cox 1987a, pp. 73–116

Ritson, B. 1986. Merits of simple intervention. See Miller & Heather 1986, pp. 375–87

Rodin, J., Maloff, D., Becker, H. S. 1984. Self-control: the role of environmental and self-generated cues. In *Substance Abuse, Habitual Behavior, and Self-control,* ed. P. K. Levison, 1:9–47. Boulder, Colo: Westview Press. 178 pp.

Rohsenow, D. J. 1983. Drinking habits and expectancies about alcohol's effects for self versus others. *J. Consult. Clin. Psychol.* 51:752–56

Roizen, R. 1987. The great controlled-drinking controversy. See Galanter 1987, pp. 245–82

Rollnick, S., Heather, N. 1982. The application of Bandura's self-efficacy theory to abstinence-oriented alcoholism treatment. *Addict. Behav.* 7:243–51

Rounsaville, B. J. 1986. Clinical implications of relapse research. See Tims & Leukefeld 1986, pp. 172–84

Rounsaville, B., Dolinsky, Z. S., Babor, T. F., Meyer, R. E. 1987. Psychopathology as a predictor of treatment outcome in alcoholics. *Arch. Gen. Psychiatry.* 44:505–13

Royce, J. E. 1981. *Alcohol Problems and Alcoholism.* New York: Free Press. 383 pp.

Sadava, S. W. 1987. Interactional theory. See Blane & Leonard 1987, pp. 90–130

Sanchez-Craig, M., Annis, H. M., Bornet, A. R., MacDonald, K. R. 1984. Random assignment to abstinence and controlled drinking: evaluation of a cognitive-behavioral program for problem drinkers. *J. Consult. Clin. Psychol.* 52:390–403

Sanchez-Craig, M., Lei, H. 1986. Disadvantages to imposing the goal of abstinence on problem drinkers: an empirical study. *Br. J. Addict.* 81:505–12

Saxe, L., Dougherty, D., Esty, K., Fine, M. 1983. *Health Technology Case Study 22: The Effectiveness and Costs of Alcoholism Treatment.* Washington, DC: Congr. US Office Technol. Assess. 98 pp.

Schacter, S. 1982. Recidivism and self-cure of smoking and obesity. *Am. Psychol.* 37:436–44

Schaeffer, K. W., Parsons, O. Q., Yohman, J. R. 1984. Neuropsychological differences between male familial and nonfamilial alcoholics and nonalcoholics. *Alcohol. Clin. Exp. Res.* 8:347–58

Schaps, E., DiBartolo, R., Moskowitz, J., Palley, C. S., Churgin, S. 1981. A review of 127 drug abuse prevention program evaluations. *J. Drug. Iss.* 11:17–43

Schuckit, M. A. 1983. The genetics of alcoholism. See Tabakoff et al 1983, pp. 31–46

Schuckit, M. A. 1984. Subjective response to alcohol in sons of alcoholics and controls. *Arch. Gen. Psychiatry* 41:879–84

Schuckit, M. A. 1987. Biological vulnerability to alcoholism. *J. Consult. Clin. Psychol.* 55:301–9

Schuckit, M. A., Gold, E., Risch, C. 1987a. Changes in blood prolactin levels in sons of alcoholics and controls. *Am. J. Psychiatry.* In press

Schuckit, M. A., Gold, E., Risch, C. 1987b. Plasma cortisol levels following ethanol in sons of alcoholics and controls. *Am. J. Psychiatry.* In press

Schuckit, M. A., Zisook, S., Mortola, J. 1985. Clinical implications of DSM-III diagnosis of alcohol abuse and alcohol dependence. *Am. J. Psychiatry* 142:1403–8

Shaffer, H. J. 1985. The disease controversy: of metaphors, maps, and menus. *J. Psychoact. Drugs* 17:65–76

Shapiro, A. P., Nathan, P. E. 1986. Human tolerance to alcohol: the role of Pavlovian conditioning processes. *Psychopharmacology* 88:90–95

Sher, K. J. 1985. Subjective effects of alcohol: the influence of setting and individual differences in alcohol expectancies. *J. Stud. Alcohol* 46:137–46

Sher, K. J. 1987. Stress response dampening. See Blane & Leonard 1987, pp. 227–71

Shiffman, S., Wills, T. A., eds. 1985. *Coping and Substance Use.* New York: Academic. 408 pp.

Shipley, T. E. 1987. Opponent process theory. See Blane & Leonard 1987, pp. 346–87

Siegel, S. 1983. Classical conditioning, drug tolerance, and drug dependence. In *Research Advances in Alcohol and Drug Dependence,* ed. R. Smart et al, Vol. 7, Ch. 6:207–46. New York: Plenum. 472 pp.

Silbereisen, R. K., Eyferth, K., Rudinger, G., eds. 1986. *Development as Action in Context: Problem Behavior and Normal Youth Development.* New York: Springer-Verlag. 322 pp.

Simon, E. J. 1983. Opiate receptors: properties and possible functions. See Levison et al 1983, pp. 239–60

Skinner, H. A. 1986. Alcohol dependence: How does it come about? *Br. J. Addict.* 81:193–95

Skinner, H. A., Goldberg, A. E. 1986. Evidence for a drug dependence syndrome among narcotic users. *Br. J. Addict.* 81:479–84

Sobell, L. C., Sobell, M. B. 1986. Can we do without alcohol abusers' self-reports? *Behav. Ther.* 9:141–46

Sobell, M. B., Sobell, L. C., Brochu, S., Roy, J., Stevens, J. A. 1987. Alcohol treatment outcome evaluation methodology: state of the art, 1980–1984. *Addict. Behav.* 12:113–28

Solomon, R. L. 1980. The opponent-process theory of acquired motivation: the cost of pleasure and the benefits of pain. *Am. Psychol.* 35:691–712

Southwick, L. L., Steele, C. M., Marlatt, G. A., Lindell, M. 1981. Alcohol-related expectancies: defined by phase of intoxication and drinking experience. *J. Consult. Clin. Psychol.* 49:713–21

Stabenau, J. R. 1984. Implications of family

history of alcoholism, antisocial personality, and sex differences in alcohol dependence. *Am. J. Psychiatry* 141:1178–82

Stall, R., Biernacki, P. 1986. Spontaneous remission from the problematic use of substances: an inductive model derived from a comparative analysis of the alcohol, opiate, tobacco, and food/obesity literatures. *Int. J. Addict.* 21:1–23

Stewart, J., DeWitt, H., Eikelboom, R. 1984. Role of unconditioned and conditioned drug effects in the self-administration of opiates and stimulants. *Psychol. Rev.* 91:251–68

Strug, P. L., Priyadarsini, S., Hyman, M. M., eds. 1986. *Alcohol Interventions: Historical and Sociocultural Approaches.* New York: Haworth. 218 pp.

Swinson, R. P. 1983. Genetic markers and alcoholism. See Galanter 1983, pp. 9–24

Tabakoff, B., Rothstein, J. D. 1983. Biology of tolerance and dependence. In *Medical and Social Aspects of Alcohol Abuse,* ed. B. Tabakoff, P. B. Sutker, C. L. Randall, 7:187–220. New York: Plenum

Tarter, R. E., Alterman, A. I., Edwards, K. L. 1985. Vulnerability to alcoholism in men: a behavior-genetic perspective. *J. Stud. Alcohol* 46:329–56

Tiffany, S. T., Baker, T. B. 1986. Tolerance to alcohol: psychological models and their application to alcoholism. *Ann. Behav. Med.* 8:7–12

Tims, F. M., Leukefeld, C. G., eds. 1986. *Relapse and Recovery in Drug Abuse.* NIDA Res. Monogr. 72. Rockville, Md: NIDA. 197 pp.

Tims, F. M., Ludford, J. P., eds. 1984. *Drug Abuse Treatment Evaluation: Strategies, Progress, and Prospects.* NIDA Res. Monogr. 51. Rockville, Md: NIDA. 181 pp.

Tuchfeld, B. S. 1981. Spontaneous remission in alcoholics: Empirical observations and theoretical implications. *J. Stud. Alcohol* 42:626–41

Vaillant, G. E. 1983. *The Natural History of Alcoholism.* Cambridge, Mass: Harvard Univ. Press

Vaillant, G. E., Milofsky, E. J. 1982. The etiology of alcoholism: a prospective viewpoint. *Am. J. Psychol.* 37:349–60

Valicer, L., Valicer, B., D'Angelo, N. 1984. Relationship of family history of alcoholism to patterns of drinking and physical dependence in male alcoholics. *Drug Alcohol Depend.* 13:215–23

Vanicelli, M. 1984. Treatment outcome of alcoholic women: the state of the art in relation to sex bias and expectancy effects. In *Alcohol Problems in Women: Antecedents, Consequences, and Interventions,* ed. L. J. Beckman, 13:369–412. New York: Guilford. 480 pp.

Walker, R. D., Donovan, D. M., Kivlahan, D. R., O'Leary, M. R. 1983. Length of stay, neuropsychological performance, and aftercare: influences on alcohol treatment outcome. *J. Consult. Clin. Psychol.* 51:900–11

Wallace, J. 1985a. *Alcoholism: New Light on the Disease.* Newport, RI: Edgehill. 406 pp.

Wallace, J. 1985b. Predicting the onset of compulsive drinking in alcoholics: a biopsychosocial model. *Alcohol* 2:589–95

Wanberg, K. W., Horn, J. L. 1983. Assessment of alcohol use with multidimensional concepts and measures. *Am. Psychol.* 38:1055–69

Washton, A. M., Gold, M. S. 1987. *Cocaine: A Clinician's Handbook.* New York: Guilford. 251 pp.

West, J. A., Sutker, P. B. 1987. Alcohol consumption, tension reduction, and mood enhancement. See Cox 1987b. In press

Wills, T. A., Shiffman, S. 1985. Coping and substance use: a conceptual framework. In *Coping and Substance Use,* ed. S. Shiffman, T. A. Wills, 1:3–24. New York: Academic. 408 pp.

Yamaguchi, K., Kandel, D. B. 1984. Patterns of drug use from adolescence to young adulthood. III: Prediction of progression. *Am. J. Public Health* 74:673–81

Zinberg, N. E. 1984. *Drug, Set, Setting: The Basis for Controlled Intoxicant Use.* New Haven: Yale Univ. Press

Zucker, R. A. 1979. Developmental aspects of drinking through the young adult years. In *Youth, Alcohol, and Social Policy,* ed. H. T. Blane, M. E. Chafetz, 4:91–146. New York: Plenum. 424 pp.

Zucker, R. A. 1987. The four alcoholisms: a developmental account of the etiologic process. In *Nebraska Symposium on Motivation, 1986:* Vol. 34, *Alcohol and Addictive Behaviors,* ed. P. C. Rivers. Lincoln, Neb: Univ. Nebraska Press. In press

Zucker, R. A., Gomberg, E. S. L. 1986. Etiology of alcoholism reconsidered: the case for a biopsychosocial process. *Am. Psychol.* 41:783–93

Zucker, R. A., Noll, R. B. 1987. The interaction of child and environment in the early development of drug involvement: a far ranging review and planned very early intervention. *Drugs Soc.* In press

Zucker, R. A., Noll, R. B. 1982. Precursors and developmental influences on drinking and alcoholism: etiology from a longitudinal perspective. In *Alcohol Consumption and Related Problems,* ed. Dep. Health and Human Services, 8:289–330. Washington, DC: GPO. Alcohol and Health Monogr. 1. 355 pp.

Ann. Rev. Psychol. 1988. 39:253–82

JUVENILE DELINQUENCY

Arnold Binder

Program in Social Ecology, University of California, Irvine, California 92717

CONTENTS

INTRODUCTION

People, particularly young people, have repeatedly behaved in ways that are perceived as disruptive or potentially disruptive of social expectations or processes. The behavior may injure someone; deprive another of his or her property; offend the moral values of a group of people, perhaps outrageously; or be of a type that is presumed to be indicative of future, more severe problems. In the attempt to control such behavior, small, informal groups have rules; larger, more formal organizations have rules and regulations; and

0066-4308/88/0201-0253$02.00

society as a whole has rules, regulations, and laws. In addition to specifications of proper and improper behavior, each of these mechanisms of social control carries sanctions for failure to conform; these may be implied or explicitly stated.

Criminal Behavior and Delinquency

Criminal law is aimed at controlling the most disruptive types of behavior, and is accordingly accompanied by the most severe possible sanctions and the greatest array of protections to minimize the likelihood that they are inappropriately applied. If an adult has violated a criminal code according to the judgment of a criminal court following highly structured procedures, he or she is thought of as a criminal. Similarly, if a youth has violated a criminal code according to the judgment of a juvenile court, he or she is thought of as a juvenile delinquent. The array of differences between the operations of the criminal and the juvenile justice systems ranges from the superficial (e.g., children are not technically arrested but "taken into temporary custody") to the important (e.g. "hearings" have traditionally been far less formal in juvenile court than "trials" in criminal court, although that picture has shown some change in recent years). Elsewhere I have discussed many aspects of these processes (Binder 1979, 1984, 1987a), including the origins and philosophy of the juvenile court, the conceptual and operational differences between criminal and juvenile courts, and the history of increasing procedural protections in the juvenile court.

A survey article on juvenile delinquency surely is concerned with research and theory devoted to the various aspects of the disruptive behavior of youths. But so is an article that covers such topics as child aggressiveness, adolescent violence, and child psychopathology. The critical differentiating element between juvenile delinquency and the other topics is the element of law. While aggressive or violent behavior is definable purely on the basis of observations of the interactions among people, delinquent behavior requires for its definition the evaluation of behavior in terms of laws and actual or potential legal processes. Thus, the behavior of a youngster who murdered his father would certainly be considered violent, but it would not be delinquent if a court eventually judged him not culpable.

However, a discussion of juvenile delinquency as a behavioral or social phenomenon cannot restrict its coverage to youths who have been defined as delinquent by law and adjudicated by juvenile courts. There are two primary reasons for this state of affairs: First, the juvenile justice system is highly selective at its various stages of possible or actual processing. At the outset, many juvenile offenses are not detected or not reported if detected, and many offenders are not taken into custody (arrested) when their offenses are reported. Then, there is a filtering out at each procedural stage as youths are handled by police officers, court intake or probation officers, prosecuting attorneys (in some states), and by the judge or referee in the adjudicatory hearing. While important for an understanding of juvenile justice as an operating social system, factors that determine the selection of particular youths rather than others for further processing are mostly irrelevant for the development of psychological theories of delinquency. These selective factors include: the alertness of possible observers of the offense, the mood of the complainant, the policy of the police department, the characteristics of arresting police officers and intake court officers in using their considerable discretion, and the general tolerance of youthful peccadilloes in the community.

The second reason for not restricting coverage of juvenile delinquency to youths so designated by law and adjudication is the variation over states (and other jurisdictional entities) in the substantive law governing juvenile misconduct. Therefore, if an article on juvenile delinquency depended on legal definition and appropriate adjudication to delineate its realm of coverage, youthful offenders with similar social histories and identical offenses might be included or excluded on the basis of the jurisdiction in which their behavior occurred.

I come now to the uncomfortable necessity of specifying coverage in positive terms. Appropriate for inclusion in a survey article like this one are all research studies and theoretical discussions of a psychological nature that focus on youths under the age of 18 who have behaved in a manner prohibited by a criminal code in the jurisdiction where it occurred. They may have indicated the behavior on a self-study questionnaire, they may have been arrested for the behavior, they may have been adjudicated in juvenile courts or convicted as criminals in criminal courts, they may have been institutionalized, or they may have been diverted from further processing in the system by referral to a mental health or similar community agency.

I conclude this section by distinguishing among the expressions "delinquency," "antisocial conduct," and "deviance." Confusion among them leads to such misleading positions as the condemnation of the practice of defining "delinquency in legal rather than psychological terms" (Arbuthnot et al 1987). As stated above, it is not possible to define juvenile delinquency in a manner independent of the laws that anchor and bound it. This does indeed create problems for psychologists who must deal with an array of behaviors woven together by the whims of legislators and jurists—in the words of Rice (1956, p. 10) the behaviors encompassed by juvenile delinquency "have about as much in common as the words quail, deliquescence, pique, and cumquat— all of which can be said to be similar because each contains the letter 'q.' " But the solution cannot be arbitrary redefinition. [A reasonable solution has been developed by Quay (1987c), who assumes that among delinquents there are identifiable subgroups that are reasonably homogeneous on certain behavioral and psychological characteristics.]

The expression "antisocial conduct," on the other hand, is used by psychologists to designate behavior that is assumed to have harmful consequences for society but is not necessarily illegal. Finally, "deviance," used mostly by sociologists, refers to behavior that violates a social norm so greatly that social control responses are mobilized. Delinquent behavior is clearly deviant from the perspective of the broader society, but it may not be deviant from the perspective of one of its subcultures. Indeed, several theorists have explained delinquent and criminal behavior in terms of conformity to subcultural norms (see e.g. Cohen 1955; Wolfgang & Ferracuti 1967).

Status Offenses, Parens Patriae, and Delinquency

In 1838, the Pennsylvania Supreme Court (in the decision *Ex parte Crouse*, 4 Wharton 9), set a critical precedent in its ruling that the state had the right to take charge of the lives of children, including the right to place them in institutions, for such offenses as "incorrigibility," "viciousness," and "moral depravity." Such offenses came to be called "status offenses" because they could be committed only by people of a certain status—below the age of legal maturity. Status offenses were not included in criminal codes or the common law defining criminal acts, and so a need for a special law that applied only to children arose; that law did evolve during the 19th century. The new law was anchored in a concept derived from English Chancery law, *parens patriae*, which justified intervention on the basis that the state (formerly the king—the original expression was *pater patriae*), as superparent, had ultimate responsibility for the welfare of all children in the country.

Since decisions under *parens patriae* were presumably made by a solicitous parent for the child's benefit, the usual constitutional protections, such as the right to trial by jury, were declared unnecessary (in the *Crouse* and many subsequent decisions of state supreme courts). That *quid pro quo* notion and jurisdiction over status as well as criminal offenses were incorporated as essential elements when the first juvenile court was established by state law in Chicago in the year 1899. While the criminal court was punitive, the juvenile court was supposed to operate on behalf of the youngster in an informal manner aimed at prescribing rehabilitative measures for behavior that ranged from serious crime to insolence. Indeed, over subsequent years, such behavior as the following was proscribed for children (see Hutzler & Sestak 1977): "habitually deports himself in a manner that is injurious to himself or others" (Iowa), "persistently runs away from the home of his parents or legal guardian" (Massachusetts), and "repeatedly associates with thieves, prostitutes, pimps or procurers" (Michigan).

Incidentally, the attitude of *quid pro quo* in the juvenile court, *parens patriae* for constitutional rights, remained firmly entrenched in juvenile justice until the years 1966–1967 when the US Supreme Court entered the scene for the first time. The feeling of the Court regarding treatment of youths in juvenile court under the *quid pro quo* notion is well summarized in the following statement from its decision *In re Gault* (387 US at 28, 1967): "Under our Constitution, the condition of being a boy does not justify a kangaroo court." If that case summarized the Court's attitude, why had it taken 67 years for the Court to intervene? The answers to that question, much too complex to take on here, may be found in Binder (1984).

Status offenders are not typically considered juvenile delinquents, but a general discussion of delinquency can be expected to include references to them. Many states maintain the distinction in their codes by referring to a status offender as a "child in need of supervision" or an "incorrigible child" or "a person in need of supervision," while referring to a criminal offender as a "delinquent child" or "delinquent juvenile" or the equivalent. Other state codes include both criminal and status offenders under the expression "juvenile delinquent."

Do delinquents and status offenders differ in important ways? Does status offending predispose a youngster toward later criminal offending (a theoretical position reflected in earlier state codes that referred to status offenders as "pre-delinquents")? How much concurrent involvement can one expect in delinquent behavior and status offenses? Attempts to answer these and similar questions may be found in Thomas (1976), Weis (1980), and Murray (1983). Regardless of the answers to those questions, there are many (e.g. Abadinsky 1976; Ketchum 1977) who argue that status offenders should be removed entirely from the jurisdiction of the juvenile court (for opposing positions, see Martin & Snyder 1976; Gregory 1978). And federal legislation, starting with the Juvenile Justice and Delinquency Prevention Act of 1974 (Public Law 93-415), has, by strong financial incentives, motivated most states to modify their codes so as to preclude, or at least reduce, the placement of status offenders in locked facilities (see Handler & Zatz 1982; Wadlington et al 1983).

THE QUESTION OF PRIMARY DISCIPLINARY AFFILIATION

Although psychologists contribute substantially in the area of juvenile delinquency both as scientists and as practitioners, the field is dominated by sociology. The dominance may be seen in prevalent theories, in published research, in the course offerings of academic departments, in the authorships of relevant monographs and textbooks, in the editorships of key journals, in the number of sessions devoted to the topic at professional meetings, and in the key individuals likely to serve on or as advisers to local and national committees and commissions devoted to dealing with delinquency as a social problem. As obvious as this state of affairs seems to an observer in the late 1980s, a reasonable person of the 19th century very likely, and a person of the early 20th century almost certainly, would have predicted that in 1988, juvenile delinquency (or its parent construct, criminology) would be a subfield of a discipline that focuses on the individual, like psychology or psychiatry, rather than of one that focuses on society, like sociology. Let us briefly explore how the shift came about. In our exploration, delinquency is considered equivalent to criminology during much of the 19th century since the separate focus on children as offenders is the product of that century, ending with establishment of a separate court for children in 1899 (see Binder 1984, 1987a,c).

The 19th Century and the Prominence of Psychiatry

The concept of "moral insanity" was introduced by the psychiatrist Prichard in 1835 to refer to the phenomena of disordered consciences and deviations from social norms without illusions or hallucinations. Individual factors in crime causation continued to be emphasized by other psychiatrists during the 19th century: Ray (1838) distinguished between crime on the basis of moral insanity and crime as motivated rationally; Morel (1857) explained criminal behavior in terms of degeneracy and classified types of degenerates; and Maudsley (1870) allowed for moral degeneracy but emphasized such psychological motivations for crime as overwork, overexertion, frustration, irritation, imitation, and coercion. The work in that psychiatric tradition culminated in the bioconstitutional theory of Lombroso (1876, 1912), which conceived of criminals as degenerates. According to the theory, most criminals are distinguished from noncriminals by atavistic physical characteristics such as small skull, retreating forehead, and broad cheekbones symptomatic of a reversion to the subhuman.

Early 19th-century work in the social aspects of crime, starting with the moral statisticians Guerry and Quetelet, did not gain the recognition of the psychiatric tradition. Lindesmith & Levin (1937) and Taylor et al (1973) have commented on the sociology of crime during the 19th century and its eclipse by genetic and psychological theories, particularly that of Lombroso.

The Early 20th Century and the Prominence of Psychology

American psychology came on the scene prominently early in the 20th century. Three principal forces caused it to focus directly on young offenders rather than on criminals generally. The first was the identification, toward the end of the 19th century, of adolescence as a unique stage of life in terms of general plasticity and particular vulnerability to deviant behavior. The viewpoint was represented most effectively by G. Stanley Hall who, in 1904, published his encyclopedic treatment of adolescence, including an analysis of delinquency. The second came via the intelligence-testing movement. The intelligence tests introduced by Binet and Simon were translated and popularized by Goddard and used in many comparative studies, most particularly comparisons of delinquent and nondelinquent groups.

The final impetus that brought psychology to a prominent position in the area of juvenile delinquency resulted from the efforts of the team of psychiatrist William Healy and psychologist Augusta Bronner. As stated above, the culmination of the century-long process of differentiating juvenile offenders from adult criminals came in 1899 when the first juvenile court was established. To serve the clinical needs of the youngsters handled by that court and to further research in juvenile delinquency, the Chicago Juvenile Psychopathic Institute was founded in 1909 with Healy as its director. Bronner joined him there four years later. They continued their work with juvenile offenders when they moved from Chicago to become director and assistant director of the Judge Baker Foundation in Boston.

Psychology (with the aid of psychiatry), then, had a firm grip on juvenile delinquency in the United States during the opening decades of the 20th century. In fact, that leadership, particularly of Healy and Bronner, went virtually unchallenged until the late 1920s and early 1930's (see Fink 1938; Snodgrass 1972) when the ecological formulations regarding delinquency of the Chicago school of sociology became widely known (see Shaw 1929; Shaw & McKay 1931).

The Later 20th Century and the Dominance of Sociology

But how did that challenge lead to such a complete conquest that juvenile delinquency (along with criminology generally) eventually became a subfield of sociology? [See Binder & Geis (1979), who set 1924 as the date of birth of modern criminology in the United States.] The question may be phrased more precisely in the following way: How did approaches to crime and delinquency that emphasize social causative factors and social relationships manage to achieve mastery over approaches that emphasize constructs of individual idiosyncrasies and the effects of environmental conditions on individuals? While a more extended attempt to answer questions of this sort may be found in Binder (1987c), a summary response is, first, that the work of the sociologists has been more imaginative than that of the individual-oriented scholars and, second, that the American intellectual culture is more receptive to theoretical positions that overtly blame society for an individual's (particularly a young individual's) transgressions than to those that seem to blame the individual. Related to the latter is the particular antipathy in American scholarship (and the culture generally) to notions of the born delinquent or even to the milder notion of individual predisposition toward delinquency. For particularly vehement criticisms of those and similar genetic positions, see Lindesmith & Levin (1937), Sutherland (1951), and Taylor et al (1973), and for an interesting analysis of the relationship between the social outlook of a country and its willingness to accept formulations like "dangerous classes," see Radzinowicz (1966).

Adelson (1986, p. 44) has lamented that delinquency and criminology fall in the "territory occupied largely by sociology and such immediate neighbors as social work," and regrets the resulting diffidence of psychology. [A related position may be found in Farrington (1985), who argues that it is just as valid to focus on individual as on social factors in the prevention of delinquency.] As illustrative of the intolerance that the domination has produced, he points to the recent drubbing that Wilson & Herrnstein's (1985) *Crime and Human Nature* has received just because of its psychological orientation to explanations of crime. [Indeed, in his review of the book, the sociologist Gibbs (1985) advised sociologists with high blood pressure to approach it cautiously.] To most psychologists, the position of Wilson & Herrnstein (p. 43) that their theory of criminal behavior incorporates "both genetic predispositions and social learning" erected on the general bedrock of "modern behavioral psychology" is so obvious and simplistic that it would hardly seem worth mentioning. But an understanding of the possibility of cardiac arrest emerges when one considers the following statement, typical of those that may be found, in several variations, widely in the sociological literature: "No one is intrinsically criminal: criminality is a definition applied by individuals with the power to do so, according to illegal and extra-legal as well as legal criteria" (Turk 1969, p. 10). (Turk is a conflict theorist and was a recent president of the American Society of Criminology.) Sociologically acceptable explanations of delinquency are expected to use peer characteristics, social class, race, economic opportunities, neighborhood features, the reactive effect of the justice system, sex, and the repressive tendencies of those who make and implement the law. The use of constructs based on individual differences is not well received and may be dismissed with a deprecatory phrase like "psychologizing."

CHARACTERISTICS OF JUVENILE OFFENDERS

Intelligence

As stated above, Goddard introduced the Binet-Simon tests into the United States, and in the process of using them became a leading advocate of a close relationship between mental deficiency and delinquency. Among the studies mentioned in his book (1914), the percentages of the feebleminded found among institutionalized delinquents ranged from a high of 89% to a low of 28%. By the time the sociologist Sutherland reviewed the state of knowledge of the relationship in 1931, there had been about 350 studies of the intelligence of delinquents in the United States. Sutherland noted that, as the tests and the testers became more sophisticated, the percentage of mental defectives in samples of institutionalized delinquents decreased. Using four periods from 1910 to 1928 he found (1931, p. 358) that the percentage of feebleminded individuals in the median study decreased as follows: 51, 28, 21, 20. He conjectured that the downward trend would continue. Among the early problems he pointed out were the difficulty of defining just what a feebleminded person was (some early testers defined the criterion cut-off in terms of the maximum mental age scores found in institutions for the retarded) and the likelihood that young offenders were selected for institutionalization because of their feeblemindedness.

Several reviewers (e.g. Hirschi & Hindelang 1977; Wilson & Herrnstein 1985) remarked that Sutherland's influential negative comments led to a virtual ban in delinquency textbooks on comments about intelligence as a factor in delinquency. The reviewers noted the prestige of Sutherland within sociology as a factor in that reaction but also indicated a general receptivity in the discipline to any position that distances sociology from concepts based on individual differences.

Another milestone in the saga of intelligence and delinquency came in 1947 when Merrill reported the results of a 10-year research project that compared the characteristics of youngsters referred to a juvenile court with those of nondelinquents. On the basis of mixed results, she concluded that more delinquents referred to court are mentally defective than are school children in general, but the conclusion was presented with the following cautions: The defective child is more likely to be caught than the normal child; the defective child is less likely to have a supportive home environment, making court referral more likely; and the defective child is more likely to be a truant or school misfit, again making court referral more likely. In regard to the relationship between IQ and type of offense, one would expect forgery to be an offense of brighter youngsters, truancy and vagrancy to be offenses of duller youngsters—and Merrill so found. But most offenses involved stealing, a category where she found no relationship with IQ. [A review of studies of that era which reported on the relation between intelligence and type of crime may be seen in Metfessel & Lovell (1942).]

To illustrate other results, in their study of 105 delinquents and 105 nondelinquents who were siblings of the delinquents, Healy & Bronner (1936) found no difference in the distributions of intelligence over the two groups. However, in the three clinics where referrals by the juvenile court were sent and the research conducted, mentally defective children were not accepted. Moreover, as Hirschi & Hindelang (1977) point out, using matched siblings necessarily reduced potential differences in intelligence because of the relatively high correlation of intrafamilial intelligence. On the other hand,

Reiss & Rhodes (1961) examined over 9000 juvenile court records and found the association of IQ and offense rate to be greater than the association of rate and occupational status of head of household. A survey of research in the area by Woodward (1955) and Caplan (1965) led to the conclusion that the average IQ of delinquents was about 92—that is, about 8 points below the average of nondelinquents. But both researchers believed the difference could be accounted for by the operation of related cultural factors (particularly SES) rather than by a direct or mediated effect of intelligence.

In 1977, Hirschi & Hindelang published their important review of the literature on delinquency and intelligence and concluded (p. 576) that "IQ is related to official delinquency and that, in fact, it is as important in predicting official delinquency as social class or race." Official delinquency concerns offenses that have come to the attention of authorities—cases where action, from arrest to institutionalization, has been taken. What about the relationship of intelligence to delinquent behavior that never comes to official attention, that may never have been detected? The question moved out of the metaphysical realm as the method of assessing delinquency by the self-report method developed.

The self-report approach to assessing delinquency was introduced in a systematic manner by Short & Nye in 1957. In a questionnaire or interview a series of offenses are presented to youngsters, who indicate which offenses they have committed over a specific period. The method depends for its accuracy on two characteristics of reporting youngsters: good memory and reasonable honesty. Doubts have been expressed about both characteristics, particularly the latter in view of the phenomena being assessed (see e.g. Reiss 1975).

In general, the self-report technique has passed various tests of reliability and validity (see particularly Hindelang et al 1981), and so it provides a means of relating intelligence to delinquency without the nuisance requirements of detection and official action. To illustrate the method, Hirschi & Hindelang (1977), using data from the research of Hirschi (1969), reported percentages of youths, over five categories of intelligence, admitting two or more delinquent acts on a self-report questionnaire. Percentages decreased as intelligence rose, for white and black males separately. For whites, twice the percentage admitted two or more delinquent acts in the lowest IQ category as in the highest category. For blacks, that ratio was 3:2. Other evidence of a relationship between intelligence and self-reported delinquency may be found in West & Farrington (1977).

On the basis of the entire array of results surveyed, those that used official records as well as those that used self-report assessments, Hirschi & Hindelang (1977, p. 577) conclude that, contrary to the predominant position in sociology ("a relation between IQ and delinquency is routinely denied in sociological textbooks"), intelligence is at least as strongly related to delinquency as are class and race (which are "the major bases of most sociological theories of delinquency"). They do not assume that IQ has a direct effect in producing delinquency but that the effect is mediated through school performance and school adjustment. Low IQ leads to poor performance in school and a concomitant poor attitude toward school, which makes the youngster more likely to commit a delinquent act. [For a challenging response in the sociological literature to the position of Hirschi & Hindelang regarding a link between intelligence and delinquency, see Menard & Morse (1984).]

Quay (1987b) agrees that there is a substantial difference (about 8 points) between the average IQs of delinquents and nondelinquents but is not convinced that the effect is mediated through the schools. After discussing several studies using Wechsler tests (primarily WISC-R) that compared delinquents and nondelinquents on the patterning of Verbal IQ, Performance IQ, and subtests of these scales, he concluded that the 8-point difference is due primarily to the inferiority of delinquents on tests requiring verbal skills. Using that conclusion and earlier findings that school failure may actually follow antisocial behavior, he argued that lower intelligence, particularly in the verbal realm, puts a child at general disadvantage in social interactions which, in turn, leads to early troublesome, and eventually, delinquent behavior. The process encourages school failure and is, in turn, exacerbated by school failure. [See also Loeber & Stouthamer-Loeber (1987) for a summary of the evidence linking IQ, educational achievement, and delinquency.]

Learning Disabilities

Wilson & Herrnstein (1985) agree that the effect of intelligence on delinquency is not mediated by school failure. They add a supporting argument with an ironic twist, namely that such special learning disabilities as dyslexia and aphasia (which, they argue, are not correlated with intelligence) produce profound levels of failure in school, without accompanying delinquency. The irony lies in the fact that the controversy regarding the relationship between learning disabilities and delinquency is almost as great as the controversy over the relationship between intelligence and delinquency.

The impetus for the assumption of a link between learning disabilities and delinquency came, according to Murray (1976), from the world of practitioners—school counselors, court psychologists, and correctional personnel—rather than from academic research. These practicing specialists observed children with serious behavior problems, including delinquency, and noted a high rate of school failure among them for reasons other than intellectual deficit. Early studies (see e.g. Mulligan 1969) did find supporting evidence for the linkage. That was the state of knowledge during the mid-1970s when the federal government took special interest in the problems of delinquency [as discussed at various other points in this article; and see Binder (1979); Binder & Binder (1982)]. Hope that the proclaimed association would lead to a relatively easy path toward delinquency reduction (certainly easier than eliminating poverty or social class distinctions), the US Department of Justice, through its National Institute for Juvenile Justice and Delinquency Prevention (NIJJDP), commissoned several approaches to examining the possibility that learning disability leads to delinquency. In addition, the General Accounting Office (GAO) took on a study of the extent of learning problems among institutionalized delinquents, the efforts of schools to iden-tify children with learning problems, and the extent of federal involvement in the learning-problem area.

One of the recipients of NIJJDP funding, Murray (1976), conducted a careful survey of theory and knowledge on the link between delinquency and learning disabilities and concluded that the evidence supporting the link was feeble. He answered the direct federal concern as follows (p. 65). "The notion that programs to diagnose and treat learning disabilities early will actually *prevent* delinquency is not supported by any data at all." Another recipient of NIJJDP funding was the National Center for State Courts; the assignment in this case was to obtain hard empirical data. The investigators at the National Center did so in seemingly solid cross-sectional and longitudinal studies, but the published analyses and conclusions are utterly bewildering. Zimmerman et al (1981) found no difference between the learning-disabled and normal children in actual delinquent behavior, while Dunivant (1982a, 1984) con-cluded that learning disability significantly increased the frequency and seriousness of delinquent behavior (as evaluated by official and self-reported measures). Zimmerman et al (1981) suggested that learning-disabled children were more likely to find themselves in the arms of the juvenile justice system because of differential selection rather than different behavior, while Duni-vant (1982a, 1984) argued that the greater delinquency among the learning disabled resulted directly from accompanying cognitive and social im-pairments. [For an attempt at resolution of the differences, see Dunivant (1982b).]

Other indications that the issue did not die with the reports of Murray (1976) and Zimmerman et al (1981), as Wilson & Herrnstein (1985) imply, is the report, based on the GAO study, of the Comptroller General of the United States to the Senate and House of Representatives (1977), and such more recent studies as Satterfield et al (1982) and Reilly et al (1985). All argue for some association between learning disability and delinquency while recogniz-ing that a "causal" link has not yet been established. Finally, see Post (1981) and Winter (1983) for indications of how firmly entrenched the link is among lawyers and judges. According to Post (1981, p. 61), "If the conclusion reached [after psychological testing] is that the child is suffering from a previously undetected LD, it should serve as a complete defense [in a delinquency action]."

Personality

MULTIFACTORAL APPROACHES Healy (1915) set the stage for this approach to the study of delinquency. He considered delinquency an individual phenomenon from which one could infer clusters of causes based on types but not a general theory. Accordingly, understanding required analysis of the multitude of factors that could be studied by clinical methods. [A recent derivative of that attitude may be found in Lamson (1983).]

Such an approach was followed by Healy & Bronner (1926) in their case studies of 4000 repeat juvenile offenders in Chicago and Boston. Among the "conditions directly causative of delinquency" (pp. 179–81) they listed "adolescent instability and impulses," "extreme social suggestibility," and "love of adventure." Greater methodological sophistication was shown in their report (1936) comparing the case histories of 105 juvenile offenders with those of nondelinquent siblings (see above). Almost one half of the delinquents were described as hyperactive, extremely aggressive, or excessively impulsive while not a single control was so characterized. Marked differences were also found between the groups in gregariousness, ascendant tendencies, and feelings of inferiority, where a greater proportion of delinquents showed these characteristics. The most profound difference was in the area of emotional discomfort—inner stress; 91% of the delinquents as opposed to 13% showed the disturbance, leading to the conjecture it played a major role (1936, p. 121) "in the origin and growth of their delinquent tendencies."

The Gluecks (1950, 1968, 1974) began their longitudinal study of 500 incarcerated juvenile offenders in the late 1930s. As a control group, they used a sample of nondelinquent boys matched on age, IQ, ethnic background, and residential neighborhood. Personality assessment was by psychiatric interview and the Rorschach test. They found the delinquents to be far less conventional, more assertive, more extraverted, less goal oriented, low in such feelings as anxiety and insecurity, less concerned about relations with others, more inclined to satisfy their needs immediately, and far more hostile and destructive.

Conger & Miller (1966) evaluated a large array of factors in their study of 184 delinquent boys and 184 matched nondelinquents. They used information available in school files about student behavior prior to the time personality tests were given in the tenth grade. The investigators found differences in personality between future delinquents and nondelinquents from the earliest school years. In general, the delinquents were egocentric, inconsiderate, demanding, anxious, uncooperative, and disrespectful. But, perhaps most importantly, Conger & Miller (1966) found that the differences in personality between the two groups varied over social-class/IQ subgroupings. [For a more recent study on the relationship between teacher ratings and later delinquency see Magnusson et al (1983), where aggressiveness was the key indicator of later delinquency.]

The Cambridge Study in Delinquent Development started in 1961–1962 when 411 boys, born during the period 1951–1954 and living in a working-class area of London, were selected for study. The first report of the study appeared in 1969 (West), the second in 1973 (West & Farrington), and the third in 1977 (West & Farrington). The last of these was based on interviews and a test of social attitudes with 389 of the original group during the years 1971–1973, when the youths were 18 or 19 years of age. By the date of their interviews, 101 had an official conviction for one or more offenses. The personality characteristic that most differentiated the convicted delinquents from the other youths, in both interview and test results, was aggressiveness, even though the convictions were mostly for nonviolent offenses. While fighting was widely reported for all youths, the delinquents far exceeded the nondelinquents in fight frequency and intensity, the use of weapons, and the extent of brutality. The information obtained by interviewing and testing about aggressive behavior and attitudes among the delinquents was confirmed by official records, especially police reports. Like others in this category, West & Farrington's study evaluated many characteristics of the youths besides personality attributes, including drinking, smoking, gambling, use of illegal drugs, sexual activity, family relationships, participation in gang activities, employment, and leisure activities. Consideration of that array of features is of consequence in appreciating the importance of the following position (West & Farrington 1977, pp. 159–60): "Without in any way contradicting the importance of social and cultural factors in determining the incidence of delinquency, the results of the present study demonstrate, unfashionably but irrefutably, that the individual characteristics of the offender also play a large part."

COMPARISONS BASED ENTIRELY ON PERSONALITY TESTS   In 1931, Courthial reported the results of a study in which 78 delinquent and 78 matched nondelinquent girls were compared using several objective personality tests. Courthial characterized the delinquents as more emotional, less controlled, poorly adjusted socially, and more individualistic. Studies over succeeding years led to the following conclusions: Delinquents in comparison with nondelinquents tend to be more sadistic and less compassionate (Hawthorne 1932), less mature emotionally (Durea 1937), less aware of the feelings of others (Reusser 1933), and more hyperactive in developmental history (Childers 1935). A thorough survey of personality (and other) differences between delinquents and nondelinquents over the years 1930–1940 may be found in Metfessel & Lovell (1942).

The year 1950 was as significant in the realm of personality and delinquency as 1931 had been in the realm of intelligence and delinquency [see the discussion above of the article by Sutherland (1931)]. In 1950, the sociologists Schuessler & Cressey reviewed 25 years of assessing the personalities of criminals (including delinquents) by formal tests. They concluded that, owing to selective sampling, weaknesses in methodology, and inconsistencies of results over studies, there was no basis for inferring a contribution by personality to criminal behavior. Indeed, they argued, the distributions of personality characteristics over offender and nonoffender groups was so great that the use of personality-test results to predict delinquency was all but impossible.

The work of Schuessler & Cressey (1950) was updated in 1967 when Waldo & Dinitz published their review of studies relating criminality and personality over the years 1950–1965, and then again in 1977 when Tennenbaum published his review for the period 1966–1975. Over the three reviews, more than 100 different tests, objective and projective, were used in more than 250 studies. Particularly noteworthy among these was the work, based on the use of the Minnesota Multiphasic Personality Inventory (MMPI) in the schools of Minnesota, reported by Hathaway & Monachesi (1953, 1957), Wirt & Briggs (1959), and Monachesi & Hathaway (1969). In two testings, one in 1948 and one in 1954, the MMPI was administered to over 15,000 children in the ninth grade. Police and court records were searched in succeeding years for the names of the youths who were tested. The results indicated that high scores on three scales of the MMPI, those measuring psychopathic deviancy, schizophrenia, and hypomania, were associated with later delinquency. See also Hindelang (1972) and Widom et al (1983)—but note that Rathus & Siegel (1980) found significant reductions in the correlations between MMPI scales and delinquency when control is introduced for the response set of faking (F scale).

There have been many other studies using the MMPI, usually along with other psychological and social information, in the prediction of delinquent behavior and its recurrence. An early review of this work was presented by Briggs & Wirt (1965); recent reviews may be found in Loeber & Dishion (1983) and Loeber & Stouthamer-Loeber (1987).

Another personality test used a good deal with delinquents is the California Psychological Inventory (CPI). Using the CPI, delinquents and delinquency-prone youths have been differentiated from nondelinquents and delinquency-resistant youths on the Responsibility and Socialization scales (see e.g. Hindelang 1972, and the comprehensive review by Laufer et al 1982).

PSYCHOLOGICALLY HOMOGENEOUS SUBGROUPS   Despite the production of "interesting and conceptually meaningful results" in the comparisons of delinquent and nondelinquent personality profiles, Quay (1965b, p. 166) emphasized that "greater rewards will come from the detailed study of more homogeneous subgroups" of delinquents. Following that sort of reasoning, Jenkins & Glickman (1947) used a trait-clustering schema to divide institutionalized male delinquents on the basis of case records into three personality categories: unsocialized aggressive, socialized, and disturbed. A bit over two thirds of the youths could be placed in one or more of the categories. When other behavioral traits were correlated with categories, a consistency in configurations was obtained. Confirmation of those results came in a study by Quay (1964a) where factor analysis was used to determine clusters of traits derived from the case histories of institutionalized delinquents. Most of the variance was accounted for by three factors, called "unsocialized-psychopathic," "sub-cultural-socialized," and "neurotic-disturbed." In a similar study, using behavioral ratings by custodial officers rather than case history data, Quay (1964b) obtained comparable results, allowing for the fact that subcultural socialization was not measured by the behavioral ratings.

A third path toward the determination of clusters of personality traits among delinquents has been by means of responses to questionnaire items. In an effort of that sort, Peterson et al (1961) factor-analyzed the responses (of both institutionalized delinquents and high-school students) to a large number of questionnaire items—including 33 from the MMPI that were related to delinquency. There were two distinct personality factors found: psychopathic (basically amoral and rebellious) and neurotic (of low self-esteem with moodiness and anxiety).

Two interesting and important theoretical positions well illustrate potential ultimate products of the determination of personality constellations among delinquents. First, Jessor et al (1968) measured personality variables and interrelated them to attain summarizing constructs, measured the sociocultural environment and used the results to form social constructs, then combined individual and social constructs to test and further develop a theory of deviant behavior based primarily on social-learning principles. And second, Wilson & Herrnstein (1985) presented an elaborate theory of criminal behavior based on characteristics of individuals in the use of rewards and punishments. In their approach, a boy who gets a high score on the psychopathic deviate scale of the MMPI or a low score on the socialization scale of the CPI would be more likely to commit a criminal act because he lacked inner sources of stress or punishment (guilt) to balance potential rewards.

ATTRIBUTION OF PERSONALITY CHARACTERISTICS   In contrast to the empirical determinations of personality constellations in the preceding sections, the attributions discussed in this section stem more or less directly from theories of behavior that range in elaboration from sets of loosely interrelated constructs to the comprehensiveness of psychoanalytic theory. Indeed the comprehensiveness of psychoanalysis has led to the attribution of a broad array of personality characteristics to juvenile offenders—e.g. they are affectionless owing to early deprivation of maternal love (Bowlby 1946), they operate under the pleasure principle in the need for immediate gratification (Friedlander 1947), they have gaps or "lacunae" in their superegos (Johnson 1959), they have an unconscious need for punishment (Glover 1960), and they have intrapsychic conflicts (Abrahamsen 1960).

Other personality characteristics that have been associated with delinquents by deduction from theoretical frameworks are: high level of impulsiveness (Wilson & Herrnstein 1985); low self-esteem (Kaplan 1980); great need for stimulation (Farley & Sewell 1976; White et al 1985); the use of a wide array of mechanisms, including hyperactivity, in the avoidance of unpleasant memories (Stott 1980); and extraversion (Eysenck 1977).

A more complete discussion of this topic may be seen in Arbuthnot et al (1987) under the heading "Univariate Personality Constructs." Critical evaluation of the constructs derived from psychoanalytic theory is contained in Feldman (1969).

THE MORE COMPREHENSIVE PSYCHOLOGICAL THEORIES

It is interesting to note at the outset of this discussion that to account for the failure of psychological methods and principles to be accepted in mainstream crime and delinquency literature, Laufer & Day (1983b) indicated various weaknesses in theorizing by psychologists. This occurs in the introduction to a book aimed at stimulating and enhancing creative psychological theory.

Classical Conditioning

The developer and leading proponent of the approach to theory via classical conditioning is Eysenck. His theory was offered in preliminary form in 1962; more current presentations are in Eysenck (1977) and Eysenck (1983). The latter summarizes the relevant theoretical material and adds references not available at the earlier writing. Unflattering comments on the theory may be found in articles by fellow Englishmen (Farrington et al 1982; Trasler 1987).

The theory's basic premise is that conscience is produced by a process of avoidance conditioning. People like parents and teachers who are responsible for socializing children punish unacceptable (including antisocial) behavior, and the pairing leads eventually to a response of pain, fear, or anxiety to the conditioned stimulus of unacceptable behavior. The thoughts preceding the behavior become similarly conditioned, as do related thoughts by the process of generalization. The net result is a conscience that deters an individual from engaging in certain types of behavior.

Accepting such an assumption regarding the formation of conscience, delinquency can be expected to result if a child is inadequately subjected to the conditioning contingencies or if the child is resistant to conditioning. These two alternatives provide, respectively, a social and a biological basis for delinquency. The biological structure depends on an elaboration of the theory that encompasses genetic, physiological, and personality variables. It is constructed as follows. Three major personality factors are associated with delinquent behavior: extraversion, emotional instability (or neuroticism), and psychoticism [as used by Eysenck & Eysenck (1976) to encompass such characteristics as troublesomeness, cruelty, and lack of empathy]. Personality differences, particularly along the dimension introversion-extraversion, are associated with differences in conditionability, with extraverts being more resistant to conditioning than introverts. These differences arise from lower cortical arousal and higher inhibitory reaction on the part of the extraverted. Thus delinquents tend to have a personality constellation that includes extraversion and to be more difficult to condition in the process of socialization.

Moral Development—The Cognitive Developmental Approach

Moral development theory is based on the early work of Piaget (1948) and the subsequent elaborations of Kohlberg (1976). According to the theory, there are three major levels, with two stages at each level, in the development of moral judgment: the preconventional, the conventional, and the postconventional. At the preconventional level, characteristic of nonoffenders in the age range 9–11, moral standards are understood in terms of "do" and "don't" with accompanying reward or punishment. The conventional level represents the moral understanding of the average adolescent or adult who upholds social rules and values. Only a minority of adults reach the postconventional level where concepts like universal moral principles and abstract human rights and duties enter the picture.

Assessment is accomplished by various measures of the stage at which development has ceased for a given individual—that is, of how the individual constructs the moral aspects of the environment. Delinquency is associated with moral viewpoints that are relatively primitive (immature) on a continuum that extends from crude to very sophisticated in a developing value system emphasizing views of justice, fairness, and human rights.

But is it reasonable to assume a connection between values as expressed on a test or during an interview and actual behavior on the streets? Attempts to wrestle with this issue have included studies that compare delinquents and nondelinquents on moral stage, and studies of subgroups of delinquents where the theory predicts a particularly high likelihood of retardation in moral development. For example, Hudgins & Prentice (1973) found that adolescents with official records exhibited a lower moral-developmental level than adolescents with no records of law violation, and Jurkovic & Prentice (1977) found that psychopathic delinquents reasoned at lower moral levels than delinquents who were not psychopathic. For summaries of research that generally affirmed the relationship between moral level and delinquency despite conflicting results, see Jennings et al (1983) and Arbuthnot et al (1987). Skepticism about this relationship, and about other aspects of the theory, may be found in Kurtines & Greif (1974), Feldman (1977), and Wilson & Herrnstein (1985).

Interpersonal Maturity

Warren (1983) presents interpersonal maturity theory as a general theory of personality development with seven levels representing progress from the immaturity (in interpersonal relations) of an infant to an ideal of full social maturity. Within each level, moreover, are a number of subtypes. The importance of the theory has not been in relating delinquency to immature levels, in the manner of moral development theory, but in providing a method for assessing appropriate intervention strategies. On the other hand, Harris (1983) does argue, with supporting evidence, for a relationship between patterns of personality identified by the Interpersonal Maturity (I-level) Classification System and delinquency, and is not willing to dismiss the possibility of some relationship between stage of maturity and delinquency [as posited by the original presenters of the theory, Sullivan et al (1957)].

Despite the considerable amount of research using the I-level system in the analysis of the personalities of delinquents (see also Werner 1975; Warren & Hindelang 1979; Heide 1983), it has become known primarily as the theoretical framework for an approach to treating juvenile offenders, initiated by the Youth Authority of California. Quay (1987c), however, in one of his arguments for thinking of delinquents in terms of patterns of behavioral subtypes rather than as a legal class, does indicate the potential value of the system in more general terms.

TREATMENT

My discussion here is restricted to cases where a youth has come into contact with the juvenile justice system for a criminal or status offense. In conformity with other parts of the review, this excludes the treatment of youths for antisocial conduct (no matter how disruptive or socially harmful) that involves no violation of law. In addition, it excludes youths who are treated for behavior that is prohibited by law but where no official action by the justice system has been taken. The recent article by Arbuthnot et al (1987) provides broader perspective, with coverage that includes treatment of youths defined purely in psychological terms as aggressive children, behavior-disordered adolescents, impulsive children, violent adolescents, and youths with conduct problems. To complete the picture even further, Lorion et al (1987) and Snyder & Patterson (1987) have written equally comprehensive articles on the methods of primary prevention, and Moffitt (1983) has discussed deterrence in terms of a learning model of punishment.

Pre-Adjudicatory Treatment

Juvenile law typically gives police broad jurisdiction in decisions about whether or not to take a youth into custody and what to do with him or her once so taken. Taken into custody, the youth may be released without further processing by the justice system. That release is usually accompanied by an admonition for future rectitude (hence the common expression "warned and released" for the process) and may also be accompanied by referral to a mental health clinic, a child guidance clinic, a family service agency, a counseling center, or an equivalent agency. Similarly, if a juvenile is referred to court intake by the police, the intake officer (usually a probation officer) may release him or her with or without admonition and with or without referral to a treatment facility. In addition, in almost all jurisdictions the youth may be put on a program of informal supervision—informal in the sense that it is not court-ordered—where a probation officer requires certain behaviors of the youth, including regular school attendance, obedience to a curfew, and participation in a treatment program at an agency to which the youth is referred [see Binder (1983) for a summary of justice-system operations and Binder & Binder (1982) for a discussion of the constitutional questions involved in such restrictions of freedom without a court hearing].

References to the use of such informal arrangements in juvenile justice occur as early as 1904 (see Wallace & Brennan 1963), just five years after the system was established; but several developments during the 1960s led to an enormous expansion of the efforts, as discussed by Binder & Binder (1982) and Binder (1988). Uppermost among these was the report of the President's Commission on Law Enforcement and Administration of Justice (1967), which recommended increased pre-adjudicatory handling of youths by means of new service bureaus established in neighborhoods. A primary goal was to move youths out of the path that leads from arrest to court hearing in order to minimize the stigmatization that, according to labeling theory, led to the escalation of delinquent careers (see in particular Lemert 1971). Labeling theory was then at a high point in its popularity in sociology, and many sociologists were on the staff of and consultants to the Commission. Since the purpose of informal handling of youths was to divert them from the justice system, various forms of that verb were used to describe the process, and "diversion" became the widely accepted identifying noun. The federal government, following the advice of the Commission, provided a great deal of money to further what became a diversion mandate, and the enterprise flourished.

As prime providers of treatment services, and also as leading practitioners of evaluation methodology, psychologists became leaders in juvenile diversion. Moreover, since behavior-change methods were in the ascendancy when the diversion movement was taking off during the early 1970s, they became central elements in the overall enterprise. The behavioral methods brought with them a focus on the family as change agent (see Snyder & Patterson 1987), a focus that was enhanced as family therapy approaches developed. Examples of diversion efforts using these and other methods are: Baron et al (1973), Alexander & Parsons (1973), Binder et al 1976, Binder & Newkirk (1977), Quay & Love (1977), Henderson (1980), Whitaker & Severy (1984), and Binder et al (1985).

The proliferation of diversion programs brought with it considerable concern about their effectiveness, and expression of that concern in a series of generalized evaluations based on earlier evaluation reports. Unfortunately, due perhaps in part to the fulminations of Martinson that "nothing works" in corrections (Martinson 1976), the emphasis in these evaluations has been on whether or not diversion "works" rather than on, as recommended by Palmer (1976) and Binder (1977), "what works for whom and under what conditions." The point is that diversion is an essential component in the American juvenile justice system—the system simply cannot operate without the police, probation officers, and even prosecuting attorneys having the option of seeking services for youngsters without formal court processing. If the services are to include those of a psychological sort, we need more creative contributions than those shown in the many surveys from 1975 (that of Higgins) to 1987 (that of Gottschalk et al), even when they use the latest analytic fad.

Another result of the expansion of diversion services, a result not unrelated to the one just described, was a marked and persistent reaction of antipathy toward the whole undertaking by sociologists—that is, by the very group that was so centrally responsible for the expansion in the first place. Examples of the expressions of that antipathy are the arguments that diversion programs create as much delinquency by labeling as the justice system (e.g. Bullington et al 1978) and that there is too much primary prevention in diversion efforts. [The cliché "widening the net" is used as a pejorative description of the process by people like Klein (1976), implying that referral to a center for psychological services is equivalent to keeping a youngster in the justice system.]

Why all that antipathy to what, at least on the surface, seems like a benign attempt to help youngsters? Binder & Geis (1984) have analyzed the reaction in some detail and offered several explanations. Perhaps most relevant for present purposes is their argument that diversion became largely the domain of psychology in the efforts to change individuals rather than social arrangements, a shift distasteful to sociologists. A clear demonstration of the effects of that disciplinary difference may be seen in the debate between Binder (1987b) and Decker (1987).

It does appear, however, that sociologists have been less successful in stopping modern diversion than they were in launching it. See, for example, the recently reported program evaluations of Severy & Whitaker (1984) and Davidson et al (1987), and the discussions of behavioral methods in diversion by Binder & Binder (1986) and by Binder (1988). Finally, note that a leading text on behavior therapy (O'Leary & Wilson 1987) now has a chapter on juvenile delinquency, and that much of its discussion is devoted to diversion programs.

Post-Adjudicatory Treatment

If the allegations of the petition are sustained in the adjudicatory hearing of the juvenile court (the equivalent of a finding of guilty in the criminal court), the court has several dispositional alternatives (see Binder 1983), from release to parents with a recommendation for treatment, to placement in a secure institution. Under historical juvenile court philosophy, the basis of choice was rehabilitation of the youth, but that position has been undergoing considerable change in recent years (see Wadlington et al 1983). However, whether or not the pure rehabilitative ideal is maintained (see also Binder 1984), it is clear that changing behavior will remain a central mission of post-adjudicatory processing.

TREATMENT IN THE COMMUNITY   As pointed out in an earlier section of this article, focus on the treatment of young offenders in the community after referral by a court dates at least to 1909 when the Chicago Juvenile Psychopathic Institute was founded. From that time until the present, mental health clinics, child guidance clinics, family service centers, counseling centers, and similar agencies have treated adjudicated delinquents by the typical array of approaches associated with them. While behavior therapy has become most prominent on the scene in recent decades, as in the case of diversion [perhaps because behavior-change specialists tend to be academicians who must publish rather than practitioners (see Binder & Binder 1983)], virtually every conceivable approach to treatment has been used over the years. For example, a quaint guidebook for the treatment of delinquents in child guidance clinics by Davidoff & Noetzel (1951) stressed individual and group psychotherapy with distinct psychoanalytic leanings, but encouraged such ancillary techniques as occupational therapy, social casework, and special tutoring.

In 1961, California initiated an experiment aimed at testing the effectiveness of treating in the community youngsters who had been committed to its Youth Authority (CYA) by juvenile courts (see Warren 1970). It was a true experiment in that eligible boys and girls were randomly assigned to the community program or to one of the regular institutions of CYA. The experiment was called, appropriately, the Community Treatment Project (CTP). The particular treatment approach used in the community was determined by classification on the basis of the I-level system described above. CTP was eventually run in three phases, ending in 1976 (Warren 1983). The general conclusion was that the various personality types could be treated successfully in the community but that it was important to match the personalities of youths with the characteristics of settings.

The most extensively studied, best known, and most widely copied example of behavioral intervention with adjudicated youths in a community setting is Achievement Place (see Wolf et al 1976; Kirigin et al 1982; Quay 1987d). The youngsters live in a home-like environment with surrogate parents highly trained in the methods of behavior modification. The program is based on rules and consequences, using a token economy, but residents are active in the development and governance of the project. Targeted behaviors encompass the array of maintenance, academic, social, and administrative behaviors that are expected of a youth in his or her parental home, and so treatment results are anticipated to be generalizable. While the program is often presented as a model for the effective use of behavior therapy in community settings, recent studies indicate serious questions about its long-range effect on behavior (Kirigin et al 1982) and its cost-effectiveness (Weinrott et al 1982).

TREATMENT IN CUSTODIAL INSTITUTIONS   According to the Bureau of Justice Statistics (1985), during each day of 1985 there were about 35,000 youths in public institutions as a result of court commitments. (Approximately another 15,000 were held in detention—that is, prior to adjudication—in equally secure facilities.) Moreover, there were almost 100,000 admissions of committed juveniles to institutions in 1984, with an average stay of just over five months. Considering that rehabilitation is the uppermost theme in juvenile justice, and that there may be a constitutionally based right to treatment for young offenders (see Rubin 1985; Binder et al 1988), the demands for psychological services among the institutionalized are clearly great.

Moreover, numbers alone do not convey the enormous difficulties of the task. To approach the actual picture of complexity, one must be aware that several developments over the past 20 years have led to the selective institutionalization of a group of youths who are most committed to crime and who have been adjudicated for the most serious offenses. Those developments include the following, all discussed above: expansion of diversionary efforts, the opening of many residential facilities like Achievement Place (other examples are the House of Umoja, VisionQuest, and Ocean Tides), the deinstitutionalization of status offenders as a result of the 1974 federal law, and the movement of juvenile court hearings from informal to adversarial, with representation by defense attorneys (see Rubin 1985). The complexity, too, is created by the widespread appeal of substituting a "just-deserts" model for the rehabilitative emphasis that has been traditionally associated with juvenile justice. That reaction stems mostly from a widespread discouragement with the promise of 1899 (when the first juvenile court was established) that the special treatment of juveniles would lead to cures, much like those achieved by medicine with diseases. The discouragement is expressed on a general level by Martinson's (1976) position that in corrections "nothing works." Implementation of a just-deserts approach may be seen in the considerable hardening of state codes dealing with juvenile offenders, including the introduction of a punitive philosophy, the shift of original jurisdiction for offenders as young as 13 from the juvenile to the criminal court, and the increased use of waivers to the criminal court even when original jurisdiction is with the juvenile court (see Flicker 1977; Davis 1980)

Quay (1987d) assessed, for juvenile corrections, the validity of the general disillusionment with treatment in institutions. In the process, he reviewed several approaches, including the use of I-level classification as the basis for assigning treatment, and their evaluations. He pointed out, as indeed several others had pointed out previously, that the issue of treatment effectiveness was unresolved because of the lack of program integrity and inadequacy of design in many of the evaluations. Moreover, he emphasized, as did Binder (1977) in the area of diversion, that many youths in institutions are being treated, and will continue to be treated, regardless of continuing outcries that nothing works. The task for psychologists is to analyze the components in the total treatment program, which includes informal staff-client interactions as well as such formal methods as Transactional Analysis, Guided Group Interaction, and Reality Therapy, and to evaluate their differential effectiveness over clients. See Ross & Gendreau (1980) and Palmer (1984) for detailed arguments about the importance of differential treatment over clients and settings.

CONCLUDING STATEMENT

Instead of a summary of previously reported material, as is usually expected at this point in a review, this concluding statement will provide a summary of important material that was not reported above. One important omission is the empirical theory that relates constitutional factors to juvenile delinquency. What many may consider a domain that died with Lombroso, Hooton, the Gluecks, and Sheldon is actually very much alive. For example, constitutional elements occur in the theoretical positions of Eysenck (1977) and Wilson & Herrnstein (1985), and are central to the theoretical position of Cortés & Gatti (1972). Moreover, Hartl et al (1982) have presented an empirical study that strongly supports the importance of somatotype in the determination of delinquency (and to the modes of treating delinquents).

The second major omission involves biological explanations of delinquent behavior. The efforts range from twin studies aimed at the genetics of delinquency (e.g. Christiansen 1977) to studies of sex chromosome abnormalities (e.g. Kahn et al 1976) and psychophysiological reactivity (e.g. Siddle et al 1976). Comprehensive summaries of theory and research in these areas may be seen in Shah & Roth (1974), Shah (1976), Mednick & Christiansen (1977), and Trasler (1987); a bibliographic listing of biological (and other) factors in delinquency is offered in Denno & Schwartz (1985).

Finally, I did not attempt to integrate the theories of sociologists into the discussion even when there are strong psychological elements in those theories. That includes such diverse efforts as the expression of Sutherland's differential association theory in the terms of operant conditioning (Burgess & Akers 1966) and the synthesis of Hirschi's social control theory and social learning (Conger 1976).

Literature Cited

Abadinsky, H. 1976. The status offense dilemma: coercion and treatment. *Crime Delinq.* 22:456–60

Abrahamsen, D. 1960. *The Psychology of Crime.* New York: Columbia Univ. Press

Adelson, J. 1986. Back to criminal psychology. *Commentary* 81:44–46

Alexander, J. F., Parsons, B. V. 1973. Short term behavioral intervention with delinquent families. *J. Abnorm. Psychol.* 81:219–25

Arbuthnot, J., Gordon, D. A., Jurkovic, G. J. 1987. Personality. See Quay 1987a, pp. 139–83

Baron, R., Feeney, F., Thornton, W. 1973. Preventing delinquency through diversion. *Fed. Probation* 37(1):13–18

Binder, A. 1977. Diversion and the justice system: evaluating the results. In *Criminal Justice. Planning and Development,* ed. A. W. Cohn, pp. 117–31. Beverly Hills, Calif: Sage

Binder, A. 1979. The juvenile justice system. Where pretense and reality clash. *Am. Behav. Sci.* 22:621–52

Binder, A. 1983. Juvenile justice and juvenile offenders. *Couns. Psychol.* 11(2):65–67

Binder, A. 1984. The juvenile court, the U.S. Constitution, and when the twain shall meet. *J. Crim. Justice* 12:355–66

Binder, A. 1987a. An historical and theoretical introduction. See Quay 1987a, pp. 1–32

Binder, A. 1987b. A systemic analysis of Decker's "A systematic analysis of diversion: net widening and beyond." *J. Crim. Justice* 15:255–60

Binder, A. 1987c. Criminology and interdisciplinarity. *Iss. Integrative Stud.* In press

Binder, A. 1988. Juvenile diversion: history and current status. In *Juvenile Justice Policies, Programs and Services,* ed. A. R. Roberts. Chicago: Dorsey. In press

Binder, A., Binder, V. L. 1982. Juvenile diversion and the Constitution. *J. Crim. Justice* 10:1–24

Binder, A., Binder, V. L. 1983. Juvenile diversion. *Couns. Psychol.* 11(2):69–77

Binder, A., Binder, V. L. 1986. Behavioral treatment in the juvenile justice network. In

Advances in Adolescent Mental Health, ed. R. A. Feldman, A. R. Stiffman, pp. 173–89. Greenwich, Conn: JAI Press

Binder, A., Geis, G. 1979. Editors introduction. *Am. Behav. Sci.* 22:613–20

Binder, A., Geis, G. 1984. Ad populum argumentation in criminology: juvenile diversion as rhetoric. *Crime Delinq.* 30:309–33

Binder, A., Geis, G., Bruce, D. D. 1988. *Juvenile Delinquency: Historical, Cultural, and Legal Perspectives.* New York: Macmillan. In press

Binder, A., Monahan, J., Newkirk, M. 1976. Diversion from the juvenile justice system and the prevention of delinquency. In *Community Mental Health and the Criminal Justice System,* ed. J. Monahan, pp. 131–40. New York: Pergamon

Binder, A., Newkirk, M. 1977. A program to extend police service capability. *Crime Prevent. Rev.* 4(3):26–32

Binder, A., Schumacher, M., Kurz, G., Moulson, L. 1985. A diversionary approach for the 1980's. *Fed. Probation* 49(1):4–12

Bowlby, J. 1946. *Forty-Four Juvenile Thieves.* London: Baillière, Tindall & Cox

Briggs, P. F., Wirt, R. D. 1965. Prediction. See Quay 1965a, pp. 170–208

Bullington, B. J., Sprowls, J., Katkin, D., Phillips, M. 1978. A critique of diversionary juvenile justice. *Crime Delinq.* 24:59–71

Bureau of Justice Statistics. 1985. *Children in Custody. Public Juvenile Facilities, 1985.* Washington, DC: US Dep. Justice

Burgess, R., Akers, R. 1966. A differential association-reinforcement theory of criminal behavior. *Soc. Problems* 14:128–47

Caplan, N. S. 1965. Intellectual functioning. See Quay 1965a, pp. 100–38

Childers, A. T. 1935. Hyper-activity in children having behavior disorders. *Am. J. Orthopsychiatry* 5:227–43

Christiansen, K. O. 1977. A review of studies of criminality among twins. A preliminary study of criminality among twins. See Mednick & Christiansen 1977, pp. 45–108

Cohen, A. K. 1955. *Delinquent Boys: The Culture of the Gang.* New York: Free Press

Comptroller General of the United States. 1977. *Learning Disabilities: The Link Should be Determined, but Schools Should Do More Now.* Washington, DC: US GPO

Conger, J. J., Miller, W. C. 1966. *Personality, Social Class, and Delinquency.* New York: Wiley

Conger, R. D. 1976. Social control and social learning models of delinquent behavior: a synthesis. *Criminology* 14:17–40

Cortés, J. B., Gatti, F. M. 1972. *Delinquency and Crime. A Biopsychosocial Approach.* New York: Seminar Press, Harcourt Brace Jovanovich

Courthial, A. 1931. Emotional differences of delinquent and non-delinquent girls of normal intelligence. *Arch. Psychol. NY* 20:No. 133

Davidoff, E., Noetzel, E. S. 1951. *The Child Guidance Approach to Juvenile Delinquency.* New York: Child Care Publ.

Davidson, W. S. II, Redner, R., Blakely, C. H., Mitchell, C. M., Emshoff, J. G. 1987. Diversion of juvenile offenders: an experimental comparison. *J. Consult. Clin. Psychol.* 55:68–75

Davis, S. M. 1980. *Rights of Juveniles. The Juvenile Justice System.* New York: Clark Boardman

Decker, S. H. 1987. Blind faith and the juvenile justice system: a response to Binder. *J. Crim. Justice* 15:261–63

Denno, D. W., Schwartz, R. M. 1985. *Biological, Psychological, and Environmental Factors in Delinquency and Mental Disorder: An Interdisciplinary Bibliography.* Westport, Conn: Greenwood Press

Dunivant, N. 1982a. *The Relationship Between Learning Disabilities and Juvenile Delinquency. Executive Summary.* Williamsburg, Va: Natl. Ctr. State Courts

Dunivant, N. 1982b. *A Note on Differences Between Learning-Disabled and Non-Learning-Disabled Teenagers in Delinquent Behavior: Addendum to* Some Observations and Further Observations *Reports.* Williamsburg, Va: Natl. Ctr. State Courts

Dunivant, N. 1984. *A Causal Analysis of the Relationship Between Learning Disabilities and Juvenile Delinquency.* Williamsburg, Va: Natl. Ctr. State Courts

Durea, M. A. 1937. The emotional maturity of juvenile delinquents. *J. Abnorm. Soc. Psychol.* 31:472–81

Eysenck, H. J. 1962. Conditioning and personality. *Br. J. Psychol.* 53:299–305

Eysenck, H. J. 1977. *Crime and Personality.* London: Routledge & Kegan Paul. 3rd ed.

Eysenck, H. J. 1983. Personality, conditioning and antisocial behavior. See Laufer & Day 1983a, pp. 51–80

Eysenck, H. J., Eysenck, S. B. G. 1976. *Psychoticism as a Dimension of Personality.* London: Hodder & Stoughton

Farley, F. H., Sewell, T. 1976. Test of an arousal theory of delinquency. *Crim. Justice Behav.* 3:315–20

Farrington, D. P. 1985. Delinquency prevention in the 1980's. *J. Adolescence* 8:3–16

Farrington, D. P., Biron, L., LeBlanc, M. 1982. Personality and delinquency in London and Montreal. In *Abnormal Offenders, Delinquency and the Criminal Justice Sys-*

tem, ed. J. Gunn, D. P. Farrington, pp. 153–201. New York: Wiley

Feldman, D. 1969. Psychoanalysis and crime. In *Delinquency, Crime and Social Process*, ed. D. R. Cressey, D. A. Ward, pp. 433–42. New York: Harper & Row

Feldman, M. P. 1977. *Criminal Behaviour: A Psychological Analysis*. London: Wiley

Fink, A. E. 1938. *Causes of Crime. Biological Theories in the United States 1800–1915*. New York: Barnes

Flicker, B. D. 1977. *Standards for Juvenile Justice. A Summary and Analysis*. Cambridge, Mass: Ballinger

Friedlander, K. 1947. *The Psycho-analytical Approach to Juvenile Delinquency*. New York: International Universities Press

Gibbs, J. P. 1985. Review essay. *Crime and Human Nature* by Wilson and Herrnstein. *Criminology* 23:381–88

Glover, E. 1960. *The Roots of Crime*. London: Imago

Glueck, S., Glueck, E. T. 1950. *Unraveling Juvenile Delinquency*. New York: The Commonwealth Fund

Glueck, S., Glueck, E. 1968. *Delinquents and Nondelinquents in Perspective*. Cambridge, Mass: Harvard Univ. Press

Glueck, S., Glueck, E. 1974. *Of Delinquency and Crime. A Panorama of Years of Search and Research*. Springfield, Ill: Thomas

Goddard, H. H. 1914. *Feeblemindedness: Its Causes and Consequences*. New York: Macmillan

Gottschalk, R., Davidson, W. S. II, Gensheimer, L. K., Mayer, J. P. 1987. Community-based interventions. See Quay 1987a, pp. 266–89

Gregory, J. D. 1978. Juvenile court jurisdiction over noncriminal misbehavior: the argument against abolition. *Ohio State Law J.* 39:242–72

Hall, G. S. 1904. *Adolescence: Its Psychology and Its Relations to Physiology, Anthropology, Sociology, Sex, Crime, Religion and Education*, 2 Vols. New York: Appleton

Handler, J. F., Zatz, J., eds. 1982. *Neither Angels nor Thieves: Studies in Deinstitutionalization of Status Offenders*. Washington, DC: Natl. Acad. Press

Harris, P. W. 1983. The interpersonal maturity of delinquents and nondelinquents. See Laufer & Day 1983a, pp. 145–64

Hartl, E. M., Monnelly, E. P., Elderkin, R. D. 1982. *Physique and Delinquent Behavior. A Thirty-Year Follow-Up of William H. Sheldon's Varieties of Delinquent Youth*. New York: Academic

Hathaway, S. R., Monachesi, E. D. 1953. *Analyzing and Predicting Juvenile Delinquency with the MMPI*. Minneapolis, Minn: Univ. Minnesota Press

Hathaway, S. R., Monachesi, E. D. 1957. The personalities of predelinquent boys. *J. Crim. Law, Criminol. Police Sci.* 48:149–63

Hawthorne, J. W. 1932. A group test for the measurement of cruelty-compassion: a proposed means of recognizing potential criminality. *J. Soc. Psychol.* 3:189–211

Healy, W. 1915. *The Individual Delinquent*. Boston: Little, Brown

Healy, W., Bronner, A. F. 1926. *Delinquents and Criminals*. New York: Macmillan

Healy, W., Bronner, A. F. 1936. *New Light on Delinquency and Its Treatment*. New Haven, Conn: Yale Univ. Press

Heide, K. M. 1983. An empirical assessment of the value of utilizing personality data in restitution outcome prediction. See Laufer & Day 1983a, pp. 251–77

Henderson, J. Q. 1980. Teaching children not to steal: four natural environment case studies. *J. NZ Psychol. Serv.* 5:4–16

Higgins, J. 1975. Juvenile delinquency: seeking effective prevention. *Public Affairs Rep.* 16(6):1–7

Hindelang, M. J. 1972. The relationship of self-reported delinquency to scales of the CPI and MMPI. *J. Crim. Law, Criminol. Police Sci.* 63:75–81

Hindelang, M. J., Hirschi, T., Weis, J. G. 1981. *Measuring Delinquency*. Beverly Hills, Calif: Sage

Hirschi, T. 1969. *Causes of Delinquency*. Berkeley, Calif: Univ. Calif. Press

Hirschi, T., Hindelang, M. J. 1977. Intelligence and delinquency: a revisionist review. *Am. Sociol. Rev.* 42:571–87

Hudgins, W., Prentice, N. M. 1973. Moral judgments in delinquent and nondelinquent adolescents and their mothers. *J. Abnorm. Psychol.* 82:145–52

Hutzler, J. L., Sestak, R. M. 1977. *Juvenile Court Jurisdiction Over Children's Conduct: A Statutes Analysis*. Pittsburgh, Penn: Natl. Ctr. Juvenile Justice

Jenkins, R. L., Glickman, S. 1947. Patterns of personality organization among delinquents. *Nerv. Child* 6:329–39

Jennings, W. S., Kilkenny, R., Kohlberg, L. 1983. Moral-development theory and practice for youthful and adult offenders. See Laufer & Day 1983a, pp. 281–355

Jessor, R., Graves, T. D., Hanson, R. C., Jessor, S. L. 1968. *Society, Personality and Deviant Behavior*. New York: Holt, Rinehart & Winston

Johnson, A. M. 1959. Juvenile delinquency. In *American Handbook of Psychiatry*, ed. S. Arieti, 1:840–56. New York: Basic Books

Jurkovic, G. J., Prentice, N. M. 1977. Relation of moral and cognitive development to dimensions of juvenile delinquency. *J. Abnorm. Psychol.* 86:414–20

Kahn, J., Reed, F. S., Bates, M., Coates, T., Everitt, B. 1976. A survey of Y chromosome variants and personality in 436 borstal lads and 254 controls. *Br. J. Criminol.* 16:233–44

Kaplan, H. B. 1980. *Deviant Behavior in Defense of Self.* New York: Academic

Ketchum, O. W. 1977. Why jurisdiction over status offenders should be eliminated from juvenile courts. *Boston Univ. Law Rev.* 57:645–62

Kirigin, K. A., Braukmann, C. J., Atwater, J. D., Wolf, M. M. 1982. An evaluation of teaching-family (Achievement Place) group homes for juvenile offenders. *J. Appl. Behav. Anal.* 15:1–16

Klein, M. W. 1976. Issues and realities in police diversion programs. *Crime Delinq.* 22:421–27

Kohlberg, L. 1976. Moral stages and moralization: the cognitive-developmental approach. In *Moral Development and Behavior: Theory, Research, and Social Issues,* ed. T. Lickona, pp. 31–53. New York: Holt, Rinehart & Winston

Kurtines, W., Greif, E. B. 1974. The development of moral thought: review and evaluation of Kohlberg's approach. *Psychol. Bull.* 81: 453–70

Lamson, A. 1983. *Psychology of Juvenile Crime.* New York: Human Sciences Press

Laufer, W. S., Day, J. M., eds. 1983a. *Personality Theory, Moral Development, and Criminal Behavior.* Lexington, Mass: Lexington Books/D. C. Heath

Laufer, W. S., Day, J. M. 1983b. Introduction. See Laufer & Day 1983a, pp. xiii–xviii

Laufer, W. S., Skoog, D. K., Day, J. M. 1982. Personality and criminality: a review of the California Psychological Inventory. *J. Clin. Psychol.* 38:562–73

Lemert, E. M. 1971. *Instead of Court: Diversion in Juvenile Justice.* Washington, DC: US GPO

Lindesmith, A., Levin, Y. 1937. The Lombrosian myth in criminology. *Am. J. Sociol.* 42:653–71

Loeber, R., Dishion, T. J. 1983. Early predictors of male delinquency: a review. *Psychol. Bull.* 94:68–99

Loeber, R., Stouthamer-Loeber, M. 1987. Prediction. See Quay 1987a, pp. 325–82

Lombroso, C. 1876. *L' Uomo Delinquente.* Milan: Hoepli

Lombroso, C. 1912. *Crime: Its Causes and Remedies.* Boston: Little, Brown

Lorion, R. P., Tolan, P. H., Wahler, R. G. 1987. Prevention. See Quay 1987a, pp. 383–416

Magnusson, D., Stattin, H., Duner, A. 1983.

Aggression and criminality in a longitudinal perspective. In *Prospective Studies of Crime and Delinquency,* ed. K. T. Van Dusen, S. A. Mednick, pp. 227–301. Boston: Kluwer-Nijhoff

Martin, L. H., Snyder, P. R. 1976. Jurisdiction over status offenses should not be removed from the juvenile court. *Crime Delinq.* 22:44–47

Martinson, R. 1976. What works?—Questions and answers about reform. In *Rehabilitation, Recidivism, and Research,* pp. 7–39. Hackensack, NJ: Natl. Council Crime Delinquency

Maudsley, H. 1870. *Body and Mind.* London: Macmillan

Mednick, S. A., Christiansen, K. O., eds. 1977. *Biosocial Bases of Criminal Behavior.* New York: Gardner Press, Wiley

Menard, S., Morse, B. J. 1984. A structuralist critique of the IQ-delinquency hypothesis: theory and evidence. *Am. J. Sociol.* 89:1347–78

Merrill, M. A. 1947. *Problems of Child Delinquency.* Boston: Houghton Mifflin

Metfessel, M., Lovell, C. 1942. Recent literature on individual correlates of crime. *Psychol. Bull.* 39:133–64

Moffitt, T. E. 1983. The learning theory model of punishment. *Crim. Justice Behav.* 10:131–58

Monachesi, E. D., Hathaway, S. R. 1969. The personality of delinquents. In *MMPI: Research Developments and Clinical Applications,* ed. J. N. Butcher, pp. 207–19. New York: McGraw-Hill

Morel, B. A. 1857. *Traité des Dégénérescences Physiques, Intellectuelles et Morales de l' Espèce Humaine; et des Causes qui Produisent ces Varietes Maladives.* Paris: Baillière

Mulligan, W. 1969. A study of dyslexia and delinquency. *Acad. Ther. Q.* 4:177–87

Murray, C. A. 1976. *The Link Between Learning Disabilities and Juvenile Delinquency. Current Theory and Knowledge.* Washington, DC: US GPO

Murray, J. P., ed. 1983. *Status Offenders: A Sourcebook.* Boy's Town, Neb: Boy's Town Center

O'Leary, K. D., Wilson, G. T. 1987. *Behavior Therapy. Application and Outcome.* Englewood Cliffs, NJ: Prentice-Hall

Palmer, T. 1976. Martinson revisited. In *Rehabilitation, Recidivism, and Research,* pp. 41–62. Hackensack, NJ: Natl. Council Crime Delinquency

Palmer, T. 1984. Treatment and the role of classification: a review of basics. *Crime Delinq.* 30:245–67

Peterson, D. R., Quay, H. C., Tiffany, T. L. 1961. Personality factors related to delinquency. *Child Dev.* 32:355–72

Piaget, J. 1948. *The Moral Judgment of the Child*. New York: Free Press. (Orig. publ. 1932, London: Routledge & Kegan Paul)

Post, C. H. 1981. The link between learning disabilities and juvenile delinquency: cause, effect and "present solutions." *Juvenile Fam. Court J.* 32(1):58–68

President's Commission on Law Enforcement and Administration of Justice. 1967. *The Challenge of Crime in a Free Society*. Washington, DC: US GPO

Prichard, J. C. 1835. *A Treatise on Insanity and Other Disorders Affecting the Mind*. London: Sherwood, Gilbert & Piper

Quay, H. C. 1964a. Dimensions of personality in delinquent boys as inferred from the factor analysis of case history data. *Child Dev.* 35:479–84

Quay, H. C. 1964b. Personality dimensions in delinquent males as inferred from the factor analysis of behavior ratings. *J. Res. Crime & Delinq.* 1:33–37

Quay, H. C., ed. 1965a. *Juvenile Delinquency. Research and Theory*. Princeton, NJ: Van Nostrand

Quay, H. C. 1965b. Personality and delinquency. See Quay 1965a, pp. 139–69

Quay, H. C., ed. 1987a. *Handbook of Juvenile Delinquency*. New York: Wiley

Quay, H. C. 1987b. Intelligence. See Quay 1987a, pp. 106–17

Quay, H. C. 1987c. Patterns of delinquent behavior. See Quay 1987a, pp. 118–38

Quay, H. C. 1987d. Institutional treatment. See Quay 1987a, pp. 244–65

Quay, H. C., Love, C. T. 1977. The effect of a juvenile diversion program on rearrests. *Crim. Justice Behav.* 4:377–95

Radzinowicz, L. 1966. *Ideology and Crime: A Study of Crime in its Social and Historical Context*. London: Heinemann Edutional

Rathus, S. A., Siegel, L. J. 1980. Crime and personality revisited. *Criminology* 18:245–51

Ray, I. 1838. *A Treatise on the Medical Jurisprudence of Insanity*. Boston: Little, Brown

Reilly, T. F., Wheeler, L. J., Etlinger, L. E. 1985. Intelligence versus academic achievement. Juvenile delinquents and special education classifications. *Crim. Justice Behav.* 12:193–208

Reiss, A. J. 1975. Inappropriate theories and inadequate methods as policy plagues: self-reported delinquency and the law. In *Social Policy and Sociology*, ed. N. J. Demerath III, O. Larsen, K. F. Schuessler. New York: Academic

Reiss, A. J., Rhodes, A. L. 1961. The distribution of juvenile delinquency in the social class structure. *Am. Sociol. Rev.* 26:720–32

Reusser, J. L. 1933. Personal attitudes of delinquent boys. *J. Juvenile Res.* 17:19–34

Rice, R. 1956. *The Business of Crime*. New York: Farrar, Straus, & Cudahy

Ross, R. R., Gendreau, P. 1980. *Effective Correctional Treatment*. Toronto: Butterworths

Rubin, H. T. 1985. *Juvenile Justice: Policy, Practice and Law*. New York: Random House. 2nd ed.

Satterfield, J. H., Hoppe, C. M., Schell, A. M. 1982. A prospective study of delinquency in 110 adolescent boys with attention deficit disorder and 88 normal adolescent boys. *Am. J. Psychiatry* 139:795–98

Schuessler, K. F., Cressey, D. R. 1950. Personality characteristics of criminals. *Am. J. Sociol.* 55:476–84

Severy, L. J., Whitaker, J. M. 1984. Juvenile diversion and system impact: Memphis-Metro Youth Diversion Project. *Child Welfare* 63:269–77

Shah, S. A. 1976. The 47,XYY chromosomal abnormality: a critical appraisal with respect to antisocial and violent behavior. In *Issues in Brain/Behavior Control*, ed. W. L. Smith, A. Kling, pp. 49–67. New York: Spectrum

Shah, S. A., Roth, L. H. 1974. Biological and psychophysiological factors in criminality. In *Handbook of Criminology*, ed. D. Glaser, pp. 101–73. Chicago: Rand McNally

Shaw, C. R. 1929. *Delinquency Areas*. Chicago: Univ. Chicago Press

Shaw, C. R., McKay, H. D. 1931. *Social Factors in Juvenile Delinquency. Report on the Causes of Crime*, Vol. II. National Commission on Law Observance and Enforcement, Rep. 13. Washington, DC: US GPO

Short, J. F., Nye, F. I. 1957. Reported behavior as a criterion of deviant behavior. *Soc. Problems* 5:207–13

Siddle, D. A. T., Mednick, S. A., Nicol, A. R., Foggitt, K. H. 1976. Skin conductance recovery in anti-social adolescents. *Br. J. Soc. Clin. Psychol.* 15:425–28

Snodgrass, J. 1972. *The American criminological tradition: portraits of the men and ideology in a discipline*. PhD thesis. Univ. Penn.

Snyder, J., Patterson, G. 1987. Family interaction and delinquent behavior. See Quay 1987a, pp. 216–43

Stott, D. H. 1980. *Delinquency and Human Nature*. Baltimore, Md: University Park Press. 2nd ed.

Sullivan, C. E., Grant, M. Q., Grant, J. D. 1957. The development of interpersonal maturity: applications to delinquency. *Psychiatry* 20:373–85

Sutherland, E. H. 1931. Mental deficiency

282   BINDER

and crime. In *Social Attitudes*, ed. K. Young, pp. 357–75. New York: Holt

Sutherland, E. H. 1951. Critique of Sheldon's *Varieties of Delinquent Youth*. *Am. Sociol. Rev.* 16:10–14

Taylor, I., Walton, P., Young, J. 1973. *The New Criminology: For a Social Theory of Deviance*. London: Routledge & Kegan Paul

Tennenbaum, D. J. 1977. Personality and criminality. A summary and implications of the literature. *J. Crim. Justice* 5:225–35

Thomas, C. W. 1976. Are status offenders really so different? A comparative and longitudinal assessment. *Crime Delinq.* 22:438–55

Trasler, G. 1987. Biogenetic factors. See Quay 1987a, pp. 184–215

Turk, A. T. 1969. *Criminality and Legal Order*. Chicago: Rand McNally

Wadlington, W., Whitebread, C. H., Davis, S. M. 1983. *Children in the Legal System. Cases and Materials*. Mineola, NY: The Foundation Press

Waldo, G. P., Dinitz, S. 1967. Personality attributes of the criminal: an analysis of research studies, 1950–1965. *J. Res. Crime & Delinq.* 4:185–202

Wallace, J. A., Brennan, M. M. 1963. Intake and the family court. *Buffalo Law Rev.* 12:442–51

Warren, M. Q. 1970. The Community Treatment Project. In *The Sociology of Punishment and Correction*, ed. N. Johnston, L. Savitz, M. E. Wolfgang, pp. 671–83. New York: Wiley

Warren, M. Q. 1983. Applications of interpersonal-maturity theory to offender populations. See Laufer & Day 1983a, pp. 23–50

Warren, M. Q., Hindelang, M. J. 1979. Current explanations of offender behavior. In *Psychology of Crime and Criminal Justice*, ed. H. Toch, pp. 166–82. New York: Holt, Rinehart & Winston

Weinrott, M. R., Jones, R. R., Howard, J. R. 1982. Cost-effectiveness of teaching family programs: results of a national evaluation. *Eval. Rev.* 6:173–201

Weis, J. G. 1980. *Jurisdiction and the Elusive Status Offender: A Comparison of Involvement in Delinquent Behavior and Status Offenses*. Rep. Natl. Juvenile Justice

Assessment Centers. Washington, DC: US GPO

Werner, E. 1975. Relationships among interpersonal maturity, personality configurations, intelligence and ethnic status. *Br. J. Criminol.* 15:51–68

West, D. J. 1969. *Present Conduct and Future Delinquency*. London: Heinemann Educational

West, D. J., Farrington, D. P. 1973. *Who Becomes Delinquent?* London: Heinemann Educational

West, D. J., Farrington, D. P. 1977. *The Delinquent Way of Life*. London: Heinemann Educational

Whitaker, J. M., Severy, L. J. 1984. Service accountability and recidivism for diverted youth. A client and service-comparison-analysis. *Crim. Justice Behav.* 11:47–74

White, H. R., Labouvie, E. W., Bates, M. E. 1985. The relationship between sensation seeking and delinquency: a longitudinal analysis. *J. Res. Crime & Delinq.* 22:197–211

Widom, C. S., Katkin, F. S., Stewart, A. J., Fondacaro, M. 1983. Multivariate analysis of personality and motivation in female delinquents. *J. Res. Crime & Delinq.* 20:277–90

Wilson, J. Q., Herrnstein, R. J. 1985. *Crime and Human Nature*. New York: Simon & Schuster

Winter, B. 1983. Learning disability. The young offender's curse. *Am. Bar Assoc. J.* 69:427

Wirt, R. D., Briggs, P. F. 1959. Personality and environmental factors in the development of delinquency *Psychol. Monogr. 73* (Whole No. 485)

Wolf, M. M., Phillips, E. L., Fixsen, D. L., Braukmann, C. J., Kirigin, K. A., et al. 1976. Achievement Place: the teaching family model. *Child Care Q.* 5:92–103

Wolfgang, M. E., Ferracuti, F. 1967. *The Subculture of Violence: Towards an Integrated Theory in Criminology*. London: Tavistock

Woodward, M. 1955. The role of low intelligence in delinquency. *Br. J. Delinq.* 5:281–303

Zimmerman, J., Rich, W. D., Keilitz, I., Broder, P. K. 1981. Some observations on the link between learning disabilities and juvenile delinquency. *J. Crim. Justice* 9:1–17

Ann. Rev. Psychol. 1988. 39:283-99

THE FAMILY AND PSYCHOPATHOLOGY

Michael J. Goldstein

Department of Psychology, University of California, Los Angeles, California
90024-1563

CONTENTS

INTRODUCTION

At present there is a resurgence of interest in family relationships as they relate to the major mental disorders. In the period from the early 1950s to the late 1960s research on the family proliferated, particularly in regard to one disorder, schizophrenia (for review see Riskin & Faunce 1972; Goldstein & Rodnick 1975; Jacob 1975; Liem 1980). However, the late 1960s to the late 1970s represents a kind of Dark Ages in research on psychopathological family conditions. Publication in this area diminished markedly, and enthusiasm for what could be learned from direct observation waned. In order to appreciate the current state of family research related to the major mental disorders, it is helpful to contrast the assumptions and methods of the 1950s and 1960s with those of the present.

The earlier studies summarized in the reviews cited above were cross-sectional, involving families in which mental disorder was present in some member, usually a young adult, often for a considerable period before the

283

research was carried out. These earlier studies assumed that direct observation contrasting families with and without a mental disorder could provide clues to the psychological precursors of that disorder. These earlier studies were further guided by an ambitious family–system theoretical organization which assumed (a) that disturbances in family relationships were the major cause of mental disorders in general and (b) that each mental disorder resulted from distinctive patterns of family dynamics.

The major barrier to testing these assumptions was that families were studied long after a major mental disorder in a member had affected the family system. The cross-sectional family interaction data collected obviously reflected a complex amalgam of family processes, some of which may indeed have antedated the onset of the disorders while others represented diverse forms of accommodation by family members to the presence of disorder. The great difficulties in replicating findings across studies (see Helmerson 1983; Jacob 1975; Liem 1980) characteristic of this earlier period were due in part to the fact that each sample varied in the pattern of pre- and post-onset family adaptations. Other factors that limited replicability were wide variations from sample to sample in the criteria used to diagnose mental disorder, the methods for eliciting interactional data, and the coding systems used to reduce the data to quantifiable units. Gradually, researchers recognized that cross-sectional studies carried out after a mental disorder had been present for some time were limited in their ability to reveal etiological processes.

The decline in family research in the late 1960s was not due entirely to the above issue. During this same period, convincing evidence appeared of strong genetic predisposition to a number of major mental disorders such as schizophrenia, bipolar and unipolar affective disorders, and alcoholism. These findings, combined with powerful evidence of the efficacy of pharmacotherapy for these disorders, challenged the underlying paradigm of previous family studies in which intrafamilial transactions were hypothesized to be the predominant etiological agents and family therapy a potent model for intervention.

Current investigators recognize that a more complex etiological model is needed to guide research. Most studies in the last ten years have been guided by the vulnerability-stress model (Rosenthal 1970; Zubin & Spring 1977). According to this model a predisposition to a disorder such as schizophrenia is inherited and forms the basis for various indexes of vulnerability to the disorder. This vulnerability is modified by all life events, particularly those in family life, which in turn modifies the likelihood of expression of the disorder later. The stress-vulnerability model is also applicable to the post-onset stage of psychiatric disorder as vulnerability to future episodes of the disorder is modified by recurrent life events within and outside the family.

The implications of the vulnerability-stress model for family interaction research are profound. This model implies that researchers must investigate the *interaction* between intrafamilial relationships and indexes of vulnerability to a particular psychiatric disorder. Ideally, researchers should have available one or more established vulnerability markers that can be investigated in the context of different family environments, some of which may be provocative of and others protective against the expression of a disorder.

Unfortunately, despite numerous efforts to define such vulnerability makers—and there are now some promising leads [with regard to schizophrenia see Nuechterlein & Dawson (1984)]—none have a secure status yet. The best risk marker for most mental disorders is still the rather crude index of being an offspring of a parent with that disorder. Nevertheless, the recognition of the vulnerability-stress model has stimulated a new sense of purpose and vigor among family researchers during the last ten years. They have recognized that tests of this model, from a family perspective, required longitudinal prospective designs in which family relationships are observed prior to the onset of a disorder, either in its prodromal or active forms, followed by careful evaluations of targeted offspring over subsequent years as they pass through the risk period for the disorder. Studies using the "high risk" paradigm have reinvigorated the field of family research.

I noted above that earlier cross-sectional studies could not separate pre-onset from post-onset patterns of family dynamics. Studies now make a clear distinction between two models regarding family factors as they relate to the major mental disorders, the etiological model and the maintenance model. Research on the etiological model involves longitudinal-prospective studies in which intrafamilial relationships are studied well before the initial onset of a psychiatric disorder.

The maintenance model refers to family relationships that alter the course of a disorder once an initial episode has occurred. Research on the maintenance model also involves longitudinal-prospective studies, but these are typically initiated at the time of an index episode and follow through a period of remission to determine whether and how family relationships affect the likelihood of reappearance of the acute symptoms of the disorder. Note that research on family factors associated with the maintenance of psychiatric disorder need not assume these relationships are continuous with those related to the onset. One can assume, as some investigators have done (Leff & Vaughn 1985), that family factors related to the maintenance of disorder contain no information concerning determinants of the initial onset.

In this review, I distinguish studies that have etiological implications (i.e. describe events antedating the initial onset of disorder) from those relating primarily to maintenance. I stress studies that attempted to use the vulnerability-stress model and that measured family relationships directly. I focus on two major mental disorders—schizophrenia and the affective disorders—because they have been investigated intensively by contemporary family researchers. I begin with schizophrenia. This is still the disorder most heavily investigated from a family perspective—an ironic fact, as this is also the disorder for which powerful evidence exists of genetic and biochemical determinants.

SCHIZOPHRENIA

Etiological Studies

Three major studies bear on this topic, the UCLA High Risk Study (Goldstein 1985), the Israeli High Risk Study (Marcus et al 1987), and the Finnish Adoption Study (Tienari et al 1987). Each fits the vulnerability-stress model, in which family relationships are or will be observed before the onset of the disorder. Two of the studies (Marcus et al and Tienari et al) follow the classic high risk design in that they study the offspring of schizophrenics; the third started with a cohort of mildly to moderately disturbed teenagers, defined as being at risk by virtue of their failure to master the developmental tasks of adolescence.

THE UCLA HIGH RISK STUDY   This study began with a cohort of 64 intact families that contained at least one teenager referred for help to a psychology clinic for mild to moderately severe emotional problems. None of the teenagers were psychotic or borderline psychotic at the time of original referral. At the time of the original contact the teenagers were subdivided into four groups on the basis of the form of their behavioral difficulties (Goldstein et al 1968), and two of these groups were hypothesized to be at greater risk than the others. This study also involved intensive investigation of intrafamilial processes. Two types of variable suggested as stressful for a vulnerable person were extracted from these data: (*a*) communication deviance (CD) (Wynne et al 1977); and (*b*) a negative affective climate in the family, termed high expressed emotion (high EE) (Vaughn & Leff 1976) or, as indexed in direct interaction, a negative affective style (AS) (Doane et al 1981).

The sample of offspring, and subsequently those siblings who developed major mental disorders, were followed up for the next 15 years with two intensive assessments at 5 and 15 years. Blind diagnostic appraisals were done at both times, and the most severe disorder for the index child and sibling were used as outcome measures. Fifty-four cases had usable outcome data. Diagnostic outcomes were grouped in a fashion similar to that used in the Danish Adoption Studies (Kety et al 1968), in which cases of schizophrenia and related disorders (borderline schizophrenia, schizoid and paranoid personality, etc) were considered an extended spectrum of schizophrenic disorders.

This study had two major objectives: first, to determine whether patterns of disturbance were predictive of the likelihood of developing a schizophrenia-spectrum disorder; and second, whether CD or EE/AS alone or in combination could identify those family units at risk for subsequent schizophrenia. The form of behavior problem had little or no predictive value (Goldstein 1985). However, the evidence with regard to the family measures was positive. The incidence of schizophrenia and schizophrenia-spectrum disorders was highest in families classified as high in CD during the assessment carried out 15 years previously. In fact, there were no cases of schizophrenia or related disorders in low-CD families. The combination of high CD and a measure of negative affect on climate (high EE or negative AS) sharpened the ability to identify those family units likely to manifest schizophrenia-spectrum disorders in the follow-up period (Goldstein 1987).

When the dependent variable was the probability of a schizophrenia-spectrum disorder in any child in the family (index or sibs), the percentages were, by CD level in the family, low CD = 8%; intermediate CD = 21%; high CD = 50%.

These data indicate that certain patterns of disturbed communication and affect in the family antedate the onset of schizophrenia; however, they do not indicate how these family patterns arise or interact with the vulnerability of the child at risk.

THE ISRAELI HIGH RISK STUDY   The high risk offspring in this study (Marcus et al 1987; Kugelmass et al 1985; Marcus et al 1985a, b; Nagler et al 1985) were 50 children of schizophrenics, and the control group were 50 offspring of parents who had no mental illness. In each group of 50 children, half were raised on a kibbutz and half in a traditional family setting in a town. The matched control groups were selected from the same classroom as the index children and were matched for age, ethnic origin, family size, parental educational level, and cultural level. The majority (38) of high risk children were offspring of schizophrenic mothers. The children ranged in age from 8.1–14.8 (mean age = 11.3) at the time of the original study in 1967, and the sample was reassessed (only 90 were followed up) for psychiatric status approximately 13 years later. Many but not all of the children had entered the risk period for schizophrenia at the time of the second assessment.

The major focus of this project was on measures of neuropsychological function that might reveal in the children certain early signs of vulnerability to the disorder. However, some effort was made to evaluate the rearing environment in the family; parents were rated, based on reports by parents and social workers, on overinvolvement, inconsistency, and hostility. Families notable in any or all of these attributes were rated as poor parenting environments. Note that no direct observational data of the type described for the Goldstein (1985) study were obtained.

At the time of the 13-year follow up, 26 subjects received DSM-III diagnosis, 22 in the high risk group and 4 in the control group, with a higher percentage in the kibbutz- (16) than the town-reared group. Of these cases, 5 were diagnosed schizophrenic, and 4 as having a schizophrenia-spectrum disorder. The only cases of schizophrenia-spectrum disorder were found in the offspring of schizophrenics, and all 9 cases had ratings of poor parenting environment. Thus, no cases of schizophrenia were observed when adequate parenting was observed.

The children who broke down had also showed signs of neuropsychological anomalies at the time of the initial assessments, and the combination of child (neuropsychological anomalies) and family attributes were present in all schizophrenia-spectrum disorders. This raises the question of the direction of effects in these data, as it is unclear how neuropsychological deficits influence parent-child interaction and vice versa. Also, it should be kept in mind that this study is still in progress. Not all the children have gone through the risk period for the disorder yet, and subsequent findings may change the rates of disorder markedly.

THE FINNISH ADOPTION STUDY   This study by Tienari et al (1983) in Finland considers vulnerability to schizophrenia by contrasting the psychiatric status of adopted-away offspring of nonpsychiatric cases. The cases were drawn from a nationwide sample of schizophrenic women and matched controls, all of whom gave away offspring for adoption to a nonrelative.

While this study is still under way, as of April 1985 (Tienari et al 1987) a total of 47 adoptive families (112 index and 135 controls) have been studied. This study attempts to investigate both genetic and environmental factors in the development of schizophrenia as it assesses the incidence of schizophrenia in offspring as a function of the quality of the rearing environment. Ratings of the interactional patterns in the family are based upon (a) a joint interview with the whole family; (b) a joint interview with the parents only; (c) a family interaction task based on the conjoint Rorschach procedure; and (d) ratings on the Interpersonal Perception Methods (Laing et al 1966). In addition the adoptive parents receive an individual interview, Rorschach test, and portions of the Wechsler Adult Intelligence Test (Wechsler 1981).

To date, these various measures of family relationships have been reduced to categorical ratings ranging from healthy to severely disturbed. While ratings of measures used in the Goldstein et al study cited previously (CD, EE, AS) are available from the data collected in the Tienari et al study, they have not been completed yet.

The data reported so far (Tienari et al 1987) strongly support the role of genetic factors in schizophrenia. Of the 10 psychotic offspring in the sample, 8 were found in the adopted-away offspring of schizophrenic mothers

(7.14%) while the population base rate was found in the control families (2/135 = 1.48%).

However, the data support a vulnerability-stress model as well. All of the schizophrenic cases in the 92 families rated thus far occurred in families rated as disturbed. In fact, the rates in the adopted-away offspring of schizophrenics with rearing environments rated as "healthy" have rates of schizophrenia at or below the general population rates.

These data also weaken the argument against a purely environmental etiology of schizophrenia. Similar patterns of family disturbance did not relate to a notable incidence of schizophrenia in the adopted-away offspring of normal biological parents.

CONCLUSION   These three studies indicate that variations in the rates of schizophrenia are predictable in part from prior estimates of disturbances in the intrafamilial environment. Two of these studies provide strong support for the vulnerability-stress model, as family stress was only associated with schizophrenia when putative genetic risk was present in the form of schizophrenia in at least one biological parent. The association between antecedent family stress and subsequent schizophrenia-spectrum disorder does not indicate the direction of effect, as we cannot reconstruct the impact of child on parent and vice versa from these limited longitudinal data.

Maintenance Studies

These studies, as indicated above, have focused on the role of the family in the course of schizophrenia after an initial episode has occurred. A vulnerability-stress model has been used in this area as well, since it is hypothesized that variations in the vulnerability to relapse interact with family stress to alter the likelihood of an exacerbation of schizophrenia. Most of the research in recent years has been focused on one type of family stress, termed high expressed emotion (high EE) by the British investigators [see Leff & Vaughn (1985) for a comprehensive review of the construct, its measurement, and validity studies]. While the present review focuses on stressful events within the family, other factors (stressful life events occurring outside the family) have also been hypothesized to be major risk factors in relapse (Brown et al 1972; Ventura et al 1986).

While most research has focused on the affective climate of the family, many schizophrenic patients are either estranged from or in minimal contact with their families and therefore their clinical course cannot be explained by family stress factors. Further, the best predictor of risk for relapse or poor clinical course is noncompliance with antipsychotic medication, and all studies on psychosocial stress factors must be considered within the context of medication compliance.

RESEARCH ON EXPRESSED EMOTION   The concept of expressed emotion evolved from a series of studies carried out at the MRC Social Psychiatry Unit in London over the last 30 years. The studies were designed to determine why some discharged schizophrenic patients survived in the community and others did not. An excellent description of the evolution of this research is contained in Brown (1985) and Leff & Vaughn (1985).

This research, which began before the widespread application of anti-psychotic medication, started with the observation, not since replicated, that patients who returned to family homes relapsed more frequently than patients who went to other living arrangements (Brown 1959). This led to an investigation of attributes of the family environment that might potentiate relapse in an already vulnerable person who had suffered a recent schizophrenic episode. Observations of families resulted in the notion that high levels of tension and emotion (originally termed "emotional involvement") characterized those family units with the most relapse-prone patients (Brown 1985, p. 19). This research was facilitated by the development of an interview procedure by Rutter & Brown (1966), the Camberwell Family Interview (CFI). This interview focuses on the three-month period prior to the onset of an episode of schizophrenia, various types of events in families (quarrels, how often household tasks were done, amount of face-to-face contact, etc), and the psychiatric history, irritability, and clinical symptoms of the patient in that same three-month period. The main intention of the interviewing procedure is to get respondents to express themselves in ways that reflect their inner feelings. The whole interview is rated on a series of scales (warmth, hostility, emotional overinvolvement), and the critical comments and positive remarks made about the patient are counted.

The original study (Brown et al 1962) found that 76% of patients returning to homes high on criticism and/or emotional overinvolvement relapsed, while only 28% of those returning to low-emotional-involvement homes did so. (High and low involvement are now called high and low EE.)

Since this original study, a number of replications have been carried out (Brown et al 1972; Jenkins et al 1986; MacMillan et al 1986; Nuechterlein et al 1986; Vaughn & Leff 1976; Vaughn et al 1984), all of which have confirmed the original trends. However, two reports exist of nonreplication (Hogarty 1985; Dulz & Hand 1986). Hogarty notes an important point: Most of the replications have high EE status predictive for *male* schizophrenic patients predominantly.

The 1976 Vaughn & Leff paper indicated that high EE status interacted with the patient's level of compliance with antipsychotic medication and the amount of face-to-face contact. Recent studies have not supported these findings and have shown instead that medication and family EE status are independent and *additive* predictors of clinical course (Vaughn et al 1984;

Jenkins et al 1986; MacMillan et al 1986). The contact effect has not been replicated.

The interpretation of these findings and their implications regarding the direction of effects are controversial. Both in the 1962 and 1972 Brown et al studies, relationships were found between relapse and ratings of patient "behavioral disturbance" in the three-month prehospitalization period. However, when this patient attribute was entered into a prediction equation with EE status, it failed to add predictive value. The 1976 Vaughn & Leff study found that ratings of the severity of psychopathology at discharge were unrelated to EE status, a finding subsequently confirmed by Miklowitz et al (1983) in the United States.

It might be expected that the patient's premorbid history would relate to the EE attitudes of relatives. Relatives faced with a socially ineffective offspring or spouse (a poor premorbid patient), might be more critical and/or emotionally overinvolved after a schizophrenic breakdown, since the breakdown might be experienced as still another sign of dysfunction. Miklowitz et al (1983) failed to find such a relationship for relatives defined as high EE on the basis of the criticism criterion, but relatives rated as high EE on the basis of emotional overinvolvement did have a schizophrenic offspring with a poor premorbid history.

Also investigating a possible link between EE status of relatives and the history of the patient's illness, MacMillan et al (1986) reported an association between preadmission duration of illness (the time between the reported initial signs of the first episode of schizophrenia and first lifetime hospital admission for the disorder) and EE status, with longer history associated with a greater probability of high-EE attitudes. These authors further concluded, from logistic regression analyses, that EE was not a significant predictor of relapse when duration of illness was also entered as a predictor.

A recent report by Nuechterlein et al (1986) of preliminary data from a comparable sample of recent-onset, predominantly first-admission schizophrenic patients failed to replicate the association between EE status of relatives and duration of illness.

The relationship between relatives' EE status and relapse in schizophrenic patients does not clarify the nature of the mediating mechanism between family attitude and patient response. A number of studies have attempted to address this problem by observing interactional patterns among patients and relatives. Four studies (Valone et al 1983; Miklowitz et al 1984; Strachan et al 1986; Hahlweg et al 1987) have indicated that high-EE relatives do express more negative affect [coded by the affective-style coding system of Doane et al (1981)] in experimentally induced interactional sessions. Further, the types of negative affective messages parallel the subtypes of high-EE attitudes: Relatives classified as high EE on criticism express more criticism; those who are labeled as high EE on the basis of emotional overinvolvement are instead more intrusive.

These verbal interchanges are paralleled by increasing psychophysiological arousal and reactivity (Tarrier et al 1979; Sturgeon et al 1981) in the patient. In one study with disturbed teenagers hypothesized to be at risk for schizophrenia, arousal and reactivity increased in both parents and offspring (Valone et al 1983). These data suggest that a negative affective climate in the family may enhance the likelihood of relapse by raising the level of arousal in the patient beyond the limits of his vulnerable post-psychotic coping mechanisms.

That the affective climate of the family may be causally related to relapse has been investigated within the framework of the Falloon et al (1982) aftercare intervention study. This research contrasted a behavioral family management program with a comparable one focused on individual patients, where all patients received regular maintenance antipsychotic medication. The direct interaction task used in the Miklowitz et al (1983) study was repeated two times in the Falloon et al study, before entry into the study and after three months of intensive treatment. The parental data were coded by the affective style system at both times. Pre-post comparisons (Doane et al 1985, 1986) indicated not only that the family management program on the average produced a greater reduction of negative affect in the family than the intervention focused on individual patients, but also that those families where this reduction occurred were least likely to experience a relapse by their young adult schizophrenic offspring by the nine-month follow-up point.

Similar findings were recently reported by Hogarty et al (1986) using the original Camberwell Family Interview method of EE assessment before and after one year of either family management, social skills training for the patient, a combination of the two, or regular maintenance drug therapy. All families in these studies were originally selected as being high EE. The rate of change from high- to low-EE status was greatest in the family treatment groups (family alone or family and social skills) and lowest in the drug-only condition. However, regardless of the assigned treatment condition, when relatives did shift to a low-EE status, patient relapse rate was 0%, whereas where this did not occur, the rate averaged 40%.

CONCLUSION   While studies carried out to date suggest that relatives' affective attitudes towards a recently discharged schizophrenic patient may play some role in the subsequent course of the patient's disorder, there are still a number of unanswered questions in this area. First, while there is little evidence that high-EE attitudes are simply reactions to variations in the clinical state of the patient, many of the direct interaction studies have not carefully examined the more subtle aspects of how patients relate to their family members. Given that EE is measured when family members are going through a major crisis involving either the hospitalization or rehospitalization of a spouse or offspring, there may be attributes of the crisis or its history, as suggested by MacMillan et al (1986), that can help us understand variations in these responses to the patient's disorder. It is likely that high-EE attitudes and negative affective behaviors towards patient relatives have complex origins, as suggested by Leff & Vaughn (1985), and that investigators should go beyond the convenient high/low-EE typology in order to understand not only the natural history of a schizophrenic disorder, but also the natural history of relatives' varying efforts to cope with the many difficult demands of a close relative with schizophrenia residing in or near their home.

AFFECTIVE DISORDERS

A recent review of the area of depression from a family perspective (Coyne et al 1987) concludes, "Yet, there is a puzzling lack of research involving actual observations of how depressed persons interact with the people who are significant in their lives" (p. 509). Generally I agree with this conclusion, although there have been signs of increased activity in the last five years.

Etiological Studies

In recent years there has been a trend to use the high risk methodology to investigate the role of the family as a source of psychosocial (in addition to the well-documented evidence for genetic) transmission of major depression and bipolar disorders. A major barrier to these studies was the lack of solid knowledge concerning the risk for affective disorders in the offspring of affectively disordered parents, the type of knowledge that existed for a long time in the area of schizophrenia. However, recent studies (Beardslee et al 1983; Orvaschel et al 1980) have documented that a substantial risk for affective disorder exists for these offspring, so it is now appropriate to investigate familial precursors of affective disorders using the same type of high risk designs used with schizophrenia.

Two major programs of research have begun in this area, one directed by Radke-Yarrow at NIMH and another at UCLA under the direction of Hammen. Neither of these studies has followed the offspring into the risk period for adult affective disorder yet, so we cannot evaluate how well family variables predict the likelihood of affective disorder in adulthood. However, each of these studies evaluates the psychiatric status of offspring in ways that permit the identification of precursors of affective disorders in children.

THE NIMH STUDY   Following an initial series of reports of a pilot study of the offspring of families of parents with manic depressive disorder constrasted with the offspring of families of normal, nonpsychiatrically disturbed parents (Zahn-Waxler et al 1984; Zahn-Waxler et al 1987), the team at NIMH headed by Radke-Yarrow began a larger-scale study contrasting families where one parent had either a bipolar (manic depressive), a unipolar, or no psychiatric disorder (Radke-Yarrow & Sherman 1987). At the time of the initial study each family had a child around 2 years of age and a sibling 5–8 years of age. Most of the sample to date (42 normal, 51 unipolar, 15 bipolar parental units) is middle to upper-middle class and caucasian, although a small, lower-SES., black sample is present as well.

A central objective of this study was to identify the distinguishing features of the child-rearing environments of young children of depressed and nondepressed parents. Intensive analyses of parent-child interaction (mainly mother-child interaction) were carried out in a simulated apartment environment in which parents and children were asked to carry out a series of tasks typical of ordinary family life. These analyses revealed many differences in the interaction styles of mothers with a history of depression (either unipolar or bipolar) such that these mothers were found, compared to well mothers, to be ineffective in controlling their child (Kochanska et al 1987), less able to handle stressful situations with the child (Breznitz & Sherman 1987), and more negative in affective expression (Radke-Yarrow et al 1988). Their children, on the other hand, were found to show deviant, particularly anxious-insecure patterns of attachment at the time of initial assessment (Radke-Yarrow et al 1985) and less social competence at a subsequent follow-up period four years later. The degree of negative affect expressed reciprocally in the mother-child relationship related to the level of social competence and directly to the degree of diagnosable psychopathology in both index child and sibling at the four-year follow-up (Radke-Yarrow et al 1988).

This study is still in progress and there are no reports as yet of differences in parent-child relationship or intermediate-term outcomes when offspring of unipolar or bipolar parents are contrasted.

THE HAMMEN STUDY   This study (Hammen et al 1987a), guided partially by Beck's cognitive-behavioral therory (Beck et al 1979), investigates the links between mother-child interaction, the development of depressive self-schema, and clinical symptomatology in the offspring of unipolar and bipolar parents. The study is longitudinal and prospective. It investigates variations in maternal diagnosis, severity of maternal psychopathology, mother-child interaction, and offspring symptomatology at the time of initial assessment and at later assessment periods. A unique aspect of this study was the use of two normal control groups, one of which had been under considerable stress although not psychiatrically impaired. The sample consists of 13 unipolar depressive mothers with 19 children, 9 bipolar mothers with 12 children, and a second comparison group of 14 mothers with medical disorders with 18 children, and 22 normal mothers with 35 children (8 considered under high and 14 under low stress at the time of assessment). The psychiatrically ill parents were generally chronic: The unipolar had an average of 2.1 hospitalizations for depression and the bipolar 5.9 admissions for bipolar disorder.

The design of the study involved an initial session with the mother, a family session with mother and child 2–4 weeks later, and regular follow-ups at 6-month intervals. The direct interaction procedures used were a game and a conflict-discussion task.

The preliminary results from the study indicate that offspring of affectively disordered parents were at high risk for affective disorder. Independent psychiatric assessment revealed that 42% of the offspring of unipolar and 25% of the offspring of bipolar parents received a diagnosis of major depressive disorder. It is worth noting that the rate for bipolar disorder did not differ from that noted for high-stress families (23%) (Hammen et al 1987b).

Using a coding system for the direct interactional data similar to the affective style system cited earlier, both bipolar and unipolar parents were coded as more negative, but only the unipolar mothers were significantly different in this quality from the various comparison groups. Further, the degree of what the authors termed "negative feedback" in the maternal-child interaction predicted the child's psychiatric and social functioning.

Obviously in both this study and the aforementioned NIMH study, the real test of the significance of the family interaction data will come from the longitudinal outcome data on these children as they enter the risk period for the adult forms of affective disorder.

CONCLUSION   Longitudinal prospective studies of offspring with affective disorders have just begun. Despite the lack of ultimate outcome data in adulthood, the intermediate outcome data on the two studies reviewed support the findings for schizophrenia. Variations in family interaction are associated with the level of offspring psychopathology within a group at risk for affective disorder based on parental psychopathology. As with the schizophrenia literature, the direction of effects is difficult to estimate. We require more precise vulnerability markers for unipolar and bipolar disorder to test for vulnerability-stress interactions over time.

Maintenance Studies

In the original Vaughn & Leff study (1976) on EE it was reported that this factor predicted the course of depressive disorders as well as schizophrenia, although the cutting score for high EE was lower for depressive disorder (2 criticisms vs 6 for schizophrenia). The depressive sample in this study were spouses (in the schizophrenic sample, parental and spousal families were both included). Recently, these findings were replicated (Hooley et al 1986) for a sample of Research Diagnostic Criteria–diagnosed major depressive disorder patients who had been hospitalized for this disorder. In this replication study, optimum prediction of relapse was found with a lower score than with relatives of schizophrenics. It is unclear whether this lower sensitivity to relative's criticism is related to depression per se or reflects the dynamics of the marital as compared with the parent-child relationship.

A unique aspect of the Hooley study was the collection of direct interactional data on these couples (Hooley 1986), which documented (as did previously cited studies of schizophrenia) that high-EE relatives were more negative, both verbally and nonverbally in direct interaction with their depressed relative. Patients, however, did not respond differentially to high- and low-EE relatives, so the patterns were not reciprocal.

Recently, Miklowitz et al (1986) investigated whether the affective climate of the family related to the course of bipolar disorder in recent-onset manic patients. He found that a combination of high-EE attitudes and negative AS behavior observed in direct interaction was highly predictive of relapse over the nine-month follow-up period after discharge from an index episode of the disorder. These family variables were predictive of relapse independent of compliance with maintenance lithium medication. The sample in this study was small (N = 23), and replication efforts are clearly warranted. This is the first evidence that psychosocial factors may relate to the course of bipolar disorder.

CONCLUSION   Paralleling the data for schizophrenia, there is increasing evidence that the affective quality of the family environment predicts the short-term course of a major affective disorder. These findings have been replicated for major depression, and the preliminary findings for bipolar disorder require replication. It now appears reasonable to consider family intervention studies, as have been developed for schizophrenia, to test whether modification of these intrafamilial attributes can alter the course of major depression and bipolar disorder in more favorable directions. Such studies can also clarify the nature of the interactional processes that connect the family environment and the subsequent exacerbation of an affective disorder in an already vulnerable individual.

ACKNOWLEDGMENTS

Preparation of this review was greatly facilitated by a grant from NIMH (MH08744) and a grant from the John D. and Catherine T. MacArthur Foundation for the Network on Risk and Protective Factors in the Major Mental Disorders.

Literature Cited

Beardslee, W. R., Bemporad, J., Keller, M., Klerman, G. L. 1983. Children of parents with major affective disorder: a review. *Am. J. Psychiatry* 140:825–32

Beck, A. T., Ward, C. H., Mendelson, N., Mock, J., Erbaugh, J. 1979. *Cognitive Therapy of Depression.* New York: Guilford

Breznitz, Z., Sherman, T. 1987. Speech patterning of natural discourse of well and depressed mothers and their young children. *Child Dev.* In press

Brown, G. W. 1959. Experiences of discharged chronic schizophrenic mental hospital patients in various types of living group. *Millbank Mem. Fund Q.* 37:105–31

Brown, G. W. 1985. The discovery of expressed emotion: induction or deduction? In *Expressed Emotion in Families,* ed. J. Leff, C. Vaughn, pp. 7–25. New York: Guilford

Brown, G. W., Birley, J. L. T., Wing, J. K. 1972. Influence of family life on the course of schizophrenic disorders: a replication. *Br. J. Psychiatry* 121:241–58

Brown, G. W., Monck, E. M., Carstairs, G. M., Wing, J. K. 1962. Influence of family life on the course of schizophrenic illness. *Br. J. Prev. Soc. Med.* 16:55–68

Coyne, J. C., Kahn, J., Gotlib, I. H. 1987. Depression. In *Family Interaction and Therapy,* ed. T. Jacob, pp. 509–33. New York: Plenum

Doane, J. A., Falloon, I. R. H., Goldstein, M. J., Mintz, J. 1985. Parental affective style and the treatment of schizophrenia: predicting course of illness and social functioning. *Arch. Gen. Psychiatry* 42:34–42

Doane, J. A., Goldstein, M. J., Miklowitz, D. J., Falloon, I. R. H. 1986. The impact of individual and family treatment on the affective climate of families of schizophrenics. *Br. J. Psychiatry* 148:279–87

Doane, J. A., West, K. L., Goldstein, M. J., Rodnick, E. H., Jones, J. E. 1981. Parental communication deviance and affective style: predictors of subsequent schizophrenia spectrum disorders in vulnerable adolescents. *Arch. Gen. Psychiatry* 38:679–85

Dulz, B., Hand, I. 1986. Short-term relapse in young schizophrenics: Can it be predicted and affected by family (CFI), patient and treatment variables? An experimental study. In *Treatment of Schizophrenia: Family Assessment and Intervention,* ed. M. J. Goldstein, I. Hand, K. Hahlweg. Berlin/Heidelberg: Springer-Verlag

Falloon, I. R. H., Boyd, J. L., McGill, C. W., Razani, J., Moss, H. G., Gilderman, A. 1982. Family management in the prevention of exacerbations of schizophrenia: a

controlled study. *N. Engl. J. Med.* 306: 1437–40

Goldstein, M. J. 1985. Family factors that antedate the onset of schizophrenia and related disorders: the results of a fifteen year propsective longitudinal study. *Acta Psychiatr. Scand.* 71:7–18

Goldstein, M. J. 1987. The UCLA High Risk Project. See Goldstein & Tuma 1987

Goldstein, M. J., Judd, L. L., Rodnick, E. H., Alkire, A .A., Gould, E. 1968. A method for the study of social influence and coping patterns in the families of disturbed adolescents. *J. Nerv. Ment. Dis.* 147:233–51

Goldstein, M. J., Rodnick, E. H. 1975. The family's contribution to the etiology of schizophrenia. *Schizophr. Bull.* 14:48–63

Goldstein, M. J., Tuma, H., eds. 1987. Special issue on high risk research. *Schizophr. Bull.* In press

Hahlweg, K., Nuechterlein, K. H., Goldstein, M. J., Magana, A., Doane, J. A., Snyder, K. S. 1987. Parental expressed emotion, attitudes, and intrafamilial communication behavior. In *Understanding Major Mental Disorder: The Contribution of Family Interaction Research,* ed. K. Hahlweg, M. J. Goldstein. NY: Family Process Press. In press

Hammen, C., Gordon, D., Burge, D., Adrian, C., Jaenicke, C. 1987a. Communication patterns of mothers with affective disorders and their relationship to children's status and social functioning. In *Understanding Major Mental Disorder: The Contribution of Family Interaction Research,* ed. K. Hahlweg, M. J. Goldstein. New York: Family Process Press. In press

Hammen, C., Gordon, D., Burge, D., Adrian, C., Jaenicke, C., Hiroto, D. 1987b. Maternal affective disorders, illness, and stress: risk for children's psychopathology. *Am. J. Psychiatry.* In press

Helmerson, P. 1983. *Family Interaction and Communication in Psychopathology: An Evaluation of Recent Perspectives.* London: Academic

Hogarty, G. E. 1985. Expressed emotion and schizophrenic relapse: implications from the Pittsburgh study. In *Controversies in Schizophrenia,* ed. M. Alpert, pp. 354–65. New York: Guilford

Hogarty, G. E., Anderson, C. M., Reiss, D. J., Kornblith, S. J., Greenwald, D. P., Javna, C. D., Madonia, M. J. 1986. Family psychoeducation, social skills training, and maintenance chemotherapy in the aftercare treatment of schizophrenia. *Arch. Gen. Psychiatry* 43:633–42

Hooley, J. M. 1986. Expressed emotion and depression: interactions between patients and high- versus low-expressed emotion spouses. *J. Abnorm. Psychol.* 95:237–46

Hooley, J. M., Orley, J., Teasdale, J. D. 1986. Levels of expressed emotion and relapse in depressed patients. *Br. J. Psychiatry* 148:642–47

Jacob, T. 1975. Family interaction in disturbed and normal families: a methodological and substantive review. *Psychol. Bull.* 82:33–65

Jenkins, J. H., Karno, M., de la Selva, A., Santana, F., Telles, C., Lopez, S. J. 1986. Expressed emotion, maintenance pharmacotherapy, and schizophrenic relapse among Mexican-Americans. *Psychopharmacol. Bull.* 22:621–27

Kety, S. S., Rosenthal, D., Wender, P. H., Schulsinger, F. 1968. The types and prevalence of mental illness in the biological and adoptive families of adopted schizophrenics. In *The Transmission of Schizophrenia*, ed. D. Rosenthal, S. S. Kety, pp. 345–62. Oxford: Pergamon

Kochanska, G., Kuczynski, L., Radke-Yarrow, M., Welsh, J. D. 1987. Resolutions of control episodes between well and affectively ill mothers and their young children. *J. Abnorm. Child Psychol.* In press

Kugelmass, S., Marcus, J., Schmueli, J. 1985. Psychophysiological reactivity in high-risk children. *Schizophr. Bull.* 11:66–73

Laing, R. D., Philipson, H., Lee, A. E. 1966. *Interpersonal Perception: A Theory and a Method of Research.* London: Tavistock

Leff, J., Vaughn, C. 1985. *Expressed Emotion in Families.* New York: Guilford

Liem, J. 1980. Family studies of schizophrenia: an update commentary. *Schizophr. Bull* 6:429–55

MacMillan, J. F., Gold, A., Crow, T. J., Johnson, A. L., Johnstone, E. C. 1986. Expressed emotion and relapse. *Br. J. Psychiatry* 148:133–43

Marcus, J., Hans, S. L., Byhouwer, B., Norem, J. 1985a. Relationships among neurological functioning, intelligence quotients, and physical anomalies. *Schizophr. Bull.* 11:101–6

Marcus, J., Hans, S., Lewow, E., Wilkinson, L., Burack, C. 1985b. Neurological findings in the offspring of schizophrenics: childhood assessment and 5-year follow-up. *Schizophr. Bull.* 11:85–100

Marcus, J., Hans, S. L., Nagler, S., Auerbach, J. G., Mirsky, A. F., Aubrey, A. 1987. A review of the NIMH Israeli Kibbutz-City study. See Goldstein & Tuma 1987

Miklowitz, D. J., Goldstein, M. J., Falloon, I. R. H. 1983. Premorbid and symptomatic characteristics of schizophrenics from families with high and low levels of expressed emotion. *J. Abnorm. Psychol.* 92:359–67

Miklowitz, D. J., Goldstein, M. J., Falloon, I. R. H., Doane, J. A. 1984. Interactional correlates of expressed emotion in the families of schizophrenics. *Br. J. Psychiatry* 144:482–87

Miklowitz, D. J., Goldstein, M. J., Snyder, K. S., Doane, J. A. 1986. Expressed emotion, affective style, and lithium compliance, and relapse in recent onset mania. *Psychopharmacol. Bull.* 22:628–32

Nagler, S., Marcus, J., Sohlberg, S. C., Lifshitz, M., Silberman, E. K. 1985. Clinical observation of high-risk children. *Schizophr. Bull.* 11:107–11

Nuechterlein, K. H., Dawson, M. E. 1984. A heuristic vulnerability/stress model of schizophrenic episodes. *Schizophr. Bull.* 10:300–12

Nuechterlein, K. H., Snyder, K. S., Dawson, M. E., Rappe, S., Gitlin, M., Fogelson, D. 1986. Expressed emotion fixed-dose fluphenazine deconoate maintenance, and relapse in recent-onset schizophrenia. *Psychopharmacol. Bull.* 22:633–39

Orvaschel, H., Weissman, M., Kidd, K. 1980. Children and depression: the children of depressed parents, the childhood of depressed patients. *J. Affect. Disord.* 2:1–16

Radke-Yarrow, M., Cummings, E. M., Kuczynski, L., Chapman, M. 1985. Patterns of attachment in two and three year olds in normal families and families with parental depression. *Child Dev.* 56:884–93

Radke-Yarrow, M., Richters, J., Wilson, W. E. 1988. Child development in a network of relationships. In *Individuals in a Network of Relationships*, ed. R. Hinde, J. Stevenson-Hinde. Cambridge: Cambridge Univ. Press. In press

Radke-Yarrow, M., Sherman, T. 1987. Hard growing children who survive. In *Risk and Protective Factors in the Development of Psychopathology*, ed. J. Rolf, A. Masten, D. Cicchetti, K. Nuechterlein, S. Weintraub. Cambridge: Cambridge Univ. Press. In press

Riskin, J., Faunce, E. 1972. An evaluative review of family interaction research. *Fam. Proc.* 11:365–456

Rosenthal, D. 1970. *Genetic Theory and Abnormal Behavior.* New York: McGraw-Hill

Rutter, M., Brown, G. W. 1966. The reliability and validity of measures of family life and relationships in families containing a psychiatric patient. *Soc. Psychiatry* 1:38

Strachan, A. M., Leff, J. P., Goldstein, M. J., Doane, J. A., Burtt, C. 1986. Emotional attitudes and direct communication in the families of schizophrenics: a cross-national replication. *Br. J. Psychiatry* 149:279–87

Sturgeon, D., Kuipers, L., Berkowitz, R., Turpin, G., Leff, J. 1981. Psychophysiological responses of schizophrenic patients to high and low expressed emotion relatives. *Br. J. Psychiatry* 138:40–45

Tarrier, N., Vaughn, C., Lader, M. H., Leff, J. P. 1979. Bodily reactions to people and events in schizophrenia. *Arch. Gen. Psychiatry* 36:311–15

Tienari, P., Sorri, A., Lahti, I., Naarala, M., Wahlberg, K., et al. 1987. Interaction of genetic and psychosocial factors in schizophrenia. The Finnish Adoptive Family Study: a longitudinal combination of the adoptive family strategy and the risk research strategy. See Goldstein & Tuma 1987

Tienari, P., Sorri, A., Naarala, M., Lahti, I., Pohjola, J., et al. 1983. The Finnish adoptive family study: adopted-away offspring of schizophrenic mothers. In *Psychosocial Intervention in Schizophrenia*, ed. H. Stierlin, L. C. Wynne, M. Wirsching, pp. 21–34. Berlin: Springer-Verlag

Valone, K., Norton, J. P., Goldstein, M. J., Doane, J. A. 1983. Parental expressed emotion and affective style in an adolescent sample at risk for schizophrenia spectrum disorders. *J. Abnorm. Psychol.* 92:399–407

Vaughn, C. E., Leff, J. P. 1976. The influence of family and social factors on the course of psychiatric illness: a comparison of schizophrenic and depressed neurotic patients. *Br. J. Psychiatry* 129:125–37

Vaughn, C. E., Snyder, K. S., Jones, S., Freeman, W. B., Falloon, I. R. H. 1984. Family factors in schizophrenic relapse: replication in California of the British research on expressed emotion. *Arch. Gen. Psychiatry* 41:1169–77

Ventura, J., Nuechterlein, K. H., Lukoff, D., Hardesty, J. 1986. *Stressful life events and schizophrenic relapse.* Presented at the 139th Ann. Am. Psychiatric Assoc. Conv., Washington, DC, May, 1986

Wechsler, D. 1981. *Manual for the Wechsler Adult Intelligence Scale.* New York: Psychological Corp.

Wynne, L. C., Singer, M. T., Bartko, J., Toohey, M. L. 1977. Schizophrenics and their families: research on parental communication. In *Developments in Psychiatric Research*, ed. J. Tanner, pp. 254–86. London: Hodder & Stoughton

Zahn-Waxler, C., Cummings, E. M., McKnew, D. H., Radke-Yarrow. 1987. Affective arousal and social interactions in young children of manic-depressive patients. *Child Dev.* In press

Zahn-Waxler, C., McKnew, D. H., Cummings, E. M., Davenport, Y., Radke-Yarrow, M. 1984. Problem behavior and peer interactions of young children with a manic depressive parent. *Am. J. Psychiatry* 141:236–40

Zubin, J., Spring, B. J. 1977. Vulnerability: a new view of schizophrenia. *J. Abnorm. Psychol.* 86:103–26

Ann. Rev. Psychol. 1988. 39:301–48
Copyright © 1988 by Annual Reviews Inc. All rights reserved

EXPERIMENTAL PSYCHOLINGUISTICS

Donald J. Foss

Department of Psychology, University of Texas at Austin, Austin, Texas 78712

CONTENTS

In 1921 Erwin Esper's review, "The psychology of language," appeared in the *Psychological Bulletin*. He examined work from 1917 through 1921 on such topics as vocabulary development in children, the origin of speech, and the language of "primitive" people. Esper's paper had 17 references. He remarked (p. 490), "Such a review, incomplete though it may be, is yet

301

0066-4308/88/0201-0301$02.00

sufficient to indicate that this field is not being extensively worked by psychologists. . . . [I]t seems highly important that language receive more attention from those whose proper business is to investigate the fundamental principles underlying human behavior."

Esper's wish came true. By 1929 there was enough work on the topic to merit a special issue of the *Psychological Bulletin*. In their summary article in that issue Adams & Powers cited 114 papers on a very wide variety of topics (e.g. language and thought, foreign language learning and its effects) using a wide variety of methods including such modern-sounding ones as eye movements and the presentation of visual materials one item at a time on a "continuously moving chain." Subsequent reviews in the *Bulletin* (e.g. McGranahan 1936; Pronko 1946) and in the *Annual Review* attest to the continuing interest in language and to the variety of intellectual frameworks from which psychologists have attempted to elucidate its fundamental psychological principles.

Fillenbaum's (1971) review first reflected the great impact of Noam Chomsky on the psychological study of language. And while neither Johnson-Laird (1974) nor Danks & Glucksberg (1980) cite a single paper by Chomsky, much of the work they do cite was influenced by Chomsky's ideas. The hegemony of Chomsky's (1965) "standard theory" is long past in both linguistics and psycholinguistics, but both fields continue to be profoundly affected by Chomsky's ideas. And both are vigorous. More than 1,600 abstracts in the PsycINFO data base contain the word "syntax," over 11,000 the word "comprehension," and nearly 2,000 the word "psycholinguistics."

From such a cornucopia one must pick ruthlessly if not always wisely. Thus, the present review concentrates on work done with adults, and on studies using normal subjects rather than language-impaired individuals. At the end of this paper I provide pointers into the literature for some topics on which I have not focused.

How are language skills represented psychologically, how is such knowledge used in production and comprehension, and how are the relevant skills acquired? How do we represent information derived from linguistic input and how does such information interact with and influence the general knowledge system? These basic questions have been at the heart of the field for some years. In the 1980s they continue to be addressed, but with some changes in emphasis. The recent literature has seen a blossoming of interest in larger units of comprehension such as texts and stories; an increase in work on language production as well as comprehension; an increase in the number of studies on spoken language comprehension, including a concern for the effects of intonation on comprehension; and laudible attention to how details of experimental techniques affect the conclusions drawn about the fundamental processes of interest. In addition, there has been a great deal of discussion about issues of "modularity" (the extent to which components of the language processing system are independent of one another) and "connectionism" (a framework for modelling that eschews the rule-based perspective that has guided most work in psycholinguistics in the past quarter century).

While the "natural" modality of language is the oral-aural channel (with the exception of signing among the deaf), there is also great interest in reading. A large fraction of work relevant to general issues presents stimuli to the visual channel. Although much that is of central concern may be common to both modalities, each has its unique characteristics, so students and new investigators must be wary of generalizations across the two. Such generalizations are not theory neutral. As we will see, the techniques used in investigating the general processes also affect the observed results in important ways. Happily, the last few years have seen progress in our understanding of some common tasks and how they interact with the basic processes of interest.

THE MENTAL LEXICON

We know the input to the comprehension mechanisms, but their product is mysterious. An explanation of comprehension requires a specification of this product and of the processes that yield it. Appropriate visual or acoustic stimuli initiate the processes that constitute comprehension. As a first approximation, the early stages of processing yield a word, word stem, or morpheme—in general, a lexical item. While the lexical item is only a way station en route to comprehending the message, it merits (and has received) a good deal of attention. The lexicon is important because it is the place in the language processing system where disparate information types (or codes) come together. That is, the lexical item must have associated with it information about its phonetic or phonological composition, information about its spelling, a specification of its syntactic category or categories, and other information as well. Given that such diverse information is available from the lexical item, there is a sense in which the lexicon is the lingua franca of the language processing system. It is the place where these diverse codes can communicate.

Gaining Access to the Mental Lexicon: Word Recognition

Most of the major theories of word recognition or lexical access[1] have been around since the 1970s, signalling the difficulty of conducting the crucial experiment and the malleability of the models. Recent years have seen

---

[1]Word recognition is sometimes used to refer to the initial contact between the stimulus and a stored item, while lexical access is used to refer to that point at which the information stored with the item becomes available to other processing mechanisms. I do not systematically honor this distinction here; context will permit the reader to tell what is meant.

additions and variations to the list but (with perhaps one exception) no subtractions from it. Older views have, of course, been changed.

THEORIES OF WORD RECOGNITION   Morton has modifed his logogen theory (e.g. Jackson & Morton 1984), though its essentials remain close in spirit to the 1969 formulation. The model assumes that each lexical entry has an associated counter sensitive to both perceptual and semantic information. When input from the perceptual system is consistent with the word, its count increments; likewise, when a semantically related word occurs the count is increased via communication within a lexical network. Each item has a threshold associated with it, and the word is recognized when the count exceeds the threshold.

Forster, too, has modified somewhat his "search model" of lexical access (e.g. Forster & Davis 1984), without changing its essentials. Forster holds that lexical access is achieved through a search process. Early stages of word recognition result in orthographic or phonological codes. These are then compared to entries in the mental lexicon. The comparison is done via a frequency-ordered search—i.e. higher frequency words are compared to the input before lower frequency words. In addition, lexical items that are semantically related to earlier words are made part of a second search set. This set is searched in parallel with the frequency-ordered search, and the input is recognized whenever a match is found in either list.

Becker (1980) has presented data consistent with his verification model. According to that view, sentence context makes available a set of candidate words, as does the initial part of the sensory input. The latter set is organized by frequency. The context set is searched first to see if it matches the input (i.e. candidates are verified with the stimulus). Thus, search time should be a function of the size of the semantic set. If the item is not found in that set, then the sensory set is searched in a frequency-ordered fashion. The verification model has probably had the most difficulty with the empirical literature, especially when sentence-level context effects are considered (see e.g. Stanovich & West 1983).

The cohort theory was introduced by Marslen-Wilson and Welsh (1978) and has stimulated considerable work over the past few years (see Marslen-Wilson 1984 for a partial review). According to cohort theory, the initial 200 msec segment of speech (this model is strongly oriented toward speech input) leads to the activation of all lexical items consistent with that speech segment—the cohort. Items then drop out of the cohort set when they are found to be inconsistent with either further input from the speech perception system or the semantic context of the sentence. When all words but one have dropped out, that word is recognized. Quite recently, Marslen-Wilson (1987) has modified his model to reduce semantic context (top-down) effects and to permit word frequency to influence early stages of the recognition process.

These theories of lexical access have been critically summarized by Norris (1986), who presented another one, the checking model. Norris assumes that word recognition is strictly a data-driven, bottom-up process. Each word has an associated threshold, as in the logogen model. Early in the process a number of candidates are made available (this part is similar to the cohort theory). Each candidate is then evaluated against the context and its threshold adjusted up or down. Thus, thresholds for lexical items are dynamically changed during processing. If the word is plausible in the context, its threshold will be lowered and less perceptual information will be required to recognize it. Frequency plays the same role here as in the logogen model—the chronic threshold is lower for more frequent items.

The TRACE theory of McClelland & Elman (1986) is also based on a set of interconnected nodes. In TRACE there are low-level nodes corresponding to features, and higher-level nodes corresponding to phonemes and words. The nodes are richly interconnected. When a node reaches threshold, others at its level in the hierarchy of node types are inhibited, while those nodes above and below it in the hierarchy are excited. This model is oriented toward spoken-word recognition, and is a variant of McClelland & Rumelhart's (1981) interactive activation model for written-word recognition. Though sometimes said to be free of rules, the units in the model are borrowed from linguistic work where they have been justified by the role they play in rule-based explanatory systems. Thus, there is a sense in which the TRACE model relies upon rules.

The LAFS (Lexical Access From Spectra) model of Klatt (1980) is a speech-based model which supposes that recognition occurs by matching spectral representations of the input with stored representations. Klatt's model addresses itself to a number of problems of speech recognition (indeed, his description of the problems of recognizing connected speech is an excellent one). In general it does so by encoding the possible variants of segments into the stored representations. The model has been critically discussed by Foss et al (1980).

EXPERIMENTAL STUDIES OF WORD RECOGNITION   Empirical work on lexical access can be divided conveniently into three subgroups, defined by the variables investigated: experiential, structural, and contextual. Each of the above-mentioned theories is evaluated, in part, by how well it accounts for these empirical phenomena. Experiential variables refer to those that arise from language experience but which seemingly do not play a role in the syntactic or semantic description of the lexical item. The latter I dub structural variables. The examples par excellance of experiential variables are the frequency and recency with which one has heard a word. Examples of structural variables include the morphological constitution of the item, the number of meanings it has, how it is subcategorized, and the thematic roles into which it enters. The immediate context within which a word appears might be considered a "local" or momentary experiential variable, but the effects of such context may depend upon structural factors like the organization of the mental lexicon. So local context effects—as exemplified by priming phenomena—can be categorized as either experiential or structural. To finesse the issue I handle context as a separate variable.

Experiential variables   Across a variety of tasks subjects are able to respond faster to high-frequency words than to words of lower frequency. Too, words presented recently are responded to more rapidly than those presented earlier (the repetition priming effect). Initially, some suggested that the frequency effect might itself be a recency effect, and consequently that the frequency-ordered structure of the lexicon postulated by Forster must constantly be changing. However, there is some evidence to support alternative interpretations. Feustel et al (1983) and Salasoo et al (1985) have produced evidence that the repetition effect is substantially due to an episodic memory trace (e.g. a trace of the particular experimental event) and not to a more structural change in the mental lexicon itself. Among other things, Feustel et al showed that there are repetition effects for nonwords, which of course do not have entries in the mental lexicon to be affected. (See Johnston et al 1985 for a critique of the episodic interpretation.) Forster & Davis (1984) have shown that the repetition effect is constant for high- and low-frequency words when the first stimulus (the prime) is masked, which supposedly precludes building an episodic trace of the prime, but also precludes the "frequency is recency" view. Kirsner et al (1983) have shown repetition effects for both high- and low-frequency words across modalities (auditory to visual). These investigators concluded that word frequency effects occur at a lexical stage and not at earlier encoding stages, and suggested that both Forster's and Morton's models are challanged by their data. To conclude, while the repetition effect is not yet fully understood, and while such data have implications for models of access, the work has not had a critical impact on theories of lexical access and organization.

Word frequency or word familiarity has a significant effect on language processing, but exactly how and when it has its effect is still an intensely studied question. Many studies of word familiarity, like other research on word recognition, have used the lexical decision task (LDT). In the LDT subjects are presented a string of letters and asked to push one button if the string composes a word and a different button if it does not. Reaction time (RT) and error rate are the two dependent variables of interest. RT is longer for low-frequency than for high-frequency words.

It has long been known that the nature of the nonwords can affect RT in this task; the times are longer when the nonwords are pronounceable (more wordlike) than when they are not. This finding suggests that the decision criterion adopted by subjects has been changed in the two conditions. (Subjects in such an experiment must not only process the stimulus, they must also make a decision about its status as a word.) Gordon (1983), among others, has suggested that a change in decision criterion can account for the word-frequency effect observed when using LDT. Gordon presented words of varying frequencies in lists that either mixed the frequencies or blocked them (a blocked list is composed of words in a single frequency range). He showed that RTs for high-frequency words were faster in the blocked condition than in the mixed condition, while there was little or no difference for the low-frequency words across these conditions. Gordon argued that this result was difficult to reconcile with Forster's search model. A frequency-ordered search ought first to find the high-frequency words in either list (therefore predicting no difference between lists in the high-frequency case), but might be able to skip the high-frequency items in a blocked list of low-frequency words (thereby suggesting that a difference would be observed across lists for the low-frequency items). According to Gordon, subjects can lower their decision thresholds when only high-frequency items are presented without risking much in the way of increased errors.

Balota & Chumbley (1984) have extended this line of reasoning and proposed a model of lexical decision with two criterion values. In their model some items will quickly be determined to be very familiar, others will quickly be determined to be very unfamiliar, while still others will fall in between. The latter will require more extensive processing. Balota & Chumbley argue that threshold-setting operations can account for data they gathered as well as that of Gordon and others. O'Connor & Forster (1981) found higher error rates in the LDT for nonwords that are misspelled versions of high-frequency words than for misspellings of low-frequency words (e.g. MOHTER led to more incorrect "word" responses than did BOHTER). This result is consistent with a criterion-bias explanation for the frequency effect since MOHTER is likely to lead to above-threshold activation for the high-frequency (low-threshold) word "mother," thus leading subjects to respond positively in LDT. O'Connor & Forster went on to argue that a criterion-bias model itself makes incorrect predictions in a spelling decision task (is this item a word, a misspelled word, or a nonword). However, the times in the spelling decision task tended to be somewhat longer than in the LDT; until that task is better understood it is not clear that the criterion-bias model was falsified by the spelling detection data. Recently, Bradley & Forster (1987) have suggested that the frequency-organized search model can account for the data if other activities important for the response are occurring in parallel. As they note, this view needs further clarification and empirical support.

A second technique that has been used extensively in the word recognition literature is reaction time to pronounce a word, the naming latency (NL) task. There is evidence that subjects do in fact access the lexical representation when carrying out the naming task, though the decision part of this task is much reduced (West & Stanovich 1982; Hudson & Bergman 1985). Word frequency or familiarity has been shown to have significant effects on NL, although Balota & Chumbley (1985) have argued that some (indeed, most) of the effect may be due to the influence of frequency on time to begin the pronunciation after the word has been accessed. In related work, Geffen & Luszcz (1983) have shown that pause duration is longer before speaking low-frequency words than before high-frequency words. They did not find any effect of frequency on the duration of the spoken words themselves, only on the pauses preceding them.

Word frequency also affects the processing of sentences. In a study of fixation durations during reading, Rayner & Duffy (1986) found that fixation time on infrequent words was longer than on frequent ones (with length controlled); in addition, fixation duration was longer on the following word, suggesting post-access effects of word frequency. Thus, while these data show that frequency has an effect during sentence processing, they do not provide unequivocal evidence that the locus of the effect is at the point of lexical access.

Before leaving the topic of frequency one must take note of an important observation made by Gernsbacher (1984). She noted that a large number of studies over a 20-year period had found interactions between frequency and a disparate set of variables—interactions that had generated much theorizing. Since the directions of the interactions varied, theorists were pressed to creative efforts of explanation. Gernsbacher showed that many of the interactions were due to sampling error in the norms for the low-frequency words. When ratings of "experiential familiarity" were gathered and new experiments conducted, the interactions disappeared. The methodological importance of this work is clear and should regularly be taken into account.

Structural variables   Lexical items differ along a number of linguistically important dimensions. Some of them may affect ease of accessing the word, or they may affect the processing that occurs subsequent to lexical access. Cutler (1983) has reviewed a substantial amount of work on lexical complexity. As she notes, semantic, syntactic, and morphological complexity may all influence comprehension difficulty. The results from a large number of studies suggest the following generalization: The syntactic and semantic complexity of a word does not affect the time to access it in the mental lexicon. (There is some evidence compatible with the hypothesis that morphological structure of a word influences lexical processing—e.g. Taft 1984.) The Rayner & Duffy (1986) study confirms this conclusion. They examined processing time for words by measuring eye fixation times during reading. The times were no different for factive verbs than for nonfactives. (A verb is factive when it presupposes the truth of the following complement—e.g. *know* vs *believe* in such sentences as *The man knew/believed the child was lying*.) Likewise, causative verbs did not differ in fixation time from noncausatives (e.g. *The actor cooked/tasted the chicken noodle soup*). And verbs with an implicit negative (e.g. *avoided*) did not differ from those without this characteristic (e.g. *praised*). (Cutler 1983, also reports new studies on implicit negatives.) Finally, while ambiguous words did not always differ from their unambiguous controls, there was a difference when the interpretations were equally likely in the context. (I return below to studies of ambiguity.)

While the above results are compatible with the hypothesis that lexical complexity (as determined in theoretical linguistics) affects comprehension (see below), a proper conclusion appears to be that lexical complexity does not affect time to access the item. This is a reasonable result from many perspectives. If verb complexity had an impact on lexical access, then our theories of access would require a very substantial top-down component— else how could, say, the factive status of a verb affect how it is accessed? As it is, models that emphasize bottom-up processes, search mechanisms, and changes in thresholds as a function of recent experience can account well for most facts of lexical access.

There is a second type of structural variable, one that is more stimulus bound, that apparently does affect lexical access. The phonetic (or orthographic) organization of a word, and its relation to other words in the lexicon, may affect access time. Evidence gathered in testing the cohort model of word recognition can be interpreted in this way. Marslen-Wilson (1984) has shown, for example, that RT in a word-monitoring task is determined by the "uniqueness point" of a word—the point where all other items in the cohort have been eliminated (this model assumes left-to-right processing of the speech signal).

Aspects of the cohort model, and other issues in perception, have been studied using the "gating task" developed by Grosjean (1980). In the gating task subjects are presented with a very small initial segment of an auditory stimulus (typically the first 50 msec of a word) while the rest of the stimulus for the word is replaced with noise. On the second trial the auditory "gate" is opened wider (typically another 50 msec) so that the subject hears the first 100 msec of the stimulus followed by noise. The process continues until the entire stimulus has been presented with no noise component. Tyler (1984) has examined predictions from the cohort model using the gating paradigm. Although much of the work concerns context effects (see next section), word-frequency effects have been demonstrated. For example, Taft & Hambly (1986) have shown in an auditory lexical decision task that a frequency effect exists when high- and low-frequency items are matched on their point of unique identity. [It is worth pointing out that Luce (1986, p. 155) has found in his sample of 20,000 words that "the frequency-weighted probabilty of a word's diverging from all others . . . prior to the last phoneme was only .39."] As Tyler noted, the cohort model did not have a way of incorporating a frequency effect. According to the standard version of the model, time to access a word is a function of the sensory input and the relation of the word to its cohort. Neither frequency of the word itself, nor frequencies of cohort members, should affect lexical access. However, S. Marcus (1984; see also Taft & Hambly 1986) has presented a modified version of cohort theory in which activation thresholds have been added to the theoretical mechanisms of the model. Marslen-Wilson (1987) has also incorporated frequency in a recent revision of the model.

Investigators have also examined the role of prosodic (rhythmic) structure on lexical access. Bisyllabic nouns and verbs tend to have different stress patterns (nouns are trochaic, *CONtract,* while verbs are iambic, *conTRACT*). While we know that stress influences speed of lexical access, there is little evidence that the more-or-less reliable stress pattern of bisyllabic English words is used in recognizing (isolated) words (Cutler & Clifton 1984). This is not to say that stress syllables are not important in word recognition. A number of investigators (Diehl et al 1987; Grosjean & Gee 1987) have proposed that stressed syllables are important access points into the mental lexicon. Indeed, this view may merit inclusion as a theory of word recognition. The implications of this approach for such models as cohort and search need to be better addressed.

Lexical ambiguity, another structural variable, affects comprehension; furthermore, it may do so at the point of lexical access. As many investigators have noted, ambiguity is ubiquitous in the language but is little noticed by language users. The processing system deals with it often and effectively—so much so that understanding how this occurs would undoubtedly tell us a lot about comprehension in general. Simpson (1984) has reviewed much of the literature on lexical ambiguity. In that review he remarks on the desirability of integrating studies of ambiguity with models of lexical access, and he relates the work he reviews to some of the theories noted above.

Views on the access of lexically ambiguous words can be divided roughly into three groups: One claims that context determines which interpretation of an ambiguity is accessed; a second claims that the more common interpretation of an ambiguity is accessed and only discarded if found to be inappropriate in the context; and a third claims that all known interpretations are accessed and a decision made among them on the basis of contextual fitness. The first of these views is a special case of the phenomena discussed in the section below on priming. The third view, as Simpson notes, seems at first glance unintuitive. However, a number of investigators have argued that the "exhaustive access" model can contribute to the overall efficiency of the language processing system. Furthermore, a reasonable amount of evidence is consistent with that model, although the frequency-ordered view also has its proponents. One of the important advances made in the past few years is an increased understanding of the importance of short temporal intervals in ambiguity processing.

Onifer & Swinney (1981) and Seidenberg et al (1982) are representative studies. Both used the cross-modal task in which subjects listen to a sentence and, sometime during it, are presented with a visual stimulus and asked to carry out the lexical decision or naming tasks. In the critical cases the visually presented word is related to one or the other of the interpretations of the ambiguity (e.g. when *mint* was presented audibly by Onifer & Swinney, *candy* or *coin*—and control items—were visually presented). Onifer & Swinney varied the degree of bias among the interpretations of the ambiguity and the degree of bias provided by the sentence context. When the visual test word was presented immediately after the ambiguous auditory word they found that subjects responded more rapidly to either of the words related to the ambiguous item than to control words. However, if the visual test item was delayed 1.5 sec then the only words that were facilitated were those related to the contextually relevant meaning of the ambiguity. Onifer & Swinney argue that the data support the exhaustive access model and the autonomy of the lexical system. Initially, all interpretations are activated by the stimulus, but then the contextually relevant one is chosen. Kintsch & Mross (1985) provide a replication and extension of this effect.

Seidenberg et al also used cross-modal priming and varied further the times between onset of the ambiguity and the onset of the visually presented words. When sentence context was neutral, the evidence indicated that all interpretations were accessed and a choice made within 200 msec. When the context sentence contained words highly related to one of the interpretations of the ambiguity (thereby exemplifying the priming paradigm), that interpretation may have been the sole one activated. The latter finding held for noun-noun ambiguities though not for noun-verb ambiguities, however. This phenomenon has not been explored in subsequent work.

Idioms and metaphors   That a discussion of idioms occurs in a section on structural variables and lexical processing tips one's hand about a theoretical decision. An idiomatic expression like *tipped his hand* might be comprehended by first accessing the standard interpretation of *tip, his,* and *hand,* putting them together syntactically, calculating the meaning of the phrase, discovering that the meaning does not make sense in context, and finally finding a stored entry for the phrase itself along with its idiomatic semantic interpretation. If that is the normal course of events, then understanding the conventional, idiomatic interpretation ought to take longer than understanding the literal interpretation. Swinney & Cutler (1979) dubbed this view the idiom list hypothesis and contrasted it with an alternative, the lexical representation hypothesis. According to that view, the conventional interpretation is stored in the lexicon and is accessed in parallel with (though perhaps more quickly than) the literal interpretations of its component words.

Using a task in which subjects were asked to judge whether a phrase was meaningful, Swinney & Cutler found evidence in favor of the lexical representation hypothesis. This effect was replicated and extended by Glass (1983), Gibbs & Gonzales (1985), and by Estill & Kemper (1982). The latter investigators used contexts biased toward either the literal or figural interpretations, and they employed on-line reaction time tasks. Times were faster in all contexts for idioms as compared to controls, a result consistent with the lexical representation view.

There is an analogous set of hypotheses about metaphors—i.e. that they are understood either by first deriving a literal interpretation or by interpreting them directly. Glucksberg et al (1982) and Inhoff et al (1984) have argued that metaphors are understood without the necessity of deriving the literal interpretation. They argue that discourse-level processes (see below) are affecting the immediate semantic interpretation of both metaphorical and literal sentences.

Priming and Lexical Processes

The priming phenomenon is one of the most thoroughly studied effects in recent experimental psychology. Priming refers to the fact that the time to respond to a word (in LDT, NL, or other tasks) is sometimes affected when that word is preceded by another, related word or words. The temporal and structural aspects of this task have been studied extensively (see Seidenberg et al 1984b for a review). The priming phenomenon has been used to support views about lexical access, the organization of the mental lexicon, and the flow of information within it and into it. In particular, one important theoretical issue addressed via priming has to do with the modularity of the processing systems. Forster (1979, 1981) and others (e.g. Cairns et al 1981; Cowart 1982; Gough et al 1981) have argued that information from higher-level processing (e.g. syntactic analysis, the overall message system) does not influence the process of lexical access; rather, it influences a post-access integration process. Lexical access is claimed to be a separable, autonomous, and "impenetrable" (Fodor 1983) module of the language processing system. Others who emphasize the interactive nature of sentence processing (e.g. Marslen-Wilson & Tyler 1980) have argued that lexical access itself is speeded when it receives higher-level contextual support.

The processing of a word is often affected by its context; this holds for words both in lists and in sentence contexts. Some of the work on ambiguity is an instance of this phenomenon. Schuberth & Eimas (1977) and others showed in (unambiguous) sentence contexts that RT to a target word using the LDT is speeded if the target is a highly likely completion of the priming sentence ("facilition dominance") and slowed if the target is anomolous in the context of the sentence ("inhibition dominance"). A substantial amount of research has tried to unravel the locus of the priming effect and the kinds of contexts that lead to facilitation vs inhibition.

One important variable that must be kept in mind when assessing results in the priming literature is the task employed. Two tasks have predominated in this area: lexical decision and naming. In a typical experiment subjects are presented with a context sentence and asked to respond to a word in the sentence (typically the last word). West & Stanovich (1982) found that LDT is not only responsive to associative relations between the priming words and the target, but also appears to reflect the ease with which the target can be integrated with the prior sentential material [a "postrecognition judgment of the relatedness of word and context," as Seidenberg et al (1984b) put it]. Naming latency appeared to be responsive to the former variable. Whether it also reflects the integration process is a matter of concern that I return to below.

Theorists have been concerned to predict which contexts lead to facilitation of the target and which lead to interference with it. Resolving such issues depends in part upon decisions about a technical detail, namely what constitutes a "neutral" context against which to compare the others. Candidates for "neutrality" have included strings of Xs, the word "blank," sequences like "the the the," "the next word will be," and others. These matters have been discussed by de Groot et al (1982), Kinoshita et al (1985), Stanovich & West (1983, especially experiments 2 and 9), and in a review by Jonides & Mack (1984). West & Stanovich (1986, p. 109) have wisely reminded us that "the appropriateness of a neutral condition depends upon the specific research question being addressed. There is no such thing as a truly neutral condition when embedded within any experiment." Stanovich & West (1983) have shown that, across a large number of neutral conditions, a pattern of facilitation dominance is observed when using sentence contexts and the NL task. Also, Lorch et al (1986) found inhibition effects with unrelated primes when they used LDT but not when they used NL. Evidence for a genuine inhibition effect on lexical access is sparse. Inhibition seems to occur after the target is recognized and not before.

Much theorizing about priming has been influenced by Posner & Snyder's (1975) two-factor theory of attention. According to that view, when a word is accessed in the lexicon, activation automatically spreads from it to its related items. Automatic activation does not require processing resources. A second, slower, and attention-requiring process then occurs; it leads to facilitation for expected items and to inhibition for items not expected. In particular, the work of Stanovich & West (1981, 1983; West & Stanovich 1982) has been conducted within that framework. However, as Stanovich & West (1983) note, their results are also in general compatible with Forster's (1981) search model of lexical access. According to that model at least the first of the two processes (automatic spreading activation) can occur entirely within the lexicon. (These investigators also found an interaction between context effects and stimulus quality such that the effects of context were greater when the target word was more difficult.) My attempt to handle matters of access and matters of representation somewhat separately gets substantially more difficult when talking about the priming phenomena. This expository strategy can be misleading if it suggests to readers that these are separate issues. Clearly, processing assumptions depend upon a theory of representation, and vice versa.

If priming plays a role in normal language comprehension, then it should be a robust phenomenon. In one sense it is; the basic effect has been replicated dozens of times. In another sense, though, it may be fragile. A controversy exists on this matter. For example, in an extensive series of studies Lupker (1984) has shown that "semantic" priming may be limited in scope. Words that are associatively related to one another resulted in priming, but when the priming and target words named members of the same semantic category (e.g. DOG and PIG), Lupker observed no facilitation when he used the NL task. He further showed that shared category membership did not add an effect when words were associates; and he replicated an earlier finding that semantic effects are observed when using the LDT. Thus, except for a small class of items, automatic activation did not appear. [However, Seidenberg et al (1984b, experiment 4) did find some facilitation in the NL task for semantically related items. The reason for this discrepancy remains to be seen.] In a conceptually similar study, de Groot (1983) found that a priming item facilitated the processing of words "one step" away in an associative network, but she found no evidence for priming two steps away. Balota & Lorch (1986) replicated de Groot's findings when they used the LDT; however, they did find mediated priming when they used NL. They found a smaller effect for mediated than for direct priming as would be expected by spreading activation.

Other results also suggest that there are strong limits on the usefulness of the priming phenomena when interpreted as an aid to lexical access. For example, Gough et al (1981) found that priming was very short lived in lists. When related items were separated by a single intervening item, the amount of facilitation dropped to zero. And while Koriat (1981) showed associative facilitation in the "backwards" direction (e.g. from FRUIT to APPLE as well as from APPLE to FRUIT) in the LDT, the effect did not replicate when the NL task was used (Seidenberg et al 1984b, experiment 3). In addition, Foss & Ross (1983) have reported some evidence that adjacent, semantically related words need not always lead to priming.

Researchers have also examined the effects of priming when the overall number of related items in the experiment is varied (e.g. Fischler & Bloom 1985; Schwanenflugel & Shoben 1985). While such effects can be demonstrated, they take time to manifest themselves; Fischler & Bloom conclude that such effects are unlikely to have a significant role in normal reading.

NONLEXICAL "PRIMING"   A more theoretically significant class of variables is concerned with nonlexical priming. If facilitation of lexical access can be observed when the prior material is syntactically (but not semantically) related to the target, or when the semantic relationship must be derived from the message processor and not just from the lexicon, then the algorithm for access would have to be responsive to variables other than such "surface" matters as frequency or morphological structure. Goodman et al (1981) reported that unassociated pairs that form a syntactic constituent (e.g. HE - SENT) were facilitated in the LDT. However, Seidenberg et al (1984b) did not observe a comparable effect when the NL task was used. Therefore, in a now familiar line of argument, they attributed the Goodman et al results to a postlexical stage of processing. Gurjanov et al (1985a,b) drew similar conclusions from their work on inflected Serbo-Croatian nouns preceded by reliable syntactic cues. Wright & Garrett (1984) used LDT and found that modal verb contexts facilitated the response to main verbs, and prepositional context facilitated the response to nouns as compared to when the priming and target contexts were reversed (e.g. preposition to main verb, and modal to noun). Unlike other effects that have tended to disappear when tried with the NL task, however, Wright & Garrett's result appears to be robust across tasks (West & Stanovich 1986). West & Stanovich found the syntactic priming effect in both tasks using the same stimuli. Importantly, they observed that the priming effect was inhibitory relative to a neutral control ("the next word will be"). As they noted, this finding means one of two things. Either there is a genuine effect of syntactic context on lexical access (one that inhibits access to syntactically impermissible items), or else the NL task is responsive to postlexical effects. The latter conclusion saves the modularity position and will probably be adopted by its proponents. This is a reasonable move and perhaps a correct one. However, if NL is sensitive to postlexical processes, then the LDT and NL tasks do not distinguish postlexical from prelexical effects after all. That will be unfortunate.

There is evidence that semantic relatedness effects are long lived during sentence processing. Foss (1982) showed that target-word processing was facilitated if semantically related items (not always associates) occurred 12 words prior to it. The same effect did not occur when the related items occurred in lists that were word-level anagrams of the sentences. Foss used the phoneme monitoring paradigm, which had earlier been shown to be responsive to priming-like effects. The amount of facilitation did not appear to differ with the distance between the "priming" words and the critical one. Thus, the results cannot be explained by a within-lexicon model of spreading activation. Two alternatives suggest themselves. Either lexical facilitation occurs from discourse-level "schemata" to individual lexical entries and access is actually facilitated, or the observed effect is due to such postlexical processes as syntactic and semantic integration. Foss & Ross (1983) have discussed these options and presented further relevant data.

To summarize, the bulk of the evidence suggests that there can be facilitation from one lexical item to associated items, but that at normal rates of listening and reading there is little if any contextual influence on lexical access. When access is difficult for any one of a number of reasons (e.g. poor stimulus quality, difficult words, poor reading ability) then attention-demanding processes may come into play to help with processing. This view has been well articulated by Stanovich & West in their "interactive-compensatory" framework. Given the degrees of freedom in the candidate models for lexical access, most can accommodate to the priming data, especially since many of the "priming" effects may be located at the point of integration rather than access.

To this point we have stressed the processes involved in accessing information in the mental lexicon, the theories of access, and the variables that affect it. A significant fraction of experimental psycholinguistics in the 1980s has been concerned with these issues. While we have grown in methodological sophistication and have learned some important things about lexical processing, the topic of lexical access is not at the heart of the psycholinguistic enterprise. In truth, and without intending a bad pun, it is a peripheral issue, one that may not merit all the attention it has received. To convince oneself of that, it is only necessary to imagine what would be involved in constructing a computer-based language processor that simulates human behavior. We could bypass the access problem, including such genuinely hard subproblems as determining where word boundaries are located in running speech, and still have most of the psycholinguistic enterprise in front of us. I except from this generalization problems of selecting (or creating) interpretations of the items. Let's turn then to work concerned with determining what information is stored in the mental lexicon and how it is used in accomplishing comprehension.

THE PRODUCTS OF COMPREHENSION

When a lexical item is accessed, what is recovered? A representation of a concept, information about its relations to other concepts, information about the syntactic category of the item, information about the extension of the term (its referents) if it has one, information that is used when the item combines with others, information about its pronunciation and spelling, etc? These types of information are needed to meet the goals of a semantic theory of the lexicon. Such goals have been perspicuously reviewed by Johnson-Laird et al (1984). According to them, there are four major goals: to specify the form of one's mental representation so that the distinction between the intension and extension of a term is captured; to explain intensional phenomena; to explain extensional phenomena; and to explain the inferences people draw on the basis of the meanings of words. To a first approximation, extensional semantics is concerned with how words and expressions relate to the world (their referents), and thus extensional semantics is related to the concept of truth ["To know the meaning of a (declarative) sentence is to know what the world would have to be like for the sentence to be true," Dowty et al (1981, p. 4)]. Intensional semantics is concerned with such relations between words (or expressions) as synonymy, ambiguity, and contradictories.

Perhaps the most pervasive framework within which theorists have sought to capture diverse relational information has been that of network theories (e.g. Anderson & Pirolli 1984). Such theories can be designed to represent relationships among concepts (e.g. class inclusion, synonymy, antonymy). This information can in principle then be used by further processing mechanisms to discover when sentences are self-contradictory, redundant, etc [but cf the work of Clark (1983), discussed below]. Chaffin & Herrmann (1984) have noted, however, that the actual variety of semantic relations has been underrepresented in such models (and they briefly review earlier work on this topic). Johnson-Laird et al (1984) evaluate network models in light of the above list of goals for semantic theory. They note that network theories have led to the discovery of new empirical phenonema (presumably they have in mind some of the facts of priming). However, they also note that such models do not properly treat the facts of reference and extension—network models are not well connected to models of the world. This leads to a set of problems they discuss. For example, consider the phrase *on the left of*. This phrase would seem to epitomize a transitive relation and thus would be handled well by a processing model that had access to the relevant lexical items and a rule of transitive inference. However, if A is on the left of B, B is on the left of C, and so on through E is on the left of F, it need not necessary follow that A is on the left of F. If the reference situation is such that A,B, . . . ,F are card players at a round table, then A will be on F's immediate right. Johnson-Laird et al use such arguments to show the necessity for a model of extension.

Johnson-Laird et al do not conclude that network models are inadequate. Indeed, they argue the class of such models is so unrestricted as to be unfalsifiable unless constraints are imposed on their form. Satisfactory revisions would make the resulting network model quite different from any of the existing ones. A revision would have to make room to represent the extensions, and such a model [dubbed a mental model by Johnson-Laird (1983)] would "have a structure that corresponds to the perceived or conceived structure of [the] state of affairs [described by the relevant sentence]" (Johnson-Laird et al 1984, p. 311). The program proposed is captured by the following quotation from the same source: "If mental models are to be constructed from sentences, the meanings of words have to specify the conditions that must be satisfied in the model for the word to apply truthfully to it. The lexical semantics must therefore capture the contribution that the word makes to the truth conditions of any assertion in which it occurs." Clearly this set of demands on the representations in the lexicon is very different from those derived from the empirical phenomena of priming. Johnson-Laird (1983, 1987) has described some experiments that examine part of his program, but they are initial attempts and much clearly needs to be done. [See Smith (1985) for a more detailed review of Johnson-Laird's book.]

I emphasize this approach here—although it has not yet stimulated much empirical work—because I think that Johnson-Laird has identified a set of "results" that must be computed by any comprehension system. To date there is no effective procedure for carrying out those computations. He has suggested an approach to representation—his mental models—that needs further test.

When lexical items are accessed, they then must be combined so that a semantic interpretation of the utterance results. Most psycholinguists, either explicitly or implicitly, agree with Frege's Principle, otherwise known as the Principle of Compositionality: "The meaning of the whole is a function of the meaning of the parts and their mode of combination," (Dowty et al 1981, p. 8). If one accepts this principle, then the lexical representations that one proposes must make available some means for a "mode of combination." Judgments of similarity, speed of classifying words as exemplars of a category, and other empirical phenomena are important sources of constraint on lexical representations or the processes that work on them. However, a successful theory of semantics requires that such representations be harmonious with representations and processes that are required for compositionality.

The principle of compositionality has been challenged in a provocative paper by Clark (1983). He argues that many expressions do not possess a finite number of senses (intentions), so that comprehenders cannot be thought of as making a selection from a stored list. For example, the phrase *steam iron* in *Steam irons never have any trouble finding roommates,* can be construed to refer to "young women who own steam irons" when read in a satirist's column reporting on a daughter's travails in finding a roommate. Further, Clark argues (p. 298) that lexical items cannot be assigned their possible senses by any rule. "Each expression of this sort . . . has only a *nonce sense,* a sense 'for the nonce.' " If that is the case, there can then be no rules for combining intentions according to the Fregian program. I return to this matter below. First, however, I discuss some further work in the tradition of compositionality—the role of syntactic organization in sentence processing.

SYNTAX AND COMPOSITIONALITY

The understanding of a sentence is built on an understanding of its parts and the relationships among them. The syntax of a language specifies some of the principles by which words combine to make legal sentences, based on such constructs as constituency, subcategorization, etc. Thus syntax is typically construed to be an important aspect of compositionality [see M. Marcus (1984) for a recent defense of the necessity of syntax]. Ever since psycholinguists began to be influenced by Chomsky's conceptions of language, there has been a debate about the proper role of syntactic rules and structures in models of language use. This debate has continued, with scholars such as Berwick & Weinberg (1983a,b) attempting to clarify the relationship between grammars and (mental) parsers. They argued that a version of transformational grammar is compatible with performance models if one permits computations to occur in parallel rather than serially. Garnham (1983b) replied that the common view is untestable until more is known about other aspects of the comprehension system.

The resurgence of interest in the psychology of syntax has been driven in part by investigations of the "modularity thesis." As noted earlier, this thesis holds that the language processing system can appropriately be divided into subsystems, each of which operates by its own principles, uninfluenced by the processes occurring in neighboring modules. According to this view, language is not simply an instance of our general cognitive abilities. There are two camps, each with its satellites. Some believe that modularity has been shown to be compatible with the facts of comprehension, or that one should hold on to that thesis as long as possible, in part for methodological reasons (e.g. Forster 1979; Tanenhaus et al 1985; Cairns 1984). Others believe that language processing is so suffused with general cognitive operations that modularity does not provide an explanatory framework (e.g. Marslen-Wilson & Tyler 1980). Members of the modular camp are likely to believe that there is a processing module that eventuates in the syntactic structure of input sentences, though they are not committed to the view that this module is embedded in series with other modules; parallel architectures consistent with modularity are possible and have been proposed. Believers in modularity will typically hold that on-line measures of comprehension are important, for only by using such measures can one observe the effects of such subsystems.

With respect to the structural nature of the products of comprehension, psycholinguists have often turned to linguistic theory for guidance. There are presently a number of influential approaches to describing the structures of sentences and the principles that determine those structures. It is beyond the scope of this chapter to review the major contenders. Sells (1985) has provided a helpful overview of three contemporary systems: the Government-Binding theory (GB) espoused by Chomsky, Generalized Phrase-Structure Grammar (GPSG) associated with Gazdar, and the Lexical-Functional Grammar (LFG) forwarded by Bresnan & Kaplan. Each has influenced some psycholinguistic work.

Another general issue that motivates work on syntax is the desire to explicate the mechanisms of compositionality. Psycholinguists need to construct a theory of compositionality that fits with constraints on memory and other processing limitations. Much of the empirical work is discussed in terms of its implications for both issues. I do not uniformly draw out the implications for them both as I mention each study.

Empirical Work on Syntax

English provides many examples of "local structural ambiguities," some of which have been used in research on syntactic processing. For example, consider *Since Keith always jogs a mile and a half this seems like a short distance to him* and compare it to *Since Keith always jogs a mile and a half seems like a short distance to him.* The local ambiguity arises from the fact that the phrase *a mile and a half* can potentially be syntactially attached to either the first or the second clause of the sentence. The second example may lead the reader down the garden path, yielding a momentary misinterpretation owing to improper attachment. Frazier & Rayner (1982) presented evidence that the first example is easier to process than the second. They recorded eye movements while subjects read such sentences and found shorter reading times per letter for the first example. Further, evidence from fixation durations and regressive eye movements was compatible with that result. They interpreted the data as being consistent with a general syntactic processing strategy in which comprehenders continue to attach new material to existing substructures as long as they can (dubbed the late closure hypothesis). Kennedy & Murray (1984) replicated this finding using word-by-word reading times on a CRT, and discussed important methodological issues relevant to such work.

A second structural matter investigated by Frazier & Rayner (and others) is called the minimal attachment hypothesis. This hypothesis [due to Frazier & Fodor (1978)] states that new material will be added to sentences such that the minimal number of nodes will have to be added to the sentence's syntactic structure. A sentence like *Susan ate the cereal with the spoon* requires one fewer nodes than does *Susan ate the cereal with the raisins*. In the latter case an additional NP *the cereal with the raisins* is required. Frazier & Rayner found that minimally attached constructions took less time to read (though the effect was only present when test sentences were somewhat longer than those given above). Ferreira & Clifton (1986) investigated the minimal attachment hypothesis in cases where the minimally attached version resulted in a semantically anomolous interpretation. Ferreira & Clifton also used the on-line measure of eye movement fixation duration as their dependent variable. They argued that, according to modularity, subjects initially opt for the minimally attached structure even when there is semantic information present to make that interpretation incorrect. Of course, the comprehenders eventually get the correct interpretation; the semantic or pragmatic variables do have an impact on the final analysis of the sentence. The crucial argument of modularity is that the initial interpretation is guided by syntactic factors alone. The eye movement data observed by Ferreira & Clifton were consistent with the modularity position. Rayner et al (1983) found similar results. Speer et al (1986) also found some evidence consistent with minimal attachment when two other on-line tasks were used. And Holmes (1984) also argued that sentence interpretations are initially based on parsing principles even when discourse context leads to odd interpretations when those principles are followed. (It should be noted that Holmes used an after-the-fact measure of comprehension when she got those results, a somewhat surprising finding.)

On the other side of the ledger, Crain & Steedman (1985, p. 321) "argue for the proposal . . . that the primary responsibility for the resolution of local syntactic ambiguities . . . rests not with structural mechanisms, but rather with immediate, almost word-by-word interaction with semantics and reference in the context." They distinguish between strong and weak forms of the interaction hypothesis. The former is completely nonmodular in that semantics influence which syntactic structures are considered; while according to the latter, "syntactic processing independently 'proposes' alternatives, either serially or in parallel, while semantics 'disposes' among these alternatives" (p. 325). The weak form (which they favor on the basis of experimental data) is more or less consistent with modularity, though if the units proposed are small enough the weak and strong forms become difficult to disentangle, as Crain & Steedman note. The data they report are not gathered on-line, so a modular interpretation of them is likely to be possible. Consistent with their interactionist position, Tyler & Marslen-Wilson (1977) concluded that context influences structure assignment as well as lexical access. They argued that the immediate analysis of such phrases as *landing planes* (which can be a gerundive, as in *Landing planes is fun,* or a plural noun phrase, as in *Landing planes are dangerous*) can be influenced by the preceding context. Cowart & Cairns (1988) have recently presented evidence against the interaction interpretation of these data.

To editorialize, some of the experimental effort devoted to supporting and refuting modularity is not being efficiently spent. The content of the thesis is presently not sharp (efforts like those of Crain & Steedman may help, but they also tend to show that versions of these two different views can have similar empirical consequences). I suspect that the important work over the next few years will be involved in testing more precise models of parsing rather than in trying to settle this issue. We need more point predictions and less hypothesis testing in this area.

Other work has emphasized the influence of lexical expectations on parsing, especially verb-based expectations about sentence structure. Such effects may be based on thematic relations (e.g. the verb requires an agent or a theme) or on the types of complements verbs can take (e.g. the verb is obligatorily [or typically] transitive, the verb is obligatorily [or typically] intransitive). Studies based on the lexical preference assumption fit well with the emphasis in current linguistic theories. "It is interesting," Wasow (1985, p. 204) states, "that contemporary syntactic theories seem to be converging on the idea that sentence structure is generally predictable from word meanings." He goes on to note how contemporary theories differ from the naive view of the matter and declares that linguists "have isolated certain kinds of grammatical information that are not predictable from lexical semantics, and have developed theories to permit them to be expressed compactly." Contemporary theories differ in the types of lexically based information they take as primitive (e.g. Bresnan and her colleagues take as primitive functional information such as "subject," while Chomsky's GB theory does not).

Ford et al (1983) argued that the structural preferences of Frazier & Fodor's model are really verb based. They presented sentences like *The woman wanted the dress on that rack* and *The woman positioned the dress on that rack.* The preferred interpretation was determined by the verb rather than by the minimal-attachment principle. In the former case the verb *want* was assigned the phrase *the dress on that rack* as its object, while in the latter case the verb *position* was assigned a complement having an object, *the dress,* and a locative phrase, *on that rack.* Clifton et al (1984) followed up this work showing that verb preference (transitive vs intransitive) influenced time to respond to a secondary stimulus during a reading task. When the sentence form corresponded with the verb preference, response times were faster. Mitchell & Holmes (1985) also found evidence for verb-based preferences in structure assignment using an on-line reading task. To facilitate further work on this topic, Connine et al (1984) have provided normative data for 127 verbs, giving the frequencies of 19 different syntactic categories of the verb phrase complementizers.

A pervasive phenomenon in English is the presence of "gaps" in the surface form of sentences. A common example occurs in sentences with relative clauses—e.g. *The boy the girl liked ___ kissed her*. This sentence has two transitive verbs each of which must have an object. The object of *liked* is in some sense missing from the surface form of the sentence (the position underlined is the missing or gapped element). A correct understanding requires that *the boy* be used to fill the gap; it is the filler. Fodor (1978) and numerous others have proposed that comprehenders take account of the subcategorization requirements (or preferences) and thereby know that a gap is present in the input. Investigators have looked at filler-gap relations and have attempted to specify the principles according to which the correct fillers are found for each gap. For example, Frazier et al (1983) found that gaps tend to be filled with the most recent candidate, though this tendency is, they propose, an instance of a more general one: Assign the most salient potential filler to the gap. In addition, Frazier et al found that some assignments of fillers to gaps are made despite the fact that certain "control" properties of verbs are violated. As Clifton (1988) has noted, these data suggest that subparts of the syntactic module are themselves modular.

The work of Freedman & Forster (1985) can also be interpreted in support of a syntactic module with close ties between grammatical and mental operations. (These investigators use a sentence-matching technique that may require further study before conclusions based upon it are secure.) Freedman & Forster found that subjects apparently process certain ungrammatical strings more quickly than they do others. Those in the former set are ungrammatical though potentially generable in Chomsky's binding theory; those in the latter set are nongenerable. Freedman & Forster entertain again the nearly three-decade-old hypothesis that there may be a "direct correspondence between formal grammatical *operations* and mental *computations*" (p. 125, italics in original).

In the realm of spoken language, Scott & Cutler (1984) have shown that syntactic structure can be cued by certain aspects of segmental phonology. They noted that the application of certain segmental rules (e.g. palatalization) is neutralized by phrase boundaries in some dialects (American English) and not in others (British English). Speakers of the former dialect used these rules in comprehension while speakers of the latter did not. This observation leads us to a more general consideration of prosody.

Prosody and Comprehension

One notable aspect of spoken language is its prosodic structure, the changes in pitch and rhythm that occur across sentences. The 1980s have seen a reawakening of interest in this topic. Cutler & Ladd (1983) presented a survey of recent work on both models of prosody and its measurement. Topics of interest include the role of stress on lexical access, the role of prosody in organizing utterances (and its relation to syntactic structure and parsing), and the role of prosody in signalling semantic and pragmatic information, as when words are given emphatic stress to signal which information is given and which is new.

In English, stressed and unstressed syllables tend to alternate, creating the stress foot; listeners perceive that English is rhythmic, with the intervals between onsets of stressed syllables approximately equal (isochrony). Fowler (1983) proposed that the perception of isochrony has a physical basis; it depends upon the timing sequence of vowels as they are produced. Importantly for our present purposes, there are further groupings into prosodic phrases and utterances. These are determined by a number of factors. For example, the fundamental frequency of the speaker's voice is thought to drop at the ends of phrases, a fact that might be used as a cue to syntactic organization. [See Cooper & Sorenson (1981), Hirst (1983), Liberman & Pierrehumbert (1984), and Lieberman et al (1985) for somewhat differing views on this matter.] A number of descriptive mechanisms have been proposed for rhythmic phenomena, many in the spirit of Martin's (1972) pioneering efforts [see Cutler & Ladd (1983), Fowler (1983), and Liberman & Pierrehumbert (1984) for references].

The rhythmic structure of speech does not always correspond to its syntactic structure. Gee & Grosjean (1983) looked at the relation between pause duration and syntactic structure, concluding that phrase length modifies this relation. Martin (1979) and Buxton (1983) showed that predictability of temporal organization influences time to perceive segments. Too, contrastive and emphatic stress may be placed on a word in order to signal pragmatic importance or to signal new information (e.g. Brown 1983). In general, the relation between temporal organization and recovery of lexical, syntactic, and semantic relations is ripe for further work.

Anaphora

A topic the resides at the intersection of syntax and the wider discourse context is that of pronoun and anaphor resolution. A pronoun may be bound to an entity already introduced in the sentence, in which case it is an anaphoric pronoun, or it may be used to introduce a new entity. On many occasions either is possible; in those cases the pronoun is ambiguous. One contribution of linguistic theory is to specify when pronouns *cannot* be anaphors. Consider, for example, the problem of assigning an interpretation to the pronoun in the following sentences: *1. Somehow Mary tripped when she was singing; 2. Somehow she tripped when Mary was singing; 3. Somehow when she was singing, Mary tripped; and 4. Somehow when Mary was singing, she tripped.*

In examples 1, 3, and 4 the pronoun *she* can (though it need not) refer to *Mary*, but in example 2 it cannot. The anaphoric interpretation is blocked. This restriction seems not to be due to semantic considerations nor to the fact that the anaphor *she* occurs before the coindexed noun *Mary* (it occurs first in example 3 as well). Instead there is a structural relation that precludes *she* from being interpreted as *Mary* in example 2. In the Government-Binding theory of Chomsky the restriction can be stated in terms of the branching relations in the structural description.[2]

While there are syntactic constraints on the interpretation of pronouns, semantic and pragmatic knowledge also influences the interpretation given to pronouns (and other anaphors). For example, *I took my dog to the vet yesterday. He {bit/injected} him.* The resolution of *he* and *him* in the second sentence switches when we change the verb, and depends upon our knowledge about the typical behavior of dogs and veterinarians [example modified from Tyler & Marslen-Wilson (1982)]. One goal of work in this area is to specify what knowledge sources are used to resolve anaphors, when they are used, and how (these issues are obviously related to concerns about modularity as well).

It seems apparent that such matters as gender and number of antecedent noun will affect the interpretation of the pronoun (e.g. *Sue told Steve a joke and then {he/she} laughed).* Too, there may be considerations of recency as in the filler-gap situation. In the end, consistency with the discourse and with world knowledge will dominate, but the route by which that happens is not clear. Corbett & Chang (1983; see also Corbett 1984) investigated this issue by presenting sentences like *Jack threw a snowball at Phil, but he missed* and asking whether the pronoun *he* led readers to access or reinstate just *Jack* (the semantically appropriate antecedent) or both *Jack* and *Phil*. They (Corbett & Chang, not Jack & Phil) presented subjects with a test word immediately after the sentence and instructed them to decide quickly whether the test word was in the sentence. Response times were consistent with the interpretation that the pronoun had momentarily reinstated both proper nouns, not just the appropriate one. Using a reading time task, Frederiksen (1981) had previously formulated the reinstatement hypothesis and suggested a set of "prioritizing rules" for the selection of the single referent from among the candidates. McKoon & Ratcliff (1980) and Dell et al (1983) have shown that other concepts in the same proposition as the referent are activated when the anaphor occurs, though the activation of these other terms is relatively short

---

[2]Roughly, if the pronoun c-commands the lexical item, they cannot corefer. The relation of c-command can be defined, again roughly, as follows: α c-commands β if and only if every branching node dominating α dominates β. See Sells (1985) for a further explication of c-command and its related construct, government. Incidentally, c-command may also be involved in the assignment of fillers to gaps; the principle is nearly the reverse of the one just stated: To be a filler a constituent must c-command the gap.

lived. [See O'Brien et al (1986) for a discussion of methodological issues.] Work using eye-movement data has shown that fixations on anaphoric pronouns are longer when the antecedent occurs farther back in the test materials than when it is closer by (Ehrlich & Rayner 1983), a result that may bear on the selection process involved if the reinstatement hypothesis is correct.

Investigators with the interactionist perspective agree, of course, that a number of knowledge sources are used to choose the correct referent for an anaphor. They argue that the evidence to date does not support the claim that there is, say, a syntactic module used in anaphor resolution prior to the use of other modules. Tyler & Marslen-Wilson (1982) interpreted some of their data to mean that readers always check whether the resolution of the anaphor makes pragmatic sense. They claim that the need to make a pragmatic inference does not add to the resolution time. Kerr & Underwood (1984) report that fixations are longer when the pronoun violates a sex stereotype (e.g. *she* when the antecedent is *engineer*). The latter study is consistent with the interaction position, as is the work of Murphy (1985).

The resolution of an anaphoric constituent may depend upon the representation and organization of the discourse. I now turn to the burgeoning literature on that topic.

DISCOURSE STUDIES

Earlier I referred to the principle of compositionality when discussing the semantic interpretation of the sentence (i.e. the meaning of a sentence is determined, at least in part, by the meanings of its words.) Similarly, the interpretation of a discourse or conversation is in part a function of the semantic interpretation of its constituent sentences. In addition, the role of the ongoing discourse interpretation may be significant in resolving uncertainties about the meaning of its sentences. But what is a discourse? Not every collection of well-formed sentences makes a well-formed discourse. Johnson-Laird (1983) suggests that we have a true discourse when there is referential coherence in the interpretation of the sentences and when they can be given a plausible interpretation within a framework of general causal knowledge. The notions of referential coherence, plausibility, causal frameworks, and discourse organization have all stimulated theoretical and empirical work in the 1980s. Of course, many theorists were concerned about discourse before then; de Beaugrande (1980) summarizes European work on discourse and text structure, including a bibliography of nearly 125 items.

Referential Coherence

Speakers and writers use a variety of devices to maintain referential coherence. Anaphora is one of them. The type of device used appears to be a function of the organization of the discourse and the location of the antecedent within it. For example, Marslen-Wilson et al (1982) analyzed a story into a hierarchy of episodes and events within episodes. Not surprisingly, they found that the storyteller used more explicit referential devices (e.g. a name plus a description) when introducing a character into the story, but later used either names alone, pronouns, or even zero anaphora (e.g. no explicit marking of the subject, as in a phrase like . . . *and then ____ hit the ball . . .,* where the zero anaphor is indicated by the gap). The degree of explicitness of the referential device was related to the point in the hierarchy where the referent had last been mentioned. The use of zero was common within events, especially when the actor was "in focus." Indeed, Marslen-Wilson et al note that an anaphoric pronoun not only refers but also signals the beginning of a new action sequence in the story—it signals a new event. (These investigators also argued that an inference process is always used in matching a pronoun to its antecedent, a view consistent with their interactionist perspective.) Fletcher (1984) also showed that subjects were likely to interpret an unmarked form such as a zero anaphor as coreferential with the immediately preceding topic. (See also Fletcher 1985.)

Hobbs (1979) noted that the interpretation of an anaphoric pronoun is not a problem that stands alone; rather, it happens during the computation of coherence relations—a ubiquitous process, as I've indicated. Coming from the perspective of workers in artificial intelligence, Grosz (1981) and Sidner (1983; Grosz & Sidner 1986) have proposed that the construct of "focus" or "attentional space" is necessary for determining coherence relations among elements in a text. According to Grosz, the focus space of a comprehender is a subset of all the knowledge relevant to a discourse and encoded in a database (memory). The focus space is meant to constrain the search for antecedents when a pronoun or other anaphor occurs. Grosz & Sidner suggest that there is a set of focus spaces and a set of rules for adding and deleting such spaces. These are needed to account for how comprehenders deal with complex discourse that may include interruptions—one focus space is put on a "memory stack" from which it can later be recovered. Focussing is the process of manipulating such spaces.

Related to the construct of focus is that of prominence. Morrow (1985a,b) has argued that cues such as verb aspect and preposition are used to make parts of a description prominent, and that the prominent elements are likely to be picked as the appropriate antecedents for pronouns. For example, if *John {walked/was walking} past the living room into the kitchen* is followed by a phrase referring to location (e.g. *there*), the choice of antecedent (living room vs kitchen) is influenced by the verb aspect. Grosz & Sidner note that coherence is determined by many variables. "The overall processing model must be one of constraint satisfaction that can operate on partial information"

(p. 188). I have noted that lexical and syntactic factors may play a role in determining coherence, but that the discourse representation and the visible world are also sources of such constraint. The question is, how do these combine in actual comprehension, what mechanisms are used, and what is the time course of their operation?

Grosz & Sidner do not relate their work to that of Kintsch & van Dijk (1978; van Dijk & Kintsch 1983), who have also worked on mechanisms of coherence and who have emphasized the importance of a psychologically motivated equivalent of a focus space. They have suggested a mechanism by which certain information in a discourse stays active in working memory. According to their model, the incoming message is broken down into its constitutent propositions. Certain elements of the propositions are held in a working memory. When an element from the next set of propositions matches one in working memory, coherence has been established and comprehension proceeds apace. If no match is found, then longer-term memory (or another part of the focus stack, to use Grosz's framework) must be searched or an inference made in order to obtain coherence. (Kintsch, van Dijk, and their colleagues propose another important mechanism as well; I turn to it momentarily.)

One difficulty with using propositions to account for coherence has been pointed out by Johnson-Laird (1983). He notes that it can be disastrously misleading to assume that overlap in propositional elements is the same as overlap in reference. Johnson-Laird points out that in the text *Roland's wife died in 1928. He married again in 1940. His wife now lives in Spain*, it would be a significant error to assume coreference between the two wives. He and others have argued that additional theoretical mechanisms are needed. This was recognized to a large extent by van Dijk & Kintsch (also 1983), who added a second level of representation—a "situation model"—to their theory. It is related to the construct of a mental model discussed below.

STORY GRAMMAR   The resurgence of interest in discourse has brought with it a variety of approaches that attempt to account for coherence and organization as well as the causal structure of stories and other genres. One influential approach has been that of the story grammar (e.g. Mandler & Johnson 1977, 1980). This approach attempts to state the essential components of a story and to specify the relations among them. The assumption is that stories contain natural subunits and that these are divided into a variety of types (e.g. settings, events, goals). Further, the claim is made that certain stories have a structure that is invariant across their content. Stein & Policastro (1984) have summarized a variety of approaches to the "concept of a story" and have described work on how that concept may change with development. Empirical evidence cited in support of the story grammar approach includes work on the organization of recall and work on comprehension. For example, Mandler & Goodman (1982) argued that the organization of a story affects reading times. They found that the first sentences of story constituents were slower to read and recall than the second (a result that has been replicated by others). They claimed further that the faster reading times for the second sentences could not be accounted for in terms of simple overlap in lexical items. (This claim may be questioned since the control items were presented in short, two-sentence versions taken from the longer stories.)

Garnham (1983a) and Johnson-Laird (1983) join Black & Wilensky (1979), Sanford & Garrod (1981), and others in pointing out inadequacies of the story grammar approach. Garnham's major criticism is that the analogy between grammars for sentences and for stories does not hold. In a grammar for sentences a finite set of lexical items can be looked up in a (mental) dictionary and information about them can be used in parsing and otherwise comprehending the sentence. However, since the story grammars have propositions as their basic elements, and since there is an unlimited number of propositions, no look-up procedure is possible. Garnham and other critics do not deny that stories have structures; they deny that the mechanisms of story grammars are necessary to capture those structures. Garnham again appeals to such notions as referential coherence and plausibility to account for the organization of stories.

SCHEMAS AND MACROPROPOSITIONS   Another major approach to discourse is that of the schema. According to Kintsch & van Dijk, schematic knowledge is used in conjunction with "macrorules" to yield a macrostructure for a text, a topic around which the information is organized. Macrorules yield a summary of the text and act to keep relevant information in working memory—where it can be used in anaphoric processes, for example—while discarding irrelevant information. A number of investigators (e.g. Cirilo 1981) have found evidence consistent with the claim that higher-level materials play a special role in comprehension. Much of the relevant work is summarized in van Dijk & Kintsch (1983). Subsequently, Guindon & Kintsch (1984) presented evidence that subjects form macroproposilons during reading. After reading paragraphs, they were given a word recognition test in which two words from summarizing statements were presented on successive trials. Even when the summarizing statements had not occurred explicity, words from the macropropositons yielded a higher false-alarm rate than thematically related distractor words. Graesser (1981) has described a schema-pointer-plus-tag model in order to account for the recall of stories, among other facts. According to Graesser, memory traces have pointers to general schematic knowledge, plus tags for moderately typical items and other tags for atypical items.

On the other side of the ledger, critics have pointed out that our knowledge is often used to understand material for which we have no obvious script; that the real problem amounts to determining how we decide what information in memory is relevant to understanding the present story or discourse; and that van Dijk & Kintsch have not provided the macrorules in detail (a state of affairs they recognize).

MENTAL MODELS   Johnson-Laird (1983) has championed the mental model approach to understanding discourse. His theory of comprehension assumes that two levels of representation are required, a relatively superficial level of propositions, and a deeper level, that of the mental model. According to him, understanding fiction involves essentially the same process as understanding true assertions ["The way you understand, say, *War and Peace,* is much the same as the way you understand an obvious work of fiction such as your daily newspaper" (p. 246)]—namely, a mental model is constructed. This model contains elements standing for the entities introduced in the discourse; it is a single representative sample from the set of models that could be built consistent with the assertions in the discourse. According to Johnson-Laird, "The coherence of prose depends primarily on its pattern of co-reference" (p. 371). He is fond of pointing out a fact well known to students of semantics: Quite different propositions, descriptions, and even names can be used to refer to the same entity in the discourse model. For example, *the shark* and *the ferocious fish* may be used to refer to the same entity. The latter may be used to keep the former "in focus" as the discourse goes on. The interpretation of the latter phrase will depend upon the referent of the former one in the discourse model, according to Johnson-Laird. The importance of the referent (the *extension,* in the parlance of semantics) is stressed extensively by Johnson-Laird. As mentioned above, van Dijk & Kintsch have also emphasized the extension in their more recent writing. Important work on the representation of discourse referents has been carried out by philosophers such as Kamp (1981) and Barwise & Perry (1983). To date these have not been well integrated into psycholinguistic work.

The processing of individual words is affected by the discourse context in which they occur (e.g. Foss 1982). Other workers have found related phenomena—e.g. that facilitation of a word occurs only when a sentence prime preceding it is understood in its context (Auble & Franks 1983). Hannigan et al (1980) presented subjects with sentences, then later gave test items in white noise and asked subjects to repeat them. The sentences were difficult to relate to one another unless a framework was presented in which the relations among the actions could be interpreted sensibly. For example, one sentence was *The man cut the basketball in half.* This could be interpreted in the Desert Island scenario as an attempt to find a container for water. One interesting result is that novel sentences that could be understood in terms of the framework were better repeated than sentences not fitting the framework. Too, Murphy (1984) has shown that establishing a new discourse referent takes time, as does accessing two vs one antecedents in the discourse (or mental model). In addition, Greenspan & Segal (1984) have argued that the discourse referents strongly influence the representation of visually presented nonlinguistic events.

CAUSAL RELATIONS   Earlier I indicated that coherence in discourse requires coreference and a framework of general causal knowledge. That is, a coherent discourse not only refers to a set of actors but also has them act in an interpretable way. When listeners or readers do not have the cultural or technical knowledge that enables them to make sense of the activities in the discourse, it will not be understood even if the same referents are used again and again. Often the correct, relevant background information is the naive physics and psychology shared by most members of the culture. Some workers in the 1980s have been concerned with specifying the types of causal relations that are important in discourse and how they are used to build a coherent representation of a discourse. Trabasso et al (1984) have specified a set of criteria for judging the existence of a causal relation between events. They presuppose a "causal field," a possible world (mental model?) within which the discourse takes place. In that model, events become linked together in a causal model or causal chain by application of the criteria. Trabasso et al provide evidence that the events in a story linked by more causal connections are better recalled than events with fewer such connections. Indeed, they found a linear relation between recall and causal connectedness. Trabasso & Sperry (1985) found that judgments of event importance in a folktale were also predicted by the causal network analysis. And Trabasso & van den Brock (1985) assessed the extent to which causal chains, causal network, story grammar, and "hierarchical problem solving" approaches predict data such as recall, summarization, and judged importance of events. This approach is compatible with a mental-model approach, augmented with rules of inference. Others have also obtained data on the effects of causal relatedness. Keenan et al (1984) showed that reading time for a sentence was affected by the degree of causal relatedness to its predecessor, the times being shorter when the relationship was more transparent. Similarly, Haberlandt & Bingham (1984) found that passages are read more rapidly when material is presented consistent with the causal order in the underlying events [though see Dixon (1982) for a somewhat different finding].

Although I have stressed the importance of causal cohesion in the understanding and representation of discourse, there is evidence that people frequently are not good at determining the logical structure of what they hear.

Epstein et al (1984) have shown that subjects often do not detect contradictory material in texts, even when instructed to do so. As one might expect, the likelihood of detecting a contradiction is a function of the importance of the material and its recency. Other workers have investigated when inferences are made during comprehension (e.g. McKoon & Ratcliff 1980; Singer & Ferreira 1983; Seifert et al 1985). There is not strong evidence for "forward" or predictive inferences. This work thus coheres rather well with the body of literature on coherence.

Conversational Coherence

A discussion of referring and its role in coherence would not be complete without mention of the work of Clark and his colleagues on conversations (e.g. Clark & Wilkes-Gibbs 1986; Clark 1983; Clark et al 1983; for a summary of some of this work see Clark 1985). The major theme of this work is that the participants collaborate in finding a common ground; their interpretations of essentially all meaningful utterance elements (e.g. definite noun phrases) depend upon their success in this collaboration. Clark has argued that comprehension cannot be driven by the interpretations of lexical items that are stored, since words are often used in an extended fashion (e.g. *the ham sandwich* may be used to refer to the person who ordered such a sandwich). Clark boldly asserts that "what a speaker means bears no direct relation to the sentence meanings assigned to it in the traditional view of sentences" (1983, p. 312) In order to understand, comprehenders must reconstruct a hierarchy of goals held by the speaker, and this is a collaborative process in general. Clark's views may not be correct if taken literally (irony intended), but they have not received the response they deserve in the literature.

To summarize, there has been a great deal of activity in the 1980s looking at the organization of discourse. A number of facts about discourse organization and processing seem secure. In addition, the theories seem to be converging; they all emphasize the role of mental models (referents), causal cohesion, inference making, and the importance of a mechanism like working memory. Working out the representational and processing mechanisms is the present challange.

READING

The topic of reading has continued to spawn a substantial amount of research. Major topics include the relationship between lexical access in the auditory and lexical access in the visual modalities, the relationship between reading comprehension and other cognitive skills, the mechanisms associated with the reading disability known as dyslexia, and the use of accurate on-line measurements of eye movements during reading to elucidate the reading process. I emphasize access codes and eye tracking though neither gets the attention it deserves (for recent summaries of many issues see Gough 1984; Just & Carpenter 1987; Perfetti 1985; Kieras & Just 1984; Mitchell 1982).

Access Codes

Alphabetic writing systems like the one used with English provide a more-or-less direct relation between the spoken and written forms of the language (the complexities of this relation for English are substantial and often remarked upon). Such a relation permits one to entertain the view that reading is mediated by the existing system of comprehension, including nearly the same process of lexical access. That could happen if there is an early stage in silent reading at which the letters (graphemes) are converted into a phonological representation. After that, the process of understanding would be the same as it is in the auditory mode. Nonalphabetic systems prove that lexical access can occur by another, nonphonologically mediated route. One question concerns how access does in fact occur in English. McCusker et al (1981) summarized work up to that time, concluding (p. 217) that "the data point to a dual access model in which high-frequency words enjoy high-speed access via a visually based representation, whereas low-frequency words are accessed using a slower, phonological recoding process." The dual access model says that both phonologically mediated and nonmediated access occurs.

If high-frequency words are directly accessed, there is no doubt that a phonological representation is made available once access occurs (this is necessary in order to read aloud, and to account for the experience of "hearing" words that one reads silently. Read (1983) showed that the phonological representation is what is scanned internally when carrying out the following task: Read the next sentence and count the number of instances of the letter F within it: FINISHED FILES ARE THE RESULT OF YEARS OF SCIENTIFIC STUDY COMBINED WITH THE EXPERIENCE OF YEARS. The majority of adults get the incorrect answer (the modal response is three when the correct number is six). The missing Fs are always those in the highly frequent word OF. OF, of course, is pronounced with a /v/, suggesting strongly that the item is missed because the phonetic representation is examined rather than a representation of the printed word. That is a powerful effect, given that the stimulus is in front of the subject at the time the Fs are counted.

One reason why spelling-to-sound rules have been thought necessary is that readers of English can pronounce novel words (like *glushko)* and pseudowords. These cannot have been learned by rote. Glushko (1979) and others have challenged the view that spelling-to-sound rules are used in lexical access at any point, even for pseudowords, arguing instead that the pronunciation of such items is carried out by analogy to similar real words. Thus, *jie* is graphemically similar to *tie, pie,* etc, and will be pronounced similarly as well. Rosson (1983) found evidence that the pronunciation of a pseudoword like *louch* can be influenced by which of two analogous words (e.g. *touch, couch*) is primed. If *sofa* is presented immediately before *louch,* then the latter is pronounced to rhyme with *couch,* presumably because *sofa* primes *couch* by spreading activation and then that item is chosen as the analogous one. Rosson (1985) later found that the influence of an analogous lexical item was tempered by the strength of the grapheme-to-phoneme rules and the frequency of use of the item.

However, as Gough & Tunmer (1986), Rosson (1985), and others have noted, the "analogy" model may beg the question, for it is not clear in general how to pick an analogous lexical item. Generally, analogies can be evaluated only with respect to some set of principles. Thus, the notion of analogy appears to presuppose the construct of rules. The model of McClelland & Rumelhart (1981) and other connectionist approaches may be subject to the same criticism.

Seidenberg & Tanenhaus (1979) found evidence consistent with the somewhat unintuitive conclusion that the orthographic code is activated during auditory word recognition. Subjects in an auditorily presented rhyme detection task were faster when the test word was orthographically similar to the cue word (e.g. *pie - tie)* than when it was not (e.g. *rye - tie).* This led them to conclude that multiple codes are activated during word recognition and that priming occurs to words that are either orthographically or phonologically similar. Subsequently, Seidenberg (1985a) and his colleagues (Seidenberg et al 1984a; Waters & Seidenberg 1985) proposed a parallel interactive model of word recognition dubbed the "time course" model. Although it resembles the dual access model, there is an important difference. In the time course model both orthographic and phonological information are always activated upon the presentation of a visual stimulus, but there are different rise times associated with the two types of activation, orthography generally being faster. Phonological effects occur "whenever the duration of processing exceeds the latency of phonological code activation. Thus, phonological effects should be found for lower frequency words and for poorer readers . . ." (Waters & Seidenberg 1985, p. 557). Norris & Brown (1985) have critiqued the time course model, and Seidenberg (1985b) has replied effectively.

However it occurs, decoding the visual stimulus in order to recover the lexical item and the information associated with it is clearly a key element in reading. One of the boldest approaches to the theory of reading—the "simple view" (Gough & Tunmer 1986)—conjectures that what is unique to reading is *simply* the decoding of words; after that, reading comprehension is essentially equivalent to listening comprehension. Thus, one cannot be a good decoder, a good listener, and a poor reader. For related work, see Palmer et al (1985). Since the early days of reading research there has been a controversy over whether the shape of a word is used in lexical access. Underwood & Bargh (1982) and others have found evidence that the visual route to access is used only when word-shape information is present. However, among fluent readers Paap et al (1984) found no effects of shape frequency on tachistoscopic recognition and lexical decision latency.

Eye Tracking

Word shape (more accurately, word length) is used, though, in deciding where to place the next fixation during normal reading (Rayner 1983a,b). For readers of English, the perceptual span has been found to be approximately 4 characters to the left of the fixation point and 12–15 characters to its right (with those beyond six characters primarily used to determine where to fixate next). This result has come from studies of eye tracking, an area that has burgeoned in the past 10 years. The advent of accurate eye trackers permits very fine measures of where the reader is looking during reading (each millisecond the fixation point can be known to within 10 minutes of arc—i.e. to within half a character for normal text). In addition, computer-controlled displays have permitted precise control over when information is presented to the eye, including displays that change during the saccadic eye movements.

In the above sections of this review I have often cited works whose dependent variables were obtained by measuring one or another aspect of eye movement. I've assumed that readers of this review understand the basic facts about saccadic eye movements in reading [see Foss & Hakes (1978) for a brief summary]. Here I mention only a few additional issues. This is not meant to slight work with eye tracking devices. I believe that significant advances in our understanding of reading (and language processing generally) are likely to arise from the eye tracking laboratories.

Using eye trackers, researchers measure the likelihood that a word has been fixated, the fixation duration, regressive eye movements, the total time a word is examined (gaze duration), and other variables—indeed, the import of the various measures has not been settled. Just & Carpenter (1980, 1984) have proposed and defended the "immediacy" and the "eye-mind" assumptions. Immediacy says that a reader tries to interpret each word as he or she encounters it, and eye-mind says that the interpretation of a word occurs while that word is being fixated. Rayner & Carroll (1984) argue that the eye-mind hypothesis is not correct *in toto,* that there is some "cognitive lag." In their study of pronoun assignment, Ehrlich & Rayner (1983) concluded that comprehension processes outlast the fixation on the pronoun of interest. With computer-controlled displays and the use of masking stimuli, it is possible to control exactly when the reader gets the visual input. McConkie et al (1985) and others have delayed information to the foveal and parafoveal areas and examined the absolute times at which stimulus information is used by the reader. Among other observations, McConkie et al found data consistent with the cognitive lag hypothesis. Finally, McClelland & O'Regan (1981a,b) have argued that information from sentence context combines interactively with information in parafoveal vision to speed lexical access [see Rayner & Slowiaczek (1981) for a critique]. Work of the type cited in this paragraph will help build a bridge to the future cognitive neuropsychology. Other methodological advances have been made in studying the reading process; see Kieras & Just (1984) for a survey.

LANGUAGE PRODUCTION

Research on production is becoming more common, though it still is much scarcer than work on comprehension and acquisition. Dell (1985) estimates that only 5% of published papers deal with production. This may be surprising, since produced language is measureable in a way that comprehended language is not. Of course, in the case of production we do not know the input to the language production mechanisms, only the output. Thus, determining the operation of the input-to-output processes is as unconstrained as in the case of comprehension, where we are in the opposite position. Theorizing about production has been influenced strongly by research on dysfluencies and other errors as much as by error-free products of speech. [See Butterworth (1980a) for a review of some techniques of studying production.]

At low levels the units of speech production may overlap—e.g. the well-known coarticulation effects. But at higher levels speech is "linear"; one clause at a time is emitted. Thus speakers must encode information so that listeners can understand it when receiving just one word at a time. Levelt (1982) distinguishes conceptualizing from formulating the linguistic message. The former includes "the development of communicative intentions, the selection of the appropriate information from the knowledge base, and the linearization of this information." The latter "give[s] form to the generated intentions and contents. Among the activities involved will be the choice of surface structure and of lexical units, the specification of morphological structure, the programming of phonological and prosodic patterns, and the construction of an articulatory program" (pp. 201–2). Levelt also states a theoretical preference based on modularity. "I would like to see as much as possible work done by the conceptual preliminaries, so that the formulating mechanism can operate in a highly automatized fashion on highly specified conceptual input" (p. 202). The goal of much of the work reviewed here has been to describe "how we recruit our knowledge of language structure in order to build sentences, given some rather specific representation of message content" (Garrett 1982, p. 19).

The Linearization Problem

One of the issues addressed recently concerns the determinants of order of mention—the linearization problem. A number of perspectives have been brought to bear on this issue. One is the given-new distinction, which says that the given is mentioned before the new because given information is more readily available in the speaker's memory—a circumstance that also helps the listener to retrieve the appropriate memory location for the addition of new information. The question of when lexical units and surface structures are chosen, and of the relation between these, is a chestnut in psychology, tying into a version of the Whorf-Sapir hypothesis that thought is determined by language. Can linearization occur without knowledge of the inventory of lexical items available to the speaker? The absence of a particular lexical item to express a "communicative intention" may require that a phrase be constructed to express that intention.

Bock (1982) has provided an extensive review of the "cognitive psychology of syntax." She argues that linearization does not take place at the level of conceptual planning; instead there are interactions between syntactic and lexical processing. In favor of this conclusion are data suggesting that when lexical items are more easily retrievable, they tend to occur first in the surface form of the utterance. There is even evidence (Pinker & Birdsong 1979) that speakers prefer to place shorter words in front of longer ones (most idioms instantiate this preference—e.g. *salt* before *pepper, bread* before *butter*). Bock thus concludes that syntactic and lexical processes take place at the same time and interact. Bock & Warren (1985) have argued that what is influenced by ease of accessibility is the assignment of grammatical relations (subject, direct object, indirect object) rather than linearization per se.

Levelt & Maassen (1981) addressed the same issue in a study in which subjects were asked to describe moving figures using more-or-less easily retrievable names for them. No effect of difficulty of lexical search was observed on order of mention, and the authors concluded that their speakers decided on order of mention irrespective of difficulty of lexical retrieval. They also found evidence that speakers can change syntactic "frames" during speech if there is difficulty retrieving an appropriate lexical item (e.g. can switch from a structure in which NPs are coordinates to one in which sentences are coordinates). This is consistent with a view that lexicalization can affect some aspects of syntactic planning, but that ease of lexical retrieval does not influence decisions about order of mention. This matter is far from resolved by the few relevant studies. In related work, Kempen & Huijbers (1983) carried out studies in which subjects described simple scenes. They found evidence for the view that the lexicon is consulted twice, once when matching an item to the semantic and syntactic requirements of the phrase, and again to recover morphological and phonological information.

Speech Errors and Hesitation Phenomena

Models of production rely heavily on the existence of hesitation phenomena and speech errors. Indeed, the models proposed have tended to concentrate on one or another of these sources of data. Garrett (1982) reviews such efforts and makes an initial attempt to examine and contrast their assumptions. With respect to the selection and insertion of lexical items into speech he continues to make use of his well-known model that distinguishes between "message," "functional," and "positional" levels (see also Garrett 1980a,b). The functional level is a planning stage at which the conceptual identity of lexical items is selected, and their phrasal roles determined. Multiple phrases (two, according to Garrett) may be present simultaneously at this stage. The positional level is a planning stage during which serial order for a single phrase is determined and a phrase-level stress assignment is made. All models of production must explain the fact that some speech errors appear to be meaning based (an error at the functional level) and some sound based (an error at a later stage, whose location Garrett and others have debated extensively).

Nearly everyone accepts Garrett's idea the slips occur when elements are present simultaneously so that they may "computationally interact." Shattuck-Hufnagel (1979, 1983) has proposed that insertion is carried out by a "scan-copier" that serially selects segments and inserts them into a suprasegmental framework. Thus, segments are fitted into a set of slots. Errors can occur when elements exchange. However, there are strong constraints on the types of exchanges, such that the characteristics of the frameworks must be honored. This is used to explain certain well-known facts—e.g. that initial segments interchange with initial segments and never with final ones in exchange errors. [Shattuck-Hufnagel notes, following Cutler (1980), that misassignment of stress within words may be due to the incorrect item being retrieved from the lexicon rather than a late error involving the exchange of stress values.]

Dell (1986) has made an ambitious effort to account for speech errors within an interactive activation framework. He has two basic types of mechanisms, one involving categorical rules that result in a frame (similar in spirit to Shattuck-Hufnagel's proposal), and one involving insertion rules. The latter requires a network of nodes at various levels of linguistic abstraction (e.g. phonology, morphology, whole words) and connections between the nodes. Activation spreads among the nodes both "upwards" and "downwards." In Dell's model, elements are inserted into the framework when they have the highest level of activation. Errors occur when incorrect items win this battle. When an item has been inserted it is tagged and its activation level goes to zero. In that way various types of exchange errors are accounted for. Dell builds into his model the assumption that items at the syntacic level can only compete with others sharing the same syntactic class. His model is subject to the criticism that it presupposes all of the units and structures devised by others—i.e. that its organization is ad hoc. He does, though, make predictions—e.g. that lexical bias should increase as speech is slowed—and finds evidence to support those predictions.

The role of lexical bias in speech errors has been studied experimentally by Motley et al (1982; Motley et al 1983). These authors argue that errors of anticipation, perseveration, and exchange occur (perhaps at levels specified by Garrett) and that an editing mechanism verifies the linguistic integrity (though not necessarily the message-level soundness) of planned speech and prevents output that violates that integrity. These authors devised a technique for stimulating speech errors in lists of words and have shown that errors are more likely to be produced when they are linguistically legitimate than when they are not. They have also demonstrated a higher frequency for socially acceptable than for socially taboo errors, a conclusion suggesting that there is a message-level editor as well. The matter of output editing has been discussed in detail by Levelt (1983), and I return to his work below.

At some point during the production process a representation at the message level is formed, perhaps with order of mention determined and abstract, prephonological lexical items selected. The message level is then transformed into a linguistic level, with its associated prosodic form and phonologically defined lexical items. Evidence concerning hesitation phenomena has typically been used to support models at this level. Garrett (1982) reviewed the evidence deriving from this tradition. Since the work of Goldman-Eisler (1968) data have accumulated supporting the idea that hesitations reflect a stage of planning for the phrasal, clausal, or multiclausal production of speech. In addition, hesitations reflect the overall difficulty of planning the message ("decision-making minicrises," in Garrett's apt term) and word-finding difficulties [see papers in Dechert & Raupach (1980) for representative work; see also Beattie (1980)]. Garrett has summarized the work noting that hesitations may reflect three modes: "Don't bother me, I'm busy" (long-range multilevel planning that has absorbed all the speaker's resouces); "Wait till the boat's loaded" (the planning-unit account); and "It's in the mail" (hesitation due to the necessity to coordinate all units including within-phrase word-finding difficulties). Obviously, with so many sources of hesitation, such data will rarely be able to refute any proposal about the production process.

Gee & Grosjean (1983) have proposed an explicit algorithm to account for pauses. They devised the term "performance structures" to refer to the sentence structures derived from experimental data such as pause durations. The algorithm is based on the construct of a phonological phrase (F-phrase), an intermediate level between the word and the syntactic phrase. The production system operates in part on "smallish, rhythmical chunks, bigger than a single lexical item, but smaller than the typical phrase . . ." (p. 454). In any syntactic phrase, all the material up to and including the head is an F-phrase. Essentially, it is a stress group. These elements are assembled into larger units, intonational phrases or I-phrases. It is important to note that the algorithm makes essential use of syntactic constructs. Gee & Grosjean report high correlations between the predications of their model and pause data.

Rhythmic factors affect sentence production and must be incorporated into a model of production. McNeill (1985) argued that gestures and speech are part of the same psychological structure. Using Garrett's analogy, gestures and speech share a computational stage. McNeill provides evidence that in both "referential and discourse oriented gestures . . . the hands function as symbols that are closely connected to the speech channel in terms of both time and semantic and pragmatic function" (p. 350). Thus, gestures are not "nonverbal."

One interesting paradigm to emerge in recent work on production is that of self-repairs. Levelt (1983) has studied this problem and tied the process of self-repair to more general issues in production. A self-repair occurs when one notes an error in one's own speech (thereby implicating a self-monitoring process). When this happens the typical chain of events is to interrupt oneself, to pause (usually including a filler phrase such as "uh" or "no"), and to make the repair. Levelt observed the point at which the error was detected in order to examine the monitoring process and he noted the ways repairs are made. With respect to monitoring, Levelt concluded that one does not have access to the language-production process; rather one parses one's own inner (or overt) speech. He made the important discovery of a regularity in the repair process. When an error is detected and signalled, there are constraints on how the repair is carried out. Levelt's well-formedness rule for errors is associated with how structures are coordinated. Thus, for example, the utterance *Did you go right, uh go left?* is associated with the syntactically correct form, *Did you go right and go left?* On the other hand, *Did you go right, uh you go left?* is associated with the incorrect form, *Did you go right and you go left?* An error of the former type was observed, not the latter.[3] Levelt also noted that the features of the repairs "make it in principle possible for the listener to predict the insertion . . . relation between the repair proper and the original utterance no latter than upon the first word after restart" (p. 95)—clearly an advantage. For another approach to disfluencies, see Fay (1980a,b) and Stemberger (1982).

In this review I have focussed upon the high-level determinants of produc-

---

[3]More specifically, Levelt's rule is: A repair $<\alpha\gamma>$ is well formed if and only if there is a string β such that the string $<\alpha$ β and $\gamma>$ is well formed, where β is a completion of the constituent directly dominating the last element of α.

tion, not the interesting and important processes of motor control. The latter are discussed in such works as MacNeilage (1983), Meyer & Gordon (1985), and Shaffer (1984). I have not discussed the important topics of acquisition [see Wanner & Gleitman (1982) and Maratsos (1983) for summaries] neurolinguistics, reading disabilities, aphasia, animal "language," etc. Many works in these areas bear directly on issues discussed explicitly here. (But, as my mother used to say, what else can you scratch but the surface?) Clearly, Esper would be amazed.

ACKNOWLEDGMENT

Preparation of this chapter was made possible by a generous grant (of time) from my family. They are not responsible for most of the errors or omissions.

Literature Cited

Adams, S., Powers, F. F. 1929. The psychology of language. *Psychol. Bull.* 26:241–60
Anderson, J. R., Pirolli, P. L. 1984. Spread of activation. *J. Exp. Psychol.:Learn. Mem. Cognit.* 10:791–98
Auble, P., Franks, J. J. 1983. Sentence comprehension processes. *J. Verb. Learn. Verb. Behav.* 22:395–405
Balota, D. A., Chumbley, J. I. 1984. Are lexical decisions a good measure of lexical access? The role of word frequency in the neglected decision stage. *J. Exp. Psychol.:Hum. Percept. Perform.* 10:340–57
Balota, D. A., Chumbley, J. I. 1985. The locus of word-frequency effects in the pronunciation task: Lexical access and/or production? *J. Mem. Lang.* 24:89–106
Balota, D. A., Lorch, R. F. 1986. Depth of automatic spreading activation: Mediated priming effects in pronunciation but not in lexical decisions. *J. Exp. Psychol.:Learn. Mem. Cognit.* 12:336–45
Balota, D. A., Pollatsek, A., Rayner, K. 1985. The interaction of contextual constraints and parafoveal visual information in reading. *Cognit. Psychol.* 17:364–90
Barwise, J., Perry, J. 1983. *Situations and Attitudes*. Cambridge, Mass: MIT Press
Beattie, G. W. 1980. The role of language production processes in the organisation of behaviour in face-to-face interaction. See Butterworth 1980b, pp. 69–107
Becker, C. A. 1980. Semantic context effects in visual word recognition: an analysis of semantic strategies. *Mem. Cogn.* 8:493–512
Berwick, R. C., Weinberg, A. S. 1983a. The role of grammars in models of language use. *Cognition* 13:1–61
Berwick, R. C., Weinberg, A. S. 1983b. Reply to Garnham. *Cognition* 15:271–76
Black, J. B., Wilensky, R. 1979. An evalua-

tion of story grammars. *Cognit. Sci.* 3:213–30
Bock, J. K. 1982. Toward a cognitive psychology of syntax: Information processing contributions to sentence formulation. *Psychol. Rev.* 89:1–47
Bock, J. K., Warren, R. K. 1985. Conceptual accessibility and syntactic structure in sentence formulation. *Cognition* 21:47–67
Bouma, H., Bouwhuis, D. G., eds. 1984. *Attention and Performance, Vol. 10: Control of Language Processes*. Hillsdale, NJ: Erlbaum
Bradley, D. C., Forster, K. I. 1987. A reader's view of listening. *Cognition* 25:103–34
Brown, G. 1983. Prosodic structure and the given/new distinction. See Cutler 1983, pp. 67–77
Butterworth, B. 1980a. Evidence from pauses in speech. See Butterworth 1980b, pp. 155–176
Butterworth, B., ed. 1980b. *Language Production. Vol. 1: Speech and Talk*. London: Academic
Buxton, H. 1983. Temporal predictability in the perception of English speech. See Cutler 1983, pp. 113–21
Cairns, H. S. 1984. Current issues in research in language comprehension. In *Recent Advances in Language Sciences*, ed. R. Naremore. San Diego: College Hill Press
Cairns, H. S., Cowart, W., Jablon, A. D. 1981. Effect of prior context upon the integration of lexical information during sentence processing. *J. Verb. Learn. Verb. Behav.* 20:445–53
Chaffin, R., Herrmann, D. J. 1984. The similarity and diversity of semantic relations. *Mem. Cogn.* 12:134–41
Chomsky, N. 1965. *Aspects of the Theory of Syntax*. Cambridge, Mass: MIT Press

Cirilo, R. K. 1981. Referential coherence and text structure in story comprehension. *J. Verb. Learn. Verb. Behav.* 20:358–67

Clark, H. H. 1985. Language use and language users. In *Handbook of Social Psychology, Volume II,* ed. G. Lindzey, E. Aronson, pp. 179–231. New York: Random House. 3rd ed.

Clark, H. H. 1983. Making sense of nonce sense. See Flores D'Arcais & Jarvella 1983, pp. 297–331

Clark, H. H., Schreuder, R., Buttrick, S. 1983. Common ground and the understanding of demonstrative reference. *J. Verb. Learn. Verb. Behav.* 22:245–58

Clark, H. H., Wilkes-Gibbs, D. 1986. Referring as a collaborative process. *Cognition* 22:1–39

Clifton, C. Jr. 1988. Sentence processing: the early stages. In (Title unknown), ed. R. Hoffman, D. Palermo, Hillsdale, NJ: Erlbaum. In press

Clifton, C. Jr., Frazier, L., Connine, C. 1984. Lexical expectations in sentence comprehension. *J. Verb. Learn. Verb. Behav.* 23:696–708

Cole, R. A., ed. 1980. *Perception and Production of Fluent Speech.* Hillsdale, NJ: Erlbaum

Connine, C., Ferreira, F., Jones, C., Clifton, C., Frazier, L. 1984. Verb frame preferences: descriptive norms. *J. Psycholinguist. Res.* 13:307–19

Cooper, W. E., Sorenson, J. M. 1981. *Fundamental Frequency in Sentence Production.* Berlin/Heidelberg/New York: Springer

Cooper, W. E., Walker, E. C. T., ed. 1979. *Sentence Processing: Psycholinguistic Studies Presented to Merrill Garrett.* Hillsdale, NJ: Erlbaum

Corbett, A. T. 1984. Prenominal adjectives and the disambiguation of anaphoric nouns. *J. Verb. Learn. Verb. Behav.* 23:683–95

Corbett, A. T., Chang, F. R. 1983. Pronoun disambiguation: accessing potential antecedents. *Mem. Cogn.* 11:283–94

Cowart, W. 1982. Autonomy and interaction in the language processing system: a reply to Marslen-Wilson & Tyler. *Cognition* 12:109–17

Cowart, W., Cairns, H. S. 1988. Evidence for an anaphoric mechanism within syntactic processing: Some reference relations defy semantic and pragmatic constraints. *Mem. Cogn.* In press

Crain, S., Steedman, M. 1985. On not being led up the garden path: the use of context by the psychological syntax processor. See Dowty et al 1985, pp. 320–58

Cutler, A. 1980. Errors of stress and intonation. See Fromkin 1980, pp. 67–80

Cutler, A. 1983. Lexical complexity and sentence processing. See Flores D'Arcais & Jarvella 1983, pp. 43–79

Cutler, A., Clifton, C. C. 1984. The use of prosodic information in word recognition. See Bouma & Bouhuis 1984, pp. 183–92

Cutler, A., Ladd, D. R. 1983. *Prosody: Models and Measurements.* Berlin/New York: Springer-Verlag

Danks, J. H., Glucksberg, S. 1980. Experimental psycholinguistics. *Ann. Rev. Psychol.* 31:391–417

de Beaugrande, R. 1980. Text and discourse in European research. *Discourse Processes* 3:287–300

Dechert, H. W., Raupach, M., eds. 1980. *Temporal Variables in Speech. Studies in Honour of Frieda Goldman-Eisler.* New York: Mouton

de Groot, A. M. B., Thomassen, A J. W. M., Hudson, P. T. W. 1982. Associative facilitation of word recognition as measured from a neutral prime. *Mem. Cogn.* 10:358–70

de Groot, A. M. B. 1983. The range of automatic spreading activation in word priming. *J. Verb. Learn. Verb. Behav.* 22:417–36

Dell, G. S., McKoon, G., Ratcliff, R. 1983. The activation of antecedent information during the processing of anaphoric reference in reading. *J. Verb. Learn. Verb. Behav.* 22:121–32

Dell, G. S. 1986. A spreading-activation theory of retrieval in sentence production. *Psychol. Rev.* 93:283–321

Dell, G. S. 1985. Putting production back in psycholinguistics. Review of *Language Production, Vol. 2: Development, Writing, and Other Language Processes,* ed. B. Butterworth. *Contemp. Psychol.* 30:129–30

Diehl, R. L., Kluender, K. R., Foss, D. J., Gernsbacher, M. A., Parker, E. M. 1987. Vowels as islands of reliability. *J. Mem. Lang.* In press

Dixon, P. 1982. Plans and written direction for complex tasks. *J. Verb. Learn. Verb. Behav.* 21:70–84

Dowty, D., Kartunnen, L., Zwicky, A., eds. 1985. *Natural Language Parsing: Psychological, Theoretical, and Computational Perspectives.* New York: Cambridge Univ. Press

Dowty, D. R., Wall, R. E., Peters, S. 1981. *Introduction to Montague Semantics.* Dordrecht, Holland: Reidel

Ehrlich, K., Rayner, K. 1983. Pronoun assignment and semantic integration during reading: eye movements and immediacy of processing. *J. Verb. Learn. Verb. Behav.* 22:75–87

Epstein, W., Glenberg, A. M., Bradley, M. 1984. Coactivation and comprehension: contribution of text variables to the illusion of knowing. *Mem. Cogn.* 12:355–60

Estill, R. B., Kemper, S. 1982. Interpreting idioms. *J. Psycholinguist. Res.* 11:559–68

Esper, E. A. 1921. The psychology of language. *Psychol. Bull.* 18:490–96

Fay, D. 1980a. Performing transformations. See Cole 1980, pp. 441–68

Fay, D. 1980b. Transformational errors. See Fromkin 1980, pp. 111–22

Ferreira, F., Clifton, C. 1986. The independence of syntactic processing. *J. Mem. Lang.* 25:348–68

Feustel, T. C., Shiffrin, R. M., Salasoo, A. 1983. Episodic and lexical contributions to the repetition effect in word identification. *J. Exp. Psychol.:Gen.* 112:309–46

Fillenbaum, S. 1971. Psycholinguistics. *Ann. Rev. Psychol.* 22:251–308

Fischler, I. S., Bloom, P. A. 1985. Effects of constraint and validity of sentence contexts on lexical decisions. *Mem. Cognit.* 13:128–39

Fletcher, C. R. 1984. Markedness and topic continuity in discourse processing. *J. Verb. Learn. Verb. Behav.* 23:487–93

Fletcher, C. R. 1986. Strategies for the allocation of short-term memory during comprehension. *J. Mem. Lang.* 25:43–58

Flores D'Arcais, G., Jarvella, R. J., eds. 1983. *The Process of Language Understanding.* Chichester: Wiley

Fodor, J. A. 1983. *The Modularity of Mind: An Essay on Faculty Psychology.* Cambridge, Mass: Bradford

Fodor, J. A. 1978. Parsing strategies and constraints on transformations. *Linguist. Inquiry* 9:427–74

Ford, M., Bresnan, J., Kaplan, R. 1983. A competence-based theory of syntactic closure. In *The Mental Representation of Grammatical Relations,* ed. J. Bresnan, pp. 727–96. Cambridge, Mass: MIT Press

Forster, K. I. 1979. Levels of processing and the structure of the language processor. See Cooper & Walker 1979, pp. 27–85

Forster, K. I. 1981. Priming and the effects of sentence and lexical contexts on naming time: evidence for autonomous lexical processing. *Q. J. Exp. Psychol.* 33A:465–95

Forster, K. I., Davis, C. 1984. Repetition priming and frequency attenuation in lexical access. *J. Exp. Psychol.:Learn. Mem. Cognit.* 10:680–98

Foss, D. J. 1982. A discourse on semantic priming. *Cognit. Psychol.* 14:590–607

Foss, D. J., Hakes, D. T. 1978. *Psycholinguistics: An Introduction to the Psychology of Language.* Englewood Cliffs, NJ: Prentice-Hall

Foss, D. J., Harwood, D. A., Blank, M. A. 1980. Deciphering decoding decisions: Data and devices. See Cole 1980, pp. 165–99

Foss, D. J., Ross, J. R. 1983. Great expectations: Context effects during sentence processing. See Flores D'Arcais & Jarvella 1983, pp. 169–91

Fowler, C. A. 1983. Converging sources of evidence on spoken and perceived rhythms of speech: Cyclic production of vowels in monosyllabic stress feet. *J. Exp. Psychol.:Gen.* 112:386–412

Frazier, L., Clifton, C., Randall, J. 1983. Filling gaps: Decision principles and structure in sentence comprehension. *Cognition* 13:187–222

Frazier, L., Fodor, J. D. 1978. The sausage machine: A new two-stage model of the parser. *Cognition* 6:291–325

Frazier, L., Rayner, K. 1982. Making and correcting errors during sentence comprehension: Eye movements in the analysis of structurally ambiguous sentences. *Cognit. Psychol.* 14:178–210

Frederiksen, J. R. 1981. Understanding anaphora: Rules used by readers in assigning pronominal referents. *Discourse Processes* 4:323–47

Freedman, S. E., Forster, K. I. 1985. The psychological status of overgenerated sentences. *Cognition* 19:101–31

Fromkin, V. A., ed. 1980. *Errors in Linguistic Performance.* New York: Academic

Garnham, A. 1983a. What's wrong with story grammars. *Cognition* 15:145–54

Garnham, A. 1983b. Why psycholinguists don't care about DTC: A reply to Berwick and Weinberg. *Cognition* 15:263–69

Garrett, M. 1980a. Levels of processing in sentence production. See Butterworth 1980b, pp. 177–220

Garrett, M. 1980b. The limits of accommodation. See Fromkin 1980, pp. 263–71

Garrett, M. F. 1982. Production of speech: Observations from normal and pathological language use. In *Normality and Pathology in Cognitive Functions,* ed. A. W. Ellis, pp. 19–76. London: Academic

Gee, J. P., Grosjean, F. 1983. Performance structures: A psycholinguistic and linguistic appraisal. *Cognit. Psychol.* 15:411–58

Geffen, G., Luszcz, M. A. 1983. Are the spoken durations of rare words longer than those of common words? *Mem. Cognit.* 11:13–15

Gernsbacher, M. A. 1984. Resolving 20 years of inconsistent interactions between lexical familiarity and orthography, concreteness, and polysemy. *J. Exp. Psychol.:Gen.* 113:256–81

Gibbs, R. W. Jr., Gonzales, G. P. 1985. Syntactic frozenness in processing and remembering idioms. *Cognition* 20:243–59

Glass, A. L. 1983. The comprehension of idioms. *J. Psycholing. Res.* 12:429–40

Glucksberg, S., Gildea, P., Bookin, H. B. 1982. On understanding nonliteral speech: Can people ignore metaphors? *J. Verb. Learn. Verb. Behav.* 21:85–98

Glushko, R. J. 1979. The organization and activation of orthographic knowledge in reading aloud. *J. Exp. Psychol.:Hum. Percept. Perform.* 5:674–91

Goldman-Eisler, F. 1968. *Psycholinguistics.* London: Academic

Goodman, G. O., McClelland, J. L., Gibbs, R. W. Jr. 1981. The role of syntactic context in word recognition. *Mem. Cognit.* 9:580–86

Gordon, B. 1983. Lexical access and lexical decision: Mechanisms of frequency sensitivity. *J. Verb. Learn. Verb. Behav.* 22:24–44

Gough, P. B. 1984. Word recognition. In *Handbook of Reading Research,* ed. P. D. Pearson, pp. 225–53. New York: Longman

Gough, P., Alford, J. A., Holley-Wilcox, P. 1981. Words and context. In *Perception of Print,* ed. O. J. L. Tzeng, H. Singer, pp. 85–102. Hillsdale, NJ: Erlbaum

Gough, P. B., Tunmer, W. E. 1986. Decoding, reading, and reading disability. *Remedial Spec. Educ.* 7:6–10

Graesser, A. C. 1981. *Prose Comprehension Beyond the Word.* New York: Springer-Verlag

Greenspan, S. L., Segal, E. 1984. Reference and comprehension: A topic-comment analysis of sentence-picture verification. *Cognit. Psychol.* 16:556–606

Grosjean, F. 1980. Spoken word recognition processes and the gating paradigm. *Percept. Psychophys.* 28:267–83

Grosjean, F., Gee, J. P. 1987. Prosodic structure and spoken word recognition. *Cognition* 25:135–56

Grosz, B. J. 1981. Focusing and description in natural language dialogues. In *Elements of Discourse Understanding,* ed. A. Joshi, B. Webber, I. Sag, pp. 84–105. New York: Cambridge Univ. Press

Grosz, B. J., Sidner, C. L. 1986. Attention, intention, and the structure of discourse. *Comput. Linguist.* 12:175–204

Guindon, R., Kintsch, W. 1984. Priming macropropositions: Evidence for the primacy of macropropositions in the memory for text. *J. Verb. Learn. Verb. Behav.* 23:508–18

Gurjanov, M., Lukatela, G., Lukatela, K., Savíc, M. 1985a. Grammatical priming of inflected nouns by the gender of possessive adjectives. *J. Exp. Psychol.:Learn. Mem. Cognit.* 11:692–701

Gurjanov, M., Lukatela, G., Moskovljevíc, J., Savíc, M. 1985b. Grammatical priming of inflected nouns by inflected adjectives. *Cognition* 19:55–71

Haberlandt, K., Bingham, G. 1984. The effect of input direction on the processing of script statements. *J. Verb. Learn. Verb. Behav.* 23:162–77

Hannigan, M. L., Shelton, T. S., Franks, J. J., Bransford, J. D. 1980. The effects of

episodic and semantic theory on the identification of sentences masked by white noise. *Mem. Cognit.* 8:278–84

Hirst, D. 1983. Structures and categories in prosodic representation. See Cutler 1983, pp. 93–109

Hobbs, J. 1979. Coherence and co-reference. *Cognit. Sci.* 3:67–82

Holmes, V. M. 1984. Parsing strategies and discourse context. *J. Psycholing. Res.* 13:237–57

Hudson, P. T. W., Bergman, M. W. 1985. Lexical knowledge in word recognition: Word length and word frequency in naming and lexical decision tasks. *J. Mem. Lang.* 24:46–58

Inhoff, A. W., Lima, S. D., Carroll, P. J. 1984. Contextual effects on metaphor comprehension in reading. *Mem. Cognit.* 12:558–67

Jackson, A., Morton, J. 1984. Facilitation of auditory word recognition. *Mem. Cognit.* 12:568–74

Johnson-Laird, P. N. 1974. Experimental psycholinguistics. *Ann. Rev. Psychol.* 25:135–60

Johnson-Laird, P. N. 1983. *Mental models: Toward a cognitive science of language, inference, and consciousness.* Cambridge, Mass: Harvard Univ. Press

Johnson-Laird, P. N. 1987. The mental representation of the meaning of words. *Cognition* 25:189–211

Johnson-Laird, P. N., Herrmann, D., Chaffin, R. 1984. Only connections: A critique of semantic works. *Psychol. Bull.* 96:292–315

Johnston, J. C., van Santen, J. P. H., Hale, B. L. 1985. Repetition effects in word and pseudoword identification: Comment on Salasoo, Shiffrin, and Feustel. *J. Exp. Psychol. Gen.* 114:498–508

Jonides, J., Mack, R. 1984. On the cost and benefit of cost and benfit. *Psychol. Bull.* 96:29–44

Just, M. A., Carpenter, P. A. 1980. A theory of reading: From eye fixations to comprehension. *Psychol. Rev.* 87:329–54

Just, M. A., Carpenter, P. A. 1984. Using eye fixations to study reading comprehension. See Kieras & Just 1984, pp. 151–82

Just, M. A., Carpenter, P. A. 1987. *The Psychology of Reading and Language Comprehension.* Boston: Allyn & Bacon

Kamp, H. 1981. A theory of truth and semantic representation. In *Formal Methods in the Study of Language,* ed. J. Groenendijk, et al, pp. 277–322. Amsterdam: North Holland.

Keenan, J. M., Baillet, S. D., Brown, P. 1984. The effects of causal cohesion on comprehension and memory. *J. Verb. Learn. Verb. Behav.* 23:115–26

Kempen, G., Huijbers, P. 1983. The

lexicalization process in sentence production and naming: Indirect election of words. *Cognition* 14:185–209

Kennedy, A., Murray, W. S. 1984. Inspection times for words in syntactically ambiguous sentences under three presentation conditions. *J. Exp. Psychol.:Hum. Percept. Perform.* 10:833–49

Kerr, J. S., Underwood, G. 1984. Fixation time on anaphoric pronouns decreases with congruity of reference. *Theoretical and Applied of Eye Movement Research*, ed. A. Gale, F. Johnson, pp. 195–202. NY: Elsevier

Kieras, D. E., Just, M. A., eds. 1984. *New Methods in Reading Comprehension Research*. Hillsdale, NJ: Erlbaum

Kinoshita, S., Taft, M., Taplin, J. E. 1985. Nonword facilitation in a lexical decision task. *J. Exp. Psychol.:Learn. Mem. Cognit.* 11:346–62

Kintsch, W., van Dijk, T. A. 1978. Toward a model of text comprehension and production. *Psychol. Rev.* 85:363–94

Kintsch, W., Mross, E. F. 1985. Context effects in word identification. *J. Mem. Lang.* 24:336–49

Kirsner, K., Milech, D., Standen, P. 1983. Common and modality-specific processes in the mental lexicon. *Mem. Cognit.* 11:621–30

Klatt, D. 1980. A new look at the problem of lexical access. See Cole 1980, pp. 243–48

Koriat, A. 1981. Semantic facilitation in lexical decision as a function of prime-target association. *Mem. Cognit.* 9:587–98

Levelt, W. J. M. 1982. Linearization in describing spatial networks. In *Processes, Beliefs, and Questions*, ed. S. Peters, E. Saarinen, pp. 199–220. Dordrecht, Holland: Reidel

Levelt, W. J. M. 1983. Monitoring and self-repair in speech. *Cognition* 14:41–104

Levelt, W., Maassen, B. 1981. Lexical search and order of mention in sentence production. In *Crossing the Boundaries in Linguistics*, ed. W. Klein, W. Levelt, pp. 221–52. Dordrecht, Holland: Reidel

Liberman, M., Pierrehumbert, J. 1984. Intonational invariance under changes in pitch range and length. In *Language Sound Structure*, ed. M. Aronoff, R. T. Oehrle, pp. 157–233. Cambridge, Mass: MIT

Lieberman, P., Katz, W., Jongman, A., Zimmerman, R., Miller, M. 1985. Measures of the sentence intonation of read and spontaneous speech in American English. *J. Acoust. Soc. Am.* 77:649–57

Lorch, R. F. Jr., Balota, D. A., Stamm, E. G. 1986. Locus of inhibition effects in the priming of lexical decisions: pre- or post-lexical access? *Mem. Cognit.* 14:95–103

Luce, P. 1986. A computational analysis of

uniqueness points in auditory word recognition. *Percept. Psychophys.* 39:155–58

Lupker, S. J. 1984. Semantic priming without association: A second look. *J. Verb. Learn. Verb. Behav.* 23:709–33

MacNeilage, P. F., ed. 1983. *The Production of Speech*. New York: Springer-Verlag

Mandl, H., Stein, N. L., Trabasso, T., eds. 1984. *Learning and Comprehension of Text*. Hillsdale, NJ: Erlbaum

Mandler, J. M., Goodman, M. S. 1982. On the psychological validity of story structure. *J. Verb. Learn. Verb. Behav.* 21:507–23

Mandler, J. M., Johnson, N. S. 1977. Remembrance of things parsed: Story structure and recall. *Cognit. Sci.* 9:111–51

Mandler, J. M., Johnson, N. S. 1980. On throwing out the baby with the bathwater: A reply to Black and Wilensky's evaluation of story grammars. *Cognit. Sci.* 4:305–12

Maratsos, M. 1983. Some current issues in the study of the acquisition of grammar. In *Handbook of Child Psychology, Vol. III: Cognitive Development*, ed. J. H. Flavell, E. M. Markman, pp. 707–86. Chichester: Wiley

Marcus, M. P. 1984. Some inadequate theories of human language processing. In *Talking Minds: The Study of Language in Cognitive Science*, ed. T. G. Bever, J. M. Carroll, L. A. Miller, pp. 253–78. Cambridge, Mass: MIT Press

Marcus, S. M. 1984. Recognizing speech: On the mapping from sound to word. See Bouma & Bouwhis 1984, pp. 151–63

Marslen-Wilson, W. D. 1984. Function and process in spoken word recognition. See Bouma & Bouwhis 1984, pp. 125–50

Marslen-Wilson, W. D. 1987. Functional parallelism in spoken word-recognition. *Cognition* 25:71–102

Marslen-Wilson, W. D., Levy, E., Tyler, L. K. 1982. Producing interpretable discourse: The establishment and maintenance of reference. In *Speech, Place, and Action*, ed. R. J. Jarvella, W. Klein, pp. 339–78. Chichester: Wiley

Marslen-Wilson, W. D., Tyler, L. K. 1980. The temporal structure of spoken language understanding. *Cognition* 8:1–71

Marslen-Wilson, W. D., Welsh, A. 1978. Processing interactions during word-recognition in continuous speech. *Cognit. Psychol.* 10:29–63

Martin, J. G. 1972. Rhythmic (hierarchical) versus serial structure in speech and other behavior. *Psychol. Rev.* 79:487–509

Martin, J. G. 1979. Rhythmic and segmental perception are not independent. *J. Acoust. Soc. Am.* 65:1286–97

McClelland, J., Elman, J. 1986. The trace model of speech perception. *Cognit. Psychol.* 18:1–86

McClelland, J. L., O'Regan, J. K. 1981a. Expectations increase the benefit derived from parafoveal visual information in reading words aloud. *J. Exp. Psychol.:Hum. Percept. Perform.* 7:634–44

McClelland, J. L., O'Regan, J. K. 1981b. On visual and contextual factors in reading: A reply to Rayner and Slowiaczek. *J. Exp. Psychol.:Hum. Percept. Perform.* 7:652–57

McClelland, J. L., Rumelhart, D. E. 1981. An interactive activation model of context effects in letter perception: Part 1. An account of basic findings. *Psychol. Rev.* 88:375–407

McCusker, L. X., Hillinger, M. L., Bias, R. G. 1981. Phonological recoding and reading. *Psychol. Bull.* 89:217–45

McConkie, G. W., Underwood, N. R., Zola, D., Wolverton, G. S. 1985. Some temporal characteristics of processing during reading. *J. Exp. Psychol.:Hum. Percept. Perform.* 11:168–86

McGranahan, D. V. 1936. The psychology of language. *Psychol. Bull.* 33:178–216

McKoon, G., Ratcliff, R. 1980. The comprehension processes and memory structures involved in anaphoric reference. *J. Verb. Learn. Verb. Behav.* 19:668–82

McNeill, D. 1985. So you think gestures are nonverbal? *Psychol. Rev.* 92:350–71

Meyer, D. E., Gordon, P. C. 1985. Speech production: Motor programming of phonetic features. *J. Mem. Lang.* 24:3–26

Mitchell, D. C. 1982. *The Process of Reading: A Cognitive Analysis of Fluent Reading and Learning to Read.* Chichester: Wiley

Mitchell, D. C., Holmes, V. M. 1985. The role of specific information about the verb in parsing sentences with local structural ambiguity. *J. Mem. Lang.* 24:542–59

Morrow, D. G. 1985a. Prominent characters and events organize narrative understanding. *J. Mem. Lang.* 24:304–19

Morrow, D. G. 1985b. Prepositions and verb aspect in narrative understanding. *J. Mem. Lang.* 24:390–404

Motley, M. T., Baars, B. J., Camden, C. T. 1983. Formulation hypotheses revisited: A reply to Stemberger. *J. Psycholing. Res.* 12:561–66

Motley, M. T., Camden, C. T., Baars, B. J. 1982. Covert formulation and editing of anomalies in speech production: Evidence from experimentally elicited slips of the tongue. *J. Verb. Learn. Verb. Behav.* 21:578–94

Murphy, G. L. 1984. Establishing and accessing referents in discourse. *Mem. Cognit.* 12:489–97

Murphy, G. L. 1985. Processes of understanding anaphora. *J. Mem. Lang.* 24:290–303

Norris, D. 1986. Word recognition: Context effects without priming. *Cognition* 22:93–136

Norris, D., Brown, G. 1985. Race models and analogy theories: A dead heat? *Cognition* 20:155–68

O'Brien, E. J., Duffy, S. A., Myers, J. L. 1986. Anaphoric inference during reading. *J. Exp. Psychol.:Learn. Mem. Cognit.* 12:346–52

O'Connor, R. E., Forster, K. I. 1981. Criterion bias and search sequence bias in word recognition. *Mem. Cognit.* 9:78–92

Onifer, W., Swinney, D. A. 1981. Accessing lexical ambiguities during sentence comprension: Effects of frequency of meaning and contextual bias. *Mem. Cognit.* 9:225–36

Paap, K. R., Newsome, S. L., Noel, R. W. 1984. Word shape's in poor shape for the race to the lexicon. *J. Exp. Psychol.:Hum. Percept. Perform.* 10:413–28

Palmer, J., MacLeod, C. M., Hunt, E., Davidson, J. E. 1985. Information processing correlates of reading. *J. Mem. Lang.* 24:59–88

Perfetti, C. A. 1985. *Reading Ability.* New York: Oxford Univ. Press

Pinker, S., Birdsong, D. 1979. Speakers' sensitivity to rules of frozen word order. *J. Verb. Learn. Verb. Behav.* 18:497–508

Posner, M. I., Snyder, C. R. R. 1975. Attention and cognitive control. In *Information Processing and Cognition: The Loyola Symposium,* ed. R. L. Solso, pp. 55–85. Hillsdale, NJ: Erlbaum

Pronko, N. H. 1946. Language and psycholinguistics: A review. *Psychol. Bull.* 43:189–232

Rayner, K., ed. 1983a. *Eye Movements in Reading: Perceptual and Language Processes.* New York: Academic

Rayner, K. 1983b. The perceptual span and eye movement control during reading. See Rayner 1983a, pp. 97–120

Rayner, K., Carlson, M., Frazier, L. 1983. The interaction of syntax and semantics during sentence processing: Eye movements in the analysis of sematically biased sentences. *J. Verb. Learn. Verb. Behav.* 22:358–74

Rayner, K., Carroll, P. J. 1984. Eye movements and reading comprehension. In *New Methods in Reading Comprehension Research,* ed. D. E. Kieras, M. A. Just, pp. 129–50. Hillsdale, NJ: Erlbaum

Rayner, K., Duffy, S. A. 1986. Lexical complexity and fixation times in reading: Effects of word frequency, verb complexity, and lexical ambiguity. *Mem. Cognit.* 14:191–201

Rayner, K., Slowiaczek, M. L. 1981. Expectations and parafoveal information in reading: Comments on McClelland and

O'Regan. *J. Exp. Psychol.:Hum. Percept. Perform.* 7:645–51

Read, J. D. 1983. Detection of Fs in a single statement: The role of phonetic recoding. *Mem. Cognit.* 11:390–99

Rosson, M. B. 1983. From SOFA to LOUCH: Lexical contributions to pseudoword pronunciation. *Mem. Cognit.* 11:152–60

Rosson, M. B. 1985. The interaction of pronunciation rules and lexical representations in reading aloud. *Mem. Cognit.* 13:90–99

Salasso, A., Shiffrin, R. M., Feustel, T. C. 1985. Building permanent memory codes: Codification and repetition effects in word identification. *J. Exp. Psychol.:Gen.* 114:50–77

Sanford, A. J., Garrod, S. C. 1981. *Understanding Written Language: Explorations of Comprehension Beyond the Sentence.* Chichester: Wiley

Schuberth, R. E., Eimas, P. D. 1977. Effects of context on the classification of words and nonwords. *J. Exp. Psychol.:Hum. Percept. Perform.* 3:27–36

Schwanenflugel, P., Shoben, E. J. 1985. The influence of sentence constraint on the scope of facilitation for upcoming words. *J. Mem. Lang.* 24:232–52

Scott, D. R., Cutler, A. 1984. Segmental phonology and the perception of syntactic structure. *J. Verb. Learn. Verb. Behav.* 23:450–66

Seidenberg, M. S. 1985a. The time course of phonological code activation in two writing systems. *Cognition* 19:1–30

Seidenberg, M. S. 1985b. Constraining models of word recognition. *Cognition* 20:169–90

Seidenberg, M. S., Tanenhaus, M. K. 1979. Orthographic effects on rhyme monitoring. *J. Exp. Psychol.:Hum. Percept. Perform.* 5:546–54

Seidenberg, M. S., Tanenhaus, M. K., Leiman, J. M., Bienkowski, M. 1982. Automatic access of the meanings of ambiguous words in context: Some limitations of knowledge-based processing. *Cognit. Psychol.* 14:489–537

Seidenberg, M. S., Waters, G. S., Barnes, M. A. 1984a. When does irregular spelling or pronunciation influence word recognition? *J. Verb. Learn. Verb. Behav.* 23:383–404

Seidenberg, M. S., Waters, G. S., Sanders, M., Langer, P. 1984b. Pre- and postlexical loci of contextual effects on word recognition. *Mem. Cognit.* 12:315–28

Seifert, C. M., Robertson, S. P., Black, J. B. 1985. Types of inferences generated during reading. *J. Mem. Lang.* 24:405–22

Sells, P. 1985. *Lectures on Contemporary Syntactic Theories: An Introduction to Government-Binding Theory, Generalized Phrase-Structure Grammar, and Lexical-Functional Grammar.* Stanford, Calif: Cent. Study Lang. Inf.

Shaffer, L. H. 1984. Motor programming in language production. A Tutorial Review. See Bouma & Bouwhuis 1984, pp. 17–41

Shattuck-Hufnagel, S. 1979. Speech errors as evidence for a serial-ordering mechanism in sentence production. See Cooper & Walker 1979

Shattuck-Hufnagel, S. 1983. Sublexical units and suprasegmental structure in speech production planning. See MacNeilage 1983, pp. 109–36

Sidner, C. L. 1983. Focusing and discourse. *Discourse Processes* 6:107–30

Simpson, G. B. 1984. Lexical ambiguity and its role in models of word recognition. *Psychol. Bull.* 96:316–40

Singer, M., Ferreira, F. 1983. Inferring consequences in story comprehension. *J. Verb. Learn. Verb. Behav.* 22:437–48

Smith, E. E. 1985. Natural reasoning. Review of P. N. Johnson-Laird (1983), "Mental Models." *Contremp. Psychol.* 30:181–82

Speer, S., Foss, D. J., Smith, C. 1986. Syntactic and thematic contributions to sentence complexity. Presented at Ann Meet. Psychon. Soc., New Orleans

Stanovich, K. E., West, R. F. 1981. The effect of sentence context on ongoing word recognition: tests of a two-process theory. *J. Exp. Psychol.:Hum. Percept. Perform.* 7:658–72

Stanovich, K. E., West, R. F. 1983. On priming by a sentence context. *J. Exp. Psychol.:Gen.* 112:1–36

Stein, N. L., Policastro, M. 1984. The concept of a story: A comparison between children's and teacher's viewpoints. See Mandl et al 1984, pp. 113–55

Stemberger, J. P. 1982. Syntactic errors in speech. *J. Psycholing. Res.* 11:313–45

Swinney, D. A., Cutler, A. 1979. The access and processing of idiomatic expressions. *J. Verb. Learn. Verb. Behav.* 18:523–34

Taft, M. 1984. Evidence for an abstract lexical representation of word structure. *Mem. Cognit.* 12:264–69

Taft, M., Hambly, G. 1986. Exploring the cohort model of spoken word recognition. *Cognition* 22:259–82

Tanenhaus, M. K., Carlson, G. N., Seidenberg, M. S. 1985. Do listeners compute linguistic representations? See Dowty et al 1985

Trabasso, T., Secco, T., van den Broek, P. 1984. Causal cohesion and story coherence. See Mandl et al 1984, pp. 83–111

Trabasso, T., Sperry, L. L. 1985. Causal relatedness and importance of story events. *J. Mem. Lang.* 24:595–611

Trabasso, T., van den Broek, P. 1985. Causal

thinking and the representation of narrative events. *J. Mem. Lang.* 24:612–30

Tyler, L. K. 1984. The structure of the initial cohort: evidence from gating. *Percept. Psychophys.* 36:417–27

Tyler, L. K., Marslen-Wilson, W. 1977. The on-line processing of semantic context on syntactic processing. *J. Verb. Learn. Verb. Behav.* 16:683–92

Tyler, L. K., Marslen-Wilson, W. 1982. The resolution of discourse anaphors: Some on-line studies. *Text* 2:263–91

Underwood, G., Bargh, K. 1982. Word shape, orthographic regularity, and contextual interactions in a reading task. *Cognition* 12:197–209

van Dijk, T. A., Kintsch, W. 1983. *Stategies of Discourse Comprehension.* Orlando, Fla: Academic

Wanner, E., Gleitman, L. R., eds. 1982. *Language Acquisition: The State of the Art.* Cambridge, Mass: Cambridge Univ. Press

Wasow, T. 1985. Postscript. See Sells 1985, pp. 193–205

Waters, G. S., Seidenberg, M. S. 1985. Spelling-sound effects in reading: Time-course and decision criteria. *Mem. Cognit.* 13:557–72

West, R. F., Stanovich, K. E. 1986. Robust effects of syntactic structure on visual word processing. *Mem. Cognit.* 14:104–12

West, R. F., Stanovich, K. E. 1982. Source of inhibition in experiments on the effect of sentence context on word recognition. *J. Exp. Psychol.:Learn. Mem. Cognit.* 8:385–99

Wright, B., Garrett, M. 1984. Lexical decision in sentences: Effects of syntactic structure. *Mem. Cognit.* 12:31–45

Ann. Rev. Psychol. 1988. 39:349–74

PERSONNEL SELECTION AND PLACEMENT

Robert M. Guion and Wade M. Gibson

Department of Psychology, Bowling Green State University, Bowling Green, Ohio 43403

CONTENTS

INTRODUCTION

Personnel selection is a process culminating in a decision to hire one or more applicants for employment and not to hire others. The decision to hire is one of a family of personnel decisions, including promotions and terminations, that should not be made without foundation. This review is concerned with

0066-4308/88/0201-0349$02.00

the literature speaking to the foundations of such decisions and their evaluation. Most of the span of this review covers publications of 1985 and 1986,
with incursions on either side of those years.

Two major documents have appeared: new *Standards for Educational and
Psychological Testing* (American Educational Research Association [AERA]
1985), the fourth in a series, and the third edition of *Principles for Validation
and Use of Personnel Selection Techniques,* (Society for Industrial and
Organizational Psychology [SIOP] 1987). A comprehensive text on personnel
selection has appeared, a revision of *Staffing Organizations,* now by Schneider & Schmitt (1986).

Changes in these publications reflect changes in professional thought during the preceding decade. Nowhere are these changes greater than in the
treatment of validity and the general evaluation of tests and selection procedures.

EVALUATION OF SELECTION PROCEDURES

Testing experts increasingly question the sacredness of the single validity
coefficient. *Standards* treats it simply as one form of evidence of validity, and
Principles treats it as the outcome of one strategy not logically separable from
others. One mark of expertise appears to be annoyance with the treatment of
content, construct, and criterion-related validities as three different entities.

Because the notion of content validity as a unique kind of validity seems as
durable as other superstitions, a final content validity conference was held in
the Bowling Green series (Cranny 1987); participants largely agreed that
content validity, even more than the single validity coefficient, was an idea
whose time was past. Validity coefficients, judgments of content relevance,
information about appropriateness of various inferences, and other psychometric and procedural information were all considered important in
evaluating measures. The emerging theme was that validity is neither a single
number nor a single argument but an inference from all the available evidence.

Standards and *Principles* agree but also point out that quality is more
important than the number of lines of evidence. *Standards* places greater
emphasis on the value of multiple evidence, perhaps because it is more
concerned with inferences about the psychological meaning of scores. In
contrast, *Principles* identifies the "specific kind of inference" from scores on
selection tests to be "ultimately an inference about probable job behavior"
(SIOP 1987, p. 4). That is, the inference is explicitly or implicitly a prediction
of some future behavior. The difference is not trivial; we consider it useful to
distinguish psychological meaning—i.e. the validity of measuring an attribute—from the job-relatedness prediction (Guion 1986a, 1987).

Frederiksen (1986) argued that the development and validation of job-related selection tests should begin with a clearly formulated theory of criterion performance and work toward similarity of constructs in predictor and criterion. Similarly, Guion (1986a) held that, in defining a content domain to be sampled or a construct to be reflected, one in fact defines a theory of the attribute to be measured. For personnel selection, showing that an attribute has been well measured is not sufficient; showing it to be job related has a higher priority. There is no single best way.

Some psychologists and many lawyers think there is. Landy (1986) likened their legalisms to "Pharisees, checking scripture to determine if law or tradition has been violated" (p. 1184). He viewed validation as testing the hypothesis that job performance is a function of one or more variables, as measured by specific procedures. In his view, the variety of hypothesis-testing (validation) methods is limited only by the creativity and experience of the validator—surely more than three categories. The traditional three categories "no more describe the range of strategies available than a mean describes the range of scores in a distribution" (p. 1186).

Statistics in Evaluating Selection Tests

Criterion-related strategies continue to be basic to evaluating job relatedness. Sussman & Robertson (1986) examined the validity of 11 concurrent and predictive designs. Their major contributions may have been (*a*) the observation that there is no statistical correction for an unrepresentative sample and (*b*) the demonstration, perhaps for the first time, that the method and timing of the selection decision relative to data collection must be considered in research design.

Fresh looks at corrections for range restriction are needed. Lee & Foley (1986) found that the ordinary corrections overestimate population validities at high score levels and underestimate them at lower levels. They argued that corrections for range restriction must take mean scores into account as well as the comparative variances. Another criticism of the traditional equations (Gross & McGanney 1987) pointed to the assumption of no relationship between a predicted criterion score and the probability of being selected; they offered new models that do not ignore the selection process.

Fowler (1986) offered improved equations, for both random and fixed predictors, for estimating the confidence limits for population cross-validated multiple correlation. For several years, analytic formulas have been considered superior to empirical cross-validation. A differing view was presented by Mitchell & Klimoski (1986); they noted that equations for estimating shrinkage do not have parameters for taking rationality into account. Purely empirical biodata batteries had high original multiple Rs but a great deal of shrinkage; whereas rational or component-scored batteries had more modest original Rs that were more stable in cross-validation. Five formula methods over-estimated the empirical shrinkage for the rationally developed batteries and underestimated it in the empirically developed batteries.

Twenty years ago or so, one of the most exciting developments in personnel selection was the emphasis on the potential of moderator variables for improving prediction. A search for moderators ordinarily includes an interaction term in ordinary least squares (OLS) multiple regression. Over the years, results rarely supported the moderator hypothesis and enthusiasm for the idea waned. More recently, conventional wisdom has said that a search for moderators in personnel selection is unlikely to be successful, at least for cognitive predictors.

In such a zeitgeist, a discussion presented by Morris et al (1986) seems a jarring note. Possible moderators are often correlated with the principal predictor, posing collinearity problems for the interaction term; by usual methods, a weak moderator effect is often the best that can be hoped for. Their suggested remedy is principal component regression, and they provided strong evidence of moderators not detected by OLS regression, in which the "hidden linear dependencies [are] an insidious source of Type II error" (p. 288). More evaluation will surely follow; if others find similar results, researchers in personnel selection may need to reconsider their positions on a wide variety of issues about moderating effects.

Validity Generalization

The mean of several validity coefficients may be a better basis for inferring a valid relationship between predictor and criterion than any one coefficient (SIOP 1987); the evidence is usually accumulated with a form of metaanalysis known as validity generalization (VG), articulated in various publications over the last decade by Schmidt, Hunter, and their associates. In VG, distributions of coefficients are corrected for sampling error and other arti-facts. Situational specificity is rejected if artifacts account for 75% of the variance; validities are said to generalize if situational specificity is rejected or if the 90% credibility value is positive. General discussions of VG have appeared; Schmidt et al (1985b) presented and discussed 40 questions; Bangert-Drowns (1986) compared VG and four other metaanalytic methods; Linn & Dunbar (1986) discussed broad areas of debate about VG.

Three papers criticized various VG procedures and common uses of them. Algera et al (1984) argued that VG has been inappropriately applied to multiple tests and criteria; errors of classification occur in compiling data, and tests of situational specificity lack adequate power to detect and explore certain sources of situational specificity. James et al (1986) also criticized the situational-specificity work; they were able to use the 75% rule to reject situational specificity and, with different assumptions and an alternative test, to reject the opposing cross-situational consistency hypothesis—both in the same contrived distribution of validity coefficients. Finally, Campbell (1986) noted that VG corrects for statistical artifacts but not for substantive flaws in the research summarized.

Three Monte Carlo studies investigated power and Type I error rates in metaanalytic tests of the hypothesis of no difference between correlations. Of three methods evaluated by Sackett et al (1986), none had adequate power to detect small population differences—or even moderate differences when sample sizes or number of studies were small. The proportion of variance explained by artifacts (90% instead of 75% because of the Monte Carlo analysis) had the best power but at the cost of the highest Type I error rate. Spector & Levine (1987) reported similar results. Kemery et al (1987) worked from bimodal distributions with population correlations of 0 and .6. Using both the 75% rule and the 90% credibility value, they rejected situational specificity when as much as 10% of the correlations were from the $\rho = 0$ population and supported generalizability when the percentage was as high as 40%. It appears metaanalysis cannot consistently detect the presence of meaningful validity differences. When validities are bimodal, VG procedures may erroneously reject situational specificity and support generalizability.

The effect of small sample studies was investigated by Schmidt et al (1985a) by partitioning a large data base into many small studies. The simulated small-sample validities were indeed quite variable and persuasively argued against reliance on small-sample studies. Although the authors argued that the sampling error disconfirmed the situational-specificity hypothesis, we believe their contribution rests with their illustration of sampling error.

One debate centers on accuracy of VG procedures. Spector & Levine (1987) sampled correlations from a single population and found mean ratios of error to observed variance greater than 1.0 unless the number of correlations was large. Because both variances reflect only error, they interpreted the findings as indicating bias in the sampling error estimate used in VG procedures. J. C. Callender and H. G. Osburn (personal communication, December, 1986) noted a distinction between bias in the ratio and bias in the formula; mean differences (as opposed to mean ratios) between error and observed variances revealed no bias in the sampling error estimates. In a broader context, Burke et al (1986) applied five VG procedures to validity coefficient distributions and found resulting estimates of the true validity means and variances to be relatively similar. However, they expressed concern regarding the occurrence of negative true variance estimates.

McDaniel et al (1986) showed that Schmitt et al (1984) had accounted for less variance by sampling error than had previous studies because of larger mean sample sizes. Schmitt & Noe (1986) concurred with the point and suggested the use of confidence intervals rather that the proportion of variance accounted as a criterion for interpreting VG results.

Utility Analysis

Research devoted to the measurement, application, and extension of utility models continues, with continuing concern for the estimation of the standard deviation of performance in dollars (SD_y). Three methods of estimation were compared by Weekly et al (1985): a global estimation procedure (Schmidt et al 1979), CREPID (Cascio 1982), and a fixed rule of 40% of average annual salary. They found that the global estimate was substantially larger than the others. However, DeSimone et al (1986) found the global SD_y lower than an empirically computed value. They also reported moderate inter-rater reliability even though stability over six months (with ten raters) was low and nonsignificant. A problem with the CREPID method, shown by Reilly & Smither (1985) was that, despite reliability and accuracy in the estimates necessary for the procedure, standard deviations across job dimensions were fixed. Because the resulting SD_y depended only on performance-dimension intercorrelations and importance weights, they suggested a modification using a magnitude estimation procedure. They reported accurate global estimates only when performance was easily transformed into dollars. Two additional estimation techniques were introduced by Eaton et al (1985).

For many purposes, variability in SD_y estimates will not affect utility conclusions. Indeed, Burke & Frederick (1986) found that variability among five estimates did not challenge the favorable conclusions about the utility of an assessment center. The value of SD_y for breaking even was only 20–60% of the various options; the choice of an SD_y estimate would be very unlikely to change the utility conclusions.

Some purposes, such as financial planning, may require more accurate utility estimates. Cronshaw & Alexander (1985) presented five practical applications of capital budgeting to selection utility, treating human resource expenditures as investments rather than as operating costs. They argued that an investment-oriented approach would allow personnel managers to compete more effectively for investment dollars within a firm. However, Tenopyr (1987) reported that managers were unimpressed with utility estimates. We wonder if managers are showing superior insight. Murphy (1986) showed that utility estimates may be grossly inflated if rejected offers are not considered in the utility computations. Overestimation of the mean standard test score of those accepting jobs is a multiplicative factor in estimating utility. A different problem was reported by Alexander & Barrick (1987), who developed standard error formulas and found a disturbing level of uncertainty in utility estimates.

Two empirical assessments of utility appeared, comparing performance of people selected under different procedures. Cascio & Ramos (1986) compared an assessment center and a panel selection interview process used in promoting managers. Two distributions of worth estimates corresponding to the two procedures were compared. As expected, the distribution for incumbents promoted by the assessment center had a higher mean and lower SD_y. A utility analysis showed that it was a cost-effective alternative to ordinary selection procedures. Schmidt et al (1986a) measured and compared job performance for employees selected with an ability test and employees selected with nontest procedures. On the average, employees selected with tests were .487 job performance standard deviation units better than their nontest-selected counterparts.

Extensions of utility models came from Boudreau and his associates. Boudreau & Rynes (1985) included recruitment in their model, focusing on the distribution of predictor scores, service values, and service costs for the labor force in general, the applicant population, the applicant pool, and the selectees. Boudreau & Berger (1985) integrated selection and turnover in a decision-theoretic model of employee movement. Primary parameters in the model represent both quantity and quality of movers and the cost incurred to produce the movement. We believe a major value of these seminal articles is that they provide a conceptual framework within which to integrate many human resource decisions and to guide future research; in addition, they indicate a variety of questions to be asked in evaluating selection procedures.

We find the research on utility theory diverse and disjointed, and we wonder where it is leading. Should the emphasis be upon making accurate predictions of utility gains? Standard errors of utility gain estimates are so large, and the measurement issues are so complex, that we do not see this as an achievable purpose, at least at present. Should the purpose be to determine relative utilities of alternative selection procedures? We suspect that such comparisons will do little more than favor the more valid procedures over those that are less valid. Is it enough that utility models specify relevant variables and their functional forms to guide selection research and practice? Such specification should prove helpful. Clarification of purpose would help guide future utility research.

Law and Bias

Equal employment opportunity litigation and regulation remain major concerns for personnel selection. Doverspike et al (1985) reiterated the assertion that the climate of litigation in the last decade or so has led to a substantial decline in the use of tests for selection and a corresponding increase in more subjective bases for decisions. In searching for alternatives to testing, trade-offs are made—and what is usually lost is validity (Davey 1984). Judging from a survey of 12 court decisions (Kleiman & Faley 1985), this is unlikely to be a concern in litigation; claims of validity were upheld in only 5. Kleiman & Faley asserted that some judges tend to sidestep technical issues, such as how a test might have been developed or chosen, and rely instead on what they view as common sense. The obvious implication is that those who serve as expert witnesses—both those for plaintiffs and those for defendants—must be well prepared and must see their responsibilities as enlightening the court, not merely as advocates for one side or the other.

Enlightenment may not come easily when there are so many issues about which psychologists themselves are still groping for solutions and appropriate methods. Consider the comparison of validity or utility for alternative selection procedures that may vary in adverse impact. For example, Cascio & Ramos (1986) found an assessment center more cost effective than panel interviews; Schmidt et al (1986b) found greater utility for selection by tests than by nontests; Hogan & Zenke (1986) found the greatest utility in an assessment center compared with three other methods. Such comparisons can be misleading. In any research intended to compare the effectiveness of two or more treatments (such as a test and an alternative), a fair comparison requires that both treatments or variables be manipulated or measured with equivalent strength. Cooper & Richardson (1986) pointed out that equivalence must be based on both procedural equivalence and distributional equivalence; the latter point is often ignored in the search for alternatives. Truly fair comparisons are difficult to attain, but researchers have an obligation to be wholly candid in reporting lacks of equivalence in their data.

Psychometric debates about "fair selection models" have abated. The consensus seems to be that (a) the regression model (Cleary 1968; Humphreys 1952) is the appropriate test for bias and (b) bias is shown by differences in slopes—i.e. an interaction between the predictor and the potentially biasing variable. The mere fact of group differences in mean scores is not a sufficient basis for a claim of discriminatory bias (Drasgow 1987; Humphreys 1986; Thissen et al 1986). Nevertheless, the courts seem still to think of group differences alone as evidence of bias at the item level as well as at the level of a total score. In the *Golden Rule Insurance Company v. Washburn et al* settlement (discussed by Drasgow 1987), the percentages of blacks and whites getting any item right in future tests were to differ by no more than .15. Drasgow also reported that the agreement in *Allen v. Alabama State Board of Education* was worse; the differences could not be greater than .05. To whatever extent real group differences exist, these agreements were necessarily made at the cost of validity.

In more technical terms, these agreements essentially rule that future test items will be free of intercept differences, a goal that Humphreys (1986) called unrealistic. Freedom from bias, according to him, calls for similarity in slopes by having essentially equal item discrimination parameters in the different groups. Drasgow (1987), using item response theory and large samples, demonstrated empirically that a test may have many biased items with little or no total score bias. This is partly because the bias in individual items was small so that accumulated effects were small. Also, individual items were biased in either direction so that their effects cancel out in the total score.

In pointing to a claimed increase of about 136% in the numbers of blacks in managerial and official occupations in a recent 10-year period, Alderfer & Tucker (1985) pointed out that "bringing more black people into management positions . . . is not equivalent to assigning them to jobs of equal centrality and influence as those held by whites" (p. 2). They developed a program to improve upward mobility of black managers based on "intergroup theory." The theory holds that each person belongs both to an organizational group and to an "identity group"—identity being based on essentially unchanging characteristics such as race and sex. The program resulted in recommendations that would have increased minority representation; the regular personnel committee reversed enough of the special group's recommendations to have a dampening effect.

Does this mean that regular organizational processes are necessarily biased in favor of the dominant identity group (white males)? Alderfer & Tucker would answer affirmatively, but neither side of a debate on the matter would have the most useful data: unbiased information about the comparative performance of those chosen by the ad hoc procedure and those chosen by the organization's traditional procedure.

Job Analysis

Some courts insist on extensive job analysis (cf Kleiman & Faley 1985), but detailed job analyses may not be necessary. Job analysis is undertaken to gain "understanding [of] the organization's needs as they relate to the selection problem so that the researcher can formulate sound hypotheses about relationships among predictors and criteria" (SIOP 1987, p. 5). The information needed depends on the understanding the researcher already has, or can get from available information, and the gaps in that understanding. Where the test of the researcher's hypothesis is to be empirical and direct, less detail is needed than in those situations where the evidence is less direct. The *Principles* requires responsible judgments, not blind adherence to a job-analytic cookbook (cf Landy 1986).

Some purposes require more detail. It is often useful to group jobs together in families or classes for metaanalytic or other purposes; Harvey (1986) described a variety of statistical approaches to job classification. Such approaches demand systematic data collection, and the dominant instrument remains the Position Analysis Questionnaire (PAQ; McCormick et al 1972). Determining the reliability of PAQ data is a problem when a great many items have "does not apply" (DNA) responses. Harvey & Hayes (1986) reported a Monte Carlo study in which the number of such responses and the number of raters were systematically varied; they documented the problem by finding that reliability coefficients of about .50 can be obtained with as few as 15–20% DNA responses and random responses to the rest.

Patrick & Moore (1985) developed the Job Structure Profile as an "anglicization" of the PAQ; their inventory reduces the DNA problem and also the confusion caused by the many different response scales by using an "extent of use" response scale for all items. Both retest and conspect reliabilities were studied with results that, at best, were called "reasonably good."

Realistic Job Previews (RJPs)

At least three metaanalyses of the effectiveness of RJPs in reducing turnover have been reported. Guzzo et al (1985) found no mean effect from 14 studies. McEvoy & Cascio (1985) reported a small mean effect for turnover reduction, moderated by task complexity; they found a substantially greater effect of job enrichment programs. Premack & Wanous (1985), with a somewhat different set of studies, found modest mean effects for both satisfaction and turnover; a still more modest mean effect was reported for job performance, moderated by the medium used for the RJP.

RJP research has been mainly descriptive. Perhaps the best that can be said is that they work—a little bit, and sometimes. When they might be expected to work, or for whom, represents an open field for research. A start was offered by Miceli (1985) in a laboratory study based on two theories of why RJPs might work: a reduction of reality shock and the provision of informational cues. The latter seemed more strongly supported; favorable cues, even if inaccurate, were associated with higher levels of subsequent satisfaction.

RJPs can also be used for getting applicants ready for the selection procedure. A recent example is a booklet and 12-minute video developed by General Motors (R. A. Bolda, personal communication, January, 1987) as an RJP for apprentice selection tests and interviews as well as for the training program itself.

Cutting Scores

In some organizations (such as civil service jurisdictions) or for some purposes (such as competency testing), dichotomous scores seem appropriate. How to establish the score used as the dividing line is a vexing question; ultimately it is a matter of judgment. Considering court cases, the literature, and the *Standards*, Berk (1986a) identified six technical criteria for judging the adequacy of a cutting score and used them to provide a "consumer guide" to 35 methods for setting them. No one method of setting cutting scores is entirely satisfactory, but the guide provides a "frequency of despair" report for each.

Some methods provide "absolute" cutting scores; others set a passing rate. Beuk (1984) and DeGruijter (1985) have studied possible compromises. We do not know why. A desired passing rate is either a matter of policy (it might be politically unwise, for example, if no one passed a state licensing exam) or, in personnel selection, a matter of expected supply and demand. In most selection situations, however, it probably remains best to select on the basis of linear assumptions, "top" of the distribution down. Moreover, DeGruijter's (1985) comparison of three methods found no clear advantage for any; his analysis underscored the subjectivity of setting cutting scores.

Similarly, Norcini et al (1987) found little difference among three variations on a group Angoff method for setting absolute cutting scores. Many courts reject employment systems that effectively rank candidates in test score order, preferring a designated passing score (but without much guidance for making decisions among those who "pass"). Considering the essential subjectivity, the difficulty in choosing rationally between different methods, and the multiplicity of variations on the basic themes, it is rather difficult to understand why. In at least one case (*Cuesta v. NYOCA* 1987), the Court concluded that a selection test was valid; however, it represented only a limited part of the overall job, so the appropriateness of ranking candidates was questioned. The Court called for further evidence on the point; perhaps this case will signal the beginning of a new rationality about cutting scores.

PERFORMANCE

Performance may be either a job-related criterion or a predictor. The 20 widely varied papers in a symposium on performance assessment (Berk 1986b) discussed both along with other administrative uses. Most criteria are global measures of performance; apparently researchers still have not absorbed Wallace's (1965) call for testing relatively narrow hypotheses about precisely defined criteria for precisely defined purposes.

In predictive, criterion-related validation, how soon after hiring should criterion data be collected? The question implies dynamic criteria, a concept challenged by Barrett et al (1985). Their challenge deserves attention and further study but is not wholly convincing. Some kinds of evidence of change (e.g. decay of validities over time) seem to have been ignored. A special sort of performance change in routine jobs was called "the honeymoon effect" by Helmreich et al (1986). If workers are initially committed to working well, their early performance is limited only by ability and experience; when the honeymoon is over, subsequent performance may be influenced by motivation. They found that measures of motivation were not valid predictors of early performance but predicted later performance.

Most studies reviewed used ratings as the criteria. Ratings are often considered suspect, and much research on ratings and the rating process has been reported.

Ratings as Measures

Conventional wisdom of late suggests that time devoted to worrying about rating formats is poorly spent; similar statements have appeared too often in the articles reviewed to cite them all. Two contrary voices have been heard, however. Guion (1986b) reiterated his earlier view that seminal research, presumably showing the failure of format research, actually showed the value of well-informed, experienced raters. Bernardin & Villanova (1986) showed that little research on format comparisons has been done within the relevant "boundary conditions." Perhaps the most useful view is that format is one, but only one, of the factors influencing the validities of performance evaluations (Bernardin & Beatty 1984). Format comparisons continue to be offered (Kinicki et al 1985) with no clear cut conclusion of superiority. Such work should be planned or evaluated in the context of comments by Cooper & Richardson (1986) on "unfair comparisons."

Of the various psychometric error tendencies, the only current concern seems to center on halo. It was addressed by Pulakos et al (1986); they offered three alternatives to the typical but misleading measurement by standard deviation across dimensions. The dead horse of partialling out overall evaluations was given another whipping by Lance & Woehr (1986); an alternative kind of statistical control, treating overall rating as a suppressor variable, was suggested by Henik & Tzelgov (1985). Feldman's (1986) essay pointed out that, rather than statistical control, halo will be controlled only when supervisors have the appropriate schema for attending to the relevant ratee attributes and behavior. Kozlowski et al (1986) found illusory halo more likely when raters lacked job knowledge or familiarity with the ratees, but they also identified several unanswered questions on the topic.

To say that halo is more than illusory, one needs to know what the ratings *ought* to have been, and that has led to much research invoking the concepts of accuracy—not always accurately. Becker & Cardy (1986) argued persuasively that better measurements of accuracy are needed. Perhaps a moratorium on halo studies pending solution of the accuracy problem would be in order. If researchers continue to emphasize overall criteria, the question of halo will seem less significant, anyway.

Various biasing factors have been considered. Classifying the supervisor's acquaintance with the subordinate as either task-related or personal, and measuring performance with both sales records and ratings, Kingstrom & Mainstone (1985) found that either category, but especially personal acquaintance, was related to the ratings even when sales performance was controlled.

Sex bias is often suspected and, according to Shore & Thornton (1986), often found in laboratory studies; however, they found no significant sex effects in the work setting they studied. Thompson & Thompson (1985) reported neither race nor sex effects in using a performance appraisal system directly based on job analysis, although Bernardin & Beatty (1984) argued that affirmative action and hiring quotas may well be expected to increase racial differences in mean performance ratings. In a metaanalysis, Tosi & Einbender (1985) summarized 21 laboratory studies in which comparable data were given the subjects about male and female ratees. The information about ratees was evaluated as "gender salient" or not, and gender saliency indexes were computed. Overall, the more information provided, the less evidence of sex discrimination in the ratings; but the more gender-salient the information, the greater the differences in mean ratings.

Kraiger & Ford (1985) considered effects of ratee race on performance ratings; their metaanalysis included both laboratory and field studies and also analyzed each type independently. Coding black ratees as 0 and whites as 1, the mean point biserial correlation between ratings and race was .183 for white raters and −.220 for black raters; and neither distribution included zero within the 95% confidence limits. Two moderating variables were identified in those studies using white raters: (a) The effect decreases when the proportion of blacks among ratees is greater, and (b) the effect was greater in field settings than in laboratory studies. A further metaanalysis based on actual employees (Ford et al 1986) found small but significant race effects for "objective" criteria, and these were "virtually identical" to the effects with ratings. White ratees were rated somewhat higher than blacks, and they did correspondingly higher on objective criteria, but the differences were small relative to the differences in mean predictor scores usually reported. In general, we can say that problems of bias in ratings exist, but they may be less critical than, though perhaps influenced by, the more subtle kinds of error investigated in theories of social cognition.

Cognitive and Affective Processes

Most cognitive research is necessarily done in laboratory settings. A brief summary of findings includes: (a) How well the rater likes the ratee influences rater accuracy (Cardy & Dobbins 1986); (b) shared distinctiveness of group membership and group behavior is *not* a basis for explaining what happens in rating (Feldman et al 1986); (c) delayed ratings have both more halo and more accuracy than ratings made immediately after viewing a tape (Murphy & Balzer 1986); and (d) previous performance affects evaluations of present performance (is this what was once called a primacy effect?) and subsequent performance biases recall of earlier performance (recency effect?) (Murphy et al 1985, 1986a).

We give these studies short shrift because we confess to being unimpressed by their relevance to personnel selection. We are not alone. Hakel (1986) praised laboratory studies but went on to call that praise "a nice way" to say that practical fruits of the research had not appeared. Since his review, much has been published about the generalizability of laboratory research (Locke 1986). We consider this literature worth serious attention, particularly as it relates to rating processes. Banks & Murphy (1985) pointed out the gap between academic research and professional practice; the gap will not be closed until it is shown that the laboratory work leads to more reliable and predictable ratings at work or at least to testable hypotheses about the consequences of certain procedures or decisions in organizational performance evaluation. In a different setting, using metaanalysis, Murphy et al (1986b) found larger effect sizes for ratings of paper people than for ratings based on either direct or "indirect" (videotape) observation. We would like to have seen the comparison of the direct and indirect findings; we suspect that many observed effects using videotaped people would not be detectable in realistic performance rating situations.

The methods and constructs of experimental social psychology tend to ignore critical differences between the research setting and the setting to which the research should generalize—i.e. boundary conditions (Bernardin & Villanova 1986; Ilgen 1986; Ilgen & Favero 1985). These include major considerations: rating purposes, rater motivation, rater experience or understanding of the procedure, rater-ratee interdependence, or the consequences of both ratee and rater behavior—ranging from potentially pleasant or unpleasant future interactions to litigation. Bernardin & Villanova (1986) described a modal setting to which research should generalize, and they also identified factors that people in real organizations see as the major effects of appraisal accuracy.

Gordon et al (1986) reported that experimental findings based on student subjects were significantly different from those based on nonstudents in the same experimental conditions. In an understatement, they said, "Given the importance of the social content of the stimulus situation in applied behavioral research . . ., it appears that a number of background variables may influence the cognitive appraisal of the experimental task" (p. 201). Greenberg (1987) took exception to that view, arguing that "rigorous theory tests . . . require the use of investigations that are internally valid and *not* diluted with real world features" (p. 159, emphasis in original). We would respond that those real world features are too important ignore for long.

If we question the generalizability of research using students in contrived situations to employees in real work settings, the conclusions to be drawn about ratings for personnel selection research are sparse indeed. The comment is not intended to discourage laboratory research so much as to encourage those who do it to include the tests of generalizability in their agendas. Indeed, the issue is not whether such laboratory studies should be done but under what circumstance and for which research questions (Campbell 1986; Ilgen 1986).

Integration

We are uncomfortable with the presumed demise of research on rating formats and related steps that are under managerial control, and we believe that laboratory studies of process should lead to testable hypotheses about what happens in actual work settings when supervisors rate subordinates. It is with special pleasure, then, that we note the eight propositions posed by Lee (1985). She argued against the "one best way" mentality in rating research and suggested that jobs with different task characteristics may require different rating forms and processes. We have not yet seen much response, but we hope her article may initiate a new era in research on performance evaluation. Other signals of the dawning of such an integrative era can be seen. Bernardin (1986) proposed such a system, complete with a complex flowchart of data and decisions needed. Cascio (1986) identified the integration of problems of finding and communicating clear performance standards (prototypes of good performance?), organizational variables, formats, and rater motivation. A different sort of integration was proposed by Sokol & Oresick (1986) with a combination of competency-based collection of information, computer maintenance files, and separation of the fact-finding and evaluation processes. These appeared in the Berk (1986b) volume, which includes other examples. The good news is that research seems to be moving forward.

PREDICTORS

Ability and Knowledge Tests

Many kinds of predictors can be useful, such as indexes of prior habits, personality traits, and others; but abilities have the best track record. Comparing ability and motivational measures in predicting team performance, Tziner & Eden (1985) consistently found main effects for ability but not for motivation. Moreover, ability had more than an additive effect in the group; crews with all high-ability people performed far better than predicted from the individual ability levels, and replacing a member of such a crew with a low-ability person had a disproportionately negative effect on group performance.

COGNITIVE TEST   After a decade of validity generalization, it is usually accepted that cognitive tests are likely to be good predictors of job performance, and evidence continues to be reported. Hirsh et al (1986) found validity generalization for several types of cognitive tests as predictors of performance in training in law enforcement occupations.

For the development of reasoning tests, Colberg (1985; Colberg et al 1985) argued that traditional distinctions between inductive and deductive reasoning should be avoided and, further, that items should be based on principles of formal logic.

Explicitly job related test development continues to invoke the concept of content validity as a special sort of beast. A "case study" of such development for testing park and recreation directors was reported by McKinney & Greer (1985). Park et al (1985) provided a more thorough and quite impressive description of procedures used in developing a reading test for a specific job.

CONSTRUCTS OF INTELLIGENCE   Once upon a time, mental ability tests provided single, global measures of intelligence. Then came the era of multiple factor analyses seeking ever finer delineations of mental abilities. The emphasis on generality seems to be returning. An entire issue of the *Journal of Vocational Behavior* (Gottfredson 1986) has been devoted to "The *g* Factor in Employment"—i.e. to views that cognitive test validities generalize across different test types because they all have general mental ability as a common variance source, that even within occupations *g*-loaded tests have higher predictive validities than do more specific tests, or that occupations can be ordered according to the intelligence levels of their incumbents (cf Yoakum & Yerkes 1920).

In a voice of moderation, Tyler (1986) acknowledged the practical value of the general measures but asserted that it is still worthwhile to seek knowledge of variance not explained by a general factor. Smith (1985) placed the matter in a broader context. She pointed out that measurements can always be arranged along a specific-to-general continuum, that they can be constructed to fit different levels of generality of the same basic domain, and that measures at those different levels are not interchangeable but can be useful for different purposes. She argued for great specificity of measurement if the criterion to be predicted is very specific and for generality in measurement if the criterion is very global in nature. Somehow, that very sensible view seems lost in too many discussions.

PHYSICAL ABILITIES   Physical ability testing has met hard times. Despite litigation and Maher's (1984) argument that physical skills tests for police selection are not likely to be valid, many jurisdictions continue to want them. There are, of course, some occupations (not necessarily restricted to unskilled labor) where muscles are still used, and unqualified people may be injured on the job or in employment office testing. For such testing, Kroemer (1985) developed an isoinertial lift test and compared it to the more conventional and static isometric test. Not only is it less likely to result in injury, but it had a better retest reliability.

JOB KNOWLEDGE   Schmidt et al (1986a) reported a path analysis in which job knowledge was an intermediate variable between experience and ability on one hand and work sample performance and supervisory ratings on the other. Both ability and experience contributed to job knowledge; knowledge contributed more than actual skill (as measured by work samples) to ratings. We can only speculate on the reasons, but the speculation suggests much further research. Do raters give good ratings to people who "talk a good job" more readily than to those who really can do the job well? Or do standardized work samples fail to tap the variety of everyday problems solved as well as job knowledge tests do? What seems clear is that knowledge is causally related to performance, whichever measure is used, and that better performance can be expected if people are selected who either have the knowledge from experience or the aptitude for acquiring it.

Background

Seeking background information about applicants is a search for behavioral consistency. If one has been over the years something of a drifter, one *might* suddenly "catch fire" and become a goal-directed doer, but it would be rather surprising; on the other hand, one who has made achievement a habit is unlikely to stop trying to achieve (Hough 1984). Background information is assessed in a variety of ways. Ash & Levine (1985) compared four methods for global assessment of training and experience, only one of which had what they called "quasi validity." (This may have been another example of "unfair comparison.") Schmitt & Ostroff (1986) abstracted information from or about specific job behaviors to develop content-relevant tests that could be given to inexperienced people. That is, although the people were inexperienced on the job at hand, they had background experiences that reflected characteristics like those required on the job. Childs & Klimoski (1986) identified background factors in a biographical inventory that predicted self-reports of both job and career success. Howard (1986) examined college experience as a predictor of managerial performance. Only the choice of major and the extracurricular activities provided the company with evidence of the interpersonal skills deemed important to managerial behavior. Her point, probably quite generalizable, was that different background experiences may be related to behavior in different facets of a job. Excessively global assessments of backgrounds and poorly defined global job behavior may, in short, hide relationships between background behavior and subsequent performance.

Background information may identify risks of antisocial behavior at the work place, quite important in the light of the legal liability an organization has for the actions of its employees. A reasonable aim is to avoid hiring those who may be likely to harm either fellow employees or other people. To try to do so, Baley (1985) called for thorough background checks of employment histories, credit abuses, and claimed educational attainments among other things. An evaluation of such investigation lies not in the usual concepts of validity or job relatedness but in the relevance of the information to the potential for legal liability.

Personality

It is difficult to define intelligence; encapsulating personality variables in a neat phrase is better not attempted. From the perspective of personnel selection, personality may be more usefully narrowed to consistencies in behavioral patterns relevant to the work to be done. Prediction based on general personality traits has been less successful than that on cognitive measures. The "honeymoon" effect may be one reason, but Helmreich et al (1986) may also attribute their success to their measures; instead of a global scale, they measured three distinguishable and work-related components of achievement motivation.

Development of more restricted, and more clearly job-relevant scales may be a trend. Gough (1985) reported the development of a work orientation scale for the California Psychological Inventory; high scorers on it tend to be dependable, moderate, optimistic, persevering, and conservative. He hypothesized that by means of this scale, in conjunction with the managerial potential scale reported earlier (Gough 1984), probable leadership styles could be identified. A different construct—service orientation—was reported by Hogan et al (1984). Subsequently, Hogan (1986) issued the Hogan Personality Inventory with six basic scales; six other work-related scales can be derived from these (five in addition to the service orientation scale) and have been issued independently as the Hogan Personnel Selection Series (Hogan & Hogan 1986).

Noninventory methods of measurement continue to be reported. For example, Hakstian et al (1986) reported on the development of a relatively easily scored, two-scale In-Basket test that was part of a larger test battery. Higher inter-rater reliabilities were reported; validities would have to be called modest at best, but they added useful increments within the battery since they were not correlated with any of the other predictors.

Some noninventory methods are not new, have no history of validity, yet persist. One of these is graphology, which seems especially strong in Europe and Israel; a survey by Robertson & Makin (1986) found that handwriting analysis was used as often as biodata or assessment centers. Ben-Shakhar et al (1986) found little support for its use. We doubt, however, that such research will deter the use of handwriting analysis as a basis for employment decisions in those organizations that find it intriguing.

Interviewing

Nor have repeatedly discouraging summaries of their reliabilities and validities deterred the use of interviews. In a blunt statement of the problem, Hanson & Balestreri-Spero (1985) said, "all too often, the person most polished in job-seeking techniques, particularly those used in the interview process, is the one hired, even though he or she may not be the best candidate for the position" (p. 114). Interviews will be used, however, and research on interviewing continues, whether in desperation or hope.

One review (Arvey & Campion 1982) expressed hope, at least for structured interviews. Arvey et al (1987) backed up that hope with a replicated large-sample study involving many interviewers in many locations. Uncorrected validity coefficients of .34 and .51 were reported for the use of a structured, scored form in two different years.

Orpen (1985) trained 76 insurance managers in two 3-hour sessions. They were randomly assigned either to training in a "standard" conversational interviewing procedure or in a structured behavior-description procedure. Once again, the structured procedure won out—and by a nontrivial margin. How long ago was the superiority of patterned interviews first demonstrated? How often has it been pointed out? Yet most interviews continue to be haphazard conversations.

The conversational approach may explain the results of a study of college recruiters (Kinicki & Lockwood 1985). Their judgments were best predicted by a generalized impression factor combining ratings on verbal expression, appearance, job knowledge, and "level of personal drive." Interpersonal attractiveness was a distant second-best predictor. Unless the job knowledge rating was based on solid information, the recruiters simply were not getting or using truly job-relevant information.

Judgments may often be based substantially on nonverbal cues providing little job relevant information at best. In a lens model study of seven nonverbal cues observed on videotaped interviews, Gifford et al (1985) asked 18 experienced interviewers to rate the applicants. They were able to predict self-report measures of social skills but not of work motivation. Perhaps the finding could be replicated with more independent criteria. If so, one might conclude that nonverbal skills (like Howard's conclusion about college experiences) may provide useful information for some narrowly defined criteria. That kind of precise targeting of research has not appeared.

INDIVIDUAL INTERVIEWS   We have long argued (cf Guion 1965) against pooling data from groups of interviewers, believing that judgments of individual interviewers are likely to vary widely in validity. Lens model and policy capturing research is moving in that direction, with some important results. Without details, Gifford et al (1985) investigated individual as well as group policies and found individual differences in the use of nonverbal cues. More detail was provided by Dougherty et al (1986) in idiographic studies of three experienced interviewers who rated 120 real job applicants. Linear equations captured their judgment policies, and these policies (individually and aggregated) were correlated with subsequent supervisor ratings on ten scales. Judgments of one interviewer were significantly correlated with nine of the ten criterion ratings; judgments of another were significantly correlated with three of them, and judgments of the other were not significantly related to any of the criterion scales. Moreover, the aggregated judgment policy was, as one might suspect, better than the poorest interviewer but not as good as the best. Linear models of the judgment policies were more valid than the actual judgments for two interviewers, but not for the one whose actual judgments were in fact pretty good predictors. Subsequent training on three of the rating dimensions used in developing the judgment, based on models, resulted in improved predictive validities for all three interviewers, showing that training based on bootstrapping can improve even a good interviewer's judgments. This study deserves wide replication.

ATTRACTIVENESS   Much research has purported to show that interviewers favor the more "attractive" or more appropriately dressed candidates (Cash & Kilcullen 1985; Dickey-Bryant et al 1986; Forsythe et al 1985).

Research on attractiveness based on rating photographs, whether it is intended to identify biases in hiring or to develop advice for job seekers, is another example of ignoring critical boundary variables. Judgments of attractiveness in an interpersonal setting such as an interview, and surely in contact of longer duration, are likely to stem from compensatory cues going well beyond those that can be captured in a photo, including for example grooming, animation, smiling, responsiveness, evidence of interest in the person making the judgment, or similarity to that person (Byrne 1971). If this line of research is valuable enough to pursue, we think it should go beyond the paper-people paradigm.

Assessment Centers

Assessment centers are widely used both for initial selection and for promotion decisions. The research question seems not to be whether to use assessment centers but how to understand what goes on in them, how to evaluate the results, and how to make them better.

For example, how important is the group discussion among assessors, and what role does it play? Although such discussion is one of the recommendations of Byham & Thornton (1986), two British studies have questioned its value. Wingrove et al (1985) found that the discussion did not change the predictive validity of overall ratings. Heriot et al (1985) found that discussion was more likely to lower a rating than to raise it.

In a comprehensive study, Russell (1985) asked assessors to group 18 dimensions they had previously rated under four equally weighted categories. Factor analyses were done independently for each assessor; overall prediscussion ratings were most heavily related to a single factor. If this is a general impression factor, we can question whether it, and the subsequent overall rating after discussion, is as dependent on performance on specific exercises as we would like to believe. Russell concluded his discussion by pointing out that research on the cognitive processes used by individual assessors may prove fruitful. We agree but urge that such research be designed with issues of external validity carefully addressed.

A related call for research concentrated on evaluation. Attending primarily to content validity arguments, Sackett (1987) concluded that, while content analysis is clearly relevant to exercise construction, most assessment center evaluation based on content arguments is incomplete; it focuses only on exercise content and not, as one example of an omission, on scoring or rating exercise performance. His call is for research that will study the effect of various details in assessment center practices beyond the ordinary concerns for content validity or, as we have noted for "the" interview, for a mythical notion of "the" assessment center.

POSTSCRIPT

Future personnel researchers will decide whether these years have been marked by any great advances, but from this too-immediate vantage point several important advances seem to have occurred. If for nothing else, this period will be noted for new versions of the *Standards* and the *Principles*. Both documents have important implications for practice in personnel selection; both documents mark with new clarity the divergence of professional opinion from the early opinions crystallized in the *Uniform Guidelines* (EEOC 1978).

Another advance is a growing awareness that Dunnette & Borman (1979) were right: Content, construct, and criterion-related validities are not discrete, independent entities. The growing awareness that ideas of validity have been muddled has brought with it some potentially useful attempts to clarify matters.

Advancements in utility theory lie in the extension of the models. These extensions have identified complexities of utility analysis and important questions to be asked in future research and in operational decisions.

Another advance may be a pendulum swing back to reality. For several years, the use of laboratory studies, often with college students playing roles as recruiters or other decision makers, has been increasing; several authors have expressed caveats about when such studies may be appropriate and when their applicability to ordinary events is questionable. Another swing might involve searches for moderators, generally a matter of some skepticism in the last few years. In addition to the direct, single-study search using principal component regression as a potentially more fruitful way to find moderators, we note that at least five articles have criticized validity generalization and the insensitivity of traditional tests of situational specificity in looking for moderator effects.

In short, personnel selection research is becoming more thoughtful, less driven by the significance or lack of significance of a mere validity coefficient. We do not know much, however, about the translation of the thoughtful research into thoughtful selection practices.

Literature Cited

Alderfer, C. P., Tucker, R. C. 1985. Measuring managerial potential and intervening to improve the racial equity of upward mobility decisions. *Yale Sch. Organ. Manage. Work. Pap. No. 68*

Alexander, R. A., Barrick, M. R. 1987. Estimating the standard error of projected dollar gains in utility. *J. Appl. Psychol.* 72:475–79

Algera, J. A., Jansen, P. G., Roe, R. A., Vijn, P. 1984. Validity generalization: some critical remarks on the Schmidt-Hunter procedure. *J. Occup. Psychol.* 57:197–210

Am. Educ. Res. Assoc. APA, National Council Meas. Educ. *Standards for Educational and Psychological Testing.* 1985. Washington DC: Am. Psychol. Assoc. 100 pp.

Arvey, R. D., Campion, J. E. 1982. The employment interview: a summary and review of recent research. *Personnel Psychol.* 35:281–322

Arvey, R. D., Miller, H. E., Gould, R., Burch, P. 1987. Interview validity for selecting sales clerks. *Personnel Psychol.* 40:1–12

Ash, R. A., Levine, E. L. 1985. Job applicant training and work experience evaluation: an empirical comparison of four methods. *J. Appl. Psychol.* 70:572–76

Baley, S. 1985. The legalities of hiring in the 80s. *Personnel J.* 64(11):112–15

Bangert-Drowns, R. L. 1986. Review of developments in meta-analytic method. *Psychol. Bull.* 99:388–99

Banks, C. G., Murphy, K. R. 1985. Toward narrowing the research-practice gap in performance appraisal. *Personnel Psychol.* 38:335–45

Barrett, G. V., Caldwell, M. S., Alexander, R. A. 1985. The concept of dynamic criteria: a critical reanalysis. *Personnel Psychol.* 38:41–56

Becker, B. E., Cardy, R. L. 1986. Influence of halo error on appraisal effectiveness: a conceptual and empirical reconsideration. *J. Appl. Psychol.* 71:662–71

Ben-Shakhar, G., Bar-Hillel, M., Bilu, Y., Ben-Abba, E., Flug, A. 1986. Can graphology predict occupational success? Two empirical studies and some methodological ruminations. *J. Appl. Psychol.* 71:645–53

Berk, R. A. 1986a. A consumer's guide to setting performance standards on criterion-referenced tests. *Rev. Educ. Res.* 56:137–72

Berk, R. A., ed. 1986b. *Performance Assessment: Method and Applications.* Baltimore: Johns Hopkins. 544 pp.

Bernardin, H. J. 1986. A performance appraisal system. See Berk 1986b, pp. 277–304

Bernardin, H. J., Beatty, R. W. 1984. *Performance Appraisal: Assessing Human Behavior At Work.* Boston: Wadsworth. 403 pp.

Bernardin, H. J., Villanova, P. 1986. Performance appraisal. See Locke 1986, pp. 43–62

Beuk, C. H. 1984. A method for reaching a compromise between absolute and relative standards in examinations. *J. Educ. Meas.* 21:147–52

Boudreau, J. W., Berger, C. J. 1985. Decision-theoretic utility analysis applied to employee separations and acquisitions. *J. Appl. Psychol.* 70:581–612

Boudreau, J. W., Rynes, S. L. 1985. Role of

recruitment in staffing utility analysis. *J. Appl. Psychol.* 70:354–66

Burke, M. J., Frederick, J. T. 1986. A comparison of economic utility estimates for alternative SD$_y$ estimation procedures. *J. Appl. Psychol.* 71:334–39

Burke, M. J., Raju, N. S., Pearlman, K. 1986. An empirical comparison of the results of five validity generalization procedures. *J. Appl. Psychol.* 71:349–53

Byham, W. C., Thornton, G. C. III. 1986. Assessment centers. See Berk 1986b, pp. 143–66

Byrne, D. 1971. *The Attraction Paradigm.* New York: Academic. 415 pp.

Campbell, J. P. 1986. Labs, fields, and straw issues. See Locke 1986, pp. 269–79

Cardy, R. L., Dobbins, G. H. 1986. Affect and appraisal accuracy: liking as an integral dimension in evaluating performance. *J. Appl. Psychol.* 71:672–78

Cascio, W. F. 1982. *Costing Human Resources: The Financial Impact of Behavior in Organizations.* Boston: Kent. 219 pp.

Cascio, W. F. 1986. Technical and mechanical job performance appraisal. See Berk 1986b, pp. 361–75.

Cascio, W. F., Ramos, R. A. 1986. Development and application of a new method for assessing job performance in behavioral/economic terms. *J. Appl. Psychol.* 71:20–28

Cash, T. F., Kilcullen, R. N. 1985. The eye of the beholder: susceptibility to sexism and beautyism in the evaluation of managerial applicants. *J. Appl. Social Psychol.* 15:591–605

Childs, A., Klimoski, R. J. 1986. Successfully predicting career success: an application of the biographical inventory. *J. Appl. Psychol.* 71:3–8

Cleary, T. A. 1968. Test bias: prediction of grades of Negro and white students in integrated colleges. *J. Educ. Meas.* 5:115–24

Colberg, M. 1985. Logic-based measurement of verbal reasoning: a key to increased validity and economy. *Personnel Psychol.* 38:347–59

Colberg, M., Nester, M. A., Trattner, M. H. 1985. Convergence of the inductive and deductive models in the measurement of reasoning abilities. *J. Appl. Psychol.* 70:681–94

Cooper, W. H., Richardson, A. J. 1986. Unfair comparisons. *J. Appl. Psychol.* 71:179–84

Cranny, J. C. 1987. *Content Validity III: A Conference on Validity Evidence for Employee Selection Procedures.* Bowling Green, Ohio: In press

Cronshaw, S. F., Alexander, R. A. 1985. One answer to the demand for accountability: selection utility as an investment decision.

Organ. Behav. Hum. Decis. Processes 35:102–18

Cuesta v. NYOCA 1987. *83 civ. 3714 (PNL)*

Davey, B. W. 1984. Personnel testing and the search for alternatives. *Public Personnel Manage. J.* 13:361–64

DeGruijter, D. N. M. 1985. Compromise models for establishing examination standards. *J. Educ. Meas.* 22:263–70

DeSimone, R. L., Alexander, R. A., Cronshaw, S. F. 1986. Accuracy and reliability of SD$_y$ estimates in utility analysis. *J. Occup. Psychol.* 59:93–102

Dickey-Bryant, L., Lautenschlager, G. J., Mendoza, J. L., Abrahams, N. 1986. Facial attractiveness and its relation to occupational success. *J. Appl. Psychol.* 71:16–19

Dougherty, T. W., Ebert, R. J., Callender, J. C. 1986. Policy capturing in the employment interview. *J. Appl. Psychol.* 71:9–15

Doverspike, D., Barrett, G. V., Alexander, R. A. 1985. The feasibility of traditional validation procedures for demonstrating job-relatedness. *Law Psychol. Rev.* 9:35–44

Drasgow, F. 1987. Study of the measurement bias of two standardized psychological tests. *J. Appl. Psychol.* 72:19–29

Dunnette, M. D., Borman, W. C. 1979. Personnel selection and classification systems. *Ann. Rev. Psychol.* 30:477–525

Eaton, N. K., Wing, H., Mitchell, K. J. 1985. Alternate methods of estimating the dollar value of performance. *Personnel Psychol.* 38:27–40

Equal Employment Opportunity Commission (EEOC), Civil Service Commission, Department of Labor, Department of Justice. 1978. *Fed. Reg.* 43(166):38290–315

Feldman, J. M. 1986. A note on the statistical correction of halo error. *J. Appl. Psychol.* 71:173–76

Feldman, J. M., Camburn, A., Gatti, G. M. 1986. Shared distinctiveness as a source of illusory correlation in performance appraisal. *Organ. Behav. Hum. Decis. Processes* 37:34–59

Ford, J. K., Kraiger, K., Schechtman, S. L. 1986. Study of race effects in objective indices and subjective evaluations of performance: a meta-analysis of performance criteria. *Psychol. Bull.* 99:330–37

Forsythe, S., Drake, M. F., Cox, C. E. 1985. Influence of applicant's dress on interviewer's selection decisions. *J. Appl. Psychol.* 70:374–78

Fowler, R. L. 1986. Confidence intervals for the cross-validated multiple correlation in predictive regression models. *J. Appl. Psychol.* 71:318–22

Frederiksen, N. 1986. Construct validity and construct similarity: methods for use in test development and test validation. *Multivar. Behav. Res.* 21:3–28

Gifford, R., Ng, C. F., Wilkinson, M. 1985. Nonverbal cues in the employment interview: links between applicant qualities and interviewer judgments. *J. Appl. Psychol.* 70:729–36

Gordon, M. E., Slade, L. A., Schmitt, N. 1986. The "science of the sophomore" revisited: from conjecture to empiricism. *Acad. Manage. Rev.* 11:191–207

Gottfredson, L. S., ed. 1986. The g factor in employment. *J. Vocat. Behav.* 29:293–450

Gough, H. G. 1984. A managerial potential scale for the California Psychological Inventory. *J. Appl. Psychol.* 69:233–40

Gough, H. G. 1985. A work orientation scale for the California Psychological Inventory. *J. Appl. Psychol.* 70:505–13

Greenberg, J. 1987. The college sophomore as guinea pig: setting the record straight. *Acad. Manage. Rev.* 12:157–59

Gross, A. L., McGanney, M. L. 1987. The restriction of range problem and nonignorable selection processes. *J. Appl. Psychol.* 71:In press

Guion, R. M. 1965. *Personnel Testing.* New York: McGraw-Hill. 585 pp.

Guion, R. M. 1986a. *Changing views for personnel selection research.* Presented at Intl. Congr. Appl. Psychol., 21st, Jerusalem

Guion, R. M. 1986b. Personnel evaluation. See Berk 1986b, pp. 345–60

Guion, R. M. 1987. Actions, beliefs, and content: Some ABCs of validity. See Cranny 1987

Guzzo, R. A., Jette, R. D., Katzell, R. A. 1985. The effects of psychologically based intervention programs on worker productivity: a meta-analysis. *Personnel Psychol.* 38:275–91

Hakel, M. D. 1986. Personnel selection and placement. *Ann. Rev. Psychol.* 37:351–80

Hakstian, A. R., Woolsey, L. K., Schroeder, M. L. 1986. Development and application of a quickly-scored In-Basket exercise in an organizational setting. *Educ. Psychol. Meas.* 46:385–96

Hanson, T. J., Balestreri-Spero, J. C. 1985. An alternative to interviews. *Personnel J.* 64:114–23

Harvey, R. J. 1986. Quantitative approaches to job classification: a review and critique. *Personnel Psychol.* 39:267–89

Harvey, R. J., Hayes, T. L. 1986. Monte Carlo baselines for interrater reliability correlations using the Position Analysis Questionnaire. *Personnel Psychol.* 39:345–57

Helmreich, R. L., Sawin, L. L., Carsrud, A. L. 1986. The honeymoon effect in job performance: temporal increases in the predictive power of achievement motivation. *J. Appl. Psychol.* 71:185–88

Henik, A., Tzelgov, J. 1985. Control of halo

error: a multiple regression approach. *J. Appl. Psychol.* 70:577–80

Heriot, P., Chalmers, C., Wingrove, J. 1985. Group decision making in an assessment centre. *J. Occup. Psychol.* 58:309–12

Hirsh, H. R., Northrop, L. C., Schmidt, F. L. 1986. Validity generalization results for law enforcement occupations. *Personnel Psychol.* 39:399–420

Hogan, J., Hogan, R. 1986. *Hogan Personnel Selection Series: Manual.* Minneapolis: Nat. Comput. Syst. 38 pp.

Hogan, J., Hogan, R., Busch, C. M. 1984. How to measure service orientation. *J. Appl. Psychol.* 69:167–73

Hogan, J., Zenke, L. L. 1986. Dollar value utility of alternative procedures for selecting school principals. *Educ. Psychol. Meas.* 46:935–45

Hogan, R. 1986. *Hogan Personality Inventory: Manual.* Minneapolis: Natl. Comput. Syst. 45 pp.

Hough, L. M. 1984. Development and evaluation of the "accomplishment record" method of selecting and promoting professionals. *J. Appl. Psychol.* 69:135–46

Howard, A. 1986. College experiences and managerial performance. *J. Appl. Psychol.* 71:530–52

Humphreys, L. G. 1952. Individual differences. *Ann. Rev. Psychol.* 3:131–50

Humphreys, L. G. 1986. An analysis and evaluation of test and item bias in the prediction context. *J. Appl. Psychol.* 71:327–33

Ilgen, D. R. 1986. Laboratory research: a question of when, not if. See Locke 1986, pp. 257–67

Ilgen, D. R., Favero, J. L. 1985. Limits in generalization from psychological research to performance appraisal processes. *Acad. Manage. Rev.* 10:311–21

James, L. R., Demaree, R. G., Mulaik, S. A. 1986. A note on validity generalization procedures. *J. Appl. Psychol.* 71:440–50

Kemery, E. R., Mossholder, K. W., Roth, L. 1987. The power of the Schmidt and Hunter additive model of validity generalization. *J. Appl. Psychol.* 72:30–37

Kingstrom, P. O., Mainstone, L. E. 1985. An investigation of the rater-ratee acquaintance and rater bias. *Acad. Manage. J.* 28:641–53

Kinicki, A. J., Bannister, B. D., Hom, P. W., DeNisi, A. S. 1985. Behaviorally anchored rating scales vs. summated rating scales: Psychometric properties and susceptibility to rating bias. *Educ. Psychol. Meas.* 45:535–49

Kinicki, A. J., Lockwood, C. A. 1985. The interview process: An examination of factors recruiters use in evaluating job applicants. *J. Vocat. Behav.* 26:117–25

Kleiman, L. S., Faley, R. H. 1985. The implications of professional and legal guidelines for court decisions involving criterion-related validity: A review and analysis. *Personnel Psychol.* 38:803–33

Kozlowski, S. W., Kirsch, M. P., Chao, G. T. 1986. Job knowledge, ratee familiarity, conceptual similarity and halo error: An exploration. *J. Appl. Psychol.* 71:45–49

Kraiger, K., Ford, J. K. 1985. A meta-analysis of ratee race effects in performance ratings. *J. Appl. Psychol.* 70:56–65

Kroemer, K. H. 1985. Testing individual capability to lift material: Repeatability of a dynamic test compared with static testing. *J. Safe. Res.* 16:1–7

Lance, C. E., Woehr, D. J. 1986. Statistical control of halo: clarification from two cognitive models of the performance appraisal process. *J. Appl. Psychol.* 71:679–85

Landy, F. J. 1986. Stamp collecting versus science: validation as hypothesis testing. *Am. Psychol.* 41:1183–92

Lee, C. 1985. Increasing performance appraisal effectiveness: matching task types, appraisal process, and rater training. *Acad. Manage. Rev.* 10:322–31

Lee, R., Foley, P. P. 1986. Is the validity of a test constant throughout the test score range? *J. Appl. Psychol.* 71:641–44

Linn, R. L., Dunbar, S. B. 1986. Validity generalization and predictive bias. See Berk 1986b, pp. 203–36

Locke, E. A., ed. 1986. *Generalizing From Laboratory to Field Settings.* Lexington, Mass: Lexington Books. 291 pp.

Maher, P. T. 1984. Police physical ability tests: can they ever be valid? *Public Personnel Manage. J.* 13(2):173–83

McCormick, E. J., Jeanneret, P. R., Mecham, R. C. 1972. A study of job characteristics and job dimensions as based on the Position Analysis Questionnaire (PAQ). *J. Appl. Psychol.* 56:347–68

McDaniel, M. A., Hirsh, H. R., Schmidt, F. L., Raju, N. S., Hunter, J. E. 1986. Interpreting the results of meta-analytic research: a comment on Schmitt, Gooding, Noe, and Kirsch (1984). *Personnel Psychol.* 39:141–48

McEvoy, G. M., Cascio, W. F. 1985. Strategies for reducing employee turnover. *J. Appl. Psychol.* 70:342–53

McKinney, W. R., Greer, D. L. 1985. The construction and validation of the IDPRE: a personnel selection examination for Illinois directors of parks and recreation. *Public Personnel Manage. J.* 14:181–89

Miceli, M. P. 1985. The effects of realistic job previews on newcomer behavior: a laboratory study. *J. Vocat. Behav.* 26:277–89

Mitchell, T. W., Klimoski, R. J. 1986. Estimating the validity of cross-validation estimation. *J. Appl. Psychol.* 71:311–17

Morris, J. H., Sherman, J. D., Mansfield, E. R. 1986. Failures to detect moderating effects with ordinary least squares-moderated multiple regressions: some reasons and a remedy. *Psychol. Bull.* 99:282–88

Murphy, K. R. 1986. When your top choice turns you down: effect of rejected offers on the utility of selection tests. *Psychol. Bull.* 99:133–38

Murphy, K. R., Balzer, W. K. 1986. Systematic distortions in memory-based behavior ratings and performance evaluations: consequences for rating accuracy. *J. Appl. Psychol.* 71:39–44

Murphy, K. R., Balzer, W. K., Lockhart, M. C., Eisenman, E. J. 1985. Effects of previous performance on evaluations of present performance. *J. Appl. Psychol.* 70:72–84

Murphy, K. R., Gannett, B. A., Herr, B. M., Chen, J. A. 1986a. Effects of subsequent performance on evaluations of previous performance. *J. Appl. Psychol.* 71:427–31

Murphy, K. R., Herr, B. M., Lockhart, M. C., Maguire, E. 1986b. Evaluating the performance of paper people. *J. Appl. Psychol.* 71:654–61

Norcini, J. J., Lipner, R. S., Langdon, L. O., Strecker, C. A. 1987. A comparison of three variations on a standard-setting method. *J. Educ. Meas.* 24:56–64

Orpen, C. 1985. Patterned behavior description interviews versus unstructured interviews: a comparative validity study. *J. Appl. Psychol.* 70:774–76

Park, R. J., Dawis, R. V., Rengel, E. K., Storlie, R. L. 1985. The selection and validation of a reading test to be used with civil service employees. *Public Personnel Manage. J.* 14(3):275–84

Patrick, J., Moore, A. K. 1985. Development and reliability of a job analysis technique. *J. Occup. Psychol.* 58:149–58

Premack, S. J., Wanous, J. P. 1985. A meta-analysis of realistic job preview experiments. *J. Appl. Psychol.* 70:706–19

Pulakos, E. D., Schmitt, N., Ostroff, C. 1986. A warning about the use of a standard deviation across dimensions within ratees to measure halo. *J. Appl. Psychol.* 71:29–32

Reilly, R. R., Smither, J. W. 1985. An examination of two alternative techniques to estimate the standard deviation of job performance in dollars. *J. Appl. Psychol.* 70:651–61

Robertson, I. T., Makin, P. J. 1986. Management selection in Britain: a survey and critique. *J. Occup. Psychol.* 59:45–57

Russell, C. J. 1985. Individual decision processes in an assessment center. *J. Appl. Psychol.* 70:737–46

Sackett, P. R. 1987. Assessment centers and content validity. *Personnel Psychol.* 40:13–25

Sackett, P. R., Harris, M. M., Orr, J. M. 1986. On seeking moderator variables in the meta-analysis of correlational data: a Monte Carlo investigation of statistical power and resistance to Type I error. *J. Appl. Psychol.* 71:302–10

Schmidt, F. L., Hunter, J. E., McKenzie, R. C., Muldrow, T. W. 1979. Impact of valid selection procedures on work-force productivity. *J. Appl. Psychol.* 64:609–26

Schmidt, F. L., Hunter, J. E., Outerbridge, A. N. 1986a. Impact of job experience and ability on job knowledge, work sample performance, and supervisory ratings of job performance. *J. Appl. Psychol.* 71:432–39

Schmidt, F. L., Hunter, J. E., Outerbridge, A. N., Trattner, M. H. 1986b. The economic impact of job selection methods on size, productivity, and payroll costs of the federal work force: an empirically based demonstration. *Personnel Psychol.* 39:1–29

Schmidt, F. L., Ocasio, B. P., Hillery, J. M., Hunter, J. E. 1985a. Further within-setting empirical tests of the situational specificity hypothesis in personnel selection. *Personnel Psychol.* 38:509–24

Schmidt, F. L. et al; Sackett, P. R. et al. 1985b. Forty questions [and Commentary on forty questions] about validity generalization and meta-analysis. *Personnel Psychol.* 38:697–798

Schmitt, N., Gooding, R. Z., Noe, R. A., Kirsch, M. 1984. Metaanalyses of validity studies published between 1964 and 1982 and the investigation of study characteristics. *Personnel Psychol.* 37:407–22

Schmitt, N., Noe, R. A. 1986. On shifting standards for conclusions regarding validity generalization. *Personnel Psychol.* 39:849–51

Schmitt, N., Ostroff, C. 1986. Operationalizing the "behavioral consistency" approach: selection test development based on a content-oriented strategy. *Personnel Psychol.* 39:91–108

Schneider, B., Schmitt, N., eds. 1986. *Staffing Organizations.* Glenview, Ill: Scott, Foresman. 478 pp. 2nd ed.

Shore, L. M., Thornton, G. C. 1986. Effects of gender on self- and supervisory ratings. *Acad. Manage. J.* 29:115–29

Smith, P. C. 1985. *Global measures: Do we need them?* Presented at Ann. Meet. Am. Psychol. Assoc., 93rd, Los Angeles

Society for Industrial and Organizational Psychology. 1987. *Principles for the Validation and Use of Personnel Selection Procedures.* College Park, Md: Author. 3rd ed.

Sokol, M., Oresick, R. 1986. Managerial performance appraisal. See Berk 1986b, pp. 376–92

Spector, P. E., Levine, E. L. 1987. Meta-analysis for integrating study outcomes: a Monte Carlo study of its susceptibility to Type I and Type II errors. *J. Appl. Psychol.* 72:3–9

Sussman, M., Robertson, D. U. 1986. The validity of validity: an analysis of validation study designs. *J. Appl. Psychol.* 71:461–68

Tenopyr, M. L. 1987. *Policies and strategies underlying a personnel research operation.* Presented at Ann. Conf. Soc. Ind. Org. Psychol., 2nd, Atlanta

Thissen, D., Steinberg, L., Gerrard, M. 1986. Beyond group-mean differences: the concept of item bias. *Psychol. Bull.* 99:118–28

Thompson, D. E., Thompson, T. A. 1985. Task-based performance appraisal for blue-collar jobs: evaluation of race and sex effects. *J. Appl. Psychol.* 70:747–53

Tosi, H. L., Einbender, S. W. 1985. The effects of the type and amount of information in sex discrimination research: a meta-analysis. *Acad. Manage. J.* 28:712–23

Tyler, L. E. 1986. Back to Spearman? *J. Vocat. Behav.* 29:445–50

Tziner, A., Eden, D. 1985. Effects of crew composition on crew performance: Does the whole equal the sum of its parts? *J. Appl. Psychol.* 70:85–93

Wallace, S. R. 1965. Criteria for what? *Am. Psychol.* 20:411–17

Weekly, J. A., Frank, B., O'Connor, E. J., Peters, L. H. 1985. A comparison of three methods of estimating the standard deviation of performance in dollars. *J. Appl. Psychol.* 70:122–26

Wingrove, J., Jones, A., Heriot, P. 1985. The predictive validity of pre- and post-discussion assessment centre ratings. *J. Occup. Psychol.* 58:189–92

Yoakum, C. S., Yerkes, R. M., eds. 1920. *Army Mental Tests.* New York: Holt. 303 pp.

Ann. Rev. Psychol. 1988. 39:375–400

PSYCHOLOGY IN AUSTRALIA

Ronald Taft and Ross H. Day

Monash University, Clayton, Victoria, 3168, Australia*

CONTENTS

HISTORICAL AND SOCIAL CONTEXT

In 1988 Australia celebrates the bicentenary of the establishment by the United Kingdom of a settlement in Sydney to provide a prison for criminal outcasts. Subsequently, a fortunate combination of the settlers' initiative and

---

*This is one of a series of chapters about psychology in the host country of the International Congress of Psychology or the International Congress of Applied Psychology. Since one or the other congress occurs in each even-numbered year, these chapters will normally appear every two years.

0066-4308/88/0201-0375$02.00

the considerable natural resources of the country resulted in the rapid establishment of an affluent, literate, democratic, highly urbanized society. The European settlers have lived in uneasy proximity with the aboriginal population who inhabited the continent for at least 20,000 and possibly 40,000 years, in a relationship marked by population decline, misery, and resentment on the part of the aborigines.

Today, 200 years after the European settlement, there has developed a flourishing network of research and training facilities in universities and colleges and of public and private facilities for the application of psychology to issues in public life, education, commerce, social welfare, medicine, and individual adjustment. In this chapter we describe these developments, their history, and the current state of psychology in Australia. By and large, this reflects the current state of psychology in developed countries generally, but we point out any emphases that seem to us more pronounced in Australia than in other countries.

The Australian Nation

This is not the place to present a detailed account of Australian society and its physical environment, but some details may be useful for an understanding of the place occupied by psychology. The population of 16 million people occupies a continent just smaller than the United States of America. Because of the shortage of water, few people are engaged in farming, even though rural products, together with minerals, have always constituted the backbone of the economy. Sixty per cent of the present population live in the five largest cities, two thirds of them in either Sydney or Melbourne. Australia is governed by a federal, six state, and two territory legislatures (Northern Territory and Australian Capital Territory)—each of which has its own education, health, and social welfare departments—together with other administrative structures, although on the whole there is considerable uniformity throughout the whole nation.

Australia has no common land border with another country. Its distance from those with which it has any social, commercial, or professional transactions creates a feeling of relative isolation. One consequence of the "tyranny of distance" is that psychologists who visit the Northern Hemisphere on leave or to attend conferences often visit other centers en route and, thus, develop a wide network of professional contacts. This point is expanded in the section on international perspectives, below.

THE PEOPLE   Until the late 1940s the population consisted almost entirely of the descendants of migrants from the United Kingdom and Ireland, who brought institutions and styles of living from their home countries that were in turn transformed in many ways in the course of adapting to the Australian environment. Since 1947 there has been a radical change in the composition of the population as a result of a large inflow of people from all parts of Europe, and to a lesser extent from Eastern and Southern Asia. Today, a substantial minority, perhaps a quarter of the entire population, consists of non-British immigrants and their children, a fifth of whom have non-European ancestry. There is little overt conflict between ethnic groups, and in contrast to the case in many other countries of immigration, rapid upward mobility of the newcomers in education and occupational status is more typical in Australia than proletariat stagnation.

The Australian Outlook

Certain stereotypical personality characteristics, both good and bad, have been consistently attributed to Australians by foreign observers and by Australians themselves for at least the last 100 years. Australians are supposed to be open, informal, practical, generous, gregarious, fair-minded, direct, argumentative, lazy, crude, and uncultured (Taft 1962; Taylor & Taft 1977). The many subjective accounts also attribute to Australians a pragmatic, anti-intraceptive orientation with a concentration on materialism, consumerism, and leisure. Some of these speculations are supported by objective data reported by Hofstede (1980) in his comparative study of 40 nations on four work-related value dimensions. Australian respondents scored much above the mean on individualism, below the mean on power distance and uncertainty avoidance, and a little above on masculinity. On the whole, the position of Australia on these dimensions is similar to that of the United States and Britain.

In a unique contribution to the characterization of national cultures, Conway (1971, 1978), an Australian clinical psychologist, developed a neopsychoanalytic typology based on an analysis of parenting styles and parallel modes of social relations; thus the Australian way is described as having emerged from a "patrist-authoritarian" past through a "matrist-indulgent" present on its way perhaps to a "fraternalist-anarchic" future in which, in the name of self-expressive libertarianism and equality, such values as order, discipline, and loyalty are submerged. Whether there is still momentum towards the dissolution of earlier modes and their replacement by newer anarchic styles may, however, be debated.

Many commentators on Australia have referred to the derivative nature of the values and the styles of behavior and the tendency to overestimate ideas from abroad—the so-called "cultural cringe." These attitudes have also prevailed with respect to scholarly and intellectual activities, and psychology has been no exception. However, in recent decades there has developed a revival of cultural confidence in Australia that is giving rise to innovations in science and arts, resulting in identifiably Australian products. This movement towards greater autonomy may also eventually be manifested in the contributions of psychologists.

DEVELOPMENT OF PSYCHOLOGY IN AUSTRALIA

Foundations up to 1939

As with many other countries, psychology owed its genesis in Australia to philosophy. In the last decade of the 19th century, three Scottish-educated scholars were appointed to university chairs that included "Mental Philosophy" in their title: Henry Laurie in Melbourne (appointed in 1890), Francis Anderson in Sydney (1890), and William Mitchell in Adelaide (1894). These transplanted scholars brought with them the empiricist perspective, which at that time was deeply embedded in British philosophy. The emphasis on the role of experience in the nature of reality seemed to lead naturally to an interest in psychology.[1] Coming as they did from the technologically developed United Kingdom, it is perhaps not surprising that these "mental philosophers" began to promote the application of psychology, like other natural sciences, to society. They were inspired also by the post-Darwinian functionalism that found its psychological expression in the dilettante experiments of Galton on perceptual and motor performance and human abilities. In 1895 Anderson and Laurie participated with others in promoting "psychophysical and psychometrical investigation in Australia" (Turtle 1985, p. 115) and thus laid the foundation for empirical psychology in Australia. These early moves towards the acceptance of scientific psychology did not, however, evoke a quick response from the universities, and the first specialist lecturer in psychology was appointed only in 1913—Le Couteur at the University of Western Australia. The first experimental laboratory was established in 1903 in Melbourne Teachers College, not a university, by John Smyth, who had been directly inspired by a visit to Wundt's laboratory in Leipzig.

UNIVERSITY DEPARTMENTS Two undergraduate courses in psychology evolved during the 1920s: one at Sydney University, which provided the first major in psychology in 1925, under the auspices of the Philosophy Department; and the other at the University of Western Australia, deriving from Education. The first lecturer-in-charge of the independent department of psychology at Western Australia (established in 1930) was Hugh Fowler, who obtained his PhD under Spearman in London; and the first chair was filled at Sydney in 1929 by H. Tasman Lovell, who had studied at Jena. The typical

---

[1]The contribution of these early Australian philosopher-psychologists has been analyzed in some detail by O'Neil 1987, and to a lesser extent by Taft 1982 and Turtle 1985.

lecturer in psychology was an Australian-born male school teacher who studied psychology before 1939 in Germany, Britain, or the United States. Thus the courses in psychology that developed between 1910 and 1930 contained elements of the subject as it was taught in these three countries, although the most widely used textbooks were from England—for instance books by Stout, Myers, and McDougall (Turtle 1985, p. 113). In the teachers colleges the nature and measurement of individual differences were emphasized, inspired by Spearman and Thorndike, and the students attended laboratory sessions in experimental psychology, following the German model.

APPLIED PSYCHOLOGY   Many of the lecturers also offered consulting services for both children and adults in educational and counseling psychology even though they mostly lacked formal training. The services were usually offered gratis on the basis that this promoted the integration of theory and practice in psychology. A typical example was A. H. Martin, an Australian who had studied at Columbia with Woodworth. In 1927, as a lecturer in psychology at the University of Sydney, Martin founded the Australian Institute of Industrial Psychology to provide services to the public in vocational guidance and industrial selection, work analysis and training, along the lines of the National Institute of Industrial Psychology (NIIP) in London. To take another example, Elton Mayo, who was influenced by Janet, offered consulting services in clinical psychology in his position as Professor of Philosophy at the University of Queensland; but it was not until he obtained an appointment at Harvard in the late 1920s that he began the program of research into industrial motivation for which he is best known. The links established over 50 years ago between the universities and the public and between theory and practice in psychology are still strong in Australia. Many of the early university lecturers were evangelists for the application of this new science of the human mind, which promised so much for improvement in the quality of life. Many of them preached their good-news message through university extension courses and other adult education groups on such topics as the emotional adjustment of children, adolescents, and adults; how to be a good parent; career choice; leadership; and personnel work.

Psychologists who were employed outside the universities and teachers colleges were largely concerned with providing vocational guidance for adolescents and assessing the abilities of children, especially those with learning problems and general mental retardation. Thus, the state of New South Wales set up a vocational guidance bureau in 1928 that worked closely with the school authorities and used tests devised by the NIIP. It was in his capacity as Superintendent of Special Education in the state of Victoria that Stanley Porteus devised his well-known Maze Test before World War I as a substitute for the Goddard version of the Binet in the diagnosis of intellectual disabilities (Porteus 1969). Porteus emigrated to the United States in the 1920s where, from his base at the Vineland Training School and the University of Hawaii, he carried out a series of research projects with his Maze Test, including some of the earliest cross-cultural research on Australian Aborigines.

The War and Afterwards

The outbreak of war in 1939 triggered a rapid acceleration of applied psychology that has continued to the present. The faith the Australian authorities had in the potential of psychology was reflected in a strong official promotion of military and industrial psychology during the war to aid in the marshalling and training of the limited human resources available. The apparent success of these professional activities led afterwards to a rapid expansion by state governments of vocational and educational guidance, counseling and clinical services for children and adults, and the establishment of industrial psychology facilities in both government and private enterprises.

The postwar period saw a parallel spectacular growth in academic psychology. This discipline, for a long time only the stepchild of philosophy, biology, and education, was suddenly after 1950 accorded such respectability that now all the universities both old and new, with the exception of Griffith, have departments of psychology offering both undergraduate and graduate degree courses. This rush of recognition of the legitimacy of psychology as one of the core academic disciplines was undoubtedly a reflection of the already existing penetration of psychological services into the life of the general community, but it also reflected an increasing realization among academics that Australian universities were lagging behind those in Britain and the United States in the teaching of psychology. Gradually the message infiltrated into Australia that psychological scholarship had earned itself a place alongside other science disciplines; but empirical research in the subject started as late as 1950, probably as a result of the impetus from newly appointed scholars with overseas qualifications. The first PhD in psychology was awarded in 1953. (The PhD degree had been introduced in Australia in 1946).

THE CURRENT SCENE IN PSYCHOLOGY

Rosenzweig (1982) suggests that there are five discernible stages in the growth of psychology in the United States, which may be a universal pattern. After passing through Stage 1 (initial period) and Stage 2 (acceleration), Australia would seem to have been in Stage 3 (rapid growth) from about 1960 to 1980. Judging by the number of new graduates and appointments to teaching staff made in the past few years, it seems now to be in stage 4 (slowing of the rate of growth) (Over 1981) but has not yet reached stage 5 (plateau at a high level).

The Psychologists

We estimate that in 1987 there are about 5500 qualified psychologists in Australia, representing 340 for every million of the population. This is close to the median for the 44 countries analyzed by Rosenzweig (1982). However, statistics on the number of psychologists must be viewed as crude approximations because of the looseness of definitions and incompleteness of information. One marked change in Australia recently is the rapid increase in the number of female psychologists. Over (1983) reported that 75% of the undergraduate psychology students in his survey were female, and the percentage in the membership of the Australian Psychology Society (APS) has risen in the last 20 years from 22% in 1966 to 45% per cent currently. This is still below the ratios reported by Rosenzweig (1982) for many countries; few female psychologists in Australia hold senior academic and administrative positions, although a recent increase in the number now being appointed suggests a change in this respect. In 1986, approximately 750 students completed the four-year educational requirements that would qualify them for Associateship—but not Membership—of the APS (see the section on course accreditation requirements, below). Only a proportion of these graduates will undertake the further training required to become a fully qualified psychologist—perhaps not much more than 50% of them—and we estimate that only about one in twelve is likely to complete a PhD. About 50–55 psychologists obtain their PhD in Australia each year.

EMPLOYMENT IN APPLIED PSYCHOLOGY   Academic or professional positions are no longer plentiful. Over (1983) has argued that in order for all graduates to find employment as psychologists there would need to be an increase in openings for industrial/organizational psychologists. Most of the students, however, reported that they were much more interested in working in clinical and counseling than in industrial psychology. Thomas & Wearing (1986) surveyed registered psychologists in the state of Victoria in 1984 and found that 11.5% were in private practice, while about 25% were employed in universities or colleges. The others were mainly in government departments and other public instrumentalities such as schools, mental hospitals, and clinics for child guidance and family therapy; others were employed by private businesses or as consultants. As in most other countries (Rosenzweig 1982), clinical psychology and related fields of application such as counseling are the most popular areas of application, but a comparison with Stapp et al's (1985) survey of psychologists in the United States suggests that the percentage of psychologists engaged in clinical and other health-care specialties may be relatively low in Australia. Thomas & Wearing (1986) reported that a higher proportion of the psychologists in their survey were employed in education and in government departments in Australia than in the United States, and considerably fewer were employed in commerce or in universities and colleges [18.8% in tertiary-level teaching and research versus 29.3% in the United States—compiled from Stapp et al (1985), Table 4, p. 1326]. Even though there are questions about the representativeness of Thomas & Wearing's sample, their findings appear to us to reflect the general position of Australia; and the survey by Nixon (1987) of the employment of recent graduates in psychology confirms that most of them were employed in educational and clinical/counseling psychology. The following sections discuss the main types of employment for psychologists.

Clinical and counseling psychology   Each state of Australia provides a system of public mental hospitals and outpatient referral clinics, in which psychologists are employed, mainly for the assessment of patients. They also engage in some therapy, especially behavior modification. Some general hospitals also employ psychologists in their psychiatric and pediatric departments, and sometimes in neurology and general medicine, or in specialized units such as those for drug and alcohol treatment. Psychologists also work in repatriation services (i.e. veterans' affairs), departments of correction, children's courts, and other clinical services for children within departments of education, child welfare, or health. Many are employed by state governments to make psychological assessments of intellectually and physically disabled children. Psychologists provide personal counseling in educational institutions and in some government departments—e.g. in Immigration or Social Services—while many are in full-time or part-time private practice. Marriage guidance counselors mostly work in state or church-supported "marriage guidance councils," and in some cases counselors have a statutory role in the family court system.

Educational psychology   Every department of education in the six Australian states employs psychologists in various capacities ranging from research on curricula to providing consulting services to teachers; but for the main part they engage in testing, counseling, and guiding of individual students on their schooling and their careers. Unlike the US practice, no distinction is made between school psychologists and school counselors. Mention should be made of the special role played in the application of psychology to education by a nongovernmental organization, the Australian Council for Educational Research (ACER). The Council was established in 1930 with the help of funds from the Carnegie Corporation of New York to promote the scientific study of education and to provide advisory services and information on curriculum, educational assessment, and other aspects of the learning process. The ACER has been, and still is, the major constructor and disseminator in Australia of tests for measuring abilities and educational achievement.

Organizational and industrial psychology   The Commonwealth Employment Service (a federal government agency) has a large establishment of psychologists who provide a free career guidance service. The Commonwealth Public Service Board and some of the State Boards have their own psychologists, as do some of the larger public enterprises such as Telecom, Australia Post, and state electricity commissions. Some of the larger private corporations also have their own psychologists, but most personnel and organizational psychologists are employed by private consultants. The three armed services have maintained establishments since World War II for the selection of recruits, for consulting on training, and for providing clinical and counseling services. Some work in ergonomics is also done by psychologists in such areas as road and industrial safety, aviation, and housing (See the section on research, below).[2]

Professional Organizations

Organizations for psychologists in Australia started essentially as study circles for interested participants that gradually evolved into more formal associations devoted to the study and practice of psychology. The Australian Branch of the British Psychological Society (BPS) was formally constituted in 1945 and was replaced by the Australian Psychological Society (APS) in 1966 by mutual agreement with the BPS as a rather belated response to the growing sense of independence of Australia from Britain. [A full account is given of the history and role of the APS by Gray (1984).]

The APS has laid down precisely formulated and strictly applied entry requirements that attest to the professional status of the members. To be eligible for membership, candidates must complete a minimum of six years of a combination of approved training and experience; graduates with four years of approved training may become Associate Members but are not regarded as qualified psychologists until they have completed a postgraduate course or have obtained approved work experience under supervision. The APS had 3242 Members and 645 Associate Members in June 1986 and each year the membership increases by 200–250, a rate that has been steady for the last few years. We estimate that 60–65% of the eligible psychologists in Australia are members, and that the proportion is somewhat higher for practitioners than for academic psychologists.

---

[2]The application of psychology to various aspects of life in Australia is described in more detail in Nixon & Taft 1977, Parts 4 and 5.

The APS is registered with the state of New South Wales as a nonprofit company and its Memorandum of Association sets out its threefold direction in the following statement of its objects: "To advance the scientific study and professional practice of psychology and enhance the contribution of psychology to the promotion of the public welfare. . . ." Thus, the APS has a community relations function as well as catering to the needs of both academic and professional psychologists. It does not engage in negotiations over wages and working conditions. The APS coordinates with outside bodies, facilitates the development of psychology in Australia, and exercises a control function over it. It has two divisions: one for Scientific Affairs, and one for Professional Affairs. The latter has the following constituent Boards: Clinical, Clinical Neuropsychology, Community, Counseling, Educational and Developmental, Forensic, and Occupational Psychology. The APS publishes two refereed journals, the *Australian Journal of Psychology* and the *Australian Psychologist;* it also produces a monthly bulletin and a set of abstracts for professional psychologists, while some branches and boards also publish bulletins. Because of the relatively small membership of the psychological community in Australia, the two major journals are comprehensive in scope, and many Australian psychologists prefer to publish in international journals catering to their special fields. The annual conferences of the Society, which also tends to be general in its orientation, attract attendances of between 300 and 600 psychologists, depending on the location.

PROFESSIONAL ETHICS   From its inception, the APS set up a standing committee to deal with ethical matters and adopted a set of guidelines based on the APA model. After much discussion, the Society has now adopted a Code of Professional Conduct (1986) that lays down standards for the following areas: assessment procedures, consulting relationships, teaching, supervision and training, research, public statements, and professional relationships. Compared to earlier versions, the current document contains more on ethics in research and less on professional relationships. Where serious breaches of professional ethics by members of the APS have been established, reprimands and even expulsion have occurred, but no sanctions other than a complaint to a State Registration Board can be applied to nonmembers.

ETHICS IN RESEARCH   In response to public concern about the treatment of animal and human subjects, universities and research institutes have set up committees to monitor and control the protection of the subjects' safety and dignity. The minimization of pain and discomfort is the basis for the guidelines for research on animals, and informed consent for research on humans. The National Health and Medical Research Council requires guaranteed conformity with its guidelines before it will release its research funds.

However, some doubts have been expressed by Australian psychologists about whether medically oriented guidelines for research with human subjects are fully applicable to nonphysiological research, especially the requirements for informed consent. Consequently, the current APS code of ethics specifies that, where prior informed consent is impossible by reason of experimental design, the researcher must ensure that the dignity of the participants is protected and distress minimized. Participants also must be informed of the nature and purpose of the investigation at appropriate stages wherever this is possible.

OTHER PROFESSIONAL ORGANIZATIONS   The more focused interests of psychologists are catered to by informal groups and study circles allied to but not affiliated with the APS. There is one such group for experimental psychology and another for social psychology, as well as several more specialized smaller ones—e.g. language and speech, behavior modification, and clinical psychologists in private practice. Many psychologists are active in scientific and professional associations that cater also to other disciplines; a listing of these seems to support the contention that Australians are a nation of joiners. Here are just a few examples of the topics: child development, family therapy, brain impairment, hypnosis, pain, mental deficiency, animal behavior, and ergonomics. Psychologists also participate in the Australian and New Zealand Association for the Advancement of Science (ANZAAS).[3]

The Academies

Twenty five psychologists are fellows of the Academy of Social Sciences in Australia. There are four "learned" academies: the Academies of Science, Social Sciences, Humanities, and Technology and Engineering Sciences. By informal agreement psychology comes within the orbit of the Academy of Social Sciences, even though a particular fellow may specialize in experimental, biological, or mathematical psychology. From time to time, this arrangement complicates mutual relationships with academies in other countries and with the International Council of Scientific Unions (ICSU); however, after a period of reluctance to do so, the Academy of Science has recently sponsored a National Committee to promote and coordinate psychological research and scholarship and to act as a liaison with the International Union of Psychological Science (IUPsyS) and other international bodies.

International Perspectives

How does the work of scholars in a small, isolated country like Australia get noticed? Australians have always been conscious of their isolation and prob-

---

[3]Further information on specific organizations may be obtained from either author.

ably are readier than residents of most other countries to pursue international contacts actively. The generous arrangements for study leave that Australian academics value and protect have sometimes been treated by university administrators more as a duty than a privilege: Lecturers should go abroad and keep up-to-date with their fields. This self-effacing attitude seems to be declining, along with the "cultural cringe" (see above). Many Australian psychologists have undertaken their graduate studies abroad—including both authors of this chapter—and thus have established academic contacts. During their study leave, academics have often taken paid employment in a university or other institution in another country, seizing an opportunity to participate in what Russell (1977) has called the "communication system of psychology." Most study leave is taken in the United States or the United Kingdom with Canada the third choice; but because Australian psychologists increasingly come from non-English backgrounds and, as a consequence, are bilingual, it is becoming more common for them to develop professional contacts with other countries and thus slightly dent the anglophonic monopoly of the discipline.

Russell (1977) indicated various other ways in which Australian psychologists attempt to overcome their communication disadvantages: Apart from visits to overseas departments while on study leave, Australians attend conferences in disproportionately large numbers, contribute substantially to leading scholarly journals, publish textbooks through publishers that distribute internationally, and engage widely in private correspondence on academic matters. Much fruitful exchange occurs when graduate students come from overseas and when scholars make short visits or come on sabbatical leave. Also it is common for non-Australian nationals to be appointed to tenured positions. Exchanges have been aided by international conferences in Australia, and the culmination will be the XXIV International Psychology Congress in Sydney in August, 1988.

Australia joined the IUPsyS in 1957 when the Society was still a branch of the BPS, and there has been an Australian on the Executive Committee for 21 of the last 24 years. There has been a similar presence of Australians on other international committees over the past 20 years—e.g. the IAAP Executive and the IACCP. Nevertheless, despite the efforts Australian authors make to overcome the communication disadvantages of being a small and isolated community, the rate of citation of their work in the international psychological literature is lower than their relative rate of publication would indicate (Over & Moore 1979)—especially citation of papers or books published only in Australia or bearing an Australian address. Australian psychologists publish 7–10 serious psychology books each year, but only 9% of the texts used in the country's psychology courses are Australian, while 77% are American and 14% British (Nixon 1987).

TRAINING PSYCHOLOGISTS

Higher Education and Professional Training

Higher education in Australia is organized on a three-tiered system consisting of Universities; Colleges of Advanced Education (CAEs), which offer bachelor's and master's degrees; and Technical and Further Education (TAFE) Colleges, which do not grant degrees. With a few minor exceptions, all institutions are publicly controlled and funded, and tuition fees are nominal for students who are Australian residents (currently about $US200 per annum). For most students the minimum requirement for admission to universities and CAEs is a good pass standard in a public examination at the 12th year level of schooling, and entry is competitive between eligible candidates. Approximately one quarter of the school population continue as full-time students at University or CAE after completing their secondary schooling. Very few students enroll in an out-of-state institution even for graduate studies.

A bachelor's degree in Arts, Science, or Economics at the "Pass" level typically requires three years of study in one, or in some cases two, major fields, while a bachelor's degree with "Honours," which is available in universities only, requires four years of focused study. A bachelor's degree in professional courses takes four or more years, and students may enter courses such as Medicine, Law, and Engineering direct from secondary school. Undergraduate courses in Australia require less concentration on one discipline than in England but are less diverse than in the United States.

GRADUATE STUDIES   Postgraduate studies may lead to a one-year professional diploma, a master's degree (which usually takes two years), or, for more academic students, a doctorate, which is given by universities only. The diplomas and master's courses include some combination of professional training and research experience, and these now provide an increasing proportion of the training given to new entrants into the profession in contrast to on-the-job training. Doctorates and research master's degrees are usually based solely on the assessment of a dissertation reporting on a substantial program of research conducted under supervision. In order to maintain high standards, it is customary for at least one of the examiners of the dissertation to be external to the university. Admission to candidature requires completion of basic studies in the relevant discipline up to the equivalent of honors level, after which formal course work tends to be minimal since it is assumed that by this stage students know how to study independently. Currently 18 Australian universities offer doctoral programs in psychology.

University Teaching Staff

Most university faculty above the rank of tutor enjoy de facto tenure, if not de jure. Although the possession of a PhD degree is not usually compulsory, it is almost universal in new appointments. Vacancies are widely advertised in various parts of the English-speaking world, and are filled by open competition. Salaries and other conditions of work are standardized throughout Australia under the auspices of the Federal Government, and perhaps because of this and also because of the tenure system, there is little staff mobility between universities.

We estimate that approximately 400 psychologists hold tenured positions in universities and colleges [an estimate based on the figures in Feather (1985, p. 388), with an appropriate allowance for those in university departments other than psychology]. According to Over's (1981) survey of university psychology staff, only two thirds of them received their undergraduate education in Australia; of these, 39% were graduates of the University of Sydney. Turtle reports (1985) that recruitment from overseas has increased in the past decade, presumably because of the high standard of some of the unplaced psychology graduates throughout the world.

The Training of Psychologists

The structure of the education and training required to become a qualified psychologist is based on the "scientist-practitioner" model. There is widespread acknowledgment of the policy of integrating theory and practice which, as we have already pointed out, is a traditional part of psychology courses in Australia. The courses are based on three pedagogical assumptions: Psychologists should have a grounding in general psychology and theory before commencing their training in practical skills; experience with psychological practice and research can illuminate theory; and some training in other disciplines at the undergraduate level helps to provide a context for the understanding of psychology. As a rule, training in professional skills is not introduced until the fourth year and then only to a limited degree.

COURSE ACCREDITATION REQUIREMENTS   The training of psychologists is regulated in three different ways: by the universities and colleges, which decide their own curricula and examining; by boards for the registration of psychologists, which have been set up by five of the six state governments (New South Wales is the exception); and by the APS, which accredits courses that conform to a set of published guidelines. The structure and content of the courses vary among universities, but the three sources of control have converged to a position at which they reinforce and complement each other. To qualify as a psychologist, and to be eligible for membership of the APS, requires six years of training at the tertiary level, consisting of four years of basic education in psychology and at least two years of postgraduate training or supervised practical experience. The APS guidelines for the accreditation of courses (APS Bulletin 1983a, 1985a,b) specify that the basic training should consist mainly of four years of sequential studies in psychology, which must include, inter alia, the study of general psychological processes, individual differences in capacity and behavior, experimental design and research methodology, statistics, and considerable practical experience of working with human subjects. All accredited postgraduate courses in professional psychology include, in addition to a training in practical skills, the relevant theory, awareness of ethical and general professional issues, training in research methods, and the actual conduct of a research project. The Board of Clinical Psychology has laid down additional training requirements for its members (APS 1982, 1983b) but it is the only Bulletin Board of the APS to do this and the issue is still controversial within the Society.

RESEARCH

University departments of psychology or their equivalents—i.e. departments or schools of behavioral science—account for most basic and applied psychological research in Australia. This is evident from the papers presented at national and international conferences, published research papers, and books and monographs.

Research Funding

Most funds for research in psychology come from federal government sources, either directly through the two major funding bodies, the Australian Research Grants Scheme (ARGS) and the National Health and Medical Research Council (NH&MRC), or indirectly through individual university budgets. There are also smaller governmental grants and private sources of funding that usually support research in areas relevant to their specific interests—e.g. the Society for Research on Mental Retardation, the Asthma Research Foundation, the Anti-Cancer Council of Victoria, and the Tobacco Research Foundation. In her recent review, Nixon (1987) reported that in 1983 ARGS and NH&MRC together accounted for 54% of the funding for psychological research, internal university funds for 30%, and the other sources for 16%.

Universities in Australia are almost entirely financed through an annual government grant. The acceptance of the principle that the conduct of research is a responsibility of universities is attested by the inclusion in each grant of an amount earmarked for research that is distributed at the discretion of the institution itself.

The ARGS and the NH&MRC are the major channels through which federal government funds are allocated to individuals, research groups, and research centers for specific projects. Grants are made annually, but they may be more or less guaranteed for three years, and in exceptional cases for longer. The system is competitive, and the allocation is based only on the criteria of the reputation or potential of the investigator and the quality of the project as assessed by local and overseas referees. The NH&MRC favors research that bears on human health, and most of the funds are allocated to medically dominated institutions. The scope, however, is liberally interpreted so that, for example, research by psychologists on sensory systems, the neuropsychology of normal speech, or the study of family interaction would be considered.

Most of the funding of psychological research comes from the ARGS, and already two of the chairmen of the committee of this body have been professors of psychology. In the period 1981–1986 the year-by-year totals allocated to projects in psychology (in Australian dollars) were respectively about 898,000; 1,196,000; 1,192,000; 1,502,000; 1,614,000, and 1,094,000. Colleagues in the United States have commented that the amounts allocated to individual projects seem small. However, unlike the case in many countries, some of the equipment, technical and computing services, and salaried personnel are usually provided by the university department without charge to the project.

Research in General

The research preeminence of university departments of psychology over CAEs is due to various factors. Included are the funding arrangements made by federal agencies; the charters for research as well as teaching held by the universities; the policy of universities to select staff with research potential and achievement, and the requirement of a research record as the main criterion for academic promotion.

The primary responsibility of the CAEs is professional and vocational training. As a consequence research in applied disciplines such as speech therapy, occupational therapy, and orthoptics (generally taught in the CAEs) is much less active than is desirable. However, research is by no means discouraged, and work of significance is possible and has been undertaken even when not supported by internal or external funding.

Research is also undertaken by departments in universities other than departments of psychology, in CAEs, and in a variety of government-funded research organizations. Each of these warrants brief comment. In Australia, as presumably elsewhere, research is undertaken by psychologists working in sociology, politics, psychiatry, medicine, business, and education. For example, a section of the Faculty of Education at Monash University has over the last decade or so made significant contributions in social psychology, the psychology of instruction, and professional issues. It is relevant to point out that at one stage three former presidents of the APS were members of this faculty. Departments of education in other universities have also carried out noteable research, especially in regard to psychological measurement.

Research of marked relevance to psychology is also undertaken by nonpsychologists in cognate disciplines. These include departments of sociology, social work, politics, physiology, pharmacology, zoology, and behavioral biology. In this regard the work on visual structures and processes in the John Curtin School of Medical Research and in developmental neurobiology in the Department of Behavioural Biology in the Australian National University is particularly noteworthy.

A good deal of mission-oriented research concerned with human factors and ergonomic problems is carried out by government research organizations with specific terms of reference. Notable among these are the Australian Road Research Board (ARRB), the Aeronautical Research Laboratories (ARL), and the Defence Research Laboratories (DRL). Some divisions of the Commonwealth Scientific and Industrial Research Organization (CSIRO) also undertake ergonomic and human factors research. Research in the 1950s and 1960s by ARL led to the development of the T-VIS visual guidance system for aircraft landings, which has since been adopted as the international standard. The ARRB, which is jointly funded by both state and federal departments of roads and transport, has made significant contributions to research on road-user behavior, perceptual problems associated with driving, and road illumination and signing. Much of the research from these government laboratories is published in in-house reports with wide circulation among national and international authorities engaged in similar work.

Apart from the human factors research bodies, important national organizations cover other aspects of psychological research—e.g. the Australian Council for Educational Research (ACER, see above) and the Institute of Family Studies, a government-funded body for the study of family interactions and their effect on the individual adjustment of family members and on society, which publishes booklets and issues reports and other public statements on the results of its investigations. In addition some important research is conducted by psychologists working in hospitals and other health settings, such as drug and alcohol centers and the Anti-Cancer Council of Victoria.

REVIEWS OF RESEARCH   Psychological research in Australia was reviewed about ten years ago by Day (1977) as part of a general account of psychology in Australia (Nixon & Taft 1977). On the basis of an analysis of publications by Australian authors in five journals, Day drew attention to the role of the universities in psychological research and to trends since 1945 in the topics studied. He noted that between 1945 and 1972 there had been a 12-fold increase in productivity, with interest directed primarily to the same main areas of experimental psychology as were attracting research effort in Europe and North America. These impressions have been supported by two more recent analyses of publications by Australian psychologists. White et al (1983) analyzed the content of the *Australian Journal of Psychology* over three decades (1949–1978) and reported that a steep rise in the number of laboratory studies occurred up to 1965, but after that the proportion of all studies of this type remained steady at about 50%. Experimental studies on human subjects were the most popular topics, followed by personality/ intelligence. Over the 30-year period, articles on social psychology have also increased while nonempirical papers on general psychology and psychometrics declined markedly. Nixon (1987) reports similar findings based on a survey of psychological research in Australian universities and CAEs and an analysis of articles in 21 publications (1974–1982). Experimental psychology and social psychology were predominant but, partly as a result of including CAEs and partly because her data were more recent, she reported much more research in educational and applied psychology (22% of the published papers) than in the previous analyses of topics.

THE ACADEMY REVIEW OF RESEARCH   Research in specific areas of psychology was recently reviewed in detail and evaluated by a group of leading contributors. This undertaking was sponsored by the Academy of the Social Sciences in Australia (ASSA) to mark, along with similar reviews in other social sciences, the Australian bicentenary in 1988. The book *Australian Psychology: Review of Research,* edited by Feather (1985), is a comprehensive and detailed account of research in five areas—basic processes, psychometric and mathematical psychology, clinical psychology, imagery and hypnosis, organizational and occupational psychology, and wider social issues. The collection contains 15 papers. The book aims "to achieve a 'state of the art' report that would accurately present the major trends in Australian research in psychology in the mid-1980s." In summarizing the current state of affairs as revealed by this material Feather states:

> The research contributions that are reviewed in this book are all in the mainstream of international psychology. One could not say that there is a distinctive Australian psychology that is markedly different from psychological theorizing and research in other countries. Australian psychologists draw upon overseas developments, especially from North America and Great Britain. The publication record indicates that the research being conducted is timely and keeps pace with the best overseas work. Like scientists everywhere psychologists in Australia are influenced by the theories and procedures developed by a small group of leading figures who command the attention of the scientific community. While Australian society may suggest some distinctive questions that require answers, the theories and techniques used to deal with these questions are predominantly those that are in the repertoire of psychologists world-wide, irrespective of their national affiliations (Feather 1985, p. 388).

All of this is fair comment. Of course, the problems associated with mind and behavior, which is the business of contemporary psychology, can not be expected to be much different in Australia from those elsewhere except in minor details. The difficulties faced by immigrants; the nature of perception, cognition, learning, and motivation; and the personal problems of individuals in modern society are likely to be basically the same in Australia as in other countries. Likewise, the methods of tackling these problems and developing theories would be expected to be broadly similar. It would be most surprising if they were not. What Feather's (1985) volume does make clear is that psychological research in Australia is well developed, sophisticated, and vigorous. Compared to the research scene in North America and Europe the difference is essentially one of scale, not of kind or standard.

O'Neil's book on psychology in Australia (in preparation) includes a shrewd commentary on the history of psychological research and the current research scene. It is notable for its identification of the main figures associated with research and the nature of their contributions. It is likely to serve as an authoritative source for the foreseeable future.

Survey of Psychology Departments

For the purpose of this review the heads of the 18 psychology departments in universities were invited to comment on the main thrust, directions, and achievements of current research in their departments. Replies were received from 17 departments. A useful distinction can be made between those in which both teaching and research activities extend over a broad spectrum and those in which they are concentrated as a matter of policy into fewer areas. Most departments of psychology fall into the first category and three into the second: those in James Cook, Monash, and Deakin Universities. Apart from deliberate policy, the range of research activities is also determined by the number of staff members and their specific interests. The specific research activities of university staff is listed in research reports issued annually by the universities.

ANALYSIS OF RESEARCH FIELDS   To render the content of the responses from heads of departments more meaningful, research activities have been classified in terms of 11 main categories, 7 of which have been divided into subcategories. The results of this analysis are shown in Table 1. Entries indicate simply the number of departments of psychology in which research in a particular category or subcategory is being undertaken. Thus the entries indicate the distribution of research interests and areas of concentration rather than the number of personal projects or the volume of output.

The most strongly represented categories in Table 1 are experimental, developmental, social psychology and personality, abnormal and clinical

Table 1 Number of departments of psychology in universities undertaking research in eleven categories and six subcategories in 1986.

Categories	Subcategories	Departments
Experimental Psychology	Perception, cognition, memory	11
	Learning & performance	9
	Behavioral states	5
Comparative Psychology	Laboratory studies	7
	Field studies	1
Developmental Psychology	Infancy	6
	Childhood	7
	Aging & lifespan	3
Social Psychology & Personality	Social psychology	11
	Personality	8
Abnormal & Clinical Psychology	Abnormal	3
	Clinical	7
	Counseling	4
	Medical & Health	12
Psychobiology	Neuropsychology	6
	Psychopharmacology	7
	Psychophysiology	9
Mathematical & Statistical Psychology		4
Applied Psychology	Human Factors	5
	Organizational	2
	Industrial & Occupational	1
Methodology & Theory		5
Psychological Assessment		8
History of Psychology		2

psychology, and psychobiology. In the first of these, the subcategories perception, cognition and memory, and performance appear with the highest frequency; in the second, infancy and childhood; in the third, social psychology including cross-cultural psychology; and in the fourth clinical and medical psychology. In psychobiology, the three subcategories of neuropsychology, psychopharmacology, and psychophysiology occur with about the same frequency. None of this is surprising; judging from recent psychological literature problems and issues in all five fields of enquiry are the current stock-in-trade of academic psychology.

What is perhaps surprising is the low representation of comparative psychology, especially field studies. It might be expected that in a country rich in unique species there would be greater interest in their behavior and sensory capacities. This is not so and never has been. With a few exceptions research psychologists have shown little interest in the study of native animals. The task has been left largely to zoologists and behavioral biologists whose work in both universities and government research laboratories is noteworthy. Lack of interest by psychologists is to be regretted. Not only are research techniques peculiar to psychology not being applied, but honors and graduate students are not encouraged by example to investigate problems of considerable interest and potential significance.

Cross-cultural psychology is fairly well represented in Australia. In Nixon's survey (1987) 5% of all research topics were in this field, and Australians came fourth in rank (after the United States, Israel, and Canada) in the nationality of authors in the *Journal of Cross-Cultural Psychology* (Lonner 1980). However, an analysis of the ethnicity of the research subjects suggests that the studies were prompted more by the recent immigration to Australia than by the presence of an aboriginal population. Just as the indigenous fauna have been relatively neglected by psychologists, so have the indigenous people.

RESEARCH IN APPLIED PSYCHOLOGY   It is evident from Table 1 that research in traditional applied psychology—human factors, organizational, and industrial and occupational psychology—is relatively rare in universities. This is also surprising given Australia's industrial and commercial maturity, although it should be pointed out that numerous government research laboratories (see above) are responsible for extensive research programs concerned with human factors in driving, aviation, and the design and operation of man-machine systems. The data from departments of psychology indicate that much of the current research in medical and social psychology is directed towards issues of immediate concern to society. These include, for example, unemployment, drug addiction, psychological consequences of disease, family relationships, social and political attitudes, tourism, and the study of special groups, notably women and immigrants. New areas of application, especially in medical and social psychology, are receiving a good deal of attention. Indeed, there is evidence in the statements from university departments of a decided trend towards research of greater social relevance and potential application and less concern with basic research. While this trend is not in itself undesirable we feel bound to emphasize here the importance of a strong base in fundamental research. It is hardly necessary to point out that applications frequently spring unheralded from such work.

In addition to the applied research conducted in universities and colleges, considerable short- and medium-term research is carried out in corporations, agencies, clinics, and government departments, especially in the fields in which most professional psychologists are employed—e.g. clinical, health and community psychology, education, employment, and marketing. However, the emphasis in these areas is mainly on applications, and it is rare for practitioners in these fields to produce research reports of publishable standard.

CENTERS OF EXCELLENCE   Achievement and reputation in research tend to be associated with particular people rather than places, although the size and research policy of the institution make their contribution to the output. The outstanding research scholars in Australia constitute that relatively small proportion of the university community whose reputation derives not only from their own work but also that of their students and associates. In turn, they attract both visitors and additional funding which add to their stature. In this way centers of excellence are generated.

Such centers tend to develop as a result of the initiative and leadership of individual scholars rather than as a result of university policy. Lack of flexibility in salaries and rigid methods of financial control make it difficult for universities deliberately to build up centers of excellence, and, in any case, to do so would run counter to the widely supported principle of collegial egalitarianism. It is thus rare in Australia for a university to try to build up research strength in an aspect of psychology by trying to attract a selected scholar to move from one institution to another.

SOME MAJOR RESEARCH PROGRAMS   In a number of departments of psychology notable programs of research have been in progress for some years. These programs typically represent the work carried out over a period of time by loosely organized groups; in Australia, they are seldom substantial enough to warrant the name "center of excellence" in the sense defined above. We list here programs from psychology departments that appear to us to be of especial interest. Our information is based mainly on the survey returns from the departments, and we have tried to concentrate on programs that appear to be substantial rather than simply to catalog all of the research activities of the academic staff. On the whole we have confined our account to programs active currently and have not attempted to describe those that may have been important historically for a particular department. The order of our listing is geographical, beginning from the West of Australia.

At the University of Western Australia, research on the visual system and visual processes is a major strength. The work has ranged over a number of problems including spatial and pattern vision, movement, image analysis, and the developmental neurobiology of visual structures. In the same department there are highly productive programs concerned with the involvement of the kinesthetic system in motor control and the development of motor skills in childhood. The programs concerned with the distinctive cognitive capacities of aboriginal children and cognitive development are also noteworthy, together with one on mental imagery. At Murdoch University, also in Perth, considerable effort has been devoted to developing research programs on the aged and the deaf, including cognitive, personality, environmental, and adjustment factors.

Visual information processing has for long been a focus of interest in the University of Adelaide. As well as experimental work the research has been concerned with the theory of information processing and its applications, especially in relation to mentally handicapped individuals. A second enterprise in this department is a program concerned with family processes and the development of a test for the study of family interactions. The School of Social Sciences in Flinders University has developed strongly in the related fields of social psychology and personality. The work is both fundamental and applied and encompasses a diversity of topics including the effects of unemployment, attitudes, decision making, leadership, and causal attribution. As a result of this continuing effort the School has grown into the main center for research in social psychology in Australia. There are also notable experimental projects concerned with hemispheric specialization for language and speech, and with motor control and motor programming of skilled performance.

Each of the three universities in Melbourne has established distinctive research programs, some of which have resulted in collaborative enterprises between centers. Thus for over a decade there has been a close sharing of research interests in psycholinguistics between the University of Melbourne and Monash University. A similar situation has grown up between Monash and La Trobe universities in the field of perceptual development in infancy, and this has led to the formation of a jointly administered and funded laboratory. The University of Melbourne has pursued an active program in both research and teaching in clinical neuropsychology. Other substantial programs in the department include one of long standing involving a pool of boys whose development is being studied longitudinally and another concerned with the adjustment of immigrant school children. In La Trobe University work in diverse areas of psychobiology has been sustained and vigorous. These include biological rhythms, the neurophysiology of memory, the neuroendocrinology of sleep, and occupational stress. Interest in human development has extended to behavioral pathology in childhood, with recent emphasis on devising ways of assessing temperament in childhood. The Monash department is organized into semiautonomous research groups concerned with specific areas of experimental psychology. These are psycholinguistics (as noted above), the neural bases of hearing, asymmetry of cerebral functioning, behavior genetics, human factors in transport and health care, and perception and perceptual development. Each has continued over some years to attract visitors and strong support from funding bodies and the output has been high. At Deakin University in Geelong, Australia's newest university, research directions are still in the process of developing. Nevertheless, a lively and productive program of research on auditory localization is now evident and has attracted wide interest.

In the University of Tasmania the work on sleep—in particular, its restorative and energy-conserving functions—is marked by concentration on physical factors such as exercise, physical fitness, and body type as determinants of sleep.

The department of psychology in the Australian National University in Canberra has developed strongly over the last decade or so in social psychology—in particular, the adaptation of immigrants, social structure, and social adjustment. There are also strong programs in cognitive structures and in developmental psychology. The latter is directed mainly towards the development of perception in infancy.

Two research programs in the University of Sydney warrant comment, one concerned with sensory processes and perception and the other encompassing a diversity of issues in the field of psychophysiology. The first is particularly notable for research on perceptual illusions and the second for work on vestibular mechanisms and processes, and behavioral neurophysiology and neuropharmacology. The last of these programs is extensive and has been strongly supported by funding bodies. This department continues to pursued a lively interest in history and philosophy of psychology. The School of Behavioral Science at Macquarie University has directed considerable effort to social congition and the effect of family and cultural context on both child and adult development. Parent-child and intrafamily relationships, social cognition, attitudes, and personal values are among the main topics of current concern. The School of Psychology in the University of New South Wales has been active in a broad range of research interests. Subjects of current research include sleep and sleep disorders; addiction; reading, speech, and lexical access; perceptual and cognitive development; assessment and rehabilitation of the brain-injured; social cognition and affect; and cross-cultural transition.

Two of the three universities in New South Wales situated outside Sydney, the Universities of Newcastle and New England (Armidale), share a longstanding interest in mathematical psychology. Both are concerned with the mathematical modeling of psychological processes as well as with the development of techniques for data analysis. At Newcastle there is also a program of cross-cultural psychology concentrating on South-East Asian countries, and at New England there is research on the reaction of viewers to television programs, and on occupational hearing loss. In the University of Wollongong strong interest has been directed to personal-construct theory and the development of procedures for objectifying personal experience.

Research programs at the University of Queensland range over a wide variety of problems including cognitive development; imagery, suggestibility, and hypnosis; perception and perceptual development; family interactions; and language and ethnicity. James Cook University (Townsville) has chosen to concentrate research on issues associated with aborigines, tourism, the impact of disasters, and community psychology.

ENVOI

Psychology in Australia was founded by philosophers from Britain who were appointed to universities in the late 19th century; professional psychological services for the public developed early, but there were no academic departments until the late 1920s; until the 1950s, empirical psychology mainly consisted of measurement of individual differences, but since then, experimental, social, developmental, and other types of psychology have surged ahead, together with the rapid establishment of both academic and professional facilities, so that today Australia rates as one of the more advanced countries in psychology despite its smallness and isolation.

The orientation is both academic and applied, and, although these two facets of psychology seem to be becoming increasingly disparate, there is still a widespread recognition that the academics and practitioners have certain interests in common—e.g. the need for the professional image to be respected by governments and the public. These common interests have so far led to the retention of the majority of psychologists, both academic and professional, among the members and active participants in the Australian Psychological Society.

Within academic departments a similar degree of ecumenicalism seems to hold despite the increasing diversification and intensification of research specialties. Most departments conform to the 'broad spectrum' curriculum pattern, and, consistent with the Australian anti-intraceptive style, an eclectic rather than a dogmatic spirit prevails. However, recently there have been signs that the spectrum in some departments is contracting and that increasing specialization in teaching and research is replacing the broad spread.

Acknowledgments

We acknowledge assistance in the preparation of this chapter through the generous provision of unpublished material by Dr. Mary Nixon, Professor W. M. O'Neil, and Dr. Alison Turtle. We also thank the chairmen of psychology departments in universities and colleges too numerous to list, for providing information about the numbers of their students and the research emphases of their departments. We thank colleagues with whom we have discussed aspects of the chapter.

Literature Cited

Conway, R. 1971. *The Great Australian Stupor: An Interpretation of the Australian Way of Life.* Melbourne: Sun Books. 282 pp.

Conway, R. 1978. *Land of the Long Weekend.* Melbourne: Sun Books. 372 pp.

Day, R. H. 1977. Psychological research in universities and colleges. See Nixon & Taft 1977, pp. 54–68

Feather, N. T., ed. 1985. *Australian Psychology: Review of Research.* Sydney: Allen & Unwin. 412 pp.

Gray, K. C. 1984. The Australian Psychological Society. In *Issues in Psychological Practice,* ed. M. C. Nixon, pp. 1–25. Melbourne: Longman Cheshire

Hofstede, G. H. 1980. *Culture's Consequences: International Differences in*

Work-Related Values. Beverly Hills, Calif: Sage. 475 pp.

Lonner, W. J. 1980. A decade of cross-cultural psychology. *J. Cross-Cult. Psychol.* 11:7–30

Nixon, M. C. 1987. Australian psychology in the 1980's: Origins, developments and issues. In *International Handbook of Psychology*, ed. A. R. Gilgen, C. K. Gilgen. Westport, Conn: Greenwood. In press

Nixon, M. C., Taft, R., eds. 1977. *Psychology in Australia: Achievements and Prospects*. Sydney: Pergamon. 318 pp.

O'Neil, W. M. 1987. *A Century of Psychology in Australia*. Sydney: Sydney Univ. Press. In press

Over, R. 1981. Impending crises for psychology departments in Australian universities. *Aust. Psychol.* 16:221–33

Over, R. 1983. Training and career preferences of undergraduates majoring in psychology. *Aust. Psychol.* 18:377–84

Over, R., Moore, D. 1979. Citation statistics for psychologists in Australian universities: 1975–77. *Aust. Psychol.* 14:319–27

Rosenzweig, M. R. 1982. Trends in develop-

ment and status of psychology: an international perspective. *Int. J. Psychol.* 17:117–40

Russell, R. W. 1977. Australian psychologists in the world context. See Nixon & Taft 1977, pp. 286–98

Stapp, J., Tucker, A. M., VandenBos, G. R. 1985. Census of psychological personnel: 1983. *Am. Psychol.* 40:1317–51

Taft, R. 1962. The myth and the migrants. In *Australian Civilization,* ed. P. Coleman, pp. 191–206. Melbourne: F. W. Cheshire

Taft, R. 1982. Psychology and its history in Australia. *Aust. Psychol.* 17:31–39

Taylor, K. F., Taft, R. 1977. Psychology and the Australian zeitgeist. See Nixon & Taft 1977, pp. 35–51

Thomas, S. A., Wearing, A. J. 1986. Human resources survey of registered psychologists. *Aust. Psychol.* 21:307–18

Turtle, A. M. 1985. Psychology in the Australian context. *Int. J. Psychol.* 20:11–28

White, K. D., Sheehan, P. W., Korboot, P. J. 1983. The Australian Journal of Psychology: The first 30 years. *Aust. Psychol.* 18:261–72

Ann. Rev. Psychol. 1988. 39:401–34

SYSTEMS OF FAMILY TREATMENT:
Substance or Semantics?

Richard L. Bednar, Gary M. Burlingame, and Kevin S. Masters

Department of Psychology, Brigham Young University, Provo, Utah 84602

CONTENTS

Even the most insouciant are likely to have serious misgivings about the prospects of interpreting the progress of the family therapies in a single chapter. If we cheerfully accept the charge of approaching this task constructively, and refrain from limiting our analyses to the more traditional "do's" and "don'ts" of theory building and hypothesis testing, these misgivings can become acute. Nevertheless, our intent is to provide an analysis of the research foundations of the family therapies. We can only address the more fundamental research issues of these treatment systems, but we strive to do this with precision and clarity.

We aim to avoid gratuitous praise or condemnation and emphasize instead what we perceive to be the problems and advances in the field. Our report

401

0066-4308/88/0201-0401$02.00

summarizes the conclusions these disciplines have developed and then offers a critique of the scientific merit of these conclusions. In most cases, we do not summarize or discuss individual research reports. Instead, we emphasize patterns of findings and major conclusions central to the development of the discipline.

Because we intend to emphasize the "scientific" merit of much of the research in these disciplines, we begin by discussing the conceptual pillars and supporting foundations of (a) science, and (b) the family therapies before proceeding with our analyses. We then review the "systemic" and "behavioral" approaches to family therapy.

SCIENCE: BASIC CONSIDERATIONS

The transcendent goal of science is the generation of new knowledge. It is generally accepted that scientific knowledge is less fallible than other recognized methods of developing knowledge (formal logic, intuition, experience). The distinguishing feature in the development of scientific knowledge is the demonstration of an acceptable level of correspondence between facts generated by careful observation and scientific propositions (formal assumptions about relationships between events). Three ingredients are basic to this process: (a) the clarity and precision of scientific propositions, (b) the methods and procedures used in observation and/or experimentation, and (c) the interpretive integrity of research results used to support theory development. Robust scientific inquiry requires adequacy in all three areas.

In most disciplines, the scientific method is synonymous with the hypothetico-deductive method.[1] This procedure is based on a scientist starting with a hypothesis or scientific proposition from which consequences are either directly observed or logically deduced (Boring 1950). If the predicted observation is verified, the original hypothesis is strengthened because the results were correctly deduced.

Our review focuses on assessing the degree to which the family therapies have made progress toward establishing scientific knowledge about their treatment approaches. However, philosophers of science have warned us that the detection of lawful relations in the social sciences will be far more difficult than in the natural sciences (Levine 1974; Popper 1975; Ravetz 1975). This

---

[1]The authors are aware that there are a number of critics of the hypothetico-deductive approach as an appropriate method for the social sciences, and that it has been argued that unambiguous logical connections between theory and observations are problematic (e.g., Kuhn, 1970). However, given that this method is the dominant one represented in the current literature, the alternate paradigms being advocated are clearly embryonic in development, and it would be impossible to enter into a thorough ontological argument on alternate methods of inquiry within our page limitation, we selected to focus our discussion of science within the hypothetico-deductive method of inquiry. Hence, we will use the terms "scientific knowledge" and the "hypothetico-deductive method" synonymously in this paper except where specifically indicated.

view becomes more germane when one considers the multifaceted, interactional nature of families. We must, therefore, carefully evaluate the
degree to which family researchers have been able to advance scientific
knowledge in their discipline. This task can best be accomplished by considering (a) the level of semantic and measurement precision family researchers have achieved in their discipline, (b) the match between the modal
methods of inquiry and the level of conceptual development in the field, and
(c) the role research results play in enhancing theory development and clinical
services. In the hopes of helping the reader understand how we reached our
conclusions and recommendations in this review, we first briefly discuss each
of these criteria.

Semantic and Measurement Precision

The success any method of inquiry may have in discovering lawful scientific
propositions is directly related to the clarity with which the central conceptual
elements in the field are defined and measured. It is unreasonable to expect
scientific propositions to have their origins in a conceptual quagmire. Because
of the accepted and preeminent requirement for semantic, conceptual, and
measurement precision in the development of scientific knowledge, we review the developmental steps of scientific maturation for a growing discipline. We suggest that these steps appear invariant across disciplines.

The first and most basic step of scientific inquiry is punctilious observation.
The law of gravity could not have been discovered without the preliminary
observation that the motion of the planets was synchronized and orderly.
However, observation is not a unitary phenomenon; it has many levels of
specificity and rigor (cf Burlingame et al 1984). It can range from the
informal methods that often precede creative hunches (Bondi 1975), to structured case-study methods (Yin 1984), to the observational techniques of
qualitative inquiry (Miles & Huberman 1984), to the rigorous quantification
of theoretical constructs (Nunnally 1978).

Important products of astute observations include the development of
descriptive taxonomies that define, describe, differentiate, and order crucial
variables in a subject of inquiry. This advances a discipline from simple
observation to a nominal level of measurement (Nunnally 1978). For example, the phylogenetic scale is a descriptive taxonomy that represents a
hierarchical ordering of different species. The initial observations that led to
its development revolved around the basic similarities and differences between and among different species. The explicit criteria inherent in this
taxonomy virtually insured semantic and measurement precision because no
two species could have the same name and, equally important, members of
the same species could not have different names. The emergence of robust
classification schemes represents the second step in the gradual maturation of
scientific disciplines. The increase in conceptual clarity inherent in descrip-

tive taxonomies increases a discipline's potential for reliable observations and provides the basis for meaningful programmatic research. Conversely, when crucial variables are not defined or classified with precision, the potential of discovering valid relationships between and among these variables is fundamentally compromised. This is why we examine the definitional clarity of central research variables and the degree to which measurement techniques accurately reflect their conceptual qualities in the family therapy literature.

After reliable classification is achieved, the third developmental step is refinement in the measurement of central variables in the subject of inquiry. For example, once family therapy has been clearly defined, we are in a position to start quantifying the treatment elements of each treatment approach. These refinements in measurement generally produce ordinal and interval levels of scaling, and allow us to assess the degree to which various treatment components are present or absent in a variety of treatment settings. The ability to measure variables reliably and validly at an interval level of scaling dramatically improves the precision of the scientific propositions that can be deduced or tested.

As a discipline develops methods of quantifying the basic elements within its taxonomies, it is able to advance to the fourth step of scientific maturation. This is the establishment of empirical relationships between and among the variables contained in the different taxonomies. The simplest illustration for the mental health profession would include several taxonomies that define and measure (a) types of clients and problems, (b) psychological treatments and their common and unique components, and (c) psychological change reflecting different dimensions of client improvement. With these fundamental building blocks developed, it would then be possible to study the empirical relationships between different types of client change and specific treatments and clients.

As the data base that describes empirical relations among psychological events (e.g. Treatment A differentially influences client types C and D) grows, the scientist can start developing theories to explain these empirical relationships. This is the point at which theory development[2] is now guided

---

[2]While there is unanimity regarding the importance of theory development in the advancement of science (Bondi 1975), the social science literature contains basic disagreements over the types of theories and methods that might be the most fruitful in the social sciences (Polkinghorne 1984; Manicas & Secord 1983; Shontz & Rosenak 1985). These authors dialectically present approaches to the development of theories that: (a) function in a convergent versus divergent fashion (Shontz & Rosenak 1985), (b) are based upon hypothetico-deductive versus a realist perspective (Manicas & Secord 1983), or (c) stem from a standard or received view of science versus more recent alternative modes of inquiry (e.g. systemic theories). The common thesis across all authors is that the manner in which one theorizes about an object of inquiry will affect the methods of inquiry, and that the social sciences should entertain alternative philosophical stances. Although this is an intriguing issue, space limitations allow us only to raise this for the reader's consideration.

and corrected by empirical data and signifies the fifth level of scientific maturation. This is where the symbiotic relationship between research methods and theory becomes vital (Kaul & Bednar 1986).

Methods of Inquiry

Reviewers must clearly distinguish between the conceptual fabric of a discipline and the methods of inquiry used to test scientific propositions (Rychlak 1977, 1981a,b). Evaluating conceptual definitions involves an examination of the clarity, precision, and logic of the models and concepts central to the subject of inquiry. The evaluation of methods involves an analysis of measurement and methodological adequacy. We suggest that a discipline's modal methods of inquiry should be appropriately matched to the level of conceptual development in the field. Generally speaking, description and measurement are prerequisites to rigorous experimentation.

For example, in young disciplines, "crucial" experiments are not even imaginable owing to the boundaries imposed by conceptual and measurement limitations. Crucial experiments are generally preceded by major advances in measurement precision (Bondi 1975). This in turn contributes to more fastidious refinements of the theoretical elements central to the discipline. In sum, increased measurement precision generally leads to increased fidelity between measurement technology and the major conceptual elements in the subject of inquiry.

Similarly, design rigor is limited in a young discipline by the more naturalistic and applied observations inherent in "early" research endeavors (Dies 1985). This issue is addressed by Cook & Campbell (1979) in their discussion of validity. Support for these views can be found in Shontz & Rosenak's (1985)[3] section regarding the match between theory building and methodological approaches.

Our thesis is that methods of inquiry need to be carefully matched with the level of conceptual development in the field. If methods of inquiry are used that are more advanced (e.g. experimentation) than the conceptual understanding of the subject of inquiry, precise results (due to methodological rigor) are obtained that may have no meaning beyond the immediate experiment (Kaul & Bednar 1986). This in turn can lead to the belief that we know more than we really do. On the other hand, perseveration in descriptive methods has seldom led to significant scientific advances. Therefore, one focus in our analysis is an assessment of the fidelity between measurement and methodological techniques, and the major conceptual elements in marriage and family literature.

---

[3]The interested reader is referred to Shontz & Rosenak's (1985) excellent discussion of how one might match methods of inquiry with approaches to theory development. Although these authors do not take the same developmental perspective proposed in this paper, their "models for clinically relevant research" clearly complement such a perspective.

Function of Achieved Results

Our final evaluative criterion in assessing the scientific progress of these disciplines is the function research results play in the profession's development. Results can function in two distinct ways. First, they contribute to theory development. Contrary to popular opinion, good scientific theories tend to destroy themselves quickly. The logic of this point of view is simple enough: (*a*) A good theory's scientific propositions will be specific enough to allow empirical evaluation; (*b*) empirical evaluation will generate new results, which rarely (really never) provide more than limited support for the ideas being tested, and (*c*) revisions in the original theory will be required to account for these new empirical findings. The demise of a good theory is guaranteed by its power to generate new empirical findings that almost always require theoretical revisions.

The basic momentum of scientific knowledge, then, is maintained by a continuing process of trying to explain what is known (empirical findings) by revising the unknown (theoretical constructs). Hence, one of the most revealing criteria for recognizing major research achievements is the contribution the data offers to the conceptual foundations that guide a profession's theory development. In evaluating the family therapies, we attend especially to the degree to which integrative reviews attempt to advance theory by collectively reviewing research findings.

The second function research results can serve is shaping treatment practices. In spite of the well-documented chasm between research findings and clinical practices (Dies 1985; Fuhriman et al 1984; Kaul & Bednar 1986), we have two reasons for suggesting this as an important consideration. The first is our ethical obligation to improve the quality of client services with the most efficacious treatment practices available. The second is the demand for accountability. We must demonstrate robust treatment practices to both the professional community and the general public.

Conclusion

Although previous reviews of the marital and family therapy research often begin by using the number of research reports as an index of scientific progress, we submit this is a misleading index. In fact, high rates of publication can hinder the maturation of a discipline. It is possible for research reports to contain no substantive contribution because of unsound data interpreted by incoherent arguments that lead to vacuous conclusions (Ravetz 1975). Furthermore, some authors (Popper 1975) have expressed concern that the current publication explosion may actually kill good ideas by submerging them in a flood of barren research reports. More to the point, however, is the assertion that quality research is the keystone of scientific progress. Because of this, our review and analysis of the family therapy literature focuses on the criteria most generally assumed to facilitate the orderly advancement of knowledge in scientific disciplines.

FAMILY THERAPIES: BASIC CONSIDERATIONS

Early theoretical notions, now common to the family therapies, may be found in the works of Sullivan (1953), Horney (1939), and Fromm (1941). Conceptually, the family therapies are unique in that they tend to emphasize personal relationships rather than intrapsychic conflict or medical considerations. These therapies are based on models from general systems theory, cybernetics, and social-learning approaches. Because of this, we provide a discussion of the conceptual properties of these treatments to set the stage for our analysis of the research literature. We discuss what we consider to be the most unique elements of these treatments.

In principle, at least, the family therapies were conceived to be fundamentally different from the various forms of individual psychotherapy. We therefore discuss the elements of these treatments that seem to differentiate them most clearly from individual psychotherapy. Two conceptual and treatment considerations seem unique to some forms of family treatment. These two elements are so unique (relative to most psychological treatment forms), and have such far-reaching theoretical and applied implications, that they provide a reasonable and durable basis for our discussion.

First, all of the therapies we discuss here are highly "interactive" treatment systems that almost always take place in an ongoing "social system" that is both active and authentic (family or marriage). Within these treatments, participants' perceptions, communication patterns, interpersonal styles, and influence on the social system can be openly discussed by all members of that system. A number of terms are used to refer to this phenomenon, but all of them reflect the assumption that an individual's behavior within a social system will ultimately reveal the essence of maladaptive behavior, the function it serves for the individual, and the social conditions under which it tends to appear or disappear.

Virtually any psychological treatment system that attends to events as they occur can be expected to have moments of high psychological "immediacy and intensity." It is not at all uncommon in the interactive treatment approaches we are discussing to invite, and perhaps even subtly require, clients to deal with personal problems and interpersonal conflicts in front of all members of the social system, and directly with the participants involved in the conflict. It is at these moments that the higher levels of psychological immediacy and intensity associated with "doing it," as compared to "talking about it," are most obvious. The fact that the family therapies all tend to deal with human behavior (a) as it occurs in an active and authentic social system and (b) at higher than usual levels of psychological immediacy and intensity is one of the unique features of these therapies.

The second element these therapies share is their acknowledgment and integration of multiple sources of psychological influences within a single-treatment approach. While virtually all forms of psychological treatment pay at least lip service to the reality that clients are simultaneously influenced by multiple social peers (significant others, family, therapist, etc), most consider the therapeutic experiences within the client-therapist relationship to be the most potent curative factor. In all of the therapies we discuss here, we find a generous use of conceptual analyses based on multiple and simultaneous sources of psychological influence.

Family practitioners, for example, must continuously try to understand how family processes affect individuals within the family system and how different individuals affect family processes. This is a classic illustration of the concept of reciprocal determinism in which every member of the social system, as well as the system's psychological organization (norms, roles), can be influenced by, and influences, every other member of the system in a never-ending cycle. A psychological event in a family system cannot be understood without taking into account the simultaneous psychological influences that shaped it.

For example, Alice's aggressive behavior will be affected by (a) family influences (pressure to conform), (b) relationship influences (attraction between family deviants), and (c) intrapsychic influences (conflict avoidance). Alice in turn affects other group members and the group's psychological organization. Each source of influence describes the same psychological event, but at different levels of analysis. And each level of analysis makes a unique and vital contribution to our ability to describe, explain, understand, predict, and enhance the theory and practice of family therapy.

This entire phenomenon is best understood as a highly interactive system of reciprocal determinism that takes place in a multidimensional context. The multiple and interacting sources of psychological influence operating in the family therapies is the second unique conceptual element that distinguishes these psychological treatments from other forms of treatment.

These considerations are far from trivial. They suggest the wisdom, if not the absolute necessity, of having the family therapies based on psychological and treatment principles (a) that reflect multiple levels of psychological influence, (b) with variables that can be conceptually defined and empirically measured, (c) that capture the essence of personal, interpersonal, group, and systemic influences within any active social system, (d) at higher than usual levels of psychological immediacy and intensity, (e) that are derived from methods of measurement and data analyses that can identify reciprocal influences among interacting variables, (f) that will eventually define and describe the principles that regulate human behavior in complex social systems.

Even the most seasoned researcher and practitioner should feel overwhelmed by the complexity of the phenomena we are discussing. It would certainly be unreasonable to expect to find many studies in the contemporary literature that can accommodate even a modest portion of the conceptual elements we have discussed. What we can do is examine the existing literature as a means of identifying the methods and trends that would suggest progress in these areas of prime importance.

SYSTEMS THEORY RESEARCH

Systems theory has had a dramatic influence on family therapy. This point of view has been adopted, or is eagerly represented, in most family therapy training programs. Additionally, a systemic approach is one of the cornerstones upon which separate training programs have developed new research journals and professional societies. Many of the research reports in these journals are introduced with a summary of the major tenets of systems theory and the revolutionary effects this approach has had on our understanding of dysfunctional behavior and its treatment.

The clinical effectiveness of these new family therapies has been a major research focus of this discipline for the last decade. We can all be pleased with the emphasis the family therapies are directing toward outcome studies. Both professional and ethical considerations require service professions to be conscientiously involved in the evaluation of their treatment methods. This obligation is undeniable when it involves the delivery of professional services based on public trust. And nowhere is the need for rigorous evaluation more obvious than in the applied mental health professions. A guided tour through the therapeutic history of these professions reveals the frequency with which well-meaning practitioners have subjected their clientele to such antiquated treatments as cold-water immersions, imprisonment, primal screams, and physical abuse as a means of offering aid and assistance. All of these treatments have had a loyal following in their time, and most of them eventually found their rightful place in our therapeutic museums. Nevertheless, it is only through a rigorous and dispassionate evaluation of its treatment practices that a profession can make legitimate claims of social and professional responsibility (Bednar & Kaul 1978).

Research Trends

In 1961, Parloff stated that there was little rigorous family therapy research and that conclusions seemed to be drawn with a maximum of vigor and a minimum of rigor. Some subsequent reviewers agreed (Goodman 1973; Olson 1970; Winter 1971). Others expressed cautious optimism about the efficacy of the family therapies based on reported improvement rates similar to those demonstrated in individual therapy (Beck 1975; Gurman 1971, 1973a,b; Lebedun 1970; Wells et al 1972). These reviews called for controlled investigations, multidimensional change measures, treatment specificity, and increased methodological rigor.

By several years later, decidedly more optimistic literature reviews had begun to appear. Reviewers boldly suggested that the family therapies had demonstrated their clinical effectiveness. The publication of major reviews by Gurman & Kniskern (1978c) and Pinsof (1981) signalled that empirical research had established its role in guiding the development of the profession. Major reviewers of this rapidly growing literature now seem to agree to the following conclusions:

1. Family therapies that are theoretically derived from systemic approaches to treatment are based on concepts, assumptions, and procedures radically different from those of traditional psychotherapy (Foster & Hoier 1982; Gurman et al 1986; Gurman & Kniskern 1978c; Haley 1984; Jacobson & Bussod 1983; Russell et al 1983; Stanton 1975).

2. Family therapies have become an acceptable method of treatment for a variety of mental health problems (Gurman et al 1986; Gurman & Kniskern 1978c, 1981; Jacobson & Bussod 1983; Russell et al 1983).

3. Family therapies generally are at least as effective as other therapeutic techniques (e.g. individual therapy) (Beck 1975; DeWitt 1978; Gurman et al 1986; Gurman & Kniskern 1978c, 1981).

4. It is unclear whether behavioral or nonbehavioral techniques are more effective (Baucom & Hoffman 1985; Gurman et al 1986; Jacobson & Bussod 1983; Jacobson & Weiss 1978).

5. Deterioration in marital therapy occurs at approximately the same rate as it does in other therapies (Gurman et al 1986; Gurman & Kniskern 1978a,b; Jacobson & Bussod 1983).

6. Much more research is needed to determine the mechanisms of change and the process of therapy (Baucom & Hoffman 1985; Gurman et al 1986; Gurman & Kniskern 1978c, 1981; Jacobson & Bussod 1983).

A synthesis of these conclusions suggests the following three dominant themes: (a) Family therapy is an effective treatment modality (b) that is based on radically new treatment procedures, concepts, and assumptions (c) whose efficacy compares favorably with other forms of psychotherapy.

We wish to alert the reader to the fact that we are far less optimistic about the legitimacy of these general conclusions than are most of our colleagues. Our thesis is that:

1. The conceptual elements that differentiate systemic approaches from other forms of psychotherapy are defined in only the vaguest of terms, if at all.
2. Attempts to operationally define systemic approaches to family therapy and to differentiate them from other forms of psychotherapy are virtually absent in the current evaluation research.
3. Methodological limitations would make it difficult to interpret the existing literature *even if* the family therapy variables being studied were clearly defined and measured in the evaluation research.

After outlining the substantive basis for these views, we suggest a new set of conclusions we believe to be more congruent with the evidence.

Semantic and Measurement Precision

Review of the introductory comments of published reports revealed that the efficacy of family therapy was the central concern of this discipline. However, when we sought to determine how family therapy was being defined and how its effects were being measured, we encountered a serious problem.

While most reports introduced their research with a brief discussion of the recent growth of family therapy and a summary of the evidence suggesting its effectiveness, few discussed its nature. Consideration of features unique to family treatments was sparse, as was discussion of the elements shared with other forms of psychological treatment. More important, family therapy was generally not operationally defined or measured. For the most part, family therapy was assumed to be whatever the particular sample of therapists did; whatever the therapists did was considered to be family therapy as long as family members were present. It appears that the defining characteristic of family treatments was the presence of family members in the treatment room rather than any psychotherapeutic considerations unique to families.

As a means of further exploring the conceptual and/or operational adequacy of the family therapy research, we classified the frequency with which reports (a) provided a description of the intended family treatment, (b) provided specific training for the intended family treatment, (c) provided a treatment manual for the intended family treatment, and (d) actually measured or rated therapist behavior on "systemic" treatment factors. We realize that these categories are neither inclusive nor mutually exclusive; nevertheless, the results of our rating studies are revealing. A summary of these ratings is contained in Table 1.[4] Inspection of Table 1 reveals that all studies (100%) did provide a written description of the intended treatment, with fewer providing specific training (62%), treatment manuals (23%), or ratings of therapist behaviors (15%). What is most revealing is the virtual absence of any study in which a measured treatment variable was drawn from the general "systemic" literature or from among the factors we suggested as relatively unique to this treatment approach.

With such scant evidence defining what constitutes family therapy in these reports, we have little reason to conclude or, for that matter, even assume that family therapy, as discussed in the general systemic theoretical literature, has

[4]*Explanation of Tables 1 and 2*. In order to locate the studies for inclusion in Tables 1 and 2, we first consulted earlier reviews of the literature. Principal among these are the reviews of Gurman & Kniskern (1978a,b,c, 1981), Gurman et al (1986), Wells & Dezen (1978a,b), Baucom & Hoffman (1985), Jacobson (1978a, 1985), Jacobson & Bussod (1983), Jacobson & Martin (1976), and Jacobson & Weiss (1978). We then conducted a computer search that covered 1983 through 1986, and included published material in the English language and the major journals in the field. We did not intend to locate dissertations, unpublished manuscripts, articles in lesser-known journals, or articles in other languages. There may be studies we missed owing to publication lag and the fact that earlier reviews may not have been all-inclusive. We believe, however, that these omissions are few and would not substantially alter the status of this literature. We located 140 studies.

Once the articles were located, the first step in developing the tables was to classify them in terms of the primary treatment under investigation. The categories of behavioral, systemic, and miscellaneous were formed for this purpose. This is in keeping with other reviewers (e.g. Gurman et al 1986) who have used these or similar categories in their analyses. We decided on the placement of articles after considering the author's intent (as described in the introduction and discussion sections of the studies), and by analysis of the therapeutic methods employed by the participating therapists. While studies that relied on reinforcement, modeling, contracting, or other techniques commonly associated with behavioral interventions were easily classified as being behavioral, it was more difficult to classify systemic articles. Thus, the systemic table includes a wide variety of treatments and is linked primarily by theoretical purpose, not technique. In a small number of cases, articles that included both behavioral and systemic interventions were placed in both tables. We have not listed the 42 miscellaneous studies; however, their references are available upon request.

The purpose of these tables was to assess the stringency by which investigators had defined and operationalized their independent variables. The columns across the top of the tables represent methods researchers may have used to ensure that their independent variables were implemented in the study as planned. They are ordered from left to right in terms of increasing stringency. It can be seen that actually measuring therapists' in-session behavior is considered the most rigorous whereas merely describing the treatment as it was to be employed is considered less reliable. Studies that offered supervision to the therapists, but did not actually observe them in session, were coded under the heading "Therapists Trained."

We adopted a liberal attitude while searching for these elements of the studies. If the authors of a study listed a topical citation for the treatment approach but did not describe the treatment in their article, we still counted that as a described treatment. Similar examples could be cited for the other categories. Thus, if we erred, we likely did so by giving authors the benefit of the doubt, thereby creating false positives.

been represented in the empirical literature. The evidence does not support the conclusion that the favorable outcomes reported in these studies are attributable to any specific systemic factors (or for that matter to any specific psychotherapeutic factors). This body of literature represents a form of psychological treatment with a clear and distinctive title that has limited substantive meaning.

This conceptual ambiguity seems to have played a major role in compromising the interpretive integrity of much of this literature. It has been suggested by many major reviewers (Beck 1975; DeWitt 1978; Gurman et al 1986; Gurman & Kniskern 1978c, 1981) that family therapy has been demonstrated to be at least as effective as other forms of psychotherapy. This is a puzzling conclusion.

Individual and family therapies obviously share many common elements, including, for example, catharsis, support, introspection, clarification, and interpretation. Thus the claim that the improvement rates for family therapy are approximately the same as those for individual psychotherapy can be interpreted in two contradictory ways. Either the equivalent successes of individual and family therapy are a function of the elements they share, or the two treatments are different but equally effective. The available data does not prove either alternative. That is the problem. In the absence of evidence demonstrating that family therapy includes unique treatment components, and lacking measures of the degree to which these components influence client outcome, comparative claims of success are meaningless.

This interpretive error is the result of conceptual vagueness more than methodological weakness. Even if the research designs employed in this research were impeccable (which they are not), the same interpretative problems would exist.

Methods of Inquiry

Other serious interpretative problems result from methodological flaws. For the most part, the treatment effects of individual and family therapy have not been systematically compared with a clientele that has been randomly assigned to each treatment. Any comparison between individual and family therapy that does not meet this condition has little substantive value. Improvement rates vary substantially among different types of clientele, whether they are receiving psychological assistance or not. The comparative effectiveness of individual and family psychotherapy cannot be assessed unless (*a*) similar clients are randomly assigned to each treatment, or (*b*) the outcome effects of either treatment can be adjusted to accommodate the base rates for improvement inherent in different treatment populations.

There are other more generic methodological problems we want to

Table 1 Systems Studies

Study	Treatment Described	Therapists Trained	Treatment Manual	Therapist Behavior Measured/ Observed	Multiple Sources of Influences	Systems Treatment Variables			
						Personal, Interpersonal, Group, or Systemic Level of Analysis	Level of Immediacy and Intensity	Reciprocal Influences	All Other Systemic Influences
Beal & Duckro (1977)	x	x							
Boelens, Emmelkamp, Mac-Gillavry & Markvoort (1980)	x	x							
Cadogan (1973)	x								
Donner & Gamson (1968)	x								
Druckman (1979)	x								
Epstein & Jackson (1978)	x	x							
Esterson, Cooper & Laing (1965)	x								
Fitzgerald (1969)	x	x							
Friedman (1975)	x								
Garrigan & Bambrick (1975)	x	x		x					
Garrigan & Bambrick (1977)	x	x	x	x					
Goldstein, Rodnick, Evans, May & Steinberg (1978)	x								

Reference					
Hardcastle (1977)	x				
Johnson & Greenberg (1985a)	x	x	x		x
Johnson & Greenberg (1985b)	x	x	x	x	
Klein, Parsons & Alexander (1977)	x	x	x	x	
Leff, Kuipers, Berkowitz, Eberlein-Vries & Sturgeon (1982)	x	x			
Reiter & Kilmann (1975)	x		x		
Safer (1966)	x				
Santa-Barbara, Woodward, Levin, Goodman, Streiner & Epstein (1979)	x	x			
Schreiber (1966)	x	x			
Scovern, Bukstel, Kilmann, Laual, Busemeyer & Smith (1980)	x	x	x		
Seeman, Tittler & Friedman (1985)	x	x			
Szapocznik, Kurtines, Foote, Perez-Vidal & Hervis (1983)	x	x			
Wellisch & Ro-Trock (1980)	x	x			
Wellisch, Vincent & Ro-Trock (1976)	x	x			

summarize. In their 1978 review, Gurman & Kniskern provided the following general description of family therapy outcome research:

> The modal study can be characterized as using only one evaluative perspective, usually that of the therapist or client(s), and a single change index; among the marital studies, this was a global measure of change or marital satisfaction; among the family studies, it was either identified patient behavior or symptomatology or overall family functioning (1978c, p. 822).

In a more recent review, Jacobson & Bussod stated:

> Most of the major theoretical models reviewed . . . have been subjected to few if any controlled investigations of treatment efficacy. Much of the outcome research that has been conducted is limited by a variety of methodological flaws including the absence of appropriate control groups, the lack of adequate follow-up data, the use of questionable, poorly validated measures of treatment outcome, and treatment procedures that are so vaguely and poorly specified that they are virtually unreplicable (1983, p. 623).

We concur with these depictions, and would add the following points. First, approximately one third of the studies cited by Gurman & Kniskern (1978c) are either unpublished manuscripts or doctoral dissertations. These sources, while not necessarily inferior, are relatively inaccessible and, therefore, difficult to evaluate. Second, most studies have been conducted by those aligned with the treatment under investigation. Meta-analyses in other areas (Berman et al 1985; Smith et al 1980) have demonstrated that theoretical allegiance of the researcher is often a significant factor in predicting the results of outcome investigations. While we do not fault researchers for investigating treatments to which they have an allegiance, we believe they must be mindful of their theoretical position when forming conclusions about these areas of inquiry.

Function of Achieved Results

We consider semantic/measurement precision and an appropriate match between the methods of inquiry and levels of knowledge development to be prerequisites if research is to enhance clinical practice and theory development. These prerequisites have not been met in the existing systemic outcome research. The modal study is based on constructs whose conceptual and treatment properties are poorly defined. Additionally, experimental outcome studies have generally preceded the most basic descriptive studies that would define family therapy, family systems, family pathology, and family health. Under these conditions, research findings have little value for theory development or clinical practice.

Conclusions and Recommendations

The conclusions of a number of the reviewers already cited are unwarranted in some cases and premature in others. Our reading of this literature suggests that:

1. The conceptual ingredients that are assumed to be central to theories of family therapy have not been represented in the evaluation research. Most of these theoretical concepts are defined in general terms, failing to delineate family therapy. Until these definitional problems yield to a rigorous theoretical analysis, the variables most essential to a systemic point of view cannot be submitted to scientific scrutiny. Until then, it is implausible to suggest that (a) family therapy is a unique treatment modality (b) at least as efficacious as individual therapy.

2. The most distinguishing feature of family therapy is that multiple family members attend the treatment sessions. From a structural point of view, this is an important observation. It suggests that families may profit from therapy, not because of any new treatment considerations, but simply because all family members are present in a discussion about family problems. If the family therapies wish to verify scientifically that they represent a unique and effective treatment modality, they must (a) define their treatment factors and demonstrate how they are unique, and (b) determine what portion of outcome variance can be accounted for by these unique treatment factors. We realize these are difficult problems in the social sciences. Nevertheless, conclusions suggesting that a new treatment has been demonstrated to be effective presuppose an accumulation of reasonably rigorous supporting evidence. The fact is, we know little about what systemic family therapy is, how it is different from other forms of therapy, and what desirable treatment effects can reasonably be attributed to any unique treatment considerations in this new form of treatment.

3. Finally, the research efforts of this discipline are out of harmony with what would normally be expected from such a young discipline. The outcome literature we have summarized attempts to establish empirical relations among the crucial variables in this field. A high level of scientific maturation usually precedes such an ambitious undertaking. We suggest that the family therapies are in desperate need of more fundamental descriptive information before proceeding with such an undertaking. This would include: (a) increased ability to recognize, define, and differentiate crucial variables; (b) more descriptive research (development of taxonomies), and emphasis on the development of measurement techniques that will adequately represent the conceptual qualities described in their taxonomies (types and basis for different family systems); and (c) the eventual development of research designs

that will link highly interactive treatment considerations across time to changes in family system structures as well as individual clients within the family system.

BEHAVIORAL MARITAL AND FAMILY THERAPY RESEARCH

Behavioral marital and family therapy (BMFT) is the primary conceptual alternative to systems-oriented approaches for the treatment of dysfunctional marriages and families. The behavioral approaches, like their systems-oriented counterparts, attend to social interaction patterns among family members, and to some degree emphasize the interdependence of family behaviors. Although differences exist among BMFT approaches (e.g. varying attention upon individual vs family behavior patterns), BMFT models can be distinguished from systemic therapies by their molecular analyses of the family system. These in turn suggest a treatment package of interventions matched to specific target behaviors.

The molecular emphasis of BMFT stems from its conceptual roots in behaviorism and social-learning theories. Generally, theoreticians espousing these approaches propose specific, operationalizable, observable, and empirically verifiable propositions. Hence, most reviewers (Baucom & Hoffman 1985; Gurman et al 1986; Gurman & Kniskern 1978c, 1981; Jacobson & Bussod 1983; Jacobson & Martin 1976; Jacobson & Weiss 1978) suggest that BMFT approaches have no peer with regard to the quantity or quality of research they have generated. The following conclusions are suggested by these reviewers regarding the BMFT literature:

1. BMFT produces improvement at a better-than-chance rate, although a large proportion of patients appear to be distressed at the end of therapy (Gurman et al 1986; Jacobson et al 1984; Jacobson & Weiss 1978).
2. It is unclear whether behavioral or systemic techniques are more effective (Baucom & Hoffman 1985; Gurman et al 1986; Jacobson & Bussod 1983; Jacobson & Weiss 1978).
3. Whether the entire treatment package is used, or only components of it, there seem to be no major differences in the overall effectiveness of BMFT. Additionally, the order in which the procedures are presented does not appear to affect outcome (Baucom & Hoffman 1985; Gurman et al 1986).

Semantic and Measurement Precision

Does BMFT claim to have a unique form of treatment? If such a claim is asserted, has BMFT demonstrated this uniqueness empirically? In addressing these questions, we first examine the semantic clarity of the conceptual elements of BMFT.

CONCEPTUAL ELEMENTS   Social learning (Thibaut & Kelly 1959) and operant exchange theories (Homans 1961) provide the infrastructure for the conceptual elements and techniques employed by BMFT therapists (Foster & Hoier 1982; Gurman & Knudson 1978; Jacobson & Martin 1976; Jacobson & Weiss 1978). Specifically, BMFT therapists intervene by clearly describing the family system from which target behaviors are identified along with the stimuli and contingencies that regulate these behaviors. Thus, the primary focus is upon individual actions and the manner in which family members control the contingencies for those actions.

Marital and family problems are conceptualized as the result of (*a*) inadequate or inappropriate stimulus control and its behavioral consequences, or (*b*) individuals' lack of the knowledge or skills necessary for participation in a healthy family system. Treatment techniques often utilize the cognitive-behavioral approaches of Beck (Beck et al 1979), Meichenbaum (1977), and Mahoney (1974), along with expanded classical and operant conditioning strategies (e.g. token economies, prompting, modeling, skill training, reinforcement & pinpointing contingencies). In addition to these treatment elements, the notion of reciprocal determinism is also elucidated by BMFT. In fact, since BMFT incorporates both the systemic and behavioral components necessary for the articulation of reciprocal determinism, this concept plays a more critical role here than in the behavioral approaches from which it originated.

CLARITY AND UNIQUENESS   The semantic clarity and developmental maturity of the conceptual elements in BMFT clearly surpass those of the systems-oriented approaches. BMFT practitioners and researchers appear careful in specifying what they are treating, how they expect change to occur, and what they want to change. This greater specificity, of course, stems from a substantive heritage in the behavioral tradition which stresses observable and well-defined target behaviors that, in turn, serve as outcome criteria. Although various behavioral approaches have been criticized for the semantic circularity of their conceptualizations, we believe BMFT fares well on our criteria of semantic precision.

From its inception, behaviorism has been concerned with the effects of various external stimuli on the behavior of people. For BMFT to specify these stimuli as the members of a family does not represent a major conceptual revolution. It may be argued that training parents to be therapists with their children is a novel form of therapy. The parents are now the agents of change. Of course, Freud (1959) suggested a similar approach many years ago with the case of Little Hans. Moreover, since the methods used by the parents consist primarily of interventions firmly grounded in social learning theory (e.g. modeling, contingency contracting, role playing), there is nothing theoretically new within BMFT conceptualizations. Therefore, to the extent that BMFT is effective in the treatment of marital and family problems, it represents a validation of the concepts drawn from behavioral approaches generalized to a new population, as well as a blending of systems thinking with behavioral techniques, rather than an introduction of new conceptual elements.

Methods of Inquiry

Our review of the methods sections of BMFT reports was, as before, designed to ascertain (*a*) the fidelity between the operational definition and measurements employed, and the principal conceptual elements of the treatment; and (*b*) the match between method of inquiry and the maturity of the conceptual knowledge base. The reports delineated in Table 2 guided our examination.

FIDELITY OF METHODS   An inspection of Table 2 reveals that of the 72 studies that employed behavioral interventions, all described the intended treatment. In addition, training was provided for therapists in 65% of these studies, and 25% used treatment manuals. More importantly, 24% of the studies made some attempt to measure therapist behaviors regarding the implementation of treatment. Assessment of therapist behaviors included: pretreatment behavioral compliance (Alexander et al 1976), live or videotape observation of treatment (Alexander & Parsons 1973; Jacobson 1984; Patterson et al 1982; Patterson et al 1975; Reisinger et al 1976), supervision of sessions and/or direct delivery of treatment (Barton et al 1985; O'Farrell & Cutter 1984), behavioral ratings of session videotapes (Johnson & Greenberg 1985a; O'Leary & Turkewitz 1981), and inventories completed at the end of treatment (Margolin & Weiss 1978; O'Leary & Turkewitz 1981).

Although assessment of treatment fidelity is not endemic to the BMFT literature, the fact remains that approximately one quarter of the BMFT studies specifically defined treatment in measurable propositions, and then assessed whether the treatment delivered matched these propositions. This method leads to more certainty not only regarding the treatment being examined but also about the conclusions derived from such. Nevertheless, significant interpretive problems exist in the remaining 76% of studies where nothing was done to ensure appropriate treatment implementation. Of course, those studies that provided no training to therapists (35%) are even more problematic.

The greater precision of operationalization found in BMFT and the greater clarity inherent in the conceptual elements of treatment warrant a more careful inspection of the type and quality of measures used in BMFT than was done in the analysis of systemic therapies. Eighty measures were used to assess treatment process and outcome variables in the aforementioned BMFT studies. Most studies incorporated more than one outcome measure drawn from more than one vantage point (e.g. parent, spouse, child, therapist, rater), suggesting a fair amount of methodological rigor.

As one might expect, self-report measures made up the largest proportion of instruments used (72%). Many of these self-report measures appear to have been homemade, specifically developed for the study, and consisted of symptom/problem checklists (e.g. bedwetting), straightforward questions (e.g. "Are you still living together?"), or a rating of specific behavior (e.g. number of arguments). Although reliability coefficients are often reported, the lack of normative data for many of these measures makes it difficult to make comparisons between studies and impossible to make generalizations beyond the sample tested.

The remaining measures consisted of observation ratings systems (18%), ratings by professionals (8%), and archival records (3%). Although observation rating systems were occasionally used to objectify assessment of treatment outcome, these measures were primarily used to assess therapist compliance with treatment implementation. Ratings by professionals and archival records were used infrequently despite their potential for providing descriptively rich data regarding the process and outcome of treatment.

MATCH OF METHODS   The primary methods of inquiry used in BMFT studies were experimental or quasi-experimental designs. Most studies had appropriate control or comparison groups and adequate assessment procedures. For example, typical studies employed multiple measures and sampled across different vantage points and response domains (e.g. Baucom 1982; Fleischman & Szykula 1981; Mathews et al 1977). A minority of studies (e.g. Fleischman & Szykula 1981; Jacobson 1977; Patterson 1974) have included follow-up assessment of up to one year with one line of research (Klein et al 1977) having a follow-up that extended for three and one half years. Moreover, BMFT studies generally examined treatments of equal length, used random assignment of subjects, and assessed pre-to-posttreatment change. These factors taken together represent a commendable standard of methodological rigor.

In contrast to the systems-oriented treatments, there appears to be a more appropriate match between the maturity of the knowledge base and the preferred method of inquiry in the BMFT approaches. Given the level of conceptual clarity in BMFT, the investigator is equipped to delineate distinctive treatment components, examine their presence or absence, and relate

Table 2 Behavioral studies

| Study | Treatment Described | Therapists Trained | Treatment Manual | Therapist Behavior Measured/ Observed | Outcome Measures | | | | |
					Self-Report	Observation	Parent Rating	Professional Rating	Archival
Alexander, Barton, Schiavo & Parsons (1976)	x	x	x	x		U[a]			x
Alexander & Parsons (1973)	x	x	x	x					x
Arnold, Levine & Patterson (1975)	x	x				N			
Arzin, Besalel, Bechtel, Michalicek, Mancera, Carroll, Shuford & Cox (1980)	x		x		N,U				
Arzin, Naster, & Jones (1973)	x		x		U				
Baucom (1982)	x	x			N,U	N			
Baucom & Aiken (1984)	x				N,U				
Barlow, O'Brien & Last (1984)	x				N,U	U			
Barton, Alexander, Waldron, Turner & Warburton (1985)									
Replication 1	x	x		x		U			x
Replication 2	x	x							x
Replication 3	x	x							x
Beach & Broderick (1983)	x				N,U				
Blechman & Olson (1976)	x	x				N	N		
Boelens, Emmelkamp, Mac-Gillavry & Markvoort (1980)	x	x			U	N			
Bogner & Zielenbach-Coenen (1984)	x	x			U				

Study								
Chamberlain, Patterson, Reid, Kavanaugh & Forgatch (1984)	x	x			U			
Cobb, Mathews, Childs-Clarke & Blowers (1984)	x	x		U	U			
Crowe (1978)	x	x		U	U		U	
Diament & Colletti (1978)	x	x	x	N,U	U			
Doane, Falloon, Goldstein & Mintz (1985)	x	x		N,U	N,U	U	U	
Emmelkamp & deLange (1983)	x	x		U	U			
Emmelkamp, Van Der Helm, Mac-Gillavry & Van Zanten (1984)	x		x		U	U		
Epstein & Jackson (1978)	x		x	U	U	U		
Eyberg & Johnson (1974)	x		x		U			
Falloon, Boyd, McGill, Razani, Moss & Gilderman (1982)	x			U	U	U		
Falloon, Boyd, McGill, Williamson, Razani, Moss, Gilderman & Simpson (1985)	x	x		U	U	U	U	x
Ferber, Keeley, & Shemberg (1974)	x			U				
Fleischman (1981)	x				N			
Fleischman & Szykula (1981)	x	x	x		N	U		
Hahlweg, Revenstorf & Schindler (1984)	x				N			
Hahlweg, Schindler, Revenstorf & Brengelmann (1984)	x			U,N	N			
Harrell & Guerney (1976)	x			U,N	N			

Table 2 Behavioral studies *(continued)*

Study	Treatment Described	Therapists Trained	Treatment Manual	Therapist Behavior Measured/Observed	Outcome Measures				
					Self-Report	Observation	Parent Rating	Professional Rating	Archival
Hedberg & Campbell (1974)	x				U				
Horne & VanDyke (1983)	x					N,U			
Huber & Milstein (1985) (cognitive-behavioral)	x				N,U				
Jacobson (1977)	x	x	x		N,U	N			
Jacobson (1978b)	x	x		x	N,U	N			
Jacobson (1979)	x	x	x		N,U	U			
Jacobson (1984)	x	x	x	x	N,U				
Jacobson & Follette (1985)	x		x		N,U				
Johnson & Greenberg (1985a)	x	x	x	x	N,U		N		
Karoly & Rosenthal (1977)	x	x			U	N			
Klein, Alexander & Parsons (1977)	x	x	x	x					x
Leff, Kuipers, Berkowitz, Eberlein-Vries & Sturgeon (1982)	x	x			U			U	
Margolin & Weiss (1978)	x	x		x	N,U	N			
Mathews, Teasdale, Munby, Johnston & Shaw (1977)	x	x	x		U	U			
Mayadas & Duehn (1977)	x					U			
McLean, Ogston & Grauer (1973)	x				N,U	U		U	x
Mehlman, Baucom & Anderson (1983)	x	x			N,U	N			
Milton & Hafner (1979)	x				N				

Study							
O'Farrell & Cutter (1984)	x		U	N		x	
O'Farrell, Cutter & Floyd (1985)	x		N,U	U	U	x	
O'Leary & Turkewitz (1981)	x	x	N,U		U	x	
Oltmanns, Broderick & O'Leary (1977)	x		N				
Parsons & Alexander (1973)	x	x		N		x	
Patterson (1974)	x	x				x	
Patterson, Chamberlain & Reid (1982)	x	x		N	U	x	
Patterson, Hops & Weiss (1975)	x	x		N		x	
Patterson & Reid (1973)	x	x			U		x
Peed, Roberts & Forehand (1977)	x	x		U	N,U		
Reisinger, Frangia & Hoffman (1976)	x	x		U		x	
Revenstorf, Schindler & Hahlweg (1983)	x	x	N,U	N			
Ross, Baker, & Guerney (1985)	x	x	N,U				
Salzinger, Feldman & Portnoy (1970)	x	x			U		
Schindler, Hahlweg & Revenstorf (1983)	x	x	N,U	N			
Stuart (1969)	x		U				
Taplin & Reid (1977)	x	x		N			
Tsoi-Hoshmand (1976)	x	x	N,U				
Valle & Marinelli (1975)	x	x	N,U				
Walter & Gilmore (1973)	x		U	N			
Weathers & Liberman (1975)	x	x	U	U		x	x
Wieman, Shoulders & Farr (1974)	x	x	N			x	x

aN = Normed; U = Unnormed. [Many of these studies contained more than one measure of a particular type (i.e. normed or unnormed). Our rating indicates only that at least one of these measures was found.] We made no attempt to assess the adequacy of the normative samples.

them to specific treatment outcomes. However, it should be noted that the measurement problems discussed above can severely limit the external validity of conclusions drawn from BMFT investigations. Another limiting factor is the narrow range of subjects that have typically been employed in BMFT research. Samples often consist of mildly disturbed individuals or recruited subjects, which makes generalization to more severely disturbed clinical populations tenuous at best.

Function of Achieved Results

Although the current BMFT literature clearly surpasses the systems-oriented literature in potential for improving both conceptual understanding and treatment practice, few investigators have engaged in the programmatic research necessary to achieve these goals. This state of affairs is somewhat disappointing, given the historical emphasis that behavioral treatments have placed on the empirical demonstration of treatment efficacy. By anchoring research within theory, BMFT investigators have a far greater potential for establishing a reciprocal network in which advances or refinements in measurement and research lead to advances or refinements in theory. Furthermore, the proclivity of BMFT investigators toward clear descriptions and operational specificity more easily enables practitioners to replicate treatments in their office. A few quality examples of the reciprocity between theory and research can be found in the literature—e.g. James Alexander, Gerald Patterson, and Neil Jacobson. We consider only one to illustrate this process.

Alexander's work with juvenile delinquents and their families provides an excellent four-phase research program that exemplifies the developmental stages of science (Alexander 1973; Alexander & Barton 1976; Alexander & Parsons 1973; Klein et al 1977; Parsons & Alexander 1973). In phase one, Alexander (1973) empirically identified and measured the theoretical constructs of defensive and supportive communication among members of delinquent and nondelinquent families. As predicted, the two groups differed along these dimensions, providing support for both the measurement process and the theoretical constructs. Phase two (Alexander & Parsons 1973; Parsons & Alexander 1973) was designed to modify the reciprocal processes of supportive and defensive communication by using the earlier results to modify intervention strategies. The results of these investigations indicated that interventions aimed at altering maladaptive communication patterns could produce change in a relatively short period. Families of delinquent children who received short-term behavioral family treatment increased supportive communication patterns.

However, improvement in communication does not guarantee improvement in outcome. Thus, phases three and four addressed the issue of client improvement. Phase three focused on recidivism rates, while phase four investigated sibling delinquency. It was hypothesized that if the family system had experienced positive change, then younger siblings should reap the benefits and not become delinquent. Both recidivism and sibling measures demonstrated the superiority of a behavioral-system treatment over both a no-treatment condition and a client-centered approach (Alexander & Barton 1976; Klein et al 1977). Although the theoretical basis for much of Alexander's work was systemic, the actual treatment employed included specific, targeted behavioral techniques (e.g. contingency contracting, reinforcing, and modeling). This program of research not only demonstrates a synthesis of the two approaches, but also shows how careful observation and explication can significantly affect conceptual understanding and practice.

Conclusions

Overall, we were decidedly more optimistic about the behavioral approaches than about the systemic theories. Our analysis suggests the following conclusions about the BMFT literature:

1. The conceptual elements that define and differentiate BMFT are precise and measurable and represent a synthesis of a behavioral treatment applied within a systemic orientation. While not representing a major conceptual advance over existing therapeutic interventions, BMFT has become a useful form of treatment.
2. Since the methodological operations employed by BMFT researchers are more rigorous, one can place greater confidence in their conclusions than in those of the systems-oriented approaches. However, the lack of rigor in measurement attenuates the potency of these conclusions.
3. Applied, theoretical, and empirical advances are closely matched in this field. There are examples of BMFT investigators who have established an appropriate model of scientific inquiry wherein theory and research interact in a reciprocal fashion.

CONCLUDING COMMENTS

During the last decade, we (Bednar & Kaul 1978; Bednar & Lawlis 1971; Bednar & Moeschel 1981; Kaul & Bednar, 1986) have reviewed and analyzed the "interactive" treatment approaches to small groups and families. We have assessed thousands of research reports representing more than 50 years of published research. These efforts have been intellectually sobering. Our comprehension of the extraordinarily difficult issues these disciplines face has become more realistic. We have come to understand that patience is more essential to progress than many of us knew. But, most importantly, we have begun to see more clearly the common and underlying obstacles to scholarly progress in these complex disciplines.

Over a decade ago, Bednar & Kaul (1978) described the symbiotic relation that must develop between conceptual clarity and methodological rigor in systems of interpersonal influence. They wrote:

Serious investigations . . . have increased at a geometric rate. It is reasonable to anticipate that such concerted effort on the part of so many would have led to clearly discernible progress. One would expect that the fundamental phenomena would have been identified and elaborated, that a systematic integration of the phenomena would be apparent, and that the areas of ambiguity would be amenable to empirical attack.

At one level, a review of the contemporary literature does not support the conclusion that these reasonable expectations have been met. In an absolute sense, the basic concepts and propositions . . . are remarkable in their ambiguity. This lack of clarity is manifest when authors employ the same term to denote two or more distinct phenomena and, conversely, when different terms are used to label identical events. When intelligent and well-trained investigators cannot agree on the meaning of basic terms, it is not surprising that the aggregate value of their work may be compromised. Nor is it surprising that this aggregate is resistant to integration and translation to clinical practice. Even though individual researchers have controlled for many sources of variance, conceptual imprecision has unnecessarily limited the value of much of the contemporary research. Evidence of a fact in isolation is important to scientific progress. But even if all the individual facts are undeniable, without an integrating conceptual framework, they carry no more thematic power than a telephone directory (p. 810).

These views seem at least as germane today as they were a decade ago. Similarly, Kaul & Bednar (1986) recently repeated their pleas for observance of the most fundamental steps involved in advancing knowledge. They wrote:

In his philosophy of science classes at the University of Minnesota, Herbert Feigl use to say that there are only two questions worth asking a scientist: "What do you mean? and How do you know?" The former refers to definitions and descriptions, the latter to the methods employed in searching for knowledge. . . . Our guess is that if research is to progress beyond a nearly futile repetition of noncumulative efforts, we will be best served by beginning with more rigorous attention to the nature of our fundamental concepts (p. 711).

Later, they noted that:

Step one in science is careful observation and description. Ironically, those processes seem more valued in the more well-developed sciences than in what Meehl (1978) has called the soft sciences, a relationship that may be more causal than casual. The meetings and publications of the hard sciences accommodate the reports of careful observations and descriptions with as much respect as the results of experiments. They understand, it appears, that while explanation is the crown jewel of science, description is its base (p. 711).

We see at least two morals to this story. First, the most generic elements of scientific inquiry have been accepted because their utility has been demonstrated across time and disciplines. And second, substantive advances in the family therapies are most prominent where the influence of these scientific principles are the most obvious. The cumulative effects of the next decade of research in the family therapies will probably be dependent on the care with which researchers ask: "What does this mean?" and "How do we know?"

Literature Cited

Alexander, J. F. 1973. Defensive and supportive communications in normal and deviant families. *J. Consult. Clin. Psychol.* 40:223–31

Alexander, J. F., Barton, C. 1976. Behavioral systems therapy for families. In *Treating Relationships,* ed. D. H. L. Olson, pp. 167–88. Lake Mills, Iowa: Graphic Publishing

Alexander, J. F., Barton, C., Schiavo, R. S., Parsons, B. V. 1976. Systems-behavioral intervention with families of delinquents: therapist characteristics, family behavior, and outcome. *J. Consult. Clin. Psychol.* 41:656–64

Alexander, J. F., Parsons, B. V. 1973. Short-term behavioral intervention with delinquent families: impact on family process and recidivism. *J. Abnorm. Psychol.* 81:219–25

Arnold, J. E., Levine, A. G., Patterson, G. R. 1975. Changes in sibling behavior following family intervention. *J. Consult. Clin. Psychol.* 43:683–88

Arzin, N. H., Besalel, V. A., Bechtel, R., Michalicek, A., Mancera, M., Carroll, D., Shuford, J., Cox, J. 1980. Comparison of reciprocity and discussion-type counseling for marital problems. *Am. J. Fam. Ther.* 8:21–28

Arzin, N. H., Naster, B. J., Jones, R. 1973. Reciprocity counseling: a rapid learning-based procedure for marital counseling. *Behav. Res. Ther.* 11:365–82

Barlow, D. H., O'Brien, G. T., Last, C. G. 1984. Couples' treatment of agoraphobia. *Behav. Ther.* 15:41–58

Barton, C., Alexander, J. F., Waldron, H., Turner, L. W., Warburton, J. 1985. Generalizing treatment effects of functional family therapy: three replications. *Am. J. Fam. Ther.* 13:16–26

Baucom, D. H. 1982. A comparison of behavioral contracting and problem-solving/communications training in behavioral marital therapy. *Behav. Ther.* 13:162–74

Baucom, D. H., Aiken, P. A. 1984. Sex-role identity, marital satisfaction, and response to behavioral marital therapy. *J. Consult. Clin. Psychol.* 52:438–44

Baucom, D. H., Hoffman, J. A. 1985. The effectiveness of marital therapy: current status and application to the clinical setting. In *Clinical Handbook of Marital Therapy,* ed.

N. Jacobson, A. Gurman, pp. 597–620. New York: Guilford

Beach, S. R., Broderick, J. E. 1983. Commitment: a variable in women's response to marital therapy. *Am. J. Fam. Ther.* 11:16–24

Beal, D., Duckro, P. 1977. Family counseling as an alternative to legal action for the juvenile status offender. *J. Marriage Fam. Couns.* 3:77–81

Beck, A. T., Rush, A. J., Shaw, B. F., Emery, G. 1979. *Cognitive Therapy of Depression.* New York: Guilford

Beck, D. F. 1975. Research findings on the outcomes of marital counseling. *Soc. Casework* 56:153–81

Bednar, R. L., Kaul, T. J. 1978. Experiential group research: current perspectives. In *Handbook of Psychotherapy and Behavior Change,* ed. S. L. Garfield, A. E. Bergin, pp. 769–815. New York: Wiley. 2nd ed.

Bednar, R. L., Lawlis, F. 1971. Empirical research in group psychotherapy. In *Handbook of Psychotherapy and Behavior Change,* ed. A. E. Bergin, S. L. Garfield, pp. 812–38. New York: Wiley

Bednar, R. L., Moeschl, M. J. 1981. Conceptual and methodological considerations in the evaluation of group psychotherapies. In *Advances in Psychological Assessment,* ed. P. McReynolds, 5:393–423. San Francisco: Jossey-Bass

Berman, J. S., Miller, R. C., Massman, P. J. 1985. Cognitive therapy versus systematic desensitization: Is one treatment superior? *Psychol. Bull.* 97:451–61

Blechman, E. A., Olson, D. H. L. 1976. The family contract game: description and effectiveness. See Alexander & Barton 1976, pp. 133–49

Boelens, W., Emmelkamp, P., MacGillavry, D., Markvoort, M. 1980. A clinical evaluation of marital treatment: reciprocity counseling versus system-theoretic counseling. *Behav. Anal. Modification* 4:85–96

Bogner, I., Zielenbach-Coenen, H. 1984. On maintaining change in behavioral marital therapy. In *Marital Interaction: Analysis and Modification,* ed. K. Hahlweg, N. S. Jacobson, pp. 27–35. New York: Guilford

Bondi, H. 1975. What is progress in science? In *Problems of Scientific Revolution,* ed. R. Harre. Oxford: Claredon

Boring, E. G. 1950. *A History of Experimental Psychology.* New York: Appleton-Century-Crofts. 2nd ed.

Burlingame, G., Fuhriman, A., Drescher, S. 1984. Scientific inquiry into small group processes. *Small Group Behav.* 15(4):440–76

Cadogan, D. A. 1973. Marital group therapy in the treatment of alcoholism. *Q. J. Stud. Alcohol.* 34:1187–94

Chamberlain, P., Patterson, G., Reid, J., Kavanagh, K., Forgatch, M. 1984. Observation of client resistance. *Behav. Ther.* 15:144–55

Cobb, J. P., Mathews, A. M., Childs-Clarke, A., Blowers, C. M. 1984. The spouse as co-therapist in the treatment of agoraphobia. *Brit. J. Psychiatry* 144:282–87

Cook, T. D., Campbell, D. T. 1979. *Quasi-Experimentation.* Boston: Houghton Mifflin

Crowe, M. J. 1978. Conjoint marital therapy: a controlled outcome study. *Psychol. Med.* 8:623–36

DeWitt, K. N. 1978. The effectiveness of family therapy: a review of outcome research. *Arch. Gen. Psychiatry* 35:549–61

Diament, C., Colletti, G. 1978. Evaluation of behavioral group counseling for parents of learning-disabled children. *J. Abnorm. Child Psychol.* 6:385–400

Dies, R. R. 1985. A multidimensional model for group research: elaboration and critique. *Small Group Behav.* 16(4):427–46

Doane, J. A., Falloon, I. R. H., Goldstein, M. J., Mintz, J. 1985. Parental affective style and the treatment of schizophrenia: predicting course of illness and social functioning. *Arch. Gen. Psychiatry* 42:34–42

Donner, J., Gamson, A. 1968. Experience with multifamily, time-limited, outpatient groups at a community psychiatric clinic. *Psychiatry* 31:126–37

Druckman, J. M. 1979. A family-oriented policy and treatment program for female juvenile status offenders. *J. Marriage Fam.* 41:627–36

Emmelkamp, P. M. G., de Lange, I. 1983. Spouse involvement in the treatment of obsessive-compulsive patients. *Behav. Res. Ther.* 21:341–46

Emmelkamp, P., Van Der Helm, M., MacGillavry, D., Van Zanten, B. 1984. Marital therapy with clinically distressed couples: a comparative evaluation of system-theoretic, contigency contracting, and communication skills approaches. See Bogner & Zielenbach-Croenen 1984, pp. 36–52

Epstein, N., Jackson, E. 1978. An outcome study of short-term communication training with married couples. *J. Consult. Clin. Psychol.* 46:207–12

Esterson, A., Cooper, D. G., Laing, R. D. 1965. Results of family-oriented therapy with hospitalized schizophrenics. *Brit. Med. J.* 2:1462–65

Eyberg, S. M., Johnson, S. M. 1974. Multiple assessment of behavior modification with families: effects of contigency contracting and order of treated problems. *J. Consult. Clin. Psychol.* 42:594–606

Falloon, I. R. H., Boyd, J. L., McGill, C. W., Razani, J., Moss, H. B., Gilderman, A. M. 1982. Family management in the prevention of exacerbations of schizophrenia: a controlled study. *N. Engl. J. Med.* 306:1437–40

Falloon, I. R. H., Boyd, J. L., McGill, C. W., Williamson, M., Razani, J., Moss, H. B., Gilderman, A. M., Simpson, G. M. 1985. Family management in the prevention of morbidity of schizophrenia: clinical outcome of a two-year longitudinal study. *Arch. Gen. Psychiatry* 42:887–96

Ferber, H., Keeley, S. M., Shemberg, K. M. 1974. Training parents in behavior modification: outcome of and problems encountered in a program after Patterson's work. *Behav. Ther.* 5:415–19

Fitzgerald, R. V. 1969. Conjoint marital psychotherapy: an outcome and follow-up study. *Fam. Process* 8:260–71

Fleischman, M. J. 1981. A replication of Patterson's "Intervention for boys with conduct problems." *J. Consult. Clin. Psychol.* 49:342–51

Fleischman, M. J., Szykula, S. A. 1981. A community setting replication of a social learning treatment for aggressive children. *Behav. Ther.* 12:115–22

Foster, S. L., Hoier, T. S. 1982. Behavioral and systems family therapies: a comparison of theoretical assumptions. *Am. J. Fam. Ther.* 10:13–23

Freud, S. 1959. Analysis of a phobia in a five-year-old boy. In *Sigmund Freud: Collected Papers,* ed. E. Jones (Transl. A. Struckey, J. Struckey), 3:147–289. New York: Basic (Original work published 1909)

Friedman, A. S. 1975. Interaction of drug therapy with marital therapy in depressive patients. *Arch. Gen. Psychiatry* 32:619–37

Fromm, E. 1941. *Escape from Freedom.* New York: Farrar & Rinehart

Fuhriman, A., Paul, S., Burlingame, G. 1984. Eclectic time-limited therapy. In *Handbook of Eclectic Psychotherapy,* ed. J. Norcross. New York: Brunner-Mazel

Garrigan, J. J., Bambrick, A. F. 1975. Short-term family therapy with emotionally disturbed children. *J. Marriage Fam. Couns.* 1:379–85

Garrigan, J. J., Bambrick, A. 1977. Family therapy for disturbed children: some experimental results in special education. *J. Marriage Fam. Couns.* 3:83–93

Goldstein, M. J., Rodnick, E. H., Evans, J.

R., May, P. R. A., Steinberg, M. R. 1978. Drug and family therapy in the aftercare of acute schizophrenics. *Arch. Gen. Psychiatry* 35:1169–77

Goodman, E. S. 1973. Marriage counseling as science: some research considerations. *Fam. Coord.* 22:111–16

Gurman, A. S. 1971. Group marital therapy: clinical and empirical implications for outcome research. *Int. J. Group Psychother.* 21:174–89

Gurman, A. S. 1973a. Marital therapy: emerging trends in research and practice. *Fam. Process* 12:45–54

Gurman, A. S. 1973b. The effects and effectiveness of marital therapy: a review of outcome research. *Fam. Process* 12:145–70

Gurman, A. S., Kniskern, D. P. 1978a. Behavioral marriage therapy: II. Empirical perspective. *Fam. Process* 17:139–48

Gurman, A. S., Kniskern, D. P. 1978b. Deterioration in marital and family therapy: empirical, clinical, and conceptual issues. *Fam. Process* 17:3–20

Gurman, A. S., Kniskern, D. P. 1978c. Research on marital and family therapy: progress, perspective, and prospect. See Bednar & Kaul 1978, pp. 817–901

Gurman, A. S., Kniskern, D. P. 1981. Family therapy outcome research: knowns and unknowns. See Broderick & Schrater 1981, pp. 742–75

Gurman, A. S., Kniskern, D. P., Pinsof, W. M. 1986. Research on marital and family therapies. In *Handbook of Psychotherapy and Behavior Change*, ed. S. L. Garield, A. E. Bergin, pp. 565–624. New York: Wiley. 3rd ed.

Gurman, A. S., Knudson, R. M. 1978. Behavioral marriage therapy: I. A psychodynamic-systems analysis and critique. *Fam. Process* 17:121–38

Hahlweg, K., Revenstorf, D., Schindler, L. 1984. Effects of behavioral marital therapy on couples' communication and problem-solving skills. *J. Consult. Clin. Psychol.* 52:553–66

Hahlweg, K., Schindler, L., Revenstorf, D., Brengelmann, J. C. 1984. The Munich marital therapy study. See Bogner & Zielenbach-Coenen 1984, pp. 3–26

Haley, J. 1984. Marriage or family therapy. *Am. J. Fam. Ther.* 12:3–14

Hardcastle, D. R. 1977. A mother-child, multiple-family, counseling program: procedures and results. *Fam. Process* 16:67–74

Harrell, J., Guerney, B. 1976. Training married couples in conflict negotiation skills. See Alexander & Barton 1976, pp. 151–65

Hedberg, A. G., Campbell, L. III. 1974. A comparison of four behavioral treatments of alcoholism. *J. Behav. Ther. Exp. Psychiatry* 5:251–56

Homans, G. C. 1961. *Social Behavior: Its Elementary Forms.* New York: Harcourt Brace

Horne, A. M., VanDyke, B. 1983. Treatment and maintenance of social learning family therapy. *Behav. Ther.* 14:606–13

Horney, K. 1939. *New Ways in Psychoanalysis.* New York: Norton

Huber, C. H., Milstein, B. 1985. Cognitive restructuring and a collaborative set in couples' work. *Am. J. Fam. Ther.* 13: 17–26

Jacobson, N. S. 1977. Problem-solving and contingency contracting in the treatment of marital discord. *J. Consult. Clin. Psychol.* 45:92–100

Jacobson, N. S. 1978a. A review of the research on the effectiveness of marital therapy. In *Marriage and Marital Therapy*, ed. T. Paolino, B. McCrady, pp. 395–444. New York: Brunner/Mazel

Jacobson, N. S. 1978b. Specific and nonspecific factors in the effectiveness of a behavioral approach to the treatment of marital discord. *J. Consult. Clin. Psychol.* 46:442–52

Jacobson, N. S. 1979. Increasing positive behavior in severely distressed marital relationships: the effects of problem-solving training. *Behav. Ther.* 10:311–26

Jacobson, N. S. 1984. A component analysis of behavioral marital therapy: the relative effectiveness of behavior exchange and communication/problem-solving training. *J. Consult. Clin. Psychol.* 52:295–305

Jacobson, N. S. 1985. Family therapy outcome research: potential pitfalls and prospects. *J. Marital Fam. Ther.* 11:149–58

Jacobson, N. S., Bussod, N. 1983. Marital and family therapy. In *The Clinical Psychology Handbook*, ed. M. Hersen, A. E. Kazdin, A. S. Bellack, pp. 611–30. New York: Pergamon

Jacobson, N. S., Follette, W. C. 1985. Clinical significance of improvement resulting from two behavioral marital therapy components. *Behav. Ther.* 16:249–62

Jacobson, N. S., Follette, W. C., Revenstorf, D., Baucom, D. H., Hahlweg, K., Margolin, G. 1984. Variability in outcome and clinical significance of behavioral marital therapy: a reanalysis of outcome data. *J. Consult. Clin. Psychol.* 52:497–504

Jacobson, N. S., Martin, B. 1976. Behavioral marriage therapy: current status. *Psychol. Bull.* 83:540–56

Jacobson, N., Weiss, R. L. 1978. Behavioral marriage therapy: III. The contents of Gurman et al. may be hazardous to our health. *Fam. Process* 17:149–63

Johnson, S. M., Greenberg, L. S. 1985a. Differential effects of experiential and problem-solving interventions in resolving marital conflict. *J. Consult. Clin. Psychol.* 53:175–84

Johnson, S. M., Greenberg, L. S. 1985b. Emotionally-focused couples therapy: an outcome study. *J. Marital Fam. Ther.* 11:313–17

Karoly, P., Rosenthal, M. 1977. Training parents in behavior modification: effects on perceptions of family interaction and deviant child behavior. *Behav. Ther.* 8:406–10

Kaul, T. J., Bednar, R. L. 1986. Experiential group research: results, questions, and suggestions. In *Handbook of Psychotherapy and Behavior Change*, ed. S. L. Garfield, A. E. Bergin, pp. 671–714. New York: Wiley. 3rd ed.

Klein, N. C., Alexander, J. F., Parsons, B. V. 1977. Impact of family systems intervention on recidivism and sibling delinquency: a model of primary prevention and program evaluation. *J. Consult. Clin. Psychol.* 45:469–74

Kuhn, T. S. 1970. *The Structure of Scientific Revolutions.* Chicago: Univ. Chicago Press. 2nd ed.

Lebedun, M. 1970. Measuring movement in group marital counseling. *Soc. Casework* 51:35–43

Leff, J., Kuipers, L., Berkowitz, R., Eberlein-Vries, R., Sturgeon, D. 1982. A controlled trial of social intervention in the families of schizophrenic patients. *Brit. J. Psychiatry* 141:121–34

Levine, M. 1974. Scientific method and the adversary model. *Am. Psychol.* 29(9):661–77

Mahoney, M. J. 1974. *Cognition and Behavior Modification.* Cambridge, Mass: Ballinger

Manicas, P. T., Secord, P. F. 1983. Implications for psychology of the new philosophy of science. *Am. Psychol.* 38(4):399–413

Margolin, G., Weiss, R. L. 1978. Comparative evaluation of therapeutic components associated with behavioral marital treatments. *J. Consult. Clin. Psychol.* 46:1476–1786

Mathews, A., Teasdale, J., Munby, M., Johnston, P., Shaw, P. 1977. A home-based treatment program for agoraphobia. *Behav. Ther.* 8:915–24

Mayadas, N. S., Duehn, W. D. 1977. Stimulus-modeling (SM) videotape for marital counseling: method and application. *J. Marriage Fam. Couns.* 3:35–42

McLean, P. D., Ogston, K., Grauer, L. 1973. A behavioral approach to the treatment of depression. *J. Behav. Ther. Exper. Psychiatry* 4:323–30

Meehl, P. E. 1978. Theoretical risks and tabu-

lar asterisks: Sir Karl, Sir Ronald, and the slow progress of soft psychology. *J. Consult. Clin. Psychol.* 46:806–34

Mehlman, S. K., Baucom, D. H., Anderson, D. 1983. Effectiveness of co-therapists versus single therapists and immediate versus delayed treatment in behavioral marital therapy. *J. Consult. Clin. Psychol.* 51:258–66

Meichenbaum, D. H. 1977. *Cognitive Behavior Modification.* New York: Plenum

Miles, M. B., Huberman, A. M. 1984. *Qualitative Data Analysis.* Beverly Hills: Sage

Milton, F., Hafner, J. 1979. The outcome of behavior therapy for agoraphobia in relation to marital adjustment. *Arch. Gen. Psychiatry* 36:807–11

Nunnally, J. 1978. *Psychometric Theory.* New York: McGraw Hill

O'Farrell, T. J., Cutter, H. S. 1984. Behavioral marital therapy for male alcoholics: clinical procedures from a treatment outcome study in progress. *Am. J. Fam. Ther.* 12:33–46

O'Farrell, T. J., Cutter, H. S. G., Floyd, F. J. 1985. Evaluating behavioral marital therapy for male alcoholics: effects on marital adjustment and communication from before to after treatment. *Behav. Ther.* 16:147–67

O'Leary, K. D., Turkewitz, M. 1981. A comparative outcome study of behavioral marital therapy and communication therapy. *J. Marital Fam. Ther.* 7:159–69

Olson, D. H. 1970. Marital and family therapy: integrative review and critique. *J. Marriage Fam.* 32:501–38

Oltmanns, T. F., Broderick, J. E., O'Leary, K. D. 1977. Marital adjustment and the efficacy of behavior therapy with children. *J. Consult. Clin. Psychol.* 45:724–29

Parloff, M. B. 1961. The family in psychotherapy. *Arch. Gen. Psychiatry* 4:445–51

Parsons, B. V. Jr., Alexander, J. F. 1973. Short-term family intervention: a therapy outcome study. *J. Consult. Clin. Psychol.* 41:195–201

Patterson, G. R. 1974. Interventions for boys with conduct problems: multiple settings, treatments, and criteria. *J. Consult. Clin. Psychol.* 42:471–81

Patterson, G. R., Chamberlain, P., Reid, J. B. 1982. A comparative evaluation of a parent-training program. *Behav. Ther.* 13:638–50

Patterson, G. R., Hops, H., Weiss, R. L. 1975. Interpersonal skills training for couples in early stages of conflict. *J. Marriage Fam.* 37:295–303

Patterson, G. R., Reid, J. B. 1973. Intervention for families of aggressive boys: a replication study. *Behav. Res. Ther.* 11:383–94

Peed, S., Roberts, M., Forehand, R. 1977.

Evaluation of the effectiveness of a standardized parent-training program in altering the interaction of mothers and their noncompliant children. *Behav. Mod.* 1:323–50

Pinsof, W. M. 1981. Family therapy process research. See Broderick & Schrader 1981, pp. 699–741

Polkinghorne, D. E. 1984. Further extensions of methodological diversity for counseling psychology. *J. Couns. Psychol.* 31:416–29

Popper, K. 1975. The rationality of scientific revolutions. See Bondi 1975

Ravetz, J. R. 1975. '. . . Et Augebitur Scientia.' See Bondi 1975

Reisinger, J. J., Frangia, G. W., Hoffman, E. H. 1976. Toddler management training: generalization and marital status. *J. Behav. Ther. Exp. Psychiatry* 7:335–40

Reiter, G. F., Kilmann, P. R. 1975. Mothers as family change agents. *J. Consult. Clin. Psychol.* 22:61–65

Revenstorf, D., Schindler, L., Hahlweg, K. 1983. Behavioral marital therapy applied in a conjoint and a conjoint-group modality: short- and long-term effectiveness. *Behav. Ther.* 14:614–25

Ross, E. R., Baker, S. B., Guerney, B. G. 1985. Effectiveness of relationship enhancement therapy versus therapist's preferred therapy. *Am. J. Fam. Ther.* 13:11–21

Russell, C. S., Olson, D. H., Sprenkle, D. H., Atilano, R. B. 1983. From family symptom to family system: review of family therapy research. *Am. J. Fam. Ther.* 11:3–14

Rychlak, J. F. 1977. *The Psychology of Rigorous Humanism.* New York: Wiley-Interscience

Rychlak, J. F. 1981a. Will psychology ever appreciate the method-theory distinction? *Acad. Psychol. Bull.* 3:13–20

Rychlak, J. F. 1981b. *A Philosophy of Science for Personality Theory.* Melbourne, Fla: Krieger. 2nd ed.

Safer, D. J. 1966. Family therapy for children with behavior disorders. *Fam. Process* 5:243–55

Salzinger, K., Feldman, R. S., Portnoy, S. 1970. Training parents of brain-injured children in the use of operant conditioning procedures. *Behav. Ther.* 1:4–32

Santa-Barbara, J., Woodward, C. A., Levin, S., Goodman, J. T., Streiner, D., Epstein, N. B. 1979. The McMaster family therapy outcome study: an overview of methods and results. *Int. J. Fam. Ther.* 1:304–23

Schindler, L., Hahlweg, K., Revenstorf, D. 1983. Short- and long-term effectiveness of two communication training modalities with distressed couples. *Am. J. Fam. Ther.* 11:54–64

Shontz, F., Rosenak, C. 1985. Models for clinically relevant research. *Prof. Psychol.* 6(2):296–304

Schreiber, L. E. 1966. Evaluation of family group treatment in a family agency. *Fam. Process* 5:21–29

Scovern, A. W., Bukstel, L. H., Kilmann, P. R., Laual, R. A., Busemeyer, J., Smith, V. 1980. Effects of parent counseling on the family system. *J. Couns. Psychol.* 27:268–75

Seeman, L., Tittler, B. F., Friedman, S. P. 1985. Early interactional change and its relationship to family therapy outcome. *Fam. Process* 24:59–68

Smith, M. L., Glass, G. V., Miller, T. I. 1980. *The Benefits of Psychotherapy.* Baltimore, Md: Johns Hopkins Univ. Press

Stanton, M. D. 1975. Psychology and family therapy. *Prof. Psychol.* 6:45–49

Stuart, R. B. 1969. Operant-interpersonal treatment for marital discord. *J. Consult. Clin. Psychol.* 33:675–82

Sullivan, H. S. 1953. *Interpersonal Theory of Psychiatry.* New York: Wiley

Szapocznik, J., Kurtines, W. M., Foote, F. H., Perez-Vidal, A., Hervis, O. 1983. Conjoint versus one-person family therapy: some evidence for the effectiveness of conducting family therapy through one person. *J. Consult. Clin. Psychol.* 51:889–99

Taplin, P. S., Reid, J. B. 1977. Changes in parent consequences as a function of family intervention. *J. Consult. Clin. Psychol.* 45:973–81

Thibaut, J. W., Kelly, H. H. 1959. *The Social Psychology of Groups.* New York: Wiley

Tsoi-Hoshmand, L. 1976. Marital therapy: an integrative behavioral-learning model. *J. Marriage Fam. Couns.* 2:179–91

Valle, S. K., Marinelli, R. P. 1975. Training in human relations skills as a preferred mode of treatment for married couples. *J. Marriage Fam. Couns.* 1:359–65

Walter, H. I., Gilmore, S. K. 1973. Placebo versus social learning effects in parent training procedures designed to alter the behavior of aggressive boys. *Behav. Ther.* 4:361–77

Weathers, L., Liberman, R. P. 1975. Contingency contracting with families of delinquent adolescents. *Behav. Ther.* 6:356–66

Wellisch, D. K., Ro-Trock, G. K. 1980. A three-year follow-up of family therapy. *Int. J. Fam. Ther.* 2:169–75

Wellisch, D. K., Vincent, J., Ro-Trock, G. K. 1976. Family therapy versus individual therapy: a study of adolescents and their parents. See Alexander & Barton 1976, pp. 275–302

Wells, R. A., Dezen, A. E. 1978a. Ideologies, idols (and graven images?): rejoinder to Gurman and Kniskern. *Fam. Process* 17:283–86

Wells, R. A., Dezen, A. E. 1978b. The results of family therapy revisited: the nonbehavioral methods. *Fam. Process* 17:25–74

Wells, R. A., Dilkes, T., Trivelli, N. 1972. The results of family therapy: a critical review of the literature. *Fam. Process* 7:189–207

Wieman, R. J., Shoulders, D. I., Farr, J. A. 1974. Reciprocal reinforcement in marital therapy. *J. Behav. Ther. Exper. Psychiatry* 5:291–95

Winter, W. D. 1971. Family therapy: research and theory. In *Current Topics in Clinical and Community Psychology*, ed. C. D. Speilberger, 3:95–121. New York: Academic

Yin, R. F. 1984. *Case Study Research*. Beverly Hills: Sage

Ann. Rev. Psychol. 1988. 39:435–73

PERCEPTUAL DEVELOPMENT

Richard N. Aslin

Department of Psychology and Center for Visual Science, University of Rochester, Rochester, New York 14627

Linda B. Smith

Department of Psychology, Indiana University, Bloomington, Indiana 47405

CONTENTS

The two 'dreary' topics in the history of experimental psychology, so convention has it, are nativism and empiricism, on the one hand, and psychophysics, on the other. Certainly the endless pages of futile talk—one of psychology's least happy inheritances from its parent philosophy—are dull, but psychophysics, which got somewhere, is not dreary, if one ignores the futilities, nor is the interminable argument about nativism and empiricism tiresome, if one forgets the talk and studies the events as an example of man's effort to see himself clearly in the dark.

Edwin G. Boring (1942)

The study of children is often the only means of testing the truth of our mental analyses.

James Mark Baldwin (1895)

0066-4308/88/0201-0435$02.00

INTRODUCTION

The topic of perceptual development has not been covered in a single chapter of the *Annual Review of Psychology,* although several chapters in the past decade have dealt with issues in perceptual development, both in humans (Haith & Campos 1977; Masters 1981; Cairns & Valsiner 1984; Hay 1986) and nonhumans (Movshon & Van Sluyters 1981). In addition, perceptual development has not received a comprehensive review since the classic text by E. J. Gibson (1969), although partial reviews have been provided by Bower (1974, 1982) and Rosinski (1977). Despite the obvious need for an extensive updating, space limitations preclude such an effort. The present chapter is a very selective treatment of theoretical issues and empirical findings reported since E. J. Gibson's review nearly 20 years ago.

Readers interested in more extensive reviews and discussions of issues in perceptual development during infancy are directed to chapters in Mussen's *Handbook of Child Psychology* by Gibson & Spelke (1983), Banks & Salapatek (1983), and Aslin et al (1983); to chapters in Osofsky's *Handbook of Infant Development* by Aslin (1987) and Rose & Ruff (1987); as well as to entire volumes edited by Gottlieb & Krasnegor (1985), Trehub & Schneider (1985), Salapatek & Cohen (1987a,b), Yonas (1987), McKenzie & Day (1987).

Readers interested in perceptual development beyond infancy are faced with a dilemma. Although earlier research on perceptual learning and selective attention in children formed the core of the literature on perceptual development (see Pick & Pick 1970), two factors appear to have reduced the impact of these topics in the past decade. First, as greater perceptual competencies in young infants were revealed, interest in the origins of perceptual abilities shifted naturally to younger and younger children. Second, perceptual tasks with preschoolers and older children are potentially influenced by cognitive- and language-related factors, even though the task itself may not entail a verbal response. Thus, the dividing line between perceptual processes and cognitive/language processes appears less clear-cut than it does in preverbal children. As a result, we seem to have progressed little from the state of exasperation expressed by Lipsitt & Eimas (1972) in their *Annual Review* chapter: "Research on perceptual processes of children is of such a diffuse and unprogrammatic nature, and the character of the stimulating conditions utilized is so varied, as to defy coherent organization or critical analysis" (p. 12). One of our goals in the present chapter is to clarify the distinction between perception and cognition/language in an effort to foster additional research on perceptual development beyond infancy.

Theories and Approaches

The study of perception in infants maintained a small but influential place in experimental psychology, beginning with studies of infant vision in Hering's laboratory at the turn of the century and extending to the reports from Gesell's laboratory in the 1930s. However, it was not until the late 1950s that suitable methods were developed to study infant perceptual development in a rigorous way. Fantz (1958) introduced the two-choice visual preference technique, Walk & Gibson (1961) developed the visual cliff, and Salapatek & Kessen (1966) perfected the corneal-reflection method for precise measures of visual scanning. Of course, a scattering of studies in the preceding decades had employed a number of other techniques, including orienting, conditioning, reaching, and physiological responses (see review by Kessen et al 1970). However, these earlier studies seemed to lack an important ingredient: precise control of stimulus variables. As the techniques introduced in the 1960s were used more widely, it became evident that proper interpretations of data gathered from infants required systematic stimulus manipulations. This trend reached its zenith in the past decade as a number of researchers studying infants began to employ a psychophysical approach to investigate perceptual development (see reviews by Banks 1985; Schneider & Trehub 1985).

At the same time, a growing number of researchers studying infant perception were attracted to the principles of ecological perception espoused by J. J. Gibson (1950, 1966, 1979). A recent summary of that viewpoint (Gibson & Spelke 1983) characterized perception as "obtaining information about the environment from an array of potential stimulation" (p. 58) via the processes of "exploration, discovery, and differentiation" (p. 59). There is an obvious tension between the psychophysical approach and the ecological approach. Psychophysics demands precise manipulation of a specified parameter (e.g. wavelength, intensity, or duration), whereas the ecological approach emphasizes the rich contextual or configurational nature of stimulation, particularly stimulation that carries meaning (affordances) for the organism. Thus, the psychophysical approach promotes precision at the risk of reductionism, and the ecological approach promotes investigations of real-world events at the risk of unmanageable stimulus interactions. The challenge to the psychophysicist is to eventually relate the organism's perception of basic stimulus variables, presented in isolation, to the multidimensional nature of stimulation contained in complex objects and events. The challenge to the ecological perceptionist is to specify those higher-order invariants that enable perception of complex stimuli when, as is often the case, one of several simpler stimulus variables may be sufficient to account for detection, discrimination, or identification.

Although a number of J. J. Gibson's ideas have gained wide acceptance, his notion of *affordance* remains controversial (see also E. J. Gibson 1982, and the prefatory Chapter of this Volume). Affordances refer to the meanings of events in the world—that is, stimulus information that serves some function for the organism. J. J. Gibson proposed that affordances are perceived directly rather than constructed from initially arbitrary elements of sensation. Although there has been considerable debate about precisely what is meant by direct perception (see Ullman 1980), we believe that few would dispute the claim that the meanings of objects and events (i.e. affordances) are perceived immediately. At issue in the present context is the process by which affordances develop.

Perhaps the primary purpose of J. J. Gibson's theory of direct perception was to argue that proximal stimulation (i.e. stimulation available at the receptor level) is not what is perceived by the organism, even in earliest infancy. Rather, the organism perceives distal stimulation (i.e. information about objects and events in the world), which is only partially specified by any given "time-slice" of proximal stimulation. This postulate would also not be disputed by most modern perceptual theorists. In fact, the "tricks" played on the perceiver by limiting proximal stimulation to a single time-slice or unchanging viewpoint form the basis for virtually all of the classic perceptual illusions. We agree with J. J. Gibson's contention, perhaps not fully appreciated until his books were published, that static proximal stimulation is not sufficient to account for perception, and that dynamic proximal stimulation provides a rich source of information that could enable veridical distal perception. However, it remains unclear how proximal stimulation comes to specify objects and events in the world. That is, how does potential stimulation become effective stimulation (Rosinski 1977)?

The particular perspective that guides our review is the belief that potential stimulation becomes effective stimulation at the level of perceptual representation, a level that is explicitly absent from J. J. Gibson's theory. By *representation* we mean a transformation of proximal stimulation into a neural code that refers to distal objects and events. By *perceptual* representation we mean that level of representation that is accessible in real-time. Thus, we believe it is useful to postulate a system of representations whose most elementary level is that of perception. We agree with J. J. Gibson's claim that perception is not necessarily mediated (determined) by higher levels of information (cognition). However, we believe that these higher levels can influence or constrain perception. We also agree with J. J. Gibson's claim that elementary sensations (proximal stimuli) are not primary, but we believe that positing a level of representation transformed from sensory input is logically and empirically justified. The alternative to such a view is (in our opinion) a system with innately determined mechanisms for the perception of every possible object or event, and some as yet unspecified decision rule for activating those object and event mechanisms. Such a Platonic view of perceptual development is actually *adevelopmental* in that stimulation simply triggers internal perceptual resonators.

Consistent with J. J. Gibson, we believe that in order to access information about elementary sensations they must be transformed to the level of perceptual representation. That is, perceptual representations require as input one or more elementary perceptual units or sensory primitives that correspond to traditional elements of sensation, such as brightness or line orientation in the visual domain and intensity or frequency in the auditory domain. However, these sensory primitives are not directly accessible to perceptual report because they do not correspond to stimulus information that is directly relevant to the extraction of perceptual information about real-world objects and events. In other words, sensory primitives do not comprise the relevant units at the level of perceptual representation.[1]

What Develops?

The view of perception just summarized proposes three different structural levels: (*a*) sensory primitives, (*b*) perceptual representations, and (*c*) higher-order representations (e.g. cognition and language). Because sensory primitives are necessary (though not sufficient) for perception, their development or emergence must influence perceptual development. For example, if the young infant were incapable of discriminating auditory frequencies that were easily discriminated by adults, and this deficit resulted from immaturities in the peripheral auditory system (e.g. at the level of the cochlea), then pitch perception would be deficient not because of a difference in the representation of pitch information, but because of an intrinsic limitation in the input (sensory primitives) to the level of perceptual representation.

Cognition and language can also influence perceptual development by placing stimulation in a particular specialized mode of perception. For example, orthographic characters take on a special status for adults by activating word meanings in a real-time task like reading (e.g. Gibson & Levin 1975). However, this special status obtains only if the letters are viewed in the appropriate (upright) orientation. Similar effects occur for other highly familiar stimuli such as faces (Carey & Diamond 1977).

Finally, perceptual development could consist of changes at the level of perceptual representation itself, independent of lower- or higher-order influences. For example, repeated exposures to initially arbitrary "squiggles" can lead to more fine-grained perceptual representations that have not been

---

[1]Our use of the term *representation* is synonymous with Marr's (1982) definition, but the term *sensory primitive* in our usage refers to both the *primal sketch* and the $2\frac{1}{2}$-*D sketch* as outlined by Marr.

influenced by improved sensory primitives or by the construction of new conceptual or linguistic representations (Gibson & Gibson 1955).

Although all three of the foregoing structural levels could influence perceptual development, there are additional *processes* that could contribute to perceptual development. For example, except under very reduced conditions, more than a single sensory primitive is present at a given time. Thus, the processes of (*a*) filtering or selecting, (*b*) segmenting or parsing, and (*c*) transforming or integrating the sensory primitives affect the development of perceptual representations. These processes are often dependent on task demands, explicit or implicit, as well as on spontaneous strategies that undergo change with experience. For example, if young children do not alter their fixations in a visual search task to encode key features of a complex stimulus, they will show deficiencies in perceptual performance (Vurpillot 1976). Of course, the deployment of attention does not always require eye movements, as in the perception of a green egg as both "green" and "an egg" or the perception of the brief acoustic event [baet] as the word *bat*. The processes of selective attention, segmentation, and integration must be guided by strategies that in turn influence the formation of perceptual representations. Thus, immaturities at the level of perceptual representation may lead to observed deficiencies in one or more of these underlying processes, or immaturities in these underlying processes may prevent the formation of veridical perceptual representations.

Another factor that may affect perceptual representations is *processing efficiency*. Because perception of objects and events in the natural environment is a real-time task, it is possible for a child to have mature sensory primitives and a full complement of processing skills that do not function rapidly enough to enable the formation of mature perceptual representations. It is clear from studies of perceptual processing in adults (e.g. Shiffrin & Schneider 1977) that with practice an effortful process can become extremely efficient. In addition, there are clear examples of perceptual deficits in young children that are simply the result of processing inefficiencies (e.g. Vurpillot 1976). Frankly, we find these examples to be rather uninteresting because they reveal no fundamental reorganization of the perceptual system, either at the structural or process levels. Thus, without denying the practical importance of processing efficiency for perceptual development, we will not consider this factor in the present review.

To summarize our position, we have postulated a hierarchy of at least three structural levels: (*a*) sensory primitives, (*b*) perceptual representations, and (*c*) higher-order (knowledge) representations. For perception, the level of perceptual representation is primary because it is immediately accessible and because it refers to distal, not proximal stimulation.

The "initial state" of the infant is presumed to consist of perceptual representations that are based on the bundling of one or more sensory primitives. For example, some primitives are in one-to-one correspondence with the level of perceptual representation, as in the case of line orientation. Other perceptual representations, such as color, are composed of more than a single sensory primitive (e.g. hue, saturation, and brightness). A multi-primitive representation like color does not allow for direct access to the component sensory primitives because the primitives are bundled (modularized) at the representational level and because these particular primitives must be spatially coincident. In contrast, a multi-primitive representation of object shape does not involve spatially coincident primitives, thereby allowing for easier access of component primitives (e.g. line orientation). However, accessing a shape primitive requires analysis, and this extra analytic process illustrates the primacy of the level of perceptual representation (i.e. object shape).

Development from the initial state, therefore, involves the reorganization of sensory primitives at the level of perceptual representation. This process of reorganization occurs for a variety of reasons: (*a*) maturation of sensory primitives, (*b*) influences from knowledge structures, (*c*) and strategies of filtering and segmenting primitives into candidate bundles that are "validated" by contact with redundant environmental input from multiple sensory modalitities.

The foregoing view of perceptual development is descriptive rather than explanatory. Thus, before proceeding to our review, we address a recurrent theme in perceptual development: What is the *mechanism* that propels development? Sometimes, it is helpful to consider an analogous issue in a different content area to provide a broader context for evaluating that issue unencumbered by data and historical bias. We have chosen to reflect on the question of grammatical development in language acquisition. The essential problem in this area can be summarized as a set of propositions. First, a child's native language must be acquired at least in part from language input (i.e. "Italian" infants do not acquire Russian). Thus, some minimal amount of auditory input in the form of native language utterances must be available in the child's listening environment. Second, the structure of one's native language is much more complex than the structure embodied in the sample of utterances actually presented to any given child. Thus, because we know that the child's language faculty is generative, in that rules once acquired are applied in many different contexts, the child must induce these rules from a limited database. Third, induction of syntactic rules can lead to errors because of false projections. That is, if the child hears several instances of the word *green* before words like *shirt, ball,* and *carpet,* the child could induce the correct rule that *green* is an adjective or the incorrect rule that *green* is an article (like *a, an,* or *the*). Similarly, the semantics of object names is ambiguous. For example, when an adult looks at and points to a book and labels it for the child as *book*, it seems perfectly obvious that the child should know that the word *book* refers to that object (the book). However, the child could just as easily (and logically) infer that *book* refers to the shape, texture, or color of that particular book. The point here is that the process of induction must be constrained to prevent the generation of incorrect grammatical rules and incorrect inferences about word meanings. These constraints must either be built into the organism or provided by the consistency of environmental input to enable language development to proceed at the rapid pace we observe in the real world of children, who receive very little "instruction" on how to acquire their native language.

By analogy, then, we can view the mechanisms that must operate in perceptual development. First, perception requires stimulus input. Sensory deprivation results in long-lasting deficits in perception (von Senden 1960; Movshon & Van Sluyters 1981; Mitchell & Timney 1984; Boothe et al 1985), and partial recovery may only occur because of transfer of information from other sensory modalities or to other neural structures. Second, the sensory input available to the organism at any time is limited. For example, in the visual modality high spatial resolution is limited to images falling on the fovea in each eye, which must move via changes in eye and head position to sample the entire visual field. Similarly, the observer can occupy only one position in space at a time and must therefore sample the visual field from a single station-point. As a result, proximal retinal stimulation must somehow lead to the perception of distal objects and events by an inductive process. Third, the potential number of objects and events consistent with proximal stimulation is much larger than the set of actual (and possible) objects and events in the world. Thus, for inductive errors to be prevented, there must be a set of constraints that eliminates or severely reduces the number of false percepts.

These propositions do not imply certain things that J. J. Gibson attributed to similar propositions raised by Helmholtz. First, to say that perception involves an inductive process does not necessarily mean that it is conscious or, if unconscious, that it builds on the perception of elementary sensations (e.g. brightness or static images). Such an inductive proposition simply means that proximal stimulation is often ambiguous in specifying which of several possible distal events is veridical. The organism must use an as yet unexplained mechanism to "choose" the appropriate distal percept. Recent treatments of the ambiguity associated with the so-called correspondence problem in motion perception (Ullman 1986) and stereopsis (Poggio & Poggio 1984) suggest strongly that "assumptions" or biological constraints (e.g. the rigidity assumption or the assumption of continuous change in disparity) must be present in the neural machinery underlying these percepts to explain why "false" percepts are not more commonly reported.

Second, although induction involves some sort of comparative process to evaluate whether, from moment to moment, proximal stimulation is consistent with the presumptive distal event, we do not have to assume that this comparison necessitates a memory trace in the information-processing tradition. Rather, as J. J. Gibson himself proposed, comparisons across time and space must be made to extract invariants. J. J. Gibson emphasized the dynamic pick-up of information for affordances, whereas constructivists emphasize the "models" of the world that act as mediators of meaning. In our view, this debate is largely semantic and likely to be essentially unresolvable. We may never have access to that part of the nervous system that provides a "readout" of affordances or meanings. Therefore, we prefer to gather the kernels of wisdom from both ecological and constructivist perspectives and go about the task of collecting sufficient empirical data to account for the development of specific perceptual skills.

VISUAL PERCEPTION

In this section, the largest part of our review, we attempt to illustrate the view of perceptual development outlined in the preceding section. Our strategy is to show how perceptual representations undergo development because of (*a*) emerging sensory primitives, (*b*) reorganizations of sensory primitives, and (*c*) cognitive operations on current perceptual representations.

Development of Sensory Primitives

The perception of two- and three-dimensional visual patterns is perhaps the most studied topic in perceptual development. Unfortunately, a comprehensive account of pattern perception has not been provided for the mature visual system, and models of pattern perception in infants and children are no more advanced. Much of the research on infant vision has been directed to the *emergence* of perceptual abilities, a reasonable first step in attempting to provide an explanation of perceptual development. If basic capacities (sensory primitives) have not emerged, then veridical perception of patterns may be impossible. This seemingly obvious fact was not appreciated until recently, in part because of methodological difficulties, and in part because a general framework for characterizing visual stimuli was not transferred from the literature on adult vision to the literature on infant vision. Methodological difficulties centered on the fact that data collected from infants must always be viewed as a conservative estimate of their actual capacity because attentional and motivational factors are not easily controlled. Thus, early failures to demonstrate a particular visual ability in young infants were often attributed to basic perceptual deficits, only to be followed a few years later by data gathered with a new measurement technique documenting the presence of that same ability. The problem of stimulus characterization centered on the linear-systems approach developed in the literature on adult vision (Cornsweet 1970; see also DeValois & DeValois 1980). One outcome of this approach (summarized in detail below) was the realization that the visual system is sensitive to only a limited range of pattern sizes. Because this band-limited property of the visual system was found to be more restricted in young infants than in adults, the same visual stimulus may "appear" quite different to the mature visual system than to the immature visual system.

TWO-DIMENSIONAL SPATIAL VISION   Perhaps the most basic set of sensory primitives are those that enable the visual system to detect the presence of elements of pattern (i.e. local transitions in luminance that define a contour). Over a decade of research was directed to estimating precisely the size of the smallest pattern element to which the developing infant was sensitive. Such an estimate for pattern elements of maximum contrast is called visual acuity, and it has been charted over the first postnatal year using a variety of techniques (see review by Dobson & Teller 1978). Although acuity estimates vary somewhat depending on the measurement technique (see Norcia & Tyler 1985, for a recent treatment of this controversy), there is at least a 3- to 4-fold improvement between birth and 1 year of age. The obvious implication of these findings on acuity development is that visual stimuli containing pattern elements that are not resolvable by the infant visual system cannot provide inputs to the level of perceptual representation.

Limitations in visual acuity, perhaps because they were known from the very early work of Fantz et al (1962), were incorporated into the design of most studies of infant vision by using large pattern elements. However, the lateral interactions among pattern elements, and therefore the visibility of these elements, could not be predicted simply from estimates of acuity. For example, a thin white vertical line surrounded by two thin black lines is much more difficult to see than that same thin white line surrounded by two thick black lines. The scheme developed to more completely characterize visual stimuli, such as the lateral interaction between pattern elements, is based on the decomposition of patterns into a set of sine wave gratings (stripes). This scheme, long used in the auditory domain, capitalizes on the mathematical property of Fourier's theorem, which states that any complex waveform can be completely characterized by the sum of a set of sine waves of appropriate frequency and amplitude that are combined in appropriate phase. In the visual domain, spatial frequency refers to the number of cyclical modulations in luminance per visual degree, contrast refers to the luminance difference between dark and light bars of the sine wave, and phase refers to the relative position of the component sine waves. An additional parameter in the visual domain is the orientation of the bars created by the sine wave.

Several studies have now provided estimates of the contrast sensitivity of the infant visual system to sine wave gratings of different spatial frequencies (see reviews by Banks & Salapatek 1983; Banks & Dannemiller 1987). As shown in Figure 1, adult contrast sensitivity (the minimal detectable difference in luminance between the dark and light bars of a grating) is optimal at medium spatial frequencies, with a fall-off in sensitivity at both high (narrow bars) and low (wide bars) spatial frequencies. The high-frequency cut-off (the point where no amount of contrast allows for detection) is the estimate of visual acuity. Thus, it is apparent that visual acuity alone provides an impoverished estimate of the sensitivity of the visual system to pattern elements across a wide range of sizes. Figure 1 also illustrates the remarkable contrast insensitivity of the young infant's visual system at all spatial frequencies, as well as the restricted range of spatial frequencies that fall below the acuity limit. In other words, if we consider the contrast sensitivity function to be an estimate of a sensory primitive for spatial vision, then the infant visual system passes only a fraction of the total stimulus information that is available to the adult visual system on to the level of perceptual representation.

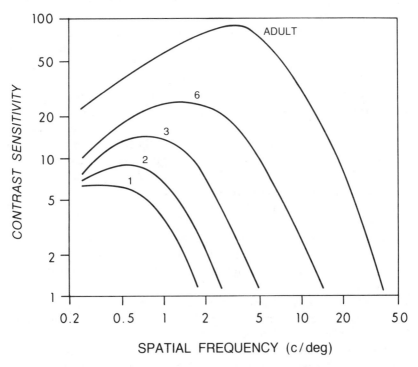

Figure 1   Schematized contrast sensitivity functions for infants and adults illustrating the improvement with age in contrast sensitivity at all spatial frequencies. Functions labeled 1, 2, 3, and 6 correspond to age in months. (Reprinted from Aslin 1987.)

The linear-systems approach has proven quite useful in bringing some semblance of order to several confusing issues in infant visual development. First, it provides a metric for evaluating whether the combination of pattern elements (or features) is actually available to the infant visual system. For example, a number of studies have reported that young infants do not prefer to fixate a facial stimulus with appropriately arranged facial features (e.g. eyes, nose, mouth) over a facial stimulus with misarranged facial features (see review by Maurer 1985). Similarly, young infants do not appear to scan the internal features of a face, but rather fixate the external features (e.g. hairline, chin, ears; see Maurer & Salapatek 1976; Haith et al 1977; Hainline 1978). Both of these findings appear to be accounted for, at least in part, by the inability of the young infant's visual system to detect the presence of small, stationary pattern elements located within a larger pattern.

Analogous evidence, labeled the *externality effect,* has been reported for nonfacial (geometric) patterns (Salapatek 1975; Milewski 1976; Maurer 1983). Because the smaller internal pattern elements were chosen to be above infant acuity values, and because infants fixated and discriminated changes in these small pattern elements when they were presented in isolation, spatial vision per se was not thought to be involved in young infants' preferences for external pattern elements. Although young infants will fixate and discriminate changes in internal pattern elements if these elements are flashed, moved, or increased in contour density (Bushnell 1979; Ganon & Swartz 1980), thereby increasing their relative salience, the linear-systems approach predicts that small pattern elements located adjacent to larger pattern elements become less visible if the visual system is not sensitive to high spatial frequencies (the small elements are essentially blurred). In addition, the ability to detect differences in contrast (as in the subtle shading that characterizes the features of a face) is quite poor in young infants (Stephens & Banks 1987). Thus, for both geometric patterns and facial stimuli, it appears that the linear-systems approach predicts several of the failures of pattern processing observed in young infants.

The linear-systems approach has also provided an account of numerous pattern preference studies in the infant perception literature. One of the difficulties that confronted the area of infant pattern vision in the early 1970s was the absence of a single organizational scheme for characterizing the myriad of possible paired-comparisons of different patterns. Although some feature-based schemes were proposed (Fantz et al 1975; Karmel & Maisel 1975), either they were limited to certain types of pattern features or they ignored stimulus contrast. The scheme developed by Banks & Salapatek (1981), with subsequent elaborations by Banks & Stephens (1982), Gayl et al (1983), Banks & Ginsburg (1985), and Slater et al (1985), proposes that the visual system "filters" the visual stimulus by an age-appropriate contrast sensitivity function. That is, each component spatial frequency in the stimulus is multiplied by the sensitivity of the visual system to that spatial frequency (i.e. by the relative height of one of the functions shown in Figure 1). After this "weighting" operation, the resultant transformed stimulus indicates what information is actually passed on to the level of perceptual representation.

Because the literature on pattern preferences contained examples of paired stimuli that differed on many dimensions (e.g. number, size, and arrangement of elements), it was now possible to analyze the "filtered" stimulus for a given infant age to determine if some property(s) of the transformed stimulus accounted for pattern preferences. Surprisingly, a single parameter, the maximum contrast of the "filtered" stimulus, predicted pattern preferences across a wide range of experiments. As shown by Banks & Ginsburg (1985), for infants up to 3 months of age, this scheme predicted pattern preferences with a correlation of 0.96.

A third example of the usefulness of the linear-systems approach concerns an apparent paradox in the literature on infant accommodation. The classic study by Haynes et al (1965) reported that young infants did not alter their focus appropriately to changes in object distance. Moreover, newborns and 1-month-olds appeared to have a fixed focal distance of approximately 19 cm. Given adult spatial resolution, the inability to accommodate would lead to blurred images for any object located at a distance other than the optimal focal distance of 19 cm, and this implication was drawn for infant vision as well. The first hint that this implication was incorrect came from a study by Salapatek et al (1976), who showed that visual acuity in young infants (who presumably do not focus accurately) did not vary as a function of viewing distance. Banks (1980) subsequently showed that infant accommodation is poor precisely because spatial resolution is poor. That is, the stimulus that drives accurate accommodation is the detection of contrast differences resulting from blur. Blur detection is primarily dependent on high spatial frequencies that are not detectable by the young infant's visual system. Thus, inaccurate accommodation does not *lead* to poor spatial resolution (even optimal image quality does not overcome the deficits in spatial vision measured in infants), but rather inaccurate accommodation is the *result* of poor spatial resolution. Without the linear-systems approach, such a shift in interpretation would not have occurred.

Despite these successes, the linear-systems approach does not provide a complete account of infants' perception of two-dimensional patterns. First, it cannot account for the effects of habituation unless a set of feature detectors (or bandpass channels) are postulated as undergoing fatigue when a stimulus is presented repeatedly (see the debate by Dannemiller & Banks 1983, 1986; Slater & Morison 1985). Second, it cannot account for the fact that older infants seem to prefer discrepancies in visual patterns, particularly when these discrepancies are defined by local areas of reduced stimulus contrast. Third, it does not account for the preferences of infants older than 2 or 3 months of age because pattern arrangement seems to emerge as a critical variable. For example, Kleiner (1987) reported that newborns' preferences for face-like and non-face-like patterns was determined by the amplitude spectrum (the amount of contrast at each orientation). However, Kleiner & Banks (1987) reported for these same stimuli that 2-month-olds preferred the face-like patterns regardless of differences in their amplitude spectrum. The critical aspect of these patterns that gave them a face-like appearance was the phase spectrum (the relative position of contrasts). These results suggest either that young infants' preferences are determined by stimulus contrast (the amplitude spectrum) or that phase-sensitivity does not emerge until approximately 2 months of age. This latter explanation is supported by results from Braddick et al (1986), who demonstrated for combinations of sine wave gratings that 1-month-olds are apparently insensitive to phase information. Additional support for the emergence of phase as potent information controlling infant preferences has been provided by Dannemiller & Stephens (1987), who showed that a face-like stimulus is preferred over its phase-reversed counterpart (where black and white regions are exchanged), but only in 12-week-olds and not in 6-week-olds.

In summary, the linear-systems approach has provided a particularly powerful scheme for characterizing the two-dimensional spatial primitives that are operative in the young infant visual system. This approach offers a universal metric for describing visual stimuli, it allows for the assessment of the "filtering" properties of the early stages of the visual system, and it predicts a variety of infant preference data for both simple and complex stimuli. Although the approach appears to be limited to younger infants (i.e. less than 3 months of age), it has sensitized researchers of infant vision to the pitfall of assuming that a visual stimulus provides identical information to both the immature and the mature visual system.

THREE-DIMENSIONAL SPATIAL VISION AND MOTION PERCEPTION
Although two-dimensional spatial vision is obviously essential for pattern vision, nearly all objects in the natural environment have the properties of three-dimensionality and motion. The perception of three-dimensionality is determined by a number of types of visual information, including kinetic, binocular, and pictorial cues (see reviews by Yonas & Granrud 1985; Yonas & Owsley 1987; Yonas et al 1987b). Similarly, the perception of object motion is determined by several types of information, including retinal image motion, retinal image displacement (apparent motion), and observer motion (eye, head, and body movements) (see review by Nelson & Horowitz 1987).

In the present context, the question is whether the development of depth and motion perception can be accounted for solely by the emergence of sensory primitives. For depth perception, the candidate sensory primitive is the neural mechanism that supports stereopsis. Stereopsis refers to the appreciation of depth based solely on retinal disparity. Retinal disparity refers to the discrepancy in the images projected to the two eyes because of their separation in the skull. Retinal disparity is defined in angular terms and, therefore, is dependent on both viewing distance and interocular separation (the latter increases by 50% during postnatal development).

Several studies (Fox et al 1980; Held et al 1980; Petrig et al 1981; Birch et al 1982) have provided compelling evidence that stereopsis does not emerge until the fourth postnatal month. This convergence across studies is remarkable given the use of different measurement techniques and different stimulus displays. Although not all potential nonbinocular explanations for the failure of younger infants to show stereopsis have been ruled out, it now seems clear that acuity, contrast sensitivity, and ocular alignment are not critically important (see Birch et al 1983). Thus, the prevailing interpretation of the absence of measureable stereopsis in infants under 4 months of age is a deficient or nonfunctional neural substrate (presumably cortical) for stereopsis. As a result, any aspect of visual perception that requires stereopsis (see section below on *Representations*) will also show deficiencies unless alternate depth information can be utilized.

It is interesting to note that data on other aspects of binocular vision are consistent with the hypothesis that an underlying neural mechanism emerges in the fourth postnatal month. Birch et al (1985) reported that infants do not prefer to fixate a fusable pattern (identical images in both eyes) over a rivalrous pattern (different images in the two eyes) until the fourth postnatal month. Similarly, Shimojo et al (1986) reported that infants younger than 4 months, presented with a rivalrous pattern that when combined contained more contours than a fusable pattern, preferred to fixate the rivalrous pattern. Thus, although there is evidence of some relatively low-level binocular functions prior to 4 months of age (Shea et al 1985; Slater et al 1983), the onset of functional stereopsis, fusion, and rivalry does not appear to emerge until the fourth postnatal month.

Unlike binocular vision, motion perception in infants has received relatively scant attention. Because motion is defined as a change in spatial location over time, both spatial resolution and temporal resolution are critical for motion perception. However, except for small objects and slow speeds, temporal sensitivity is the primary determinant (sensory primitive) for motion perception. For example, poor spatial resolution implies that an object traveling slowly will traverse fewer receptive fields per unit time. If this rate of motion does not exceed the noise associated with stimulation of receptive fields by a stationary object, then no reliable motion signal will be present. Studies of vernier (offset) acuity have shown that this type of spatial resolution is much poorer in young infants than in adults (Manny & Klein 1984, 1985; Shimojo et al 1984; Shimojo & Held 1987). Thus, in the limit, motion thresholds are determined by spatial resolution. For a more rapidly moving object, however, the relative loss in signal-to-noise ratio due to poor spatial resolution is minimal, and estimates of speed can be based on the differences in time taken to traverse a given number of receptive fields. Thus, the ability to resolve small differences in time is the more important sensory primitive for suprathreshold motion perception.

Consistent with these postulates, motion thresholds in infants are several times poorer than in adults (Volkmann & Dobson 1976; Kaufmann et al 1985; Freedland & Dannemiller 1987). However, rapid stimulus motions do not appear to be significantly degraded in 1- and 3-month-olds (Kaufmann et al 1985). This latter finding is consistent with evidence on flicker detection in 2-month-olds (Regal 1981), suggesting very little difference in temporal sensitivity compared to adults. Unfortunately, there are no data from infants on the perception of stimulus velocity, other than the indirect finding that smooth-pursuit eye movements are severely velocity-limited in the first 3 postnatal months (Aslin 1981).

In summary, sensory primitives for stereopsis and motion perception appear to undergo considerable development during the first four months after birth. Because these sensory primitives act as constraints on the transmission of stimulus information to higher levels of the visual system, they undoubtedly influence the characteristics of perceptual representations. In the next section, we consider examples of perceptual abilities that are not limited by sensory primitives, but which appear to involve the emergence or reorganization of new perceptual representations.

Development of Representations

The foregoing summary of emerging sensory primitives captures what seem to be clear examples of low-level constraints on perceptual development. However, once sensory primitives are mature, it is problematic to demonstrate clearly whether an emerging perceptual ability is the result of perceptual mechanisms or cognitive operations. In this section, we summarize three examples that capture the development of perceptual representations per se. Of course, we cannot be certain that cognitive operations are totally uninvolved in the development of the examples we have selected, but we are fairly certain that prototypical cognitive influences are minimal in each case.

PICTORIAL CUES TO DEPTH   For several centuries, artists have known that distance information can be depicted on a two-dimensional surface using a set of static "cues," such as linear perspective, shading, and interposition. Yonas, Granrud, and their colleagues reported a series of experiments that examined sensitivity to these pictorial cues to depth in 5–7-month-olds. The basis of these experiments was the discovery that once infants begin to reach for objects (typically at 4 months of age), they reliably reach for the nearer of two simultaneously presented objects (Granrud et al 1984). By eliminating binocular information for depth using an eye patch and presenting two objects at the same actual distance, they could determine whether a pictorial depth cue led to preferential reaching for the apparently nearer of two objects.

Using this procedure, Yonas et al (1978) demonstrated that 7-month-olds, but not 5-month-olds, reached for the apparently nearer edge of an Ames window display. The poor performance of the 5-month-olds was not simply the result of a lack of preference for the apparently nearer edge because under binocular conditions they reached for the nearer edge of an object that was actually slanted in depth. Moreover, Kaufmann et al (1981) showed that 5-month-olds are unresponsive to the pictorial depth information presented in an Ames window display when it conflicts with actual depth information (e.g. motion parallax), whereas 7-month-olds are more strongly influenced by the pictorial cues. Thus, it appears that the use of pictorial depth cues contained in the Ames window (relative size, linear and angular perspective, and shading) emerges between 5 and 7 months of age.

Subsequent experiments examined individual pictorial cues to depth, and the same shift in reaching performance between 5 and 7 months of age was documented for *relative size* (Yonas et al 1985), *familiar size* (Yonas et al 1982; Granrud et al 1985a), *interposition* (Granrud & Yonas 1984), *shading* (Granrud et al 1985b), and *linear perspective* (Yonas et al 1986). Thus, the preferential reaching technique has provided compelling evidence for a reorganization of proximal stimulus information between 5 and 7 months of age, and this reorganization is consistent with an emerging representation of distal object distance based on the pictorial cues to depth.

SIZE CONSTANCY   Changes in viewing distance, induced either by object motion or by observer motion, result in a variable retinal image size for an object with invariant actual size. As early as Cruikshank's (1941) investigation, researchers have been attempting to determine the age at which size constancy emerges as well as its underlying mechanism. A recent study by Granrud (1986) appears to have clarified at least some of the controversy surrounding past reports of the success and failure of size constancy in young infants. A habituation procedure was used to familiarize 4-month-olds with a single object presented at several viewing distances, thereby exposing each infant to a range of retinal image sizes. Posthabituation test trials consisted of either the same object that was presented during habituation or an object identical in appearance but different in actual size from the habituation object. Because the range of retinal image sizes on the test trials fell within the range of retinal image sizes presented during habituation, the proximal cue of retinal image size could not lead to differential fixation on the test trials. Four-month-olds showed a significant increase in fixation to the novel-sized object but no recovery to the familiar-sized object. However, this evidence of size-constancy was present only for those 4-month-olds who on a pretest showed reliable evidence of stereopsis [using the procedure developed by Held et al (1980)].

From these results by Granrud (1986), it appears that stereopsis provides sufficient information about object distance to allow for the extraction of an invariant relation between object identity and retinal image size. However, it is unclear why stereopsis was required for estimating object distance, particularly because motion parallax is an effective monocular cue to relative depth. Either stereopsis is a particularly good source of information for object distance or the measurement technique used by Granrud (1986) was not optimal. The latter explanation has received support from a study of newborns (Granrud 1987). Rather than searching for differential posthabituation recovery of fixation, Granrud simply measured the rate of habituation. If newborns have size constancy, then they should habituate more slowly to a series of otherwise identical objects varying in actual size than to the same object varying in retinal size. Because the newborns who viewed the objects varying in actual size failed to habituate within six 20-sec trials, whereas the infants who viewed the single object varying in retinal size did habituate, it appears that even newborns possess rudimentary size constancy.

The implication of these data on size constancy for the reorganization of perceptual representations is twofold. First, the identity of an object, even in earliest infancy, appears to be based on distal stimulus information. If it were not, then newborns would rely on proximal information (retinal size). Second, distal stimulus information about object size depends on available information about object distance. If the data on the emergence of stereopsis at 4 months of age are correct, then newborns must utilize some other type of information to specify object distance (e.g. motion parallax). Thus, the perceptual representation of object size would seem to undergo reorganization as more finely tuned sensory primitives for distance and depth emerge during the first several postnatal months.

SHAPE PERCEPTION   As discussed in our introductory section, a classic question in perceptual development is whether infants attend to proximal or distal information. Illustrations of this interpretive dilemma were summarized in the preceding sections on stereopsis and size constancy. Although there is compelling evidence for the emergence of stereopsis in the fourth postnatal month, a skeptic could argue that these experiments have only provided evidence for infants' detection of the proximal information (retinal disparity) that underlies stereoscopic depth perception. As pointed out by Yonas & Pick (1975), evidence for the use of distal information for depth must come either from quantitative behavioral adjustments appropriate to changing levels of apparent depth (as in distance-appropriate reaching) or from the transfer of information from one type of depth cue to another (e.g. from disparity to linear perspective).

Several experiments have employed this transfer-of-cues paradigm to determine whether infants perceive the 3-dimensional shape of an object or whether they perceive the proximal information correlated with object shape. Owsley (1983) habituated 4-month-olds under monocular conditions to a solid object, thereby eliminating binocular information for object shape. Posthabituation recovery was shown to a novel solid object viewed under binocular conditions. However, this recovery was only present for infants habituated to a moving object. Thus, static views of an object were apparently insufficient for the extraction of object shape, whereas dynamic monocular information (i.e. changes in texture gradients, shading, and linear perspective) enabled 4-month-olds to perceive object shape. Subsequent experiments reduced the dynamic monocular information for object shape by presenting either shading and linear perspective (Kellman 1984) or linear perspective alone (Kellman & Short 1987). These studies showed that 4-month-olds are capable of discriminating those dynamic proximal cues that are correlated with differences in object shape.

Shaw et al (1986) also eliminated all dynamic monocular information for object shape except changes in linear perspective. In a post-habituation test, they presented two actual solid objects under binocular viewing conditions. One test object was identical to that depicted in the 2-dimensional habituation display and the other was a novel object. Six-month-olds, but not 4-month-olds, preferentially fixated the novel test object, indicating transfer of object shape information from a single, dynamic, monocular cue (changes in linear perspective) to multiple, static, monocular and binocular cues. Yonas et al (1987a) conducted a similar transfer experiment with 4-month-olds, except that the post-habituation test objects were specified stereoscopically. As in the Granrud (1986) study of size constancy, only those 4-month-olds who had stereopsis showed a novelty preference on the post-habituation test trials. Thus, for those infants with stereopsis, information about object shape transferred from one type of cue (dynamic, monocular, linear perspective) to another cue (binocular disparity).

Kellman et al (1987) examined a different aspect of infants' perception of 3-dimensionality using the transfer paradigm. Four-month-olds were habituated to a triangular array of three lights (in an otherwise dark room) that each moved toward and away from the center of the array. This pattern of motion could result either from movement of the three lights on a surface or from movement of the surface itself in depth. Post-habituation test trials (in an illuminated room) presented either three lights that moved on a textured surface or three lights fixed to a textured surface that moved in depth. Infants showed greater recovery of fixation to the nondepth display. If this recovery is based on novelty, then the dynamic motion information presented during habituation must have specified a surface that varied in depth.

Finally, Kaufmann-Hayoz et al (1986) reported that 3-month-olds, who were habituated to a 2-dimensional shape specified solely by the coherent motion of a subregion of texture within a larger textured array, showed a novelty response to a change in object shape specified by luminance contours.

The results of these transfer experiments are important for two reasons. First, they demonstrate that by 4 months of age infants have a representation of the distal properties of objects and surfaces. Second, they demonstrate that this distal representation is based on several different sources of proximal information. Thus, it appears that proximal information, if discriminable, automatically acts as input to the level of perceptual representation, at least by 4 months of age.

Development of Part-Whole Relations

A classic controversy in perception concerns whether whole objects are built from elementary features and attributes or whether objects are perceived as unitary wholes, with features and attributes derived secondarily from those wholes. Resolution of this controversy would seem to require careful consideration of the possibility that developmental change may reside in the sensory primitives, in their bundling to form perceptual representations, or in a restructuring of perceptual representations at a more cognitive level.

INFANCY: FROM PARTS TO WHOLES   Our introductory discussion of possible developmental changes in sensory primitives and perceptual representations would seem to favor the view that percepts of whole objects are built up from sensory primitives; that is, from prior analyses of features or attributes. Both logic and empirical evidence offer compelling support for this view. The comparison of one "whole" to another, essentially a similarity judgment, has been argued to be logically impossible without analyses in terms of constituent features or attributes (Goodman 1951; see also L. Smith 1987). Evidence in adult perception, such as Treisman & Gelade's (1980) findings of illusory conjunctions, also favors the view that whole objects are built up from the prior processing of features or attributes. For example, adults shown a red square and a blue circle sometimes report the perception of a red circle and a blue square. This dissociation of color from form implies that spatially unitary wholes are constructed from their attributes.

Empirical evidence from several studies of infants fits well with this characterization of perception as proceeding from parts to wholes. In general, younger infants seem sensitive to parts (features and attributes), and only with maturation or experience do they seem to represent the separate parts as conjoined wholes (correlations among attributes). Thus, for example, 6-week-olds appear to encode the orientation of the separate line segments that make up an angle, whereas 3-month-olds encode the angles regardless of the orientation of the line segments (Cohen & Younger 1984). A similar generalization of line-element configuration across orientation has been reported by Quinn & Eimas (1986) for 3- and 4-month-olds.

Other evidence also suggests that younger infants perceive separate attributes whereas older infants perceive correlations among attributes. For example, Cohen et al (1971) reported that 4-month-olds perceive colored forms only in terms of their separate components, whereas Fagan (1977) reported that 5-month-olds perceive compounds of color and form. However, Bushnell & Roder (1985) reported that 4-month-olds preferentially attend to novel combinations of familiar color and form components. That is, they perceive color-form compounds by recognizing a red square as having the attributes of both redness and squareness. The slight discrepancy in age-of-onset for infants' perception of color-form compounds appears to be the result of reduced memory demands in the paradigm used by Bushnell & Roder. Even with reduced memory demands, however, Burnham (1987) has shown that 4-month-olds do not perceive color-form compounds if the stimuli are undergoing oscillatory movement. Apparently, movement acts as an inhibitor of the process of analyzing an object into its constituent properties.

Stronger evidence of a developmental shift in infants' perception of parts vs wholes comes from the use of more complex stimuli. Younger & Cohen (1983, 1986) have shown that 4-month-olds attend to specific featural information whereas 10-month-olds attend to the correlations among attributes (i.e. the whole object). Seven-month-olds responded like 4-month-olds when there were irrelevant variations in other stimulus attributes, but they responded like 10-month-olds when these irrelevant variations were eliminated. In general, therefore, infants appear to show an increasing ability to synthesize features into represented wholes—a trend that follows from the notion that wholes are built up from their parts.

One thorny interpretive problem associated with these studies of infants centers on the difficulty of instructing the infant to attend to the level of the whole rather than attending to local features that are independent of the global stimulus configuration. For example, Van Giffen & Haith (1984) reported that 3-month-olds direct their fixations to a discrepant local element within an array of elements making up a square or a circle, whereas 1-month-olds do not. These results suggest that 3-month-olds detect the relation between the *properties* of the elements and the *arrangement* of the elements. However, the failure of the 1-month-olds may have resulted from (a) attention to the elements and not their arrangement, or (b) an inability to detect local differences in element-properties.

One type of stimulus information that appears extremely powerful (perhaps necessary) in directing infants' attention to wholes rather than parts is motion. Studies of partially occluded objects (Kellman & Spelke 1983; Kellman et al 1986) have demonstrated that parts of objects that move together, even if grossly different in shape, are treated as a single object by 4-month-olds. In addition, depth information for object segregation appears less important than relative motion information as measured by the reaching responses of 5-month-olds (von Hofsten & Spelke 1985). Thus, the developmental shift from processing objects as parts to processing objects as wholes appears to involve, at least in part, a shift in the kinds of stimulus information to which infants spontaneously attend.

A second interpretive problem with studies of infants' perception of part-whole relations (see Kemler 1981), and one shared by any description of parts and wholes *across* development, is that what seems to be the level of parts or wholes as defined by the experimenter may not conform to the level of parts or wholes as utilized by the child. Consider for illustrative purposes a task in which adults are shown rectangles and asked to make separate judgments of height and width. Adults typically have considerable difficulty in attending selectively to one of these dimensions and ignoring the other, suggesting that adults perceive rectangles wholistically. In fact, there is evidence that adults perceive rectangles in terms of two quite separate dimensions—shape and area (Shepard 1964; Beals et al 1986). Thus, it is possible to conclude erroneously that adults employ wholistic perception simply because the dimensions under investigation were chosen incorrectly (Cheng & Pachella 1984; Kemler-Nelson 1987).

The important theoretical issue here, particularly for researchers studying infants, is that conclusions about the developmental primacy of parts over wholes is determined largely by the prior definition of the composition of the stimulus. Without a clear definition of the sensory primitives as well as the structure of perceptual representations, it is possible that a developmental trend from parts to wholes is actually a shift from one part to another part or from one whole to another whole. As Kemler (1981) suggested, young infants who appear to extract individual features may be learning that wholes are composed of more than a single feature. In addition, the similarity relations between represented wholes in early infancy may differ from the similarity relations between represented wholes in later infancy because the sensory primitives that make up those wholes have changed. Conversely, older infants may not learn about combinations of features as suggested by Cohen & Younger (1984), but rather they may represent objects in terms of a single feature that is different from the feature used to represent that same object in earlier infancy. To resolve this interpretive dilemma, estimates must be made of the sensory primitives, the structure of represented wholes, and the changes in these structures with development.

CHILDHOOD: FROM WHOLES TO PARTS   The status of features as sensory primitives necessary for the level of perceptual representation does not mean that constituent features are primary and wholes are secondary at all levels of analysis. In our everyday lives, we interact with objects as wholes and not as free-floating attributes. Thus, as we have argued earlier and as many others have proposed, the perceptual system operates primarily at the level of wholes. Indeed, in most contexts it would be advantageous if at the level of perceptual representation the whole were somehow simpler than the constituent parts. Evidence from both the adult and child literatures is consistent with this view.

The developmental trend during childhood is quite the opposite of that observed during infancy in that children under 6 years of age easily and naturally succeed on tasks that require attention to the whole but have great difficulty on tasks that require attention to constituent parts (e.g. Kemler 1983). Beyond 6 years of age there is an emerging ability to compare objects on the basis of their constituent parts. For example, on speeded tasks, children under 6 years of age have great difficulty attending selectively to one dimension whereas older children do not (e.g. Shepp & Swartz 1976). In classification tasks, younger children group objects by their simultaneous similarities on all varying dimensions, whereas older children group objects by their similarity on each dimension separately (e.g. Smith & Kemler 1977). In embedded-figures tasks, young children have difficulty detecting even simple forms, whereas older children can quite easily detect complex forms (Vurpillot 1976). In discriminative-learning tasks, young children learn rules about whole objects, whereas older children learn rules about attributes and dimensions (e.g. Tighe & Tighe 1978). In sum, across a variety of different tasks, young children seem to interact with objects at the level of wholes more readily than at the level of parts, implying that the whole is developmentally primary. This robust trend from wholes to parts has even taken on the status of a principle of development—development proceeds from being wholistic to being differentiated (Werner 1957; Wohlwill 1962; E. J. Gibson 1969; Vurpillot 1976).

Despite the foregoing evidence, the trend from wholes to parts in childhood is not all-or-none. Preschool children can, under simplified circumstances, compare and classify objects by single dimensions and constituent parts (e.g. Caron 1969; Odom 1978; Kemler 1983; L. Smith 1983, 1984; Prather & Bacon 1986). Furthermore, under certain circumstances adult perception is "wholistic." Adults who are able to compare objects using single dimensions and constituent features perform just like young children when their perform-ance is placed under severe time constraints or limited by the addition of a concurrent task or by high stimulus complexity (J. D. Smith & Kemler-Nelson 1984; L. Smith 1981; Ward 1983). J. D. Smith & Kemler-Nelson (1984) have suggested that whole-object perception dominates whenever processing time or capacity is limited, and this limitation seems to character-ize both the young child under most circumstances and older children and adults under conditions of high task demand. Perceptual operations on objects as wholes seem to involve simpler, or at least less demanding, processing than perceptual operations directed to attributes and dimensions.

FROM PARTS TO WHOLES TO PARTS   The developmental trend in the domain of part vs whole perception seems to be curvilinear: Parts dominate during infancy, parts become organized into wholes during early childhood as parts become relatively inaccessible, and finally parts reemerge as analyzable constituents of whole objects. This curvilinear developmental trend is certain-ly consistent with the three potential influences on perception summarized earlier—sensory primitives, perceptual representations, and cognitive influ-ences on perception. We have proposed that percepts are accessible only at the level of perceptual representations, even though deficient sensory primi-tives and cognitive operations on perceptual representations can influence our percepts.[2] Thus, the trend from parts to wholes in infancy may reflect the developmental joining of spatially coincident features or attributes into whole objects. Based on her work with adults, Treisman (1987) suggested that attention is required to "glue" the attributes of one object together into a whole. It may be that this glue is initially fragile in infancy and gradually strengthens as features are bundled into consistent perceptual representations.

The trend in early childhood from wholes to parts may reflect developmen-tal changes in cognitive operations on well-formed and perhaps rigidly stable wholes. For all perceivers beyond infancy, perceptual representations of spatially unitary wholes may be processed most rapidly, with the least cogni-tive demand, and result in the most typical representation of a distal stimulus. For example, a cup in its entirety may be the primary perceptual unit, only strategic cognitive operations on this representation enabling the size, color, shape, etc to emerge as separate accessible representations. What develops in childhood, then, may not be a structural change in the perceptual repre-sentations themselves but a set of strategic and cognitively motivated

---

[2]We are not suggesting that infants perceive features, children perceive wholes, and adults perceive dimensions. Rather, we suggest at all levels of development that what is perceived is the representation. What changes during development is the quality of that representation and the available operations that can be performed on it.

operations on basic units of perception that are largely intact during later infancy as the sensory primitives reach maturity (Smith & Evans 1987).

These conclusions are not meant to suggest that perceptual representations rarely change beyond infancy. The human perceptual system is highly flexible and sensitive to the effects of experience, either via general exposure or specific learning. Changes in perceptual representations themselves as well as cognitive operations on those representations may be common. There are clear examples of improvements in perceptual performance with training (Gibson & Gibson 1955). It seems likely that at least part of this improvement involves the formation of new units at the level of perceptual representation, perhaps through a process of extracting task-relevant correlations between sensory primitives after repeated exposures.

SPEECH PERCEPTION

The development of speech perception is an intriguing topic of study for several reasons. First, speech perception in adults has traditionally been viewed as involving mechanisms beyond those accounted for by basic auditory psychophysics (Liberman et al 1957). Thus, relatively little attention has been directed to the purely auditory component of speech discrimination and categorization until relatively recently. Second, speech perception in adults seems so natural and effortless that it is hard to imagine a situation in which word meanings were not extracted automatically. As a result, empirical findings from infants and children have typically been interpreted as if an identical mechanism operated at all ages. Although many empirical findings are consistent with this hypothesis of a developmentally invariant underlying mechanism for speech perception, alternative mechanisms are both possible and justified.

Speech perception provides an interesting counterpoint to the theoretical issue in visual perception between proximal versus distal information. In vision, proximal stimuli are events at the level of the retina that are correlated with distal stimuli, which correspond to objects and events in the external world. In speech, proximal stimuli are events at the level of the external ear that are correlated with a different type of distal stimuli: the meanings conveyed by the perception of phonemes, syllables, and words. In contrast to visual perception, in which distal stimuli seem to comprise the primary level of perceptual representation, speech perception seems to undergo an intermediate level of development as configurations of strictly auditory events emerge as units of perception prior to the attachment of meanings to these events. The puzzle resides in the process by which these auditory units are formed and appropriate meanings attached.

Development of Sensory Primitives

Since the pioneering study of infant speech perception by Eimas et al (1971), we have learned that by 6 months of age infants can discriminate virtually any acoustic difference that signals a phonologically relevant speech contrast used in natural languages (see reviews by Jusczyk 1981; Aslin et al 1983; Aslin 1987; Kuhl 1987). The Eimas et al study, and its many replications and extensions, also demonstrated that speech discriminability is nonlinear; that is, equal physical differences in acoustic dimensions do not correspond uniformly to equal psychological differences. This nonlinearity, called categorical perception, was initially hailed as proof that speech is processed by a specialized mode of perception (Mattingly et al 1971). However, subsequent research on adults' (Miller et al 1976; Pisoni 1977; Pisoni et al 1983) and infants' (Jusczyk et al 1980, 1983) categorical perception of nonspeech sounds and nonhumans' categorical perception of human speech sounds (Kuhl & Miller 1975, 1978; Kuhl & Padden 1982, 1983) provided compelling evidence that a specialized mode of perception for speech, though consistent with the data from infants, was not a necessary conclusion from those data.

Despite a continuing controversy concerning the uniqueness of speech sounds in the infant's processing of complex acoustic events, it seems safe to conclude that the sensory primitives that enable speech discrimination are quite mature in early infancy. Of course, these sensory primitives may not function in the same way during infancy, childhood, and adulthood if processing efficiency improves (which seems likely). For example, all studies of infant speech perception have presented syllables in isolation rather than in the real-time format of fluent speech. Thus, it is not clear whether infants, even with mature sensory primitives, can effectively deploy their perceptual capacities to segment fluent speech into words and to discriminate these words for subsequent comprehension. The bundling of sensory primitives for speech sounds, along with lexical and semantic influences, certainly must alter the level of perceptual representation for speech during a lengthy period of early development.

Development of Representations

There is convincing evidence from infants' comprehension and production that word meanings begin to emerge by the end of the first postnatal year (Benedict 1979; Oviatt 1980; Thomas et al 1981). Of course, the 1-year-old may not perceive speech in exactly the same manner as adults, and it seems unlikely that word meanings are as finely differentiated as they will become in mature speaker/listeners of a natural language.

Even before the emergence of word meanings in infants' production and comprehension of speech, there is evidence that exposure to complex acoustic events can induce differential preferences and maintain differential discriminative abilities. Newborns prefer to listen to their own mother's voice over that of a strange female (DeCasper & Fifer 1980), and auditory preferences can be experimentally induced by controlled auditory exposure during the last trimester of pregnancy (DeCasper & Spence 1986; Panneton 1985). Newborns also prefer the prosodic characteristics of their native language over that of a nonnative language (Mehler et al 1988). In addition, although infants seem capable of discriminating nonnative speech contrasts (Lasky et al 1975; Streeter 1976; Trehub 1976; Eilers et al 1979; Aslin et al 1981; Werker et al 1981), there is a precipitous loss of these nonnative discriminative abilities between 6 and 12 months of age (Werker & Tees 1984). The presence of these nonnative speech discrimination abilities in early infancy implies that there are innately determined universal acoustic categories. The loss of these nonnative speech discrimination abilities suggests either that acoustic categories can be altered by the absence of exposure or that the acquisition of word meanings activates attention to those acoustic categories that underlie phonemic contrasts in the native language.

As in the case of visual pattern perception, the trend in infancy from parts to wholes and the trend in children from wholes to parts seems to characterize the development of speech perception (Studdert-Kennedy 1986). As summarized earlier, by 6 months of age infants seem capable of discriminating virtually any segmental contrast in any syllable position. However, in communicative settings, children as old as 7 years of age do not readily attend to contrasts in voicing (Graham & House 1971; Barton 1980) and do not tend to detect mispronunciations in medial and final syllable position (Cole 1981; Walley 1987). Evidence from other tasks, such as classification, selective attention, and learning (Liberman et al 1974; Treiman & Baron 1981; Walley et al 1986), provide consistent evidence that young children perform poorly when required to make judgments about individual phonemes. These findings from young children have been interpreted as evidence that smaller and smaller segmental units (words, syllables, and finally phonemes) are extracted from speech as words enter into the child's lexicon (Waterson 1971; Ferguson 1978; Menyuk & Menn 1979; Kent 1980; Locke 1983; Eimas et al 1987; Jusczyk 1985, 1986).

This curvilinear trend in the development of speech perception—from an apparent overanalysis of speech into segments during infancy, followed by an apparent underanalysis of words—implies that the tasks used to assess infant speech perception may not involve the real-time processing demands required to perceive fluent speech as meaningful units. That is, infants could "solve" a simple phonemic discrimination task by detecting the acoustic variations that underlie phonemic contrasts. As suggested by Jusczyk (1985, 1986), phonetic segments may not achieve any linguistic function, and may not be represented as such, until the infant discovers the unique relation that exists between sounds and meanings. Because the word is the primary unit of speech used to convey differences in meaning (Menyuk & Menn 1979), the developmental emergence of smaller linguistic units may only be required as the number of words in the lexicon grows rapidly.

The general trend from parts to wholes in infancy does not mean that young infants always analyze speech sounds into phonetic segments. Bertoncini & Mehler (1981) and Jusczyk & Derrah (1987) have provided evidence that the syllable is a more salient perceptual unit than the phonetic segment in early infancy. In a study analogous to that of color-form compound perception in visual development (see Bushnell & Roder 1985), Miller & Eimas (1979, 1983) provided evidence that 2- to 4-month-olds can attend to combinations of phonetic features that make up a syllable. However, most evidence on young infants' perception of speech sounds suggests that any available acoustic information is discriminated unless such information is rendered task-irrelevant. One technique that appears to bias infants to ignore discriminable acoustic differences involves the presentation of multiple exemplars that differ along an acoustic dimension irrelevant to the task. Using this technique and the operant head-turning procedure, Kuhl and her colleagues (Kuhl 1979, 1983, 1985; Hillenbrand 1983, 1984) have shown that some kinds of acoustic information are more easily used for categorization of speech sounds by 6-month-olds than others.

Another aspect of speech perception that implies the integration of separable acoustic cues into a wholistic phonetic percept has been termed *trading relations* (Repp 1982). Different acoustic cues, each of which alone can signal a given phonetic distinction, can combine to yield an invariant phonetic category. The operation of trading relations has been demonstrated in 5-year-olds (Morrongiello et al 1984), but similar attempted demonstrations in infants have been limited because of the absence of a measure of speech-sound identification. However, results from several discrimination experiments (Morse et al 1982; Eimas 1985; Levitt et al 1988) suggest that young infants treat different acoustic cues as if they signal the same phonetic category. Unfortunately, discrimination data alone are not sufficient to conclude that infants perceive the acoustic correlates of a phonetic category as a linguistic unit.

Beginning at about 2 years of age, there is a dramatic spurt in vocabulary growth that lasts for several years. During this period, 10–20 words are added to the child's lexicon each day (Miller 1977; Benedict 1979; McCune-Nicolich 1981). Eimas et al (1987), Jusczyk (1985, 1986), and Walley (1987) have suggested that this spurt may cause words to be represented at a segmental rather than a wholistic level. That is, efficient storage and retrieval of words from the lexicon may require a representation based on a small set of phonemes. Charles-Luce & Luce (1986) have shown that as the size of the lexicon grows, the acoustic similarity of words increases dramatically. Thus, for a small lexicon, rapid word recognition should be possible even if words are represented wholistically and matched wholistically to the auditory input of speech, whereas for a large lexicon, a more segmental representation and analytic process of partial matching would be more efficient.

In summary, the trend outlined for the perception of parts and wholes in visual perception seems to apply as well to speech perception. Infants appear biased to analyze complex acoustic events like speech into the smallest discriminable unit. It remains unclear whether this analysis is based solely on acoustic mechanisms, although such an interpretation is consistent with the majority of the findings in the area of infant speech perception until language-specific losses become evident in the second 6 postnatal months (see Werker & Tees 1984). Because this evidence of language-specificity in speech perception coincides with the precursors to lexical development, it seems likely that words take on a different type of significance during this period of development. Thus, the remarkably sophisticated perceptual skills demonstrated in the laboratory with young infants may indicate a latent capacity that is not utilized in the real-time task of associating sounds with meanings from the fluent speech of adults. Only in the course of acquiring a well-differentiated lexicon may these sophisticated perceptual skills become activated. In addition, the development of reading skills may foster the reemergence of parts as salient units of speech perception (Rozin & Gleitman 1977).

PERCEPTION BETWEEN MODALITIES

There are two kinds of cross-modal abilities. First, inputs from two or more sensory modalities can provide information about the identity of an object or event, as in the case of touching, hearing, and seeing a particular dog. Second, inputs from two or more sensory modalities can be compared on one or more dimensions that are modality-independent, as in the case of perceiving the similarity between a loud sound and a bright light. For both kinds of cross-modal abilities, the critical theoretical issue has centered on whether the comparison process between modalities is based on a modality-specific representation or on an amodal representation. Those who argue for an amodal representation believe that the task of cross-modal comparison is simplified because no mediating process is required (E. J. Gibson 1969; Gibson & Spelke 1983).

A voluminous literature on cross-modal abilities in infants obviates an extensive review in the present chapter. Excellent summaries have been provided by Bushnell (1981), Gottfried & Rose (1986), Rose & Ruff (1987), and Spelke (1987). It is now clear that infants are capable of recognizing the match between object properties specified by information from different modalities, either in a transfer task or in a matching task. However, demonstrations of these cross-modal abilities are subject to a number of subtle assessment variables which suggests that these abilities are not robust in early infancy. Moreover, some types of stimulus information (e.g. shape) are not as readily transferred between modalities as others (e.g. texture).

The second type of cross-modal ability—recognizing the similarity of modality-independent information—has received little developmental study. In fact, as noted by E. J. Gibson (1969), one can ask whether such correspondences are truly perceptual rather than conceptual and whether they are innate or acquired. Although these questions are by no means resolved, Marks (1978) has amassed a variety of findings that support a sensory basis for at least some of these perceived correspondences between modalities. If correct, such a perceptually based correspondence between modalities would be important because of the possibility that such "abstract" concepts as "twoness," intensity, and extent may be fundamental aspects of perception rather than derived from conceptual analysis.

Marks et al (1987) have pursued this possibility by investigating the development of cross-modal correspondences between pitch and brightness, loudness and brightness, and pitch and size. When asked to match lights and sounds or sizes and sounds, children as young as 4 years of age readily make cross-modal matches between pitch and brightness and between loudness and brightness. Older children also make these cross-modal matches, and they do so on verbal tasks as well. In addition, children older than 6 years rate high-pitched sounds as brighter than low-pitched sounds, bright lights as higher pitched than dim lights, etc. Thus, there is a gap between the emergence of cross-modal abilities on a matching task and the emergence of these same abilities on a verbal report task. This delay suggests that cross-modal correspondences are perceived prior to the age at which they become incorporated into the child's language system. The final piece of evidence is the very late emergence of the correspondence between pitch and size, an ability that does not appear until 11 years of age on both the matching and the verbal report tasks. Marks et al (1987) suggest that this pitch-size correspondence may be learned through experience rather than provided innately as in the other perceptually based correspondences.

Marks (1978; see also Marks & Bornstein 1987) has proposed that perceptually based cross-modal correspondences reflect the existence of abstract amodal dimensions that are based on neural processes located in sensory areas of cortex. Although direct evidence of such an amodal neural code is lacking, the point here is that some underlying neural mechanism appears to organize diverse sensory inputs into "natural" combinations. Perhaps these natural combinations provide a perceptually based explanation for metaphorical relations. Support for the innateness (or at least the absence of verbal mediation) of an amodal code has been provided by Lewkowicz & Turkewitz (1980) and Wagner et al (1981) in their demonstrations of cross-modal matching of intensity in newborns and "metaphorical" mapping of changing auditory and visual events in 11-month-olds.

Smith et al (1986) have also provided evidence that very young children can make cross-modal correspondences. Children as young as 2 years of age consistently grouped big and loud objects together, small and quiet objects together, big and dark objects together, and small and light objects together. These results were interpreted as evidence for an abstract dimension of "moreness" that transcends and organizes other dimensions of magnitude (see also Smith 1987).

Two aspects of the results from Smith et al (1986) merit further comment. First, evidence of cross-modal correspondence was obtained only in a perceptual matching task and not in a verbal report task. Nevertheless, even young children who lacked a full understanding of the words "dark" and "big," for example, never confused these terms by picking the "dark" object when asked to pick the "big" object. Thus, consistent with the findings from Marks et al (1987), cross-modal correspondences do not appear to have their origin in language. Second, the consistent mapping of big onto loud and small onto quiet in the perceptual matching task increased with age. In contrast, the mapping of dark onto big and light onto small decreased with age, yielding no consistent mapping of dark onto big in adults.

Smith et al (1986) interpreted these developmental trends as evidence for an abstract dimension of "moreness" that is functional early in development but is subject to strengthening or weakening as a result of specific experiences. Thus, the loud-big correspondence is strengthened by the real-world correlation (though imperfect) between big objects and loud sounds. In contrast, the dark-big correspondence, if it exists initially, may be weakened by the absence of a strong correlation between these attributes in the real world. Moreover, the dark-big correspondence may be further weakened by the real-world correlation between bright lights and light surfaces. Although this recent work on cross-modal correspondences suggests an important role for perceptually based amodal codes in the formation of conceptual and linguistic abilities, there are many relations left unstudied (e.g. pitch and loudness). Nonetheless, preliminary results raise the possibility that perceptual mechanisms may play a critical role in constraining the possible outcomes of cognitive and language systems.

SUMMARY AND CONCLUSION

Our selective review of perceptual development has attempted to highlight three different structural levels: sensory primitives, perceptual representations, and higher-order operations. Each of these levels appears to undergo considerable development. Moreover, both within- and between-level developments appear to influence the emergence and form of perceptual abilities. The distinction between levels is often elusive, defined more by task than by logic. As a result, some distinctions seem clearer than others. First, the emergence of sensory primitives, particularly in the visual modality, may severely constrain the quality of perceptual representations. Despite these constraints, however, there is strong support for the hypothesis that distal stimulation is primary at the level of perceptual representation. Second, perceptual representations, particularly in the domain of speech sounds, appear to undergo considerable reorganization that cannot be attributed to the emergence of sensory primitives. Although some of this development in perceptual representations can be attributed to representational changes per se, much of this reorganization at the level of perceptual representations appears to be mediated by emerging cognitive operations and linguistic processes. Unfortunately, an evaluation of reorganizational factors (e.g. familiarity) that are potentially independent of higher-order cognitive and language influences is confounded by the co-occurrence of postnatal experience with the emergence of more mature cognitive and language abilities. Obviously, to disentangle the effects of experience from the effects of higher-order processes on perceptual development, it would be necessary either to eliminate these higher-order processes or to accelerate their potential influence. Controlled experiments of this sort are difficult or impossible to conduct with humans, although suitable animal models of some aspects of perceptual development may be possible.

Current and future research on perceptual development appears to be directed toward three general goals. First, the ecological and psychophysical perspectives appear headed for a marriage that will enhance both the richness and the utility of these two approaches. Second, computational techniques appear to offer a new level of sophistication that should force developmentalists to sharpen their hypotheses and to make point predictions rather than simple directional predictions. Third, the search will continue for methods to assess the role of higher-order processes.

ACKNOWLEDGMENTS

Preparation of this chapter was made possible by NIH research grants EY-05976 and HD-20286 to R. N. Aslin and by NIH research grant HD-19499 and NIH Research Career Development Award HD-00589 to L. B. Smith. The helpful critical comments provided by Sandy Shea, Amanda Walley, Al Yonas, Larry Marks, Peter Jusczyk, and Emily Bushnell are gratefully acknowledged.

Literature Cited

Aslin, R. N. 1981. Development of smooth pursuit in human infants. In *Eye Movements: Cognition and Visual Perception*, ed. D. F. Fisher, R. A. Monty, J. W. Senders, pp. 31–51. Hillsdale, NJ: Erlbaum

Aslin, R. N. 1987. Visual and auditory development in infancy. See Osofsky 1987, pp. 5–97

Aslin, R. N., Pisoni, D. B., Hennessy, B. L., Perey, A. J. 1981. Discrimination of voice onset time by human infants: new findings and implications for the effects of early experience. *Child Dev.* 52:1135–45

Aslin, R. N., Pisoni, D. B., Jusczyk, P. W. 1983. Auditory development and speech perception in infancy. See Haith & Campos 1983, pp. 573–687

Baldwin, J. M. 1895. *Mental Development in the Child and the Race.* New York: Macmillan

Banks, M. S. 1980. The development of visual accommodation during early infancy. *Child Dev.* 51:646–66

Banks, M. S. 1985. How should we characterize visual stimuli? See Gottlieb & Krasnegor 1985, pp. 31–51

Banks, M. S., Dannemiller, J. L. 1987. Infant visual psychophysics. See Salapatek & Cohen 1987a, 1:115–84

Banks, M. S., Ginsburg, A. P. 1985. Early visual preferences: a review and new theoretical treatment. In *Advances in Child Development and Behavior*, ed. H. W. Reese, pp. 207–46. New York: Academic

Banks, M. S., Salapatek, P. 1981. Infant pattern vision: a new approach based on the contrast sensitivity function. *J. Exp. Child Psychol.* 31:1–45

Banks, M. S., Salapatek, P. 1983. Infant visual perception. See Haith & Campos 1983, pp. 435–571

Banks, M. S., Stephens, B. R. 1982. The contrast sensitivity of human infants to gratings differing in duty cycle. *Vision Res.* 22:739–44

Barton, B. 1980. Phonemic perception in children. In *Child Phonology*, ed. G. H. Yeni-Komshian, J. F. Kavanagh, C. A. Ferguson, 2:97–116. New York: Wiley

Beals, R., Krantz, D. H., Tversky, A. 1968. Foundations of multidimensional scaling. *Psychol. Rev.* 75:127–42

Benedict, H. 1979. Early lexical development: comprehension and production. *J. Child Lang.* 6:183–200

Bertoncini, J., Mehler, J. 1981. Syllables as units in infant speech perception. *Infant Behav. Dev.* 4:247–60

Birch, E. E., Gwiazda, J., Held, R. 1982. Stereoacuity development for crossed and uncrossed disparities in human infants. *Vision Res.* 22:507–13

Birch, E. E., Gwiazda, J., Held, R. 1983. The development of vergence does not account for the onset of stereopsis. *Perception* 12:331–36

Birch, E. E., Shimojo, S., Held, R. 1985. Preferential-looking assessment of fusion and stereopsis in infants aged 1–6 months. *Invest. Ophthalmol. Visual Sci.* 26:366–70

Boothe, R. G., Dobson, V., Teller, D. Y. 1985. Postnatal development of vision in human and nonhuman primates. *Ann. Rev. Neurosci.* 8:495–545

Boring, E. G. 1942. *Sensation and Perception in the History of Experimental Psychology.* New York: Irvington

Bower, T. G. R. 1974. *Development in Infancy.* San Francisco: Freeman

Bower, T. G. R. 1982. *Development in Infancy.* San Francisco: Freeman. 2nd ed.

Braddick, O. J., Atkinson, J., Wattam-Bell, J. R. 1986. Development of the discrimination of spatial phase in infancy. *Vision Res.* 26:1223–39

Burnham, D. K. 1987. The role of movement in object perception by infants. See McKenzie & Day 1987

Bushnell, E. W. 1981. The ontogeny of intermodal relations: vision and touch in infancy. In *Intersensory Perception and Sensory Integration*, ed. R. D. Walk, H. A. Pick, pp. 5–36. New York: Plenum

Bushnell, E. W., Roder, B. J. 1985. Recognition of color-form compounds by 4-month-old infants. *Infant Behav. Dev.* 8:255–68

Bushnell, I. W. R. 1979. Modification of the externality effect in young infants. *J. Exp. Child Psychol.* 28:211–29

Cairns, R. B., Valsiner, J. 1984. Child psychology. *Ann. Rev. Psychol.* 35:553–77

Carey, S., Diamond, R. 1977. From piecemeal to configural representation. *Science* 195:312–13

Caron, A. J. 1969. Discrimination shifts in three-year-olds as a function of dimensional salience. *Dev. Psychol.* 1:333–39

Charles-Luce, J., Luce, P. A. 1986. Some structural properties of words in young children's lexicons. In *Progress Report: Research on Speech Perception*, 10:323–44. Bloomington, Ind: Speech Res. Lab.

Cheng, T. W., Pachella, R. G. 1984. A psychophysical approach to dimensional separability. *Cognit. Psychol.* 16:279–304

Cohen, L. B., Gelber, E. R., Lazar, M. A. 1971. Infant habituation and generalization to repeated visual stimulation. *J. Exp. Child Psychol.* 11:379–89

Cohen, L. B., Salapatek, P., eds. 1975a. *In-*

fant Perception: From Sensation to Cognition. Basic Visual Processes, Vol. 1. New York: Academic.

Cohen, L. B., Salapatek, P., eds. 1975b. Infant Perception: From Sensation to Cognition. Perception of Space, Speech and Sound, Vol. 2. New York: Academic

Cohen, L. B., Younger, B. A. 1984. Infant perception of angular relations. Infant Behav. Dev. 7:37–47

Cole, R. A. 1981. Perception of fluent speech by children and adults. Ann. NY Acad. Sci. 379:92–109

Cornsweet, T. N. 1970. Visual Perception. New York: Academic

Cruikshank, R. M. 1941. The development of visual size constancy in early infancy. J. Genet. Psychol. 58:327–51

Dannemiller, J. L., Banks, M. S. 1983. Can selective adaptation account for early infant habituation? Merrill-Palmer Q. 29:151–58

Dannemiller, J. L., Banks, M. S. 1986. Testing models of early infant habituation. Merrill-Palmer Q. 32:87–91

Dannemiller, J. L., Stephens, B. R. 1987. A critical test of infant pattern preference models. Child Dev. In press

DeCasper, A. J., Fifer, W. P. 1980. Of human bonding: Newborns prefer their mothers' voices. Science 208:1174–76

DeCasper, A. J., Spence, M. J. 1986. Prenatal maternal speech influences newborns' perception of speech sounds. Infant Behav. Dev. 9:133–50

DeValois, R. L., DeValois, K. K. 1980. Spatial vision. Ann. Rev. Psychol. 31:309–41

Dobson, V., Teller, D. Y. 1978. Visual acuity in human infants: a review and comparison of behavioral and electrophysiological studies. Vision Res. 18:1469–83

Eilers, R. E., Gavin, W., Wilson, W. R. 1979. Linguistic experience and phonemic perception in infancy: a cross-linguistic study. Child Dev. 50:14–18

Eimas, P. D. 1985. The equivalence of cues in the perception of speech by infants. Infant Behav. Dev. 8:125–38

Eimas, P. D., Miller, J. L., Jusczyk, P. W. 1987. On infant speech perception and the acquisition of language. In Categorical Perception, ed. S. Harnad. New York: Cambridge Univ. Press, pp. 161–95.

Eimas, P. D., Siqueland, E. R., Jusczyk, P., Vigorito, J. 1971. Speech perception in infants. Science 171:303–6

Fagan, J. F. 1977. An attentional model of infant recognition. Child Dev. 48:345–59

Fantz, R. L. 1958. Pattern vision in young infants. Psychol. Rec. 8:43–47

Fantz, R. L., Fagan, J. F., Miranda, S. B. 1975. Early visual selectivity. See Cohen & Salapatek 1975a, 1:249–345

Fantz, R. L., Ordy, J. M., Udelf, M. S. 1962.

Maturation of pattern vision in infants during the first six months. J. Comp. Physiol. Psychol. 55:907–17

Ferguson, C. A. 1978. Learning to pronounce: the earliest stages of phonological development in the child. In Communicative and Cognitive Abilities: Early Behavioral Assessment, ed. F. D. Minifie, L. L. Lloyd, pp. 273–97. Baltimore, Md: Univ. Park Press

Fox, R., Aslin, R. N., Shea, S. L., Dumais, S. T. 1980. Stereopsis in human infants. Science 207:323–24

Freedland, R. L., Dannemiller, J. L. 1987. Detection of stimulus motion in 5-month-olds. J. Exp. Psychol.: Hum. Percept. Perform. 13:566–76

Ganon, E. C., Swartz, K. B. 1980. Perception of internal elements of compound figures by one-month-olds. J. Exp. Child Psychol. 30:159–70

Gayl, I. E., Roberts, J. O., Werner, J. S. 1983. Linear systems analysis of infant visual pattern preferences. J. Exp. Child Psychol. 35:30–45

Gibson, E. J. 1969. Principles of Perceptual Learning and Development. New York: Appleton-Century-Crofts

Gibson, E. J. 1982. The concept of affordances in development: The renascence of functionalism. In The Minnesota Symposium in Child Psychology: The Concept of Development, ed. W. A. Collins, 15:55–81. Hillsdale, New Jersey: Erlbaum.

Gibson, E. J., Levin, H. 1975. The Psychology of Reading. Cambridge, Mass: MIT Press

Gibson, E. J., Spelke, E. S. 1983. The development of perception. In Handbook of Child Psychology: Cognitive Development, ed., J. H. Flavell, E. Markman, 3:1–76. New York: Wiley. 4th ed.

Gibson, J. J. 1950. The Perception of the Visual World. Boston: Houghton-Mifflin

Gibson, J. J. 1966. The Senses Considered as Perceptual Systems. Boston: Houghton-Mifflin

Gibson, J. J. 1979. The Ecological Approach to Visual Perception. Boston: Houghton-Mifflin

Gibson, J. J., Gibson, E. J. 1955. Perceptual learning: differentiation or enrichment? Psychol. Rev. 62:32–41

Goodman, N. 1951. The Structure of Appearance. Cambridge, Mass: Harvard Univ. Press

Gottfried, A. W., Rose, S. A. 1986. Cross-modal functioning in infancy: a symposium. In Advances in Infancy Research, ed. L. Lipsitt, C. Rovee-Collier, 4:161–245. Norwood, NJ: Ablex

Gottlieb, G., Krasnegor, N. A., eds. 1985. Measurement of Audition and Vision in the

First Year of Postnatal Life: A Methodological Overview. Norwood, NJ: Ablex

Graham, L. W., House, A. S. 1971. Phonological oppositions in children: a perceptual study. J. Acoust. Soc. Am. 49:559–66

Granrud, C. E. 1986. Binocular vision and spatial perception in 4- and 5-month-old infants. J. Exp. Psychol.: Hum. Percept. Perform. 12:36–49

Granrud, C. E. 1987. Size constancy in newborn human infants. Suppl. Invest. Ophthalmol. Visual Sci. 28:5

Granrud, C. E., Haake, R. J., Yonas, A. 1985a. Infants' sensitivity to familiar size: the effect of memory on spatial perception. Percept. Psychophys. 37:459–66

Granrud, C. E., Yonas, A. 1984. Infants' perception of pictorially specified interposition. J. Exp. Child Psychol. 37:500–11

Granrud, C. E., Yonas, A., Opland, E. A. 1985b. Infants' sensitivity to the depth cue of shading. Percept. Psychophys. 37:415–19

Granrud, C. E., Yonas, A., Pettersen, L. 1984. A comparison of monocular and binocular depth perception in 5- and 7-month-old infants. J. Exp. Child Psychol. 38:19–32

Hainline, L. 1978. Developmental changes in visual scanning of face and nonface patterns by infants. J. Exp. Child Psychol. 25:90–115

Haith, M. M., Bergman, T., Moore, M. J. 1977. Eye contact and face scanning in early infancy. Science 198:853–55

Haith, M. M., Campos, J. J. 1977. Human infancy. Ann. Rev. Psychol. 28:251–93

Haith, M. M., Campos, J. J., eds. 1983. Handbook of Child Psychology: Infancy and Developmental Psychobiology, Vol. 2. New York: Wiley. 4th ed.

Hay, D. F. 1986. Infancy. Ann. Rev. Psychol. 37:135–62

Haynes, H., White, B. L., Held, R. 1965. Visual accommodation in human infants. Science 148:528–30

Held, R., Birch, E. E., Gwiazda, J. 1980. Stereoacuity of human infants. Proc. Natl. Acad. Sci. USA 77:5572–74

Hillenbrand, J. 1983. Perceptual organization of speech sounds by infants. J. Speech Hear. Res. 26:603–12

Hillenbrand, J. 1984. Speech perception by infants: categorization based on nasal consonant place of articulation. J. Acoust. Soc. Am. 75:1613–22

Jusczyk, P. W. 1981. Infant speech perception: a critical appraisal. In Perspectives on the Study of Speech, ed. P. D. Eimas, J. L. Miller, pp. 113–64. Hillsdale, NJ: Erlbaum

Jusczyk, P. W. 1985. On characterizing the development of speech perception. In Neonate Cognition: Beyond the Blooming Buzz-

ing Confusion, ed. J. Mehler, R. Fox, pp. 199–229. Hillsdale, NJ: Erlbaum

Jusczyk, P. W. 1986. Toward a model of the development of speech perception. In Invariance and Variability in Speech Processes, ed. J. S. Perkell, D. H. Klatt, pp. 1–35. Hillsdale, NJ: Erlbaum

Jusczyk, P. W., Derrah, C. 1987. Representation of speech sounds by young infants. Dev. Psychol. In press

Jusczyk, P. W., Pisoni, D. B., Reed, M., Fernald, A., Myers, M. 1983. Durational context effects in the processing of nonspeech sounds by infants. Science 222:175–77

Jusczyk, P. W., Pisoni, D. B., Walley, A., Murray, J. 1980. Discrimination of relative onset time of two-component tones by infants. J. Acoust. Soc. Am. 67:262–70

Karmel, B. Z., Maisel, E. B. 1975. A neuronal activity model for infant visual attention. See Cohen & Salapatek 1975a, 1:77–131

Kaufmann, F., Stucki, M., Kaufmann-Hayoz, R. 1985. Development of infants' sensitivity for slow and rapid motions. Infant Behav. Dev. 8:89–98

Kaufmann, R., Maland, J., Yonas, A. 1981. Sensitivity of 5- and 7-month-old infants to pictorial depth information. J. Exp. Child Psychol. 32:162–68

Kaufmann-Hayoz, R., Kaufmann, F., Stucki, M. 1986. Kinetic contours in infants' visual perception. Child Dev. 57:292–99

Kellman, P. J. 1984. Perception of three-dimensional form by human infants. Percept. Psychophys. 36:353–58

Kellman, P. J., Short, K. R. 1987. The development of three-dimensional form perception. J. Exp. Psychol.: Hum. Percept. Perform. 13:545–57

Kellman, P. J., Spelke, E. S. 1983. Perception of partly occluded objects in infancy. Cognit. Psychol. 15:483–524

Kellman, P. J., Spelke, E. S., Short, K. R. 1986. Infant perception of object unity from translatory motion in depth and vertical translation. Child Dev. 57:72–86

Kellman, P. J., von Hofsten, C., Soares, J. 1987. Concurrent motion in infant event perception. Infant Behav. Dev. 10:1–10

Kemler, D. G. 1981. New issues in the study of infant categorization: a reply to Husaim and Cohen. Merrill-Palmer Q. 27:457–63

Kemler, D. G. 1983. Wholistic and analytic modes in perceptual and cognitive development. In Perception, Cognition, and Development: Interactional Analyses, ed. T. Tighe, B. E. Shepp, pp. 77–102. Hillsdale, NJ: Erlbaum

Kemler-Nelson, D. G. 1987. The nature and occurrence of wholistic processing. In Object Perception: Structure and Process, ed.

B. E. Shepp, S. Ballesteros. Hillsdale, New Jersey: Erlbaum. In press

Kent, R. D. 1980. Articulatory and acoustic perspectives on speech development. In *The Communication Game: Perspectives on the Development of Speech, Language, and Non-verbal Communication Skills,* ed. A. P. Reilly, pp. 38–43. Skillman, NJ: Johnson & Johnson Baby Products Co. Pediatric Round Table Series

Kessen, W., Haith, M. M., Salapatek, P. H. 1970. Infancy. See Mussen 1970, pp. 287–445

Kleiner, K. A. 1987. Amplitude and phase spectra as indices of infants' pattern preferences. *Infant Behav. Dev.* 10:49–59

Kleiner, K. A., Banks, M. S. 1987. Stimulus energy does not account for 2-month olds' face preferences. *J. Exp. Psychol.: Hum. Percept. Perform.* 13:594–600

Kuhl, P. K. 1979. Speech perception in early infancy: perceptual constancy for spectrally dissimilar vowel categories. *J. Acoust. Soc. Am.* 66:1668–79

Kuhl, P. K. 1983. Perception of auditory equivalence classes for speech in early infancy. *Infant Behav. Dev.* 6:263–85

Kuhl, P. K. 1985. Methods in the study of infant speech perception. See Gottlieb & Krasengor 1985, pp. 223–51

Kuhl, P. K. 1987. Perception of speech and sound in early infancy. See Salapatek & Cohen 1987b, 2:275–382

Kuhl, P. K., Miller, J. D. 1975. Speech perception by the chinchilla: voiced-voiceless distinction in alveolar plosive consonants. *Science* 190:69–72

Kuhl, P. K., Miller, J. D. 1978. Speech perception by the chinchilla: identification functions for synthetic VOT stimuli. *J. Acoust. Soc. Am.* 63:905–17

Kuhl, P. K., Padden, D. M. 1982. Enhanced discriminability at the phonetic boundaries for the voicing feature in macaques. *Percept. Psychophys.* 32:542–50

Kuhl, P. K., Padden, D. M. 1983. Enhanced discriminability at the phonetic boundaries for the place feature in macaques. *J. Acoust. Soc. Am.* 73:1003–10

Lasky, R. E., Syrdal-Lasky, A., Klein, R. E. 1975. VOT discrimination by four to six and a half month old infants from Spanish environments. *J. Exp. Child Psychol.* 20:215–25

Levitt, A., Jusczyk, P. W., Murray, J., Carden, G. 1988. Context effects in two-month-old infants' perception of labiodental/interdental fricative contrasts. *J. Exp. Psychol: Hum. Percept. Perform.* In press

Lewkowicz, D. J., Turkewitz, G. 1980. Cross-modal equivalence in early infancy:

auditory-visual intensity matching. *Dev. Psychol.* 16:597–607

Liberman, I. Y., Shankweiler, D., Fischer, F. W., Carter, B. 1974. Explicit syllable and phoneme segmentation in the young child. *J. Exp. Child Psychol.* 18:201–12

Liberman, A. M., Harris, K. S., Hoffman, H. S., Griffith, B. C. 1957. The discrimination of speech sounds within and across phoneme boundaries. *J. Exp. Psychol.* 54:358–68

Lipsitt, L., Eimas, P. D. 1972. Developmental psychology. *Ann. Rev. Psychol.* 23:1–50

Locke, J. 1983. *Phonological Acquisition and Change.* New York: Academic

Manny, R. E., Klein, S. A. 1984. The development of vernier acuity in infants. *Curr. Eye Res.* 3:453–62

Manny, R. E., Klein, S. A. 1985. A three alternative tracking paradigm to measure vernier acuity of older infants. *Vision Res.* 25:1245–52

Marks, L. E. 1978. *The Unity of the Senses: Inter-relations Among the Modalities.* New York: Academic

Marks, L. E., Bornstein, M. H. 1987. Sensory similarities: classes, characteristics, and cognitive consequences. In *Cognition and Symbolic Structures: The Psychology of Metaphoric Transformation,* ed. R. E. Haskell. Norwood, NJ: Ablex. In press

Marks, L. E., Hammeal, R. J., Bornstein, M. H. 1987. Perceiving similarity and comprehending metaphor. *Monogr. Soc. Res. Child Dev.* 52 (Whole No. 215). In press

Marr, D. 1982. *Vision.* San Francisco: Freeman

Masters, J. C. 1981. Developmental psychology. *Ann. Rev. Psychol.* 32:117–51

Mattingly, I. G., Liberman, A. M., Syrdal, A. K., Halwes, T. 1971. Discrimination in speech and non-speech modes. *Cognit. Psychol.* 2:131–57

Maurer, D. 1983. The scanning of compound figures by young infants. *J. Exp. Child Psychol.* 35:437–48

Maurer, D. 1985. Infants' perception of facedness. In *Social Perception in Infants,* ed. T. M. Field, N. A. Fox, pp. 73–100. Norwood, NJ: Ablex

Maurer, D., Salapatek, P. 1976. Developmental changes in the scanning of faces by young infants. *Child Dev.* 47:523–27

McCune-Nicolich, L. 1981. The cognitive bases of relational words in the single word period. *J. Child Language* 8:15–34

McKenzie, B. E., Day, R. H., eds. 1987. *Perception in Infancy: Problems and Issues.* Orlando, Fla: Academic

Mehler, J., Jusczyk, P. W., Lambertz, G.,

Amiel-Tison, C., Bertoncini, J. 1988. A precursor of language acquisition in the four-day-old infant. *Cognition*. In press

Menyuk, P., Menn, L. 1979. Early strategies for the perception and production of words and sounds. In *Language Acquisition: Studies in First Language Development*, ed. P. Fletcher, M. Garman, pp. 49–70. Cambridge: Cambridge Univ. Press

Milewski, A. E. 1976. Infants' discrimination of internal and external pattern elements. *J. Exp. Child Psychol.* 22:229–46

Miller, G. A. 1977. *Spontaneous Apprentices*. New York: Seabury Press

Miller, J. D., Wier, C. C., Pastore, R., Kelly, W. J., Dooling, R. J. 1976. Discrimination and labeling of noise-buzz sequences with varying noise-lead times: an example of categorical perception. *J. Acoust. Soc. Am.* 60:410–17

Miller, J. L., Eimas, P. D. 1979. Organization in infant speech perception. *Can. J. Psychol.* 33:353–67

Miller, J. L., Eimas, P. D. 1983. Studies on the categorization of speech by infants. *Cognition* 13:135–65

Mitchell, D. E., Timney, B. 1984. Postnatal development of function in the mammalian visual system. In *Handbook of Physiology: The Nervous System*, ed. J. M. Brookhart, V. D. Mountcastle, 3:507–55. Bethesda, Md: Am. Physiol. Soc.

Morrongiello, B. A., Robson, R. C., Best, C. T. 1984. Trading relations in the perception of speech by 5-year-old children. *J. Exp. Child Psychol.* 37:231–50

Morse, P. A., Eilers, R. E., Gavin, W. J. 1982. The perception of the sound of silence in early infancy. *Child Dev.* 53:189–95

Movshon, J. A., Van Sluyters, R. C. 1981. Visual neuronal development. *Ann. Rev. Psychol.* 32:477–522

Mussen, P. H., ed. 1970. *Carmichael's Manual of Child Psychology*, Vol. 1. New York: Wiley. 3rd ed.

Nelson, C. A., Horowitz, F. D. 1987. Visual motion perception in infancy: a review and synthesis. See Salapatek & Cohen 1987b, 2:123–53

Norcia, A. M., Tyler, C. W. 1985. Spatial frequency sweep VEP: visual acuity during the first year of life. *Vision Res.* 25:1399–1408

Odom, R. D. 1978. A perceptual salience account of decalage relations and developmental change. In *Alternatives to Piaget*, ed. L. S. Siegel, C. J. Brainerd, pp. 111–30. New York: Academic

Owsley, C. 1983. The role of motion in infants' perception of solid shape. *Perception* 12:707–17

Osofsky, J., ed. 1987. *Handbook of Infant Development*. New York: Wiley. 2nd ed

Oviatt, S. L. 1980. The emerging ability to comprehend language: an experimental approach. *Child Dev.* 51:97–106

Panneton, R. K. 1985. *Prenatal auditory experience with melodies: effects on postnatal auditory preferences in human newborns.* PhD thesis. Univ. North Carolina, Greensboro. 72 pp.

Petrig, B., Julesz, B., Kropfl, W., Baumgartner, G., Anliker, M. 1981. Development of stereopsis and cortical binocularity in human infants: electrophysiological evidence. *Science* 213:1402–5

Pick, H. L., Pick, A. D. 1970. Sensory and perceptual development. See Mussen 1970, pp. 773–847

Pisoni, D. B. 1977. Identification and discrimination of the relative onset of two component tones: implications for voicing perception in stops. *J. Acoust. Soc. Am.* 61:1352–61

Pisoni, D. B., Carrell, T. D., Gans, S. J. 1983. Perception of the duration of rapid spectrum changes in speech and nonspeech signals. *Percept. Psychophys.* 34:314–22

Poggio, G. F., Poggio, T. 1984. The analysis of stereopsis. *Ann. Rev. Neurosci.* 7:379–412

Prather, P. A., Bacon, J. 1986. Developmental differences in part/whole identification. *Child Dev.* 57:549–58

Quinn, P. C., Eimas, P. D. 1986. Pattern-line effects and units of visual processing in infants. *Infant Behav. Dev.* 9:57–70

Regal, D. M. 1981. Development of critical flicker frequency in human infants. *Vision Res.* 21:549–55

Repp, B. H. 1982. Phonetic trading relations and context effects: new experimental evidence for a speech mode of perception. *Psychol. Bull.* 92:81–110

Rose, S. A., Ruff, H. A. 1987. Cross-modal abilities in human infants. See Osofsky 1987, pp. 318–62

Rosinski, R. R. 1977. *The Development of Visual Perception*. Santa Monica, Calif: Goodyear

Rozin, P., Gleitman, L. R. 1977. The structure and acquisition of reading: II. The reading process and the acquisition of the alphabetic principle. In *Toward a Psychology of Reading*, ed. A. S. Reber, D. L. Scarborough, pp. 55–141. Hillsdale, NJ: Erlbaum

Salapatek, P. 1975. Pattern perception in early infancy. See Cohen & Salapatek 1975a, 1:133–248

Salapatek, P., Bechtold, A. G., Bushnell, E. W. 1976. Infant visual acuity as a function of viewing distance. *Child Dev.* 47:860–63

Salapatek, P., Cohen, L., eds. 1987a. *Hand-*

book of Infant Perception: From Sensation to Perception, Vol. 1. New York: Academic

Salapatek, P., Cohen, L., eds. 1987b. Handbook of Infant Perception: From Perception to Cognition, Vol. 2. New York: Academic

Salapatek, P., Kessen, W. 1966. Visual scannings of triangles by the human newborn. J. Exp. Child Psychol. 3:155–67

Schneider, B. A., Trehub, S. E. 1985. Infant auditory psychophysics: an overview. See Gottlieb & Krasnegor 1985, pp. 113–26

Shaw, L., Roder, B., Bushnell, E. W. 1986. Infants' identification of three-dimensional form from transformations of linear perspective. Percept. Psychophys. 40:301–10

Shea, S. L., Doussard-Roosevelt, J. A., Aslin, R. N. 1985. Pupillary measures of binocular luminance summation in infants and stereoblind adults. Invest. Ophthalmol. Visual Sci. 26:1064–70

Shepard, R. N. 1964. Attention and the metric structure of the stimulus space. J. Math. Psychol. 1:54–87

Shepp, B. E., Swartz, K. B. 1976. Selective attention and the processing of integral and nonintegral dimensions: a developmental study. J. Exp. Child Psychol. 22:73–85

Shiffrin, R. M., Schneider, W. 1977. Controlled and automatic human information processing. II. Perceptual learning, automatic attending, and a general theory. Psychol. Rev. 84:127–90

Shimojo, S., Bauer, J. Jr., O'Connell, K. M., Held, R. 1986. Pre-stereoptic binocular vision in infants. Vision Res. 26:501–10

Shimojo, S., Birch, E. E., Gwiazda, J., Held, R. 1984. Development of vernier acuity in infants. Vision Res. 24:721–28

Shimojo, S., Held, R. 1987. Vernier acuity is less than grating acuity in 2- and 3-month-olds. Vision Res. 27:77–86

Slater, A., Earle, D. C., Morison, V., Rose, D. 1985. Pattern preferences at birth and their interaction with habituation-induced novelty preferences. J. Exp. Child Psychol. 39:37–54

Slater, A., Morison, V. 1985. Selective adaptation cannot account for early infant habituation: A response to Dannemiller and Banks. Merrill-Palmer Q. 31:99–103

Slater, A., Morison, V., Rose, D. 1983. Locus of habituation in the human newborn. Perception 12:593–98

Smith, J. D., Kemler-Nelson, D. G. 1984. Overall similarity in adults' classification: the child in all of us. J. Exp. Psychol.: Gen. 113:137–59

Smith, L. 1981. The importance of the overall similarity of objects for adults' and children's classifications. J. Exp. Psychol.: Hum. Percept. Perform. 7:811–24

Smith, L. 1983. Development of classification: the use of similarity and dimensional relations. J. Exp. Child Psychol. 36:150–78

Smith, L. 1984. Young children's understanding of attributes and dimensions: a comparison of conceptual and linguistic measures. Child Dev. 55:363–80

Smith, L. 1987. From global similarities to kinds of similarities: the construction of dimensions in development. In Similarity and Analogy, ed. S. Voniadou, A. Ortony. Cambridge: Cambridge Univ. Press. In press

Smith, L. B., Evans, P. M. 1987. Similarity, identity, and dimensions: perceptual classification in children and adults. In Object Perception: Structure and Process, ed. B. E. Shepp, S. Ballesteros. Hillsdale, NJ: Erlbaum. In press

Smith, L., Kemler, D. G. 1977. Developmental trends in free classification: evidence for a new conceptualization of perceptual development. J. Exp. Child Psychol. 24:279–98

Smith, L., Sera, M., McCord, C. 1986. Relations of magnitude in children's object comparison and language. Presented at Ann. Meet. Psychonomic Soc., 27th, New Orleans

Spelke, E. S. 1987. The development of intermodal perception. See Salapatek & Cohen 1987b, 2:233–73

Stephens, B. R., Banks, M. S. 1987. Contrast discrimination in human infants. J. Exp. Psychol.: Hum. Percept. Perform. 13:558–65

Streeter, L. A. 1976. Language perception of 2-month-old infants shows effects of both innate mechanisms and experience. Nature 259:39–41

Studdert-Kennedy, M. 1986. Sources of variability in early speech development. In Invariance and Variability in Speech Processes, ed. J. S. Perkell, D. H. Klatt, pp. 58–76. Hillsdale, NJ: Erlbaum

Thomas, D. G., Campos, J. J., Shucard, D. W., Ramsay, D. S., Shucard, J. 1981. Semantic comprehension in infancy: a signal detection analysis. Child Dev. 52:798–803

Tighe, T. J., Tighe, L. S. 1978. A perceptual view of conceptual development. In Perception and Experience, ed. R. D. Walk, H. L. Pick, 1:387–416. New York: Plenum

Trehub, S. E. 1976. The discrimination of foreign speech contrasts by infants and adults. Child Dev. 47:466–72

Trehub, S. E., Schneider, B. A., eds. 1985. Advances in the Study of Communication and Affect: Auditory Development in Infancy, Vol. 10. New York: Plenum

Treiman, R., Baron, J. 1981. Segmental analysis ability: development and relation to reading ability. In *Reading Research: Advances in Theory and Practice*, ed. T. G. Waller, G. E. MacKinnon, 3:159–98. New York: Academic

Treisman, A. M. 1987. Properties, parts, and objects. In *Handbook of Perception and Performance*, ed. K. Boff, L. Kaufman, J. Thomas. New York: Wiley

Treisman, A. M., Gelade, G. 1980. A feature integration theory of attention. *Cognit. Psychol.* 12:97–136

Ullman, S. 1980. Against direct perception. *Behav. Brain Sci.* 3:373–415

Ullman, S. 1986. Artificial intelligence and the brain: computational studies of the visual system. *Ann. Rev. Neurosci.* 9:1–26

Van Giffen, K., Haith, M. M. 1984. Infant visual response to Gestalt geometric forms. *Infant Behav. Dev.* 7:335–46

Volkmann, F. C., Dobson, M. V. 1976. Infant responses of ocular fixation to moving visual stimuli. *J. Exp. Child Psychol.* 22:86–99

von Hofsten, C., Spelke, E. S. 1985. Object perception and object-directed reaching in infancy. *J. Exp. Psychol.: Gen.* 114:198–212

von Senden, M. 1960. *Space and Sight.* Transl. P. Heath. New York: Methuen

Vurpillot, E. 1976. *The Visual World of the Child.* New York: International Univ. Press

Wagner, S., Winner, E., Cicchetti, D., Gardner, H. 1981. "Metaphorical" mapping in human infants. *Child Dev.* 52:728–31

Walk, R. D., Gibson, E. J. 1961. A comparative and analytical study of visual depth perception. *Psychol. Monogr.* 75:15 (Whole No. 519)

Walley, A. C. 1987. Young children's detections of word-initial and -final mispronunciations in constrained and unconstrained contexts. *Cognit. Dev.* 2:145–67

Walley, A. C., Smith, L. B., Jusczyk, P. W. 1986. The role of phonemes and syllables in the perceived similarity of speech sounds for children. *Memory Cognit.* 14:220–29

Ward, T. B. 1983. Response tempo and separable-integral responding: evidence for an integral-to-separable processing sequencing in visual perception. *J. Exp. Psychol.: Hum. Percept. Perform.* 9:103–12

Waterson, N. 1971. Child phonology: a prosodic view. *J. Linguist.* 7:179–211

Werker, J. F., Gilbert, J. H. V., Humphrey, K., Tees, R. C. 1981. Developmental aspects of cross-language speech perception. *Child Dev.* 52:349–55

Werker, J. F., Tees, R. C. 1984. Cross-language speech perception: evidence for

perceptual reorganization during the first year of life. *Infant Behav. Dev.* 7:49–63

Werner, H. 1957. The concept of development from a comparative and organismic point of view. In *The Concept of Development: An Issue in the Study of Human Behavior*, ed. D. B. Harris, pp. 125–48. Minneapolis: Univ. Minn. Press

Wohlwill, J. 1962. From perception to inference: a dimension of cognitive development. *Monogr. Soc. Res. Child Dev.* 72:87–107

Yonas, A., ed. 1987. *Perceptual Development in Infancy: The Minnesota Symposium on Child Psychology*, Vol. 20. Hillsdale, NJ: Erlbaum. In press

Yonas, A., Arterberry, M. E., Granrud, C. E. 1987a. Four-month-old infants' sensitivity to kinetic and binocular information for three-dimensional object shape. *Child Dev.* 58:910–17

Yonas, A., Arterberry, M. E., Granrud, C. E. 1987b. Space perception in infancy. In *Annals of Child Development*, ed. R. Vasta, 4:1–34. London: J. A. I. Press

Yonas, A., Cleaves, W., Pettersen, L. 1978. Development of sensitivity to pictorial depth. *Science* 200:77–79

Yonas, A., Granrud, C. E. 1985. The development of sensitivity to kinetic, binocular and pictorial depth information in human infants. In *Brain Mechanisms and Spatial Vision*, ed. D. Ingle, M. Jeannerod, D. Lee, pp. 113–45. Dordrecht: Nijhoff

Yonas, A., Granrud, C. E., Arterberry, M. E., Hanson, B. L. 1986. Infants' distance perception from linear perspective and texture gradients. *Infant Behav. Dev.* 9:247–56

Yonas, A., Granrud, C. E., Pettersen, L. 1985. Infants' sensitivity to relative size information for distance. *Dev. Psychol.* 21:161–67

Yonas, A., Owsley, C. 1987. Development of visual space perception. See Salapatek & Cohen 1987b, 2:79–122

Yonas, A., Pettersen, L., Granrud, C. E. 1982. Infants' sensitivity to familiar size as information for distance. *Child Dev.* 53:1285–90

Yonas, A., Pick, H. L. 1975. An approach to the study of infant space perception. See Cohen & Salapatek 1975b, 2:3–31

Younger, B. A., Cohen, L. B. 1983. Infant perception of correlations among attributes. *Child Dev.* 54:858–67

Younger, B. A., Cohen, L. B. 1986. Developmental change in infants' perception of correlations among attributes. *Child Dev.* 57:803–15

Ann. Rev. Psychol. 1988. 39:475–543

MEASURES OF MEMORY

Alan Richardson-Klavehn and Robert A. Bjork

Department of Psychology, University of California, Los Angeles, California 90024-1563

CONTENTS

We review here a body of work that is at once a natural outgrowth of a hundred years' empirical research on human memory and a revolution in the

475

0066-4308/88/0201-0475$02.00

way we measure and interpret the influence of past events on current experiences and behavior. The crucial research tool consists of examining interrelationships among different memory measures, a technique we refer to as *task-comparison methodology.*

There is nothing new in task-comparison methodology, per se. Comparisons between traditional free recall, cued recall, and recognition measures fueled theoretical developments in the 1970s; and, in an earlier era, comparisons of cued recall, modified-modified free recall, and matching-recognition were central to theories of interference. What *is* new, and critical to the work we review here, is that task comparisons have been extended to include a new set of measures that differ markedly from traditional measures in the demands they make on the subject and in the picture they provide of the impact of a prior episode.

FORMS OF MEMORY AND METHODS OF TESTING

Although the relationships between cued recall, free recall, and recognition are highly complex, these three memory tests share an essential property: Success in them is predicated upon the subject's knowledge of events that occurred when he/she was personally present in a particular spatiotemporal context. Because the task instructions make explicit reference to an episode in the subject's personal history, such tasks have been referred to as *autobiographical* (Jacoby & Dallas 1981), *direct* (Johnson & Hasher 1987), *episodic* (Tulving 1972, 1983), *explicit* (Graf & Schacter 1985; Schacter 1985a,b, 1987), or *intentional* (Jacoby 1984) memory tests.

These traditional measures of memory do not, however, exhaust the possible memorial manifestations of personal experiences. Another set of tasks, classified as *implicit* (Graf & Schacter 1985; Schacter 1985a,b, 1987), *indirect* (Johnson & Hasher 1987), or *incidental* (Jacoby 1984) tests of memory, involve no reference to an event in the subject's personal history but are nonetheless influenced by such events. For example, prior experience with a particular word might later improve a subject's ability to identify that item under conditions of perceptual difficulty, restore deleted letters in order to complete that item, or make a decision concerning that item's lexical status. In general, such tasks require the subject to demonstrate conceptual, factual, lexical, perceptual, or procedural knowledge, or to make some form of affective or cognitive judgment. The measures of interest reflect change in performance (e.g. change in accuracy and/or speed) as a function of some form of prior experience (e.g. experience with the task, with the test stimuli, or with related stimuli). When the prior experience occurs within the experimental context, it is possible to compare such measures of behavioral change with traditional measures of memory for the events causing that change.

The extension of task-comparison methods to encompass measures of behavioral change has generated considerable excitement in the field, largely because a number of striking dissociations between these measures and traditional measures have been demonstrated. For example, behavioral change caused by an event is sometimes observed in the absence of the ability to recall or recognize that event as having occurred. The occurrence of such dissociations permits the minimal conclusion that the two types of measure can reveal different aspects of memory function: Measures of behavioral change are better suited than are the traditional memory measures to support Ebbinghaus's claim that prior episodes can "give indubitable proof of their continuing existence even if they themselves do not return to consciousness at all" (1885/1964, p. 2).

The underlying assumption of task-comparison methods is that different tasks make different informational demands on the subject. Based on patterns of dissociations and parallel effects across tasks as a function of critical independent variables, inferences can be made about the similarities and differences between the mental states and processes necessary to comply with the informational demands of the respective tasks. This methodology is therefore central to one of the fundamental aims of cognitive science—to determine how much heterogeneity in mental structures and processes is necessary to account for the complexity of experience and behavior.

The potential payoff of this new application of task-comparison methods is, from a theoretical standpoint, enormous. In the limit, it may prove possible to integrate theories of encoding, storage, and retrieval of personal experiences with theories of organization and retrieval of knowledge (i.e. conceptual, factual, lexical, perceptual, and procedural knowledge). These cognitive subareas have traditionally remained somewhat separate, each being associated with a particular set of paradigms and associated theoretical constructs.

Direct and Indirect Measures

Here we adopt Johnson & Hasher's (1987) use of the terms *direct* and *indirect* to characterize the two classes of memory measures outlined above. As we define them, these terms classify memory tests with respect to task instructions and measurement criteria. The direct/indirect nomenclature therefore involves minimal a priori assumptions concerning the mental states and processes involved in performing the tasks.

DIRECT MEMORY TESTS   We define as *direct* those tasks in which the instructions at the time of the memory test make reference to a target event (or target events) in the personal history of the subject (e.g. by mentioning the spatiotemporal context—time of day, date, environment—in which the event occurred). The subject is deemed successful in such tasks when she/he gives behavioral evidence of knowledge concerning that event. A typical target event is the presentation of a list of words, pictures, or sentences, although it could be an event in the subject's preexperimental personal history. In a recognition test, the subject is required to discriminate stimuli that were present during the target event from stimuli that were not present. In recall tests, the subject is required to produce—with or without the aid of cues— items that formed part of the target event. When cues are presented at test, they might form part of the stimuli presented during the target event (*intralist cues*—e.g. Nelson & McEvoy 1979b; Tulving & Thomson 1973), or they might be *extralist cues* that are related in some way to the target item (semantically—e.g. Nelson & McEvoy 1979b; Thomson & Tulving 1970; phonemically—e.g. Fisher & Craik 1977; Nelson & McEvoy 1979b; or graphemically—e.g. Blaxton 1985; Nelson & McEvoy 1979b; Roediger & Blaxton 1987a).

INDIRECT MEMORY TESTS   We define as *indirect* those tests requiring the subject to engage in some cognitive or motor activity, when the instructions refer only to the task at hand, and do not make reference to prior events. The measures of interest reflect a change (typically a facilitation) in task performance observed by comparing performance with relevant prior experience to performance without such experience (a control condition). The term *indirect* is particularly suitable because the relevant tasks do not "direct" the subject at a target event, and because it implies that such measures of memory are generally *derived* by comparing at least two separate data points. Indirect measures fall into four categories: (*a*) tests of factual, conceptual, lexical, and perceptual knowledge; (*b*) tests of procedural knowledge (i.e. skilled performance, problem solving); (*c*) measures of evaluative response; and (*d*) other measures of behavioral change, including neurophysiological response and conditioning measures.

Conceptual, factual, lexical, and perceptual knowledge   Tasks in this category have traditionally been used by researchers attempting to specify structures and processes involved in the retrieval of permanent knowledge. In the factual and conceptual domains, subjects have been required to retrieve items of general knowledge (e.g. Blaxton 1985; Roediger & Blaxton 1987a; Roediger et al 1983), generate members of a semantic category (e.g. Brown 1981; Gardner et al 1973; Graf et al 1985; Kihlstrom 1980), generate associates to stimulus words (e.g. Chumbley & Balota 1984; Kihlstrom 1980; Schacter 1985a; Shimamura & Squire 1984), verify category membership (e.g. Balota & Chumbley 1984; Collins & Quillian 1970; Hampton 1984; Gruenenfelder 1986), and categorize or classify stimuli (e.g. Durso & Johnson 1979; Higgins et al 1985; Kroll & Potter 1984; Metcalfe & Fisher 1986). In the lexical domain, tasks include lexical decision (e.g. Scarborough et al 1977), word naming or pronunciation (e.g. Balota & Chumbley 1985; de Groot 1985;

Lupker 1984; Seidenberg et al 1984), word retrieval (generating a word from a definition—e.g. Bowles & Poon 1985; Brown 1979), word completion (producing a word that fits a three-letter stem—e.g. Graf et al 1982; Graf et al 1984), fragment completion (supplying deleted letters to complete a word— e.g. Roediger & Blaxton 1987a,b; Tulving et al 1982; Squire et al 1987), and spelling of auditorily presented homophones (Eich 1984; Jacoby & Witherspoon 1982). Perceptual tasks include perceptual identification of words (e.g. Feustel et al 1983; Jacoby & Dallas 1981), pictures (e.g. Carroll et al 1985; Jacoby & Brooks 1984; Warren & Morton 1982), and faces (e.g. Bruce & Valentine 1985); picture naming (e.g. Brown 1981; Carroll et al 1985; Durso & Johnson 1979); and identifying fragmented pictures (e.g. Roediger & Weldon 1987; Warrington & Weiskrantz 1968; Weldon & Roediger 1987). A number of other perceptual tasks are summarized by Weiskrantz (1985).

In these types of task the measures of interest are accuracy, or latency of a correct response. Prior exposure to test stimuli generally increases accuracy and/or decreases latency, a phenomenon known as *direct* or *repetition priming* (Cofer 1967). In paradigms in which subjects are to generate any response they wish to the test stimulus (e.g. generating category members, generating associates to words, word completion, homophone spelling), prior study of items increases the likelihood that those items will be generated as responses at test.

Changes in test performance are also observed when information that is related to test stimuli is presented prior to test. The typical example is the decrease in lexical decision latency consequent on presenting associatively or semantically related words prior to the test stimulus, a phenomenon known as *associative* or *semantic priming* (e.g. Fischler 1977; Meyer & Schvaneveldt 1971). Effects of prior presentation of stimuli that are graphemically and phonemically related to test items have also been studied (e.g. Bowles & Poon 1985; Brown 1979; Evett & Humphreys 1981; Forster & Davis 1984; Feustel et al 1983; Hillinger 1980; Mandler et al 1986; Shulman et al 1978), as have effects of presenting morphologically related words (e.g. Fowler et al 1985; Henderson et al 1984; Kempley & Morton 1982; Murrell & Morton 1974; Stanners et al 1979; for a summary, Henderson 1985). *Indirect priming* is any change in performance resulting from the presentation of information related in some way (associatively, semantically, graphemically, phonemically, or morphologically) to test stimuli.

Procedural knowledge   Studies of skill learning and problem solving typically examine changes in performance as a function of degree of practice with the task. Perceptual-motor tasks such as pursuit rotor and mirror drawing have been studied (for summaries see Baddeley 1982; Cohen 1984; Moscovitch 1982; Squire & Cohen 1984). However, of particular interest in the current context are studies of the development of cognitive skills, such as proofread-

ing (e.g. Levy 1983; Levy & Begin 1984) and reading geometrically transformed text (e.g. Graf & Levy 1984; Horton 1985; Kolers 1979, 1985; Kolers
& Roediger 1984; Masson 1986; Moscovitch et al 1986). Problem-solving
tasks that have been studied include solving jigsaw puzzles (Brooks &
Baddeley 1976), the Tower of Hanoi puzzle (Cohen 1984; Cohen & Corkin
1981; Cohen et al 1985; Simon 1975), and control tasks, such as learning a
rule relating size of work force to factory production output (Berry & Broadbent 1984). Other problem-solving tasks are summarized by Moscovitch
(1982) and Weiskrantz (1985).

Evaluative response   A number of researchers have investigated effects of
exposure to stimuli upon evaluative responses to those stimuli. The classic
studies by Zajonc and coworkers show that exposure to stimuli increases
affective preference for those stimuli (for a summary see Zajonc 1980; see
also Gordon & Holyoak 1983; Johnson et al 1985; Mandler & Shebo 1983;
Seamon et al 1984 for follow-ups). Cognitive judgments are also influenced
by stimulus exposure; for example, prior exposure to statements (or components of statements) increases the rated truth of those statements (e.g.
Bacon 1979; Begg et al 1985). Other types of cognitive judgment have been
studied by Jacoby (1987), Lewicki (1986), and Mandler et al (1987), among
others.

Other measures of behavioral change   Effects of prior exposure to stimuli
can be revealed in changes in physiological response, such as galvanic skin
response (e.g. Rees-Nishio, cited in Moscovitch 1985) and event-related
potentials (e.g. Rugg 1987). Conditioning measures, such as eye-blink conditioning (Weiskrantz & Warrington 1979), can also be included as indirect
tests of memory; measurements of interest simply reflect acquisition of a
behavioral response to an originally neutral stimulus. Similarly, Schacter &
Moscovitch (1984) have argued that habituation and novelty-preference paradigms used in studies of infant memory "can be conceptualized in terms of
facilitated processing of old (familiar) stimuli, rather than in terms of gaining
access to information about the prior occurrence of the familiar stimulus in the
experimental context" (p. 184). Finally, measures of savings in relearning
repeated items (e.g. Ebbinghaus 1885/1964; Nelson 1978) qualify as indirect
memory measures, under the assumption that subjects are merely told to learn
a list at test, with no indication as to whether or not that list has been presented
before.

Explicit and Implicit Forms of Memory

Schacter's work (e.g. 1985a,b, 1987; Graf & Schacter 1985, 1987; Schacter
& Graf 1986a,b) represents a major theoretical and empirical contribution to
research comparing direct and indirect memory measures. His explicit/

implicit memory distinction is currently more widely used as a task taxonomy than is the direct/indirect distinction that we use here. However, we deviate from current usage because the terms direct and indirect clearly refer to tasks and methods of measurement; they do not lend themselves to use as labels for hypothetical forms of memory underlying test performance. We agree with Tulving (1985b) that it is not possible to define and classify memory tasks without making some minimal assumptions about the mental states of the subject. However, there is a fine but very important line between mental states whose involvement in a task can be reasonably assumed a priori, given that the subject understands the task instructions, and mental states whose involvement in a task must be ascertained empirically through the use of verbal reports and/or behavioral data.

The terms *implicit memory* and *explicit memory* can be used interchangeably to refer to tasks and methods of measurement, or to hypothetical forms of memory (where *form of memory* is a term descriptive of mental content) whose existence must be inferred from behavioral data. For example, Schacter (1985b) states that "implicit memory is revealed on tasks that do not require reference to a specific prior episode" (p. 353). This definition is a task-based one, similar to that for indirect measures given above. By contrast, Graf & Schacter (1985) state that "implicit memory is revealed when performance on a task is facilitated in the absence of conscious recollection" (p. 501). This definition implies that implicit memory is *inferred* from a dissociation between two measures of memory; implicit memory, in this sense, is a term referring to a hypothetical form of memory (where "hypothetical" simply means "not directly observable").

Similarly, direct memory tests have been defined as "requiring conscious recollection of previous experiences" (Graf & Schacter 1985, p. 501) and requiring "conscious awareness of the learning episode for successful performance" (Roediger & Blaxton 1987a, p. 351). "Conscious recollection" or "awareness" can be taken as implying (*a*) awareness, based on task instructions, that the test refers to a prior episode and consequent intention to retrieve material from that episode, or (*b*) that the subject has a particular form of subjective awareness of the episode (e.g. reexperiencing the episode) in performing the task successfully. Once again, the former of these definitions is task-based, whereas the latter refers to mental states whose existence must be inferred from data.

It might be argued that the logical distinctions we make are too fine to be of empirical importance. However, there are at least four important negative consequences of using the terms explicit and implicit memory to refer to both tasks and hypothetical forms of remembering:

1. If direct memory (i.e. intentional retrieval of material from a prior event) is conflated with explicit memory (i.e. a form of subjective awareness

of a prior event), we definitionally rule out cases in which a subject becomes aware of a prior event without having consciously intended to do so. Such cases of *involuntary explicit memory* (Schacter 1987) were noted by Ebbinghaus (1885/1964), who pointed out that "mental states once present in consciousness return to it with apparent spontaneity and without any act of the will; . . . we at once recognise the returned mental state as one that has been previously experienced" (p. 2). The conflation of intentional retrieval and awareness of remembering in current memory studies has obscured the possible role of involuntary explicit memory in performance on indirect tests of memory (as noted by Schacter 1987).

2. Unwarranted assumptions are often made about the mental states or processes involved in performing a task. This difficulty is particularly acute in the case of direct memory measures. Of course, the task instructions in such tests refer to a prior episode; if the subject understands the instructions he/she is "aware of the prior episode" in the sense of being aware *that* the study episode occurred, and that she/he must recall or recognize material presented as part of that episode in order to achieve success in the task. However, these minimal assumptions about the task leave considerable slack with respect to the states of consciousness and memory processes involved in achieving success at the task: For example, it is well known that direct test performance involves a blend of reproductive and constructive, semantically based processes. Correct performance on a test of "conscious" memory therefore does not require as a precondition that the subject is conscious of the learning episode in the sense of reexperiencing that episode. For example, repeating an item results in improved free recall of that item but poorer memory for the specific details of that item's individual presentations (Watkins & Kerkar 1985). Similarly, Cermak (1984; Cermak & O'Connor 1983) argues that one amnesic's memory for his personal history represents "retrieval from a very personal base of semantic knowledge" (1984, p. 57); Brewer (1986) distinguishes between *personal memory, autobiographical fact,* and *generic personal memory*; and Tulving (1985c) distinguishes direct memory performance based on "remembering" versus "knowing" that an item was on a list of words. A review of contributions to Rubin's (1986) volume *Autobiographical Memory* confirms our conclusion concerning the complexity of the experiences and mental processes involved in direct tests. By ignoring this complexity, we limit our ability to interpret empirical relationships between direct and indirect measures.

3. It is sometimes assumed that a particular method of testing reveals only one underlying form of memory, and that different methods of testing necessarily reveal different forms of memory. For example, with reference to direct and indirect tests, Graf & Schacter (1987) state that they "have used the labels explicit and implicit to describe the forms of memory indexed by these two

types of tests" (p. 45). This assimilation of forms of memory to methods of testing cannot be justified: The hypothesis that different testing methods reveal different forms of memory can be entertained only when *dissociations* between those methods of measurement are observed (Schacter 1985b). However, our review below shows that direct and indirect measures are sometimes influenced similarly by variables of interest. In these cases, we cannot be sure (*a*) whether two fundamentally different underlying forms of memory are affected similarly by a particular variable, or (*b*) whether the same form of memory is being engaged by both types of task. Distinguishing between these alternative explanations of parallel effects is a matter of considerable theoretical importance.

4. Confusion results when researchers suggest that performance on implicit memory tasks can be mediated by explicit remembering. For example, Schacter (1985b) argues that "there are two distinct ways to perform word completion tasks, one of which is independent of the capacity for explicit recollection and one of which makes use of this capacity" (p. 359). On the task-based definition of implicit memory, of course, this suggestion embodies a contradiction, because "implicit memory" refers to a facilitation in task performance regardless of the cause of such facilitation; the suggestion only makes sense when "explicit remembering" is taken as referring to a hypothetical form of memory that can manifest itself in both explicit and implicit memory tasks.

In this context it is also worth considering that implicit or less aware memory processes could influence performance on direct tests of memory: For example, Lockhart et al (1976) argue that effects of prior events are revealed in the way probe items are encoded, or interpreted, in a recognition memory test, and that such encoding processes are critical in determining the success of recognition attempts. A related proposal (Jacoby 1987; Jacoby & Brooks 1984; Jacoby & Dallas 1981; Johnston et al 1985; Masson 1984) is that subjects are led to attribute "oldness" to recognition probes when encoding of those probes is facilitated by implicit memory processes. In memory-disordered subjects, cued recall performance is much better when to-be-remembered response words are semantically related to the stimulus words than when they are unrelated (e.g. Graf & Schacter 1985; Schacter 1985a; Shimamura & Squire 1984; Winocur & Weiskrantz 1976). Despite the fact that cued recall is a direct memory test, the advantage for pairs whose members are related has been attributed to implicit memory; presentation of a related pair at study is assumed to prime the pair as a unit, increasing the probability that the unit will be redintegrated given a partial cue (Graf et al 1984; Mayes et al 1987; Schacter 1985a; Shimamura & Squire 1984).

A Taxonomy of Forms of Memory and Methods of Testing

The above considerations suggest that distinctions between tasks must necessarily be made independently of distinctions between hypothetical forms of memory. In the current article we use the terms *direct* and *indirect* to distinguish memory tests, based on instructions and method of measurement; we use the terms *implicit* and *explicit memory* to refer to the effects of an episode that are expressed without awareness of remembering, and with awareness of remembering, respectively. Following Ebbinghaus (1885/1964) and Schacter (1987), explicit memory can be intentional or involuntary: Reexperiencing of an episode, or reconstruction of its contents, that occurs as a result of a conscious, strategic attempt to remember that episode is termed *intentional explicit memory;* reexperiencing or reconstruction of an episode that occurs spontaneously is termed *involuntary explicit memory*. Our view of the relationship between measures of memory and forms of memory is summarized in Table 1. The cells of the table indicate the relative frequency with which a given form of memory is involved in a particular type of test, based on the evidence reviewed here. Because the pattern of mnemonic performance across direct and indirect tests differs so markedly between amnesic and normal subjects (as reviewed below), we treat these categories of subject separately.

Table 1 Frequency with which a given form of memory contributes to performance in direct and indirect tests of normal and amnesic subjects

Type of test (Type of subject)	Form of memory		
	Explicit: intentional	Explicit: involuntary	Implicit
Direct			
(normals)	always	occasionally?[a]	sometimes[b]
(amnesics)	sometimes[c]	occasionally?[c]	sometimes[d]
Indirect			
(normals)	sometimes[e]	sometimes[f]	usually
(amnesics)	never	never	always

[a] As in hypermnesia (Erdelyi & Becker 1974).
[b] As in the influence of implicit memory on encoding of recognition probes (e.g. Lockhart et al 1976; Jacoby & Dallas 1981).
[c] Depending on factors such as severity of amnesia and difficulty of test.
[d] As in cued recall with pairs whose members are related, where good performance in amnesics can be attributed to an implicit priming effect (Graf et al 1984; Schacter 1985a; Shimamura & Squire 1984; Winocur & Weiskrantz 1976).
[e] As when subjects spontaneously treat an indirect memory test, such as word completion, as a direct memory test.
[f] As when identification or generation of an item is followed by recognition of that item as having occurred previously.

THEORETICAL APPROACHES

There has been general agreement that some type of classificatory distinction between forms of memory is necessary, such as the distinction between memory with and without awareness (Jacoby & Witherspoon 1982) or the distinction between implicit and explicit memory (Graf & Schacter 1985). Schacter (1987) finds a number of precedents for the distinction between implicit and explicit forms of memory in philosophy, neurology, psychology, and psychical research, dating as far back as Descartes. In another historical survey, Herrmann (1982) found 34 precedents for a distinction between memory for personal experiences and other forms of memory such as habits, skills, and general knowledge (for a similar survey and a modern approach to classification, see Brewer & Pani 1983). Modern research confirms the validity of such typologies by demonstrating dissociations between direct and indirect measures of memory.

While agreeing that there are different forms of memory, theorists disagree concerning the degree of heterogeneity in memory structures and processes necessary to explain these forms. We identify three general approaches to the relationship between less aware, or implicit, and more aware, or explicit, forms of memory.

Abstractionist Positions

Abstractionist positions view implicit memory as reflecting modification of the state of abstract lexical, semantic, or procedural knowledge structures; by contrast, explicit memory is assumed to depend on formation and retrieval of memory traces representing specific experiences. Abstractionists are often neuroscientifically oriented, using brain lesion data to constrain their theories. Of particular interest are findings that amnesic patients are selectively impaired on direct tests of memory but show normal learning as measured by some indirect tests (reviewed below). These deficits are ascribed to an impairment of the system responsible for memory of specific experiences. In neuroscience, modularity of systems is the rule rather than the exception: If one accepts a straightforward relationship between brain systems and cognitive systems, the hypothesis of multiple memory systems is a logical extension of current knowledge (Cohen 1984; Oakley 1983; for discussion, see Cohen 1985; Olton 1985; Schacter 1986).

Tulving's (1972) heuristic distinction between *episodic* and *semantic* forms of memory was later developed into a multiple-system theory (Schacter & Tulving 1982a,b; Tulving 1983, 1984a). Episodic memory "deals with unique, concrete, personal, temporally dated events," while semantic memory "involves general, abstract, timeless knowledge that a person shares with others" (1986, p. 307). In recent versions of the theory (Tulving 1984b,c;

1985a,b,c; 1986) episodic memory is viewed as a specialized subsystem of semantic memory, with both systems embedded within a procedural memory, an arrangement Tulving terms *monohierarchical*. This position was designed to facilitate conceptualization of Tulving's (1983) hypothesis of the phylogenetic evolution of episodic from semantic memory, and to account for recent arguments that whereas indirect memory measures reveal evidence of memory early in human ontogeny, the capacity to perform direct memory tasks first emerges only at 8–9 months of age (Schacter & Moscovitch 1984).

There are a number of other multiple-system formulations that are somewhat analogous to the episodic-semantic distinction (e.g. Halgren 1984; Johnson 1983; Oakley 1983; O'Keefe & Nadel 1978; Olton et al 1979; Schacter & Moscovitch 1984; Warrington & Weiskrantz 1982). One of these deserves special note: Morton's (1969, 1970, 1979, 1981) multisystem theory differs from Tulving's in that conceptual and factual knowledge, as well as personal or episodic memories, are dealt with by the same system (the *cognitive system*); a separate system contains abstract representations for words *(logogens)* that are responsible for lexical access.

Other theorists regard the distinction between procedural and declarative (or propositional) memories (accepted by Tulving) as sufficient to explain the observed dissociations between direct and indirect measures (e.g. Baddeley 1984; Cohen 1984; McKoon et al 1986; Squire & Cohen 1984). The procedural/declarative distinction was originally formulated by workers in artificial intelligence as a distinction between types of knowledge (e.g. Barr & Feigenbaum 1981; Winograd 1975), but it has been extended into a multiple-system viewpoint (Cohen 1984; Squire & Cohen 1984). Procedural memory involves "reorganization or other modification of existing processing structures or procedures," whereas declarative memory "represents explicitly new data structures derived from the operation of any process or procedure" (Cohen 1984, pp. 96–97). Although procedural memory can be revealed only when a task reengages prior processing operations, it is abstract in the sense that it does not record the specific prior events that caused those processing operations to be modified. The declarative system is considered to be responsible for conscious access to facts and past experiences; it is necessary for performance of direct memory tests, and is impaired in amnesia. An approach analogous to the procedural/declarative distinction is proposed by Mishkin (Mishkin et al 1984; Mishkin & Petri 1984), who distinguishes between a *memory* system and a *habit* system.

The distinction between *activation* and *elaboration* (Graf & Mandler 1984; Mandler 1980; Mandler et al 1986) is a process-oriented viewpoint; it differs from other abstractionist positions in being neutral with respect to the issue of memory systems. Activation of a preexisting mental representation "strengthens the relations among its components and increases its accessibility" (Graf

& Mandler 1984, p. 553); elaborative processing is necessary in order to retain new relationships and relate stimuli to the context in which they were presented. Activation alone is sufficient to result in processing facilitation that is revealed in indirect memory tests, whereas elaboration is necessary for direct tests of memory. A similar concept of *trace activation* has been proposed by Diamond & Rozin (1984; see also Mortensen 1980).

Nonabstractionist Positions

Nonabstractionists are unified by their disagreement with the necessity to distinguish abstract representations from memory traces that preserve information from specific experiences. They are typically mainstream cognitive psychologists who concern themselves primarily with the behavior of normal human subjects.

Kolers (e.g. 1979, 1985; Kolers & Roediger 1984; Kolers & Smythe 1984) has attacked the distinction between procedural and declarative (or propositional) knowledge, arguing that "statements or declarations . . . do not fail of procedural representation" (Kolers & Roediger 1984, p. 437). When a subject displays knowledge, he/she is assumed to be engaging in a form of skilled performance. Knowledge is regarded as being specific to the processes by which that knowledge is acquired: Rather than offering a "unitary" theory in opposition to multisystem approaches, Kolers suggests that mentation consists of a multiplicity of processes whose properties are poorly correlated. Memory is revealed to the extent that processing operations at study and test overlap (the principle of *transfer-appropriate processing*, Bransford et al 1979). Dissociations between direct and indirect measures of retention are to be expected when members of the two classes of task make different processing requirements, and not otherwise [see also Moscovitch et al (1986) for a similar viewpoint].

Jacoby (1983b), Blaxton (1985), and Roediger & Blaxton (1987a,b) have used the terms *conceptually driven* and *data-driven* as a taxonomy of the processing demands of memory tests. Direct memory tests typically involve more conceptually driven than data-driven processing because the subject uses associative information to reconstruct the study episode mentally; indirect memory tests typically involve more data-driven than conceptually driven processes because the subject focusses on external stimuli (e.g. a fragment of a word) at test. Dissociations between data-driven and conceptually driven memory tests would be expected as a function of the type of information (semantic-associative vs perceptual) encoded in a prior episode.

Jacoby (1982, 1983a,b, 1984, 1987; Jacoby & Brooks 1984; Jacoby & Dallas 1981; Jacoby & Witherspoon 1982) argues that implicit and explicit memory are reflections of "different aspects of memory for whole prior processing episodes" (1983a, p. 21). The aware and unaware aspects of memory for episodes are assumed to result from differences in information provided by test cues, and possibly accompanying differences in retrieval processes (see Whittlesea 1987 for a similar position).

Hybrid Positions

Like abstractionist positions, hybrid positions accept a distinction between abstract representations and memory traces preserving information about specific events. However, hybrid approaches assume that episodic memory traces can be accessed either explicitly/with awareness, or implicitly/without awareness. This dual-access assumption differentiates hybrid approaches from abstractionist views postulating that explicit, or strategically based, memory sometimes influences performance on indirect memory tests (e.g. Clarke & Morton 1983; Cohen 1984; den Heyer 1986; Diamond & Rozin 1984; Forster & Davis 1984; Fowler et al 1985; Graf et al 1984; Johnson et al 1985; Monsell 1985; Oliphant 1983; Squire et al 1987).

Feustel et al (1983) and Salasoo et al (1985) propose a model of perceptual identification in which both abstract lexical codes and episodic memory images contribute to identification. Presence of a lexical unit corresponding to a stimulus confers an advantage on that stimulus in identification; however, repetition priming effects are attributed to episodic images from prior presentations of items. As in Jacoby's view, different test cues result in different modes of access to the episodic information, permitting an accounting of dissociations between direct and indirect memory tests.

In contrast to Feustel et al, Schacter (e.g. 1985a,b, 1987) regards repetition priming as critically dependent on activation of unitized memory structures; however, he also proposes that newly acquired information influences the extent of priming, differentiating his view from simple activation views described above. To account for effects of newly acquired information on implicit memory, Schacter (1985a) proposes that unitized structures can be *locally modified* by the episodic contexts in which they occur. By contrast, explicit memory for newly acquired information is supported by *nested* structures, which are accessible only through contextual cues. However, it is not clear whether this type of model is identifiably different from a modified version of the Feustel et al model in which implicit memory results either from activation of unitized structures or from implicit access to episodes, and explicit memory depends on explicit access to those same episodes.

DISSOCIATIONS ACROSS MEASURES

A number of variables are strongly associated with performance on direct memory tests but are not associated with memory as revealed by indirect tests. As direct tests are held to reveal memory for past episodes, this evidence can be taken to suggest that indirect tests do not reflect memory for episodes;

rather, they can be held to reflect alteration of the state of abstract and relatively stable lexical, semantic, or procedural memory structures. The validity and replicability of a number of dissociations of this type reported by Tulving (1983, 1984a) has been questioned by McKoon et al (1986; Ratcliff & McKoon 1986). While we can agree with McKoon et al that dissociations between direct and indirect measures are not a completely general phenomenon (as reviewed below), a more extensive review indicates that dissociations produced by a number of critical variables are rather stable across studies.

Memory-Disordered Subjects

Chronic global amnesia is characterized by "a clinically significant deficit in new learning of verbal and nonverbal material irrespective of stimulus modality [that is] disproportionate to other cognitive impairment" (Corkin et al 1985, p. 10). Etiologies of organic amnesia include chronic alcohol abuse (Korsakoff's syndrome), bilateral resection of the medial temporal lobe (e.g. case H. M.), herpes simplex encephalitis, cerebral anoxia, closed head injury, ruptured aneurysm of the anterior communicating artery, and bilateral stroke. Studies comparing direct and indirect memory tests have used amnesics from all of these etiologic categories; other memory-disordered patients used in such studies include a nonglobal amnesic (case N. A.; Cohen & Squire 1980; Squire & Cohen 1982; Zola-Morgan et al 1983) with damage to the dorsomedial thalamic nucleus (and probably other structures, Weiskrantz 1985), patients receiving electroconvulsive therapy (ECT; e.g. Squire et al 1978, 1984, 1985), and patients with progressive dementia of Alzheimer's type (e.g. Martone et al 1984; Moscovitch et al 1986; Shimamura et al 1987).

A matter currently receiving intensive discussion is whether observed differences in memory performance across these categories of patient reflect fundamentally dissimilar memory deficits, or whether there is a core memory deficit differing in severity between patients, together with differences in superimposed nonobligatory intellectual deficits (e.g. Albert & Moss 1984; Corkin et al 1985; Mayes 1986; Morris & Kopelman 1986; Moscovitch 1982; Shimamura et al 1987; Squire 1982; Squire & Cohen 1984; Squire & Shimamura 1986; Weiskrantz 1985). This issue is beyond the scope of this paper; however, we note that results often differ across patient groups, so that comparisons across studies using different classes of memory-disordered patients must be made with caution.

Numerous studies have shown preserved memory in memory-disordered patients as indexed by indirect tests of memory (where "preserved" means "at a level not worse than controls") together with impaired memory as indexed by direct tests (where "impaired" means "at a level significantly worse than controls"). In addition, there are a number of more informal demonstrations of learning in amnesics (e.g. studies in which only one memory task was studied, or no control group was included). Reviews of this material are available (e.g. Baddeley 1982; Cohen 1984; Moscovitch 1982, 1984, 1985; Schacter 1985a,b, 1987; Schacter & Graf 1986b; Shimamura 1986; Squire 1986; Squire & Cohen 1984; Weiskrantz 1985) so we restrict ourselves to recent examples relevant to the theoretical discussion below.

SEMANTIC AND LEXICAL KNOWLEDGE   In an extension of the classic studies by Warrington & Weiskrantz (1968, 1970, 1974, 1978) and Weiskrantz & Warrington (1970), Graf et al (1984) found normal priming effects in memory-disordered patients of various etiologies in the word-completion paradigm. In this paradigm the subject is asked to complete each of a list of three-letter word stems (e.g. REA_____) with the first English word that comes to mind; there are generally about ten appropriate completions. Prior study of a word significantly increased the probability of generating that word as a completion to the appropriate stem (relative to baseline words with no prior study). This priming effect was equivalent in amnesics and control subjects; additionally, the advantage for primed words declined over time at the same rate for both groups, being absent by about 2 hr after presentation. By contrast, when subjects were told to use the stems to retrieve study-list words (a direct memory test) amnesics were severely impaired relative to normals. A number of studies have replicated preserved priming of word completion in amnesics in conjunction with impaired performance on direct tests of memory (Diamond & Rozin 1984; Graf & Schacter 1985; Graf et al 1985; Shimamura & Squire 1984; Shimamura et al 1987; Squire et al 1987, Expt. 1).

Similar patterns of results have been found with a variety of other indirect memory tests. Gardner et al (1973) and Graf et al (1985) report that studying category exemplars enhanced the likelihood that those exemplars would be given in response to category cues in a generation task. This priming effect was equivalent in amnesic and control subjects; however, when asked to use category cues to retrieve studied words (Gardner et al 1973), or to freely recall studied words (Graf et al 1985), amnesics were impaired relative to controls. Shimamura & Squire (1984) found that study of a pair such as *table-chair* more than doubled the probability (relative to baseline) that the studied response *(chair)* would be given as a response to the stimulus *(table)* in a free-association test. Free-association priming was equivalent in Korsakoffs and controls, whereas Korsakoffs were impaired relative to controls on a cued-recall test with the same materials. Schacter (1985a) reports a similar dissociation in amnesics of diverse etiologies using idiomatic phrases such as *sour grapes* and *small potatoes* as the studied items. Moscovitch (1984, 1985) obtained normal repetition-priming effects in memory-disordered patients in a lexical-decision task, in conjunction with poor or chance performance on a recognition memory test. Cermak et al (1985, Expt. 1) found preserved priming in perceptual identification of words by Korsakoff patients, together with impaired recognition memory performance. Finally, Jacoby & Witherspoon (1982) had Korsakoff patients and controls spell auditorily presented homophones at test; some of these homophones had earlier been presented in a biasing context that required the least common of the two or more meanings of the homophone to be selected. Biased homophones were more likely than new homophones to be spelled according to their least common interpretation; this priming effect was larger for Korsakoffs than controls, whereas Korsakoffs were severely impaired relative to controls on a subsequent recognition memory test.

PROCEDURAL KNOWLEDGE   The early literature demonstrated that amnesics could acquire and retain a number of perceptual-motor skills, such as pursuit rotor and mirror drawing, and show benefits of practice on problem-solving tasks, such as solving a jigsaw puzzle and learning a mathematical rule (for reviews: Baddeley 1982; Cohen 1984; Moscovitch 1982; Squire & Cohen 1984; Weiskrantz 1985). In the present paper we focus on indirect tests that are more amenable to comparison with direct memory measures.

An important property of studies of reading degraded or geometrically transformed script is that they permit general benefits from increased practice to be separated from specific benefits accruing to repeated groups of words or sentences (by comparison of repeated and nonrepeated items as practice progresses). Initial studies of speed of reading mirror-reversed script (Cohen & Squire 1980; Martone et al 1984) found a general practice effect in amnesics, as well as an item-specific repetition effect; however, whereas the general practice effect was preserved in amnesics, the item-specific effect was not as large in amnesics as in normals. This impairment was paralleled by the amnesics' impairment in recognizing old items.

Moscovitch et al (1986) argue that the impairment on repeated items occurred because the difficulty of reading mirror-reversed script encourages normal subjects to use explicit memory to speed reading of repeated items (for a similar argument see Horton 1985), a resource not available to the amnesic patients. In their Experiment 2, they used speeded reading of normally oriented masked words and sentences to reduce possible influences of explicit memory on reading speed; item-specific repetition effects were now preserved in a heterogeneous group of memory-disordered patients (including early Alzheimer's sufferers), whereas these patients were severely impaired on a recognition test for the same materials.

As in studies of normal subjects (e.g. Kolers 1976), practice effects in reading geometrically transformed text are quite durable in memory-disordered patients: Moscovitch et al (1986, Expt. 1) found both general and item-specific effects at intervals from 4 days through 2 weeks following initial training, using sentences whose letters were rotated 180 degrees around their vertical axis. In Cohen & Squire (1980), both general and item-specific effects persisted at a delay of 3 months. Interestingly, mirror-reading skill acquired before a course of ECT treatments persisted after those treatments, despite retrograde amnesia for the words read during acquisition of the skill (Squire et al 1984).

   A most impressive demonstration of acquisition of problem-solving ability in amnesics has been provided by Cohen et al (1985; see also Cohen 1984; Squire & Cohen 1984), using the Tower of Hanoi puzzle. This puzzle is complex (requiring solution of a series of nested subproblems), and practice effects are predicated on the recursive nature of the problem being reflected in subjects' solution strategies. A heterogeneous group of amnesics showed completely preserved practice effects (measured in terms of reduction in number of moves to solution) over 16 attempts to solve the problem (4 per day for 4 days). A direct memory test was constructed by presenting the puzzle in intermediate stages of solution. Some of these configurations were on the optimal 31-move solution path and would have been encountered previously; others were not on the optimal path and would not have been encountered previously. On this recognition test, amnesics' discrimination performance was close to chance, whereas control subjects performed at levels well above chance. As in studies of reading transformed text, practice effects on the Tower of Hanoi puzzle are apparently very persistent: Patient H. M. demonstrated large savings over initial performance levels one year after last solving the puzzle (Cohen 1984). Curiously, Butters et al (1985) failed to replicate normal learning of the Tower of Hanoi puzzle in diencephalic (e.g. Korsakoff syndrome) amnesics; they attribute this failure to a impairment in "initiating and ordering of problem-solving strategies," so that "failure to acquire the . . . solution does not necessarily indicate an impairment in procedural learning" (pp. 741–742).

EVALUATIVE RESPONSE   Following up on anecdotal evidence of Claparède (1911/1951), Johnson et al (1985) studied acquisition of affective reactions in Korsakoff patients. In one experiment, Korsakoffs were found to rate melodies that they had heard before in the experiment as more pleasant than new melodies; this affective bias was the same in Korsakoffs and controls, whereas recognition of old melodies was significantly impaired in Korsakoffs compared to controls.

   In another experiment, subjects were given biographical information about two males depicted in photographs; one stimulus person was described in positive terms, the other in negative ones. Later they were asked to indicate preference for one or the other of the two men. In this situation, amnesics did not show as extreme a bias in favor of the positively characterized stimulus person as did controls. Johnson et al attributed this failure to find equivalence in the preference test (an indirect test) to the control subjects' conscious use of specific biographical information to determine affective response; by contrast, information of this type was not available to control subjects in the case of melodies, limiting the influence of reflective retrieval processes on the affective ratings.

Temporary Change in Brain State

Effects of drugs and hypnosis have been cited as dissociating direct and indirect tests (e.g. Hashtroudi et al 1984; Kihlstrom 1980; Parker et al 1983; Williamsen et al 1965); however the validity and replicability of these studies have been questioned [McKoon et al (1986); but see also Nissen et al (1987) for more recent drug work, and Kihlstrom (1985) for more recent hypnosis work]. We refer instead to another striking demonstration of this type of dissociation by Squire et al (1985). They administered study-test trials at different times in the recovery period following individual treatments in a course of bilateral ECT, using word completion priming and three-choice recognition memory as dependent measures. Priming recovered at a much faster rate than did recognition memory performance: At 45 min following ECT, priming was normal in comparison to non-ECT controls, whereas recognition memory was at chance. Recognition memory took 9 hr to return to a level approaching that shown by controls.

Normal Subjects

LEVEL AND ELABORATION OF PROCESSING, DIFFICULTY OF PROCESSING, AND STUDY-TIME EFFECTS   There are now numerous demonstrations that traditional encoding manipulations, while producing strong effects on performance in a direct test, do not affect the extent of repetition effects in an indirect test. In Jacoby & Dallas (1981), manipulating the level of processing (LOP) of study words did not change the size of the repetition priming effect in perceptual identification, but it produced large effects on recognition memory (semantically processed words yielding better performance than phonemically or orthographically processed words). In subsequent studies, null effects of study LOP on repetition priming have been found for word completion (Graf & Mandler 1984; Graf et al 1982), lexical decision (Kirsner et al 1983, Expts. 2 & 3; Monsell 1985), picture naming latency (Carroll et al 1985, Expts. 1–3), and perceptual identification of pictures (Carroll et al 1985, Expt. 4). Further, Begg et al (1985) found that LOP at study did not influence the advantage of repeated over nonrepeated statements in ratings of credibility. In each of the studies cited, a direct memory test (across studies, free recall, cued recall, and recognition) showed a large effect of LOP for the same items. An exception to this general trend is Squire et al (1987, data from control subjects), in which an LOP effect on fragment completion priming was found; the authors attribute this finding to the spontaneous use of explicit memory for deeply processed items in the indirect test.

Increasing elaborative processing at study enhances direct memory performance (e.g. Bradshaw & Anderson 1982) but does not appear to influence repetition priming. Richardson & Bjork (1982) had subjects rehearse auditorily presented words imaginally in a prefamiliarized speaker's voice; rehearsal was either rote or elaborative. Priming was equivalent for the two types of rehearsal in a subsequent auditory perceptual identification test; however, elaborative rehearsal produced better recognition memory than did rote rehearsal. Consistent with this result, Graf & Schacter (1985) and Schacter & Graf (1986a) showed that elaborative processing (e.g. generating a sentence including the study word) did not increase the amount of direct priming obtained in word completion, in comparison with a condition in which study words were orthographically processed. Similar results were obtained in free-association priming with common idioms and highly related word pairs as study materials (Schacter & Whitfield 1986). Finally, Greene (1986) found no effect on word completion priming of intention to learn at study (presumed to influence elaborative activity). In the latter four studies large effects of amount of elaboration on cued recall were observed.

Jacoby & Dallas (1981) investigated effects of difficulty of encoding and study time. They showed that reading a word resulted in as much priming of later perceptual identification as did producing that word as a solution to an anagram; by contrast, solving anagrams produced much better recognition memory for studied items than did reading. Similarly, increasing study time (by slowing rate of presentation of study words) enhanced recognition memory but did not affect the magnitude of priming. Consistent with the latter result, Richardson and Bjork (1982) found no effect of duration of rehearsal in an imagined voice on priming of auditory perceptual identification (for both rote and elaborative types of rehearsal), and Greene (1986) obtained a null effect of rehearsal duration on word completion priming. Increasing rehearsal duration in these studies resulted in significant improvements in recognition and in cued recall, respectively.

DEVELOPMENTAL DISSOCIATIONS   Schacter & Moscovitch (1984; Schacter 1984; Moscovitch 1985) reinterpreted the data on the early development of memory as showing that there are "early" and "late" memory systems, the latter beginning to emerge only 8–9 months after birth. Before the emergence of the late system, "behavior may be modified but without any recollection of a previous episode" (Moscovitch 1985, p. 80). They regard data on infant search errors as reflecting memory deficits associated with inability to recollect episodes (for a similar view, see Bjork & Cummings 1984). Performance on indirect memory tests (habituation, novelty preference, certain types of conditioning tasks) would not be expected to show a developmental trend from 8–12 months; performance on direct tests (object search, other types of conditioning) would show such a trend as the late system developed. Here again a variable is associated with performance on direct tests, but not with performance on indirect tests.

Schacter & Moscovitch (1984) argued that the late system is impaired in amnesia. To support this argument, they showed that memory-disordered patients (including early Alzheimer's patients and amnesics) perform poorly on the type of object search task originally used by Piaget in his investigations of object permanence. The poor performance of memory-disordered subjects was due to intrusions of responses made in prior trials in which the object was hidden at a different location than the current one (a phenomenon they term *mnemonic precedence*); however, such intrusions could not be attributed to perseveration associated with frontal lobe pathology (e.g. Moscovitch 1982) because patients with frontal lobe damage performed well at the task.

Stochastic Independence

A supplementary strategy to generating functional dissociations has been to test for stochastic independence between direct and indirect tests. The principal demonstrations of independence/nonindependence are summarized first. That summary is followed by a discussion of the effects that can contaminate such analyses—effects that themselves must be accounted for before theoretical implications can be attributed to independence or dependence across measures.

OBSERVED INDEPENDENCE AND DEPENDENCE   In the face of objections to his use of functional dissociations of the type described above to support the episodic-semantic distinction (e.g. Hintzman 1984; Roediger 1984), Tulving (1985a) has emphasized the importance of stochastic independence between different measures of memory, arguing that this type of independence places tighter constraints on theory. He points out that functional independence or dissociation can be explained by assuming that one or more processing stages is common to different tasks, but that others are used for one task but not for the other (as in generation-recognition models of recognition and recall—e.g. Anderson & Bower 1972). On the other hand, "as long as there is any overlap in those operating components that are responsible for differences in what is retrieved, some positive dependence between measures should appear. Perfect stochastic independence implies complete absence of such overlap" (1985a, p. 395).

The classic examples of stochastic independence are studies by Jacoby & Witherspoon (1982) and Tulving et al (1982). In the former study, the probability of recognizing a primed homophone as having been studied was no greater when calculated as a proportion of those words spelled in the biased fashion than when calculated without regard to spelling status. This result held for both normals and Korsakoff amnesics, even though their overall rates of correct recognition differed by about 50%. Jacoby & Witherspoon obtained similar results from the perceptual identification-recognition paradigm, using word stimuli: The probability of perceptual identification given recognition was equivalent to the simple probability of perceptual identification across 12 conditions that differed in overall rate of identification. Tulving et al (1982) found that probability of recognition conditionalized on successful fragment completion was equivalent to the overall proportion of words recognized, for four conditions that differed in overall recognition probability.

Tulving (1985a) presents further more recent examples from his laboratory of stochastic independence between recognition and indirect memory tasks. In Chandler's (1983) master's thesis, fragment completion and recognition were studied under 32 different conditions, including conditions in which the relation between the word fragments and the study list words was pointed out to subjects at test. Other indirect memory tasks used by Tulving's students were anagram solution and identifying the presence of a face in an ambiguous drawing. Probability of recognition conditionalized on fragment completion, anagram solution, or face identification was essentially equivalent to the simple recognition probability across 39 conditions. These conditions varied in simple probability of recognition between .03 and .88 (approximate values). Additional examples of stochastic independence are given by Eich (1984) and Light et al (1986).

A number of exceptions to stochastic independence have been observed. For example, dependence was found when nonword stimuli were used in perceptual identification (Jacoby & Witherspoon 1982), when subjects were instructed to use word fragments to help retrieve study-list words (G. Hayman, unpublished observations cited in Schacter 1985b), and when a completion test preceded a recognition test (Light et al 1986; Shimamura & Squire 1984; Tulving et al 1982). The first two examples might be explained by assuming that subjects used explicit memory in both the direct and indirect tests (e.g. Schacter 1985b). The latter example brings up the important issue of intertest biases, which we consider next.

CONTAMINATING EFFECTS   Some critics have argued that stochastic independence (and sometimes dependence) is often an artifact produced by the influence of the first test on the second test (e.g. Mandler et al 1986; Shimamura 1985). This problem is fundamental and formidable. The stochastic-independence logic requires that a given subject be tested on the same item in more than one way. It is simply an implausible assumption that the item exposures and subject reactions that comprise a first test leave the memory system unaltered and ready to give an uncontaminated picture of the influence of the study episode on a second test of some type. Shimamura (1985) presents examples illustrating that independence can appear when dependence is in fact the case, and vice versa, depending on the nature of the two tests and the presumed influence of the first test on the second test. When a completion test occurs before a recognition test, stochastic dependence is likely to result because the completion test represents an additional study trial for items successfully completed (Tulving et al 1982). This dependence could occur even when the information tapped by the two tests was in fact uncorrelated. More important, when a recognition test precedes a completion test, and the recognition test boosts later completion performance, the interest bias is towards independence, even when dependence between measures exists in fact.

At a more advanced stage of theory development, tests of stochastic independence may prove to be more important and useful. When our theories of memory as revealed in direct and indirect tests are complete enough, and quantitative enough, to account for the effects of one test on another, such effects can potentially be partialled out of tests for stochastic independence [e.g. Flexser & Tulving (1982) attempt to model the priming of subsequent recall attributable to an item's exposure on a prior recognition test]. Even now, there are cases in which we can specify with some confidence whether the effect of one test on another should work towards producing independence or dependence. Given that the observed outcome is in the opposite direction, we may be relatively safe in attaching theoretical significance to the result.

Although some current examples of independence and dependence may be statistically interpretable, difficulties remain in drawing theoretical implications from such results. Tulving's critics do not agree that stochastic independence between direct and indirect measures represents convincing evidence for multiple memory systems, or even for absence of process overlap between tests, arguing instead that independence could result from absence of overlap in the information provided by different test cues (e.g. Flexser & Tulving 1978; Shoben & Ross 1986). It is not possible to discriminate between the opposing interpretations because none of the currently viable theories is precisely specified enough to permit deduction of dependence or independence between direct and indirect measures from its premises. A consequence of this problem is that findings of stochastic independence and dependence play little role in discriminating between competing theories of the relationship between direct and indirect measures.

PARALLEL EFFECTS ACROSS MEASURES

Repetition Effects

Using a study-test procedure, Jacoby & Dallas (1981, Expts. 4a,4b) found that presenting items twice at study resulted in greater priming of perceptual identification than did presenting them once (if the presentations of twice-presented items were spaced); this repetition effect mirrored that found in recognition memory. (Of course, the positive effects of repetition in direct memory tests are well known; see Crowder 1976, Ch. 9). Feustel et al (1983) extended this result using a continuous identification procedure and somewhat different measures of perceptual identification performance: Across a number of experiments perceptual identification performance was enhanced monotonically as a function of the number of presentations of an item (1, 2, or 3). Effects of repetition on word completion and recognition have also been found to be parallel (Graf & Mandler 1984).

Feustel et al (1983) confirmed the similarity between the effects of repetition on recognition and perceptual identification by presenting words that were different in meaning from previously repeated words, but highly similar in orthography (e.g. *huge* presented following prior repetition of *hug*). Identification of these *derived words* was improved by prior presentation of the words from which they were derived (an indirect priming effect); additionally, subjects made more false positive responses to the derived words than to underived new words in a recognition memory test.

Level of Attention at Encoding

Experiments reviewed above suggested that manipulations of orienting task at encoding did not affect the strength of repetition priming, but strongly influenced performance on direct tests. The insensitivity of repetition priming to the nature of encoding processes seemed to be confirmed by demonstrations of effects of prior exposure in the absence of attentional encoding. In studies by Zajonc and colleagues (e.g. Kunst-Wilson & Zajonc 1980; Wilson 1979; Zajonc 1980) stimuli were presented for initial study under conditions that led to chance recognition memory performance in a later test (e.g. visual presentation at extremely brief durations, or auditory presentation on an unattended channel in dichotic listening). Despite their inability to recognize "old" stimuli, subjects displayed affective preference for those stimuli over "new" stimuli. Similar results were obtained using visual presentation by Seamon et al (1983a,b, 1984; but see also Mandler & Shebo 1983). Eich (1984) combined the dichotic listening technique with Jacoby & Witherspoon's (1982) homophone spelling paradigm; biasing primes were presented over the unattended channel in the study phase. At test, subjects showed a spelling bias for primed homophones in conjunction with chance recognition for "old" items. In sum, when conscious or attentional processing in the initial exposure phase is difficult or impossible, the behavior of normals seems to mimic that of amnesics under attentional encoding conditions (e.g. Jacoby & Witherspoon 1982; Johnson et al 1985).

Although studies of this type permit the conclusion that attentional encoding is not necessary for prior-exposure effects to occur, they typically do not include a control condition in which stimuli are attentionally encoded at study. This omission prevents the conclusion that the indirect measure in question is insensitive to a manipulation of level of attention to which a direct measure is sensitive. In short, studies that do not manipulate level of attention at study cannot be said to have demonstrated dissociations between direct and indirect measures analogous to those found in comparisons of amnesics and normals, or in manipulations of orienting task at encoding.

Studies of affective preference that include appropriate manipulations have yielded mixed results. Seamon et al (1983a) compared a condition in which subjects shadowed an auditory message during initial brief visual presentations to a condition in which no shadowing was performed. In one experiment, affective preference was greater for attended than for unattended stimuli, and a similar advantage for attended stimuli was found in recognition memory. Results from two other experiments were less clear-cut, but in no case did the shadowing variable interact with the type of test (preference vs recognition), as would be expected if level of attention dissociated the two tests. A different pattern was obtained by Seamon et al (1984), who manipulated stimulus exposure duration in the study phase. At test, the effect of prior exposure on affective judgments was little influenced by exposure duration (from 2 msec through 48 msec); by contrast, items exposed for 24 msec at study were recognized much better than those exposed for 8 msec.

By contrast, studies in the lexical domain give much stronger evidence for the role of attention in priming effects. Eich (1984) presented biasing homophones over an unattended or an attended channel. As expected, recognition memory performance was much better for attended than for unattended study items; however, attended primes also biased later spelling to a greater extent than did unattended primes. Jacoby & Brooks (1984) had subjects search for members of a target semantic category in a series of words presented rapidly (300 msec/item) in one position on a CRT screen. Half of the items in the series were target-category exemplars; the remainder were members of the same nontarget category. In a later perceptual identification test, old members of the target category were identified better than new members of the same category. The difference between old and new items for nontarget-category items was much smaller than that for target-category items. This study is flawed because target items (but not nontarget items) were recalled following the study phase (perhaps accounting for their superior identifiability), and because no comparison of direct memory for targets and nontargets was made to permit assessment of differential versus parallel effects across a direct and an indirect test. However, the results are suggestive of an effect on perceptual identification that parallels the effect of comparable manipulations in direct memory studies (e.g. Fisk & Schneider 1984).

Similar results have been obtained in lexical decision studies. In a study by Oliphant (1983), repeated words received their first presentation either as part of the typewritten instructions for the lexical decision task, or as stimuli in the lexical decision task. Only the latter condition resulted in repetition priming; reading words as part of the instructions conferred no benefit on later lexical decisions concerning those words. This result can be given an attentional interpretation: Individual items receive less attentional processing when they are presented as part of a coherent body of text than when they are presented as individual items in the lexical decision task. This reasoning is confirmed by the results of Monsell & Banich (in Monsell 1985), who found weaker repetition priming in lexical decision when primes were read as part of sentences than when they were presented as stimuli in the lexical decision task. Finally, Forster & Davis (1984) found that the frequency-attenuation effect in lexical decision was eliminated when the first presentation of to-be-repeated items was masked so that the prime was minimally available to awareness. The *frequency-attenuation effect* refers to the finding that low-frequency words benefit more from repetition than do high-frequency words, so that repetition attenuates the usual superiority of high-frequency words (e.g. Jacoby & Dallas 1981; Kirsner et al 1983; Nelson et al 1984; Scarborough et al 1977, 1979). When primes were masked, repetition conferred equal benefits on subsequent processing of low- and high-frequency words; this result suggests that attentional encoding plays an important role in producing the repetition effect for low-frequency words.

Reinstating List Context

Jacoby (1983a) showed that the magnitude of the repetition priming effect in perceptual identification was positively related to the ratio of the numbers of primed and unprimed words on the test list. The priming effect was larger when primed words constituted 90% of the test list than when they constituted only 10% of the test list. In another experiment, subjects received study-test trials on five consecutive days. Words studied on the fifth day were identified better when they alone constituted the old times on the test list than when they were mixed with old items from previous days. According to Jacoby these results show that repetition priming is sensitive to contextual reinstatement in the same way that direct tests of memory are. Jacoby (1983a; see also Jacoby & Witherspoon 1982) also investigated the influence on priming of match between environmental contexts at study and test, with generally negative results. However, since null effects of incidental environmental context have been obtained in recognition memory (e.g. Godden & Baddeley 1980; Smith et al 1978) and recall (Bjork & Richardson-Klavehn 1987; Eich 1985; Fernandez & Glenberg 1985), failure to obtain effects on priming measures cannot be taken to imply that indirect measures are less sensitive to environmental context than are direct measures.

Influence of New Associations

In their critique of the episodic-semantic distinction, McKoon et al (1986; Ratcliff & McKoon 1986) place considerable emphasis on studies comparing indirect priming effects in lexical decision and recognition memory tasks. In the context of task-comparison methods there are two questions of interest: (a) Are lexical decision and recognition influenced similarly or differently by presentation of information that is semantically related to the target word (semantic priming), and (b) are lexical decision and recognition influenced similarly or differently by the presentation of an item that was first associated with the target in the experimental context (episodic priming)? McKoon et al base their arguments on the assumption of similarity of effects across the direct and indirect tasks. However, studies investigating these questions have produced mixed results, with some showing dissociative effects (e.g. Carroll & Kirsner 1982; Neely & Durgunoğlu 1985) and others suggesting parallel effects (e.g. McKoon & Ratcliff 1986; McKoon et al 1985; Ratcliff & McKoon 1981; Ratcliff et al 1985). Durgunoğlu & Neely (1987) have shown that differences in experimental procedures are responsible for the apparent inconsistencies in the results; in particular, episodic priming of lexical decision occurs only when numerous experimental conditions are conjointly satisfied. The procedural complexities of such studies are too great to permit a detailed treatment here.

We refer instead to work of Graf & Schacter (1985, 1987; Schacter 1985a,b; Schacter & Graf 1986a,b), which clearly demonstrates that performance in an indirect test can be influenced by new associations. In the basic experiment, word pairs are presented, the stimulus and response terms of each pair bearing no preexperimental relationship to each other (e.g. window-REASON). The subject must generate a meaningful association between the two words. In the word completion test, subjects are given three-letter stems accompanied by a stimulus word that is the same as at study (same-context condition—e.g. window-REA_____), or different, but also normatively unrelated to the response word (different-context condition—e.g. officer-REA_____). Although priming (relative to baseline completion performance) is observed in the different-context condition, preserving the stimulus word from the study list (same-context condition) significantly increases the probability that the subject will generate a list word. The difference between the same- and different-context conditions represents an episodic priming effect due to the retention of a new association. Moscovitch (1984, 1985; Moscovitch et al 1986) has obtained similar results in studies of reading transformed and degraded script. Increases in reading speed for pairs of words whose members have been read before are greater for test pairs whose members were previously read together as a pair (old pairs) than for test pairs consisting of words that were read as parts of different pairs in the study phase (recombined pairs). Again, the results show the influence on an indirect memory measure of an association formed during prior exposure to the test materials.

As would be expected, direct tests also reveal the influence of new associations. In the experiments of particular interest here (Schacter & Graf 1986a, Expts. 1 & 2), deliberate recall of study-list words using the word stems as cues (*letter-cued recall*, a form of direct test) was influenced in the same way as word completion priming by the contextual manipulation. Same-context responses were recalled significantly more often than were different-context responses. These cued-recall results mirrored previous results in recognition memory: DaPolito et al (1972) showed that words studied in the context of two other unrelated words were recognized better when the context words were reinstated at test than when the context words were removed or replaced with different words. In sum, cued recall and recognition were influenced in the same way as was word completion by the formation of new associations.

Graf & Schacter (1985; see also Schacter & Graf 1986b) showed normal episodic priming effects on word completion in amnesic subjects; the same subjects were subsequently severely impaired in a test of cued recall for the response terms of studied pairs (a direct test for associations formed during study). Moscovitch (1984, 1985; Moscovitch et al 1986) also demonstrated normal retention of new verbal associations in memory-disordered patients, even though these patients were severly impaired when asked to discriminate old from recombined pairs of words. These demonstrations of the acquisition of verbal associations complement prior demonstrations of eye-blink (Weiskrantz & Warrington 1979) and galvanic skin response (Rees-Nishio, in Moscovitch 1985) conditioning in memory-disordered patients. The results in memory-disordered patients suggest that retention of new associations as revealed by indirect tests is not due to explicit retrieval of associations; they therefore support McKoon et al's (1986) claim that episodic priming is automatic/unconscious.

Memory for Facts Versus Memory for Experiences

Anterograde amnesia in memory-disordered patients is not limited to performance on tests whose instructions make explicit reference to a prior episode. Learning of new facts (e.g. Cermak & O'Connor 1983; Schacter et al 1984;

Shimamura & Squire 1987) and vocabulary (Gabrieli et al 1983; Glisky et al 1986a) is impaired, although memory-disordered patients are able to acquire and use some new information relating to particular domains when learning and testing techniques are appropriately contrived (e.g. Glisky & Schacter 1987; Glisky et al 1986a,b; Schacter & Glisky 1986; Schacter et al 1985). Memory-disordered patients also exhibit retrograde amnesia, although the severity and temporal extent of retrograde impairment vary considerably across patients with different etiologies (for a summary, see Butters & Cermak 1986). To the extent that retrograde impairment occurs, however, it covers memory for past public events and figures, and for past television shows (e.g. Albert et al 1979; Butters & Albert 1982; Cohen & Squire 1981; Meudell et al 1980; Squire & Cohen 1982).

Tests of factual information, vocabulary, and remote memory for public information meet only some of the criteria for inclusion as indirect tests. Their task instructions do not typically make explicit reference to a prior episode in the history of the individual; on the other hand, the measures involved are not derived from comparison of two or more data points, and an individual is necessarily aware of remembering in some sense when performing some of these tests. Nonetheless, such tests are clearly not direct tests, and the data from such tests therefore represent an exception to the generalization that memory-disordered patients show deficits only in direct tests of memory.

COMPLEX PATTERNS ACROSS MEASURES

Recent research has shown that patterns of dissociations and parallel effects across direct and indirect measures of memory vary systematically as a function of certain critical variables.

Conceptually Driven Versus Data-Driven Tests

Performance in indirect tests is often more dependent on match between perceptual conditions at study and test (such as modality of presentation) than is performance in direct tests. Sensitivity to match between study and test context is one of the criteria used to determine whether a test involves retrieval of episodic information. Such dissociations therefore seem paradoxical because indirect measures of memory have traditionally been assumed to reflect modification of an abstract (context-free) representation, whereas direct measures have been assumed to depend on information about spatiotemporal context.

Following up on an argument made by Roediger (1984), Blaxton (1985) and Roediger & Blaxton (1987a) have proposed that the apparent generality of such dissociations is an artifact of a failure to consider a wide enough range of direct and indirect memory tests. Most indirect tests can be classified as *data-driven* because the subject is required to operate on perceptual information provided by the experimenter (e.g. fragment completion, perceptual identification); the data-driven nature of most indirect tests accounts for their sensitivity to perceptual context. On the other hand, direct tests usually involve a significant amount of *conceptually driven* processing because the subject must mentally reconstruct the study episode (e.g. in free recall). However, the data-driven/conceptually driven and indirect/direct taxonomies are by no means coextensive. Indirect tests can be conceptually driven (e.g. retrieval of facts and general knowledge), and direct tests can be data-driven (e.g. cued recall with extralist cues that are graphemically similar to studied items). Recognition memory tests usually involve a blend of data-driven and conceptually driven processing; the subject operates on perceptual data provided by the experimenter, but must often reconstruct the study episode in order to perform accurately.

In the context of the data-driven/conceptually driven taxonomy the literature on perceptual and linguistic context effects shows a remarkable degree of consistency: Manipulations of similarity between linguistic or perceptual context at study and test affect data-driven tasks similarly, regardless of direct/indirect status; manipulations of elaboration at study affect conceptually driven tasks similarly, regardless of direct/indirect status. Tests of recognition memory align themselves either with data-driven or with conceptually driven tasks, depending on the types of processing permitted by the specific experimenatal circumstances.

THE GENERATION EFFECT   The term *generation effect* (Slamecka & Graf 1978) refers to the advantage—in terms of later recall or recognition performance—of generating rather than reading information in the study phase. In Jacoby's (1983b) study, reading a word produced greater priming of later perceptual identification than did generating that word in response to a related word; by contrast, study words that were read were more poorly recognized than study words that were generated. Blaxton (1985, Expt. 1) replicated this dissociation using free recall and fragment completion as the direct and indirect tests, respectively. Winnick & Daniel (1970, Expt. 2) and Clarke & Morton (1983, Expt. 1) obtained similar dissociations between free recall and visual duration threshold (VDT). Generating a word from a definition led to better free recall than did reading a word; however, reading a word reduced its later VDT significantly, whereas generating the word did not. This crossover interaction occurred despite the fact that type of test was within-subjects in both studies, with free recall preceding the identification test. Completing this general pattern, Monsell & Banich (cited in Monsell 1985) found priming in a visual lexical decision task only when tested words had previously been read, but not when they had been generated from a definition or as a completion to a proverb; in auditory lexical decision the generation condition resulted in significant priming, but priming in this condition was attenuated compared to the read condition. On indirect tests in these studies, amount of priming was positively related to similarity of the perceptual form of a word at study and test. In contrast, a generation advantage occurred for a visual test of recognition memory, even though generating a word at study meant that the word was not visually presented until test (Jacoby 1983b).

In support of the data-driven/conceptually driven taxonomy of tests described above, Blaxton (1985; see also Roediger & Blaxton 1987a) has shown that the generation effect dissociates some pairs of direct and indirect tests but produces parallel effects on other pairs. In her experiment, subjects either generated a study word from a cue (e.g. *tin-C_____*) or read the word in the absence of a meaningful context (e.g. *XXX-COPPER*). Two direct memory tests were used: free recall, and cued recall with extralist cues that were graphemically similar to to-be-remembered items (e.g. *CHOPPER* was a cue for *COPPER*). The two indirect tests were fragment completion and a general knowledge test (e.g. "What metal makes up 10% of yellow gold?"). Generating the study word produced better performance than did reading it for the free recall test and for priming in the general knowledge test; by contrast, reading the study word was superior to generating it for the graphemically cued recall test and for fragment completion priming. In sum, dissociations between direct and indirect tests were observed in comparisons of free recall with fragment completion (replicating the dissociations reported by Jacoby 1983b and others), and graphemic cued recall with general knowledge retrieval; however, parallel effects were observed in comparisons of free recall with general knowledge retrieval and graphemic cued recall with fragment completion. With respect to the direction of the generation effect, then, the tests group themselves according to the data-driven/conceptually driven taxonomy, and not according to the direct/indirect taxonomy.

PICTURE-WORD EFFECTS   Studies that have manipulated whether an item is presented for study in its pictorial or its verbal form have yielded patterns of results very similar to those in studies of the generation effect. A large literature demonstrates the superiority of pictorial over verbal presentation in free recall, cued recall, and recognition memory tests (for a summary, see Roediger & Weldon 1987). By contrast, priming in indirect tests is often greater when items are presented for study as words than when they are presented as pictures. Winnick & Daniel (1970, Expt. 2) found the standard picture superiority effect in free recall; however, VDTs were lower for items studied in verbal form than for those studied as pictures. This crossover interaction between test type and mode of presentation occurred despite the fact that the free recall test was administered to subjects before the VDT test.

The picture-word variable produces similar dissociations between recognition memory and lexical decision (Scarborough et al 1979), cued recall (with semantically related extralist associates) and fragment completion (Roediger & Weldon 1987, Expt. 3), and free recall and fragment completion (Weldon & Roediger 1987, Expt. 1). Additionally, naming and semantic categorization latencies for words are reduced more when primes are presented as words than when they are presented as pictures (Durso & Johnson 1979; Durso & Sullivan 1983; Kroll & Potter 1984).

As with the generation effect, performance in recognition is better when physical cues at study and test are different (picture at study, word at test) than when they are the same (word at study, word at test); by contrast, the indirect tests that have been studied are highly sensitive to match/mismatch between the physical cues at study and test. However, picture superiority is not an intrinsic property of direct memory tests. Roediger & Weldon (1987, Expt. 2) showed that the picture superiority effect was eliminated in a direct test when subjects were given fragments of studied items and told to use them to retrieve studied words (a data-driven test). Similarly, word superiority is not intrinsic to indirect tests. When the indirect test consists of naming a picture (Durso & Johnson 1979), categorizing a picture (Durso & Johnson 1979; Kroll & Potter 1984), identifying a tachistoscopically presented picture (Warren & Morton 1982), or identifying a fragmented picture (Weldon & Roediger 1987, Expt. 4), picture primes produce more facilitation than do word primes.

Roediger & Weldon (1987) suggest that picture-word effects can best be conceptualized in terms of the interaction of study conditions and test demands. Additional support for their position comes from a study by Blaxton (1985, Expt. 3). She had subjects form mental images corresponding to certain study words; for other study words subjects simply read the word silently. Consistent with the results on depth and elaboration of processing described above, performance was better under imagery conditions than under no-imagery conditions for free and cued recall tests, but the imagery manipulation did not affect fragment completion priming. However, imagery at study also improved priming on a general knowledge test (an indirect conceptually driven test) but did not affect performance on a graphemically cued recall test (a direct data-driven test). With respect to imagery effects, therefore, memory tests honor the data-driven/conceptually driven distinction, and not the direct/ indirect distinction.

EFFECTS OF LANGUAGE   Kirsner & Dunn (1985) review six studies of repetition priming in bilingual subjects (across studies subjects spoke English as one language and in addition either French, Hindi, Italian, Spanish, or Turkish). Language of items at study and test was manipulated such that a concept presented in a particular language at study was tested either in the same or in a different language. Tests used were fragment completion (Watkins & Peynircioğlu 1983), lexical decision (Cristoffanini et al 1986; Kirsner et al 1984; Scarborough et al 1984), and semantic classification (R. Harvey, unpublished observations). Conditions in which words in the different languages were cognates (e.g. *publicidad* vs *publicity*) or in which they differed only in script but not in phonology or reference (as in certain words used in both Hindi and Urdu, Brown et al 1984) were excluded. To permit comparison of data from different tests and conditions, Kirsner & Dunn computed a *relative priming* ratio by dividing the amount of priming (performance on old items minus performance on new items) obtained in the different-language condition by the amount of priming obtained in the same-language condition. Averaged over nine conditions the relative priming ratio was .05 ± .09 SD, indicating essentially no cross-language priming. Kolers (1975) has obtained similar effects. Studying a sentence in normally oriented French primed later reading of the same sentence in geometrically inverted English less than did reading that sentence in normally oriented or inverted English. At longer lags between initial study and test, reading a sentence in French resulted in no transfer at all.

The test used by Watkins & Peynircioğlu (1983) was treated by Kirsner & Dunn (1985) as fragment completion; however, by the classification criteria given above, it should be considered a graphemically cued recall test (a direct data-driven test), because subjects were told to use word fragments to help recall study words. Surprisingly, language context effects with graphemic fragment cues do not seem to depend on whether or not the test instructions refer to the study episode: Durgunoğlu & Roediger (1987; see also Roediger & Blaxton 1987a) also failed to obtain cross-language priming in an indirect fragment completion test. The important implication of these two studies taken together is that linguistic context effects are observed in data-driven tests, regardless of whether such tests are direct (Watkins & Peynircioğlu 1983) or indirect (Durgunoğlu & Roediger 1987).

Durgunoğlu & Roediger (1987) also included the critical intraexperiment comparison between the effects of language (Spanish vs English) on direct and indirect tests. In the conditions of interest, study words were presented twice, either in the same language on each presentation (e.g. *caballo, caballo; horse, horse*), or in a different language (e.g. *caballo, horse*). Presenting a word in Spanish produced no significant priming for a fragment completion test given in English; however, presenting it in English or in mixed languages did produce significant priming. These results are completely consistent with those of the studies reviewed by Kirsner & Dunn (1985). In a free recall test, the mixed language condition produced better recall than the pure language conditions, but there was no difference between the English-English and Spanish-Spanish conditions. In a recognition memory test conducted in English, words studied in Spanish were recognized well above chance, but not as well as words studied in English, and mixed language words were recognized best. The superiority of mixed language words in recall and recognition can be attributed to the positive effects of encoding variability (e.g. Melton 1970). The absence of an effect of language on free recall is difficult to interpret, since subjects were allowed to recall words in Spanish or English, so test language was not controlled as in the other two tests.

In sum, a change in language context attenuates priming in indirect tests (fragment completion, lexical decision, semantic classification) and produces performance decrements in some direct tests (recognition, recall with graphemic cues). These direct and indirect tests share data-driven components. The effect of language context on conceptually driven tests, such as free recall and general knowledge retrieval, remains to be established in conditions in which language of input and output is systematically manipulated.

MODALITY EFFECTS   A considerable number of studies have shown that priming in indirect tests is attenuated by a change in modality of presentation between study and test. For both auditory and visual tests, the manipulation of interest is whether items are studied in the visual or the auditory modality. In all 24 experiments from the 14 studies we reviewed, priming was significantly reduced when input and test modalities mismatched (i.e. visual priming for auditory test, or auditory priming for visual test), compared to the case in which input and test modalities matched.

Modality effects have been demonstrated in visual tests of fragment completion (Blaxton 1985, Expt. 2; Roediger & Blaxton 1987b, Expts. 1 & 2), lexical decision (Kirsner et al 1983, Expts. 2 & 3; Kirsner & Smith 1974; Monsell & Banich, in Monsell 1985), perceptual identification (Clarke & Morton 1983, Expts. 2 & 3; Jacoby & Dallas 1981; Jacoby & Witherspoon 1982; Kirsner et al 1983, Expts. 1, 4–8; Postman & Rosenzweig 1956), and word completion (Graf et al 1985). Additionally, Kolers (1975) reports that speed of reading a geometrically inverted sentence is not facilitated as much by prior auditory presentation of that sentence as it is by prior reading of that sentence in either normal or inverted form. Similarly, Levy (1983) found that exposure to a passage facilitated later detection of typographical errors in that passage in a proofreading task, but that this facilitatation effect was smaller when initial exposure to the passage was auditory than when it was visual. Auditory tests of lexical decision (Kirsner & Smith 1974; Monsell & Banich, in Monsell 1985) and perceptual identification (Ellis 1982; Jackson & Morton 1984; Postman & Rosenzweig 1956) also show modality effects, with auditory presentation of study words producing greater priming than visual presentation.

In most of the experiments we reviewed, performance in the different-modality condition, though attenuated in comparison to the same-modality condition, was still better than performance on new items; however, a few studies have failed to obtain such cross-modality priming. Clarke & Morton (1983, Expt. 2), Jacoby & Dallas (1981), and Postman & Rosenzweig (1956) found no significant effect of auditory study on later visual perceptual identification; Monsell & Banich (in Monsell 1985) obtained a similar null effect in a visual lexical decision test. Ellis (1982) found no transfer from visual study to auditory perceptual identification, and Kirsner & Smith (1974) found very little transfer from visual study to auditory lexical decision. In all these cases there are counterexamples in which significant cross-modality priming was obtained using the same type of test (visual perceptual identification: Clarke & Morton 1983, Expt. 3; Kirsner et al 1983; visual lexical decision: Kirsner et al 1983; auditory perceptual identification: Jackson & Morton 1984; auditory lexical decision: Monsell & Banich, in Monsell 1985). The reason for this discrepancy between studies is currently unclear.

Kirsner & Dunn (1985) reviewed the results of six of the studies of modality effects in lexical decision and perceptual identification discussed above. Across 16 conditions from the six studies, mean relative priming (the ratio of priming in the different-modality condition to priming in the same-modality condition) was .38 ± .24 SD, indicating that priming effects were attenuated considerably by a change in modality, but not eliminated. The results of their survey are therefore consistent with those of ours, which includes a larger range of indirect tests.

Only a few studies have directly compared modality effects in direct and indirect tests; these studies indicate that modality is generally a less important factor in direct than in indirect tests. Graf et al (1985) obtained no difference between visual and auditory presentation for a free recall test, in conjunction with a significant effect of modality on word completion; Blaxton (1985) obtained the same pattern of results across tests using free recall and fragment completion. Advantages of auditory over visual presentation in recall seem to occur only at relatively short retention intervals and with particular experimental procedures, although it is now clear that they persist over longer durations than once thought (e.g. Conway & Gathercole 1987; Greene 1985).

Results have been more mixed with respect to recognition memory than with respect to free recall: Kirsner et al (1983, Expts. 1–3) found no effect on recognition memory of modality match versus mismatch between study and test, in conjunction with a significant modality effect on lexical decision; this pattern of results was duplicated by Roediger & Blaxton (1987a) using recognition and fragment completion tests. Modality effects have sometimes been observed in recognition memory, but they vary in size (e.g. compare Jacoby & Dallas 1981 to Kirsner 1974). The variable results with recognition memory can be understood under the assumption that different study and test conditions lead to variations in the amount of conceptually driven processing possible at test. Effects of modality would be observed in cases in which subjects could not make use of elaborative processes at study or test, or both. In the Jacoby & Dallas (1981) work, items were presented for study at a 1-sec rate, probably accounting for the large effect of modality observed.

As with effects of other forms of context reviewed here, tests group themselves according to the data-driven/conceptually driven distinction where modality effects are concerned. Priming of general knowledge retrieval is not modality dependent (Blaxton 1985, Expt. 2), whereas both intralist (Nelson & McEvoy 1979a) and extralist (Blaxton 1985, Expt. 2) graphemically cued recall are modality dependent.

EFFECTS OF CASE, SCRIPT, TYPEFONT, TYPOGRAPHY, AND VOICE   A number of studies have investigated effects on indirect test performance of match versus mismatch of rather subtle aspects of perceptual context. As in studies of modality effects, the comparison of interest is between a condition in which the perceptual form of an item (case, script, typefont, typography, or voice) is the same at study and test, and a condition in which it is changed between study and test. Our review indicates that effects of reinstating these types of context, though generally small and rarely significant at the level of the individual experiment, are consistent across studies using different tests and different types of contextual manipulation. We therefore simply indicate whether the difference between same- and different-context conditions was in the direction expected under the hypothesis of a context effect. To the degree that such effects exist, however small, they are important theoretically, as we indicate in the final section of this review.

Changing letter case (upper to lower, lower to upper) between study and test has been associated with small reductions of priming in perceptual identification (Feustel et al 1983, Expts. 1 & 3; Jacoby & Hayman 1987; Jacoby & Witherspoon 1982) and in lexical decision for words (Scarborough et al 1977, Expts. 1 & 2), compared with conditions in which case was preserved between study and test. Masson (1986, Expt. 3) studied reading of geometrically transformed script using words presented in mixed case (e.g. *KeTtLe*). The positive effect of prior exposure on reading time was significantly greater when the mixed-case form of a word matched between study and test (e.g. *KeTtLe* at both study and test) than when it mismatched (e.g. study *KeTtLe*, test *kEtTlE*). (For related results in a visual search task, see Brooks 1977.)

Changing script (handwritten to typewritten, typewritten to handwritten) resulted in small decrements in priming in fragment completion (Roediger & Blaxton 1987b, Expts. 1 & 2) and perceptual identification (Clarke & Morton 1983, Expt. 1). Brown et al (1984) used a particularly extreme manipulation of script in their lexical decision study. They used words that have the same phonology and reference in Hindi and Urdu but are written very differently in the two languages. For subjects bilingual in Hindi and Urdu, the repetition priming effect was about 20 msec larger when scripts matched than when they mismatched.

Levy (1983) found improvements in error detection in a proofreading task as a result of prior experience with the test passage; however, this improvement due to repetition occurred only when the typefont of the passage (IBM Script or Prestige-Elite) was the same on first and second presentations. Kolers et al (1980) showed that the positive effects of naming geometrically inverted letters on later reading of geometrically inverted text are specific to the typefont used for practice and test; however, it should be noted that the study materials were generated from different text pages than were the test materials, so the possible influence of typefont on item-specific effects (i.e. direct priming effects) in this type of reading task remains to be discovered.

Kolers (1975) had subjects read geometrically inverted sentences at test. Some of these had previously been read in normal form; others had been read in inverted form. Both forms of prior experience increased reading speed at test, but reading sentences in inverted form resulted in a larger increase than did reading sentences in normal form. Based on these data, Kolers argues that information concerning the perceptual characteristics of specific items mediates the effects of repetition in reading. Horton (1985) has questioned this claim, arguing that the advantage for sentences first read in inverted form occurred because such sentences received more extensive semantic processing at study than did sentences first read in normal form. To equate semantic processing at study, Horton had subjects read study sentences in two different geometric transformations; sentences were later tested either in the same or in a different transformation. In contrast to Kolers's findings, the positive effects of repetition were largely independent of the similarity between study and test transformations; however, repetition effects in different-typography conditions were consistently slightly (nonsignificantly) smaller than those in same-typography conditions across three experiments. Horton's findings therefore fall into the general pattern of small effects noted here.

Jackson & Morton (1984) used an auditory perceptual identification test in which words were spoken by a female voice. Study words were presented to one group of subjects in that female voice, and to another in a male voice. After statistical correction for performance differences between groups, there was a small advantage for items studied in the same voice as the test voice. However, a condition in which half the study items were presented in the female voice and the remaining half were presented in the male voice produced no decrement relative to the same-voice condition.

Evidence concerning the effects of these types of perceptual context on tests of recognition memory yields a similar pattern. Kirsner (1973) found a small but significant advantage of preserving letter case between study and test, and Roediger & Blaxton (1987a) found a small nonsignificant advantage for compatibility between study and test script (handwritten vs typewritten). Sentence recognition experiments have revealed significant effects of compatibility between study and test typography (e.g. Kolers & Ostry 1974; Masson & Sala 1978; Masson 1984). Effects on auditory recognition of compatibility between speaker's voice (male vs female) at study and test have been relatively easy to obtain (e.g. Craik & Kirsner 1974; Geiselman & Glenny 1977). As would be expected of recognition, effects of speaker's voice are obtained only when semantic-elaborative processing is suppressed at study, minimizing the role of conceptually driven processing at test (Geiselman & Bjork 1980).

Consistent with the trends presented above, sensitivity to factors such as letter case and typefont is better predicted by the data-driven/conceptually driven distinction than by the direct/indirect distinction. Blaxton (1985, Expt. 3) found no effect of typefont (uppercase italic vs lowercase elite) on priming in general knowledge retrieval; however, she found small effects of typefont on word fragment completion priming and graphemically cued recall.

NONSEMANTIC SET-SIZE AND DATA-DRIVEN TESTS   The similarity in retrieval processing between direct and indirect data-driven tasks is confirmed by D. L. Nelson and coworkers (e.g. Nelson 1981; Nelson & McEvoy 1979a,b; Nelson & McEvoy 1984; Nelson et al 1984). In their experiments, subjects are presented with word endings (e.g._____ESS, _____USK) and asked to write the first word that comes to mind that rhymes with each ending. The *nonsemantic set size* of the ending is defined as the number of different rhyming words generated to a given ending (e.g._____ESS rhymes with 20 items, whereas _____USK rhymes with only 5). In cued recall tests with endings as cues (a form of graphemically cued recall), endings that define smaller nonsemantic sets produce better recall than those that define larger sets (Nelson & McEvoy 1979b; Nelson & McEvoy 1984); similarly, in a perceptual identification test, words that come from smaller nonsemantic sets are easier to identify than those that come from larger nonsemantic sets (Nelson et al 1984). As noted above, intralist graphemically cued recall also parallels perceptual identification and other data-driven tests in the way it responds to changes in modality between study and test (Nelson & McEvoy 1979a).

Relationships Between Implicit Associative Memory, Explicit Associative Memory, and Repetition Priming

As reviewed above, one type of indirect test for a newly formed association requires the subject to complete a stem corresponding to the response word of a studied pair of words when the stimulus member of the studied pair is either present or absent. Superior word-completion priming when the stimulus term of the pair is present (same-context condition), compared to when it is not (different-context condition), indirectly reveals the formation of a new association. (For example, if *window-REASON* was studied, priming is greater when *window-REA*_____ is presented at test, than when *officer-REA*_____ is presented.) Word completion performance in the different-context condition (e.g. *officer-REA*_____) yields a measure of repetition priming (i.e. priming resulting simply from prior presentation of the response term).

Comparisons of amnesic and normal subjects (Graf & Schacter 1985; Schacter 1985b; Schacter & Graf 1986b), manipulations of the way word pairs are encoded at study (Graf & Schacter 1985; Schacter & Graf 1986a), and interference manipulations (e.g. Graf & Schacter 1987) have demonstrated a complex pattern of similarities and differences between repetition priming, indirect memory for new associations, and direct memory for new associations.

IMPLICIT VERSUS EXPLICIT ASSOCIATIVE MEMORY

Evidence from amnesic subjects   Preliminary evidence from a small number of amnesic subjects shows that severity of amnesia (as indexed by standard tests, such as the Wechsler Memory Scale) is correlated with memory for new associations as revealed by an indirect test. Patients defined as "mildly amnesic" are more likely to show indirect memory for new associations than are patients defined as "severely amnesic" (Schacter 1985b; Schacter & Graf 1986b). Since severe amnesics would be expected to show poorer memory than mild amnesics on a direct test for new associations, this result is suggestive of a parallel effect of severity of amnesia on direct and indirect measures of association [but see also Moscovitch et al (1986), who found memory for new associations in severely memory-disordered patients, using a reading-speed measure].

This result might be taken to imply that indirect memory for new associations relies on explicit retrieval of associations; such explicit retrieval would be more likely to occur in mild amnesics than in severe amnesics. However, amnesics who perform normally on an indirect test of a new association can show floor-level performance on a direct test of recall for the same association (Graf & Schacter 1985, data from unrelated pairs). Additionally, normals (and also amnesics, if they are given study pairs whose members are related) produce a substantial number of responses in cued recall that they did not produce in the same-context condition in a previous test of word completion. This result suggests that indirect tests of association are not simply more sensitive tests than are direct tests of association, because success on a less sensitive test (e.g. cued recall) implies that a more sensitive test could also be passed (Graf & Schacter 1985). New associations can be termed "implicit" when indirect measures of those associations are dissociated in this manner from direct measures for the same associations.

Encoding and interference effects   An indirect test will reveal an association between two previously unrelated words only when the subject has encoded those words semantically and in a meaningful relation to one another. It will not reveal an association if the encoding task consists of (*a*) comparing the members of the pair with respect to some structural feature, such as number of vowels (Graf & Schacter 1985); (*b*) processing each word semantically (e.g. pleasantness rating), but not in relation to the other member of the pair (Schacter & Graf 1986a); or (*c*) reading the pair of words as part of an anomalous sentence, such as "the *ROCK* was returned to the *CANDLE*" (Schacter & Graf 1986a). Memory for an association as revealed in a direct test is also poor if the to-be-remembered response word is not processed in a meaningful relation to the stimulus word (Graf & Schacter 1985; Schacter & Graf 1986a); in this respect direct and indirect tests of new associations behave similarly.

However, direct and indirect tests of new associations are dissociated when the degree of semantic elaboration of the relationship between the members of a pair of words is manipulated. The advantage of the same- over the different-context condition in word completion remains the same (*a*) whether the subject generates a single word or a complete sentence linking the members of a pair, and (*b*) whether the subject rates a sentence according to how well it relates the two words or generates a sentence linking the words. By contrast, when told to use stems of response words to retrieve studied responses (a direct test), the subject benefits much more from reinstatement of the stimulus term of the pair when she/he previously generated a complete sentence relating the two items than when she/he generated a word linking the items or read a sentence linking the items (Schacter & Graf 1986a).

Indirect and direct measures of memory for new associations are also dissociated by proactive and retroactive interference manipulations. In a study by Graf & Schacter (1987), subjects either learned two associations to the same stimulus term (e.g. *window-REASON* and *window-OFFICER*) or they learned one association (e.g. *window-REASON* or *window-OFFICER*). In a completion test in which response stems were provided (e.g. *REA_____*, or *OFF_____*), reinstating the stimulus member of a pair *(window)* enhanced the likelihood of generating a studied response word to the same extent whether subjects had associated one or two responses with that stimulus. By contrast, when subjects were told to use word stems to retrieve studied responses, the positive effects of reinstating the stimulus term were much weaker when two responses had been associated with a stimulus than when one response had been associated with a stimulus (i.e. standard proactive and retroactive interference effects were obtained). This selective effect of interference on a direct test for new associations also occurred when the direct test was a pair-matching test or a modified-modified free-recall test.

REPETITION PRIMING VERSUS ASSOCIATIVE MEMORY   As noted above, severely amnesic patients were impaired on both direct and indirect tests of memory for new associations (Schacter 1985b; Schacter & Graf 1986b), whereas mildly amnesic patients were impaired only on direct tests of new associations; by contrast, both severely and mildly amnesic patients showed intact repetition priming effects. Repetition priming effects also differ from direct and indirect manifestations of associative memory in that the same amount of priming is obtained regardless of LOP or degree of elaborative or associative processing at study (Graf & Schacter 1985; Schacter & Graf 1986a; see review above). However, repetition priming seems to share immunity to interference with indirect tests of associative memory. Jacoby (1983a) found no reduction in perceptual identification priming across five study-test trials conducted on consecutive days (i.e. there was no proactive interference); additionally, the number of study-test trials intervening between study and test of a list did not influence the magnitude of priming (i.e. there was no retroactive interference). Perceptual identification priming also does not appear to be susceptible to intralist interference effects (list-length effects). Merickle (unpublished data cited in Jacoby 1987) found no difference in priming between a condition in which 500 words were studied and a condition in which 100 words were studied.

Although direct priming effects do not seem to be susceptible to interference in the traditional sense of the word (i.e. interference between items encoded in a similar spatiotemporal context), interference might occur between items encoded similarly on dimensions other than spatiotemporal ones. For example, if a subject studied *OFFEND* on a first list and *OFFICER* on a second list, then later completed the stem *OFF_____*, it seems likely that the two primed words would compete as responses to the same cue, inhibiting priming in comparison to a single-list control condition. Mayes et al (1987) provide intriguing results relating to this hypothesis. They presented A–B (e.g. *bee-WASP*) and A–C (e.g. *bee-HONEY*) lists to amnesic and control subjects. In one condition, subjects received a cued-recall test for A–C pairs following presentation of the two lists; in another condition, a free-association test was given (e.g. *bee-???*). Consistent with past results, production of C responses in cued recall was better for controls than for amnesics, and amnesics' poor performance could be attributed to intrusions of B responses. By contrast, both amnesics and controls performed similarly under free-association instructions, both producing similar numbers of B ("intrusions") and C ("correct") responses. This result suggests (*a*) that cued recall performance in amnesics reflects implicit memory, because amnesics suffered the same amount of proactive interference under cued recall and free-association instructions, and (*b*) that two high associates of a cue word, when both primed, will compete as responses to the cue word in a free association test in both normal and amnesic subjects.

Role of the Linguistic Unit

Comparisons of stimuli that possess memorial representations prior to the experiment with those that do not are occupying an increasingly central position in research on the relation between implicit and explicit memory. Examples are the comparison of word and nonword stimuli, and the comparison of two-word compounds that behave linguistically as a unit (e.g. nominal compounds like *stumbling block*) with those that do not (e.g. noun phrases like *copper block*). Stimuli that have preexperimental representations are assumed to be *chunked* (e.g. Wickelgren 1979), *codified* (Salasoo et al 1985), or *unitized* (e.g. Hayes-Roth 1977; Schacter 1985a). A codified representation "responds as a single unit to a set of features and serves to label, code, name, or identify those features" (Salasoo et al 1985, p. 51). A number of studies now indicate that the occurrence or nonoccurrence of dissociations between direct and indirect measures depends critically on whether the stimuli used possess codified representations. These data have important implications for the debate between abstractionist and nonabstractionist views of implicit memory.

Comparisons of repetition priming with word and nonword stimuli have been numerous. Lexical decision studies (which necessarily include both word and nonword stimuli) have yielded inconsistent results, some showing nonword repetition effects (e.g. Dannenbring & Briand 1982; Kirsner & Smith 1974; Moscovitch 1985; Scarborough et al 1977) and others failing to find such effects (e.g. Forbach et al 1974; Ratcliff et al 1985). When nonwords do show a repetition effect in lexical decision, it is smaller than that observed for words, and it decays rapidly as the interval between the two presentations of the item increases. Since nonwords have no memorial representation prior to the experiment, this pattern of findings has been taken to imply that repetition priming with words primarily reflects modification of the state of a stable lexical representation and that nonword repetition effects, when they are observed, reflect contamination from nonlexical factors (e.g. Monsell 1985). Indeed, the original connotation of the term "priming" was that the primed item possesses a memorial representation prior to the priming event (Jacoby & Brooks 1984).

In contrast to the lexical decision results, it has been known for some time that repetition of pseudoword stimuli enhances perceptual identification of those stimuli (e.g. Feustel et al 1983; Jacoby & Witherspoon 1982; Johnston et al 1985; Postman & Rosenzweig 1956; Solomon & Postman 1952). Feustel et al (1983) argued that the discrepancy between the lexical decision and identification paradigms results from an inherent property of lexical decision: Repeated nonwords are to be rejected by the subject as nonwords; however, repetition may confer word-like properties upon nonwords, so that there would be conflicting tendencies to accept repeated nonwords as words and reject them as nonwords. Consistent with this hypothesis is the McKoon & Ratcliff (1979) finding of inhibition for repeated nonwords in lexical decision [see also Forster & Davis (1984) for a similar small effect]. Monsell (1985) found a nonword repetition effect in lexical decision when the interval between the decision response and the presentation of the next item was 1 sec, but not when it was 0.5 sec. He argued that subjects learned the relationship between the specific nonword and the "no" response better in the former condition than in the latter. Thus it is possible that the inconsistency of nonword repetition effects in lexical decision is the result of a varying trade-off between improved response learning and increasing word-likeness of the stimuli. In sum, the difference between word and nonword priming effects in lexical decision does not support the notion that repetition priming primarily reflects alteration in the state of a preexisting memory representation.

Feustel et al (1983) developed a latency measure of perceptual identifiability by having subjects terminate a gradually clarifying stimulus when they believed they could identify it (*continuous threshold latency identification,* CTLI). In CTLI, words were identified faster than pseudowords, and both words and pseudowords benefitted approximately equally from repetition in the experiment, over a small range of number of repetitions (1, 2, or 3 presentations/item). Using Sternberg's (1969) logic, Feustel et al argued that this approximate additivity ruled out the idea that the locus of the repetition effect was a preexisting memory representation; instead, processes common to the identification of words and pseudowords must produce the repetition effect. The overall superiority of words over pseudowords was attributed to the presence of a unitized code that made a response readily available.

The unitized-code concept also accounts for the variation in the difference between word and pseudoword performance as a function of the type of identification task. The advantage of words over pseudowords in accuracy is large in the traditional perceptual identification situation, in which the stimulus is briefly presented before a mask. By contrast, when the stimulus is gradually clarified before presentation terminates, the word advantage is reduced (Feustel et al 1983; Salasoo et al 1985). Feustel et al (1983) argue that the presence of a discrete and automatic identification response to a stimulus is important in the former situation because perceptual information decays rapidly while the subject is trying to construct a response. When the stimulus is gradually clarified, perceptual information is constantly restored while the subject attempts to construct a response, so the presence of a ready response to a stimulus is not so important.

Feustel et al's argument for the noninvolvement of unitized representations in repetition priming has difficulty dealing with the data on word and nonword repetition in memory-disordered subjects. When these subjects study a pseudoword, such as *numdy,* they show no priming when later given *num* and asked to generate a completion (Diamond & Rozin 1984), and their later perceptual identification of that item is not significantly facilitated (Cermak et al 1985). In sum, the memory disorder produces parallel impairments on indirect and direct tests when nonword stimuli are used. If the processes producing repetition priming are common to words and nonwords, there is no reason to expect impaired priming when nonwords are used.

Consistent with the word/nonword data from amnesics, Rugg (1987) found that changes in event-related potentials that occur with repetition of specific stimuli were different for words and nonwords in normal subjects. Additionally, dependence between recognition memory and perceptual identification is found in normal subjects when nonword stimuli are used (Jacoby & Witherspoon 1982; Johnston et al 1985), when independence is found with the same procedure (test order etc) with word stimuli. This result suggests that priming effects with nonword stimuli rely on some of the same processes that are recruited by direct tests of memory; amnesics, who are impaired on direct tests, would then be expected to be impaired on nonword priming.

Schacter (1985a,b; Glisky et al 1986a,b; Schacter & Glisky 1986) has argued that preserved priming in amnesics is critically dependent on the provision at test of a part of a stimulus that has a unitized memorial representation. Glisky et al (1986a) presented subjects with the definition of a target word; the subject was then given a stem corresponding to that word and asked to generate the appropriate response. As trials progressed, memory-disordered subjects learned to produce the appropriate response with fewer and fewer letters of the response word provided. However, they experienced inordinate difficulty (compared with controls) in making the transition from producing the word with one letter provided to producing it with no cue letters. When the task consisted of learning pairs of unrelated words using this *method of vanishing cues,* the difficulty in making the transition from the one-letter stem to no letters was even more acute than with definitions (Schacter 1985a).

Schacter's arguments are more directly confirmed by studies of cued recall and free-association priming with unitized and non-unitized word pairs. In a study by Schacter (1985a; see also 1985b), unitized pairs were common idioms, such as *sour grapes* and *small potatoes;* non-unitized pairs were created by re-pairing the elements of the idioms (i.e. *sour potatoes, small grapes*). After studying unitized and non-unitized pairs, subjects were given a free-association test, then a cued recall test. In free association with unitized pairs severe amnesics displayed the same level of priming as did matched controls; in the subsequent cued recall test the amnesics produced no more responses than they had produced in free association, whereas controls produced twice as many in cued recall as in free association. By contrast, both controls and amnesics produced essentially no list-words in free association for the non-unitized pairs. Amnesics were also unable to produce any responses from these pairs in cued recall, whereas controls were able to recall a substantial proportion of the responses. Amnesics demonstrate knowledge of an association between two previously unrelated words only when the stem of the response word is provided and the test for the association is indirect (Graf & Schacter 1985; Schacter & Graf 1986b). When memory-disordered patients perform quite well on cued recall tests, the members of the pairs must be highly related, and the patients do not produce any more list words than they produce in an indirect test such as word completion or free association (e.g. Diamond & Rozin 1984; Graf et al 1984; Mayes et al 1987; Schacter 1985a; Shimamura & Squire 1984).

Non-unitized word pairs also present an exception to the generalization that repetition priming is independent of study LOP or elaboration in normal subjects. When North American subjects were tested with unfamiliar British idioms (e.g. *curtain lecture*) or unrelated word pairs, the likelihood of producing a list-word was higher for elaborative than for nonelaborative study processing for both free-association and cued recall tests. By contrast, free-association priming is independent of study processing for familiar idioms and highly related paired associates (Schacter & Whitfield 1986). As with dependence between recognition and perceptual identification for nonwords, these data could be taken to imply that indirect test performance (in this case free association) with non-unitized stimuli relies on processes that are used in direct tests.

The important role of preexisting linguistic units in priming is further emphasized by Osgood & Hoosain's (1974) results with nominal compounds. They used nominal compounds (e.g. *stumbling block*), noun phrases (e.g. *copper block*), and nonsense phrases (e.g. *sympathy block*). Nominal compounds resemble the idioms used by Schacter in that the meaning of the compound cannot be predicted from knowledge of the meaning of either of its parts in isolation. Osgood & Hoosain initially demonstrated that visual duration thresholds (VDTs) for nominal compounds were the same as those of single words matched in length and frequency, suggesting that nominal compounds behave as units in identification. In the experiment of most interest here, initial identification of compounds was best for nominal compounds, next best for noun phrases, and worst for nonsense phrases. In the next phase, individual words from previously presented compounds were presented. In contrast to the results for whole-compound identification, VDTs for individual words were higher for words from nominal compounds than for words from noun phrases or nonsense phrases (thresholds for the latter two phrase types were not different). In a subsequent free-recall test, nominal compounds and noun phrases were equally well recalled, and both were better recalled than nonsense phrases.

The dissociations observed among VDTs for compounds, VDTs for individual words, and free recall mean that the superiority of noun phrases and nonsense compounds over nominal compounds in priming of VDTs for individual words cannot be explained by differences in identifiability or recallability of the compounds themselves. It is also important to note that the similarity between the physical form of the stimulus between initial presentation of a compound and later test of its components was identical for all three types of compounds; therefore views of priming that emphasize the role of perceptual similarity between study and test stimuli (e.g. Jacoby 1983b; Roediger & Blaxton 1987a,b) are not sufficient to explain the results. Instead, it seems that the additional notion of codified representations is necessary.

Transfer between study of unitized compounds and tests of their subunits and between study of subunits and tests of compounds seems to be asymmetrical. Whereas study of nominal compounds does not reduce later VDTs for components of those compounds, study of the components does reduce later VDTs for the entire compound (Osgood & Hoosain 1974). Similarly, studying one of the component nouns of a compound noun facilitates a later lexical decision concerning the entire compound (Monsell & Conrad, in Monsell 1985), whether that compound is transparent (e.g. *beanpole*), opaque (e.g. *butterfly*), or a pseudocompound (e.g. *boycott*). Such asymmetries are again difficult to account for with the notion of sensory-perceptual overlap, because the overlap between study and test cues is identical. For example, study of *stock market* and test of *market* involves the same degree of study-test overlap as does study of *market* and test of *stock market*.

Transfer is sometimes found between words that are structurally but not morphologically or semantically related, such as words that share graphemes (e.g. Evett & Humphreys 1981; Feustel et al 1983; Shulman et al 1978) or phonemes (Hillinger 1980; Mandler et al 1986). However, it seems unlikely that the literature on priming between morphologically related words can be explained in terms of overlap between perceptual or structural features; instead, morphemic codes must be postulated that are common to the words that facilitate each other (e.g. Feldman & Fowler 1987; Fowler et al 1985; Henderson et al 1984; Kempley & Morton 1982; Murrell & Morton 1974; Stanners et al 1979; for a summary, see Henderson 1985).

Additional support for the role of codified representations in priming comes from priming studies in which there was no perceptual overlap between study and test cues (Shimamura 1986): In free association, studying a strong associate (e.g. *chair*) of a test cue *(table-?)* enhances the likelihood of generating that associate to the cue, even if the cue was not itself studied with the associate in the priming phase (Shimamura & Squire 1984). A similar effect is obtained in category generation when category exemplars are studied in the absence of the category label, and the category label is used as a test cue (Graf et al 1985).

The contrast between Schacter's (1985a) results with idioms and Osgood & Hoosain's results with nominal compounds is suggestive of an interesting dissociation between priming measures that results from the interaction of the type of priming unit with the type of testing unit. When the test permits subjects to redintegrate a compound (as in free association), priming is found with prior study of unitized compounds and not with prior study of nonunitized compounds (Schacter 1985a). By contrast, when the test depends on redintegration of subunits of compounds (such as in individual word identification) prior study of non-unitized compounds yields superior priming to study of unitized compounds (Osgood & Hoosain 1974).

Retention Interval and Cuing Conditions

Retention interval effects have been cited as providing a basis for differentiating direct from indirect tests of memory (e.g. Jacoby & Dallas 1981; Tulving 1983, 1984a). Such claims are often based on instances in which priming shows no significant decrease over a particular retention interval, whereas a direct memory measure shows a significant decrease in performance over the same interval. Some of these instances involved manipulations of interval between study and test presentations within an experimental session (e.g. perceptual identification: Feustel et al 1983; lexical decision: Moscovitch 1985; Scarborough et al 1977). In other instances study and test phases took place in different sessions and the intervals involved were large, such as 24 hr (perceptual identification: Jacoby & Dallas 1981), and 7 days (fragment completion: Komatsu & Ohta 1984; Tulving et al 1982).

However, priming measures rarely defy the law of forgetting over periods of days or weeks. Jacoby (1983a) and Salasoo et al (1985) found decreases in perceptual identification priming over 24 hr, and Scarborough et al (1977) found a 24-msec repetition effect in lexical decision after 2 days, whereas the within-session repetition effect was 64 msec. Decreases in fragment completion priming have been reported over 7 days (Roediger & Blaxton 1987a,b), and from 7 days to 5 weeks (Komatsu & Ohta 1984). Moreover, whether within-session lag effects are observed can depend on the lags considered. Repetition priming in lexical decision shows a very short-term facilitation that decays when one or two other items intervene between the presentations of an item, leaving a longer-term priming effect that is relatively constant across within-session lags (Monsell 1985; Ratcliff et al 1985) but declines slightly over large values of lag (e.g. Scarborough et al 1977). In sum, immunity to forgetting for indirect measures is not well replicated and depends on the particular range of intervals considered in the study.

Indirect measures often seem to show slower decay over a particular retention interval than do direct measures; however, interpretation of these cases is complicated by scale differences between the two types of measure. There are only a few cases in which an argument for the direct comparability of measurement scales might be made, such as in lexical decision/recognition comparisons, in which the same stimuli and response sets are used, and the dependent variable is always reaction time. Unless measurement scales are directly comparable, only a limited subset of the possible interactions between test and retention interval (e.g. crossover interactions) can be taken as evidence for differential forgetting between tests (for a list of such interactions, see Loftus 1978).

One might rely on the more qualitative argument that tests of indirect memory show very persistent effects, in contrast to the typical lability of memory as revealed by direct tests. In all the above studies, priming effects were still significant at the longest interval studied. Effects of prior exposure on affective preference persisted at a week (Seamon et al 1983b). Savings in reading geometrically transformed text have been found at 2 weeks (Moscovitch et al 1986) and at 3 months (Cohen & Squire 1980) in memory-disordered subjects, and at a year in normal subjects (Kolers 1976). Savings in maze learning, jigsaw puzzle assembly, and pursuit rotor performance persisted at a week in Korsakoff amnesics (Brooks & Baddeley 1976), and patient H. M. displayed savings in the Tower of Hanoi puzzle after a year (Cohen 1984).

However, extreme persistence of memory as revealed in indirect tests is not general. Repetition priming in free association and in word completion (in which stems can be completed as at least 10 different words) has consistently been found to decay rapidly, reaching baseline at about 2 hr in both normal and amnesic subjects (e.g. Diamond & Rozin 1984; Graf & Mandler 1984; Graf et al 1984; Mayes et al 1987; Shimamura & Squire 1984; Squire et al 1987). In the same studies, tests of recognition memory given to normal subjects still show well-above-chance performance at a 2-hr delay. Salasoo et al (1985) found no advantage of old over new words in perceptual identification a year after initial study, even though old words were still recognized at above-chance level.

In sum, the most that can be said based on retention interval data is that direct and indirect measures are sometimes independent as a function of retention interval; that is, one type of measure sometimes shows evidence of memory at a particular retention interval when the other type does not. However, a general classification of the different measures based on resistance to forgetting is not possible (*a*) because scale differences often preclude comparison of forgetting rates across direct and indirect measures, and (*b*) because forgetting rates within the two classes of measures are extremely variable.

Factors accounting for variability in persistence of priming in indirect tests have not been extensively investigated, although knowledge of such factors is critical to explanations of priming. However, a few extremely interesting results suggest the importance of encoding conditions, materials, and cuing conditions at test:

1. Forster & Davis (1984) masked the first presentations of repeated stimuli in the lexical decision paradigm, reducing the role of attention in the initial encoding of an item. Priming decayed rapidly as a function of the number of items intervening between first and second presentations of a word, reaching chance when 17 items intervened. This decline in priming over a short interval is in contrast to the persistence of priming over similar or much larger lags observed in other lexical decision studies (e.g. Kirsner & Smith 1974; Monsell 1985; Ratcliff et al 1985; Scarborough et al 1977) and suggests the role of attention at encoding in producing long-lasting priming effects.

2. In perceptual identification, Salasoo et al (1985) found that old pseudowords that had received numerous repetitions at initial study were identified better than new pseudowords in a test given a year after initial study. As noted above, no repetition effects over a year were obtained with words in the same study; both old and new words were identified as well as old pseudowords. This result suggests that study procedures that lead to codification of previously poorly integrated items will produce long-lasting differences between studied and nonstudied items, because nonstudied items do not have the advantage of codification.

3. Schacter & Graf (1986a) obtained above-chance word completion priming in a 24-hr test by reinstating a word that had been associated with the to-be-completed word when it was studied. When the associate of the to-be-completed word was not reinstated, no priming was observed, as would be expected based on the word completion data discussed above. This result suggests that reinstatement of local contextual conditions present at encoding can retard the decay of priming.

The role of cuing conditions in retention interval effects has been systematically investigated by Squire et al (1987). They hypothesized that the persistence of priming in completion tests (such as word completion and fragment completion) was inversely related to the number of possible completions of the test cue. Using the word stems that are typically used in word completion studies (which have at least 10 possible completions) they obtained the typical pattern, with priming at chance 2 hr after study. With word stems (e.g. JUI_____ for JUICE) or word fragments (e.g. A___A___IN for ASSASSIN) susceptible to only one completion, priming effects in normal subjects persisted at 4 days (although a decrease in priming was observed from an immediate to a 4-day test).

This result is plausible, given that graphemic cues that define smaller nonsemantic sets are more effective in both perceptual identification and graphemically cued recall (Nelson & McEvoy 1979b, 1984; Nelson et al 1984); however, it is complicated by the fact that LOP effects were observed in both word and fragment completion for normal subjects (with a semantic orienting task yielding superior performance to a nonsemantic task), suggesting the involvement of conscious retrieval strategies in the completion tests. Squire et al (1987) claim that their data show that long-lasting priming effects depend on conscious retrieval strategies, such as those used in recall. However, this claim is at variance with the large number of results showing that semantic processing is not necessary for long-lasting priming effects (reviewed above). Indeed, study activities that emphasize the perceptual characteristics of study items are beneficial for tests such as fragment completion, whereas they often result in poor performance in direct tests (e.g. Blaxton 1985; Jacoby 1983b; Roediger & Blaxton 1987a).

The Squire et al results from amnesics are much more impressive, since the indirect-test performance of amnesics is rarely, if ever, influenced by explicit memory. Priming declined to chance at 2 hr after study regardless of whether a test cue could be completed ten different ways or just one way. These results stand in marked contrast to the long-lasting priming effects obtained in other studies using normal subjects and cues that were susceptible to only one completion (e.g. Komatsu & Ohta 1984; Roediger & Blaxton 1987a,b; Tulving et al 1982). It appears, therefore, that long-lasting priming effects in normal subjects can be based on a form of information that is not available to amnesics. However, this conclusion does not imply that the form of information in question also supports performance in tests such as recognition and free recall. Instead, it is possible that normals gain implicit access to such information via graphemic or perceptual cues, and that such access is uncorrelated with access to the study episode in the sense in which it is required in recall and recognition. We elaborate on this view of priming effects below.

CONCLUSIONS

Interpreting the Data Pattern

The results reported above support Shoben & Ross's (1986) claim that "any successful theory must account for the pattern of dissociations and failures to obtain dissociations" (p. 569). As they point out, the debate between abstractionist theorists and their critics has to some extent involved stacking dissociations between direct and indirect measures (which are assumed to support abstractionist positions) against nondissociations (which are assumed to call abstractionist positions into question). An example is the McKoon et al (1986) critique of the episodic-semantic distinction, in which one strategy employed is to question the validity and replicability of dissociations reported by Tulving (1983, 1984a). Our review suggests that this strategy is misconceived, because abstractionist positions derive support from parallel effects as well as dissociations, and nonabstractionist positions derive support from dissociations as well as parallel effects. For example, the deficit obtained in both recognition and perceptual identification in amnesic subjects when pseudoword stimuli are used supports abstractionist positions. This parallel effect is predicted because priming is assumed to depend on activation of an abstract representation, which is lacking for pseudoword stimuli. On the other hand, when priming tests show greater sensitivity to match between the precise physical form of study and test stimuli than do direct tests (a dissociation), abstractionist theories of priming are undermined because information about events resulting in priming is assumed to be lost, and direct tests are assumed to rely on recovery of study context.

DIRECT/INDIRECT AS A PREDICTOR   Both abstractionist and nonabstractionist theories regard the distinction between direct and indirect measures as important. The direct/indirect distinction is useful in understanding differences between tasks and forms of measurement; further, recent comparisons of direct and indirect tests are of great importance to attempts to integrate theory across cognitive subdomains. Our review suggests, however, that the direct/indirect distinction performs poorly as a predictor of dissociations and nondissociations. Although there are a number of clear dissociations between direct and indirect tasks, there are at least as many examples of parallel effects, and of complex patterns in which the occurrence/nonoccurrence of dissociations varies systematically as a function of a critical variable.

The complexity of the data pattern across direct and indirect tests is complemented by an equally complex picture of dissociations and parallel effects within the direct and indirect classes of test. Dissociations between recognition and free recall measures (e.g. Anderson & Bower 1972, Expt. 3) and between recognition and cued recall measures (e.g. Tulving & Thomson 1973; Tulving & Wiseman 1975) were central to the classical theories of performance on direct tests (namely, generation-recognition theory and the encoding specificity principle). Comparisons of free recall, cued recall, and recognition have subsequently revealed a highly complex pattern of interrelations. For example, Tulving (1983, Ch. 11) summarized experiments that show dissociations between cued recall and free recall, and Gillund &

Shiffrin (1984) offered a comprehensive quantitative model of the effects on recognition and recall of a number of traditional independent variables, some producing parallel effects on the two measures, others producing dissociative effects. Most pertinent to the issues discussed here, contextual manipulations dissociate free and semantically cued recall from graphemically cued recall (as reviewed above; Blaxton 1985; Roediger & Blaxton 1987a). Additionally, Hirst et al (1986) found that amnesics were impaired in comparison to controls on a recall test, even when recognition performance between amnesics and controls was experimentally equated.

Research on lexical and conceptual organization has relied increasingly on task comparisons. Most prominent are comparisons of lexical decision and naming latencies (e.g. de Groot 1985; Hudson & Bergman 1985; Lupker 1984; Seidenberg et al 1984; for a summary, see Johnson & Hasher 1987). Other tasks compared with lexical decision include category verification (e.g. Balota & Chumbley 1984; Smith 1984), free association (Chumbley & Balota 1984), object and reality decision (e.g. Kroll & Potter 1984), and word retrieval (Bowles & Poon 1985). The relationships between these measures are again complex. Given this background, we should not be surprised by instances of dissociations between different measures of priming (Witherspoon & Moscovitch, cited in Moscovitch et al 1986), between priming and skill learning (Butters 1987), between cognitive skills such as reading and naming the letters of inverted text (Kolers & Magee 1978), and between objective task performance and verbalizable knowledge about that task (e.g. Berry & Broadbent 1984; Cohen et al 1985; Lewicki 1986). To this list of dissociations between indirect measures, we can add those between fragment completion and general knowledge retrieval (Blaxton 1985; Roediger & Blaxton 1987a), between word-fragment and picture-fragment completion (Roediger & Weldon 1987; Weldon & Roediger 1987), and between repetition priming and priming by new associates (Schacter & Graf 1986a,b), all described above.

As more and more comparisons between measures of memory are made, the complexity of the overall data pattern increases enormously and the important aspects of the data become more difficult to assimilate. On the other hand, we come closer to forming an overall image of the functioning of the memory system. Our task could be likened in some respects to finding the important dimensions of variation in a set of data, as in multivariate analysis. Isolating substages of different tasks must become increasingly important in determining which dissociations and parallel effects are of theoretical importance. As Shoben & Ross (1986) point out, simply enumerating dissociations and parallel effects is unlikely to result in progress unless we gain some insight into the nature of the processes that are being differentially or similarly affected.

Shoben & Ross suggest that progress on this enterprise might be made by combining dissociation methodology with additive-factors methodology to specify the locus of differential effects. Unfortunately, use of additive-factors methods assumes that the tasks being compared possess directly comparable measurement scales. As pointed out above, this assumption is rarely, if ever, justified in task-comparison experiments. Nevertheless, the emphasis on analysis of component processes that can be found in work on semantic priming and lexical access (e.g. attempts to untangle automatic and strategic contributions to semantic priming; comparisons of lexical decision and naming) could profitably be incorporated into work comparing direct and indirect memory measures. In this vein, it is urgent that explicit (strategically based) and implicit contributions to repetition-priming effects be teased apart, because our knowledge of the relative contributions of these factors is critical to our theoretical interpretation of parallel effects on direct and indirect memory tests.

PROBLEMS IN INTERPRETING PARALLEL EFFECTS   As we noted at the outset, there are two ways of interpreting parallel effects on direct and indirect memory tasks. The first is to assume that both implicit and explicit forms of memory are affected in a similar way by particular variables. This seems to be the conclusion that Jacoby (1983a, 1987; Jacoby & Brooks 1984) wants to make; the point of demonstrating that direct and indirect tasks are affected similarly by variables such as repetition, attention, and list context was to demonstrate that both explicit and implicit forms of memory depend on memory for prior episodes. However, this conclusion is underdetermined by the data unless explicit memory is identified with performance on direct tests and implicit memory is identified with performance on indirect tests. We have argued that this assimilation of forms of memory to methods of testing is inappropriate and begs important questions.

The occurrence of parallel effects is equally compatible with a second interpretation, namely that direct and indirect tests sometimes share a form of memory that is being affected by the manipulation that is producing the parallel effect. For example, Schacter's (1985b) interpretation of Jacoby's (1983a) list-context data is that the manipulation of proportion of old words on the test list affected the likelihood that subjects would spontaneously use conscious retrieval strategies to enhance identification performance for old items. Similarly, effects of repetition and attention at encoding could be seen as influencing the likelihood that subjects notice repetitions of stimuli at test; noticing such repetitions might lead them to invoke conscious strategies to enhance processing of repeated items. The superiority of generation over reading in recall and general knowledge tests (Blaxton 1985; Roediger & Blaxton 1987a) could be explained by assuming that subjects spontaneously used explicit memory for studied items to arrive at answers on the general knowledge test.

A number of other investigators have argued that observed repetition-priming effects can be due to implicit memory but that use of a conscious strategy can increase the amount of priming observed (e.g. Clarke & Morton 1983; Cohen 1984; Diamond & Rozin 1984; Forster & Davis 1984; Fowler et al 1985; Graf et al 1984; Johnson et al 1985; Monsell 1985; Moscovitch et al 1986; Squire et al 1987). Such arguments are often used to explain cases in which a memory disorder is associated with parallel deficits on a direct and an indirect task; that is, it can be assumed that the deficit shown by memory-disordered patients on the indirect memory test is due not to a deficit in implicit memory processes but to the spontaneous use of conscious retrieval strategies by control subjects that are not available to memory-disordered patients (e.g. Cohen 1984; Moscovitch et al 1986; Schacter 1985b; Squire et al 1987). Demonstrating impaired indirect test performance in memory-disordered subjects involves the use of two etiologic groups, of which one shows normal indirect test performance and the other shows impaired performance (e.g. Shimamura et al 1987).

Views that attribute priming in normals to a combination of implicit and explicit forms of memory have problems handling the data showing interactions between encoding manipulations and test conditions. Elaboration and LOP at study produce strong effects on direct tests but no effect on indirect tests. Generating study items as opposed to reading them improves free recall but reduces priming in perceptual identification (Jacoby 1983b) and fragment completion (Blaxton 1985; Roediger & Blaxton 1987a). If priming sometimes involved access to conscious memories, why would priming effects not be larger for words that are well remembered on direct tests of memory (i.e. deeply processed and generated items) than for items that are poorly remembered? Additionally, Jacoby's perceptual identification studies (1983a,b; Jacoby & Dallas 1981; Jacoby & Witherspoon 1982) have consistently revealed very low rates of intrusion errors due to the production of study-list words. In the 1983a study, the probability of giving a list word as an incorrect response was .003, both in the condition in which 90% of test words had been studied, and in the condition in which only 10% of test words had been studied. These results rule out crude guessing interpretations of the contribution of conscious strategies to priming (but see Ratcliff & McKoon 1988 for a sophisticated bias theory of priming).

The data on parallel effects will remain difficult to interpret until we know more about the contribution of intentional explicit memory to performance on indirect tests. One possible strategy would be to look for stochastic independence or dependence in cases in which parallel effects are observed. If a parallel effect was accompanied by stochastic dependence between measures, it would suggest that the parallel effect was the result of a form of memory that was contributing to performance in both tests. If independence was observed, it would suggest that the manipulated variable was producing similar effects on different forms of memory. Such an analysis presumes, of course, that one can work around the effects (discussed above) that currently contaminate analyses of stochastic independence.

Evaluation of Theoretical Positions

Schacter (1985a, 1987) presents incisive criticisms of abstractionist and nonabstractionist accounts of implicit and explicit memory. We briefly list the deficiencies and strengths of each position, borrowing liberally from his treatments, then outline what we take to be the essential components of an adequate position.

ABSTRACTIONIST POSITIONS   These positions share the assumption that implicit memory results from a form of representation that is *ahistorical* (Monsell 1985) or *synchronic* (Henderson 1985); that is, it does not maintain information about the events that formed or modified that representation. Explicit memory depends on the formation of memory traces that encode specific details of prior experiences. The ahistorical form of representation is described as activation of a lexical or semantic representation (semantic/episodic system view; logogen model; activation/elaboration view), or as formation and modification of cognitive and perceptual-motor procedures (procedural/declarative distinction).

Views that attribute implicit memory to activation of preexisting abstract lexical or semantic representations account well for dissociations in which a variable exerts a strong influence on a direct test but not on an indirect test (e.g. effects of LOP of study words in repetition priming). All that is necessary for priming is that a permanent representation is activated in the study phase. Activation views also account well for demonstrations of the importance of preexisting linguistic units in priming. For example, priming in amnesics depends critically on provision at test of a portion of a stimulus that has a preexisting memory representation, and does not occur with nonword stimuli.

When performance on a direct or an indirect test reveals the influence of newly acquired information, this influence, *ex hypothesi,* cannot be attributed to implicit memory; it must therefore be attributed to explicit memory. Activation views would therefore attribute nonword priming effects in normal subjects to explicit memory; however, they could not account for implicit memory for new associations in amnesics, or any other demonstrations of preserved memory for new information in amnesics (such as in studies of conditioning, and of cognitive and perceptual-motor skill learning). These views also do not account for the dissociative effects of interference and degree of elaboration on direct and indirect tests for new associations in normals.

Because the notion of activation connotes the idea of autonomous decay over time, activation views fail to predict variability in the persistence of priming as a function of cuing conditions. Activation theorists might point to the Squire et al (1987) finding that priming in amnesics decayed to chance at 2 hr, regardless of the nature of the test cues. Priming in normal subjects that persists for days or years would then be attributed to the influence of explicit memory. However, this explanation runs afoul of the numerous cases in normal subjects in which a variable exerts a large effect on a direct test but not on an indirect test. It was this type of dissociation that initially suggested the plausibility of an activation account. Additionally, there are examples of long-lasting item-specific priming in amnesics (e.g. Cohen & Squire 1980; Moscovitch et al 1986).

The episodic-semantic distinction attributes memory for facts to the semantic system and memory for personal experiences to the episodic system; memory for personal experiences and memory for facts should therefore be dissociable. As numerous critics of the episodic-semantic distinction have pointed out, there is little evidence for such a dissociation. To cite two counterexamples to this prediction, priming in general knowledge retrieval is influenced in the same way as free and semantically cued recall by experimental manipulations (Blaxton 1985; Roediger & Blaxton 1987a), and memory for facts as well as for personal experiences is disrupted in both anterograde and retrograde amnesia (as reviewed above).

The procedural-propositional distinction suggests that memory for both experiences and facts should be impaired in amnesia, since both forms of knowledge are assumed to be propositional. It also accounts for dissociations in normals between task performance and verbalizable knowledge about that task. Unlike activation views, it accounts for new learning of cognitive and perceptual-motor skills in amnesics. Priming is treated as reflecting modification of the procedures used to deal with specific stimuli. Dissociations between skill learning and priming in memory-disordered subjects (Butters 1987) therefore cannot be accommodated, since these two classes of memory phenomena are supposed to reflect the operation of the same memory system. The absence of nonword priming in amnesics is also not predicted, because there is no reason why the procedures used to identify nonwords should not be modified by experience.

All abstractionist positions have difficulty dealing with effects on priming of match between study and test context, because the representations support-ing priming are assumed to lose information about the priming episode. Activation models have been modified to account for some of these effects (e.g. Allport & Funnell 1981; Clarke & Morton 1983; Jackson & Morton 1984; Kirsner & Dunn 1985; Monsell 1985; Morton 1979, 1981). Modality effects in priming can be handled by postulating separate auditory and visual logogens. The superiority of reading over generating for later perceptual identification can be handled by assuming that generating material at study involves firing production logogens but not the receptive logogens that are later involved in identifying test words. This proliferation of modular input and output systems in response to data may be independently justifiable on philosophical grounds (e.g. Fodor 1983, 1985). However, even the modified logogen model cannot handle effects of subtle aspects of context on priming, such as typeface, letter case, etc. Activation theorists have often attempted to "explain away" such findings, which are generally nonsignificant at the level of the individual study but rather consistent across studies. We believe that it is no longer possible to ignore the consistent, if small, influence of subtle aspects of perceptual context on priming effects.

NONABSTRACTIONIST POSITIONS   As Schacter (1987) points out, the strengths and weaknesses of Jacoby's episodic perspective and Kolers & Roediger's procedural perspective can be described as a mirror reflection of those of activation views. Priming of nonwords in normal subjects, effects of match between study and test context on priming, and dependence of priming on new associations are all accommodated. Further, the distinction between data-driven and conceptually driven tasks permits an account of the effects of perceptual and linguistic context that accommodates both parallel and dissociative effects across direct and indirect memory tests. Because forgetting in both direct and indirect tests is construed as being *cue-dependent* (Tulving 1974), these positions can account for the variability in persistence of memory as revealed by different direct and indirect memory tests. In particular, they can account for greater persistence of completion priming with cues that uniquely specify their completions than with cues that can be completed multiple ways. The former type of cue results in more unique feature overlap between the test cue and the study episode than does the latter. Uniqueness of cue-trace feature overlap is an important determinant of memory in direct tests (e.g. Craik & Jacoby 1979; Eysenck 1979; Fisher & Craik 1977; Jacoby & Craik 1979).

Difficulties for the Jacoby and Kolers & Roediger positions are created by the important role of preexisting linguistic units in priming. For example, it is not clear why free-association priming should be found for unitized phrases but not for non-unitized phrases. It is also not clear why preserved priming in amnesics should be so dependent on provision of part of a preexisting unit at test, and why amnesics do not show priming with nonwords. If priming in amnesics results from implicit access to traces that are specific to particular episodes, it is not clear why amnesics, unlike normals, show the same decay rates in completion priming whether cues can be completed multiple ways or only one way. Finally, it is not clear why implicit memory for new associations is elaboration dependent, when repetition priming is not so dependent. This finding argues strongly against the view that effects of new associations in word completion and other indirect memory tests are simply due to reinstatement of a perceptual gestalt that was present at study.

Ratcliff & McKoon (1988) have proposed a nonabstractionist model [adapted from the recognition model of Gillund & Shiffrin (1984)] designed to handle effects of new associations on performance in indirect and direct memory tests. The model assumes that context cues and target stimuli are combined into a compound cue. When context cues and target items are experimentally or preexperimentally related, the familiarity of this compound cue is higher than when context and target are residually related; and performance is consequently facilitated. This model accommodates McKoon & Ratcliff's (1979, 1986; McKoon et al 1986; Ratcliff & McKoon 1981, 1986) claims concerning the similarity (time course, automaticity) of episodic and semantic priming effects. The debate over episodic priming effects in direct and indirect memory tests (e.g. Carroll & Kirsner 1982; Durgunoğlu & Neely 1987; Neely & Durgunoğlu 1985) is supposed to address McKoon & Ratcliff's claim that direct and indirect tests rely on the same type of information.

However, our review suggests that this debate is based on mistaken premises, for two reasons. First, priming by new associations definitely occurs, and can be implicit (i.e. unconscious/automatic) because it occurs in amnesics (although for methodological reasons it may be difficult to demonstrate in lexical decision with normal subjects). Second, what is really at issue is whether the representations and processes that support priming due to a new association in an indirect test *are the same as those that support retrieval of that same association in a direct test,* such as cued recall. It remains to be seen whether the Ratcliff & McKoon (1988) model can accommodate the differential effects of amnesia, interference, and degree of elaboration on retention of new associations as measured by direct (e.g. cued recall) and indirect (e.g. word completion) tests. It is also not clear that Ratcliff & McKoon's (1988) bias explanation of repetition priming could handle the effects of perceptual and linguistic context on repetition priming.

Components of an Adequate Theoretical Position

The complexity of the current data pattern suggests that an adequate explanation of the relationship between implicit and explicit memory needs to incorporate components of both abstractionist and nonabstractionist theory. In particular, it seems necessary to postulate at least two sources of implicit memory—ahistoric traces that depend on preexisting codified representations, and historic traces that incorporate contextual information. Whether the latter, "episodic," type of trace supports explicit or implicit memory depends on task demands and the nature of the retrieval cues available (cf the dual-access position of Jacoby and others).

These two components of implicit memory seem necessary to account (*a*) for the rapid decay of priming under some conditions, and for the dependence of priming on preexisting codified units; and (*b*) for the persistence of priming under other conditions, for priming with new information (nonwords, new associations), for the contextual specificity of priming, and for the variations in performance on direct and indirect tests as a function of the type of test processing (data-driven vs conceptually driven). In overall character, such a hybrid position seems to us to be closest to that proposed by Schacter (1985a), although it is couched in somewhat different terminology.

Proposing a hybrid position that combines "activation" (abstractionist) and data-driven/conceptually driven processing (nonabstractionist) perspectives is an obvious but less than satisfying response to Schacter's (1987) observation that the virtues and shortcomings of the two perspectives are mirror-images of each other. It is less than satisfying because a hybrid position, simply by incorporating more theoretical constructs than the simpler positions, is bound to fit the data better than either simpler position does. Even with those constructs, however, significant difficulties remain with the hybrid position as outlined above. It would seem natural, for example, to attribute the absence of nonword priming in amnesics, and the rapid decay of word-completion priming in amnesics, to a deficit in the formation or utilization of episodic traces. If the component of implicit memory that depends on episodic traces is impaired in amnesics, however, it is difficult to explain the acquisition of new associations by amnesics as revealed by indirect tests, and the highly persistent priming effects sometimes shown by amnesics, such as those found in reading geometrically inverted script.

Despite the current theoretical turmoil, a conclusion that can be made with considerable force, based on current task-comparison data, is that human memory is not a monolithic entity, revealing itself in similar ways regardless of the way we choose to test memory. Indirect measures are not simply sensitive memory tests that can reveal "weak" memory traces that evade direct tests—a type of "monolith" theory ruled-out conclusively by those cases in which manipulations produce opposite effects on direct and indirect measures. By contrast, the complex relationships between direct and indirect measures suggest that memory is multifaceted and highly versatile. As our sophistication in interpreting such relationships evolves, we can expect increasingly rich characterizations of the interplay of mental representations and processes that we call "memory."

ACKNOWLEDGMENTS

Preparation of this review was facilitated by Grant 3186 from the Committee on Research, University of California, to the second author. We thank Larry L. Jacoby, Gail McKoon, Roger Ratcliff, Henry L. Roediger III, Daniel L. Schacter, and Arthur P. Shimamura for access to manuscripts in press or submitted for publication. Special thanks to Greta Mathews for reading prior drafts of this paper, and to Thomas D. Wickens for helpful discussions. The first author is indebted to Gordon S. Claridge, Gillian Cohen, Eric Eich, Ronald P. Fisher, Janet Metcalfe, James S. Nairne, and Nancy C. Waugh for past help and encouragement.

Literature Cited

Albert, M. S., Butters, N., Levin, J. 1979. Temporal gradients in the retrograde amnesia of patients with alcoholic Korsakoff's disease. *Arch. Neurol.* 36:211–16

Albert, M. S., Moss, M. 1984. The assessment of memory disorders in patients with Alzheimer disease. See Squire & Butters 1984, pp. 236–46

Allport, D. A., Funnell, E. 1981. Components of the mental lexicon. *Philos. Trans. R. Soc. London B Ser.* 295:397–410

Anderson, J. R., Bower, G. H. 1972. Recognition and retrieval processes in free recall. *Psychol. Rev.* 79:97–123

Bacon, F. T. 1979. Credibility of repeated statements: memory for trivia. *J. Exp. Psychol.: Hum. Learn. Mem.* 5:241–52

Baddeley, A. D. 1982. Amnesia: a minimal model and an interpretation. See Cermak 1982, pp. 305–36

Baddeley, A. D. 1984. Neuropsychological evidence and the semantic/episodic distinction. *Behav. Brain Sci.* 7:238–39

Balota, D. A., Chumbley, J. I. 1984. Are lexical decisions a good measure of lexical access? The role of frequency in the neglected decision stage. *J. Exp. Psychol.: Hum. Percept. Perform.* 10:340–57

Balota, D. A., Chumbley, J. I. 1985. The locus of word-frequency effects in the pronunciation task: lexical access and/or production? *J. Mem. Lang.* 24:89–106

Barr, A., Feigenbaum, E. A., eds. 1981. *The Handbook of Artificial Intelligence,* Vol. 1. Los Altos, Calif: William Kaufmann

Begg, I., Armour, V., Kerr, T. 1985. On believing what we remember. *Can. J. Behav. Sci.* 17:199–214

Berry, D. C., Broadbent, D. E. 1984. On the relationship between task performance and associated verbalizable knowledge. *Q. J. Exp. Psychol.* 36A:209–31

Bjork, E. L., Cummings, E. M. 1984. Infant search errors: stage of concept development or stage of memory development. *Mem. Cognit.* 12:1–19

Bjork, R. A., Richardson-Klavehn, A. 1987. *On the puzzling relationship between environmental context and human memory.* Presented at Flowerree Mardi Gras Symp. Cognit., Tulane Univ., New Orleans

Blaxton, T. A. 1985. *Investigating dissociations among memory measures: support for a transfer-appropriate processing framework.* PhD thesis. Purdue Univ.

Bower, G. H., ed. 1983. *The Psychology of Learning and Motivation,* Vol. 17. New York: Academic

Bowles, N. L., Poon, L. W. 1985. Effects of priming in word retrieval. *J. Exp. Psychol.: Learn. Mem. Cognit.* 11:272–83

Bradshaw, G. L., Anderson, J. R. 1982. Elaborative encoding as an explanation of levels of processing. *J. Verb. Learn. Verb. Behav.* 21:165–74

Bransford, J. D., Franks, J. J., Morris, C. D., Stein, B. S. 1979. Some general constraints on learning and memory research. See Cermak & Craik 1979, pp. 331–54

Brewer, W. F. 1986. What is autobiographical memory? See Rubin 1986, pp. 25–49

Brewer, W. F., Pani, J. R. 1983. The structure of human memory. See Bower 1983, pp. 1–38

Brooks, D. N., Baddeley, A. D. 1976. What can amnesic patients learn? *Neuropsychologia* 14:111–22

Brooks, L. R. 1977. Visual pattern in fluent word identification. In *Toward a Psychology of Reading,* ed. A. S. Reber, D. L. Scarborough, pp. 143–81. Hillsdale, NJ: Erlbaum

Brown, A. S. 1979. Priming effects in semantic memory retrieval processes. *J. Exp. Psychol.: Hum. Learn. Mem.* 5:65–77

Brown, A. S. 1981. Inhibition in cued retrieval. *J. Exp. Psychol.: Hum. Learn. Mem.* 7:204–15

Brown, H., Sharma, N. K., Kirsner, K. 1984. The role of script and phonology in lexical representation. *Q. J. Exp. Psychol.* 36A:491–505

Bruce, V., Valentine, T. 1985. Identity priming in the recognition of familiar faces. *Br. J. Psychol.* 76:373–83

Butters, N. 1987. *Procedural learning in dementia: a double dissociation between Alzheimer and Huntington's disease patients on verbal priming and motor skill learning.* Presented at Int. Neuropsychol. Soc., Washington, DC

Butters, N., Albert, M. S. 1982. Processes underlying failures to recall remote events. See Cermak 1982, pp. 257–74

Butters, N., Cermak, L. S. 1986. A case study of the forgetting of autobiographical knowledge: implications for the study of retrograde amnesia. See Rubin 1986, pp. 253–72

Butters, N., Wolfe, J., Martone, M., Granholm, E., Cermak, L. S. 1985. Memory disorders associated with Huntington's disease: verbal recall, verbal recognition and procedural memory. *Neuropsychologia* 23:729–43

Carroll, M., Byrne, B., Kirsner, K. 1985. Autobiographical memory and perceptual learning: a developmental study using picture recognition, naming latency, and perceptual identification. *Mem. Cognit.* 13:273–79

Carroll, M., Kirsner, K. 1982. Context and repetition effects in lexical decision and recognition memory. *J. Verb. Learn. Verb. Behav.* 21:55–69

Cermak, L. S., ed. 1982. *Human Memory and Amnesia.* Hillsdale, NJ: Erlbaum

Cermak, L. S. 1984. The episodic-semantic distinction in amnesia. See Squire & Butters 1984, pp. 55–62

Cermak, L. S., Craik, F. I. M., eds. 1979. *Levels of Processing in Human Memory.* Hillsdale, NJ: Erlbaum

Cermak, L. S., O'Connor, M. 1983. The anterograde and retrograde retrieval ability of a patient with amnesia due to encephalitis. *Neuropsychologia* 21:213–34

Cermak, L. S., Talbot, N., Chandler, K., Wolbarst, L. R. 1985. The perceptual priming phenomenon in amnesia. *Neuropsychologia* 23:615–22

Chandler, C. 1983. *Does retrieval strategy determine the relation between episodic recognition and semantic priming?* Master's thesis. Univ. Toronto

Chumbley, J. I., Balota, D. A. 1984. A word's meaning affects the decision in lexical decision. *Mem. Cognit.* 12:590–606

Claparède, E. 1911. Recognition and "meness." *Arch. Psychol. Genève* 11:79–90. Transl. D. Rapaport, 1951, in *Organization and Pathology of Thought,* ed. D. Rapaport,

pp. 58–75. New York: Columbia Univ. (From French)

Clarke, R., Morton, J. 1983. Cross-modality facilitation in tachistoscopic word recognition. *Q. J. Exp. Psychol.* 35A:79–96

Cofer, C. N. 1967. Conditions for the use of verbal associations. *Psychol. Bull.* 68:1–12

Cohen, N. J. 1984. Preserved learning capacity in amnesia: evidence for multiple memory systems. See Squire & Butters 1984, pp. 83–103

Cohen, N. J. 1985. Levels of analysis in memory research: the neuropsychological approach. See Weinberger et al 1985, pp. 419–32

Cohen, N. J., Corkin, S. 1981. The amnesic patient H. M.: learning and retention of a cognitive skill. *Soc. Neurosci. Abstr.* 7:235

Cohen, N. J., Eichenbaum, H., Deacedo, B. S., Corkin, S. 1985. Different memory systems underlying acquisition of procedural and declarative knowledge. *Ann. NY Acad. Sci.* 444:54–71

Cohen, N. J., Squire, L. R. 1980. Preserved learning and retention of pattern analyzing skill in amnesics: dissociation of knowing how and knowing that. *Science* 210:207–10

Cohen, N. J., Squire, L. R. 1981. Retrograde amnesia and remote memory impairment. *Neuropsychologia* 19:337–56

Collins, A. M., Quillian, M. R. 1970. Facilitating retrieval from semantic memory: the effect of repeating part of an inference. *Acta Psychol.* 33:304–14

Conway, M. A., Gathercole, S. E. 1987. Modality and long-term memory. *J. Mem. Lang.* 26:341–61

Corkin, S., Cohen, N. J., Sullivan, E. V., Clegg, R. A., Rosen, T. J., Ackerman, R. H. 1985. Analyses of global memory impairments of different etiologies. *Ann. NY Acad. Sci.* 444:10–40

Craik, F. I. M., Kirsner, K. 1974. The effect of speaker's voice on word recognition. *Q. J. Exp. Psychol.* 26:274–84

Craik, F. I. M., Jacoby, L. L. 1979. Elaboration and distinctiveness in episodic memory. In *Perspectives in Memory Research,* ed. L.-G. Nilsson, pp. 145–66. Hillsdale, NJ: Erlbaum

Cristoffanini, P., Kirsner, K., Milech, D. 1986. Bilingual lexical representation: the status of Spanish-English cognates. *Q. J. Exp. Psychol.* 38A:367–93

Crowder, R. G. 1976. *Principles of Learning and Memory.* Hillsdale, NJ: Erlbaum

Dannenberg, G. L., Briand, K. 1982. Semantic priming and the word repetition effect in a lexical decision task. *Can. J. Psychol.* 36:435–44

DaPolito, F., Barker, D., Wiant, J. 1972. The effect of contextual changes on component recognition. *Am. J. Psychol.* 85:431–40 de Groot, A. M. B. 1985. Word-context effects in word naming and lexical decision. *Q. J. Exp. Psychol.* 37A:281–97

den Heyer, K. 1986. Manipulating attention-induced priming in a lexical decision task by means of repeated prime-target presentations. *J. Mem. Lang.* 25:19–42

Diamond, R., Rozin, P. 1984. Activation of existing memories in anterograde amnesia. *J. Abnorm. Psychol.* 93:98–105

Durgunoğlu, A. Y., Neely, J. H. 1987. On obtaining episodic priming in a lexical decision task following paired-associate learning. *J. Exp. Psychol.: Learn. Mem. Cognit.* 13:206–22

Durgunoğlu, A. Y., Roediger, H. L. III. 1987. Test differences in accessing bilingual memory. *J. Mem. Lang.* In press

Durso, F. T., Johnson, M. K. 1979. Facilitation in naming and categorizing repeated pictures and words. *J. Exp. Psychol.: Hum. Learn. Mem.* 5:449–59

Durso, F. T., Sullivan, C. S. 1983. Naming and remembering proper and common nouns and pictures. *J. Exp. Psychol.: Learn. Mem. Cognit.* 9:497–510

Ebbinghaus, H. 1885. *Memory: A Contribution to Experimental Psychology.* Transl. H. A. Ruger, C. E. Bussenius, 1913. 2nd ed. 1964. New York: Dover (From German)

Eich, E. 1984. Memory for unattended events: remembering with and without awareness. *Mem. Cognit.* 12:105–11

Eich, E. 1985. Context, memory, and integrated item-context imagery. *J. Exp. Psychol.: Learn. Mem. Cognit.* 11:764–70

Ellis, A. W. 1982. Modality-specific repetition priming of auditory word recognition. *Curr. Psychol. Res.* 2:123–28

Erdelyi, M. H., Becker, J. 1974. Hypermnesia for pictures: incremental memory for pictures but not for words in multiple recall trials. *Cognit. Psychol.* 6:159–71

Evett, L. J., Humphreys, G. W. 1981. The use of abstract graphemic information in lexical access. *Q. J. Exp. Psychol.* 33A:325–50

Eysenck, M. W. 1979. Depth, elaboration, and distinctiveness. See Cermak & Craik 1979, pp. 89–118

Feldman, L. B., Fowler, C. A. 1987. The inflected noun system in Serbo-Croatian: lexical representation of morphological structure. *Mem. Cognit.* 15:1–12

Fernandez, A., Glenberg, A. M. 1985. Changing environmental context does not reliably affect memory. *Mem. Cognit.* 13:333–45

Feustel, T. C., Shiffrin, R. M., Salasoo, A. 1983. Episodic and lexical contributions to the repetition effect in word identification. *J. Exp. Psychol.: Gen.* 112:309–46

Fischler, I. 1977. Semantic facilitation without association in a lexical decision task. *Mem. Cognit.* 5:335–39

Fisher, R. P., Craik, F. I. M. 1977. The interaction between encoding and retrieval operations in cued recall. *J. Exp. Psychol.: Hum. Learn. Mem.* 3:701–11

Fisk, A. D., Schneider, W. 1984. Memory as a function of attention, level of processing and automatization. *J. Exp. Psychol.: Learn. Mem. Cognit.* 10:181–97

Flexser, A. J., Tulving, E. 1978. Retrieval independence in recognition and recall. *Psychol. Rev.* 85:153–71

Flexser, A. J., Tulving, E. 1982. Priming and recognition failure. *J. Verb. Learn. Verb. Behav.* 21:237–48

Fodor, J. A. 1983. *The Modularity of Mind.* Cambridge, Mass: Bradford

Fodor, J. A. 1985. Précis of *The Modularity of Mind. Behav. Brain Sci.* 8:1–5

Forbach, G. B., Stanners, R. F., Hochhaus, L. 1974. Repetition and practice effects in a lexical decision task. *Mem. Cognit.* 2:337–39

Forster, K. I., Davis, C. 1984. Repetition priming and frequency attenuation in lexical access. *J. Exp. Psychol.: Learn. Mem. Cognit.* 10:680–98

Fowler, C. A., Napps, S. E., Feldman, L. 1985. Relations among regular and irregular morphologically related words in the lexicon as revealed by repetition priming. *Mem. Cognit.* 13:241–55

Gabrieli, J. D. E., Cohen, N. J., Corkin, S. 1983. Acquisition of semantic and lexical knowledge in amnesia. *Soc. Neurosci. Abstr.* 9:28

Gardner, H., Boller, F., Moreines, J., Butters, N. 1973. Retrieving information from Korsakoff patients: effects of categorical cues and reference to the task. *Cortex* 9:165–75

Geiselman, R. E., Bjork, R. A. 1980. Primary versus secondary rehearsal in imagined voices: differential effects on recognition. *Cognit. Psychol.* 12:188–205

Geiselman, R. E., Glenny, J. 1977. Effects of imagining speakers' voices on the retention of words presented visually. *Mem. Cognit.* 5:499–504

Gillund, G., Shiffrin, R. M. 1984. A retrieval model for both recognition and recall. *Psychol. Rev.* 91:1–67

Glisky, E. L., Schacter, D. L. 1987. Acquisition of domain specific knowledge in organic amnesia: training for computer-related work. *Neuropsychologia.* In press

Glisky, E. L., Schacter, D. L., Tulving, E. 1986a. Learning and retention of computer-related vocabulary in memory-impaired patients: method of vanishing cues. *J. Clin. Exp. Neuropsychol.* 8:292–312

Glisky, E. L., Schacter, D. L., Tulving, E.

1986b. Computer learning by memory-impaired patients: acquisition and retention of complex knowledge. *Neuropsychologia* 24:313–28

Godden, D. R., Baddeley, A. D. 1980. When does context influence recognition memory? *Br. J. Psychol.* 71:99–104

Gordon, P. C., Holyoak, K. J. 1983. Implicit learning and generalization of the "mere exposure" effect. *J. Pers. Soc. Psychol.* 45:492–500

Graf, P., Levy, B. A. 1984. Reading and remembering: conceptual and perceptual processing involved in reading rotated passages. *J. Verb. Learn. Verb. Behav.* 23:405–24

Graf, P., Mandler, G. 1984. Activation makes words more accessible, but not necessarily more retrievable. *J. Verb. Learn. Verb. Behav.* 23:553–68

Graf, P., Mandler, G., Haden, P. E. 1982. Simulating amnesic symptoms in normals. *Science* 218:1243–44

Graf, P., Schacter, D. L. 1985. Implicit and explicit memory for new associations in normal and amnesic subjects. *J. Exp. Psychol.: Learn. Mem. Cognit.* 11:501–18

Graf, P., Schacter, D. L. 1987. Selective effects of interference on implicit and explicit memory for new associations. *J. Exp. Psychol.: Learn. Mem. Cognit.* 13:45–53

Graf, P., Shimamura, A. P., Squire, L. R. 1985. Priming across modalities and priming across category levels: extending the domain of preserved function in amnesia. *J. Exp. Psychol.: Learn. Mem. Cognit.* 11:386–96

Graf, P., Squire, L. R., Mandler, G. 1984. The information that amnesic patients do not forget. *J. Exp. Psychol.: Learn. Mem. Cognit.* 10:164–78

Greene, R. L. 1985. Constraints on the long-term modality effect. *J. Mem. Lang.* 24:526–41

Greene, R. L. 1986. Word stems as cues in recall and completion tasks. *Q. J. Exp. Psychol.* 38A:663–73

Gruenenfelder, T. M. 1986. Relational similarity and context effects in category verification. *J. Exp. Psychol.: Learn. Mem. Cognit.* 12:587–99

Halgren, E. 1984. Human hippocampal and amygdala recording and stimulation: evidence for a neural model of recent memory. See Squire & Butters 1984, pp. 165–82

Hampton, J. A. 1984. The verification of category and property statements. *Mem. Cognit.* 12:345–54

Hashtroudi, S., Parker, E. S., DeLisi, L. E., Wyatt, R. J., Mutter, S. A. 1984. Intact retention in acute alcohol amnesia. *J. Exp. Psychol.: Learn. Mem. Cognit.* 10:156–63

Hayes-Roth, B. 1977. Evolution of cognitive structures and processes. *Psychol. Rev.* 84:260–78

Henderson, L. 1985. Towards a psychology of morphemes. In *Progress in the Psychology of Language*, ed. A. W. Ellis, 1:15–72. London: Erlbaum

Henderson, L., Wallis, J., Knight, D. 1984. Morphemic structure and lexical access. In *Attention and Performance*, ed. H. Bouma, D. Bouhuis, 10:211–26. London: Erlbaum

Herrmann, D. J. 1982. The semantic-episodic distinction and the history of long-term memory typologies. *Bull. Psychonom. Soc.* 20:207–10

Higgins, E. T., Bargh, J. A., Lombardi, W. 1985. Nature of priming effects on categorization. *J. Exp. Psychol.: Learn. Mem. Cognit.* 11:59–69

Hillinger, M. L. 1980. Priming effects with phonemically similar words: the encoding-bias hypothesis reconsidered. *Mem. Cognit.* 8:115–23

Hintzman, D. L. 1984. Episodic versus semantic memory: a distinction whose time has come—and gone? *Behav. Brain Sci.* 7:240–41

Hirst, W., Johnson, M. K., Kim, J. K., Phelps, E. A., Risse, G., Volpe, B. T. 1986. Recognition and recall in amnesics. *J. Exp. Psychol.: Learn. Mem. Cognit.* 12:445–51

Horton, K. D. 1985. The role of semantic information in reading spatially-transformed text. *Cognit. Psychol.* 17:66–88

Hudson, P. T. W., Bergman, M. W. 1985. Lexical knowledge in word recognition: word length and word frequency in naming and lexical decision tasks. *J. Mem. Lang.* 24:46–58

Jackson, A., Morton, J. 1984. Facilitation of auditory word recognition. *Mem. Cognit.* 12:568–74

Jacoby, L. L. 1982. Knowing and remembering: some parallels in the behavior of Korsakoff patients and normals. See Cermak 1982, pp. 97–122

Jacoby, L. L. 1983a. Perceptual enhancement: persistent effects of an experience. *J. Exp. Psychol.: Learn. Mem. Cognit.* 9:21–38

Jacoby, L. L. 1983b. Remembering the data: analyzing interactive processes in reading. *J. Verb. Learn. Verb. Behav.* 22:485–508

Jacoby, L. L. 1984. Incidental versus intentional retrieval: remembering and awareness as separate issues. See Squire & Butters 1984, pp. 145–56

Jacoby, L. L. 1987. Memory observed and memory unobserved. In *Real Events Remembered: Ecological Approaches to the Study of Memory*, ed. U. Neisser, E. Winograd. Cambridge: Cambridge Univ. In press

Jacoby, L. L., Brooks, L. R. 1984. Nonanalytic cognition: memory, perception, and concept learning. In *The Psychology of Learning and Motivation*, ed. G. H. Bower, 18:1–47. New York: Academic

Jacoby, L. L., Craik, F. I. M. 1979. Effects of elaboration of processing at encoding and retrieval: trace distinctiveness and recovery of initial context. See Cermak & Craik 1979, pp. 1–22

Jacoby, L. L., Dallas, M. 1981. On the relationship between autobiographical memory and perceptual learning. *J. Exp. Psychol.: Gen.* 110:306–40

Jacoby, L. L., Hayman, C. A. G. 1987. Specific visual transfer in word identification. *J. Exp. Psychol.: Learn. Mem. Cognit.* 13:456–63

Jacoby, L. L., Witherspoon, D. 1982. Remembering without awareness. *Can. J. Psychol.* 36:300–24

Johnson, M. K. 1983. A multiple-entry, modular memory system. See Bower 1983, pp. 81–123

Johnson, M. K., Hasher, L. 1987. Human learning and memory. *Ann. Rev. Psychol.* 38:631–68

Johnson, M. K., Kim, J. K., Risse, G. 1985. Do alcoholic Korsakoff's syndrome patients acquire affective reactions? *J. Exp. Psychol.: Learn. Mem. Cognit.* 11:22–36

Johnston, W. A., Dark, V. J., Jacoby, L. L. 1985. Perceptual fluency and recognition judgments. *J. Exp. Psychol.: Learn. Mem. Cognit.* 11:3–11

Kempley, S. T., Morton, J. 1982. The effects of priming with regularly and irregularly related words in auditory word recognition. *Br. J. Psychol.* 73:441–54

Kihlstrom, J. F. 1980. Posthypnotic amnesia for recently learned material: interactions with "episodic" and "semantic" memory. *Cognit. Psychol.* 12:227–51

Kihlstrom, J. F. 1985. Posthypnotic amnesia and the dissociation of memory. In *The Psychology of Learning and Motivation*, ed. G. H. Bower, 19:131–78. New York: Academic

Kirsner, K. 1973. An analysis of the visual component in recognition memory for verbal stimuli. *Mem. Cognit.* 1:449–53

Kirsner, K. 1974. Modality differences in recognition memory for words and their attributes. *J. Exp. Psychol.* 102:579–84

Kirsner, K., Dunn, J. 1985. The perceptual record: a common factor in repetition priming and attribute retention. In *Attention and Performance*, ed. M. I. Posner, O. S. M. Marin, 11:547–65. Hillsdale, NJ: Erlbaum

Kirsner, K., Milech, D., Standen, P. 1983. Common and modality-specific processes in the mental lexicon. *Mem. Cognit.* 11:621–30

Kirsner, K., Smith, M. C. 1974. Modality effects in word identification. *Mem. Cognit.* 2:637–40

Kirsner, K., Smith, M. C., Lockhart, R. S., King, M. L., Jain, M. 1984. The bilingual lexicon: language-specific units in an integrated network. *J. Verb. Learn. Verb. Behav.* 23:519–39

Kolers, P. A. 1975. Specificity of operations in sentence recognition. *Cognit. Psychol.* 7:289–306

Kolers, P. A. 1976. Reading a year later. *J. Exp. Psychol.: Hum. Learn. Mem.* 2:554–65

Kolers, P. A. 1979. Reading and knowing. *Can. J. Psychol.* 33:106–17

Kolers, P. A. 1985. Skill in reading and memory. *Can. J. Psychol.* 39:232–39

Kolers, P. A., Magee, L. E. 1978. Specificity of pattern-analyzing skills in reading. *Can. J. Psychol.* 32:43–51

Kolers, P. A., Ostry, D. J. 1974. Time course of loss of information regarding pattern analyzing operations. *J. Verb. Learn. Verb. Behav.* 13:599–612

Kolers, P. A., Palef, S. R., Stelmach, L. B. 1980. Graphemic analysis underlying literacy. *Mem. Cognit.* 8:322–28

Kolers, P. A., Roediger, H. L. III. 1984. Procedures of mind. *J. Verb. Learn. Verb. Behav.* 23:425–49

Kolers, P. A., Smythe, W. E. 1984. Symbol manipulation: alternatives to the computational view of mind. *J. Verb. Learn. Verb. Behav.* 23:289–314

Komatsu, S., Ohta, N. 1984. Priming effects in word-fragment completion for short- and long-term retention intervals. *Jpn. Psychol. Res.* 26:194–200

Kroll, J. F., Potter, M. C. 1984. Recognizing words, pictures, and concepts: a comparison of lexical, object, and reality decisions. *J. Verb. Learn. Verb. Behav.* 23:39–66

Kunst-Wilson, W. R., Zajonc, R. B. 1980. Affective discrimination of stimuli that are not recognized. *Science* 207:557–58

Levy, B. A. 1983. Proofreading familiar text: Constraints on visual processing. *Mem. Cognit.* 11:1–12

Levy, B. A., Begin, J. 1984. Proofreading familiar text: Allocating resources to perceptual and conceptual processes. *Mem. Cognit.* 12:621–32

Lewicki, P. 1986. Processing information about covariations that cannot be articulated. *J. Exp. Psychol.: Learn. Mem. Cognit.* 12:135–46

Light, L. L., Singh, A., Capps, J. L. 1986. Dissociation of memory and awareness in young and older adults. *J. Clin. Exp. Neuropsychol.* 8:62–74

Lockhart, R. S., Craik, F. I. M., Jacoby, L. L. 1976. Depth of processing, recognition and recall: some aspects of a general memory system. In *Recognition and Recall*, ed. J. Brown, pp. 75–102. London: Wiley

Loftus, G. R. 1978. On interpretation of interactions. *Mem. Cognit.* 6:312–19

Lupker, S. J. 1984. Semantic priming without association: a second look. *J. Verb. Learn. Verb. Behav.* 23:709–33

Lynch, G., McGaugh, J. L., Weinberger, N. M., eds. 1984. *Neurobiology of Learning and Memory*. New York: Guilford

Mandler, G. 1980. Recognizing: the judgment of previous occurrence. *Psychol. Rev.* 87:252–71

Mandler, G., Graf, P., Kraft, D. 1986. Activation and elaboration effects in recognition and word priming. *Q. J. Exp. Psychol.* 38A:645–62

Mandler, G., Nakamura, Y., Van Zandt, B. J. S. 1987. Nonspecific effects of exposure on stimuli that cannot be recognized. *J. Exp. Psychol.: Learn. Mem. Cognit.* In press

Mandler, G., Shebo, B. J. 1983. Knowing and liking. *Motiv. Emotion* 7:125–44

Martone, M., Butters, N., Payne, M., Becker, J. T., Sax, D. S. 1984. Dissociations between skill learning and verbal recognition in amnesia and dementia. *Arch. Neurol.* 41:965–70

Masson, M. E. J. 1984. Memory for the surface structure of sentences: remembering with and without awareness. *J. Verb. Learn. Verb. Behav.* 23:579–92

Masson, M. E. J. 1986. Identification of typographically transformed words: instance-based skill acquisition. *J. Exp. Psychol.: Learn. Mem. Cognit.* 12:479–88

Masson, M. E. J., Sala, L. S. 1978. Interactive processes in sentence comprehension and recognition. *Cognit. Psychol.* 10:244–70

Mayes, A. R. 1986. Learning and memory disorders and their assessment. *Neuropsychologia* 24:25–39

Mayes, A. R., Pickering, A., Fairburn, A. 1987. Amnesic sensitivity to proactive interference: its relationship to priming and the causes of amnesia. *Neuropsychologia* 25:211–20

McKoon, G., Ratcliff, R. 1979. Priming in episodic and semantic memory. *J. Verb. Learn. Verb. Behav.* 18:463–480

McKoon, G., Ratcliff, R. 1986. Automatic activation of episodic information in a semantic memory task. *J. Exp. Psychol.: Learn. Mem. Cognit.* 12:108–15

McKoon, G., Ratcliff, R., Dell, G. S. 1985. The role of semantic information in episodic retrieval. *J. Exp. Psychol.: Learn. Mem. Cognit.* 11:742–51

McKoon, G., Ratcliff, R., Dell, G. S. 1986. A critical evaluation of the semantic-episodic distinction. *J. Exp. Psychol.: Learn. Mem. Cognit.* 12:295–306

Melton, A. W. 1970. The situation with respect to the spacing of repetitions and memory. *J. Verb. Learn. Verb. Behav.* 9:596–606

Metcalfe, J., Fisher, R. P. 1986. The relation between recognition memory and classification learning. *Mem. Cognit.* 14:164–73

Meudell, P. R., Northern, B., Snowden, J. S., Neary, D. 1980. Long-term memory for famous voices in amnesic and normal subjects. *Neuropsychologia* 18:133–39

Meyer, D. E., Schvaneveldt, R. W. 1971. Facilitation in recognizing pairs of words: evidence of a dependence in retrieval operations. *J. Exp. Psychol.* 90:227–34

Mishkin, M., Malamut, B., Bachevalier, J. 1984. Memories and habits: two neural systems. See Lynch et al 1984, pp. 65–77

Mishkin, M., Petri, H. L. 1984. Memories and habits: some implications for the analysis of learning and retention. See Squire & Butters 1984, pp. 287–96

Monsell, S. 1985. Repetition and the lexicon. In *Progress in the Psychology of Language*, ed. A. W. Ellis, 2:147–95. London: Erlbaum

Morris, R. G., Kopelman, M. D. 1986. The memory deficits in Alzheimer-type dementia: a review. *Q. J. Exp. Psychol.* 38A:575–602

Mortensen, E. L. 1980. The effects of partial information in amnesic and normal subjects. *Scand. J. Psychol.* 21:75–82

Morton, J. 1969. Interaction of information in word recognition. *Psychol. Rev.* 76:165–78

Morton, J. 1970. A functional model for memory. In *Models of Human Memory*, ed. D. A. Norman, pp. 203–54. New York: Academic

Morton, J. 1979. Facilitation in word recognition: experiments causing change in the logogen model. In *The Processing of Visible Language*, ed. P. A. Kolers, M. E. Wrolstad, H. Bouma, pp. 259–68. New York: Plenum

Morton, J. 1981. The status of information-processing models of language. *Philos. Trans. R. Soc. London B Ser.* 295:387–96

Moscovitch, M. 1982. Multiple dissociations of function in amnesia. See Cermak 1982, pp. 337–70

Moscovitch, M. 1984. The sufficient conditions for demonstrating preserved memory in amnesia: a task analysis. See Squire & Butters 1984, pp. 104–14

Moscovitch, M. 1985. Memory from infancy to old age: implications for theories of normal and pathological memory. *Ann. NY Acad. Sci.* 444:78–96

Moscovitch, M., Winocur, G., McLachlan, D. 1986. Memory as assessed by recognition and reading time in normal and memory-impaired people with Alzheimer's disease and other neurological disorders. *J. Exp. Psychol.: Gen.* 115:331–47

Murrell, G. A., Morton, J. 1974. Word recognition and morphemic structure. *J. Exp. Psychol.* 102:963–68

Neely, J. H., Durgunoğlu, A. Y. 1985. Dissociative episodic and semantic priming effects in episodic recognition and lexical decision tasks. *J. Mem. Lang.* 24:466–89

Nelson, D. L. 1981. Many are called but few are chosen: the influence of context on the effects of category size. In *The Psychology of Learning and Motivation*, ed. G. H. Bower, 15:129–62. New York: Academic

Nelson, D. L., McEvoy, C. L. 1979a. Effects of retention interval and modality on sensory and semantic trace information. *Mem. Cognit.* 7:257–62

Nelson, D. L., McEvoy, C. L. 1979b. Encoding context and set size. *J. Exp. Psychol.: Hum. Learn. Mem.* 5:292–314

Nelson, D. L., McEvoy, C. L. 1984. Word fragments as retrieval cues: letter generation or search through nonsemantic memory? *Am. J. Psychol.* 97:17–36

Nelson, D. L., McEvoy, C. L., Bajo, M. T. 1984. Retrieval processes in perceptual recognition and cued recall: The influence of category size. *Mem. Cognit.* 12:498–506

Nelson, T. O. 1978. Detecting small amounts of information in memory: savings for nonrecognized items. *J. Exp. Psychol.: Hum. Learn. Mem.* 4:453–68

Nilsson, L.-G., Archer, T., eds. 1985. *Perspectives on Learning and Memory*. Hillsdale, NJ: Erlbaum

Nissen, M. J., Knopman, D., Schacter, D. L. 1987. Neurochemical dissociation of memory systems. *Neurology* 37:789–94

Oakley, D. A. 1983. The varieties of memory: a phylogenetic approach. In *Memory in Humans and Animals*, ed. A. R. Mayes, pp. 20–82. Wokingham, UK: Van Nostrand Reinhold

O'Keefe, J., Nadel, L. 1978. *The Hippocampus as a Cognitive Map*. London: Oxford Univ.

Oliphant, G. W. 1983. Repetition and recency effects in word recognition. *Aust. J. Psychol.* 35:393–403

Olton, D. S. 1985. Memory: neuropsychological and ethopsychological approaches to its classification. See Nilsson & Archer 1985, pp. 95–113

Olton, D. S., Becker, J. T., Handelmann, G. 1979. Hippocampus, space, and memory. *Behav. Brain Sci.* 2:313–65

Osgood, C. E., Hoosain, R. 1974. Salience of the word as a unit in the perception of language. *Percept. Psychophys.* 15:168–92

Parker, E. S., Schoenberg, R., Schwartz, B.

S., Tulving, E. 1983. Memories on the rising and falling blood alcohol curve. *Bull. Psychonom. Soc.* 21:363

Postman, L., Rosenzweig, M. R. 1956. Practice and transfer in the visual and auditory recognition of verbal stimuli. *Am. J. Psychol.* 69:209–26

Ratcliff, R., McKoon, G. 1981. Automatic and strategic priming in recognition. *J. Verb. Learn. Verb. Behav.* 20:204–15

Ratcliff, R., McKoon, G. 1986. More on the distinction between episodic and semantic memories. *J. Exp. Psychol.: Learn. Mem. Cognit.* 12:312–13

Ratcliff, R., McKoon, G. 1988. A retrieval theory of priming in memory. *Psychol. Rev.* In press

Ratcliff, R., McKoon, G., Hockley, W. 1985. Components of activation: repetition and priming effects in lexical decision and recognition. *J. Exp. Psychol.: Gen.* 114: 435–50

Richardson, A., Bjork, R. A. 1982. *Recognition versus perceptual identification: effects of rehearsal type and duration.* Presented at Ann. Meet. Psychonom. Soc., Minneapolis

Roediger, H. L. III. 1984. Does current evidence from dissociation experiments favor the episodic/semantic distinction? *Behav. Brain Sci.* 7:252–54

Roediger, H. L. III, Blaxton, T. A. 1987a. Retrieval modes produce dissociations in memory for surface information. In *Memory and Cognitive Processes: The Ebbinghaus Centennial Conference*, ed. D. S. Gorfein, R. R. Hoffman, pp. 349–79. Hillsdale, NJ: Erlbaum

Roediger, H. L. III, Blaxton, T. A. 1987b. Effects of varying modality, surface features, and retention interval on word fragment completion. *Mem. Cognit.* In press

Roediger, H. L. III, Neely, J. H., Blaxton, T. A. 1983. Inhibition from related primes in semantic memory retrieval: a reappraisal of Brown's (1979) paradigm. *J. Exp. Psychol.: Learn. Mem. Cognit.* 9:478–85

Roediger, H. L. III, Weldon, M. S. 1987. Reversing the picture superiority effect. In *Imagery and Related Mnemonic Processes: Theory, Individual Differences, and Applications*, ed. M. A. McDaniel, M. Pressley, pp. 151–74. New York: Springer

Rubin, D. C., ed. 1986. *Autobiographical Memory*. Cambridge: Cambridge Univ.

Rugg, M. D. 1987. Dissociation of semantic priming, word and nonword repetition effects by event-related potentials. *Q. J. Exp. Psychol.* 39A:123–48

Salasoo, A., Shiffrin, R. M., Feustel, T. C. 1985. Building permanent memory codes: codification and repetition effects in word identification. *J. Exp. Psychol.: Gen.* 114:50–77

Scarborough, D. L., Cortese, C., Scarborough, H. S. 1977. Frequency and repetition effects in lexical memory. *J. Exp. Psychol.: Hum. Percept. Perform.* 3:1–17

Scarborough, D. L., Gerard, L., Cortese, C. 1979. Accessing lexical memory: the transfer of word repetition effects across task and modality. *Mem. Cognit.* 7:3–12

Scarborough, D. L., Gerard, L., Cortese, C. 1984. Independence of lexical access in bilingual word recognition. *J. Verb. Learn. Verb. Behav.* 23:84–99

Schacter, D. L. 1984. Toward the multidisciplinary study of memory: ontogeny, phylogeny, and pathology of memory systems. See Squire & Butters 1984, pp. 13–24

Schacter, D. L. 1985a. Priming of old and new knowledge in amnesic patients and normal subjects. *Ann. NY Acad. Sci.* 444:44–53

Schacter, D. L. 1985b. Multiple forms of memory in humans and animals. See Weinberger et al 1985, pp. 351–379.

Schacter, D. L. 1986. A psychological view of the neurobiology of memory. In *Mind and Brain: Dialogues in Cognitive Neuroscience,* ed. J. E. Ledoux, W. Hirst, pp. 265–69. New York: Cambridge Univ.

Schacter, D. L. 1987. Implicit memory: history and current status. *J. Exp. Psychol.: Learn. Mem. Cognit.* 13:501–18

Schacter, D. L., Glisky, E. L. 1986. Memory remediation: restoration, alleviation, and the acquisition of domain-specific knowledge. In *Clinical Neuropsychology of Intervention,* ed. B. Uzzell, Y. Gross, pp. 257–82. Boston: Martinus Nijhoff

Schacter, D. L., Graf, P. 1986a. Effects of elaborative processing on implicit and explicit memory for new associations. *J. Exp. Psychol.: Learn. Mem. Cognit.* 12:432–44

Schacter, D. L., Graf, P. 1986b. Preserved learning in amnesic patients: perspectives from research on direct priming. *J. Clin. Exp. Neuropsychol.* 8:727–43

Schacter, D. L., Harbluk, J. L., McLachlan, D. R. 1984. Retrieval without recollection: an experimental analysis of source amnesia. *J. Verb. Learn. Verb. Behav.* 23:593–611

Schacter, D. L., Moscovitch, M. 1984. Infants, amnesics, and dissociable memory systems. In *Infant Memory: Its Relation to Normal and Pathological Memory in Humans and Other Animals,* ed. M. Moscovitch, pp. 173–216. New York: Plenum

Schacter, D. L., Rich, S. A., Stampp, M. S. 1985. Remediation of memory disorders: experimental evaluation of the spaced retrieval technique. *J. Clin. Exp. Neuropsychol.* 7:79–96

Schacter, D. L., Tulving, E. 1982a. Amnesia and memory research. See Cermak 1982, pp. 1–32

Schacter, D. L., Tulving, E. 1982b. Memory, amnesia, and the episodic/semantic distinction. In *The Expression of Knowledge,* ed. R. L. Isaacson, N. E. Spear. New York: Plenum

Schacter, D. L., Whitfield, S. 1986. *Implicit memory for unitized and nonunitized information.* Presented at Ann. Meet. Psychonom. Soc., New Orleans

Seamon, J. G., Brody, N., Kauff, D. M. 1983a. Affective discrimination of stimuli that are not recognized: effects of shadowing, masking, and cerebral laterality. *J. Exp. Psychol.: Learn. Mem. Cognit.* 9:544–55

Seamon, J. G., Brody, N., Kauff, D. M. 1983b. Affective discrimination of stimuli that are not recognized: II. Effect of delay between study and test. *Bull. Psychonom. Soc.* 21:187–89

Seamon, J. G., Marsh, R. L., Brody, N. 1984. Critical importance of exposure duration for affective discrimination of stimuli that are not recognized. *J. Exp. Psychol.: Learn. Mem. Cognit.* 10:465–69

Seidenberg, M. S., Waters, G. S., Sanders, M., Langer, P. 1984. Pre- and postlexical loci of contextual effects on word recognition. *Mem. Cognit.* 12:315–28

Shimamura, A. P. 1985. Problems with the finding of stochastic independence as evidence for multiple memory systems. *Bull. Psychonom. Soc.* 23:506–8

Shimamura, A. P. 1986. Priming effects in amnesia: evidence for a dissociable memory function. *Q. J. Exp. Psychol.* 38A:619–44

Shimamura, A. P., Salmon, D. P., Squire, L. R., Butters, N. 1987. Memory dysfunction and word priming in dementia and amnesia. *Behav. Neurosci.* 101:347–51

Shimamura, A. P., Squire, L. R. 1984. Paired-associate learning and priming effects in amnesia: a neuropsychological approach. *J. Exp. Psychol.: Gen.* 113:556–70

Shimamura, A. P., Squire, L. R. 1987. A neuropsychological study of fact memory and source amnesia. *J. Exp. Psychol.: Learn. Mem. Cognit.* 13:464–73

Shoben, E. J., Ross, B. H. 1986. The crucial role of dissociations. *Behav. Brain Sci.* 9:568–71

Shulman, H. G., Hornak, R., Sanders, E. 1978. The effects of graphemic, phonetic, and semantic relationships on access to lexical structures. *Mem. Cognit.* 6:115–23

Simon, H. A. 1975. The functional equivalence of problem solving skills. *Cognit. Psychol.* 7:268–88

Slamecka, N. J., Graf, P. 1978. The generation effect: delineation of a phenomenon. *J. Exp. Psychol.: Hum. Learn. Mem.* 4:592–604

Smith, L. C. 1984. Semantic satiation affects category membership decision time but not lexical priming. *Mem. Cognit.* 12:483–88

Smith, S. M., Glenberg, A. M., Bjork, R. A. 1978. Environmental context and human memory. *Mem. Cognit.* 6:342–53

Solomon, R. L., Postman, L. 1952. Frequency of usage as a determinant of recognition thresholds for words. *J. Exp. Psychol.* 43:195–201

Squire, L. R. 1982. The neuropsychology of human memory. *Ann. Rev. Neurosci.* 5:241–73

Squire, L. R. 1986. Mechanisms of memory. *Science* 232:1612–19

Squire, L. R., Butters, N., eds. 1984. *The Neuropsychology of Memory.* New York: Guilford

Squire, L. R., Cohen, N. J. 1982. Remote memory, retrograde amnesia, and the neuropsychology of memory. See Cermak 1982, pp. 275–303

Squire, L. R., Cohen, N. J. 1984. Human memory and amnesia. See Lynch et al 1984, pp. 3–64

Squire, L. R., Cohen, N. J., Zouzounis, J. A. 1984. Preserved memory in retrograde amnesia: sparing of a recently acquired skill. *Neuropsychologia* 22:145–52

Squire, L. R., Shimamura, A. P. 1986. Characterizing amnesic patients for neurobehavioral study. *Behav. Neurosci.* 100:866–77

Squire, L. R., Shimamura, A. P., Graf, P. 1985. Independence of recognition memory and priming effects: a neuropsychological analysis. *J. Exp. Psychol.: Learn. Mem. Cognit.* 11:37–44

Squire, L. R., Shimamura, A. P., Graf, P. 1987. Strength and duration of priming effects in normal subjects and amnesic patients. *Neuropsychologia* 25:195–210

Squire, L. R., Wetzel, C. D., Slater, P. C. 1978. Anterograde amnesia following ECT: an analysis of the beneficial effects of partial information. *Neuropsychologia* 16:339–48

Stanners, R. F., Neiser, J. J., Hernon, W. P., Hall, R. 1979. Memory representation for morphologically related words. *J. Verb. Learn. Verb. Behav.* 18:399–412

Sternberg, S. 1969. The discovery of processing stages: extensions of Donders' method. *Acta Psychol.* 30:276–315

Thomson, D. M., Tulving, E. 1970. Associative encoding and retrieval: weak and strong cues. *J. Exp. Psychol.* 86:255–62

Tulving, E. 1972. Episodic and semantic memory. In *Organization of Memory,* ed. E. Tulving, W. Donaldson, pp. 381–403. New York: Academic

Tulving, E. 1974. Cue-dependent forgetting. *Am. Sci.* 62:74–82

Tulving, E. 1983. *Elements of Episodic Memory.* New York: Oxford Univ.

Tulving, E. 1984a. Précis of *Elements of Episodic Memory. Behav. Brain Sci.* 7:223–38

Tulving, E. 1984b. Relations among components and processes of memory. *Behav. Brain Sci.* 7:257–63

Tulving, E. 1984c. Multiple learning and memory systems. In *Psychology in the 1990's,* ed. K. M. Lagerspetz, P. Niemi, pp. 163–84. North Holland: Elsevier

Tulving, E. 1985a. How many memory systems are there? *Am. Psychol.* 40:385–98

Tulving, E. 1985b. On the classification problem in learning and memory. See Nilsson & Archer 1985, pp. 67–94

Tulving, E. 1985c. Memory and consciousness. *Can. Psychol.* 26:1–12

Tulving, E. 1986. What kind of hypothesis is the distinction between episodic and semantic memory? *J. Exp. Psychol.: Learn. Mem. Cognit.* 12:307–11

Tulving, E., Schacter, D. L., Stark, H. 1982. Priming effects in word-fragment completion are independent of recognition memory. *J. Exp. Psychol.: Hum. Learn. Mem.* 8:336–42

Tulving, E., Thomson, D. M. 1973. Encoding specificity and retrieval processes in episodic memory. *Psychol. Rev.* 80:352–73

Tulving, E., Wiseman, S. 1975. Relation between recognition and recognition failure of recallable words. *Bull. Psychonom. Soc.* 6:79–82

Warren, C., Morton, J. 1982. The effects of priming on picture recognition. *Br. J. Psychol.* 73:117–29

Warrington, E. K., Weiskrantz, L. 1968. New method of testing long-term retention with special reference to amnesic patients. *Nature* 217:972–74

Warrington, E. K., Weiskrantz, L. 1970. Amnesic syndrome: consolidation or retrieval? *Nature* 228:628–30

Warrington, E. K., Weiskrantz, L. 1974. The effect of prior learning on subsequent retention in amnesic patients. *Neuropsychologia* 12:419–28

Warrington, E. K., Weiskrantz, L. 1978. Further analysis of the prior learning effect in amnesic patients. *Neuropsychologia* 16:169–77

Warrington, E. K., Weiskrantz, L. 1982. Amnesia: a disconnection syndrome? *Neuropsychologia* 20:233–48

Watkins, M. J., Kerkar, S. P. 1985. Recall of a twice-presented item without recall of either presentation: generic memory for events. *J. Mem. Lang.* 24:666–78

Watkins, M. J., Peynircioğlu, Z. F. 1983. On the nature of word recall: evidence for linguistic specificity. *J. Verb. Learn. Verb. Behav.* 22:385–94

Weinberger, N. M., McGaugh, J. L., Lynch, G., eds. 1985. *Memory Systems of the Brain.* New York: Guilford

Weiskrantz, L. 1985. On issues and theories of the human amnesic syndrome. See Weinberger et al 1985, pp. 380–415

Weiskrantz, L., Warrington, E. K. 1970. A study of forgetting in amnesic patients. *Neuropsychologia* 8:281–88

Weiskrantz, L., Warrington, E. K. 1979. Conditioning in amnesic patients. *Neuropsychologia* 17:187–94

Weldon, M. S., Roediger, H. L. III. 1987. Altering retrieval demands reverses the picture superiority effect. *Mem. Cognit.* In press

Whittlesea, B. W. A. 1987. Preservation of specific experiences in the representation of general knowledge. *J. Exp. Psychol.: Learn. Mem. Cognit.* 13:3–17

Wickelgren, W. A. 1979. Chunking and consolidation: a theoretical synthesis of semantic networks, configuration in conditioning, S-R versus cognitive learning, normal forgetting, the amnesic syndrome, and the hippocampal arousal system. *Psychol. Rev.* 86:44–60

Williamsen, J. A., Johnson, H. J., Eriksen, C. W. 1965. Some characteristics of posthypnotic amnesia. *J. Abnorm. Psychol.* 70:123–31

Wilson, W. R. 1979. Feeling more than we can know: exposure effects without learning. *J. Pers. Soc. Psychol.* 37:811–21

Winnick, W. A., Daniel, S. A. 1970. Two kinds of response priming in tachistoscopic word recognition. *J. Exp. Psychol.* 84:74–81

Winocur, G., Weiskrantz, L. 1976. An investigation of paired-associate learning in amnesic patients. *Neuropsychologia* 14:97–110

Winograd, T. 1975. Frame representations and the declarative-procedural controversy. In *Representation and Understanding: Studies of Cognitive Science,* ed. D. G. Bobrow, A. M. Collins, pp. 185–210. New York: Academic

Zajonc, R. B. 1980. Feeling and thinking: preferences need no inferences. *Am. Psychol.* 35:151–75

Zola-Morgan, S., Cohen, N. J., Squire, L. R. 1983. Recall of remote episodic memory in amnesia. *Neuropsychologia* 21:487–500

Ann. Rev. Psychol. 1988. 39:545–82

HUMAN RESOURCE TRAINING AND DEVELOPMENT

Gary P. Latham

Department of Management and Organization, and Department of Psychology, University of Washington, Seattle, Washington 98195

CONTENTS

It may become a tradition in this journal for the authors of the chapter on training and development to lament both the lack of attention to theory and the lack of research influencing practice evident in the practitioner literature on

0066-4308/88/0201-0545$02.00

this topic. Certainly this was an underlying theme of the chapters written by Campbell (1971), Goldstein (1980), and Wexley (1984). What is puzzling about this theme is that it is equally applicable to the practice of selection and placement, organization behavior, specifically the exercise of leadership, and organization development. Nevertheless, the intensity with which this theme pervades the previous chapters on training and development is missing from the chapters dealing with these other content domains. One explanation may lie in the number of practitioner-oriented magazines devoted to the subject of training and development as opposed to selection or organization behavior. These magazines were usually included in the literature searches conducted by the previous authors of this chapter.

There are also practitioner-oriented journals devoted to the topic of organization development. Perhaps, then, a second explanation to this puzzle is that the gap between the researchers and practitioners in the field of organization development is relatively small compared to the gap between the psychologists who conduct research on training, and the training practitioners who appear unfazed by this research. A fertile field of study in any of the behavioral sciences is the diffusion of scientific knowledge to the practitioner. Such research would broaden the scope of transfer of training to transfer of learning that brings about a relatively permanent change in the behavior of practitioners.

To break the theme of despair that underlies the preceding chapters on training and development, the objectives of the present chapter were narrowed, namely, to summarize and integrate articles on training and development published in scientific journals from 1983 through March of 1987, and to communicate the results in such a way that they will affect the thinking, if not the behavior, of researchers. Restricting this review to scientific journals allowed the omission of articles that often agitate researchers who read topics of interest in lay magazines; the advantage of writing this chapter for colleagues is that it provided motivation for reviewing the scientific literature without worrying about any lack of impact on a lay audience.

One conclusion of Campbell's (1971) chapter was the need to focus on observable behavioral outcomes. A wish expressed in both Campbell's (1971) and Goldstein's (1980) chapters was to break away from training fads. A need identified in Campbell's (1971), Goldstein's (1980), and Wexley's (1984) chapters was to focus on training theory. All three wishes have been fulfilled to various extents in the period between 1983 and 1987. What remains elusive is the ability of training research to bring about relatively permanent changes in the behavior of the practitioner. The optimistic conclusion from reading this trend line, however, is that theory and/or research will exist on this topic before the next chapter on training and development is written.

In addition to a tone of optimism, the present chapter differs from its predecessors in two ways. First, emphasis is given to training research conducted in countries other than the United States. Second, emphasis is given to studies that focused on the training of people for leadership positions. The chapter is similar to the other three in its attention to the identification of training needs and the evaluation of training programs.

The chapter begins with a brief history of training. This is followed by a discussion on needs analysis—namely, identifying the objectives of the organization, identifying the tasks that must be performed to attain these objectives, and identifying who needs training on how to perform these tasks. Because the accuracy of a needs analysis is dependent upon the objectivity of the rater, training programs for raters are reviewed. This is followed by a discussion of the progress made in the evaluation of training interventions. Attention then shifts to training that has been conducted in and on other cultures, and the training that is done for leadership positions. The chapter concludes with a brief review of research on ways of maximizing trainee learning.

HISTORICAL BACKGROUND

One might have expected that advances in training and development in Euro-American countries would have progressed at approximately the same rate as industrial growth since the Industrial Revolution. That it did not, explained Downs (1983), was because of 18th and 19th century views of the work force. The prevalent view of that time was that "the lower orders are innately idle and depraved except when they are goaded by the spur." This philosophy influenced social legislation in England from the reign of Elizabeth I to the revival of liberalism in England in 1906.

Such ingrained attitudes which discouraged formal training activities, noted Downs, might have changed faster if there had been any prolonged labor shortage. However, the Enclosure movement in England from 1760 to the Act of 1845, accelerated population movements from rural communities to cities. Consequently, labor costs were low because workers were plentiful. High employee turnover reinforced the attitude that any expenditure on training workers would be wasteful.

An additional factor that contributed to an attitude of indifference toward training, according to Downs, was the efficiency of new machinery, with which the labor force was compared to its discredit. However, this view of workers changed rapidly with the advent of scientific management. Taylor (1911) advocated the selection of the best workers for each task, followed by extensive training. Training was viewed as critical for breaking the practice of allowing employees to acquire inappropriate work habits.

Paralleling Taylor was the research of Munsterberg (1913). His work promoted a range of activity in selection and training of both military and civilian personnel during World War I. Between the wars, research was conducted in the United Kingdom by organizations such as the Industrial Health Research Board and the National Institute of Industrial Psychology. The outbreak of World War II again accelerated research on both selection and training.

The continuing need in England after the war for systematic training was recognized by the Industrial Training Acts of 1964 and 1973. The government felt that both skill shortages and lack of adaptability to change would arise as a result of insufficient training (Downs 1983). Training was defined by the UK Department of Employment (1971) as the systematic development of the attitude-knowledge-skill behavior patterns required by an individual in order to perform adequately a given task or job. This definition is useful for the present chapter, and is not appreciably different from that promulgated by Wexley & Latham (1981).

Parallel developments in North America during the past 50 years have resulted in a push-pull philosophy between selection and training (Hinrichs 1970). The selection or early identification philosophy stresses identifying individuals with strong potential and grooming them for positions to which they are likely to be promoted. In the case of a training philosophy, the organization is primarily interested in identifying and overcoming existing performance deficiencies for employees on their present jobs. In a survey of Canadian organizations, Mealiea & Duffy (1985) found that regardless of size of the organization, the primary emphasis today is on the latter philosophy.

In the United States, training (which is now a multibillion-dollar activity) is inextricably tied to selection through Title VII of the 1964 Civil Rights Act. Admission into training, as well as promotions, demotions, transfers and the like that are based on training performance, are considered employment decisions. Apprenticeship training programs are specifically covered in section 703d of the Act. Thus, before training is conducted in the United States, an understanding of Title VII is required.

Russell (1984) summarized case law affecting the field of training in the United States. In brief, training performance must correlate significantly with job performance if successfully completing training is to be used as a criterion for the validation of the selection device. In addition, there now are definite guidelines for demonstrating pay differentials based on training programs.

Conclusions

1. The emphasis that organizations place on training originated relatively recently.
2. The current emphasis in North America and the United Kingdom on a training as opposed to a selection philosophy may be attributed to a

decline in voluntary labor turnover. As is discussed in a subsequent section, Japanese companies located in Hong Kong and Singapore give high turnover as a reason for a low investment in off-the-job training activities. Cammock & Inkson (1985) reported that most engineering apprentices in New Zealand intend to pursue other careers overseas following qualification. It will be interesting to see whether apprenticeship training declines in that country over the next 3–5 years.

IDENTIFYING TRAINING NEEDS

The traditional trichotomy for needs assessment (McGhee & Thayer 1961)—organization analysis, task analysis, and person analysis—does not capture completely the writing that has occurred in this area since 1984. Several articles that have appeared between 1983 and 1987 have been macro in nature in that they assess the needs of populations of individuals (e.g. women, people over 40) from a policy level rather than from the standpoint of the individual employee within an organization. Thus a fourth category has been added to this subsection: demographic analysis.

Organizational Analysis

Two themes underlie research in this area. First, training needs must be linked to corporate strategy. Second, organizations have an ethical responsibility for developing training programs that minimize the technical obsolescence of their employees.

With regard to the first theme, Brown & Read (1984) concluded that the productivity gap between UK and Japanese companies can be closed by taking a strategic view of training policies. This should be done by ensuring that the training plan is constructed in the same context and by the same process as the business plan, and more importantly, that it is viewed in direct relationship to it. Thus achievement of training goals should be regularly monitored and subjected to a thorough annual review alongside the business plan.

Hussey (1985), too, argued that training objectives, especially for management development, should be reviewed by top management whenever a major switch in strategic emphasis is planned. However, his survey of UK companies revealed that only one third of the respondents saw the necessity for doing so. Most managers felt that training objectives should be tailored to the individual rather than to corporate needs. Hussey argued for a shift in thinking regarding the purpose of training. Training should not be for the improvement of the individual with the hope that it will benefit the organization; training should be for the benefit of the firm, knowing that this in turn will benefit the individual. Such training should ensure that strategy is communicated and implemented effectively throughout the organization.

Hall (1986) argued that an organizational analysis must focus on future objectives rather than present ones. Only in this way can the development and training of senior executives prove effective.

Picking up on a point raised by Wexley (1984), Russell et al (1985) included in their organizational analysis climate variables that might facilitate or impede store-wide training interventions in 62 retail stores. Specifically, they focused on supervisory (e.g. the instructions I receive are clear and easy to understand) and merchandising (e.g. scheduled use of trained part-time help) support. No interactions were found between training and climate variables. Supervisory support was not significantly related to any criterion variables. Merchandising support correlated with ratings of store image, but not with sales volume per employee. On the basis of the preceding studies reviewed here, it is likely that the wrong climate/support variables were measured. Organizational support for training should be operationally defined as the extent to which training objectives are linked to organizational objectives, the extent to which the training objectives change as soon as there is a change in the organization's strategic emphasis, and the extent to which training progress is viewed together with the progress made in achieving the business plan.

The second theme in organizational analysis is a relatively new one: the objective of minimizing technical obsolescence. The plight of displaced workers in the United States has exposed business to considerable political attack in the past four years. For example, Congress nearly passed a law regulating plant shutdowns. In a *Business Week* (1986) editorial, Randolph Hale, Vice President of the National Association of Manufacturers, was quoted as stating that retraining workers is one way for business to cool down this issue. In addition to reducing political pressure, retraining workers should foster corporate loyalty and make the work force more flexible and adaptable. The *Business Week* editorial, sympathetic to this viewpoint, pointed out that Ford Motor Company and General Motors Corporation even train displaced workers who must seek jobs elsewhere. Hansen (1984) provided an excellent description of a Ford-UAW approach to retraining that included adult basic education, vocational training, and job-search skills training.

Task Analysis

Downs (1985) conducted a survey across British industry to determine the most relevant and difficult areas related to retraining. Not surprisingly, the data indicated that the jobs of the future will require less memorizing of facts and procedures, fewer physical skills, and far more conceptual ability. A review of the literature (Arvey et al, unpublished; Fossum et al 1986) showed that while it is replete with descriptions of job change, little has been done to apply existing technology to measure these changes. One such procedure is to compare job descriptions over time. But the precision of this method is dependent upon the kind of job analysis method used and the type of information needed [e.g. tasks; behaviors; knowledge, skills, abilities (KSAs)]. Another procedure would be to have managers "nominate" jobs where significant change is likely. Research is needed on the reliability and validity of these techniques if significant strides are going to be made to minimize technical obsolescence.

Hall (1986) described ways of strengthening the links among the management succession process, individual executive learning, and business strategy. The first step is to conduct a future-oriented job analysis. The purpose of this analysis is to link future strategic organizational objectives with future executive job requirements. To do this, the future mission and future goals of the organization must be made explicit. Unfortunately, this is often not possible.

Arvey et al (unpublished) advocated the concept of updating. This concept is similar to a future job analysis. However, as Arvey et al admitted, the concept is a fuzzy one. The authors urged a more comprehensive and precise description and measurement system than currently exists for these kinds of behaviors. From examples provided by Arvey et al, it would appear that a present-oriented critical incident methodology would lend itself to the development of behavioral observation scales for measuring the extent to which a person engages in updating behaviors (e.g. keeps abreast of technical journals, periodicals, and in-house publications; allocates working time for developmental purposes; volunteers for special assignments and tasks that represent a change in present job assignments).

Several studies have appeared on ways of evaluating training content as opposed to training outcome. Ford & Wroten (1984) applied procedures used by Lawshe (1975) to derive content validity ratios for each training course element in order to derive an overall content validity index for the course. A matching procedure linking course content to training needs was then applied to determine representativeness. This approach, based on an earlier paper, was described in detail by Wexley (1984). An alternative method has been suggested by Goldstein (1986). Job analysis information, based on the rated importance of KSAs, is correlated with time devoted to each in training. The correlation reflects the degree of relatedness. Which method is better is a subject for future research.

Faley & Sandstrom (1985) demonstrated a post hoc empirical method for evaluating the representativeness of the behavioral content of a training program for police patrol officers. The method involves comparing the training program with the job for which the training is intended, using the position analysis questionnaire (PAQ). In that study, training program analysts used the PAQ to analyze the training program as if it were a job. Similarly, job incumbents independently analyzed the job itself using the PAQ. The technique thus allowed the identification of important job behaviors that the program under- or overemphasized. The profile comparison indicated substantial overlap of the technical content of the training program and the job. This constitutes post hoc evidence of content representativeness of the training program in terms of job behavior. Essential to the method is the use of analysts who have no inherent interest in finding the training program similar to the job.

Michener & Kesselman (1986) developed a training evaluation procedure for determining the representativeness and job relevance of both training program content and post-training tests. The latter is essential when post-training scores are used for making selection and promotion decisions.

In brief, subject matter experts (SMEs) first linked each training element of a job with a job analysis element. Where a linkage was not possible, the training element was said to be irrelevant. Where a linkage was possible, Lawshe's (1975) method for determining content validity ratios was used. In a similar manner, SMEs linked each post-training test item to a training item. The results showed that the post-training test was much lower in terms of content validity indexes (CVIs) than those for the training course. If only test score CVIs had been calculated, the training program might have undergone expensive and unfounded revisions when only a reconstruction of the written exam items was required.

Person Analysis

Various methodologies continue to be discussed for assessing who needs training. These include intensive interviewing with key informants, group meetings with training specialists and relevant managers, use of the critical incident technique to determine areas for improvement, and telephone and mail surveys. The mail survey appears to be the most popular, probably because it is cost effective with large samples.

Regardless of the methodology used, a continuing problem in needs analysis concerns the ambiguous nature of the word "need." Need can be an expression of preference or demand, and not an observable discrepancy in performance produced by a lack of skill (Mitchell & Hyde 1979). In order to minimize this problem, Swierczek & Carmichael (1985) developed a survey that requested information only about skills-related actions, and scaled for need and priority. However, the interobserver reliability and construct validity of these self-reports were not investigated. Tucker's (1985) self-reporting questionnaire was revised and refined following a review of the literature and discussions with trainers and job incumbents. A critique of the questionnaire was made in terms of content validity, clarity of instructions, and relationship of the questions to the purpose of the study. A "jury" of 12 senior training professionals was used to further analyze the questions for content validity.

Research is needed on the interobserver reliability and construct validity of self-ratings with regard to person analysis. For example, in a study of hospital employees, McEnery & McEnery (1987) found that employee and supervisor needs assessments were not significantly related. Employees' own needs assessments resulted in three independent factors while supervisors' needs assessments of subordinates resulted in only one general factor. In addition, the authors found that supervisors projected their own needs when identifying subordinates' needs.

Similar findings were obtained by Staley & Shockley-Zalabak (1986). In a survey of 122 female professionals and 80 of their direct supervisors (92% of whom were male), females and their supervisors agreed on only 3 of 15 competency areas: business writing, oral presentations, and communications technology. Correlation coefficients for proficiency in such areas as group decision-making processes and leadership management techniques indicated virtually no agreement between female professionals and their supervisors.

Demographic Analysis

Demographic studies have been conducted to identify the training needs of populations of workers. For example, Tucker's (1985) survey focused on perceptions of workers 40 years of age and older in order to determine their training needs in the technological and management areas within the US Geological Agency of the Department of the Interior. The younger age group, 40–49, preferred management training; the upper age group, 50–59, preferred training in technological areas; while the age-60-and-above group showed little interest in any kind of training.

Bernick et al (1984) used management hierarachy to determine the audience to which training courses should be directed. Through the use of factor analysis, 28 training courses were reduced to 6 factors. First-line supervisors had as their highest need technical factors (e.g. record keeping, written communications), mid-level managers rated human resource courses as most important for meeting their needs (e.g. leadership skills, performance appraisal), and upper management rated conceptual courses (e.g. goal setting, planning skills) as most important for their development.

Berryman-Fink (1985) focused on male and female managers' views of the communication needs and training needs of women in management. Both male and female managers identified four communication skills for which women managers need training: assertiveness, confidence building, public speaking, and dealing with males. Male managers need training in listening, verbal skills, nonverbal communication, empathy, and sensitivity. However, in her survey of government workers, Tucker (1985) found no significant difference between women's and men's expressions of training needs. Nevertheless, her study demonstrated the need for human resource planning with regard to organizational analysis. Such planning, she showed, reveals the necessity for discouraging the early retirement of older workers from the US Department of the Interior because fewer people are entering the work force.

Lester (1985) identified demographic correlates with graduation from a police training academy. The study showed that whites and males were more likely to graduate than were nonwhites and females. Steps to correct this problem were not offered. Age was not a correlate of graduation.

Streker-Seeborg et al (1984) investigated whether training economically disadvantaged women for male-dominated occupations increases the probability of their achieving employment. The results showed that despite training, they were much less likely than their male counterparts to become employed in male-dominated occupations.

Conclusions

1. The research emphasis since 1984 with regard to organizational analysis has been on identifying training needs on the basis of corporate strategy. Part of the organization's strategy must include recognition of the growing pressure from government to attend to the needs of workers who have been displaced by structural shifts in the economy, geographic relocation of jobs, international competition, technological changes, and the convergence of market activities prompted by both technological change and industry deregulation (Sonnenfeld & Ingols 1986). Research on ways of minimizing job obsolescence should increase over the next five years.

2. Task analysis may be shifting from an emphasis on what is currently required to what will in future be required to be effective on the job. The overriding emphasis is on preventing skills obsolescence at the white- (e.g. Hall 1986) as well as the blue-collar levels (e.g. Fossum et al 1986). The reliability and predictive validity of these techniques will need to be tested.

3. The newfound emphasis on evaluating the content validity of both training content and the subsequent test scores is excellent. However, as Goldstein (1986) pointed out, using this approach should not be viewed as a substitute for evaluating training outcomes. A crucial question is whether training produces a relatively permanent change in the employee's behavior. Content validity with regard to task analysis cannot answer this crucial question. It can only address the issue of training relevance to the job.

4. Needs analysis continues to be dominated by self-report measures. The necessity for determining the reliability and validity of these ratings is as great here as it is in the area of performance appraisal. In addition, psychological variables affecting rating accuracy should be studied. Bandura's (1986) concepts of self-efficacy and outcome expectancies would appear especially worthy of study in this regard.

5. Person analysis remains a quandary. There appears to be no agreement between employee and supervisor evaluations. This is especially true when the supervisor is male and the subordinate is female. Given the reliability and validity of peer evaluations for appraisal purposes (Latham & Wexley 1981; Latham, 1986), and given the probability that peers include males and females, this should perhaps be considered an alternative methodology. In an innovative study, Ash & Levine (1985) used peer assessments of coworkers' performance "should they be promoted" as means of assessing the "quasi validity" of different methods of evaluating worker education and training for selection and promotion purposes. Another alternative would be to use a multi-trait multi-rater matrix to identify who needs training.

6. Noe (1986) pointed out that currently there is no research on trainee reaction to skill-assessment feedback. If the person analysis is conducted by sources other than self, measures of trainee belief regarding accuracy of the assessment and satisfaction with the method should be taken. Research is needed on the extent to which different needs-assessment procedures result in an improvement in trainee understanding of their skill-based strengths and weaknesses, and on their subsequent motivation to obtain training.

7. Advances in the field of needs assessment may occur as a result of research on career development. For example, Morrison & Hock (1986) described a six-step process in this regard: (a) identifying career goals in the form of target positions; (b) analyzing those key positions for tasks, roles, and associated personal characteristics; (c) identifying positions that could provide the development required to perform effectively in the target position; (d) establishing a hierarchy of the positions from step c; (e) analyzing the content and context of the positions in step c; and (f) designing a sequence of positions as a career pattern that focuses on development and provides effective alternative choices at each level. Two technologies must be developed before further progress can be made (Morrison & Hock 1986). First, techniques for designing sequences of work assignments (career ladders) are needed to provide a systematic, developmental approach. Second, job-analysis methodology must enable the identification and analysis of roles and role behaviors that need to be learned.

TRAINING OF RATERS

Because the accuracy of a needs analysis is dependent upon the objectivity of the rater, the training of raters could have been reviewed as a subpart of the previous section. However, research conducted in this area since 1983 has focused almost exclusively on performance appraisal rather than needs analysis per se. Three things have gone wrong during the 1980s with this area of training. First, the myth arose that reducing psychometric rating errors such as leniency or halo has virtually no effect on rating accuracy. This is a myth because there is evidence that reducing rating errors with an effective training program can improve predictive validity coefficients (Pursell et al 1980). The myth arose because researchers reported Bernardin's (Bernardin & Pence 1980) early work in this area and ignored the follow-up article by Bernardin & Buckley (1981).

As most readers of this chapter know, Bernardin (Bernardin & Pence 1980) described candidly the limitations of the demand effects inherent in his training program—namely, that people will not rate others highly on all criteria if they are instructed that it is inappropriate to do so. Compliance with this demand/instruction was labeled "avoidance of leniency error." Instructing/demanding raters not to rate a person the same way on all criteria will also result in compliance in a laboratory setting. This compliance was labeled "avoidance of halo error." However, as Bernardin & Buckley later (1981) pointed out, these instructions are not always appropriate. Some leaders, for example, excel on both task and interpersonal criteria. Giving these leaders the same (erroneously called halo) high (erroneously called leniency) rating on both criteria would be accurate rather than inaccurate. Thus blind adherence to the heuristic admonishing against the use of the high end of a rating scale, or against giving the same rating across performance dimensions, can lead to a decrease rather than an increase in rating accuracy. Nevertheless, rather than concluding that inappropriate training can be worse than no training, many researchers have argued that any training program designed to reduce psychometric rating errors is incorrect.

A second limitation of research in this area is that people have continued to use so-called "true scores" to evaluate the effectiveness of their training programs. The problems with the use of true scores have been described in detail in an earlier Annual Review chapter (Zedeck & Cascio 1984).

A third limitation of research in rater training is that most researchers have eschewed parsimonious explanations of rating inaccuracy in favor of complex ones. For example, outcome expectancies of raters for rating accurately have yet to be explored systematically (Latham 1986). Instead researchers have looked to attribution and implicit personality theories to develop a unified model of rater information processing (e.g. DeNisi et al 1984; Lord 1985).

Weekley & Brush (unpublished) tested the hypotheses that raters can be trained to use information processing strategies when observing rater behavior, and that these information processing strategies can later be used as cues in testing the origins of memories of prototypic behavior. Their study assessed the effectiveness of frame-of-reference training (FOR), rater observation-recall training (ROR), and the two approaches combined into one training package.

The objective of FOR is to standardize raters by providing them with a common schemata of effective and ineffective performance (Bernardin & Beatty 1984). ROR is designed to teach people how to minimize recall for inferred but unobserved performance information, thereby reducing false positive errors in recall (Lord 1985).

Contrary to the admonition of Zedeck & Cascio (1984), true scores were used to assess accuracy. In addition, measures based on signal detection theory were employed—i.e. hit rates and false-alarm rates. The study failed to support the efficacy of either FOR or ROR. FOR actually decreased rating accuracy when viewed from a signal-detection-theory perspective.

The rating scale used by Weekley & Brush was a behaviorally anchored rating scale (BARS). Silverhart & Dickinson (1985) obtained essentially the same findings with regard to FOR using the mixed standard rating scale format (MSS). Again, true scores were used as the criterion for assessing accuracy. FOR did not significantly improve ratings on any one of five measures of rating quality.

Like Pursell et al (1980), Dickinson & Silverhart (1986) argued that the so-called accuracy criteria used in most rater training programs are not a substitute for examining rater validity. They compared four training programs and a control group within the context of a multi-trait-multi-method design using BARS and MSS. The results showed that regardless of training method or rating scale, training resulted in ratings with both convergent and discriminant validity.

Fay & Latham (1982) found that in the absence of training, rating errors occur regardless of whether the scale format is based on traits or observable behavior. However, subsequent to training, there were no appreciable differences between behavioral observation scales (BOS) and BARS with regard to rating errors; both were superior to trait scales. The training principles stressed that performance-related dimensions of behavior are, in reality, often correlated. Negatively skewed distributions are not necessarily an indication of leniency error. Ratings should by no means always form a normal distribution. Ratings at about the same level across dimensions and within raters are not necessarily an indication of halo error. Raters should be trained simply to record what they see.

Pulakos (1986) argued that training should be tailored to the rating scale. BOS require the reporting of the occurrence of specific behaviors while BARS require extracting evaluative judgments from observed behaviors. Consequently, FOR training should increase accuracy with the use of BARS as opposed to BOS because it provides an understanding of the performance dimensions and the behaviors representative of different effectiveness levels within each. Training raters to use common standards for evaluating behavioral effectiveness would not be an optimal strategy for increasing training accuracy with BOS. Rather, training with the use of BOS should focus on ensuring that the behaviors of interest are recognized quickly and reported efficiently. Again, true scores were developed as criterion measures.

Pulakos's hypotheses were supported. Accuracy was greater for congruent instrument and training combinations than for incongruent and controlled training conditions. Considering the observational task alone, only observational training was effective for increasing accuracy. Use of an evaluative training strategy with the observational instrument had no effect whatsoever on any of the accuracy components. For those required to make evaluative judgments, evaluative training produced greater accuracy than observational training.

Conclusions

What must we as researchers start doing, stop doing, or consider doing differently?

1. We must convey unequivocally to the practitioner that behavioral instruments are better (resistant to rater error) than trait scales given that the person is properly trained in their use (Fay & Latham 1982). The effectiveness of rater training will increase if the training is tailored to the use of the instrument (Pulakos 1986).

2. We must establish the external validity of the training methods. Generalizability may not be an issue (Locke 1986); but saleability (Smith 1976) of the training to the practitioner should be as important a concern to researchers as are concerns with reliability, validity, and freedom from bias. Most of the rater training conducted since 1984 has been limited to laboratory settings.

3. The time to abandon the so-called true scores as criterion measures (Zedeck & Cascio 1984) is long overdue especially since practical alternatives exist. One alternative is to adopt the approach used by Latham et al (1975) where true scores were at most manipulation checks. For example, several hundred people were used to establish the arithmetic mean for the rating of three video tapes used to test contrast effects. These scores were not used to evaluate the effectiveness of the training. One group of trainees rated an "outstanding" person on videotape followed by an "average" person. Another group of trainees rated an "incompetent" person on videotape before rating the same "average" person. To evaluate whether the training was effective, trainees who rated the "average" tape were required to give approximately the same score regardless of whether the preceding tape was of an outstanding or incompetent employee. If the control group rated the "average" tape significantly different than the training group, the training was considered effective.

A second alternative would be to use validity coefficients. This would prove especially saleable to practitioners in the area of interviewer training. Much of the present research in this area had as its genesis the work of Wexley et al (1973), which focused on the interviewer.

4. Researchers need to reexamine their hypotheses about rater accuracy. Rather than look to answers in experimental psychology, which in general ignores the scientific-practitioner model in favor of a scientific one only, we should look at concepts in clinical psychology such as social learning theory (Bandura 1977, 1986). The study of outcome expectancies and affect of raters may provide a parsimonious explanation for why rater inaccuracy can occur even after exposure to an effective training program (Latham 1986). A similar conclusion has been reached by Goldstein (1986; Goldstein & Musicante 1986). Of further interest would be to identify differences, if any, in self-efficacy and outcome expectancies within raters regarding needs-analysis decisions, versus interviewing decisions, versus performance-appraisal decisions.

EVALUATING TRAINING PROGRAMS

Once assessors/raters have been trained in ways to increase their objectivity, attention can be given to ways of evaluating the effectiveness of training programs. Bruwelheide & Duncan (1985) described two methods that can be used together for evaluating training results in terms of observable changes in trainee behavior. The two methods are self-report behavioral checklists and analogue testing. In the latter, trainees observe a prerecorded dramatized interaction between two actors. At a critical moment in the interaction, the presentation is halted and the trainees are asked to carry the interaction forward by writing on an answer sheet a response that would complete the interaction. By using stop-action videotaping, an in vivo situation can be closely approximated with time allowances at critical moments for responses. This was done to evaluate a labor relations training course for first- and second-level supervisors. Agreement between the two sources of data were viewed by the authors as an indication of convergent validity.

The value of this approach relative to the use of simulations or role-playing exercises is not clear. Nevertheless, Campbell (1971) should be pleased regarding the attention researchers are giving to the rigorous evaluation of training outcomes. This attention is not restricted to behavioral scientists. Even people in industrial relations (e.g. Haveman & Saks 1985) have concluded that both good evaluations and good institutions form the necessary elements of the best employment and training policies.

Economists too (e.g. Bassi 1984; Bloom 1984; Ashenfelter & Card 1985; Simpson 1984) have shown a strong interest in evaluating the effects of training. This should please Wexley (1984) in that the economists have been concerned with the way the outside environment in which an organization operates affects the organization, which in turn affects training needs. For example, Simpson (1984) in his study of training practices in Canada found that neither minimum wages nor unions have significant negative effects upon training. Turnover, however, discourages specific training but encourages general training. Government assistance has the opposite effect.

Further reason for optimism regarding the emphasis given to evaluation is the strong recognition by economists of the necessity for control groups with random assignment. They (e.g. Ashenfelter & Card 1985) appear to be as upset as psychologists when they find that control groups are lacking.

What would disappoint Campbell as well as this writer is that rather than looking at employee behavior, the economists focus exclusively on performance outcome variables such as employment or earnings as criteria for evaluating training programs. Such variables are so highly contaminated that they usually preclude meaningful conclusions (Campbell et al 1970; Latham & Wexley 1981).

Arvey et al (1985) examined the sample sizes needed to achieve various levels of statistical power using post-test only, gain score, and analysis of covariance designs in evaluating training interventions. They found that the power to detect true effects differs according to the type of design, the correlation between the pre- and post-test, and the size of the effect due to the training program. ANCOVA was shown almost always to be at least as powerful as either the post-test only or the gain-score designs. However, as the authors noted, in nonequivalent control group designs, the use of a covariate can produce biased, misleading results.

Burke & Day (1986) used metaanalysis to evaluate the effectiveness of managerial training. The results indicated that managerial training is, on the average, effective. Of importance here was their finding that criterion reliability, degree of range restriction, sample characteristics, and a thorough description of the methodology were missing from many studies.

Little has appeared on the utility or cost effectiveness of training programs per se. It may be noteworthy that the economists themselves have not embraced this methodology as advocated by psychologists. What is troublesome about work in this area is that the standard deviation of performance in dollars is almost always based on a primitive estimate (Landy et al 1982). Dreher & Sackett (1983) have taken a skeptical view by pointing out that (a) there is no evidence that a rational estimate approach to assessing the standard deviation of performance approximates the true value; (b) agreement among job experts is not a guarantee that the estimates are valid; and (c) the procedure lacks face validity in that the basis of each supervisor's judgment is unknown. As is the case with performance appraisal (Latham 1986), the question arises of who in the organization is requesting information on the monetary value of conducting in-house training programs? More appropriate may be to ask "What does upper management take into account when determining the value of in-house training?" A major impediment to management support for training may be the failure of managers to see how training has a positive effect on a subordinate's behavior with regard to the attainment of organizational or task objectives. The hypothesis offered here is that seeing a positive behavior change on the part of subordinates will result in upper management treating training seriously—more seriously than if presented with dollar estimates that justify time spent on training. Research is needed on client reactions and behaviors in response to observable behavior change versus dollar estimates.

Conclusions

1. Psychologists have been joined by economists and people in industrial relations in emphasizing the need for rigorous training evaluation. Psychologists, however, to borrow a phrase from Peters & Waterman (1982), need to "stick to their knitting" and not be persuaded to regress to a search for reliable and valid outcome variables. Such variables may not exist (Ronan & Prien 1971). The article by Smith & Kendall (1963) is seminal not because of the research that it stimulated on behavioral expectation scales, but rather because it returned organizational psychologists to the roots of our discipline by reminding us that psychology is the systematic study of behavior. Behavior, rather than an economic construct, is in most instances the dependent variable of interest in organizational psychology (Latham 1988).

2. The sample size required to achieve various levels of statistical power is affected complexly by the evaluation design used (Arvey et al 1985). Designs that covary any measure of preexisting individual differences will usually lower the standard error of the relevant statistic and thus increase power.

3. Researchers need to improve their reports evaluating training and development interventions. At a minimum, criterion reliability must be reported.

4. An implicit assumption is that, having conducted a utility analysis, a company will eliminate fewer personnel programs (e.g. training) during an economic hardship than it would have before. This assumption needs to be tested. The reason why Brogden & Taylor's (1950) work on the dollar criterion has been largely ignored for 38 years may be that the customer has not asked for it.

5. The concern for rigorous evaluation of training is not exclusive to North American researchers. The Indian Institute of Management makes the same point. In a survey of human resource development interventions in India, Rao & Abraham (1986) reported with concern that the need for

post-training follow-up is completely ignored. In the section below, research on training in and on other cultures is reviewed.

TRAINING IN AND ON OTHER CULTURES

Mendenhall & Oddou (1985) reviewed empirical research on dimensions of expatriate acculturation. They concluded that little is known of the cognitive dynamics that lead to correct and incorrect attributional or evaluative processing in cross-cultural settings.

It would appear that research in North America on cross-cultural training is now stagnant compared to its state in the late 1960s and 1970s when studies were being conducted on the cross-cultural assimilator (e.g. Fiedler et al 1971). An exception to this stagnation is the study by Earley (1987), who used a two factor, cross-factorial design to study the effects of documentary and interpersonal training methods. In documentary training, trainees were given literature contrasting the United States with the target country on such things as politics, religion, food, and male-female relationships. The interpersonal training involved role-playing exercises (e.g. a simulated cocktail party). Among the dependent variables were a supervisory rating in the foreign locale prior to the person's return to the United States, a self-rating, and a self-report measure of cultural adaptation. The self-assessment composite correlated significantly with the supervisory composite rating. The effects of the two training methods were additive and comparable in strength. Earley concluded that the key element to preparing a person successfully for entry into a new culture is clarifying that person's expectations concerning the future culture relative to his or her home culture. Most of the trainees in Earley's study were male. Research is now needed on training North American women to manage effectively in male-dominated societies such as Japan.

In the early 1980s, much was written about Japanese management practices (e.g. Tanaka 1980; Hatvany & Pucik 1981; Rehder 1983). In the latter part of this decade interest has shifted to the Chinese. For example, at the National University of Singapore Putti and his colleagues (Putti & Chong 1986; Putti & Yoshikawa 1984) have studied the transferability of Japanese training and development practices to Singapore, a country where 76% of the population is Chinese. Through the use of surveys and follow-up interviews, he found that Singaporeans were hired for specific job positions where little or no provision was made for job rotation. There was no socialization process for new recruits. Training took place largely on the job. There was no special staff specifically assigned for the purpose of training and development.

The explanation by the Japanese of the discrepancy between their human resource practices in Japan and those in Singapore included the higher turnover in Singapore, the interpretation of Japanese values for which there are no

English explanations, and Singaporean statutory requirements of high compulsory company contributions to the Central Provident and Skills Development Funds. The latter exists to ensure a highly skilled work force in Singapore.

Putti & Yoshikawa (1984) concluded that the transferability of the Japanese training and development model to Singapore is neither feasible nor desirable. Singaporeans are highly competitive and individualistic. This works against the Japanese values of "groupism." Because Singaporeans are consistently looking for opportunities to better themselves, they are highly mobile, making voluntary turnover rates high and the emphasis on group values low.

Suzuki (1986) quashed the widespread belief that Japanese management systems, and in particular training and promotion systems, are culturally derived and therefore stable. In fact, his survey showed they are changing rapidly. This is because it is becoming increasingly difficult to maintain the seniority-based promotion system within the framework of lifelong employment. As a result, Japanese companies are beginning to require the satisfactory completion of a training program as indicated by passing a comprehensive exam as a prerequisite for promotion. Employees are accepting this practice without much resistance. This is partly attributable to the fact that a test is viewed as an objective basis for making promotion decisions. However, Suzuki speculated that as the training test score becomes the prerequisite for promotion rather than seniority, the result may be the destruction of holistic values fostered by a group-oriented system that has hitherto enabled a company to maximize loyalty and productivity.

Latham & Napier (1987) studied Chinese human resource management practices in Hong Kong and Singapore. In Hong Kong, 98% of the people are Chinese. Education and training in both countries are revered among the Chinese as the means for increasing one's status. The emphasis the individual places on education and the belief that knowledge leads to advancement explain why respondents in both countries strongly preferred working for North American rather than Chinese or Japanese firms. A common response of the Chinese was that "the Americans and Canadians will teach you anything; they are outgoing and gregarious; all you need to do is ask." The Japanese are viewed as secretive and clannish. Moreover, the Chinese do not like being kept at the same job level for many years. Training and the subsequent promotion of Chinese to top management positions are common in North American–owned companies in Hong Kong and Singapore. People who join Chinese and Japanese companies are those who value job security. But Chinese companies are viewed by the Chinese as stifling training and advancement. "If I know 10 things, I teach you 9 is said to be the practice in Chinese companies.

Lindsay & Dempsey (1985) described process outcomes of a training program they developed in Bejing to teach Chinese business people Western management techniques. The topics included motivation, group process, negotiation tactics, and leadership and power. The topics were taught through the use of lecture, group discussion, role playing, and business games. The Chinese managers participated readily in group discussions but not in decision making. The latter reflected their desire to avoid public conflict. Informal group meetings that were set up by the instructors as egalitarian help sessions were not viewed in that way by the Chinese. They continued to see the trainers as authority figures who required "correct answers." Feedback sessions were viewed by the Chinese as synonymous with their concept of group criticism *(hsiao-tsu)*. Thus the emphasis was on accusation with few suggestions of alternatives. Consequently, what the US trainers saw as a kind of t-group was viewed by the Chinese as an opportunity both for obtaining an admission of guilt and for the punishment of incorrect actions and thoughts.

Group leaders were appointed through random assignment by the trainers. At the end of group process meetings, people were asked to rank one another's contribution to the group. In each group each member asked to be ranked last. The person who protested loudest "won the honor" of being designated the worst. Each group then nominated the assigned group leader as first in the ranking. The group leader would decline the nomination several times before modestly accepting it.

The fight for last place is a face-saving ritual performed for the benefit of the lowest group member. It is designed to create an atmosphere in which the worst member will feel comfortable. More importantly, it allows the worst member to "win" the title of lowest rank.

In one instance, the appointed leader had actually contributed little to the group. As soon as the trainer was absent the other group members started a fistfight with the appointed leader. It appears that when authority is absent, the need to behave in the "proper fashion" also disappears. The Chinese culture has retained from the philosophy of Mencius the "right of rebellion" against authorities who fail to fulfill the obligations of their roles.

Several articles have been written on the need to study training from a policy level. As noted earlier, training is an integral part of the Singaporean government's policy to attract multinational corporations and ensure high employment (Latham & Napier 1987). The Skills Development Fund (SDF) has existed since 1979 to encourage employer-supported training. The SDF levies a payroll tax on companies in order to achieve a nation of highly skilled workers who will concomitantly attract multinational corporations. Financial incentives ranging from 30 to 90% of training costs are given back to employers who offer training in computer-related skills, craft skills, technical skills, management and supervisory skills, etc. The MBA program in the National University of Singapore is subsidized by the SDF. The government requires all undergraduate students to take at least one course in human resource management.

Haveman & Saks (1985) wrote an essay on transatlantic lessons for training policy. The Swedish government has argued that training should be emphasized rather than deemphasized during an economic recession so that skilled workers will be available during a recovery to relieve inflationary pressures and rapidly expand the industries. Thus training is expanded to include some 5% of the labor force during the peaks of recessions by paying companies to expand in-house training.

The German Federal Employment Institute also carries out its activities countercyclically with the economy. A primary objective in weak labor markets is to provide training for meeting probable skill bottlenecks when expansion again occurs.

Brown & Read (1984) studied Japanese practices that might be applied to the United Kingdom. They found that the investment in training in Japanese companies is five to six times that of many UK companies. In all the companies visited, training plans were used as the vehicle not only for inculcating knowledge and skills, but also as the means by which the general aims, intentions, and culture of a company are conveyed.

Conclusions

1. Interest in conducting empirical research on cross-cultural training has declined in North America since the late 1960s and 1970s. This may reflect the growing emphasis in North American companies and host countries on hiring and promoting locals. Such practices lend themselves to intriguing research questions. After years of local management, is a split likely to develop between the corporate office and the affiliate? Will host-country managers perceive that they will remain on the job with no possibility for promotion to corporate headquarters? If so, how does this affect their performance? How does one continue to develop local top management? It is generally true that Japanese owned companies in the United States hire Americans with an understanding on both sides that the Americans are not candidates for senior positions in Tokyo even if they are fluent in Japanese (Adams 1985). Will this type of policy in turn lead to job boredom and a concentration on building name and reputation in the local community by local managers? Will turnover be high among these people?

2. Interest in Japanese human resource practices is not limited to the United States. Researchers in the United Kingdom and Singapore are also interested in the transferability of these practices to other cultures. Brown & Read (1984) emphasized the point that many Japanese prac-

tices are far from traditional. Their origin is in post–World War II Western theories of management. For example, before 1930 Japanese employers were as cavalier in their attitudes toward hiring and firing as were their Western counterparts.

3. The American faddishness of gushing over the strong points of one culture (e.g. Sweden) and then another (e.g. Japan) seems to be fading. Much to their credit, Japanese writers are debunking much of the naiveté in the writing of American scholars about Japan. In place of this American folly, there appears to be genuine interest throughout the world research community in how people in different countries cope with training and development issues. In short, the emphasis is on learning rather than adulation.

4. It would appear that there are few if any training techniques or methodologies that are not well known in Europe, North America, or Asia (Brown & Read 1984; Latham & Napier 1987). Differences in training success are generally attributable to the planning, execution, control, and evaluation of the training arrangements.

5. Some countries and some companies within some countries do an excellent job of linking training to strategy. The message for trainers is that this key step, probably more than any utility analysis based on "guesstimates," will ensure their lifelong employment. The rather obvious message for strategic planners is that the best-conceived plan will fail if people lack the training to implement it.

6. Katz & Kahn (1968) developed a four-fold typology of motivation: internalization of corporate goals, job identification, instrumentality, and legal compliance. Much has been studied and written in North America with regard to the first three. Legal compliance, however, appears to be an anathema to scholars in North America. Yet it is legal compliance, the desire to do something because it is right, and its concomitant, responsiveness to authority, that appear to distinguish the Asian worker from the European or North American. A primary reason for this legal compliance is the high degree of trust between Chinese superiors and subordinates. Likewise there is a high degree of trust between Japanese superiors and subordinates. The training of leaders in Euro-American companies is reviewed in the section below. The issue of trust between leaders and subordinates is only discussed tangentially in the review of Graen's work. It would appear that trust between the formal leader and followers and legal compliance need to become major dependent variables of interest to behavioral scientists. Researchers who are interested in pursuing this area should read Brief & Motowidlo's (1986) discussion of prosocial behaviors.

LEADERSHIP TRAINING

Research and training for managerial positions in foreign countries have declined; but training programs, well grounded in theory, for developing leaders in Euro-American companies continue to be refined and evaluated. Wexley & Baldwin (1986a) reviewed the literature on management development. Management development was defined as the process through which individuals learn, grow, and improve their abilities to perform professional management tasks. A critical task of professional managers is leadership. In this section leadership training is reviewed.

Self-Regulation

A theory that continues to receive increasing attention in the literature with regard to self-leadership (Manz 1986) is Bandura's social learning theory. This is a social cognitive theory with self-efficacy and outcome expectancies as key cognitive variables (Bandura 1986). The theory states that people who judge themselves low in self-efficacy have difficulty in coping with environmental demands. They dwell on their personal deficiencies. They imagine potential difficulties as more formidable than they really are. People who have a strong sense of self-efficacy, on the other hand, focus their attention and effort on the demands of the situation. They are spurred to greater effort by obstacles.

How can we increase self-efficacy in a training program? One important variable is active participation that leads to accomplishments, or what is called enactive mastery (Gist 1986). Bandura (1982, 1986) has found that self-efficacy increases when experiences fail to validate fears and when the skills acquired allow mastery over situations once felt as threatening. However, if in the process of completing a task, trainees encounter something unexpected and intimidating, or if the experience highlights the limitations of their present skills, self-efficacy decreases, even if performance was "successful." Only as people increase their ability to predict and manage perceived threats do they develop a robust self-assurance that enables them to master subsequent challenges. It would appear imperative that trainers arrange subject matter in such a way that the trainees know in advance what they will be taught, and experience success in that arena through active participation with the subject matter.

A second important variable for increasing self-efficacy is extrinsic reinforcement. Extrinsic incentives are especially important for fostering interest in an activity that people would otherwise disregard. However, the extrinsic incentives must be given for performance accomplishments that reflect personal efficacy. Loggers who are paid on a piece-rate basis for cutting trees day in, day out are unlikely to develop a growing fondness for their work. But a logger who receives money contingent upon felling a tree with minimum breakage may begin to see him- or herself as an expert. As involvement and skills in an activity increase, social, symbolic, and self-evaluative rewards become incentives, and the need for extrinsic reinforcers decreases (Bandura 1977, 1986). By making self-satisfaction contingent upon a certain level of performance mastery, people create self-incentives for their efforts. Thus a third variable that affects self-efficacy is goal setting.

Goal setting is important for increasing self-efficacy because without goals people have little basis for judging how they are doing. Self-motivation is sustained by adopting specific attainable subgoals that lead to large future goals. Subgoal attainment provides clear markers of progress, which in turn verifies a growing sense of self-efficacy. Thus it is important for a trainer to coach trainees not only to set goals, but also to ensure that they are difficult but attainable for the trainee.

Trainers must realize that trainees measure the adequacy of their performance against their own personal standards. Depressive reactions can arise from stringent standards of self-evaluation. Trainees who are prone to giving up are often those who self-impose high performance demands and then devalue their accomplishments because they fall short of their exacting goals (Bandura 1982).

What can be done to increase acceptance of and commitment to realistic self-set goals? F. Kanfer's (1980) work in self-management suggests at least two steps. One is the development of an explicit contract with oneself that specifies the conditions for self-administering rewards and punishments, and the second is self-monitoring.

Tangible and evaluative consequences affect behavior separately, but they are not independent. Goal attainment that results in tangible benefits usually activates positive self-evaluations. And self-evaluative reactions acquire and retain their rewarding and punishing value through correlation with tangible consequences.

Why is it that some trainees do not accept goals or do not respond to self-management techniques? Social learning theory distinguishes between two judgmental sources of futility. Trainees can give up because they do not believe they can do what is being taught. This would be an example of low self-efficacy. On the other hand, people high in self-efficacy also may experience feelings of futility because they do not believe the environment will be responsive to their efforts. This belief is referred to as a low outcome expectancy.

Conditions that result in perceptions of high self-efficacy and low outcome expectancies typically generate resentment, protest, and efforts to change existing practices within the organization. Should change be difficult to achieve, the trainees are likely to desert environments they perceive as unresponsive to their efforts, and pursue their activities elsewhere (Bandura 1982).

Thus a key role of trainers is to teach significant others outside of training to look for and reinforce desired change. For example, if a person labeled as a problem employee continues to be seen as a problem employee, why should the person exert considerable effort to change? In addition, trainers need to teach people strategies for making the environment responsive or ways to cope effectively in a hostile environment.

Brief & Hollenbeck (1985) surveyed salespersons to measure the extent to which self-regulatory activities occur in the absence of training. Self-regulation was operationalized in terms of three components: goal setting, self monitoring, and self-rewarding or self-punishing contingent upon the magnitude of the discrepancy between one's behavior and one's goal. The results showed that most people do not actively regulate their own job performance. The benefit of such training was shown in a study by Frayne & Latham (1987).

Based on work by Kanfer (1980), Frayne & Latham trained unionized state government employees to increase their attendance at the work site. The training consisted of goal setting, a behavioral contract, self-monitoring, and the selection and self-administration of rewards and punishments. Compared to a controlled condition, training in self-regulatory skills taught employees how to manage personal and social obstacles to job attendance, and it raised their perceived self-efficacy. Consequently, employee attendance was significantly higher in the training than in the control group. The higher the perceived self-efficacy, the better the subsequent job attendance. A follow-up study (Latham & Frayne, unpublished) showed that the increase in job attendance held over 12 months. The subsequent training of the control group lent support to a self-efficacy-based theory of job attendance.

Gist (1986) studied the self-efficacy of government administrators. She found that it could be increased significantly if training included positive feedback and cognitive modeling experiences for handling intrapersonal inhibitors discussed in the lecture.

A second aspect of Bandura's (1986) social learning theory that continues to be investigated in the training literature is behavior modeling. Decker (1983) showed that videotaped feedback and the presence of one observer enhanced reproduction skills. Mann & Decker (1984) found that when creating a behavior-modeling display, attaching learning points closely to the key behavior performed (especially for key behaviors that are not naturally distinctive) enhances both the recall and the acquisition of these behaviors. Subjects were unable to identify key behaviors from simply observing the model. As was the case in the Latham & Saari (1979) study, giving trainees the learning points in the absence of the model did not affect trainee behavior.

That the absence of learning points can have unintended and undesirable effects on trainees was discovered serendipitously by Manz & Sims (1986). The exposure to a reprimanding model inadvertently led to a decrease in goal-setting and positively reinforcing behaviors.

Hogan et al (1986) showed that trainees should not be restricted to the use of learning points written by trainers, even if trainer-generated points are assessed by SMEs to be of higher quality than trainee-generated learning points. Their study revealed that when trainees developed their own rule mnemonics in organizing the material presented via modeling and displays, better performance occurred on a generalization test one week later than was the case when trainees were restricted to learning trainer-generated rules. This may be because trainee-developed rules facilitate the development and retention of clear cognitive generalized scripts (Gioia & Manz 1985). The study of scripts may introduce new insights into research on transfer of training.

Meyer & Raich (1983) evaluated the outcome of behavior-modeling training in terms of sales performance. Those who received the training increased their sales by an average of 7% during the ensuing six-month period, while their counterparts in the control group showed a 3% decrease in average sales.

Davis & Mount (1984) compared the effectiveness in the teaching of appraisal skills of (*a*) using computer assisted instruction (CAI) and (*b*) using computer assisted instruction plus behavior modeling. The CAI training alone was as effective as the CAI plus modeling in terms of performance on a multiple-choice test. However, the CAI plus the modeling was found to improve significantly employee satisfaction with the way their managers conducted the appraisal discussion. The CAI training was no more effective than the control group in this regard.

That behavior-modeling training is not always effective was found by Russell et al (1984). The reasons remain unclear. One hypothesis the authors offered is that the post-training environment did not allow for adequate reinforcement of the modeled behaviors. Regardless of the reasons, a metaanalysis of 70 studies on the effectiveness of management training found that behavior modeling was among the most effective (Burke & Day 1986). One reason for this superiority is that modeling affects self-efficacy as an intervening variable affecting performance. However, different training methods may be needed for persons with high and low self-efficacy. In a study involving the use of computer software, Gist et al (1987) found that modeling increased performance for people whose pretest self-efficacy was in the moderate-to-high range. For those with low self-efficacy, a one-on-one tutorial was effective.

It would appear that a needs analysis should take into account a person's self-efficacy for the task(s). Mitchell (1979) expressed doubt over the wisdom of pursuing personality variables as moderators in organizational behavior research. It may be time to treat variables such as self-efficacy, self-esteem, and need for achievement as dependent variables in their own right, given that their measurement is both reliable and valid. For a review of self-efficacy implications for organizational behavior see Gist (1987).

Leader Match

Self-management training teaches people how to increase their perceived self-efficacy in mastering a given situation. Leader Match training teaches people how to change the situation so that it is favorable to them. Unlike training in self-management, Leader Match continues to be attacked vehemently by researchers. The attacks are surprising because the training program, like self-management, is based on theory (i.e. Fiedler 1967; 1978), and continues to be evaluated in different organizational settings. Moreover, a metaanalysis showed that Leader Match training with respect to behavioral measures generalizes across situations (Burke & Day 1986). The authors concluded that on the basis of these results, as well as the cost effectiveness of this training relative to other leadership training programs, this method is to be encouraged. Nevertheless, Jago & Ragan (1986a) attacked its theoretical underpinnings by showing that the measurement instrument used in Leader Match can be expected to classify almost one fourth of those using it in a manner inconsistent with the theory. Chemers & Fiedler (1986) responded by attacking the assumptions underlying the Jago & Ragan study. Jago & Ragan (1986b), not surprisingly, defended their assumptions.

It is not clear whether the debate added to our understanding of leadership behavior. In the interim, research on Leader Match continues. Frost (1986) used a pre/post control group design with randomization to conditions. The study showed that experienced managers who received the training not only changed their situational control, but did so in accordance with Leader Match prescriptions. The Leader Match training was evaluated against an alternative training method and a control group. In the alternative method, trainees were taught ways of changing their situational control, but they were not informed of their Least Preferred Coworker score (LPC). If the performance of these trainees in this alternative condition had improved, one would have concluded that the results were due simply to increases in the leaders' confidence. If their performance had not increased, the results would have supported Fiedler's contention that feedback on leadership style (LPC) is critical to Leader Match training effectiveness. The dependent variables included behaviors measured on BOS. Unfortunately, the results showed that performance in both training groups was essentially the same as that of the control group. Frost pointed out that most previous evaluations of Leader Match involved leaders who had joined new groups or were new to their positions at the time of training. He concluded that for experienced leaders in established situations, behavior modeling may be more effective in improving their performance.

In a study of mine productivity and safety, Fiedler et al (1984) acknowledged that although Leader Match emphasizes the need to change situations to match one's leadership style, behavior-modeling training usually teaches leadership actions that are required of every leader regardless of the situation (e.g. Latham & Saari 1979). These include, for example, correcting undesirable work behavior, disciplining subordinates, and orienting new employees. With no attempt to ascertain the additive or interactive effects of the two types of training, Fiedler and his colleagues found that the two together increased productivity and decreased accidents. A five-year follow-up evaluation showed that the use of both types of training continued to have a positive effect on productivity and safety (Fiedler et al 1988).

Managerial Role Motivation Training

In a review of research on managerial role motivation training, Miner (1988) argued that the intervening variable explaining the effectiveness of training programs such as behavior modeling and Leader Match is the motivation to manage others. This is because each approach sensitizes trainees to the managerial role. Miner's training is unique in emphasizing the necessity as well as the techniques of dealing with ineffective performance in a subordinate. A person's motivation to manage is usually measured by a projective technique such as the Miner Sentence Completion Scale. The dependent variables usually include observable behavioral measures. Miner concluded his article with a request for comparative research analysis.

Leader Member Exchange

Another approach to dealing with the performance of subordinates is Graen's training in leader-member exchange. A critique of the leader-member exchange (LMX) theory was provided by Dienesch & Liden (1986). In brief, the authors questioned the operationalization and psychometric properties of the LMX scale and argued for the measurement of a multidimensional construct. Measurement issues aside, the LMX approach focuses on an aspect of leadership that has been overlooked, namely the formation of in-groups and out-groups as a result of the leader-member exchange. The result is lack of productivity and satisfaction among out-group members even though performance prior to formation of these two groups would have been equal. The leadership training program is designed to enable and encourage supervisors to correct the situation by teaching them to analyze and act upon major positive and negative elements of their relationship with each subordinate.

Scandura & Graen (1984) compared this training with a placebo control condition. LMX training resulted in significant increases in the degree of supervisor support and member availability perceived by the initially LMX out-group compared to the in-group. The outcome was an increase in both productivity (weekly output records) and job satisfaction.

Graen & Scandura (1986) argued that managers and subordinates can be expected to collaborate on tasks that allow growth opportunities for the subordinate if gain is desired by both parties. This is because the LMX model states that interdependence between a manager and a subordinate is necessary for both the offer and the acceptance of opportunities of growth on the job. To test this assertion, Graen et al (1986) manipulated growth opportunities by a vertical collaboration offer based on the LMX model. As predicted, only employees high in growth need strength (GNS) responded to the growth opportunity as defined behaviorally by actual collaboration over time on tasks by the subordinate with the manager. The result was an increase in quantity and quality of output on the part of high-GNS people. This was not true of low-GNS people. It would be interesting in subsequent studies to see whether training in role motivation theory would significantly affect growth need strength.

Double-Loop Learning

In a survey of the supervisory training programs conducted in Fortune 500 companies, Alpander (1986) discovered a paradox. Most of the organizations surveyed espouse a participative management philosophy, but about two thirds of the companies train their supervisors more in technical skills than in interactive and conceptual ones. Resolving such paradoxes is a primary objective of double-loop learning (Argyris 1987).

A central theme of Argyris's training program is to overcome the need to defend against embarrassment or threat, be it at the individual, small group, intergroup, or organizational level. Such defensive reactions prevent learning and are not productive (Argryris & Schon 1986). The thrust of the double-loop learning training program is to make people aware of the discrepancy between their espoused theories and their actions so that they can reduce it.

In one study (Argyris 1986), OD professionals wrote case analyses of the problems they encounter with clients, including the solutions they should employ. The cases were analyzed within subgroups to see if their theory-in-use matched their espoused theory. The next step was for the OD practitioner to use their new ideas and skills in actual client situations.

Argyris has continued to prod the scientific community with regard to his views on evaluating training. An example of model 1 behavior in science is to take steps to minimize threats to internal and external validity, which may result, he stated (Argyris, 1987) in generalizations that have the features of mixed messages and defensive routines. To overcome this dilemma, his prescription is for researchers to combine description with intervention. The intervention becomes the context for testing the description.

Job Simulation

Kaplan et al (1985) pointed out that a simulation is an excellent method for bringing about team development because it allows for the direct observation of people at work rather than relying on interviews, questionnaires, and follow-up group discussion. Moreover, a simulation is a more effective way than natural observation for both team members and trainers to observe behavior. The simulation is not based on theory but rather organization and task analysis, concepts reviewed at the beginning of this chapter. Their "Looking Glass, Inc." simulation includes an annual report, financial data, and product information. During the simulation, 20 positions are filled in the top four levels of the simulated company. The training involves one day in the simulation, one day of individual and group feedback, and one day of applying the feedback. However, a six-month follow-up evaluation underscored the necessity for developing structures for supporting the behaviors acquired during training on the job.

Conclusions

1. The scientific leadership training literature is not dominated by fads. Applications of self-regulation techniques, Leader Match, role motivation theory, LMX, and double-loop learning have been systematically evaluated for more than a decade, and their evaluation is on-going. The importance of this sentence is three-fold. First, these leadership training programs are grounded in theory; second, the training programs have been subject to repeated investigations; and third, the training has been evaluated empirically. Many of the evaluations included follow-up data collected from three months to five years subsequent to the training. Moreover, the dependent variables for evaluating the training programs included observable behaviors. Campbell, Goldstein, and Wexley should be pleased.

2. Investigators have not been content simply to show the causal relationship between training and performance. Intervening variables such as self-efficacy, leadership style, motivation to manage, leader-member exchange, growth need strength, and a reduction in defensiveness have been studied to determine why these training programs are effective. Miner (1988) may be right in his belief that what all five of these training programs have in common is a process of sensitization to the managerial role that can interact with the basic personalities of people to increase their motivation to manage. The conditions that can make for change in motivation to manage, he might argue, appear to exist within

four of these five training procedures. Double-loop learning, the exception, should increase the learning potential of people regardless of their desire to manage others.

3. Like Campbell (1977) in the United States, Stewart (1984) in the United Kingdom has argued the need to understand what leaders do. She concluded that the background of academicians in business schools may have led to an overrating of management as a "knowing" rather than a "doing" occupation. The above theories of training focus on what leaders do to be successful, and on the psychological processes that make this "doing" a reality. For example, role motivation focuses on what people need to do to increase their motivation to manage others. Self-management training focuses on what people need to do to regulate their own behavior. Behavior modeling focuses on what people need to do in regulating the behavior of others. LMX focuses on what people need to do to prevent "we-they" behavioral patterns in dyadic situations. Leader Match focuses on what people need to do to change the situation in which they are operating so that it is favorable to them. Double-loop learning teaches people what they need to do to minimize defensiveness.

4. The psychometric properties of LMX have been questioned as has been the LPC scale in Leader Match. Role motivation theory uses projective tests. Social learning theory includes operant methodology. Double-loop learning eschews orthodox evaluation techniques. Thus each has a potential red flag for different subgroups within the scientific community. It would be fascinating to discover why Leader Match is singled out year after year for attack from the scientific community. What is it about this training that lowers the affect level of so many researchers?

5. Researchers are beginning to use combinations of training programs to form a treatment package to affect change (e.g. Fiedler et al 1984; 1988). A treatment-package approach analogous to what is done in clinical psychological settings (Azrin 1977) may be more appropriate than trying to tease out the additive or interactive effects of each, especially in light of the difficulty in making fair comparisons (Cooper & Richardson 1986). The latter is especially problematic if the components of the treatment package are designed to change different rather than the same target behaviors.

6. The wide-eyed naiveté that plagued research in previous years regarding the diminished effects of training over time seems to be disappearing. What is needed now is explicit research on the psychological and structural variables needed to maintain what is learned in training on the job. For example, Wexley & Baldwin (1986b) tested the hypothesis that after completing a training program, trainees should have specific be-

havioral goals, and should monitor their goal achievement as a way to get them to apply what was learned on the job. They found that relative to the control condition, both assigned and participatively set goals were equally effective in bringing about transfer of training as measured two months after the training program. Goldstein (1986) and Newstrom (1986) provided lists of organizational factors that may facilitate or constrain positive transfer of learning. For a traditional approach to this topic of transfer of training, see Fotheringhame (1984, 1986).

MAXIMIZING TRAINEE LEARNING

This chapter closes with a potpourri of subject matter not treated elsewhere yet important for ensuring that employee learning of job-related behavior is relatively permanent. These topics include the training environment, learning strategies, and individual differences.

With regard to training environment, Rosengren & Albert (1986) studied American, British, and Spanish students who were undergoing training as merchant marine engineering officers. The Americans were exposed to a military-like social environment and transoceanic cruises each summer. The British were exposed to a collegial relationship with faculty as well as shipboard training. The Spanish received highly abstract theory with no shipboard training. Yet the Spanish, followed by the British, had the most positive attitudes and the lowest turnover intentions toward their future profession. This result can be explained in terms of outcome expectancy (Bandura 1986). Seagoing jobs on Spanish vessels are currently plentiful, with comparatively large rewards; the US merchant marine has been steadily shrinking since the end of World War II.

Downs & Perry showed how learning strategies can be improved. Downs (1985) argued that the powerful media of interactive computers and videos enabled people to meet their own learning needs when and where they wish to do it and at their own pace; but the software for these programs must be designed not just to impart and check facts, but to match the ways of learning and prior knowledge of individuals. Downs & Perry (1984) developed a workshop to teach supervisors skill in training groups of trainees to be aware of and improve learning skills. Perry & Downs (1985) summarized three learning strategies: internalized acts of learning (e.g. self-questioning), activities and behaviors (e.g. recording, documenting, interpreting), and products (e.g. a report or project). They reviewed evidence indicating that initially poor learners can learn and use effectively those strategies employed by better learners.

The subject of how individual differences in cognitive abilities, achievement motivation, and creativity affect the design of educational programs was reviewed by Snow (1986). Less able learners do better when instruction is tightly structured and lessons are broken down into a sequence of simplified units. Computer assisted instruction, because it is highly structured, results in better learning in highly anxious students.

Because of projections of a lack of qualified personnel in male-dominated technical jobs, the West German Ministry of Science instigated a large-scale study on the apprenticeship of women in mechanical-technical occupations. Schuler (1986) found that the training could develop job-relevant aptitudes for women but could not diminish the initial differences that existed between males and females prior to training.

Gordon et al (1986) found that trainees with greater seniority tended to require more time than standard to complete training than did people with less seniority. Interjob similarity, not surprisingly, was a strong predictor of training time.

Noe (1986) presented a comprehensive model for studying how trainees' attributes and attitudes affect training effectiveness. The model posits four conditions necessary for learning: Trainees must believe that the assessment of their strengths and weaknesses is accurate, they must believe that they can master the training content and that mastery is related to the attainment of desired outcomes, they must value effective job performance, and they must view their work setting as providing the necessary resources to perform the job well.

Conclusion

To maximize training effectiveness, this writer has been influenced by Bandura's (1977, 1982, 1986) concepts of self-efficacy and outcome expectancies. They explain the results obtained by Rosengren & Albert (1986) regarding American, British, and Spanish merchant marines. They are among those variables that should be targeted when developing learning strategies, and they are important individual difference variables that should be taken into account when evaluating training interventions.

SUMMARY

There is no reason to be complacent over the quality of scientific research on training and development, nor is there reason for despair. Fads do not dominate the scientific literature on training and development; advancement in theory and empirical research is ongoing. What troubles some people is the extent to which practitioners and practitioner journals appear to be unaffected by these advancements. Overcoming this problem is certainly an area for research. One solution may be simply to translate one's scientific articles for a lay audience. This is currently being done in India (e.g. Rao 1984; Rao & Abraham 1986).

ACKNOWLEDGEMENTS

Barbara Finnegan and William Silver, doctoral students in the University of Washington's Business School, were invaluable in the preliminary work they performed for writing this chapter. Drs. Goldstein and Wexley provided invaluable critiques of an earlier draft of this chapter. Preparation of this chapter was funded in part by the Ford Motor Company Affiliate Research grant to the author.

Literature Cited

Adams, F. Jr. 1985. Developing an international work force. *Columbia J. World Bus.* 20:23–25

Alpander, G. G. 1986. Conceptual analysis of supervisory training programs in major U.S. corporations. Presented at Natl. Acad. Manage. Meet., Chicago

Argyris, C. 1986. Reasoning, action strategies, and defensive routines: the case of OD practitioners. In *Research in Organizational Change*, ed. W. Pasmore, R. Woodman, 1:89–128. Greenwich, Conn: JAI Press

Argyris, C., Schon, D. A. 1986. Reciprocal integrity. Paper presented at the symposium on functioning of executive integrity. Weatherhand School of Management, Case Western Reserve Univ., October

Argyris, C. 1987. Crafting a theory of practice: the case of organizational paradoxes. In *Paradox and Transformation: Towards a Theory of Change in Organization and Management*, ed. R. Quinn, K. Cameron. Boston, Mass: Pitman

Arvey, R. D., Cole, D. A., Hazucha, J. F., Hartanto, F. M. 1985. Statistical power of training evaluation designs. *Personnel Psychol.* 38:493–508

Arvey, R. D., Fossum, J. A., Robbins, N., Paradise, C. 1984. Skills obsolescence: psychological and economic perspectives. Unpublished manuscript

Ash, R. A., Levine, E. L. 1985. Job applicant training and work experience evaluation: an empirical comparison of four methods. *J. Appl. Psychol.* 70:572–76

Ashenfelter, O., Card, D. 1985. Using the longitudinal structure of earnings to estimate the effect of training programs. *Rev. Econ. Stat.* 67:648–60

Azrin, N. H. 1977. A strategy for applied research: learning based outcome oriented. *Am. Psychol.* 32:140–49

Bandura, A. 1977. Self-efficacy: toward a unifying theory of behavior change. *Psychol. Rev.* 84:191–215

Bandura, A. 1982. Self-efficacy mechanism in human agency. *Am. Psychol.* 37:122–47

Bandura, A. 1986. *Social Foundations of Thought and Action.* Englewood Cliffs, NJ: Prentice-Hall

Bassi, L. J. 1984. Estimating the effect of training programs with non-random selection. *Rev. Econ. Stat.* 66:36–43

Bernardin, H. J., Beatty, R. W. 1984. *Performance Appraisal: Assessing Human Behavior at Work.* Boston, Mass: Kent

Bernardin, H. J., Buckley, M. R. 1981. Strategies in rater training. *Acad. Manage. Rev.* 6:205–12

Bernardin, H. J., Pence, E. C. 1980. Effects of rater training: creating new response sets and decreasing accuracy. *J. Appl. Psychol.* 65:60–66

Bernick, E. L., Kindley, R., Pettit, K. K. 1984. The structure of training courses and the effects of hierarchy. *Pub. Personnel Manage.* 13:109–19

Berryman-Fink, C. 1985. Male and female managers' views of the communication skills and training needs of women in management. *Publ. Personnel Manage.* 14: 307–13

Bloom, H. S. 1984. Estimating the effect of job-training programs, using longitudinal data: Ashenfelter's findings reconsidered. *J. Hum. Res.* 19:544–56

Brief, A. P., Hollenbeck, J. R. 1985. An exploratory study of self-regulating activities and their effects on job performance. *J. Occup. Behav.* 6:197–208

Brief, A. P., Motowidlo, S. J. 1986. Prosocial organizational behaviors. *Acad. Manage. J.* 11:710–25

Brogden, H. F., Taylor, E. K. 1950. The dollar criterion—applying the cost accounting concept to criterion construction. *Personnel Psychol.* 3:133–54

Brown, G. F., Read, A. R. 1984. Personnel and training policies—some lessons for Western companies. *Long Range Plan.* 17(2):48–57

Bruwelheide, L. R., Duncan, P. K. 1985. A method for evaluating corporation training seminars. *J. Organ. Behav. Manage.* 7(1/2):65–94

Burke, M. J., Day, R. R. 1986. A cumulative study of the effectiveness of managerial training. *J. Appl. Psychol.* 71:232–46

Business Week. Sept. 29, 1986. Automation needs a speedup and so does retraining, p. 132

Cammock, P., Inkson, K. 1985. The aspirations of trade apprentices and their implications for apprenticeship. *J. Occup. Psychol.* 58:49–55

Campbell, J. P. 1977. The cutting edge of leadership: an overview. In *Leadership: The Cutting Edge*, ed. J. G. Hunt, L. L. Lawson. Carbondale, Ill: Southern Illinois Press

Campbell, J. P. 1971. Personnel training and development. *Ann. Rev. Psychol.* 22:565–602

Campbell, J. P., Dunnette, M. D., Lawler, E. E., Weick, K. E. 1970. *Managerial Behavior, Performance, and Effectiveness.* New York: McGraw-Hill

Chemers, M. M., Fiedler, F. E. 1986. The trouble with assumptions: a reply to Jago and Ragan. *J. Appl. Psychol.* 71:560–63

Cooper, W. H., Richardson, A. J. 1986. Unfair comparisons. *J. Appl. Psychol.* 71:179–84

Davis, B. L., Mount, M. K. 1984. Effectiveness of performance appraisal training using computer assisted instruction and behavior modeling. *Personnel Psychol.* 37:439–52

Decker, P. J. 1983. The effects of rehearsal group size and video feedback in behavior modeling training. *Personnel Psychol.* 36:763–74

DeNisi, A. S., Cafferty, T. P., Meglino, B. M. 1984. A cognitive view of the performance appraisal process: a model and research propositions. *Organ. Behav. Hum. Perform.* 33:360–96

Dickinson, T. L., Silverhart, T. A. 1986. Training to improve the accuracy and validity of performance ratings. Presented at Ann. Am. Psychol. Assoc. Conv., 94th, Washington, DC

Dienesch, R. M., Liden, R. C. 1986. Leader Member Exchange model of leadership: a critique and further development. *Acad. Manage. Rev.* 11:618–34

Downs, S. 1985. Retraining for new skills. *Ergonomics* 28:1205–11

Downs, S. 1983. Industrial training. In *Using Personnel Research*, ed. A. P. O. Williams. Aldershot, Hants, England: Gower

Downs, S., Perry, P. 1984. Developing learning skills. *J. Eur. Ind. Train.* 8:21–26

Dreher, G. F., Sackett, P. R., eds. 1983. *Perspectives on Employee Staffing and Selection.* Homewood, Ill: Irwin

Earley, P. C. 1987. Intercultural training for managers: a comparison of documentary and interpersonal methods. *Acad. Manage. J.* In press

Faley, R. H., Sandstrom, E. 1985. Content representativeness: an empirical method of evaluation. *J. Appl. Psychol.* 70:567–71

Fay, C. H., Latham, G. P. 1982. Effects of training and rating scales on rating errors. *Personnel Psychol.* 35:105–16

Fiedler, F. 1967. *A Theory of Leadership Effectiveness.* New York: McGraw-Hill

Fiedler, F. E. 1978. The contingency model and the dynamics of the leadership process. In *Advances in Experimental Social Psychology*, ed. L. Berkowitz, pp. 59–112. New York: Academic

Fiedler, F. E., Bell, C. H., Chemers, M. M., Patrick, D. 1984. Increasing mine productivity and safety through management training and organization development: a comparative study. *Basic Appl. Soc. Psychol.* 5:1–18

Fiedler, F. E., Mitchell, T. R., Triandis, H. C. 1971. The culture assimilator: an approach to cross-cultural training. *J. Appl. Psychol.* 55:95–102

Fiedler, F. E., Wheeler, W. A., Chemers, M. M., Patrick, D. 1988. Structured management training in underground mining: a five year follow-up. *Train. Dev. J.* In press

Ford, J. K., Wroten, S. P. 1984. Introducing new methods for conducting training evaluation and for linking training evaluation to program redesign. *Personnel Psychol.* 37:651–66

Fossum, J. A., Arvey, R. D., Paradise, C. A., Robbins, N. E. 1986. Modeling the skills obsolescence process: a psychological/economic integration. *Acad. Manage. Rev.* 11:362–74

Fotheringhame, J. 1984. Transfer of training: a field investigation of youth training. *J. Occup. Psychol.* 57:239–48

Fotheringhame, J. 1986. Transfer of training: a field study of some training methods. *J. Occup. Psychol.* 59:59–71

Frayne, C. A., Latham, G. P. 1987. The application of social learning theory to employee self-management of attendance. *J. Appl. Psychol.* 72:387–92

Frost, D. E. 1986. A test of situational engineering for training leaders. *Psychol. Rep.* 59:771–82

Gioia, D. A., Manz, C. C. 1985. Linking cognition and behavior: a script processing interpretation of vicarious learning. *Acad. Manage. J.* 10:527–39

Gist, M. E. 1987. Self-efficacy: implications for organizational behavior and human resource management. *Acad. Manage. Rev.* 12:472–85

Gist, M. E. 1986. The effects of self-efficacy training on training task performance. *Acad. Manage. Best Pap. Proc.* 46:250–54

Gist, M. E., Schwoerer, C., Rosen, B. 1987. Modeling vs. non-modeling: the impact of self efficacy and performance in computer training for managers. *Acad. Manage. Best Pap. Proc.* 47:122–26

Goldstein, I. L. 1980. Training in work organizations. *Ann. Rev. Psychol.* 31:229–72

Goldstein, I. L. 1986. *Training in Organizations: Needs Assessment, Development, and Evaluation.* Monterey, Calif: Brooks/Cole 2nd ed.

Goldstein, I. L., Musicante, G. R. 1986. From the laboratory to the field: an examination of training models. In *The Generalizability of Laboratory Experiments: an Inductive Survey,* ed. E. A. Locke. Lexington, Mass: D.C. Heath

Gordon, M. E., Cofer, J. L., McCullough, P. M. 1986. Relationships among seniority, past performance, interjob similarity, and trainability. *J. Appl. Psychol.* 71:518–21

Graen, G. B., Scandura, T. A. 1986. Toward a psychology of dyadic organizing. In *Research in Organizational Behavior,* ed. B. M. Straw, L. L. Cummings, Vol. 9. Greenwich, Conn: JAI

Graen, G. B., Scandura, T. A., Graen, M. R. 1986. A field experimental test of the moderating effects of growth need strength on productivity. *J. Appl. Psychol.* 71:484–91

Hall, D. T. 1986. Dilemmas in linking succession planning to individual executive learning. *Hum. Res. Manage.* 25:235–65

Hansen, G. B. 1984. Ford and the UAW have a better idea: a joint labor-management approach to plant closings and worker retraining. *Ann. Am. Acad. Pol. Soc. Sci.* 475:158–74

Hatvany, N., Pucik, V. 1981. An integrated management system: lessons from the Japanese experience. *Acad. Manage. Rev.* 6:469–80

Haveman, R. H., Saks, D. H. 1985. Transatlantic lessons for employment and training policy. *Ind. Relat.* 24:20–36

Hinrichs, J. R. 1970. Two approaches to filling the management gap. *Personnel J.* 49:1008–14

Hogan, P. M., Hakel, M. D., Decker, P. J. 1986. Effects of trainee-generated versus trainer-provided rule codes on generalization in behavior-modeling training. *J. Appl. Psychol.* 71:469–73

Hussey, D. E. 1985. Implementing corporate strategy: using management education and training. *Long Range Plan.* 18(5):28–37

Jago, A. G., Ragan, J. W. 1986a. The trouble with Leader Match is that it doesn't match Fiedler's contingency model. *J. Appl. Psychol.* 71:555–59

Jago, A. G., Ragan, J. W. 1986b. Some assumptions are more troubling than others: rejoinder to Chemers and Fiedler. *J. Appl. Psychol.* 71:564–65

Kanfer, F. H. 1980. Self-management methods. In *Helping People Change: A Textbook of Methods,* ed. F. H. Kanfer, A. P. Goldstein. New York: Pergamon. 2nd ed.

Kaplan, R. E., Lombardo, M. M., Mazique, M. S. 1985. A mirror for managers: using simulation to develop management teams. *J. Appl. Behav. Sci.* 21:241–53

Katz, D., Kahn, R. L. 1968. *The Social Psychology of Organizations.* New York: Wiley

Landy, F. J., Farr, J. L., Jacobs, R. R. 1982. Utility concepts in performance measurement. *Organ. Behav. Hum. Perform.* 30:15–40

Latham, G. P. 1986. Job performance and appraisal. In *International Review of Industrial and Organizational Psychology,* ed. C. L. Cooper, I. T. Robertson. Chichester: Wiley

Latham, G. P. 1988. The influence of Canadian researchers on organizational psychology. *Can. Psychol.* In press

Latham, G. P., Napier, N. 1987. Chinese human resource management practices in Hong Kong and Singapore. Int. Personnel and Hum. Resource Manage. Conf., Singapore, December

Latham, G. P., Saari, L. M. 1979. The application of social learning theory to training supervisors through behavior modeling. *J. Appl. Psychol.* 64:239–46

Latham, G. P., Wexley, K. N. 1981. *Increasing Productivity Through Performance Appraisal.* Reading, Mass: Addison-Wesley

Latham, G. P., Wexley, K. N., Pursell, E. D. 1975. Training managers to minimize rating errors in the observation of behavior. *J. Appl. Psychol.* 60:550–55

Lawshe, C. H. 1975. A quantitative approach to content validity. *Personnel Psychol.* 28:563–75

Lester, D. 1985. Graduation from a police training academy: demographic correlates. *Psychol. Rep.* 57:542

Lindsay, C. P., Dempsey, B. L. 1985. Experience in training Chinese business people to use U.S. management techniques. *J. Appl. Behav. Sci.* 21:65–78

Locke, E. A. 1986. *Generalizing from Laboratory to Field Settings: Research Findings from Industrial-Organizational Psychology, Organizational Behavior, and Human Resource Management.* Lexington, Mass: Heath Lexington

Lord, R. G. 1985. Accuracy in behavioral measurement: an alternative definition based on raters' cognitive schema and signal detection theory. *J. Appl. Psychol.* 70:66–71

Mann, R. B., Decker, P. J. 1984. The effect of key behavior distinctiveness on generalization and recall in behavior modeling training. *Acad. Manage. J.* 27:900–9

Manz, C. C. 1986. Self leadership: toward an expanded theory of self influence processes in organizations. *Acad. Manage. Rev.* 11:585–600

Manz, C. C., Sims, H. P. 1986. Beyond imitation: complex behavioral and affective linkages resulting from exposure to leadership training models. *J. Appl. Psychol.* 71:571–78

McEnery, J., McEnery, J. M. 1987. Self-rating in management training needs assessment: a neglected opportunity. *J. Occup. Psychol.* 60:49–60

McGehee, W., Thayer, P. W. 1961. *Training in Business and Industry.* New York: Wiley

Mealiea, L. W., Duffy, J. 1985. Contemporary training and development practices in Canadian firms. Presented at Ann. Meet. Atlantic Sch. Bus., Halifax

Mendenhall, M., Oddou, G. 1985. The dimensions of expatriate acculturation: a review. *Acad. Manage. J.* 10:39–47

Meyer, H. H., Raich, M. S. 1983. An objective evaluation of a behavior modeling training program. *Personnel Psychol.* 36:755–62

Michener, S. E., Kesselman, G. A. 1986. Content-related validation technique applied to training evaluation. Presented at Ann. Am. Psychol. Assoc. Conv., 94th, Washington, DC

Miner, J. B. 1988. Managerial role motivation training. *J. Manage. Psychol.* In press

Mitchell, E., Hyde, A. 1979. Training demand assessment: three case studies in planning training programs. *Public Personnel Manage.,* Nov-Dec., pp. 360–73

Mitchell, T. R. 1979. Organizational behavior. *Ann. Rev. Psychol.* 30:243–81

Morrison, R. F., Hock, R. R. 1986. Career building: learning from cumulative work experience. In *Career Development in Organizations,* ed. D. T. Hall. San Francisco: Josey-Bass

Munsterberg, H. 1913. *Psychology and Industrial Efficiency.* Boston: Houghton Mifflin

Newstrom, J. 1986. Leveraging management development through the management of transfer. *J. Manage. Dev.* 5(5):33–45

Noe, R. A. 1986. Trainees' attributes and attitudes: neglected influences on training effectiveness. *Acad. Manage. Rev.* 11:736–49

Perry, P., Downs, S. 1985. Skills, strategies,

and ways of learning. *Program. Learn. Educ. Technol.* 22:177–81

Peters, T. J., Waterman, R. H. Jr. 1982. *In Search of Excellence.* New York: Harper & Row

Pulakos, E. D. 1986. The development of training programs to increase accuracy with different rating tasks. *Organ. Behav. Hum. Decision Process* 38:76–91

Pursell, E. D., Dossett, D. L., Latham, G. P. 1980. Obtaining validated predictors by minimizing rating errors in the criterion. *Personnel Psychol.* 33:91–96

Putti, J. M., Chong, T. 1986. Human resource management practices of Japanese organizations. *Singapore Manage. Rev.* 8:11–19

Putti, J., Yoshikawa, A. 1984. Transferability—Japanese training and development practices. In *Proc. Acad. Int. Bus. Int. Meet., Singapore,* pp. 300–10

Rao, T. V., Abraham, E. 1986. Human resource development: practices in Indian industries—a trend report. *Man. Labour Stud.* 2(2):73–85

Rao, T. V. 1984. Role of training in human resources development. *Ind. J. Train. Dev.* 15:118–22

Rehder, R. R. 1983. Education and training: have the Japanese beaten us again? *Personnel J.* 42–47

Ronan, W. W., Prien, E. P. 1971. *Perspectives on the Measurement of Human Performance.* New York: Appleton-Century-Crofts

Rosengren, W. R., Albert, A. 1986. Training environments, work attitudes, and turnover intention. *Sociol. Inquiry* 56:477–97

Russell, J. S. 1984. A review of fair employment cases in the field of training. *Personnel Psychol.* 37:261–76

Russell, J. S., Terborg, J. R., Powers, M. L. 1985. Organizational performance and organizational level training and support. *Personnel Psychol.* 38:849–63

Russell, J. S., Wexley, K. N., Hunter, J. E. 1984. Questioning the effectiveness of behavior modeling training in an industrial setting. *Personnel Psychol.* 37:465–82

Scandura, T. A., Graen, G. B. 1984. Moderating effects of initial leader-member exchange status on the effects of a leadership intervention. *J. Appl. Psychol.* 69:428–36

Schuler, H. 1986. Females in technical apprenticeship: development of aptitudes, performance, and self concept. In *Human Assessment: Cognition and Motivation,* ed. S. E. Newstead, S. H. Irvine, P. L. Dann, pp. 351–957. The Hague: Nijhoff

Silverhart, T. A., Dickinson, T. L. 1985. Training to improve ratings with the mixed standard scale: an investigation of cognitive strategy and rater accuracy training. Presented at Ann. East. Psychol. Assoc. Conv., Boston

Simpson, W. 1984. An econometric analysis of industrial training in Canada. *J. Hum. Res.* 19:435–51

Smith, P. C. 1976. Behaviors, results, and organizational effectiveness: the problem of criteria. In *Handbook of Industrial and Organizational Psychology*, ed. M. D. Dunnette. Chicago: Rand McNally

Smith, P. C., Kendall, L. M. 1963. Retranslation of expectations: an approach to the construction of unambiguous anchors for rating scales. *J. Appl. Psychol.* 47:149–55

Snow, R. E. 1986. Individual differences and the design of educational programs. *Am. Psychol.* 41:1029–39

Sonnenfeld, J. A., Ingols, C. A. 1986. Working knowledge: charting a new course for training. *Organ. Dynam.* 15(2):63–79

Staley, C. C., Shockley-Zalabak, P. 1986. Communication proficiency and future training needs of the female professional: self-assessment vs. supervisors' evaluations. *Hum. Relat.* 39:891–902

Stewart, R. 1984. The nature of management? A problem for management education. *J. Manage. Stud.* 21:323–30

Streker-Seeborg, I., Seeborg, M. C., Zegeye, A. 1984. The impact of nontraditional training on the occupational attainment of women. *J. Hum. Resources* 19:452–71

Suzuki, N. 1986. Problems and prospects of Japanese companies' training programmes. *Asia Pac. J. Manage.* 3:110–20

Swierczek, F. W., Carmichael, L. 1985. Assessing training needs: a skills approach.

Public Personnel Manage. 14:259–74

Tanaka, H. 1980. The Japanese method of preparing today's graduate to become tomorrow's manager. *Pers. J.* 109–12

Taylor, F. W. 1911. *The Principles of Scientific Management.* New York: Harper

Tucker, F. D. 1985. A study of the training needs of older workers: implications for human resources development planning. *Publ. Personnel Manage.* 14:85–95

U. K. Dept. Employment. 1971. *Glossary of Training Terms.* London: HMSO

Weekley, J., Brush, D. H. 1987. The effects of rater training on performance rating accuracy and rater attributions.

Wexley, K. N. 1984. Personnel training. *Ann. Rev. Psychol.* 35:519–51

Wexley, K. N., Baldwin, T. T. 1986a. Management development. In *1986 Yearly Review of Management of the Journal of Management*, ed. J. G. Hunt, J. D. Blair, 12(2):277–94

Wexley, K. N., Baldwin, T. T. 1986b. Posttraining strategies for facilitating positive transfer: an empirical exploration. *Acad. Manage. J.* 29:503–20

Wexley, K. N., Latham, G. P. 1981. *Developing and Training Human Resources in Organizations.* Glenview, Ill: Scott, Foresman

Wexley, K. N., Sanders, R. E., Yukl, G. A. 1973. Training interviewers to eliminate contrast effects in employment interviews. *J. Appl. Psychol.* 57:233–36

Zedeck, S., Cascio, W. F. 1984. Psychological issues in personnel decisions. *Ann. Rev. Psychol.* 35:461–518

Ann. Rev. Psychol. 1988. 39:583–607
Copyright © 1988 by Annual Reviews Inc. All rights reserved

ADOLESCENT DEVELOPMENT

Anne C. Petersen

Department of Individual and Family Studies, The Pennsylvania State University, University Park, Pennsylvania 16802

CONTENTS

INTRODUCTION

This is a propitious time for the first article on adolescence in this series. Although scholars have written about adolescents for centuries, and a developmental phase called adolescence was identified at the beginning of this century, research on adolescence has been meager. Currently, however, many

583

scientists are at work on topics relevant to adolescent development. The great societal interest in adolescence and youth in the late 1960s and early 1970s may have helped to stimulate this activity. For example, an increase in the number of textbooks on the subject presumably reflects an increase in the number of courses on adolescence. The current cohort of adolescence researchers are likely to have been in college or graduate school during the years of peak societal interest. Current adolescence researchers, few of whom had mentors who studied adolescence, have brought to this topic rigorous expertise in other relevant areas.

One index of the nature and significance of prior research on adolescence is the coverage of this topic in previous *Annual Review of Psychology* volumes. The present article is the first devoted entirely to adolescence. Only a few previous articles devoted enough discussion to adolescence to warrant a heading. This lack of attention was perhaps appropriate, given the nature and quantity of research. Most relevant earlier research fell into one of two categories: (*a*) studies on behavioral or psychological processes that happened to use adolescent subjects, or (*b*) descriptive accounts of particular groups of adolescents, such as high school students or delinquents.

Basic theoretical and empirical advances in several areas have permitted the advance of research on adolescence. Some areas of behavioral science from which adolescence researchers have drawn are life-span developmental psychology, life-course sociology, social support, stress and coping, and cognitive development; important contributing areas in the biomedical sciences include endocrinology and adolescent medicine. The recent maturation to adolescence of subjects in major longitudinal growth studies (e.g. Baumrind 1985; Block & Gjerde 1987) has also contributed to the topic's empirical knowledge base.

Certain forces have impeded the scientific study of adolescence as well. Belief in the importance of early experience focused attention for decades on infancy and early childhood (e.g. Brim & Kagan 1980; Clarke & Clarke 1976). In addition, powerful beliefs about adolescence have undermined systematic work. For example, adolescents are often portrayed in the media as noisy, obnoxious, dirty, inarticulate, rebellious, and so forth. Such portrayals not only communicate to adolescents how they are expected to behave but also create expectations in the research community. The problems of psychology in gaining credibility as a science, presumably reflecting the belief that psychological science only consists of providing evidence for what your grandmother always knew, are all floridly manifested in research on adolescence. Despite the paucity of research on this topic, most people believe they know what adolescence is like and are unreceptive to findings that challenge their beliefs (Brooks-Gunn & Petersen 1984).

Major Areas of Current Scientific Activity

In order best to communicate the flavor of current research on adolescence, I focus on a few of the many areas in which there is important new work. This approach necessitates omitting several areas of research, but fortunately there are good textbooks and handbooks on adolescence for readers who would like to see a comprehensive review or who have interests in a topic omitted here (e.g. Adelson 1980; Conger & Petersen 1984; Santrock 1987; Steinberg 1985; Van Hasselt & Hersen 1987).

Three major areas in which there has been a great deal of recent psychological research on adolescence include: (a) adjustment or turmoil, (b) puberty and its effects, and (c) adolescent-family relations. All three areas have long traditions of work, though in each case the current work is of a different nature, in part because of technological advances. For example, research on the biological changes of puberty was advanced by the development of radioimmunoassay as a technique for measuring hormones; psychological research on puberty was then stimulated by the exciting biological findings. Similarly, parent-adolescent interaction research has been aided by audio and video technology, especially when accompanied by computer monitoring and storage of information on-line.

It is important to note that current research on adolescence is inherently interdisciplinary. Perhaps related to the increasing incorporation of other disciplinary perspectives into psychology over the past 20 years, the field of adolescent psychology has developed with important contributions from biology, sociology, anthropology, and applied areas such as medicine (especially psychiatry and pediatrics). There is exchange and cross-fertilization of ideas among multidisciplinary researchers of adolescence in our research meetings and publications. This has surely arisen because of prevailing conceptual perspectives, such as that from life-span (e.g. Baltes et al 1980) and ecological (Bronfenbrenner 1979) perspectives on developmental psychology, drawing our attention to the multifaceted nature of lives and their contexts.

Definitions and Key Concepts

Age is the most convenient marker for developmental changes and phases but, as many have noted (e.g. Featherman & Peterson 1986; Neugarten 1979; Wohlwill 1973), chronological age does not appropriately index many developmental phenomena. Therefore, for each developmental domain, researchers typically identify the best developmental markers, and individual change is considered within the framework of each set of markers. For example, beginning puberty is a major developmental milestone of adolescence, considered by many as the developmental change that signals one's transition into adolescence from childhood (e.g. Brooks-Gunn & Petersen

1984). Thus, we might conclude that pubertal change is the best way to index adolescent development. It is probably not appropriate, however, to consider pubertal development as sole developmental marker in adolescence because of the strong organization of the period accomplished by the school in our society. This largely age-graded institution emphasizes the importance of chronological age, regardless of any other developmental status. In view of the salience of the social organization of schooling, and despite the great individual variability in various developmental statuses, such as puberty or cognitive development, it is convenient to identify some span of years as the scope of this discussion of adolescence. Although a great many conventions are used by writers and researchers, I focus primarily on the second decade of life.

A concept central to much current developmental research, particularly on adolescence, is developmental transition. A developmental transition is a period of life in which there is a great deal of change, both within the individual and within the social environment (Eichorn et al 1981). Although the debate continues among developmentalists regarding the dominance of continuity versus discontinuity over the life course (e.g. Brim & Kagan 1980; Rutter 1987), an emerging perspective (e.g. Rutter 1986) focuses on the importance of considering both aspects. Within this framework, developmental transitions are thought to involve more discontinuity and less continuity than other periods. The movement from childhood to adolescence and from adolescence to adulthood have both been considered developmental transitions (Connell & Furman 1984; Petersen & Ebata 1987).

HISTORY OF RESEARCH ON ADOLESCENCE

Although some have claimed that adolescence is a twentieth-century invention (e.g. Aries 1962), reference to behavior stereotypic of adolescents may be found in the writings of both Plato (1953 translation) and Aristotle (1941 translation). After the regressive views on development characteristic of the Middle Ages, in which children were thought to be small adults, Rousseau (1911 translation) renewed the life-phase concepts of Plato and Aristotle, describing two phases that encompass our current view of adolescence.

Adolescence in the Twentieth Century

Hall (1904) is usually credited with being the first to identify adolescence as an important period in life and with the first writings on the psychology of adolescence. Hall's descriptions of adolescents were not based on research and were probably not representative of adolescence even at that time. Nevertheless, Hall's views of adolescence, which included the concept of storm and stress, had great influence on all writing about adolescence for the next 50 years or so. Hall (1904), influenced by Darwin's concepts of evolution, believed that development recapitulated evolution, with the developmental phase of adolescence recapitulating the period of emerging civilization. He generated particular controversy at the time with his view that physical development in adolescence was saltatory rather than continuous, and with his related view linking saltatory physical change to psychological turmoil (storm and stress). Although his views prevailed, both ideas were strongly challenged by other prominent psychologists of that time (e.g. Hollingworth 1928; Thorndike 1904).

Other psychologists included adolescence in their theoretical perspectives and often elaborated on Hall's concepts. Lewin (1939), for example, developed the analogy between adolescence and marginality in the society. Psychoanalytic writers, such as A. Freud (1958), amplified Hall's emphasis on turmoil as a necessary aspect of adolescent development.

Mid-Century Research on Adolescence

By mid-century, scholars had begun to integrate more positive aspects of development into their stage theories. A prime example is Piaget's work on cognitive development, which involves the development of abstract reasoning during adolescence (Inhelder & Piaget 1958). Erikson's (1950, 1968) concept of stages involving key crises over the life span emphasized the development of an identity as a central task of adolescence. Mead's (1950, 1953) research on growing up in Samoa and New Guinea was also influential in promoting the view that the adolescent transition was not necessarily tumultuous.

The most important research on adolescents prior to the current period was probably that emanating from the major US growth studies, such as the California studies (e.g. Eichorn et al 1981) and the Fels Longitudinal Study (e.g. Kagan & Moss 1962). These studies focused less on specific age periods and their particular problems and phenomena than on more general aspects of growth and development (e.g. physical growth, social growth, intellectual growth, etc). They nevertheless provided a great deal of basic information about adolescence. For example, Bayer & Bayley (1959) described the adolescent growth spurt and the development of secondary sex characteristics. The psychological and social correlates of these changes and their relative timing were described in a series of articles (e.g. Jones & Bayley 1950; Jones & Mussen 1958; Mussen & Jones 1957).

Current Research on Adolescence

Current research on adolescent development differs from earlier research in important respects. First, the quantity has dramatically increased, as evidenced by (*a*) the number of researchers identifying themselves with this area; (*b*) the existence of a new professional society, the Society for Research on

Adolescence; and (c) the increased numbers of journal articles, new journals, and edited volumes on adolescence.

More important, and perhaps explaining the quantitative increase, are the qualitative changes in adolescent research. As with much developmental research, there has been a shift in adolescent-development research from stage-oriented approaches to process-oriented approaches (e.g. Keating 1987). For example, many developmental domains, from secondary sex characteristic development to cognitive development, were conceptualized as involving a series of invariant stages. Although the validity of some of these progressions has not been questioned [e.g. secondary sex characteristic development or "Tanner staging" (Tanner 1974)], validity has been an issue in other domains (e.g. identity development). Even with developmental change such as secondary sex characteristic development, the underlying process is assumed to involve fairly continuous, progressive changes, rather than transformations from one qualitative stage to another. Development in many areas is now conceptualized as involving more continual change, often even involving regressions as a typical aspect. This is true even with pubertal development, in which regressions are infrequent but possible.[1] Furthermore, with some stage conceptions there is little evidence of any progression through stages, as with identity development (e.g. Marcia 1980). Although there is still some controversy on the issue of the underlying course of development—qualitative stages versus more quantitative progressions (with possible regressions)—there seems to be accumulating evidence that stages inaccurately depict the processes involved in some domains, and in others represent at best a categorical abstraction of what is actually a more continual process.

The more process-oriented approaches of current research on adolescent development also recognize that these processes must involve interactions between the individual and other people and contexts (e.g. Lerner 1981). A return to recognition of the person-environment interaction is probably attributable to the significant contributions of the life-span and ecological perspectives on human development (e.g. Baltes et al 1980; Bronfenbrenner 1979). To fully understand even a biological developmental process such as puberty it is important to know about the effects of nutrition, exercise, and the norms of the broader society regarding weight and body shape (e.g. Attie et al 1987). Similarly, after decades of neglecting the situation and environment, work in cognitive development is currently turning toward context effects to explain developmental findings (e.g. Keating 1987). With processes such as

---

[1]In precocious puberty, for example, the goal of treatment is to reverse the development of secondary sex characteristics that has taken place prematurely. The reversibility of these processes through intervention is likely to have a natural analog, albeit in milder form (Warren 1980). For example, different rates of maturation of the two breasts are sometimes seen, with occasional regression of the more mature one (E. J. Susman, personal communication).

social development, the importance of the family, peers, and the broader social environment is even clearer. Current adolescence research reflects an emphasis on context effects. Three areas exemplifying current research are reviewed next.

ADOLESCENT ADJUSTMENT VS TURMOIL

Hall and the psychoanalytic theorists (e. g. Blos 1962; A. Freud 1958; Hall 1904) had pervasive influence on the research on adolescent mental health. These theoretical perspectives established the still prevalent belief in normative turmoil during adolescence—that is, the belief that significant difficulties during adolescence represent normal healthy development. As a result, difficulties during adolescence were not investigated and typically were not treated in any extensive way when they occurred.

In the 1960s and early 1970s, several research reports appeared that challenged the previous beliefs and the resulting research and treatment practices. These studies documented the absence of significant psychological difficulties among at least some, if not the majority, of adolescents (Bandura 1964; Douvan & Adelson 1966; Grinker et al 1962; Offer 1969; Offer & Offer 1975). The Offers (1975), in particular, went beyond verifying that there existed adolescents without significant difficulties, to specify the developmental routes taken by the boys they studied. Three routes typified most boys: continuous growth, surgent growth (characterized by alternating periods of difficulties and easier times), and tumultuous growth. Roughly 23% of the boys were characterized as continuous, 35% as surgent, and 21% as tumultuous. Thus, a minority of boys showed the pattern thought previously to typify the period.

At the same time, research demonstrated that difficulties manifested in adolescence often continued into adulthood. Two studies (Rutter 1980; Rutter et al 1976; Weiner & DelGaudio 1976) reported evidence that these difficulties frequently developed into serious mental illness. It was clearly inappropriate to assume that psychological difficulties in adolescence were normal and something that young people grew out of.

Early Adolescence

By the mid-1970s an interest in early adolescence had emerged (e.g., Hamburg 1974; Lipsitz 1977). It was thought that the studies described above had not identified normative turmoil because it occurred earlier as a result of the effects of pubertal hormones (e.g. Kestenberg 1968). This hypothesis was consistent with the research identifying a dip in self-esteem in early adolescence (Simmons et al 1973).

The early adolescent turmoil hypothesis led to a set of new studies examining the development of mental health in relation to the social and biological changes of early adolescence. The first research program addressing this question was begun by sociologist Simmons, recently culminating in a volume written with Blyth (Simmons & Blyth 1987). A second research program begun in 1978 by the present author, initially in collaboration with psychiatrist Offer, is also nearing completion (Ebata & Petersen submitted; Petersen 1987a,b; Petersen & Ebata 1987). Other studies are now elaborating the conceptualizations and replicating basic findings (e.g. Nottelmann et al 1987a).

This research has demonstrated that although early adolescence may be a challenging life period, young people traverse it with varying degrees of difficulty, just as in later periods of life. For example, we find that about 11% of young adolescents have serious chronic difficulties, 32% have more intermittent and probably situational difficulties, while 57% have basically positive, healthy development during early adolescence (Ebata 1987; Petersen & Ebata 1987). These percentages, when compared to percentages describing the extent of psychological difficulties among high school youth and older youngsters (e.g. Offer & Offer 1975), suggest that development during early adolescence is characterized by fewer rather than more difficulties. Because these studies used different measures and statistical analyses, definitive conclusions await further replication.

Given the belief that adolescence is characterized by moodiness, it is odd that there is little research on this topic. Larson and colleagues (Larson et al 1980), using a method of random time sampling with automatic paging devices, found more mood variability among high school students than among adults. In his current research, Larson (personal communication) finds a linear increase in mood variability from the fifth to the ninth grade among girls but not boys. Thus, in the little extant research on moodiness, there appears to be no support for the hypothesis that early adolescence involves more normative turmoil and difficulties than other life phases.

There is still a great deal to be learned about the development of mental health or psychological difficulties during adolescence. If not all adolescents experience difficulties, which ones do develop problems? Gender differences appear to be important here. We find, for example, that adolescent boys with psychological difficulties are likely to have had problems in childhood; girls, in contrast, are more likely to first manifest psychological difficulties in adolescence (Ebata 1987). As others have found (e.g. Rutter 1986), girls appear to increase in depressive affect over the adolescent period, so that by age 17 they have significantly poorer emotional tone and well-being, and more depressive affect than boys (Petersen et al 1987b). The causes of different developmental patterns for boys and girls remain to be elucidated; but genes, hormones, and environmental stressors have been implicated (Rutter 1986).

One hypothesis that may encompass the findings is that anxiety plays a role in the development of depression. Suomi (1987) has proposed that challenging situations together with greater arousal in such situations may produce anxiety; individuals who feel little control or efficacy may subsequently become depressed. Both situational factors (e.g. uncontrollable situations) and personal response styles [e.g. negative expectancies (Seligman & Peterson 1986) or low perceived self-efficacy (Bandura 1982, 1987)] may play important causal roles in this process. To relate this hypothesis to the findings cited above, it has been found previously that achievement situations are more likely to produce anxiety responses in males whereas interpersonal situations are more likely to produce anxiety in females (Frankenhaeuser 1983). Girls are more likely than boys to experience particular challenging situations of pubertal change accompanied by simultaneous school change or parental divorce (Petersen & Ebata 1987). Experiencing more challenge and responding less positively to challenge (e.g. Peterson & Seligman 1984) may render girls more susceptible to anxiety, and thus to depressive affect, in adolescence. Other behavioral indexes suggest girls' greater susceptibility to affective disturbance. For example, Kirmil-Gray et al (1984) found that significantly more adolescent girls than boys reported sleep problems, and poor sleepers exhibited more cognitive and behavioral signs of daytime stress than good sleepers. Poor sleep, then, may be a marker of greater difficulties in adolescent girls. The gender difference in negative self-appraisal is widely found by middle adolescence (e.g. Gove & Herb 1974; Kandel & Davies 1982; Petersen et al 1987b; Weissman & Klerman 1977). Thus, the anxiety hypothesis for depressive feelings is consistent with the findings on gender differences in developmental patterns during adolescence.

Development of Mental Health in Adolescence: Discrepant Views

Although the more recent normative research on adolescent mental health reveals that some, if not most, adolescents traverse the period without significant psychological difficulties, and that indicators such as self-esteem become steadily more positive over adolescence (e.g. Damon & Hart 1982), the statistics on various other indicators make it clear that the proportion of young people who experience difficulties increases during the adolescent decade of life. For example, the prevalence of suicide, of various kinds of substance abuse, and of diagnoses of several other psychological disorders increases with age during adolescence (e.g. Green & Horton 1982; Petersen & Hamburg 1986). The percentage of young people with diagnosable difficulties increases from childhood to adolescence (Kaplan et al 1984; Rutter et al 1976; Weiner 1980). The rosy picture of increasingly positive development over adolescence from representative samples of subjects seems at odds with the statistics on increasing casualties of the period. How can these two pictures be reconciled?

The answer probably lies in the nature of the samples. Although the statistics document that troubles for some youth increase with age, none of the indicators identify a majority of adolescents with difficulties. Similarly, although the psychoanalytic and clinical literatures frequently describe the kind of adolescent we have known, worked with, or perhaps been, such portraits represent a biased sampling of the population.

The representative samples are not without problems either. They are probably not useful for identifying or understanding those subgroups of youngsters who develop difficulties during adolescence. The minority of adolescents with psychological difficulties may become lost in the overall group patterns and statistics. Indeed, statistics describing central tendencies in the overall distributions may represent no one in particular. Our findings indicate an increasing divergence over the adolescent decade between those who can cope with the challenges of adolescent transition and those who cannot (Petersen & Ebata 1987; Petersen et al 1987a). The latter group may internalize their difficulties in depression or externalize them in delinquent behavior or substance abuse. Thus, the pictures of adolescence derived from clinical and normative developmental studies may describe two distinct groups of young people. The emerging field of developmental psychopatholo-gy (e.g. Cicchetti 1984; Rolf et al 1987; Rutter 1986) may help to integrate clinical and developmental perspectives on adolescent mental health.

PUBERTY AND ITS EFFECTS IN EARLY ADOLESCENCE

During the mid-1970s two reports focused on the potential importance of early adolescence, the transition from childhood to adolescence; puberty plays a central role in this transition. Hamburg (1974) first drew attention to the possibility that early adolescence represented a critical transition. Shortly thereafter, Lipsitz (1977) reported on this age period for the Ford Foundation. (Calling attention to the dearth of programs for, and research on, this age group, Lipsitz titled her volume *Growing Up Forgotten.*) These two pieces stimulated a great deal of research that included puberty as a central variable.

Pubertal Change

The development of radioimmunoassay methodology in the late 1960s made it possible to study the hormones presumably responsible for gender differentia-tion and reproductive maturation (Faiman & Winter 1974). Growth studies had already documented the increased rate of growth characteristic of puberty (e.g. Bayer & Bayley 1959); but until the 1960s the endocrine basis for differences between men and women had not been demonstrated, and the endocrinology of pubertal change had not been described.

Yet pubertal hormones were hypothesized to cause adolescent behavior, turmoil, moodiness, difficulties in parent-adolescent relationships, and hypersexuality (e.g. Kestenberg 1968). It became important, particularly in the social climate of the late 1960s and early 1970s, to test these hypotheses.

Endocrine studies documented the increases in pubertal hormones that generally paralleled changes in the development of secondary sex characteristics (e.g. Gupta et al 1975). The most exciting work in pubertal endocrinology has investigated the mechanisms that control puberty (e.g. Grumbach et al 1974). Research on precocious puberty (e.g. Comite et al 1987), a problem in which children as young as four or five develop secondary sex characteristics such as breasts or pubic hair, revealed that the mechanisms that control pubertal change develop prenatally. An apparent test of the system, involving the attainment of adult endocrine values, occurs just prior to birth (e.g. Grumbach et al 1974). These high levels are then suppressed until, in normal children, pubertal hormone levels begin increasing around seven years of age, with visible somatic changes typically appearing four or five years later. These somatic changes appear a year or two earlier in girls than in boys, depending on the specific characteristic examined (Marshall & Tanner 1969, 1970).

Pubertal change is a universal characteristic of adolescence and involves the most extensive and rapid change in postnatal life (Grave 1974). Perhaps more important than the physical changes themselves are the responses of the self and others to the physical changes. Adolescents are acutely aware of their changing selves.

Two aspects of pubertal change may be important to psychological functioning: *pubertal status,* the changes experienced by every individual as he or she matures physically; and *pubertal timing,* the timing of these changes relative to same-aged peers. Pubertal status effects could be direct, or they could be indirect effects mediated by social and psychological responses of the individual or of others in the social environment (Petersen & Taylor 1980). Although timing effects could have a direct biological origin (e.g. if earlier pubertal timing produced changes different from those of later timing),[2] they are most likely to result from the interaction between the timing of puberty relative to that of peers and the psychological and social responses of the individual and others.

Other processes may have an impact on psychological outcomes as well. Extreme asynchrony among the pubertal changes could produce anxiety in the

---

[2]There is some evidence, for example, that late developers have longer limbs, resulting from longer prepubertal growth of the long bones (e.g. Tanner 1974).

individual and perhaps physical difficulties as well (Eichorn 1975). For example, feet typically grow before other limbs, producing a clumsy individual for a time (Tanner 1974).

Puberty and Psychological Functioning

Research linking pubertal change and psychological status has thus far found little evidence for pervasive pubertal effects on psychological difficulties. Puberty seems to affect several psychological variables, but these effects are specific and proximal. They are not uniformly negative but may enhance functioning as well. Finally, the effects on boys and girls are different.

Only a few studies have examined the hypothesis that pubertal change increases psychological difficulties. In our research, which controls for age effects, we found that advancing pubertal status was related to enhanced body image and improved moods for boys, but decreased feelings of attractiveness for girls (Crockett & Petersen 1987). As pubertal status advanced, both boys and girls became more interested in the other sex, and conflict increased in girls' relationships with their parents. In analyses of pubertal timing effects (Petersen & Crockett 1985), we found improved psychological adjustment for later-developing boys and girls.

These results correspond well with those of others, as long as pubertal status is not confounded with chronological age. For example, Simmons & Blyth have found that early pubertal development is related to better body-image and higher self-esteem for boys (Blyth et al 1981), whereas for girls later development is associated with these positive psychological outcomes (Simmons et al 1979). These researchers hypothesize (Simmons et al 1983) that pubertal change is most stressful when it puts the early adolescent in a deviant status relative to his or her peers or when the changes are not seen as advantageous or desirable. Early maturing boys tend to be more muscular, and this leads to social benefits such as strength and athletic ability. In contrast, the pubertal changes manifested by girls (e.g. weight gain) are in conflict with desired goals of this time (e.g. thinness). In a similar vein, Brooks-Gunn & Warren (1988), in their study of girls, found that pubertal events noticeable by others (e.g. height and breast development) are more likely to affect psychological functioning than nonpublic changes (e.g. pubic hair growth). Furthermore, early maturers and those unprepared for menarche were most likely to have negative psychological outcomes (Ruble & Brooks-Gunn 1982).

While many researchers acknowledge the importance of the social forces that mediate between pubertal development and psychological outcomes, other more direct links are possible. In a study of early adolescent boys, Rutter (1980) reported that almost none of the prepubescent sample reported any depressive feelings, whereas almost one third of the postpubescent boys did. The pubescent boys were intermediate in comparison to these groups. Rutter suggested that puberty rather than age may be the crucial factor in the development of psychological disorders; however, he acknowledged that "whether this means an endocrine influence or the effects of the psychological adaptations which are consequent upon sexual maturation" (p. 21) remains to be discovered. Other research has attempted to address this issue.

Nottelmann et al (1987b) approach the issue from a biological perspective by focusing on endogenous variables such as hormone levels. They report that, especially for boys, adjustment problems were associated with a profile that may reflect later maturation (i.e. for boys, low sex steroid levels, lower pubertal stage, and higher adrenal androgen levels in combination with greater chronological age). For both boys and girls, relatively high levels of adrenal androgen were associated with adjustment difficulties. Because adrenal androgen level is responsive to environmental stressors, the profile of lower levels of sex steroids and higher levels of both adrenal androgen and adjustment problems was interpreted as reflecting stress-related processes. In this case, the stress of later maturation may result from self-comparisons with same-age peers or from the effects of adrenal and gonadal hormones.

Therefore, research suggests that puberty does not bring psychological turmoil. Pubertal hormones may affect the behavior of boys, particularly aggression (Olweus 1979; Susman et al 1987). They may also affect sexual interest (e.g. Meyer-Bahlburg et al 1985; Udry et al 1985, 1986). Most of the observed effects, however, appear to be mediated by or interact with social and psychological factors (Brooks-Gunn & Warren 1987). Becoming pubertal has meaning for one's emerging status as an adult, socially and sexually. Cultural standards for attractiveness in women, particularly the emphasis on thinness, appear to be implicated in the negative relationship between becoming pubertal and body image in girls (e.g. Faust 1983; Garner & Garfinkel 1980). Otherwise, developing adolescents like most pubertal changes.

These general findings do not apply to certain subgroups of adolescents, for whom puberty may hold liabilities. For example, Simmons and colleagues (Zakin et al 1984) have found that attractive girls were more anxious about becoming pubertal than were less attractive girls. Adolescents whose occupational goals involve a particular body shape may be distressed when puberty produces some other shape. Young women who aspire to be models or dancers, and both boys and girls who engage in particular sports (e.g. runners, wrestlers), may find that puberty brings disappointment, and perhaps subsequent psychological difficulties. Patterns of intense exercise together with restriction of food intake during puberty appear to influence body shape. Brooks-Gunn & Warren (1985) found, for example, that ballet dancers had longer limbs and later menarche than their nondancing mothers and sisters.

Future research on puberty will continue to elucidate the mechanisms of its effects on specific subgroups. The literature is already sufficient to suggest several hypotheses. For example, it seems reasonable to hypothesize that children who are having difficulties with issues of control, particularly if they are struggling to attain greater control of their lives, would be likely to have negative reactions to pubertal change, a process typically beyond the control of the individual. On the biological side of the process, newer methods of endocrine assay afford the possibility of specifying the hormones most responsible for effects, both physical and psychological. Social factors can be examined with pubertal change as well, to identify which family, peer, or cultural contexts produce which kinds of developmental processes (e.g. Magnusson et al 1985; Magnusson 1987).

ADOLESCENT-FAMILY INTERACTIONS

Although the relationship of adolescents to their families has been of interest for some time, the recent research has benefited from the increase in attention to adolescence as a period of life and from technological advances (e.g. computer-linked audio or video capability, which permits more efficient access to family interactions). Recent adolescent-family research is very much in the tradition of contextually based life-span psychology (e.g. Baltes et al 1980; Bronfenbrenner 1979; Lerner & Spanier 1978), examining the reciprocal effects of the family on the developing individual (e.g. Block et al 1986; Cooper et al 1983; Hauser et al 1984) and of the developing individual on family processes (e.g. Steinberg 1981; Steinberg & Hill 1978). In addition to its consistency with the life-span perspective on human development (e.g. Lerner 1984), the nature of the current adolescent-family research is also consistent with recent conceptualizations of parent-child relationships (e.g. Maccoby & Martin 1983).

Adolescent-Family Conflict

The traditional belief is that adolescents and their parents suffer from a "generation gap." Research has shown this belief to be incorrect (e.g. Lerner et al 1975). For example, Kandel & Lesser (1972) found that parents and their children had more similar values and attitudes than did adolescents and their friends. Adolescent-peer similarities are typically found in areas of "adolescent culture" (e.g. dress, music).

The view that adolescent-parent relationships are inevitably stormy has been advanced primarily by psychoanalytic theorists (e.g. Adelson & Doehrman 1980; Blos 1970), but it has not been supported by the research (see Montemayor 1983 for a review). The origins of adolescent-parent conflict were once thought to be adolescent difficulties, needs, or developmental changes (e.g. Blos 1962; Erikson 1968; Hall 1904), but parental factors, too—e.g. parents' midlife status (Chilman 1968; Hill 1980) and maternal control (Turner 1980)—have now been identified as playing a role in adolescent-parent stress.

Most recently it is typical to consider the family system in relation to the developmental status of family members. In particular, the developmental changes and needs in the adolescent are thought to disrupt the functioning of the family system, requiring a readjustment to achieve a new homeostasis. The limited existing research suggests that there is an increase in parent-adolescent conflict during early adolescence, with subsequent declines until the adolescent leaves the parental home (Montemayor 1983; Smetana 1987). The manifestations of parent-adolescent conflict have changed little over the past century (e.g. Caplow & Bahr 1979; Lynd & Lynd 1929), involving primarily the mundane aspects of life (e.g. chores, hours). The potentially explosive issues (e.g. sex) tend not to be discussed.

The hypothesis that parent-adolescent conflict is basically healthy is also unsupported by the findings. High levels of conflict are related to the adolescent's moving away (Gottlieb & Chafetz 1977), running away (Blood & D'Angelo 1974; Shellow et al 1967), joining a religious cult (Ullman 1982), marrying or becoming pregnant early (McKenry et al 1979), dropping out of school (Bachman et al 1971), developing psychiatric disorders (Rutter et al 1976), attempting suicide (Jacobs 1971), and abusing drugs (e.g. Kandel et al 1978; McCubbin et al 1985).

New Adolescent-Family Research: Some Examples

Cooper & Grotevant (Cooper et al 1983; Grotevant & Cooper 1985, 1986) have been investigating an old construct from psychoanalytic theory—individuation (e.g. Blos 1979)—in a new and interesting way. They define individuation in the family context as involving a balance between connectedness and individuality. Connectedness is conceptualized as mutuality (i.e. showing sensitivity or respect in relating to others) and permeability (i.e. expressing responsiveness and openness to others' ideas), while individuality is conceptualized as self-assertion (i.e. the expression of one's own views) and separateness (i.e. the expression of differences in views between self and others). These constructs were analyzed by discourse analysis, that is, the analysis of family conversations. The first 300 utterances in a family interaction task formed the data base. In a sample of high school seniors and their families, the investigators found that individuation, including both connectedness and individuality, was favorable for adolescent development in role-taking skill and identity development (Cooper et al 1983; Grotevant & Cooper 1985).

In similar research, Hauser and colleagues (Hauser et al 1984) have linked the use of enabling discourse (e.g. problem solving, empathy) to higher ego development in adolescents and their parents, while lower ego development was related to more constraining discourse (e.g. devaluing, withholding). The nature of adolescent patterns of discourse (i.e. whether discourse sequences progressed positively, regressed, terminated, or changed focus) was also related to the adolescent's level of ego development and to overall patterns of family interaction. These investigators are now attempting to study the longer-term development of family conversational style, adolescent ego development, and, especially, their interactions.

Pubertal Change and Family Interaction

One of the interesting areas of research integrating those discussed thus far concerns the effects on family interaction of a child's becoming pubertal. The primary hypothesis is that pubertal change signals emerging adult size, shape, and reproductive potential and that this new status affects the nature of the child's interactions with mother and father. The theoretical perspectives that have been used as the framework for examining this set of relationships range from sociobiology (e.g. Savins-Williams et al 1981; Steinberg 1981), to family process (e.g. Papini & Datan 1983), to gender role relationships (e.g. Hill et al 1985a,b).

The results show that in families with two biological parents present, boys engage in more conflict with parents as they reach the middle of the pubertal process (e.g. Hill et al 1985a,b; Steinberg 1981; Steinberg & Hill 1978). For girls results are mixed. Although results like those with boys were obtained in one study (Papini & Datan 1983). In other studies, girls experienced decreased levels of conflict and control with mothers as they reach the pubertal apex (Anderson et al 1986; Hill et al 1985a). Despite these gender variations, there is disequilibrium in the parent-child relationship for both boys and girls at the pubertal apex.

More research is needed to identify the aspects of the parent-child relationships that change, and why, but a common interpretation of these studies is that with the adolescent's increasing maturity and impending adult status, the adolescent-parent relationship needs to change. It is functional to begin to have more autonomy and responsibility within the family as one proceeds through adolescence, and puberty is an appropriate signal for the timing of this change.

This research has identified a normative period of adolescent-parent conflict that is earlier than the stereotype. The peak of pubertal change is roughly around 12 years of age in girls and 13 years in boys. The stereotype of peak adolescent-parent conflict is with the already mature and fully grown high school student. It may be that difficulties in renegotiating the relationship in early adolescence (e.g. if parents are authoritarian and unwilling to grant more autonomy) lead to increased conflict over the next few years, escalating into major difficulties by mid-adolescence.

Research with families involving stepparents or single parents suggests that pubertal effects on the adolescent-parent relationship are conditional on parental composition. For example, Hetherington and colleagues (Anderson et al 1986) found that the patterns were entirely different with stepfathers and single or remarried mothers. For both boys and girls in single-mother or mother/stepfather families, there was less mother-child conflict at the pubertal apex and a generally more quiescent transition. The authors interpret this result in terms of other results on the effects of divorce: Children in divorced families are expected to behave more maturely and responsibly than children in nondivorced families. A transformation in the parent-child relationship, like that otherwise occurring with puberty, may have taken place soon after the divorce. No relationship between pubertal status and conflict with stepfathers was seen; in general, stepfathers appeared to be disengaged from their stepchildren. Because these remarriages all took place within a year of data collection, the authors reason that pubertal effects were suppressed by the more potent process of incorporating the stepfather into the family. These results suggest that the family context at puberty's onset influences the nature and intensity of adolescent-parent interactions. The strong effects of parental composition have been seen in other research as well (e.g. Dornbusch et al 1985).

OTHER AREAS OF ACTIVE WORK

Three additional areas merit brief summaries: (*a*) cognition and achievement, (*b*) social development and peer relationships, and (*c*) problem behavior.

Cognition and Achievement

There has always been a substantial amount of research on the cognitive development and achievement of adolescents (e.g. Bayley 1949; Inhelder & Piaget 1958). Recent research has provided new information on developmental trends. School achievement, in terms of marks assigned by teachers, appears to decline over the adolescent years (e.g. Schulenberg et al 1984; Simmons & Blyth 1987). Grade decline is generally believed to result from increasingly stringent grading practices. In contrast, cognitive development and cognitive abilities increase over the adolescent years, with particular increase in the capacity to think abstractly (e.g. Keating & Clark 1980; Martorano 1977; Petersen 1983). Growth in mental age, or intelligence, is typically thought to slow during adolescence (Sternberg & Powell 1983).

The possibility that cognitive change in adolescence is linked to pubertal change has been repeatedly examined (e.g. Kohen-Raz 1974; Shuttleworth

1939). Interestingly, a recent metaanalysis of the relationship between pubertal timing and IQ test performance supports the view that early maturers have a small but consistent advantage (Newcombe & Dubas 1987). Waber's intriguing hypothesis (1976, 1977) that the earlier pubertal timing of girls produced sex differences in cognition has not been supported by subsequent work (reviewed by Linn & Petersen 1985; Newcombe & Dubas 1987). There may be a small effect of pubertal timing on spatial abilities, such that later maturers are more spatially adept, particularly on tasks that require disembedding (Newcombe & Dubas 1987). Explanations for these maturation effects remain inconclusive.

Social Development and Peer Relationships

Adolescence involves systematic changes in social development and the nature of peer relationships. The peer group increases in size and complexity (Crockett et al 1984), with adolescents spending and enjoying more time with chosen friends than with classmates (Csikszentmihalyi & Larson 1984). Adolescents, relative to children, are more involved and intimate with peers, increasingly sharing thoughts and feelings (Camarena et al submitted; Hartup 1983; Youniss & Smollar 1985).

Gottman & Mettetal's (1987) analysis of adolescents' conversations provides interesting and rich data on the processes involved with friendship. Their results led them to hypothesize that "developmental change in friendships occurs because of changes in the affective competence demands of the ecological niches children are forced by our culture to occupy and to maneuver within" (p. 193). Salient ecological niches of adolescents are school as well as the cross-sex and same-sex peer cultures. These researchers further propose that qualitative change in cognitive competence accompanies the increasing social competence involved with friendship change.

Problem Behavior

As noted earlier, several kinds of behavior thought to be problematic increase over the adolescent period. Research has focused especially on drug and alcohol use, cigarette smoking, sexual behavior, and delinquency (e.g. Jessor & Jessor 1977). Most of these behaviors would not be alarming in adults but are perceived as inappropriate for youngsters (Petersen 1982). Excessive engagement in many behaviors, of course, can be problematic at any age.

In a very interesting program of research, Silbereisen and colleagues (e.g. Silbereisen et al 1986, 1988) have proposed that these so-called problem behaviors are in fact purposive, self-regulating, and aimed at coping with problems of development. Therefore, they play a constructive developmental role, at least over the short term (Kaplan 1980; Silbereisen et al 1988). Early sexual activity and even early childbearing may have a similar function (Petersen et al 1987a). Nevertheless, the negative consequences of these behaviors over the longer term, often with lasting developmental effects, can be clearly documented (e.g. Baumrind & Moselle 1985; Furstenberg et al 1987).

CONCLUDING COMMENT

This sampling of recent research on adolescence cannot do justice to the large and varied body of current work. At most, a sampling can convey that there is systematic work addressing questions of both scientific and practical significance. Current research on adolescence will not only aid understanding of this particular phase of life, it also may illuminate development more generally. Because there is so much change during adolescence, and these changes require effective coping on the part of the individual, the processes involved are likely to be ones needed to respond to challenges throughout life. Furthermore, one could hypothesize that adolescence differs from earlier years in the nature of challenges encountered and in the capacity of the individual to respond effectively to challenge. If this hypothesis is correct, adolescence will be the first phase of life requiring, and presumably stimulating, mature patterns of functioning that persist throughout life. Conversely, failure to cope effectively with the challenges of adolescence may represent deficiencies in the individual that bode ill for subsequent development. Continued research on the biological, psychological, and social factors that affect the developmental course over adolescence will surely inform future knowledge on these questions.

ACKNOWLEDGMENTS

Preparation of this paper was supported in part by grant number MH30252/38142. The assistance of Joy Barger, Phame Camarena, Cleo Campbell, Pamela Sarigiani, Nina White, and especially Julie Graber is gratefully acknowledged. I also thank all of the colleagues who shared their recent articles as well as Albert Bandura, J. Brooks-Gunn, Richard Lerner, Michael Rutter, and Rainer Silbereisen for their helpful suggestions on an earlier draft.

Literature Cited

Adelson, J., ed. 1980. *Handbook of the Psychology of Adolescence*. New York: Wiley. 624 pp.

Adelson, J., Doehrman, M. J. 1980. The psychodynamic approach to adolescence. See Adelson 1980, pp. 99–116

Anderson, E. R., Hetherington, E. M., Clingempeel, W. G. 1986. *Pubertal status and its influence on the adaptation to remarriage.* Presented at Soc. Res. Adol., 1st, Madison, Wis.

Aries, P. 1962. *Centuries of Childhood: A Social History on Family Life*. Transl. R.

Baldick. New York: Random House (Vintage Books)

Aristotle. 1941. Ethica nicomachea. In *The Basic Works of Aristotle*, ed. R. McKeon, Transl. W. D. Ross. New York: Random House

Attie, I., Brooks-Gunn, J., Petersen, A. C. 1987. A developmental perspective on eating disorders and eating problems. In *Handbook of Developmental Psychopathology*, ed. M. Lewis, S. M. Miller. New York: Plenum. In press

Bachman, J. G., Green, S., Wirtanen, I. D.

1971. *Youth in Transition:* Vol. 3: *Dropping Out—Problem or Symptom.* Ann Arbor, Mich: Inst. Soc. Res. 250 pp.

Baltes, P. B., Reese, H. W., Lipsitt, L. P. 1980. Life-span developmental psychology. *Ann. Rev. Psychol.* 31:65–110

Bandura, A. 1964. The stormy decade: fact or fiction? *Psychol. Schools* 1:224–31

Bandura, A. 1982. Self-efficacy mechanism in human agency. *Am. Psychol.* 37:122–47

Bandura, A. 1987. Self-regulation of motivation and action through goal systems. In *Cognition, Motivation, and Affect: A Cognitive Science View,* ed. V. Hamilton, G. H. Bower, N. H. Fryda. Dordrecht:Martinus Nijhof. In press

Baumrind, D. 1985. Familial antecedents of adolescent drug use: a developmental perspective. In *Etiology of Drug Abuse: Implications for Prevention (NIDA Res. Monogr. No. 56),* ed. C. L. Jones, R. J. Battjes, pp. 13–44. Rockville, Md: Natl. Inst. Drug Abuse

Baumrind, D., Moselle, K. A. 1985. A developmental perspective on adolescent drug abuse. *Adv. Alcohol & Subst. Abuse* 4:41–67

Bayer, L. M., Bayley, N. 1959. *Growth Diagnosis.* Chicago: Univ. Chicago Press

Bayley, N. 1949. Consistency and variability in the growth of intelligence from birth to eighteen years. *J. Genet. Psychol.* 75:165–96

Block, J. H., Block, J., Gjerde, P. F. 1986. The personality of children prior to divorce: a prospective study. *Child Dev.* 57:827–40

Block, J. H., Gjerde, P. F. 1987. Depressive symptomatology in late adolescence: a longitudinal perspective on personality antecedents. See Rolf et al 1987

Blood, L., D'Angelo, R. 1974. A progress research report on value issues in conflict between runaways and their parents. *J. Mar. Fam.* 36:486–91

Blos, P. 1962. *On Adolescence: A Psychoanalytic Interpretation.* New York: Free Press. 269 pp.

Blos, P. 1970. *The Young Adolescent.* New York: Free Press. 252 pp.

Blos, P. 1979. *The Adolescent Passage.* New York: International Universities Press. 521 pp.

Blyth, D. A., Simmons, R. G., Bulcroft, R., Felt, D., VanCleave, E. F., Bush, D. M. 1981. The effects of physical development on self-image and satisfaction with body-image for early adolescent males. In *Research in Community and Mental Health,* ed. R. G. Simmons, 2:43–73. Greenwich, Conn: JAI Press

Brim, O. G., Kagan, J. 1980. *Constancy and Change in Human Development.* Cambridge, Mass: Harvard Univ. Press. 754 pp.

Bronfenbrenner, U. 1979. *The Ecology of Human Development: Experiments by Nature and Design.* Cambridge, Mass: Harvard Univ. Press. 330 pp.

Brooks-Gunn, J., Petersen, A. C., eds. 1983. *Girls at Puberty: Biological and Psychosocial Perspectives.* New York: Plenum. 341 pp.

Brooks-Gunn, J., Petersen, A. C. 1984. Problems in studying and defining pubertal events. *J. Youth Adol.* 13:181–96

Brooks-Gunn, J., Warren, M. P. 1985. Effects of delayed menarche in different contexts: dance and nondance students. *J. Youth Adol.* 14:285–300

Brooks-Gunn, J., Warren, M. P. 1987. *Biological contributions to affective expression in young adolescent girls.* Presented at Bien. Meet. Soc. Res. Child Dev., Baltimore

Brooks-Gunn, J., Warren, M. P. 1988. The psychological significance of secondary sexual characteristics in 9- to 11-year-old girls. *Child Dev.* In press

Caplow, T., Bahr, H. M. 1979. Half a century of change in adolescent attitudes: replication of a Middletown survey by the Lynds. *Publ. Opin. Q.* 1:17

Chilman, C. S. 1968. Families in development at mid-stage of the family life cycle. *Fam. Coord.* 17:297–331

Cicchetti, D. 1984. The emergence of developmental psychopathology. *Child Dev.* 55:1–7

Clarke, A. M., Clarke, A. D. B., eds. 1976. *Early Experience: Myth and Evidence.* New York: Free Press

Coates, T. J., Petersen, A. C., Perry, C., eds. 1982. *Promoting Adolescent Health: A Dialog on Research and Practice.* New York: Academic. 483 pp.

Comite, F., Prescovitz, O. H., Sonis, W. A., Hench, K., McNemar, A., Klein, R. P., Loriaux, D. L., Cutler, G. B. Jr. 1987. Premature adolescence: neuroendocrine and psychosocial studies. See Lerner & Foch 1987, pp. 155–72

Conger, J. J., Petersen, A. C. 1984. *Adolescence and Youth.* New York: Harper and Row. 732 pp. 3rd ed.

Connell, J. P., Furman, W. 1984. The study of transitions: conceptualization and methodological considerations. In *Continuity and Discontinuity in Development,* ed. R. Emde, R. Harmon. New York: Plenum Press. 418 pp.

Cooper, C., Grotevant, H., Condon, S. 1983. Individuality and connectedness in the family as a context for adolescent identity formation and role-taking skills. In *Adolescent Development in the Family,* ed. H. Grotevant, C. Cooper, pp. 43–60. San Francisco: Jossey-Bass. 116 pp.

Crockett, L. J., Losoff, M., Petersen, A. C.

1984. Perceptions of the peer group and friendship in early adolescence. *J. Early Adol.* 4:155–81

Crockett, L. J., Petersen, A. C. 1987. Pubertal status and psychosocial development: findings from the Early Adolescence Study. See Lerner & Foch 1987, pp. 173–88

Csikszentmihalyi, M., Larson, R. 1984. *Being Adolescent.* New York: Basic Books

Damon, W., Hart, D. 1982. The development of self-understanding from infancy through adolescence. *Child Dev.* 53:841–64

Dornbusch, S. M., Carlsmith, J. M., Bushwall, S. J., Ritter, P. L., Leiderman, H., Hastorf, A. H., Gross, R. T. 1985. Single parents, extended households, and the control of adolescents. *Child Dev.* 56:326–41

Douvan, E., Adelson, J. 1966. *The Adolescent Experience.* New York: Wiley

Ebata, A. T. 1987. *A longitudinal study of psychological distress during early adolescence.* PhD thesis. Penn. State Univ.

Eichorn, D. H. 1975. Asynchronizations in adolescent development. In *Adolescence in the Life Cycle: Psychological Change and Social Context,* ed. J. E. Dragastin, G. H. Elder Jr. Washington, DC: Hemisphere

Eichorn, D. H., Mussen, P. H., Clausen, J. A., Haan, N., Honzik, M. P. 1981. Overview. In *Present and Past in Middle Life,* ed. D. H. Eichorn, J. A. Clausen, N. Haan, M. P. Honzik, P. H. Mussen, pp. 411–34. New York: Academic. 500 pp.

Erikson, E. H. 1950. *Childhood and Society.* New York: Norton. 397 pp.

Erikson, E. H. 1968. *Identity: Youth and Crisis.* New York: Norton. 336 pp.

Faiman, C., Winter, J. S. D. 1974. Gonadotropins and sex hormone patterns in puberty: clinical data. See Grumbach, et al 1974, pp. 32–55

Faust, M. S. 1983. Alternative constructions of adolescent growth. See Brooks-Gunn & Petersen 1983, pp. 105–26

Featherman, D. L., Peterson, T. 1986. Markers of aging: modeling the clocks that time us. *Res. Aging* 8:339–65

Frankenhaeuser, M. 1983. The sympathetic-adrenal and pituitary-adrenal response to challenge: comparison between the sexes. In *Biobehavioral Bases of Coronary Heart Disease,* ed. T. M. Dembroski, T. H. Schmidt, G. Blümchen, pp. 91–105. Basel, Switzerland: S. Karger

Freud, A. 1958. *Adolescence: Psychoanalytic Study of the Child,* Vol. 13. New York: Academic

Furstenberg, F. F., Jr., Brooks-Gunn, J., Morgan, S. P. 1987. *Adolescent Mothers in Later Life.* New York: Cambridge Univ. Press. In press

Garner, D. M., Garfinkel, P. E. 1980. Sociocultural factors in the development of anorexia nervosa. *Psychol. Med.* 10:647–56

Gottlieb, D., Chafetz, J. S. 1977. Dynamics of familial generational conflict and reconciliation. *Youth Soc.* 9:213–24

Gottman, J., Mettetal, G. 1987. Speculations about social and affective development: friendship and acquaintanceship through adolescence. In *Conversations of Friends,* ed. J. M. Gottman, J. Parker. New York: Cambridge Univ. Press. In press

Gove, W. R., Herb, T. R. 1974. Stress and mental illness among the young: a comparison of the sexes. *Soc. Forces* 53:256–65

Grave, G. D. 1974. Introduction. See Grumbach et al 1974, pp. xxiii–iv

Green, L. W., Horton, D. 1982. Adolescent health: issues and challenges. See Coates et al 1982, pp. 23–43

Grinker, R. R. Sr., Grinker, R. R. Jr., Timberlake, I. 1962. Mentally healthy young males (homoclites). *Arch. Gen. Psychiatr.* 6:311–18

Grotevant, H., Cooper, C. 1985. Patterns of interaction in family relationships and the development of identity exploration in adolescence. *Child Dev.* 56:415–28

Grotevant, H., Cooper, C. 1986. Individuation in family relationships. *Hum. Dev.* 29:82–100

Grumbach, M. M., Grave, G. D., Mayer, F. E., eds. 1974. *Control of the Onset of Puberty.* New York: Wiley. 484 pp.

Gupta, D., Attanasio, A., Raaf, S. 1975. Plasma estrogen and androgen concentrations in children during adolescence. *J. Clin. Endocrinol. Metabl.* 40:636–43

Hall, G. S. 1904. *Adolescence: Its Psychology and Its Relations to Physiology, Anthropology, Sociology, Sex, Crime, Religion, and Education,* Vols. 1,2. New York: Appleton-Century-Crofts. 591, 784 pp.

Hamburg, B. A. 1974. Early adolescence: a specific and stressful stage of the life cycle. In *Coping and Adaptation,* ed. G. V. Coelho, J. E. Adams. New York: Basic Books

Hartup, W. W. 1983. Peer relations. See Hetherington 1983, pp. 103–96

Hauser, S. T., Powers, S. I., Noam, G. G., Jacobson, A. M., Weiss, B., Follansbee, D. J. 1984. Familial contexts of adolescent ego development. *Child Dev.* 55:195–213

Hetherington, E. M., ed. 1983. *Socialization, Personality, and Social Development,* Vol. 4. 1043 pp. In *Handbook of Child Psychology,* ed. P. H. Mussen. New York: Wiley

Hill, J. 1980. The family. In *Toward Adolescence: The Middle School Years,* ed. M. Johnson, pp. 32–55. Chicago: Univ. Chicago Press

Hill, J., Holmbeck, G., Marlow, L., Green, T., Lynch, M. 1985a. Menarcheal status and parent-child relations in families of seventh-grade girls. *J. Youth Adol.* 14:301–16

Hill, J., Holmbeck, G., Marlow, L., Green, T., Lynch, M. 1985b. Pubertal status and parent-child relations in families of seventh-grade boys. *J. Early Adol.* 5:31–44

Hollingworth, L. S. 1928. *The Psychology of the Adolescent.* Englewood Cliffs, NJ: Prentice-Hall. 259 pp.

Inhelder, B., Piaget, J. 1958. *The Growth of Logical Thinking From Childhood to Adolescence.* New York: Basic Books

Jacobs, J. 1971. *Adolescent Suicide.* New York: Wiley. 147 pp.

Jessor, R., Jessor, S. L. 1977. *Problem Behavior and Psychological Development.* New York: Academic. 281 pp.

Jones, M. C., Bayley, N. 1950. Physical maturing among boys as related to behavior. *J. Educ. Psychol.* 41:129–48

Jones, M. C., Mussen, P. H. 1958. Self-conceptions, motivations, and interpersonal attitudes of early and late maturing girls. *Child Dev.* 29:491–501

Kagan, J., Moss, H. A. 1962. *Birth to Maturity: The Fels Study of Psychological Development.* New York: Wiley. 381 pp.

Kandel, D. B., Davies, M. 1982. Epidemiology of depressive mood in adolescents. *Arch. Gen. Psychiatr.* 39:1205–12

Kandel, D. B., Kessler, R., Margulies, R. 1978. Adolescent initiation into stages of drug use: a developmental analysis. In *Longitudinal Research on Drug Use: Empirical Findings and Methodological Issues*, ed. D. B. Kandel. Washington, DC: Hemisphere-Wiley

Kandel, D. B., Lesser, G. S. 1972. *Youth in Two Worlds.* San Francisco: Jossey-Bass. 217 pp.

Kaplan, H. B. 1980. *Deviant Behavior in Defense of Self.* New York: Academic. 255 pp.

Kaplan, S. L., Hong, G. K., Weinhold, C. 1984. Epidemiology of depressive symptomatology in adolescents. *J. Am. Acad. Child Psychiatr.* 23:91–98

Keating, D. P. 1987. Structuralism, deconstruction, reconstruction: the limits of logical reasoning. In *Reasoning, Necessity, and Logic: Developmental Perspectives*, ed. W. F. Overton. Hillsdale, NJ: Erlbaum. In press

Keating, D. P., Clark, L. V. 1980. Development of physical and social reasoning in adolescence. *Dev. Psychol.* 16:23–30

Kestenberg, J. 1968. Phase of adolescence with suggestions for correlation of psychic and hormonal organizations. Part III. Puberty growth, differentiation, and consolidation. *J. Am. Acad. Child Psychiatr.* 6:577–614

Kirmil-Gray, K., Eagleston, J. R., Gibson, E., Thoresen, C. E. 1984. Sleep disturbance in adolescents: sleep quality, sleep habits, beliefs about sleep, and daytime functioning. *J. Youth Adol.* 13:375–84

Kohen-Raz, R. 1974. Physiological maturation and mental growth at preadolescence and puberty. *J. Child Psychol. Psychiatr.* 15:199–213

Larson, R., Csikszentmihalyi, M., Graef, R. 1980. Mood variability and the psychosocial adjustment of adolescents. *J. Youth Adol.* 9:469–90

Lerner, R. M. 1981. Adolescent development: scientific study in the 1980s. *Youth Soc.* 12:251–75

Lerner, R. M. 1984. *On the Nature of Human Plasticity.* New York: Cambridge Univ. Press. 208 pp.

Lerner, R. M., Foch, T. T., eds. 1987. *Biological-Psychosocial Interactions in Early Adolescence: A Life-Span Perspective.* Hillsdale, NJ: Erlbaum. 394 pp.

Lerner, R., Karson, M., Meisels, M., Knapp, J. R. 1975. Actual and perceived attitudes of late adolescents: the phenomenon of the generation gaps. *J. Genet. Psychol.* 126:197–207

Lerner, R. M., Spanier, G. B. 1978. A dynamic interactional view of child and family development. In *Child Influences on Marital and Family Interaction: A Life-Span Perspective*, ed. R. M. Lerner, G. B. Spanier. New York: Academic. 360 pp.

Lewin, K. 1935. *A Dynamic Theory of Personality.* New York: McGraw-Hill. 286 pp.

Lewin, K. 1939. Field theory and experiment in social psychology: concepts and methods. *Am. J. Sociol.* 44:868–97

Lewin, K. 1951. *Field Theory and Social Science.* New York: Harper & Row. 346 pp.

Linn, M., Petersen, A. C. 1985. Gender differences and spatial ability: emergence and characterization. *Child Dev.* 56:1479–98

Lipsitz, J. 1977. *Growing Up Forgotten: A Review of Research and Programs Concerning Early Adolescence.* Lexington, Mass: D. C. Heath. 267 pp.

Lynd, R. S., Lynd, H. M. 1929. *Middletown: A Study in Contemporary American Culture.* New York: Harcourt, Brace

Maccoby, E., Martin, J. 1983. Socialization in the context of the family: parent-child interaction. See Hetherington 1983, pp. 103–96

Magnusson, D. 1987. *Individual Development in an Interactional Perspective*, Vol. 1. In *Series Paths Through Life*, ed. D. Magnusson. Hillsdale, NJ: Erlbaum

Magnusson, D., Stattin, H., Allen, J. L. 1985. Biological maturation and social development: a longitudinal study of some adjustment processes from mid-adolescence to adulthood. *J. Youth Adol.* 14:267–83

Marcia, J. E. 1980. Identity in adolescence. See Adelson 1980, pp. 159–87

Marshall, W. A., Tanner, J. M. 1969. Variations in the pattern of pubertal changes in girls. *Arch. Dis. Childhood* 44:291–303

Marshall, W. A., Tanner, J. M. 1970. Variations in the pattern of pubertal changes in boys. *Arch. Dis. Childhood* 45:13–23

Martorano, S. C. 1977. A developmental analysis of performance on Piaget's formal operations tasks. *Dev. Psychol.* 13:666–72

McCubbin, H. I., Needle, R. H., Wilson, M. 1985. Adolescent health risk behaviors: family stress and adolescent coping as critical factors. *Fam. Rel.* 34:51–62

McKenry, P. C., Walters, L. H., Johnson, C. 1979. Adolescent pregnancy: a review of the literature. *Fam. Coord.* 28:16–28

Mead, M. 1950. *Coming of Age in Somoa.* New York: New American Library

Mead, M. 1953. *Growing Up in New Guinea.* New York: New American Library. 297 pp.

Meyer-Bahlburg, H. F. L., Ehrhardt, A. A., Bell, J. J., Cohen, S. F., Healey, J. M., Feldman, J. F., Morishima, A., Baker, S. W., New, M. J. 1985. Idiopathic precocious puberty in girls: psychosexual development. *J. Youth Adol.* 14:339–53

Montemayor, R. 1983. Parents and adolescents in conflict: all families some of the time and some families most of the time. *J. Early Adol.* 3:83–103

Mussen, P. H., Jones, M. C. 1957. Self-conceptions, motivations, and interpersonal attitudes of early and late maturing boys. *Child Dev.* 28:243–56

Neugarten, B. L. 1979. Time, age, and lifecycle. *Am. J. Psychiatr.* 136:887–94

Newcombe, N., Dubas, J. S. 1987. Individual differences in cognitive ability: Are they related to timing of puberty? See Lerner & Foch 1987, pp. 249–302

Nottelmann, E. D., Susman, E. J., Blue, J. H., Inoff-Germain, G., Dorn, L. D., Loriaux, D. L., Cutler, G. B., Chrousos, G. P. 1987a. Gonadal and adrenal hormonal correlates of adjustment in early adolescence. See Lerner & Foch 1987, pp. 303–24

Nottelmann, E. D., Susman, E. J., Inoff-Germain, G., Cutler, G. B., Jr., Loriaux, D. L., Chrousos, G. P. 1987b. Developmental processes in early adolescence: relations between adolescent adjustment problems and chronological age, pubertal stage, and puberty-related serum hormone levels. *J. Pediatr.* 110:473–80

Offer, D. 1969. *The Psychological World of the Teenager: A Study of Normal Adolescent Boys.* New York: Basic Books. 286 pp.

Offer, D., Offer, J. 1975. *From Teenage to Young Manhood: A Psychological Study.* New York: Basic Books. 262 pp.

Olweus, D. 1979. Stability of aggressive reaction patterns in males: a review. *Psychol. Bull.* 86:852–75

Papini, D., Datan, N. 1983. *Transition into adolescence: an interactionist perspective.* Presented at Bien. Meet. Soc. Res. Child Dev., Detroit, Michigan

Petersen, A. C. 1982. Developmental issues in adolescent health. See Coates et al 1982, pp. 61–72

Petersen, A. C. 1983. Pubertal change and cognition. See Brooks-Gunn & Petersen 1983, pp. 179–98

Petersen, A. C. 1987a. The nature of biological-psychosocial interactions: the sample case of early adolescence. See Lerner & Foch 1987, pp. 173–88

Petersen, A. C. 1987b. Pubertal change and psychosocial development. In *Life-Span Development and Behavior,* Vol. 9, ed. P. Baltes, D. L. Featherman, R. M. Lerner. New York: Academic. In press

Petersen, A. C., Crockett, L. J. 1985. Pubertal timing and grade effects on adjustment. *J. Youth Adol.* 14:191–206

Petersen, A. C., Ebata, A. T. 1987. Developmental transitions and adolescent problem behavior: implications for prevention and intervention. In *Social Prevention and Intervention,* ed. K. Hurrelmann. New York: de Gruyter. In press

Petersen, A. C., Ebata, A. T., Graber, J. A. 1987a. *Coping with adolescence: the functions and dysfunctions of poor achievement.* Presented at Bien. Meet. Soc. Res. Child Dev., Baltimore, Maryland

Petersen, A. C., Ebata, A. T., Sarigiani, P. 1987b. *Who expresses depressive affect in adolescence?* Presented at Bien. Meet. Soc. Res. Child Dev., Baltimore, Maryland

Petersen, A. C., Hamburg, B. A. 1986. Adolescence: a developmental approach to problems and psychopathology. *Behav. Ther.* 17:480–99

Petersen, A. C., Taylor, B. 1980. The biological approach to adolescence: biological change and psychosocial adaptation. See Adelson 1980, pp. 117–55

Peterson, C., Seligman, M. E. P. 1984. Causal explanations as a risk factor for depression: theory and evidence. *Psychol. Rev.* 91:347–74

Plato. 1953. Laws. In *The Dialogues of Plato,* Vol. 4. Transl. B. Jewett. New York: Oxford Univ.

Rolf, J. E., Masten, A., Cicchetti, D., Nuechterlein, K. H., Weintraub, S., eds. 1987. *Risk and Protective Factors in the Development of Psychopathology.* New York: Cambridge Univ. Press. In press

Rousseau, J. J. (1911) 1969. *Emile.* Transl. London: Dent-Everyman's

Ruble, D. N., Brooks-Gunn, J. 1982. The

experience of menarche. *Child Dev.* 53: 1557–66

Rutter, M. 1980. *Epidemiological-longitudinal approaches.* Presented at Minn. Symp. Child Psychol., Minneapolis

Rutter, M. 1980. *Changing Youth in a Changing Society: Patterns of Adolescent Development and Disorder.* Cambridge, Mass: Harvard Univ. Press. 323 pp.

Rutter, M. 1986. The developmental psychopathology of depression: issues and perspectives. See Rutter et al 1986, pp. 3–30

Rutter, M. 1987. Continuities and discontinuities from infancy. In *Handbook of Infant Development,* ed. J. Osofsky, pp. 1256–96. New York: Wiley. 2nd ed.

Rutter, M., Graham, P., Chadwick, O., Yule, W. 1976. Adolescent turmoil: fact or fiction? *J. Child Psychol. Psychiatr.* 17:35–56

Rutter, M., Izard, C., Read, P., eds. 1986. *Depression in Young People: Developmental and Clinical Perspectives.* New York: Guilford Press. 550 pp.

Santrock, J. W. 1987. *Adolescence: An Introduction.* Dubuque, Iowa: William C. Brown Publishers. 725 pp. 3rd ed.

Savins-Williams, R. C., Small, S. A., Zeldin, R. S. 1981. Dominance and altruism among adolescent males: a comparison of ethological and psychological methods. *Ethol. Sociobiol.* 2:167–76

Schulenberg, J. E., Asp, C. E., Petersen, A. C. 1984. School from the young adolescent's perspective: a descriptive report. *J. Early Adol.* 4:107–30

Seligman, M. E. P., Peterson, C. 1986. A learned helplessness perspective on childhood depression: theory and research. See Rutter et al 1986, pp. 223–49

Shellow, R., Schamp, J., Liebow, E., Unger, E. 1967. Suburban runaways of the 1960s. *Monogr. Soc. Res. Child Dev.* 32:Ser. No. 111. 51 pp.

Shuttleworth, F. K. 1939. The physical and mental growth of girls and boys age six to nineteen in relation to age at maximum growth. *Monogr. Soc. Res. Child Dev.* 4:(3, Ser. No. 22)

Silbereisen, R. K., Noack, P., Eyferth, K. 1986. Place for development: adolescents, leisure settings, and developmental tasks. In *Development as Action in Context,* ed. R. K. Silbereisen, K. Eyferth, G. Rudinger, pp. 87–108. New York: Springer-Verlag. 322 pp.

Silbereisen, R. K., Noack, P. 1988. On the constructive role of problem behavior in adolescence. In *Person and Context: Developmental Processes,* ed. N. Bolger, A. Caspi, G. Downey, M. Moorhouse. Cambridge: Cambridge Univ. Press. In press

Simmons, R. G., Blyth, D. A. 1987. *Moving into Adolescence: The Impact of Pubertal Change and School Context.* New York: Aldine. In press

Simmons, R. G., Blyth, D. A., McKinney, K. L. 1983. The social and psychological effects of puberty on white females. See Brooks-Gunn & Petersen 1983, pp. 229–72

Simmons, R. G., Blyth, D. A., VanCleave, E., Bush, D. 1979. Entry into early adolescence: the impact of school structure, puberty, and early dating on self-esteem. *Am. Sociol. Rev.* 44:948–67

Simmons, R. G., Rosenberg, M. F., Rosenberg, M. C. 1973. Disturbance in the self-image at adolescence. *Am. Sociol. Rev.* 38:553–68

Smetana, J. G. 1987. Adolescent-parent conflict: reasoning about hypothetical and actual family conflict. In *21st Minnesota Symposium on Child Psychology,* ed. M. R. Gunnar. Hillsdale, NJ: Erlbaum & Assoc. In press

Steinberg, L. D. 1981. Transformations in family relations at puberty. *Dev. Psychol.* 7:833–40

Steinberg, L. D. 1985. *Adolescence.* New York: Alfred A. Knopf

Steinberg, L. D., Hill, J. P. 1978. Patterns of family interaction as a function of age, the onset of puberty, and formal thinking. *Dev. Psychol.* 14:683–84

Sternberg, R. J., Powell, J. S. 1983. The development of intelligence. In *Handbook of Child Psychology: Cognitive Development,* ed. J. H. Flavell, E. M. Markman, 3:341–419. New York: Wiley. 4th ed. 942 pp.

Suomi, S. 1987. *Individual differences in rhesus monkey behavioral and adrenocortical responses to social challenge: correlations with measures of heart rate variability.* Presented at Bien. Meet. Soc. Res. Child Dev., Baltimore, Maryland

Susman, E. J., Inoff-Germain, G., Nottelmann, E. D. 1987. Hormones, emotional dispositions, and aggressive attributes. *Child Dev.* In press

Tanner, J. M. 1974. Sequence and tempo in the somatic changes in puberty. See Grumbach et al 1974, pp. 448–70

Thorndike, E. L. 1904. The newest psychology. *Educ. Rev.* 28:217–27

Turner, R. J. 1980. *Social support as a contingency in psychological well-being.* Presented at the Am. Soc. Assoc. Meet., New York

Udry, J. R., Billy, J. O. G., Morris, N., Groff, T., Raj, M. 1985. Serum androgenic hormones motivate sexual behavior in adolescent boys. *Fertil. Steril.* 43:90–94

Udry, J. R., Talbert, L. M., Morris, N. M. 1986. Biosocial foundations for adolescent female sexuality. *Demography* 23:217–30

Ullman, C. 1982. Cognitive and emotional antecedents of religious conversion. *J. Person. Soc. Psychol.* 43:183–92

Van Hasselt, V. B., Hersen, M., eds. 1987. *Handbook of Adolescent Psychology.* New York: Pergamon Press

Waber, D. P. 1976. Sex differences in cognition: a function of maturation rate? *Science* 192:572–74

Waber, D. P. 1977. Sex differences in mental abilities, hemispheric lateralization, and rate of physical growth at adolescence. *Dev. Psychol.* 13:29–38

Warren, M. P. 1980. The effects of exercise on pubertal progression and reproductive function in girls. *J. Clin. Endocrinol. Metab.* 51:1150–57

Weiner, I. B. 1980. Psychopathology in adolescence. See Adelson 1980, pp. 447–71

Weiner, I. B., DelGaudio, A. 1976. Psychopathology in adolescence. *Arch. Gen. Psychiatr.* 33:187–93

Weissman, M. M., Klerman, G. L. 1977. Sex differences and the epidemiology of depression. *Arch. Gen. Psychiatr.* 34:98–111

Wohlwill, J. F. 1973. *The Study of Behavioral Development.* New York: Academic. 413 pp.

Youniss, J., Smollar, J. 1985. *Adolescent Relations with Mothers, Fathers, and Friends.* Chicago: Univ. Chicago Press. 201 pp.

Zakin, D. F., Blyth, D. A., Simmons, R. G. 1984. Physical attractiveness as a mediator of the impact of early pubertal changes for girls. *J. Youth Adol.* 13:439–50

Ann. Rev. Psychol. 1988. 39:609–72

INTERPERSONAL PROCESSES IN CLOSE RELATIONSHIPS

Margaret S. Clark

Department of Psychology, Carnegie-Mellon University, Pittsburgh, Pennsylvania 15213-3890

Harry T. Reis

Department of Psychology, University of Rochester, Rochester, New York 14627

CONTENTS

INTRODUCTION

The last time the *Annual Review of Psychology* dealt with the psychology of relationships was in 1978, when Huston & Levinger discussed recent advances in the study of attraction and relationships. Eighty percent of that research, they maintained, involved subjects who were "personally irrelevant" to each other, in the sense that they had never met before, did not expect to see each other in the future, and might not come face-to-face during the study. Perhaps because this paradigm seemed to many psychologists limited in its usefulness for understanding relationships, and perhaps because William Proxmire's bestowal of a "Golden Fleece" award upon some of the best work in this area made such research politically problematic, research activity waned in the late 1970s and early 1980s. Fortunately, with a turn toward more realistic laboratory and naturalistic research designs, this decline has been reversed in recent years, so that in the ebb and flow of research productivity, close relationships are once again riding a wave of growing enthusiasm.

Signs of this trend are abundant. Journal articles reporting new theoretical positions and empirical findings appear with increasing frequency; a new journal devoted exclusively to the study of relationships, the *Journal of Personal and Social Relationships,* was inaugurated in 1984; two international, interdisciplinary societies for the study of relationships have been formed, one in 1984 and one in 1987; at least two continuing series of edited volumes reporting and commenting on relationship research have been initiated; and countless edited volumes dealing with relationship phenomena in one form or another have been published.

In this review we discuss what we believe to be some of the most important developments in this new era of relationship research. Our review is specifically organized around interpersonal processes that affect the course and conduct of interpersonal relationships, rather than, as is common in the literature, relationship types (e.g. friendship, marriage). We take this approach because we believe that interpersonal processes, when broadly construed, offer principles that can enhance our understanding of almost every type of relationship. We discuss three processes: interdependence, emotion, and intimacy. The recent literature on adult close relationships largely focuses on friendship and romance, and these three processes describe much of what is important not only in these particular relationships, but, we are confident, in many other types of close relationships as well. Although our coverage is necessarily selective, we endeavor to describe those studies that from our vantage point have the most potential for increasing our knowledge and suggesting new research.

This chapter is divided into six parts. Our first three sections review new developments in interdependence, emotion, and intimacy. The fourth section discusses recent studies of love, a reemerging topic of intrinsic importance to the study of close relationships. Through the example of love, we show how general processes of interdependence, emotion, and intimacy may apply to specific interpersonal states and relationships. Next, we examine research on individual differences, an area with promising new findings and paradigms yet largely unrealized potential for providing important insights about interpersonal processes. Finally, we describe recent methodological innovations well suited for expanding the range of ideas that can be studied empirically, and for enhancing the technical quality of our research.

INTERDEPENDENCE

Definitions of Relationships and of Closeness

An important book in the relationship field, *Close Relationships,* by Kelley, Berscheid, Christensen, Harvey, Huston, Levinger, McClintock, Peplau, and Peterson, appeared in 1983. Central to this volume are definitions of relationship and close relationship. According to Kelley et al, if two people's behaviors, emotions, and thoughts are mutually and causally interconnected, the people are interdependent and a relationship exists. A relationship is defined as close to the extent that it endures and involves strong, frequent, and diverse causal interconnections.

Kelley et al's definitions denote the tasks of our discipline—to describe and understand the nature of interdependence within pairs of people. That is, we seek to describe the events in which pairs are involved, the causal connections between those events, and the enduring environmental and social conditions that alter the nature of interdependence in such relationships. We also attempt to summarize event patterns over time in order to identify general properties of interdependence. Most importantly, we aim to identify the nature of interdependence in ongoing relationships of different types, in different situations, and at different points in relationship development. Kelley et al's definition of closeness, although not the only one possible, helps indicate the kind of relationships in which we believe researchers in our field ought to be primarily interested. It defines the heretofore elusive construct of closeness in a manner that captures some of the meaning that people wish to convey when describing relationships as close, and it includes those relationships—both friendly and hostile—that are most important to people. It also permits empirical tests of the implications of closeness. For instance, as will be seen below in the section on emotion, such closeness substantially affects the experience of emotion in relationships.

Kelley et al's framework encourages researchers to conceptualize interdependence broadly, in terms of ongoing chains of mutual influence between two people. Most research has instead been confined to particular components of the larger process. For example, aspects of interdependence are involved in maintaining self-evaluation (Swann & Read 1981; Tesser 1987), making joint decisions (Gottman et al 1979), solving conflicts (Gottman et al 1977), and deciding to maintain or dissolve dissatisfying relationships (Rusbult et al 1982; Rusbult & Zembrodt 1983). Rather than reviewing all such work, we concentrate on advances in outcome interdependence, a topic long of interest to social psychologists. That is, what are the processes involved in the giving and acceptance of benefits in relationships, and how does adherence to such processes relate to satisfaction with the relationship? We focus on studies that examine these processes in romantic relationships and friendships, and that deal with need satisfaction. This research relates closely to emotion and intimacy, two interdependent processes that are discussed next.

Norms Governing the Giving and Acceptance of Benefits

The questions of when and how people benefit one another have generated a great deal of empirical and theoretical work for almost 30 years, stimulated initially by Thibaut & Kelley (1959) and Walster et al (1973). We see no slowing of this trend in recent years. If anything, interest in this area, particularly in what norms are considered just or fair, has expanded, as evidenced by a great many recent edited volumes and relevant review articles (e.g. Bierhoff et al 1986; Cook & Hegtvedt 1983; Gergen et al 1980; Greenberg & Cohen 1982; Folger 1984; Lerner & Lerner 1981; Masters & Smith 1987; Messick & Cook 1983; McClintock et al 1984; Mikula 1980; Pruitt & Rubin 1985) as well as by numerous empirical studies.

Continuing the trend begun in the 1960s, some new work tests the applicability of the equity norm to understanding interdependence (e.g. Hatfield et al 1985). A more recent trend emphasizes the diversity of distributive and procedural justice norms (e.g. Deutsch, 1985), although only norms of equality and of needs have actually received much attention in empirical work. In addition to traditional research concerning the applicability of norms governing the giving and acceptance of resources among superficial acquaintances or hypothetical others, some researchers now examine the nature of interdependence in giving and accepting resources in close, intimate, ongoing social relationships such as friendships, romantic relationships, and marital relationships (e.g. Berg 1984; Berg & McQuinn 1986; Hatfield & Traupmann 1980) or in situations in which subjects are led to expect and/or desire a close relationship with another (e.g. Clark & Mills 1979).

Other related changes have also taken place. These include: (a) increased theorizing about and empirical work regarding need-based norms for giving and receiving benefits (e.g. Clark & Mills 1979; Kelley 1979; Miller & Berg 1984; Schwinger 1986); (b) greater reliance on field-based, survey, or interview work using correlational designs, in addition to laboratory experiments (e.g. Berg 1984; Berg & McQuinn 1986; Rook 1987a); and (c) a shift toward more descriptive work (e.g. Hays 1985; see especially Chapter 2 of Kelley et al 1983).

CONTINUING WORK ON EQUITY   The direction of equity theory research provides a clear example of two of the trends mentioned above—toward supplementing laboratory experiments with correlational studies, and toward examining ongoing, close relationships. Earlier equity studies almost exclusively featured laboratory interactions between strangers who did not expect to see each other again. This work, reviewed by Walster et al (1978), indicates that in such circumstances people tend to follow an equity norm (i.e. the ratio of each person's inputs relative to their outcomes should be equivalent). The results of some more recent surveys of ongoing close relationships by equity theorists are also consistent with equity propositions. For instance, people who hold global impressions that their relationships are equitable are more confident than those who do not of staying together in the future (Hatfield et al 1985; Sabatelli & Cecil-Pigo 1985), report being more content in the relationship (Hatfield et al 1985), are less likely to have extramarital sexual affairs (Hatfield et al 1985), report more liking for the others with whom they have such relationships (Rees & Segal 1984, see results for Team 1), evaluate outcomes derived from their marriage more favorably (Sabatelli & Cecil-Pigo 1985), and report more positive affect and less negative affect in their relationships (Sprecher 1986).

Other findings by equity theorists have been unexpected but not in conflict with equity theory. Hatfield et al (1985) found that women are more distressed with being overbenefited in close relationships than men are, whereas men are more distressed by underbenefit. Sprecher (1986) demonstrated that global impressions of inequity explain more variance in men's than women's emotions and that for men inequity is equally related to positive and negative emotions whereas for women inequity is more related to negative emotions. Finally, Berg (1984) reported that women perceive their relationships with other women to be more equitable than men perceive their relationships with other men.

Still other findings do not support equity theory. For instance, Hatfield et al (1985) note the absence of evidence for relationships' becoming more equitable over time, as predicted by equity theory; and more recent studies find either no change (Berg & McQuinn 1986) or decreases in roommates' perceptions of equity over time (Berg 1984). Further, a number of studies in which both global impressions of equity and the total number of benefits have been assessed suggest that the total number of benefits received predicts success in that relationship better than equity does. For instance, Cate et al

(1985) gave dating couples questionnaires that included measures of global equity and global equality (Hatfield's measures) as well as of the absolute levels of rewards received. Only absolute reward level successfully discriminated stable relationships from those that did not last. Neither equity nor equality distinguished stable and unstable relationships after reward level was controlled. Similarly, Michaels et al (1984) examined the effects of both equity (rated globally and on a dimension-by-dimension basis) and benefits received in close, opposite-sex relationships. Although measures of equity and equality did account for significant variance in relationship satisfaction in this work, these proportions were small compared to those accounted for by overall level of positive outcomes.

Berg reports two additional studies suggesting that overall reward level may be a better predictor of relationship success than perceived equity is (Berg 1984; Berg & McQuinn 1986). In the first, pairs of same-sex roommates were surveyed soon after meeting and again later in the year. The best predictors of liking and satisfaction were rewards received and comparison levels for alternatives. Perceived equity did not predict liking and satisfaction. In addition, roommates who planned to stay together increasingly met each other's needs and desires as the year progressed, whereas those who planned to separate showed no such increase. Once again, levels of equity or changes in equity did not discriminate these two groups. Berg's second study involved members of opposite-sex romantic relationships surveyed early in their relationship and again four months later. Couples still dating at the second point in time demonstrated greater love, more relationship-maintaining behaviors, more favorable evaluation of the relationship, and more self-disclosure than did those who had broken up. Perceived equity did not differentiate continuing and noncontinuing relationships at either point in time. Finally, other studies have also shown that total benefits received predict friendship development (e.g. Hays 1985), although equity was not assessed in this work.

The fact that total benefits received (or total desires met) predicts relationship success has led some to suggest that a simple reinforcement hypothesis best accounts for the data (e.g. Michaels et al 1984). However, recently reported results argue against this interpretation. A reinforcement approach also predicts that costs should be negatively correlated with satisfaction and success, and benefits minus costs should predict success best. However, although some studies have shown such a relationship (Rusbult 1980a, Study 2; 1980b), other studies have shown no relationship between costs and relationship success (Rusbult 1980a, Study 1; Hays 1985). Furthermore, in his longitudinal study of ongoing relationships, Hays found that an index of benefits *plus* costs was a better predictor of relationship success than was an index of benefits *minus* costs. We return to this finding in the next section.

NORMS OTHER THAN EQUITY   Findings such as those reviewed above notwithstanding, some theorists have argued that equity norms apply to diverse situations—including intimate, ongoing relationships—if the characteristics considered to be inputs and outcomes are changed according to the situation and relationship (for example, by redefining inputs and outcomes in terms of needs). Critics have replied that equity theory cannot accommodate such findings without becoming so flexible that the concept of equity is no longer useful (Folger 1986; Furby 1986; Reis 1984). As a result, researchers have tried to identify more specific justice rules and personality and situational factors that influence choices among them. Alternative norms that might apply include mutual responsiveness to needs and equality (Deutsch 1975), and indeed up to 11 (Deutsch 1975) or even 17 (Reis 1984) alternative justice rules (e.g. one's own needs should be met first, power should determine distribution of benefits) have been proposed. Researchers have further argued, and provided supporting evidence, that such norms are differentially applicable to relationships depending upon various situational factors and individual differences, such as the type of relationship between partners (Clark & Mills 1979; Lerner et al 1976), gender (Kahn et al 1980; Major 1987; Major et al 1984), orientations toward relationships (Clark et al 1987a,b; Major & Adams 1983; Murstein & Azar 1986; Swap & Rubin 1983), and how allocation tasks are defined (Reis 1984).

Where have such arguments led? Only two justice norms other than equity actually have received much empirical attention—need (benefits should be distributed according to people's needs) and equality (benefits should be distributed equally). To us, the growing focus on these norms reflects interdependence researchers' increased attention to ongoing close relationships. After all, need and equality are more likely to apply in such relationships than in economic exchanges or in encounters between strangers (Deutsch 1985).

Several researchers have examined the social context of need-based and equality norms in contrast to equity. For example, Deutsch (1975, 1985) suggested that norm preferences depend on people's goals in a particular relationship. According to Deutsch, equity norms predominate when maximizing economic productivity is the goal. When cooperation or positive socioemotional bonds are more salient, however, equality or need-based rules tend to prevail (see also Mikula 1980). Other researchers have emphasized the nature of ongoing types of relationships rather than situational goals as determinants of rule preference. Clark & Mills (1979; Mills & Clark 1982), for example, distinguished between exchange relationships, in which benefits are expected in response to past benefits or in anticipation of future comparable benefits, and communal relationships, in which members feel mutual responsibility for each other's welfare and give benefits either in response to needs or to demonstrate concern for the other. Communal relationships often occur between family members, romantic partners, and friends, whereas exchange relationships are frequent between strangers meeting for the first time, acquaintances, or business associates. Mikula & Schwinger (1978) have also emphasized the impact of relationship type on rule preferences. They postulated that relationships characterized by neutral affect follow a contributions (equity) rule, those with positive affect follow an equality rule, and those with very positive affect follow a need-based rule. It should be noted, however, that the Clark/Mills and Mikula/Schwinger conceptualizations are quite distinct. Communal relationships are not always characterized by positive affect, nor are exchange relationships necessarily characterized by neutral affect.

Finally, in connection with the shift toward emphasizing the importance of needs, a new development in Kelley and Thibaut's theorizing about the nature of interdependence should be mentioned (Kelley 1979; Kelley & Thibaut 1978). In their original work, Thibaut & Kelley (1959) assumed that people were motivated to maximize their own rewards while minimizing their costs. In more recent work, they emphasize that transformations of outcome matrixes may take place such that, for example, one person may feel personally rewarded when the other's needs are met. The idea that such transformations take place is, of course, consistent with the theories cited in the preceding paragraph, which specify when such transformations will occur.

Empirical research has confirmed the relevance of equality and need-based rules to understanding interaction in certain ongoing relationships. Austin (1980), for example, had pairs of college roommates and strangers work together on a task and receive a joint reward. One member of each dyad was put in charge of dividing the reward between both partners. Roommates tended to overlook input differences in contributions and allocate the reward equally, whereas strangers chose merit when they themselves excelled and equality when they performed poorly. In two role-playing studies, Lamm & Schwinger (1980, 1983) asked subjects how they would allocate money to friends (or to people to whom they were highly attracted) versus strangers. Subjects were especially likely to take needs into account with friends and with others to whom they were highly attracted.

The most extensive program of research on need-based norms has been conducted by Clark & Mills and their colleagues. Mills & Clark (1982), for example, reported a series of experiments in which expected relationship type was varied. Some subjects were led to anticipate that an attractive other was interested in befriending new, similar others (communal conditions); other subjects were led to expect that the other was not available for new relationships (exchange conditions). When exchange relationships were expected, subjects followed equity principles—that is, they reacted positively to immediate compensation for favors and to requests for repayment of accepted favors (Clark & Mills 1979), kept track of individual inputs on jointly rewarded tasks (Clark 1984), and felt exploited when their help was not reciprocated (Clark & Waddell 1985). In contrast, when communal relationships were anticipated, subjects reacted negatively to immediate compensation for favors (Clark & Mills 1979), did not keep track of individual inputs on joint tasks (Clark 1984), and did not feel exploited by unrequited help (Clark & Waddell 1985). Instead, they were more likely to keep track of the other's needs even when there was no opportunity for repayment (Clark et al 1986), help others, and respond to their sadness with increased helping (Clark et al 1987a). These researchers have also outlined types of communications likely to lead to feelings of exploitation in communal and exchange relationships (Mills & Clark 1986) and have provided some evidence that these findings will apply not only when subjects are led to expect communal relationships but in ongoing friendships as well (Clark 1984, Studies 2 & 3).

It is noteworthy that the evidence reviewed earlier indicating that benefits received predict satisfaction in friendship and romance relations is consistent with research on need-based norms. Moreover, Hays's (1985) finding that benefits plus costs predicted relationship success better than benefits minus costs can be explained if one assumes that members of such relationships feel responsible for each other's needs. That is, the more each person feels responsible for the other, the more benefits each receives as the other meets his or her needs *and* the more costs each incurs in meeting the other's needs.

OTHER FINDINGS RELEVANT TO OUTCOME INTERDEPENDENCE   Other recent advances in our understanding of interdependence deal with changes in interdependence over time and with the nature of resources given and received in different types of relationships. Looking at the latter question first, in contrast to the predictions of several theories of relationship development (e.g. Altman & Taylor 1973), recent studies suggest that patterns of outcome interdependence differentiate relationships destined to become close from those not so destined soon after they are initiated. Berg, for example, collected descriptions of exchange patterns (e.g. indexes of rewards received, companionship, consideration, and affection) in same-sex (Berg 1984) and opposite-sex (Berg & McQuinn 1986) relationships during the first weeks of a relationship's life and approximately four months later. The early exchange measures predicted ratings of satisfaction and desires to continue the relationship at four months virtually as well as the later measures did. Hays (1984, 1985) reported similar findings. He showed that in friendships destined to become close, giving of goods, services, and support increased sharply during the first six weeks of a relationship and then leveled off. On the other hand, relationships that remained distant showed steady declines in benefits given from early stages until the end of the study at 12 weeks. [Berg & Clark (1986) discuss this issue more extensively.]

These studies also suggest that as relationships develop, the nature of benefits received may become more important than the total quantity. For example, Berg's (1984) study found a significant correlation between brand new roommates' reports of the number of benefits received from the other, but no correlation in their reports of receiving the specific benefits they thought would help them most. Later in the year, this pattern was reversed. Berg suggests that this change indicates that balancing the total benefits given and received matters early in a relationship, but that meeting each other's needs becomes more important as partners grow close. Relatedly, Hays (1984, 1985) showed that friendship intensity ratings continued to rise even after ratings of the total number of benefits received had peaked.

We have also learned more about the types of resources exchanged between friends. Hays (1984), for example, reported that emotional support and the provision of a confidant differentiated close and nonclose friendships. Other studies have examined the relevance of Foa & Foa's (1980) resource typology in various types of relationships. Foa & Foa specified six categories of resources: love, status, information, services, goods, and money. Lloyd et al (1982) found that in casual friendship, receipt of status predicted relationship satisfaction, whereas in romantic couples, information and love but not status related to satisfaction. Törnblom & Fredholm (1984) provided similar results. Their data indicated that exchange of love and information led to perceptions of greater friendship than did exchanges of goals, money, and services, whereas exchanges of status led to perceptions of less friendship. Finally, Berg & McQuinn (1986), using Foa & Foa's (1980) classification of resources along dimensions of particularism/universalism (the extent to which the value of a resource depends on who provides it) and symbolism (how tangible the resource is), found that exchange of particular and symbolic rewards increased as romantic relationships deepened.

Considerable progress has occurred in identifying and describing norms governing outcome interdependence in friendship and romance. In the future it will be important also to conduct research on such patterns in other types of ongoing relationships (e.g. between teachers and students, or in exploitive relationships). Research on the moderating impact of situational and personality variables would also be useful, as would research specifying the manner in which different patterns of outcome interdependence affect relationship development and functioning.

EMOTION

Much of the emotion people experience arises in the context of social relationships, particularly close or intimate relationships (Averill 1983; Berscheid

1983; Bowlby 1969; Csikszentmihalyi & Larson 1984; DeRivera 1984; Scherer et al 1983; Schwartz & Shaver 1987; Trevarthen 1984). However, researchers primarily interested in emotion have typically studied it in nonsocial contexts, examining processes that seem more *intra* than *inter*personal (see, for instance, much of the research discussed in Clark & Fiske 1982). Moreover, until recently, relationship researchers have tended to neglect emotion, in large part owing to the tendency, noted earlier, to study initial encounters between strangers—interactions characterized by little emotion.

With the recent upswing in studies of close relationships, interest in emotion has grown. Some researchers have considered the impact of perceivers' emotions on initial impressions of others (e.g. Forgas & Moylan 1987). Other investigators have examined the role of a person's expressed emotion in determining observers' impressions of and subsequent behavior toward him or her (e.g. Sommers 1984; Clark et al 1987b). Additional (and we believe some of the most important) work has focused on the occurrence and patterning of emotion in ongoing relationships.

Still other researchers, coming from a variety of distinct theoretical backgrounds, conceive of emotion as involving complex patterns of concerns, appraisals, and action tendencies. They have begun to conduct empirical work identifying the characteristic, often social, antecedents and consequences of specific emotions (e.g. Averill 1982, 1983; Scherer et al 1986; Schwartz & Shaver 1987; Shaver et al 1987). For example, Shaver et al examined prototypes of various emotions relevant to relationships, including fear, sadness, anger, joy, and love. Finally, several researchers have begun to explore the implications of existing social psychological theories for understanding emotion in relationships (Bradbury & Fincham 1987; Kelley et al 1987; Salovey & Rodin 1984; Sprecher 1986; Tesser 1987).

Perceivers' Emotions, Impressions of Others, and Social Interest

We first consider recent work showing that perceivers' emotions influence impressions of others. Bower (1981) demonstrated that subjects hypnotized to feel angry were more likely than subjects induced to feel happy to interpret pictures of people in a negative manner. Further, Forgas et al (1984) found that subjects hypnotized to feel good believed that they and their interview partners had displayed more positive, prosocial actions. In contrast, subjects in negative moods judged themselves to have exhibited more negative actions, and their partners to have shown approximately the same number of positive and negative behaviors. [See Forgas & Bower (1987) for further evidence consistent with these findings.]

Because these particular studies lacked a neutral-mood condition, we cannot tell whether negative mood, positive mood, or both are responsible for these effects. Fortunately, other studies have included neutral-mood control conditions, and these studies, taken together, reveal both evidence for positive moods' increasing the favorability of judgments of others (e.g. Fiedler et al 1986; Clark & Waddell 1983; Schiffenbauer 1974; Forgas & Moylan 1987) and evidence for negative moods' decreasing the favorability of judgments of others (e.g. Griffitt 1970), social interest in others (Crandall 1978), and perceptions of the amount of social support available from others (Procidano & Heller 1983). However, it should be noted that studies that have included *both* positive and negative mood conditions as well as control conditions often have found only effects for positive moods (e.g. Clark & Waddell 1983; Forgas & Moylan 1987). This suggests that the effect of mood on judgments about others may be stronger for positive than for negative moods, an idea further supported by consideration of the broader literature on the effects of moods on judgment (see Isen 1985).

Finally, a few studies have identified boundary conditions regarding these effects. Positive moods do not always enhance impressions of others, such as when there is little positive information about the other [see Forgas & Moylan (1987) regarding judgments of drunk drivers and heroin traffickers]. Moreover, it appears that arousal accompanying strong inductions of positive emotion sometimes can be misattributed to repulsion from physically unattractive targets, as well as attraction toward physically attractive targets (White et al 1981). Further, turning to boundary conditions for the effects of negative moods, it is similarly the case that arousal accompanying strong inductions of negative emotion may sometimes be misattributed to attraction to a physically attractive target, as well as repulsion from a physically unattractive target (White et al 1981). Overall, however, research on moods and judgments most generally indicates that positive moods often and negative moods sometimes influence impressions of self and others in a way that makes judgments congruent with moods.

Future research is needed to determine when and which moods influence such judgments—a task that should be aided by current efforts to identify mechanisms behind such effects (see, for instance, Bower 1981; Isen 1984; Schwarz & Clore 1983). Still another important task will be to consider how perceivers' moods influence impressions of interaction partners and behavior toward them. That moods can have powerful effects on behavior is amply demonstrated by an older literature showing that both positive (e.g. Isen 1970) and negative (e.g. Cialdini et al 1973) moods increase helping, as well as by a more recent literature confirming that such effects occur and examining possible underlying mechanisms (see, for instance, Batson et al 1981; Fultz et al 1986; Cialdini et al 1987; Isen 1984). Little is known, however, about effects of moods on other social behaviors of potential importance to developing, maintaining, and dissolving relationships; and we believe such research has considerable promise. For example, a recent study by Cunningham (1987) demonstrates that happiness increases the happy person's tendency to self-disclose to a partner. In that self-disclosure predicts satisfaction in dating relationships (Berg & McQuinn 1986) and friendship formation (Cohen et al 1986), moods may set off interactive chains of events, perhaps in the manner of self-fulfilling prophecies, that determine whether or not relationships are initiated and developed.

TARGETS' EMOTIONS AND IMPRESSIONS OF TARGETS   We next consider how a target person's expressed emotions influence others' impressions of and behavior toward him or her, a topic about which only a small amount of experimental evidence is available. Sommers (1984) asked respondents what emotions they and others experienced on typical days, and then assessed independent observers' reactions to expression of these emotions. Positive emotions were judged to be more typical than negative emotions, and targets who predominantly experienced positive affect were seen as more sociable, conventional, popular, and likeable than others. Sommers' results also revealed that females who expressed negative affect were seen as more unsociable and unpopular than males who expressed the same affect.

Other research suggests that the impact of expressed emotions on others' impressions may depend upon the type of relationship. Clark & Muchant (1987) found that if a communal relationship was expected, expression of emotion produced more positive impressions of the other than if an exchange relationship was expected. Further, Clark et al (1987a, Study 2) found that if a potential donor of help expected a communal relationship with the recipient, that recipient's sadness increased the amount of help offered. In contrast, if an exchange relationship was expected, the recipient's sadness had no effect.[1] Although experimental research on reactions to others' emotions is scarce, given that people react strongly to others' emotions in everyday life, additional experimental studies identifying reactions to a variety of distinct emotions are needed.

EMOTION IN INTERDEPENDENT RELATIONSHIPS   The studies described so far investigate emotional processes in relatively simple laboratory paradigms. Other researchers have theorized about and examined emotional interdependence in the more complex context of ongoing relationships. Berscheid (1983; Berscheid et al 1984), for example, recently proposed a model of emotional interdependence in close relationships. Adopting Kelley et al's

[1]Although clinical depression involves more than just negative affect, readers interested in people's reactions to a target person's emotional states may also find research by Coyne (1976; Strack & Coyne, 1982) and other depression researchers (e.g. Hammen & Peters 1978; Howes & Hokanson 1979) to be informative.

(1983) framework, described earlier, she views relationships as existing when changes in the cognitive, physiological, or behavioral state of one person influence those states in another person, and vice versa. The relationship is close, furthermore, to the extent that members have frequent, strong, and diverse impact on each other over a long period. Berscheid views emotion as autonomic arousal caused by interruptions in well-practiced, organized action sequences, coupled with cognitive appraisal of that arousal. Putting these points together, Berscheid suggests that emotion in relationships is a direct function of the nature of interdependence in those relationships. If two people are not close, their organized action sequences tend to be independent. Neither has much power to interrupt the other; there should be few interruptions, little resulting arousal, and little emotion in that relationship. In contrast, in close relationships, members' action sequences are closely intertwined. They consequently are especially capable of interrupting each other's well-practiced action sequences and eliciting arousal and emotion. When such interruptions take place, emotion is experienced; when they do not, there is little emotion. Emotions are negative when interruptions block goal attainment and positive when they facilitate reaching a goal or when they are interpreted as benign.

Berscheid's conceptualization is important for several reasons. First, it allows for hypotheses linking relationship closeness (interdependence) to emotional experience. Second, it generates specific predictions regarding emotional activity in different phases of relationships, such as during termination. Dissolution of superficial relationships should produce little emotion. However, if the relationship was close, regardless of prior levels of satisfaction or whether positive or negative emotion was common, termination should produce considerable emotion. Thus, one can understand grief reactions not only in couples who had experienced considerable joy, but also in emotionally quiet (but still intertwined) and intensely negative relationships. The model also explains why satisfying but largely unmeshed relationships may produce little emotion upon termination, as well as why relationships that are quickly replaced (thereby allowing organized action sequences and goal attainment to continue) should yield less emotion.

Simpson (1987) tested some of these ideas. He first determined the length and closeness of ongoing relationships, relationship satisfaction, and perceived ease of finding new relationships. Three months later he assessed emotional distress among those whose relationships had ended. As expected, the greater the interdependence (as indicated by closeness and length) and perceived difficulty of replacement, the greater the distress. Also, counterintuitively but not contrary to Berscheid's theory, earlier feelings of satisfaction with the relationship did not predict distress.

Other researchers have taken on the important task of characterizing emotional interaction that takes place in marriage. For example, Levenson & Gottman (1983) videotaped couples in three situations: waiting together, discussing events of the day, and discussing marital problems. During these times they collected a variety of physiological measures. Spouses later returned separately and, while viewing the videotapes, rated the emotions they had felt throughout the earlier session. Among the major findings were that "physiological linkage" (interrelatedness of spouses' physiological reactions) was higher among distressed than among nondistressed couples, but only during problem discussions. Indeed, 60% of the variance in marital satisfaction could be accounted for by such linkage, far more than has been accounted for in past studies or with other measures. Levenson & Gottman interpreted this as evidence that when distressed couples attempt to solve problems, they often feel "locked into" the interaction, are unable to "step back," and hence fall into a pattern of conflict reflected in their physiological reactions. Also, relative to happy marriages, unhappy marriages were characterized by less positive affect, more negative affect, and more reciprocity of negative affect (see also Margolin & Wampold 1981).

Three years later, Levenson & Gottman (1985) conducted a follow-up study with the same subjects. The more aroused a couple had been in the earlier study, the more marital satisfaction had declined since then. Thus, the earlier arousal may have indicated the couple's past affective experience, summarized over the history of the relationship. Interestingly, dissatisfaction at the time of the original study and declines in satisfaction as measured in the follow-up study were predicted by males' emotional withdrawal and females' emotional involvement, both in terms of negative emotion (presumably used to express dissatisfaction) and positive emotion (presumably used to draw the husband back into the relationship).

Related research by Gaelick et al (1985) adds more information about emotional interdependence in marital interaction. After conversations about marital problems had been videotaped, spouses were asked to describe their own intentions and reactions during those conversations, as well as their perceptions of their partner's intentions, reactions, and perceptions of themselves in return. Gaelick et al found that participants reciprocated the degree of love and hostility they perceived their partner to convey. Spouses also believed that their own expressions of emotion were reciprocated by their partners. However, perceptions were not always accurate, and only hostility, not love, was actually reciprocated. Sternberg & Barnes (1985) found related results in a study of actual and ideal love partners. Relationship success was more closely linked to perceptions of the other than to actual characteristics of the other.

Sex differences were also observed in Gaelick et al's (1985) study. Expressed hostility affected women's satisfaction more than men's. In addition, women, but not men, perceived their partner's lack of hostility as an indication of love, whereas men, but not women, perceived their partner's lack of love as an indication of hostility. In other words, women exhibited a positive bias in interpreting ambiguous communication whereas men's bias was negative—a pattern also evident in a study of decoding errors in nonverbal communication by Noller (1980). Noller likewise found differences between satisfied and dissatisfied couples in emotional communication. Well-adjusted couples were better able to communicate emotion nonverbally than couples low in adjustment, largely because husbands from happy marriages sent clearer messages and made fewer decoding errors than husbands in unhappy marriages.

To summarize, emotion clearly plays an important role in natural interdependence. More research on the nature of emotional interdependence in different situations, different types of relationships, and at different stages of relationships is needed.

LAY UNDERSTANDING AND PROTOTYPES OF EMOTION   A somewhat different approach with considerable potential for helping us understand the role of emotion in relationships deals with people's accounts of their own emotional experiences (e.g. Averill 1982, 1983; Scherer et al 1986; Schwartz & Shaver 1987). Researchers in this area come from a variety of theoretical backgrounds but share the assumption that to understand emotion fully we must understand the (often social) antecedents and consequences that comprise emotional experience. One example of such research comes from Averill (1982, 1983), a social constructivist, who asserts that emotions are complex "syndromes" of physiological, cognitive, and social responses, no single subset of which is necessary or sufficient to define the emotion in question. Emotion is seen as arising from social situations and as serving social functions. (For example, anger might be caused by another person blocking one's goals, and it might be expressed in order to stop that person from blocking one's goals in the future.) Averill has focused primarily on anger and has collected people's descriptions of their own experiences expressing emotion and being the target of another person's expressed emotions. Among the questions he has asked are "At whom do people become angry?" "What events cause anger?" and "What are the consequences of anger?" In the majority of cases, anger is expressed at well-known and well-liked targets rather than at disliked others or strangers. Anger generally arises in response to a perceived misdeed by another person and it is thought to be voluntary, intentional, and preventable. In addition, targets of anger reported that the consequences of the anger were sometimes positive (e.g. it made them realize their own faults or strengths) and often interpersonal in nature (e.g. anger can strengthen relationships).

Another example of this approach to understanding emotion, not derived from a social constructivist perspective, is provided by Shaver, Schwartz, and their colleagues (Schwartz & Shaver 1987; Shaver & Schwartz 1987; Shaver et al 1987). In their view, emotion is an organizational construct that links various components, such as concerns, appraisals, and action tendencies, in a functionally meaningful way. Using a paradigm and techniques originally developed by Rosch (e.g. Rosch 1978; see also Fehr & Russell 1984), these researchers identified "emotion prototypes," that is, people's implicit understanding of and beliefs about emotions. By cluster analyzing descriptions of actual emotional experiences, Shaver et al identified prototypical scripts—antecedents, responses, and self-control procedures—of anger, fear, sadness, joy, and love. Sadness, for example, begins with perception of loss, harm, or defeat, often in the realm of social relationships (e.g. social rejection or death of a loved one), and leads to responses such as withdrawal, reduced talking, and crying. Self-control procedures include attempts to alter or eradicate existing circumstances, such as, in the case of sadness, energetic activity, denial, or hopeful optimism.

Analyses of lay conceptions of emotion should prove valuable in increasing our knowledge of emotional processes in relationships. They provide many hypotheses about elicitation and expression of emotion in relationships, how people react to such emotion, when and how they try to control emotions, and how emotional expression influences the future course of a relationship. All of these issues are at the core of understanding the role of emotion in close relationships.

IMPLICATIONS OF EXISTING THEORIES FOR EMOTION IN RELATIONSHIPS
We turn finally to research that derives principles for thinking about emotional processes in relationships from theories of other social psychological phenomena. A good example is Self-Evaluation Maintenance theory (Tesser 1987). This theory holds that people are motivated to maintain positive self-evaluations; it proposes two processes through which self-evaluation may be influenced by others—"comparison" and "reflection." On tasks relevant to self-definitions, people compare their performance to that of their partners. When comparison favors the other, self-evaluation decreases. This decrease is greater to the extent that people feel close to the other. [Unlike Kelley et al (1983), Tesser defines closeness as the extent to which people see themselves belonging with the other.] On the other hand, when someone we feel close to performs well on tasks not relevant to our self-evaluation, we "bask in their reflected glory," and self-evaluation increases. The implications of the theory for emotion are clear. When self-evaluation improves, positive emotions should be experienced; when it deteriorates, negative emotions should predominate.

Research largely supports this derivation. Considering comparison processes first, Salovey & Rodin (1984) found that when subjects received feedback that similar others had outperformed them on a relevant dimension, feelings of jealousy, depression, and anxiety were highest, and liking and desire for friendship were lowest (similarity promotes perceptions of belonging with the other in Tesser's view). When the dimension was irrelevant to the self, or if the other was not similar, such effects dropped off. Nadler et al (1983) found that receiving help twice from a friend on a task of high self-relevance produced more negative affect than receiving help once on a relevant task from a friend, help on any kind of task from a stranger, or help on an irrelevant task from anyone. Finally, Tesser et al (1987) found, in one study, that being outperformed by close others on relevant tasks produced greater arousal than being outperformed on the same task by someone who is not close (arousal is interpreted as evidence of negative affect). In another study, in which subjects received feedback about their own and a partner's performance on a high-relevance task, Tesser et al (1987) observed a reduction in facial pleasantness expressed to a friend (relative to a stranger) when the other began to perform better than the self.

Existing studies also support the predicted influence of reflection processes on emotion. Moore & Tesser (1987) found that on self-irrelevant tasks, subjects felt better when outperformed by a friend than when their performance equaled that of a friend or when their partner was a stranger. In addition, Tesser et al (1987) found that being outperformed by close others on irrelevant tasks increased arousal relative to being outperformed by others who are not close on the same tasks (in this case arousal was interpreted as evidence of positive affect). In a second study, they found that low-relevance tasks produced increased facial pleasantness expressed to a friend (relative to a stranger) as the other began to perform better than the self.

Others, working outside the self-evaluation maintenance framework, have also applied social comparison theory to emotional processes in relationships. For example, Rosenhan et al (1981) demonstrated that one's own joy increased helping. However, thinking about another person's joy decreased helping. The reverse held true for sadness. When experienced for the self it decreased helping, but thinking about another person's sadness increased helping (Thompson et al 1980). Apparently, thinking about another person's feelings elicits social comparison. If the other feels worse than oneself, helping increases; if the other feels better, helping decreases.

The implications of equity theory for emotion in relationships have also been explored. Researchers have begun to examine the implications of global feelings of inequity for the experience of specific emotions such as depression (Schafer & Keith 1980) and guilt, hurt, resentment, sadness, and satisfaction

(Sprecher 1986). Like earlier researchers interested in global measures of distress (e.g. Walster et al 1978), these researchers found evidence that perceived inequity is related to the experience of negative emotions.

A final example is provided by Kelley's recent theory of interdependence (Kelley 1979; Kelley et al 1987). Kelley and his colleagues had subjects play matrix games varying in the degree and symmetry of interdependence between partners, commonality versus conflict of interest, and fate control or behavior control—in other words, games representing some of the basic patterns of interdependence identified earlier (Kelley & Thibaut 1978). After playing the games, subjects were asked questions about how likely the various types of interdependence were to generate emotion. Not surprisingly, high-conflict situations were seen as very likely to generate anger, whereas low-conflict situations were described as pleasant and as unlikely to evoke emotion. Low symmetry was seen as creating the possibility of anger in one person and guilt in the other.

Kelley (1984) has also discussed the importance of emotion in "intersituational transitions." According to Kelley, emotions summarize recent experiences in terms of both the specific outcomes obtained in interdependent situations and reactions to the partner's "transformation tendencies." Receiving rewards from interaction with another person, for example, may make one feel happy. Further, if the other is considerate—a transformation tendency in which the other gives importance to one's outcomes as well as the other's own—the experience of happiness and gratitude may be enhanced all the more. In addition, emotion orients people toward future interdependent situations by determining what situations they are likely to enter, what specific actions they will take, and what transformations they will make. For instance, happy people may be more willing to enter a situation in which their outcomes depend upon another person, may be more likely to behave cooperatively, and may be more likely to make prosocial transformations of their own. Kelley's work begins to tell us how various patterns of interdependence produce specific emotions, but further work is needed in which subjects' actual emotional reactions are assessed, rather than their perceptions of what emotions are likely to be elicited. More work on the impact of emotion on behavior in interdependent situations, choices of situations, and transformational tendencies would also be valuable.

The studies summarized in this section indicate considerable progress in understanding the role played by emotions in close relationships. We believe this progress will continue, and that such research will be increasingly tied to interdependence, as discussed above, and intimacy, the process to which we turn next.

INTIMACY

If nothing else, recent research on intimacy is notable for ushering in a broader conceptualization, one that is more nearly commensurate with lay usage, and with psychologists' implicit theoretical understanding of the construct. Using publication of Altman & Taylor's (1973) *Social Penetration* theory as a reference point, a decade and a half ago the casual reader of the literature would have concluded that intimacy referred to the willingness to disclose information about normatively private topics to another person or, alternatively, to interaction that was physically proximate or nonverbally engaging. [Recall Hall's (1966) use of the term *intimate zone* to describe interactions in which participants were placed 18 inches or less from each other.] Since then, the operational definition of intimacy has been expanded and refined, so that it encompasses a broader set of phenomena and processes and, more importantly, possesses greater construct and ecological validity. For present purposes, intimacy is defined as a process in which one person expresses important self-relevant feelings and information to another, and as a result of the other's response comes to feel known, validated (i.e. obtains confirmation of his or her world view and personal worth), and cared for. This definition is developed and extended by Reis & Shaver (1988).

Components of Intimacy

The fact that early definitions were too narrow is indicated in two studies that examined spontaneous accounts of what people mean by "intimacy" (Helgeson et al 1987; Waring et al 1980). In both, affection and emotional expressiveness were mentioned at least as prominently as disclosure. Other characteristics were also central: support, cohesiveness, and sexuality, for example. Lay accounts need not be definitive parameters for rigorous theorizing and research, of course, but in this instance they were closer than research was to many influential theoretical positions, such as those of Sullivan, Erikson, and Rogers.

Morton (1978), in one of the first self-disclosure studies taking emotion into account, distinguished between descriptive self-disclosure (revealing facts about oneself) and evaluative self-disclosure (revealing personal feelings about one's life). She found these factors to be conceptually and empirically distinct, and the combination of descriptive and evaluative intimacy to be more common among spouses than strangers. Another study (Berg & Archer 1982) further suggested that early evidence for the importance of descriptive intimacy might be traced to the fact that subjects typically were strangers instructed to seek and convey accurate impressions of each other. This setting seems likely to maximize the value of informational disclosure. Berg & Archer compared an explicit information-seeking condition with another condition in which subjects were instructed to converse as they might in the "real world" and create a favorable impression. In the former condition, rates of evaluative and descriptive disclosure were about equal. In the latter, when confederates disclosed intimately, subjects responded by increasing their own levels of evaluative but not descriptive intimacy.

Other, more recent studies also suggest that emotional openness is a more important component of self-revelation than informational disclosure. Pennebaker & Beall (1986) found that disclosing feelings about traumatic events in one's life led to decreased health problems six months later. In contrast, subjects whose disclosure was limited to the facts of those events were no better off than control subjects who discussed trivial topics. Marital communication and satisfaction are also more strongly influenced by disclosure of feelings than by disclosure of information (Fitzpatrick 1987). The direction of this influence may be positive or negative, depending on the nature of the feelings revealed and the manner in which couples cope with them.

The notion that emotional self-expression might lie at the heart of the disclosure component of intimacy helps to integrate this literature with its traditional counterpart, nonverbal involvement. Heretofore, nonverbal engagement, such as through physical closeness, eye contact, and touch, has generally been shown to enhance perceived intimacy, but these factors have rarely been unified with verbal self-disclosure in a comprehensive theoretical model. Because nonverbal channels are prominent in emotional communication (Ekman et al 1972; Izard 1977; but see Brown 1987 for a somewhat different point of view), it seems reasonable to expect that emotional self-revelation includes nonverbal components. Patterson (1982, 1984) has suggested such an integration, proposing that nonverbal factors be thought of as "involvement" behaviors—forms of engagement that enhance or diminish partners' impact on each other. Involvement behaviors may serve many functions, two of which are pertinent here: expressing intimacy (feelings of openness and/or union with another person) and communicating personal information. Thus, one might examine how nonverbal behaviors influence these functions.

Although little research has explored the interface between nonverbal and verbal components of intimacy, there are notable exceptions (Montgomery 1981, 1984; Schwartz et al 1987). Montgomery examined several components of open communication simultaneously, including verbal content, nonverbal openness, emotional openness, and verbal immediacy (i.e. paralinguistic cues such as use of the active voice and "I" statements). In one study of self-revealing conversations (1981), communication style was shown to be an important and independent dimension of self-revelation, over and above content and topic of disclosure. In another study (1984), Montgomery demonstrated that sender and receiver judgments of openness were both predicted better by communication style variables than by content variables. [See also Hornstein's (1985) study of the importance of paralinguistic cues in intimate communication.] Schwartz et al (1987) found that males tend to respond to conversations about highly intimate topics by withdrawing nonverbally, whereas females tend to approach.

Intimacy, then, involves both verbal and nonverbal communication of personally relevant information and emotions. Recent conceptualizations, however, as well as more traditional views, suggest that these processes may be necessary but not sufficient to foster intimate bonds. Chelune et al (1984), for example, propose that the next step involves metacognition, arising from appraisal of revealed information that evolves into shared, reciprocal understandings: coming "to know the innermost, subjective aspects of another, and [becoming] known in a like manner" (p. 14). Acitelli & Duck (1987) also discuss the importance of metacognitions in intimate relationships. Reis & Shaver (1988) go further. Drawing on the theories of Sullivan, Erikson, and Rogers, they posit that the fundamental characteristics of intimacy are the discloser's feelings of being understood, validated, and cared for. Derlega (1984; Derlega et al 1987b) also focuses on the role of self-validation in intimacy.

Although to date validation and caring have received less attention than self-disclosure in studies of intimacy, their relevance has nevertheless received support. For example, mutual validation has been shown to be more common in the problem-focused communication of happy than of distressed couples (Gottman 1979). With regard to caring, Sprecher (1987) demonstrated that liking for a dating partner was correlated with perceived disclosure by that partner, a finding that is consistent with Archer et al's (1980) laboratory study of self-disclosure by new acquaintances. Moreover, significant self-disclosure seems unlikely if listeners are perceived to be disinterested or uncaring (Reis & Shaver 1988). Berg & Archer (1980) found that recipients of high self-disclosure were liked better when they gave concerned responses (acknowledgment plus sympathy) than when they replied with reciprocally high self-disclosures of their own. Because these processes appear repeatedly in theories of intimacy (see Perlman & Fehr 1987, for a review, or Fisher & Stricker's 1982 collection of various perspectives), and especially because lay accounts focus on affection, validation, and support as much as they do on disclosure (Helgeson et al 1987; Waring et al 1980), the view of intimacy emerging from future research seems likely to continue expanding its conceptual breadth.

Examining Intimacy on Different Levels

Existing research has for the most part discussed intimacy as if it were a unitary phenomenon. Yet different researchers have examined different aspects of the phenomenon, so that at times the emergent picture depends very much on the perspective adopted. It may not be coincidental, then, that three recent reviews likened intimacy to the proverbial elephant (Acitelli & Duck, 1987; Montgomery, 1984; Reis & Shaver 1988). At this point, a fully integrated picture seems premature. Nevertheless, in the interest of clarifying research results that often appear not to fit together, it may be useful to identify and discuss various perspectives that have received empirical attention in recent years. Three viewpoints will be discussed: processes involved in intimate interaction, the nature of intimate relationships, and individual differences in capacities and preferences for intimacy.

EXAMINING INTIMACY AS A PROCESS   Nearly all early social-psychological research into self-disclosure and nonverbal engagement concerned intimacy processes—namely the mechanisms by which intimacy (within this more narrow definition) arises, develops, and influences subsequent interaction. As discussed earlier, it now seems more appropriate to view intimacy as a multicomponent process, including disclosure of personally relevant facts and feelings, affection and caring, and validation. But the legacy of early research is such that in the recent literature self-disclosure still receives the lion's share of attention.

Advances in our understanding of self-disclosure processes have been modest. As early as 1973, Altman & Taylor, and Rubin were able to summarize existing research with two general principles that, in more recent reviews, still endure as the most apt generalizations (e.g. Berscheid 1985): (a) disclosure becomes more intimate as partners become better acquainted, and vice versa (social penetration); and (b) disclosure levels tend to be mutual (reciprocity). Even so, useful additions and qualifications to our knowledge have appeared. For example, with regard to social penetration, research by Hays (1984, 1985) indicates that disclosure levels may reach asymptote as early as six weeks into the development of a new relationship. Also, Prager (1986) found that individuals who have not attained a close primary relationship disclose highly and equally to both strangers and close friends. Perhaps the failure to differentiate levels of self-disclosure as a function of closeness contributes to the inability to develop ongoing intimate relationships, since close friends usually prefer that their disclosure to each other is unique and personalized (Derlega & Grzelak 1979; Jones & Archer 1976). With regard to relationship termination, although it was originally assumed that dissolution would involve progressively decreasing levels of disclosure (Altman & Taylor 1973; Taylor & Altman 1987), recent studies suggest that this may not be so. Tolstedt & Stokes (1984), for example, demonstrated that as married couples became less close, the depth of their disclosure to each other increased, presumably because they were working through the failure of their relationship.

The fact that self-disclosure tends to be reciprocal has also been specified more precisely in recent research. Miller & Kenny (1986), employing Social Relations Analysis (see Methodology section, below) separated dyadic effects (reciprocity unique to particular relationships) from individual effects (reciprocity due to the tendency of people who generally disclose equivalently, or who are generally disclosed to equivalently, to prefer interacting with each other). No evidence for individual effects was found, but strong dyadic effects appeared, suggesting that self-disclosure reciprocity is rooted in specific relationships. Moreover, high self-disclosure is not always reciprocated, such as when attributions for the cause of disclosure are unflattering or deindividuating (Derlega et al 1987a), when reactance is induced (Archer & Berg 1978), or when the recipient wants to avoid becoming involved with the speaker (Davis et al 1986). It is also clear that reciprocity is displayed less often in established close relationships than in new or developing relationships (e.g. Morton 1978; Won-Doornick 1979). This may be because reciprocity is observable only over longer time spans in ongoing relationships, or because exchange norms do not apply to communal relationships (Mills & Clark 1982).

An additional novel approach to the study of self-disclosure processes bears noting. Self-disclosure is frequently examined as a response to environmental or relational conditions. In contrast, Miell & Duck (1986) and Miller & Read (1987) independently proposed that disclosing behavior be viewed as an intentional strategy for accomplishing interpersonal goals and plans. Thus, disclosure levels not only reflect normative and relational conditions, they also represent deliberate strategies for steering intimacy levels in one or another direction. This approach seems promising, not only because it might identify the intentional substructure of self-disclosing communication, but also because it might resolve inconsistencies in the existing literature attributable to subtle, often unmentioned, differences in subjects' goal orientation.

EXAMINING INTIMATE RELATIONSHIPS   Intimate relationships are those relationships typically or frequently characterized by the processes described above. Individual intimate episodes are of course not necessarily affected by the same factors that influence ongoing, intimate relationships (Duck & Sants 1983). Most studies of self-disclosure have been conducted in one-time laboratory encounters between strangers, leading Berscheid to conclude that "next to nothing is known of its role in ongoing relationships of some duration and little is known of its role in naturalistic, nonlaboratory contexts" (1985, pp. 469–470). This gap has not gone unnoticed by the field and, as a result, recent research suggests that Berscheid's precis may soon be outdated. Much of this research examines or extends principles derived in laboratory studies of initial encounters to ongoing relationships. For example, Fitzpatrick (1987) demonstrated that disclosure of feelings, more than of facts, affects marital satisfaction, perhaps in part because prior personal knowledge moderates the impact of factual self-disclosure. Other studies in the marital arena address other components of the intimacy process, such as validation and affection (e.g. Gottman 1979; Noller 1984), generally demonstrating their importance for relationship satisfaction.

Outside of marriage, studies of ongoing relationships are fewer but still forthcoming. In a study of same-sex friendships, Hays (1984, 1985), as noted earlier, found that levels of intimacy, defined in terms of companionship, communication, affection, and consideration, reached maximum levels six weeks after partners became acquainted. Similarly, a short-term longitudinal study by Berg & McQuinn (1986) indicated that higher levels of self-disclosure early in a dating relationship predicted later continuity, and, in a prospective study, Cohen et al (1986) found that self-disclosure predicted changes in perception of tangible, appraisal, and belonging support as well as in the number of friends acquired during students' first year at college. As for the later stages of relationships, a recent review by Baxter (1987) concluded that intimate disclosure often increases as relationships dissolve, especially when such disclosure concerns facts and feelings about the relationship itself. In sum, although it is apparent that process-oriented research involving sustained relationships is in a nascent state, theoretically useful findings have begun to appear.

A key distinction to be emphasized concerns the difference between intimacy processes and behaviors occurring in intimate relationships. Many of the studies described in the preceding section examined the operation of intimacy processes in intimate relationships. The existence of an intimate relationship, however, indicates only that a particular kind of connection exists; it does not necessarily implicate intimacy processes per se in every behavior that occurs, because many other activities and processes are also present within intimate relationships. For example, many studies examine attribution processes in marriage, sometimes ascribing attributional differences between married persons and strangers to the impact of intimacy. It is possible, however, that the findings are due to other processes operating in close relationships, such as denial of responsibility, deception, or division of labor. Such studies are generally not informative about the nature of intimacy as a process; rather, the existing intimate relationship is simply one contextual factor underlying the phenomenon of interest.[2]

This issue sometimes arises in research deriving from Erikson's (1950,

---

[2]To some extent, this difficulty arises because "intimate" is frequently used as a synonym for "close," or worse, for the existence of a marriage. Although such usage is consistent with everyday definitions, it does not lend itself to conceptual or operational rigor. We suggest that the term "intimate relationship" should be reserved for relationships that fulfill the psychological conditions of intimacy processes.

1968) conceptualization of intimacy. Consistent with his focus, researchers developed questionnaires assessing intimacy status—the presence or absence of an intimate relationship (e.g. Orlofsky 1987; Ochse & Plug 1986). Intimacy status is then related to a variety of demographic, individual-difference, and outcome measures (e.g. personality development, mental health). Although this subdiscipline is developing useful core concepts of its own, the fact of an intimate relationship and the impact of its existence might be attributable to environmental circumstances, preferences, goals, and demographic factors, in addition to the personality and relational processes described in Erikson's theory. Consequently, the relevance of these findings to process-oriented studies and theories remains unclear. Rapprochement is desirable.[3]

EXAMINING INDIVIDUAL DIFFERENCES   The third level of analysis, which only in the past decade has become the object of systematic empirical attention, concerns individual differences in preferences and capacities for intimacy. Research on this topic is needed for two reasons: First, and obviously, it elucidates the influence of personality variables on intimacy processes; and, second, it allows researchers to observe the impact and operation of these processes among persons who possess and display those characteristics most strongly (Snyder & Ickes 1985). Thus, studies of individual dispositions toward intimacy are an increasingly valuable source of knowledge about intimacy processes per se.

Although early studies examined dispositional variables related to it, intimacy was never discriminated from other traits in the affiliation/nurturance cluster. For example, elements of intimacy can be found in Murray's (1938) needs for affiliation, nurturance, rejection, and succorance. Recently, primarily through the work of McAdams and his colleagues, a differentiated concept of intimacy motivation has been articulated and operationalized. According to McAdams, "the intimacy motive is a recurrent preference or readiness for experiences of close, warm, and communicative exchange with others" (1984, p. 45). McAdams's studies are based on a projective measure of intimacy motivation—content analyses of Thematic Apperception Test (TAT) responses—and constitute a sophisticated program of research on the effects of intimacy motivation on social interaction and personal well-being. For example, relative to low scorers, persons high in intimacy motivation express greater trust in and concern for friends; self-disclose more emotional,

---

[3]Erikson's theorizing was also very different from that of earlier studies that focused on self-disclosure and nonverbal communication, but this may have been a limitation of those studies. The reconceptualization of intimacy to include notions of validation and affection, as discussed earlier, relies with increasing emphasis on points made by Erikson.

personal, and relational content (McAdams et al 1984a); and have more frequent and more affectively positive interpersonal thoughts in daily interaction (McAdams & Constantian 1983). They also are perceived as more likable and noncompetitive by peers (McAdams & Powers 1981); smile, laugh, and engage eye contact more often in an interview (McAdams et al 1984b); and, in a longitudinal study, report greater marital enjoyment and better personal adjustment 17 years after intimacy motivation was assessed (McAdams & Vaillant 1982). It is noteworthy that these effects are demonstrably independent of the need for affiliation, a broader social motive with a more instrumental flavor (McAdams & Constantian 1983; McAdams & Powers 1981).

Research employing this and related measures has for the most part been limited to studies of dispositional and contextual factors that affect intimate behavior. Yet because individuals differ in their desire for, and appreciation of, intimacy, it seems apparent that full understanding of the nature of intimacy in everyday life requires a person × situation approach (Snyder & Smith 1986). One need only scan the literature to realize the potential impact a moderator-variable approach might have on the formulation of interesting hypotheses. Do persons high in intimacy motivation respond differently to circumstantial disruptions of their social network than those low in intimacy motivation? Does the impact of emotionally charged self-revelation depend on the listener's preferred level of intimacy? Does the effect of intimate self-disclosure on marital conflict depend on partners' predispositions for intimacy?

Individual-difference variables have also been related to Erikson's (1950, 1968) concept of intimacy status. Such studies examine personality factors that distinguish persons who have achieved an intimate relationship from those who have not. The extent to which these findings speak directly to intimacy processes is not clear, because, as noted earlier, the presence or absence of an intimate relationship may be attributable to many causes, some relevant to the theory and others not. Nevertheless, a useful view of personality factors influencing the capacity for intimacy is beginning to emerge. Bellew-Smith & Korn (1986) and Tesch & Whitbourne (1982) empirically confirmed Erikson's proposition that a resolved, stable identity is prerequisite to establishing intimate relationships. In a study of college women, Levitz-Jones & Orlofsky (1985) found relatively more severe attachment and separation-individuation problems and heightened defensiveness among subjects experiencing problems in attaining truly intimate relationships. Developmental studies suggest that disturbances in infant-caregiver attachment relations ought to predict intimacy problems in later life (Hazan & Shaver 1987; Main et al 1985; Ricks 1985), presumably because early relationships establish prototypic motives, needs, goals, and fears that tend to persist

(Bowlby 1969; see Reis & Shaver 1988). The longest longitudinal studies available to date (e.g. Sroufe 1987) indicate that early attachment difficulties adversely affect middle-childhood peer relations in a manner that may foretell intimacy problems in adulthood (cf Buhrmester & Furman 1986; Kohlberg et al 1984).

Sex Differences

If any subarea of intimacy research has yielded inconsistent, difficult to reconcile findings, it is the area of sex differences. The general thrust of these findings is that females are likely to express greater interpersonal intimacy than males do. Some studies indicate either no difference or greater intimacy among males, however (see Cozby 1973 or Hill & Stull 1986 for reviews). Because of these contradictions, research has turned in the direction of identifying potential moderator variables, and recent studies suggest principles that may prove helpful in reconciling past results. First, sex differences indicating greater intimacy among females than males appear stronger in same-sex interaction than in opposite-sex interaction (Caldwell & Peplau 1982; Reis 1986), perhaps because societal norms inhibit intimacy in all-male dyads more than in other sex pairings. Second, although intimacy typically serves expressive purposes, males may increase intimacy more than females do in situations that allow intimacy to serve goal-oriented, instrumental functions. For example, Derlega et al (1985) found that males paired with newly met female partners disclosed more intimately than males with male partners or females with partners of either sex, presumably because they were trying to create favorable impressions. Third, studies that examine intimacy motivation or interest in intimate friendship tend to show few sex differences, whereas laboratory observations and self-reports of existing and past interactions tend to reveal greater intimacy among females. This may indicate greater behavioral inhibition by males than by females with equivalent preferences for intimate interaction (Reis et al 1985). Other moderator variables have also been proposed, such as sex-role identity (Hill & Stull 1986; Wheeler et al 1983), questionnaire differences (Hill & Stull 1986), and conversation topics (Rubin et al 1980). It seems clear that a moderator-variable approach, incorporating notions discussed elsewhere in this review, is needed to resolve these inconsistencies.

Is Intimacy All Good?

Most, if not all, empirical studies and theoretical analyses of intimacy are grounded in the assumption that intimacy has many positive effects on human well-being, and indeed, much existing research supports this assumption. For example, recent studies have linked greater intimacy to the absence of loneliness (Wheeler et al 1983), the perception of social support (Hobfoll et al

1986), better psychosocial adjustment (McAdams & Vaillant 1982), fewer symptoms of illness (Pennebaker & Beall 1986; Reis et al 1985), and higher levels of ego development (Loevinger 1976). Nevertheless, intimacy may also have negative consequences. Rook's (1984, 1988) studies of social support, for example, demonstrate that psychological well-being may be affected adversely by problems and conflicts stemming from intimate interaction. Fitzpatrick's (1987) research suggests that intimate self-disclosure and open communication may be harmful for married couples who define their relationships in an emotionally distanced manner [which is, incidentally, a more common definition of marriage in earlier eras (Gadlin 1977) and in other cultures (Dion & Dion 1988)]. Disclosure and discussion of fearful feelings can also, at least in the short run, aggravate anxiety and interfere with coping (Costanza et al 1987).

Intimacy might also produce comparison problems, given that intimate partners are likely to see themselves as close and similar. Tesser's creative studies of self-esteem maintenance (summarized in Tesser 1987) indicate that when two individuals are close, superior performance by one on self-relevant tasks may threaten the other's self-esteem and lead to negative emotions (see Emotion section, above). Such threat can be managed in various ways, but all seem detrimental: distancing from the partner, self-depreciation, and loss of interest in the task, for example. Finally, harmful effects that arise in the context of intimate relationships are discussed often in the clinical literature. These effects include negative feelings and growth-inhibiting states such as enmeshment, exploitation, vulnerability, loss of individuality, and fear of abandonment (Fisher & Stricker 1982; Hatfield 1984). To us, the fact that both positive and negative consequences of intimacy have been observed points to the need to distinguish intimacy as a process from other phenomena that occur in the context of intimate relationships. It does not seem appropriate to describe the consequences of fighting or emotional withholding in a marriage, for example, as a negative effect of intimacy, because it is precisely the failure to adequately provide components of the intimacy process per se that is problematic. Fuller understanding of the manner in which intimacy may be detrimental therefore requires distinguishing relationship context from processes that are causally responsible for observed effects. Further research along the lines suggested above, and in the concluding section of this review, may be useful in supplying such information and in helping to integrate our understanding of positive and negative consequences of intimacy.

LOVE

We have focused on three processes in this review: interdependence, emotion, and intimacy. These processes were selected in the belief that they apply to most types of close, personal relationships, and that our understanding of particular relationships will be enhanced by considering the operation of these processes within them. This logic seems especially pertinent to the study of love. Love was a fertile topic for social psychological research during the mid-1970s, but then, both because political pressure deemed love "unscientific" and because empirical studies had to that point failed to capture the essence of romantic love (Berscheid 1988; Rubin 1988), research activity abated. Love has reemerged in conceptually broader form as a productive area of inquiry in the mid-1980s. Much new theory and research examines interpersonal processes that affect the experience of love in human relationships, and we focus on this material. Because the resurgence of love research is still new, theoretical statements have outpaced empirical findings, and many of the most interesting propositions remain to be tested. Nevertheless, in reviewing this material, it became apparent to us that intimacy, emotion, and outcome interdependence were critical to most theories of love. Consequently, our understanding of love may be enhanced by considering the operation of these three processes in the context of existing love research and theory.

Before turning to process-oriented accounts of love, it may be helpful to discuss descriptive studies that seek to establish the nature of love.

Descriptions of Love: Prototypes and Varieties

Two conceptual frameworks dominated the first wave of love research. First, Rubin's (1973) model conceived of love as an attitude comprised of three components: attachment (needing), caring, and intimacy (willingness to self-disclose). Berscheid & Walster (1974, 1978), in a second approach, proposed two distinct types of love, companionate and passionate. Companionate love referred to affection felt for others with whom we are deeply intertwined. Passionate love dealt with intense feelings of absorption in another person, and arose from heightened physiological arousal labeled as love (in the manner of Schachter's two-factor theory of emotion). Although both approaches bore reasonable empirical fruit, they were ultimately dissatisfying in their failure to describe the many varieties and richness of human loving experiences (McClelland 1986) and in their inability to account for many causal antecedents and consequences of love.

The need for a broader view was noted by Kelley (1983a), who argued that a full theoretical account of love must include four kinds of information: identification of observable phenomena, notions about current causes of these phenomena, their historical antecedents, and their future consequences. A number of descriptive studies have focused on the first aspect of Kelley's mandate. Shaver et al (1987), for example, sought to identify prototypic conceptions of love. Relying on cluster analyses of emotion words and of written accounts of love experiences, they found that love was characterized primarily in companionate terms (e.g. adoration, affection, fondness), although a more passion-oriented secondary cluster (e.g. desire, lust) also emerged. The most prototypical antecedents were also companionate in nature—believing the loved other provides something the person needs or wants, realizing that one is appreciated by the other, communicating openly, and finding the other attractive. Responses to love included expression of positive feelings; physical affection; being obsessed with thoughts about the other; and feeling self-confident, happy, and secure about the relationship.

Other descriptively oriented studies have also examined prototypic accounts of love, with similar results. Davis & Todd (1982) suggested that a cluster of affectionate-companionate traits characterizes love in general (e.g. in relationships with siblings, children, close friends, etc) and that passionate arousal is added to this core to differentiate the special case of romantic relationships. Fehr (1987) had subjects rate how central each of 68 attributes (generated from spontaneous descriptions of love) was to the concept of love. Trust, caring, honesty, and friendship were seen as most central, whereas passion and attraction were more peripheral. Fehr & Perlman (1987) extended the prototype logic by demonstrating that central traits covaried more closely with perceptions of the degree of love than peripheral traits did. Thus, affectionate qualities seem more characteristic of lay conceptions of love, generically defined, than passionate qualities do. Still, Fehr & Perlman's data indicate that passionate arousal—lust, to use Berscheid's (1988) term—is an important secondary feature of romantic love in particular. The dynamic properties of passionate love have received little research attention, however, and are not well understood (Berscheid 1988).

An alternate tack to describing the phenomenon of love is taken by researchers who identify and define different types of love. Such studies begin with the assumption that there are demonstrably different and conceptually distinct styles of loving, as reflected both in individual tendencies to repeatedly prefer one or more of these love styles, and in systematic variations from one kind of relationship to another. Perhaps the best known of these efforts is Lee's (1973, 1988) "colors of love" typology, which was recently converted into a self-report questionnaire by Hendrick & Hendrick (1986). Lee's typology posits three primary classes of love—Eros (passionate love), Ludus (game-playing love), and Storge (companionate love)—and three secondary classes, blending all possible pairs of the primary types: Mania (possessive, dependent love), Pragma (logical, practical love), and Agape (selfless love). By and large, Lee's typology is confined to simple description and includes little theorizing about the dynamic properties of different types of love. As a result, research using his framework has been limited to documenting attitudinal, personality, and gender-related correlates of the various types. For example, women have been shown to be more manic, storgic, and pragmatic, and less ludic and erotic than men (Hendrick et al 1984). Also, erotic and agapic lovers tend to self-disclose more to their lovers and see sex as a communal act, whereas ludic lovers have more permissive sexual attitudes, see sex as an egocentric, hedonic act, and disclose less (Hendrick & Hendrick 1987).

Other researchers offer different taxonomies. Kelley (1983a), for example, suggests three primary types of love: passionate, pragmatic, and altruistic. Berscheid (1983, 1988) proposes four varieties: eros, friendship, attachment-affection, and altruistic love. Hazan & Shaver (1987), drawing on attachment theory, advance three categories: securely attached, anxious/ambivalent, and avoidant. Sternberg's (1986) triangular theory of love uses the presence or absence of each of three factors—intimacy, passion, and commitment—to yield eight possible combinations: nonlove, romantic love, liking, fatuous love, infatuation, companionship, empty love, and consummate love. No doubt other and more differentiated classification schemes can and will be conceived. If they are to have theoretical value, they must go beyond simple description of face-valid types to suggest new understandings of the causal dynamics of love. That is, the primary gain to be realized from taxonomies of love is in pointing the way to differences in causal antecedents, moderators, mediating processes, and consequences among the sundry varieties of love (Berscheid 1988; Kelley 1983a). When used in this manner, taxonomies have the potential to enhance our knowledge about processes involved in the phenomenon of love. We now turn to research that has examined such processes.

Interpersonal Processes in the Experience of Love

In our opinion, the most exciting developments in the resurgence of love research concern its constituent processes. Different researchers have, of course, advocated different theoretical positions. Nevertheless, our sense is that they all involve, in one form or another, the three interpersonal processes reviewed earlier in this chapter. Thus, love research demonstrates how relationship researchers repeatedly rely on aspects of these three core processes.

One promising model that has received a great deal of popular attention is offered by Sternberg (1986). He proposes that love has three component processes: intimacy, passion, and commitment. Intimacy refers to feelings that promote closeness, such as affection, positive regard, self-disclosure, and supportiveness. Sternberg hypothesizes that the intimacy component is large-ly emotional, so that it follows Berscheid's (1983) account of emotional processes (discussed above). The passion component deals with arousal, some of it sexual and some of it stemming from other sources of motivation such as needs and traits. This factor, evident in intense feelings of attraction to another person, is presumed to operate in the manner of opponent-processes (Solomon 1980). That is, quickly developing positive drives are balanced by more slowly developing (and more slowly fading) negative drives. The final component of Sternberg's model consists of two elements, short-term decisions that one loves another person, and long-term commitment to maintain that love. Decision/commitment is primarily a function of relationship duration and success, although research suggests that other factors are also relevant [e.g. availability of alternative partners (Simpson 1987)].

Sternberg's model is primarily a structural model of love. Focusing on the intimacy component, Sternberg & Grajek (1984) compared three plausible alternative models of love: a "Spearmanian" model, which conceptualizes love as a single undifferentiated entity; a "Thomsonian" model, which regards love as a unified composite that can be decomposed into several closely related but distinct components; and a "Thurstonian" model, which views love as a set of independent factors, each of which contributes to the overall experience of love. Based on cluster and factor analyses of various love scales, their data supported the Thomsonian model most closely. Moreover, the structure of intimacy in love that emerged did not vary appreciably from one type of loving relationship to another. Sternberg & Grajek suggest that the nature and role of intimacy may be relatively stable in different relationships, but that passion and commitment are more likely to fluctuate depending on relationship type.

Sternberg also uses the visual heuristic of depicting love as a triangle, in which each vertex represents one of the three primary components. Thus, as with a triangle, the form of the whole depends upon how the three parts connect. Some support for this proposition was provided by Sternberg (1987). The three components varied systematically across different relationships (e.g. mother-child, lovers, siblings) in rated characteristicness and importance, and in their correlations with one another. Sternberg & Wright (1987) demonstrated that the intimacy and commitment components were seen as somewhat more important to various love relationships than passion was.

We see value in Sternberg's theory for at least two reasons. First, in describing both structures and processes involved in love, it is more comprehensive than most existing models. Second, it proposes specific process mechanisms for each component, thereby affording fuller possibilities for developing hypotheses about antecedents and consequences. As yet, however, the validity of these processes for understanding love has not been established empirically, and the fit of these processes to each component is not clear. For example, Sternberg (1986) used Berscheid's theory of emotion to explain intimacy but not passion, yet Berscheid herself used this selfsame theory to account for passionate love (1983, 1988). Further, although couching intimacy as an emotional process is consistent with the role of emotional self-disclosure noted in our review of intimacy research, several aspects of this factor seem likely to appear in the absence of emotional experience (e.g. mutual understanding and regard, dependability). It will therefore be necessary in coming years to provide tests of the process components of Sternberg's model.

Processes of emotion, intimacy, and outcome interdependence are also prominent in another important new theory of love advanced by Hazan & Shaver (1987; Shaver & Hazan 1987; Shaver et al 1988). In their view, derived from Bowlby's (1969) theory, romantic love is best conceptualized as an attachment process. They describe love in two ways: as a momentary emotional state and as a readiness to experience that state with regard to another person. When used in the latter, more dispositional meaning, romantic love between adults bears striking similarities to the affectional bonds that promote attachment between infants and their caregivers. That is, love refers to an enduring affectional bond that involves strong and diverse feelings, as well as the behaviors and behavioral tendencies associated with those feelings. Satisfying bonds evoke a sense of security, contentment, and joy, whereas the absence of such bonds or threats to their continuity produce negative emotions—e.g. anxiety, anger, depression—and behavior designed to restore them or cope with their absence. Continuities between childhood attachment and adult romantic love are further emphasized by the developmental nature of Hazan & Shaver's model. Using Bowlby's term, they propose that "inner working models" (i.e. prototypes that include expectations, beliefs, and defenses about relatedness) are established in the infant-caregiver bond, which later influence desires for and evaluations of adult relationships.

In a pair of studies designed to test these propositions, Hazan & Shaver (1987) derived predictions about adult love relationships from childhood attachment research and then examined adult self-reports of love experiences and beliefs about love for evidence of these effects. Results supported their predictions and the relevance of attachment theory. For example, in secure infant-caregiver relationships, the caregiver provides a "secure base," allowing infants to feel more confident and safe exploring the environment, and happier in general. Similar feelings were promoted by secure adult love relationships. In contrast, adults whose love relationships tended to be insecure showed problems paralleling the behavior of infants with problematic attachment. That is, persons whose love relationships were characteristically avoidant found closeness uncomfortable and believed that "true love" rarely lasts. Anxious-ambivalent lovers reported falling in love quickly and easily, but felt that their desire for merger and union with their lover was rarely reciprocated.

Three aspects of Hazan & Shaver's approach seem especially noteworthy. First, they take a developmental perspective, highlighting similarities and continuities in people's orientation to close relationships across the life span (although, to be sure, they acknowledge that romantic love differs from childhood attachment in several important ways, such as in terms of sexuality and reciprocity). Their model locates the origins of adult love preferences and behaviors in early developmental experiences and proposes mediating processes—cognitive-emotional structures called inner working models—that both account for stability of early relational patterns into adulthood and, at the same time, allow possibilities for later modification and change. Second, partly because it is a broad process-oriented theory, a wide array of relatedness phenomena are housed under a single conceptual roof. In their research and theorizing, such phenomena as love, lovesickness, grief and reactions to loss, loneliness, caregiving and nurturance, and personal well-being are considered and integrated. Third, the same general concepts are used to explain insecure and secure relationships, adding parsimony and wholeness to the question of love "types." Earlier accounts of extreme forms of love, particularly of the anxious/ambivalent type, tended to describe them in isolation, with minimal consideration of more generally applicable processes or of the relationship between secure and insecure forms of love (e.g. Hindy & Schwarz 1984; Peele 1975, 1988; Tennov 1979). As with Sternberg's model, further research is needed to extend empirical support for their approach beyond existing preliminary evidence.

Hazan & Shaver's approach is also socioevolutionary. They assert: "Romantic love is a biological process designed by evolution to facilitate attachment between adult sexual partners who, at the time love evolved, were likely to become parents of an infant who would need their reliable care" (1987, p. 523). The notion that romantic love might have evolved because of its reproductive advantages has recently been proposed by Buss (1988a), Kenrick & Trost (1986), and Mellen (1981), among others. According to this position, because feelings and actions associated with romantic love lead adults to attract and retain mates, reproduce with them, and invest in their offspring's survival, reproductive success is likely to be enhanced among persons experiencing, and acting upon, romantic love. Activities designed to attain proximate goals related to romantic love, such as resource display and sharing, desires for commitment and exclusivity, sexual and emotional intimacy, and parental investment, are therefore likely to help fulfill the distal goal of reproductive success (Buss 1988a).

Although socioevolutionary accounts of such processes typically do not lead to testable propositions in humans, two recent papers by Buss and his colleagues offer an exception. First, in two studies of mate preferences, Buss & Barnes (1986) found that cues suggestive of investment in the marital bond and in the survival of offspring were more highly ranked than other potential bases for mate choices. Sex differences corresponding to socioevolutionary predictions emerged as well. Males preferred more attractive women (presumably because attractiveness cues such as youth, health, and weight signal reproductive fitness), whereas females preferred males with more education and earnings potential. Second, Buss (1988b) examined tactics used by males and females to attract members of the opposite sex. Males more frequently relied on resource displays (e.g. bragging about accomplishments, demonstrating strength), whereas females were more likely to focus on appearance (e.g. using cosmetics, dieting, dressing provocatively). Of course, because such propositions also might be generated by other theoretical frameworks, the predictive uniqueness of socioevolutionary concepts remains to be demonstrated. Nevertheless, recent accounts, such as those of Buss (1988a) and Hazan & Shaver (1987), are promising because they integrate evolutionary considerations with more proximate interpersonal processes.

A few additional studies have examined other aspects of emotion processes involved in love. White et al (1981) provided the clearest evidence to date that physiological arousal, regardless of its source, can be misattributed to romantic love in the manner derived by Berscheid & Walster (1974, 1978) from Schachter's two-factor theory of emotion. In two experiments, they demonstrated that arousal produced by exercise or listening to humorous or distressing audiotapes increased males' romantic attraction to an attractive female but not to an unattractive female. Relatedly, Seligman et al (1980) showed that attending to extrinsic reasons for a relationship led partners to report less love for each other. In a very different vein, Harvey et al (1986) examined descriptions of past love relationships that had been terminated for at least six months. The most vivid memories focused on affect and emotional arousal experienced in the relationship, in its break-up, or in subsequent encounters. Moreover, the more depressed respondents currently were, the more vivid and "flashbulb-like" their accounts were, suggesting that emotional by-products of the lost love relationship were still evident.

Intimacy processes have also been investigated in recent studies of love. Steck et al (1982), for example, compared the relative salience of care, need, and trust in subjects' conceptions of love, attraction, and friendship for romantic partners. They found that caring was most prototypic of love, needing was more representative of attraction, and trust was more characteristic of friendship. McAdams (1980) reported comparable findings in a study of TAT protocols provided by in-love and not-in-love matched controls. In their descriptions of the depicted relationships, in-love persons featured greater positive affect, union, and harmony, and were more likely to describe relationships as happy refuges from outside stress. Because companionate love is in many ways comparable to intimacy (Hatfield 1988), and because the most consistent and central prototypic features of love involve intimacy (as discussed earlier), the need for additional research investigating the operation of intimacy processes within the domain of love is clear.

Finally, although research on interdependence in love relationships has been rarer, a number of useful points have been advanced. Kelley (1983b), for example, proposed that one infers a partner's love from beneficial acts one believes are motivated by the partner's dispositional caring for oneself. Some support for this notion was provided by Rempel et al (1985). They correlated three aspects of trust with love, as measured by Rubin's (1973) scale: predictability (expectations based on the other's past behavior), dependability (dispositional inferences based on the other's past behavior), and faith (dispositional inferences that go beyond available evidence). Love was uncorrelated with predictability, moderately correlated with dependability, and strongly correlated with faith.

A number of studies (reviewed in the section on Interdependence, above) apply equity and other exchange norms to dating relationships and marriage. In a recent review of some of these studies, Hatfield et al (1985) concluded that love relationships in which global impressions of equity are high are more stable and satisfying. There is also evidence (reviewed above in the Interdependence section) that commitment to and satisfaction in adult romantic relationships increase as outcome levels increase and as availability of alternative partners decreases (see especially Rusbult 1980a, 1983; Rusbult et al 1986; Simpson 1987). Nevertheless, we do not know much about how outcome interdependence affects the experience of love, either globally or, as seems more likely, differentiated into its various types. For example, need-based norms might predominate in companionate and securely attached relationships, but equity norms might prevail in avoidant or ludic relationships. As the field begins to examine love in dyadic terms, interdependence processes are likely to grow in importance.

In conclusion, researchers are increasingly aware of the importance of studying interpersonal processes involved in love. The processes described earlier may prove fruitful in enhancing our understanding of this complex and stirring phenomenon.

INDIVIDUAL DIFFERENCES IN RELATIONSHIP PROCESSES

The study of individual differences has great potential for contributing to our knowledge about relationship processes. Although this potential is, as yet, largely unrealized, some recent programs of research have provided important new findings and, as such, illustrate the promise of systematic studies of dispositional differences. First, to show how systematic study of individual differences can help us understand interpersonal processes in close relationships, we review recent studies of self-monitoring in social relations conducted by Snyder and his colleagues. Second, because relationships depend not on the character of one person but on the interaction of two predispositions, we discuss research by Ickes that examines pairings of people with specifiable individual differences. Third, we briefly and selectively review new personality measures of particular relevance to relationship researchers. We highlight these measures because they have already yielded interesting results and, if used in comprehensive programs of research on relationships, seem likely to bear greater intellectual fruit.

Systematically Relating Personality Variables to Relationships: The Case of Self-Monitoring

According to Snyder (1974, 1987), high self-monitors strive to be the kind of person called for by social and interpersonal cues. In contrast, low self-monitors typically try to display their own dispositions and attitudes no matter what the situation. Thus, the behavior of high self-monitors varies from situation to situation and does not necessarily correspond to underlying attitudes, whereas attitude-behavior correspondence is closer among low self-monitors.

What are the implications of this distinction for relationships? Considering friendship first, Snyder et al (1983) examined how people choose activity partners from their own social networks. High self-monitors tended to select partners skilled at the activity in question regardless of how well liked those partners were (presumably because they wanted a partner who would facilitate performance). In contrast, low self-monitors tended to select well-liked partners regardless of their abilities in particular activities (presumably because they could "be themselves" with such others). Such choices leave high self-monitors with highly compartmentalized social networks and low self-monitors with simpler, more integrated networks.

Later studies expanded on these initial findings. For example, content analyses of friendship descriptions revealed that high self-monitors focus primarily on shared activities whereas low self-monitors stress mutual nurturance and compatibility (Snyder & Smith 1986). Moreover, friendship is generally preferred with others of similar self-monitoring levels (Snyder & Smith 1986), perhaps because similarity facilitates goal attainment and smooth interaction. Two high self-monitors, for example, would not feel obliged to interact with each other or provide mutual nurturance beyond situational dictates. Other researchers have also investigated this process. Shaffer et al (1987) found that when future interaction was anticipated, only high self-monitors reciprocated a partner's level of disclosure (a partner's disclosure is a situational cue); lows did not, relying more on their own thoughts and feelings to determine self-disclosure levels. Interestingly, when no future interaction was expected (and therefore no relationship was possible) both high and low self-monitors reciprocated their partner's disclosure.

These findings suggest that high self-monitors might form close, enduring romantic relationships less frequently than low self-monitors, and, indeed, Snyder & Simpson (1984) report evidence to this effect. Compared to low self-monitors, high self-monitors report greater willingness to change partners, more dating partners in the last year, less time in their current relationship, and less of a link between relationship length and intimacy. Additionally, in contrast to low self-monitors, high self-monitors pay relatively more attention to a potential date's physical attractiveness than to enduring personality characteristics, both when initially acquiring information and when actually choosing dating partners (Snyder et al 1985). Glick (1985) found that in choosing a romantic setting for a first date, high self-monitors were particularly influenced by the other's physical appearance, whereas low self-monitors were influenced more by the other's personality. These studies indicate that the choice of interaction partners is broadly influenced by self-monitoring tendencies.

Interestingly, Snyder's research suggests a note of caution to relationship researchers with regard to collecting and interpreting measures based on self-reports of numbers of friends, romantic partners, or significant others [e.g. social network measures, such as that used by Stokes (1983)]. That is, just who qualifies for description as a friend or partner depends on the meaning attributed to those categories of relationships, and people differ systematically in the criteria they use in these judgments.

Examining Interaction Between People with Specified Dispositions

Research by Ickes and his colleagues demonstrates that interaction patterns are often affected by the unique pairing of two individuals, each with specifiable dispositions. In a representative study, using the Unstructured Interaction Paradigm (see the Methodology section, below) Ickes and his colleagues observed pairs of opposite-sex (Ickes & Barnes 1978) or same-sex (Ickes et al 1979) subjects in spontaneous interaction. All subjects had been pretested with the Bem Sex Role Inventory and fit into the masculine, feminine, or androgynous category. Opposite-sex dyads revealed less attraction and behavioral involvement (e.g. less verbalization and fewer directed gazes and expressive gestures) when masculine males were paired with feminine females than when either or both members was androgynous. In same-sex dyads, behavioral involvement was greatest when androgynous subjects were paired, and less when the dyad involved at least one sex-typed person. Apparently, interaction between two sex-typed individuals is likely to be inflexible, distant, and stalemated. In contrast, when both partners were androgynous, each was sufficiently flexible to permit adaptation to the other, facilitating successful interaction. When one member of a dyad was androgynous and the other sex-typed, only opposite-sex pairs had enjoyable interactions; same-sex pairs were stalemated. Ickes accounts for this difference by suggesting that androgynous persons follow the other's lead in same-sex interaction, so that only expressive or instrumental behavior is represented, producing stalemates. On the other hand, in opposite-sex pairs following the other's lead allows androgynous persons the flexibility to adopt behaviors appropriate to their own sex or that of the opposite sex.

Ickes's approach might profitably be applied to other personality and individual-difference variables. How, for example, might pairs of people varying in self-esteem interact? Will people with the same general orientation to relationships interact more successfully than those with mixed orientations? Would shy persons come out of their shell when paired with a socially skilled other? Like Kenny's studies with the Social Relations Model (see the Methodology section, below), Ickes's work nicely illustrates how certain important phenomena emerge only in dyadic contexts. Ickes's approach should not be limited to studies of strangers, however (as he acknowledges; Ickes 1985). We also need to know how particular pairings of dispositional traits influence various relational processes during the development, maintenance, and dissolution stages of ongoing relationships.

New Individual-Difference Measures

Many new individual-difference measures seem particularly relevant to the study of relationship processes. These include: loneliness (Rubenstein & Shaver 1980; Russell et al 1980); shyness (i.e. acute awareness of oneself as a social object, low self-esteem, and tense and awkward feelings with others) and sociability (i.e. preferences for affiliating with others as opposed to being alone) (Cheek & Buss 1981); an "Opener's" scale designed to assess tendencies to elicit self-disclosure from others (Miller et al 1983); intimacy motivation (McAdams 1984); social reticence (Jones & Russell 1982); social anxiety (Leary 1983); and trust and fear of rejection (Reis et al 1982).

Other new measures focus on generalized orientations toward relationships. For instance, Swap & Rubin (1983) presented a measure of "Interpersonal Orientation" (IO). High IOs are interested in and reactive to other people, whereas low IOs are less interested in others and more socially fearful. Clark et al (1987a) and Clark et al (1987b) developed independent measures of "communal" and "exchange" orientations toward relationships. The communal scale assesses the desire to give and receive benefits on the basis of needs or to demonstrate concern for others. It also measures the desire for the other to follow the same rules. The exchange scale assesses the desire to give benefits with the expectation of specific repayment or in response to specific benefits received in the past, as well as the desire for the other to follow the same rule. A somewhat similar "exchange orientation" scale was reported by Murstein & Azar (1986). Their measure concerns the tendency to keep tabs on who does what for whom and to keep benefits and favors balanced in relationships.

For the most part, these scales have demonstrated adequate reliability and at least preliminary evidence for construct validity. Moreover, early studies have yielded interesting results. For example, research with Cheek & Buss's shyness and sociability scales has shown that in free interaction, shy-sociable subjects talk less, avert their gaze more, and engage in self-manipulation more often than people who are not shy, or than people who are shy but not sociable. Apparently, the quality of interaction decreases only when people are both strongly motivated to be with others *and* at the same time socially fearful (Cheek & Buss 1981). Murstein and his colleagues found that exchange orientation was positively related to friendship intensity (Murstein et al 1977), poorer marital adjustment (Murstein & McDonald 1983), and greater incompatibility with roommates (Murstein & Azar 1986). The latter two findings fit well with a point noted earlier: People expecting a communal relationship react negatively when others follow exchange norms (e.g. Clark & Mills 1979). However, the friendship intensity finding (Murstein et al 1977) remains a puzzle.

Miller et al (1983) examined the impact of a target's chronic responsiveness to self-disclosure on a discloser's willingness to reveal intimate information. They found that although high "Openers" do not increase disclosure levels from subjects dispositionally inclined to self-disclose frequently, they elicit greater disclosure from partners low in the tendency to self-disclose. Finally, Reis et al (1982) found that among males, fear of rejection by opposite-sex (but not same-sex) others was negatively correlated with their own physical attractiveness. There were no significant correlations between fear of rejection and attractiveness among females. Reis et al (1982) also found that among females, trust of opposite-sex (but not same-sex) others was negatively correlated with their own physical attractiveness. There were no significant correlations between trust and attractiveness for males.

To date, extensive programs of research relating personality characteristics and other individual differences to relationship phenomena remain rare. However, the success of programs investigating self-monitoring (Snyder 1987), intimacy motivation (see the Intimacy section, above; McAdams 1980), and loneliness (Perlman & Peplau 1981) ought to encourage researchers to explore dispositional factors more extensively, both with the new measures cited above and with older, more established instruments. In the latter category, for instance, Hansson et al (1984) suggest that assertiveness

(Rathus 1973), introversion (Morris 1979), and self-esteem (Stroebe et al 1977) should prove particularly useful in helping researchers understand people's social worlds. Traits such as public and private self-consciousness and social anxiety (Fenigstein et al 1975) hold similar potential. Insofar as dispositional characteristics describe what a person brings to a relationship, such research is an important, but as yet understudied component of relationship processes.

Neglected Areas

In the area of personality factors relevant to interpersonal processes, the predominant research activity involves developing new scales. Although some of these measures have led to considerable attention and findings, others deserve more attention. We see several fruitful directions in which personality-relationship research might progress. For one, with few exceptions (e.g. Glick 1985), we know little about the interaction of personality traits and situational factors, as they pertain specifically to relationship development. Personality traits may affect interaction and relationship development differently depending on the situation. For instance, being high in desire for social approval might lead young adults to select physically attractive, ebullient partners when interacting with peers (who presumably value these attributes), but to choose polite, hardworking, well-bred partners when socializing with family. Or, it might be the case that shy people will interact smoothly with freely chosen partners but awkwardly with others with whom they are forced to converse. Situational norms may also affect the emergence of personality effects. As Ickes (1982) has noted, personality factors are most likely to affect behavior when situational cues and requirements are weak. If we assume, for example, that there are fewer norms regarding acquaintanceship than employer-employee relations, we should expect personality to influence the former type of relationship more than the latter.

Second, we know little about how personality factors interact with relationship types, even though varying relationship characteristics ought to make different personality traits more or less salient. The nature and degree of interdependence, for example, may influence interaction in different ways, depending on the personalities of the persons involved. One might imagine that two individuals differing in the need for dominance might have similar relationships with a distant third person. However, if they were to become more closely involved with the third person, their diverging needs for dominance ought to produce very different relationships with the third person. As yet, person-relationship interactions have received little research. To extend this logic further, we also know little about personality × situation × relationship interactions. For example, people dispositionally high in communal orientation may express more emotion than those low in communal orientation when interacting with family members at home. However, when interacting with family members in public settings, or with superficial acquaintances in any setting, they may suppress emotion displays and consequently appear not to differ from those low in communal orientation. Such research seems likely to advance our understanding of the impact of personality factors on relationship functioning.

METHODOLOGY

Is theoretical necessity the mother of methodological invention, or do new methodologies make their mark by suggesting novel and more differentiated questions? We suspect both propositions are correct. Methodological advances not only allow us to address questions that have resisted earlier research strategies, they also suggest new ways of thinking about phenomena, thereby expanding the conceptual range within which research activity takes place. Because the central phenomena in the new field of interpersonal relations are interactional in their essence, methodological expansion is especially valuable (Hinde 1981; Kelley 1986). Paradigms focusing on the behavior of individuals in isolation need to be supplemented by paradigms focusing on interdependence, relationships, and influence (Kenny 1988). Development of such procedures will no doubt be part of the definition of this discipline.

Relationship researchers already have at their disposal an ever-growing and diverse collection of techniques, strategies, and paradigms. Our review selectively focuses on recently developed or expanded procedures that offer opportunities for enhancing the range of the field's vision. We nevertheless believe that no single approach is likely to suffice for any research question. Triangulation is the best strategy for discovering the essence of a phenomenon. That is, systematic integration of experiments, quasi-experiments, and surveys, of laboratory and field settings, of self-report and observational methods, and of objective and subjective indicators will allow us to rule out alternative explanations and artifacts, and ultimately will yield the least method-bound, and hence most valid, understandings. In other words, the multimethod approach advocated by Campbell & Fiske (1959) three decades ago remains the metastrategy of choice.

In both laboratory experiments and field studies of social interaction and relationships, two general methods have traditionally predominated and still do: self-reports (self-administered questionnaires, behavioral records, interviews, and narrative records) and observer reports (partner accounts, and judges' assessments). Self-report methods remain the most common research tool for several reasons. First, often the people involved are the only ones having access to all information relevant to the researchers' questions. Second, many important phenomena concern subjective meanings ascribed to objective events (e.g. relationship expectations, perceived intimacy), to which, again, only the involved individuals have access. Third, despite the many criticisms leveled at self-report measures, their generic validity is often adequate, as demonstrated both by explicit studies of this issue and by the predictive and theoretical utility of findings generated by self-reported data (see Harvey et al 1983, for fuller discussion of these issues). Because Harvey et al (1988) review self-report methods particularly relevant to interpersonal relations researchers, including various new measures of relationship satisfaction and evaluation, interpersonal processes, and individual differences, and because many are described in the personality section of this review, they are not discussed here.

Observational studies have become more comprehensive and sophisticated in recent years, in part because technological advances in videotaping and data management via microcomputers permit collection and analysis of more information, differentiated into finer and finer components (both in terms of time and processes). For example, Duncan & Fiske (1985) examined a great variety of verbal, nonverbal, and paralinguistic cues associated with every attempted exchange of the speaking role in lengthy two-person conversations. These procedures are far more labor-intensive than self-report methods, a factor that undoubtedly contributes to their underutilization. They nevertheless can be a rich source of data, especially when independent judgments of behavioral events are compared to self-reports (see Gottman 1979; Montgomery 1981, 1984; Ickes et al 1986; and Reis et al 1985, for examples of this approach).

In the remainder of this section, we selectively review a few new methodological advances that offer novel perspectives or data collection approaches, grouped into two categories: new research design strategies and new procedures and techniques.

New Research-Design Strategies

THE SOCIAL RELATIONS MODEL   One of the most important new procedures available to interpersonal relations researchers is the Social Relations Model (SRM) developed by Kenny and his colleagues. Heretofore, researchers have been unable to distinguish effects attributable to characteristics of individual interactants from effects that characterize unique features of their relationship. For example, John's disclosure of personal feelings to Mary may be due to John's general tendency to self-disclose, Mary's general tendency to elicit self-disclosure from others, or something unique about their relationship (i.e. John's tendency to disclose only to Mary, and Mary's tendency to receive disclosure only from John). The difficulty of distinguishing these effects compelled researchers to skirt many of the more interesting questions about dyadic interaction: What makes one relationship different from another? How does one partner's behavior depend on the other's? How does relationship context affect expression of individual predispositions?

The SRM explicitly takes into account the interactive nature of behavior in relationships by apportioning variance in a given behavior to one of five components: the tendency of all people to display that behavior (i.e. the grand mean); the tendency of one partner to display that behavior to all partners *(actor effect);* the tendency of a partner to elicit that behavior from all actors *(partner effect);* the tendency of actors to display that behavior only to a specific partner *(relationship effect);* and instability or error. (If data are collected only from a single point in time, the latter two components are combined, adding ambiguity.) SRM research designs require crossing subjects so that they interact with multiple partners, thereby permitting distinction of general and relationship-specific interaction tendencies. Fuller descriptions of SRM can be found in Kenny & LaVoie (1984) and Kenny (1987a).

SRM's ability to unconfound individual- and dyadic-level effects and thereby generate theoretically important findings has already been demonstrated. Often, SRM analysis has uncovered, or at least more appropriately specified, conclusions that previously had been obscured or imprecisely inferred from analyses overlooking the individual-dyad distinction. For example, Sabatelli et al (1986) found that the bulk of the variance in nonverbal communication accuracy among married couples was due to sender skill and unique relationship effects, with little evidence of receiver decoding ability effects. Another example is provided by Kenny & LaVoie (1982), who speculated that prior researchers' failure to find evidence of increasing reciprocity of attraction over time might have been a statistical artifact of measures that confounded individual- and dyadic-level effects. When they differentiated these two levels of measurement, strong and increasing within-dyad reciprocity correlations were observed.

SRM has also shown considerable versatility in providing new analytic strategies for old problems, and in illuminating new ways of conceptualizing relationship issues. Three uses are especially noteworthy. First, Kenny (1987b; Kenny & Albright 1987) suggests that SRM be used to isolate precisely specified components of person perception accuracy, a need originally identified by Cronbach (1958) that had heretofore remained methodologically elusive. DePaulo et al (1987) have done so, finding that subjects were inaccurate judges of which partners liked them best, but were successful in estimating how different partners' impressions of them changed over time. Second, SRM might be useful in personality × situation research (Malloy & Kenny 1986). In this scheme, dispositional factors are actor effects (e.g. do low self-esteem persons smile at everyone more than high self-esteem persons do?); situational variations induced by another person's behavior are partner effects (e.g. does a warm face elicit smiles from everyone more than dour faces do?); and interactions are relationship effects (e.g. do low self-esteem persons smile only at warm faces?). Third, it has often proved difficult to specify exactly how interaction in "special" relationships (e.g. marriage, parent-child, employer-employee, coach-athlete) is different from interaction among strangers and casual acquaintances. By dividing interaction behavior variance into precisely identified components, SRM offers a new paradigm for uncovering just what is "special" about special relationships (Kenny 1987a).

SRM is not without difficulties. It is as yet a cumbersome procedure with stringent measurement, subject, and design requirements, and data analytic software is not available on standard statistical packages. However, as a paradigm that exploits, rather than ignores or controls, interdependence among dyadic partners, SRM is a very promising tool for asking interesting and uncommon questions about relationships.

STRUCTURAL EQUATION MODELING   Another potentially useful research design for interpersonal relations researchers is structural equation modeling (SEM). This procedure, which essentially integrates confirmatory factor analysis with path analysis, evaluates the degree to which a data set fits a given theoretical model—that is, whether the observed correlations are consistent with the various associations predicted by the model. SEM has four primary advantages. First, it permits examination of causal hypotheses with nonexperimental data. Second, by utilizing multiple indicators of the same latent construct, measurement is enhanced, in terms of both internal consistency and generalizability. Third, by focusing on models of the interrelationship among a set of variables rather than myriad simultaneous bivariate correlations, more sophisticated theoretical understandings are likely to emerge. Fourth, and finally, SEM facilitates explicit and direct tests of mediating processes (Judd & Kenny 1981), which have in the past only been assumed or examined indirectly. (It should be noted, however, that the same logic of mediation can also be tested in many instances with simpler regression analyses.)

Although interpersonal process researchers have not yet seized upon SEM with the same enthusiasm as researchers in other areas, there are exceptions. For example, Shaver et al (1985) developed a model of the impact of social skills, network changes, and trait loneliness on changes in state loneliness during the transition to college. Certainly the reluctance of researchers to attempt SEM is due both to its stringent statistical requirements and to needed technical prowess. Nevertheless, programs such as LISREL and EQS are becoming more accessible, so that mathematical novices need not be overly daunted. In our view, increased reliance on SEM is desirable, not only because of its power to answer questions of the sort listed above, but also because it encourages conceptualization in terms of full theoretical models rather than multiple one-to-one associations. An excellent overview of the applicability of SEM can be found in a special section of *Child Development* devoted to this topic (Connell & Tanaka 1987). More comprehensive instruction is provided by Long (1983a,b).

OTHER STRATEGIES   Two additional design strategies are noteworthy. The first, meta-analysis, summarizes effects that cross-cut multiple studies in a rigorous quantitative, rather than descriptive, fashion. Meta-analytic procedures have been developed by Glass et al (1981), Cooper (1984), and Rosenthal (1984), among others, as a formal technique for accumulating the results (and effect sizes) of many studies and for resolving inconsistent findings. Two important advantages are (*a*) that meta-analysis aggregates data collected in numerous settings using diverse paradigms and measures, thereby enhancing confidence that findings are not unique to particular methods or situations, and (*b*) that possible distortions due to impressionistic reviews are eliminated.

The literature now contains many meta-analytic summaries relevant to relationships. For example, Borys & Perlman (1985) reviewed 28 studies of sex differences in loneliness. Although only six showed significant sex differences or trends (males were lonelier in all), when the data were aggregated, males were reliably lonelier than females ($p < .01$). Meta-analytic procedures can also confirm the impact of moderator variables, either by correlating effect sizes with levels of the moderator variable (Rosenthal 1984) or by separate tabulations of findings categorized by moderators. Mediating processes can be evaluated similarly. For example, Harris & Rosenthal (1985) conducted 31 separate meta-analyses of different variables thought to mediate interpersonal expectancy effects. Sixteen of these variables provided significant evidence of mediation, whereas 15 did not.

Time-series designs are also growing in popularity and accessibility, although they remain underutilized. These designs allow researchers to examine regular cycles and other action-response patterns in interpersonal data. For example, one might ask whether the probability of a nasty comment is greater immediately after receipt of an insult than it was before. A number of researchers have used time-series designs effectively. Gottman (1979) found that validating responses were more likely to follow problem expression in happy than in unhappy married couples. Duncan & Fiske (1985) identified nonverbal turn-taking rules by examining partner responses to various nonverbal signals. Useful introductions to time-series designs are provided by Bakeman & Gottman (1986) and Gottman (1981).

New Procedures and Techniques

THE ROCHESTER INTERACTION RECORD   Self-report methods typically ask respondents to select and summarize various aspects of past social experiences. Several sources of bias—memory, aggregation, and sampling, for instance—are possible with such methods. That is, events become more or less memorable over time, and the rules by which subjects decide which events to describe and how to summarize them are unclear. To eliminate these problems, Wheeler & Nezlek developed the Rochester Interaction Record (RIR; 1977; Nezlek et al 1983). The RIR is a diary-like procedure in which respondents use standardized rating scales to describe every social encounter lasting ten minutes or longer that occurs during a fixed period (usually one to two weeks). Rating dimensions are chosen on the basis of theoretical interest, and subjects are asked to describe each interaction as soon after it occurs as is feasible. The data are then aggregated statistically, both overall and within relational categories of theoretical or descriptive interest (e.g. with same-sex partners, with best friends or lovers, or in groups). Thus, detailed descriptions of spontaneous social participation in everyday life are obtained.

RIR studies have assessed both quantitative (e.g. number of different partners, time spent interacting per day) and qualitative dimensions (e.g. intimacy, pleasantness) of social participation. For example, Reis and his colleagues (Reis et al 1980; Reis et al 1982) found that one's own physical attractiveness related to increased opposite-sex interaction for males, but not for females, contrary to folk wisdom. Attractive persons of both sexes reported more intimate and satisfying interactions with either sex. Milardo et al (1983) found that as primary close relationships deepened, the frequency and duration of contact with other close friends and kin remained unchanged, but contact with intermediate friends and acquaintances lessened. Wheeler et al (1983) showed that loneliness related more closely to lesser intimacy than to deficiencies in interaction frequency. Finally, Cutrona (1986), using a modification of the RIR diary, demonstrated that stress elicits specific behavioral events from others—listening, advice, and caring—that produce feelings of social support, suggesting that support perceptions are rooted in actual interaction and not in global evaluations of a relationship.

THE EXPERIENCE SAMPLING METHOD   Another naturalistic technique for studying ongoing social activity is the Experience Sampling Method (ESM; Csikszentmihalyi & Larson 1984; Hormuth 1986; Larson & Csikszentmihalyi 1983). In contrast to the RIR, which assesses all interactions of a given length during a fixed period, the ESM randomly samples representative moments in people's lives. Subjects carry electronic pagers or portable, preprogrammed beepers (e.g. modified digital wristwatches) and are sporadically and unpredictably signaled during the day. When cued, subjects complete a brief questionnaire describing their current activities, as well as any impressions or ratings in which researchers are interested. Aggregated over time (e.g. one week), these reports provide a detailed and representative portrait of an individual's typical thought, behavior, and affect.

Csikszentmihalyi & Larson's (1984) study of adolescent activity is the most comprehensive ESM analysis to date. Seventy-five high school students were beeped 40 to 50 times over the course of one week. At each instance, they indicated where they were, what they were doing, whom they were with, and what their affective state was (in terms of positivity and activation). The resulting description of adolescent behavior, particularly with regard to social interaction, is extensive and revealing. For example, when compared to other age groups (assessed in other ESM studies), adolescents show greater drops in mood when they leave the company of others, and greater uplifts when rejoining them. Solitude also has benefits for adolescents, however. Those who reported intermediate and high rates of being alone showed better psychological adjustment and school performance. McAdams & Constantian (1983) also used the ESM to advantage. They demonstrated that high intimacy motivation is associated with having more interpersonal thoughts and experiencing more positive affect in interpersonal situations.

These studies, as well as those using the RIR, demonstrate that accurate, well-differentiated descriptions of social participation in everyday life are feasible, and that such measures can be useful in evaluating theoretically driven hypotheses.

THE UNSTRUCTURED INTERACTION PARADIGM   A complaint often voiced about studies of dyadic interaction is that laboratory contexts, cues, and demand characteristics provided by the experimenter, and/or a confederate's narrowly scripted activities constrain and shape the subject's behavior, producing findings with limited generalizability. In response to this criticism, Ickes developed the Unstructured Interaction Paradigm (UIP; 1982). This technique involves surreptitiously videotaping whatever interaction spontaneously occurs between two persons waiting by themselves in a room. Typically, partners are unacquainted individuals with known characteristics (e.g. sex role, birth order) who are left alone by an experimenter for five minutes. Upon the experimenter's return, they are separated and asked a variety of questions concerning their impressions and feelings about the prior interaction. Behavioral assessments coded from their verbal and nonverbal interaction (or lack thereof) during the observation period are also collected. Because use of surreptitious videotapes might produce ethical problems, Ickes has developed a number of precautionary procedures (e.g. allowing subjects to erase their tapes, if they choose, before anyone else sees them).

The UIP elicits spontaneous, unstructured dyadic interaction in a format minimizing experimenter cues about appropriate or desired behavior. Its flexibility is particularly well suited to studying the impact of personality factors on social interaction (see Individual Differences section, above), in that any pairing of preexisting personal characteristics or traits is possible. For example, Ickes & Turner (1983) demonstrated that individuals with older, opposite-sex siblings were likely to have more rewarding interactions with opposite-sex strangers. The technique can also be used for process-oriented research, as Ickes et al (1982) did in a study of reactions to pre-interaction expectancies. They found that expecting one's partner to behave in a positive, friendly manner led subjects to accept and reciprocate friendly behavior, whereas negative expectations led them to discount friendly behavior and react in a distrustful fashion. In a different study examining naturally occurring social cognition, Ickes et al (1986) combined this technique with Cacioppo & Petty's (1981) thought-listing method. Immediately after the five-minute UIP period, participants watched videotapes of their interaction and recorded all thoughts and feelings that they recalled having at that time. This addition seems promising in that it expands the range of phenomena that can be considered in Ickes's paradigm to include more covert variables. They found, for example, that persons high in private self-consciousness increased their conversational involvement by adopting metaperspectives more often (i.e. A's thoughts about B's thoughts about A).

PSYCHOPHYSIOLOGY   Although psychophysiological constructs have been of interest to interpersonal process researchers since the 1920s, recent advances in instrumentation and understanding of physiological processes have greatly enhanced the appeal of such measures as skin conductance and resistance, heart rate, and facial electromyogram (EMG) activity (Cacioppo & Petty 1983, 1986). Psychophysiological measures have at least three distinct advantages: (a) on a purely methodological level, they provide information about individual responses relatively unaffected by many biases inherent in self-reports; (b) they help illuminate the manner in which physiological processes influence social relations (and vice versa); and (c) they enable researchers to isolate and identify component processes of social behavior. To illustrate this latter point, Cacioppo & Petty (1986) analyzed many psychophysiological studies of social facilitation and cognitive dissonance. They concluded that a single underlying process of general or autonomic arousal was less likely than a two-stage process involving assessment of potential negative consequences for oneself, followed by "effortful striving."

A study by Levenson & Gottman (1983), described earlier, exemplifies the potential of psychophysiological measures for interaction research. They constructed an index of "physiological linkage" (i.e. close parallel responses between husband and wife) in married couples from four measures: heart rate, pulse transmission time, skin conductance, and general somatic activity. As they predicted, linkage was correlated with marital satisfaction during conversations about conflictful issues but not about events of the day. Levenson & Gottman interpreted this result as indicating that spouses in distressed marriages are "locked into" a pattern of negative affect reciprocity that discourages enjoyable marital interaction and constructive problem solving. More relevant to present purposes, physiological linkage and self-reported affect reciprocity accounted for independent variance in marital satisfaction.

We suspect that in the near future, psychophysiological indicators will gain popularity among researchers generally interested in interpersonal relations, and particularly in the three processes we have featured—emotion, intimacy, and outcome interdependence. This may be especially true for facial EMG, which assesses muscular activity in various regions of the face. The face is debatably the dominant channel for communicating emotions in humans and animals (Izard 1977), so that any procedure capable of detecting both gross and subtle variations associated with different emotional experience and expression has great potential for studying emotional reactions to, and interdependence with, others.

OTHER PROCEDURES   Two additional procedural innovations bear note. The first of these, simulation methodologies, have been used to investigate implications of varying assumptions or conditions inherent in social psychological theories. For example, Kelley (1985) programmed "robots" to play numerous payoff matrix games under different assumptions (e.g. metaperspectives—thinking about what the other actor is thinking about you). Changes in their payoff outcomes demonstrate the impact of these assumptions for dyadic interdependence. For example, metaperspectives reduced the likelihood that Kelley's robots would exploit their game partners in order to enhance their own outcomes. In a very different realm, Kalick & Hamilton (1986) used simulation data to argue that dating partners might be roughly equivalent in physical attractiveness not because of any inherent preference for matching, but rather as an artifact of the tendency of more attractive persons to be selected first (and hence leave the pool of available partners). Although their conclusion has been challenged (Aron 1988), the value of simulations for testing the logical consequences of such assumptions is clear.

Second, in attempts to develop extensive data bases more efficiently, some institutions have initiated ongoing, collaborative services that centralize data collection, processing, and storage. Such efforts make more information available to a greater number of researchers with less total expenditure of resources and energy. Perhaps the best known example is the Computer Administered Panel Study (Latané 1987).

In closing this section, one point bears reiteration. Although these designs involve new statistical and methodological procedures, their value is less in changing the way researchers perform computations and conduct studies than it is in expanding the way researchers think about the phenomena they are studying and formulate researchable questions.

CONCLUDING COMMENTS

Although the field's vision has expanded and our understanding of many elements of relationships has grown, in the process of reviewing the literature several gaps and ambiguities became apparent. By way of concluding, we briefly discuss some of these issues.

1. Two types of research predominate in this literature: laboratory experiments involving strangers, and correlational studies or surveys of individuals in ongoing close relationships. It seems to us that, too often, advocates of each approach neglect findings generated from the other, or, worse, actively dismiss the other in their attempt to promote one particular paradigm. We believe that integration of information obtained from both strategies is essential for understanding complex and multifaceted close relationships. Certainly such integration can be difficult, given that diverging results might be due to variations in method, setting, length or type of relationship, or other substantive differences. To facilitate integration, researchers need to fill certain key gaps that permeate the literature. For example, we need laboratory experiments using ongoing relationships to contrast with similar experiments utilizing strangers; we need studies of relationships among superficial acquaintances, parents and children, cousins, coworkers, enemies, and secretaries and their bosses to contrast with existing studies of close friends and romantic partners. Through such comparisons it will be possible to distinguish relationship, situation, and method effects.

2. Our impression is that field studies of ongoing relationships tend to be descriptive, whereas tests of cause and effect tend to be confined to the laboratory. Certainly, careful and thorough descriptive research is necessary and beneficial as new topical areas emerge (Kelley et al 1983). It is nevertheless imperative, in our opinion, to test causal hypotheses about ongoing close relationships not only in the laboratory (as advocated above) but also in their natural, everyday context. Relationship context and history, in all their complexity, may be important moderators of the processes that interest researchers. For example, in day-to-day marital conflict, spouses might use the claim "I'm too busy now" as an avoidance strategy, a ploy not available in laboratory interaction. It is therefore important to verify that processes observed in the laboratory also operate in spontaneous everyday behavior. Fortunately, given the methodological advances described earlier, naturalistic studies are increasingly effective vehicles for testing causal hypotheses.

3. In laboratory studies, researchers tend to measure fine-grained components of a process, whereas in field studies, they tend to assess global and aggregated impressions. For example, laboratory tests of equity theory often examine a single allocation of one class of resource, such as money. On the other hand, field studies typically use global ratings of equity, such as the Hatfield et al (1985) measure based on a single question: "Considering what you put into your relationship, compared to what you get out of it . . . and what your partner puts in compared to what he or she gets out of it, how does your relationship 'stack up'?" Fine-grained measures and global aggregates are both valuable sources of knowledge, but it cannot be assumed that they will produce analogous results. Moreover, even if they did, the same mediating processes may not be responsible for both effects. It consequently is necessary to utilize both sorts of measures in the laboratory and in the field. At the same time, empirical comparison of these differing levels of measurement (including studies of processes that may be responsible for differences) is needed.

4. As Hinde (1981) and Duck & Sants (1983), among others, have noted, relationships are more than the sum of repeated interactions. Sustained relationships involve different features, components, and processes than single interactions do, even when summed across many episodes. We do not deny the obvious truism that relationships are built upon the substance of individual interaction. But the nature of relationships depends on the manner in which partners aggregate, process, and reflect on their interactions with each other. It should therefore be expected that principles derived from studies of single encounters will require additional empirical scrutiny and, often, elaboration and modification in order to be generalized to ongoing relationships.

5. Researchers have recently begun studying relationship development. Much of this research is cross-sectional, some of it is longitudinal. Valuable substantive findings about first impressions and initial interaction [cf Berscheid's (1983) summary] and relationship distress and conflict (cf Baxter 1987; Gottman 1979) have accumulated. However, we are struck by the relative absence of research into certain critical time periods. What happens, for instance, after first meetings, when a new contact burgeons into close friendship or romance a few weeks or months later—that is, during the period in which partners learn about each other and negotiate the terms of their friendship? We also need to know more about what might be termed the "postmortem" phase—the period following relationship dissolution—and how this stage affects development (or lack thereof) of subsequent relationships. Studies of the termination phase itself exist (summarized in Baxter 1987). Yet people maintain memories, feelings, habits, and fears that may profoundly affect the possibility and nature of subsequent relationships (e.g. Harvey et al 1986), and these processes have been little studied.

During the past decade, our knowledge about interpersonal processes affecting close relationships has grown. At the same time, as is inevitable and perhaps desirable in any scientific endeavor, our awareness of gaps and deficiencies in the literature has also grown. Close relationships are an intrinsically difficult phenomenon to investigate. Many of the most important components are inherently subjective, and others are distorted by subjective impressions, yielding data that can be difficult to interpret. Relationships are interactive, dyadic, and time-bound, necessitating special methodologies. Moreover, folk wisdom and naive psychology offer principles and advice, some of it accurate, some of it not, about almost every aspect of interaction in relationships. For these reasons and more, research conducted under the heading of interpersonal processes in close relationships may at times be reproved and at other times be discouraging. We nevertheless share Berscheid's conviction that the field must "stop to consider not only the difficulties of the task we face, but its importance to the human condition" (1986, p. 286). By doing so, researchers will be able to recognize how far our understanding has already come, and how our present activity should be designed to move us further along the path.

ACKNOWLEDGMENT

The order of authorship is alphabetical. We gratefully acknowledge the helpful comments of John Berg, Val Derlega, Judy Schwartz, and Phillip Shaver on an earlier draft of this manuscript. We are also indebted to Beth Muchant and Elizabeth Whitehead for literature searches and perseverance in the preparation of this manuscript. Margaret Clark was assisted by grant R01 MH40390 from the National Institute of Mental Health; Harry Reis received assistance from grant BNS-8416988 from the National Science Foundation and from a University of Rochester Faculty Mentor grant.

Literature Cited

Acitelli, L. K., Duck, S. 1987. Postscript: Intimacy as the proverbial elephant. In *Intimate Relationships: Development, Dynamics, and Deterioration*, ed. D. Perlman, S. Duck, pp. 297–308. Beverly Hills: Sage

Altman, I., Taylor, D. A. 1973. *Social Penetration: The Development of Interpersonal Relationships*. New York: Holt, Rinehart & Winston

Archer, R. L., Berg, J. H. 1978. Disclosure reciprocity and its limits: a reactance analysis. *J. Exp. Soc. Psychol.* 14:527–40

Archer, R. L., Berg, J. H., Runge, T. E. 1980. Active and passive observers: attraction to self-disclosing others. *J. Exp. Soc. Psychol.* 16:130–45

Aron, A. 1988. The matching hypothesis reconsidered again: comment on Kalick and Hamilton. *J. Pers. Soc. Psychol.* In press

Austin, W. 1980. Friendship and fairness: effects of the type of relationship and task performance on choice of distribution rules. *Pers. Soc. Psychol. Bull.* 6:402–8

Averill, J. R. 1982. *Anger and Aggression: An Essay on Emotion*. New York: Springer-Verlag

Averill, J. R. 1983. Studies on anger and aggression: implications for theories of emotion. *Am. Psychol.* 38:1145–60

Bakeman, R., Gottman, J. M. 1986. *Observing Interaction*. New York: Cambridge Univ. Press

Batson, C. D., Duncan, B. D., Ackerman, P., Buckley, T., Birch, K. 1981. Is empathic emotion a source of altruistic motivation? *J. Pers. Soc. Psychol.* 40:290–302

Baxter, L. A. 1987. Self-disclosure and relationship development. In *Self-Disclosure: Theory, Research and Therapy*, ed. V. J. Derlega, J. Berg. New York: Plenum

Bellew-Smith, M., Korn, J. H. 1986. Merger intimacy status in adult women. *J. Pers. Soc. Psychol.* 50:1186–91

Berg, J. H. 1984. The development of friendship between roommates. *J. Pers. Soc. Psychol.* 46:346–56

Berg, J. H., Archer, R. L. 1980. Disclosure or concern: a second look at liking for the norm-breaker. *J. Pers.* 48:245–57

Berg, J. H., Archer, R. L. 1982. Responses to self-disclosure and interaction goals. *J. Exp. Soc. Psychol.* 18:501–12

Berg, J. H., Clark, M. S. 1986. Differences in social exchange between intimate and other relationships: Gradually evolving or quickly apparent? In *Friendship and Social Interaction*, ed. V. J. Derlega, B. A. Winstead, pp. 101–28. New York: Springer-Verlag

Berg, J. H., McQuinn, R. D. 1986. Attraction and exchange in continuing and noncontinuing dating relationships. *J. Pers. Soc. Psychol.* 50:942–52

Berscheid, E. 1983. Emotion. See Kelley et al 1983, pp. 110–68

Berscheid, E. 1985. Interpersonal attraction. In *Handbook of Social Psychology*, ed. G. Lindzey, E. Aronson, 2:413–84. New York: Random House. 3rd ed.

Berscheid, E. 1986. Mea culpas and lamentations: Sir Francis, Sir Isaac, and the "slow progress" of soft psychology. In *The Emerging Field of Personal Relationships*, ed. R. Gilmour, S. Duck, pp. 267–86. Hillsdale, NJ: Erlbaum

Berscheid, E. 1988. Some comments on love's anatomy: or, whatever happened to old-fashioned lust? In *The Anatomy of Love*, ed. R. J. Sternberg, M. L. Barnes. New Haven: Yale Univ. Press

Berscheid, E., Gangestad, S. W., Kulakowski, D. 1984. Emotion in close relationships: implications for relationship counseling. In *Handbook of Counseling Psychology*, ed. S. D. Brown, R. L. Lent, pp. 435–76. New York: Wiley

Berscheid, E., Walster, E. 1974. A little bit about love. In *Foundations of Interpersonal Attraction*, ed. T. L. Huston, pp. 355–81. New York: Academic

Berscheid, E., Walster, E. 1978. *Interpersonal Attraction*. Reading, Mass: Addison-Wesley. 2nd ed.

Bierhoff, H. W., Cohen, R. L., Greenberg, J. 1986. *Justice in Social Relations*. New York: Plenum

Borys, S., Perlman, D. 1985. Gender differences in loneliness. *Pers. Soc. Psychol. Bull.* 11:63–74

Bower, G. 1981. Mood and memory. *Am. Psychol.* 36:129–48

Bowlby, J. 1969. *Attachment and Loss. Vol. 1: Attachment*. New York: Basic Books

Bradbury, T. N., Fincham, F. D. 1987. Affect and cognition in close relationships: towards an integrative model. *Cognit. Emot.* 1:59–87

Brown, R. 1987. *Social Psychology*. New York: Free Press. 2nd ed.

Buhrmester, D., Furman, W. 1986. The changing functions of friends in childhood: a neo-Sullivan perspective. In *Friendship and Social Interaction*, ed. V. J. Derlega, B. A. Winstead, pp. 41–62. New York: Springer-Verlag

Buss, D. M. 1988a. Love acts: the evolutionary biology of love. In *The Anatomy of Love*, ed. R. J. Sternberg, M. L. Barnes. New Haven: Yale Univ. Press. In press

Buss, D. M. 1988b. The evolution of human intrasexual competition: tactics of mate attraction. *J. Pers. Soc. Psychol.* In press

Buss, D. M., Barnes, M. 1986. Preferences in human mate selection. *J. Pers. Soc. Psychol.* 50:559–70

Cacioppo, J. T., Petty, R. E. 1981. Social psychological procedures for cognitive response assessment: the thought-listing technique. In *Cognitive Assessment*, ed. T. Merluzzi, C. Glass, M. Genest, pp. 309–42. New York: Guilford

Cacioppo, J. T., Petty, R. E. 1983. *Social Psychophysiology: A Sourcebook*. New York: Guilford

Cacioppo, J. T., Petty, R. E. 1986. Social processes. In *Psychophysiology*, ed. M. G. H. Coles, E. Donchin, S. W. Porges, pp. 646–79. New York: Guilford

Caldwell, M. A., Peplau, L. A. 1982. Sex differences in same-sex friendship. *Sex Roles* 8:721–32

Campbell, D. T., Fiske, D. W. 1959. Convergent and discriminant validation by the multitrait-multimethod matrix. *Psychol. Bull.* 56:81–105

Cate, R. M., Lloyd, S. A., Henton, J. M. 1985. The effect of equity, equality, and reward level on the stability of students' premarital relationships. *J. Soc. Psychol.* 125:715–25

Cheek, J. M., Buss, A. H. 1981. Shyness and sociability. *J. Pers. Soc. Psychol.* 41:330–39

Chelune, G. J., Robison, J. T., Kommor, M. J. 1984. A cognitive interactional model of intimate relationships. In *Communication, Intimacy, and Close Relationships*, ed. V. J. Derlega, pp. 11–40. New York: Academic

Cialdini, R. B., Darby, B. L., Vincent, J. E.

1973. Transgression and altruism: a case for hedonism. *J. Exp. Soc. Psychol.* 9:502–16

Cialdini, R. B., Schaller, M., Houlihan, D., Arps, K., Fultz, J., Beaman, A. L. 1987. Empathy-based helping: Is it selflessly or selfishly motivated? *J. Pers. Soc. Psychol.* 52:749–58

Clark, M. S. 1984. Record keeping in two types of relationships. *J. Pers. Soc. Psychol.* 47:549–57

Clark, M. S., Fiske, S. T., eds. 1982. *Affect and Cognition: The Seventeenth Annual Carnegie Symposium on Cognition.* Hillsdale, NJ: Erlbaum

Clark, M. S., Mills, J. 1979. Interpersonal attraction in exchange and communal relationships. *J. Pers. Soc. Psychol.* 37:12–24

Clark, M. S., Mills, J., Powell, M. 1986. Keeping track of needs in communal and exchange relationships. *J. Pers. Soc. Psychol.* 51:333–38

Clark, M. S., Muchant, C. B. 1987. Reactions to three emotions in communal and exchange relationships. Manuscript submitted for publication. Carnegie-Mellon University.

Clark, M. S., Muchant, C. B., Wesner, K. 1987a. A measure of exchange orientation. Manuscript submitted for publication

Clark, M. S., Ouellette, R., Powell, M., Milberg, S. 1987b. Relationship type, recipient mood, and helping. *J. Pers. Soc. Psychol.* 53:94–103

Clark, M. S., Waddell, B. A. 1983. Effects of moods on thoughts about helping, attraction and information acquisition. *Soc. Psychol. Q.* 46:31–35

Clark, M. S., Waddell, B. 1985. Perceptions of exploitation in communal and exchange relationships. *J. Soc. Pers. Relat.* 2:403–18

Cohen, S., Sherrod, D. R., Clark, M. S. 1986. Social skills and the stress-protective role of social support. *J. Pers. Soc. Psychol.* 50:963–73

Connell, J. P., Tanaka, J. S. 1987. Introduction to the special section on structural equation modeling. *Child Dev.* 58:2–3

Cook, K. S., Hegtvedt, K. A. 1983. Distributive justice, equity, and equality. *Ann. Rev. Sociol.* 9:217–41

Cooper, H. 1984. *The Integrative Research Review: A Social Science Approach.* Beverly Hills: Sage

Costanza, R. S., Derlega, V. J., Winstead, B. A. 1987. Positive and negative forms of social support: effects of conversational topics on coping with stress among same-sex friends. *J. Exp. Psychol.* In press

Coyne, J. C. 1976. Depression and the response of others. *J. Abnorm. Psychol.* 85:186–93

Cozby, P. C. 1973. Self-disclosure: a literature review. *Psychol. Bull.* 79:73–91

Crandall, J. E. 1978. Effects of threat and failure on concern for others. *J. Res. Pers.* 12:350–60

Cronbach, L. J. 1958. Proposals leading to analytic treatment of social perception scores. In *Person Perception and Interpersonal Behavior,* ed. R. Tagiuri, L. Petrullo, pp. 353–79. Stanford, Calif: Stanford Univ. Press

Csikszentmihalyi, M., Larson, R. 1984. *Being Adolescent: Conflict and Growth in Teenage Years.* New York: Basic

Cunningham, M. 1987. Does happiness mean friendliness?: induced mood and heterosexual self-disclosure. *Pers. Soc. Psychol. Bull.* In press

Cutrona, C. E. 1986. Behavioral manifestations of social support: a microanalytic investigation. *J. Pers. Soc. Psychol.* 51:201–8

Davis, D., Dewitt, J., Charney, A. 1986. Limitation on some rules of conversation: when responsive behavior is expected and condoned. University of Nevada. Manuscript submitted for publication

Davis, K. E., Todd, M. 1982. Friendship and love relationships. In *Advances in Descriptive Psychology,* ed. K. E. Davis, T. O. Mitchell, 2:79–122. Greenwich, Conn: JAI Press

DePaulo, B. M., Kenny, D. A., Hoover, C., Webb, W., Oliver, P. V. 1987. Accuracy in person perception: Do people know what kind of impressions they convey? *J. Pers. Soc. Psychol.* 52:303–15

Derlega, V. J. 1984. Self-disclosure and intimate relationships. In *Communication, Intimacy, and Close Relationships,* ed. V. J. Derlega, pp. 1–9. New York: Academic

Derlega, V. J., Grzelak, J. 1979. Appropriateness of self-disclosure. In *Self-disclosure: Origins, Patterns, and Implications of Openness in Interpersonal Relationships,* ed. G. Chelune, pp. 151–75. San Francisco: Jossey-Bass

Derlega, V. J., Margulis, S. T., Winstead, B. A. 1987a. A social-psychological analysis of self-disclosure. *J. Soc. Clin. Psychol.* In press

Derlega, V. J., Winstead, B. A., Wong, P. T. P., Greenspan, M. 1987b. Self-disclosure and relationship development: an attributional analysis. In *Interpersonal Processes: New Directions in Communication Research,* ed. M. Roloff, G. Miller, 14:172–87. Beverly Hills, Calif: Sage

Derlega, V. J., Winstead, B. A., Wong, P. T. P., Hunter, S. 1985. Gender effects in an initial encounter: a case where men exceed women in disclosure. *J. Soc. Pers. Relat.* 2:25–44

DeRivera, J. 1984. The structure of emotional relationships. In *Review of Personality and Social Psychology, Emotions, Relationships, and Health,* ed. P. Shaver, 5:116–45. Beverly Hills: Sage

Deutsch, M. 1975. Equity, equality, and need: What determines which value will be used as the basis of distributive justice? *J. Soc. Iss.* 31:137–49

Deutsch, M. 1985. Distributive justice: a social psychological perspective. New Haven: Yale Univ. Press

Dion, K. L., Dion, K. K. 1988. Romantic love: individual and cultural perspectives. In *The Anatomy of Love,* ed. R. J. Sternberg, M. L. Barnes. New Haven: Yale Univ. Press. In press

Duck, S., Sants, H. 1983. On the origin of the specious: are personal relationships really interpersonal states? *J. Soc. Clin. Psychol.* 1:27–41

Duncan, S., Fiske, D. W. 1985. *Interaction Structure and Strategy.* Cambridge: Cambridge Univ. Press

Ekman, P., Friesen, W. V., Ellsworth, P. C. 1972. *Emotion in the Human Face.* New York: Pergamon

Erikson, E. 1950. *Childhood and Society.* New York: Norton

Erikson, E. 1968. *Identity: Youth and Crisis.* New York: Norton

Fehr, B. 1987. Prototype analysis of the concepts of love and commitment. University of Winnipeg. Manuscript submitted for publication

Fehr, B., Perlman, D. 1987. Prototypes of love and commitment in the analysis of interpersonal relationships. University of Winnipeg. Manuscript submitted for publication

Fehr, B., Russell, J. A. 1984. Concept of emotion viewed from a prototype perspective. *J. Exp. Psychol.: Gen.* 113:464–86

Fenigstein, A., Scheier, M. F., Buss, A. H. 1975. Public and private self-consciousness: assessment and theory. *J. Consult. Clin. Psychol.* 43:522–27

Fiedler, K., Pampe, H., Scherf, U. 1986. Mood and memory for tightly organized social information. *Eur. J. Soc. Psychol.* 16:149–65

Fisher, M., Stricker, G., eds. 1982. *Intimacy.* New York: Plenum

Fitzpatrick, M. A. 1987. Marriage and verbal intimacy. In *Self-Disclosure: Theory, Research and Therapy,* ed. V. J. Derlega, J. Berg. New York: Plenum

Foa, E. B., Foa, U. G. 1980. Resource theory: interpersonal behavior in exchange. In *Social Exchange: Advances in Theory and Research,* ed. K. J. Gergen, M. S. Greenberg, R. H. Willis, pp. 77–102. New York: Plenum

Folger, R. 1984. *The Sense of Injustice: Social Psychological Perspectives.* New York: Plenum

Folger, R. 1986. Rethinking equity theory: a referent cognitions model. In *Justice in Social Relations,* ed. H. W. Bierhoff, R. L. Cohen, J. Greenberg, pp. 145–62. New York: Plenum

Forgas, J. P., Bower, G. H. 1987. Mood effects on person perception judgments. *J. Pers. Soc. Psychol.* 53:53–60

Forgas, J. P., Bower, G. H., Krantz, S. E. 1984. The influence of mood on perceptions of social interactions. *J. Exp. Soc. Psychol.* 20:497–513

Forgas, J. P., Moylan, S. 1987. After the movies: transient mood and social judgments. *Pers. Soc. Psychol. Bull.* In press

Fultz, J., Batson, C. D., Fortenbach, V. A., McCarthy, P. M., Varney, L. L. 1986. Social evaluation and the empathy-altruism hypothesis. *J. Pers. Soc. Psychol.* 50:761–69

Furby, L. 1986. Psychology and justice. In *Justice: Views from the Social Sciences,* ed. R. L. Cohen. New York: Plenum

Gadlin, H. 1977. Private lives and public order: a critical view of the history of intimate relationships in the United States. In *Close Relationships: Perspectives on the Meaning of Intimacy,* ed. G. Levinger, H. L. Raush, pp. 33–72. Amherst, Mass: Univ. Mass. Press

Gaelick, L., Bodenhausen, G. V., Wyer, R. S. 1985. Emotional communication in close relationships. *J. Pers. Soc. Psychol.* 49:1246–65

Gergen, K. J., Greenberg, M. S., Willis, R. H., eds. 1980. *Social Exchange: Advances in Theory and Research.* New York: Plenum

Glass, G. V., McGaw, B., Smith, M. L. 1981. *Meta-Analysis in Social Research.* Beverly Hills: Sage

Glick, P. 1985. Orientations toward relationships: choosing a situation in which to begin a relationship. *J. Exp. Soc. Psychol.* 21:544–62

Gottman, J. 1979. *Marital Interaction: Experimental Investigations.* New York: Academic

Gottman, J. M. 1981. *Time-Series Analysis.* New York: Cambridge Univ. Press

Gottman, J., Markman, H., Notarius, C. 1977. The topography of marital conflict: a sequential analysis of verbal and nonverbal behavior. *J. Marr. Fam.* 39:461–77

Gottman, J., Notarius, C., Markman, H., Bank, S., Yoppi, B., Rubin, Z. E. 1979. Behavior exchange theory and marital decision making. *J. Pers. Soc. Psychol.* 34:14–23

Greenberg, J., Cohen, R. L., eds. 1982. *Eq-*

uity and Justice in Social Behavior. New York: Academic

Griffitt, W. 1970. Environmental effects on interpersonal affective behavior: ambient effective temperature and attraction. *J. Pers. Soc. Psychol.* 15:240–44

Hall, E. T. 1966. *The Hidden Dimension.* Garden City, NY: Doubleday

Hammen, C. L., Peters, S. D. 1978. Interpersonal consequences of depression: responses to men and women enacting a depressed role. *J. Abnorm. Psychol.* 87:322–32

Hansson, R. O., Jones, W. H., Carpenter, B. N. 1984. Relational competence and social support. In *Review of Personality and Social Psychology, Emotions, Relationships, and Health,* ed. P. Shaver, 5:265–84. Beverly Hills: Sage

Harris, M. J., Rosenthal, R. 1985. Mediation of interpersonal expectancy effects: 31 meta-analyses. *Psychol. Bull.* 97:363–86

Harvey, J. H., Christensen, A., McClintock, E. 1983. Research methods. See Kelley et al 1983, pp. 449–85

Harvey, J. H., Flanary, R., Morgan, M. 1986. Vivid memories of vivid loves gone by. *J. Soc. Pers. Relat.* 3:359–73

Harvey, J. H., Hendrick, S. S., Tucker, K. 1988. Self-report methods in studying personal relationships. In *Handbook of Personal Relationships,* ed. S. Duck. Chichester, England: Wiley

Hatfield, E. 1984. The dangers of intimacy. See Derlega 1984, pp. 207–20

Hatfield, E. 1988. Passionate and companionate love. In *The Anatomy of Love,* ed. R. J. Sternberg, M. L. Barnes. New Haven: Yale Univ. Press. In press

Hatfield, E., Traupmann, J. 1980. Intimate relationships: a perspective from equity theory. In *Personal Relationships I: Studying Personal Relationships,* ed. S. Duck, R. Gilmour, pp. 165–78. London: Academic

Hatfield, E., Traupmann, J., Sprecher, S., Utne, M., Hay, J. 1985. Equity and intimate relations: Recent research. In *Compatible and Incompatible Relationships,* ed. W. Ickes, pp. 91–117. New York: Springer-Verlag

Hays, R. B. 1984. The development and maintenance of friendship. *J. Soc. Pers. Relat.* 1:75–98

Hays, R. B. 1985. A longitudinal study of friendship development. *J. Pers. Soc. Psychol.* 48:909–24

Hazan, C., Shaver, P. 1987. Romantic love conceptualized as an attachment process. *J. Pers. Soc. Psychol.* 52:511–24

Helgeson, V. S., Shaver, P., Dyer, M. 1987. Prototypes of intimacy and distance in same-sex and opposite-sex relationships. *J. Soc. Pers. Relat.* 4:195–233

Hendrick, C., Hendrick, S. S. 1986. A theory and method of love. *J. Pers. Soc. Psychol.* 50:392–402

Hendrick, C., Hendrick, S. S., Foote, F. H., Slapion-Foote, M. J. 1984. Do men and women love differently? *J. Soc. Pers. Relat.* 1:177–95

Hendrick, S. S., Hendrick, C. 1987. Love and sexual attitudes, self-disclosure, and sensation seeking. *J. Soc. Pers. Relat.* 4:281–97

Hill, C. T., Stull, D. E. 1986. Gender and self-disclosure: strategies for exploring the issues. In *Self-Disclosure: Theory, Research and Therapy,* ed. V. Derlega, J. Berg. New York: Plenum

Hinde, R. A. 1981. The bases of a science of interpersonal relationships. In *Personal Relationships I: Studying Personal Relationships,* ed. S. Duck, R. Gilmour, pp. 1–22. London: Academic

Hindy, C. G., Schwartz, J. C. 1984. Individual differences in the tendency toward anxious romantic attachments. Paper presented at the 2nd Int. Conf. Personal Relationships, Madison, Wisconsin

Hobfoll, S. E., Nadler, A., Lieberman, J. 1986. Satisfaction with social support during crisis: Intimacy and self-esteem as critical determinants. *J. Pers. Soc. Psychol.* 51:296–304

Hormuth, S. E. 1986. The sampling of experience *in situ. J. Person.* 54:262–93

Hornstein, G. A. 1985. Intimacy in conversational style as a function of the degree of closeness between members of a dyad. *J. Pers. Soc. Psychol.* 49:671–81

Howes, M. J., Hokanson, J. E. 1979. Conversational and social responses to depressive interpersonal behavior. *J. Abnorm. Psychol.* 88:624–34

Huston, T. L., Levinger, G. 1978. Interpersonal attraction and relationships. *Ann. Rev. Psychol.* 29:115–56

Ickes, W. 1982. A basic paradigm for the study of personality, roles and social behavior. In *Personality, Roles and Social Behavior,* ed. W. Ickes, E. S. Knowles, pp. 305–41. New York: Springer-Verlag

Ickes, W. 1985. Sex-role influences on compatibility in relationships. In *Compatible and Incompatible Relationships,* ed. W. Ickes, pp. 187–208. New York: Springer-Verlag

Ickes, W., Barnes, R. D. 1978. Boys and girls together—and alienated: on enacting stereotyped sex roles in mixed-sex dyads. *J. Pers. Soc. Psychol.* 36:669–83

Ickes, W., Patterson, M. L., Rajecki, D. W., Tanford, S. 1982. Behavioral and cognitive consequences of reciprocal versus compensatory responses to preinteraction expectancies. *Soc. Cognit.* 1:160–90

Ickes, W., Robertson, E., Tooke, W., Teng,

G. 1986. Naturalistic social cognition: methodology, assessment and validation. *J. Pers. Soc. Psychol.* 51:66–82

Ickes, W., Schermer, B., Steeno, J. 1979. Sex and sex-role influences in same-sex dyads. *Soc. Psychol. Q.* 42:373–85

Ickes, W., Turner, M. 1983. On the social advantages of having an older, opposite-sex sibling: birth order influences in mixed-sex dyads. *J. Pers. Soc. Psychol.* 45:210–22

Isen, A. M. 1970. Success, failure, attention, and reaction to others: the warm glow of success. *J. Pers. Soc. Psychol:* 15:294–301

Isen, A. M. 1984. Toward understanding the role of affect in cognition. In *Handbook of Social Cognition,* ed. R. Wyer, T. Srull, pp. 179–236. Hillsdale, NJ: Erlbaum

Isen, A. M. 1985. Asymmetry of happiness and sadness in effects on memory in normal college students: Comment on Hasher, Rose, Zacks, Sanft, and Doren. *J. Exp. Psychol. Gen.* 114:388–91

Izard, C. E. 1977. *Human Emotions.* New York: Plenum

Jones, E. E., Archer, R. L. 1976. Are there special effects of personalistic self-disclosure? *J. Exp. Soc. Psychol.* 12:180–93

Jones, W. H., Russell, D. 1982. The social reticence scale: an objective instrument to measure shyness. *J. Pers. Assess.* 46:629–31

Judd, C. M., Kenny, D. A. 1981. Process analysis: estimating mediation in treatment evaluations. *Eval. Rev.* 5:602–19

Kahn, A., O'Leary, V. E., Krulewitz, J. E., Lamm, H. 1980. Equity and equality: male and female means to a just end. *Basic Appl. Soc. Psychol.* 1:173–97

Kalick, S. M., Hamilton, T. E. III. 1986. The matching hypothesis reexamined. *J. Pers. Soc. Psychol.* 51:673–82

Kavanagh, D. J., Bower, G. H. 1985. Mood and self-efficacy: impact of joy and sadness on perceived capabilities. *Cognit. Ther. Res.* 9:507–27

Kelley, H. H. 1979. *Personal Relationships: Their Structures and Processes.* Hillsdale, NJ: Erlbaum

Kelley, H. H. 1983a. Love and commitment. See Kelley et al 1983, pp. 265–314

Kelley, H. H. 1983b. The situational origins of human tendencies: a further reason for the formal analysis of structures. *Pers. Soc. Psychol. Bull.* 9:8–30

Kelley, H. H. 1984. Affect in relationships. In *Review of Personality and Social Psychology: Emotions, Relationships and Health,* ed. P. Shaver, 5:89–115. Beverly Hills: Sage

Kelley, H. H. 1986. Personal relationships: their nature and significance. In *The Emerg-*

ing Field of Personal Relationships, ed. R. Gilmour, S. Duck, pp. 3–19. Hillsdale, NJ: Erlbaum

Kelley, H. H. 1985. A theoretical analysis, by means of computer robots, of single interaction in 2 × 2 games. *Electron. Soc. Psychol.,* Art. 8501011, 1,1

Kelley, H. H., Berscheid, E., Christensen, A., Harvey, J. H., Huston, T. L., et al. 1983. *Close Relationships.* New York: W. H. Freeman

Kelley, H. H., Gonzalez, R., Morasch, B. 1987. A computer based exercise to introduce students to patterns of interdependence and their implications. UCLA. Manuscript submitted for publication

Kelley, H. H., Thibaut, J. W. 1978. *Interpersonal Relations: A Theory of Interdependence.* New York: Wiley-Interscience

Kenny, D. A. 1988. The analysis of data from two-person relationships. In *Handbook of Personal Relationships: Theory, Relationships and Interventions,* ed. S. Duck. Chichester, England: Wiley. In press

Kenny, D. A. 1987a. What makes a relationship special? In *Methods to Study Families,* ed. T. Draper. Beverly Hills: Sage. In press

Kenny, D. A. 1987b. Interpersonal perception: a social relationships analysis. *J. Soc. Pers. Relat.* In press

Kenny, D. A., Albright, L. 1987. Accuracy in interpersonal perception: A social relations analysis. *Psychol. Bull.* In press

Kenny, D. A., LaVoie, L. 1982. Reciprocity of attraction: a confirmed hypothesis. *Soc. Psychol. Q.* 45:54–58

Kenny, D. A., LaVoie, L. 1984. The social relations model. In *Advances in Experimental Social Psychology,* ed. L. Berkowitz, 18:141–82. New York: Academic

Kohlberg, L., Ricks, D., Snarey, J. R. 1984. Childhood development as a predictor of adaptation in adulthood. *Genet. Psychol. Monogr.* 110:91–172

Kenrick, D. T., Trost, M. R. 1986. A biosocial model of heterosexual relationships. In *Males, Females, and Sexuality,* ed. D. Byrne, K. Kelly. Albany: SUNY Press

Lamm, H., Schwinger, T. 1980. Norms concerning distributive justice: Are needs taken into consideration in allocation decisions? *Soc. Psychol. Q.* 43:425–29

Lamm, H., Schwinger, T. 1983. Need consideration in allocation decisions: Is it just? *J. Soc. Psychol.* 119:205–9

Larson, R., Csikszentmihalyi, M. 1983. The experience sampling method. In *Naturalistic Approaches to Studying Social Interaction,* ed. H. T. Reis, pp. 41–56. Washington: Jossey-Bass

Latané, B. 1987. Social science should invest in infrastructure. *Soc. Sci.* 72:1–16

Leary, M. R. 1983. Social anxiousness: the construct and its measurement. *J. Pers. Assess.* 47:66–75

Lee, J. A. 1973. *The Colors of Love: An Exploration of the Ways of Loving.* Don Mills, Ontario: New Press

Lee, J. A. 1988. Lovestyles. In *The Anatomy of Love,* ed. R. J. Sternberg, M. L. Barnes. New Haven: Yale Univ. Press. In press

Lerner, M. J., Lerner, S. C., eds. 1981. *The Justice Motive in Social Behavior: Adapting to Times of Scarcity and Change.* New York: Plenum

Lerner, M. J., Miller, D. T., Holmes, J. G. 1976. Deserving and the emergence of forms of justice. In *Advances in Experimental Social Psychology,* ed. L. Berkowitz, E. Walster, 9:133–62. New York: Academic

Levenson, R. W., Gottman, J. M. 1983. Marital interaction: physiological linkage and affective exchange. *J. Pers. Soc. Psychol.* 45:587–97

Levenson, R. W., Gottman, J. M. 1985. Physiological and affective predictors of change in relationship satisfaction. *J. Pers. Soc. Psychol.* 49:85–94

Levitz-Jones, E. M., Orlofsky, J. L. 1985. Separation-individuation and intimacy capacity in college women. *J. Pers. Soc. Psychol.* 49:156–69

Lloyd, S., Cate, R., Henton, J. 1982. Equity and rewards as predictors of satisfaction in casual and intimate relationships. *J. Psychol.* 110:43–48

Loevinger, J. 1976. *Ego Development.* San Francisco: Jossey-Bass

Long, J. S. 1983a. *Confirmatory Factor Analysis.* Beverly Hills: Sage

Long, J. S. 1983b. *Covariance Structure Models: An Introduction to LISREL.* Beverly Hills: Sage

Main, M., Kaplan, N., Cassidy, J. 1985. Security in infancy, childhood and adulthood: A move to the level of representation. *Monogr. Soc. Res. Child Dev.* 50:66–104

Major, B. 1987. Gender, justice, and the psychology of entitlement. In *Sex and Gender: Review of Personality and Social Psychology,* ed. P. Shaver, C. Hendrick, 7:124–48. Beverly Hills: Sage

Major, B., Adams, J. B. 1983. The role of gender, interpersonal orientation, and self-presentation in distributive justice behavior. *J. Pers. Soc. Psychol.* 45:598–608

Major, B., McFarlin, D., Gagnon, D. 1984. Overworked and underpaid: on the nature of gender differences in personal entitlement. *J. Pers. Soc. Psychol.* 47:1399–1412

Malloy, T., Kenny, D. A. 1986. The social relations model: an integrative model for the study of personality research. *J. Pers.* 54:101–27

Margolin, G., Wampold, B. E. 1981. Sequential analysis of conflict and accord in distressed and nondistressed marital partners. *J. Consult. Clin. Psychol.* 49:554–67

Masters, J. C., Smith, W. P. 1987. *Social Comparison, Social Justice, and Relative Deprivation: Theoretical, Empirical, and Policy Perspectives.* Hillsdale, NJ: Erlbaum

McAdams, D. P. 1980. A thematic coding system for the intimacy motive. *J. Res. Pers.* 14:413–32

McAdams, D. P. 1982. Experiences of intimacy and power: relationships between social motives and autobiographical memory. *J. Pers. Soc. Psychol.* 42:292–302

McAdams, D. P. 1984. Human motives and personal relationships. See Derlega 1984, pp. 41–70

McAdams, D. P., Constantian, C. A. 1983. Intimacy and affiliation motives in daily living: an experience sampling analysis. *J. Pers. Soc. Psychol.* 45:851–61

McAdams, D. P., Healy, S., Krause, S. 1984a. Social motives and patterns of friendship. *J. Pers. Soc. Psychol.* 47:828–38

McAdams, D. P., Jackson, R. J., Kirshnit, C. 1984b. Looking, laughing and smiling in dyads as a function of intimacy motivation and reciprocity. *J. Pers.* 52:261–73

McAdams, D. P., Powers, J. 1981. Themes of intimacy in behavior and thought. *J. Pers. Soc. Psychol.* 40:573–87

McAdams, D. P., Vaillant, G. E. 1982. Intimacy motivation and psychosocial adjustment: a longitudinal study. *J. Pers. Assess.* 46:586–93

McClelland, D. C. 1986. Some reflections on the two psychologies of love. *J. Pers.* 54:334–53

McClintock, C. G., Kramer, R. M., Keil, L. J. 1984. Equity and social change in human relationships. In *Advances in Experimental Social Psychology, Vol. 17: Theorizing in Social Psychology,* ed. L. Berkowitz, pp. 183–228. New York: Academic

Mellen, S. L. W. 1981. *The Evolution of Love.* San Francisco: W. H. Freeman

Messick, D. M., Cook, K. S. 1983. *Equity Theory: Psychological and Sociological Perspectives.* New York: Praeger

Michaels, J. W., Edwards, J. N., Acock, A. C. 1984. Satisfaction in intimate relationships as a function of inequality, inequity, and outcomes. *Soc. Psychol. Q.* 47:347–57

Miell, D., Duck, S. 1986. Strategies in developing friendships. In *Friendship and Social Interaction,* ed. V. J. Derlega, V. A. Winstead, pp. 129–43. New York: Springer-Verlag

Milardo, R. M., Johnson, M. P., Huston, T. L. 1983. Developing close relationships: changing patterns of interaction between pair members and social networks. *J. Pers. Soc. Psychol.* 44:964–76

Mikula, G., ed. 1980. *Justice and Social Interaction.* New York: Springer

Mikula, G., Schwinger, T. 1978. Affective inter-member relations and reward allocation in groups: some theoretical considerations. In *Dynamics of Group Decisions,* ed. H. Brandstatter, H. J. Davis, H. Schuller, pp. 229–50. Beverly Hills: Sage

Miller, L. C., Berg, J. H. 1984. Selectivity and urgency in interpersonal exchange. See Derlega 1984, pp. 161–205

Miller, L. C., Berg, J. H., Archer, R. L. 1983. Openers: individuals who elicit intimate self-disclosure. *J. Pers. Soc. Psychol.* 44:1234–44

Miller, L. C., Kenny, D. A. 1986. Reciprocity of self-disclosure at the individual and dyadic levels: a social relations analysis. *J. Pers. Soc. Psychol.* 50:713–19

Miller, L. C., Read, S. J. 1987. Why am I telling you this? Self-disclosure in a goal-based model of personality. In *Self-Disclosure: Theory, Research and Therapy,* ed. V. Derlega, J. Berg, pp. 35–58. New York: Plenum

Mills, J., Clark, M. S. 1982. Exchange and communal relationships. In *Review of Personality and Social Psychology,* ed., L. Wheeler, 3:121–44. Beverly Hills: Sage

Mills, J., Clark, M. S. 1986. Communications that should lead to perceived exploitation in communal and exchange relationships. *J. Soc. Clin. Psychol.* 4:225–34

Montgomery, B. M. 1981. Verbal immediacy as a behavioral indicator of open communication content. *Commun. Q.* 30:28–34

Montgomery, B. M. 1984. Behavioral characteristics predicting self and peer perceptions of open communication. *Commun. Q.* 32:233–40

Moore, J., Tesser, A. 1987. Some effects of relative performance and closeness on mood. Paper presented at Ann. Meet. Am. Psychol. Assoc., New York City

Morris, L. W. 1979. *Extraversion and Introversion.* New York: Halstead

Morton, T. L. 1978. Intimacy and reciprocity of exchange: a comparison of spouses and strangers. *J. Pers. Soc. Psychol.* 36:72–81

Murray, H. 1938. *Explorations in Personality.* New York: Oxford Univ. Press

Murstein, B., Azar, J. A. 1986. The relationship of exchange-orientation to friendship intensity, roommate compatibility, anxiety, and friendship. *Small Group Behav.* 17:3–17

Murstein, B., Cerreto, M., MacDonald, M. G. 1977. A theory and investigation of the effect of exchange orientation on marriage and friendship. *J. Marr. Fam.* 39:543–48

Murstein, B., MacDonald, M. G. 1983. The relationship of the exchange-orientation and commitment scales to marriage adjustment. *Int. J. Psychol.* 18:297–311

Nadler, A., Fisher, J. D., Ben-Itzhak, S. 1983. With a little help from a friend: effect of single or multiple act aid as a function of domain and task characteristic. *J. Pers. Soc. Psychol.* 44:310–21

Nezlek, J. B., Wheeler, L., Reis, H. T. 1983. Studies of social participation. In *Naturalistic Approaches to Studying Social Interaction,* ed. H. Reis. Washington: Jossey-Bass

Noller, R. 1980. Misunderstandings in marital communication: a study of couples' nonverbal communication. *J. Pers. Soc. Psychol.* 39:1135–48

Noller, P. 1984. *Nonverbal Communication and Marital Interaction.* Oxford: Pergammon

Ochse, R., Plug, C. 1986. Cross-cultural investigation of the validity of Erikson's theory of personality development. *J. Pers. Soc. Psychol.* 50:1240–52

Orlofsky, J. L. 1987. Intimacy status: theory and research. In *Identity in Adolescence,* ed. J. E. Marcia. Hillsdale, NJ: Erlbaum. In press

Patterson, M. L. 1982. A sequential functional model of nonverbal exchange. *Psychol. Rev.* 89:231–49

Patterson, M. L. 1984. Intimacy, social control, and nonverbal involvement: a functional approach. See Derlega 1984, pp. 105–132

Peele, S. 1975. *Love and Addiction.* New York: Taplinger

Peele, S. 1988. Fools for love: the romantic ideal, psychological theory and addictive love. In *The Anatomy of Love,* ed. R. J. Sternberg, M. L. Barnes. New Haven: Yale Univ. Press. In press

Pennebaker, J. W., Beall, S. K. 1986. Confronting a traumatic event: toward an understanding of inhibition and disease. *J. Abnorm. Psychol.* 95:274–81

Perlman, D., Fehr, B. 1987. The development of intimate relationships. In *Intimate Relationships: Development, Dynamics, and Deterioration,* ed. D. Perlman, S. Duck, pp. 13–42. Beverly Hills: Sage

Perlman, D., Peplau, L. A. 1981. Toward a social psychology of loneliness. In *Personal Relationships 3: Personal Relationships in Disorder,* ed. S. Duck, R. Gilmour. New York: Academic

Prager, K. J. 1986. Intimacy status: its relationship to locus of control, self-disclosure, and anxiety in adults. *Pers. Soc. Psychol. Bull.* 12:91–110

Procidano, M. E., Heller, K. 1983. Measures of perceived social support from friends and from family: three validation studies. *Am. J. Commun. Psychol.* 11:1–24

Pruitt, D. G., Rubin, J. Z. 1985. *Social Conflict: Escalation, Stalemate and Settlement.* New York: Random House

Rathus, S. 1973. A thirty-item schedule for assessing assertive behavior. *Behav. Ther.* 4:398–406

Rees, C. R., Segal, M. W. 1984. Intragroup competition, equity and interpersonal attraction. *Soc. Psychol. Q.* 47:328–36

Reis, H. T. 1984. The multidimensionality of justice. See Folger 1984, pp. 25–61

Reis, H. T. 1986. Gender effects in social participation: intimacy, loneliness and the conduct of social interaction. In *The Emerging Field of Personal Relationships,* ed. R. Gilmour, S. Duck, pp. 91–105. Hillsdale, NJ: Erlbaum

Reis, H. T., Nezlek, J., Wheeler, L. 1980. Physical attractiveness and social interaction. *J. Pers. Soc. Psychol.* 38:604–17

Reis, H. T., Senchak, M., Solomon, B. 1985. Sex differences in the intimacy of social interaction: further exploration of potential explanations. *J. Pers. Soc. Psychol.* 48: 1204–17

Reis, H. T., Shaver, P. 1988. Intimacy as an interpersonal process. In *Handbook of Personal Relationships: Theory, Relationships and Interventions,* ed. S. Duck. Chichester: Wiley. In press

Reis, H. T., Wheeler, L., Spiegel, N., Kernis, M. H., Nezlek, J., Perri, M. 1982. Physical attractiveness in social interactions II. Why does appearance affect social experience? *J. Pers. Soc. Psychol.* 43:979–996

Reis, H. T., Wheeler, L., Kernis, M. H., Spiegel, N., Nezlek, J. 1985. On specificity in the impact of social participation on physical and psychological health. *J. Pers. Soc. Psychol.* 48:456–71

Rempel, J. K., Holmes, J. G., Zanna, M. P. 1985. Trust in close relationships. *J. Pers. Soc. Psychol.* 49:95–112

Ricks, M. H. 1985. The social transmission of parental behavior: attachment across generations. *Monogr. Soc. Res. Child Dev.* 50:221–27

Rook, K. S. 1984. The negative side of social interaction: impact on psychological well-being. *J. Pers. Soc. Psychol.* 46:1097–1108

Rook, K. S. 1987. Reciprocity of social exchange and social satisfaction among older women. *J. Pers. Soc. Psychol.* 52:145–54

Rook, K. S. 1988. Toward a more differentiated view of loneliness. In *Handbook of Personal Relationships: Theory, Relationships, and Interventions,* ed. S. Duck. Chichester: Wiley. In press

Rosch, E. 1978. Principles of categorization. In *Cognition and Categorization,* ed. E. Rosch, B. B. Lloyd, pp. 27–48. Hillsdale, NJ: Erlbaum

Rosenhan, D. L., Salovey, P., Hargis, K. 1981. The joys of helping: Focus of attention mediates the impact of positive affect on altruism. *J. Pers. Soc. Psychol.* 40:899–905

Rosenthal, R. 1984. *Meta-Analytic Procedures for Social Research.* Beverly Hills: Sage

Rubenstein, C., Shaver, P. 1980. Loneliness in two northeastern cities. In *The Anatomy of Loneliness,* ed. J. Hartog, R. Audy, Y. A. Cohen, pp. 319–37. New York: Int. Univ. Press

Rubin, Z. 1973. *Liking and Loving.* New York: Holt, Rinehart & Winston

Rubin, Z. 1988. Preface. In *The Anatomy of Love,* ed. R. J. Sternberg, M. L. Barnes. New Haven: Yale Univ. Press. In press

Rubin, Z., Hill, C. T., Peplau, L. A., Dunkel-Schetter, C. 1980. Self-disclosure in dating couples: sex roles and the ethic of openness. *J. Marr. Fam.* 42:305–17

Rusbult, C. E. 1980a. Commitment and satisfaction in romantic associations: a test of the investment model. *J. Exp. Soc. Psychol.* 16:172–86

Rusbult, C. E. 1980b. Satisfaction and commitment in relationships. *Rep. Res. Soc. Psychol.* 11:96–105

Rusbult, C. E. 1983. A longitudinal test of the investment model: the development (and deterioration) of satisfaction and commitment in heterosexual involvements. *J. Pers. Soc. Psychol.* 45:101–17

Rusbult, C. E., Johnson, D. J., Morrow, G. D. 1986. Predicting satisfaction and commitment in adult romantic involvements: an assessment of the generalizability of the investment model. *Soc. Psychol. Q.* 49:81–89

Rusbult, C. E., Zembrodt, I. M. 1983. Responses to dissatisfaction in romantic involvements: a multi-dimensional scaling analysis. *J. Exp. Soc. Psychol.* 19:274–93

Rusbult, C. E., Zembrodt, I. M., Gunn, L. K. 1982. Exit, voice, loyalty and neglect: responses to dissatisfaction in romantic involvements. *J. Pers. Soc. Psychol.* 43:1230–42

Russell, D., Peplau, L. A., Cutrona, C. E. 1980. The revised UCLA Loneliness Scale: concurrent and discriminate validity evidence. *J. Pers. Soc. Psychol.* 39:471–80

Sabatelli, R., Buck, R., Kenny, D. A. 1986. A social relations analysis of nonverbal communication accuracy in married couples. *J. Pers.* 54:513–27

Sabatelli, R. M., Cecil-Pigo, E. F. 1985. Relational interdependence and commitment in marriage. *J. Marr. Fam.* 47:931–37

Salovey, P., Rodin, J. 1984. Some antecedents and consequences of social-comparison jealousy. *J. Pers. Soc. Psychol.* 47:780–92

Schafer, R. B., Keith, P. M. 1980. Equity and depression among married couples. *Soc. Psychol. Q.* 43:430–35

Scherer, K. R., Wallbott, H. G., Summerfield, A. B., eds. 1986. *Experiencing Emotion: A Cross-Cultural Study.* Cambridge: Cambridge Univ. Press

Scherer, K. R., Summerfield, A. B., Wallbott, H. G. 1983. Cross-national research on antecedents and components of emotion: a progress report. In *Social Science Information.* Beverly Hills: Sage

Schiffenbauer, A. 1974. Effect of observer's emotional state on judgments of the emotional state of others. *J. Pers. Soc. Psychol.* 30:31–35

Schwartz, J. C., Sharpstein, D. J., Butler, J. M. 1987. Regulation of intimacy in conversations between same-sex close friends. University of Denver. Manuscript submitted for publication

Schwartz, J. C., Shaver, P. 1987. Emotions and emotion knowledge in interpersonal relations. In *Advances in Personal Relationships,* ed. W. Jones, D. Perlman, 1:197–241. Greenwich, Conn: JAI Press

Schwartz, N., Clore, G. L. 1983. Mood, misattribution and judgments of well-being: informative and directive functions of affective states. *J. Pers. Soc. Psychol.* 45:513–23

Schwinger, T. 1986. The need principle of distributive justice. In *Justice in Social Relations,* ed. H. Bierhoff, R. L. Cohen, J. Greenberg, pp. 211–25. New York: Plenum

Seligman, C., Fazio, R. H., Zanna, M. P. 1980. Effects of salience of intrinsic rewards on liking and loving. *J. Pers. Soc. Psychol.* 38:453–60

Shaffer, D. R., Ogden, J. K., Wu, C. 1987. Effects of self-monitoring and prospect of future interaction on self-disclosure reciprocity during the acquaintance process. *J. Pers.* 55:75–96

Shaver, P., Furman, W., Buhrmester, D. 1985. Aspects of a life transition: network changes, social skills and loneliness. In *The Sage Series in Personal Relationships,* ed. S. Duck, D. Perlman, 1:193–219. London: Sage

Shaver, P., Hazan, C. 1987. Being lonely, falling in love: Perspectives from attachment theory. *J. Soc. Behav. Pers.* 2:105–24

Shaver, P., Hazan, C., Bradshaw, D. 1988. Love as attachment: the integration of three behavioral systems. In *The Anatomy of Love,* ed. R. J. Sternberg, M. L. Barnes. New Haven: Yale Univ. Press. In press

Shaver, P., Schwartz, J. 1987. Cross-cultural similarities and differences in emotion and its representation: a prototype analysis. Manuscript submitted for publication

Shaver, P., Schwartz, J., Kirson, D., O'Connor, C. 1987. Emotion knowledge: further exploration of a prototype approach. *J. Pers. Soc. Psychol.* 52:1061–86

Simpson, J. A. 1987. The dissolution of romantic relationships: factors involved in relationship stability and emotional distress. *J. Pers. Soc. Psychol.* 53:683–92

Snyder, M. 1974. The self-monitoring of expressive behavior. *J. Pers. Soc. Psychol.* 30:526–37

Snyder, M. 1987. *Public Appearances and Private Realities: The Psychology of Self-Monitoring.* New York: W. H. Freeman

Snyder, M., Berscheid, E., Glick, P. 1985. Focusing on the exterior and the interior: two investigations of the initiation of personal relationships. *J. Pers. Soc. Psychol.* 48:1427–39

Snyder, M., Gangestad, S., Simpson, J. A. 1983. Choosing friends as activity partners. *J. Pers. Soc. Psychol.* 45:1061–72

Snyder, M., Ickes, W. 1985. Personality and social behavior. In *The Handbook of Social Psychology,* ed. G. Lindzey, E. Aronson, 2:883–947. New York: Random House. 3rd ed.

Snyder, M., Simpson, J. A. 1984. Self-monitoring and dating relationships. *J. Pers. Soc. Psychol.* 47:1281–91

Snyder, M., Smith, D. 1986. Personality and friendship: the friendship worlds of self-monitoring. In *Friendship and Social Interaction,* ed. V. J. Derlega, B. A. Winstead, pp. 63–80. New York: Springer-Verlag

Solomon, R. L. 1980. The opponent process theory of acquired motivation: the costs of pleasure and the benefits of pain. *Am. Psychol.* 35:691–712

Sommers, S. 1984. Reported emotions and conventions of emotionality among college students. *J. Pers. Soc. Psychol.* 46:207–15

Sprecher, S. 1987. The effects of self-disclosure *given* and *received* on affection for an intimate partner and stability of the relationship. *J. Soc. Pers. Relat.* 4:115–28

Sprecher, S. 1986. The relation between inequity and emotions in close relationships. *Soc. Psychol. Q.* 49:309–21

Sroufe, L. A. 1987. The role of infant-caregiver attachment in development. In *Clinical Implications of Attachment,* ed. J. Belsky, T. Nezworski. Hillsdale, NJ: Erlbaum. In press

Steck, L., Levitan, D., McLane, D., Kelley, H. H. 1982. Care, need, and conceptions of love. *J. Pers. Soc. Psychol.* 43:481–91

Sternberg, R. J. 1986. A triangular theory of love. *Psychol. Rev.* 93:119–35

Sternberg, R. J. 1987. Construct validation of a triangular theory of love. Yale University. Manuscript submitted for publication

Sternberg, R. J., Barnes, M. L. 1985. Real and ideal others in romantic relationships: Is four a crowd? *J. Pers. Soc. Psychol.* 49:1586–1608

Sternberg, R. J., Grajek, S. 1984. The nature of love. *J. Pers. Soc. Psychol.* 470:312–29

Sternberg, R. J., Wright, S. L. 1987. What matters when? A cross-sectional study of love across the adult life-span. Yale University. Manuscript submitted for publication

Stokes, J. P. 1983. Predicting satisfaction with social support from social network structure. *Am. J. Commun. Psychol.* 11:141–52

Strack, S., Coyne, J. C. 1982. Social confirmation of dysphoria: shared and private reactions. *J. Pers. Soc. Psychol.* 44:798–806

Stroebe, W., Eagly, A. H., Stroebe, M. S. 1977. Friendly or just polite? The effects of self-esteem on attributions. *Eur. J. Soc. Psychol.* 7:265–74

Swann, W. B. Jr., Read, S. J. 1981. Self-verification processes: How we sustain our self-conceptions. *J. Exp. Soc. Psychol.* 17:351–72

Swap, W. C., Rubin, J. Z. 1983. Measurement of interpersonal orientation. *J. Pers. Soc. Psychol.* 44:208–19

Taylor, D. A., Altman, I. 1987. Communication in interpersonal relationships: social penetration processes. In *Interpersonal Processes: New Directions in Communications Research,* ed. M. Roloff, G. Miller. Beverly Hills: pp. 257–277. Sage. 2nd ed.

Tennov, D. 1979. *Love and Limerence: The Experience of Being in Love.* New York: Stein & Day

Tesch, S. A., Whitbourne, S. K. 1982. Intimacy and identity status in young adults. *J. Pers. Soc. Psychol.* 43:1041–51

Tesser, A. 1987. Toward a self-evaluation maintenance model of social behavior. In *Advances in Experimental Social Psychology,* ed. L. Berkowitz, Vol. 20. New York: Academic. In press

Tesser, A., Millar, M., Moore, J. 1987. Some affective consequences of social comparison and reflection processes: the pain and pleasure of being close. *J. Pers. Soc. Psychol.* In press

Thibaut, J. W., Kelley, H. H. 1959. *The Social Psychology of Groups.* New York: Wiley

Thompson, W. C., Cowan, C. L., Rosenhan, D. L. 1980. Focus of attention mediates the impact of negative affect on altruism. *J. Pers. Soc. Psychol.* 39:291–300

Tolstedt, B. E., Stokes, J. P. 1984. Self-disclosure, intimacy, and the depenetration process. *J. Pers. Soc. Psychol.* 46:84–90

Törnblom, K. Y., Fredholm, E. M. 1984. Attribution of friendship: the influence of the nature and comparability of resources given and received. *Soc. Psychol. Q.* 47:50–61

Trevarthen, C. 1984. Emotions in infancy: regulators of contact and relationships with persons. In *Approaches to Emotion,* ed. K. Scherer, P. Ekman. Hillsdale, NJ: Erlbaum

Walster, E., Berscheid, E., Walster, G. W. 1973. New directions in equity research. *J. Pers. Soc. Psychol.* 25:151–76

Walster, E., Walster, G. W., Traupmann, J. 1978. Equity and premarital sex. *J. Pers. Soc. Psychol.* 37:82–92

Walster, E., Walster, G. W., Berscheid, E. 1978. *Equity: Theory and Research.* Boston: Allyn & Bacon

Waring, E. M., Tillman, M. P., Frelick, L., Russell, L., Weisz, G. 1980. Concepts of intimacy in the general population. *J. Nerv. Ment. Dis.* 168:471–74

Wheeler, L., Nezlek, J. 1977. Sex differences in social participation. *J. Pers. Soc. Psychol.* 35:742–54

Wheeler, L., Reis, H. T., Nezlek, J. 1983. Loneliness, social interaction, and sex roles. *J. Pers. Soc. Psychol.* 45:943–53

White, G. L., Fishbein, S., Rutstein, J. 1981. Passionate love and misattribution of arousal. *J. Pers. Soc. Psychol.* 41:56–62

Won-Doornick, M. J. 1979. On getting to know you: the association between the stage of a relationship and reciprocity of self-disclosure. *J. Exp. Soc. Psychol.* 15:229–41

AUTHOR INDEX

673

SUBJECT INDEX

CONTRIBUTING INDEXES

CONTRIBUTING AUTHORS, VOLUMES 35–39

A

Achenbach, T. M., 35:227–56
Alkon, D. L., 36:419–93
Amir, Y., 37:17–41
Anastasi, A., 37:1–15
Aslin, R. N., 39:435–74

B

Baer, J. S., 39:223–52
Bargh, J. A., 38:369–425
Baum, A., 36:349–83
Bednar, R. L., 39:401–34
Beer, M., 38:339–67
Ben-Ari, R., 37:17–41
Bettman, J. R., 37:257–89
Binder, A., 39:253–82
Bjork, R. A., 39:475–544
Blanchard, D. C., 39:43–68
Blanchard, R. J., 39:43–68
Borgen, F. H., 35:579–604
Boynton, R. M., 39:69–100
Brewer, M. B., 36:219–43
Browne, M. A., 35:605–25
Brugge, J. F., 36:245–74
Burlingame, G. M., 39:401–34

C

Cairns, R. B., 35:553–77
Cantor, N., 36:275–305
Cascio, W. F., 35:461–518
Chaiken, S., 38:575–630
Clark, M. S., 39:609–72
Cohn, T. E., 37:495–521
Cook, T. D., 37:193–232
Cooper, J., 35:395–426
Cross, D. R., 37:611–51
Croyle, R. T., 35:395–426
Cutting, J. E., 38:61–90

D

Dark, V. J., 37:43–75
Datan, N., 38:153–80
Day, R. H., 39:375–400
de Boer, E., 38:181–202
Deaux, K., 36:49–81
Denmark, F., 38:279–98
Diaz-Guerrero, R., 35:83–112
Donovan, D. M., 39:223–52
Dreschler, W. A., 38:181–202
Duncan, C. C., 37:291–319

E

Edelbrock, C. S., 35:227–56

F

Farley, J., 36:419–93
Feder, H. H., 35:165–200
Fischer, K. W., 36:613–48
Foss, D. J., 39:301–348
Fraisse, P., 35:1–36

G

Gescheider, G. A., 39:169–200
Gesten, E. L., 38:427–60
Gibson, E. J., 39:1–42
Gibson, W. M., 39:349–74
Goldstein, M. J., 39:283–300
Gorsuch, R. L., 39:201–22
Gould, J. L., 37:163–92
Green, B. F., 35:37–53
Grunberg, N. E., 36:349–83
Guion, R. M., 39:349–74

H

Hakel, M. D., 37:135–61
Hall, J. A., 35:37–53
Hall, W. G., 38:91–128
Harris, L. C., 35:333–60
Harvey, J. H., 35:427–59
Hasher, L., 38:631–68
Hay, D. F., 37:135–61
Heller, J. F., 38:461–89
Helzer, J. E., 37:409–32
Hendersen, R. W., 36:495–529
Higgins, E. T., 38:369–425
Holahan, C. J., 37:381–407
Honzik, M. P., 35:309–31
Horn, J. M., 39:101–34
Horton, D. L., 35:361–94
House, R., 38:669–718
Hughes, F., 38:153–80

I

Iscoe, I., 35:333–60

J

Jason, L. A., 38:427–60
Johnson, M. K., 38:631–68
Johnston, W. A., 37:43–75

K

Kaas, J. H., 38:129–51
Kamil, A. C., 36:141–69
Keesey, R. E., 37:109–33
Kessler, R. C., 36:531–72
Kihlstrom, J. F., 36:385–418
Kivlahan, D. R., 39:223–52
Klaber, M., 36:115–40
Kolligian, J., Jr., 38:533–74
Kozma, R. B., 37:611–51
Kramer, A., 36:307–48
Kramer, R. M., 36:219–43
Krantz, D. S., 36:349–83

L

Lam, Y. R., 36:19–48
Lanyon, R. I., 35:667–701
Lasley, D. J., 37:495–521
Latham, G. P., 39:545–82
Leventhal, H., 37:565–610
Loehlin, J. C., 39:101–34
London, P., 37:321–49

M

Mahoney, M. J., 35:605–25
Markus, H., 38:299–337
Marlatt, G. A., 39:223–52
Marshall, J. F., 35:277–308
Masters, K. S., 39:401–34
McGinty, D., 39:135–68
McKeachie, W. J., 37:611–51
Medin, D. L., 35:113–38
Miller, D. T., 37:291–319
Mills, C. B., 35:361–94
Mineka, S., 36:495–529
Mirsky, A. F., 37:291–319

O

Oden, G. C., 38:203–27
Oppenheim, R. W., 38:91–128
Osipow, S. H., 38:257–78

P

Panksepp, J., 37:77–107
Parloff, M. B., 37:321–49
Pervin, L. A., 36:83–114
Petersen, A. C., 39:583–608
Phillips, D. P., 36:245–74
Pintrich, P. R., 37:611–51

707

CHAPTER TITLES, VOLUMES 35–39

Annual Reviews Inc.

A NONPROFIT SCIENTIFIC PUBLISHER

 4139 El Camino Way
P.O. Box 10139
Palo Alto, CA 94303-0897 • USA

ORDER FORM
Now you can order
TOLL FREE
1-800-523-8635
(except California)

Annual Reviews Inc. publications may be ordered directly from our office by mail or use our Toll Free Telephone line (for orders paid by credit card or purchase order, and customer service calls only); through booksellers and subscription agents, worldwide; and through participating professional societies. Prices subject to change without notice. ARI Federal I.D. #94-1156476

- **Individuals:** Prepayment required on new accounts by check or money order (in U.S. dollars, check drawn on U.S. bank) or charge to credit card — American Express, VISA, MasterCard.
- **Institutional buyers:** Please include purchase order number.
- **Students:** $10.00 discount from retail price, per volume. Prepayment required. Proof of student status must be provided (photocopy of student I.D. or signature of department secretary is acceptable). Students must send orders direct to Annual Reviews. Orders received through bookstores and institutions requesting student rates will be returned. You may order at the Student Rate for a maximum of 3 years.
- **Professional Society Members:** Members of professional societies that have a contractual arrangement with Annual Reviews may order books through their society at a reduced rate. Check with your society for information.
- **Toll Free Telephone orders:** Call 1-800-523-8635 (except from California) for orders paid by credit card or purchase order and customer service calls only. California customers and all other business calls use 415-493-4400 (not toll free). Hours: 8:00 AM to 4:00 PM, Monday-Friday, Pacific Time.

Regular orders: Please list the volumes you wish to order by volume number.
Standing orders: New volume in the series will be sent to you automatically each year upon publication. Cancellation may be made at any time. Please indicate volume number to begin standing order.
Prepublication orders: Volumes not yet published will be shipped in month and year indicated.
California orders: Add applicable sales tax.
Postage paid (4th class bookrate/surface mail) by **Annual Reviews Inc.** Airmail postage or UPS, extra.

ANNUAL REVIEWS SERIES		Prices Postpaid per volume USA & Canada/elsewhere	Regular Order Please send:	Standing Order Begin with:
			Vol. number	Vol. number
Annual Review of ANTHROPOLOGY				
Vols. 1-14	(1972-1985)	**$27.00/$30.00**		
Vols. 15-16	(1986-1987)	**$31.00/$34.00**		
Vol. 17	(avail. Oct. 1988)	**$35.00/$39.00**	Vol(s). _____	Vol. _____
Annual Review of ASTRONOMY AND ASTROPHYSICS				
Vols. 1-2, 4-20	(1963-1964; 1966-1982)	**$27.00/$30.00**		
Vols. 21-25	(1983-1987)	**$44.00/$47.00**		
Vol. 26	(avail. Sept. 1988)	**$47.00/$51.00**	Vol(s). _____	Vol. _____
Annual Review of BIOCHEMISTRY				
Vols. 30-34, 36-54	(1961-1965; 1967-1985)	**$29.00/$32.00**		
Vols. 55-56	(1986-1987)	**$33.00/$36.00**		
Vol. 57	(avail. July 1988)	**$35.00/$39.00**	Vol(s). _____	Vol. _____
Annual Review of BIOPHYSICS AND BIOPHYSICAL CHEMISTRY				
Vols. 1-11	(1972-1982)	**$27.00/$30.00**		
Vols. 12-16	(1983-1987)	**$47.00/$50.00**		
Vol. 17	(avail. June 1988)	**$49.00/$53.00**	Vol(s). _____	Vol. _____
Annual Review of CELL BIOLOGY				
Vol. 1	(1985)	**$27.00/$30.00**		
Vols. 2-3	(1986-1987)	**$31.00/$34.00**		
Vol. 4	(avail. Nov. 1988)	**$35.00/$39.00**	Vol(s). _____	Vol. _____

ANNUAL REVIEWS SERIES	Prices Postpaid per volume USA & Canada/elsewhere	Regular Order Please send:	Standing Order Begin with:
		Vol. number	Vol. number

Annual Review of COMPUTER SCIENCE
Vols. 1-2	(1986-1987)...................**$39.00/$42.00**		
Vol. 3	(avail. Nov. 1988)..............**$45.00/$49.00**	Vol(s). _____	Vol. _____

Annual Review of EARTH AND PLANETARY SCIENCES
Vols. 1-10	(1973-1982)...................**$27.00/$30.00**		
Vols. 11-15	(1983-1987)...................**$44.00/$47.00**		
Vol. 16	(avail. May 1988)..............**$49.00/$53.00**	Vol(s). _____	Vol. _____

Annual Review of ECOLOGY AND SYSTEMATICS
Vols. 2-16	(1971-1985)...................**$27.00/$30.00**		
Vols. 17-18	(1986-1987)...................**$31.00/$34.00**		
Vol. 19	(avail. Nov. 1988)..............**$34.00/$38.00**	Vol(s). _____	Vol. _____

Annual Review of ENERGY
Vols. 1-7	(1976-1982)...................**$27.00/$30.00**		
Vols. 8-12	(1983-1987)...................**$56.00/$59.00**		
Vol. 13	(avail. Oct. 1988)..............**$58.00/$62.00**	Vol(s). _____	Vol. _____

Annual Review of ENTOMOLOGY
Vols. 10-16, 18-30	(1965-1971; 1973-1985)........**$27.00/$30.00**		
Vols. 31-32	(1986-1987)...................**$31.00/$34.00**		
Vol. 33	(avail. Jan. 1988)..............**$34.00/$38.00**	Vol(s). _____	Vol. _____

Annual Review of FLUID MECHANICS
Vols. 1-4, 7-17	(1969-1972, 1975-1985)........**$28.00/$31.00**		
Vols. 18-19	(1986-1987)...................**$32.00/$35.00**		
Vol. 20	(avail. Jan. 1988)..............**$34.00/$38.00**	Vol(s). _____	Vol. _____

Annual Review of GENETICS
Vols. 1-19	(1967-1985)...................**$27.00/$30.00**		
Vols. 20-21	(1986-1987)...................**$31.00/$34.00**		
Vol. 22	(avail. Dec. 1988)..............**$34.00/$38.00**	Vol(s). _____	Vol. _____

Annual Review of IMMUNOLOGY
Vols. 1-3	(1983-1985)...................**$27.00/$30.00**		
Vols. 4-5	(1986-1987)...................**$31.00/$34.00**		
Vol. 6	(avail. April 1988)..............**$34.00/$38.00**	Vol(s). _____	Vol. _____

Annual Review of MATERIALS SCIENCE
Vols. 1, 3-12	(1971, 1973-1982).............**$27.00/$30.00**		
Vols. 13-17	(1983-1987)...................**$64.00/$67.00**		
Vol. 18	(avail. August 1988)............**$66.00/$70.00**	Vol(s). _____	Vol. _____

Annual Review of MEDICINE
Vols. 1-3, 6, 8-9	(1950-1952, 1955, 1957-1958)		
11-15, 17-36	(1960-1964, 1966-1985)........**$27.00/$30.00**		
Vols. 37-38	(1986-1987)...................**$31.00/$34.00**		
Vol. 39	(avail. April 1988)..............**$34.00/$38.00**	Vol(s). _____	Vol. _____

Annual Review of MICROBIOLOGY
Vols. 18-39	(1964-1985)...................**$27.00/$30.00**		
Vols. 40-41	(1986-1987)...................**$31.00/$34.00**		
Vol. 42	(avail. Oct. 1988)..............**$34.00/$38.00**	Vol(s). _____	Vol. _____